Short Story Criticism

Guide to Gale Literary Criticism Series

For criticism on	Consult these Gale series
Authors now living or who died after December 31, 1999	*CONTEMPORARY LITERARY CRITICISM (CLC)*
Authors who died between 1900 and 1999	*TWENTIETH-CENTURY LITERARY CRITICISM (TCLC)*
Authors who died between 1800 and 1899	*NINETEENTH-CENTURY LITERATURE CRITICISM (NCLC)*
Authors who died between 1400 and 1799	*LITERATURE CRITICISM FROM 1400 TO 1800 (LC)* *SHAKESPEAREAN CRITICISM (SC)*
Authors who died before 1400	*CLASSICAL AND MEDIEVAL LITERATURE CRITICISM (CMLC)*
Authors of books for children and young adults	*CHILDREN'S LITERATURE REVIEW (CLR)*
Dramatists	*DRAMA CRITICISM (DC)*
Poets	*POETRY CRITICISM (PC)*
Short story writers	*SHORT STORY CRITICISM (SSC)*
Literary topics and movements	*HARLEM RENAISSANCE: A GALE CRITICAL COMPANION (HR)* *THE BEAT GENERATION: A GALE CRITICAL COMPANION (BG)* *FEMINISM IN LITERATURE: A GALE CRITICAL COMPANION (FL)* *GOTHIC LITERATURE: A GALE CRITICAL COMPANION (GL)*
Asian American writers of the last two hundred years	*ASIAN AMERICAN LITERATURE (AAL)*
Black writers of the past two hundred years	*BLACK LITERATURE CRITICISM (BLC-1)* *BLACK LITERATURE CRITICISM SUPPLEMENT (BLCS)* *BLACK LITERATURE CRITICISM: CLASSIC AND EMERGING AUTHORS SINCE 1950 (BLC-2)*
Hispanic writers of the late nineteenth and twentieth centuries	*HISPANIC LITERATURE CRITICISM (HLC)* *HISPANIC LITERATURE CRITICISM SUPPLEMENT (HLCS)*
Native North American writers and orators of the eighteenth, nineteenth, and twentieth centuries	*NATIVE NORTH AMERICAN LITERATURE (NNAL)*
Major authors from the Renaissance to the present	*WORLD LITERATURE CRITICISM, 1500 TO THE PRESENT (WLC)* *WORLD LITERATURE CRITICISM SUPPLEMENT (WLCS)*

ISSN 0895-9439

Volume 156

Short Story Criticism

Criticism of the
Works of Short Fiction Writers

Jelena Krstović
Project Editor

GALE
CENGAGE Learning

Detroit • New York • San Francisco • New Haven, Conn • Waterville, Maine • London

Short Story Criticism, Vol. 156

Project Editor: Jelena O. Krstović

Editorial: Dana Ramel Barnes, Sara Constantakis, Kathy D. Darrow, Kristen A. Dorsch, Dana Ferguson, Jeffrey W. Hunter, Michelle Kazensky, Michelle Lee, Marie Toft, Lawrence J. Trudeau

Content Conversion: Katrina D. Coach, Gwen Tucker

Indexing Services: Tonya Weikel

Rights and Acquisitions: Margaret Chamberlain-Gaston

Composition and Electronic Capture: Gary Oudersluys

Manufacturing: Cynde Lentz

Product Manager: Mary Onorato

For product information and technology assistance, contact us at **Gale Customer Support, 1-800-877-4253.**
For permission to use material from this text or product, submit all requests online at **www.cengage.com/permissions.**
Further permissions questions can be emailed to **permissionrequest@cengage.com**

Gale
27500 Drake Rd.
Farmington Hills, MI, 48331-3535

LIBRARY OF CONGRESS CATALOG CARD NUMBER 88-641014

ISBN-13: 978-1-4144-7166-2
ISBN-10: 1-4144-7166-1

ISSN 0895-9439

Printed in the United States of America
1 2 3 4 5 6 7 15 14 13 12 11

Contents

Preface

Short Story Criticism (SSC) presents significant criticism of the world's greatest short-story writers and provides supplementary biographical and bibliographical materials to guide the interested reader to a greater understanding of the authors of short fiction. This series was developed in response to suggestions from librarians serving high school, college, and public library patrons, who had noted a considerable number of requests for critical material on short-story writers. Although major short-story writers are covered in such Gale series as *Contemporary Literary Criticism (CLC)*, *Twentieth-Century Literary Criticism (TCLC)*, *Nineteenth-Century Literature Criticism (NCLC)*, and *Literature Criticism from 1400 to 1800 (LC)*, librarians perceived the need for a series devoted solely to writers of the short-story genre.

Scope of the Series

SSC is designed to serve as an introduction to major short-story writers of all eras and nationalities. Since these authors have inspired a great deal of relevant critical material, *SSC* is necessarily selective, and the editors have chosen the most important published criticism to aid readers and students in their research.

Approximately three to six authors, works, or topics are included in each volume, and each entry presents a historical survey of the critical response to the work. The length of an entry is intended to reflect the amount of critical attention the author has received from critics writing in English and from foreign critics in translation. Every attempt has been made to identify and include the most significant essays on each author's work. In order to provide these important critical pieces, the editors sometimes reprint essays that have appeared elsewhere in Gale's Literary Criticism Series. Such duplication, however, never exceeds twenty percent of an *SSC* volume.

Organization of the Book

An *SSC* entry consists of the following elements:

- The **Author Heading** cites the name under which the author most commonly wrote, followed by birth and death dates. Also located here are any name variations under which an author wrote, including transliterated forms for authors whose native languages use nonroman alphabets. If the author wrote consistently under a pseudonym, the pseudonym will be listed in the author heading and the author's actual name given in parentheses on the first line of the biographical and critical introduction. Uncertain birth or death dates are indicated by question marks. Single-work entries are preceded by the title of the work and its date of publication.

- The **Introduction** contains background information that introduces the reader to the author and the critical debates surrounding his or her work.

- The list of **Principal Works** is ordered chronologically by date of first publication and lists the most important works by the author. The first section comprises short-story collections, novellas, and novella collections. The second section gives information on other major works by the author. For foreign authors, the editors have provided original foreign-language publication information and have selected what are considered the best and most complete English-language editions of their works.

- Reprinted **Criticism** is arranged chronologically in each entry to provide a useful perspective on changes in critical evaluation over time. All short-story, novella, and collection titles by the author featured in the entry are printed in boldface type. The critic's name and the date of composition or publication of the critical work are given at the beginning of each piece of criticism. Unsigned criticism is preceded by the title of the source in which it appeared. Footnotes are reprinted at the end of each essay or excerpt. In the case of excerpted criticism, only those footnotes that pertain to the excerpted texts are included.

- Critical essays are prefaced by brief **Annotations** explicating each piece.

- A complete **Bibliographical Citation** of the original essay or book precedes each piece of criticism. Source citations in the Literary Criticism Series follow University of Chicago Press style, as outlined in *The Chicago Manual of Style*, 15th ed. (Chicago: The University of Chicago Press, 2006).

- An annotated bibliography of **Further Reading** appears at the end of each entry and suggests resources for additional study. In some cases, significant essays for which the editors could not obtain reprint rights are included here. Boxed material following the further reading list provides references to other biographical and critical sources on the author in series published by Gale.

Indexes

A **Cumulative Author Index** lists all of the authors that appear in a wide variety of reference sources published by Gale, including *SSC*. A complete list of these sources is found facing the first page of the Author Index. The index also includes birth and death dates and cross references between pseudonyms and actual names.

A **Cumulative Nationality Index** lists all authors featured in *SSC* by nationality, followed by the number of the *SSC* volume in which their entry appears.

An alphabetical **Title Index** lists all short-story, novella, and collection titles contained in the *SSC* series. Titles of short-story collections, separately published novellas, and novella collections are printed in italics, while titles of individual short stories are printed in roman type with quotation marks. Each title is followed by the author's last name and corresponding volume and page numbers where commentary on the work is located. English-language translations of original foreign-language titles are cross-referenced to the foreign titles so that all references to discussion of a work are combined in one listing.

In response to numerous suggestions from librarians, Gale also produces an annual paperbound edition of the SSC cumulative title index. This annual cumulation, which alphabetically lists all titles reviewed in the series, is available to all customers. Additional copies of this index are available upon request. Librarians and patrons will welcome this separate index; it saves shelf space, is easy to use, and is recyclable upon receipt of the next edition.

Citing *Short Story Criticism*

When citing criticism reprinted in the Literary Criticism Series, students should provide complete bibliographic information so that the cited essay can be located in the original print or electronic source. Students who quote directly from reprinted criticism may use any accepted bibliographic format, such as University of Chicago Press style or Modern Language Association (MLA) style. Both the MLA and the University of Chicago formats are acceptable and recognized as being the current standards for citations. It is important, however, to choose one format for all citations; do not mix the two formats within a list of citations.

The examples below follow recommendations for preparing a bibliography set forth in *The Chicago Manual of Style*, 15th ed. (Chicago: The University of Chicago Press, 2006); the first example pertains to material drawn from periodicals, the second to material reprinted from books:

Morrison, Jago. "Narration and Unease in Ian McEwan's Later Fiction." *Critique* 42, no. 3 (spring 2001): 253-68. Reprinted in *Short Story Criticism*, Vol. 57, edited by Jelena Krstovic, 212-20. Detroit: Gale, 2003.

Brossard, Nicole. "Poetic Politics." In *The Politics of Poetic Form: Poetry and Public Policy*, edited by Charles Bernstein, 73-82. New York: Roof Books, 1990. Reprinted in *Short Story Criticism*, Vol. 57, edited by Jelena Krstovic, 3-8. Detroit: Gale, 2003.

The examples below follow recommendations for preparing a works cited list set forth in the *MLA Handbook for Writers of Research Papers*, 7th ed. (New York: The Modern Language Association of America, 2009); the first example pertains to material drawn from periodicals, the second to material reprinted from books:

Morrison, Jago. "Narration and Unease in Ian McEwan's Later Fiction." *Critique* 42.3 (Spring 2001): 253-68. Rpt. in *Short Story Criticism*. Ed. Jelena Krstovic. Vol. 57. Detroit: Gale, 2003. 212-20. Print.

Brossard, Nicole. "Poetic Politics." *The Politics of Poetic Form: Poetry and Public Policy*. Ed. Charles Bernstein. New York: Roof Books, 1990. 73-82. Rpt. in *Short Story Criticism*. Ed. Jelena Krstovic. Vol. 57. Detroit: Gale, 2003. 3-8. Print.

Suggestions are Welcome

Readers who wish to suggest new features, topics, or authors to appear in future volumes, or who have other suggestions or comments are cordially invited to call, write, or fax the Product Manager:

Mary Onorato, Product Manager, Literary Criticism Series
Gale
27500 Drake Road
Farmington Hills, MI 48331-3535
1-800-347-4253 (GALE)
Fax: 248-699-8054

Acknowledgments

The editors wish to thank the copyright holders of the excerpted criticism included in this volume and the permissions managers of many book and magazine publishing companies for assisting us in securing reproduction rights. Following is a list of the copyright holders who have granted us permission to reproduce material in this volume of *SSC*. Every effort has been made to trace copyright, but if omissions have been made, please let us know.

COPYRIGHTED MATERIAL IN *SSC*, VOLUME 156, WAS REPRODUCED FROM THE FOLLOWING PERIODICALS:

American Imago, v. 57.3, fall 2000. Copyright © 2000 Johns Hopkins University Press. Reproduced by permission of the publisher.—*ANQ*, v. 22.1, winter 2009. Copyright © 2009 Taylor & Francis. Reproduced by permission of the publisher.—*Arkansas Review*, v. 4.2, 1995. Copyright © 1995 by Arkansas Review. Reproduced by permission of the publisher.—*ATQ*, v. 15, March, 2001. Copyright © 2001 *American Transcendental Quarterly (ATQ)*. Reproduced by permission of the publisher.—*Boundary 2*, v. 27.2, Summer 2000. Copyright © 2000 by Duke University Press. Reproduced by permission of the publisher.—*Chasqui*, v. 20.2, 1991. Copyright © 1991 Chasqui. Reproduced by permission of the publisher.—*Children's Literature Association Quarterly*, v. 19.1, 1994. Copyright © 1994 Children's Literature Association. Reproduced by permission of the publisher.—*Consciousness, Literature, and the Arts*, v. 5.3, 2004 for "Maharishi Vedic Science and Literary Theory" by Terry Fairchild. Copyright © 2004 Terry Fairchild. Reproduced by permission of the author. —*Discurso*, v. 9.2, 1992 for "Repression and Violence in Selected Contemporary Argentine Stories" by Joseph Tyler. Copyright © 1992 University of West Georgia. Reproduced by permission of the author.—*Edgar Allan Poe Review*, v. 3, fall, 2002; v. 4, fall, 2003; v. 6, spring, 2005. Copyright © 2002, 2003, 2005 Penn State Berks-Lehigh Valley College. All reproduced by permission.—*Explicacion de Textos Literarios*, v. 32.1-2, 2003-2004, "Cortazar, a Writing Inspiration" by Gaetan Brulotte. Copyright © 2003-2004 by University of South Florida Press. Reproduced by permission of the author.—*Hispania*, v. 80.2, 1997. Copyright © 1997 by Hispania. Reproduced by permission of the publisher.—*Hispanic Journal*, v. 11.1, Spring 1990. Copyright © 1990 Hispanic Journal. Reproduced by permission of the publisher.—*Interdisciplinary Literary Studies*, v. 11.2, Spring 2010 for "Poe's Portrait of Mathematics in 'The Purloined Letter': Some Historical Context" by Lynne L. Doty. Copyright © 2010 Penn State. Reproduced by permission of the author.—*Iowa Review*, v. 12.4, 1981. Copyright © 1981 The Iowa Review. Reproduced by permission of the publisher.—*Journal of the Fantastic in the Arts*, v. 12.2, 2001. Copyright © 2001 International Association for the Fantastic in the Arts. Reproduced by permission of the publisher.—*Latin American Literary Review*, v. 32; v. 37. Copyright © Latin American Literary Review. All reproduced by permission of the publisher.—*Literature and Medicine*, v. 26.2, fall 2007. Copyright © 2007 Johns Hopkins University Press. Reproduced by permission of the publisher.—*MLN*, v. 101.5, 1986. Copyright © 1986 Johns Hopkins University. Reproduced by permission of the publisher.—*Mythlore*, v. 12, autumn, 1985; v. 26, spring, 2008; v. 28, spring, 2010. Copyright © 1985, 2008, 2010 *Mythlore*. All reproduced by permission.—*New Literary History*, v. 19.3, 1988. Copyright © 1988 by Johns Hopkins University. Reproduced by permission of the publisher.—*Nineteenth-Century Literature*, v. 64.3, December 2009. Copyright © University of California Press. Reproduced by permission of the publisher.—*Pacific Coast Philology*, v. 38, 2003. Copyright © 2003 by Pacific Ancient and Modern Language Association. Reproduced by permission of the publisher.—*Revista de Estudios Hispanicos*, v. 21, 1994. Copyright © 1994 Universidad de Puerto Rico Recinto de Rio Piedras. Reproduced by permission of the publisher.—*Revista/Review Interamericana*, v. 25.1-4, 1995. Copyright © by Revista/Review Interamericana. Reproduced by permission of the publisher.—*Romance Languages Annual*, v. 5, 1993. Copyright © 1994 Purdue Research Foundation. Reproduced by permission of the publisher.—*Studies in Romanticism*, v. 47.2, summer 2008. Copyright © 2008 Studies in Romanticism and Center for Puerto Rican Studies. Reproduced by permission of the publisher.—*Studies in Short Fiction*, 1990. Copyright © University of Guelph and Studies in Short Fiction, Inc. Reproduced by permission of the publisher.—*Studies in the Humanities*, v. 23.1, June 1996. Copyright © 1996 University of Illinois at Urbana-Champaign. Reproduced by permission of the publisher.—*Style*, v. 40.3, fall 2006. Copyright © 2006 *Style Magazine*. Reproduced by permission of the publisher.—*Tolkien Studies*, v. 6, 2009 for "Clinamen, Tessera, and the Anxiety of Influence: Swerving from and Completing George MacDonald" by Josh B. Long. Copyright © 2009 Tolkien Studies. Reproduced by permission of the author.

COPYRIGHTED MATERIAL IN *SSC*, VOLUME 156, WAS REPRODUCED FROM THE FOLLOWING BOOKS:

Alliot, Bertrand. From *Tolkien's Shorter Works: Proceedings of the 4th Seminar of the Deutsche Tolkien Gesellschaft and Walking Tree Publishers Decennial Conference*. Walking Tree Publishers, 2008. Copyright © Walking Tree Publish-

Gale Literature Product Advisory Board

Julio Cortázar
1914-1984

(Also wrote under the pseudonym Julio Denís) Argentine short story writer, novelist, poet, and author of nonfiction.

The following entry provides an overview of Cortázar's short fiction. For additional information on his short fiction career, see *SSC,* Volumes 7 and 76.

INTRODUCTION

Credited with playing a key role in the growth of twentieth-century Latin American literature, Cortázar is hailed as an important innovator of the short story format. Together with writers like Jorge Luis Borges, Gabriel García Márquez, and Carlos Fuentes, Cortázar helped bring Latin American literature and politics to international prominence. Stylistically, Cortázar was a constant experimenter and a member of the literary avant-garde. His stories probe the connections between the real and surreal as well as the ordinary and extraordinary. Although Cortázar advocated socialism in his works and vocally supported the Cuban and Nicaraguan revolutions, he also upheld the need for individual freedom. Strongly influenced by the works of the French surrealists, Cortázar's tales counter staid, conventional logic by fostering a childlike sense of wonder in the reader, transforming the everyday world into a space of enchanting and sometimes terrifying sublimity.

BIOGRAPHICAL INFORMATION

Cortázar was born in Brussels, Belgium, the son of Argentine citizens Maria Scott and Julio Cortázar. In 1918 he moved with his parents to their native Argentina, where they settled in Banfield, a suburb of Buenos Aires. An excellent student, Cortázar began writing at a young age, completing a novel by the time he was nine years old. After earning a teaching degree, he taught high school from 1937 to 1944. During this time he began writing short stories and poetry, and in 1938, under the pseudonym Julio Denís, he published *Presencia,* a book of sonnets exhibiting the influence of French symbolist poet Stéphane Mallarmé. In 1944 and 1945 Cortázar taught French literature at the University of Cuyo in Mendoza. He resigned from his

post after participating in demonstrations against Argentine president Juan Perón. He moved to Buenos Aires and began working for a publishing company. Shortly thereafter he published his first short story, "Casa tomada" ("House Taken Over"), in *Los anales de Buenos Aires,* an influential literary magazine edited by Borges. Between 1946 and 1948, he studied law and languages to earn a degree as a public translator. In 1951 he published *Bestiario,* his first collection of short stories, and also received a scholarship to study in Paris, where he became a translator for the United Nations Educational, Scientific, and Cultural Organization (UNESCO). In 1953, collaborating with his wife, Aurora, he completed translations into Spanish of Edgar Allan Poe's prose works. Throughout his life Cortázar traveled extensively—primarily to Argentina, Cuba, Nicaragua, and the United States—often lecturing on social reform in Latin America. He died of leukemia and heart disease in Paris.

MAJOR WORKS OF SHORT FICTION

Cortázar's short fiction often establishes an ordinary world that becomes overrun with extraordinary events and creatures. For example, in "Carta a una señorita en París" ("Letter to a Young Lady in Paris"), the sickly male protagonist begins to vomit living, healthy rabbits. However, as is typical in Cortázar's fantastic tales, the character is not perplexed by this turn of events. The bunnies begin to come with increasing frequency until they have overtaken his apartment. The titular letter is a suicide note that explains why the protagonist jumped from the balcony after first throwing all of the rabbits to the pavement below. Fernando, the first-person narrator of "Silvia," begins to see the imaginary playmate of his friends' offspring. He continues to observe the beautiful and mysterious Silvia until the children finally deny her existence, at which point Fernando is left to ponder the reality of his vivid hallucinations. Autobiographical and fantastic elements commingle in "La noche boca arriba" ("The Night Face Up"), in which the protagonist suffers a motorcycle accident identical to an accident endured by the author in real life. In the story, the narrator is given an anesthetic at the hospital and dreams that he is a Moltec Indian being captured by Aztec pursuers. As the man drifts in and out of sleep, his real-life situation begins to resemble the dream world:

while he lies on the operating table, the man dreams that he is being held down as the Aztecs prepare to sacrifice him to the gods.

Cortázar's tales are also known for featuring characters that cross the line between fantasy and reality. In "La isla a mediodía" ("The Island at Noon"), an airline attendant becomes fascinated by a Greek island, Xiros, which his plane passes over every midday. His obsession with the island grows until he finally quits his job and settles there. One day while strolling the beach, he watches a plane crash into the ocean. He is able to recover only one body from the crash—his own. The protagonist of "Continuidad de los parques" ("Continuity of Parks") is seated in a high-backed, green-velvet armchair while reading a murder mystery. The man and woman in the mystery are planning to kill the woman's husband. As the murderers proceed to the victim's house, they find him seated in a high-backed, green-velvet armchair, reading a book. The reader discovers that the protagonist himself is, in fact, the victim in the story. Another tale that merges imagination and reality, "Fin de etapa" ("A Leg of the Journey"), features Diana, a woman touring a museum filled with paintings of the same empty room. Diana leaves the museum and enters a house in the adjacent village to smoke a cigarette. She returns to the museum to find that one of the paintings now depicts the scene of her smoking in the formerly empty room. A tale of the fantastic takes a nightmarish turn in "La escuela de noche" ("The School at Night"). Two students, Nito and Toto, break into their school one night. Once inside, they find a group of school officials and teachers engaging in acts of sexual perversion and bizarre sadism. Toto escapes and threatens to reveal what he has witnessed, but Nito, now brainwashed by the evil school officials, warns Toto that his life will be in danger if he speaks out.

Many of Cortázar's stories display a deep understanding of the troubled human psyche. For example, "House Taken Over" concerns a middle-aged brother and sister who live in comfort in the large home they have inherited. Their inheritance also provides an ample income, so neither sibling works. One day the brother, who narrates, hears a noise in an adjoining room and realizes that "they" have invaded the house. He bolts the door to seal off that portion of the building. As the attacks from "them" continue to intensify, the siblings become increasingly cut off from reality and eventually flee the house. An example of Cortázar's psychological realism, "Tango de vuelta" ("Return Trip Tango") focuses on Matilde, a married woman who leaves her husband, Emilio, and seeks out her true love, Germán. Matilde and Germán have a son and live together for many years. One day, while Germán is away on business, Emilio shows up and be-

gins a strategic infiltration of Matilde's life. He befriends her son and seduces her maid, thus gaining entrance into the house. After several years of terror, Matilde kills Emilio during an attack, only to subsequently die from an overdose of pills that she had taken two hours earlier. "Ahí pero dónde, cómo" ("There But Where, How") emphasizes the psychological trauma at the center of many of Cortázar's stories. The story deals with the author-narrator's obsession with Paco, a friend who died thirty years earlier. Paco keeps haunting him in his dreams and memories, and the author-narrator warns that the reader, too, will likely have one death that will remain lodged in his or her psyche. The characters in "El perseguidor" ("The Pursuer") attest to Cortázar's interest in the dichotomous nature of man. Johnny is a jazz musician who feels time slip away when he performs; Bruno is Johnny's biographer, an analytical man jealous of the musician's freedom from daily routine. Although Bruno characterizes Johnny's talent as a kind of communication with God, Johnny rejects this description as a narrow, convention-bound perspective on artistic expression. A stylistic experiment in narrative perspective, "Grafitti" ("Graffiti") also serves as a tale of urban political violence. Inspired by the troubles surrounding the military dictatorship of Argentina, the story begins in second person as the anonymous narrator tells of a graffiti artist whose sketches express the anguish of a city imprisoned by its government. When a female correspondent of the graffiti artist is arrested and beaten by the police, the artist begins to draw her damaged face next to his work. At this point it is revealed that the narrator is the correspondent, recently released by the government.

CRITICAL RECEPTION

Cortázar's stories have consistently been held in high esteem among critics. In particular, reviewers have lauded the psychological aspect of his short fiction, applying the theories of Carl Jung to the archetypal characterizations in "Silvia" and reading "The Night Face Up" as a study of the effect of anesthetics on the dream state. Critics have compared the merging of the psychological and physical worlds in "A Leg of the Journey" to a similar psychological ambiguity in Vladimir Nabokov's "The Visit to the Museum," while underscoring the conflict between the protagonist and his/her "shadow" self in several of Cortázar's tales. As scholar Luis F. González-Cruz has argued, "[A] number of Cortázar's characters seem doomed to get involved, to fight, to try to conquer chaos, or the dark forces of the universe, only to realize that they have failed because they do not constitute a center of harmony, but—in Jungian terms—they are torn by the opposite drives of [self] and shadow, a primary source of universal disruption." Furthermore, commentators have studied the philosophical component of Cortázar's stories, illuminating the influence of Jean-Paul Sartre's existentialist philosophy on his early work. According to critic Rubén Noguera, Cortázar's use of fantastic elements signals his desire to move away from the strict logic of Western philosophy. "Cortázar's mission," Noguera writes, "seems to be to remind us that there is more out there than meets the eye, and he does this in his stories by inserting such 'fantastic' elements as dreams, imagination, creativity, nightmares, fears. . . . Thus, Cortázar is ultimately trying to distance himself (and his readers) from traditional Western philosophy, which tends to rely too much on logical reason."

From a textual perspective, scholars have focused on the linguistic intricacies of "Continuity of Parks," the use of an unreliable narrator in "Silvia," and the relationship between reader and story in "House Taken Over." The political nature of Cortázar's stories has elicited positive comparisons to fellow Argentine writer Luisa Valenzuela's short fiction, and commentators have noted Cortázar's ambivalent feelings toward Buenos Aires in "There But Where, How" and "The School at Night." Some reviewers have discussed the subtextual references to gender in "Graffiti," while others have likened the story to the public art of Liliana Porter. Regardless of the specific critical approach to his work, most scholars have concurred with Gaetan Brulotte's conclusion that Cortázar "illustrates the importance of literature and creativity in our world." As Brulotte wrote, "[His stories] help create a higher state of consciousness; they give a different meaning to life and generate forms of solidarity among people."

PRINCIPAL WORKS

Short Fiction

Bestiario 1951
Final del juego [*End of the Game, and Other Stories*; also published as *Blow-Up, and Other Stories*] 1956
Las armas secretas 1959
Cuentos 1964
Todos los fuegos el fuego [*All Fires the Fire, and Other Stories*] 1966
Relatos 1970
La isla a mediodía y otros relatos 1971
Reunión 1973
Octaedro [*A Change of Light, and Other Stories*] 1974

Antología 1975
Los relatos. 3 vols. 1976
Queremos tanto a Glenda [*We Love Glenda So Much, and Other Tales*] 1980
Deshoras [*Unreasonable Hours*] 1982
Nicaragua tan violentamente dulce [*Nicaraguan Sketches*] 1983
Cuentos completos. 2 vols. 1995
Diario de Andrés Fava [*Diary of Andres Fava*] 1995

Other Major Works

Presencia [as Julio Denís] (poetry) 1938
Los premios [*The Winners*] (novel) 1960
Rayuela [*Hopscotch*] (novel) 1963
62: Modelo para armar [*62: A Model Kit*] (novel) 1968
Último round (nonfiction) 1969
Libro de Manuel [*A Manual for Manuel*] (novel) 1973
El examen [*Final Exam*] (novel) 1986

CRITICISM

Rob Rix (essay date 1987)

SOURCE: Rix, Rob. "Visions of Blighted Youth: Buenos Aires Remembered in the Tales of Julio Cortázar." In *A Face Not Turned to the Wall: Essays on Hispanic Themes for Gareth Alban Davies,* edited by C. A. Longhurst, pp. 257-76. Leeds, England: Department of Spanish and Portuguese, University of Leeds, 1987.

[*In the following essay, Rix comments on the troubling and mysterious aura surrounding the author's remembrance of Buenos Aires in "There But Where, How" and "The School at Night."*]

Julio Cortázar lived in Argentina for most of the first half of his life, after an early infancy in Europe. His childhood, youth and early manhood were spent in Buenos Aires; two years teaching at the University of Cuyo in the Andean city of Mendoza were followed by a return to Buenos Aires before he travelled to Europe, where he was to live until his death in Paris in 1984. While his life and work had other perspectives and settings ranging from the Indian subcontinent (his interest in Zen and mandalas, texts such as 'Turismo aconsejable' from *Ultimo Round, Prosa del observatorio*) to Cuba, Chile, Nicaragua and the U.S.A., he returned periodically in person or in writing to the city which he left behind immediately after the publication of his first book of tales, *Bestiario* (1951). His occasional visits were, it seems, disturbing; he once described how he had felt "como un fantasma entre los vivos, lo que es horrible, o como un vivo entre los fantasmas, lo que es todavía peor." The experience of return to Buenos Aires was like a nightmare "en la que nos sentimos atraídos y rechazados al mismo tiempo, en la que quisiéramos alcanzar un rostro o un recuerdo y se nos resuelve en otra cosa, en una inevitable diferencia, en una distancia como de humo."[1] This estrangement is framed in a story from the collection *Final del juego* (1964), '**La puerta condenada**', in which a lonely traveller, haunted by an archetypal scene (crying child comforted by mother) is at once separated from and tormented by an obsession which is manifested only on the other side of a locked, never-used door in his hotel room.

Distanced from the environment of his childhood and youth by a self-imposed exile, Cortázar stands apart from a host of Latin American writers who have lived and worked abroad (including Carlos Fuentes, Gabriel García Márquez and Mario Vargas Llosa) in that his novels and stories are not primarily set in his country or continent of origin. Most volumes of his stories since *Bestiario* offer a predominance of themes and scenarios which cannot be easily or exclusively defined as Argentinian or Latin American, and the only novel which can be entirely related to life in Buenos Aires, *Los premios,* is located on board a ship cruising somewhere in the South Atlantic. Elsewhere the Argentinian background of the author is presented as just one side of reality, contrasted with the cosmopolitan world without frontiers of his life as an expatriate, and ultimately left behind, remembered fondly or rejected.

The two stories from Cortázar's later work chosen for discussion in this paper return to the haunts of the writer's youth which remained unexplored in any other texts, in that they deal neither with remembrances of early childhood (like '**Los venenos**') nor with the mature adult world of Buenos Aires re-visited in many tales from *Final del juego* (for example '**Las ménades**'), *Todos los fuegos el fuego* (for example, '**El otro cielo**') or other collections. Both '**Ahí pero dónde, cómo**' and '**Escuela de noche**' look back in time, near the end of a writing career characterised by the themes of exile, nostalgia, escape and liberation, to scenes and moments whose mysterious, equivocal and disturbing force lay at the heart of Cortázar's conflicts and obsessions as a writer. Core experiences of rejection and betrayal produced the crisis of loyalty and the quest for an ethical freedom in exile which became major preoccupations in every novel and volume of stories published by the writer who came to represent the essential Argentinian expatriate in Europe, whose final words in the posthumous volume of poetry *Salvo el crepúsculo* (1984) reflect on the dangers of his situation:

Desde luego, como Orfeo, tantas veces habría de mirar hacia atrás y pagar el precio. Lo sigo pagando hoy; sigo y seguiré mirándote, Eurídice Argentina.

(p. 345)

Cortázar's last visit to the city of his childhood took place shortly before his death and in the aftermath of the military dictatorship which slaughtered the nation's children in the *guerra sucia,* the war of repression with its host of *desaparecidos,* and later in the Malvinas débâcle. Greeted with indifference by the official literary and political world of his *ex-patria,* he was welcomed effusively by his readers for many of whom he represented an international voice of solidarity who had used his freedom from the nightmare they had endured to denounce the horrors of the tyranny at every opportunity and in all possible arenas.[2] In *Argentina: años de alambradas culturales* he refers to the condition of exile as "eje y motor de una denuncia constante de los crímenes de la junta militar", and presents a selection of the texts and speeches he had produced in response to what he saw as "las obligaciones de un intelectual en este momento de la historia latinoamericana" (Barcelona, 1984, p. 8). Many of his stories from the last few years ('**Segunda vez**', '**Apocalípsis de Solentiname**', '**Recortes de prensa**', etc.) gave literary expression to the task of denunciation, and while his political and human rights campaigning perhaps forestalled the writing of further novels after *Libro de Manuel* (1972), the flow of stories was constant, with four major collections appearing in eight years: *Octaedro* (1974), *Alguien que anda por ahí* (1977), *Queremos tanto a Glenda* (1981), and *Deshoras* (1982). These volumes demonstrate the range and variety of Cortázar's work as a *cuentista,* with themes which recur throughout his writing (*doppelgängers,* children with mysterious powers, strange encounters, persecutions, aesthetic and ideal projections of reality, nightmares, metamorphoses, eroticism and death) treated in settings and situations which may be historically real or autobiographically true, invented or simply fantastic, and using modes of discourse from the recollected and reproduced *lunfardo* notable in many early tales to the cultivated cosmopolitanism of characters who embody Cortázar's multilingual and multicultural interests and experience.

In all of these books Cortázar engages the reader in mysteries, revelations and changes, setting nostalgia, absurd humour, tenderness and normality as traps in which we may find ourselves face to face with the writer enmeshed in the web of his own fictions. We are led to the brink of madness or utopia and, sometimes gently, sometimes violently, we are thrust through the curtain of the texts into a new and unexpected kind of sanity. We emerge from his stories like dreamers awakening to a more delicate and fragile world, a world of alienation but also of reconciliations. While the stories wrench and shake the consciousness of readers we sense that they discharged the author of energies, burdens, debts and the poison of certain experiences, as he often hinted in referring to the quasi-automatic process of creation, and as he explicitly avowed in the case of his earliest *cuentos*.

Cortázar achieved, in this final phase of his work, a complete coherence in his texts. Tone, voice and register are rarely those of a neutral, detached narrator, but, as in many passages and chapters of *Rayuela*, they create an answer to the tensions of form and structure to conduct the experience which is discovered and communicated in the tale. The lack of perceptible separation between author, narrator and protagonist in many of these stories reduces the critical need for autobiographical exegesis and ideological interpretation. The tales are not so much accounts of experience (lived in the material world or lived imaginatively) transmuted into fiction, nor are they deliberated messages conveyed through fables; they are the life of the author, transcribed in the various languages of creative writing which he had mastered. Cortázar engaged in the literary praxis which carried out his own project of creating 'revolutionary literature', "la revolución de la literatura y no la literatura de la revolución." The values embodied in his writing are not detachable from his entire personal history; neither can they be set aside from their means of expression in the form of abstract mental or historical constructs for analysis as evidence of Cortázar's 'bourgeois sensibilities', 'liberal yearnings' or, for that matter, 'socialist principles'. His work exudes commitment, and not solely the literary *compromiso* of the creative writer but engagement with his own history. Made conscious in the 1960s, from the moment of his contact with Cuba (which coincided with the publication of *Rayuela*) of his need to rediscover and identify with the lives of his brothers and sisters, the *pueblo latinoamericano*, Cortázar has always returned in his work to the task of recreating moments from his *viajes*, whether from Buenos Aires to Paris, from Paris to Cuba or Nicaragua, from Europe to India or from the Mediterranean to the River Plate. Cortázar was the complete traveller, not the frustrated *porteño* who bears the name like a millstone in *Rayuela* but the true *viajero* defined by Cristina Peri Rossi:

> Se viaja para contar. Cada viajero se convierte en un narrador, es decir, alguien que ordena *la visión* en un tiempo y en un espacio que es el del relato. El viajero mira desde el ángulo del narrador, con ojos dobles: el de que *está* en el tiempo y en el espacio visitado y el par de ojos de quien ya ha regresado (o nunca se fue) y

testimonia a los demás la experiencia del viaje. Por eso la condición imprescindible del viaje es—mucho más que el lugar al que se llega—el regreso.[3]

Cortázar's journeys were simultaneously outward and return, 'de ida y vuelta'; Paris and Buenos Aires are twinned in his life and work to such an extent that, as indicated by the definition of Paris as "acá" in *Rayuela*, both cities are his starting point and destination.

A mid-century expatriate, Cortázar had left behind him in Argentina a clutch of personal neuroses (exorcised through the writing of his stories), friendships and memories from childhood, youth and his literary adolescence on the fringes of the *Sur* group, and above all the stifling effect of Peronism, which had mounted a crude attack on the aesthetic values and cultural activities of the Argentinian intellectual elite. His own writings to date had consisted of a book of sonnets and a verse drama (*Los reyes*) written under the influence of European Romantic and Symbolist poets, a few literary articles and reviews, and the *cuentos fantásticos* of **Bestiario**. His wide reading in foreign literature gave him access to Gothic themes, the monsters, tortured fantasies and agonies of the whole nineteenth-century European and North American poetic traditions; his discovery and use of two variants of Argentine speech, the *lunfardo* of the *porteño* lower classes and the domestic exchanges of the middle-class family, cliché-ridden and laden with euphemisms, set the scene for dénouments of extraordinary tension. The complete breakdown of normality was registered in most cases 'not with a bang but a whimper', leading not to release but to a kind of whimsical nostalgia combined with lingering guilt feelings about scenarios from which the writer could feel he had narrowly escaped on the boat which took him to France. The monstrous presences which invaded and occupied his characters were arbitrary, uncontrollable and impervious to counter-attack. The victims could only flee, be taken over completely, or seek refuge in the "zona sagrada" identified by the critic Noé Jitrik in his study of **Bestiario**.[4] Referring to the moment in the tales in which "la llamada 'zona sagrada' emerge de la interioridad en la que estaba guardada," Jitrik explains: ". . . en ese momento es un apestado, un intocable, un privilegiado. El personaje así afectado busca entonces un igual y constituye con él un grupo que es esencialmente defensivo . . ." (p. 21). Cortázar's protagonists, due to their heightened sensibility, their innocence and self-consciousness tempered by tenacity or visionary awareness, are able to form discreet support groups which can resist raids on their persons or psyches by others, by society at large, or by unknown forces. Jitrik identifies their need to "cuidar la 'zona sagrada' de los 'otros' que no la admiten, de aquellos frente a quienes al sustraerse se experimenta sin embargo una sensación de orgullosa culpabilidad a la cual no se quiere renunciar" (p. 22). Public and private life held untold dangers for the vulnerable individual, haunted at home or hunted down in the open where society had become a savage beast of conformity, hysteria and vengeance on the conspicuous eccentric or outsider. With little possibility of freedom in such circumstances, Cortázar's characters are faced with negative options; in Jitrik's words, "la renuncia . . . abandonar la casa . . . aislarse . . . el suicidio . . . emergentes de los triunfos indirectos de los 'otros', de los que encarnan la persecución, con los que la integración es imposible" (p. 22). Jitrik notes the value of these tales as denunciations of "los otros", "su estúpida dureza y arbitrariedad frente al alumbramiento que supone la aparición de una 'zona sagrada'" (p. 24).

The stories of **Bestiario,** however effective, suggest that their author had failed to resolve the conflicts and anxieties at the heart of the tales, but had managed to rid himself of their most painful and disturbing symptoms by writing them and subsequently by getting out of the city and the nation in which they had developed. Cortázar found refuge in anonymity in Paris, and spent the rest of his life discovering and propounding the positive aspects of an exile which, if voluntary at first, would be virtually enforced during the years of the military *junta*. In *Argentina: años de alambradas culturales* he analysed the condition which he had tried to "asumir . . . como positividad, como un valor y no como una privación" (p. 40). Aligning himself with a younger generation of "innumerables protagonistas de la diáspora" he encouraged them to see "una analogía entre el maravilloso viaje cultural de antaño y la expulsión despiadada del exilio: la posibilidad de esa re-visión de nosotros mismos en tanto que escritores arrancados a nuestro medio" (p. 23). Faced with a real *desarraigo* which left his compatriots stranded in Europe (which for Cortázar was always a "catalizadora de fuerzas y talentos todavía en embrión") he recommended the following course of action:

> En vez de concentrarnos en el análisis de la idiosincrasia, la conducta y la técnica de nuestros adversarios, el primer deber del exiliado debería ser el de desnudarse frente a ese terrible espejo que es la soledad de un hotel en el extranjero y allí, sin las fáciles coartadas del localismo y de la falta de términos de comparación, tratar de verse como realmente es.
>
> (pp. 23-24)

Through the story of Horacio Oliveira in *Rayuela* Cortázar had tackled in his own work a fundamental challenge: "plantear la condición del exilio en términos que superen su negatividad, a veces inevitable y terrible, pero a veces también estereotipada y esterilizantes" (p. 18). In countering the usual tendencies of

the exile ("una nostálgica búsqueda de la patria perdida"), and attempting to "reconquistar esta patria", Cortázar delivered a final message to "Todo aquel que no haya renunciado a esa voluntad de regreso": "Por más crueles que puedan parecer mis palabras, digo una vez más que el exilio enriquece a quien mantiene los ojos abiertos y la guardia en alto" (p. 20; pp. 106-107). This insistence was founded on his own experience in Europe, which from the very start had encouraged a process of self-examination and produced a series of challenges which were of greater importance than any feelings of regret or nostalgia, as Cortázar recalled in conversation with Ernesto González Bermejo:

> Llegar a Europa significó justamente, la necesidad de confrontar todo ese sistema de valores mío, mi manera de ver, mi manera de escuchar. La experiencia europea, en muy pocos años, fue una sucesión de choques, desafíos, dificultades, que no me había dado el clima infinitamente más blando, apacible, de Buenos Aires.[5]

The immediate task of coming to terms with this new life had begun with a re-examination of the last years in Argentina with the advantages of distance and hindsight and under different pressures to those released in *Bestiario*. Some of the products of this retrospection, notably **'La banda'** and **'Final del juego'**, were included in his second collection of tales, entitled *Final del juego* (First edition 1956). His next book, *Las armas secretas* (1959), related more directly to the problems, the lessons and the crises of Cortázar's first years in Europe. The first story in this collection, **'Cartas de mamá'**, examined the question of expatriation from a new perspective; the direction of the author's gaze was no longer towards Europe and exile from Argentina, but back towards the abandoned homeland from a precarious Parisian freedom, or rather a conditional freedom, as he noted at the beginning of the story. True freedom involves a long and complex process, not merely the act of escape, which is only a first step towards independence. Luis, the protagonist of **'Cartas de mamá'**, is tied to the past and to Argentina by the apron-strings of his mother's letters, which continually disrupt the security and freedom of his new life in Paris. They are a persistent reminder which can only be appeased by habitual replies, the antidotes from the realm of independence:

> Cada nueva carta insinuaba por un rato (porque después él las borraba en el acto mismo de contestarlas cariñosamente) que su libertad duramente conquistada, esa nueva vida recortada con feroces golpes de tijera en la madeja de lana que los demás habían llamado su vida, cesaba de justificarse, perdía pie, se borraba como el fondo de las calles, mientras el autobús corría por la rue de Richelieu.
>
> (*Relatos,* Buenos Aires, 1972, pp. 213-214)

Still insecure in the transitional process of becoming a citizen of Paris, Luis is suddenly thrown into confusion by one of his mother's letters. The letter mentions Nico, the younger brother whose death from tuberculosis preceded Luis's marriage to Laura (formerly Nico's *novia*) and their subsequent escape to Europe. Nico is presented as a personification of innocence who haunts Luis as, with a show of cynicism and hardened experience, he attempts to reject the past. This attempt is hindered by the guilt feelings which the letters, in speaking of Nico as if he were still alive, resurrect. Yet although they are problematic, the letters provide an essential contact with the past:

> . . . si le hubieran faltado habría sentido caer sobre él la libertad como un peso insoportable. Las cartas de mamá le traían un tácito perdón (pero de nada había que perdonarlo), tendían el puente por donde era posible seguir pasando.
>
> (p. 214)

The letters sublimate the past for Luis and Laura, who never speak of Nico; yet Nico is always between them, he forms an important and mysterious part of their relationship. The resuscitation of the past in the letters exposes the nerve-endings of their marriage and the falsity of an existence which Luis has been so careful to compose and construct:

> La carta de mamá lo metía, lo ahogaba en la realidad de esos dos años de vida en París, la mentira de una paz traficada, de una felicidad de puertas para afuera, sostenida por diversiones y espectáculos, de un pacto involuntario de silencio en que los dos se desunían poco a poco como en todos los pactos negativos.
>
> (p. 225)

Laura's nightmares are another area of exposure to the past, another negative and destructive force threatening their new life. The story ends with the reintegration of a *ménage à trois*; Nico is accepted as a presence in their relationship who, if not recognised, would cause a rift between them. The equation of freedom through escape with guilt-feelings replaced any conventional notion of nostalgia in Cortázar's approach to the problems of exile. Luis is conscious of the brutality of his decision to leave his family and Argentina:

> Todo había sido brutal en esos días: su casamiento, la partida sin remilgo ni consideraciones para con mamá, el olvido de todos los deberes sociales, de los amigos entre sorprendidos y desencantados. No le había importado nada. . . .
>
> (p. 218)

That decision is seen in retrospect as a betrayal of his dying brother, a betrayal implicit in the rejection of "ese orden que el había repudiado una noche en el jardín después de oir una vez más la tos apagada, casi humilde de Nico" (p. 219). Having fled the country and the recriminations of the family Luis and Laura are unable to come to terms with their responsibility for this betrayal, which insidiously undermines their future together:

> Luis había agradecido a Laura que jamás hiciera referencia al pobre fantoche que tan vagamente había pasado de novio a cuñado. Pero ahora, con un mar de por medio, con la muerte y dos años de por medio, Laura seguía sin nombrarlo, y él se plegaba a su silencio por cobardía, sabiendo que en el fondo ese silencio lo agraviaba por lo que tenía de reproche, de arrepentimiento, de algo que empezaba a parecerse a la traición.
>
> (pp. 221-222)

The story portrays Nico as a silent presence, inexorably exacting a price for freedom in the conscience of Luis. Every reference to him outside of mother's letters evokes images of silent suffering and the inevitable drift towards death:

> Luis sentía otra vez la presencia de Nico en el jardín de Flores, escuchaba su tos discreta preparando el más perfecto regalo de bodas imaginable, su muerte en plena luna de miel de la que había sido su novia, del que había sido su hermano.
>
> (p. 222)

> Callado, tan poca cosa el pobrecito, Nico se había ido quedando atrás, perdido en un rincón del patio, consolándose con el jarabe pectoral y el mate amargo.
>
> (p. 226)

> Allí esperaría, tendido de espaldas, fumando también él su cigarrillo, tosiendo un poco, riéndose con una cara de payaso como la cara de los últimos días, cuando no le quedaba ni una gota de sangre sana en las venas.
>
> (pp. 236-237)

'Cartas de mamá' presents an elaborate explanation, if not yet an expiation, of the guilt associated with voluntary expatriation and the severance of links with the past. Involving as it does the death from tuberculosis of a loved one who is betrayed by the act of escape the story also carries a troubled undercurrent of feeling which can be associated with the literary figures and fantasies analysed by Susan Sontag in her study *Illness as Metaphor* (London, 1979); her work suggests a wealth of interpretations which can be applied as clarifications of a later story by Cortázar which is foreshadowed by 'Cartas de mamá', 'Ahí pero dónde, cómo' from *Octaedro* (Madrid, 1974). The problem faced by Luis and Laura to some extent contains the germ of a phenomenon outlined by Sontag as follows: "Contact with someone afflicted with a disease regarded as a mysterious malevolency inevitably feels like a trespass; worse, like the violation of a taboo" (p. 6). This feeling is compounded in '**Cartas de mamá**' by a transgression which is implicitly sexual, but which also, and more potently, involves the theft of an identity or role (Nico's relationship to his former *novia* and to his own brother is violated) and, in consequence, the haunting of the transgressors by the victim of disease and betrayal.

In two other stories written earlier and included in the volume *Final del juego* Cortázar broached an aspect of departure from the past which relates to the problems of Luis. In '**Los amigos**', a very short story of betrayal and revenge in the setting of *el hampa*, Buenos Aires low-life, old friends whose ways have parted long ago are reunited in a murder scene, as killer and victim; no remorse is indicated in the hit-man's tranquil observation: "Manejando sin apuro, el Número Tres pensó que la última visión de Romero había sido la de un tal Beltrán, un amigo del hipódromo en otros tiempos" (*Relatos,* p. 317). In this scenario, however, Beltrán has forfeited his own identity by betraying his former friend. The theme is developed in a totally different setting in the disturbing and confusing tale '**Relato con un fondo de agua**' (*Relatos,* pp. 51-58). From the deranged memories of the protagonist who attempts to explain a mysterious sequence of events to another friend from bygone days emerges an understanding of friendship as a kind of judgement or reproach. In a troubled consciousness images recur in dreams of the death of a friend by drowning. The protagonist is haunted by his friend who is also, in his dreams, a doppelgänger, who accuses: "Hasta eso me has robado, hasta mi deseo más secreto; porque yo he deseado un sitio así, yo he necesitado un sitio así. Has soñado un sueño ajeno" (p. 57). The metaphysical anguish resulting from this confusion of identities and destinies can only be lifted, the story suggests, by a final reconciliation in death: ". . . alguna noche me llevará con él. Me llevará, te digo, y el sueño cumplirá su imagen verdadera . . . el sueño estará al fin completo" (p. 58). In this rather tentative oneiric fantasy one phrase, which indicates the problems of this kind of writing at the same time as it attempts to counter them, echoes through the volumes of Cortázar's stories: "No invento nada, Mauricio, la memoria sabe lo que debe guardar entero" (p. 53). In '**Ahí pero dónde, cómo**' the same notion is put forward, now as a direct challenge to the reader: "Y vos que me leés creerás que invento; poco importa, hace mucho que la gente pone en la cuenta de mi imaginación lo que de veras he vivido, o viceversa" (p. 92). From a technical concession to the suspension of disbelief Cortázar had evolved a complete identification of creative consciousness with the act and the product of writing; there is no longer a distance between author and story, no longer any perceptible line or point of separation between imagination and experience and the communication of both.

At the start of the tale an indication is given of the cultural and autobiographical territory within which or from which the story operates, with the mention of Magritte's painting 'Esto no es una pipa' which establishes the equivocal surreality of the text, and the citation of the dedication in *Bestiario*: "A Paco, que gustaba de mis relatos." These two *lemas* mark the poles of Cortázar's creative imagination: his own background of personal relationships in Buenos Aires and the European cultural and intellectual ambience which he both inherited and joined in his exile. The text is a sustained meditation on the invasion of the writer's consciousness by the presence of a friend long dead. Paco appears in dreams which refuse to subside in the course of present time, "este presente sucio, lleno de ecos de pasado y obligaciones de futuro" (p. 83). Memories of the death and burial of his friend haunt not only Cortázar's memory, they invade his whole person and, he suggests, against or outside of his will, dictate the process and the very practice of his writing:

> Te digo, esos treinta y un años no son lo que importa, mucho peor es este paso del sueño a las palabras, el agujero entre lo que todavía sigue ahí pero se va entregando más y más a los nítidos filos de las cosas de este lado, al cuchillo de las palabras que sigo escribiendo y que ya no son eso que sigue ahí pero dónde, cómo.
>
> (p. 85)

In the midst of other nightmares ("las noticias de Chile, esa otra pesadilla que ningún dentífrico despega de la boca" [p. 84]) the image of Paco, alive and dying, imposes an ultimate mystery on the crowded life of the author. In attempting to sieze and understand the strange knowledge which only Paco's presence brings, Cortázar faces the essential frustrations which accompany the creative urge. Meticulously defining the nature of Paco's visitations ("Paco no es un fantasma", "con Paco es como si se despertara también conmigo") Cortázar struggles to express the inexpressible:

> Lo que entonces sé es que haber soñado no es más que parte de algo diferente, una especie de superposición, una zona otra, aunque la expresión sea incorrecta pero también hay que superponer o violar las palabras si quiero acercarme, si espero alguna vez estar.
>
> (pp. 86-87)

The dream of Paco is then a kind of threshold experience, holding out a possibility of access to some other reality, just the other side of each meeting, each *cita*.

Paco, like Nico in 'Cartas de mamá', died of TB. In many of Cortázar's early stories about children, illness, especially asthma (from which the author suffered as a child), is an important element in the psychological traumas suffered by the young protagonists whose heightened consciousness is their one defence against the forces which threaten them. 'Bestiario', 'Los venenos' and 'Final del juego' all share to some extent what Sontag has referred to as "the romantic view . . . that illness exacerbates consciousness" (p. 36). In charting the history of literary expressions of disease the American writer launched a powerful critique of literary myths, such as "the Victorian idea of TB as a disease of low energy (and heightened sensibility)" and "the inveterate spiritualizing of TB and the sentimentalizing of its horrors", but also underlined some of the most potent creative uses of "Illness as Metaphor": which can help to explain the nature of Paco's influence on Cortázar the writer (p. 62, p. 41). For example, the problematic references to the passage and simultaneity of time in the text can be related not only to the processes of dream and memory but also to the very ravages of Paco's sickness: as Sontag notes, "TB is a disease of time; it speeds up life, highlights it, spiritualizes it" (p. 14). In Cortázar's story it is Paco's illness which seems to set him apart from any of those referred to by the writer as "mis otros muertos" and which gives him the special power at the heart of the text: "la enfermedad lo ciñe, lo fija en esa última apariencia que es mi recuerdo de él hace treinta y un años; así está ahora, así es" (p. 89). If other old friends are remembered in different circumstances and places (Alfredo, for example, appears in "cualquiera de sus tantas imágenes, de las opciones del tiempo y de la vida . . . casándose con Zulema, saliendo conmigo del normal Mariano Acosta para ir a tomar un vermut en *La Perla* del Once" [p. 85]). Paco is always the same, in his room in the house on Rivadavia or in any other setting:

> Paco es solamente la pieza desnuda y fría de su casa, la cama de hierro, la bata de esponja blanca, y si nos encontramos en el café y está con su traje gris y la corbata azul, la cara es la misma, la terrosa máscara final, los silencios de un cansancio irrestañable.
>
> (p. 86)

TB, as Susan Sontag notes, is "the disease that individualizes, that sets a person in relief against the environment" (p. 37). The presence of Paco is not only static and set in relief, it is also obsessive; tortured by his illness, suffering in silence but "levantándose con esfuerzo para que no me dé cuenta de que está tan enfermo, . . . pidiéndome el cigarillo que le tienen prohibido" he provokes a reaction of shunning, of rejection:

> Cada noche que he vuelto a soñarlo ha sido lo mismo, las variaciones del tema; no es la recurrencia la que po-

dría engañarme, lo que sé ahora ya estaba sabido la primera vez, creo que en París en los años cincuenta, a quince años de su muerte en Buenos Aires. Es verdad, en aquel entonces traté de ser sano, de lavarme mejor los dientes; te rechacé, Paco. . . .

(p. 87)

Cortázar records in the text how the persistence of Paco's memory has led him to accept the burden and seek access to a form of reconciliation with an aspect of his own past defined in the terms of Paco's illness and death. Many elements of this process are again clarified by Sontag's argument:

> TB was understood, like insanity, to be a kind of one-sidedness: a failure of will or an overintensity. However much the disease was dreaded, TB always had pathos. Like the mental patient today, the tubercular was considered to be someone quintessentially vulnerable, and full of self-destructive whims.
>
> (p. 63)

The features and traits of the inhabitants of Cortázar's *Bestiario* from the Buenos Aires of the 1940s are fused in the enduring image of Paco, the youth blighted by a disease which has a long literary pedigree.

In establishing parallels between the fancies associated with tuberculosis and insanity Sontag strikes a rich vein; her insights can be cited to identify the nature and force of Paco's enduring influence on Cortázar's subconscious. Firstly, she notes that sufferers from both kinds of illness enter "a duplicate world with special rules" (p. 36). Cortázar's stories are full of such worlds, inhabited by various Nicos, Pacos, *cronopios* and wondrous individuals who persistently occupy the consciousness of the writer in his own disconsolate routine reality. Eternally locked in *ahí* where his destiny repeats itself Paco reaches out to Cortázar, to one kind of exile from another: "ya no su imagen percibida con la cruel precisión lenticular del sueño . . . sino la certidumbre de que impensablemente sigue ahí y que sufre" (pp. 92-93). As Susan Sontag explains, both TB and insanity are, in their way, kinds of exile: "The metaphor of the psychic voyage is an extension of the romantic idea of travel that was associated with tuberculosis. To be cured, the patient has to be taken out of his or her daily routine" (p. 36). Cortázar insists that although even seers would think him demented he knows that Paco is not dead, that they are bound together inexorably:

> Sólo puedo creer en lo que sé, seguir por mi vereda como vos por la tuya empequeñecido y enfermo ahí donde estás, sin molestarme, sin pedirme nada pero apoyándote de alguna manera en mí que te sé vivo, en ese eslabón que te enlaza con esta zona a la que no pertenecía pero que te sostiene vaya a saber por qué, vaya a saber para qué. Y por eso, pienso, hay momen-

tos en que te hago falta y es entonces que llega Claudio o que de golpe te encuentro en el café donde jugábamos al billar. . . .

(p. 91)

Paco is the writer's access to his own youth in Buenos Aires, but also the source of an indomitable "alegría deslumbrada" which does not evaporate on waking, a joy whose essence is hope:

> y la alegría dura y está aquí mientras escribo, y no contradice la tristeza de haberte visto una vez más tan mal, es todavía la esperanza, Paco, si escribo es porque espero aunque cada vez sea lo mismo . . . la esperanza de que alguna vez sea de otra manera. . . .

(p. 91)

Cortázar works at his text in the hope that once and for all he might help Paco to be cured, or to die; hope and exasperation, the two sides of the coin of writing, are also the *cara y cruz* of illness and of exile, an exile dogged by the memories and claims of past loyalties and friendships, abandoned but not forgotten because they tenaciously exact a price for freedom. Paco can not be assimilated into the experience of sustained exile composed by Cortázar into the mythical, universalized cosmopolitan metropolis, 'la ciudad', Cortázar's personal Paris or Europe of the imagination which formed the setting of *62: modelo para armar* and other miscellaneous texts, because Paco exists in a previous life and city of Cortázar's subconscious and conscious self, in pre-1950s Buenos Aires:

> Mirá, a Paco no lo encontré nunca en la ciudad de la que he hablado alguna vez, una ciudad con la que sueño cada tanto, y que es como el recinto de una muerte infinitamente postergada, de búsquedas turbias y de imposibles citas. Nada hubiera sido más natural que verlo ahí, pero ahí no lo he encontrado nunca ni creo que lo encontraré. El tiene su territorio propio, gato en su mundo recortado y preciso, la casa de la calle Rivadavia, el café del billar, alguna esquina del Once.

(p. 92)

Paco is the presiding genius and spirit of place in the territory renounced by the writer in exile.

In the final lines of the tale the author suggests, reminding us that its writing was not voluntary but the result of necessity, that the text is like the stories of *Bestiario* a form of exorcism, or at least an expiation; only in the telling can the experience be creatively assumed:

> simplemente tenía que decirlo y esperar, decirlo y otra vez acostarme y vivir como cualquiera, haciendo lo posible por olvidar que Paco sigue ahí, que nada termina porque mañana o el año que viene me despertaré sabiendo como ahora que Paco sigue vivo, que me llamó porque esperaba algo de mí, y que no puedo ayudarlo porque está enfermo, porque se está muriendo.

(p. 93)

The country of Cortázar's childhood and youth, the country which he left to become a writer, endures in his most intimate work as a place where the individual, dying (really or metaphorically) from TB or contemplating the ravages of 'the disease of the sick self', the 'disease that isolates one from the community', must suffer in silent desperation or escape to another dimension. The escapist finds himself pursued by the memory of those abandoned, betrayed or left to perish. The pull of his country and his past, exerted earlier in his work by the 'cartas de mamá', tugs at Cortázar's sleeve and conscience in the shape of Claudio, forever "pidiéndome que vaya a verte" (p. 91). The sentiments of the text are not those of guilt or even regret, nor is nostalgia a keynote; in response to the call of the past the writer seeks conciliation through recognition and acceptance of the immutability of the past and of its hold over us, along with a conviction (and knowledge) that writing not only releases but reveals and even intensifies consciousness, and thereby exercises a transforming potential. If the past can not be changed through re-living, if Paco's death-in-life eternally recurs in some dimension of being which is not just memory or dream, both writer and reader are changed, however subtly, by the uncompromising presence of Paco, whether Paco is understood to be a real historical identity, a symbol of lost youth or the sick self, or the personification of Cortázar's ill-defined sense of indebtedness to the human and geographical location of his youthful years, his close friends and their Buenos Aires haunts. Our normal perceptions and understanding of our relationship to the past, and particularly to the irrecuperable dead who stay with us in images and inner visions which have their own force independently of our conscious will, are not able to account for Paco's presence as manifested in this text. He will not be explained away as simple memory, dream-image or even ghost; he is the very essence of the self which Cortázar cast off, along with friends, family and familiar places and scenes, when he made the momentous and definitive move to Europe in 1951. Just as Traveler, Oliveira's best friend who becomes a threat to the latter's identity, a *doppelgänger,* after their reunion in the second part of *Rayuela,* was the personification of what Oliveira (and Cortázar) might or would have become without the experience of Paris, so Paco lives out in Cortázar's imagination, and in his entire creative consciousness, the consequences of remaining in Buenos Aires. If his illness is a metaphor then his vulnerability, his isolation and resignation, and his drift toward annihilation, relate closely to the predicament of many of the victims in the *Bestiario* of 1951. The innocent monsters of those tales, children of the Cortazarian Minotaur (in *Los reyes*), respond to their particular circumstances in diverse ways, all of which to some degree involve a withdrawal, retreat or escape into a "zona sagrada" which in some cases implies an element of mutual support or complicity. Paco, who occupies his own sacred zone of life-in-death, continues to beckon; "mi camarada de estudios, mi mejor amigo" whose presence is both inexplicable and unavoidable impels Cortázar on his quest through the act of writing: "si un día, si ahora mismo en cualquier momento alcanzo a manotear más lejos" (pp. 86-87). Like the betrayed brother of **'Cartas de mamá'** and even the crippled Leticia of **'Final del juego'** Paco has been left behind but continues to condition the exile's liberation.

In many other stories from **Bestiario** and **Final del juego** Cortázar turned from the fate of the individual in terms of personal obsessions, neuroses and illness (the sick self) to accounts of the vulnerability of isolated characters in settings and circumstances where society at large, particularly in its conglomerate role, threatened their identity and even survival. In **'Omnibus'**, **'Las ménades'**, **'La banda'** and **'Las puertas del cielo'** characters are faced with different kinds of exposure and alienation in situations involving the behaviour of groups or crowds. Manifestations of group hysteria and vulgar (valueless) or meaningless rituals demanding conformity leave the bewildered and defenceless outsiders of these stories sickened, impossibly lonely and, in the case of Lucio Medina in **'La banda'**, driven to exile. Like **'Casa tomada'** these stories contain elements which encourage their reading as fables referring to some of the most disconcerting aspects of the rise of Peronism in Argentina and its exploitation of cultural phenomena; in **'La banda'** we are told that in September of 1947, by which time the Peronist revolution had taken hold of the nation, the narrator discovered that Lucio Medina, whose equivocal and unsettling experience he has related, "había renunciado a su profesión y abandonado el país" (*Relatos,* p. 439). Some thirty years later Cortázar wrote **'La escuela de noche'**; included in his very last volume of stories, *Deshoras* (Madrid, 1982, pp. 103-122), this tale returns to the plight of an innocent individual exposed to the irrational nightmare of what is now presented explicitly as a fascistic rite. The opening lines of the story closely parallel the presentation of Paco in **'Ahí pero dónde, cómo'**, as does the setting of the story in the author's days as a student at the *Escuela Normal* which he attended in Buenos Aires, "la escuela anormal (lo decíamos para jorobar y por otras razones más sólidas)":

> De Nito ya no sé nada ni quiero saber . . . Más vale no pensar en él, solamente que a veces sueño con los años treinta en Buenos Aires, los tiempos de la escuela normal y claro, de golpe Nito y yo la noche en que nos metimos en la escuela, después no me acuerdo mucho de los sueños, pero algo queda siempre de Nito como

> flotando en el aire, hago lo que puedo para olvidarme, mejor que se vaya borrando de nuevo hasta otro sueño, aunque no hay nada que hacerle, cada tanto es así, cada tanto vuelve como ahora.
>
> (p. 105)

Tied to Nito by the loyalties of friendship, their *alianza* as schoolmates, vaguely curious but passively drawn along by Nito's obsession with the school under cover of darkness, the narrator, Toto, agrees to enter a nightmare world:

> Nito se acordaba de pesadillas donde cosas instantáneamente borradas por un despertar violento habían sucedido en galerías de la escuela, en el aula de tercer año, en las escaleras de mármol; siempre de noche, claro, siempre él solo en la escuela petrificada por la noche, y eso Nito no alcanzaba a olvidarlo por la mañana, entre cientos de muchachos y de ruidos.
>
> (p. 80)

The two adolescents lead uneventful lives in the streets and in 'La Perla del Once' (a bar also mentioned in the story of Paco): "leíamos como locos de día pero a la noche vagábamos los dos—a veces con Fernández López, que murió tan joven—" (p. 79); their adventurous incursion into the unfamiliar realms of their school at night is a pointless act of trespass and transgression which holds only incidental promises of vandalism, at worst, and at best daredevilry. Once inside the night school they stumble across an unsuspected hidden curriculum of terrors. In the staff room, that forbidden territory which is the seat of pedagogical power and mystification, they are initiated into an orgy of vice, violence and regimentation; the most unsavoury of their fellow pupils, in league with the sinister headmaster, Rengo and other dubious characters on the staff, indulge in a series of masquerades and rituals involving transvestism, sexual degradation and militaristic bullying. In a surrealistic amalgamation of the Buenos Aires underworld (*el hampa*) and the brutalising environment of a military academy reminiscent in its atmosphere of the institution exposed in Mario Vargas Llosa's *La ciudad y los perros,* Cortázar's innocent interlopers run a labyrinthine gauntlet of force which demands blind obedience and submission, the covert reality of school:

> los por qué nos faltaban a esa altura, Nito que me seguía callado miraba el largo zaguán en penumbras y era otra vez cualquiera de las pesadillas que tenía con la escuela, ahí donde nunca había un por qué, donde solamente se podía seguir adelante, y el único por qué posible era una orden de Fiori, ese cretino vestido de milico que de golpe se sumaba a todo lo otro y nos daba una orden, valía como una orden pura que debíamos obedecer, un oficial mandando y andá a pedir razones. Pero esto no era una pesadilla, yo estaba a su lado y las pesadillas no se sueñan de a dos.
>
> (p. 89)

Separated from his companion, Toto is subjected to a humiliating masturbatory initiation rite by the only female teacher in the establishment, "la señorita Maggi"; the sexually vulnerable youth is degraded and expelled into further scenes of bestial torture which culminate in orchestrated incantations:

> —Se procederá a enunciar el decálogo—dijo el profesor Iriarte—. Primera profesión de fe. . . . Monótonamente, casi sílaba a sílaba, el cuadro enunció:
>
> —Del orden emana la fuerza, y de la fuerza emana el orden.
>
> —¡Corolario!—mandó Iriarte.
>
> —Obedece para mandar, y manda para obedecer—recitó el cuadro.
>
> (p. 97)

Fortuitously making his escape ("De todo eso me acuerdo poco, yo no era más que mi propia fuga") Toto abandons his companion Nito in the depths of the night school (p. 98). When they are eventually reunited at the school gates on Monday morning Nito, it soon emerges, has been changed by his experience. Now successfully recruited to the night school, he attempts in his turn to persuade Toto to join the conspiracy; Toto, unwilling to acquiesce and sensing the estrangement of his erstwhile friend ("Era él, claro, pero fue como si de repente no lo conociera") is threatened with dire consequences if he does not remain silent about the scenes he has witnessed (p. 100).

The story ends on a note of apocalyptic foreboding; the night school's activities are understood to be preparations for the bloodbath unleashed in Argentina decades later, when (in **'Recortes de prensa'**, from *Queremos tanto a Glenda* [Madrid, 1980, pp. 65-82]) Noemí and her sculptor friend would meet in a Parisian studio to seek together an artistic response to man's cruelty to man only to find that they were "una vez más dos argentinos dejando subir la marea de los recuerdos, la cotidiana acumulación del espanto a través de cables, cartas, repentinos silencios" (p. 66). Toto may have escaped personal implication in the brutalism being hatched in the darkness of his school, but Nito and the others are waiting:

> para que lo otro, lo que importaba de veras, se fuera cumpliendo poco a poco, así como poco a poco se habían ido enunciando para él las profesiones de fe del decálogo, una tras otra, todo eso que iría naciendo alguna vez de la obediencia al decálogo, todo eso que había aprendido y prometido y jurado esa noche y que alguna vez se cumpliría para el bien de la patria cuando llegara la hora y el Rengo y la señorita Maggi dieran la orden de que empezara a cumplirse.
>
> (p. 101)

'Escuela de noche' derives its impact from the sense of devastation with which Toto received the betrayal by his friend Nito, who succumbs to the forces of his own nightmares, forces which lurk in the darkest regions of his social and cultural environment. Gratuitous violence and chauvinist tendencies, channeled by systematic brutalisation, are welded into preceptive norms of behaviour for deployment by tyrants against any opponent in the name of patriotic abstractions.

If **'Ahí pero dónde, cómo'** represents Cortázar's final recognition in fiction of an outstanding debt to his virtuous friend Paco, who died of TB, the disease which as Susan Sontag points out "claimed the likes of Keats, Poe, Chekhov, Simone Weil, Emily Brontë, and Jean Vigo" and which was "as much an apotheosis as a verdict of failure" (p. 49), the story **'Escuela de noche'** is a final revindication of his exile from a society which, sick with a disease for which Argentina would find no cure before it had wreaked terrible ravages, was headed for a disaster of monstrous proportions. Both stories reach back into his own adolescence to express on the one hand his commitment to the creative transformation and communication of experience through art, that essentially irrational process because it cannot be contained, confined or explained by mere reason, and on the other hand the scourge of man's irrationality and inhumanity when subjected to the unscrupulous exercise of power through intimidation, repression and the imposition of divisive creeds.

Both stories recreate and testify to the embattled innocence of youth, blighted in one instance by a disease whose ravages informed the consciousness of the creative writer as conceived by Cortázar, heir to a literary tradition of universal dimensions, and voracious reader, in his youth and thereafter, of the victims of an illness borne by a friend and companion who would not be forgotten or confined to a purely metaphorical existence. In the second case, the **'Escuela de noche'** can be construed as a vision of Argentina which, as the youthful protagonist suspected and as the ageing writer saw confirmed, would engulf its own children in a tragic ritual of arbitrary brutality. Cortázar's nightmare of a community initiated into an orgy of torture and destruction was enacted historically in the Argentina of the *guerra sucia* and the *desaparecidos* during the final years of his life.

Notes

1. Cortázar quoted by Mireya Bottone, 'Cortázar en el testimonio', *Boletín de literaturas hispánicas*, No. 6 (1966), p. 86.

2. For details of Cortázar's last visit to Buenos Aires see Martín Prieto, 'Largo desencuentro con Buenos Aires', *El País,* 14.2. 1984, p. 31, and a letter from Julio Cortázar to Mario Muchnik, dated "París, 12 de diciembre de 1983", published in *Cambio 16*, No. 658 (9.7. 1984), p. 93.

3. Cristina Peri Rossi, '13 años después', *El País*, 24.6. 1985, p. 9.

4. Noé Jitrik, 'Notas sobre la "zona sagrada" y el mundo de los "otros" en *Bestiario* de Julio Cortázar' in *La vuelta a Cortázar en nueve ensayos*, edited by Sara Vinocur de Tirri & Nestor Tirri (Buenos Aires), 1968, pp. 13-30.

5. *Conversaciones con Cortázar* (Barcelona, 1978), p. 14.

Luis F. González-Cruz (essay date spring 1990)

SOURCE: González-Cruz, Luis F. "Disruptive Tensions: *Ego* and *Shadow* in Julio Cortázar's Narrative." *Hispanic Journal* 11, no. 1 (spring 1990): 147-55.

[*In the following essay, González-Cruz explores the confrontation with the psychological double or alter ego in Cortázar's stories.*]

The theme that most frequently appears in Cortázar's short stories is that of "man" and "the other" in an exuberant display of fictional possibilities. The reader may feel that each story is a new original piece while, in reality, the same topic is presented in many of them, What makes Cortázar a master of disguise is his ability to endow the same theme with innumerable variants, introducing characters and plots that each time astonish the reader, causing him to forget, for a while at least, that the subject matter in question is essentially the same as in so many other of his stories. Today, when his lifetime work can be seen in perspective, one can identify such a recurring theme as a duplication of man's reality or, better, the splitting up of the individual into at least two well-defined separate beings.

This aspect of Cortázar's narrative must, of course, be placed within the tradition of the "double" in modern literature, a tradition exemplified by Poe, Dostoevski, Conrad and Borges, among others. But Cortázar's approach to this well-known theme should also be seen in the light of those views with which contemporary psychology has enriched our understanding of the processes of the human mind; we refer specifically to Carl Jung's notion of the *shadow*, that other which is the embodiment of certain unconscious features of our individual personality, and which "can also consist—in the words of a noted Jungian—of collective factors that stem from a source outside the individual's personal life."[1] The difficulty of integrating the *shadow* into the realm of the conscious, with the aid of the Self—a difficulty contemplated by Jungian psychology (Franz, 182)—, that is, to attain a sense of personal

wholeness, and therefore, to establish a harmonious relationship with outside reality, lies at the heart of Cortázar's constant use of the figure of the "double." We will return to this point in the conclusion.

We do not intend to cover here all of the stories that illustrate our proposition, but, rather, to outline Cortázar's technique in accomplishing his goal and to consider especially those complex allegories which have not been treated in as much detail as others.

The theme of "self" in relation to "other" is evident in **"The Night Face Up," "A Yellow Flower," "Axolotl,"** and **"Island at Noon."**[2] At the same time, in these four texts, there is a well-marked difference between the realities in which the two interconnected beings exist—except, perhaps, for **"A Yellow Flower."**

In **"A Yellow Flower,"** the man who one day finds Luc—the boy that he believes had been put on earth to take his place whenever he died—, shares with his double the same reality; its sordidness, which the man does not want Luc to continue experiencing, is what prompts him to kill the child. The role which time plays is merely to place Luc on this earth a little too soon but, it does not delimit different realities as it does in **"The Night Face Up."** As for space, it becomes relevant to the plot only in the sense that the man and Luc (or, more precisely, "the man" and his "other self") meet in a bus where chance has brought them together. Reality encompasses the same miseries for both: insurmountable limitations, unavoidable illness, an existence of boredom, confined by the common space of the big and busy city.

In **"The Night Face Up,"** on the other hand, realities are distinctly separated by time and space: the man who suffers the accident and is hospitalized, and the "Motec" [sic] Indian he dreams about (or vice versa), occupy different worlds in time and space. In addition, the worlds they live in, although similar on the surface—the characters are near death, victims of their respective social practices or ways—are essentially different: one is "civilized," the other "barbaric."

In both **"A Yellow Flower"** and **"The Night Face Up"** there is a sort of *majic moment* that conjues up the *alter ego*: the encounter with Luc in the bus and the unexplained gap between the accident and the time when the main character regained consciousness, respectively. In **"The Night Face Up"** Cortázar writes:

> He saw himself leaving the hotel again, wheeling out the cycle. Who'd have thought that it would end like this? He tried to fix the moment of the accident exactly and it got him very angry to notice that there was a void there, an emptiness he could not manage to fill.
>
> (72-73)

This emptiness is the point in which two different men (or the same in two distant realities) can converge or identify with each other. Several other stories have one added feature in common which operates as a clear symbol: the two realities are separated by a piece of glass or, simply, a window. In **"Axolotl"** and **"Island at Noon"** the two modes of existence which the protagonist experiences are divided by the glass of the aquarium, in the first instance, and by that of the airplane window, in the second. How can one keep from being reminded of Lewis Carroll's *Through the Looking-Glass?* What man sees on the other side of the glass in these two texts is that "other" who soon ends by becoming "himself." In **"Axolotl,"** as by an act of magic, the reality of the observer transgresses spatial limits and changes into the reality of the axolotl on the other side:

> My face was pressed against the glass of the aquarium, my eyes were attempting once more to penetrate the mystery of those eyes of gold without iris, without pupil. I saw from very close up the face of an axolotl immobile next to the glass. No transition and no surprise, I saw my face against the glass, I saw it on the outside of the tank, I saw it on the other side of the glass. Then my face drew back and I understood.
>
> (8)

Graciela de Sola, referring to **"Island at Noon,"** mentions the significance of the dividing glass. Her comments could be applied to both **"Island at Noon"** and **"Axolotl"** because the passive, detached, and ancestral life of the axolotl is very much like the one which lures the steward whenever he flies over the island of Xiros. She explains:

> He is the one who looks through the glass, the one who wishes to cross to the other side, but he is also, in the story, capable of actually transcending linear chronology, setting himself in a mythical time, a timeless, unchangeable island that can offer him the only possible happiness by rescuing him from duration and corrosion.[3]

The glass, as in *Through the Looking-Glass,* is not an element that isolates two universes but, rather, the doorway which communicates one with the other, even if the glass, as in the case of **"Island at Noon,"** only serves *to show* the protagonist the alternate universe he is attracted to—a sort of preview or anticipation of things to happen. For, in truth, the *two men* in that story coexist only from the moment of the plane crash until *the first steward,* now vacationing in the island, sees his *alter ego* die on the shore after dragging him out of the water. The interpretation of this phenomenon, if one wants to find a rational explanation to a *magic* occurrence, is offered by David Lagmanovich in an incisive commentary:

> If we look for an explanation to what happens with Marini and his island, we could interpret it as a case of premonition (Marini foresees his visit to the island as

well as the accident in which he dies, all of it while looking through the airplane window), or as a series of images displayed in the very instant the airplane falls (a superimposition of chronological time and the sheer duration experienced by his consciousness), or, finally—and this is the most practical interpretation—as another example of the fulfillment, simultaneous or not, of the several potential forms of life that coexist within a single person.[4]

The conclusion of the story is as controversial as that of **"The Night Face Up,"** and, no matter what argument we use, we could never be certain that we are right. Does the man in the hospital in **"The Night Face Up"** die? Perhaps we could *assume* that he does if we look at one of the several possible theories: if he and his Indian double are living parallel lives and the Indian cannot escape the execution, then the man in the hospital must also die. The principle of parallelism cannot be fully applied to **"Island at Noon"** because here we could see the first man *saved* the island and made symbolically eternal—like the man absorbed by (or converted into) an axolotl. Looking at it this way, the man now in the island actually sees the death of that "other" man he abhors. As a matter of fact, there is a clear reference in the story to his intention: "It wouldn't be easy to kill the former man," but "he felt the enterprise was possible" (99). The man who dies is the man he does not want to be again, someone who was ruled by civilized mores, trivial love affairs, and who could not be part of a reality which had always seemed foreign to him, even if the ending realistically suggests that with the death of the steward both selves die in one single body. In a first reading of the text one could assume that the existence of the man in the island is only illusory, since at the end we are told that the people of that island were, as always, "alone on the island" and the only new thing for them was "the open-eyed corpse" (100). On this point, however, we must look for a more profound symbolism than the one suggested by the simplistic ending which merely unites both entities into the one dead body. Just before this apparently clear ending, we are told how the children in the island, surrounding the corpse, could not figure out how a man bleeding so profusely had the strength not only to swim from the place of the crash, but to drag himself to the point where he was found. We, the readers, however, have the answer: the dead man's *alter ego,* whether he existed or not in a carnal form to the islanders, pulled his twin out of the water.

If one looks carefully at another of Cortázar's classic stories, **"End of the Game,"** one can realize that the plot resembles, in its essential traits, the plot of **"Island at Noon,"** only that in **"End of the Game"** the story is told from the perspective of the stationary characters, instead of that of the passerby.

In **"Island at Noon,"** the steward flies over Xiros repeatedly. His perspective of the island is that of an observer. From his airplane he looks at the universe below. It is only at the end, when he is finally on the island, that the two realities merge as the airplane comes down. Very much the same happens in **"End of the Game."** Ariel, every time he rides the train, sees through the window Letitia and the other girls wearing costumes and pretending to be statues. It is one of the girls, from her "static" point of view, who tells the story. And yet, despite the different narrative perspective here, the outcome of the plot is similar to that of **"Island at Noon"**; Ariel's discovery through the train window of a fascinating new universe prompts him to get off one day and meet the girls, entering, thus, into that foreign reality, or, rather, causing the two realities to intersect.

Although there is, again, a disconcerting conclusion to the plot in **"Island at Noon"**—disconcerting because we cannot rationally explain the disappearance of the vacationer unless we accept in simple terms that both men unite in the body of the steward or that the man on the island never existed and was nothing more than a dream—we could assume that one of the two selves who compose the steward—or his spirit in search of a more natural and pure life—symbolically survives to thrive in the island. Nevertheless, had the vacationer, in fact, remained alive, most probably he would not have stayed there permanently. No matter how much he rejected civilization, he was part of it, and only a dream or an illusion could have permitted him to belong in such an alien world as that of the fishermen.[5] In a similar manner, in **"End of the Game,"** Ariel must abandon the *precarious* paradise he has found where the unspoiled girls play; he does so after getting a mysterious letter from Letitia, the one he has fallen in love with. Letitia does not show up on this occasion so that Ariel would not discover that she is partially paralyzed.

At this point, it becomes evident that in all these stories, the merging of two different realities always has catastrophic consequences, as if one could only be safer (or happier) in one's own "here and now." Ariel brings destruction to the girls, and to Letitia in particular, in many ways. It is because of his intrusion that the game ends, never to be played again. He, like the spider that may appear in one's shoe, as the narrator says in **"Blow Up"**—the spider symbolizing Nichel's interfering with the seduction that was bound to happen had he not meddled in the affair—, comes to disrupt the daily routine of the girls' life which consists of playing their make-believe scenes for those who passed by on the train.

Ariel, furthermore, by announcing his visit, creates a crisis that disturbs the girls' reality. Because Letitia is partially paralyzed, she makes the best statues of the three. But how could she face Ariel and reveal the truth? The love he felt for her at first sight would be destroyed were he to see her as she really is. The irony of it all, Cortázar seems to imply, is that the girl chosen by Ariel was the only one who could not satisfy the young man's expectations. And more cruel still is the fact that the train that transported Ariel was, perhaps, the only gift which life had to offer to Letitia. The train, obviously, functions as a symbol: it is happiness passing Letitia by, leaving her behind. Letitia would appear only once more before the eyes of Ariel, in an elaborate disguise prepared by the other girls, giving her most accomplished performance ever, which turns out to be the end of the game.

One must bear in mind that **"The Night Face Up,"** **"A Yellow Flower,"** and **"Island at Noon,"** conclude with a far more catastrophic event than the one just examined, i.e. the death of at least one of the complementary selves which, consequently, abolishes one of the two existential realities (or perhaps even both of them, as it has been suggested above).

"Continuity of Parks" follows the same pattern. Once more it is through a window that two similar situations are connected. The man reading the novel in his study, which has windows overlooking a wooded park, reads of a pair of lovers who, beyond the great windows, are plotting to kill the woman's husband. The murderer enters the study of the man who is reading—supposedly coinciding with the latter's reading of the same occurrence in the plot of the novel—knife in hand, and the assassination is about to take place near "the light from the great windows" (65). This last detail disquietingly links the "true" world to the fictional one, and the reader of the novel with "the other" about whom he has been reading, for both, it is assumed, will be simultaneously killed.

"Blow Up" is probably the most complex of the stories that deal with different levels of reality and the fragmentation of the main character's identity. This is because, in addition to Cortázar's frequent dichotomies, he adds one more distinction between the two realities he now introduces: one represents good, the other evil. The clear-cut, well-defined sides of the protagonist are not so evident in **"Blow Up,"** except for the fact that one can see him as a photographer and as a writer. At the beginning, however, the main character (and narrator) points to a multiplicity of *alter egos*, giving the story at the same time ambiguity and objectivity:

> It'll never be known how this has to be told, in the first person or in the second, using the third person plural or continually inventing modes that will serve for nothing.
>
> (114)

Further on he adds: "One of us all has to write if this is going to get told" (115). The protagonist, as one of his several hypostases, will tell the story. Throughout the first part of the narrative, the character refers to himself as someone "who is dead" and at the same time, "who is alive," introducing, thus, two more *forms* of this multiple and yet individual being.

Julio Matas has clearly defined how the core of the story is the struggle between good and evil. Matas writes:

> When Michel imagines the details of what awaits the boy, he concludes: "the awakening in hell." This "angel with mussed hair" who has fled, vanishing *like a gossamer filament of angel-spittle,* to be substituted by "devil-spit," also seems to him "the perfect victim who aids in bringing about his catastrophe," condemned, in Michel's present view, to "wake up in hell." The insistent opposition between the angelic and the diabolic in the narrative's choice of expressions, a rhetoric deliberately pseudotheological, reveals once more the archetypal dichotomy of Good and Evil as perceived by Cortázar.[6]

As in **"The Night Face Up,"** there is one distinct moment in which the two realities are brought together, joined as a couple of Siamese twins, or the two faces of Janus. It is at that instant that he clicks his camera, capturing another dimension, a metareality. Normally—and Cortázar is very explicit in the commentary which we quote below—a photographer kills life, freezes it, unless, like a skillful magician, he chooses the "essential imperceptible fraction" of time that captures life, as Michel, the photographer-writer, does. We read:

> I raised the camera, pretended to study a focus which did not include them, and waited and watched closely, sure that I would finally catch the revealing expression, one that would sum it all up, life that is rhythmed by movement but which a stiff image destroys, taking time in cross sections if we do not choose the essential imperceptible fraction of it. I did not have to wait long.
>
> (123)

From that moment on his camera is, literally, impregnated by the scene captured; it is carrying a life within. That life becomes apparent to Michel once he enlarges the photograph. Now he has access to both realities, inside and outside the picture, or, stated in other terms, he can cross the threshold leading to "the other side." He can actually pass from his room into the living picture in the fashion of Alice walking through the looking-glass. And the enlarged photo, a rectangle on the wall, serves the same function as the many windows we have seen. The catastrophe has also taken place. Michel remains in the prison he has found in his studio; the "other reality" is even worse. The char-

acter admits to be dead (and paradoxically, alive), and his sacrifice—for the purpose of saving the boy from corruption—will amount to a failure. Cortázar suggests that the paradise of "goodness" which Michel, through his intercession, has created for the child, will not last:

> For the second time he'd escaped them, for the second time I was helping him to escape, returning him to his precarious paradise.
>
> (130-131)

The texts presented here show how "self" and "other" coexist, problematically, in different realities. In some of Cortázar's stories, the unfolding of diverse shapes of the same entity sets off a malevolent destiny that rules man to failure, or worse, to his own death. This is a rather pessimistic vision of man, for a number of Cortázar's characters seem doomed to get involved, to fight, to try to conquer chaos, or the dark forces of the universe, only to realize that they have failed because they do not constitute a center of harmony, but—in Jungian terms—they are torn by the opposite drives of and shadow, a primary source of universal disruption.

Notes

1. M. L. von Franz, "The Process of Individuation," in *Man and his Symbols* (New York: Dell, 1974), 174.

2. We have used English translations from the Spanish by Paul Blackburn for all of Cortázar's stories (*End of the Game and Other Stories* [New York: Harper & Row, 1978]), except for "Island at Noon," translated by Suzanne Jill Levine (Anne Fremantle, editor, *Latin American Literature Today* [New York: New American Library, 1977], 94-100).

3. The original Spanish of the quotes we have translated to assist the English reader is provided here in notes 4 and 6.

> Es él el que mira a través de un cristal, el que desea pasar al otro lado, pero es también, en el cuento, el que es capaz de salir realmente fuera del tiempo, de instalarse en un tiempo mítico, en una isla eterna y sin devenir que depara la única forma posible de felicidad al rescatar al hombre de la duración y la corrosión.

(Graciela de Sola, *Julio Cortázar y el hombre nuevo* [Buenos Aires: Editorial Sudamericana, 1968], 67-68).

4. Si buscamos uan explicación, el "qué" de lo que ocurre en la relación de Marini con su isla puede interpretarse como un caso de premonición (Marina anticipa tanto su visita a la isla como el accidente en que muere, todo ello mientras mira

por la ventanilla del avión), o como una serie de imágenes que ocurren en el momento mismo de la caída del avión (en uan superposición del tiempo cronológico y la pura duración experimentada por su conciendia), o, en rinde mejores resultados— como un ejemplo más de la realización, simultánea o no, de las distintas posibilidades que coexisten, como vidas susceptibles de ser realizadas, dentro e una misma persona. (David Lagmanovich, "Acotación a 'La isla a mediodía.'" *Revista Iberoamericana,* vol. 39, numbers 84-85/643)

5. The dichotomy between civilized and primitive worlds is here a variation of that presented in "The Night Face Up." We know that the reality of the "Motec" Indian is the dreamed one—it is unlikely that the Indian could dream in so much detail about a way of life that would not exist for centuries. Equating both stories one would have to see the steward's visit to the island as a dream, and his death as the most likely probability. But the complex narrative construction leaves doors open to several conclusions.

6. Cuando Michel imagina los pormenores de lo que aguarda al muchacho, concluye así: . . . "el despertar en el infierno." Este "ángel despeinado," que ha huido antes perdiéndose *como un hilo de la Virgen* para ser sustituido por "Las babas del diablo," le parece también "la perfecta victima qye ayuda a la catástrofe," condenado según lo ve ahora, a "despertar en el infierno." Esta frecuente oposición de lo angélico y lo diabólico y lo diabólico en los giros verbales escogidos, intencionado juego pseudoteológico, revela una vez más la estrica dicotomía del Bien y del Mal como la siente, arquetípicamente, Cortázar. (Julio Matas, "Lección moral de Cortázar," *La cuestión del género literario* [Madrid: Gredos, 1979], 149).

Gordana Yovanovich (essay date fall 1990)

SOURCE: Yovanovich, Gordana. "Character Development and the Short Story: Julio Cortázar's 'Return Trip Tango.'" *Studies in Short Fiction* 27, no. 4 (fall 1990): 545-52.

[*In the following essay, Yovanovich treats the importance of the reader as a character in "Return Trip Tango."*]

To make characters believable and interesting within the narrow compass of a short story is perhaps the most challenging problem afforded by the genre.
—Valerie Shaw

A study of characters in a short story, and especially in a story of the twentieth century, is unusual. The analysis that follows is not an enumeration of charac-ter traits, nor is it a study of character development in time; the article focuses on a specific relationship between the reader and the character—the reader being the most important character, an alive amalgamation of characters in the story.

Cortázar's **"Return Trip Tango"** is easy to read but very difficult to understand. If we attempt to interpret the story only on the basis of probability we discover a number of forking paths and the unity of the story escapes us. However, we must search for unity if we are to understand the story. Seymour Chatman says: "I must simply respect my need for a coherence, however sketchy, and follow its promptings. Afterwards, perhaps, I can enjoy the space-ship ride among Barthes' galaxy of signifiers. For the moment simple coherence is my imperative" (27). If we must look for coherence, a theoretical discussion on the question of character from Julio Cortázar's novel *Hopscotch* may provide us with a clue. Wong, one of the characters of *Hopscotch,* summarizes Morelli's (and Cortázar's) specific concern:

> The novel that interests us is not one that places characters in a situation, but rather one that puts the situation in the characters. By means of this the latter ceases to be character and becomes people.
>
> (478)

Analogously, on a higher level, if we place Cortázar's story (situation) in our own experience, the reader's experience, we discover that the characters of **"Return Trip Tango"** are embodiments of that experience. The characters then become alive through us, the reader, and the story becomes meaningful because it is a reflection of our reality.

According to Mary Louise Pratt, we always read a short story in the context of something bigger: "facts about the novel are necessary to explain facts about the short story" (180) she says. In other words, the short story exceeds its written discourse, at least in the reading practice of it. The story a reader of the short story reconstructs on the basis of the discourse written by the author is much larger than the written text. Similarly, the characters in the story are much more developed than in the discourse. They grow into the reader through whom they become alive. The relationship between the characters and the reader in Cortázar's short story is not, however, a simple question of identification.

Cortázar explains that in his fiction he searches for "another order, more secret and less communicable" (27). He captures a moment, or a single character, but, through the reader "flings open a much wider reality" (28) not so much through the novelistic literary tradition, as Pratt says, but through a specific relationship of his characters and the reader. Let us examine Cortázar's short story. The text of **"Return Trip Tango"** deals with some highly improbable situations, but in the most usual language and style. The language, style and above all the emphasis on details from everyday life draw the reader into the story and make him or her believe that the story actually took place. We know that Matilde did not really kill Milo, that with the help of friends and bribes she has only had him declared dead in Argentina (a country famous for its *desaparecidos*). Because of this, she could have been living in fear that the truth may be uncovered, and when Simón waits for Flora in front of her window, Matilde in panic confuses him with Milo. Furthermore, Flora and Simón's social position is probably similar to Matilde and Milo's: most likely, Matilde was a servant herself. She has to conceal her past in order that her husband maintain his social status "because Germán wasn't a man to accept anything else, Germán and his career, his colleagues and his club and his parents" (64). Now bored and reminded of Milo by Simón, out of fear and frustration, Matilde confuses fantasy and reality. Therefore, when she believes that Simón-Milo is making love to Flora, out of jealousy or mere frustration, Matilde mistakenly murders Simón and kills herself, leaving Flora free to meet the narrator who works in a hospital and who obviously becomes very close to Flora and her "little breasts that in the end would be more in life for her than any feather duster or good manners" (61)—as Matilde's breasts were a road to wealth for her.

The similarity between Flora's and the narrator's situation to that of Matilde, Milo and Germán suggests further interpretation. Together with other apparently incongruous elements in the short story, the similarity leads the reader to look for, as Cortázar says, "another order, more secret and less communicable." In order to make sense of the story we must, as in metaphoric texts, synthesize the two simultaneously similar and different levels on a third level. The point of departure in our interpretation is the familiar that we develop further in the memory of our own experience.

In her book *The Short Story: A Critical Introduction*, Valerie Shaw points out that Anton Chekhov's greatness as a story teller stems directly from his concern with characters. She says further that "Chekhov's ability to convey simultaneously the inner reality and the typicality of characters like Olga in 'The Butterfly' (1894) and 'Ariadne' (1895) has never been surpassed" (20). In his short story **"Return Trip Tango,"** Cortázar, like Chekhov, not only emphasizes the human aspect of the story, but conveys simultaneously the typicality of his characters and their inner reality. Typical elements and incidents are essential for the ex-

perience and the understanding of the particular; the typical is the link between the character and the reader. The reader has to identify with the character first in order to be able to follow him into his particular fictional world.

The main character of **"Return Trip Tango,"** Matilde, is a typical upper-middle class woman, married to a businessman but knowing nothing about his work. While her husband is away she meets with her girlfriends, goes to the movies, talks on the telephone and paints her nails. Most of the story describes meals, telephone calls, conversations about shopping, etc. The language used in the story is everyday language and the story is written in a manner that suggests direct speech rather than narrative. In other words, a typical woman, in a typical situation is described in everyday (typical) language and style.

Beyond the apparent reality and developing out of it, there is another, deeper, inner reality. The typicality of the situation reminds the reader of his behavior in situations similar to those Matilde is in, and allows him to intuit Matilde's relationship with Milo and interpret this story. Milo appears at a moment when Matilde is sitting at the window, her husband away: "Matilde was bored without the car" (63). We are told that she misses the car more than her husband, who is always away on business trips "and she didn't understand those business matters" (63). On another occasion, we are told, casually, that Matilde married her husband, Germán, because he was rich and had a respectable family name. Page 66 is a reflection of what goes on around Matilde and through her mind at a moment in time: Flora, the servant, is complaining that Matilde's spoiled son Carlitos refuses to take a bath, Matilde debates whether or not to call her friend Perla (because she does not wish to go out with Perla) and she recalls "the Recanatis' mother," obviously a gossiper, who has never accepted Matilde as Germán's wife. We are also indirectly told that Germán is not a good and warm person because he puts his son to bed downstairs, in a room close to the living room (he cannot stand Carlitos crying in the morning). Flora and Matilde do not eat together because "Carlitos would have told Germán and Germán the discourse and respect" (72).

Reading about the situation Matilde is in, the reader begins to desire an escape. How? By remembering more interesting situations and sympathetic people. It is logical that at this point Matilde sees Milo under her window; her recollection of a happier relationship with her boyfriend allows her to escape her unhappy relationship with her husband. Matilde's memory, nonetheless, is not presented as a subjective experience separate from her surrounding; the dividing line between the subjective and objective world is erased. When Matilde sees Milo, who probably is Flora's boyfriend, Simón, the narrator describes Matilde's supper in great detail, giving the situation the most natural tone, as if nothing unusual is taking place:

> She threw the mushrooms out the window while Flora prepared the tray with the dessert, she heard her coming up with that rhythm like a sleigh or a runaway colt that Flora has when she came up the stairs, told her that the mushrooms were delicious, praised the color of the pumpkin dessert, asked for a double cup of strong coffee, and for her to bring her up another pack of cigarettes from the living room. It's hot tonight, Miss Matilde, we'll have to leave the windows open wide.
>
> (72)

The scene develops in front of the reader's eyes as if he were watching it on television. The narrator does not interrupt the scene with comments, such as "he said," "she said." The emphasis on detail around Matilde gives the impression that something is actually happening to her and the reader is able to watch it with her. At the same time, however, the reader has been told that the story is mostly a subjective experience, imagined by the narrator. The narrator tells us at the outset: "The day came when it would have been impossible for me to distinguish between what Flora was telling me and what she and I myself had been putting together" (62). When he describes Milo he says, "there was nothing of the ghost about him" (85). In other words, while Milo is imagined, he is perceived as real because "when I write," the narrator tells us, "I see what I'm writing, I really see it, I'm seeing Emilio Díaz" (62). Similarly, the characters see what they imagine, and the reader experiences the text as if the story is actually taking place. In the scene in which Milo is supposed to have entered the house:

> She (Matilde) didn't hear the street door open but it didn't matter, it was absolutely clear that the main door was being opened or was going to be opened and nothing could be done, she couldn't go out.
>
> (73)

It is possible that nothing actually does take place outside the narrator's and the character's mind. Even though the story appears real it differs from a realistic story. We are told that Matilde "killed" her first husband Milo in Mexico before she fled to Buenos Aires and married Germán. The word "kill," however, is used figuratively because Matilde only had him declared dead. Therefore, the reader must pay attention not only to the literal but to the figurative meaning of words. And since there are not enough explicit reasons for Matilde to kill Milo again or to commit suicide, and since the story does not emphasize that the man under Matilde's window is, in fact, Milo, the reader concludes that Matilde kills Milo and herself only in the figurative sense of the word.

The story is not a nineteenth-century Realistic story but one that reflects a new, subjective realism. Cortázar does not use the words "kill" and "murder" in the same way we normally use them nor are they used symbolically because they do not point to another, independent reality. Cortázar often complained about the limitations of language and the need for a new tool of communication. He stretches the meaning of words here and suggests that Matilde does not actually kill Milo at the end of the story but that she has an imagined sexual relationship with him. At the critical moment the emphasis falls not on her reasons for killing Milo but on her search for a novel that contains her fate. There is no way out for Matilde: she is trapped in the situation. The only thing left for her are dreams and desires. Therefore, "She pulled off the clothing that clung to her body; naked, she rolled onto her side on the bed and looked for the bottle of pills" (74). What follows is a detailed description of the moment when Simón takes Flora's virginity. The conversation between Flora and Simón is not written in the form of dialogue but as one long sentence forming part of the main text. It leads us to believe that the dialogue is imagined by Matilde and that it belongs with all the fantasies that pass through her head:

> She was sure that the door had opened downstairs, that Milo had come into the house, into Flora's room, was probably talking to Flora or had already begun to undress her, because for Flora that had to be the only reason Milo was there, gaining access to her room in order to undress her and undress himself, kissing her, let me, let me stroke you like this, and Flora resisting and not today, Simón, I'm afraid, let me, but Simón in no hurry, little by little he'd laid her crosswise on the bed and was kissing her hair, looking for her breasts under her blouse, resting a leg on her thighs and taking off her shoes as if playing, talking into her ear and kissing her closer and closer to her mouth, I want you, my love, let me undress you, let me see you, you're so beautiful, moving away the lamp and unwrapping her in shadows and caresses, Flora giving in with a first whimper, the fear that something will be heard upstairs, that Miss Matilde or Carlitos, but no, speak low, leave me like this now, the clothes falling just anywhere, the tongues finding each other, the moans, Simón, please don't hurt me, it's the first time, Simón, I know, stay just like that, be quiet now, don't cry out, don't cry out.
>
> (75)

The sentence starts as a speculation: "[the visitor] was probably talking to Flora or had already begun to undress her" but ends as if the seduction is actually taking place: "Flora giving in with a first whimper, the fear that something will be heard upstairs, that Miss Matilde or Carlitos, but no." The incident is imagined and takes place at the same time. This contradiction leads the reader to the following interpretation. Left alone at home, trapped in a marriage without warmth and understanding, perhaps sexually frustrated, Matilde remembers when she lost her virginity to Milo. Simón and Flora are only objective correlatives of Matilde's desires and memories, and the author's device to present Matilde's emotions realistically, in an illustrative, not abstract way. The scene with two naked bodies, Matilde's and Milo's, with a knife stuck in Milo's body produces an erotic image analogous to Simón's forceful piercing of Flora's hymen, a scene described only a moment earlier. Hence the conclusion that Matilde does not actually kill Milo but imagines a sexual relationship with him. The word "kill" acquires the poetic meaning "to make love," "to have an orgasm." Had the author presented Matilde's memory only as memory the story would have lacked intensity because it would not show simultaneously Matilde's external and internal life; more importantly, it would not allow the reader to share the experience with the character and to be as confused as is the sexually frustrated Matilde.

A distinguished Italian writer, Alberto Moravia, says that "characters in short stories are the product of lyrical intuition" (150). This is certainly true of the characters in Cortázar's **"Return Trip Tango."** The text is written as it develops in the narrator's and the reader's mind, which is why the present progressive tense is used in the opening sentence: "One goes along recounting things ever so slowly" (60). What we see, however, is not lyrical emotions but a succession of objective correlatives of the character's/narrator's/reader's feelings, as if the brain were replaying a movie. The relationship between the text and the reader, the surface and the deeper structure of the story, is based on intuition. The text describes typical scenes that in everyday language stimulate the reader's memories and his intuitive (emotional) internal world. Speaking about the nature of the short story in general, Mary Rohrberger says:

> The short story derives from the romantic tradition. The metaphysical view that there is more to the world than that which can be apprehended through the senses provides the rationale for the structure of the short story which is a vehicle for the author's probing of the nature of the real. As in the metaphysical view, reality lies beyond the ordinary world of appearances, so in the short story, meaning lies beneath the surface of the narrative. The framework of the narrative embodies symbols which function to question the world of appearances and to point to a reality beyond the facts of the extensional world.
>
> (81)

Mary Rohrberger is right when she says that "in short stories, meaning lies beneath the surface of the narrative." When Milo appears under Matilde's window, given the situation she lives in, we suspect what she

may do from our own experiences of boredom and dissatisfaction: we remember or imagine our happier moments. This also explains the narrator's obsession at the beginning of the story: he makes Flora tell him what had happened again and again and makes her story his as he probably is not sure of his own position with Flora. Is she with him, as Matilde was with Germán, only because of his position and money? Does she cry each time she tells him the story because she pities Matilde's fate or because she misses Simón? Other readers may see other reasons for suspicion and insecurity.

Thematically, Cortázar's **"Return Trip Tango"** is very similar to Jorge Luis Borges's "The Circular Ruins." In Borges's story, a dreamer dreams a new person to find out that he too is a product of someone's creative imagination. In **"Return Trip Tango,"** Matilde imagines that Milo comes back. She dreams that he visits Flora and comes up to her room where she kills him. In turn, Flora, we are told at the beginning, takes Matilde's story and together with the narrator integrates it into her own context. What at the beginning is someone else's story becomes the narrator's story because he sees himself at the end calling an ambulance. On a higher level, the narrator and Flora's story, **"Return Trip Tango,"** is interpolated into the reader's context on the basis of his reading experience. Cortázar knows at the outset that his reader, like the narrator, will make the story his reality as he fills in the gaps. Therefore he teasingly mentions "that baroque necessity of the intelligence that leads it to fill every hollow" (61).

Despite the shortness of the genre, and the lyrical nature of characters, through his active participation the reader has a relationship with characters of **"Return Trip Tango"** as if they actually were real people. In fact, the story has unity and meaning only when the reader intuits a part of himself in the story. In his essay, "Some Aspects of the Short Story," Cortázar says that "Every enduring story is like the seed in which the giant tree lies sleeping. That tree will grow in us, will cast its shadows across our memory" (3). **"Return Trip Tango"** does exactly this: its typical character in a typical situation awakens reality in us and through the typical makes the reader conscious of his individual reality (interpretation) which is analogous to the character's reality. This relationship between the reader and the character allows the characters of the short story to be as developed as the characters of the novel may be.

Works Cited

Chatman, Seymour. "The Rhetoric of Difficult Fiction: Cortázar's 'Blow-up.'" *Poetics Today* 1: 4 (1980): 23-57.

Cortázar, Julio. *Hopscotch.* Trans. Gregory Rabassa. New York: Pantheon, 1966.

————. "Return Trip Tango." *We Love Glenda So Much and A Change of Light.* Trans. Gregory Rabassa. New York: Vintage, 1984: 60-81.

————. "Some Aspects of the Short Story." *The Review of Contemporary Fiction* 3 (1983): 27-34.

Moravia, Alberto. "The Short Story and the Novel." *Short Story Theories.* Ed. Charles E. May. [Athens]: Ohio UP, 1976: 147-52.

Pratt, Mary Louise. "The Short Story: The Long and The Short of It." *Poetics* 10 (1981): 175-94.

Rohrberger, Mary. "The Short Story: A Proposed Definition." *Short Story Theories.* Ed. Charles E. May. [Athens]: Ohio UP, 1976: 80-83.

Shaw, Valerie. *The Short Story: A Critical Introduction.* New York: Longman, 1983.

Julia Cruz (essay date 1990)

SOURCE: Cruz, Julia. "Todorov's Pure Fantastic in a Story by Julio Cortazar." In *The Shape of the Fantastic: Selected Essays from the Seventh International Conference on the Fantastic in the Arts,* edited by Olena H. Saciuk, pp. 75-83. New York: Greenwood Press, 1990.

[*In the following essay, Cruz analyzes the fantastical elements in "The Island at Noon" according to the critical tenets established by philosopher and literary theorist Tzvetan Todorov.*]

"The Island at Noon" ("La isla a mediodia"), a short story by Julio Cortazar, was published in 1966 as part of ***All Fires the Fire*** (***Todos los fuegos el fuego***). This is one of the most representative stories of what has been called the "pure Fantastic" genre (Todorov). This story is well populated by doppelgängers and elements of duality that provide the story's main themes.

The story's plot is rendered according to the structure described by Tzvetan Todorov as the required one for the true pure fantastic story: from the very beginning of the story, the order of our real world is established by the description in Cortazar's story of a typical day for Marini, an airline steward, work routine and all. His job routine consists of the required amiability toward the passengers, including flirting with the foreign lady passengers, as well as his regular steward duties.

His plane's route is Rome-Tehran. What seems to break the monotony of his routine is a small Greek island (Xiros) which catches the protagonist Marini's eye.

That island, unknown to him, stirs his curiosity and in the process becomes part of his daydreams. He starts making vacation plans to go to that island, which he soon identifies as Xiros. Since his relationships with women seem to be superficial in nature, his main source of interest becomes more and more his trip to Xiros.

It becomes an obsession. Practically from one moment to the next, he arrives at Xiros and, almost immediately, he decides to move there for good and start a new life. On his way to the beach, just before noon, he meets Klaios's son. Klaios is the patriarch of the island's only hamlet. They go swimming. Although neither Marini nor Klaios's son, Ionas, speaks the other's language, some communication in the form of gestures and smiles is established.

On his way back, after having said goodbye to Ionas, Marini suddenly hears a motor. It is now noon and, according to his normal schedule, "his" plane is flying overhead. He tries to evade the memories of his useless and routine-oriented life which he had decided to leave behind, but this is just not possible. He hears the jet's turbine engines falter and then watches as the plane plummets to the sea nearby. It appears that there is one lone survivor. He tries to save him and reaching the beach with him in tow, Marini notices that his efforts were in vain. The man has a fatal wound in his throat and dies.

Klaios and his sons come running to the beach but they find only a corpse. Klaios looks toward the sea for any survivors. There are none. Between them and the sea, there is nothing "new" save the dead body. They are alone as before.

The protagonist Marini wanted to escape from his routine-oriented and meaningless existence by way of his daydreams. The Greek island over which the plane regularly flew attracted him from the very first moment he spotted it. His first glance at it did not provide very much detail except for the impression that it looked like a turtle climbing out of the sea. The island even looked as if it were deserted, except for a grey spot.

Each time the plane flies over that island, Marini drops everything in order that he may focus his attention on it. On one occasion he tries to photograph it but the picture is "blurred." The thought of the island and the possibility of going there on his vacation is so tantalizing that he starts living just for the moment his dream will come true. The island of Xiros becomes an ideal.

The "grey spot" soon becomes a few scattered houses. It is just as he had imagined it. The hamlet represents to him a different sort of life: the quiet village on a scarcely inhabited island, away from Marini's harried yet routine existence. It is also interesting to note the image's neutral color, grayish. Neutral colors indicate ambiguity. The image is undefined, that is, the "grayish spot" suggests another way of life, another reality.

Xiros, with its simple life-style, offers Marini a better life from his point of view. The aspiration to find a way to give meaning and sense to his life finally seems within his reach. His vacation is the break from the overwhelming routine.

The noon hour is an important element because within the context of a clock's time and the day's cycle, it divides the day in two; the morning as the past and the afternoon as the future of that very moment, the noon hour. It is also the point in time when the plane flies over the island, which is Marini's illusion of the non-routine. That is why the protagonist interrupts his routine by neglecting his duties and giving Xiros his undivided attention. The noon hour breaks with time (just as midnight does). It is the zero hour; the hour of transition of one order into another. The clock reinitiates its cyclic path of twelve hours. The new cyclic order could be interpreted as a new order of life. The detailed view of the island makes it more real and enhances his daydreams even better.

Marini's mental idealization plus the blurred photograph that he took of Xiros foreshadow the reality Marini is bestowing on the island. It is the idea of the island, an image of the other, that which is the different and unknown as opposed to our overfamiliar reality. With regard to the noon hour's description as zero and its function of dividing two orders of time, the idea of timelessness is projected. The noon hour in the literary text is the moment when Marini is physically spaceless. While flying over Xiros, Marini is "suspended" in space; he is on a plane. He is in the air between heaven and earth, halfway on the clock's path and on the horizontal path between Rome and Tehran.

The more the island is visually discerned, the more real it becomes. By opposition, the more Marini's daydreams are transformed into his conscious reality, the more his routine chores are neglected by him. Even his superficial relationships with other people fall by the wayside: "He was unaware about the day of the week; sometimes it was Tania in Beirut, sometimes Phyllis in Tehran, almost always his younger brother in Rome, everything seemed blurred and facile and stupid" (122). The blurring, of course, suggests the lack of reality which his "normal" life, his daily routine, is acquiring.

One day, flying over Xiros, Marini notices a black dot which he suspects must be a fisherman, and Marini decides that he can no longer postpone his trip to Xiros. From the moment of this decision, Marini starts making concrete plans: how to fund his trip; how he will be there in three days.

The language, through the very tenses, inserts the element of the uncanny within the action of the story in the following manner. In an ambiguous present, defined as such by the noon hour and Marini's physical presence on the plane at midflight, the protagonist's reality loses its significance because his "look" is directed, not at his immediate reality which is his airline steward duties and the passengers around him on the airplane, but rather, at the island—the island which, for Marini, at that moment of his decision, signifies a possible future. Through the use of the conditional verb tense, the daydream acquires its potentiality, that is, the possibility of being made "real." Projecting himself in his imagination toward that very near realization of his daydreams, Marini sees himself already in Xiros.

Immediately, the story narration is transformed from the conditional to the abstract and impersonal of the gerund which bears the stamp of timelessness—the suspension of defined time and, therefore, the conjugated verb tense. The noon hour is represented thus on the semantic level and on that of the action. The phrases expressed in the conditional tense are followed immediately by the timelessness of the impersonal anacoluthon: "Once decided, nothing was difficult; a night time, the first boat, another old and dirty boat, the stopover at Rynos, the endless bargaining with the felucca's captain, the night on the deck, close to the stars, the taste of anise and lamb, dawn among the islands" (123).

In the linguistic transition between the verb tenses indicated above, the transmutation of time and space on the level of the action was effected. This is the unexplainable, the irrational. However, the problem of time and space might still have a rational explanation, as the story has not ended at this point.

Marini is happy in his new environment. Xiros has not disappointed him. The protagonist makes friends right away with Klaios the patriarch and his sons. He settles in his room quickly and then goes to the beach. The clock's hands have begun to mark time. There is a definite present; it is now ten o'clock in the morning and Marini is aware of it. There is a specific location: Marini's physical presence on the island of Xiros.

Here the narration holds an element of foreshadowing. "He knew without a shadow of a doubt that he would not leave the island, that somehow he would remain on the island forever" (124).

However, this element of foreshadowing has a double function. On the one hand, the foreshadowing creates the illusion that Marini has finally found his authenticity in the life he has chosen on Xiros. On the other hand, it hints at the true outcome; it foreshadows Marini's fate. The phrase "somehow he would remain on the island forever" points to his appointment with death at the end of the story.

In the following sentence, there is another element of foreshadowing also with a dual function. What is suggested here is manifested more discreetly: "He went down to the houses where two women looked at him fearfully before running away to hide behind their closed doors" (124). The first impression is that to these women Marini represents the alien or other; thus his presence is to be interpreted as a kind of violation of the hamlet's established order. But this scene also suggests the supernatural quality of the protagonist's figure. At the same time, the text gives evidence of Marini's physically real presence on the island.

At eleven o'clock, concrete time indicated by the text in Marini's awareness, he is with Ionas and they go into the sea for a swim. Marini, again, to himself, starts to make plans to stay to live on Xiros among these people. This is still another element of foreshadowing that tries to convey the idea of permanence to the new life Marini has found there. The activities that Ionas and Marini share imply the motion of time toward the noon hour.

Upon his return alone, the image of the "grey spot" reappears once more in the narration. The first time, the "grey spot" was presented from the top view, from the airplane as he looks down on it and imagines himself climbing to the top of it. This image reflects Marini's hopeful view with regard to his trip to Xiros. The repetition of this image is described from a closer view, the reality of tangible Nature and the senses. Paradoxically, it suggests a fantastic relationship: the fusion of the visible in the herbs with the invisible of the heat, the breeze, the scent by means of the senses.

The narration insists on sustaining, on the level of the action and that of represented reality, an awareness of time: "Marini looked at his watch and then, with an impatient gesture, tore it from his wrist and put it in his swimming trunks pocket. No, it would not be easy to do away with the old man" (125). The watch's image inevitably points to the idea of time in motion, moving toward the noon hour. But Marini's act of removing his watch suggests his wish to annul time. Doing away with the "old man" means leaving his former life behind, forgotten. Upon disposing of the watch, he symbolically forsakes his past, the harried and boring life of contemporary civilization. To do away with the "old man" is to become free of him in order to start a new life, one in communion with Nature and his neighbor, and thus be "another," the "new man." The past like the morning is already behind Marini.

Suddenly, the protagonist hears the engine of the plane. He rebels against his memories, which the noise stirs in him. It is "his" plane's engine that is meeting its schedule on flying over Xiros at noon. He shuts his eyes to eradicate the images from his past which the plane's presence is causing. He cannot erase them. The plane's presence is too strong a link between his present reality and that of his past. He views his previous reality of the daily routine as "the worst in me."

With this last phrase, the existence of another "I" in Marini is proposed. The present Marini on the island would be "the best" in the protagonist. This underscores a duality in Marini's character. It might be the duplication of the fantastic double or the accepted duality that is recognized in the human condition of good and evil in everyone.

From the repetition in the story narration, time in Marini's island reality has arrived at the noon hour. The plane's schedule with regard to Xiros shows that it must fly over it at that particular moment. That schedule belonged to Marini's airline steward's past reality. By being on time, the plane's presence establishes the noon hour, placing it within the context of the world outside of the island's own, that is, outside the world of the ideal. This means that the times of both the real and the ideal worlds have converged, fusing into one.

If, upon fleeing his routine-oriented existence of reality, Marini managed to jump into his daydream reality, the ideal in the future, and thus make a past from it, then one can admit to a possible duplication of time. By this, we mean a reverse process—and this would have to be qualified as a fusion of times, since the plane's time and that of the island have become one, the noon hour.

With the fusion of time, another type of fusion becomes plausible within the narration, which the "change in the sound of the turbine engine, the almost vertical fall into the sea" (126) cause. With the plane's fall into the sea at one hundred meters from Xiros's coast, in the level of action, the two spaces also converge physically, the plane's space with that of the island.

There is another impersonal language phrase that establishes the suspension of time and that now introduces openly the irrational (uncanny) element merely hinted at before this point in the story. If doubt had been simply stirred before, here it makes itself definitely felt: "But nothing more than the soft line of the waves could be seen, an oscillating cardboard box absurdly near the place of the fall and almost at the end, when it was pointless to keep on swimming, a hand out of the water, barely an instant" (126).

The hand out of the water suggests a possible survivor. Marini tries desperately to save that man's life. But it is useless. The survivor dies right before Marini's anguished eyes. His own death is immediately insinuated. "What good could mouth to mouth resuscitation do since with each convulsion the wound seemed to open a bit more and it was just like a repugnant mouth calling out to Marini, dragging him away from his little happiness of so few hours on the island, yelling at him between spurts something *he no longer was able to hear*" (127). This last phrase which I have emphasized suggests Marini's death because if he is "no longer able to hear" what the dying man was saying, it is only because the dead are unable to hear. Besides this, the story's last paragraph hints at it, when Klaios cannot find any other survivors. There is only one corpse. This observation is of great significance because it implies Marini's and his double's death. When Klaios and his sons arrive at the beach, according to the text, there is no one else save the corpse. The text confirms that there is no one alien to the community except for the cadaver. In other words, Marini's and his double's fusion is suggested at the moment of death; that is why there is only one body, one Marini, "the only new thing among them and the sea."

The story has a surprise ending and the reader is left with hesitation and doubt, unable to choose an explanation either natural or supernatural. One contradicts the other.

The first and easiest explanation to eliminate is the realistic one. It is not possible for Marini to be in two places at once. Nor is a jump in time from the present into the future realistically possible in our order of the "normal"; nor from a daydream into its "real-ization" or materialization, just as the suspension of time is inadmissible in our reality.

Nor can Marini's presence on the island be attributed to the mere illusion of a daydream; that is to say, that he was in Xiros only in his imagination, in a daydream, and therefore he was never physically present in Xiros, for there is textual proof that Marini was materially present in Xiros—as there is of just the opposite: that he was never there.

If we try to render a supernatural explanation, the attempt will end in frustration. If, on a supernatural plane, it becomes possible for Marini to have made

the jump in time into the future, with the two Marinis' respective deaths, their corresponding time (Marini of the island's future and Marini of the airplane's present) fuses into one, that is, the two realities, the ideal and the realistic, become one. Klaios and his sons are placed textually and by name within the ideal reality just as they are, in similar manner, placed textually within the fused reality and the final one in the narration. Then, the reader asks himself, how could Marini have known the inhabitants of a reality independent from his fantasy by their true names? Within the context of the daydream it *is* possible to move forward in time and space in order to "create" a subjective reality. However, when such reality entails the material presence of an image that is unknown to the daydreamer, it is impossible to extract real and verifiable data in true reality from a world of fantasy in order to confirm its existence in the real world.

No explanation is possible even after having finished reading the text which leaves us, as we stated before, in doubt before just what *did* happen in **"The Island at Noon."** We are before what Todorov calls the "pure Fantastic."

Two kinds of doubt coincide in **"The Island at Noon."** However, in this case, one of the doubts is related to the uncertainty before the unexplained event in the narration (the transmutation, duplication, and fusion of planes). And this fits perfectly Todorov's concept of the fantastic element. This kind of doubt complies strictly with Todorov's theory. All of this categorizes this story as one of the pure fantastic.

On the other hand, there is also another element of doubt. This one has to do with the narrative mode. **"The Island at Noon"** has a problem related to its omniscient narrator. He is the *only* narrator. The narration contains two possible realities that converge at the story's end. From just such a fusion of realities, the explicit reader is besieged by doubt incited by this fusion of realities. Outside of the text, such a reader asks himself, why two realities and their convergence at the end of the story? We can only guess that the narrative mode of **"The Island at Noon"** is closely related to the author's intent, one that would integrate all in order to create a more complete reality, and one of course a more authentic one. This would be from the perspective of Cortazar, the writer, not from that of Todorov, the theoretician. This explanation is feasible because the material author's intention is extraliterary, like the explicit reader and his doubt.

In summary, the development of the fantastic literature that Cortazar represents today is not satisfied with providing a fantastic effect within the space of the literary text. This effect must now be sustained beyond the reading experience of the text.

"The Island at Noon" contains several literary themes and two metaphysical ones, at the very least. The literary themes are at the service of the metaphysical themes. The ontological themes are the search for an authentic reality, and death.

As we have observed in this story, everything, at the linguistic level, converges on the problem of reality. The story proposes the existence of more than one reality, yet none in its singularity is the one and only solution.

The literary figure of the double is just one of this story's themes. In **"The Island at Noon"** the double represents several relationships of duplication or division, such as those of time, space, the literary character, and reality itself. The reverse process of these literary devices is the fusion of the temporal, spatial, the character, and of the planes of reality which are all present here.

Another distinctive element of **"The Island at Noon"** must be pointed out, too: the metaphysical perspective of contemporary man's condition. The point of view in this story is very much influenced by existentialism à la Camus, Sartre, or Onetti, that is, the anguished point of view.

The theme of death, not infrequent in Cortazar's work, is ever present in **"The Island at Noon."** The protagonist's efforts to go back to becoming a part of man's natural environment end in frustration. The noon hour, that of zero, nothing, indicates every man's inevitable fate: his appointment with death. The noon hour, then, is death's double in this story.

All action in the story leads in the direction of the protagonist's encounter with death. Its presence is felt in the timelessness and spacelessness of the described reality. Death, too, is the impersonal, timeless, and spaceless, or just nothingness. It is an alien experience to all living man. As a great unknown, death is a violation of our established order of life. Once death becomes one with man, the process of death alters his destiny irreversibly and eternally. It is the ultimate and most definite disruption of his life. For Cortazar in this story, death is the end. After encountering it, no possible restoration of order is possible. For this reason, one might state that the point of view of man's fate in **"The Island at Noon"** is a negative one.

Man's routine-oriented and alienated existence even when he is surrounded by other people is the main theme of **"The Island at Noon."**

Because of Julio Cortazar's recurrent themes at the metaphysical level, it is difficult to attempt to give a new, different interpretation to his work. It is at the level of the treatment he gives these themes, and corresponding literary figures, that one notices the variation. The magical sleight-of-hand tricks with the language that Cortazar performs offer a very fertile and broad area for future study.

In conclusion, the role of the fantastic in Cortazar's story upholds Todorov's theoretical model of the pure fantastic. The structure of this story is homologous to that postulated by Todorov as the fantastic structure: 1) The establishment at the beginning of the story of a realistic setting, a world we can readily recognize as our own; 2) the introduction of the fantastic element into that world; and 3) the effect of uncertainty on the reader provoked by the fantastic element which remains unexplained beyond the end of the story. It is precisely this irresolution of the fantastic effect on the reader beyond the text that proves that Cortazar's story is a vindication of Todorov's theory of not just the fantastic in general, but rather specifically of the pure fantastic.

Works Cited

Cortazar, Julio. "La isla a mediodia." *Todos los fuegos el fuego.* Buenos Aires: Sudamericana, 1966. Translation of the story title, "The Island at Noon," the book title, *All Fires the Fire,* and all quotations from same contained in this essay are my own.

Todorov, Tzvetan. *The Fantastic: A Structural Approach to a Literary Genre.* Ithaca: Cornell Univ. Press, 1975.

Richard Callan (essay date November 1991)

SOURCE: Callan, Richard. "Cortázar's Story 'Silvia': The Hero and the Golden Hoard." *Chasqui* 20, no. 2 (November 1991): 46-53.

[*In the following essay, Callan notes the influence of analytical psychologist Carl Jung's notion of the hero archetype in "Silvia."*]

Fernando, the narrator [**"Silvia"**] and Argentine writer-intellectual living in France, is captivated by his visions of the imaginary girl Silvia. In describing himself as an ill-mannered loner who keeps human relationships at a minimum and who thinks his intellectual views are not of great value, he appears to be typical of the successful middle-aged man who has lost spontaneity and feeling due to his absorption with the world and intellect. He needs an energizer, something to restore the spark in life, and throughout history man has often sought rejuvenation from a girl or a young woman.[1] Fernando's strange yet common experience parallels Carl Jung's psychological theory of the hero archetype which depicts an irruption of the neglected unconscious for the purpose of effecting a rebirth of energy and feeling, an archetype treated in Cortázar's first novel, *Los premios* (Callan).[2]

The validity of this theory was clearly acknowledged by Cortázar in conversations with Ernesto González Bermejo when the author initiated six specific references to his works and their relationship to the archetypal concept of Jung. For example, his remarks on **"Casa tomada,"** equally suitable to **"Silvia,"** directly support the value of a psychological analysis: ". . . creo que el interés que tiene la gente con ese cuento tiene que ver, no solamente con el placer literario que pueda producirle, sino con algo que toca sus propias experiencias profundas. Lo que decíamos de Jung y el inconsciente colectivo" (140). Still on the literary significance of Jungian thought, he refers to critiques of his stories made along Freudian and Jungian lines, both of which are fascinating to him, "sobre todo en la línea yungiana que me parece que se adapta mucho más al universo de la creación literaria" (32). In an interview with Evelyn Picón Garfield, he said of his frequent use of labyrinths that they are "uno de mis temas arquetípicos, la rayuela, y allí está Jung para explicarlo probablemente" (*Cortázar por Cortázar* 95).

Perhaps his most enlightening comment on the archetypal unconscious in his stories follows:

> Si algunos se salvan del olvido es porque he sido capaz de recibir y transmitir sin demasiadas pérdidas esas latencias de una psiquis profunda, y el resto es una cierta veteranía para no falsear el misterio, conservarlo lo más cerca posible de su fuente, con su temblor original, su balbuceo arquetípico.
>
> *Ultimo Round* 42

The quotation describes the two essential factors in great writers: they are makers (*poietes*) who put together their art by means of "una cierta veteranía," and seers (*vates*) whose inspiration originates in the hidden forces of the "psiquis profunda." In concluding this introduction on the profoundly psychological vein in the Argentine's works, the words of Picón Garfield on **Bestiario** seem fitting for a study of **"Silvia."** She writes that it is in the dark realm, "created and nurtured by man's imagination and subconscious alone, that Cortázar reveals the complex depths of reality, one that too often ignores the 'nocturnal' side of man's life" (*Julio Cortázar* 29).

The plot opens with Fernando trying to write about Silvia and thereby conjure forth again the phantasm he saw at a cookout given by his only friends, the Mayers. They arranged the party so that his admirer, Jean

Borel, a French professor of Latin American literature, and his wife Liliane could meet him. Another couple, Javier and Magda, were also there together with the couples' children, Graciela, Lolita, Alvaro, and Renaud. During the twilight meal in the tree-lined garden, the children were "playing Indians" with their make-believe older friend Silvia, whom Fernando actually saw. After an evening of intellectual conversation, the narrator invited the group to his house for a cookout the following week. On that occasion he is once more enraptured with the sight of Silvia, this time sleeping in his bedroom. The party ended, it is unlikely that he will see her again because two of the families are leaving the region, and he believes that Silvia is only present in the company of the other children.

The following psychological study is rather technical in nature because of Cortázar's amazingly detailed portrayal of the hero archetype and its effects precisely as Jung describes them. Inasmuch as Fernando's experience and its imagery are archetypal, a literary criticism influenced by Jung can be useful. We think that Cortázar would agree for he attributes reader appeal in some of his stories to "una especie de eco de su subconsciente y, si Jung tiene razón y compartimos un inconsciente colectivo, es bastante lógico que sea así" (Gonzâlez 57).

The psyche consists of masculine consciousness and the feminine unconscious with an equilibrium between them essential to mental health. The balance is achieved by a rapport of consciousness with the affective, instinctual values of the unconscious. Fernando's success through the use of reason, the predominate function of consciousness, has subtly disconnected him from the feminine and its capacity for feeling and human relationships. As Jung says, "nothing endangers this connection more in a man than a successful life; it makes him forget his dependence on the unconscious" (*Symbols of Transformation* 298).

What consciousness depends on is the psychic energy of life originating in the unconscious, also referred to as libido but unlike Freud's restriction of the term to sexual desire, for Jung it includes a range of motivations. The dynamism of libido or psychic energy results from its flow between the psychic opposites. If movement is blocked, the ego seeks renewal at the source by regressing to the unconscious "realm of the mothers," a return which activates positive and negative images of the ambivalent feminine archetype (Jung, *Symbols* 355). In this regression the weakened ego may be tempted to abandon life's struggle and sleep in the mother's embrace, but since the sleep of consciousness is death, the psyche presents this lure as a threat to be overcome.

The dual motivation of desire and fear during the return appears in mythology as hero facing a dragon in order to free a captive maiden or to gain a golden treasure guarded by the monster. Psychologically the mother dragon is the unconscious possessing the treasure or damsel (libido) and only releasing it if the ego-hero holds fast to his diminished consciousness and defeats the beast. Mother-dragon-treasure-damsel are one and the same: the unconscious. Jung's term for the maiden is the anima, "the *archetype of life itself*," and "were it not for the leaping and twinkling of the soul [anima], man would rot away in his greatest passion, idleness" (*The Archetypes and the Collective Unconscious* 32, 27).

Silvia is Fernando's twinkling soul, first appearing against a forest backdrop like a wood nymph, the sylvan form of the anima and appropriately named Silvia (Jung, *Archetypes* 25). With the narrator's arrival at sunset in the Mayer's garden, the scene is prepared for his struggle toward rebirth. The fiery sun is a major mythological example of the ego-hero and his libido "because our source of physical energy and life actually *is* the sun," and like this star sinking into the maternal earth or sea for renewal, so is Fernando's waning energy receding into the unconscious (Jung, *Symbols* 122, 210-213). Fernando employs fire metaphors when he says that "la noche inventó el fuego del asado" whose light first revealed Silvia "entonada en fuego." In the second vision "el fuego fue otra vez fugazmente Silvia," and the third time she appeared her profile was "como encendido por las brasas" (*Ultimo Round* 83, 84, 87). The anima is a flame (libido), and throughout the story Silvia is associated with fire or its color, for example, golden hair and breasts (Jung, *Archetypes* 26).

Fernando's infatuation with Silvia suggests that she may become a phantom lover, but "the anima . . . appears, at first, mingled with the mother-image" (Jung, *Archetypes* 82). The girl continually cares for the children, feeding and washing Renaud, changing his diapers, tending his cuts and bruises, and consoling him with a toy; she helps them cut their meat and assists Graciela to find her way downstairs from Fernando's bathroom.

Silvia's physical description in each vision reveals maternal associations: twice she squats next to Renaud in her miniskirt, emphasizing her thighs; bending over the children, her waist length hair draws attention to her abdomen; in the final vision the narrator notes her calves, thighs, rump, waist, and lastly her small breasts. The lower anatomy symbolizes man's basic experience of woman as the giver of life or, in psychologist Erich Neumann's term the elementary character of the feminine archetype. In ancient art and ritual

the Great Mother is often represented sitting on the earth. This "sedentary" character, in which the buttocks form the antithesis to the feet, . . . represents a close bond with the earth. . . . Even where she stands, her center of gravity draws her downward toward the earth. . . . The woman's motherliness resides not only in the womb but also in the seated woman's broad expanse of thigh, her lap on which the newborn child sits enthroned.

The Great Mother 98

The maternal is also stressed in repeated references to nature and its nourishing products. The two barbecues take place in a garden surrounded by woods with people eating under a linden tree. Trees are mother symbols, such as the sheltering linden, and Silvia was "como un álamo de bronce" (Jung, *Symbols* 351; *Ultimo Round* 90). There are poplar and cherry trees, chrysanthemums and pansies, meat, figs, apples, pears, yogurt, candy, and cheese. Silvia tends the children around their green tent, an enclosure or shelter which is a prime symbol of the mother, with green the color of life (Neumann, *Great Mother* 282).

If Fernando can free his energy from the mother, it will surface as a coequal person, a helpmate and guide to the world of feeling; but so far the mother archetype dominates the ego, and there can be no equality with a divine figure larger than life. Since Fernando has been unsuccessful in detaching the anima from the mother, all females remain mothers: Liliane's shadow, cast by the grill's fire, interposes itself between Fernando and Silvia, fusing the two maternal figures, and the three adult mothers, Liliane, Nora, and Magda curiously resemble each other because of a kind of rhythm they share in common (87, 82-83). Rhythm (movement) is a manifestation of psychic energy, the feminine treasure (Jung, *Symbols* 154, 144).

Even the wise Graciela, dubbed "la sabelotodo," is motherly toward the passive narrator by the fact of her authoritarian manner and her several criticisms of his "silly" behavior (84). Furthermore, her hands are covered with mother earth from the mud ball weapons of the Indian game, and her kiss has the smell of yogurt (milk) and apple, two predominately feminine foods with the positive and negative implications of life-giving nourishment and forbidden fruit.

The psychological problem is that the masculine consciousness of the narrator has cut its life line to the feminine unconscious and may suffer dire consequences. The kite episode is an example. Alvaro and Lolita brought it to Fernando's barbecue and he helps the boy fly it. Kite, like sky, wind, flying, wings, and birds, is a symbol for the ego, the upper region of consciousness. Fernando, long familiar with this region, erroneously but understandably thinks that Alvaro did not need Silvia for this male activity. When Lolita joins them, criticizing Fernando's handling of the kite and cautioning him not to pull the string too much, Alvaro rebukes her "en rápida alianza masculina" and tells her to go play with Graciela (89).

As in the myth of Icarus, ego-consciousness must not soar too high from its source of strength, the unconscious as mother earth, and the kite's string is the umbilical cord connecting these opposites. If it is severed, the tension between them ends, and the ego, devoid of energy, plummets back to the mother, in this case not for rebirth but extinction. Alvaro alludes to the danger in saying that one must be careful or the kite will fall on the poplar trees. Silvia was a poplar, a tree symbolically positive and negative due to its contrastive leaf coloring, and the mother is the tree of life and death, i.e., vegetation and coffin (90; Cirlot, *Diccionario de símbolos tradicionales* 77; Jung, *Symbols* 233). Silvia will soon be seen in her deadly or coffin guise.

The kite scene's masculine accent stands out in contrast to numerous mother nature symbols: cherry trees, the chrysanthemums stepped on by the children, and three references to Graciela's pansies. It is also significant in this masculine context that Alvaro, a boy, invented Silvia. His mother called him a "mitómano," a word popularly meaning "liar" but literally "one with a mania for myths," and the feminine god is a major figure in the ancient mythologies created by men (86).

Fernando's emotional reaction to Silvia has been intensifying ever since the ambivalent disquiet he felt as she faded from view after her first appearance, and there are increasing intimations of the negative mother as the destroyer of consciousness. In a light but compassionate vein Raúl warns Fernando that he will go mad if he listens to the children, a warning later repeated with pity: "te va a costar caro . . . te vas a arrepentir, hermano" (86, 89). Nora thought him "una víctima nata," which Fernando might well be of the terrible mother due to his diminished contact with the unconscious, a deterioration apparent when he is "luchando contra . . . el absurdo o la pesadilla o el retardo mental" just before his last vision (87, 90).

The inner strife of opposites is metaphorically expressed in the children's Indian war waged in the feminine garden/battlefield, and Silvia is involved in the game because she is the mother who contains the conflictive opposites. A mythic parallel for her would be Aphrodite, the divinity of love and war (Neumann, *Great Mother,* 172). For Cortázar games have "the power and function of rites of passage to the 'sacred zone' of authentic reality lying hidden beneath the surface of daily existence" (Picón Garfield, *Julio Cortázar* 27). The game is a form of the hero myth: Lolita is the captive of Alvaro, Bisonte Invencible, the beast whom Graciela must conquer in order to rescue the girl (maiden-dragon-hero). The hero's gender is of no consequence. Cortázar's game and Jung's mythic parallel are actually symbolic representations of life's daily conflicts, a fact implicit in Fernando's comment that when the game ended and adult conversation began, "la batalla cambió de naturaleza . . ." (82).

What now remains is Fernando's battle against the dragon for the maiden or treasure, i.e., against the threatening mother to win his feminine energy, and of course both are Silvia. The fiendish aspect may be difficult to imagine in the case of Silvia, but she is the Medusa, the monster with serpents for hair who is vanquished by Perseus the hero, and must again be overcome by Fernando. The enchanting girl's hair is mentioned four times, twice "como una medusa de oro," presumably meaning curly blond (81, 90).

The final scene with Silvia depicts the regressing ego's confrontation with Medusa (Jung, *Symbols* 372-374). Monster and maiden are identical; they are libido in the unconscious which the ego must heroically enter if he is to regain the treasure of life. Inasmuch as the unconscious appears as the mother, the feat of entering is colored with incestuous symbolism. Jung explains that "the fear of incest [the dragon] must be conquered if one is to gain possession of . . . the treasure hard to attain" and "it is not the real mother who is symbolized, but the libido of the son . . ." (*Symbols* 294, 222).

Silvia is asleep in Fernando's bedroom. Although clothed, she first appears to him as naked, suggesting that an amorous embrace may follow. It would be a union with the mother, not the maiden, because he is returning to the dark and ancient unconscious for rebirth. She lies on his red bedspread with her black sandals, miniskirt, and blouse. Red or black are the principal colors of the dark, primitive earth mother, and Neumann mentions red as the predominate color on prehistoric depictions of gods to symbolize mana-libido (Jung, *Archetypes* 185; *Great Mother* 106). The ancient or primitive unconscious is also conveyed in the thought that the Sioux were Silvia's "territorio natural," even though contextually Fernando meant that she was possibly as young as the seven-year-olds who played Indians. The Red race, primitive for many, has a burnished complexion as does Silvia, and brownish gold is the earth tone of the chthonic mother (83).

As he approaches Silvia with her golden Medusa hair, the poetic language used to describe his wild feelings also summarizes the archetypal meaning of his experience: "aquí hay huecos y látigos, un agua que corre por la cara cegando y mordiendo, un sonido como de profundidades fragosas, un instante sin tiempo, insoportablemente bello" (90). Jung writes that "emptiness is a great feminine secret," and hollows, cavities, and the like are ancient symbols for the womb, the place of the treasure; whips are the weapons of the Terrible Mother; water is the feminine unconscious both as giver of life and as the Stygian river of death (*Archetypes* 98; *Symbols* 364; 373; 369; 218-219; 389). The waters have risen to Fernando's head and eyes, blinding consciousness and drowning him in the mother. It is "the dangerous moment when the issue hangs between annihilation and new life. For if the libido gets stuck in the wonderland of this inner world, then for the upper world man is nothing but a shadow, he is already moribund or at least seriously ill" (Jung, *Symbols* 293).

The water also bites because it is a snake: "snake and water are mother attributes" rightly associated with the Medusa reptile (Jung, *Symbols* 350, 374, 312). The "thundering depths" are the waters of the unconscious, the flowing libido which Fernando must free in the form of the anima. But to heroically enter the proscribed region means a readiness to risk one's consciousness. In Jung's language the feat is a symbolic death "commonly regarded as an entry into the mother's womb (for rebirth)," or as Cortázar has it, a moment when time ceases (*Symbols* 238). It is "a beautiful moment" because of the anticipated union with the lovely sylvan form of the unconscious, but more especially because an imminent victory over the fierce mother inspires the narrator, and inspiration is implicit in the concept of beauty.

Despite the narrator's desire for Silvia, he senses the negative mother behind the attractive girl, and, paralyzed by fear, does nothing. In fact, he is "incapaz de toda palabra," a fitting expression in that "word" (logos)—speech, breath—stands for the masculine consciousness he cannot muster (Jung, *Symbols* 359; *Archetypes* 96). The scene ends with Graciela calling for Silvia to show her the way downstairs from the bathroom. She wakes at the call and passes Fernando without looking at him. He has not gained the anima; she is still the mother responding to a child's call for help.

However, there are indications in this scene and elsewhere that the narrator may yet untap his psychic energy. For example, while he observes Silvia's lower body as he did a week earlier, he now refers for the first time to her "pequeños senos imperiosos y rubios" (91). Previous quotations from Neumann explained the childbearing region as symbolic of the elementary character of the mother archetype, but there is also a

transformative character, the anima sphere or upper body, where "tiny, barely suggested breasts reinforce the—unconscious—tendency to surpass the elementary and corporeal" (106, 47n). Silvia's breasts are "imperious" because like all archetypes the anima is an authority figure; they are golden like her serpentine hair and the fire that illuminates her because she is the golden hoard of libido. Apropos this linking of gold-fire-libido-snake, Jung writes that "gold and fire are essentially similar"; that the serpent of death who guards the treasure "is of a fiery nature," and libido is "fire, flame, and a snake" (*Symbols* 104, 374, 373, 96).

Another encouraging note follows after Raúl and Nora have laughed at Fernando's seriousness over the "nonexistent" girl. Their comments have wounded his self-image of an intellectual, an identification built up over the years at the expense of his affective, playful side. Due to pride he momentarily accepts their joking although he realizes it might mean loss of access to the world of Silvia (87). Reason and pride usually reject Silvias as foolish phantasms, but Fernando clearly needs that world because "after the middle of life . . . permanent loss of the anima means a diminution of vitality, of flexibility, and of human kindness. The result, as a rule, is premature rigidity . . ." (Jung, *Archetypes* 71). Fernando must recognize Silvia as his own inner femininity and avoid "attempting to situate her within a conceptual framework of time and space . . . trying to subject her to reason or logical inquiry" (Gyurko 36).

At this moment of embarrassment and confusion for Fernando, Borel invites him to a roundtable discussion at the university. He declines, inwardly blaming Silvia for his decision. But if his friends were right and she was only foolishness, then he should have agreed to join the university group, Cortázar's fitting example of reason in action. His refusal means that he is listening to Silvia and has not rejected nor lost the anima. Here the psychic opposites of consciousness and the unconscious are fully activated: a mature, accomplished thinker preoccupied with a foolish phantasy about a young girl.

Yet both friends and narrator are correct about the ambivalent archetype: she is a pixie, "a mischievous being who crosses our path in numerous transformations and disguises, playing all kinds of tricks on us, causing happy and unhappy delusions, depressions and ecstasies . . . ," while at the same time "something strangely meaningful clings to her, a secret knowledge or hidden wisdom, which contrasts most curiously with her irrational elfin nature" (Jung, *Archetypes* 26, 30).

Another positive sign concerns Borel's question to Fernando about a statue from the Cyclades Islands in the Aegean Sea which he felt responsible to answer. Oddly, just before the question the phantasm had appeared again and Fernando was reflecting that Silvia's nose and lips were like those of an ancient statue (84). For Neumann the Cycladean statues have an abstract form and spiritual associations which exemplify the transformative character of the feminine with the upper area of head and face representing the anima (113, 103-112, 123). Elsewhere he adds that "the positive femininity of the womb appears as a mouth; that is why 'lips' are attributed to the female genitals, and on the basis of this positive symbolic equation the mouth, as 'upper womb,' is the birthplace of the breath and the word, the Logos" (168). That Fernando, now drawn to the positive feminine, should feel responsible for the Cycladean question is psychologically understandable: he must assimilate the anima from the mother.

Immediately following the Cycladean question the narrator reflects: "Sentí que si alguna cosa deseaba saber en ese momento era Silvia, saberla de cerca y sin los prestigios del fuego, devolverla a una probable mediocridad de muchachita tímida o confirmar esa silueta demasiado hermosa y viva como para quedarse en mero espectáculo" (84). The repeated verb is "saber" not "conocer." Fernando wants to know what she is at first hand, to return the archetype and its numinous charge of libido to human form as his own anima and energy, or in his words, to see her as "an average timid girl." Since the anima is part of his personality, "timid" describes her well. Finally, he desires to make the shadowy phantom real because it is too beautiful and dynamic to remain forever a figure projected on a stage.

The above theatrical allusion implies that Silvia should not be an actor on a stage, unrelated to Fernando, but a real person playing a role in his own drama. In discussing rebirth symbolism in the Mass and other dramas, Jung writes that too often such experiences

> represent an action in which the spectator becomes involved though his nature is not necessarily changed. . . . The most beautiful and impressive dreams often have no lasting or transformative effect on the dreamer. He may be impressed . . . , but he does not necessarily see any problem in them. The event . . . remains 'outside,' like a ritual action performed by others.
>
> *Archetypes* 118

In contrast to this passive attitude toward archetypal experiences, Fernando wants to do something in order to realize the meaning of his visions. What he does is to write about them, a positive action for understanding anything.

In fact the *raison d'être* of Cortázar's story is Fernando's attempt to write about Silvia so as to bring her into reality (81). Writing is a form of "active imagina-

tion," a therapeutic process by which the projected archetypes are eventually perceived as parts of oneself, and the drama is then no "spectacle" but one's own inner reality:

> Take the unconscious in one of its handiest forms, say a spontaneous fantasy . . . and operate with it. Give it your special attention. . . . For what is now happening is the decisive rapprochement with the unconscious. . . . It is very important to *fix this whole procedure in writing* at the time of its occurrence, for you then have ocular evidence that will effectively counteract the ever-ready tendency to self-deception. (Emphasis added.)
>
> Jung, *Mysterium Coniunctionis* 526, 529, 496

Symbols convey psychic energy and are vehicles for transformation. While Fernando has not yet understood his, he is pursuing their meaning through active concentration on the intriguing Silvia. Whether or not the author intended an understanding of the hero myth according to Jungian terms, it is a commonplace that the creative imagination draws inspiration from the fertile unconscious.

Notes

1. Studies of the story are scarce, but that of Lanin A. Gyurko sees Fernando as an adult seeker of the ideal found in the child's world. Joseph Tyler discusses the adolescent and the adult in Fernando, emphasizing the erotic.

2. Jungian thought has also been applied to some of his stories by Lilia Dapaz Strout, Harry L. Rosser, Rhonda Dahl Buchanan, and Daniel R. Reedy (see "Works Cited" for samples).

Works Cited

Buchanan, Rhonda Dahl. "El juego subterráneo en 'Manuscrito hallado en un bolsillo.'" *Los ochenta mundos de Cortázar: ensayos.* Ed. Fernando Burgos. Madrid: EDI-6, S.A., 1987, 167-176.

Callan, Richard J. "Cortázar's *Los premios*: A Journey of Discovery." *Revista de estudios hispánicos* XV, Número 3 (Oct. 1981): 365-375.

Cirlot, Juan-Eduardo. *Diccionario de símbolos tradicionales.* Barcelona: Luis Miracle, 1958.

Cortázar, Julio. *Ultimo Round.* México: Siglo XXI Editores, 1969.

Dapaz Strout, Lilia. "Casamiento ritual y el mito del hermafrodita en 'Omnibus' de Cortázar." *Anales de literatura hispanoamericana* Núm. 2-3. Madrid (1973-74): 533-553.

González Bermejo, Ernesto. *Conversaciones con Cortázar.* México: Editorial Hermes, 1978.

Gyurko, Lanin A. "Cortázar's Fictional Children: Freedom and its Constraints." *Neophilologus* LVII, No. 1 (Jan. 1973): 24-41.

Jung, C. G. *The Archetypes and the Collective Unconscious.* Trans. R. F. C. Hull. *Collected Works* 9, pt. I. Princeton: Princeton UP, 1971.

———. *Mysterium Coniunctionis: An Inquiry into the Separation and Synthesis of Psychic Opposites in Alchemy.* Trans. R. F. C. Hull. *Collected Works* 14. Princeton: Princeton UP, 1977.

———. *Symbols of Transformation: An Analysis of the Prelude to a Case of Schizophrenia.* Trans. R. F. C. Hull. *Collected Works* 5. Princeton: Princeton UP, 1962.

Neumann, Erich. *The Great Mother: An Analysis of the Archetype.* Trans. Ralph Manheim. Princeton: Princeton UP, 1970.

Picón Garfield, Evelyn. *Cortázar por Cortázar.* México: Universidad Veracruzana, 1978.

———. *Julio Cortázar.* New York: Frederick Ungar, 1975.

Reedy, Daniel R. "The Symbolic Reality of Cortázar's 'Las babas del diablo.'" *Revista hispánica moderna* XXXVI, Núm. 4 (1970-71): 224-237.

Rosser, Harry L. "The Voice of the Salamander: Cortázar's 'Axolotl' and the Transformation of the Self." *Kentucky Romance Quarterly* 30, No. 4 (1983): 420-427.

Tyler, Joseph. "El elemento infantil en la ficción de Julio Cortázar." *Los ochenta mundos de Cortázar: ensayos.* Ed. Fernando Burgos. Madrid: EDI-6, S.A., 1987. 157-165.

Joseph Tyler (essay date 1992)

SOURCE: Tyler, Joseph. "Repression and Violence in Selected Contemporary Argentine Stories." *Discurso* 9, no. 2 (1992): 87-97.

[*In the following essay, Tyler underscores the reflection of oppressive Argentine political regimes in the stories of Cortázar and Luisa Valenzuela.*]

> I think the works you refer to were all attempts to communicate on different levels. Journalism, the novel, the popular song—finally they're all activities involving the word; they are attempts to communicate with one's fellow creatures.
>
> Augusto Roa Bastos, "An Interview", *Salmagundi*, 72 (Fall 1986): 25

The repressive political cycles experienced by the Argentine people since the days of Rosas have been recorded in works such as the novel *Amalia,* and more

recently by a film entitled *Camila.* Indeed, history seems to repeat itself over and over. Fortunately in our times we have a better sense of justice, and the many atrocities committed during the last decade in Argentina are finally coming to an end. Now, after due process, the guilty are being punished accordingly. In a recent newspaper article on this subject, we read that "General Ramon Camps, the former police chief who ordered the torture of Argentine newspaper editor Jacobo Timerman, was sentenced to 25 years in prison . . . for massive human rights crimes"[1]. The same UPI account also informs that

> Timerman, founder of the daily newspaper *La Opinion,* described Camps in 1983 as "a lunatic, paranoid assassin". In a book that became a world-wide best seller, Timerman detailed his torture and the network of clandestine prisons where victims of the military government were taken before they "disappeared" in secret executions. Former Police Chief Gen. Olvidio Richeri, who succeeded Camps under the military government that ruled Argentina from 1976 to 1983, was sentenced to 14 years on 20 counts of torture. Former Police Commisary Gen. Miguel Etchecolatz was convicted of 91 counts and sentenced to 23 years. Police Cpl. Norberto Cozzani was convicted of four counts of torture and given a four-year term, and Dr. Jorge Berges, a former police physician accused of evaluating the limits of endurance of torture victims, was sentenced to six years' imprisonment.[2]

In light of the above news media report, I would like to argue for the propriety of using political interpretation more often for literary texts. And since this paper deals with repression during the most recent period of violence in Argentina, I intend to primarily cite and discuss selected stories from the works of Julio Cortázar and Luisa Valenzuela. Detractors may quickly misinterpret these literary pieces and brand them political pamphlets, but shortly we will learn to appreciate their artistic value. No one can deny, on the other hand, that these stories, with all their artistry, were intended as literary accusations with a very definite target in mind. For as we know, today these manifestations, together with the protests of other groups, the mothers of Plaza de Mayo, among others, finally brought about a change for the better. In 1983, with the inception of the democratic government of President Raúl Alfonsin, censorship restrictions were eliminated, and the doors of democracy were opened anew.

I originally had intended to use Luisa Valenzuela's "Los mejor calzados" as the point of departure, but I have changed my mind in order to emphasize the logic and cause and effect. I will begin instead with the stories by Julio Cortázar.

While lecturing at UC-Berkeley, Cortázar incisively contrasted the realistic short story with the fantastic tale, and he went on to draw a distinction between the purely anecdotic narrative, commonly told by unseasoned storytellers, and the realistic story. Paradigmatically Cortázar then stated:

> En América Latina, en las circunstancias actuales de muchos de nuestros países, los escritores que tienen una participación en la historia y cuya literatura quiere llevar en muchos casos, un mensaje y transmitir ideas útiles en ese campo, los cuentos realistas mejores, los cuentos realistas perdurables, por debajo de lo que cuentan y sin decirlo nunca, contienen siempre de alguna manera una denuncia. Una denuncia de un estado de cosas, una denuncia de un sistema en crisis, una denuncia de una realidad humana que es vista como negativa, como retrógrada. Todos los cuentos realistas que se están escribiendo ahora, y son muchos en América Latina que merecen recordación, contienen prácticamente todos ese tipo de denuncia. Y lo que es curioso, es que no siempre el autor tiene una plena conciencia de esa denuncia, pero el solo hecho de haber escogido un tema determinado y ser un escritor que sabe por qué lo ha escogido, por qué lo ha elegido con respecto a otros, aunque no lo haya hecho por razones de denuncia, está dándole al cuento esa carga que después va a llegar al lector si lo analiza, si lo piensa, si lo vive un poco por debajo.[3]

As an illustration of a realistic short story, Cortázar offered a summary of **"Second Time Around"** (**"Segunda vez"**)[4]. This narrative, according to its author, tells of a young girl from Buenos Aires who is summoned, for an unknown reason, to a ministry located on a certain street in Buenos Aires for questioning. The girl, who is shown as a very simple and ingenious character, knows that this summons has to do with a bureaucratic matter, and so she goes, arrives at the office at the indicated time, and enters a long hall where she sees a second door and a group of people waiting. The second door is the entrance to the office. Soon she has to sit down to wait her turn, for there are many scheduled to enter before she does. As it usually happens in these instances, she begins conversing with those around her. In the group she finds a young man with whom she gets along. He quickly tells her that already this is his second time around because there is a first summons during which one must fill out papers and answer questions, and then there is a second call. He is appearing, indeed, for a second time around; the girl, on the other hand, is there for the first time. As they continue to talk about these matters, the others continue going in succession. These people remain in the office five or ten minutes, and then come out again. There are only two doors: the one to gain entrance to the office, and the other one leading to the stairs through the hall. At a given moment, the young man's turn comes up. Because the two are more or less of the same age, and they have had time to chat a bit, smoke a cigarette, tell one another about the area of the city they live in and what sort of work they do,— it's evident that a most cordial relationship has begun

between the two—the girl trusts him to go in and come out of the office, promptly, to speed things up, so she too can go in right away.

Two or three minutes go by; the door opens, but instead of the young man coming out, there appears one of the employees who motions her to enter. She is left a bit surprised because there was only that one door, and everyone had come out through there. All four who previously had gone in also had come out through the same door, and they had said good-bye. Then, the girl thinks that perhaps the young man is still in the office, attended by another employee, and that perhaps his affairs are a bit more complex. But when she enters the office—which is quite spacious, in fact, with many tables—she looks around, and doesn't see him. In the meantime they call her to a table where she has to fill out some lengthy forms, as is always the case in this type of office. But she continues to worry, nevertheless; it all seems very strange to her. She thinks perhaps there might be another door which she didn't notice, and that maybe they instructed him to leave through that alternate door. After all, she remembers at that moment, he was coming for a second time around, and she for the first time. Perhaps, she thinks, it's possible that those who come for a second time around are forced to leave through another door. She looks around, but she still cannot see another exit. Finally, they take her completed forms, and she is told to leave. They tell her that she'll be called again, that she will have to come a second time around. As she leaves, she slowly descends the stairs, and goes out into the streets searching for him and asking herself where the young man could possibly be. She pauses and remains standing there, waiting for him a bit longer, for she had taken a liking to him. But then, woman that she is, she feels uneasy waiting there for a man whom she hardly knows, and she leaves.

Basically, this is the gist of the story. Cortázar wrote it at the time in which Argentina was beginning to feel the effects of one of the most sinister and infamous forms of repression known as "las desapariciones" ("disappearances"). Naturally, the publication of **"Second Time Around"** was prohibited almost immediately by the Argentine government; eventually, this story appeared in Mexico, along with another forbidden tale, **"Apocalypsis in Solentiname"**, as part of the collection *Alguien que anda por ahí*.

As one can see, the narrative just summarized belongs to the traditional, straight-forward tale recounting the mysterious disappearance of someone who went into an office and never came out. Or, conceivably, he did come out, and the girl, perchance distracted, did not see him; however, that couldn't possibly be the case given the description of the hall. Perhaps, Cortázar tells us, there was a second door, hidden behind posters, and the girl didn't see it. The story really doesn't explain what happens, precisely because disappearances at that time could not be explained. Thus the tale serves as a summary of events, and yet, the author skillfully hides from us the fact that he purposely chose one of the government's agents to tell his tale. The following opening lines begin to illustrate their ironic nature:

> We just waited for them, each one had his date and his time, but there was no rush about it, smoking slowly, every so often Nigger Lopez would come by with coffee and then we'd stop working and talk about what was new, almost always the same things, the boss's visit, the changes higher up, the races at San Isidro. They, of course, had no way of knowing that we were waiting for them, what's called waiting, things like that without worrying, the boss's word, he would repeat it every so often just in case, you people just go ahead nice and easy, when you come down to it, it was easy, if there was a slip they wouldn't take it out on us, the ones responsible were higher up and the boss was okay, just rest easy, boys, if there's any trouble here I'll take responsibility, the only thing I ask is that you don't get your subjects mixed up on me, an investigation first so you don't get involved where you shouldn't, and then you can go right ahead.
>
> (*STA* ["**Second Time Around**"], pp. 199-200)

In spite of this narrative concealment, Cortázar did comment on what he intended to accomplish when he wrote this story; as he told his audience,

> El cuento entonces, en mi espíritu, cuando lo escribí, contenía una denuncia, pero no hay absolutamente ninguna referencia concreta, salvo el hecho que eso sucede en Buenos Aires, ninguna referencia concreta a ese tipo de desapariciones. Es simplemente un pequeño episodio burocrático en una oficina, pero es el lector el que, en su segunda lectura del cuento, verá hasta qué punto ese mecanismo, tan pedestremente realista, puede tener un enriquecimiento desde abajo, en este caso, bastante horrible. Un enriquecimiento . . . mostrar que la realidad es mucho más compleja y mucho más complicada, de lo que parecería por la simple anécdota, el simple relato.[5]

The second story by Julio Cortázar I wish to discuss is entitled "**Graffiti**". This tale, like "De noche soy tu caballo" by Luisa Valenzuela, is based on a process of communication with a twofold addresser and addressee. In this instance the persecuted and oppressed are two graphic artists, one professional, the other, amateur. The persecution, this time, is sort of generic; by that I mean it could have occurred in any country in Latin America. Here, as in most societies, graffiti appears, no doubt as a peripheral type of art form[6]. Those who are caught scribbling graffiti are incarcerated, and some are brutally punished. During a state of siege, as is the case here, any attempt at clandestine

communication is instantaneously suppressed. The story, delivered in monologue form by a woman-narrator, is addressed to her platonic lover. It is another sad case of *fait accompli,* for we know he has witnessed her arrest.

"**Graffiti**" has all the mechanics of a deadly game. It begins with the drawing of two sketches; one is created by an occasional artist, a man who sketches on public walls late at night, just for kicks, while the other design is drawn by a female insurgent as an act of rebellion to protest "the menacing prohibition against putting up posters or writing on walls"[7]. These symbolic acts become tokens of love as well as badges of courage—emblems of freedom. For in this totalitarian state of prohibition, graffiti or any other source of communication—even the most innocent and harmless sketches—are quickly effaced from the walls. The narrator leads us to believe that perhaps neither the clean-up crew nor the police suspects the media to be the message: "One night you saw her first sketch all by itself; she'd done it in red and blue chalk on a garage door, taking advantage of the worm-eaten wood and the nail heads. It was more than ever she—the design, the colors—but you also felt that sketch had meaning as an appeal or question, a way of calling you" (*G* ["**Graffiti**"], p. 35).

Graffiti, the plural form of the word graffito which is an inscription, slogan, drawing, etc. crudely scratched or scribbled on a wall or other public surface[8], is one of the oldest attempts at communication, and their effectiveness here is well founded. In spite of its sordid denouement, "**Graffiti**" ends with a light shade of hope, clearly discernible because the last sketch hasn't been erased yet, "the agitation in the suburbs (you'd heard the news reports) had taken the urban patrols away from their routine . . ." (*G,* pp. 37-38), and there is the strong possibility that the passive sketcher, without a cause of his own, may join the struggle, as the final lines in the story seem to suggest:

> You saw the orange oval and the violet splotches where a swollen face seemed to leap out, a hanging eye, a mouth smashed with fists. I know, I know, but what else could I have sketched for you? What message would have made any sense now? In some way I had to say farewell to you and at the same time ask you to continue. I had to leave you something before going back to my refuge where there was no mirror anymore, only a hollow to hide in until the end in the most complete darkness, remembering so many things and sometimes, as I had imagined your life, imagining that you were making other sketches, that you were going out at night to make other sketches.
>
> (*G,* p. 38)

If we consider the first story, "**Second Time Around**" by Julio Cortázar, as an accusation protesting the many disappearances that occurred in Argentina during the repressive governments prior to the coming to power of Raúl Alfonsin, then Luisa Valenzuela's "Los mejor calzados" is nothing less than an outcry for justice. This narrative, told in a Buñuelesque fashion, is an expression of another nameless narrator, this time an outsider, someone who, like the rest of his ilk, the numerous beggars, lives on the very periphery of both city and society. These *forgotten people* of the suburbs in Buenos Aires have suddenly found a new way of making a living by plundering on the dead. In Luisa Valenzuela's equally powerful story, dead bodies (those "desaparecidos") are found surfacing in the undesirable suburbs of the city. Indeed, the beggars have started to make a modest living out of the accessories they retrieve from human refuse. For example, the corpses are found, for the most part, dressed in the best pairs of shoes. The whole process is told in a kind of gruesome, but metonymic description: ". . . zapatos sobran. Eso sí, en ciertas oportunidades hay que quitárselo a alguna pierna descuartizada que se encuentra entre los matorrales y sólo sirve para calzar a un rengo"[9]. This ironic description, using synecdoche *pars pro toto* is certainly most frequently the norm. However, the narrator adds, "a menudo, en general se encuentra el cadáver completito con los dos zapatos intactos" (*LMC*, p. 147). The dump and its environs, then, become the final destination for the unfortunate "desaparecidos". Word has gotten around that the beggars are running a sort of "flea market", a place where relatives can come in search of clues, an identifiable sign, such as a pair of shoes or a single show, to determine the fate of its original owner. From the start, the narrator expounds ironically on the systematic violence inflicted upon these poor souls by the police and/or the military. This is well understood when the beggar-narrator explains that, although the shoes come to them almost intact, "En cambio las ropas sí están inutilizadas. Suelen presentar orificios de bala y manchas de sangre, o han sido desgarradas a latigazos, o la picana eléctrica les ha dejado unas quemaduras muy feas y difíciles de ocultar" (*LMC*, p. 147). This dehumanizing description is enough to make us realize the awful, prevalent violence experienced by a great number of families in those confines. The narrative reflects and synthesizes all the unfortunate anguish suffered by both the living and the dead. Furthermore, it shows quite poignantly the carnage that systematically devastated, physically and mentally, one of the most progressive societies in the southern cone.

A second story by Luisa Valenzuela, "De noche soy tu caballo", exemplifies a diverse, but no less devastating, kind of anguish caused by a similar repression, aggravated even more by persecution. The story unfolds with one of the nocturnal visits received by the main protagonist. "De noche soy tu caballo" borrows its title from a popular Brazilian song sung, we are told, by Gal Costa: *"A noite eu so teu cavallo"*. Both media titles produce a totally controlling equestrian metaphor which graphically delivers a restless, and yet unsurpassed, amorous longing for an absent lover. It also serves as a symbol of humans' intimate relations, truncated by the ups and downs of political persecution. The story is part of the deadly game of hide and seek between oppressor and oppressed.

* * *

The ephemeral circumstances shown taking place in "De noche soy tu caballo" turn into a haunting experience for both readers and narrator. Is the lover's clandestine visit "factual" or illusory? Is it the naked truth, or is it simply a dreamy event experienced by the main protagonist? One thing is certain: the tale is a charming fantasy imbedded in a true house of horrors. It really doesn't matter whether these events are taken as true or false; the fact is that the story is used to describe a mixture of tender moments enmeshed in acts of persecution and violence. The lovers find solace, though fleetingly and under very trying circumstances. The narrator's loving ambiguity lingers on in the repetitive use of the verbal phrase: "Te hacía" ("I thought you were") pronounced after the moments when he stealthily rings at her door. Before their surprising encounter, the narrator tells Beto, her insurgent lover, that she had imagined him in a series of polarizing situations. At times she had seen him in dynamic participation, fighting, castigating, and eliminating the enemy; in other instances she had pictured him docile, in passive incarceration, tortured, or even dead. She tells him in an almost perfect monologue:

> Te hacía peleando en el norte
> te hacía preso
> te hacía en la clandestinidad
> te hacía torturado y muerto
> te hacía teorizando revolución
> en otro país.[10]

Considering this text from its narrative point of view, we see very quickly, as in Cortázar's **"Graffiti"**, a truly semiotic structure. We recognize in this narrative, and in all the rest discussed earlier, a basic paradigm in communication. The *ab(normal)* pattern is as follows: first, at the story's onset, Beto, arrives at the narrator's apartment and gains entrance to her apartment using a paralinguistic code: the systematic ringing of the door bell. Next, we perceive through the music of the record and the bottle of rum, sure signs of Beto's previous whereabouts. This is followed by affective language, which allows for a more direct mode of communication—the few furtive phrases uttered by the fugitive, "—Callate, chiquita de qué te sirve saber en qué anduve? Ni siquiera te conviene"

(p. 106). And finally, the bursting of emotions, the musical sounds ("De noche soy tu caballo"), and their love-making, are all transposed into a sort of fleeting liberation. In the end, we know that, after another series of rings, this time emitted by the telephone, the protagonist has been tricked. We know of her arrest after the ensuing communication: "—Lo encontraron a Beto, muerto. Flotando en el río cerca de la otra orilla. *Parece que lo tiraron vivo desde un helicóptero.* Está muy hinchado y descompuesto después de seis días en el agua, pero casi seguro es él" (*DNSC*, p. 108).

In passing, it's not hard to recognize the connotative value of the above italicized phrase as a reminder of similar coercive interrogative practices employed by the military in Viet-Nam. But this is just a minor ideological communiqué on the part of both author and narrator. Finally, the story ends with an epilogue: the female protagonist's final soliloquy addressed not so much to Beto as to the readers:

> Beto, ya lo sabés, Beto, si es cierto que te han matado o donde andes, de noche soy tu caballo y podés venir a habitarme cuando quieras aunque yo esté entre rejas. Beto, en la cárcel sé muy bien que te soñé aquella noche, sólo fue un sueño. Y si por loca casualidad hay en mi casa un disco de Gal Costa y una botella de cachaza casi vacía, que por favor me perdonen: decreté que no existen.
>
> (*DNSC*, p. 109)

This epilogue more likely turns into an epitaph.

To conclude, I have tried to show in these few pages how two concerned writers have teamed up, each in his/her own way, to artistically tell some of the most condemning acts of a dirty war. Artistically, these paradigms appear as inventions of the soul, but I believe we all know the meaning involved in the interpretation of these signs.

Notes

1. "Police in Argentina convicted of Torture", *The Atlanta Constitution* (December 3, 1986), p. 3A.

2. "Police in Argentina convicted of Torture", p. 3A.

3. Julio Cortázar, *UC-Berkeley Lectures.*

4. Julio Cortázar, "Second Time Around", in *We Love Glenda So Much and a Change of Light,* trans. Gregory Rabassa (New York: Vintage Books, 1984). All references to this edition appear parenthetically within the text.

5. Julio Cortázar, *UC-Berkeley Lectures.*

6. For another approach to this story, see my essay "El vanguardismo en algunas obras de Julio Cortázar", en *Prosa hispánica de vanguardia,* Fernando Burgos, ed. (Madrid: Editorial Orígenes, S.A., 1986), pp. 163-171.

7. Julio Cortázar, "Graffiti", in *We Love Glenda So Much and a Change of Light,* pp. 33-45. All references to this edition appear parenthetically within the text.

8. *New World Diccionary of the American Language,* 2nd. college ed., p. 606.

9. Luisa Valenzuela, "Los mejor calzados", ("The Best Shod Ones") in *El cuento hispánico,* Edward S. Mullen and John F. Garganigo, eds. (New York: Random House, 1984), pp. 147-148.

10. Luisa Valenzuela, "De noche soy tu caballo", *Cambio de Armas* (Hannover, N.H.: Ediciones del Norte, 1982), p. 106. All references to this edition appear parenthetically within the text.

Kathleen O'Gorman (essay date 1993)

SOURCE: O'Gorman, Kathleen. "The Textual Body in Cortázar's 'Carta a una señorita en París.'" *Romance Languages Annual* 5 (1993): 491-94.

[*In the following essay, O'Gorman suggests that the letter in Cortázar's short story inscribes a patriarchal power dynamic that coincides with the writer's suicide.*]

In Julio Cortázar's **"Carta a una señorita en París,"** an unnamed man writes a letter to a friend, Andrea, who has given him the use of her apartment for several months while she is in Paris. The man writes with a certain equanimity of an unusual experience he has had which, of late, has repeated itself with distressing frequency. He vomits up little bunnies. In order to accommodate the bunnies and to keep Andrea's housekeeper, Sara, from discovering them and their destruction of Andrea's home, the writer hides his creations in his bedroom by day and tends to their needs by night. When the writer vomits up his eleventh bunny, he writes, "En cuanto a mí, del diez al once hay como un hueco insuperable" (33). The letter ends with his enigmatic anticipation of his own suicide:

> Está este balcón sobre Suipacha lleno de alba, los primeros sonidos de la ciudad. No creo que les sea difícil juntar once conejitos salpicados sobre los adoquines, tal vez ni se fijen en ellos, atareados con el otro cuerpo que conviene llevarse pronto, antes de que pasen los primeros colegiales.
>
> (33)

What has occupied the attention of most who have written about Cortázar's story is the question of the writer's sanity and the correlative question of the kind of world the reader has entered. Do we accept the bunnies as real—that is, perceptible to others in flesh and blood—or do we read them as markers of the writer's losing touch with reality? I want to shift the focus somewhat, considering that problematic figuration in the larger context of the position of the female in the story and with regard to epistolary form *per se*.

The writer of the letter appears to occupy a subject position that is decidedly, disturbingly that of the feminine, despite his biological sex. He writes literally from the place of the female, having taken over Andrea's apartment in her absence, even given his own disclaimers: "Andrée, yo no quería venirme a vivir a su departamento" (19). He defines himself in terms of entrapment in the maternal body, giving birth to little bunnies against his will. And, more abstractly, the writer appropriates for himself the traditional markers of the feminine, depicting himself in terms of cultural constructions of gender: he is disruptive, defining himself insistently against the order he finds in Andrea's place; he is confined by his need to tend to his creations, while Andrea is free to move in a much wider world, unconstrained by domestic obligations. He is *re*active, moving from one place to another depending on his friend's actions; his is the world of the nocturnal, allowing him to care for the bunnies without disturbing Sara, while Andrea's is the world of light—the writer imagines "[S]ería sórdido que el correo se la entregara alguna clara mañana en París" (32). He marginalizes himself as mad—"loco de sueño" (30)—while Andrea is associated with reason and order. As such constructions suggest, the writer configures himself in terms of binary oppositions: in the first paragraph of the letter, in fact, he states, "Ah, querida Andrée, qué difícil oponerse, aun aceptándolo con entera sumisión del propio ser, al orden minucioso que una mujer instaura en su liviana residencia" (20). And, at the end of that same paragraph, "Y yo no puedo acercar los dedos a un libro, ceñir apenas el cono de luz de una lámpara, destapar la caja de música, sin que un sentimiento de ultraje y desafío me pase por los ojos" (20). I will return to those oppositions, but first I want to examine in greater depth the representation of masculine and feminine at the level of narrative incident in the text.

Andrea's place—her apartment—serves as a locus of her displacement in the story. Not only does the writer occupy her home; he goes to great lengths to re-present it to Andrea as he perceives it, at once identifying it with her—"como una reiteración visible de su alma" (19)—and noting its suffocating sense of order. His representation, where none would seem to be needed, substitutes image for reality, discursive construct for integral materiality. That construct is decidedly masculine: it is marked by order and rationality *against* which its current occupant identifies himself. There is no visible world of female culture even noted within this ostensibly female space. With an excess of speci-

ficity, we are told of the cultural markers of that space: a portrait of Miguel de Unamuno, a bust of Antinoös, books by Giraudoux, Gide, and López, music by Ravel, Mozart, Benny Carter, and Franck, among others. The writer creates this space in terms of his own choosing: that is, highlighting those cultural artifacts he alone decides to represent. He determines its contours from an incontrovertible position of empowerment, presenting it with a decidedly masculine cast.

Figuring the spatial dislocation of Andrea is critical to the writer's purpose: our "translator" transforms a female womb-like place into a site of male creation. It is telling, then, that the writer usurps the generative function of the womb—vomitting up little bunnies—while simultaneously effacing the sexual body of the female. That which would most conspicuously announce her sexuality—the pregnant body—is repressed, while the procreative function *per se* is made present in a radical, obsessive, and ultimately terrifying form. Woman's body is made an abstraction, "disappears into its representative function" (Irigaray, *Sex* 186), while the male engenders himself. If giving birth is configured in terms of "committing women to an imprisoning biological destiny that denies the autonomy of the self . . . obliterating the very boundaries of self" (Kahane 347), then the terror the writer experiences in Cortázar's **"Carta"** [**"Carta a una señorita en París"**] is grounded in the denial of intentionality to the maternal subject, played out in terms of a kind of mad alterity, a radical otherness. The body becomes a matrix of indeterminacy, encoded on the one hand in terms of the maternal function and on the other in terms of male primacy.

The bunnies themselves, as well as their disgorgement, function in a variety of ways in the story. Associated with the female and with prodigious reproduction, even *their* generative and regenerative functions are usurped by this translator. Benign creatures in nature, they become threatening as elements in an *un*natural process.[1] That process at once contravenes the natural order while participating in an order of its own. It is not so much the fact of vomiting up bunnies that upsets the writer. In fact, he speaks of this disturbing phenomenon in surprisingly casual terms:

> Justo entre el primero y segundo piso sentí que iba a vomitar un conejito. Nunca se lo había explicado antes, no crea por deslealtad, pero naturalmente uno no va a ponerse a explicarle a la gente que de cuando en cuando vomita un conejito. . . . No es razón para no vivir en cualquier casa, no es razón para que uno tenga que avergonzarse y estar aislado y andar callándose.
>
> (21-22)[2]

It is instead the very mathematical progression and inevitability of the bunnies' birth that ultimately defeats him: "[P]orque decir once es seguramente doce, Andrée, doce que será trece" (33). That progression, that order, suggests in a different mode the suffocating order against which the writer has defined himself from the story's inception. It is not the bunnies themselves or the vomitting up of bunnies that so disturbs: it is the inevitability of the next in the linear sequence of numbers. The mind's impulse is to order, to keep at bay the obliterating recognition of the essential falsehood of its constructs, whether in the arts, in mathematical systems, or in the design of one's living space, for example. "[E]l conejo . . . como un poema" (24) is at once part of an artificial order and the embodiment of that which subverts all order.[3]

Appropriating the generative powers of the womb and positing a metaphoric link with literary creation—"el conejo . . . como un poema" (24)—the writer simultaneously inscribes himself as a god: "[Y]o quisiera verlos quietos—un poco el sueño de todo dios, Andrée, el sueño nunca cumplido de los dioses" (28) and "[E]s casi hermoso ver cómo les gusta pararse, nostalgia de lo humano distante, quizá imitación de su dios ambulando y mirándolos hosco" (30). Finally, "[E]stuvieron en círculo bajo la luz de la lámpara, en círculo y como adorándome" (32-33). For all of his essentialist and constructivist appropriations of the feminine, however, for all of his concomitant attempts to portray Andrea in terms of the masculine, the writer nevertheless situates himself even at the level of narrative perception within a hierarchy predicated on patriarchal constructs.

What occurs at the level of narrative incident—the privileging of the masculine and the disempowerment of the feminine—occurs at the level of discursive practice as well. The letter, "the traditional realm of the feminine" (Benstock 260), becomes, in Cortázar's text, a critical locus of her displacement. The epistolary form itself situates the female unequivocally within patriarchal discourse, within a discursive field which defines a phallic order: that is, an order predicated on a singular, totalizing entity which posits itself as the primary, privileged referent against which difference is measured.[4] The writer himself notes that the bunnies, like a poem, exist in a "llano mundo blanco tamaño carta" (24)—a world whose contours he alone defines.

As the addressee, Andrea is constituted exclusively by the anonymous writer; she has no possibility of self-representation, no way to articulate herself. To use Irigaray's formulation, she "is always already transformed for/by the projected representation of the father" (*Speculum* 345). The male occupies the subject position—the position of privileged, primary referent—by virtue of his authorship of the letter. There are more subtle ways in Cortázar's **"Carta"** in which the male assumes that position as well.

In her discussion of epistolary form, Janet G. Altman notes the intermediary nature of a letter and represents its function in terms of binary oppositions. An emblem of separation, the letter nevertheless mediates presence and absence, intimacy and abandonment (13-14, 43). It can emphasize either the distance between the writer and addressee or its function as a connector, a bridge between the two. It can also demonstrate the gap between self and world, enacting a dialectic of private and public in its elements of plot as well as in its textual strategies.

The writer of this letter draws attention to many of the epistolary attributes Altman isolates. In negotiating the relation between presence and absence, he repeatedly refers to Andrea's being elsewhere—in Paris—even as he insists with an excess of specificity on her presence, in the artifacts and ambience of her apartment, "como una reiteración visible de su alma" (19). More significantly, he anticipates his own absence made present to Andrea when she returns to the apartment to read his letter after his suicide. In effect, the writer takes the two elements which motivate epistolary mediation—time and place which are not shared by writer and reader—and reconstitutes them, reinforcing rather than dissolving what Linda Kauffman calls "the hierarchies of active writer and passive reader" (293). In refusing "total presence (reunion)" and opting instead for "total absence (death)" (Altman 150), the writer abandons Andrea with an absoluteness that diminishes by any comparison her abandonment of him.

The writer's abandonment of Andrea is enacted in a curious dialectic of private and public. He attempts to hide his bunnies from Sara, the housekeeper, exposing them to public view only at the instant of their destruction: "No creo que les sea difícil juntar once conejitos salpicados sobre los adoquines, tal vez ni se fijen en ellos" (33). In a letter which ought to be private, he suggests the conditions leading up to a disturbing—and disturbingly public—spectacle. That spectacle itself—a body splattered on the ground—in its own way invites a violation of the letter's privacy. Suicide letters circulate in a more public domain than most others—they are part of police investigations, coroners' inquiries—and the writer's decision to leave the letter in the apartment rather than send it through the postal system fairly ensures its scrutiny in a much more public domain than that which it acknowledges. The writer transgresses the very private space of Andrea's apartment to violate the very public space of the sidewalk below—the space of the wider world in which Andrea and others move. In reversing what Janet Altman terms "a transfer[ence] from the level of *action* . . . to the epistolary mode's essential level of *communication*" (60), subverting the letter's promise of private communication with the letter writer's very public act of self-annihilation, the story alternates between intimacy and exposure with important consequence. The writer's act compels the reader to "focus on *social* construction, culture, discourse, the *public* sphere of women's activities and . . . den[ies] the relevance of their 'other'—the private sphere of women's activities, 'real' biological bodies, nature, the non-discursive" (Threadgold 26). It makes public Andrea's abandonment of the writer, situates her irrevocably *in terms of the male*. She becomes the "inscriptional space for . . . the 'masculine' unconscious" (Irigaray, *Speculum* 111), left as she is to answer for that to which she returns.

The writer uses the signifying potential of an inscriptional space in a much more subversive way in the text when he considers the issue of representation *per se* and its inadequacies. At a critical juncture in the text, he notes,

> Un trozo en blanco de la página será para usted el intervalo, apenas el puente que une mi letra de ayer a mi letra de hoy. Decirle que en ese intervalo todo se ha roto, donde mira usted el puente fácil oigo yo quebrarse la cintura furiosa del agua. . . .
>
> (31-32)

By foregrounding the representational blank, by interrogating it and the language which determines it, and by reading that blank in two different ways, the writer in effect destabilizes the possibility of absolute meaning in the very text which he himself authors. He makes legible the repressed subtext of female desire and associates it with the positing of alternative readings, allowing for the multifariousness and diffuseness of female sexuality/textuality. The blank becomes the space in which meaning itself is created, the mediation of language—a letter written by a translator—ultimately failing in its representational function.

The writer disrupts the authority of his own position vis-à-vis the text in a rather different way as well: he fails to sign the letter. At the narrative level, that might figure in the problematics of identity noted above; as Altman suggests, "The ritual of opening and closing a letter imposes upon the writer a gesture of self-definition vis-à-vis the addressee" (146), a gesture this writer would predictably have difficulty enacting. At the discursive level, it "subverts the ideology of authorship . . . , radically challenging conventional notions of a text's paternity, lineage, geneology, genre" (Kauffman 23). The failure to sign "augments tension rather than producing resolution" (Altman 159).

Still, there is a resoluteness in the writer's suicide, in what Janet Altman terms the "motivated renunciation of writing . . . [which] assures the strongest closure

in this kind of narrative" (161)—a resoluteness which carries greater narrative and discursive weight than the text's strategies of subversion can claim. Despite those strategies, **"Carta a una señorita en París"** reinscribes patriarchal structures in ways that allow no change. If a "carta" is a letter, it is also a map.[5] In this case, the writer's discursive practices map the subject positions available to the female, subject positions which are always elsewhere: she is off-stage, in Paris, and will receive this letter when any response of hers to the writer will have been silenced absolutely. Especially striking in the refusal of such subjectivity is the fact that a letter *ought* to accommodate a reciprocal utterance. A letter traditionally compels a response, enabling the addressee to constitute herself in a discourse of her own. In Cortázar's **"Carta,"** the female cannot articulate herself.

At the most critical juncture of the text, in what amounts literally to his own death sentence, the writer identifies self with other—abolishes the self in the name of the Other—effacing the sexual and textual body in a single gesture. In configuring his self-destruction in terms of an oppositional relation, the writer "guarantees and reproduces the patriarchal order" (Weedon 66), inscribes in the representational apparatus the structures of patriarchy that the text in other ways attempts to subvert.

Notes

1. One thinks of Gregor Samsa in Kafka's *Metamorphosis,* whose transmogrification into a gigantic insect might be compared to this narrator's plight. Notably, Samsa's horror is tied to a creature more easily associated with the grotesque than little bunnies. The very incongruity here intensifies the letter writer's upset.

2. I am indebted to Kate Halischak for the observation that the writer's descriptions of the bunnies' disgorgement is in many ways similar to bulemics' strikingly casual descriptions of their obsessive behaviors. A study of this story in terms of bulemia, most frequently a problem of middle- to upper-class females, and its companion issues would, I suspect, engage a variety of rich interpretive possibilities.

3. One thinks, of course, of the end of the essay "Avatares de la tortuga," by Jorge Luis Borges: "[H]emos soñado el mundo. Lo hemos soñado resistente, misterioso, visible, ubicuo en el espacio y firme en el tiempo; pero hemos consentido en su arquitectura tenues y eternos intersticios de sinrazón para saber que es falso" (136).

4. I use Irigaray's notion of phallic order here and elsewhere in my discussion.

5. Altman notes this with a slightly different emphasis but in terms which also might be applicable to
a reading of this text: "The *I* of epistolary discourse always situates himself vis-à-vis another. . . . To write a letter is to map one's coordinates—temporal, spatial, emotional,
intellectual—in order to tell someone else where
one is located at a particular time and how far one
has traveled since the last writing. Reference
points on that map are particular to the shared
world of writer and addressee" (119).

Works Cited

Altman, Janet Gurkin. *Epistolarity: Approaches to a Form.* Columbus: Ohio State UP, 1982.

Benstock, Shari. "From Letters to Literature: *La Carte Postale* in the Epistolary *Genre.*" *Genre* 18 (Fall 1985): 257-95.

Cortázar, Julio. *Bestiario.* Escollo, Mexico: Nueva Ima-gen, 1987.

Irigaray, Luce. *Speculum of the Other Woman.* Trans. Gillian C. Gill. Ithaca: Cornell UP, 1985.

———. *This Sex Which Is Not One.* Trans. Catherine Porter. Ithaca: Cornell UP, 1985.

Kahane, Claire. "The Gothic Mirror." *The (M)other Tongue: Essays in Feminist Psychoanalytic Interpreta-tion.* Ithaca and London: Cornell UP, 1985. 334-51.

Kauffman, Linda S. *Discourses of Desire: Gender, Genre, and Epistolary Fictions.* Ithaca and London: Cornell UP, 1986.

Threadgold, Terry. "Introduction." *Feminine, Mascu-line, and Representation.* Ed. Terry Threadgold and Anne Cranny-Francis. Boston: Allen & Unwin, 1990. 1-35.

Weedon, Chris. *Feminist Practice & Poststructuralist Theory.* Oxford and New York: Blackwell, 1987.

Rubén Noguera (essay date 1994)

SOURCE: Noguera, Rubén. "The Fantastic in the Sto-ries of Julio Cortazar." *Revista de Estudios Hispánicos* 21 (1994): 221-34.

[*In the following essay, Noguera views Cortázar's par-ticular appropriation of the fantastic as an attempt by the author to move away from the logical reality pos-ited by Western philosophy and toward a more meta-physical view of life.*]

Roger Caillois, in his book *Images, Images . . . ,* makes a distinction between what he calls the "mar-velous" and the "fantastic" in literature.[1] To him, the marvelous deals with beings and events that are liter-ally out of this world; that is, they belong in another space and time, a completely different world from ours. The fantastic, on the other hand, deals with be-ings and events that are of this world but that interrupt the "natural" or normal flow of events in it; they are like unsettling or unknown pauses in the midst of our everyday routines, of our complacency. He explains it thus:

> The universe of *the marvellous* is naturally populated
> by dragons, by unicorns and by fairies; the miracles
> and the metamorphoses are continuous there; the magi-
> cal wand, of common use; the talismans, the genies,
> the elves and the thankful animals are abundant; the
> fairy godmothers immediately satisfy the desires of de-
> serving orphans . . . In *the fantastic,* on the contrary,
> the supernatural appears as a rupture of universal co-
> herence. The wonder here turns into a prohibited ag-
> gression, threatening, which breaks the stability of a
> world in which the laws till then were considered to be
> rigorous and immutable. It is the impossible suddenly
> erupting into a world where the impossible is exiled by
> definition.[2]

Many of the short stories of the Argentine writer, Julio Cortázar, have been described as belonging to the lit-erary genre of the fantastic, perhaps in the sense that Caillois has described it. In most of his stories, Cortázar interrupts everyday reality with doses of what might be called separate realities, or the unknown pro-truding into the known.

Much like another well-known Argentine writer of the fantastic—Jorge Luis Borges—, Cortázar himself adopted the designation of literature of the fantastic—"for lack of a better name," according to him—to cat-egorize his short stories. According to the critic Jaime Alazraki, both Borges and Cortázar "were using the term [fantastic] in a wide sense in order to set it against literary realism and to distinguish thus two modes of perception and two styles of configuration."[3] Alazraki goes on to state that "[t]he distinctive trait of the genre, in which everyone appears to coincide, must consist in its capacity to generate fear or horror."[4] Or, at least in Cortázar's case, the fantastic generates uncertainty or enigma. Alazraki is merely summarizing here the con-sensus of critics of the fantastic and does not necessar-ily agree with them that the fantastic should necessar-ily inspire fear or horror. Another critic who thinks that fear or horror is not necessarily an ingredient or a result of the fantastic is Tzvetan Todorov, who wrote a book on the subject; in it, he analyzes and summarizes previous studies of the genre and offers his own view:

> In a world which is very much ours, the one we know,
> without devils, sylphs, nor vampires, an event occurs
> which cannot be explained by the laws of this familiar
> world. The one who perceives the event must opt for

one of two possible solutions: or it deals with an illusion of the senses, of a product of the imagination, and the laws of the universe remain as they are (*the strange*); or the event has really taken place, is an integral part of reality, but now this reality is dictated by laws with which we are not familiar (*the marvelous*). Or the devil is an illusion, an imaginary being, or he really does exist, like other living beings. The fantastic occupies the length of time of this uncertainty; as soon as we choose one answer or the other, we get out of the fantastic in order to enter into a neighboring genre, the strange or the marvelous. The fantastic is the vacillation experienced by a being who knows nothing but the natural laws and who is suddenly confronted with an event of supernatural appearance.[5]

As we shall see further on, the characters in Cortázar's stories, all apparently "rational" or commonsensical beings, are suddenly or gradually confronted with events that are out of the ordinary, that make both they and the reader pause to consider these extraordinary events and perhaps ask the question: what is really happening here? What is reality?

Nevertheless, despite the two rather lucid and profound analyses of the literature of the fantastic by Caillois and Todorov quoted above, Alazraki asserts that writers such as Kafka, Borges and Cortázar do not fall easily under the rubric of the fantastic, as is traditionally understood. The critic asks the question: "What are we to do with some of the narrations by Kafka, Borges or Cortázar, of indisputable fantastic ancestry, which dispense with genies, horror and technology [a reference to Caillois's three stages in the development of the genre: the fairy story, the fantastic proper and science fiction]?"[6] Alazraki proposes the name of "neo-fantastic" to some of the contemporary fantastic literature which does not, in his view, quite fit the mold of the traditional fantastic. He states: "If for the literature of the fantastic horror and fear constituted the route of access to *the other,* and the story was organized around that route, the neofantastic story dispenses with fear because *the other* emerges from a new postulation of reality, from a new perception of the world, which modifies the organization of the story, its functioning, and whose purposes differ considerably from those followed by the fantastic."[7]

Cortázar himself made a distinction between his brand of the fantastic and historical or traditional fantastic. While acknowledging his dues to master writers of the fantastic of the past, he placed his stories within a different category which, while owing to the past, opened a new perception and a different set of poetics:

> The traces of writers like Poe are undeniably in the most profound levels of my stories, and I believe that without "Ligeia," without "The Fall of the House of Usher," I would not have had that inclination toward the fantastic which assaults me in the most unexpected

moments and which spurs me to write as a unique way of crossing certain limits, of putting me in the territory of *the other.* But something indicated to me since the beginning that the road toward that otherness was not, as far as the form, in the literary devices on which the traditional fantastic literature depends for its celebrated "pathos," which was not found in the verbal staging which consists of disorienting the reader from the beginning, conditioning him with a morbid climate in order to obligate him to accede easily to mystery and fear . . . The irruption of *the other* occurs in my case in a manner markedly trivial and prosaic, without premonitory warnings, plots *ad hoc* and appropriate atmospheres like in gothic literature or in the present fantastic stories of bad quality . . . We arrive thus at a point in which it is possible to acknowledge my idea of the fantastic within a wider and more open register than the predominant one in the age of gothic novels and of the stories whose attributes were ghosts, werewolves and vampires.[8]

For the French philosopher Jean Paul Sartre, 20th century writers of the fantastic, such as Kafka or Blanchot (and, one might add, Borges or Cortázar), "have stopped depending on extraordinary beings; for them there is no more than one fantastic subject: man."[9] Man is thus placed at the center of a perplexing universe, one that has not totally been explained away by science. While 20th century science and technology have largely discounted or ridiculed the supernatural beings and events recounted in traditional literature of the fantastic, they have largely not dealt with the philosophical idea of man's enigmatic presence within a puzzling reality, perhaps the central premise of "neofantastic" literature. In other words, science and technology have raised more questions than answers about man and reality. Some contemporary fiction writers, such as Kafka, Borges and Cortázar, have tried—each in his own unique style—to reflect and ask these lingering questions of man's place in the universe, of the mind's problematic relation to reality, whatever the latter may be. One of their common threads seems to be that reality is interpreted by the mind in infinite ways, that it is perceived in unique and sometimes strange ways by the mind which, paradoxically, also conceives it. Thus, the lull that rational thinking places on the mind is sometimes broken by the mind's brief and sudden excursions into the irrational, into the unknown or unknowable. In a sense, then, the mind creates reality or realities; but since it is so often numbed or deceived by its routine empirical observations and manipulations of the world (science and technology), it is often shocked or puzzled when it confronts different, startling realities ("the other"). According to Alazraki, in order to bring these other realities to light and life, the contemporary writer has had to create a new language and a different style of writing ("a new set of poetics"): "If the world, as Nietzsche writes, is an invention, a meager sum of observations, the neofantastic is an attempt to reinvent it starting from a new language, starting from a transgression of the names of things: it is infinitely more important to know the names of things than to know what they are . . . It is sufficient to coin new names, new appraisements and new probabilities in order to create also 'new things' in the long run."[10]

As Cortázar suggests in his bizarre stories, the idea that ordinary reality is solid or always the same, is false. At times certain things occur that destroy the concept of the continuity of sameness. At times we are faced with events that baffle us, that "yank" us out of our complacent routine. Cortázar says in effect that these extraordinary interruptions of the ordinary, the subject matter of the neofantastic—to adopt Alazraki's terminology—, are like, in the author's words, "openings to estrangement or exile, instances of an ungluing, the result of which is an unnerving of the usual because nothing is customary as soon as it is subjected to a silent and sustained scrutiny."[11] Again, then, the implication is that the mind—in a sense—takes stock of itself and reality and "decides" that routine reality is not always what it seems to be, that there is something more that is infinitely more complex and "strange" than what the "usual" tells us there is. Time for Cortázar and other writers of the "unusual" is not a straight-line *continuum,* but a record of multi-layered, multi-perspective changes which nevertheless occur simultaneously, or parallel with ordinary reality. It is also circular and cyclical, repeating itself from time to time. As Malva Filer puts it, "Cortázar, in a manner analogous to Robbe-Grillet, looks for the way in which the literary work will develop in a temporal complex in which present, past and future will come to be realized in the unity of consciousness."[12] Time then for a writer like Cortázar is, in his own words, "a diachrony which is sufficient by itself to disadjust all submission to city [or clock] time. Time that is more inward or deeper: encounters in the past, appointments of the future with the present, verbal probes which simultaneously penetrate the before and now and annul them."[13]

As the title of one of his books—*La vuelta al día en ochenta mundos (Around the Day in Eighty Worlds)*—implies, a day in the life of a "Cronopio," an imaginative and creative individual, is like an incursion into numerous different realities or worlds. Cortázar typically inverts an idea, in this case the title of a famous book by Jules Verne, to get his point across that the inward or mental journey of a man is infinitely richer and more complex, and thus more fraught with perils and joys of different sorts, than mere external or physical journeys, though these can also be made more exciting by introspection or imagination, or can serve to stimulate the creative powers of the mind. As Cortázar

himself has said, "[n]o one can know how many worlds there are in the day of a *cronopio* or a poet."[14] His worlds are thus "surrealistic," though he takes care not to identify himself too closely with surrealism as a literary movement. According to Filer, ". . . when Cortázar speaks of the presence of surrealism [in his works], he is not referring to the existence of a school, ideology or organized group. What interests him is the diffused presence of surrealism, its vitality as an active element incorporated to the vanguard movement."[15] The author's surrealistic vision is, according to him, "a lived experience that is the most open possible to the world, and the result of that opening, of that porosity in front of circumstance, translates itself as the annihilation of the more or less conventional barriers that reasoning reason tries to establish between what it considers real (or natural) and what it qualifies as fantastic (or supernatural), including in the first all that tends to repetition, accepts causality and submits itself to the categories of the understanding, and considering as fantastic or supernatural all that which manifests itself with the character of exception, marginal, unusual."[16]

Another way of looking at Cortázar's stories is that of unreality living alongside reality. At any moment, at any place, reality—according to the author—can and is at times interrupted by the irruption of unreality, that is, by beings and events that are not ordinarily found in everyday reality. In her aptly-named article, "The Unreality in the Narrative of Cortázar," Rosa Boldori observes that if it is true that some of Cortázar's stories like **"Los venenos" ("The Poisons"), "Reunión" ("Reunion")** and **"Final del juego" ("End of the Game")** can be classified as realistic, none of the stories of this author can, on the other hand, be considered totally fantastic.[17] The unusual or fantastic elements erupt within the confines of reality, they are of and in this world, but usually out of sight, hidden in the backs of our minds, in the individual and collective psyche or unconscious. The unreal, then, is like a beast within which surfaces at will, though it usually decides to remain hidden. It is often a reminder of our mortality and shakes up the complacent view that we have of the world and our place in it.

Malva Filer, in her book *Los mundos de Cortázar (The Worlds of Cortázar)*, divides the author's stories into two categories. She writes: "To one of them would correspond those stories in which the author describes a situation, scene or circumstance such as can probably be produced in day-to-day reality, within its temporal and spatial limits, even though the interpretation of the same [the situation, scene or circumstance] might be subtle, in general."[18] In this first group, Filer includes such stories as **"Las puertas del cielo" ("The**

Doors of Heaven"), "Los venenos" ("The Poisons"), "Las ménades" ("The Maenads"), "La banda" ("The Band"), "Los amigos" ("The Friends"), "El móvil" ("The Mobile"), "Torito" ("Little Bull"), "Después del almuerzo" ("After Lunch"), "Final del juego" ("End of the Game"), "Los buenos servicios" ("The Good Services"), "El perseguidor" ("The Persecutor"), "La salud de los enfermos" ("The Health of the Sick"), "Reunión" ("Reunion") and "La señorita Cora" ("Miss Cora").[19] The second category would include, according to Filer, those stories in which "an irrational, perturbing element is introduced," or in which "the planes of reality and fantasy, or reality and dreams, crisscross and mix."[20] In this second category might belong such stories as "La noche boca arriba" ("The Night Lying Face Up"), "Casa tomada" ("House Taken Over"), "La puerta condenada" ("The Condemned Door"), "La isla al mediodía" ("The Island at Noon"), "Las babas del diablo" ("The Droolings of the Devil"), "Axolotl," "Las armas secretas" ("The Secret Weapons"), "Continuidad de los parques" ("Continuity of the Parks") and others like these. Needless to say, it is in the second group that the fantastic or unreal elements are the most obvious, although, as has been mentioned before, they are also expressed—perhaps in more subtle, sinister ways—in the first group.

There are various themes of importance in Cortázar's stories. For example, there is the theme of the double popularized by Robert Louis Stevenson's *Dr. Jekyll and Mr. Hyde*—in "Lejana" ("Far Away"). This story deals with a skinny woman of Buenos Aires who at certain moments has a kind of vision that she is not only in Buenos Aires but also in another country far away, in which everything is very different; she is also a poor woman, a beggar. Little by little, she sketches the idea of who that other dreamed-up woman could be and, finally, she goes out to look for her. She finds her on a bridge and they embrace each other. It is there that the change in the interior of the double is produced and the beggar woman goes away in the wonderful body covered with furs, while the skinny one is left on the bridge as a raggedy beggar. The theme of the double is also evident in "Los pasos en las huellas" ("The Footsteps in the Tracks") and in "Una flor amarilla" ("A Yellow Flower"), in which the protagonist encounters a child who is he himself in an earlier stage. It is also evident, in a way, in "La noche boca arriba" ("The Night Lying Face Up"), in which the protagonist is both the dreamer and the dreamed, the motorcyclist dying in a hospital and the prisoners of the Aztecs about to be sacrificed. At the end, Cortázar inverts the story and makes the dreamed into the dreamer, adding a new twist to the theme.

In an interview he did with Ernesto González Bermejo, Cortázar speaks of his own personal experience with the idea of the double:

> Once I split into two. It was the biggest horror that I've had in my life, and luckily it only lasted a few seconds. A doctor had given me an experimental drug for migraines . . . derived from lysergic acid, one of the strongest hallucinogens. I took the pills, felt strange, but I thought: 'I have to get used to it'.
>
> One sunny day like today—the fantastic occurs in very common and normal conditions—I was walking on the *rue de Rennes* and at one given moment I discovered, without daring to look, that I myself was walking at my side; something of my eyes must have seen something because I, with a sensation of frightening horror, felt my physical doubling. At the same time I was reasoning very lucidly: I went into a bar, asked for a very strong cup of coffee and drank it all at once. I remained waiting and suddenly I understood that I could look again, that I was no longer at my side.[21]

There is no doubt that in this case, Cortázar's doubling effect was brought about, at least partially, by a drug, but the characters in a few of his stories "split" into two under normal conditions, that is, unaided by synthetic chemicals or drugs. The mind splits into two under certain personal or universal stimuli, whether they be escapist—such as in "Lejana"—or regressive—as in "Una flor amarilla"—, or dream-like, as in "La noche boca arriba".

Another recurrent and unusual theme that some critics have discerned in Cortázar's stories is that of incest, such as in the story "Bestiario", for example. But the one story which the author mentions specifically in his interview with González Bermejo as containing explicitly the theme of incest is "Casa tomada" ("House Taken Over"). He says: "It deals with a brother and a sister but at some point it says 'that simple, matrimony of siblings', an image which has a lot to do with the relationship they live out . . . The two have enclosed themselves in the house and live lives of bachelors. It is not by any means a consummated incest but there exists an ambiguous relationship between the two siblings; that is evident."[22] While the incest theme has little to do *per se* with the fantastic proper, it is an unusual subject to deal with, especially in "neofantastic" fiction, and especially since society considers it a taboo subject. Cortázar has usually dealt with it in his stories in a subtle way, that is, in its platonic overtones rather than as physical consummation.

Returning to the biggest theme of all in the author's stories, that of the fantastic proper (or neo-fantastic, if one prefers), once again we find that a definitive definition of it is difficult to come by. Cortázar himself refuses to define it because he thinks that all that can be done is "to try to look for the notion of the fantastic

. . ."[23] He goes on to state: "[The fantastic] is something very simple, that can occur in the midst of quotidian reality, in this sunny mid-day . . . The fantastic can come about without there being a spectacular modification of things . . . For me the fantastic is simply the sudden indication that, at the edge of Aristotelian laws and of our reasoning mind, there exist mechanisms perfectly valid, in force, that our logical cerebrum does not grasp but which at certain moments irrupt and make themselves felt. A fantastic act occurs once and it is not repeated; there will be another one, but the same one is not produced again."[24] The author attributes his heightened awareness of the fantastic to a child-like hypersensibility to the world.[25] In other words, the fantastic calls out to what is child-like in us; only as a child, or with the eyes of a child, can we truly perceive the wonders of the world. As adults, we often lose this marvellous way of seeing reality and become bogged down in boring or repetitive routines. But, as Cortázar's stories would seem to imply, at certain given moments we recapture—in essence—our childhood and see the world in a new light again, magically and fantastically. At times these revelations frighten us because we are not used to them, but they are mainly reminders of the magical heritage of which we are part.

This child-like way of looking at the world is at the very heart of the author's fiction. He sees literature basically as play or game, a serious one at times: "If we made a scale of values of games, that went from the most innocent to the most refined intentional ones, I believe that we would have to put literature (music, art in general) among those of the highest, most desperate (without attaching a negative value to this word) expressions."[26] Aptly enough, Cortázar's stories are populated with children, and in many, he assumes the point of view of a child. He explains his child-like propensities thus:

> . . . [W]hen I started to write, toward the end of adolescence, in first youth, all of those layers [of child-like sensibilities] that had apparently been left behind came back in the form of characters, of half-confessions, as is the case in the story **"Los venenos"** [**"The Poisons"**] and as is the case in **"Bestiario"** [**"Bestiary"**]. The depth of sensibility of the child Isabel of **"Bestiario"** is mine, and the child of **"Los venenos"** is I. In general the children that circulate through my stories represent me in some way.[27]

Some of the other stories in which children play predominant roles are **"Final del juego"** (**"End of the Game"**), **"Después del almuerzo"** (**"After Lunch"**), **"La puerta condenada"** (**"The Condemned Door"**), and some others. Many critics have concluded that the literary treatment of children by Cortázar in his stories and novels is efficacious, that he feels them very close, and that he makes them speak and live without artificiality.

Another important element in Cortázar's stories are animals. Some of his stories are like zoos, populated with all kinds of animals, some exotic, some not. His first collection of short stories, and the leading story in this collection, are named—appropriately enough—*Bestiario* (*Bestiary*). Another story is named **"Axolotl,"** the scientific denomination of an exotic Mexican fish. In this story, the protagonist identifies himself so strongly with the odd fish that he "becomes" one at the end. In turn, the animal that the author personally identified with the most is the cat: "I consider the cat to be my totemic animal and cats know it because I have confirmed this many times when I go to the house of friends who have dogs and cats: the dogs are indifferent to me, but the cats look for me right away."[28] Often also in his stories, human beings are seen as animals or are considered from the angle of an animal; there are certain areas in which they are seen zoologically. Why this fascination with animals? Cortázar's answer has an element of the fantastic or the unusual: ". . . [A]n animal moves (or lives) outside of time—given that history is given in a temporal context—, it repeats to the infinite the same movements, and for what? Why?: those are human notions that have no value for an insect. We say that the animal works, but the notion of work is invented by us."[29]

One of the major fantastic themes in Cortázar's stories is time. As has been mentioned before, time is a problematic element in the author's stories and is often annulled or broken (in its linear continuity) by experiences which seem to be either out of time or which seem to occur simultaneously or circularly. For example, in the story **"El perseguidor"** (**"The Persecutor"**), the protagonist Johnny is keenly aware of the fracture of linear time when he says at one point, ". . . I'm touching this tomorrow," or when he tells that in the subway between stations he suddenly realizes that he has been thinking in a few moments a series of things that if he were to unravel in ordinary time would take him much longer. Here then is the idea that psychological time is really timeless when compared to clock time because it is not measurable and has no notion of linear, measured time. Psychological time is really then a timeless break in the continuity of clock time.

Another story where psychological time plays a major role is **"Liliana llorando"** (**"Lillian Crying"**), the first story of the collection *Octaedro*. In this story, there is an irruption of a time different from that of clock time. A dying man thinks about the future life of his wife Lillian, spanning several months, which in clock time occurs in two or three days writing in the clinic. The irony is that he does not die but the future he foresaw for his wife, which included another man, is fulfilled in another plane of time, but fulfilled nevertheless. In **"La autopista del sur" ("The South Freeway")**, a group of people caught up in a huge traffic jam enters a dimension out of the ordinary where time passes quickly: there are seasonal changes, loves, deaths, pregnancies, etc., which all suddenly come to an end when the traffic jam is broken and the people return to their ordinary lives.

The idea of psychological time in Cortázar's stories is closely connected to intuition or a sixth sense, and the ones most attuned to this are, according to the author, the common people: ". . . the more I deal with the common people, people that are not very educated, the more I'm amazed at their capacity for intuition and at the openness that they have for certain things which the erudite and the hyperintellectuals do not always have."[30] This is in tune with the idea that logic or reasoning (the tool of the intellectuals) is usually opposed to intuition and therefore subject to linear time, whereas intuition works outside of ordinary time.

How does Cortázar get his "fantastic" effects across? What are the techniques, the style of writing that insinuate or reproduce those unusual elements of reality? One more or less obvious way is through language, that is, the words and syntax he employs in his stories. The author manipulates these in such a way that they create an atmosphere that is familiar yet strange, an effect which Nicolas Bratosevich has described as *extrañamiento,* or astonishment.[31] The critic, in a prologue to his anthology of Cortázar's stories, sees the element of astonishment as being effected through language and hyperbole:

> . . . [T]he problematization is double, that of acts and words, because the language of technification, when applied to a reality so predictable as climbing a stairway surprises itself as a language, parodying itself, and thus denounces the excesses of an age that runs the risk of losing its freshness when it loses its freedom of movement, boxing it all in. The other modality of astonishment is the *narrative hyperbole,* by which is forced into the improbable a situation which is in itself an ordinary one, such as for example a traffic jam in the highways of access to a big city. In **"La autopista del sur,"** that incident is stretched to the period of a year, which leads the characters isolated in their cars to disalienate themselves from their individualism . . . : by virtue of the pressure of the circumstances, all or almost all discover a distinct form of society, marked by communitarian concerns, and they realize it.[32]

Cortázar's language could be described as "skeletal," devoid of flowery or superfluous words. He owes this somewhat laconic technique to Jorge Luis Borges, an-

other Argentine writer of the fantastic. Cortázar has often acknowledged this technical debt to Borges. On one occasion, he said: "My readings of the stories and essays of Borges, in the period in which he published *El jardín de senderos que se bifurcan* [*The Garden of Forking Paths*] showed me a language of which I had no idea . . . The first thing that surprised me reading the stories of Borges was an impression of 'dryness'. I asked myself: 'what is going on here? This is admirably told, but it would seem that more than an addition of things it's rather about a continuous subtraction.'"[33] Thus, according to Omar Prego, there are three main elements in the author's stories: 1) an economy (Borges-like) of words; 2) the structural notion of the story which, according to the author, coincides also with his structural notion of language; 3) music,[34] about which the author says: "For me, writing is a musical operation. We have already said this many times: it is the notion of rhythm, of euphony, not euphony in the sense of pretty words, of course not, but rather the euphony which comes out of syntactic drawing (we are not talking of language) which, having eliminated everything unnecessary, everything superfluous, demonstrates pure melody."[35]

Another stylistic or literary technique which Cortázar uses in his stories is that of understatement, which is closely tied with his economy of words. For example, in **"Casa tomada,"** the protagonists, a brother and a sister, are slowly invaded in their house by something unknown, but they accept this invasion and their total displacement nonchalantly, not even bothering to investigate or speculate about the strange event; they merely accept it as fate, there's no alarm or fear. The same is true of **"Carta a una señorita de París" ("Letter to a Lady of Paris")**, in which the vomiter of little rabbits nonchalantly describes the unusual experience which drives him to suicide; again, the tone is one of understatement, without alarm or fear, unquestioning. One could say that the characters who undergo these strange, unusual experiences are under a state of shock, in this case literary shock, and thus seem to accept these events without questions, alarm or fear; the understated tone of the narrators of these stories would seem to support this theory. Or it could also be that Cortázar does not want to give the whole story away by too many explanations, but rather wants to leave it up to the reader to draw his own conclusion. A third possibility is that these strange, sinister events are just not explainable, they are part of the unknown, of the mystery and enigma of existence. The open-ended technique used by the author, in which the narrator is no longer omniscient but limited in what he knows or sees, is also evident in such enigmatic stories as **"Continuidad de los parques,"** where the man who reads a novel is at the same time the protagonist of that same novel—without his (or the narrator's, perhaps) knowledge; at the end of the story, he may perhaps suffer the consequences of this identification. In this, as in many other stories by the author, the ending is insinuated but never clearly articulated.

Cortázar may perhaps employ the device of literary shock to make the reader aware of the absurd dichotomy of reality in Western philosophy. Because reality does not only consist of repetitive everyday routine or the logic that supports this, but also of the myriads of mental experiences we have while going through these routines. Which is real? I believe that Cortázar would say that both are real, or that everything is real, or that the question is absurd because no one has a cornerstone on reality. Reality, for Cortázar, is an unknown complexity and it is absurd to believe only in the empirical, rational observations and explanations of science. We must consider everything experience everything, because the totality of it all is reality. Cortázar perceives the dichotomy between reality and fantasy, waking and dreaming, science and literature, to be meaningless. For example, in the story **"La isla al mediodía"** (**"The Island at Noon"**), the steward in the airplane flying over the island every day at noon finally fulfills his desire to retire on the island but, in apparent contradiction, the corpse that appears floating on the sea after the plane crashes, is his. Puzzling? Yes. Here the story splits into two parallel levels: that of the steward bored literally to death of his professional routine, and that of the steward who has realized his dream of living on an island paradise—they are both played out by the steward Marini and neither one can be diminished as being fictitious; they are both valid in Cortázar's literary world.

Similarly in **"Sobremesa"** (**"After-Dinner Chat"**), one of a group of friends shares with the others an experience which, however, the rest will not have shared with him, nor will they ever, because one of them dies before the reunion can be realized. Again, the parallelism between the "fictitious" and the "real", dreams and life, brings up the enigma of reality itself and momentarily suspends our logical certainties as well as our system of values, because as the saying goes, "up and down don't mean a great deal when one no longer knows where one is." One of the apparent motives of this and other similar stories seems to be to turn our world upside down—or to turn the tables on us—, in order for us to reexamine and question our complacent views of reality and make us glimpse other ways of perceiving. In **"Todos los fuegos el fuego"** (**"All the Fires the Fire"**), the oddity of the title ushers in another bizarre experience: two characters, apart in time by centuries, share—without knowing it—an event which draws them and their experiences into one: the burning catastrophe. Comments the critic Bratosevich:

"The title of the story universalizes both situations till he converts all deaths into one unanimous death; and along the same line, all lives."[36]

While **"Todos los fuegos el fuego"** merely suggests the idea of reincarnation, **"Las armas secretas"** (**"The Secret Weapons"**) is somewhat more explicit. In this story, the protagonist feels himself more and more invaded by a dead man whom he ignores and who is avenging in him the loss of the woman who had a love relationship with both, in different situations and different times. However, it is in the story **"Una flor amarilla"** (**"A Yellow Flower"**), where the idea of reincarnation reaches full "bloom," so to speak: its protagonist discovers that he is part of a link of a series of infinite reincarnations, which condemn him thus to a kind of cyclical immortality: "'The worst thing is that Luc would die in turn and another man would repeat the figure of Luc and his own figure till he dies, so that another man would in turn enter into the wheel . . .'"[37] But the most vertiginous example yet of this "karmic wheel" or cosmic kaleidoscope of life is given in **"Las babas del diablo"** (**"The Droolings of the Devil"**), perhaps Cortázar's most enigmatic story. In it, the photographer Michael ends up identifying himself with his own photographic camera in such a way that, in a first instance, he recognizes himself as a "double": both the man who is alive writing his own story and, at the same time, the lens of his camera, which is immobilized in an unrecoverable eternity, from which it is always focusing on the sky, registering the time of the clouds and the doves—a kind of death from which the lives of others are detected. But life and death, temporality and still eternity, are not all that disconcert Michael the narrator. Since what is in play is his own identity, he needs to include in his story the complication of how to write it because it is no longer clear who is definitely telling the story, the man or the camera or . . . : "One will never know how to tell this, if in the first or second person, or using the third plural, or continuously inventing forms that will serve no purpose."[38] Perceiving the uselessness of trying to determine the identity of the narrator (i.e., his own identity), Michael—the literary alter ego of Cortázar—suggests that it is Time itself, the illusion of change and movement in a constant, eternal Cosmos, which is telling the story, his story and that of all others. Comments Bratosevich: "Evidently here the duplicity [of the narrator] seems to have been atomized till it becomes a multiplicity to the infinite, since Michael—the "I"—, the camera and the blond woman, and finally all of the grammatical persons, the singular and the plural, serve as the identification of the true narrator."[39]

The cosmic implications of **"Las babas del diablo"** may perhaps serve as concluding reflections on Julio

Cortázar's preoccupation with the so-called fantastic and on his overall motives, intentions or purposes in dealing with extraordinary mental phenomena in his short stories. The author is truly wrestling with the ontological questions of Reality, Being and Time: What is reality? What does it mean to be alive or dead? What is time and how does it affect us as individuals (or is there such a thing as individuality in an impersonal cosmos)? These and similar questions are truly metaphysical explorations into the enigmas of existence, life and death. By inserting bizarre experiences into what are otherwise ordinary lives, Cortázar is asking his readers to ponder the big questions, to break their dull routines and try to glimpse into the unknown, into the Cosmos. Literature is thus for him an exploration into the Mind, the creator of all conceptions and perceptions about the Universe. What makes us sentient, thinking beings is this universal awareness of phenomena, be they "ordinary", be they bizarre. The problem that we all have is that we tend to dull our minds, our consciousness, only with the immediate acts of everyday survival—basic things such as eating, working, sleeping and reproducing—that we forget or neglect the metaphysical, cosmic heritage of which we are all part. Cortázar's mission seems to be to remind us that there is more out there than meets the eye, and he does this in his stories by inserting such "fantastic" elements as dreams, imagination, creativity, nightmares, fears and, ultimately, the splitting of the "I" into double or multiple beings living in multi-layered times and spaces who are finally absorbed into the Cosmic Energy of Time. Thus, Cortázar is ultimately trying to distance himself (and his readers) from traditional Western philosophy, which tends to rely too much on logical reason, and embrace Eastern or Oriental philosophy, which sees men or individuals as "waves" of the Cosmic Ocean or as infinite spokes of the infinite Wheel of Life.

Notes

1. Roger Caillois, *Images, Images.* . . . París: José Cortí, 1966. Spanish translation: Buenos Aires: Sudamericana, 1970.

2. Caillois, 5.

3. Jaime Alazraki, *En busca del unicornio: The Stories of Julio Cortázar* (*In Search of the unicorn: The Stories of Julio Cortázar*). Madrid: Editorial Gredos, 1983, IX.

4. Alazraki, 18.

5. Tzvetan Todorov, *Introduction à la litterature fantastique*. Paris: Seuil, 1970, 40.

6. Alazraki, 25.

7. Alazraki, 28.

8. Julio Cortázar, "Algunos aspectos del cuento" ("Some Aspects of the Short Story"). *Casa de las Américas,* 15-16 (1962), 3.

9. Jean Paul Sartre, *Situations I*. Paris: Gallimard, 1947, 12.

10. Alazraki, 44.

11. Julio Cortázar, *La vuelta al día en ochenta mundos* (*Around the Day in Eighty Worlds*). México: Siglo XXI, 1967, 25.

12. Malva E. Filer, *Los mundos de Julio Cortázar* (*The Worlds of Julio Cortázar*). Nueva York: Las Américas Publishing Co., 1970, 19-20.

13. Cortázar, *La vuelta al día.* . . . , 67.

14. Cortázar, Ibid., 210.

15. Filer, 22.

16. Julio Cortázar, "Sobre el surrealismo" ("On Surrealism"), *Realidad,* 15 (1949), 349-50.

17. Rosa Boldori, "La irrealidad en la narrativa de Cortázar" ("Unreality in the Narrative of Cortázar"), *Boletín de Literaturas Hispánicas,* 6 (1966), 15-16.

18. Filer, 26.

19. Filer, 26-27.

20. Filer, 27.

21. Ernesto González Bermejo, *Conversaciones con Cortázar.* Barcelona: EDHASA, 1978, 35.

22. González Bermejo, 36-37.

23. González Bermejo, 41.

24. González Bermejo, 42.

25. González Bermejo, 46-47.

26. González Bermejo, 49.

27. González Bermejo, 50.

28. González Bermejo, 52.

29. González Bermejo, 54-55.

30. González Bermejo, 63.

31. Nicolás Bratosevich, ed., *Julio Cortázar: Antología.* Buenos Aires: EDHASA, 1978, 21.

32. Bratosevich, 22-23.

33. Omar Prego, *La fascinación de las palabras: Conversaciones con Julio Cortázar.* Barcelona: Muchnik Editores, 1985, 59-60.

34. Prego, 24.

35. Prego, 61.

36. Bratosevich, 42.

37. Bratosevich, 43.

38. Bratosevich, 43-44.

39. Bratosevich, 44.

Martin Wasserman (essay date January 1995)

SOURCE: Wasserman, Martin. "Julio Cortázar's 'The Night Face Up': Literary Support for Federn's Ideas on Anesthetic Dreams." *Revista/Review Interamericana* 25, nos. 1-4 (January 1995): 116-27.

[*In the following essay, Wasserman illustrates how Cortázar's short story supports physician Paul Federn's analysis of the egoless dream state experienced while under anesthetic.*]

In 1944, the eminent psychoanalyst, Paul Federn, wrote an article on the nature and function of anesthetic dreams based on a surgical experience he had undergone in the late 1930s. Towards the end of the article, he urged other surgical patients to publish the results of their anesthetic dreams to see if they supported his views on the subject (Federn 1952:114). Interestingly enough, validation for Federn's ideas came from the writings of one of the most important Latin American authors of the twentieth century—Julio Cortázar. In 1952, Cortázar had a motor scooter accident for which he needed immediate surgery under general anesthesia. Four years later, Cortázar had his anesthetic dream published as **"La noche boca arriba" ("The Night Face Up")** in the short-story collection, ***Final del juego***.[1] It is the purpose of this essay to now show that Cortázar's oneiric experience during surgery, as well as his approach to writing subsequent to his operation, can be considered strong support for Federn's stated beliefs on the nature and function of anesthetic dreams.

FEDERN

Paul Federn (1871-1950), a Viennese physician, joined Freud's psychoanalytic circle in 1904. When Freud discovered he had cancer, in 1924, Federn became his deputy and continued in that capacity until he emigrated to the United States in 1938. His study of the ego, especially in dreams, neuroses, and schizophrenia, permitted him to develop important concepts—at times at variance with those of Freud—which eventually were applied in new methods of therapy (Roazen 1975:304-310).

Based upon his work with clients, as well as with student-trainees in the Viennese Psychoanalytic Society, Federn developed a great desire to understand the manifestation of the ego as it showed itself in dreams (Weiss 1966:148). It was for this reason that he wrote about his dream experience under general anesthesia.

Shortly after Federn arrived in the United States, in 1938, he required dental surgery. During his surgery, an inhalant anesthetic was applied which caused Federn to achieve a very intense dream state. When the effects of the anesthesia ultimately wore off, Federn was able to have vivid recall of his dream. He then concerned himself with analyzing the special nature of his oneiric experience as well as determining its specific purpose.[2]

In Federn's dream, he was both chief commander and statesman of a country that resembled Greece. By taking decisive action in the dream, he was able to successfully defend his country against invading hordes from the north. He did so, not by military power, but by the strength of his own personality. According to Federn (1952:100), in the anesthetic dream, his life was a glorious struggle without any conceit or show; his entire being was governed by the motto, "do what you have to do."

Examining his oneiric experience after the dental surgery had been completed, Federn believed that he had never been more alive than in his dream. Federn (1952:101) claimed that during his anesthetic dream he not only struggled for his ideals, but that he himself had become his own ideal. Federn describes this phenomenon as the loss of both a mental and a bodily ego. He asserts that in ordinary dreams we frequently transfer our mental ego to another figure but we always retain our bodily ego, in that we recognize ourselves as the dreamer. The purpose of this retention is that, by being "housed" in our own bodies, we obtain a certain sense of security and the sleep process can continue unabated throughout the night; in other words, we do not automatically wake up whenever we start to dream. However, according to Federn ((1952:106), since the anesthetic dream state is one of deep unconsciousness offering no chance whatsoever of waking up, it then becomes possible not only to transfer our thoughts to another figure but to, also, literally become that other figure in our dream. On this score, Federn believed that in his own anesthetic dream the disappearance of his ego was so complete that he had indeed become the chief commander and statesman of a foreign country.

As far as the meaning of his dream was concerned, Federn (1952:101-102) interpreted the content as providing him with a cosmic connection since, by observing a personal event from the past, it gave him an opportunity to see what, specifically, had to be done with his life in the future. Thus, for Federn, his anesthetic dream satisfied the purpose of wish fulfillment. Federn interpreted his dream in this light based on his current circumstances. He had come to the United States in 1938 to escape Nazi oppression. The German military had already overrun Austria, his home country, and it was Federn's estimation that the country resembling "Greece" in his dream represented all the European nations that Hitler would like to conquer.[3] By placing himself in the dream as a "chief commander and statesman" who was successful at repelling the German military, Federn (1952:102) believed that, in a sense, he had engaged in a role which prevented Nazi tyranny from spreading throughout Europe.

However, for Federn, the special information contained in his anesthetic dream was viewed as much more than a personal data source from which to generate a research hypothesis; this kind of dream material was also viewed as the informational basis by which the dreamer could change his or her behavior to lead a more rewarding life. On this matter, Federn asserted that in real life the dream ego should be willed "toward an action or thought, and not a mere foreknowledge of the action, thought, or planning that is going to occur" (Weiss 1952:18).

In Federn's case (1952:101), he knew that his "exile" status prevented him from actively participating as a member of the military in the struggle against the Nazis, so he made his contribution to the war effort as an intellectual. He temporarily put aside his major research interest which was how the ego manifested itself in dreams, neuroses, and schizophrenia, and, instead, focused on writing an article about sustaining the mental health of the Allied soldiers who were presently engaged in fighting against the Nazis. This article was based on Federn's own experience as an army physician during World War I.[4]

Federn (1952:114), as part of his concluding essay statement on the function of anesthetic dreams, urged other surgery patients to report their particular oneiric experiences in order to determine whether or not his personal research findings would be validated. It will now be shown that confirmation of Federn's ideas on anesthetic dreams did indeed come approximately fifteen years later from the writings of the Argentine novelist and author of short stories, Julio Cortázar.

CORTÁZAR

Julio Cortázar (1914-1984) has been recognized as one of the most important Latin American writers of the twentieth century. Commenting upon Cortázar's skill as a short-story writer, Frank Magill (1994:540), the editor of *Masterpieces of Latino Literature,* states: "Cortázar perhaps more than any other writer of his

day easily crossed boundaries, cultures, and ideologies. His influence on world literature has been enormous. . . . He wrote masterpieces in virtually every short-story genre."

In a personal essay written by Cortázar (1984:161), on the special approach he took to formulate his best short stories, he remarked emphatically that they "are products of neurosis, nightmares, or hallucinations neutralized through objectification and translated to a medium outside the neurotic terrain." Cortázar (1978:30), in a lecture, speaking specifically about the nightmare and dream aspects found in his short stories, commented: "Many of my fantastic stories were born in an oneiric territory and I had the good fortune that in some cases the censorship was not merciless and permitted me to carry the content of the dreams into words."

Cortázar's story, **"La noche boca arriba"** (**"The Night Face Up"**), is one such example of a specific work that came to him in a dream. According to Cortázar, in 1952 he had the misfortune to be in a motor scooter accident on the streets of Paris and, as a result, he was taken to a hospital for immediate surgery since some of his injuries were considered serious. Just before the surgery, Cortázar was given an anesthetic and it is at this point that his dream began. Throughout the operation and even after surgery was completed, when Cortázar, in an anesthetic haze was taken back to his hospital bed to convalesce, his dream continued to unfold. Cortázar asserts that, ultimately, it was to be the specific content of this dream which would serve as his source material for **"The Night Face Up."**[5]

In **"The Night Face Up,"** a modern man who is seriously injured in a motor scooter accident has surgery performed under the influence of anesthesia. While in surgery, and during convalescence, he has a dream about a Moteca Indian fleeing from the Aztecs. The Moteca is caught and imprisoned before he is to be sacrificed. However, at the end of the story as the Moteca is about to be killed, he ceases being a figure in a dream and now becomes a corporeal being. The Moteca then projects into the future and sees a figure riding a strange device through the avenues of an astonishing city.

It will now be argued that Cortázar's anesthetic dream, as reported in **"The Night Face Up,"** appears to confirm Federn's ideas, previously presented, on the special phenomenal experience, as well as the important purpose provided by such dreams. Like Federn, Cortázar's bodily and mental egos disappeared altogether. In an interview, Cortázar clearly stated that as far as his anesthetic dream was concerned, the Moteca Indian had become real and the modern man riding the motor scooter (Cortázar himself) had turned into a figure from a projected dream (Prego 1985:65-66). Here we see an obvious parallel between Federn literally becoming the character in his dream—a chief commander and statesman—and Cortázar actually becoming the character in his dream—a Moteca.

With regard to the purpose of anesthetic dreams, here, too, there is a strong confirmation in Cortázar's dream of Federn's statements on the subject. According to Federn, the anesthetic dream provides the person with a connection to the past which, in turn, serves the purpose of wish fulfillment because it gives the dreamer a glimpse of what has to be done in one's life to achieve a more rewarding future. Based on conversations with Cortázar, this same conclusion about anesthetic dreams sustaining a definite continuity from past to future was drawn by the literary critic, Luis Harss, who states that **"The Night Face Up"** helped Cortázar find "a lost self—a vanished unity in others" (Harss and Dohmann 1967:239). The next section of this essay will explain how Cortázar used the "continuity" aspect of his anesthetic dream to achieve wish fulfillment in his own life.

Cortázar's Relation to the Moteca

Just as Federn gained wish fulfillment by dreaming of a civilization that had ancient roots, namely Greece, so, too, did Cortázar dream of an ancient world, but the civilization which he dreamt about was that of pre-Cortesian Mexico. The figure that Cortázar had become in his anesthetic dream was a Moteca, and it is this quite specific self-projection which eventually allowed Cortázar to accomplish his goal of wish fulfillment.

The word, *Moteca,* in the Nahuatl language—the language spoken by the Aztecs and by almost all other indigenous people in the central highlands of Mexico— means "to spread revenants himself" (Bierhorst, *A Nahuatl-English Dictionary* 1985:219,227). The term "revenants" refers to "the return of a departed one," so a Moteca was an individual who would spread the knowledge and wisdom of one who had already departed this world (Bierhorst, *Cantares Mexicanos* 1985:219-221). The specific departed one whose legacy was disseminated by a Moteca was the Toltec priest and culture-giver, Topiltzin Quetzalcoatl (*ibid.*; 1974:63-66). Topiltzin Quetzalcoatl was a personage who believed that the truth on earth could only be discovered through the arts and, most importantly, through the art of writing (Soustelle 1964:129; Brotherson 1979:280).

That Cortázar would have had access to the specific meaning of the concept, *Moteca,* is indicated by the type of work he performed when he emigrated to Paris

in 1951. Cortázar was employed by UNESCO as a professional translator. This job was responsible for shaping much of the experience behind *62: Modelo para amor* (*62: A Model Kit*), an autobiographical novel which was first published in 1968.[6] In this work, Cortázar (1952:6) wrote about his obsessive need to quickly and correctly translate material from one language to another since he was "a good interpreter accustomed to the instant liquidation of all problems of translation in that struggle against time and silence." It seems likely, therefore, that when Cortázar remembered the term, *Moteca,* from his anesthetic dream he would have looked up its definition in a Nahuatl-to-Spanish dictionary.[7] It also seems likely that once he became aware of the definition, he would have looked in the anthropological literature to ascertain how the Moteca functioned in pre-Cortesian Mexico.[8] Adding further strength to the argument that these specific research tasks were actually performed by Cortázar is the pronouncement by Cortázar himself that upon emigrating to Paris he had become particularly drawn to books dealing with the subject of anthropology (Garfield 1975:8; Harss and Dohmann 1967:218).

Further evidence that Cortázar's anesthetic dream was viewed in a manner similar to Federn's—that is, as a wish which needed to be fulfilled in order to find meaning in life—came from Cortázar's good friend, the Mexican novelist, Carlos Fuentes. According to Fuentes (1984:331), when Cortázar visited Mexico late in his life, he was "enthralled by the constant affirmations of the coexistence of culture and nature." Fuentes goes on to say that Cortázar's happiness in his country came as no surprise to the Argentine writer because, in a sense, Cortázar "had been in Mexico before—. . . in the dream of a man on an operating table in a Parisian hospital who sees himself being sacrificed."

Cortázar's joy in Mexico at re-experiencing a coexistence between culture and nature was merely a continuation of what the Moteca Indian of Cortázar's dream would have tried to achieve during his lifetime. Like all Nahuatl writers, this Moteca would have used the imagery of nature as the raw material from which to create his symbolism (Nicholson 1959:139). Although the natural beauty of Moteca writings retained the physical shapes of nature, the total effect would have been extremely abstract, far removed from the physical circumstances of time and place (*Ibid.*:145).

Cortázar (1984:166-167), after his motor scooter accident, came to believe very much the same thing about his own writing. In his work he tried to show that the "extraordinary" had become the rule without displacing the "ordinary" formations of nature. Cortázar, on this matter, compared his writing to a certain type of cloud formation which would allow highly observant persons to see not only the clouds but to also discover that Beethoven's profile had formed between the clouds.

For Nahuatl writers, like the Moteca, natural objects served as a smaller, yet manageable, representation of some greater abstract truth. It was a way for them to remake a profound cosmic absolute into a format perceptible to a person's senses (Nicholson 1959:147).

This great abstract truth conveyed by the Moteca was that persons have to detach themselves from the temporary pleasures of life because the things of this world are only an illusion; one, instead, has to explore one's inner self to find the real world which is absolute and everlasting. By doing so, an individual will be able to replace a physical face and heart, which was brought into this world with a metaphysical face and heart which identifies enduring peace and happiness not with life on earth, but with a greater reality found in the innermost of heavens (Nicholson 1968:8-9; León-Portilla 1963:133). Thus, for the Moteca, the logical positivism of Western philosophy would be contradictory to their way of thinking about the truth in the universe.

Cortázar's thoughts on this matter can be considered a continuation of Moteca writings because, like the Moteca, Cortázar believes that absolute truth cannot be found by adopting an empirical viewpoint. On this score, Cortázar has stated that the ideas found in his short stories "oppose the false realism that consists of believing that all things can be described and explained according to the philosophical and scientific optimism of the eighteenth century, that is, as part of a world ruled more or less harmoniously by a system of laws" (Garfield 1975:12).

Cortázar adheres to a non-empirical viewpoint of the absolute truth because, similar to the Moteca, he believes the reality of things in this world should be taken only as an illusion. Speaking on this subject, he claims: "We are all illusions in each other's minds; . . . everything can be wiped out in a flash because it has no real existence; its reality exists only, one might say, at the expense of our unreality" (Harss and Dohmann 1967:219).

As was mentioned previously in this essay, Federn used the wish-fulfillment aspect of his anesthetic dream to achieve a more meaningful life. He did so by temporarily changing the subject matter of his writing in an intellectual effort to ward off Nazi oppression. Cortázar, too, after his anesthetic dream, used his writing in the service of wish fulfillment because, like Federn, the beliefs that he conveyed in his works provided him with a rewarding and purposeful existence. Furthermore, as will now be shown, these beliefs can be considered a meaningful continuation of Moteca ideology.

Cortázar, like the Moteca in the Aztec world, subscribed to a more genuine reality than life on earth. He called it a "marvelous" reality because our daily life tends to obscure it (Alazraki 1978:9). According to Cortázar, the distorted notions which obstruct one's access to this marvelous reality are the Western perceptions of death and two of the most established concepts in the Western grasp of reality—time and space. It is because of these distortions that Cortázar claims it is legitimate for him to "renounce mortality" (Harss and Dohmann 1967:219).

Similar to the Moteca of the fifteenth-century Aztec world, Cortázar came to believe, and indicated likewise in his writings, that eternal happiness could only be achieved when one is released from the bondage of the physical world and is raised "to a higher plane where freedom begins.'" Like the Moteca, this higher metaphysical plane which is a more genuine form of reality, is depicted by Cortázar in his works as a place of everlasting peace, for it is "a state of immanence, where opposites meet and one simply is." Also, just like the Moteca who understand the metaphysical plane as being somewhere in the farthest reaches of the cosmos, Cortázar, through his writings, locates his "marvelous" reality at the "far shore of eternity, . . . that sort of final island where man would at last find himself reconciling his inner differences and contradictions." One sees, therefore, that this farthest metaphysical plane serves Cortázar in a way which is equivalent to the Moteca's "innermost of heavens," since it is obviously a sacred locale where one can find enduring happiness.

SUMMARY

This essay has argued that Julio Cortázar, like Paul Federn before him, used his anesthetic dream for the purpose of wish fulfillment which, in turn, enabled Cortázar to achieve a more rewarding existence. It has been shown that Federn's personal dissociative experience gained through his anesthetic dream, as well as the wish fulfillment function provided by his dream, were confirmed by Cortázar's autobiographical short story, **"La noche boca arriba"** (**"The Night Face Up"**). Here, Cortázar's bodily ego vanished entirely after being given an anesthetic during surgery, and he became the Moteca Indian projected in this dream. Cortázar later acted on the content of his anesthetic dream by formulating, through his writing, a metaphysical system based on the pre-Cortesian Moteca way of viewing the universe.

Notes

1. *Final del juego* was first published in Mexico, by Los Presentes, in 1956. This short-story collection was translated into English, in 1963, and published as *The End of the Game and Other Stories*.

"La noche boca arriba" was included in the English edition as "The Night Face Up." When the English edition of the book came out as a paperback, in 1968, the publisher decided to change its title to *Blow-Up and Other Stories* based on the success of the film, *Blow-Up*.

2. Federn first published the content and interpretation of his anesthetic dream as a journal article in 1944. It was later republished, in 1952, as part of a posthumous collection of Federn's most important works, entitled *Ego Psychology and the Psychoses*.

3. At the time Federn actually had his anesthetic dream, Greece was not yet conquered by the Nazis (*Ibid.*, p. 102). This country was eventually overrun by German forces in April of 1941.

4. Federn published his article entitled "Some Suggestions on the Mental Hygiene of Soldiers," in 1942, in the journal, *Mental Hygiene*. This periodical encouraged contributions dealing with the psychological effects of war. Thus, in the same issue as Federn's article can be found the following essays: "The Refugee Child: A Task for Mental Hygiene"; "The Prevention of Panic"; and "Mental Health Problems in a War Production Area."

5. Cortázar relates the events which surrounded his motor scooter accident, along with his subsequent surgery under the influence of anesthesia, in the following sources: José Amicola, *Sobre Cortázar* (Argentina: Editorial Escuela, 1969), p. 143; Evelyn Picon Garfield, *Julio Cortázar* (New York: Frederick Ungar Publishing Company, 1975), p. 31; Terry J. Peavler, *Julio Cortázar* (Boston: Twayne Publishers, 1990), pp. 34-35; and Omar Prego, *La fascinación de las palabras: Conservaciones con Julio Cortázar* (Barcelona, Spain: Muchnik Editores, 1985), pp. 65-66.

6. Alfred J. Macadam, "Cortázar on Cortázar: A Literary Anthology," *Review* (Winter 1972), pp. 35-41. *62: Modelo para amor* was first published in 1968. Four years later, in 1972, the English translation of this work was published as *62: A Model Kit* (New York: Pantheon Books).

7. In the early 1950s, when Cortázar wrote "La noche boca arriba," there would have been available to him at least eight dictionaries that translated Nahuatl words into a modern European language and, of these, at least four would have translated Nahuatl terms into Spanish. On this matter, see John Bierhorst, *A Nahuatl-English Dictionary and Concordance to the Cantares Mexicanos with an Analytic Transcription and Grammatical Notes* (Stanford, CA: Stanford University Press, 1985), pp. 740-751.

8. The concept of Moteca is found most prominently in the pre-Cortesian Nahuatl work, *Cantares Mexicanos*. When Cortázar recounted his anesthetic dream in "La noche boca arriba," excerpts from this Nahuatl work, which explained the function of the Moteca, had already been translated into both English and Spanish. On this matter, see John Bierhorst, *Cantares Mexicanos: Songs of the Aztecs* (Stanford, CA: Stanford University Press, 1985).

9. All the quoted material in this paragraph comes from an interview Cortázar gave to the literary critic, Luis Harss, on the philosophy behind his unique way of viewing the writer's task. (Luis Harss and Barbara Dohmann, *Into the Mainstream: Conversations with Latin American Writers* [New York: Harper and Row, 1967], p. 219).

References Cited

Alazraki, Jaime. 1978. "Introduction: Toward the Last Square of the Hopscotch." In *The Final Island: The Fiction of Julio Cortázar*, ed. Jaime Alazraki and Ivar Ivask. Norman, OK: University of Oklahoma Press. 3-18.

Amicola, José. 1969. *Sobre Cortázar*. Argentina: Editorial Escuela.

Bierhorst, John. 1974. *Four Masterworks of American Indian Literature*. Tucson, AZ: University of Arizona Press.

———. 1985. *Cantares Mexicanos: Songs of the Aztecs*. Stanford, CA: Stanford University Press.

———. 1985. *A Nahuatl-English Dictionary and Concordance to the Cantares Mexicanos with an Analytic Transcription and Grammatical Notes*. Stanford, CA: Stanford University Press.

Brotherson, Gordon. 1979. *Image of the New World: The American Continent Portrayed in Native Texts*. London: Thames and Hudson.

Cortázar, Julio. 1956. *Final del juego*. México: Los Presentes.

———. 1968. *Blow-Up and Other Stories*. New York: Collier Books.

———. 1972. *62: A Model Kit*. New York: Pantheon Books.

———. 1978. "The Present State of Fiction in Latin America." *The Final Island: The Fiction of Julio Cortázar*. Ed. Jaime Alazraki and Ivar Ivask. Normal, OK: University of Oklahoma Press. 26-36.

———. 1984. *Around the Day in Eighty Worlds*. San Francisco, CA: North Point Press.

Federn, Paul. 1942. "Some Suggestions on the Mental Hygiene of Soldiers." *Mental Hygiene* 26:554-559.

———. 1952. *Ego Psychology and the Psychoses*. New York: Basic Books.

Fuentes, Carlos. 1984. "Julio Cortázar, 1914-1984: The Simón Bolívar of the Novel." *Contemporary Literary Criticism Yearbook 1984*. Ed. Sharon K. Hall. Detroit, MI: Gale Research Company. 330-331.

Garfield, Evelyn Picon. 1975. *Julio Cortázar.* New York: Frederick Ungar.

Harss, Luis, and Barbara Dohmann. 1967. *Into the Mainstream: Conversations with Latin American Writers.* New York: Harper and Row.

León-Portilla, Miguel. 1963. *Aztec Thought and Culture.* Norman, OK: University of Oklahoma Press.

Macadam, Alfred J. 1972. "Cortázar on Cortázar: A Literary Anthology." *Review* (Winter), 35-41.

Magill, Frank N. 1994. *Masterpieces of Latino Literature.* New York: Harper and Collins.

Nicholson, Gail. 1959. *Firefly in the Night: A Study of Ancient Mexican Poetry and Symbolism.* London: Faber and Faber.

———. 1968. *A Guide to Mexican Poetry: Ancient and Modern.* Mexico, D. F.: Minutiae Mexicana.

Peavler, Terry J. 1990. *Julio Cortázar.* Boston: Twayne Publishers.

Prego, Omar. 1985. *La fascinación de las palabras: conversaciones con Julio Cortázar.* Barcelona, Spain: Muchnik Editores.

Roazen, Paul. 1975. *Freud and His Followers.* New York: Alfred A. Knopf.

Soustelle, Jacques. 1964. *Daily Life of the Aztecs.* Harmondsworth, Middlesex, England: Pelican Books.

Weiss, Edoardo. 1952. "Introduction." In Paul Federn, *Ego Psychology and the Psychoses.* New York: Basic Books.

———. "Paul Federn." 1966. In F. Alexander, S. Eisenstein, and M. Grotjahn, eds., *Psychoanalytic Pioneers.* New York: Basic Books.

Marshall Bruce Gentry (essay date fall 1995)

SOURCE: Gentry, Marshall Bruce. "Gender Dialogue and Ventriloquism in Julio Cortázar's 'Graffiti.'" *Arkansas Review* 4, no. 2 (fall 1995): 229-41.

[*In the following essay, Gentry focuses on the ambiguous attitude toward the female gender evidenced by the questionable sex of the narrating voice in "Graffiti."*]

In the introduction to their anthology *Our Mutual Room: Modern Literary Portraits of the Opposite Sex,* Emily Ellison and Jane B. Hill suggest that one of the signs of "vitality" in contemporary fiction is the frequency with which we see "cross-gender writing" (v), writing using a point of view by which the author enters the perspective of the opposite sex. Their anthology responds to an article by Reynolds Price in which he bemoans what he calls "the increasing rarity" of such writing (16).[1] One might reasonably ask how thoroughly a contemporary male fiction writer like the late Julio Cortázar takes advantage of the various strategies for introducing the perspectives of women into his work. This essay explores a fascinating late story by Cortázar, "Graffiti," in which the gender of the narrating voice is one of the major puzzles. The story can be read as one in which the treatment of women is admirable, but it can also be read as a story in which the treatment of women is extremely sinister, in which women exist to be silenced. This story raises the issue of the extent to which a story's vitality may depend on its balancing of progressive and retrograde stances on gender issues.

I would like to think Cortázar would agree with Wendy Lesser when, in *His Other Half: Men Looking at Women Through Art,* she talks about male artists whose work "evokes the human figure and its surrounding world":

> For me, the highest criterion on which such art can be judged is the extent to which the artist succeeds in freeing his creations, his human figures, rather than retaining possession of them as puppets of his own ideas and desires . . . Fairness—not in the sense of total objectivity . . . and not in the sense of rigidly observed evenhandedness (as if gender quotas prevailed in art), but in the sense of true open mindedness, true willingness to tolerate difference and disagreement and disobedience—that kind of fairness is essential. . . .
>
> (266)

Such sentiments call to mind the theories of M. M. Bakhtin, for whom the novel as dialogue (as a field of play in which characters may rival their authors for authority) is the height of modern literary art; yet, Bakhtin himself has something of a blind spot with regard to feminism (Booth 154). I consider it important to ask how successfully the crossing of the gender line on the part of an author like Cortázar produces the freedom for females that would constitute a Bakhtinian dialogue of genders. The opposite of a gender dialogue, for my purposes here, I will call ventriloquism, that situation in which characters are merely ventriloquists' dummies, mouthing only those words prescribed for them by the hand of the monologic author or narrator.

The standard conception of the "plot" of "Graffiti," a story narrated primarily in second person, is easy to summarize. The narrator addresses a graffiti artist (presumably male) in a totalitarian atmosphere where the police prohibit even abstract graffiti. Through much of the story, the narrator describes the artist's actions and thoughts, even those that are most secret. One day additional drawings begin to appear next to those produced by the graffiti artist, who imagines that these drawings are produced by a female artist, and the two carry on a wordless dialogue of sorts until she is apparently arrested and tortured. At the end of the story comes a reversal of sorts achieved by a shift into first person. Commentators generally say they discover at the end of the story that the female artist (who has barely survived her torture) is the narrator (Cochran 9, Peavler 91), and her final words are that she will no longer communicate with the graffiti artist but she wants him to continue to draw graffiti. Maurice Hemingway and Frank McQuade say that "the whole narration belongs to the woman and what seems to have been the man's speculation about her turns out to be her speculations about him" (57). Hemingway and McQuade almost make **"Graffiti"** a romantic love story:

> [T]he woman has been describing her fate in . . . a nobly detached way and . . . we realize that, hiding herself away, she has been speculating about the graffiti artist's reactions to her. This then is an original and unusual setting for a kind of political *Romeo and Juliet,* and the reader feels a sense of loss, a sense that delicate human feelings, symbolized by the graffiti, have been violated by a regime of terror.
>
> (57-58)

Commentators generally agree that the story is both political and politically advanced. Mary Lusky Friedman mentions a *New York Times* article about graffiti in Buenos Aires to support her claim that Cortázar's story protests "the censorship of art" (35). Hemingway and McQuade say that they can arrive at a "precise" reading because they know the story was "written after the military coup in Argentina in March 1976" (50); the state's "brutality" is opposed to the victims' "humanity" (56).[2] Terry J. Peavler says it is significant that Cortázar himself placed **"Graffiti"** in the volume of his complete stories that contains other realistic stories about politics (93). One might also note that **"Graffiti"** was the only story from the collection *We Love Glenda So Much and Other Tales* to be published in English (in *Mother Jones*) outside of its publication in the collection, and the only story from the collection to be selected for the posthumous collection *Textos Politicos.*

Nevertheless, serious questions have been raised about Cortázar's politics when it comes specifically to gender. Martha Paley Francescato was among the first to question Cortázar's treatment of his female characters. Perhaps the most thorough indictment of Cortázar's politics of gender comes from Ana Hernández del Castillo. In discussing works Cortázar published by

the mid 1970s, this critic analyses his "profound uneasiness regarding women, which [is] reflected in the nonhuman or mythical representation of the Feminine in his works . . ." (6). Hernández del Castillo charges that Cortázar typically fails to confront "the symbolic figures that are born through him"—his most significant refusal having to do with the central female figure in *Hopscotch* (91). Hernández del Castillo concludes, "The line of development drawn by Cortázar's works points to an integration that has not yet occurred" (114); presumably, late works like **"Graffiti"** could give Cortázar's career a successful shape. In discussing the stories that appear in *We Love Glenda So Much and Other Tales,* two male critics suggest again that there may be problems with Cortázar's handling of gender. E. D. Carter, Jr., says, "There is always an undercurrent of violence and male domination in Cortázar's eroticism, and the author consistently maintained . . . that all erotic activity contains an element of sadism" (25-26). Paul Zweig connects the *Glenda* [*We Love Glenda So Much*] stories to Poe, saying, "Almost every story contains a preternatural, maybe dangerous woman who both eludes the author and fascinates him" (37). The comparison to Poe is surely justified, for Cortázar translated all of Poe's prose into Spanish in 1953 with the help of his first wife (Peavler xi, 2). Ana Hernández del Castillo, furthermore, makes a strong case that Poe heavily influenced Cortázar; she compares Cortázar's *Hopscotch* to those Poe stories in which "the hero paradoxically expresses his love through the destruction of its object" (38).

The best argument in favor of Cortázar's handling of gender comes from John Turner. While he says that Cortázar constantly associates the male's "eroticism with violence, with behavior which in real life we call sexist or worse" (44), Turner, who analyzes two stories other than **"Graffiti,"** concludes as follows:

> I suspect that, whatever conscious messages may be derived from these stories, our unconscious view of male sexuality is shaken up in the act of reading them and that, if we read with our minds open, the experience is as therapeutic for the reader as Cortázar felt it was for the writer.
>
> (54)

I read **"Graffiti"** in a manner Turner might endorse—as a story conveying conflicting messages—and I think it is necessary to acknowledge the conflict in order to derive what may be the story's "therapeutic" pleasures.

While I have encountered little specific discussion of the gender politics of **"Graffiti,"** the commentaries I have found say little that would not fit into a reading in which Cortázar breaks with Poe, in which Cortázar's openness toward the perspectives of women is remarkable, in which the voice of a woman succeeds in taking over the story. Nor does the presumably male graffiti artist in the story clearly feel anything other than affection for the woman who undergoes torture. At this point I would like to retrace and analyze more carefully some of the twists and turns in the experience of reading **"Graffiti"** (for myself and some other readers) in order to clarify the basis for the standard interpretation of the story—as a gender dialogue producing love and good politics—and also in order to clarify other possibilities, including an interpretation in which the story displays a particularly sneaky form of ventriloquism, with a male ventriloquist and a female dummy.

While reading **"Graffiti,"** one has to make several adjustments in one's notion of who is addressing whom. A first impression may be that the author is speaking directly to the reader, at least through the first few words: "So many things begin and perhaps end as a game, I suppose that it amazed you" (33). Such an initial response is likely, I would suggest, among both naive readers (who may not catch that this is a work of fiction) and sophisticated readers on the lookout for postmodern trickery. By the story's end, one realizes that such a reading is correct in a sense, that, among other things, the story is indeed about the relationship between Cortázar and the reader.

By the time one finishes the first sentence of the story, one probably decides that the reader is not being addressed after all, that instead a graffiti artist is being addressed. It may seem that the speaker is the author, or—if one wishes to explain who produced the second sketch mentioned in the story's first sentence—one may decide that the speaker is another graffiti artist. The reader does not know the gender of either the speaker or the listener at this point. Reading further, one will think that the gender of both speaker and listener has become clear, but by the end, one will be back almost at the starting point, almost entirely unsure about gender.

Soon after starting to read **"Graffiti,"** the reader "discovers" that the other graffiti artist is a woman:

> When the other one [sketch] appeared next to yours you were almost afraid, suddenly the danger had become double, someone like you had been moved to have some fun on the brink of imprisonment or something worse, and that someone, as if it were of no small importance, was a woman.
>
> (34)

One may decide that the speaker is this woman, even though it seems peculiar that the speaker should know so much about a listener she may never have met; one

assumes for the moment that the woman has come to know the listener by looking at the listener's graffiti, or that the two artists have come to know each other after the events of the story but prior to the telling of this story. Or perhaps the narrator is a third party, not one of the graffiti artists.

The next adjustment to one's theory about who is talking to whom in **"Graffiti"** seems to become necessary when the woman is carried away by the police for sketching an answer to one of the listening artist's sketches: "you saw the struggle, black hair pulled by gloved hands, the kicks and screams, the cut-off glimpse of blue slacks before they threw her into the wagon and took her away" (36). The reader presumes the police will torture and kill her. If the reader has theorized that the woman graffiti artist is the speaker, it is difficult to explain how she continues to tell the listener what the listener is doing and thinking; one may decide that the all-knowing, loving female speaker is actually the creation of the listener she seems to know so well. Perhaps the woman who narrates the story does not exist. On the other hand, if the reader has been comfortable with the idea that the author is narrating, the woman's death is less disturbing to our theories; some readers may be relieved to think her dead, because her death might simplify the story.

The sense that one has finally figured out that the woman graffiti artist exists only in the listener's mind is shaken in the final sentences of the story. After the listener manages to overcome the loss of the woman sufficiently to draw another sketch, it receives an answering sketch, perhaps from the woman, who presumably is not quite dead. The final sketch—drawn supposedly by the woman—is a grotesque drawing of a battered, distorted face, the description of which leads into lines in which it is possible to imagine at least three different voices speaking.

The lines are "I know, I know, but what else could I have sketched for you? What message would have made any sense now?" (38). There are at least three ways to read these questions. Perhaps the woman artist is saying to her listener, "I know it's a horrible drawing, but how else can I draw the truth of my situation and tell you that you must reach out to others?" Or, if one recalls that the pronoun "I" has disappeared since the beginning of the story, when one may have thought the author was speaking, one may decide now that the author is reappearing, saying to the reader something like "I know that this is a confusing, distressing story, but how else am I to tell the truth?" A third possibility is that for the first time in the story, the listener becomes a speaker, saying to the fantasy woman he has created something like "I realize now that I'm the one who was drawing *all* of the graffiti on the walls, and I know you want it to be beautiful, but how else can I show you that I share your pain?" Going through the story's final lines, the reader can easily imagine the two graffiti artists telling each other to carry on despite a world of problems and the author telling the reader to do likewise. Of course, this description of how one might read **"Graffiti"** is affected by my multiple readings of the tale. Everyone I have talked to about the story relates a series of false starts and confusions that my complicated description may still have oversimplified.

After arriving at some set of conclusions about who may be talking to whom in the story, one may proceed to ask other questions. If one decides that a female graffiti artist narrates, the story probably appears to achieve gender dialogue; Cortázar succeeds in adopting the viewpoint of his female character and emphasizing the pathos of her situation in a world ruled by men. But even if the reader decides that a male graffiti artist narrates, **"Graffiti"** does not necessarily become a horror story. One way to read it that I like is that this is a story in which we learn that the life of the artist, male or female, is inherently isolated and solipsistic, but that being an artist is a kind of solipsism that cures itself. In this reading, the listener, as he expresses his irresistible urge to be creative, creates the female, which one might understand as the female part of his own psyche, or as a lover, or both. Even his retreat into a world entirely of his own making, into a world that has little connection to the world of real people, is ultimately a movement that will result in his return to caring for the suffering humanity around him. The final lines of the story refer to the need to have the making of sketches continue, to have sketches produced even though they will have to find a different and presumably larger audience than the sketches have found before. The possibility of such an expanded audience is suggested when the man waits for the imagined woman to see the sketch he has drawn in answer to one of hers and sees many people passing by: "any one of the many women coming and going might be her" (36).

The reader can make much of the ambiguity of some words near the end of the story, "I had imagined your life" (38). One way to read this line is to say that the artist who has been listening through most of the story is now telling the imagined woman he realizes she is in his imagination; he simply wants to continue to believe in her. An alternative reading is that in which she is speaking, in which the woman, real or fantastic, claims to have created the artist who has listened to her throughout the story. Such a reading makes sense when one thinks about how little of a life the artist has without this "muse" of sorts, or about how fantasies can be more "real" than the rest of one's life. Perhaps

it is significant that the title of the story is a word the woman likes more than the graffiti artist does: "you didn't like the term graffiti, so art critic-like" (34). A third way to read the line about having "imagined your life," of course, is to consider the author the speaker again. Is Cortázar telling readers that he is creating them? It is comforting to imagine that he has anticipated the trek through his narrative labyrinth. Perhaps he is able to admit that readers can turn the tables on him, that readers can say to Cortázar that they have imagined his life as well. Some of my students have in fact done that; the biographical note at the end of the story as it appears in *Mother Jones* suggests to some readers that Cortázar has taken the easy way out, that he has run away to Paris instead of staying to fight the problems in Argentina that the story describes. But as a colleague of mine has suggested, the train of thought I have been following—in which fantasies about art sustain us despite the possible distance of art from our lives—justifies even that movement on Cortázar's part. Argentineans may need to create a Cortázar who battles for them from the fantasyland of Paris, in other words.[3] The story may lead one to a view of it in which identity is essentially shared, in which all people create each other and understand each other. The reader may take the story as gender dialogue regardless of whether the narrator is male or female.

But to read the story as a gender dialogue provides only partial understanding. What happens when one focuses on the morality of the listener's actions? Perhaps, operating in a desperate situation, the listener manages to at least fantasize the possibility of devotion to and communication with another human being. On the other hand, one might also say that in order to believe that a woman loves him, he has accepted—perhaps even required—her death. This acceptance of her death may be unavoidable due to the extreme repressiveness of the society, of course; notice that the story suggests on two occasions that even children in this culture are losing the creative urges one typically considers natural to them (34, 37). But it may also be that the death of the woman is to some extent the male artist's fault. As the man begins to create his beloved, he creates a woman who is, in many ways, merely his puppet. She is present to him only through the drawings he attributes to her—sketches he has created himself—and through the script he has written for her that he himself recites, in which all she can think about is what he might be thinking. When he makes love to her, moreover, she is given a body of his creation: "you pictured her as dark and silent, you chose lips and breasts for her, you loved her a little" (35). The word "silent" here is especially significant; it implies that the artist cannot allow a woman a full measure of freedom even in fantasy. When the woman is supposedly carried off by the police—because presumably the sight of his sketch in reply to one of her sketches is so overwhelming that she loses all caution—what he sees is necessarily only a hint of a woman, totally without specific characteristics. As one of my female students has pointed out about this passage, there is nothing in it to tell us definitely that what the artist sees is even clearly the arrest of a woman, much less the woman the artist loves. It is probably important that the artist finds a meaning he likes in the remains of the sketch she drew before her capture, a sketch which may achieve some of its value for him from the fact that it is "truncated" (36). The artist cannot afford to see so much of the woman that she becomes fully individualized.

It is also possible to argue, I believe, that the corrupt political system described in the story can be taken very seriously as a necessary precondition to the listening artist's art. He draws because the police and their workers keep the walls blank, and rather puzzlingly, his happiness while one of his sketches is allowed to stay up is compared to a "very clean space" (34). The story makes it very apparent that the drawing of sketches did not begin because of political protest, and that the artist avoids writing words because the police, rather than their underlings, the cleaning crew workers, clean those up (34). Are we then to suspect that the sketches and even their replies from the woman are in fact functions of the state's absolute control? Are we to suspect that the artist's imagined scene in which the woman is taken away unites him with the police, who can see in such a woman only a potential prisoner? Perhaps one should view this story primarily as one in which the horrors of the police state are illustrated through descriptions of the truncated art it produces. When one reaches the final scene in which the authorities do not erase the sketches, one might suspect that the artist is producing the kind of graffiti that the police like. I find troubling the artist's comfortable feeling of safety when he sees a drunk collapse before what is supposedly a sketch of "recognition and love" (37). It may be the oppressor's strategy to encourage our illusions of freedom; perhaps when we look at the story's ending, we should suspect that the multiplicity of meaning is linked to the smashing of a face.[4]

"Graffiti" points out, I believe, the dangers inherent in the process of imposing one's will on the lives of others, truncating people in order to make them fit into one's fantasy life, into one's work of art—or, for that matter, into an interpretation. While on the one hand we may look at this story as one in which several voices manage to have their say, we might also suspect, with trepidation, that the voices are all controlled by another master ventriloquist from whom they think themselves to be free—the state. Even the extreme experiment of having a story narrated by a fantasy in a listener's mind may not be sufficiently innovative to achieve freedom from the malicious authority that fiction pretends to let us escape.

Let us not underestimate that multiplicity of meaning. My students and I have determined that this may be a story in which a man and a woman exist, in which only a man exists, in which only a woman exists, in which two women exist (both homosexual), or in which two men exist (one homosexual, narrating for a heterosexual).[5] The more one examines the story, the more one notices one's inclination to wear blinders. As a male educator at an institution that primarily serves female students, I find that one of the things most valuable for me about **"Graffiti"** is that I continue to be given insights into the story by women readers. This circumstance is part of what leads me toward the acceptance of something like John Turner's position, described earlier. Even if the story does give conflicting messages, wherein some cases women are silenced, made dummies, or tortured, perhaps the story is valuable for the experience of reexamining the habits that lead to our readings. Still, I wonder. One may be puzzled about what to make of Cortázar's distinction between a "passive reader" or "female-reader," who reads in a straight-forward, unquestioning, less engaged manner, and the "accomplice-reader," presumably male (qtd. in Carter 27). Carter says that Cortázar "always insisted upon the 'open' nature of his fiction, inviting the reader to participate, to use his imagination freely, to become, in his terms, an 'accomplice-reader'" (21). The female reader does not receive as clear an invitation as the male reader does to search out the story's complicated possibilities. Is the implication here that Cortázar expects women to find only the love story narrated by a dying woman?

Notes

1. Another interesting contrast between Price's essay and the anthology introduction is that while Price sees more men than women carrying on the grand tradition that extends back at least to the beginnings of the novel (16), Ellison and Hill discover more women than men engaged in cross-gender writing (iv).

2. According to Sarah de Mundo Lo's bibliography of Cortázar, "Graffiti" first appeared in Spanish ("Grafitti") in *Queremos tanto a Glenda y otros relatos* in 1980 (20).

3. This colleague is Alice Friman, my wife.

4. For an interesting argument that the story is *more* successfully and admirably political for revealing

the political nature of what is supposedly non-political, see Terry Cochran's "Critical Action and the 'Third World.'"

5. This last reading has two special virtues: it explains why the speaker knows his arrest was not seen clearly, and it gives an interesting explanation for the speaker's decision not to be seen at the end.

Works Cited

Booth, Wayne C. "Freedom of Interpretation: Bakhtin and the Challenge of Feminist Criticism." *Critical Inquiry* 9.1 (1982): 45-76. Rpt. in *Bakhtin: Essays and Dialogues on His Work.* Ed. Gary Saul Morson. Chicago: U of Chicago P, 1986. 145-76.

Carter, E. D., Jr. *Julio Cortázar: Life, Work, and Criticism.* Fredericton, NB, Can.: York, 1986.

Cochran, Terry. "Critical Action and the 'Third World.'" *Critical Exchange* 22 (Spring 1987): 1-9.

Cortázar, Julio. "Graffiti." *Mother Jones* Apr. 1983: 35-36.

———. "Graffiti." *We Love Glenda So Much and Other Tales.* Trans. Gregory Rabassa. New York: Knopf, 1983. 33-38.

———. "Graffiti." *Textos Politicos.* Barcelona: Plaza and Janés, 1985. 83-88.

Ellison, Emily, and Jane B. Hill. Introduction. *Our Mutual Room: Modern Literary Portraits of the Opposite Sex.* Ed. Emily Ellison and Jane B. Hill. Atlanta: Peachtree, 1987. i-xxvi.

Francescato, Martha Paley. "The New Man (But Not the New Woman)." *The Final Island: The Fiction of Julio Cortázar.* Ed. Jaime Alazraki and Ivar Ivask. Norman: U of Oklahoma P, 1978. 134-39.

Friedman, Mary Lusky. "Ulterior Realities." Rev. of *We Love Glenda So Much and Other Tales,* by Julio Cortázar. *Review* 32 (1984): 35-36.

Hemingway, Maurice, and Frank McQuade. "The Writer and Politics in Four Stories by Julio Cortázar." *Revista Canadiense de Estudios Hispanicos* 13.1 (1988): 49-5.

Hernández del Castillo, Ana. *Keats, Poe, and the Shaping of Cortázar's Mythopoesis.* Purdue University Monographs in Romance Languages 8. Amsterdam: John Benjamins, 1981.

Lesser, Wendy. *His Other Half: Men Looking at Women Through Art.* Cambridge: Harvard UP, 1991.

Mundo Lo, Sarah de. *Julio Cortázar: His Works and His Critics: A Bibliography.* Urbana: Albatross, 1985.

Peavler, Terry J. *Julio Cortázar.* Twayne's World Author Series 816. Boston: Twayne, 1990.

Price, Reynolds. "Men, Creating Women." *New York Times Book Review* 9 Nov. 1986: 1, 16, 18, 20.

Turner, John H. "Sexual Violence in Two Stories of Julio Cortázar: Reading as Psychotherapy?" *Latin American Literary Review* 15 (July-Dec. 1987): 43-56.

Zweig, Paul. "Ominous People Doing Odd Things." Rev. of *We Love Glenda So Much and Other Tales,* by Julio Cortázar. *New York Times Book Review* 27 Mar. 1983: 1, 37, 38.

Terry J. Peavler (essay date 1995)

SOURCE: Peavler, Terry J. "Something Old, Something New? Cortázar's Final Fictions." In *La Chispa '95: Selected Proceedings,* edited by Claire J. Paolini, pp. 291-300. New Orleans: Louisiana Conference on Hispanic Languages and Literatures, Tulane University, 1995.

[*In the following essay, Peavler studies the thematic commingling of the visual arts and sociopolitical commentary in Cortázar's later collections.*]

Few writers of short fiction have been more concerned with the visual arts than Julio Cortázar. Dozens of essays examine the close relationship between **"Las babas del diablo,"** photography, and motion pictures, while other dozens explore the importance of painting, photography, and other forms of visual art in such novels as *62. modelo para armar* and *Rayuela,* or in such short stories as **"Siestas"** and **"Con legítimo orgullo,"** or in books dedicated to photography or painting for which Cortázar provided written texts, books such as *Territorios,* or *Silvalandia,* or even the mixed text created by Cortázar himself, *Prosa del observatorio*; such a list could go on almost indefinitely.

In recent years, attention has again turned to the presence of visual arts in Cortázar's fiction, largely because of their return to preeminence in his later works, a tendency particularly evident in his last three short story collections, **Alguien que anda por ahí** (1977), **Queremos tanto a Glenda** (1980), and **Deshoras** (1983). Significantly, these are not only texts in which non-verbal artistic forms acquire their greatest presence, but they are also the works in which Cortázar's preoccupation with social and political issues reaches its apogee. Any avid reader of the Argentine writer's fiction is well aware that political and social commentary have existed both overtly (*Los reyes* [1949], *El examen* [1950?], *Libro de Manuel* [1973]), and, more subtly perhaps, in dozens of fine stories, including **"La banda"** (1956), **"Las ménades"** (1956), **"Con legítimo orgullo"** (1967), etc., and most will be familiar with his attempt to demonstrate to Cuban revolutionaries that political statement and aesthetic excellence are not antithetical in **"Reunión"** (1966). However, the three story collections that represent the culmination of Cortázar's preoccupation with visual arts also contain the stories in which he paints his social and political concerns with the finest aesthetic brush. This is by no means to assert that all of the stories in *Alguien que anda por ahí, Queremos tanto a Glenda,* and *Deshoras* are among the author's finest, but rather that these collections contain some of his very best, and that among these are works in which Cortázar somehow managed to wed his greatest love with his greatest worry, the artistic with the social, sublimation with denunciation.

In fact, Cortázar's ability to cloak the insidious with the comic and the absurd has become, in some instances, so great that readers are almost forced to approach some stories twice—once as delightful comic narratives, and again as ominous commentaries on censorship and control. Most, for example, will have found the title story **"Queremos tanto a Glenda"** to be a captivating tale of an overly exhuberant fan club, but these same readers might suffer a chill of recognition on reading Lois Parkinson Zamora's observation: "The insistence of Glenda's fans on a single, unchanging aesthetic is implicitly related to social and political repression. The narrator speaks derisively of differences of opinion, of moral objections within the group itself . . . but he assures the reader that such 'heresy' has been eradicated" ("Movement and Stasis" 56). This echoes, on more than one level, the paradigm shift that many experience in reading the much earlier **"La banda"** (1956), the specific political undertones of which have been explained by Jaime Alazraki.

The story that is most evocative of previous Cortázar masterpieces is **"Apocalipsis en Solentiname"** (*Alguien que anda por ahí*). Here, a hardly disguised Julio Cortázar visits the revolutionary city of Solentiname, Nicaragua, where he takes still photographs of simple, child-like paintings that local townspeople create and sell to help support their struggle. After returning to his apartment in Paris, in a scene reminiscent of **"Las babas del diablo,"** the narrator projects the slides and discovers to his horror that they depict massacres and scenes of torture, including the killing of his friend, the Salvadoran poet Roque Dalton. When his female companion comes in and asks to see the pictures, the narrator leaves her to view them while he goes to the bathroom to vomit. Upon his return, she comments on how delightful the paintings are and how beautifully the slides of them turned out. As in **"Las babas"** [**"Las babas del diablo"**], the photo-

graphs clearly have an existence that is either independent of the scene photographed, or one that is projected only in the mind of the photographer.

The story also evokes **"Las babas"** in its almost metaphysical toying with the photographic process (Peavler, "Blow-Up"). Whereas in the earlier piece Cortázar "pataphysically" speculates that perhaps when one presses the shutter button the photographic process can be reversed and that the photographer may be forever captured in the act of observing the action that passes before his lens, in **"Apocalipsis"** [**"Apocalipsis en Solentiname"**], he toys with the concept of the instant camera: how can one be certain that rather than a print of the visiting dignitaries, the camera will not eject a photograph of Napoleon on his white charger? The latter story is, however, far more grim in its depiction of real, not imagined, scenes of horror: the torture, the massacre, the devastation of the Nicaraguan village, as well as the death of Roque Dalton, are very much a part of documented, "real" history, a story that photography brought into the living rooms of the world. The power of **"Apocalipsis,"** however, is not due to the author's cleverness in combining visual art with fictional narrative, for he has travelled that road many times before, nor does it stem from the obvious passion that the events in Nicaragua provoked in Cortázar, for other stories are clearly born of equal rage. **"Apocalipsis"** is, quite simply, one of Cortázar's best stories because it combines in a masterful way the radical narrative experiments of his early fiction with the realism and social commitment that are more evident in his later works.

The power of art achieves new heights in one of Cortázar's most compelling (and most repulsive) stories, **"Grafitti"** (*Queremos tanto a Glenda,* 1980). This story is even more disturbing than **"Apocalipsis"** because the horrors are not revealed through the interaction of a character's mind and a series of photographs (hence removed at least one degree from reality), but are the direct result of two artists' personal experiences. Like a number of the author's later works, **"Grafitti"** depicts the urban political violence that plagued Argentina in the 1970s. The narrator (whose identity is obscured at first) corresponds with another who is identified simply as "tú" by means of painting grafitti on public walls. Their works depict the anguish of the city's inhabitants who have become prisoners and victims of their own government. Finally the police catch and torture one of correspondents, and the walls remain clean for some time. Soon, however, "tú" renews his secret efforts, now painting the screams of the victims of oppression. One night, another work by his anonymous correspondent (the narrator) appears, a farewell message, painted by a woman whose face has been totally disfigured by police torture, and who does not want her correspondent to see the result.

According to the narrator, the narratee began painting grafitti just for the pleasure of it, without recognizing or acknowledging the seriousness of the game: "Tu propio juego había empezado por aburrimiento, no era en verdad una protesta contra el estado de cosas en la ciudad, el toque de queda, la prohibición amenazante de pegar carteles o escribir en los muros. Simplemente te divertía hacer dibujos con tizas de colores . . ." (*Relatos* 4, 7). These drawings were not political at all, but nonetheless fell under the official prohibition. But when the narrator left her own drawing alongside one of his, the game took a more dangerous turn: "Cuando el otro apareció al lado del tuyo casi tuviste miedo, de golpe el peligro se volvía doble, alguien se animaba como vos a divertirse al borde de la cárcel o algo peor, y ese alguien por si fuera poco era una mujer . . . la admiraste, tuviste miedo por ella, esperaste que fuera la única vez, casi te delataste cuando ella volvió a dibujar al lado de otro dibujo tuyo, unas ganas de reír, de quedarte ahí delante como si los policías fueran ciegos o idiotas" (8).

The two carry on an extensive dialog, almost a lover's conversation, by means of nightly drawings on dark city streets. The exchange increases in rhythm and in intensity, as does the risk for the correspondents who seek ways to catch glimpses of one another by lingering near the scenes of their crimes. Inevitably one, the woman who narrates, is captured by the police while attempting to draw yet another utterance in their pictorial dialog. "Tú" seeks solace in gin, trying to drown the imagined details of what surely is being inflicted on the "desaparecida." A month later, "tú" takes up his colored chalk once again, but this time without the innocence and without the play: "allí donde ella había dejado su dibujo, llenaste las maderas con un grito verde, una roja llamarada de reconocimiento y de amor" (10). The following night the grafitti is still in place, for the police have been distracted by trouble in the suburbs, and at three the following morning "tú" discovers that the narrator has returned:

> Te acercaste con algo que era sed y horror al mismo tiempo, viste el óvalo naranja y las manchas violeta de donde parecía saltar una cara tumefacta, un ojo colgando, una boca aplastada a puñetazos. Ya sé, ya sé, ¿pero qué otra cosa hubiera podido dibujarte? ¿Qué mensaje hubiera tenido sentido ahora? De alguna manera tenía que decirte adiós y a la vez pedirte que siguieras.
>
> (11)

"**Grafitti**" does not, in any direct way, project the power of visual art onto a metaphysical plane. Nor does it seem to suggest that painting can express the

otherwise inexpressable. Essentially, the grafitti dialog begins as a sort of game; the conversants fall (or the narrator imagines that they fall) in love; she is captured and tortured; she is released but never allows "tú" to see her now-disfigured face. Here art is born amid the sparkle of innocence, albeit against a deadly backdrop of repression, and boasts neither artistic pretension nor importance: "Simplemente te divertía hacer dibujos con tizas de colores (no te gustaba el término *grafitti*, tan de crítico de arte)" (7). That the narrator knows so much about "tú," his thoughts and his intentions, may readily be ascribed to her imagination and to the fact that just as he has done with her, she too has watched him "read" her work and create his response from a safe hiding place: "Algo tenía que dejarte antes de volverme a mi refugio donde ya no había ningún espejo, solamente un hueco para esconderme hasta el fin en la más completa oscuridad, recordando tantas cosas y a veces, así como había imaginado tu vida, imaginando que hacías otros dibujos, que salías por la noche para hacer otros dibujos" (11).

This condemnation of urban violence, violence on a level that only government institutions can attain, is echoed but carried to a far more personal level in "**Recortes de prensa**" (*Glenda* [*We Love Glenda So Much*], 1980). Here the protagonist, Noemí, a professional writer, anguishes over her inability to do anything about the horrors taking place in Argentina. She is invited by a sculptor to write a series of texts to accompany photographs of his work, sculptures that denounce violence. Together (and with the reader) they review a "real" press clipping—an open letter from an Argentine woman, now living in Mexico, denouncing the horrors inflicted on her and her family. Shortly after leaving the sculptor's studio Noemí finds a little girl sobbing in the streets. On being told "'Mi mamá' . . . 'Mi papá le hace cosas a mi mamá,'" (*Relatos* 4, 33), she accompanies the child back to her shack where she finds the nude mother bound to a bed and being slowly and systematically tortured by the father with a burning cigarette. Noemí attacks the man with a stool, releases the woman, ties the man in her place, and then helps the former victim torture her former tormentor—to death. The text she provides to the sculptor is the story of the night's events, but he reads another account of the episode in the newspaper, complete with photographs, and concludes that she based her version on it. Noemí is unable to find the scene of her crime, but she does encounter the child, who is taken into custody by a social worker.

Much has been made of the story and of its Biblical overtones (for example Zamora, "Decifering," and González-Pérez), and critics disagree strongly over whether it is to be read as fiction or reality. As in the cases of "**La banda**" and "**Queremos tanto a**

Glenda," it is difficult to read **"Recortes"** as both simultaneously. Like the classic paradigm shifts of psychology, one can see either the old woman, or the young one, but never both at once; two opposing faces or a vase. I have discussed the story elsewhere (*Julio Cortázar*, 92-93) as essentially realistic, others have argued that the torture scene takes place only in the mind of Noemí, and nearly all who have commented on the work recognize the powerful presence of both explicitly "real" details—particularly the press clipping—and the uncertainty that surrounds much of the second half of the narrative. While Noemí finds a little girl that may or may not be the one she accompanied to the gardener's shack, she can find neither the garden nor the building where the murder took place. Near the end, we discover that the story we have just read is the text written by Noemí to accompany the sculptor's work, yet the events in which she participated were reported in the newspaper. As is so often the case with Cortázar, when one attempts a purely "realistic" reading the "facts" blur into what is quite clearly the realm of the fantastic; and yet a "fantastic" reading seems to stumble constantly over stubborn bits of what is just as clearly as "real" as anything can possibly be within a work of fiction. As González-Pérez observes, both readings conflict with one another and both do violence to the text. In point of fact, it is simply impossible to decipher whether Noemí read the account in the newspaper and based her piece on it, actually participated in the events narrated, or whether the entire story takes place only in her mind, and, in fact, it hardly matters.

These three stories—**"Apocalipsis en Solentiname," "Grafitti,"** and **"Recortes de prensa"**—clearly mark a shift that is obvious in a number of other stories from Cortázar's later period. The early stories were characterized, by and large, by a fascination with and the sheer joy of telling a great story. Despite the arguable social and political content of many works written in the forties and fifties (**"La banda"** and **"Las ménades,"** for example, are both from 1956), **"Reunión,"** from 1966, may be the first story in which the author deliberately set out to accomplish both. His intent was to challenge young Cuban revolutionaries: "que se puede escribir un cuento fantástico—que es quizás el más fantástico del libro—que tenga, a la vez, un contenido revolucionario" (González Bermejo 143). In the later stories, particularly the ones discussed here, he achieved this wedding of the aesthetic with the serious—often to the point of causing anguish and depression, to a remarkable degree. Early stories, even the most serious, typically offered the respite of Cortázar's humor, if only in an oblique way. The later stories are far more ominous. In fact, only the author's joke of Napoleon coming out of the instant camera on

his charger in **"Apocalipsis"** affords us the opportunity to smile, and that appears early in the story. Some stories from the final three collections become so serious, so deadly serious, and are told with such obvious anguish and passion on the part of the author, that his hand becomes oppressive, as I have argued elsewhere (*Julio Cortázar*, Chapter 5).

These differences were apparently due to profound changes in Cortázar himself. The later Cortázar, the author who visited Solentiname and dedicated the proceeds of his works to the Nicaraguan revolution, wrote a number of stories—**"Pesadillas," "Alguien que anda por ahí," "La escuela de noche,"** etc.—that seem inconsistent with the *oeuvre* of the man who argued that: ". . . uno de los más agudos problemas latinoamericanos es que estamos necesitando más que nunca los Che Guevara del lenguaje, *los revolucionarios de la literatura más que los literatos de la revolución*" (*Revolución* 76; original emphasis). This is not to say that such works are devoid of artistic merit, nor that he abandoned his efforts to create fresh, new, sophisticated, and aesthetically pleasing fiction; the stories we have just examined prove the contrary. Nonetheless, the later Cortázar is clearly willing to be brutally direct in denouncing a variety of social and political ills.

The later Cortázar also revisited gender issues in a very significant way. After decades on the defensive for his "lector hembra" remark, and after making a great many readers squirm with his borderline misogynous scenes, such as the sodomizing of Francine in *Libro de Manuel,* and the marital rape in **"Verano"** (1971), Cortázar seems, in **"Grafitti"** and in **"Recortes de prensa,"** to have made an effort to see the world from the perspectives of sensitive, artistic, intelligent women. However, these stories apparently do not signal a change in perception, for in *Queremos tanto a Glenda,* the same collection in which these two stories appear, one finds the infamous **"Anillo de moebius,"** a story in which a young school teacher is so enthralled by being raped and murdered that her spirit seeks out her attacker before his execution and persuades him to commit suicide so that they may spend eternity in one another's arms. This story, like those we have previously examined, is masterfully written as well, which moved Alicia Helda Puleo to write: "La extraordinaria belleza formal de este texto nos invita a olvidar su contenido" (206).

The heroines of **"Grafitti"** and **"Recortes de prensa,"** then, do not signal a new sensitivity regarding gender issues on the part of Cortázar. What they do seem to signal is a new exploration of the inner self by the author. Many of the stories of the last four collections, *Octaedro, Alguien que anda por ahí, Queremos tanto* *a Glenda,* and *Deshoras,* are dark and gloomy to the extreme, for they suggest an obsession not only with the evils of the world, but those that reside within us all. Evelyn Picón Garfield, arguably Cortázar's most devoted reader, confessed that it took her months to read **Octaedro** because she found it so distressing, and she subtitled her essay "Eight Phases of Despair." Moreover, the artist-as-narrator plays a particularly prominent role in a number of these later stories, another suggestion that the author is peering within himself.

"Recortes de prensa" is clearly the most significant story in this regard, for it suggests that Cortázar, late in his life and career, began to recognize the presence of the beast that lurks within us all, not just within others, but within even liberal Argentine writers living in Paris, within even women, within even those who are outraged at the injustices and torments inflicted by others. Thus the narrator's discovery of her own culpability, whether real or imagined—and here whether the events are "real" or "fantastic" is no longer pertinent—coincides with Cortázar's discovery of his own culpability, whether real or imagined, and her words become his: "Cómo saber cuánto duró, cómo entender que también yo, también yo aunque me creyera del buen lado también yo, cómo aceptar que también yo ahí del otro lado de manos cortadas y de fosas comunes, también yo del otro lado de las muchachas torturadas y fusiladas esa misma noche de navidad . . ." (36). These words are not simply the confession of an anguished protagonist who has only just discovered that she too, like those she would condemn, is capable of torture and murder, but also the cry of an aging author peering deep within himself and recoiling in horror at the sight of his own soul.

Works Cited

Alazraki, Jaime. "Los últimos cuentos de Julio Cortázar." *Revista Iberoamericana* 51 (1985): 31-32.

Cortázar, Julio. "Literatura en la revolución y revolución en la literatura: algunos malentendidos a liquidar." *Literatura en la revolución y revolución en la literatura.* By Óscar Collazos, Julio Cortázar and Mario Vargas Llosa. 2nd. ed. Mexico: Siglo Veintiuno, 1971. 38-77.

———. *Los relatos.* 4 vols. Madrid: Alianza, 1985.

González-Bermejo, Ernesto. *Conversaciones con Cortázar.* Barcelona: Edhasa, 1978.

González-Pérez, Aníbal. "'Recortes de prensa': periodismo y ética de la escritura en Julio Cortázar." University of Puerto Rico, Río Piedras. 14 Feb. 1995.

Peavler, Terry J. "'Blow-Up': A Reconsideration of Antonioni's Infidelity to Cortázar." *PMLA* 94 (1979): 887-93.

———. *Julio Cortázar.* Twayne's World Authors Series 816. Boston: G. K. Hall, 1990.

Picón Garfield, Evelyn. "*Octaedro*: Eight Phases of Despair." *The Final Island: The Fiction of Julio Cortázar.* Ed. Jaime Alazraki and Ivar Ivask. Norman: U of Oklahoma P, 1978. 115-28.

Puleo, Alicia Helda. "La sexualidad fantástica." Saul Yurkievich et al., *Coloquio Internacional: lo lúdico y lo fantástico en la obra de Cortázar.* Madrid: Fundamentos, 1986. 206-207.

Zamora, Lois Parkinson. "Deciphering the Wounds: The Politics of Torture and Julio Cortázar's Literature of Embodiment." *Literature and the Bible.* Ed. David Bevan. Rodopi Perspectives on Modern Literature. Amsterdam: Rodopi, 1993. 179-206.

———. "Movement and Stasis, Film and Photo: Temporal Structures in the Recent Fiction of Julio Cortázar." *Review of Contemporary Fiction* 3 (1983): 51-65.

Frederic Barberà (essay date 1995)

SOURCE: Barberà, Frederic. "Pere Calders's and Julio Cortázar's Short Stories: A Comparative Study." In *Modern Catalan Literature: Proceedings of the Fourth Catalan Symposium,* edited by Josep M. Solà-Solé, pp. 7-15. New York: Peter Lang, 1995.

[*In the following essay, Barberà compares the objectification of the fantastic via narrative perspective in the stories of Cortázar and Pere Calders.*]

Many critics have dealt with either the narrative voice or the fantastic in Cortázar's short stories; in this way, Mora Valcárcel (1982) made a great effort in distributing most of these short stories by following methodically Genette's narrative categories. Concerning the fantastic element, Eyzaguirre (1986) and Gloria Cruz (1988), both made an attempt to define the nature of the fantastic in Cortázar's short stories taking Todorov's *Le Fantastique* as a starting point. And yet a very important aspect was neglected by such an effective theoretical scaffolding: the different ways in which speech through narrative uttering shapes the fantastic and makes it appear in the text through different devices in such a way that it becomes acceptable for the reader. This is, ultimately, our goal in this approach to Cortázar's short stories, but also to those by Calders to which unfortunately (or fortunately, who knows) critics have not paid as much attention.

* * *

In the case of Cortázar's short stories, many different discursive devices, the result of which is the objectivization of the fantastic, carry out a progressive acceptance of this element in the minds of the readers. In this way, those deliberate attempts of empiric observation which come through the narrative voice already in the very first realistic novels, now emerge in these short stories to make the fantastic more and more credible. This is the case of explicative interpolations like this,

(nunca sabremos como)

("Queremos tanto a Glenda")

or the recurrent use of adverbs or periphrasis of doubt, which ends up by showing the limitations of a human narrator when trying to give an empirical version of a whole set of odd facts.

Quizá el apetito fue la razón dominante, . . .

("Reunión con un círculo rojo")

. . . y supongo que gritaba como las demás, *probablemente* como yo mismo.

("Las ménades")

Debió durar un segundo, *acaso* algo más . . .

("Los pasos en las huellas")

Likewise, the use of disjunction by the narrative voice would have a similar effect.

. . . para completar un pedido *o* acaso cambiarlo *o* irse,

("Reunión con un círculo rojo")

And even sometimes a special treatment of the linguistic register being used by the narrative voice can work its way to making a very peculiar situation appear as pure routine. This is the case of the following narrative statement:

A las cinco de la mañana . . . los pongo en el armario y hago la limpieza.

("Carta a una señorita de París")

where the 1st person narrator is referring to a few live rabbits that he has just nicely vomited. Furthermore some other discursive devices make the fantastic elements become accepted by the reader not through objectivization but through bringing it nearer to him. Thus the use of adverbs the nature of which is meant to be closer to reality often comes up in the text together with the 1st narrative person and the present tense to shape different levels of reality in the fiction of the same short story. This is the effect which would come up in the reading of this passage in **"Botella al mar"**

. . . mientras *yo aquí* termin*o esta* carta y usted en algún lado, . . .

where the 1st person "yo," the adverb "aquí," the present tense "termino" and even the demonstrative "esta" work out a "more real" level of fiction in the mind of the reader in a very subtle way which is to be distinguished from the other level pointed to as more distant, more vague, by the same narrator, "usted," "en algún lado," . . . and more "unreal" as a result. And sometimes only a difference of aspect within the past tense would be enough to establish two different "realities" within the fantastic; so it occurs in the following passage of **"El otro cielo"**:

. . . y Josiane *fue* otra vez mía en su bohardilla

. . . Pero *helaba* en las calles, y las noticias de la guerra . . .

where that switch of verbal aspect is the only subtle evidence that brings the reader, along with the narrator's experiences, from 1870 Paris to early 1940s Buenos Aires.

In spite of the importance of all these different discursive devices allowing the fantastic to become either more objective or closer to the reader, many more devices of the same discursive nature are to be found in Cortázar's short stories producing ambiguity and, along with it, creating an ideal context for the fantastic to come up. This ambiguity can be achieved in different ways. Thus those devices that cause vagueness are used quite often with this purpose, from variations purely morphological that deliberately make it impossible for the reader to know about the gender of a very odd community

un*o* de nosotros . . . , la otr*a* . . .
(un*a* de nosotros prepara . . .)

un*o* de nosotros se ocupa del apare . . .

in **"Cefalea,"** to the use of vague demonstratives, both adjectives and pronouns

. . . que nunca le habían querido, que había *esa* enfermedad, . . .

. . . para librarse de *eso* que seguía aferrando la garganta de Dina, . . .

in **"Cuello de gatito negro"** where, because of them, the reader cannot figure out anything specific; to the use of substantives the meaning of which is so generic that in a general context of deliberate confusion it does not give the reader any precise information about any thing. In this way, again in **"Cefalea,"** we never get to know the mysterious job the members of that strange community were doing since it is always referred to as "la tarea,"

. . . si *la tarea* espera en los corrales

and the same happens when the reader tries to know more about the way of life of the community itself, as the set of rules they are meant to follow is always referred to as "el estatuto."

> . . . sin previo aviso, sin cumplir para nada *el estatuto*, se han ido anoche los muy hijos de puta, . . .

Another source of ambiguity is to be found in the deliberate absence of the parts of the sentence, along with the lack of expected information which that represents for the reader; we find a whole paradigm of these "absences" in **"Las fases de Severo"** where although it is obvious that something of importance is happening around the central character, Severo, we never really get to know what is going on throughout the whole short story, those absences being mainly responsible for it. In this way, when the 1st person narrative voice states

> Me hubiera gustado darle conversación . . . *para distraerla* [0].

or

> Mamá manda decir que *se preparen*.

we, readers, never get to know "de qué," in the first case, or "para qué," in the second case. Absences, blanks (informative as well as grammatical) that result in an ambiguous understanding in the reading process . . . once more, the favourable ambience for the fantastic has been created.

In Calders' short stories, the fantastic element, which appears in most of them and gives them form, also meets an effective objectivization through the narrative voice via many discursive devices leading to a progressive "acceptance" by the reader. In this way, the narrator's claims to empirical observation of facts are indeed a good weapon against what otherwise would turn out to be suspected of "fantastic." Thus, a whole set of similar formulas underlining veracity:

> . . . del que estava segur era que, . . .

> . . . se m'aparegué com absolutament indubtable.

or paradoxically getting rid of the purely imaginative or literary as unreliable

> Pot parlar-se aquí d'una força oculta, novelesca, . . . ?
> No. De cap manera.

> . . . una superfície de carn neta i viva substituïa el monyó sangonós de nervis i de tendons *que algú s'hauria imaginat*.

> (all in "Les mans del taumaturg")

Likewise, stereotyped claims to a unique truth directly opposed to the apparently fantastic,

> Però la veritat és que . . .
>
> ("Triangles màgics")

or to claim to the readers' general knowledge,

> Sabia—*ho sap tothom*—que . . .
>
> ("Un estrany al jardí")

or just the recognition of the narrative voice's own ignorance

> No he pogut saber mai si . . .
>
> ("Triangles màgics")

> . . . què sé jo quins . . .
>
> ("Les mans del Taumaturg")

—only as a means of showing the human limits of empirical observation—, all of them are different manifestations of that effective process of objectivization of the fantastic.

Certainly, there is no doubt that the fantastic element is brought nearer the reader in an effective way through devices such as the ones we have mentioned; but it is fair to say that, in Calders' short stories, neither they nor the recurrent use of the present tense as well as the 1st narrative person, which often accompanies them, are the main distinctive features of that process of "acceptance" of the fantastic. If in Cortázar, as we saw above, several discursive sources producing ambiguity were mainly responsible for the acceptance of the fantastic, far more than those other devices of objectivization which also existed in his short stories, in the case of Calders, the process of acceptance of the fantastic is mostly carried out, still from objectivization, but through humor and irony. And, also in this case, quite a few discursive devices of different nature are serving this purpose. Thus, on the one hand is the shaping of a peculiar linguistic register through using spontaneous expressions or hilarious reactions when confronting the fantastic.

> No vau preguntar-li *què hi busquen* a la Terra?

—is asked of the narrator of "El millor amic" about an alien whom he has just met; and, likewise, in "Imprevist a la casa número deu," after a terrible gas explosion in the neighbourhood, the narrative voice states:

> Cadascú rep sobre seu el munt de runes *que li pertoca*, amb resignació.

and not long after that:

> [unes veïnes] *aprofiten* el succés per a desmaiar-se

It is often the peculiar linguistic register in charge of bringing along a dissonant element which clashes humorously with the fantastic, particularly when the story is near the end. Thus when, at the end of "El millor amic" the man who met an alien reaches the conclusion that the reason why they do not come very often to Earth is because they are afraid of dogs; this being said in colloquial Catalan sounds rather hilarious.

> . . . que els gossos els fan por. . . . aquesta és la causa que no baixin més sovint!

On the other hand, some other discursive devices come up in the text through metaliterary remarks such as the following ones the apparent result of which is the parody of what is being narrated, which in this story, "Un estrany al jardí," is the appearance of a talkative soul in the garden of the narrator's friend.

> Però això requereix no tan sols un punt i a part, sinó un espai generós marcat amb asteriscos.
>
> . . . quant al curs de la present història, també ha arribat el moment d'obrir un a part final, amb un nou espai que remarqui la seqüència.

In the same way, a similar effect is achieved by the use of contrast, by juxtaposing solemn elements to hilarious actions often translated into slang terms, for instance when the narrator-character of "Un estrany al jardí" tells us about the moment when he realized that his wife was digging near where he had just found an Egyptian mummy in the garden of his old Catalan "masia," he does so in the following terms,

> Vet aquí que un dia me la vaig trobar furgant en *la parcel·la de la mòmia.*

—where the use of the word "furgar," mainly used in a low register meaning "to scrape inside one's nose" applied to an ancient mummy who, like 20th century urban citizens in Catalonia, owns a "parcel·la" (a piece of land for building purposes), all together has an immediate parodic effect on the poor mummy, but, implicitly, the same device has further implications: we, readers, even though we laugh at the poor mummy, get to believe that it is likely for an Egyptian mummy to be found in Catalonia buried in somebody's garden, as we before got to believe that a talkative soul was having a chat in somebody else's garden, or that aliens, even though they are afraid of dogs, may come to Earth from time to time.

Cortázar's and Calders' short stories: two different sides of the fantastic through narrative uttering.

Patricia V. Lunn and Jane W. Albrecht (essay date May 1997)

SOURCE: Lunn, Patricia V., and Jane W. Albrecht. "The Grammar of Technique: Inside 'Continuidad de los parques.'" *Hispania* 80, no. 2 (May 1997): 227-33.

[*In the following essay, Lunn and Albrecht present a method for demonstrating to students the complex employment of verbs and linguistic repetition in Cortázar's short story "Continuity of Parks."*]

INTRODUCTION

Julio Cortázar's **"Continuidad de los parques"** (from the 1967 collection **Final del juego**) is one of the most anthologized stories in college textbooks. Clearly, the minimalism of the story and its arresting conclusion have captured the attention of editors, teachers and students. Surprisingly, however, little critical attention has been paid to how Cortázar achieves the effects for which the story is known. This is the more surprising in view of the story's extreme brevity, which allows the author considerable technical control and which permits readers to track all of the elements of the narrative.

Lagmanovich has shown how Cortázar uses the grammatical possibilities of Spanish, especially the aspectual contrast between preterite and imperfect, to demarcate and then to merge two fictional worlds.[1] This paper goes beyond Lagmanovich's observations to define verbal aspect in accord with current linguistic research, and then to use this definition to generate an analysis of the story which reveals that its aspectual structure is parallel to its narrative structure. To the extent that this analysis is convincing, it is also an argument in favor of using grammar as a tool for understanding texts, and against the curricular separation of grammar and literature.

The story begins with a man who is sitting in a green velvet armchair and reading a novel about an adulterous couple who plan to murder the woman's husband. The story ends as the woman's lover, who has somehow escaped from the novel, creeps up behind the green armchair in which the reader/husband is sitting. Obviously, the story raises questions about the boundaries of fiction and the permeability of fictional worlds. Not so obvious, however, is just how Cortázar manages to tell this complex and mysterious story in little more than five-hundred words.

LINGUISTIC BACKGROUND

The contrast between preterite and imperfect in Spanish is not one of tense, because both forms are past tense forms. Instead, the contrast is aspectual. The linguistic category of aspect is very broad, but it is sufficient for our purposes to say that aspect is the linguistic encoding of a speaker's (or a writer's) perspective on a verbal situation. According to Comrie, the various kinds of aspect encoded in the world's languages are "different ways of viewing the internal temporal constituency of a situation" (3). The words *perspective* and *viewing* suggest that how speakers use aspect has something in common with how they manipulate visual focus, and, indeed, the visual metaphor is both inevitable and instructive.

Langacker has argued convincingly that "[l]anguage is an integral part of human cognition" (12). It follows from this view of language that the grammars of human languages are cognitive systems that exhibit numerous parallels with perception. The preterite/ imperfect contrast is a clear example of the link between aspect and perception, because the contrast depends on speaker focus. When speakers can focus on the entirety of a past situation and therefore perceive it as a whole, i.e., as having boundaries, they mark it with the preterite; when they perceive a past situation as out of focus and therefore unbounded, they mark it with the imperfect. But focus, whether linguistic or visual, depends on point of view, and speakers may adopt a point of view either consciously or unconsciously. Historians, for example, consciously adopt an objective point of view which marks foregrounded events with the preterite and the background to these events with the imperfect. Other speakers may unconsciously use the imperfect because they are too close to a situation to see it whole (as in dreams), or too far away from a situation to perceive it clearly (as in reminiscence).

Conventionally, situations that have natural definition (typically, concrete actions) are likely to be perceived as units, and situations that lack natural definition (typically, ongoing states) are unlikely to be perceived as units. These conventions are often misinterpreted (and, alas, taught to students) as "rules" of preterite/ imperfect usage. However, it is not the case that the nature of the verbal situation imposes aspectual choice on speakers. On the contrary, speakers impose aspectual encoding on situations in the act of describing them—just as artists impose perspective on scenes in the act of painting them. That is, virtually any situation can seem whole to a speaker who is at a vantage point (physical or psychological) from which it appears to be in focus, and virtually any situation can lack boundaries for the speaker who is too close or too far away (again, either physically or psychologically) to perceive its boundaries. Lunn has discussed the literary exploitation of aspectual marking: "In their aspectual choices novelists can ignore the objective characteristics of a situation and classify it according to the point of view they wish the reader to adopt, or according to the point of view they wish to impute to a character" (54).

As a particularly skilled user of Spanish and a master storyteller, Cortázar gets maximum impact out of the preterite/imperfect contrast. In **"Continuidad de los parques"** he uses patterns of aspectual contrast to distinguish the world of the reader/husband from that of the novelistic adulterers, and then to merge the two worlds. In fact, the linguistic structure of the story is mimetic to its narrative structure, with the result that the impact of the whole is enhanced.

ASPECTUAL ANALYSIS

Based on verb endings, the story can be divided into three parts: a first part in which the reader/husband settles into the act of reading, a second part in which the doubly fictional characters in the book he is reading are introduced, and a third part in which one of these characters enters his home. At the end of the story, there is a fourth part which can be defined not by verb endings, but by the absence of verbs. Significantly, what happens in each of the first three parts of the story corresponds to distinct and describable uses of verb morphology; i.e., the content of the story is mirrored in the verb forms that are used to tell it.

In the first part, in which nothing untoward has so far taken place, preterite and imperfect are used in conventional ways: discrete actions appear in the preterite ("*volvió* al libro," "se *puso* a leer"), and background states appear in the imperfect ("del estudio que *miraba* hacia el parque," "su memoria *retenía* sin esfuerzo los nombres" [emphasis throughout ours]). At this point, the story is quite unremarkable; we are invited to believe what we are reading because the scene is described in the kind of language that an ordinary observer would use to describe it. Narratively, preterite situations stand out in contrast to imperfect situations in just the way that carefully drawn figures stand out against a sketchy background. Narratively, visually and grammatically, then, everything seems normal.

At the end of the first part, the reader/husband is firmly linked to the concrete reality of his world by the use of the preterite: "*fue* testigo del último encuentro en la cabaña del monte." The use of the word *testigo*, though, suggests that he is present in the novelistic world as well. Lagmanovich (182-83) discusses the language of children's play, in which an anchoring preterite is followed by a series of imperfects which are understood to describe imagined events.

The second part of the story describes the episode in the novel in which the lovers put into action their plan to murder the woman's husband. In this part, the preterite—used to this point to mark "real" actions—does not appear at all. In the novelistic world, even discrete actions appear in the imperfect: "ahora *llegaba* el amante," "*restañaba* ella la sangre," "él *rechazaba* las caricias." The use here of the imperfect, the marker of unbounded past tense situations, is consistent with the fact that the fictional adulterers live inside their novel and outside of time. Whenever the novel is opened to a certain page, there they are, doing just what they were doing the last time that page was read. Fictional situations are ongoing and repetitive by definition, because stories are realized each time they are heard or read; the unlimited nature of such situations is perfectly congruent with the meaning of the imperfect. The use of the imperfect to narrate the novel-within-the-story marks this world as having an existence which is simultaneous to, and contingent on, the act of reading about it.

The term "co-preterite" used by the Venezuelan grammarian Andrés Bello is helpful in understanding the role played by the imperfect in narration. For Bello, the imperfect "significa la coexistencia del atributo con una cosa pasada" (163). Bello's terminology captures the fact that imperfect situations are anchored to narrative by the preterite and serve basically to fill in background information related to situations encoded in the preterite. In **"Continuidad de los parques,"** the use of the imperfect relegates the events of the novel to the background of the story, while the preterite foregrounds the reader of the novel. This aspectual marking invites readers of the story to assume that the conventions of reading are being observed: fiction is unreal but the readers of it are real. Of course, according to these conventions, the fictional reader/husband is treated as real. In this story, as in so much of his work, Cortázar both straddles and examines the fuzzy line between reality and unreality.

There is a break between the second and third parts of the story which is signalled both by a new paragraph (the only paragraph break in the story) and by a new use of the preterite. For the first time, the actions of the characters/lovers cease to appear exclusively in the imperfect and are encoded in the preterite: "se *separaron* en la puerta," "él se *volvió* un instante." Their actions, in other words, now bear the same aspectual marking as those of the reader/husband in the first section. This choice of verb form signals aspectually that the lovers have entered the husband's world. Because its basic meaning is that of past tense time span with defined limits, the preterite often adds an air of reality to the verbal situations that bear its mark. Compare, for example, *quise llamarte* with *quería llamarte*: the preterite version means that the speaker actually made an effort to call, while the imperfect version means only that the speaker had good intentions. In the same way, the use of the preterite to mark the actions of the novelistic lovers confers on them a reality that they lacked when marked with the aspectually unfocused imperfect.

Where there is just one point of view, narrative texture and character depth are minimal. Such one-dimensionality can be seen in the second section, where the lovers are generic figures seen from a detached perspective. Both linguistically and metaphorically, the lovers become two-dimensional in the third section, where they enter the short story world in which their actions have enough definition to merit preterite focus—and to influence events in that world. In Cortázar's fiction, a change in language *is* a change in events, as he himself recognized: "En todo gran estilo el lenguaje cesa de ser un vehículo de 'ideas y sentimientos' y accede a ese estado límite en que ya no cuenta como mero lenguaje porque todo él es presencia de lo expresado" (*Vuelta* 94).

On being reread, the aspectually distinct parts of the story reveal links among themselves. The following passage appears at first to be a simple description of the reader/husband's experience of reading the novel: "*Gozaba* del placer casi perverso de irse desgajando línea a línea de lo que lo *rodeaba,* y sentir a la vez que su cabeza *descansaba* cómodamente en el terciopelo del alto respaldo, que los cigarrillos *seguían* al alcance de la mano, que más allá de los ventanales *danzaba* el aire del atardecer bajo los robles." When this sentence is re-read in the light of the story's structure, the imperfects can be understood to prefigure the aspectual marking of the novel, and the husband can be seen to leave his world behind, verb by verb. Another example comes from the third part of the story, in which "Los perros no *debían* ladrar, y no *ladraron*" as the lover/assassin approaches the house. In one sentence, imperfect *debían* refers back to the novel (in which the lovers surely discussed whether the dogs would give them away) and preterite *ladraron* places the action in the world of the reader/husband. Cortázar leads us through the loop of the story visually (from the room where the reader/husband sits, through the window to the forest where the lovers meet, and back into the house), grammatically (from the use of both verb forms, to the use of only one, and back to the use of both) and narratively (from the story to the novel and back to the story). Readers who understand how this loop is designed can experience the continuity of the text.

In the last three sentences of the story, there are no verbs at all: "En lo alto, dos puertas. Nadie en la primera habitación, nadie en la segunda. La puerta del salón, y entonces el puñal en la mano, la luz de los ventanales, el alto respaldo de un sillón de terciopelo verde, la cabeza del hombre en el sillón leyendo una novela." When verbs are absent, the information that is carried by verb morphology is absent as well. The morphological categories of person and tense have thus been eliminated, with the result that the end of the story is *literally* impersonal and atemporal: the violation of reality described in the story is not specific to any person or time. There is grammatical motivation, then, for the uncomfortable feeling that the boundary between Cortázar's story and our own reality may be as permeable as that between the reader/husband and the characters he is reading about.

ADDITIONAL FEATURES OF THE TEXT

In a successful short text, every word and every grammatical recourse must successfully communicate meaning. In addition to the manipulation of the implications of the preterite/imperfect contrast already discussed, **"Continuidad de los parques"** exhibits masterful use of other features of Spanish grammar and lexicon.

There are only three subjunctives among the fifty-two conjugated verbs, but these three subjunctives are telling. Bybee has defined mood in a general and useful way: "mood is a marker on the verb that signals how the speaker chooses to put the proposition into the discourse context" (165). Terrell and Hooper's classic study showed that the indicative mood is used in Spanish to mark propositions that can be asserted and the subjunctive to mark propositions that cannot be asserted, often because they are untrue or unrealized. Clearly, most conjugated verbs—in this text and elsewhere—are intended to engage a hearer's or a reader's attention; that is why most verbs are conjugated in the indicative, the mode of assertion. The subjunctive, in contrast, serves to suggest the existence of certain situations whose status precludes assertion.[2] Once again, verb morphology provides a potential contrast which can be used to structure narrative.

The first subjunctive in the story appears in part one, in the description of the reader/husband who is sitting in his armchair "de espaldas a la puerta que lo *hubiera* molestado como una irritante posibilidad de intrusiones." No intruder has come through that door at this point in the story, but the subjunctive foreshadows the intrusion that is to come. The remaining two occurrences of the subjunctive appear on the verb *acariciar.* In part one, the reader/husband "dejó que su mano *acariciara* una y otra vez el terciopelo verde." He does not caress his wife, because someone else is doing that. The lovers' caresses in part two appear in the subjunctive as well: "el doble repaso despiadado se interrumpía apenas para que una mano *acariciara* una mejilla." Narratively, caresses are the background to what happens in this story, and modally they are so described; for all of the characters involved, events have gone far beyond caresses.

In the context of the story's sophisticated syntax, the lexicon is notably straightforward. But, while the words themselves are simple, their disposition reveals yet another element of the continuity of the text. Of the fifty-two conjugated verbs, three appear in both parts one and two (*acariciar, empezar,* and *ser*) and three others appear in parts two and three (*correr, entrar,* and *llegar*). *Volver* appears in parts one and three. Most of the repeated verbs are verbs of motion, appropriately enough in a story in which characters and motifs arrive, enter the narrative, pass through it, and return.[3]

A look at how these verbs are used reveals links among the aspectually distinct parts of the story. For example, the first verb in the story is *había empezado,* which is pluperfect and thus connects the story with a previous past time. This same verb appears in the imperfect at the end of part two; "*Empezaba* a anochecer" describes the time of day in both worlds. In part one, the reader/husband is twice the subject of *volvió*; in part three, the lover/assassin is the subject of this verb, i.e., he performs the same action once performed by his lover's husband. The lover/assassin is the subject of imperfect *entraba* in part two, where all verbs are marked aspectually as belonging to the unreal world of the novel, and also of preterite *entró* in part three, where the fictional characters have entered the short-story world. In this case, the same character performs an action which is first aspectually blurry and then aspectually distinct.

The word *mano* appears four times, twice in part one, where the husband strokes the arm of the chair, and where cigarettes are described as being "al alcance de la *mano,*" once in part two, where the lovers' hands caress one another's cheeks, and once in part three, where the lover/assassin has "el puñal en la *mano.*" Only in the first of these instances does the noun appear with a possessive; otherwise, *mano* appears with the definite article, a word whose generic and impersonal meanings further serve to confuse and link the worlds of the novel and of the story.

USING THE STORY IN CLASS

Because of its length and its modest vocabulary, **"Continuidad de los parques"** is often assigned to intermediate learners of Spanish. The story is only superficially easy to read, however. As we have shown, Cortázar makes very sophisticated use of the linguistic resources of Spanish, and this usage is part and parcel of the plot. Students who do not understand the grammatical choices that the author has made cannot read the clues that point to the story's conclusion. Unprepared to perceive the concrete features of the text, they must have the ending explained to them, thereby missing out on the flash of understanding that the story was designed to effect. In contrast, when the story is taught as an example of, say, how the meanings of preterite and imperfect can be manipulated, it is rendered both comprehensible and accessible.

A very simple but effective tool for guiding students to an understanding of the use of aspect in the story is to ask them to mark all preterite and imperfect verbs contrastively, e.g., underline one form and circle the other, or highlight one form with one color and the other with a different color. Based on this identification of the forms (which is not as easy a task as one might expect at this level[4]), students can see that there is a part of the story which contains only imperfect verbs, and that the end of this part coincides with the paragraph break. They can also see that the all-imperfect section segregates the part before it from the part after it.

Further insights will result from asking students to answer the following questions:

> —En la primera parte, ¿qué personaje es el sujeto de los verbos en pretérito?

> —En la segunda parte, ¿qué personajes son los sujetos de los verbos en imperfecto?

> —En la tercera parte, ¿qué personajes son los sujetos de los verbos en pretérito?

> —¿Cuántos verbos conjugados hay en las últimas tres frases del cuento?

Up to this point, students have been asked to perform analyses of a mechanical kind. Based on these analyses, though, and on an understanding of the semantic value of preterite and imperfect morphology,[5] students can go on to draw inferences from the patterns they have identified. They can answer the kinds of questions which have a number of correct answers and therefore lead to discussion:

> —En la primera parte del cuento, el uso de pretérito e imperfecto es convencional. ¿Qué nos dice el convencionalismo del lenguaje sobre el mundo descrito por este lenguaje?

> —El imperfecto es la marca de situaciones pasadas ilimitadas. Teniendo en cuenta esto, ¿cuáles son las implicaciones del uso exclusivo del imperfecto en la segunda parte?

> —En la tercera parte, los actos de los personajes novelísticos llevan la marca del pretérito. ¿Cuáles son las implicaciones de este uso del pretérito?

> —En las últimas líneas del cuento, no hay verbos y, por lo tanto, no hay marcadores de tiempo ni de persona. ¿Cuáles son las implicaciones de la falta de verbos en esta parte del cuento?

Answering these questions will induce students to understand the story. Crucially, though, this process does not *tell* students what the story means; rather, it allows them to see how the meaning of the story grows out of the language of which it is made.

CONCLUSION

As admirers of Cortázar's story will have realized, there are many critical possibilities that have not been discussed here.[6] This article is not an exhaustive treatment of the story, but a proposal for integrating grammatical analysis and the reading of literature. This integrated approach invites students to *apply* their knowledge of grammar, thus helping them to understand that all grammatical choices have meaningful consequences. It also encourages students to see literature as a modality of the language they are learning, rather than a code to which they have no access.

Far from detracting from the artfulness of literature, grammatical analysis reveals just how artful great writers are. Surely, one's appreciation for Cortázar's skill increases as one becomes aware of how he makes use of the grammatical potential of Spanish. Cortázar's comments on his own work suggest that he was aware of the kind of linguistic engineering that characterizes **"Continuidad de los parques."** Professional users of language differ in this way from other native speakers (the producers of what is misleadingly called "ordinary" speech), who are often unaware of how they create rhetorical effects. Whether literary and rhetorical effects are consciously or unconsciously achieved, though, they are analyzable linguistically. The abiding relevance of literature lies in its comprehensibility, and revealing the source of this comprehensibility is an act of homage to literature. In the case of modern Latin American literature, justly famous for its linguistic playfulness, linguistic analysis allows students access to the rules of the game.

In writing about translation[7] Gregory Rabassa has made the polemical statement that "[l]anguage learning and the study of literature are two completely different things" (27). One need not agree with his characterization of the problem to recognize that there is a contradiction inherent in the teaching of foreign languages through literature. Rabassa argues that serious discussions of literature require sophisticated language skills; this suggests (and, in fact, often results in) the use of English in the classroom. At the same time, language learners need to practice encoding and communicating ideas; this suggests that the foreign language be used in the classroom. Integrating the study of grammar with the study of literary texts provides a partial rapprochement between the goals of literary study and those of language learning.

Notes

1. The analysis in this article was developed independently of Lagmanovich's article. However, both analyses divide the story into the same four parts, which argues for the empirical basis of the division.

2. The past subjunctive in Spanish is, appropriately enough, an imperfect subjunctive. There is an inevitable semantic overlap between lack of focus and irreality, and the confluence of imperfective aspect and subjunctive mood is the morphological expression of this overlap.

3. Greimas points out that the story begins with the words "Había empezado a leer la novela" and ends with "del hombre en el sillón leyendo una novela" (32). As the title suggests, themes, settings, and characters are continuous in the story and loop back on themselves.

4. Indeed, fourth year university students not infrequently misidentify the verb "había empezado" as imperfect. Ability to mechanically identify verb endings is a useful diagnostic; surely, students who cannot pick out preterites and imperfects from a text are not ready to read that text in any ordinary sense of the word *read*.

5. Butt and Benjamin present a concise and well-documented treatment of preterite and imperfect. The relevant chapter in Lunn and DeCesaris discusses the semantic motivation of both conventional and unconventional uses of aspectual morphology.

6. Greimas, for example, links the lack of verbs in the last part of the story to aesthetic apprehension, a "purified" signifier, and Aristotelian catharsis (36). In the literary-critical mode, the story is the first step in a series of appreciations. For students, though, the story is a language-learning exercise as well as a literary text, which argues in favor of an approach that involves the examination of grammar.

7. "Continuidad de los parques" poses an interesting dilemma when translated into a language which lacks the preterite/imperfect distinction, such as English. There are several English versions that make no distinction between the two forms and translate both of them as the English past tense; in these translations, Cortázar's wordplay is lost and the story becomes a simple horror story. Linguistic analysis suggests a solution: the English present tense, which is aspectually imperfective, could be used to translate the imperfects.

Works Cited

Bello, Andrés, and Rufino J. Cuervo. *Gramática de la lengua castellana*. Buenos Aires: Anaconda, 1941.

Butt, John, and Carmen Benjamin. *A New Reference Grammar of Modern Spanish*. 2nd ed. Lincolnwood, IL: NTC Publishing Group, 1994.

Bybee, Joan L. *Morphology*. Amsterdam: Benjamins, 1985.

Comrie, Bernard. *Aspect*. Cambridge UP, 1976.

Cortázar, Julio. "Continuidad de los parques." *Ceremonias*. Barcelona: Seix Barral, 1968. 11-12.

———. *La vuelta al día en ochenta mundos*. México: Siglo XXI, 1967.

Greimas, Algirdas-Julien. "Una mano, una mejilla." *Revista de Occidente* 85 (1988): 31-37.

Lagmanovich, David. "Estrategias del cuento breve en Cortázar: Un paseo por 'Continuidad de los parques.'" *Explicación de textos literarios* 17.1-2 (1988-89): 177-85.

Langacker, Ronald W. *Foundations of Cognitive Grammar*. Vol. 1. Stanford UP, 1987. 2 vols.

Lunn, Patricia V. "The Aspectual Lens." *Hispanic Linguistics* 2 (1985): 49-61.

Lunn, Patricia V., and Janet A. DeCesaris. *Investigación de gramática*. Boston: Heinle & Heinle, 1992.

Rabassa, Gregory. "If This Be Treason: Translation and Its Possibilities." *Translation: Literary, Linguistic and Philosophical Perspectives*. Ed. William Frawley. Newark: U of Delaware P, 1984. 21-29.

Terrell, Tracy, and Joan Hooper. "A Semantically Based Analysis of Mood in Spanish." *Hispania* 57 (1974): 484-94.

Graciela P. García (essay date 2003)

SOURCE: García, Graciela P. "Time, Language, Desire: Julio Cortázar's 'The Pursuer.'" *Pacific Coast Philology* 38 (2003): 33-9.

[*In the following essay, García contends that Bruno represents logical, linear time while Johnny represents fractured, creative time in "The Pursuer."*]

Published in 1964, **"The Pursuer"** deals with art and society by exploring the paradoxical relationships that link the artist—in this case, the jazz musician as a performing artist—to his art and to his audience. By exploring the realities of the jazz performer, the music, and the public, the story involves the complex connections between the three major aspects of the artistic process, namely the creative moment, the work itself, and the reception. However, **"The Pursuer"** may also be read as a story about the multiplicity and diversity of human experience, especially the many "worlds" layering *the world,* the many chronologies of time within "the time of clocks," and the multiple orders of existence that a certain type of hegemonic Order seeks to control. Underneath all this, the story seems to evoke a struggle between two opposing forces, two "mindsets" respectively embodied by "the artist" (Johnny, the musician) and "the intellectual" (Bruno, the music critic and scholar). Key to the narrative strategy, however, is the fact that the story is told from the perspective and point of view of Bruno, and that the latter's relationship with Johnny (and with himself) is neither unilateral nor simplistic.

Cortázar, the real author, constructed the text of **"The Pursuer"** as the first-person narrative fictitiously written by Bruno, a professional jazz critic. The story line follows a series of physical and mental crises in the last two years of the tragic and quasi-chaotic life of Johnny Carter, a brilliant saxophonist openly modeled after the famous Charlie Parker. Bruno's interest in Johnny's fate is not purely personal; it is based on the fact that, as the story opens, the critic has recently published an acclaimed book dealing with Johnny's famous musical genius. It is important to note that, in the text of **"The Pursuer,"** Bruno himself makes comments about the biographical nature of his study. He remarks that such an approach has conveniently served him to avoid the truly significant questions concerning the sources of Johnny's originality, the roots of his "genius." At the same time, he admits that his use of the biographical approach has also helped him to comply with the mainstream conventions of the music critic's professional world. Therefore, whereas Bruno's book has followed the recipes for successful publishing, what he writes in the story that we actually read amounts to a confession of sorts.

It is also important to note that the text of **"The Pursuer"** is constructed as a kind of intimate diary, that is, a personal notebook containing the unofficial "dossier" privately kept by Bruno. In it, he purports to "tell the truth" about Johnny, the actual man behind his art, an approach which Johnny himself considered essential to an honest account of his music and which Bruno has admittedly avoided in his book. As it turns out, the critic ends up "telling the truth" about himself in a narrative that reaches beyond his control. Thus, the duality Bruno/Johnny parallels that of the two writings: namely the unpublished notes "behind" the published book and the book itself. The counter position Bruno/Johnny also corresponds to the unrecorded conversations between the two men, as reported and discussed by the former in his narrative. Furthermore, the rapport between the critic and the artist doubles that between discourse and music, and it constitutes the main organizing device for the construction of the story's multiple meanings. Through the complex layers of these meanings, what emerges in **"The Pursuer"** is a vision of desire as a profoundly contradictory force at the center of both personal and social human experience.

The text functions by combining several lines of obvious representations with more subtle connotations of meaning, and these combinations all hinge on the counterpoint between Bruno and Johnny. As a nonverbal form, for example, Johnny's music represents the desire to return to instinct, intuition, and magic. For the saxophonist, the true feat of humankind would be to dismiss the apparent constancy of linear time, that is, the constructed order of sequential chronology. According to Johnny, our minds cling to a simplistic notion of time as a shield from our fear of uncertainty and lack of control. But if we could accept the fluid nature of time, space, and matter, that fluidity would become part of our concept of the world and would give us access to an immense power. Therefore, to stretch beyond the limitations of fear in the mind, of a need for control, would be to fly like music into the heavens of fluid thought and into a kind of "nonreality," that is, a reality free from all preconstructed and restrictive molds. Johnny is thus characterized as a musician whose art breaks down established boundaries in pursuit of deeper truths. As the "pursuer" in the title of the story, he has a group of followers who depend on him; and this includes Bruno, who admits that he has been touched by Johnny's genius but tries to silence such a disturbing influence by confining it to a purely aesthetic dimension. Bruno, therefore, is not very different from the rest of Johnny's "groupies," in spite of his desire to separate himself from them.

According to Bruno, Johnny is thoughtless, dependent, and self-serving; yet there is an elusive pattern in the jazzman's rebellious originality that the critic recognizes. In fact, Bruno believes that he, following Johnny's comings and goings, is seriously trying to understand the metaphysical sources of the musician's originality. It may be said that, up to a certain point, Bruno "pursues" Johnny's pursuit of musical transcendence because he is intrigued by it. However, he fears the path of vital excess followed by the man behind the music. Actually, Johnny can't keep a saxophone without losing it, he can't play music without heroin. Those around him accept the paradox, the pattern of brilliant musical perfection intersected by chaotic existential unpredictability. Because of Johnny's talent, they compensate for him and make excuses for his deficiencies. But they do this for their own self-serving ends, something which Bruno clearly perceives when he writes: "Basically, we're a bunch of egotists; under the pretext of watching out for Johnny what we're doing is protecting our own idea of him" (206). Those who follow the idol will do anything for him as long as he keeps playing his fabulous improvisations. Johnny as a musician is a construct of the imagination of others: as in the case of Bruno himself, in spite of his own disclaimers, the others' pursuit of Johnny—from gig to gig and from party to party—has more to do with their own identities than with any true recognition of the jazzman as an independent individual. Here is what Bruno writes about Johnny's "fans":

> From my puritanical world—I don't need to admit it, anyone who knows me knows that I'm horrified by vice—I see them as sick angels, irritating in their irresponsibility [. . .]. I envy them, I envy Johnny, that Johnny on the other side, even though nobody knows exactly what *that* is, "the other side." I envy everything except his anguish [. . .], but even in his pain he's got to have some kind of insight into things that's denied me.
>
> (203)

Bruno can see that, when Johnny produces music, he touches the divine. In his music, Johnny's self-consciousness is momentarily annihilated and his art seems to come not from him but rather through him from somewhere else, he acting as a vessel. He brings everyone closer to beauty, but in order to pursue the truth about himself in his performances, he seems to need the people and their indulgence. What Johnny the man tells Bruno that he ultimately mourns is the fact that the aesthetic value of his music is isolated by his "fans" from the rest of what he considers "the total experience" embodied in his art, thus blinding everyone to the "truth" about him and about themselves. Yet, as the object of the critic's pursuits, the saxophonist makes Bruno uncomfortable because of the latter's perception of what that "truth" involves: namely, excess, chaos, and senselessness. Throughout the story, this obvious conflict stimulates a number of explicitly stated feelings within Bruno: jealousy, disgust, envy, and condescending affection. His fascination with Johnny's way of life resembles that of a moth fluttering about the fire, and this prompts Bruno to deal with a powerful topic in the story: namely, the link manifested in Johnny's actions between creation, destruction, and self-destruction.

As a pursuer of fine tunes, Bruno, the critic, is represented as occupying a partly understandable position within the narrative. His attending many performances makes the exceptional moments stand out for him. It is easy for the critic to make comparisons between prior versions of the same tune. For the soloist playing with changing sets of musicians, even a slight variation can make a significant difference. Particularly with jazz, every night is new, hearing truly good music is intoxicating, and being part of that moment can seem like a spiritual experience. Bruno knows all this, but as a music critic he listens, compares, and evaluates. Throughout the narrative, however, what sharply separates the critic from the artist is the open question of the link between creativity and destruction. Bruno

truly cannot understand how Johnny could do the excessive acts that he carries out, for they are thoroughly self-destructive. Bruno's anger at Johnny's self-abusive behavior functions within a number of distinct power imbalances between the two men: white versus black, critic versus artist, skill versus genius. Bruno's awareness of his position as the skilled critic—as the cerebral temperament who lacks the special type of passion and talent that Johnny has—makes him acutely insecure. In spite of this, Bruno knows that he has the very real power to make or break Johnny's career, a fact of which both men seem silently aware.

Although Johnny makes him angry on many levels, Bruno admits that he is directly profiting from the musician's genius and is therefore dependent on it. However, in his book he does not talk about the man himself, but instead about the music, which his skillful language can dissect, analyze, and reduce, thereby retaining power for himself in his control of discourse. He explains away Johnny's art: for instance, the saxophonist is good because he is black, because of his cultural determinants when he was a child, and so on. Ultimately, Bruno lies in his book; it is a lie of omission, and Johnny complains to him:

> What you forgot to put [in your book] is me. [. . .] [You did not write] [a]bout me, Bruno, about *me*. And it's not your fault that you couldn't write what I myself can't blow. When you say that my true biography is in my records, I know you think that's true and besides it sounds very pretty, but that's not how it is.
>
> (238)

Bruno's message is that the creator of amazing works does not really matter once the creation is finished, unless his or her image is useful to satisfy society's need for cultural "heroes." Because of his self-destructive way of life, Johnny is hard to make into a hero; therefore he is treated as a "chimp," an idiot who happens to possess a gift. After Johnny's death, Bruno writes:

> I decided not to touch the second edition, to go on putting Johnny forth as he was at bottom: a poor sonofabitch with barely mediocre intelligence, endowed like so many musicians, so many chess players and poets, with the gift of creating incredible things without the slightest consciousness [. . .] of the dimensions of his work.
>
> (245)

Johnny's death is quite literal in Bruno's narrative, but it also has symbolic importance as it embodies a major motif in **"The Pursuer"**: namely, the theme of the "death of the author." This concept is based on the fashionable theory of abstracting the works themselves from the practices that connect writers and artists with the products of their art. In Cortázar's story, the "death of the author" theme is treated as an idea that often serves to isolate the figure of the artist from the understanding of his or her work and to focus exclusively on the reductive interpretation of the "object" itself. By stating that Johnny's "reality" is contained in his music, Bruno dismisses the elusive question of the desire embodied in that music and tied to the musician's ungraspable identity. But while Johnny may have a point when he says that Bruno has not dealt with who he is at all, he also acknowledges that the critic could not—as Johnny says—"write what I myself can't blow" (238). The saxophonist's anguish lies in his failure to comprehend the meaning of his existence. Yet what appears to matter most to him is not his music itself but rather what he pursues when he plays. Ironically, Bruno perceives this tragic split that sweeps through Johnny's life when he writes that the jazzman's music is a vehicle for his journey toward an understanding beyond everyday reality, something that Johnny himself is unable to articulate and ultimately cannot find. This is perhaps the single most important passage in **"The Pursuer"**:

> The artist inside [Johnny] is going to blow his stack every time he hears this mockery of his desire, of everything that he had wanted to say while he was playing, the saliva running out of his mouth along with the music, more than ever alone in front of what he pursues, facing that which flees from him the more he pursues it.
>
> (220-21)

It is interesting to note that Johnny's criticism of Bruno's book reaches beyond the "death of the artist" theme into the question of what constitutes "reality" and what is the fate of someone who sees through the illusions of established order. Further confronting Bruno for the latter's language in his book, Johnny says: "I don't accept your God. [. . .] Why have you made me accept him in your book? I don't know if there is a God, I play my music, I make my God!" (239). What the musician is saying is that Bruno has made him, at least in his book, accept notions of normalcy and order, in short, mundane reality. And Johnny does, in a sense, make his own reality through his music; but music is very much a part of this world because it is very dependent on timing. Here lies the musician's paradox: he is using a real medium, the saxophone, to express something that is of another plane of existence or of a different realm of understanding. Johnny is trying to "break through to the other side," but to the other side of what? Of reality, presumably, but Johnny purports not to believe in "reality"—even though he must accept at least the illusion of reality (for instance jazz, his wife, pain, and death), enough to know he wants out of it.

Perhaps the strongest thread that runs through **"The Pursuer"** is the question of time. Bruno mentions early on in his narrative that Johnny is obsessed with time: "It is a mania of his, the worst of his manias, of which he has plenty" (185). Through Bruno's narrative and Johnny's comments, we realize that Bruno and Johnny represent two different ways of thinking—analytical and creative, respectively. They also symbolize two competing notions of time: namely, linear time and another kind of time, a non-time or a time outside of time, a time that transcends linear sequential chronology. As Johnny says: "Music got me out of time, but that's only a way of putting it. If you want to know what I think, really, I believe that music put me *into* time. But then you have to believe that this time has nothing to do with [. . .] well, with us, as they say" (189). What Johnny suggests, paradoxically, is that there are two kinds of time: linear (or unreal) and nonlinear (or real); that it is our notion of linear time that is illusory, and that "real time" only emerges through flashes of transient moments that take us away from our firm belief in linear chronology.

Johnny's moments in this absolute or "real" time seem to occur only when he is playing music with a certain degree of intensity or when he is riding the Paris *metro*. Both of these experiences pull him out of his "self" or what he knows to be his life. He says that "to ride the *métro* is like being put inside a clock; the stations are minutes, it's *now* time; but I know there is another time [. . .]" (195). It seems that at least part of what Johnny pursues is ultimately to get to a point where he would constantly be living in that state of "real" or absolute time, attaining a kind of immortality in life by stretching linear chronology to infinity. Even though he tries, he cannot access this parallel alternate time-zone at will. He is prevented from doing so by his own human limitations and by the imposition of the linear time construct to which the rest of the world subscribes.

Unlike Johnny, Bruno is a man of logic, of linear time, and of what most people call "reality." His simultaneous fascination with, and distaste for, Johnny result partly from his position as a critic, in which he is able to live vicariously a life of "depravity" (of excess) without having the more sordid aspects of Johnny's existence adversely affect his own. Johnny concretely represents the chaos that Bruno fears, particularly the disruption of everyday order, of which time is a major aspect. In the face of excessive desire, Bruno uses the linear time of discourse as a protection against the kind of time that Johnny talks about, even while he acknowledges that the musician could possibly be right about time's "elastic" nature. He needs the stability of linear time in order to exist, just as he needs the logical structure of language—also a kind of Order—to be able to write his books. In this respect, therefore,

Bruno represents us, the readers. We, too, need (or at least believe we need) a linear sense of time for our daily lives to make sense. Confronted by what Johnny proposes, our lives lived by the clock, by minutes and years, would seem absurd. But the possibilities contained within Johnny's perceptions remain with us. Even when Johnny is not with Bruno in the flesh, he is there, in Bruno's mind. Cortázar shows that the two men—and the two ways of thinking that they embody in music and in language—cannot be separated or set up as diametrically opposed. The two coexist, although somewhat uneasily, just as the story indicates that our time-bound reality perhaps exists as a mask of another mode of experiencing the world, as the screen of a timeless reality.

Work Cited

Cortázar, Julio. "The Pursuer." *Blow-Up and Other Stories.* Trans. Paul Blackburn. New York: Pantheon Books, 1985. 182-247.

Gaetan Brulotte (essay date 2003-2004)

SOURCE: Brulotte, Gaetan. "Cortázar, a Writing Inspiration." *Explicación de Textos Literarios* 32, nos. 1-2 (2003-2004): 22-35.

[*In the following essay, Brulotte describes the personal inspiration that he has drawn from Cortázar's exploration of the short story genre and credits Cortázar with balancing philosophical, political, and humanistic concerns within an experimental and self-aware aesthetic.*]

I saw Cortázar twice in Paris when I was a young student and each time by chance. The first time in a café where I used to hang out with friends in the 1970s: La Palette, rue de Seine in the 6th arrondissement, which still exists today and has not changed a bit. He was by himself, waiting for someone, and not reading or writing, as one would expect. He was just there, watching people, listening to conversations around him. The second time was in spring 1976, early in the morning on the Pont des Arts, near the Louvre. He was by himself again, simply taking a walk, and I passed by him while returning home from a night spent out. It came to my mind that he was probably wishfully wandering the streets of Paris, as the surrealists would do, receptive to the creative, and maybe erotic, potential of the city. The sun was rising over Paris and the giant man was walking with his hands in the pockets of his trench coat along the Seine River. It is the last time I saw him. That was some thirty years ago. I never spoke to him. I was too shy. And he probably never imagined being observed by a reader at such a close distance. From these two encounters I built up an image of him

of an elusive phantom, a lonely man who enjoyed solitude, independence, a meditative life and the intense presence of the surrounding reality. If I had stopped or followed him that morning through Paris, it could have ended up as a Cortázar-style story. Maybe I will write it one day. His last companion, Carol Dunlop, was the former wife of a Montreal friend of mine, François Hébert who happened to be the publisher of my first short story collection *Le Surveillant* (*The Secret Voice*). Maybe I could use François as a narrator of my eventual future story on the author of *We Love Glenda So Much.*

Although they left a memorable trace in my memory, needless to say that these elusive encounters do not make me a Cortázar scholar. I am only an enthusiastic reader of his works, and probably a bad one for that very reason, since my admiration prevents me from having the necessary critical distance to evaluate his writings in a scholarly fashion. On top of that I have read him in French translation and not in the original, although I suspect the French translations are excellent, since the author himself, who knew the language very well, probably supervised most of them. My views are therefore very limited and I am afraid what I can bring here is just a simple personal tribute to a writer who influenced a whole generation of writers such as myself, in the hope that it will encourage those who are not familiar with his work to read it. At the same time, it is also a tribute to the substantial and highly stimulating scholarly work that Cortázar generated and of which I would like to act as an echo chamber, since these numerous critics have said everything I have to say about him and in a much better fashion. Cortázar was blessed for attracting such reading and interpretative talents that give his work a different life each time. I will focus this commentary on this master's short story contributions, because, as Vargas Llosa puts it in his preface to the French edition of Cortázar's complete stories, that's where his true revolution lies. So please take this as a modest homage to the great short fiction writer he was, one of the greatest of all times, who changed the face of the genre and turned upside down the nature of fiction.

The first aspect I would like to pay tribute is Cortázar's ability to test the genre, and this by all means possible. Disregarding most literary dogmas, he wrote irreverent pieces which shook the usual passivity of the reader and pushed him/her to be surprised, puzzled, destabilized, actively involved, with his/her mind full of questions and uncertainties. Sometimes funny, often troubling or even horrifying, his stories are always disconcerting. They seem at times loose and simple, at others compact and complex, with multiple levels of meaning, so much so that one is moved to put the book down after each single story to try to sort things out. His short stories exceed their written discourse and invite the reader to build his/her own interpretation. His endings offer less a closure than an opening. With him the last word never belongs to the text.

A Cortázar short story has no fixed, "correct" form that one could reproduce as a formula. It has no pre-established design, nor one single targeted effect or meaning. He wrote without a plan, nor any particular methods, and ideally without a pause and without effort, in a trancelike condition, or so he said. A short story was for him an open form to creativity. Writing is an improvisation for him, which involves invention and beauty, as he further says (Weiss 76). This is why his style looks at times improvised, jazzy, bohemian, gropingly progressing, wandering as a vagabond, written with some kind of natural flow, while at others it is highly concerted, exact, skilful and thought through. In fact Cortázar was so creative and unconventional in his writing that he was an inventor of literary genres. His art defies the categories of literature. Many of his stories propose a blurring of distinctions between genres, emphasizing bricolage, pastiche, parody and playfulness. They artfully twist the narrative linearity, mock the conventional coding of information and its organization, and subvert the easily made up essences, the dogma of mimesis and "pure" representation. He never hesitates to use fragmented forms, discontinuous narratives, and even random-seeming collages of different materials. In just one story for instance it is possible for the narrative perspective to change thirty-four times, even in the middle of a sentence or a thought of any given character (see **"Nurse Cora"** in *All Fires the Fire*). The reader can easily get lost, and that may be an effect the author hopes to produce, such as if he/she was getting off a roller coaster. In any case writing for Cortázar was what he called "a dizzying experience", and reading his stories is one too.

His creativity definitely broke the rules and habits in story telling and often his stories are defined by their experimental edge. For instance (and I am referring here to French theoretician, Florence Goyet, who has analyzed what she labeled "classical short story" at the turn of the 19th-20th century in many European countries as well as in Japan, America and Russia), contrary to the classical tradition his stories often have no conventional plots nor action, or the plot is secondary to a mind-bugging problem that a character is trying to resolve. The stereotyped organization of the narrative, with a well-defined beginning, middle and end tends to disappear and be replaced by a softer structure such as the stream of consciousness, the epistolary format, the diary form, an improvisational flow of thoughts in the surrealist fashion of "automatic writing". His stories are not based on external action, which was the driving force of conventional story writing and many of his narratives are uneventful.

"Southern Thruway" for instance (in *All Fires the Fire*), which inspired Godard's film *Week-end*, exploits a traffic jam on a highway, as they frequently happen in France in August. In the traditional short story, authors would also exploit the maximum distance possible between the world they narrate and the reader. The narrator took pride in judging, discrediting or disqualifying the characters, so that they became exemplars of mediocre destinies, with which it is hard for the reader to identify. Such distance is not Cortázar's usual attitude towards his characters, as he rather elicits sympathy for them and even solidarity. Characters tend not to be treated from a distant, superior, authoritative stand. He portrays them as if they were ordinary human beings, which allow the readers to penetrate their fictional worlds. They engage our empathy. In an essay he wrote untitled "On the Short Story and Its Environs" (*Around the Day*), he says the primary rule is to tell the story to a small circle, in order to create a form of closeness. He avoids in the narration "those acts of distancing that constitute judgments on what is happening" (160).

With the same spirit Cortázar also stayed away as much as possible from the distant objectivity provided by cold omniscient third-person narrators, fixed narrative points of view, and clear-cut moral positions. Even when he uses a third-person narrator, he frequently exploits this device as one of the voices he represents within the text or through which he presents a character's point of view, thus creating a covert first-person perspective. The narrative situation develops from inside out, and not from outside in as it would in a traditional classic short story where an external and impersonal narrator objectifies the subject and is emblematic of power and mastery. His manner offers a more human and involved point of view on the world. It emphasizes subjectivity and relativity. And relativity is a key word here: relativity of perception, of reason, of reality itself, of facts, of truth, of existence or non-existence, of the world we live in. Nothing can be sure or clearly defined. His narrators are not representatives of Truth (with a capital T), which would be the kind of narrators we find in the traditional short story. Cortázar's are often unreliable because their narratives contain contradictions, ambiguities, hesitations, and questions. They even tell at times their own problems of interpretation, showing the reader they are themselves confused by a situation. Needless to say, the classic "monologic" stand of the traditional short story gives way here to a complex polyphony, by which the reader hears a multiplicity of voices and levels of interpretations.

CHARACTERS

Cortázar's stories are based on characters, on the minds and hearts of the characters and the narrators, more than on narrative structures, which is the reverse of traditional short stories. Characters are not only actors within a given situation, they determine the heartbeat of the story, they contain the narrative, and they constitute the story. A critic (Yovanovitch) even said that the revival of characterization is one of Cortázar's most important contributions to the development of the 20th century short story. These characters are presented with human complexity and depth, which was not always the case in the genre until him. They are not clear cut, nor defined from an external point of view, as they tended to be in the classical tradition. When they feel they have a limiting identity, they want to change it, or they are close to death. They are very often ambivalent, illogical, irrational, internally conflicting, tormented. They are not passive entities submitted to external forces and devoid of dynamism (such as Kafka's heroes). They show a great vitality and they participate in the shaping of their lives. They rely heavily on their deep desires, although they often meet deception.

The basis for his stories is the study of human beings in their relationships with themselves, with others, with the world. Relationships with others, in particular, represent a major problem to be solved and are an outstanding story generator for Cortázar. Whether these relations are based on desire, love, power, service, care, admiration, hysteria, frustration, interest, solidarity, protection, conflict, hostility, threat, aggression, paranoia, quest for justice, etc., they present some form of enigma, secret, or obstacle, either to decipher or to overcome and in any case a challenge to face or to retreat away from. Many are obsessed with extravagant projects, or unusual and magnetic objects or fantastic animals. Sometimes they throw themselves into a prison of their own making and show a pathetic inability to escape a chain of absurd events. For instance a fight with a sweater drives the protagonist to fall through an open window twelve stories above the street. They also can make farfetched links between things, like the surrealists did with their revealing coupling of elements alien to each other and which created a new look at reality.

Cortázar's characters proclaim in their own ways the author's dissatisfaction with existence and his quest for a different life: they often would like to change their reality by setting different rules in the hope of exploring new life directions. But soon they discover that play may be serious and they become victims of their own new ruling, especially if the rules that they establish are obsessive and absurdly rigid. See for instance **"Manuscript Found in a Pocket"** (*A Change of Light*; *Octaedro*), in which a madman devises an elaborate set of precise rules he must follow to meet a woman, thus limiting the chances of such a meeting to ever happen. He is surprised when it seemed to work

once, but it was an illusion. Excessive rules are for brainless losers. Chance and spontaneity, not rules, are on the side of winners, i.e. what the surrealists called objective chance, a chance internally driven by desire. He often portrays characters imprisoned in an Image that either they have built or that people around have built of them. See **"We Love Glenda So Much"**, for instance, for a striking example: it shows the passion that fans have for a star, that goes up to the point of adoration and even murder because fans don't accept that their idol change with time. Cortázar may have read Barthes who analyzed this issue in an insightful commentary published in 1978 (reproduced in *le Bruissement de la langue*). He argued in favor of something like "Image abstinence" (on the model of food abstinence); he wished that we could stop building images of others and get rid of those defining images of us made by others.

Wishful thinking of course: whether we like it or not, and that's a frequent sub-text in Cortázar's stories, the language of others always attributes to us an image, and this image can not be separated from our biography. It is part of the self. We never have the last word on our identity. **"The Pursuer"** (*End of the Game*) might be the best illustration of that issue. Bruno does not tell the truth about the jazzman's life in his biography. Confronted by the star on its inaccuracies, the narrator admits to falsification for positive reasons, and he succeeds in publishing it so that the reader will never know the real Johnny Carter and his lamentable life of promiscuity, schizophrenia, and drug use. Ultimately, the language of others defines what we are or become to be through them, and whatever the dreams we may have of purity and authenticity, especially being a public figure such as an actor, a musician, a writer, a political figure; this dependency is inevitable. A Cortázar's character can only feel trapped in such an image; it is the equivalent of being death. What is the way out? Unfortunately there is no way out except death itself or a change of identity.

And indeed the switch of identity by which a character becomes another is a permanent theme in his short fiction, even if it means for the trapped one to resort to some symbolic substitutions or poetic escapes such as metamorphosis and transmigration from human to animal or from life to art object. (See for instance, **"Axolotl," "The Night Face Up,"** in *End of the Game*, **"The Other Heaven," "The Island at Noon,"** in *All Fires* [*All Fires the Fire*] or **"Fin de etapa"** in *Deshoras*). Cortázar definitely abandoned the rational and unified subject of traditional short story in favor of a de-centered, divided, and polymorphic subject. He quite often analyzed the anxiety that this change is creating by representing characters that are isolated, alienated, uncertain, doubtful, and fearful, in a state of displacement and estrangement, left to their own mental refuge.

VISION

His inventiveness in style and narrative techniques are not separable from an engaging vision of human condition and a distinct worldview. That's another aspect of his writing that I'd like to pay homage to. He succeeded in combining playfulness with philosophical and social investigation. I think he owes that success to an original mixture of influences: besides of course the Latin American ones that he integrated into his fiction or reacted to, his short stories are a combination of substantial French influences, such as surrealism, existentialism, the New Novel, the OULIPO experimental group (as he was close to at least two of its members, Calvino and Perec), or inventive poets such as Tardieu and Michaux. This is a rare combination, which may explain his complex quest for the marvelous, the tracking of the absurd, the search for depth and authenticity, as well as for new meaning and new forms.

On one hand he says that literature is a form of play for him, a serious game that can stake one's life; but on the other hand I never felt in his writing an exclusive focus on art for art's sake, which may turn out to be rather empty. There is obviously a playful dimension to his writing by which he tried to rejuvenate literature, but this side is not all. His short stories are not futile formal exercises, but a meaningful experience with their mixture of rationality and irrationality, intelligence and sensibility, depth and originality, aesthetic achievement and human emotions to relate to. They call for a revolution beginning within us, with our look at reality and our everyday activities. Of course such an orientation is driven by some certitudes and convictions, but the outcome is uncertain and involves the dynamics of change and a plunge into the adventure of experience.

Under the obvious influence of surrealism, which he openly recognized, if only through persistent explicit tributes, dedications and epigraphs, he was stressing the impossibility of life as it is and the need for something new. In his improvisational narratives he seemed to have embraced the lyric attitude the surrealists defined, and where the story is proceeding from the subconscious and infused with a dream-like touch: "It's as if they were dictated to me a little", he says (Weiss 77). He wanted the reader to learn to rely on instinct rather than on rationality. For him writing was aimed at opening alternative cognitive windows, since not everything has a logical explanation, and at bringing reality in a new light.

TRUTH

Cortázar's short stories constantly raise the issue of the relationship of literature to Truth. Most often his narratives cast doubts about the so-called Truth and question this human concept: its relativity, its constitution, its manipulation, its function, its mythology, its definition compared to fiction. There is no such thing as Truth with a capital T. There are points of view, and some are more convincing than others. Relativity is again a key to the perception of all phenomena. "I am telling a truth, which is only my truth," says the subjective storyteller of **"Blow-Up"**. The two basic units of Truth are facts and beliefs, and art can deconstruct what was presented as a fact or a belief, and bring them into a different perspective. That's exactly what many of Cortázar's stories do. Sincerity and authenticity count more than Truth as values, even if they can be source of mistakes.

His short stories may be seen as a reaction and a form of resistance to the "Grand Narratives" such as those that believe they carry an eternal and irrefutable religious Truth (the *Bible,* the *Koran,* the *Torah*) or a political Truth (*Mein Kampf, The Red Book*) that should be imposed on everyone, and that caused so much suffering throughout history. He reacted with "mini-narratives" or "mini-texts" that capture daily situations or small portions of discourses from oppressed voices, such as confessions, lyric monologues, dreams, testimonies, press clippings, diaries, letters, and turn them against the Grand Oppressive Narratives. Those stories explain inner viewpoints, small practices, humble destinies, personal ingenuity, fugitive joys and fears, local events, rather than large-scale universal or global concepts acting as Truth.

Truth is a matter of perception. Cortázar shows this in a particularly clarifying way through characters who are struggling with this notion, like biographers: this is a type of story teller that interested him as image builders, for whom truth and fiction see their frontiers blur. We are not what we are, but what others make or try to make of us. Facts can easily become fiction or vice versa. What those biographical attempts show is that the subject is a fabricated device, a discursive effect. Everything seems to be fiction and cannot escape from it. This is an issue that contemporary theory has been addressing by showing that fiction and the referential world sometimes interfere and cannot always be separated (See Pavel, Ryan *et al,* in Grefen & Audet, for instance). In the 1970s Cortázar was certainly influenced by structuralism, which rejected the principle of a fictional world totally different from the non-fictional one, thus creating troubling marriages of reality and fiction with referential insertions (such as press clippings for example) in narratives. One of his masterpieces, **"The Health of the Sick"** (*All Fires*) exam-ines the effect of fiction on life and reality. A whole family extensively conspires to protect the mother from the news that her son was killed in an accident. They fabricate a story in which they pretend he is gone to Brazil to work and arrange with an accom-plice to act as correspondent. They invent all kinds of reasons that prevent the son from coming back. The situation gets complicated when an aunt falls ill and dies, a second piece of bad news from which they will also protect the mother by false briefings on her im-proving health. Finally comes the end for Mamá, but even after they have buried her, the fictive lives they had created were so powerful that they still believed in them and wondered how they would now break the news of his mother's death to the fictitious son.

His stories also have a tendency toward reflexivity, or self-consciousness about the production of the work of art, so that each piece calls attention to its own status. It's another way of challenging the notion of Truth. Indeed Cortázar engages in an evaluative frenzy of his own writing, either by adding notes or directions to help the reader understand his intentions (such as in **"Clone"** in *Glenda* [*We Love Glenda So Much*]) or by frequently using meta-fictional comments on the story in progress, reflecting on it, on the situation, the characters, the relationship of the narrative to Truth. See for example **"The Ferry or Another Trip to Ven-ice"** (in *Glenda*), where one of the characters evalu-ates the weaknesses of the story in-progress, thus ex-ploiting self-consciousness as a way to devaluate the utterance. Here fiction opens up, in a very transparent fashion, the uncertainties of its own assertions. And paradoxically fiction turns out to be more trust worthy than a discourse pretending to represent the Truth with absolute and arrogant certainty. Many stories deal with the power of the mind over reality. Characters hear voices when they are not supposed to, casting doubt on what is real and what is not, and on the compe-tency of our senses to inform us on reality. Reality ac-quires an unstable status in Cortázar's world. Reality that one perceives is a form of fabricated fiction. Slip-page into another level of reality or the gradual fusion of two realities is the key to many destabilizing effects of his short narratives. He creates bridges between re-alities, so that dreams or hallucinations and reality in-tertwine and exchange positions. Behind our daily routine, behind what we get as irrefutable facts of life, another universe, richer yet chaotic, lies hidden ready to be seized. He excels in detecting the unusual em-bedded in our world of habits or the absurd in a logi-cal series of events. In all this, he rejects the assump-tions of psychological and social coherence as well as the notions of causality in favor of multiplicity and in-determinacy.

By promoting undecidability, with his open endings, the many twists and turns between reality and dreams, his frequent use of shifting viewpoints, especially at the end of stories to bring about a different evaluation of things, he understood that what characterizes litera-ture in its best accomplishments is its fundamental ambiguity, as Maurice Blanchot said. It is no surprise, as many critics repeat endlessly, that his texts have generated an array of commentaries from political al-legories to psychoanalytical interpretations. There is no such thing as a single "correct" reading of Cortázar's stories; a work does not have only one meaning, it is a well of meanings and in fifty years from now these texts will generate even more inter-pretations than they have already. That's the lasting virtue of true literature.

ART

The non-dualistic in-between position he is trying to figure out in his stories could be expressed by the im-age of communicating vessels, an image used by Bre-ton, the head of surrealism in one of his books bearing that title. Already Cortázar adopted that intermediate position by being between one side of the Atlantic and the other, one hemisphere and the other, the Hispanic culture and the Francophone one, being part of the two while not completely being on one side or the other. His works also act as communicating vessels between two worlds of differences, and his stories ex-ploit many situations of linkages. One of them is the coupling of art and text. He liked to fuse the mundane reality with the visual arts, especially photographs and paintings, as well as music. In **"Clone"** (*Glenda*), which blends music and fiction, he went as far as to add at the end of his story an explanation on the musi-cal structure of his narrative, which is based on Bach's "Musical Offering".

He often uses art as a hypotext—which is the starting point of the story—to produce a hypertext, which is the finished product, resulting from the disturbing and revealing influence of art on the characters' percep-tion. Cortázar likes to question reality as we usually perceive it by confronting it with the fictive status of art. He puts an emphasis on HOW seeing (or percep-tion itself) takes place, rather than on WHAT is seen. You don't get what you see in Cortázar's world, but you get what you put in what you see. See how a simple visit to the museum transforms a female char-acter in **"Fin de etapa"** (**"End of a Stage"**, *Deshoras*) and our perception of reality, when she becomes part of a painting herself. In the tradition of Poe's "Oval Portrait" and Gautier's "La Toison d'or" where a woman becomes a painting, Cortázar seemed to have been fascinated by the effect of art on our perception of reality. For him, art acts as an acute corrector of reality; it has the power to transform it. Art is never innocent or just harmlessly entertaining, it can replace life, it may connect us with a deeper side of reality or of ourselves, it can reveal another dimension of the given, including some unimaginable hidden world beyond a first subjective impression.

COLLECTION

One aspect that has always struck me is his conception of the collection itself. He did not try to create any sort of artificial homogeneity; there is no particular underlying logic to the groupings. "A book, he said, is nothing more than the moment at which an author finished a pile of stories, put them together and sent them to be published. The separation between one book and another is false" (cited in Peavler 19). He did not insert each individual story into a superstructure that would unify them and make them more inter-dependant or force them to engage into a form of relationship. Each one has its own world and is self-sufficient. "For me, he says, the thing that signals a great story is what we might call its autonomy" (*Around the Day* 160). It comes as no surprise if for the first translated collections the groupings are different from the original, forcing scholars to perform some gymnastics in their referencing tasks. In French for instance, the first batch to be published in 1963 was a selection of three separate collections: ***End of the Game, Bestiary, Secret Weapons*** and beard the title of ***Secret Weapons*** (***Las Armas secretas***). Cortázar even published a second version of ***End of the Game*** with ten additional short stories. So it seems that, in his conception of a collection, the unit was more important than the whole and did not belong to any specific group. This may explain why he valued most highly the sphere as the metaphor for the perfect story. This image of enclosure does not contradict the openness that characterizes his stories, especially with their open endings.

CONCLUSION

I don't always agree of course with every aspect of his writing: for example, I dislike at times his treatment of women as monstrous entities or as crying little animals, the recurrent sadistic sexuality, the blind support of Castro who imprisoned writers. But this essay is in homage to his craft and my purpose is not negative judgment. I accept that such a tribute belongs to what Cortázar called idiocy. In a fascinating text in *Around the Day,* untitled "Only a Real Idiot", he describes his unbridled and unabashed enthusiasm for the creative efforts of others and for the simple marvels of life, while his surroundings look down at his lack of critical spirit. This is when he defined idiocy as "the ability to be enthusiastic all the time about anything you like". So I have to live with that verdict.

Despite his extraordinary literary achievements, Cortázar was full of self-doubts as an artist. In one of his last interviews he said: "The truth is, each day I lose more and more confidence in myself, and I am happy. I write worse and worse, from an aesthetic view point" (cited in Stavans xvi). He added that while saying he was already one of the greatest writers of the 20th century, and a monument in world literature. Twenty years later we can measure what a trailblazer he was, a pioneer who helped readers and writers to look differently at things and act accordingly, if only it were to have a refreshing view on reality. At the very least Cortázar certainly illustrates the importance of literature and creativity in our world. They help create a higher state of consciousness; they give a different meaning to life and generate forms of solidarity among people. That's a vision that I personally and deeply share with him.

I also have lots of empathy for the fact that he wrote in a different language than the one of his immediate surroundings. Cortázar kept writing in Spanish while he lived in a French environment. This situation has been analyzed by the French philosopher Gilles Deleuze, when he speaks about the natural spring of creative innovation that comes out from what he called the "de-territorialization" of a writer, citing Kafka as a great example, who wrote in German while living in Prague. Yet this situation is very challenging for any writer, and one has to spend a lot of energy to make one's native language survive within one's self, in all its subtleties, when the daily interactions are constantly in a foreign language. So, kudos to Cortázar who has joined those few displaced writers who used their exile as a platform to innovate. Through constant and risky innovations he succeeded in jazzing his way out of the profound melancholic dead-end he must have experienced in front of conventional literature. Out of the world of categories and dichotomies that structures our common thinking he tried to explore positions that were out of the box and where categories are irrelevant, and where the possibility of non-dualistic experiences can be envisioned, maybe close to what the surrealists called the sublime point, a place in-between dichotomies, a place that we still are trying to figure out what it is.

Works Cited

Alonso, Carlos J., ed. *Julio Cortázar: New Readings.* Cambridge: Cambridge University Press, 1998.

Barthes, Roland. *Le Bruissement de la langue.* Paris: Seuil, 1984.

Cortázar, Julio. *Nouvelles 1945-1982.* Edition intégrale. Trans. Laure Guille-Bataillon, Françoise Campo-Timal and Françoise Rosset. Foreword by Mario Vargas Llosa. Paris: Gallimard, 1993.

———. *Around the Day in Eighty Worlds.* Trans. Thomas Christensen. San Francisco: North Point Press, 1986.

———. *Entretiens avec Omar Prego* (*La fascinación de las palabras*). Trans. Françoise Rosset. Paris: Gallimard, 1982.

Goyet, Florence. *La Nouvelle: 1870-1925. Description d'un genre à son apogée.* Paris: PUF, 1993.

Grefen, Alexandre et René Audet, dirs. *Frontières de la fiction.* Québec: Editions Nota Bene/Presses Universitaires de Bordeaux, 2001.

Peavler, Terry J. *Julio Cortázar.* Boston: Twayne, 1990.

Picón Garfield, Evelyn, *Interview with Julio Cortázar. The Review of Contemporary Fiction* 3.3 (Fall 1983). www.centerforbookculture.org

Stavans, Ilan. *Julio Cortázar. A Study of the Short Fiction.* New York: Twayne, 1996.

Weiss, Jason. "Writing at Risk: Interview with Cortázar." In *Writing at Risk: Interviews in Paris with Uncommon Writers.* Iowa: University of Iowa Press, 1991.

Yovanovitch, Gordana. *Julio Cortázar's Character Mosaic: Reading the Longer Fiction.* Toronto: University of Toronto Press, 1991.

Brett Levinson (essay date January-June 2004)

SOURCE: Levinson, Brett. "Populism, Aesthetics, and Politics for Cortázar and for Us: Houses Taken Over." *Latin American Literary Review* 32, no. 63 (January-June 2004): 99-112.

[*In the following essay, Levinson concentrates on the signification and limits of power, and on the relationship between reader and text in "House Taken Over."*]

In this essay I want to analyze Julio Cortázar's **"Casa tomada"** [**"House Taken Over"**] as an extraordinary text that allows us to glimpse, through the force of literature, the very conditions of our intellectual life, some fifty years after the work was written. I am betting on an amazing possibility, whose door Cortázar opens: if we—retrospectively—can discover what Cortázar was doing back then, then he—proleptically—will reveal to us what we are doing right now. In the name of this possibility, I will first conduct a political reading of **"Casa tomada,"** then an aesthetic one, and finally a third exegesis that examines the stakes of casting literature as either aesthetic object or political vehicle: of reading in terms of the value of the political, the value of the aesthetic, or in terms of the competition between such values, in terms of value itself.[1]

"Casa tomada" narrates the life of two middle-aged siblings, unmarried and childless, who dwell within a large Buenos Aires house that they have inherited from the generations preceding them. The brother, who is also the narrator, ventures from the residence only occasionally, to shop and to visit bookstores in search of recent French literature. The sister appears never to abandon the home. The hours of the pair are consumed by cleaning chores—which, to judge from the account, amount to a full time job—cooking, and hobbies.

The "action" of the narrative turns on the take-over of the house, which is a two part process. In the first, the back portion, which includes the library and dining room, is usurped by unnamed, unseen, noiseless, perhaps imagined figures. The siblings lock the door dividing the abode so as to impede further incursion. In the second, the front section is appropriated: without putting up the slightest resistance, as if they were yielding not to trespassers but to new owners, the proprietors abandon the dwelling. Onto the street with no possessions or currency, they bolt the entrance and toss away the key as the tale closes.

Perhaps the easiest and most interesting entrance into the text is the one taken by numerous previous critics: political context. I am of course referring to the rise of Peronism in the 40s, the subsequent politicization of the Argentine working class, and the destabilization of the bourgeoisie.[2] The narrator hints at the issue as he explains how it is possible to live in great material comfort without an income-earning job: "We didn't have to earn our living, there was plenty coming in from the farms each month, even piling up" (12, 108).[3] The siblings are landlords; they do not simply receive money but accumulate wealth. This accumulation, in fact, has numerous parallels within the narrative. The sister amasses, without ever using, the sweaters and socks that she incessantly knits. The family accrues books and stamps. Also, the brother stockpiles cash, which fittingly he fails to retrieve as he is shut out of the home in the final scene.

The protagonists, then, compile while barely exchanging or putting their gains into circulation. By circulation I refer not to monetary expenditure. In fact, the siblings scarcely pass around the city; they have ceased mixing among friends or family; and they have withdrawn from any sexual economy—save, perhaps, from their own possible incestuous relation. It is as if the narrator and his sister had fallen so far out of a public circulation that, as they were meticulously dusting the living room, they missed a small detail, one which has only now come to their attention: a populist overturning of the state's entire political structure had taken place.

Now, these topoi of accumulation and circulation, at least when situated within a narrative about a two-some which so obviously embodies the Argentine bourgeoisie, conjure the base of Marxist theory. And in either gleaning or making this association a reader implicitly identifies the figure who takes over the house. He is the worker and/or the migrated campesino, politicized by Peronism. The laborer's efforts, in some fashion, yielded and have upheld the abode. Therefore this laborer, as he takes over, does not actually do so from the outside. Already a fundamental component of the residence, he has always dwelled by right within. Yet only now, with the advent of Peronism, is his "in-habitation" and/or cohabitation experienced.

These last points would explain an odd absence within the house: that of a servant. The typical bourgeois Argentine family of the period surely would not conduct, by itself, all the cleaning and cooking duties. It would utilize an employee to perform some of these tasks. The fact that the brother and sister do not make such a hire, choosing to occupy their daily lives with chores—and the narrator makes sure to use the language of the workplace in his description of the toil: for instance, he emphasizes his sister's punctuality—points up a desire to keep paid workers outside the household. For via the exclusion, the pair can present its household/social status not as bound to other positions—for example, to other classes—as relational or relative, hence as historical and mortal, but as one that lies beyond such ties, indeed, which transcends every bond, boundary, border, or contaminant, and which is invulnerable due to this fact.

Hence, it is the resistance to circulation which breaks down when the back part of the house is taken over, when the siblings find themselves not *in* but *as* a relation: with others, within circulation itself. But why is this significant? A not-yet-mentioned component of "Casa tomada" permits us to answer. I am alluding to the story's intentional or unintentional deployment of Freud's notion of the uncanny.[4] Freud, it is to be recalled, commences his analysis of the "Unheimlich" by defining the term as both the "familiar" and "unfamiliar," the "homely" and "foreign." And just as the word signifies the opposite of itself, so too, for Freud, can the essence of the ego be its very opponent. Herein, indeed, lies the essence of the uncanny. When the ego experiences an alien entity as its replica, and that double as its repressed essence or secret truth, it encounters the uncanny.

It is not then a particular odd image or foreign being that, for Freud, is uncanny. No object is objectively uncanny—or any could be. For when doubled the ego confronts the fact that, because it can be duplicated, because a perfect substitute exists, it is dispensable not

necessary. The true self, in fact, desires to endure as dissimilar from any copy. Only as absolutely distinct from this contingent entity does he prevail, stand as necessary, the inviolable itself. The uncanny dispels the illusion; ownmost and most alien, the *unheimlich* is not the double as such but the self's death, which doubling, repeatability, and encounter mark.

Thus, uncanny doppelgangers abound throughout "Casa tomada." The rightful occupants are doubled by the outside entities that appropriate this ownership, also by right. Idleness stands as the mimicry of work, the public as the fundament of the private, the bourgeois owners as clones of servants, siblings as the copies of spouses, the campo as omnipresent—in the form of dirt or *tierra* that, as the brother complains (13, 108), ceaselessly falls upon the furniture—within the metropolis. Death in circulation and circulation as death haunt the house's—and the bourgeoisie's—very foundation. The encounter with, and the subsequent deployment, appropriation, and overcoming of the popular or public, the withdrawal into a safe private home, is how the bourgeoisie came to be. And the same circulation among others, now recalled, announces in "Casa tomada" this class' dispossession: the end of a childless family line, the mortality of a certain social structure.

This political reading, if satisfactory, nonetheless puts itself into question as it presents "Casa tomada" as an allegory: of Peronism or populism. For if Cortázar's sole intention were to expose the vulnerability of the bourgeoisie within Peronist Argentina, and if, as we shall see, a main embodiment of this class is the high French literature that the brother covets, it is unlikely that the author would deploy the most literary or artificial of tropes, allegory, in order to carry out this dismantling project. Or is it?

The pre-capitalist nobility, we know, is defined by blood, by nature. The nobleman is noble due to lineage, not culture, wealth, or even character. The bourgeoisie's status, quite to the contrary, is not given. It is gained and it therefore can be lost. In other words class, as modernity emerges, is not fixed but earned and forfeited, constructed and transitory. The bourgeois may have obtained his position, as have the siblings in "Casa tomada," through inheritance, ancestry, and prior social structures; but neither pedigree nor assets can guarantee the sustenance of the niche.

The bourgeoisie thereby attaches to itself certain public forms by means of which it seeks to preserve its standing. These, because set off from other sorts of production—domains such fashion, popular forms of expression, work itself—emerge as the site of "culture," ultimately of a national culture: culture as in "being cultured." The bourgeois stands as the elite, protracts his class, by appropriating this "high" domain. For as appropriated, as public object turned private property, turned propriety, culture materializes as natural, as the essence and ground not only of a class but of the State and even of Being. It thereby permits the bourgeoisie, having claimed Being or essence, to situate itself in the same place, albeit in a distinct manner, as the one occupied by the nobility: as natural and as superior, as naturally superior, clear of any potential plunge.

But what distinguishes the high from low, culture from other productions? The response appears to lie in permanence. **"Casa tomada"** testifies to this possibility by positing books, in addition to the house itself, as the representatives of the family's position. One of the brother's statements speaks directly to the point: "One can reread a book but once a pullover is finished you can't do it over again, it's some kind of disgrace" (11-12, 108). The classic's value and utility, we see, do not decrease as the book circulates, as it is read and reread.

This fact renders the brother's initial reference to books as crucial as it is paradoxical: "I took advantage of these trips to make the rounds of the bookstores, uselessly asking if they had anything new in French literature. Nothing worthwhile had arrived in Argentina since 1939" (11, 107). The narrator desires both the new ("novedades") and the valuable ("valioso"). For him, the worth of the great work is tied to *novedad*—to originality but also to modes and styles: to the novel. But unlike style, the tome must also persist, stand as other than a *novedad,* as everlasting value.

The great book, over against a great painting or opera, circulates widely throughout public space. It is fingered and passed down, duplicated and discarded, cited and recited. Indeed, literature as the embodiment of "high culture" came into being precisely due to its public appearance, its publication: to the advent not of the printing press but of literary salons and cafes. Yet because it circulates alongside and even inside other forms, such as fashion, *but then vanquishes them*— fashion dies off and is replaced; a novel, while also new and fashionable, can subdue its own replaceability and mortality, take on as *great book* the merit of *culture as the modern rendering of classical art*—the literary surfaces as the marker of the eternal merit of the bourgeoisie, as value which goes public, profits from, but then surmounts its engagements so as to stand as a worth beyond others and without opposition, as priceless (in **"Casa tomada,"** as an invaluable *private collection*): as the true worth that transcends,

therefore founds, the crassness of money, of capital. The loss of access to the library during the first take-over stage in **"Casa tomada"** is therefore, for the bourgeois protagonists, the mark of the forfeiture of this, their non-transient value.

However such claims, which smoothly suture the political and the aesthetic, bypass the already-signaled contradiction. Allegorizing Peronism rather than addressing this political movement less obliquely, through, say, a social realist text, Cortázar in **"Casa tomada"** calls upon, seems to need, the literary as such. The political component consequently falls to something less than a necessity, less than essential. Indeed, the form and/or style of **"Casa tomada"** raise the question as to whether the narrative's *main* concern is Peronism at all. Could the story not just as well be one about allegory, about literature itself? Might not the few Peronist allusions found in the tale represent an *alibi* or aside for an account that is *primarily* a literary recitation: a ghost story, a yarn about perversion, an intertextual dialogue with Poe, Kafka, Borges, a statement on the fantastic with little political inclination, one that stands culpable, in *need* of an alibi, precisely due to this insufficient political engagement—a deficiency, imagined or real, for which Cortázar never ceased to feel guilty, and about which he never ceased to write?

To respond, we do well to underscore still another metaliterary component of the tale. Any reading of **"Casa tomada"** must base itself on the brother's report. The reader seemingly has no other testimony to go on: the meaning of the text turns on this sole, nameless authority. Yet the authority of this authority in fact dwindles as the story draws to a close. Indeed, when the account ends—one might say, when its door is finally slammed—meaning is entirely entrusted to the reception of the reader. The narrator, as vehicle of the author, of his authority, forfeits control and is "silenced" the instant the saga, the house, shuts down.

Reception theory might argue that this is true of any narrative. The moment a text concludes, it yields rule to its receiver. The death of the author is the birth of the reader. But in **"Casa tomada"** the idea seems especially pertinent since the brother's deadpan narration "authorizes" or empowers almost no reading at all. Or rather, the narrator offers hints that might lead to *numerous* visions but no "solid information" that would help us resolve once and for all the fundamental question of the tale: who or what invades the home and why? This intruder in fact stands, by the anecdote's finish, as a blurry figure that can be clarified by a dense quantity of speculations and opinions, all of which are more or less supported by the text—as is the Peronist reading put forth above—but none which can be proved central.

Here, we return to the issue of reception. Perhaps we should say that the house in **"Casa tomada"** is the story itself. The trespasser is thereby the reader. At the threshold of the text/home as he interprets, both proper and exterior to the house qua tale (as is any threshold), *unheimlich,* this reader gradually assumes a mandate as the story develops. Eventually, the "old" authority is locked out and the reader is at liberty to take over: to name the assailants and shed light on their obscurity. And said receiver is free to perform the act not once but many times. Indeed, at the tale's termination the narrator indicates where he has discarded the key: in the sewer. The reader can retrieve it time and again so as to enter and reenter, claim and reclaim proprietorship of the mystery: the truth.

The "death of the author," when first proclaimed, referred to a break from authority on the part of the subject-reader, and therefore to a certain notion, abstract or not, elitist or not, of liberty and transgression. Thus, as **"Casa tomada"** gives itself to the receiver, authority hands its power to the previously unlicensed or unauthorized. Here again, a possible Peronist interpretation sneaks through the sealed entrance of the metaliterary one: the reader's take-over of the dead authority figure parallels the worker's or Peronism's subsumption of the dying bourgeoisie, of the class in power.

Yet, as **"Casa tomada"** illustrates, the "death of the author" is actually about this sort of freedom only in a most complex manner. In the account the reader is indeed freed the instant the text's speaker is closed out. Yet in making a claim on or about the house's invader, in naming it, this interpreter does not actually exercise his self-determination. In fact, **"Casa tomada"** has interpellated the reader by extending to him a series of choices—none thoroughly authorized but none that is uninvited either—which, when selected, inscribe this reader precisely into the discourses of authority from which he supposedly liberated himself. For the sake of brevity, I have been emphasizing only three such slots, all thoroughly institutionalized. One is the political interpretation, which keys into the narrative through an appeal to Peronism. The second is the metaliterary analysis, which unveils **"Casa tomada"** as an account about the relation of writer and reader. A third exegesis views the story as political allegory, concerned evenly with politics *and* allegory, historical context *and* aesthetic principles. Meaning in the first perspective is grounded in the value of politics; in the second, in the worth of the aesthetic; in the third, in the merit of tolerance, neutrality, balance, and rigor. Ascribing to different, yet equally traditional ideological, intellectual, and moral positions, each of these interpretations testifies to the authority of that tradition by ascribing to its modern foundation, as capitalist as it is

metaphysical as it is aestheticist: the reduction of being to value and calculation.

The reader of **"Casa tomada"** is not compelled, by some autocratic figure, to adopt his stance. He does so of his own desire, through his self-determination. Picking among meanings the reader in fact opts for none of the above but for the highest value, the value of value, self-determination itself: himself as a free subject, transcendental via this very right to select. The overt focus of the scholar or consumer may well be structure, truth, theory, consciousness-raising, or simple enjoyment, not value. Yet the choice of any of these materialize as value, maximum value, *because* the individual selects among them, *because* choice qua a subject position qua power is itself that very value.

The reader, we noted previously, is in **"Casa tomada"** one conceivable usurper as he moves from the text's threshold at the outset to an authority or inside personage, one with the power and freedom to fill in the story's blank. Yet now we see that the moment the reader locates the key, enters the tale in this manner—as empowered but somewhat grimy—he as liberating invader surfaces simultaneously as the sullied invadee. For once he discloses the tale's truth as either/or political or aesthetic, the reader exposes his subjectivity and will to power as that truth. The certainty will thus be broken down by future readers and readings—precisely because the interpreter, by averring authority, puts that authority in circulation where, one subjective speculation and spectacle among others, it is consumed and perishes.

One might therefore contend that the "winner" upon this ideological and literary field of horror that Cortázar constructs in **"Casa tomada"** is neither the reader nor the narrator, the worker nor the bourgeoisie, politics nor aesthetics, balance nor bias, but absolute authority itself. For this authorial position, in the last instance, is not embodied by the brother who is tossed outside his domain; and it is not represented by the reader. The power is held by Cortázar who—as he so often does—has woven the interpreter into his narrative net. The reader as transcendental subject who takes over in the wake of another authority's death ultimately succumbs to the author's scam, as he is blinded by his own will to selfhood.

Among the most horrible of all of Cortázar's ghost stories, **"Casa tomada"** is therefore a ghastly ambush that induces each reader to enclose or house himself within himself, to seek that self, via the tale as mere medium, in a drive for an uninfringeable position, in a self-identification with, and self-affirmation of a figure of absolutism that this reader seems to displace and subvert but actually, in the end, constitutes.

The fall of a single and central authority, such as *the* author, does not then inevitably liberate. Fundamental to a shift from one method of domination and restraint to another, decentralization only obliges the citizen or non-citizen, now turned consumer, to select: not automatically to select this or that but just to select. The subjectivity that is gained through such choice, by its own logic, sets up every relation to the other, hence any politics or poetics, as unnecessary since what is here necessary, essential, is the subject himself, the absolute as embodied by reader or author.

Across the author's demise, intra-active or readerly interpretation—not unlike intra-active TV talk shows—thereby easily backs non-commitment to any outside or alternative, to the world itself, as that world's foundation and ideal. Indeed, it is the consumer/citizen's intra-activity, not his passivity, that stands in opposition to engagement: soliciting the participation of the individual or collective I, intra-activism constructs the value of non-engagement and non-engagement, unadulterated might without potential praxis or poeisis, as this value. Stated in contemporary Latin Americanist terms, the production of a variety of meanings and the demand for preference, which surface in the wake of the despotic authority's slippage, only reinforce the newest form of rule: the neoliberal consensus qua the market, which induces every subject to desire, therefore reproduce, the Same, the Subject himself.

Is **"Casa tomada"** in fact an allegory of Peronism? The base of populism proper, of course, is a figure, such as Juan or Eva Peron. This site lures the diverse sectors of the public into locating in the state their own proper place. The state is good for many choices, many ideologies. It, and only it, offers each a state position, a site of self-determination. The populist thus materializes as the absolute power that authorizes also alternative forces and freedoms. He/she appears, in short, as a totalizing field that precludes the very freedoms that he/she stimulates. Peronism, in **"Casa tomada,"** thus emerges as the scene of the convergence of left and right, of the reduction of the one to the other in the *figure*—the empty territory to be populated, the imaginary free and exterior-to-capital space upon which all capitalist enterprises call—in the *figure*, literary like all figures, of power.

Drawing the reader into affirming the structures of authority through his liberty to fill in its vague invader with himself, **"Casa tomada"** therefore less describes as performs populism. Populism or Peronism names a political operation that is both too centered and decentered, and that is therefore the logical precursor of its historical aftermath in Argentina: the too strong state of dictatorship and/or the too weak state of the neoliberal marketplace.

Indeed, like the figure of Peron, the figure of modern allegory (Kafka's insect in "The Metamorphosis" is a prime example) stands as the hazy core that extends an invitation to a multitude of identifications. It is at once a given text's authorial center and the vacant, passive area over which the spectator, the crowd, the reader, assumes dominion. Perhaps, therefore, we should not discuss **"Casa tomada"** as an allegory of Peronism but posit Peronism as the literary performance of the political, as itself an allegory.

In the beginning of this essay it seemed that every aesthetic view of **"Casa tomada"** would end up supporting a political interpretation. Now it appears that every political take on the text will prop, via the notion of the figure, an aesthetic or metaliterary analysis. The allegory of Peronism switches, almost by itself, into an allegory of reading or a reading of allegory. In truth the "more political" readers of **"Casa tomada"** appear, the more they affirm as necessary a trope, hence the more they foreground the aesthetic components of the tale. Likewise, the more the scholar insists on the literary value of the text, the more he discloses literature as the political tool of either class difference or its overturning, of the right or left.

Cortázar desired his texts to be themselves, without historical referent, literary precedent, or future followers. Cortázar sought, in other words, to be absolutely modern, to devise a total break, from history and even from literature, well aware that he came too late, as do all Latin American artists, for that very modernity. Conversely, as loyal if anomalous leftist Cortázar sought to address the historical positions and social institutions into which the very act of writing and publishing flung him. His texts, struggling to stand as pure creations, devoid of aesthetic or material history, *and* as historical testimonies and recitations, replete with an eerily unpretentious rather than arty mood— Cortázar's short texts are penned across the schism between these two. They take place upon the fault between aesthetic drive and political aspiration, a split that is neither: not politics and not aesthetics but the impossibility of their conjunction *and* disjunction.

The Cortázar reader, then, cannot select either aesthetics or politics without conjuring both and neither. The choice between the two, indeed, is no choice since the claim to one, uncannily, must call upon its opposite as an alternative foundation that displaces and decenters it. This pick, in other words, cannot be grounded in a reasonable assertion but only in ideology since, by that reason, the selection of one overdetermines the other: when the qualitative difference between aesthetics and politics surfaces as an unbearable demand, ideology and subject positions call upon quantitative distinctions, value conflict, so as to break the tie and affirm themselves as truth. **"Casa tomada,"** in other words, will not tend a ground for any (but it will for every) interpretation; each such exegesis is literally groundless, situated over a rift. The individual exposition of the tale is thus a willful assertion without support—not because **"Casa tomada"** is meaningless but because its sense stretches across a divide, takes in its other side, materializes as more than itself, as one truth too many.

Yet if the scholar does in fact opt for aesthetics the instant he decides for politics, and vice-versa, if his choice is no choice (he cannot take one without taking the other) and if the production and invitation to selection are the means by which the transcendental subject emerges as the consumer who backs a pure consensus—if this is all true, then the reader's drive to authority is also an exposure to the limit of choice itself: of a market that reduces meaning and sovereignty to free selection, and of the transcendental ego who liberates and empowers himself merely by reproducing and ascribing to these options.

Because Cortázar's own authority in **"Casa tomada"** could not come about if not accompanied by a demand for the reader participation that the demand itself cannot dictate, the story exposes reception and doxa, thereby mutability, exchange, and deauthorization as proper to power's very essence, as literature's and culture's double: the very double from which the bourgeoisie and literature as ruling sites—striving to affirm their value as autonomous, as essentially unbound to publication and the public, meager tastes, and subjective evaluations—must withdraw in order to stand.

Now, one name for this boundary or liminal space that binds authority to uncertified response, and by extension, culture to fashion, the bourgeoisie to the public, the aesthetic to the political, is desire. For one cannot control the force of desire; nor can one select, as would a subject, the object of desire. One can certainly *repress* desire, substitute the object of desire for an object choice, the pleasure for the reality principle. Yet repression only displaces or compresses, in any case proliferates, the desire itself. In maintaining one reading over another when every such claim enjoys only itself as foundation, in asserting himself as subject, the reader exposes his interpretation as this very exposure: of his own desire.

Interpretation, then, reflects not only the truth but the desire of empowerment. The reader makes a determination across a limit that "inseparates," renders "unselectable," politics and/or aesthetics. His pick is the disclosure of his desire, of the manacle on authority

which he has had to disavow in order to emerge as a power, as chooser. Desire is the frontier that opens Self to Other, to the ecstatic, incestuous eros that pervades the entirety of **"Casa tomada."**

"Casa tomada" thereby represents not just an assault on but an affirmation of power. The tale makes public its signs and representations, hence lends its hand to the taking of ideological positions. And it bears responsibility for these appropriations, be they by the left or right. Yet the narrative also communicates the border on or between powers, the fix between self and other that the drive for power renders not visible but readable: desire as the rift that is the condition of politics and art, but that cannot come forth in either a political claim or an aesthetic object. This bind is in fact the partition that, while making categories conceivable, is not one of them, is not itself a choice but an obligation, a responsibility. You cannot *not* have it. As interpreter you *might* opt for reading A over reading B but, either way, you *must* decide for the interval, discontinuity, the sharing that joins and disconnects the positions. Yes, the bond of forces, the communication between author and reader, teacher and student, colleague and colleague, politics and aesthetics, is also the hard boundary or dis-joint that generates selection, hence the positioning of subjects: the institutional empowerment, the consensus without negotiation, contact, or contract, the market that erases in advance unions, desires, engagements, communities, simple dialogue, indeed, plain courtesy. However, this linkage is at the same time the communication that hitches self to other, that casts strict separation as an impossibility that yields to possibility, to engagement as such.

"Casa tomada" conveys this double bind as the dual nature of power, and as the two components of both literature and society. The story is composed of signifiers that yield the subjects of representation and self-representation. Yet these signs also communicate the borders and edges which thrust each subject into an intimate relation with an Other: they communicate communication itself, encounter—ecstatic and erotic like all genuine encounters—as the core of every commitment, artistic or political. Moreover, this communication of limits or limit of communication is the condition of the transgression and freedom of which Cortázar remained forever capable, of any *powerful* engagement with or refusal of the institution, since without limits—limits to power—there is no such crossing, trespassing, or force: no liberation, break, or break in, no strength or affirmation, but solely the *resentiment* of the will to a boundless and ideal I, individual or collective (it makes no difference).

Notes

1. The original point of departure of this study was the extreme diversity of previous critical readings

of "Casa tomada." While the political component is marked in essays such as Claudio Cifuentes's "Un personaje ausente en la fantasticidad de dos relatos de Julio Cortázar: La ley de la propiedad privada" in *Coloquio internacional: Lo lúdico y lo fantástico en la obra de Cortázar, II* (Madrid: Fundamentos, 1986), 89-95, Maguelina Soifer treats the tale as a strictly metaliterary and aesthetic work in *Revista letras* 35 (1986): 173-184. Still others, such as Renato Martínez in "Fonema o grafema? El Boom y la deconstrucción de Derrida," *Torre de papel* 2, no. 1 (1992): 54-63, locate in "Casa tomada" a prototype for deconstructive reading practices. Other essays which spurred my work, given the remarkable difference of their points of view, are: Fernando Moreno Turner, "El texto en movimiento y los movimentos del texto: Nuevo asalto a 'Casa tomada' de Julio Cortázar" in *Acta literaria* 23 (1988): 69-80; "La casa de los sueños: sobre 'Casa tomada,' de Julio Cortázar," *Coloquio internacional: Lo lúdico y lo fantástico en la obra de Cortázar, II* (Madrid: Fundamentos, 1986), 97-109; María Rosenblat, "La nostalgia de la unidad en el cuento fantástico: 'The Fall of the House of Usher' y 'Casa tomada'" in *Los ochenta mundos de Cortázar, ensayos,* ed. Fernando Burgos (Madrid: EDI, 1987), 199-209; Bernard Terramorsi, "Maison occuppée de Julio Cortázar: Le demon de la solitude," *CCERL I* 9 (1984): 33-41; Jose H. Brandt Rojas, "Asedios a 'Casa tomada' de Julio Cortázar," *Revista de estudios hispánicos* 7 (1980): 75-84.

2. Andres Avellanada, in his *El habla de la ideología* (Buenos Aires: Editorial Sudamericana, 1993), offers an excellent summary of (and contribution to) the field of criticism that addresses "Casa tomada" as a political narrative about Peronism. Other scholars that tackle the issue include Juan José Sebrieli, *Buenos Aires: Vida contidiana y alienación* (Buenos Aires: Siglo Veinte, 1965), 102-105; Aníbal Ford, "Los últimos cuentos de Cortázar" in *Mundo Nuevo,* no. 5 (1966), 81-83; Nestor García Canclini, *Cortázar: Una antropología poética* (Buenos Aires: Editorial Nova, 1968); and Antún Arrufut, "Prólogo," en Julio Cortázar, *Cuentos* (La Habana: Casa de las Américas, 1964), ix. While I am indebted to these texts, I want to emphasize that my essay differs in focus from them. The above studies are efforts to demonstrate that Cortázar's politicization, above all his critique of the bourgeoisie, emerges with his earliest tales. (This thesis contrasts with those who argue that Cortázar does not become "politicized" until after the Cuban Revolution.) My essay—which, by the way, does not view "Casa tomada" as solely a critique of the bourgeoisie; it is also a critique of that critique—is not about this

particular position but about the political ramifications of taking a position at all when reading. What are the *political* ramifications, *for us today,* of taking one position over the other, in particular a political or aesthetic position, when analyzing? In short, the present essay does not investigate, much less set out to "discover," the relation of Cortázar's narratives to Peronism. It is only marginally about Cortázar and Peronism, and is therefore not actually a dialogue with the important criticism just cited.

3. All quotes are from the English *Blow Up and Other Stories,* trans. Paul Blackburn (New York: Pantheon Books, 1967). Citations include first the page number from this translation and are followed by the page number from the Spanish: Julio Cortázar, *Cuentos completos*/1 (Santanilla, S.A. Madrid, 1994).

4. Sigmund Freud, "The Uncanny," in *The Collected Papers of Sigmund Freud,* vol. 4, trans. Joan Riviere (London: Hogarth, 1957), 152-170.

Works Cited

Arrufut, Antún. "Prólogo," en Julio Cortázar, *Cuentos.* La Habana: Casa de las Américas, 1964, i-x.

Avellanada, Andrés. *El habla de la ideología.* Buenos Aires: Editorial Sudamericana, 1993.

Brandt Rojas, José H. "Asedios a 'Casa tomada' de Julio Cortázar," in *Revista de estudios hispánicos* 7 (1980): 75-84.

Cifuentes, Claudio. "Un personaje ausente en la fantasticidad de dos relatos de Julio Cortazar: La ley de la propiedad privada," in *Coloquio internacional: Lo lúdico y lo fantástico en la obra de Cortázar, II.* Madrid: Fundamentos, 1986, 89-95.

Cortázar, Julio. *Blow Up and Other Stories.* Trans. Paul Blackburn New York: Pantheon Books, 1967.

Cortázar, Julio. *Cuentos completos*/1. Santanilla, S.A. Madrid, 1994.

Ford, Aníbal. "Los últimos cuentos de Cortázar," in *Mundo Nuevo,* no. 5 (1966), 81-83.

Freud, Sigmund. "The Uncanny," in *The Collected Papers of Sigmund Freud,* vol. 4, trans. Joan Riviere (London: Hogarth, 1957), 152-170.

García Canclini, Nestor. *Cortazar: Una antropología poética.* Buenos Aires: Editorial Nova, 1968.

Martínez, Renato. "Fonema o grafema? El Boom y la deconstrucción de Derrida," in *Torre de papel* 2, no. 1 (1992): 54-63.

Moreno Turner, Fernando. "El texto en movimiento y los movimentos del texto: Nuevo asalto a 'Casa tomada' de Julio Cortázar," in *Acta literaria* 23 (1988): 69-80.

Rosenblat, María. "La nostalgia de la unidad en el cuento fantástico: 'The Fall of the House of Usher' y 'Casa tomada,'" in *Los ochenta mundos de Cortázar, ensayos,* ed. Fernando Burgos. Madrid: EDI, 1987, 199-209.

Sebrieli, Juan José. *Buenos Aires: Vida contidiana y alienación.* Buenos Aires: Siglo Veinte, 1965, 102-105.

Soifer, Miguelina. "Cortázar y la estética," in *Revista letras* 35 (1986): 173-184.

Terramorsi, Bernard. "Maison occuppée de Julio Cortázar: Le demon de la solitude," in *CCERL I* 9 (1984): 33-41.

Alice Jedličková (essay date fall 2006)

SOURCE: Jedličková, Alice. "From Otherworldliness and a Two-World Scheme to 'Heterocosmica': A Visit to a Museum with Cortázar and Nabokov." *Style* 40, no. 3 (fall 2006): 258-71.

[*In the following essay, Jedličková contrasts the psychological and physical aspects of the world in "A Leg of the Journey" with those in Vladimir Nabokov's "The Visit to the Museum," concluding that Cortázar's story ultimately resolves the ambiguous movement between these two realms.*]

1. INTRODUCTION: DISTURBING THE PEACE OF THE REPRESENTED WORLD

Apart from individual Czech attempts to expand the scope of the possible-worlds theory of fiction (especially as presented in Lubomír Doležel's *Heterocosmica*) by developing it and applying it to a nonnarrative genre (see Červenka), I have observed two major results of the impact of possible-worlds theory on Czech literary study. A number of scholars who used to apply the term *represented world* or even *depicted world,* when referring to a work of fiction in their analyses, have slightly changed their usage by replacing *depicted* with *fictional.* Unfortunately, a description of what a depicted world looks like, or what topics it represents, that is, a basically thematic reading, does not equal an examination of how a fictional world works or what principles control it. (As research tradition has it, implementing a new model does not mean just adopting a new terminological inventory but adopting a new way of thinking as well.) The other phenomenon I have been able to observe as a teacher is the mythologizing of the rationalist aspect of the theory. This results in questioning possible-worlds theory as a tool of decision-making in literary discourse. One of the most popular issues is whether the theory makes it possible to tell an anonymous fictional

text from a nonfictional one; thus it is necessary to realize that the theory was intended to provide a concept of *fictional* semantics. Rereading Marie-Laure Ryan's essay "Possible Worlds in Recent Literary Theory," which predicted the main spheres of application of possible-worlds theory and its impact some fourteen years ago, provides an occasion to reconsider her prognosis and thus the actual scope of the concept. The last option is to demonstrate its analytic power as well as interpretive limits. I had made my first attempt to do so by distinguishing the domains of the fictional world of Julio Cortázar's short story **"Silvia"** and in particular by showing how the whole structure of the story rested on the mutual accessibility of these domains ("Jak proniknout na území Silvie"). A recent attempt is my analysis "Children Would Not Talk Like That," referring to a critic's statement about a Czech short story; it employs possible-worlds theory (i.e., the theory of fictional worlds of literature) to defend specific qualities of a fictional world, and it complements my essay discussing exactly the "antimimetic" aspect of Doležel's *Heterocosmica* ("S mimezí v batohu na výlet do roznosvto"). The incentive for the present analytic attempt based on a confrontation of Cortázar's and Vladimir Nabokov's short stories was a fascinated reader's encounter with Nabokov's "The Visit to the Museum," followed by an inquiry into the search for analytic tools (and metaphors as well) performed by other scholars fascinated by Nabokov's "otherworlds."

2. THIS AND "THE OTHER" SIDE: NABOKOV'S OTHERWORLDLINESS

We should always remember that the work of art is invariably the creation of a new world, so that the first thing we should do is study that new world as closely as possible, approaching it as something brand new, having no obvious connection with the worlds we already know.

—Vladimir Nabokov

In his introduction to *Nabokov's Otherworld* (1991), Vladimir Alexandrov states the aim of his book as dismantling "the widespread critical view that Vladimir Nabokov is first and foremost a metaliterary writer, and to suggest instead that an aesthetic rooted in his intuition of a transcendent realm is the basis of his art" (3). I wholly agree with Alexandrov's intention, not only because this is a constrictive characteristic of Nabokov's poetics indeed, excluding an essential part of his oeuvre as a result, but also because of the fact, first, that a preference for examining metaliterary concepts, techniques, and devices proves quite often to be an occasion to display the critic's erudition rather than that of the examined author and, second, that it makes it possible to evidence how the examined author is like others, while backgrounding the aspects of how he is unlike them. The ironic gesture of the "anthropomorphic deity" in *Bend Sinister* offering salvation to the tortured protagonist and destroying the fictional existence of the narrated world at same time—and thus transferring a "world-constructing text" into a "self-voiding" one (cf. Doležel 24, 281)—has become an almost obligatory device of postmodern writing in the past few decades. "Disclosing" this trick will hardly be acknowledged as a profound analytical gesture anymore—even though one has to admit Nabokov's self-disclosing narrative devices are very subtle, elaborate, and distinctive compared to others. Still, I would like to state that it is more interesting to me to inquire into how fictional worlds are designed and how they work, than into how they are deprived of their existence. The particular reason to do so in Nabokov's case is not only their specific global design (in terms of Doležel's fictional-worlds theory) but also an ensemble of qualities that a reader, and I daresay even a critic, will appreciate for their psychological complexity—and, to put it in an old-fashioned way—for their sensational, even "physical" plasticity. Just imagine thumby Pnin washing the dishes after his house-warming party in a haze of dim light reminding the reader of Pieter de Hooch's paintings depicting cosy interiors. Nabokov's characters—though designated as "textual entities" quite frequently by the narrator and though apprehended as inhabitants of a fictional world by an enlightened reader—are what we were allowed to call flesh-and-blood people, prior to the invention of antimimetic theories of narrative, of course. Julian Moynahan puts it in a different way but quite appropriately: "Neither Proust nor Nabokov permits this essentially metaphysical quest to sterilize his fictional art. . . . Thirst for the eternal never alienates their loyalty to the human condition although it may constitute the deepest source of their great originality and power as stylists and fabulists" (6).

I do not find it necessary to speak in support of Nabokov's ability to create a nice illusion of a physical world in his reader, a perfect virtual reality (in that respect, his method could be called "a realistic" one); neither do I wish to object to Alexandrov's argument that Nabokov's "transcendent realm" might have been apprehended intuitively by the author. But this imaginary realm is transferred in a variety of "otherworlds constructed by texts"; thus an explanation of a crucial feature of Nabokov's aesthetics can be given employing the main arguments of fictional-worlds theory.

A "two-world model" has been employed quite frequently to elucidate the principles of Nabokov's fictional world (see Shrayer 52; he gives a record of further analyses, e.g., one by Davydov that uses the notion of "bispatiality" literally) resting upon a statement by Vera Nabokov, who had suggested the presence of "the other side" of things (*potustoronnost*) and

its significance in Nabokov's way of thinking and writing (cf. Alexandrov 3; Shrayer 17). The notion of otherworld (or otherworldliness) has been used in the analysis of Nabokov's aesthetics by Alexandrov. A number of Nabokov's short stories actually do suggest a two-world scheme as sufficient by presenting an obvious difference between the world shared by all the characters and the way it is experienced by the protagonist, or a distinct difference between the world surrounding the protagonist and his mental world, especially his memories, yearnings, and dreams.

Jonathan Borden Sisson's 1979 dissertation "Cosmic Synchronization and Other Worlds in the Work of Vladimir Nabokov" might be considered a seminal inquiry into Nabokov's oeuvre as an ensemble of possible worlds, here being referred to as "alternative realities." Sisson's position may be described as negotiating between radical principles of theoretical physics challenging the idea of a single integral world and Nabokov's concept of "cosmic synchronization." This notion originates from Nabokov's reflection of human experience as well as artistic creation and is meant to express a state of simultaneous perception of the personal mental world, that of the physical space surrounding the perceiving individual, as well as the principles that govern the universe; in his oeuvre, especially short stories, it is often connected with epiphanic moments of bliss and freedom experienced by his characters. Sisson points to the existence in Nabokov's works (giving a typical example in the short story "Terra Incognita") of "simultaneous but mutually exclusive fictional worlds presented in ambiguous contraposition in order that the reader's habits of perception are violated, thus liberating the reader's mind and stimulating it to a greater capacity of consciousness" (qtd. by Shrayer 18). I should like to object to the idea of "mutually exclusive" fictional worlds, backing my objection with fictional-worlds theory. Alternative worlds are not necessarily exclusive provided that the global design of the world of the story delivers an explanation of their possible coexistence. In "Terra Incognita," the ambivalence or indeterminacy of the situation concerned lies in the fact that the reader finds it difficult or even impossible to judge whether the protagonist is experiencing a nightmare of a tropic adventure while lying on a hospital bed or a hallucination of an European apartment while dying in a hostile jungle. To put it differently, the traditional scheme of a mundane physical world and a world of dreams or nightmares is undone: there is no "privileged" world. Maxim D. Shrayer states that we seem to be facing an oral narration by the explorer based on his written record of the adventure and arriving at the moment of his seeming death—this would entitle us to prefer the idea of a nightmare in a hospital. However, the theory of fictional worlds also allows impossible possible worlds, for example, a world where the voice of a dead explorer can be heard recounting his experience to the very last moment of his life. After that, nothing more can be told of the mundane experience, of course. Still, there remains one question to be answered: What was the incentive for the narrator to raise his voice from the world beyond and how is it possible it can be heard?

Shrayer, referring to Sisson, compares this situation with the story of a Chinese sage who wakes from his dream wondering "whether Chuang Chou dreamt he was a butterfly, or a butterfly is dreaming that he is Chuang Chou" (49). This concentrated metaphor has been developed in numerous works of fiction; a salient, elaborated metaphor that appears to tempt comparison to Nabokov's "Terra Incognita" is a short story by Cortázar, **"La noche boca arriba"** (**"The Night Face Up"**).[1] The protagonist, a young man who had been hospitalized after a traffic accident, seems to lapse into horrifying nightmares while recovering from an operation. His fellow patients try to ease his pain and to calm him down by explaining that this is quite a common occurrence in feverish patients. So far the world of modern street traffic and hospitals seems to be the privileged one, the one where the character's consciousness dwells and, being excited by the extreme physical condition, produces horrible nightmares. But the protagonist finds it more and more difficult to escape the nightmares, "to wake up," as he does not seem to sleep; on the contrary, he seems to be perfectly awake when trying desperately to escape the knives of Aztec priests who are after him in a dark jungle. Finally, the assumed world of the nightmares proves to be the original one, and we may apply the Chinese metaphor by saying "Chuang Chu finds out he is a butterfly that dreamt of being Chuang Chu." This ontological change is sealed by a significant change in focalization, a very different apprehension of things: the protagonist, now being approached by his immolators, remembers having a dream in which he had been sitting on a huge metallic buzzing insect and riding through a giant town of flaming lights of red and green.[2] Thus Cortázar's story differs from that by Nabokov in resolving the state of indeterminacy in its closure.

So far, we have encountered fictional worlds challenging the opposition of a mundane world and that of dreams with a various degree of indeterminacy; the two-world scheme seemed to match. I should like to demonstrate by confronting two further short stories—Nabokov's "Poseschchenie muzeya" ("The Visit to the Museum") and Cortázar's **"Fin de etapa"** (**"The End of a Phase"**)—and showing that even then, when the fictional world displays, at least at first sight, a duality

of worlds, the two-world scheme may not be enough to explain its logic. The intention of the following comparison is not to demonstrate thematic overlaps of both short stories, though I have to admit there are some: one of the crucial motifs of Cortázar's story (as well as its dedication to painters) reveals his fancy for creating fictional works of art and emplotting them in his stories, a preference he shares with Nabokov (see the short story "Veneziana," for example). Neither is it to search for a narrative method kindred to that of Nabokov or to challenge two "masters of otherworldliness" to compete in their ability to astonish their readers, even though in both stories the characters leave what we call the "normal" world to enter "the other" one. The point is a profound correspondence in the design of fictional worlds.

3. THE END OF A PHASE: FAMILIARIZING WITH A STRANGE WORLD

Diana, the protagonist of Cortázar's **"The End of a Phase,"** travels the French countryside without any particular destination and without paying attention to any particular qualities of her surroundings in order just to "watch things as if they were watching her." Generally, her attitude towards the world is an extremely passive or detached one: when she is walking along a street the buildings seem to be passing her, not she them. She stops in a small town and involuntarily finds her way to the local museum displaying an exhibition of a local painter. At first, she is surprised by what the narrator calls "a realistic obsession," mistaking pictures for extremely large blow-ups; she does not feel quite at ease while observing the pictures that seem not only to display almost empty rooms but also to be components of a giant tromp l'oeil, that is, rooms of an illusionary house. Certain motifs appear in all the pictures—an anonymous male silhouette facing an open door, an empty table. The protagonist refuses to pay a visit to the last room displaying a single picture as she is told by the custodian: she wishes to break the "sad tourist's rule" to see everything. On her way back she has to cope with another surprise as one of the pictures seems to have changed, or perhaps she had not observed the pictured items carefully: one of the depicted tables that she supposed to be bare is occupied by a jar filled with paintbrushes.

The reader can hardly avoid the temptation of constructing a connection between the pictures and the current situation of the protagonist after her relationship with a friend had failed and she traveled just because of a restlessness resulting from her inability to cope with the situation and to find peace—the juxtaposition of her personal, nonrecurring situation and the scenes shown in the museum implies parallels. The anonymous male silhouette in the doorway suggests a double symbolic interpretation: it might be read either as a piece of advice to realize that a man who has left is never going to come back in his search for a new way, or as the possibility of meeting someone new who might not pay attention at the moment but who might respond when being addressed. The almost empty rooms seem to offer an alternative space to be filled; the jar with paintbrushes appears as a sample of how to start by adding—creating—a new item and thus becoming active again.

After having visited the museum, the protagonist goes for a walk in the town. Coincidentally she discovers a house with a dim hallway that looks like the one depicted in the museum and, as she declined to do earlier in the museum, goes on to discover the interior. When she comes across a closed door, she is not surprised because she remembers she rejected seeing the last room in the museum and thus the last room of the depicted house. In the end, everything seems all too "geometric, inconceivable and foreseen at the same time." This point of view expresses the situation when a strange world or at least a world of strange coincidences becomes familiar. Though it remains inconceivable, its implicit logic has been accepted by the fictional character; as Doležel puts it in his discussion of Franz Kafka's short story "A Country Doctor," "The bizarre, the physically impossible, is in the midst of the human world, waiting there to be discovered or to interfere, purely by chance" (188-89).[3] After having deliberated the whole situation and having judged that it might be easier to accept it as a matter of fact without analysis, the protagonist returns to the museum to find out that the last picture depicts a lonely woman seated at a table: her remarkably quiet expression suggests the calmness of death. The protagonist begins her journey out of town, but after driving for a while, she feels she inevitably has to return to the house. She admits that—had she gone on the way she did before, traveling with no destination, staying at indistinctive places in indistinctive hotels—"one phase would appear as a copy of the previous one," a phase of an endless runaway. So, imitating the posture of the female figure in the picture, she rests at the table. The story's close is open ended. As the narrator puts it, the protagonist is free to leave as well as free to stay; we can see she has arrived at the point where she is finally able to let herself go. She may watch the situation change in time or not: the second possibility means accepting the timelessness of the pictorial world, that is, adopting the rules of the possible world designed by the pictures, to implement them in the world she is experiencing. As a result, this means accepting the possibility of her own death. The alternative world is very simple, almost empty, excluded from time and cultural context (similarly, there are

very few cues to the regional appearance and location of the town the protagonist is visiting). The paintings do not seem to depict individual objects but to represent whole classes of objects (i.e., to present images of "man," "table," and so on). This could lead to the conclusion that the reader is encouraged to produce a variety of interpretations—if it were not for the global design of the fictional world: the emptiness of the images equals the psychical "emptiness" of the protagonist's life, her indifference to the abundance of the world that she obviously reduced to a scheme after her relationship was broken (e.g., when watching hilarious card players in the local pub, she realizes she is no longer able to experience a moment of triumph or intense sensation at all).

Summarizing the point of the story, we may go back to the initial embarrassing question of whether possible-worlds theory allows us to make decisions in literary discourse. We could concede it does, when applied as fictional-worlds theory to fiction. In the case of **"The End of a Phase"** we might "decide" we do not have to bother with whether the physical alternative of the world designed by the pictures is a "fantastic" one or just a coincidence. The pictures in the museum obviously represent Diana's situation and its alternatives in a highly stylized (though at first sight very "realistic") way: this possible world makes her realize what she has been doing and what she has avoided, as well as what opportunities there are left. The physical space of the house is just a way of externalizing those alternatives and thus demonstrating the fact the protagonist cannot escape her experience, her memories, and her mental world as well as the necessity to do something or to let the world do something about her. Her decision to adopt the scene of the last picture to replace her escape from the past is a choice made of alternatives offered by the depicted space. As she did not take the chance to change her attitude to the world, she gives the world the chance to do (or not to do) something about her.

We may say, then, that the global design of the fictional world of the story is based upon a symmetry between the mental world of the protagonist and its double representation—a symbolic one (represented through objects of visual art using its specific language) and a physical one (represented through the space of a provincial house).

4. THE VISIT TO THE MUSEUM: COMPILING THE ENCYCLOPEDIA OF A FICTIONAL WORLD

The opening of Nabokov's short story "The Visit to the Museum" appears very forthcoming in giving all details of the narrator's mission to a provincial French museum as well as his secret wish to avoid it. A Russian friend in Paris asks him to examine the collection and find out if a portrait of his grandfather by a local artist could be purchased. The portrait used to belong to his grandfather's property in Paris and was sold after his death at the time of Russo-Japanese war—that is, at a time when the apartments in both St. Petersburg and Paris belonged to the same domain of well-to-do people, representing two locations equally accessible and available according to the season and wishes of their proprietor. Thus the ancestral portrait not only represents a family's history but also alludes to a part of the history of prerevolutionary Russia. While Shrayer emphasizes the fact that the narrator's friend is considered a person prone to fantasies, to the "otherworlds" (thus introducing the two-world-system we have encountered already and confronting the "mundane" world with that of the fantasies of a character [Shrayer 57]), I should like to suggest that a no less—maybe even more—important feature of the fictional world of the story is the fact that the reader is introduced into a world consisting of differently accessible domains.

The narrator is finally forced to pay a visit to the museum, due to unexpected heavy rain; he discovers the portrait during his examination of the obscure exhibition of a variety of items displayed in only two rooms. He approaches the administrator of the museum, a Mr. Godard, to negotiate the purchase of the picture; at first, Mr. Godard denies the presence of the painting in the museum. Finally, he surrenders to the narrator's persuasion and declares his willingness to sell the picture. In the museum, he keeps on putting off the purchase by fabricating a number of obstructions and urging the visitor to pay attention to further collections displayed in rooms the protagonist did not take notice of during his first visit. This seems to be a logical explanation, as he focused on the portrait located in the second room; now he is literally being dragged along by his companion to other parts of the exhibition. The atmosphere—sleepy and tedious during his first visit—is becoming peculiar: a group of young people enjoying themselves in their own way transform the visit of the museum into a grotesque scene resembling those in Alfred Kubin's novel *Die andere Seite* (1919).[4]

Finally, the narrator loses not only Mr. Godard's company but also control over the situation. Searching desperately for his way back, he finds the exhibition to be expanding so that sometimes it is difficult to tell whether he entered a room or had just been "swallowed up" in there. In the beginning, the order of the rooms and exhibited items that the narrator is forced to see mainly corresponds with a general scheme of a science and history museum, for example starting with ancient cultures or displaying a whale skeleton. Later on, unusual effects are created as a result of the manner of exhibiting (the display of steam machines with glowing signals and wet tracks is extremely realistic; finding himself at a mock-up railway station the narrator experiences an unexpected attack of anxiety and pain) or by exhibiting unusual items ("Section Fountains and Brooks" proves to be slippery and life endangering). Some parts of the exhibition resemble "samples of life" rather than mock-ups: "In front of me stretched an infinitely long passage, containing numerous office cabinets and elusive, scurrying people" (279). The museum seems to consist not of separated exhibition rooms anymore but of a number of independent spaces; the narrator does not enter all of them but cannot avoid listening to the noise coming from within (resembling numerous machines and typewriters at work, for example). I dare say just about anything could be expected in the next room or space: the museum seems to be expanding like the universe. Or, to put it in a different way, the museum as a world sui generis seems to possess the ability to compress time and space and to provide outlets into "sections" or "samples" of other worlds. The only restriction is imposed upon the narrator's actions: he cannot find his way back (we may assume, that, for some reason, he is not allowed to do so).

The reader is thus facing not only an "odd" fictional world but obviously a multiple-worlds scheme as well. According to Doležel, "Knowledge about a possible world constructed by a fictional text constitutes a fictional encyclopedia. Fictional encyclopedias are many and diverse, but all of them to a greater or lesser degree digress from the actual-world encyclopedia" (177). He later adds:

> The immensely varied fictional encyclopedias guide the recovery of implicit meaning in fictional texts. In order to reconstruct and interpret a fictional world, the reader has to reorient his cognitive stance to agree with the world's encyclopedia. . . . The actual-world encyclopedia might be useful, but it is by no means universally sufficient; for many fictional worlds it is misleading, it provides no comprehension but misreading. The readers have to be ready to modify, supplement, or even discard the actual-world encyclopedia. . . . they must background the knowledge of their actual domicile and become cognitive residents of the fictional world they visit through the act of reading.
>
> (181)

So far it has become obvious that the scheme of a history museum displaying the "progress of mankind" or that of a "world of science" known to the reader has to be altered. So one of the crucial conditions of recovering the implicit meaning in the fictional text of "The Visit to the Museum" is discovering the principles of organization (if any) of the odd museum visited by the narrator.

Why is "a gigantic mock-up of the universe" observed by "a crowd of grey-haired people with umbrellas"? Why not a group of adequately attentive or bored or restless pupils, for example? Even if we try to avoid "suspicious reading" and suppose that the mock-up of the universe does not mean anything special, just a simple reference to the conventions of a science museum, and that grey-haired people with umbrellas are far from referring to anxiety and insecurity, still the question remains of how it could be housed in a "building of modest proportions." Shrayer considers the scene an "absurdist" one. Indeed, the static situation might resemble a painting by René Magritte for example, much as the scene with the young sportsmen climbing giant ancient sculptures resembles a scene from Alfred Kubin's novel. Some other critics base their interpretation upon a reflection of modernism, especially surrealism and its preference for oneiric processes; the narration is referred to as a "phantasmagoric" one then (e.g., Liudmila Foster, cited in Shrayer 58). But such an observation would lead exactly where we do not wish to be led: to discovering intertextual bonds, similarities, and influences. Apart from the fact that this would be the type of analysis the author himself had held in scorn (though we do not have to obey the "master's" principles), it would hardly help us to understand the global design of the fictional world of the story. The text would dissipate into a conglomerate of other texts.

Having the idea of a fictional world in mind we can assume that the reader may not find it difficult to accept the specific principles of the world of the museum, to "naturalize" the fictional world, because he or she has been gradually prepared by a series of hints and innuendoes that things are going to differ from the usual state of affairs: the accidental visit to the museum and its obscure collection, Mr. Godard's odd behavior on his way to the museum, the bouncing about of the young men. But there must be a scheme hidden beyond the idea of "everything possible" in the museum. Shrayer draws the reader's attention to a number of motifs that he suggests as allusions to the history of Soviet Russia. Some of the cues are obvious (for example, the scene displaying a vivid public meeting behind the closed door of cloakroom); some cues Shrayer finds are very subtle, perhaps even depending on whether we read the Russian original or the English translation. Shayer claims that the passage where the narrator finds himself in a "greenhouse with hydrangeas and broken windowpanes" to be an allusion to the Winter Palace captured during the October Revolution, citing the original Russian text, where the greenhouse is presented as *zimnii sad* (279). In fact, a *zimnii sad* is very different from a greenhouse, as it used to be a representative part of bourgeois man-

sions, a quiet intimate space meant to provide a place to relax and contemplate; thus the scene may allude to the elegant quiet past of a high society family and thus an individual history as well. What entitles us to think so is the fact that all the items and spaces exhibited are necessarily presented in a selection; thus, for example, the whale skeleton might be mentioned not only because it is typical but because it is exactly what a very young child may also remember after his or her first visit to a science museum: a reference to the recollection of a visitor's younger days. The pain experienced by the narrator at the mock-up railway station suggests the traditional image of leaving home, saying goodbye, or losing someone. This allows us to assume some of the "alternative worlds" of the museum, and thus their seemingly "phantasmagoric" order may be adequate to the narrator's associative memory processes.

Can we imagine a world capable of comprehending a variety of incompatible objects, situations, and actions? The only world of this kind known to us (at least relatively) is the human mind, a mental world. Thus the capacity of the museum "of modest proportions" equals that of the human mind. This symmetry, that is, the capability of the museum to keep or to create innumerable parallel spaces of very different kinds and the ability of the human mind to recall and create images, may be the basic scheme of the design of this fictional world. It also explains the partly logical, partly messy succession of the rooms: sometimes it mirrors a certain order (much like our attempts to order our experience according to its chronology, importance, or sphere of our activity); sometimes the rooms follow one another in an unexpected way, much as our memories and recollections are called back by unexpected impulses and a stream of memories is triggered as a result. If the reader adopts the suggested scheme he or she has to deliberate whose mental world is reflected in the ensemble of rooms: only that of the protagonist (narrator) or that of his whimsical Russian friend or maybe that of the odd Mr. Godard? Or everyone's?

The close reveals that the predominant mental world may have been that of the narrator, as he—after having survived the bewildering and sometimes even appalling obstacles of his stray in the museum's maze—finally ends up in his native town, in a fresh snowy atmosphere that suggests a different time (but it is only when the tough Russian autumn is compared to the mild October of Southern France that the difference is made clear), only to find out he has not returned to the Russia of his past but landed in the Soviet Russia of the present, a place to which only his nightmares would usually take him.[5] As we were able to observe, the narrator found it impossible to go back in the space of the museum. Obviously, this impossibility and the scene in "real" St. Petersburg reveal that the world of the narrator's youth is accessible in space but not in time. The close (in contrast to the opening of the story) is very brief: "But enough. I shall not recount how I was arrested, nor tell of my subsequent ordeals. Suffice it to say that it cost me incredible patience and effort to get back abroad, and that, ever since, I have forsworn carrying out commissions entrusted one by the insanity of others" (281). The unwillingness of the narrator to recall this part of his experience and the subsequent disproportion in the narrative may be explained as follows: the first part of the narration tells about the life the narrator regards his own; the second part, about the life he has to live involuntarily (unable to escape our memories, we may find a way of just coping with them); the third, "non-narrated" one, about the life he has always dreaded and wished to avoid.

5. Employing the Reader's Encyclopedia: Identifying the Global Design of a Fictional World

A symmetric inner structure is the main feature the two short stories have in common, though there are numerous other parallels—or coincidences—between them (but the global design of the fictional world is exactly the notion that enables us to resolve this semantic difference). Both Nabokov's and Cortázar's protagonists enter the other world unwillingly, one of them without wanting to be involved in other people's affairs, the other one without even wanting to be involved in her own. Thus, in the beginning, both of them respond relatively passively to the strange surroundings. The coincidence of local painters being involved in the stories may be just a parallel resulting from both authors' interest in the visual arts. However, the parallel of the locations is a striking and essential one: an indistinctive, tedious provincial town offers its obscure museum as a "test space" for specific processes and experience. The fictional worlds of the stories differ in the variety and characteristics of the universe of possible worlds offered: **"The End of a Phase"** displays only three spaces—(1) the provincial town with its museum that provides a frame for (2) a virtual space, depicted on the paintings either mirroring or mirrored by (3) the physical space of a particular house—all of them given just minimalistic characteristics. Thus the encyclopedias employed in understanding the story comprehend in particular that of human psychology and its relation to art and other ways of representing the human mind.

Obversely, Nabokov's alternative worlds contain a vast number of cultural and historical emblems; in their interpretation general schemes of presenting the

development of human civilization and science intersect with Russian and Soviet history, conventional symbols, and moments of individual experience. When also the encyclopedia of the ideology of a totalitarian establishment (not necessarily only the Soviet one) is employed, the noise of the innumerable typewriters and machines may be understood easily: representing the work of millions was an important part of the propaganda aimed at displaying power and intimidating the "enemy" as a result. However the implicit meaning of some motifs is revealed not only when they are located in their cultural or historical context but also when they are detected as allusions to typical features of Nabokov's writing. The individual fictional worlds of particular short stories and novels generate "the encyclopedia of Nabokov's possible worlds," just as every single text of one author features a particular implied author and his oeuvre allows us to abstract a general implied author concept (provided that we accept the notion of implied author at all). The encyclopedia of Nabokov's (as well as Cortázar's) possible worlds comprehends a lost or never confessed love and a delayed attempt to restore the relationship, be it love for a person or homeland, for example, but the scheme crucial for "The Visit to the Museum" is the "émigré" encyclopedia, to be observed especially in his short stories. Thus the course of reading and understanding "The Visit to the Museum" might differ substantially if this were a reader's first or single attempt at Nabokov, or if the text were read backed up with a "reader's encyclopedia" of Nabokov's oeuvre. Just consider this passage: "How strangely glowed the violet signals in the gloom beyond the fan of wet tracks, and what spasms shook my poor heart! Suddenly everything changed again: In front of me stretched an infinitely long passage, containing numerous office cabinets and elusive, scurrying people" (279). And picture, then, an émigré visiting dozens of authorities and offices where hardly anyone will listen! Even the "grey-haired people with umbrellas" might then be understood as lost in the endless universe (provided that we stick to the émigré encyclopedia and the encyclopedia of traditional symbolic meanings, ignoring Nabokov's proclaimed hatred of "allegories" and "standardized symbols" [see Appel 22]).

Confronting the stories by Cortázar and Nabokov, we were able to observe a different range of encyclopedias employed in understanding, on the one hand, the fictional worlds and, on the other hand, a parallel global design of the fictional world based upon a symmetry between the mental world of the protagonist and its representation in the space of a provincial museum that—though sometimes confusing, flustering, alienating in its effect—bears in its structure a logical resemblance to the mind of the protagonist. Even though the narration may appear as a display of "phantasmagoric" scenes and cultural allusions or suggest an eerie sequence of coincidences, fictional-worlds theory offers a frame of interpretation aimed at inquiring about the crucial principle that makes these "strange" fictional worlds work.

Notes

1. As far as Hispano-American fiction and particularly imaginative or "fantastic" writing are concerned, Nabokov himself confessed his interest in Jorge Luis Borges; a comparative analysis has been done by Patricia Merivale. If Borges may be akin to Nabokov in his discursive, reflective, and sophisticated part, Cortázar may be allied to him in the vivid, sensual, emotional quality of his fiction. Apart from that, the kinship of Cortázar's writings is evident in other aspects: all-embracing nostalgia for a beloved person, a person's addiction to an image that prevails over the relationship to another person so much that it destroys the relationship, sometimes even the people involved, and so on. The English titles of Cortázar's short stories (apart from "The Night Face Up") and quotations from "The End of a Phase" are my own translations.

2. Such a possible-worlds scheme and a kind of plot based on replacing the assumed ontologically privileged world by the apparently constructed one has been employed successfully by Norwegian writer Jostein Gaarder in his novel *Sophie's World* (1991) aimed at introducing young children into the study of ontology and epistemology.

3. In fact, this type of familiarity of the bizarre or fantastic and its common presence in the "normal" human world agrees with the poetics of Hispano-American "magic realism" as represented in a variety of ways by Julio Cortázar, Jorge Luis Borges, Gabriel García Márquez, Mario Vargas Llosa, Isabella Allende, and others.

4. Literally "the other side," Kubin's title can be easily interpreted as an alternative to "the other world." *Die andere Seite* is a fiction bearing some typical features of surrealist and expressionist writing and narrating the decline of a queer utopian empire.

5. We should supplement the author's own note: "One explanatory note may be welcomed by non-Russian readers. At one point the unfortunate narrator notices a shop sign and realizes he is not in the Russia of his past but in the Russia of the Soviets. What gives that shop sign away is the absence of the letter that used to decorate the end of a word after a consonant in old Russia but is omitted in the reformed orthography adopted by the Soviets today" (Nabokov, *A Russian Beauty and Other Stories*, 1973, here quoted from the English translation in *The Stories of Vladimir Nabokov* [647]). Obviously, the author did not see any difficulty in the translation of "zimnii sad" as "greenhouse."

Works Cited

Alexandrov, Vladimir E. *Nabokov's Otherworld*. Princeton: Princeton UP, 1991.

Appel, Alfred, Jr. "An Interview with Vladimir Nabokov." Dembo 19-44.

Červenka, Miroslav. *Fikční světy lyriky*. Praha: Paseka, 2003.

Cortázar, Julio. *Změna osvětlení*. Trans. Kamil Uhlír et al. Praha: Odeon, 1990.

Dembo, L. S., ed. *Nabokov: The Man and His Work*. Madison: U of Wisconsin P, 1967.

Doležel, Lubomír. *Heterocosmica: Fiction and Possible Words*. Baltimore: Johns Hopkins UP, 1998. Published in Czech as *Heterocosmica: Fikce a možné světy*. Praha: Karolinum, 2003.

Gaarder, Jostein. *Sophie's World: A Novel about the History of Philosophy*. Trans. Paulette Müller. New York: Farrar, 1994.

Jedličková, Alice. "Jak proniknout na území Silvie: fikční domény v Cortázarově povídce." *Slovenská literatúra* 49.5 (2002): 389-98.

———. "S mimezí v batohu na výlet do roznosvětů." *Česká literatura* 53.2 (2005): 203-25.

Merivale, Patricia. "The Flaunting of Artifice in Vladimir Nabokov and Jorge Luis Borges." Dembo 209-24.

Moynahan, Julian. *Vladimir Nabokov*. Minneapolis: U of Minnesota P, 1971.

Nabokov, Vladimir. *Bend Sinister*. New York: Holt, 1947.

———. *Povídky 2: 1930-1937*. Trans. Pavel Dominik et al. Praha: Paseka, 2004.

———. *The Stories of Vladimir Nabokov*. New York: Knopf, 1996.

Ryan, Marie-Laure. "Possible Worlds in Recent Literary Theory." *Style* 26 (1992): 528-53. In Czech as "Možné světy v soudobé teorii literatury." *Česká literatura* 45.6 (1997): 570-99.

Shrayer, Maxim D. *The World of Nabokov's Stories*. Austin: U of Texas P, 1999.

Sisson, Jonathan Borden. "Cosmic Synchronization and Other Worlds in the Work of Vladimir Nabokov." Diss. University of Minnesota, 1979.

Mark D. Harris (essay date July-December 2009)

SOURCE: Harris, Mark D. "Existence, Nothingness, and the Quest for Being: Sartrean Existentialism and Julio Cortázar's Early Short Fiction." *Latin American Literary Review* 37, no. 74 (July-December 2009): 5-25.

[*In the following essay, Harris maintains that the sense of alienation in Cortázar's early short fiction corresponds to the author's interest in the existential philosophy of Jean-Paul Sartre, particularly as embodied in Sartre's novel* Nausea.]

INTRODUCTION

In 1951, the same year that Cortázar published his first short story collection **Bestiario,** he also would publish a Spanish translation of *The Existential Philosophy of Jean-Paul Sartre.*[1] Though a great many of Cortázar's short stories could be considered generally existentialist in terms of their protagonists' experiences and outlook, several of his early stories, especially those appearing in the collections of **Bestiario** and **Final del juego,** seem conspicuously so. While Cortázar recognized Rimbaud and Surrealism as major influences for him as a young poet in the thirties, the mid-century existentialists such as Sartre and Camus, whose works were enjoying a vogue in Buenos Aires of the forties, were equally important for his beginnings as a prose writer. In fact, as early as his 1941 essay on Rimbaud, Cortázar appears to indicate the role existentialism was playing in the formation of his worldview as an aspiring short story writer:

> Por haber jugado la Poesía como la carta más alta en su lucha contra la realidad odiosa, la obra de Rimbaud nos llega anegada de existencialismo y cobra para nosotros, hombres angustiados que hemos perdido la fe en las retóricas, el tono de un mensaje y de una admonición (Because of having played Poetry as the highest card in his battle against detestable reality, the work of Rimbaud arrives to us drowned out by existentialism and recovers for us, anguished men who have lost faith in mere words, the tone of a message and a warning; my translation).[2]

In 1948, however, Cortázar would make the most definitive statement concerning his stance on existentialism and reveal his particular connection to Sartre's work. In that year, Cortázar wrote a review of a recently-translated Spanish version of Sartre's novel *Nausea*[3] wherein he commented on the wide-ranging appeal the new French existentialism had in the Buenos Aires of his day:

> Hoy que sólo las formas aberrantes de la reacción y la cobardía pueden continuar subestimando la tremenda presentación del existencialismo en la escena de esta posguerra y su influencia sobre la generación en plena actividad creadora, la versión al español de la primera novela de Sartre mostrará a multitud de desconcertados y ansiosos lectores la iniciación hacia lo que el autor llamó posteriormente "los caminos de la libertad" (Today that only the aberrant forms of the reaction and cowardice can continue underestimating the tremendous presence of existentialism in this post-war scene and its influence on this generation in all creative activity, the Spanish version of Sartre's first novel will show a multitude of disconcerted and anxious readers the beginnings toward what the author previously called "the ways to freedom"; my translation).[4]

Yet while indeed a member of that generation of young Buenos Aires artists and writers, Cortázar does not simply confirm the popularity of Sartre's existentialist thought and his own affinity for it. Rather, he demonstrates a profound understanding of the inner workings of Sartre's ontology as revealed by *Nausea*: the protagonist's gradual discovery of the Sartrean notion of existence in the world around him via the nausea which culminates in his frightful encounter with the chestnut tree roots in the botanical garden; his realization that human life is completely contingent, a fact which is at the same time disconcerting and liberating; and his desire to transcend existence by entering into Being. In this way then, *Nausea* was not only a highly significant work for Cortázar in terms of its useful philosophical underpinnings (as I plan to show here with respect to his early short fiction), but also one which in general renewed the question of man's ultimate purpose—clearly a question that would serve as an overarching theme throughout Cortázar's *oeuvre*.

Thus considering Cortázar's positioning with regard to existentialism and specifically to that of Sartre, here I will suggest that Sartre's existentialist thought in particular served as a significant formative influence for him early on in his career. To that end, in this paper I will examine three of Cortázar's early short stories—"Axolotl," "Letter to a Young Lady in Paris" ("Carta a una señorita en París"), and "A Yellow Flower" ("Una flor amarilla")—in light of the salient features of Sartre's philosophy by way of *Nausea*. Overall, this paper aims at establishing a new theoretical paradigm for the early period of Cortázar's short story writing.

"AXOLOTL" AS EXISTENTIAL EPIPHANY

Critics have long considered the 1956 tale of "Axolotl" a seminal text in Latin American letters, but opinion remains divided on its interpretation. Either "Axolotl" is a work which concerns the difficulties of narrating the fantastic or one which dramatizes the return of Latin America's "lost" Other, or its pre-Columbian self. Though it is not my intention to deny the validity of these readings, I will offer yet another reading of this work, casting "Axolotl" as the story of an individual who encounters Sartre's notion of existence and with that discovery experiences an existential epiphany.

"Axolotl" tells the story of a nameless individual who describes his recent encounter with strange salamanders known as axolotls that are on display at a local Parisian aquarium. After initial contact with the creatures, he investigates their origin and discovers that a number of species are indigenous to regions of Africa. Yet despite these findings, he is convinced that they are associated with Mexico, as he indicates very early on: "That they were Mexican I already knew by looking at them and their little pink Aztec faces . . ." (4); ("Que eran mexicanos lo sabía ya por ellos mismos, por sus pequeños rostros rosados aztecas . . ." [500]).[5] In a short time the narrator's interest in the axolotls turns obsessive, bordering on the delusional: his visits to the aquarium become an everyday occurrence (and sometimes twice a day), and he believes that the axolotls are in some way connected to him: "There's nothing strange in this, because after the first minute I knew we were linked, that something infinitely lost and distant kept pulling us together" (4); ("No hay nada de extraño en esto, porque desde un primer momento comprendí que estábamos vinculados, que algo infinitamente perdido y distante seguía sin embargo uniéndonos" [500]).

Because of the narrator's seemingly deliberate attempt to associate the axolotls with Mexico and specifically with the Aztecs (mainly based on their "Aztec-like" features), recent studies have regarded the creatures as a metaphor for the inability to posit Latin America's pre-Columbian past as epistemological object. Amar-Sánchez views the "Aztec-like" axolotls as emblematic of Latin America's pre-Columbian self, contact with and understanding of which an impossibility. Hence the narrator's desire to know this Other requires his becoming an axolotl himself.[6] Levinson, in a similar way, suggests that the axolotls point up an important aspect of present-day Latin American identity: while many Latin Americans can claim partial descent from their pre-Columbian forbears, they cannot make such an historical inheritance their own property, that is, their "true" heritage. Thus for the narrator (possibly a displaced Latin American residing in France), the axolotls serve as an indelible mark of that ethnicity which is proper to him (Levinson likens the creatures to a "scar"), but at the same time that which is untranslatable and unknowable.[7]

While such post-colonialist readings are possible ways of interpreting the work, upon closer examination of the creatures, especially with respect to the ways in which the narrator attempts to understand them, quite a different picture emerges, one which seems to in-voke ontological as opposed to cultural-historical notions. In particular, the axolotls bear striking resemblance to Sartre's concept of existence, which is best illustrated in *Nausea*. In that work the protagonist Antoine Roquentin perceives everyday objects (e.g., a stone, water, and tree roots) of his world in quite an unusual way. Overall, he realizes that the objects which populate the world around him are merely examples of existence—by virtue of the fact that they are visible and present—and that all descriptive and classificatory characteristics (i.e., an apple is a round, red-colored fruit), which Sartre calls essence, reveal themselves to be subordinate to the fact that they exist. In other words, essence does not constitute epistemological truth; rather, only through acknowledging the existence of things can their true reality be known. In a similar way to Antoine Roquentin, the narrator of "Axolotl" learns that the creatures cannot truly be approached epistemologically via essence: he reads they are indigenous to Africa but intuits a New World provenance; semantically, *axolotl* and the Spanish equivalent *ajolote* offer no useful information about the animals. Likewise, scientific discourse, as yet another form of essence, appears to be of little use here. He learns that they are a larval stage of a species of salamander belonging to a specific genus (*Ambystoma*) and are capable of living on dry land for extended periods of time. From an evolutionary standpoint, they seem to occupy an ambiguous status within the animal kingdom, since they have characteristics of both fish and amphibians, a fact that the narrator points out: ". . . looking like a small lizard about six inches long, ending in a fish's tail . . ." (5); ("semejante a un pequeño lagarto de quince centímetros, terminado en una cola de pez . . ." [500]).

Thus it is not coincidental that the narrator encounters these creatures at a public aquarium, since he, like other visitors, would be sure to note the axolotls' dissimilarity to other aquatic species. As he notes: "In the standing tanks on either side of them, different fishes showed me the simple stupidity of their handsome eyes so similar to our own. The eyes of the axolotls spoke to me of the presence of a different life, of another way of seeing" (6); ("Al lado de ellos, en los restantes acuarios, diversos peces me mostraban la simple estupidez de sus hermosos ojos semejantes a los nuestros. Los ojos de los axolotl me decían de la presencia de una vida diferente, de otra manera de mirar" [501]). Because of the similarities between the axolotls of Cortázar's work and the objects of Roquentin's world, perhaps the narrator's comments regarding the creatures' ability to reveal "the presence of a different life" and "another way of seeing" amount to the fact that the axolotls are not meaningful *as* animals, *as* amphibians, or *as* larvae as he himself appears to indicate: "I think it was the axolotls' heads, that triangular pink shape with the tiny eyes of gold. That looked and knew. That laid the claim. They were not *animals*" (6); ("Yo creo que era la cabeza de los axolotl, esa forma triangular rosada con los ojillos de oro. Eso miraba y sabía. Eso reclamaba. No eran *animales*" [502]). If the axolotls are not animals as such, as the narrator suggests, what purpose do they serve?

As intimated previously, Cortázar's protagonist is faced with a similar dilemma to that of Antoine Roquentin in that the axolotls resist any attempts to be categorized and understood on the basis of essence. To put it simply, they are anomalous. But in a playful way, Cortázar adds further layers to the axolotls' anomalous status by pointing out other peculiarities about them, as if winking to readers that perhaps we should be wary of any terminology which is informed by essence: "They were larvas, but larva means disguise and also phantom" (7); ("Eran larvas, pero larva quiere decir máscara y también fantasma" [502]). To refer to something as a larva implies that it *will* become something else (e.g., a caterpillar becomes a butterfly), but this is not the case with axolotls. In actuality axolotls are one of the few animal species that exhibit neoteny, that is, they never reach an adult phase (unlike frogs, for instance). Except in rare cases, axolotls remain as larvae through adulthood and are capable of reproducing as such. As an animal that is in a perpetual state of immaturity, it seems likely that Cortázar employed the figure of the axolotl to demonstrate that which embodies a relative state of changelessness—a creature with "inexpressive features, with no other trait save the eyes . . ." (5); (sin otro rasgo que los ojos [501]). In sum, the axolotl is an amorphous, nondescript, and underdeveloped animal. If it is an animal that perpetually remains a larva—as ironic as it may sound—what can it become? It can become nothing more than the fact that it *is,* and this I believe is precisely Cortázar's point: just as Roquentin discovers in the pivotal moment of *Nausea* that the roots of a chestnut tree, when stripped of their meaning via essence—*as* roots, *as* part of a tree, *as* a living thing—become a grotesque, amorphous mass of matter (i.e., existence) which provokes a dizzying, nauseating effect in him (hence the title), the narrator of **"Axolotl"** is similarly forced to conclude that the axolotls simply are an example of existence, no more or no less, by virtue of the fact that they are present, observable. It seems that if the axolotls as "larvae" were, as the narrator so ironically puts it, a "disguise" of something, Cortázar is calling into question how language itself— here the words "larvae" and "disguise"—can serve to deceive us. Indeed, the axolotls *as* larvae are a disguise: thought of in terms of essence, they disguise their very existence.

Unlike Sartre's scenario of the chestnut tree roots, however, Cortázar's depiction of the discovery of existence is rendered artistically, depicted, as it were, with surrealist overtones. For his protagonist, existence as embodied by the axolotl stares back at him: "The golden eyes continued burning with their soft, terrible light; they continued looking at me from an unfathomable depth which made me dizzy" (6); ("Los ojos de oro seguían ardiendo con su terrible, dulce luz; seguían mirándome desde una profundidad insondable que me daba vértigo" [502]). Similar to Roquentin's discomfort and subsequent feelings of nausea at the sight of the existence of the tree roots, the narrator of Cortázar's work finds the unveiling of existence frightful: "I think that had it not been for feeling the proximity of other visitors and the guard, I would not have been bold enough to remain alone with them" (7); ("Creo que de no haber sentido la proximidad de otros visitantes y del guardián, no me hubiese atrevido a quedarme solo con ellos" [503]).

While the axolotls are important in unveiling existence to the narrator, more importantly they point to two fundamental principles of Sartre's ontology which can be seen in *Nausea*. First, there is a hint that Roquentin's own bouts of nausea at the sight of things are to demonstrate his growing awareness that he exists much in the same way as the objects he observes. Similarly, the narrator of "Axolotl" has such a realization, but in a fundamentally different way. Rather than his body serving as the vehicle for revealing his own existence (like Roquentin), it seems that the narrator sees the axolotls as a mirror image of himself, one which connotes the idea of anguish: "I imagined them aware, slaves of their bodies, condemned indefinitely to the silence of the abyss, to a hopeless meditation" (6); ("Los imaginé conscientes, esclavos de su cuerpo, infinitamente condenados a un silencio abisal, a una reflexión desesperada" [502]).

Second, the axolotls, like the objects which are the source of Roquentin's contemplation, create what Sartre referred to as an idling sense of freedom which gives rise to ontological questioning. The narrator of **"Axolotl,"** so much like his analogue, Roquentin, conspicuously does not employ freedom in the way that a normal individual does because if he did, it is likely he would not engage in such contemplation about the nature of the creatures. Rather, he would go about his normal routine and not give the animals a moment of thought. But the narrator, like Roquentin, is quite unlike every day people: his visits to the aquarium occur everyday (and sometimes twice a day) and seem not to be a matter of choice, but rather a necessity. It should be recalled that from the beginning of the tale the narrator is a man who, for all intents and purposes, is utterly alienated from his world. Lacking any form of social interaction with humans, the axolotls *are* his life. This lack of freedom created by the objects in *Nausea* and the axolotls in **"Axolotl"** serves an important purpose for Sartre's and Cortázar's projects respectively and thus has been carefully thought out. Overall, the lack of freedom is a source of existential anguish, relief from which Roquentin finds in writing and the narrator actually finds in the axolotls themselves. For Cortázar's narrator, it is thus natural that he should wish to associate himself with the axolotls since they are very much like him. As a nameless, most likely unemployed (judging from his frequent, extended visits to the aquarium) individual, he finds comfort in essentially nameless creatures that occupy an anomalous status within the animal kingdom (both geographically and scientifically). Overall, the narrator seeks relief from his existential anguish—a result of the realization of his own existence and his lack of freedom via the creatures—by relating himself to the creatures, which ultimately will lead to his desire to "transform" himself into one of them.

Sartre had suggested in *Being and Nothingness* that individuals often flee anguish "by trying to look at themselves *from outside* as *another person* or as a *thing*" (81).[8] This is specifically what occurs at the end of Cortázar's tale, which involves the "transformation" of the man into axolotl, or rather the transmigration of his consciousness, into the axolotl's body:

> I saw from very close up the face of an axolotl immobile next to the glass. No transition and no surprise, I saw my face against the glass, I saw it on the outside of the tank, I saw it on the other side of the glass . . . Outside, my face close to the glass again, I saw my mouth, the lips compressed with the effort of understanding the axolotls. I was an axolotl and now I knew instantly that no understanding was possible. He was outside the aquarium, his thinking was outside the tank (8); (Veía de muy cerca la cara de un axoltotl inmóvil junto al vidrio. Sin transición, sin sorpresa, vi mi cara contra el vidrio, en vez del axolotl vi mi cara contra el vidrio, la vi fuera del acuario, la vi del otro lado del vidrio. Entonces mi cara se apartó y yo comprendí [503]).

Therefore the transformation is not literal, that is, it is not a "reality" of the fiction. Instead, through the belief that his consciousness has entered an axolotl, the narrator affords himself respite from his existent self.[9] Such a desire to escape his existence is the case with Antoine Roquentin, and it underscores what the narrator of **"Axolotl"** hopes to achieve by "becoming" one of the animals.

At the end of *Nausea*, Roquentin implies that he might be able to attain something beyond existence—an immortality of sorts in which he will always be remembered like an ideal object, or a changeless form which

cannot be altered by the accidents of this world—through his writing: "A book. A novel. And then there would be people who would read the novel and say: 'Antoine Roquentin wrote it, a red-headed man who hung around cafés, and they would think about my life . . . as something precious and almost legendry'" (178). In a very similar way, the narrator of **"Axolotl"** also thinks about the use of writing as an escape from existence. The way he envisions it, his "former" self (the man whose body he formerly "occupied") will indirectly serve as the instrument for attaining his own immortality. It works in the following way: the man, believing he is creating a fictional work, will write a story about axolotls (the very same one which we read), thereby allowing his displaced consciousness (now believed to be in the animal) to become an ideal object very much like the way in which Roquentin hopes he will be remembered. Overall, like Roquentin's wishful thinking about escaping existence (which Sartre called "bad faith" for obvious reasons) it offers at least a glimmer of hope that there may be a better fate to be had than that which the suffering existent must endure.

"LETTER TO A YOUNG LADY IN PARIS": THE DARKER SIDE OF CONSCIOUSNESS OF EXISTENCE

One of Cortázar's more memorable works, **"Letter to a Young Lady in Paris,"** has as its focal point a peculiar fantastic element interwoven into the story's fabric unobtrusively, merely as a matter of course—the narrator's uncontrollable habit of vomiting live, miniature-sized bunnies. As many critics would agree, the reading of the entire work depends on how these rabbits are viewed: as realistic, fantastic, or hallucinatory. Naturally, I do not disagree with this approach since it also serves as the basis for my own reading. But considering the foregoing analysis that has assessed Cortázar's work along philosophical rather than principally aesthetic lines, I will suggest that the story more closely relates to the discovery of existence in objects and especially with respect to one's physical self and its associated feelings of disgust, rather than the fantastic or psychological dimensions which may also be simultaneously evoked in the story's reading.

As the title suggests, the narrator relates the tale in the form of a letter addressed to his female friend Andrea, whose Buenos Aires apartment he has agreed to occupy while she is abroad. In that letter, chief among the narrator's concerns is his inability not only to prevent the vomiting of new rabbits but also to control the ones he has already "born" and which he subsequently raises as pets. Moreover, a great deal of his anxiety stems from his fear that the housekeeper of the apartment will discover the rabbits; he thus takes the precaution of hiding them in a wardrobe during the day and only brings them out to feed and play at night while she is asleep.

To reiterate, surely the most significant aspect of the work are the rabbits themselves which, for all practical purposes, are not unlike naturally-occurring ones. The rabbits have been interpreted in a number of ways, ranging from hallucinatory manifestations of a delusional narrator to simply the penetration of the fantastic into the rational world, the latter of which can be readily seen in Cortázar's work elsewhere. Peavler, however, has suggested that readings which employ the rabbits as metaphor for something else—fantastic, delusional, or otherwise—render much of story's other details superfluous. In his opinion, the rabbits are realities in themselves, and nothing about them, save their fantastic origin, gives us any reason to suspect that they constitute a symbolic meaning.[10] Peavler's position, however, is only partially correct. Indeed, the rabbits function on *both* the symbolic and literal level. On the one hand, the rabbits are symbolic insofar as they—like Antoine Roquentin's recurrent nausea—are used to illustrate the protagonist's growing awareness of his own bodily existence. On the other hand, they are also literal manifestations of the narrator's own finite body which are visible and tangible (much like sweat or excrement would be). Thus Cortázar may well have employed *Nausea*—and especially those pivotal moments of Roquentin's realization of his physical self—to serve as inspiration for his own tale. It is certainly worth noting that Cortázar should have the narrator of **"Letter to a Young Lady in Paris"** make the following comment about his vomiting of rabbits: "Always I have managed to be alone when it happens, guarding the fact as we guard so many of our privy acts, evidences of our physical selves which happen to us in total privacy" (41); ("Como siempre me ha sucedido estando a solas, guardaba el hecho igual que se guardan tantas constancias de lo que acaece (o hace uno acaecer) en la privacía total" [170]). This comment, of course, is much in line with Sartre's ontology: Sartre had pointed out that nausea and boredom constitute the only two instances in which one may become aware of his/her bodily existence. In this way, the rabbits are "realities in themselves," as Peavler suggests, and, as such, they are, in the words of the narrator, tangible proofs of his own existence.

But Cortázar has taken the rather subtle hint of bodily existence that Roquentin exhibits and has transformed the scenario into something rather surreal, bordering on the absurd. Indeed, the protagonist not only physically vomits the rabbits, but they also constantly serve to remind him (even more so than the actual vomiting) of that existence by "communicating" it back to him:

. . . and besides they yipped, there's no word for it, they stood in a circle under the light of the lamp, in a circle as though they were adoring me, and suddenly they were yipping, they were crying like I never believed rabbits could cry (49); (. . . y también gritaron, estuvieron en círculo bajo la luz de la lámpara, en círculo y como adorándome y de pronto gritaban, gritaban como yo no creo que griten los conejos [176]).

As Curutchet has pointed out, a strong current in a great many of Cortázar's stories is the presence of a reality that overshadows the protagonists, rendering them impotent.[11] For the narrator of **"Letter to a Young Lady in Paris"** surely that reality must be the weight of existence itself, or more specifically the realization of his own existence, which takes the form of the vomited rabbits. Although the creatures are a product of himself, he neither has the power to end their lives, nor does he possess control over the frequency with which they come into the world: "I realized that I could not kill [the rabbit]. But that same night I vomited a little black bunny. And two days later another white one. And on the fourth night a tiny grey one" (44); ("Comprendí que no podía matarlo. Pero esa misma noche vomité un conejito negro. Y dos días después uno blanco. Y la cuarta noche un conejito gris" [172]).

As the typical suffering existent, the narrator has realized the fact that he, like all other things, is governed by existence, or, looked at another way, he simply occupies a state of contingency in which his capacity for self-reflection and reasoning will fail him. In many ways like the object-centered world of Roquentin which speaks to him the disconcerting truth that existence occupies a position of primacy in his world and over which he is truly unable to exert any control— hence relegating humanity to a category of secondary, or even incidental importance—the rabbits for the protagonist of **"Letter to a Young Lady in Paris"** function similarly: as a figure for existence, the rabbits govern his actions, causing him to adjust his daily routine and lifestyle. Most importantly, he is a contingent thing, and clearly *not* a being above existence. Surely he is not above it, and as a man who is unable to control the rabbits, he is like a puppet, *literally* ruled by the heavy hand of existence: the rabbits cause him to adjust his work schedule according to their "playtime"; he falls behind in his work; he socially retreats, using his poor health as an excuse for not visiting with friends; and he becomes sleep deprived due to his "double shifts" of working and caring for them.

The rabbits are also analogous in many ways to the tree roots which Roquentin observes. Inasmuch as the roots of the chestnut tree for Roquentin embody a chaotic, grotesque glimpse at bare existence, the rabbits as well represent a grotesque and chaotic notion of existence with which the narrator is unable to cope. This chaos associated with the rabbits finds expression not only by virtue of the fact that the narrator cannot stop their coming into being, but also in that they are unruly: ". . . they gnawed off the backs [of books] to sharpen their teeth—not that they were hungry, . . . They tore the curtains, the coverings on the easy chairs, the edge of Augusto Torres' self-portrait, they got fluff all over the rug . . ." (49); (". . . royeron los lomos para afilarse los dientes—no por hambre, . . . Rompieron las cortinas, las telas de los sillones, el borde del autorretrato de Augusto Torres, llenaron de pelos la alfombra . . ." [176]). In the end, we learn that the text we are reading amounts to a suicide note left for Andrea. Unable to cope with now eleven rabbits which he believes are destroying her apartment during their nocturnal playtime, and convinced he will be unable to prevent the vomiting of even more, it is implied that he throws himself off the balcony (along with the rabbits), resulting in his death in the street below: "This balcony over the street is filled with dawn, the first sounds of the city waking. I don't think it will be difficult to pick up eleven small rabbits splattered over the pavement, perhaps they won't even be noticed, people will be too occupied with the other body, it would be more proper to remove it quickly before the early students pass through on their way to school" (50); ("Está este balcón sobre Suipacha lleno de alba, los primeros sonidos de la ciudad. No creo que les sea difícil juntar once conejitos salpicados sobre los adoquines, tal vez ni se fijen en ellos, atareados con el otro cuerpo que conviene llevarse pronto, antes de que pasen los primeros colegiales" [176]). Thus the protagonist of **"Letter to a Young Lady in Paris"** takes his own life since it is the only effective means of escaping such a loathsome existence.

"A Yellow Flower": Existence or
Nothingness?, That Is the Question

Though not unusual for Cortázar, **"A Yellow Flower"** employs an intra-diegetic narrative strategy in which a first-person narrator relates a tale that he has heard in a local bar from another character who is a retired city employee. The retired man begins his story with the pronouncement "We are immortal, I know it sounds like a joke" (51) ("Parece una broma, pero somos inmortales" [447]) because of his discovery of what he believes to be a younger version of himself while riding the bus. This in turn leads the man to suggest a theory of immortality: when an individual dies, an analogue of that person is born with a different identity essentially to live and experience (with slightly different details) a similar life the former had done, and so on and so forth.

According to the man's understanding of this everpresent immortality, certainly this event on the bus is

unique; in fact, his encountering the boy should have never occurred. But through what he describes as a "crimp and doubling back in time" (53); ("un pliegue del tiempo" [448]) the boy, Luc, was born before it was his time to live, that is, before the retiree's passing. Curiosity prompts the man to investigate the matter further, which results in his befriending Luc and his family. What exactly occurs at the story's climax is unclear: Luc suddenly falls ill, and the man, entrusted with the boy's medication, appears to share complicity in the boy's demise. With Luc's death, and with the eternal chain of immortality now broken, the man becomes, in his own words, "the only mortal" (51); ("[e]l único mortal" [447]). Momentarily exhilarated to have spared the boy from the same unfulfilled life that he has led, the man's fate can only be described as bitter-sweet: while looking at a yellow flower in a garden he realizes that the flower can reproduce itself infinitely, thus possessing a kind of immortality from which he has now excluded himself.

Considering the details above, it goes without saying that the story can be (and rightfully so) regarded simply as one of Cortázar's typical explorations of the irruption of the fantastic onto the world of the real— here a tale dealing with an ordinary individual's discovery of a fantastic immortality in which all people are reincarnated *ad infinitum*. Nonetheless, in light of Sartrean existentialism, **"A Yellow Flower"** presents parallels to the notion of existence and, above all, points to Cortázar's positing of existential Nothingness. The relationship between Cortázar's work and these existential concepts will be discussed below.

The retiree's story of immortality and its culmination in deceit and murder probably should be taken with a grain of salt. It is the tale of a drunkard who "drunk enough so it didn't bother him to tell the truth" (52); ("tan borracho que no le costaba nada decir la verdad" [447]), obviously finds escape in the bottle. Up to the point of telling his story, there is indication he has been nothing but a very ordinary man, a city worker who, for all accounts, has lived a rather uneventful life. If to that life we add the recent failure of his marriage, it is possible to understand why he may have been inclined to fabricate such a tale. Insofar as the protagonist is concerned, all of this fantasy of immortality is, of course, yet another instance of being in "bad faith." As we have seen earlier, Roquentin is guilty of it; so too is the narrator of **"Axolotl."** The protagonist of **"A Yellow Flower"** is, of course, no exception. In essence, he employs his tale simply as a means of injecting substance and perhaps meaning into an otherwise unsatisfying existence.

Yet, as readers well know, Cortázar is not one necessarily inclined to happy endings, and it is clear that he is intent on showing through the protagonist of **"A**

99

Yellow Flower" that there is no rosy side to existence. Thus it could be said that Cortázar has succeeded—where Sartre had failed in his own literary work—in revealing that the myth of "bad faith" must be dispelled: existence should be accepted for what it is, and there is no reason to embellish it (or imagine escaping it) so that it might be more tolerable. Certainly for Cortázar, as a proponent of Sartrean existentialism, Being is out of reach for humanity: there can be only existence, beyond which there is Nothingness. And in the words of his protagonist, that Nothingness is expressed poetically, through the metaphor of the yellow flower: "All at once I understood *nothing*, I mean *nothingness, nothing,* I'd thought it was peace, it was the end of the chain. I was going to die, Luc was already dead, there would never again be a flower for anyone like us, there would never be anything, there'd be *absolutely nothing,* and *that's what nothing was,* that there would never again be a flower" (59; my emphasis); ("De golpe comprendí la nada, eso que había creído la paz, y término de la cadena. Yo me iba a morir y Luc ya estaba muerto, no habría nunca más una flor para alguien como nosotros, no habría nada, no habría absolutamente nada, y la nada era eso, que no hubiera nunca más una flor" [453]). Stricken with the fear of not only death without the possibility of rebirth but, more importantly, an ominous Nothingness after death, the protagonist seeks to ameliorate his situation by re-inserting himself into the immortal chain.

His attempts to re-enter immortality, as one might suspect however, are met with difficulty and frustration: he boards various busses in an attempt to find yet another analogue so that he may "protect him" (59); ("protegiéndolo" [453]), hence ensuring the continuance of the chain. Yet his searches are in vain; he shall find no such analogue. Now faced with the prospect of Nothingness, at the story's conclusion, the protagonist's stance now becomes one of resignation: he realizes (although too late) that perhaps it is better to exist as a repetition of an "imbecilic abortive life" (59); (imbécil vida fracasada [453]) rather than not to exist at all. This final point may suggest that he, like the protagonists of **"Letter to a Young Lady in Paris,"** decides to take his own life rather than to endure the sometimes painful and indeed purposeless mode of existence.

CONCLUSIONS

I have had one particular goal in mind for this project which, I hope, has been achieved at least in part: to present a number of strong parallels between Sartrean notions of existence and Being and a few of Cortázar's well-known early short stories. To that end, I contend that the foregoing analysis is compelling. If it is ad-

mitted that Cortázar's characters typically inhabit a world from which they are alienated (i.e., lacking proper names, direction, control over their lives), surely there must be theoretical underpinnings that sustain this manifold alienation characteristic of his works. By probing deeper into Cortázar's explorations of alienation as I have in the stories examined here, one discovers that his protagonists, and much like Sartre's Antoine Roquentin, invariably find themselves in an encounter with existence. For Cortázar, this encounter centers on the various ways in which his characters respond to existence: by entering into "bad faith" to escape the anguish brought on by the knowledge of it; by taking their own lives because of its extreme detestability; or by resigning themselves to the harsh fact that it is the *only* reality.

Though my analysis has suggested literary projects essentially on parallel course, two important distinctions should be drawn between Cortázar and Sartre. First, Sartre and Cortázar differ in their stance toward man's tendency to wish for Being beyond existence. Since Sartre acknowledges man's irremediable state as "unhappy consciousness," he does make allowances for man's tendency to fall into the trap of "bad faith"; in this he offers at least a modicum of hope for his protagonist in that the possibility for Being could at least be wished for. Cortázar appears to take a firmer stance with regard to this: in **"A Yellow Flower"** especially the protagonist is quickly disabused of such fanciful thinking and is brought face to face with the harsh reality of existence and particularly its end—Nothingness. Second, Sartre and Cortázar approach the detestability of existence in markedly different ways. In the former's work, the disgust brought on by the unveiling of existence functions only to bring Roquentin's attention to existence for the purposes of its contemplation and finally its acknowledgment *as* reality. For Cortázar, it appears that the very weight of existence itself is often too great for his protagonists to bear, causing them to resort to drastic measures: fleeing through metempsychosis, committing suicide, and advancing a theory of immortality.

Notes

1. Alfred Stern, trans. Julio Cortázar, *La filosofía existencial de Jean-Paul Sartre* (Buenos Aires: Iman, 1951).

2. Julio Cortázar, "Rimbaud," *Obra crítica/2*, ed. Jaime Alazraki (Buenos Aires: Suma, 2004), 27-28.

3. The work was originally published as *La nausée* (1938). For the purposes of this paper I have used the English translation, Jean-Paul Sartre, *Nausea*, trans. Lloyd Alexander (New York: New Directions, 1969).

4. The review was originally published as "*La náusea,* por Jean-Paul Sartre," in *Cabalgata: Revista Mensual* de *Letras y Artes* 2.15 (1948). It has now been reproduced in Julio Cortázar, "*La Náusea,* por Jean-Paul Sartre" *Obra crítica/2,* ed. Jaime Alazraki (Buenos Aires: Suma, 2004), 143-45.

5. All quotes in English are from Julio Cortázar, *Blow-Up and Other Stories,* trans. Paul Blackburn (New York: Pantheon, 1967). Spanish quotes are from Julio Cortázar, *Obras Completas* I, ed. Saúl Yurkeviech (Barcelona: Galaxia Gutenberg, 2003).

6. See Ana María Amar Sánchez, "Between Utopia and Inferno (Julio Cortázar's Version)," trans. M. Elizabeth Ginway, in *Julio Cortázar, New Readings,* ed. Carlos Alonso (Cambridge: Cambridge University Press, 1998), 19-35.

7. See Brett Levinson, *The Ends of Literature, The Latin American "Boom" in the Neoliberal Marketplace* (Stanford: Stanford University Press, 2001), 10-20.

8. Jean-Paul Sartre, *Being and Nothingness,* trans. Hazel Barnes (New York: Philosophical Library, 1956).

9. The protagonist's apparent "escape" into the axolotl's body in order to free himself from existential anguish was observed many years ago by Lanin Gyurko, "Destructive and Ironically Redemptive Fantasy in Cortázar," *Hispania* 56.4 (1973): 988-999. See page 994 in particular.

10. See Terry Peavler, *Julio Cortázar* (New York: Twayne, 1990), 24.

11. Juan Carlos Curutchet, *Julio Cortázar o la crítica de la razón pragmática* (Madrid: Editora Nacional, 1972), 24.

Works Cited

Amar Sánchez, Ana María. "Between Utopia and Inferno (Julio Cortázar's Version)." Trans. M. Elizabeth Ginway. *Julio Cortázar, New Readings.* Ed. Carlos Alonso. Cambridge: Cambridge University Press, 1998.

Cortázar, Julio. *Blow-Up and Other Stories.* Trans. Paul Blackburn. New York: Pantheon, 1967.

———. "*La náusea,* por Jean-Paul Sartre." *Obra crítica/2.* Ed. Jaime Alazraki. Buenos Aires: Suma, 2004, 143-45.

———. *Obras Completas* I. Ed. Saúl Yurkeviech. Barcelona: Galaxia Gutenberg, 2003.

———. "Rimbaud." *Obra crítica/2.* Ed. Jaime Alazraki. Buenos Aires: Suma, 2004, 19-30.

Curutchet, Juan Carlos. *Julio Cortázar o la crítica de la razón pragmática.* Madrid: Editora Nacional, 1972.

Gyurko, Lanin. "Destructive and Ironically Redemptive Fantasy in Cortázar." *Hispania* 56.4 (1973): 988-999.

Levinson, Brett. *The Ends of Literature, The Latin American "Boom" in the Neoliberal Marketplace.* Stanford: Stanford University Press, 2001.

Peavler, Terry. *Julio Cortázar.* New York: Twayne, 1990.

Sartre, Jean-Paul. *Being and Nothingness.* Trans. Hazel Barnes. New York: Philosophical Library, 1956.

———. *Nausea.* Trans. Lloyd Alexander. New York: New Directions, 1969.

Stern, Alfred. *La filosofía existencial de Jean-Paul Sartre.* Trans. Julio Cortázar. Buenos Aires: Iman, 1951.

Marcy Schwartz (essay date 2009)

SOURCE: Schwartz, Marcy. "The Writing on the Wall: Urban Cultural Studies and the Power of Aesthetics." In *City/Art: The Urban Scene in Latin America,* edited by Rebecca E. Biron, pp. 127-44. Durham, N.C.: Duke University Press, 2009.

[*In the following essay, Schwartz links the expression of urban space in Cortázar's "Graffiti" to Liliana Porter's public art, contending that both artists offer "new and challenging dimensions of writing the city."*]

The vibrancy of the urban world has complex multisensory dimensions. While this essay will focus on the interactions of verbal and visual urban expressions, the sonorous, kinetic, architectural, and material aspects of the urban world also participate in those expressions. Cities' structures, with all the noise and movement that surround and emanate from them, create visual horizons (it's no accident that photography originated in the city) and generate verbal products, both oral and written. Latin American urban development has often been considered a "lettered" phenomenon, as Angel Rama (1984) elaborates; however a visual dimension informs much of its written production, frequently intersects with it, and sometimes supercedes it. The semiotic coparticipation—even competition—of visual and verbal designs reminds readers and spectators of the fundamental role of aesthetics in urban representation and experience. Like Michel de Certeau's walkers in the city, those who decipher a city's cultural products as readers or spectators engage with and help construct city space. The investigation of urban public space particularly benefits from considering the aesthetics of language and visual images in the construction and use of those spaces.

Recent debates within and about cultural studies expose the unresolved disciplinary, political, and philosophical dilemmas in working with cultural materials.

Roundtable discussions, panels at academic conferences, and columns in journals devoted to the place of literature and art within the panorama of "high" and "low" or popular cultural spheres have yet to resolve the definition and categorization of what falls under the rubric of "cultural studies."[1] The use, value, and experience of urban space involves a mingling, sometimes even a bombardment, of a wide range of expressive culture, resulting in an inseparability of the supposed high and low realms to the extent that these categories become, I believe, obsolete or irrelevant. Part of the controversy in situating cultural products within their sociopolitical contexts, which has become the hallmark of cultural studies, concerns the contested and often discounted place of aesthetics in interdisciplinary approaches. This essay shifts the focus to the role of aesthetics in urban art and writing in order to rediscover the dynamics of verbal and visual art in the experience of the urban in Latin America.

When cultural studies ignores the subjective and symbolic dimensions of cultural products, it leaves gaps in interpretation as well as in sociohistoric grounding. I draw on recent work in cultural studies on urban space to contextualize examples from art and literature whose verbal and visual interactions suggest a dialogic aesthetics of the urban imagination. The political possibilities of public art by Liliana Porter and fiction by Julio Cortázar reassert the potency of aesthetics within the experience of city space and the politics of culture.

The heated discussion, critique, and defense of cultural studies has debated the materials studied and also scrutinized the methodologies applied to them. Among the shifts and tensions in these reconsiderations are a focus on popular culture and a delegitimation of "art." The cultural critics Néstor García Canclini and Beatriz Sarlo are two key figures whose work helps frame the struggle to define cultural studies and the debates over the place of art in Latin America. García Canclini's vast interdisciplinary focus, mostly grounded in sociology and anthropology but more recently focused on communications and mass media, occasionally takes art into account but mostly dismisses it. His theory of the hybrid proposes more fluid and less dichotomized notions of the modern and the traditional and questions the local and the cosmopolitan, demonstrating a confluence of these categories rather than their previously rigid separation. While his work has been key to a new understanding of urban space (such as the coexistence of historical monuments with commercial culture) and the dynamics of consumer culture in Latin America, he often relies on a false division between art and the supposedly more politicized immediacy of popular culture. For example, he identifies one of the circuits of cultural development "la cultura de élites," defined as the realm that "abarca las obras representa-

tivas de las clases altas y medias con mayor nivel educativo. . . . No es conocido ni apropiado por el conjunto de cada sociedad" (encompasses the representative works of middle and upper classes with greater education. . . . This level is not known or appropriated by the whole society) (1995a, 32-33).[2] It is not unusual for cultural studies to be wary of visual art and literature, considering them "privileged" and therefore warranting less attention. García Canclini, despite brief moments of championing visual media in urban contexts (graffiti, photography, video, painting), largely neglects art and literature in his theories on hybridity and multimedia communications.[3] Patrimony and canonicity make high art suspect, and according to John Beverley, cultural studies privileges the autonomous creativity in the sphere of consumer or popular culture that does not depend on being authorized by high culture. To the contrary, if it is authorized by high culture, it becomes denatured and loses its oppositional force (Beverley 1999, 123). Some critics still accuse cultural studies practitioners, despite their focus on popular and consumer culture, of not being far enough to the Left. In effect, by celebrating the consumer market, cultural studies may only serve to confirm the neoliberal economic policies of the past decade.[4] Tensions continue surrounding the place of art and the definition of *aesthetics* in relation to consumer and popular cultural production.

Sarlo, along with many other literary critics, contests this dismissal of the subjective and aesthetic field within cultural studies. She defends art and literature as essential expressions whose aesthetics grow out of and engage with politics and society. Although she finds García Canclini's theory of the hybrid convincing, she finds it "is not able to cover a wide enough field, and is attractive only with regard to well-chosen examples" (Sarlo 1997a, 86). In a discussion on the intersections of literary criticism and cultural studies, she expresses concern that ignoring aesthetic value leaves unresolved the relationship between artistic expression and society's symbolic dimension (Sarlo 1999). What she calls "la sociología de la cultura" definitely "ha operado como un ácido frente al esencialismo [y al] elitismo" (worked like acid to undo essentialism and elitism) (1994, 154). However, even if cultural sociology "logra desalojar una idea bobalincona de desinterés y sacerdocio estético, al mismo tiempo evacúa rápidamente el análisis de las resistencias propiamente estéticas que producen la densidad semántica y formal del arte" (manages to unseat a frivolous sense of disinterest and sacredness within aesthetics, at the same time it rapidly empties analysis of the properly aesthetic resistances that constitute art's semantic and formal density) (1994, 155-56). Attention to aesthetics in studying urban cultural production and reception reveals fundamental aspects of a society's symbolic values. Compositional strategies, discursive registers, linguistic innovations, parodic critiques and challenges to aesthetic traditions in visual art and literature respond—beyond social class association and consumer behavior—to the society's political, environmental, and institutional dramas.

Latin American urban expression, such as Cortázar's fiction and Porter's public art, highlights the integration of the aesthetic and sociopolitical dimensions of cultural products. Lois Parkinson Zamora, in her reexamination of interdisciplinarity and pedagogy, questions the "unnecessary disciplinary divisions that currently characterize the academic study of the arts" and calls for a more direct integration of art in literary studies (1999, 389). Her launching of interartistic study offers a far-reaching *ars critica combinatoria* for Latin American culture in particular. She identifies the limits of verbal and visual meaning in order to propose a mode of analysis that moves beyond an isolated medium or mode of expression. She states that interartistic criticism serves to "elucidate the work of one artist in terms of another, to weigh the expressive potential of one medium in terms of another, and to compare cultural constructions of the image in their visual and verbal media" (1999, 413). These kinds of analyses insist on the intersection of an array of interdisciplinary modes that includes the artistic and aesthetic with the market and consumer, analyses that expand the sometimes rigid limits of market reception and consumer-based studies.[5]

In fact, studies such as García Canclini's *Consumidores y ciudadanos* examine consumer culture but avoid direct discussions of art. Through the analysis of mass participation in local arts festivals, sociological attitudes on multilingualism, and access to information technology, García Canclini studies how identities are negotiated in increasingly multicultural and global contexts. Mentions of literature lead to dismissive reductionisms such as "fundamentalismo macondista" (Macondistic fundamentalism) regarding magic realism. While a number of the essays are centered around cinema, film as an art form becomes swallowed up by the "redes globalizadas de producción y circulación simbólicas" (globalized networks of symbolic production and circulation) and by the multimedia policies of each country (1995a, 108, 128). García Canclini ignores examples of canonical literature repackaged in popular productions for mass consumption. In the domain of popular music alone one could consider examples such as the lyrics to Josefito Fernández's ageless "Guantanamera" from José Martí's *Versos sencillos,* Nicolás Guillén's poem "Tengo" performed by Conjunto Céspedes, and Chico Buarque's and Caetano Veloso's interpretations of poetry in song.[6] Lisan-

dro Meza's vallenato "Canción de una muerte anunciada" pays homage to Gabriel García Márquez's novel *Crónica de una muerte anunciada,* and the novelist himself has referred to his best-known work, *Cien años de soledad* (*One Hundred Years of Solitude*), as a 450-page vallenato (Wade 2000, 137).

While cultural studies often categorizes visual art and literature as suspiciously high brow, "street art" does captivate cultural studies practitioners because it represents an aesthetic middle world that mediates between high and low cultures. This is art that challenges the aesthetic institutionalization of national monuments and museum exhibits. Visual manifestations for public consumption, such as graffiti, banners in demonstrations, and murals, play an important role in cultures now recognized as hybrid because these materials coexist with neon signs and modern architecture, and intersect with transportation systems and urban planning projects. This is art exploding into public space that is spontaneous, sometimes risky, unlawful, and aggressive.

Graffiti, a medium that inscribes the city itself, pertains to what García Canclini calls today's "perishable, transient, and evanescent" visual culture (1993, 442). This is art that challenges the static confines of a museum collection or the presumed fixity of the printed word in literature. Cortázar's short story **"Graffiti,"** from the collection ***Queremos tanto a Glenda*** (1980) brings together street art and literature in an intense urban drama.[7] **"Graffiti"** demonstrates the limitations of a rigid classification of certain cultural products—literature, in particular—as "elite" and therefore not pertinent. In fact, **"Graffiti"** accomplishes what much of cultural studies suggests only hybrid popular manifestations can: it subverts the dominant codes governing expression to reveal significant elements of urban social and political reality as part of the overt resistance to censorship and repression under dictatorship.

"Graffiti" tells the story of anonymous communication between a man and a woman through drawings on walls in an unnamed city under a repressive political regime. The two characters exchange drawings on the dangerous space of public walls until the woman is arrested and tortured by the police. After a long "silence," or lapse in their visual communication, she lets him know what happened to her before she takes refuge in "la más completa oscuridad" (the most complete darkness): "Viste el óvalo naranja y las manchas violetas de donde parecía saltar una cara tumefacta, un ojo colgando, una boca aplastada a puñetazos" (You saw the orange oval and the violet splotches where a swollen face seemed to leap out, a hanging eye, a mouth smashed with fists [1983, 38]) (1994, 2:400).

Cortázar dedicates his story to Antoni Tàpies, the Catalan painter, and a description of one of the character's drawings in the story is reminiscent of Tàpies's industrial textures: "Lo había hecho con tizas rojas y azules en una puerta de garaje, aprovechando la textura de las maderas carcomidas y las cabezas de los clavos" (She had done it in red and blue chalk on a garage door, taking advantage of the worm-eaten wood and the nail heads [1983, 35]) (1994, 2:398). Several published editions of the story have exploited the writer's recognition of Tàpies's "pintura matérica" (matter painting)[8] by overlaying the printed text on a background that exposes "aquellos aspectos más humildes y abandonados de la realidad inmediata, tales como los graffiti callejeros, objetos de desecho y otros . . . [para] reevaluar esos objetos condenados socialmente al desuso" (those most humble and abandoned aspects of immediate reality, such as street graffiti, discarded objects . . . to reevaluate those objects socially condemned to disuse) (Borja-Villel 1992, 23-24).[9] Thus art is pushed into the public domain, imitating and becoming public space. Like Tàpies's paintings, the drawings in Cortázar's story try to defy, and clearly denounce the violence of everyday life and of authoritarian regimes—repression under Francisco Franco in Catalunya for Tàpies, surveillance and disappearances during the Argentine Proceso that Cortázar observed from afar. The violence evident in the colors, detached body parts, and disconnected shapes on the walls, parallels the psychic and physical violence done to the public.[10] Public walls that serve as canvases further expose the dilemma of artistic expression under censorship. Cortázar's fictitious graffiti exposes violence and censorship on public walls, while Tàpies and other "matter" painters (see Borja-Villel 1992) convert the space of their canvases into public plazas for exposing political and sociocultural aggression.[11] Both Tàpies and Cortázar simultaneously challenge the traditional models of signification in their respective media and the political structures they embody.

Art critics have linked Tàpies's work along with other matter painters' work to graffiti. The aesthetics and the politics of graffiti corresponded to both the resistance and the emphasis on the primitive in Tàpies's work.[12] The huge size of his canvases in the matter paintings also suggests street art dimensions. In *Culturas híbridas,* García Canclini similarly recognizes the spatial and political elements of graffiti's aesthetic:

> Una escritura territorial de la ciudad, destinada a afirmar la presencia y hasta la posesión sobre un barrio. . . . Su trazo manual, espontáneo, se opone estructuralmente a las leyendas políticas o publicitarias 'bien' pintadas o impresas, y desafía esos lenguajes institucionalizados cuando los altera.
>
> (1990, 314)

> A territorial writing of the city designed to assert presence in, and even possession of, a neighborhood. . . . Its manual, spontaneous design is structurally opposed to 'well'-painted or printed political or advertising legends and challenges those institutionalized languages when it alters them.
>
> (1995b, 249)

Cortázar's story challenges institutional (in this case, the military regime's) language and control through intimate visual communication. As Anne Wilkes Tucker notes in her comments on Brassaï's experiments with graffiti, graffiti is an art form that "attracts those who harbor something for which society can be reproached, and those whose impulses can no longer be repressed" (1999, 95). Brassaï describes graffiti as "la parole y redevenait action," verbal art that takes words and turns them into action (1993, 7). He insists that carving, writing, and painting on walls is not vandalism but rather instinctual survival (1993, 18). The characters in Cortázar's story choose arbitrary walls (a garage, a gray wall), not to occupy and claim their neighborhood, but to frame the alienation and repression they work under. The whitewashing trucks antiseptically obliterate the drawings, but when the man dares to write the words, "A mí también me duele" (It hurts me, too) along with one of the drawings, "la policía en persona la hizo desaparecer" ("The police themselves made it disappear") (Cortázar 1994, 2:397; 1983, 34).[13]

This subtle reference to *desaparecidos,* or the disappeared, is part of this story's political grammar. Addressing the reader in the second person is another of Cortázar's politicizing strategies in **"Graffiti."** In speaking to "you," the story implicates the reader, immediately assigning "you" a position in the dangerous artistic exchange. The narration pulls the readers into the story as potential victims of repression and potential resisters through art and solidarity. The narrator's gender remains uncertain through most of the story. Other than one verb in the first line of the story (*supongo*), the first person is withheld until the very end, when the narration ultimately reveals that it is the female protagonist who narrates:

> Ya sé, ya sé, ¿pero qué otra cosa hubiera podido dibujarte? ¿Qué mensaje hubiera tenido sentido ahora? De alguna manera tenía que decirte adiós y a la vez pedirte que siguieras.
>
> (1994, 2:400)

> I know, I know, but what else could I have sketched for you? What message would have made any sense now? In some way I had to say farewell to you and at the same time ask you to continue.
>
> (1983, 38)

This delay in gender identification prolongs the suspense and the open-ended relationship with the reader.

Finally protected by "la más completa oscuridad," the narrator tragically asserts herself and calls out from the other side of disappearance and silence.

The temporary, precarious, and tragic nature of the fictitious drawings in Cortázar's **"Graffiti"** has both political and aesthetic messages about contemporary urban expression in its verbal and symbolic content. As ethnographic material, **"Graffiti"** is paradoxical: imagined pictures and silenced communication. The crisis of the image in this story underscores the need to reassess the role of literature. Alberto Moreiras positions literature under the umbrella of cultural studies and considers it subaltern. Reassigning literature this new subaltern function, according to Moreiras, "endows it with a forceful irruptive potential" (2001, 13). It is art's irruptive force, through its political content along with its linguistic or visual gestures, that challenges semiotic order and proposes alternative structures of behavior.

Porter's public art offers its own urban immediacy. Her mosaic series from 1994, *Alice: The Way Out,* is installed along the train platforms of the Fiftieth Street Interborough Rapid Transit (IRT) subway station in New York City. Two images frame each side of the platform (north- and south-bound) just at the edge of the wall that separates the platform from the entrance to the station. The four murals represent characters from Lewis Carroll's *Alice's Adventures in Wonderland,* specifically Alice, the Mad Hatter, the Queen of Hearts, and the Rabbit. The murals' placement along the subway platform highlights the movement already incorporated in their medium and design, and further connects them to the commuters and travelers who become their spectators.

The murals' incorporation of movement, both in their content and from the angle of the spectator, underscores the urbanity of these images. Porter inserts Alice and company into the classic nineteenth-century flâneuristic gaze. They evoke a preindustrial story (despite Carroll's writing in the height of English Victorian industrialization) where magic happens without any reliance on machines, rendering them doubly campy in their transposed context. The modernizing mechanism of urban rapid transit that frames them makes them simultaneously contemporary and anachronistic. Their physical location along the platforms of the IRT forces a postmodern self-consciousness of their perception. Just as Cortázar's story directly addresses the reader via second-person pronouns, Porter's murals impinge on and animate the viewers. As Rosalind Krauss reminds us, the wall as art's recognized and codified exhibition space has had a major role in structuring aesthetic discourse since the nineteenth century. If the salon, gallery, or museum began

to offer walls as continuous surfaces for the exchange between artists, patrons, and viewers, then the walls of the underground transport network only exaggerate that continuity. According to Krauss, "aesthetic discourse resolves itself around a representation of the very space that grounds it institutionally" (1989, 288). While Malcolm Miles finds that much of the art in public transportation systems relates more "to the static spaces of stations than the ephemeral experiences of movement" (1997, 132), Porter's murals resist being bounded by the confines of their setting. In medium and message, *Alice: The Way Out* ventures boldly into the complexities of movement. Porter exploits the incorporation of the transit system's public exhibition space into the murals to capitalize on movement, perspective and the intertextual relationship to travel.

The silhouetted figures "drawn" in blue with red highlights against the contrasting white background are positioned in movement, perhaps on *their* way out, skipping, hopping, jumping, or running with a bold and youthful gait. One of the murals pictures the Mad Hatter in the foreground, coattails flying as he runs after the Rabbit. The angular perspective on him from the bottom corner—leaning into his stride, knees bent, feet cut out of the picture—emphasizes his movement. As in a crowded subway scene, we see shoulders and coats and hats from behind but feet tend to be beneath our sight lines. The movement in these mosaic images is not motorized or mechanical, since the figures propel themselves without vehicles or transport systems. Nevertheless, they comment on the *loco*motion of mass transit as they intersect with the travelers who end up framing and entering their scenes.

A brief consideration of Porter's mosaics in their context of commuting and perceptual psychology illuminates the role of visual expression in urban experience. The medium chosen requires distance for viewing, and the murals' colors and composition not only accommodate that distance but also incorporate how to access the works given the movement of the subway.[14] The murals account for the fact that they will not only be viewed straight on from a standing position, as in a gallery, but from various angles and rates of movement. They are constructed for what E. H. Gombrich calls the "elusiveness of vision." Many viewers will experience the murals only peripherally, and according to Gombrich, "peripheral vision is extremely sketchy in the perception of shapes and colors but very responsive to movement" (1974, 206). Porter relies on stark color contrasts and large shapes so that viewers may grasp the images even while moving and through peripheral vision.

Travel and movement have become commonplaces of urban life, and recent studies that track the experience of urban movement in Latin America go beyond the demographics of regional migration and begin to consider the everyday practice of urban dislocations. One example is the study of travel in Mexico City and the urban imaginary by García Canclini and his collaborators Alejandro Castellanos and Ana Rosas Mantecón, documented in their book, *La ciudad de los viajeros*. The team presented participating groups with photographs and film clips of streetscapes, highway labyrinths, and scenes of public transportation that frequently included street art. These examples of photographic documentation chronicle urban life through its intersection with art. The movement that these images capture—streetcars passing, demonstrators marching, workers commuting, lovers meeting—triggered responses from the participants regarding their own experiences of moving through city space. The images used in the study were pulled out of context, fragmented and isolated from their original works, but reintegrated into a sociopsychological consideration of commuting and intra-urban travel in the megalopolis. Their insistence on movement and newly configured fluidity is inconsistent with the static confines of a museum collection or the presumed fixity of the printed word.

One of the images from *Alice: The Way Out* merits particular attention in this exploration of writing on the walls because it turns the wall into a page and the pictorial representations into a book. Porter positions Alice grabbing the right edge of one of the murals where it curls up into a turning page. The Rabbit stands back, apprehensive; perhaps this is the way out, or a way leading deeper into the book's mysteries and the city's underground passages.[15] Here the visual catches up to the verbal intertext, transforming the ceramic tiles into paper, wordlessly writing a page, and inviting the spectator/traveler into its subsequent tales. Porter's work is known for her ironic quoting from literary texts, such as work by Jorge Luis Borges, intermixed with icons of popular culture.[16] Often she teases at collage, graphically reproducing shreds of text, their textures, and their shadows as if they were pasted onto the canvas. She isolates fragments of verbal text within the conventions of visual art. On the subway murals, however, she inverts this practice, making pages out of tiles such that literature can be read from a moving subway car in which Alice and the Rabbit, along with contemporary commuters, travel among its pages.

Porter's murals at the Fiftieth Street station are part of the Metropolitan Transit Authority's project called Arts for Transit, begun in the 1980s to clean up and beautify the subway spaces.[17] The Federal Transit Authority wants "good design and art" to help revitalize urban neighborhoods, "make patrons feel welcome," and ultimately "create liveable cities" (quoted in Miles 1997, 144, 146). In an essay on New York City, Malcolm Miles calls it "a city worthy of narration." The essay is accompanied by a photograph of a graffiti-covered subway car whose caption identifies it as "the very icon of 1970's New York" (52). This image is precisely what Arts for Transit combats.[18] Miles bemoans the "clean up" of the last quarter of the century, mourning the loss of rough textures, grit, and pungency, and embraces the city in 2003 as it readjusts to the hard times of the current economy and post-September 11 terror.[19] Porter's mosaics may replace graffiti, but they inscribe the city with more stories by visually narrating on walls and through movement along with throngs of passengers who foreground and frame these images. Porter's mosaic murals feature not only the intersection of urban transportation and art (incorporating the people who move within and use the subway and the station's architecture) but also the integration among urban space, art, and literature. Carroll's wit, inventiveness, and playfulness do much more than brighten up the dim underground. As visual icons of verbal satire and metadiscursiveness, the figures of Alice and her gang underscore the written nature of urban space.[20] Porter's murals are both testimony to and invitations into the city as a narrative experience.

Writing, reading, painting, and moving in urban space are all practices of the city that contribute to its discourse, its grammar, its sociospatial functioning. Cortázar's **"Graffiti"** and Porter's *Alice: The Way Out* inscribe the urban, and help write the city's text while they simultaneously contest it. As Certeau writes, "The language of power is in itself 'urbanizing,' but the city is left prey to contradictory movements that counterbalance and combine themselves outside the reach of panoptic power" (1984, 95). The communicating artists in **"Graffiti"** resist the censorship and state control of urban public space, while Alice and her companions in the mosaic murals skip off the tracks, outside the cars, resist the linearity of the system, and turn the station into a book, its walls into pages to be ventured into, turned, and read.

These two examples of urban expression illustrate—ekphrastically in the case of Cortázar's story and concretely in the case of Porter's murals—new and challenging dimensions of writing the city. A published verbal text that dramatizes a prohibitive, illegal, visual form of expression and a non-verbal visual text that animates a literary classic point out the hybrid and multitextual nature of urban space in Latin American culture. The intertextual, interartistic relationships between Tàpies and Cortázar in the case of the short story **"Graffiti,"** and between Porter and Carroll in the mosaics, further exploit the textualization of the city's spatial dimension. These works go beyond exemplifying the rich possibilities of a culture's aesthetic and symbolic elements through verbal and visual expression. They inscribe city space, affect the urban imagination and insist on an active engagement on the part of the reader/viewer. These texts mesh what is often considered "elite" or "high" literature with popular street expression, challenging the boundaries that supposedly distinguish them.

According to W. J. T. Mitchell, "all art is public art" (1990a, 4). Inquiries into public art have been defined traditionally by the "relation of beauty to bureaucracy" (2), and many critics would like to see public art spur more debate, generate critique, take on the structures of power and patronage that help inaugurate them. More than decoration and embellishment, art in public space should motivate "the activation in their users of a *reflective civilized consciousness*; of their being in a place shaped both to specific uses—learning, healing, debate, diplomacy, etc.—and to those general purposes beyond immediate utility, of the human project, which include the contemplation of matters of value, the pursuit of happiness, and a sense of well-being" (emphasis added; Gooding 1998, 19-20). To what extent critical messages and political opposition can be conveyed in public art depends not only on the artist but also on the mechanisms of funding, patronage, and civic planning at a given site. Therefore, public art, or visual expression in public places (particularly in cities), is built on a paradox of opposition, wrestling between the freedom of aesthetic expression and the institutional and financial apparatuses of urban planning. While Mitchell locates public art outside the realm of galleries and museums, he cannot help but note this paradox. Although it appears to be independent of those institutional physical structures, public art "makes its way in the larger sphere of publicity—billboards, bumper stickers, postcards, and posters—yet it also seems, to use a loaded word, 'destined' to return to the gallery and museum" (1991, 438). Clearly the examples highlighted in this essay reflect the hybrid stories of their production—literary culture and its conventions in the case of Cortázar's text and the official financial backing of an urban arts institution in the case of Porter's mosaics—along with their *ars combinatoria* of the verbal and the visual.

Both texts considered here, as they underscore the paradoxes of urban institutionalization, have important implications for public space in the urban realm. Even García Canclini admits this potential, when he states that "los discursos literarios, artísticos y massmediáticos, además de documentos del imaginario compensatorio, sirven para registrar los dramas de la ciudad, de lo que en ella se pierde y se transforma" (literary, artistic and mass-media discourses not only document compensatory imagination, but also serve to register the city's dramas, what in the city is lost and

transformed) (1995a, 78). The transformation of garage walls into canvases defies censorship, denounces political violence, and helps recuperate some of the loss; the transformation of underground passageways into fantastic adventures stretches the confines of industrial structures and incorporates the commuters into its movement. Porter's murals and Cortázar's story bypass the false dichotomy between "elite" and "popular" culture by initiating new uses for urban space. They question who controls urban spatial functions and propose their own rules about who may enter and interact with it. **"Graffiti"** identifies the consequences of infringement of those controls, and *Alice: The Way Out* blends literary figures into the commuting crowds. Cortázar's and Porter's works, in their reliance on both visual and verbal signs to a degree that puts the visual at the service of the verbal or vice versa, exemplify the opportunities for a productive synthesis, not only among different media, but also between the aesthetics and the politics of cultural production.

Notes

1. Both PMLA and *Journal of Latin American Cultural Studies* have hosted a variety of views concerning the evolution of cultural studies as a practice. Special issues of the journals devoted to the topic, numerous panels at academic conferences, and even scholarly books (Moreiras 2001, for example) have taken on these controversies as academic enterprises in their own right.

2. Translations are mine unless otherwise indicated.

3. Few readers are aware that García Canclini's first book, *Cortázar, una antropología poética* (1968), proposes a structuralist anthropological discussion of Cortázar's short fiction. His article in *South Atlantic Quarterly* on aesthetic theory surprisingly recognizes the political potential for art. He frames the discussion in his usual examples of museology and indigenous craft production but finally arrives at contemporary Latin American visual art, defending it against the "ahistorical metaphysics of a present without substance" and also against indigenistic nostalgia (1993, 442-43). Encompassing both "high" and "low" cultural manifestations, here he delivers a more fully interdisciplinary message than he usually allows.

4. "If hybridization is seen as coextensive with the market, consumer choice, and possessive individualism, then despite [García] Canclini's own protestations that his work is intended as a contribution to reformulating the project of the left, there is a sense in which it is also, in principle, compatible with globalization and neoliberal hegemony" (Beverley 1999, 129). Alberto Moreiras concurs, and in his discussion of hybridity (through which

he critiques not only García Canclini's *Hybrid Cultures* but the impact of García Canclini's and others' work in this realm) notes that "the political force of hybridity . . . remains to a large extent contained within hegemonic politics." He goes as far as to call hybridity "a sort of ideological cover for capitalist reterritorialization" (2001, 264, 267).

5. Zamora's chapter in Boris Muñoz's and Silvia Spitta's volume on urban writing (2003) provides another example of how the visual and verbal intersect in Latin American urban culture.

6. See César Braga-Pinto's discussion of both Buarque and Veloso and their insertion into the literary canon: "It is well known that one of the peculiarities of Brazilian pop culture is that, at least since the 1960s, popular songs have enjoyed the status of literature. . . . What has characterized canonical popular music production in the last thirty years is precisely its relative mobility between high culture, on the one hand, and popular culture and mass production, on the other" (2000, 103).

7. This work was published in translation as *We Love Glenda So Much and Other Tales* in 1983.

8. The Barcelona branch of the Galerie Maeght's catalogue prints the story in a typewriter font over a reproduction of a Tàpies earthy, wall-like texture (Cortázar 1979). Another version appears in an art journal in Costa Rica, *Graphiti,* which prints the story on a two-page spread, including a photograph of Cortázar and interspersed with drawings by the artist Otto Apuy (Cortázar 1993). Still another example, a limited edition from Switzerland, prints the story translated into French followed by twelve color photographs by Jean-Pierre Vorlet taken "of different walls from all over the world" (Cortázar 1984, n.p.).

9. The implementation and representation of materials and surfaces traditionally considered anti-aesthetic or even unseemly is fundamental to graffiti. Brassaï, for example, "believed that the rawness of the images was derived as much from the rough-hewn qualities of the deteriorating walls into which the graffiti were typically chiseled as from the crude qualities of the drawings themselves" (Tucker 1999, 94). Tàpies's urban primitivism furthers this collaboration of materials and design by restoring, uncovering, or breaking through the "walls" of contemporary urban existence: "Tàpies llegaba para abrir, en aquella tradición tan extendida, no una ventana tradicional, sino una brecha en el muro" (Tàpies came to open up, in a long-standing tradition, not a traditional window, but a break through the wall) (Guilbaut 1992, 33).

10. Tàpies's canvases present equally disturbing, potentially brutal images in their textures, such as scratches, boot marks, indentations, and gashes.

11. See W. J. T. Mitchell's "The Violence of Public Art" for a discussion of the associations between public art and violence. Here he considers the frequent vandalism suffered by public art as well as representations of violence in public art, stating that rather than an abstract notion of violence, public art seems "encoded" with violence in its very practice and conception (1990b, 888). He outlines three forms of violence in public images, all of which coincide with "Graffiti": the image suffering demolition (in the story, the whitewashing of graffiti by the police), the image as a weapon (in the story's case, an act of resistance), and the image representing violence (the last drawing in the protagonists' exchange, which depicts a face after a beating).

12. Tàpies himself refers to prehistoric drawings and African masks along with the mention of graffiti in what for him were essential connections between modernity and primitivism (from *Por un arte moderno y progresista*; qtd. in Borja-Villel 1992, 23-24).

13. Brassaï considers the complicated role of those hired to erase or deface graffiti, and photographs the rather hieroglyphic results of black spray paint or brush strokes covering the graffiti artists' words (Brassaï 1993, 20).

14. Gombrich discusses mosaics in his treatment of still images captured by the moving eye: "The medium does not permit smooth transitions and makes it impossible to show objects smaller than the smallest tessera at the disposal of the craftsman. Go too near and you will no longer see what you are meant to see but rather individual patches" (1974, 191).

15. It is interesting to note that the original title of Carroll's book was "Alice's Adventures Underground" (1960, 44 n. 7).

16. A recent retrospective exhibition of Porter's work was titled, "Liliana Porter: Fotografía y ficción." In the catalogue of the same name, many of the essays refer to the literary associations in her work, such as those to Borges and Carroll. The essay by Mercedes MacDonnell, "The Sphinx's Suicide: Literature, Dream and Enigma in Liliana Porter's Photographs," discusses Porter's reliance on images and citations from Borges, her affinity with Wallace Stevens, and her Alice motif (MacDonnell 2003, 203-5). MacDonnell notes the dream-like unreality Porter achieves in her photographs of everyday objects, rendering them enig-

matic and offering the viewer an experience of both irony and vertigo: "Porter puts the viewer in a state similar to that which a certain English girl named Alice might have experienced. . . . It is curiosity that leads Alice to chase the rabbit, the same curiosity that leads the viewer of Porter's pieces" (203).

17. In 1981 the MTA established a program of refurbishment for the subway system. The Arts for Transit office emerged in 1985 to coordinate the installation of permanent art and the organization of periodic exhibits and performances, with funds totaling 1 percent of the station upgrading costs (in accordance with the Percent for Art policy for public works). See Miles 1997, chap. 6.

18. In the process of securing permission to reproduce photographs of Porter's murals for this book, I noticed some very telling hesitation on the part of permissions-desk staff at the Arts for Transit office. When I explained that the article was about graffiti, red flags went up and a much more concerned investigation into exactly what I was doing ensued. I was quite surprised to find that my chapter here might cause some controversy, but came to understand why Cortázar's story, indirectly, provoked a new response. I thank the Arts for Transit office for their consideration, which included a careful reading of a draft of this chapter, and for granting permission to reproduce these images.

19. "Urbanism isn't always pretty. But the broken porticoes and cracked pavements, the walls of garbage and zaftig rats, the constant recall, ironically or otherwise, of the city that scared us and made us—this is the stuff of true New York stories" (Miles 1997, 53).

20. MacDonnell finds that the objects, toys, and images that Porter portrays are "representing their own representation. . . . In Porter's work, the viewer looks at looking and, at the same time, is looked at" (MacDonnell 2003, 203).

Bibliography

Beverley, John. 1999. *Subalternity and Representation: Arguments in Cultural Theory.* Durham, N.C.: Duke University Press.

Borja-Villel, Manuel J. 1992. "Comunicación sobre el muro." In Tàpies, *Comunicació sobre el mur,* 13-31.

Braga-Pinto, César. 2000. "How to Organize a Movement: Caetano Veloso's Tropical Path." *Studies in Latin American Popular Culture* 19: 103-12.

Brassaï. 1993. *Graffiti.* Paris: Flammarion.

Carroll, Lewis. 1960. *The Annotated Alice: "Alice's Adventures in Wonderland" and "Through the Looking Glass."* Introduction and notes by Martin Gardner. New York: Bramhall House.

Certeau, Michel de. 1980. *L'invention du quotidian.* Paris: Union Général d'Editions.

Cortázar, Julio. 1979. "Grafitti." In *Tàpies: desembre 78-gener 79,* n.p. Barcelona: Galerie Maeght.

———. 1983. *We Love Glenda So Much and Other Tales.* Translated by Gregory Rabassa. New York: Knopf.

———. 1984. *Graffiti.* Translated by Laure Guille-Bataillon. Photography by Jean-Pierre Vorlet. Lausanne: Galerie Porfolio.

———. 1993. "Grafitti." *Graphiti* 4:4-5.

———. 1994. *Cuentos completos.* 2 vols. Madrid: Alfaguara.

Gombrich, E. H. 1974. "Standards of Truth: The Arrested Image and the Moving Eye." In *The Language of Images,* edited by W. J. T. Mitchell, 181-217. Chicago: University of Chicago Press.

Guilbaut, Serge. 1992. "Materias de reflexión: Los muros de Antoni Tàpies." In Tàpies, *Comunicació sobre el mur,* 33-46.

MacDonnell, Mercedes. 2003. "The Sphinx's Suicide: Literature, Dream, and Enigma in Liliana Porter's Photographs." In Porter, *Liliana Porter,* 203-5.

Miles, Malcolm. 1997. *Art, Space and the City: Public Art and Urban Futures.* London: Routledge.

Mitchell, W. J. T. 1990b. "The Violence of Public Art: *Do the Right Thing.*" *Critical Inquiry* 16, no. 4: 880-99.

Moreiras, Alberto. 2001. *The Exhaustion of Difference: The Politics of Latin American Cultural Studies.* Durham, N.C.: Duke University Press.

Muñoz, Boris, and Silvia Spitta, eds. 2003. *Más allá de la ciudad letrada: Crónicas y espacios urbanos.* Pittsburgh: Instituto Internacional de Literatura Iberoamericana.

Tucker, Anne Wilkes. 1999. "Brassaï: Man of the World." In *Brassaï: The Eye of Paris.* Houston: Museum of Fine Arts, 16-135.

Wade, Peter. 2000. *Music, Race, and Nation: Música Tropical in Colombia.* Chicago: University of Chicago Press.

FURTHER READING

Criticism

Boldy, Steven. "Cortázar's Controllers." *Bulletin of Spanish Studies* 82, nos. 3-4 (May 2005): 375-86.

Discusses themes of reification and otherness in Cortázar's short stories.

Guzmán, María Constanza. "The Spectrum of Translation in Cortázar's 'Letter to a Young Lady in Paris.'" *Íkala* 11, no. 17 (January-December 2006): 75-86.
Interprets the role of the translator in Cortázar's short story as emblematic of the author's concerns with exile, transformation, and creative mimesis.

Jedličková, Alice. "An Unreliable Narrator in an Unreliable World: Negotiating between Rhetorical Narratology, Cognitive Studies, and Possible Worlds Theory." In *Narrative Unreliability in the Twentieth-Century First-Person Novel,* edited by Elke D'hoker and Gunther Martens, pp. 281-302. Berlin: Walter de Gruyter, 2008.
Discusses "Silvia" in light of Czech literary theory regarding the processing of narrative information through an unreliable narrator, and questions the extent to which the trustworthiness of the narrator normalizes discrepancies in the text.

Rodríguez-Luis, Julio. "Cortázar's Approach to the Fantastic." In *The Contemporary Praxis of the Fantastic:* *Borges and Cortázar,* pp. 61-100. New York: Garland Publishing, Inc., 1991.
Probes the psychological origins of the fantastic in Cortázar's stories.

Schmidt-Cruz, Cynthia. *Mothers, Lovers, and Others: The Short Stories of Julio Cortázar.* Albany: State University of New York Press, 2003, 209 p.
Book-length study of Cortázar's short fiction from a feminist perspective.

Sommer, Doris. "Grammar Trouble: Cortázar's Critique of Competence." *Diacritics* 25, no. 1 (spring 1995): 21-45.
Provides a semiotic analysis of "The Pursuer."

Standish, Peter. "Delvaux and Cortázar." *Bulletin of Spanish Studies* 82, nos. 3-4 (May 2005): 363-74.
Examines image-text relations in "Siestas" and the paintings of Belgian surrealist Paul Delvaux.

Stavans, Ilan. *Julio Cortázar: A Study of the Short Fiction.* New York: Twayne Publishers, 1996, 162 p.
Analyzes Cortázar's short fiction oeuvre and the critical response to his work.

"The Purloined Letter"

Edgar Allan Poe

The following entry presents criticism of Poe's short story "The Purloined Letter" (1844). For discussion of Poe's complete short fiction career, see *SSC,* Volumes 1, 54, and 111; for discussion of the short story "The Fall of the House of Usher" (1839), see *SSC,* Volume 22; for discussion of the short story "The Tell-Tale Heart" (1843), see *SSC,* Volume 34; for discussion of the short story "The Cask of Amontillado" (1846), see *SSC,* Volume 35; for discussion of the short story "The Masque of the Red Death" (1842), see *SSC,* Volume 88.

INTRODUCTION

Poe is credited with establishing the genre of conventional detective fiction and "The Purloined Letter" is one of his most acclaimed tales of ratiocination, or the process of logical reasoning. Along with "The Murders in the Rue Morgue" and "The Mystery of Marie Rogêt," "The Purloined Letter" centers on C. Auguste Dupin, the sleuth who established the prototype for a multitude of subsequent detective characters, including Sherlock Holmes. The story differs from other detective narratives because the criminal is known at the outset; the mystery involves the location of the stolen object. At the same time, "The Purloined Letter" conveys an aura of ambiguity by refusing to reveal the contents of the titular stolen letter. This unique construction lends itself to an openness to interpretation that has made "The Purloined Letter" one of Poe's most discussed works.

PLOT AND MAJOR CHARACTERS

The story's narrator is a close associate of Dupin, the amateur detective already famous for solving the Rue Morgue murders and the case of Marie Rogêt. The two men are quietly smoking their pipes together at Dupin's apartment when they are visited by Monsieur G——, the prefect of the Paris police force. He explains that an incriminating letter has been stolen from the Queen's bedroom by a government official, Minister D——, who was seen taking the letter and who now holds the Queen in his power through his knowledge of its contents. During the minister's frequent absences from his home, the police have conducted a thorough and scientific search and have found no trace of the letter. Dupin queries the prefect closely about the extent of the search and also asks for an exact description of the letter. He suggests that the minister's rooms be searched again, and the despondent Monsieur G—— goes on his way. One month later, the prefect returns to Dupin's home and reports that the letter is still apparently in the possession of Minister D——. Knowing that a large reward has been offered for the return of the letter, Dupin asks the prefect what he would be willing to pay for it; the prefect responds with the figure of fifty thousand francs and, at Dupin's request, writes out a check for this amount. Dupin then produces the letter, which the elated prefect carries away with him. Dupin now explains to the flabbergasted narrator how he came to possess the purloined letter. He claims that his success is the result of his ability to perceptively gauge the minister's intellect and probable behavior. He knew that the minister would never hide the letter where it could easily be found. Instead he would place the letter in plain sight where it would never be noticed. Thus, Dupin concocted an excuse to visit the minister, whom he knew personally, and surreptitiously scanned the sitting room for clues. He discovered that the minister had placed the missing letter in an ordinary letter holder on the mantelpiece. By purposely leaving one of his own possessions in the minister's house, Dupin was able to return the next day under the guise of retrieving it. He arranged for a man to fire a gun loaded with blanks at a prearranged time in the street below and then easily recovered the Queen's letter—leaving a facsimile in its place—while the minister looked out the window.

MAJOR THEMES

One of the primary themes of "The Purloined Letter" is the psychological component of rational deduction. By calmly reflecting upon the psychology of the minister, Dupin is able to track down the letter with ease. On the other hand, the prefect is unable to discover the letter because he only applies abstract logic to the investigation—he focuses on discovering *where* the letter is hidden instead of *how* it is hidden. "The Purloined Letter" also raises questions about the structure and nature of the detective genre itself. By revealing the perpetrator of the crime at the beginning of the story, Poe reversed the narrative paradigm that he established in the earlier Dupin tales. Poe further complicated the foundations of the detective story by choosing not to explain why the letter wields such power over the Queen. In this manner, the story places explicit emphasis on the pure machinations of the plot, providing a solution to the mystery while simultaneously withholding the meaning of the importance of the central plot device.

CRITICAL RECEPTION

Much of the scholarly analysis surrounding "The Purloined Letter" deals with psychoanalyst Jacques Lacan's theory that the letter is a metaphor for the inscrutability and transference of linguistic meaning, and philosopher Jacques Derrida's argument against the certainty of Lacan's contention. Critics have pointed out that while Lacan and Derrida provide different readings of the story, they both agree on the seemingly mathematical, technically precise arrangement of the narrative structure. The interpretations of Lacan and Derrida also have been used to compare the subtext of semiotics in "The Purloined Letter" with that in Honoré de Balzac's "Adieu." At the same time, some reviewers have offered new ways of avoiding a Lacanian reading of the tale. Commentator Kay Stockholder has demonstrated that by reading "The Purloined Letter" as the narrator's dream, the story's underlying aggression toward women becomes manifest.

Outside of the debate surrounding Lacan's theories, critics have also noted the misogynistic undertones of the story by concentrating on the veiled references to women's reproductive rights. Scholar Dennis Porter has written that "[T]he structure which is narrativized in 'The Purloined Letter' is that of a competition between male protagonists in which a woman and her body are themselves the game by means of which they compete in narcissistic play." Furthermore, reviewers have analyzed the political implications of the story, maintaining that the themes of vengeance and undisclosed information reflect an animosity toward the capitalistic marketplace. In addition, they have credited "The Purloined Letter" with anticipating forms of twentieth-century mathematics that question the idea that math represents a closed system. Commentators have also studied the influence of Poe's story on Alfred Hitchcock's films *Murder!* and *Dial M for Murder.* They have likewise highlighted the influence of poet and literary critic Samuel Taylor Coleridge on "The Purloined Letter." While Coleridge's philosophical system entails a balanced combination of poetic imagination and faith, Poe's story, according to scholar

Alexander Schlutz, emphasizes the imagination over faith. "In performing this shift," Schlutz noted, "Poe severs the union of poetry and philosophy that was essential for Coleridge." Some critics have proposed that "The Purloined Letter" reveals Poe's consternation over his readers' failure to fully appreciate the depth of his work. According to Warren Hill Kelly, the "mirroring of Poe's critical ideas on readership within the voice of Dupin finds substantiation in the manner in which both Poe's literary technique and content reflect his attitudes toward the readers of his day."

PRINCIPAL WORKS

Short Fiction

The Narrative of Arthur Gordon Pym of Nantucket (novella) 1838
Tales of the Grotesque and Arabesque. 2 vols. 1840
*The Prose Romances of Edgar A. Poe 1843
Tales 1845
The Works of Edgar Allan Poe: Newly Collected and Edited, with a Memoir, Critical Introductions, and Notes. 10 vols. (short stories, novella, essays, poetry) 1894-95
The Complete Works of Edgar Allan Poe. 17 vols. (short stories, novella, essays, poetry) 1902
Tales of Mystery and Imagination 1928
The Complete Tales and Poems of Edgar Allan Poe (short stories, novella, poetry) 1938
The Complete Poems and Stories of Edgar Allan Poe. 2 vols. (poetry, short stories) 1946
Complete Stories and Poems of Edgar Allan Poe 1966
Collected Works of Edgar Allan Poe. 3 vols. (short stories, novella, essays, poetry) 1969
The Short Fiction of Edgar Allan Poe (short stories and novella) 1976
Poetry and Tales (poetry and short stories) 1984
Tales of Horror and Suspense 2003

Other Major Works

Tamerlane, and Other Poems (poetry) 1827
Al Araaf, Tamerlane, and Minor Poems (poetry) 1829
The Raven, and Other Poems (poetry) 1845
Eureka: A Prose Poem (poetry) 1848
The Letters of Edgar Allan Poe. 2 vols. (letters) 1948
Poe's Poems and Essays (poetry and essays) 1955
Marginalia (nonfiction) 1981
Essays and Reviews (criticism) 1984

**Contains the short stories "The Murders in the Rue Morgue" and "The Man That Was Used Up."

CRITICISM

Claude Richard (lecture date 6 December 1980)

SOURCE: Richard, Claude. "Destin, Design, Dasein: Lacan, Derrida, and 'The Purloined Letter.'" *Iowa Review* 12, no. 4 (fall 1981): 1-11.

[*In the following essay, originally delivered as a lecture on 6 December, 1980, Richard discusses the Lacanian reading of "The Purloined Letter" and Jacques Derrida's critique of that analysis, highlighting the contention of both critics that the letter serves as a metaphor for the transfer of linguistic meaning.*]

For the second time in the rich history of Franco-American misunderstanding, Edgar Allan Poe is becoming, in France, one of the most important American writers. Since cultural anger and ironical puzzlement are likely to be as strident in American Academe as they have been over the last century at Baudelaire's and Mallarmé's supposed blindness to Poe's vulgarity, I wish to emphasize at once that the new recognition of Poe situates itself on a radically non-aesthetic plane. If Poe has become so meaningful to contemporary French criticism, it is because his texts respond admirably to the new questions addressed to literature from the whole gamut of French contemporary thought. What is perhaps difficult to realize, here in America, is that in the list of contemporary writers and critics who write about or around Poe, we find practically all the major names: Poulet, Bachelard, Ricardou, Todorov, Genette, Barthes, Lacan and Derrida.

One of Poe's texts—**"The Purloined Letter"**—has become the arena where one of the fundamental debates of contemporary criticism is being held. Do not however, be worried: I am not going to give a talk about Poe. I know better than that: I have learnt that when one wants to be taken seriously in the United States, one does not give a talk about Poe. It seems that if one wants to be taken seriously, one gives a talk about contemporary French philosophy: I am not sure however that French philosophy will sound very serious to you if I elaborate on Derrida's latest pun, "connect I cut," and if I assert that *dasein* is Lacan's favorite dessert.

The basis of modernity is the seriousness of playfulness; the game is played with words and, even if, with some American critics, we blind ourselves to the brilliantly exemplified experimentations with arbitrary signifiers where pokerfaced Poe illustrated the fecundity of systematic formalization and dislocation of meaning, we shall still meet on our path many post modern Imps of the Perverse playing their game of hide and sex.

The game we are going to play today began in 1844 when Poe, having invented and exhausted the so-called genre of the detective story in **"The Murders in the Rue Morgue,"** decided to write a meta-detective story about the theft of that letter which enables one to write detective stories, made it into another allegory of the poet as priest, and forever forgot about detective stories, passing on to what he regarded as his "legitimate thesis," the Universe and to the writing of one of the unacknowledged masterpieces of modernity, *Eureka.*

Thus the riddle of the day is: "what has happened to the purloined letter" and the game of the day is "uncover the letter to recover the letter"—a game played with admirable devotion, over the last few years, in Paris and in New Haven.

The game may appear frivolous to you—as will any destabilization of an old comfortable category by word play—but, maybe, the formidable names of the players will force us into some kind of respect and help us realize that the issues at stake are crucial to nothing less than the meaning of the Lacanian "subject," the sense of Derridean deconstruction and therefore to nothing less than the relevance of the problem of meaning in communication.

Between 1845 and 1956, not much happened in the realm of the purloined letter, except that Marie Bonaparte read it—to nobody's surprise—as the "struggle between father and son . . . to seize possession . . . of the penis . . . of the mother," thus making the cheeks of the fireplace between which the letter hangs, the most famous pair of jambs, or gambs, in the history of literary criticism.

In 1956, Lacan published "The Seminar on 'The Purloined Letter'": that text however, did not actually make its full impact felt until it was placed by Lacan himself at the head of a book, *Écrits* which, over the last decade, has become a challenge and a nightmare for a whole generation of intellectuals. When *Écrits* was reprinted in the popular collection, *Points,* not only did Lacan leave "The Seminar" at the head of the book as a reminder that it was the cornerstone of his system; he also added a new introduction in which he emphasized more clearly than before the fact that an understanding of what was really happening in Poe's tale was crucial to an understanding of Lacan's central concept—the idea that "the only master is the signifier."

We are only emerging from an age that has asserted with unusual energy that we are language, nothing but language. This is the age of Saussure and Levi-Strauss before being the age of Deleuze; this is an age to subscribe to Heidegger's statement that "words and language are not wrappings in which things are packed for the commerce of those who speak and write." Lacan is the son of Saussure and Heidegger. He would certainly not deny that "it is in words and language that things first come into being and are." He would certainly go further and would probably agree that it is in the letter that men come into being and are.

What "The Seminar on 'The Purloined Letter'" contributed is both easy and impossible to state, but it is indisputably the most unequivocal assertion that language is the primal cause. Before attempting to summarize this contribution, it might be useful to dispose of the inevitable remark—which came from Yale, with the deadly industrial precision brought by American critics to the minimization of Poe—that Poe's text is only a pretext for Lacan. This is precisely where we should begin: as Lacan makes it clear, Poe's text is the pre-text. As proto-text, **"The Purloined Letter"** has verbalized, once and forever, some of the potentialities of the discourse of psychoanalysis. To be more specific, Poe in **"The Purloined Letter"** has dreamt and worded not only the relationship between the repetition automatism and the insistence of the signifying chain but also the process through which "the displacement of the subjects is determined by the place which a signifier—the purloined letter—comes to occupy" in the successive trios which constitute the intersubjective modulus. In other words, Poe's tale appears as the perfect metaphor of the discourse of psychoanalysis insofar as that discourse is a discovery of the split. Or again—and to remind you briefly of the diegesis of the tale—what Lacan points out is that the basic structure of Poe's tale is founded on the repetition of a situation involving each time three agents, that is to say on the compulsive repetition of triads: the first scene, called the primal scene, involves the Queen, the King and the Minister D—, who steals a letter addressed to the Queen. The second scene involves the Minister D—, Dupin and the police: during a visit to D—'s house, Dupin manages to steal the letter from D— and to leave, as D— did previously, a facsimile—a simulacrum of a letter—in the card-rack where the original letter had been concealed by its very gaudy exhibition, that is to say by the very fact that it was, like all signifiers, "a little too self-evident."

What essentially interests Lacan is, first that this signifier-without-a-signified (the content of the letter is never disclosed) is a *letter*, that is to say a material signifier, secondly that the fact that this unread message is retransmitted "assures us of what may, by no means, be taken for granted: that it belongs to the dimension of language."

The invisibility of the letter, which has remained undiscovered in spite of the meticulous search of the police, demonstrates its nullibility in spite of its unques-

tionable materiality as signifier. The concealed-unconcealed letter is thus shown to be truly odd (that is to say to belong to the order of the one as opposed to the imaginary order of the two) and thus to "not admit of partition." The indivisibility of the letter (you cannot talk of "some letter")—whether it be typographical character or epistle—makes it the perfect image of "the signifier—a unit in its very uniqueness, being by nature symbol only of an absence."

Lacan may now come to what he calls "the true subject of the tale"—the true subject of any tale: the purloining of a letter, the fact that its trajectory is prolonged and that it thus becomes "a letter in sufferance," in other words, the delayed (or diverted) itinerary of a signifier on the signifying chain will determine how "the subjects, grasped in their intersubjectivity . . . , will model their very being on the moment of the signifying chain which traverses them."

This is therefore man's *destin,* this is man's *destiny,* what Freud discovered with a perpetually increasing sense of shock, the awareness that "the displacement of the signifier *determines* the subjects in their acts."

Thus Poe's tragic imagination—an imagination of absence and motion as revealed by the structure of the cosmos in *Eureka*—allowed him to fictionalize the "gripping truth" according to which he who holds the letter is bound to go through a phase determined by the signifier and, more particularly, through a phase of femininity: the Queen, then D—, then Dupin will exude the oddest *odor di femina* as long as they are "in possession of the letter"; that is to say, as long as they are possessed by the letter they possess.

"What Poe's tale shows," writes Lacan in the introduction to the *Points* edition, "is that the effect of the signifier bears primarily on its post-theft possessor and that along its travels what it conveys is the very femininity which it is to have taken into its shadow."

Thus Dupin's final involvement in the "intersubjective triad" leads him to feel "a rage of manifestly feminine nature" and "to turn toward the medusoid face of the signifier"; that is to say, to be petrified and blinded when he confronts the final remaining trace written on the simulacrum of the letter, the quotation from Crébillon he had scribbled in the facsimile he has left in the rack in the place of the original letter. It reads: "Un dessein si funeste, s'il n'est digne d'Atrée est digne de Thyeste" ("so infamous a *design,* if not worthy of Atreus, is worthy of Thyestes").

It is however well known by now that Lacan, at the end of his article, misquotes both Crébillon and Poe. Twice he writes "un *destin* si funeste" ("so infamous—or baleful—a *destiny*"). In the same way as Poe is—as he liked to remind his readers—a poet to a T, *destin* is *dessein* to a T. What remains therefore is the question of the purloined letter. For Lacan's version of the quotation, in spite of the over-ingenious explanations of French and American disciples, simply means what it says: it says that the letter dictates man's destiny whereas the emphasis in Crébillon's line was on man's exercise on his free will, on his *design*; that is to say, on the human responsibility in the curse on the House of Atreus.

Lacan does comment on *destin*-destiny with unusual clarity: "so runs the signifier's answer . . . : 'You think you act *when I stir* you at the mercy of the bonds through which I knot your desires.'" What the misquotation allows him to do is to show the multiplication of the objects of desire in the case of the tragic Don Juan and to bring in the idea that "the letters on the wall that dictate his destiny [*destin*]" will "be his *feast* until the return of the stone guest." Destiny is *destin* but feast is *festin*. *Festin* is, naturally, *destin* to a D and no feast is complete without dessert: "the signifier's answer to whoever interrogates it, is [writes Lacan] 'Eat your *Dasein*.'" Destiny contradicts *Dasein* because *Dasein* denies the concept of Lacanian subject insofar as the subject is the absent product of its linguistic cause, the letter, which will always arrive at its destination because destination is the destiny of the letter.

The last few sentences you have no doubt recognized as the gist of Derrida's critique of Lacan's "Seminar" first published in 1975, immediately translated into English under the title "The Purveyor of Truth" and reprinted with many additional comments in Derrida's most recent book, *La Carte postale.*

Derrida's critique, which will eventually raise the problem of the structure of the act of communication, reaches in two directions: first, it attempts to demonstrate that Lacan eliminates "the scene of writing" because he is concerned with truth—"not any truth but the truth itself, the truth of the truth"—that Lacan's truth is castration and that, consequently, as Purveyor of Truth or, more precisely, as the postman who delivers the truth, Lacan is nothing but a belated metaphysician. His metaphysics are the eternal metaphysics of presence, that is to say, in the case of castration, the presence of an absence. His second and consequential argument concerns what seems to be at stake not only in contemporary linguistics but in the whole field of modernity, from John Barth to Thomas Pynchon; I mean the itinerary of the letter as signifier in the act of communication. To Derrida a "letter does *not always* arrive at its destination and since this belongs to its structure, it can be said that it never really arrives

there, and that when it arrives, its possibly-not-arriving torments it with an internal divergence."

The neutralization of the scene of writing is brilliantly demonstrated when Derrida shows how Lacan can isolate two repetitive triangular scenes only because he works exclusively on the *contents* of the tale, the nakedness of the Freudian *stoff,* at the expense of the act of narration and more precisely of the presence of the narrator. The exclusion of the narrator of the story—that old reflex of scholarly hermeneutics which ultimately achieves the most paradoxical evaluation of the narrator as the agency who is alien to his narration—allows Lacan to gloss over the linguistic act of telling and to present the "displacement of the signifier as a signified, as the recounted object" or subject matter in Poe's story, that is to say as the truth of the story unveiled by the discourse of Dupin-the-analyst in a Heideggerian act of *aletheia.* Thus, the truth of the story would, paradoxically, be independent of the narration, which is disposed of under the name of secondary elaboration.

In the case of **"The Purloined Letter"** it implies that if the very important role played by the "narrating narrator" (as opposed to the "narrated narrator") is taken into account, Lacan's "narrated triangular scenes" become quadrangles, in other words series of duplicated doubles or couples, brotherly or otherwise, whose dissemination saves them from the fatality of endless displacement in the enclosure of the triangular modulus.

Lacan's tendency to triangulate **"The Purloined Letter"** is dictated by a psychoanalytical-transcendental topology—which implies that, even though the signifier "has no self-identical place," it will always follow a single proper trajectory and that, in order to tread circularly back upon its own topological tracks, the letter must end up where it should be, at the place of castration, when it forces its holder to occupy the place of woman, a place where what is veiled-unveiled is a hole, a non-being. The place of the signifier, in Lacan's thought, is finally revealed to be where Marie Bonaparte had discovered it, on the immense body of the woman sprawled across the room of D—, between the cheeks or the jambs of the fireplace from whose mantelpiece it hangs. For Derrida, Lacan's ultimate truth is that "the link between femininity and truth is its ultimate signified." Thus the Truth of the Truth would be castration. As castration is what "contracts to bring the phallus, the signifier, the letter or the fetish back to their *oikos,* their familiar dwelling," the phallus may travel in peace along its transcendental Moebius strip. The Law is preserved.

What threatens the Law is dissemination and in particular dissemination of letters. As long as the post office is the law (the royal mail, a state monopoly), letters will reach their destination. Even letters in sufference, Scarlet Letters, so to speak. There exists however a Dead Letter Office and, once in a while, a scrivener prefers not to transmit the letter. So that the letters which end up in the graveyard of the post office or on the desk of Bartleby *never* reach their destination. This is the genuine *post office reform*, the taking of the letter from the mailman whose eternal function has been to deliver the letter to the female. That is the basis of Derrida's deconstruction of the all-powerful scheme of the Lacanian act of communication: if the sender succeeds in sending a letter to a receiver, even if the sender is defined as "he who receives from the receiver his own message in reverse form," what is postulated is that some literal part of the message always arrives at its destination, that is to say that the letter is the destiny of both the sender and the receiver. But the idea of destination itself, an idea Derrida equates in *La Carte postale* with the idea of death, rests entirely on the acceptance of the materiality of the letter deduced from its indivisibility, which, for Derrida, "is not found anywhere" and which can thus be properly called an idealization. Communication is seen by Lacan as a contract between two presents and even if communication does not communicate anything, it communicates itself: "the discourse represents the existence of communication . . . ; even if it denies the obvious, it affirms that the Word constitutes the Truth." If, truly, the existence of communication is the truth of communication—what Derrida very Poesquely calls "the power of the [spoken] word . . . testifying to the truth"—then the letter does arrive at its destination. But "l'écriture avant la lettre"—"writing before the letter" which has already deconstructed the totalitarian phallogocentrism of philosophy, demonstrates that **"The Purloined Letter"** is but a letter in a chain of letters and that no letter ever arrives at its destination. The proof is that the cannibalistic *dessein* (design) of the brother of Atreus has become the *destin* of the subject and that "design" has been turned into the *dasein* of the Parisian sleuth: in fact, as Derrida demonstrates, Lacan "carries *dasein* back to the subject." The letter is therefore revealed as divisible and thus loses any assurance of destination.

It can, in particular, be shared, notably by two brothers. Derrida does allude briefly to the dedoubling of the characters in **"The Purloined Letter"** ("brothers or confrères") to show how the so-called "unity" of the tale is carried into an endless drifting-off course and a labyrinth of doubles without originals. When, in the signature of his tale, Poe-Dupin alludes to the relationship between Atreus and Thyestes, he is obviously alluding to another archetypal couple, the couple of brothers, and to the curse of sameness in difference.

The organizing motif of the tale is, as a matter of fact, the brotherly couple: Atreus and Thyestes, the narrator and Dupin, D— and his brother—poet and mathematician—the King and the Prefect, and finally, Dupin and D—.

"The Purloined Letter" has bravely born the brunt of the battle fought on its ring, but no one is going to make me believe that the last word has been taken from the text and that Poe is not smirking with glee somewhere in the Hell of Humanists recently converted into Paradise for Structuralists. That Dupin and D— tend to identify throughout the tale will be obvious to anyone who is not concerned with using the tale for the construction or deconstruction of a system, even if that reader did not know that Dupin's real life model, André Marie Jean Jacques Dupin had a brother, Charles Pierre Dupin, and even if that reader had forgotten that Dupin is described as "a bi-part soul" who engages in the hunt for the Great Tawny Ape of the Rue Morgue in order to vindicate Lebon, his good side, mistaken by the blind police of Paris for his ontological brother, the hideous *monstrum horrendum* of the repressed self. It would have been enough to realize that from the vast alphabetic scale offering a paradigmatic choice of 26 letters, Poe, the master of conundrums, elected to name the Minister D, thus making him share with Dupin the signifier D, making them, therefore, different to a D, that is to say similar in their difference. The rest of the paternal name is but a syntagmatic sequel deprived of its liberty to differ by the determinism of the inaugural D.

It should be pretty obvious that the purloining of the letter stands, in the tale, as a mirror metaphor of the theft of a D. Dupin and D—, those Siamese twins in the fashion of Atreus and Thyestes or in the fashion of Chang and Eng, are linked by the flesh—the flesh of the children of Thyestes devoured in a cannibalistic *festin* (feast) or the flesh of the letter that welds them together for the worst of destinies (*destin*). To be welded to one's brother by a leash of flesh—symbolical or literal—to be, as John Barth would put it, two in one, to be at the same time "I" and "the other," to be both oneself and one's sign, to be neither one nor quite two, condemns Dupin-the-writer to "school himself in detachment" and "to lust for disjunction."

When he learns about the theft of the letter, Dupin understands that, symbolically, the Minister D— has stolen his D, depriving him of his integrity, dividing his signifier—his paternal name—which constitutes the essence or rather the letter of his identity. This may be regarded as structuralist's delirium. Let us, nevertheless, return to the letter of the text of Poe. That the whole story is concerned with the differentiation of one and two is obvious from the beginning. It is a story at the same time "simple and odd" (double d), a business which is, to quote the Prefect, "simple indeed" and it deals, among other things, with the idea developed by Dupin that "two motives, each of a given value, have not necessarily a value, when united, equal to the sum of their values apart."

With twin, or nearly twin, brothers, that is to say with the subject, whatever is simple is odd, because to be one is to be two. The subject is two-in-one like a Moebius strip, yearning for the split, longing, as Dupin himself puts it, "to be even with him," that is to say to transform the one twoness into two onenesses by recovering his D.

The Minister, indeed, has more than just stolen a D from Dupin: he has hoarded D's into the cellar of his self: he owns such an excess of letters that he can afford to leave his own letter upon the table, his hotel is called the D— hotel, all his papers show the D— sign, he has written on Differential Calculus and his large black seal bears the D— cipher. More convincingly still, he appears to Dupin as the illegal holder of a stock of illegitimate D's as he, Dupin, "reflects [like a mirror—a very envious mirror—] upon the *d*aring, *d*ashing and *d*iscriminating ingenuity of D—." I am not prepared to believe that this is not deliberate.

Dupin's design is obviously to liberate his D or to reclaim his letter because, on account of "its susceptibility of being destroyed," he is, when deprived of his D, "driven to despair." Thus, in order to "redirect" the letter, Dupin will resort to the simulacrum of writing: he will replace the letter by a facsimile and, in order to recover his property, he will "imitate the D— cipher." The last doubt we might have, will, I hope, be dispelled, when we take into consideration the signifier he uses (or is used by) to express his victory: "I bade the Minister good morning and took my *de*parture."

The Minister, who, as you have noticed, is in his turn, deprived of his D, is consequently a "desperate man" whose "downfall" is properly called a political "*de*struction." Now the destruction of the Minister D has been, we remember, achieved by Dupin through a process very properly described, by both Dupin and the narrator, as "a process of identification." The successful recovery of the D seems therefore to aim at the reconstruction of Dupin's identity which has been destroyed by the Minister D—.

By ministering to his D, Dupin reconstructs his broken identity, achieves the reunification of I and D, thereby demonstrating that oneness can be and is. The age believed in the conjunction of I and D; Poe believed in oneness.

If identity is the union of I and D, to steal the D is to reduce the I to the bare ego which is an illusion of identity begot by the ideology of presence.

Dupin however will not egoistically and gluttonously feed on his newly reconstructed I.D. He will share the feast with the narrator in the palace of imagination and together they will write a story, entitled **"The Purloined Letter,"** which shows that two brothers can share the House of Atreus as long as no D is appropriated by an I, no letter possessed by a sender, no language owned by the writer.

The function of the letter is to travel back and forth incessantly from one subject to another, to underline that there is no sender and no receiver, that we have always known, with Derrida, that Plato had been dictating to Socrates the message Socrates had received from Plato who had got it from Socrates.

In order to write, you must be two, like Deleuze and Guattari, and as each of the two is many persons, what it means is that it takes a lot of people to write a letter. That is the grand opening of Deleuze and Guattari's *Rhizome* and this is where we might conclude, if to conclude were not to attempt to arrest or put an end to a D. Thus, as I do not know how to conclude, I shall, with your permission, simply take my leave without *de*lay.

* * *

"The Purloined Letter" Dossier

1. Bonaparte, Marie. *Edgar Poe: Étude psychanalytique.* Paris: Denoël et Steele, 1933, 2 vols. (Paris: P.U.F., 3 vols.) translated by J. Rodker, London: Imago Publishing Company, 1949.

2. Lacan, Jacques. "Ouverture de ce recueil" and "Le Séminaire sur *La Lettre volée*" in *Écrits*, Paris: Le Seuil, pp. 9-10 and 11-61. (Reprinted 1971 in *Écrits*, Paris: Le Seuil, Collection "Points," pp. 19-75 with a new introduction (pp. 7-12) dated December 14, 1969.)

————. "Seminar on 'The Purloined Letter,'" translated by Jeffrey Mehlman, *Yale French Studies* 48 (1973), 38-72 (issue entitled *French Freud*) (An abridged version. Reprinted in, *Aesthetics To-Day,* revised edition, eds. Morris Philipson and Paul J. Gudel, New York: N.A.L., 1980, pp. 382-412).

3. Derrida, Jacques. "Le Facteur de la vérité," *Poétique,* 21 (1975), pp. 96-148, reprinted in *La Carte postale.* Paris: Aubier-Flammarion, 1980 (*La Carte postale* includes many allusions to "The Purloined Letter," to Lacan's "Seminar" and to B. Johnson's and F. Jameson's articles. See *infra*).

————. "The Purveyor of Truth," translated by Willis Domingo, James Hulbert, Moshe Ron and M.-L.R., *Yale French Studies* 52 (1975), 31-113 (the issue is entitled *Graphesis*).

4. Roustang, François. *Un Destin si funeste* (sic). Paris: Editions de Minuit, 1976.

5. Johnson, Barbara. "The Frame of Reference: Poe, Lacan, Derrida," *Yale French Studies* 55/56 (1977), 457-505 (the issue is entitled *Literature and Psychoanalysis*).

6. Jameson, Frederic. "Imaginary and Symbolic in Lacan: Marxism, Psychoanalytical Criticism and the Problem of the Subject," *Ibid.*, pp. 338-395.

7. Holland, Norman N. "Recovering 'The Purloined Letter,' Reading as a Personal Transaction," in Susan R. Suleiman and Inge Crosman, eds., *The Reader in the Text, Essays on Audience and Interpretation,* Princeton University Press, 1980, pp. 350-370.

8. Mehlman, Jeffrey. "Poe Pourri: Lacan's Purloined Letter," in *Aesthetics To-Day,* pp. 413-433.

9. A recent number of *Tel Quel*, LXXXVII (Spring 1981) contains incidental remarks on "The Purloined Letter" by Ph. Sollers, J. L. Giribone and an interesting article by Françoise P. Lévy, "La Lettre . . ." (pp. 64-73) which explores the implications of Lacan's neglect of the content of the letter.

Note

A lecture given at the University of Iowa on December 6, 1980, and printed with Professor Richard's permission.

John T. Irwin (essay date December 1986)

SOURCE: Irwin, John T. "Mysteries We Reread, Mysteries of Rereading: Poe, Borges, and the Analytic Detective Story; Also Lacan, Derrida, and Johnson." *MLN* 101, no. 5 (December 1986): 1168-1215.

[*In the following excerpt, Irwin demonstrates how Jacques Lacan, Jacques Derrida, and Barbara Johnson each illuminate the numerical, geometric structure of Poe's short story despite the differences in their respective readings of the text.*]

I

Let me start with a simple-minded question: How does one write analytic detective fiction as high art when the genre's basic structure, its central narrative mechanism, seems to discourage the unlimited rereading associated with serious writing? That is, if the point of an analytic detective story is the deductive solution of a mystery, how does the writer keep the achievement of that solution from exhausting the reader's interest in the story? How does he write a work that can be reread by people other than those with poor memories? I use the term "analytic detective fiction" here to distinguish the genre invented by Poe in the Dupin tales of the 1840s from stories whose main character is a detective but whose main concern is not analysis but adventure, stories whose true genre is less detective fic-

tion than quest romance, as one of the masters of the adventure mode, Raymond Chandler, implicitly acknowledged when he gave the name Mallory to an early prototype of his detective Philip Marlowe. For Chandler, the private investigator simply represents a plausible form of modern knight-errant. In his essay "The Simple Art of Murder," he says that a detective story is the detective's "adventure in search of a hidden truth, and it would be no adventure if it did not happen to a man fit for adventure."[1] The emphasis in Chandler's remarks, as in his fiction, is on the detective's character and his adventures, with the revelation of a hidden truth simply serving as a device to illuminate the former and motivate the latter. But in the pure analytic detective story the matter is otherwise. As a character, Dupin is as thin as the paper he's printed on. As for his adventures, they amount to little more than reading newspaper accounts of the crime and talking with the Prefect of police and the narrator in the privacy of his apartment. What gives the analytic detective genre its special appeal is that quality which the Goncourt brothers noted on first reading Poe. In an 1856 journal entry they described Poe's stories as "a new literary world" bearing "signs of the literature of the twentieth century—love giving place to deductions . . . the interest of the story moved from the heart to the head . . . from the drama to the solution."[2] Precisely because it is a genre that grows out of an interest in deductions and solutions rather than in love and drama, the analytic detective story shows little interest in character, managing at best to produce caricatures—those monsters of idiosyncrasy from Holmes to Poirot. In its purest form it puts all its eggs in the basket of plot, and a specialized kind of plot at that. The problem is that this basket seems to be one that can be emptied in a single reading.

Related to this difficulty is another. If the writer does his work properly, if he succeeds in building up a sense of the mysterious, of some dark secret or intricately knotted problem, then he has to face the fact that there simply exists no hidden truth or guilty knowledge whose revelation will not seem anticlimactic compared to an antecedent sense of mystery and the infinite speculative possibilities it permits. Borges, one of the contemporary masters of the analytic detective story, acknowledges this difficulty in his tale "Ibn Hakkan al-Bokhari, Dead in His Labyrinth." He says that one of his characters, "steeped in detective stories, thought that the solution of a mystery is always less impressive than the mystery itself."[3] But if in the analytic detective story the solution is always in some sense an anticlimax that in dissipating the mystery exhausts the story's interest for us, an interest in speculative reasoning which the mystery empowers, then how does one write this kind of story as a serious, that is, rereadable, literary form? How does one both present the analytic solution of a mystery and at the same time conserve the sense of the mysterious on which analysis thrives?

Given the predictable economy of a critical essay, I think the reader is safe in assuming that if I didn't consider Poe's Dupin stories to be, on the one hand, archetypes of analytic detective fiction, and on the other, serious literary works that demand and repay re-reading, there would be no reason for my evoking at this length the apparent incompatibility of these modes and thus the writer's problem in reconciling them. All of which brings me to the task of uncrumpling that much crumpled thing **"The Purloined Letter"** to consider the way that this problem of a mystery with a repeatable solution, a solution that conserves (because it endlessly refigures) the sense of the mysterious, lies at the very origin of the analytic detective story.

II

My approach to **"The Purloined Letter"** will be along what has recently become a well-worn path. I want to look briefly at three readings of the story that form a cumulative series of interpretations, each successive reading commenting both on the story and on the previous reading(s) in the series. They are Jacques Lacan's "Seminar on 'The Purloined Letter'" (1957), Jacques Derrida's "The Purveyor of Truth" (1975), and Barbara Johnson's "The Frame of Reference: Poe, Lacan, Derrida" (1978). Each of these essays presents a lengthy, complex argument in which **"The Purloined Letter"** is treated as a pretext, which is to say, read as a parable of the act of analysis. However, I am not so much interested here in following the convolutions of their individual arguments as in isolating a thread that runs through all three, a clue to conduct us through labyrinthine passages. And that thread is the position that each essay takes on what we might call the numerical/geometrical structure of the story.

Let us begin with Lacan. He says that the story consists of "two scenes, the first of which we shall straightway designate the primal scene, and by no means inadvertently, since the second may be considered its repetition."[4] The first or primal scene takes place in "the royal *boudoir*" (p. 41), the second scene in "the Minister's office" (p. 42). And according to Lacan, each of these scenes has a triangular structure: each is composed of "three logical moments" (p. 43) "structuring three glances, borne by three subjects, incarnated each time by different characters":

The first is a glance that sees nothing: the King and the police.

The second, a glance which sees that the first sees nothing and deludes itself as to the secrecy of what it hides: the Queen, then the Minister.

The third sees that the first two glances leave what should be hidden exposed to whoever would seize it: the Minister, and finally Dupin.

(p. 44)

Thus in the royal boudoir, the King does not see the incriminating letter which the Queen in her haste has hidden in the open, leaving it with its address uppermost in plain sight on a table. And the Queen, seeing that the King doesn't see the letter, mistakes his blindness for the letter's concealment, thus leaving herself vulnerable to the Minister who sees both the King's glance and the Queen's and realizes that the letter can be seized before the Queen's very eyes precisely because she dare not do anything to attract the King's attention to it. Similarly in the second scene, at the Minister's residence, the letter, having been turned inside out and readdressed in a female hand, is once again hidden in plain sight in a card rack on the mantelpiece. And this time the police, who have searched the Minister's quarters repeatedly without noticing the letter, represent that first glance which sees nothing; while the Minister, who mistakes the blindness of the police for the concealment of the letter, represents the second glance, and Dupin represents the third glance that sees what the first two miss, i.e., that the letter hidden in the open is his for the taking. The figure who participates in both these triangular scenes is the Minister, and his shifting from the position of the third glance in the initial scene to that of the second glance in its repetition exhibits the special vulnerability to self-delusion, to a blind spot, which the possession of the letter conveys.

Consider, now, Derrida's critique of this reading, keeping in mind that in his essay "The Purveyor of Truth" Derrida is motivated less by an interest in Poe or **"The Purloined Letter"** than by a desire to score points off Lacan. As Johnson points out, Derrida, in a lengthy footnote to his book *Positions,* sketches the argument that will become "The Purveyor of Truth" and cites in this context Lacan's multiple "*acts of aggression*" against him since the publication of *De la grammatologie* in *Critique* in 1965.[5] Obviously, Derrida takes the case of **"The Purloined Letter"** for one of the same reasons that Dupin did—the Minister once did Dupin "an evil turn" (Poe, 3: 993) at Vienna, and Dupin sees the affair of the letter as an opportunity to get even. The wit of Derrida's essay lies in the way that it uses Lacan's reading of **"The Purloined Letter"** against itself, for if Lacan believes that with his interpretation of the story he has, as it were, gained possession of Poe's **"Purloined Letter,"** has made its meaning his own, then Derrida will show him that the possession of that letter, as Lacan himself pointed out, brings with it a blind spot. In his essay Derrida sets out to repeat the encounter between Dupin and the

Minister with himself in the role of Dupin and Lacan in the role of the Minister.

Derrida attacks Lacan's reading of the story on a variety of points, but the one that concerns us has to do with Lacan's notion of the triangular structure of each of the two scenes in the tale. Derrida agrees that the story consists of two scenes, but not the two on which Lacan focusses. He points out that the scene in the royal boudoir and the subsequent scene at the Minister's residence are two narrated scenes within the framing artifice of the story, but that the story itself consists of two scenes of narration—the first scene being the Prefect's initial visit to Dupin during which the Prefect recounts the events in the royal boudoir, and the second scene being the Prefect's subsequent visit during which Dupin recounts the events at the Minister's residence. While the narrators of the two *narrated scenes* in the royal boudoir and at the Minister's residence are respectively the Prefect and Dupin, the narrator of the two *scenes of narration* at Dupin's lodgings is Dupin's unnamed companion. Thus, according to Derrida, Lacan reduces the four-sided structure of the scene of narration—what Derrida calls "the scene of writing"—to the three-sided structure of the narrated scene "by overlooking the narrator's position, the narrator's involvement in the content of what he seems to be recounting."[6] In ignoring the presence of the narrator of **"The Purloined Letter,"** Lacan cuts "a fourth side" out of the narrated figure "to leave merely triangles" (p. 54). And he does this, says Derrida, precisely because as a psychoanalyst, Lacan projects upon Poe's story the structure of the Oedipal triangle in his desire to read **"The Purloined Letter"** as an allegory of psychoanalysis or *"an allegory of the signifier"* (Johnson, p. 115).

Now since in his critique of Lacan's interpretation of **"The Purloined Letter"** Derrida aims to get even with Lacan by being one up on him, and since Lacan in his reading of the numerical structure of the tale has already played the numbers one, two, and three (the tale is composed of two scenes, the second of which, by repeating the triangular structure of the first, creates a sameness or oneness between the two), then being one up on Lacan means playing the next open number (four); and that is what Derrida does in arguing that the structure of the scenes is not triangular but quadrangular. However, whether Derrida arrives at this quadrangular structure by adding one to three or by doubling two is a problematic point, a point on which Johnson focusses in her critique of Lacan's and Derrida's readings of the tale's numerical structure.

As Johnson notes, Derrida objects to the triangular structure which Lacan sees in the repeated scenes because this structure, derived from the Oedipal triangle,

represents in Derrida's opinion a characteristic psychoanalytic attempt to dismiss or absorb the uncanny effects of doubling, a doubling which Derrida maintains is everywhere present in the tale. Doubling tends, of course, to be a standard element of the analytic detective story, in that the usual method of apprehending the criminal involves the detective's doubling the criminal's thought processes so as to anticipate his next move and end up one jump ahead of him. And, of course, the number associated with doubling is usually four rather than two, for what we refer to as doubling is almost always splitting and doubling. Which is to say, the figure of the double externally duplicates an internal division in the protagonist's self (but with the master/slave polarity of that division characteristically reversed), so that doubling tends to be a structure of four halves problematically balanced across the inner/outer limit of the self rather than a structure of two separate, opposing wholes. Thus in the first Dupin story, **"The Murders in the Rue Morgue,"** the narrator says that while observing Dupin in the exercise of his "peculiar analytic ability," he entertained "the fancy of a double Dupin—the creative and the resolvent" in accordance with "the old philosophy of the Bi-Part Soul" (2: 533). And in **"The Purloined Letter"** the Minister, as both poet and mathematician, is represented as having this same dual intellectual power. In matching wits with the Minister, Dupin first doubles the Minister's thought processes—a mental operation that Dupin illustrates by telling the story of the schoolboy who always won at the game of even and odd—and he then replays, that is, temporally doubles, the scene in which the Minister originally seized the letter, but with himself now in the Minister's role, thus shifting the Minister into the role played by the Queen in the original event and evoking the destabilizing reversal-into-the-opposite inherent in doubling.

As Johnson notes, Derrida thinks that "the problem with psychoanalytical triangularity . . . is not that it contains the wrong number of terms, but that it presupposes the possibility of a successful dialectical mediation and harmonious normalization, or *Aufhebung,* of desire. The three terms in the Oedipal triad enter into an opposition whose resolution resembles the synthetic moment of a Hegelian dialectic" (p. 122). But that synthetic moment, that successful dialectical mediation of desire, is precisely what the uncanny destabilizing effect of doubling constantly subverts, for in the Oedipal triangle each of the three positions functions as one pole of a mutually constitutive opposition with one of the other positions and thus each position is subject to being reversed into its opposite. There exists in the Oedipal triangle, then, no privileged position that is above or outside the uncanny effects of doubling, no exempt, objective position from which to mediate or regularize the subjective interaction of the other two positions.

As with Derrida's reading of Lacan, the wit of Johnson's reading of Derrida lies in the way that she doubles Derrida's own insights back upon themselves to make them problematic. Thus in dealing with Derrida's attempt to be one up on Lacan by playing the number four to Lacan's three, Johnson assimilates their opposed readings of the numerical structure of the tale to the game of even and odd, the game which Dupin proposed as an illustration of the way that one doubles the thought processes of an opponent in order to be one jump ahead of him. Derrida opts for a quadrangular structure, that is, he plays the even number four, in order to evoke the uncanniness, the oddness of doubling; while Lacan opts for a triangular structure by playing the odd number three, in order to enforce the regularizing or normalizing effect of the dialectical triad. In this game of even and odd, Derrida and Lacan end up as reciprocal opposites, as specular doubles of one another: Derrida asserts the oddness of evenness, while Lacan affirms the evenness of oddness. Given the destabilizing reversal-into-the-opposite inherent in doubling, Johnson sees the opposition between Derrida's and Lacan's interpretations as an "oscillation" between the former's "unequivocal statements of undecidability" and the latter's "ambiguous assertions of decidability" (p. 146).

As to Johnson's own position on **"The Purloined Letter,"** her reading of Lacan and Derrida is meant to free her from having to take a position on the numerical structure of the tale, or more exactly, to free her from having to take a *numerical* position on that structure. She does not intend, for example, to play the next open number (five); for since she has reduced Lacan's and Derrida's readings of the numerical structure of the story to the specular game of even and odd, there exist only two numerical positions that one can take on that structure—even or odd—and these, Johnson contends, have already been played by Derrida and Lacan without any clear conclusion. Johnson's strategy is to call into question the whole concern with numbers. At one point she asks, "But can what is at stake here really be reduced to a mere numbers game?", and a bit later she answers, "Clearly, in these questions, the very notion of a number becomes problematic, and the argument on the basis of numbers can no longer be read literally" (p. 121). As Johnson sees it, taking a position on the numerical structure of the tale means, for Lacan and Derrida, taking a numerical position, choosing a number, but that means playing the game of even and odd, the game of trying to be one up on a specular, antithetical double. And playing that game means endlessly repeating the structure of

"The Purloined Letter" in which being one up inevitably leads to being one down. For if the structure created by the repeated scenes in the tale involves doubling the thought processes of one's opponent in order to use his own methods against him—as Dupin does with the Minister, as Derrida does with Lacan, and as Johnson does with Derrida—then the very method by which one outwits one's opponent, by which one comes out one up on him, is the same method that will be employed against oneself by the next player in the game, the next interpreter in the series, in order to leave the preceding interpreter one down.

Is it possible, then, to interpret **"The Purloined Letter"** without duplicating in the interpretive act that reversal-into-the-opposite inherent in the mechanism of seizing the letter as that mechanism is described in the tale? Is it possible to generate an insight without a blind spot in it, a flaw that allows the insight subsequently to be turned against itself? Clearly, the desire for such an invulnerable insight is at work in Johnson's essay and accounts for the at times disconcerting level of self-consciousness which she tries to maintain regarding her own methodological stance, her own critical assumptions. For Johnson the refusal to take a numerical position on the structure of the tale, i.e., to play the next open number, is an effort to avoid the game of trying to be one up by adding the number one to the opponent's numerical position, as Derrida does in playing the number four to Lacan's three; for that game will simply turn into an oscillation between even and odd running to infinity. But is it possible for Johnson to avoid becoming involved in this numbers game simply by refusing to choose a specific number with which to characterize the geometrical/numerical structure of the tale? Doesn't the very form of her essay—as a critique of Derrida's critique of Lacan's reading of **"The Purloined Letter"**—involve her in the numbers game? In situating her essay as the third in a series of three critical readings, Johnson places herself in that third position which, in the structure governing the wandering of the purloined letter, is the position of maximum insight, but also the position in which the observer is subject to mistaking his insight concerning the subjective interaction of the other two glances for an objective viewpoint above such interaction. And indeed, how are we to describe the relationship between Johnson's interpretation and those of Lacan and Derrida? Are they linked in a triangular structure in which Lacan and Derrida face off as antithetical doubles, while Johnson, by refusing to become involved in the game of even and odd, occupies a position of "successful dialectical mediation" above them, a Hegelian synthesis of their positions? Or are they involved in a quadrangular structure in which Lacan and Derrida are reciprocal halves of one pole of a mutually constitutive opposition (i.e., the pole of trying to be one up on a specular double), while Johnson occupies the other pole of this opposition by doubling back Lacan's and Derrida's methods against them in order to avoid this game of one up? Indeed, Johnson's final comment on her own methodology invokes the image of Derrida's quadrangular frame: ". . . my own theoretical 'frame of reference' is precisely, to a very large extent, the writings of Lacan and Derrida. The frame is thus framed again by part of its content; the sender again receives his own message backward from the receiver" (p. 146).

Johnson's essay is at odds with itself, as she is the first to acknowledge. Indeed, it is precisely her strategy to present the opposed aspects of her essay—such as its explicit refusal, on the one hand, to take a numerical position on the structure of the tale, coupled with its implicit assumption, on the other hand, of a numerical position in representing its own relationship to the two earlier critical essays, a numerical position that reinscribes the question of a triangular versus a quadrangular structure present in the tale—precisely her strategy to present these opposed aspects of her essay as an aporia, as a trope of undecidability not unlike the one which Paul de Man describes in the passage Johnson uses as the epigraph to her book *The Critical Difference,* the book whose final chapter is her essay on Derrida and Lacan. In that epigraph de Man evokes the aporia between grammar and rhetoric by citing as an example the case in which Edith Bunker asks her husband Archie if he wants his bowling shoes laced over or laced under—to which the irascible Archie replies, "What's the difference?" In terms of grammar Archie's reply asks for the difference between two alternatives, but in terms of rhetoric his reply means "Whatever the difference is, it's not important enough to make a difference to me." De Man remarks, "The same grammatical pattern engenders two meanings that are mutually exclusive: the literal meaning asks for the concept (difference) whose existence is denied by the figurative meaning" (Johnson, p. v). It is in this same vein that Johnson at the end of her essay, after having described the opposition between Derrida's and Lacan's positions as "the oscillation between unequivocal statements of undecidability and ambiguous assertions of decidability," concludes, "'Undecidability' can no more be used as the last word than 'destination'. . . . The 'undeterminable' is not opposed to the determinable; 'dissemination' is not opposed to repetition. If we could be sure of the difference between the determinable and the undeterminable, the undeterminable would be comprehended within the determinable. What is undecidable is whether a thing is decidable or not" (p. 146).

Now what are we to make of these words? By which I mean not just what do these words say grammatically but what do they convey rhetorically, for what purpose are they being said in this context. I think the key lies in Johnson's statement that "'Undecidability' can no more be used as a last word than 'destination.'" At the point she says this, Johnson is nearing her own destination, the end of her essay, and is faced with the formal requirement of saying a last word and thus with the question of whether a last word can be said in the oft-renewed critical discussion of **"The Purloined Letter."** Having to say a last word, she says in effect, "The last word is that there is no last word." This type of statement which says one thing grammatically and means its opposite rhetorically occurs again and again in her essay. As we noted, it is the strategy at work when Johnson refuses to take a numerical position on the structure of the tale at the same time that she implicitly assumes a numerical position in relation to the two earlier critical readings which her own essay retrospectively groups into a series along with itself. It is at work again when she turns Derrida's insights on doubling back upon themselves to tell Derrida that it is impossible to be one up on his specular double Lacan, for though what she says on a grammatical level is that it is impossible to be one up in such an encounter, the rhetorical effect of her statement is to leave her one up on her specular double Derrida. And this strategy is at work once again when she decisively concludes, "What is undecidable is whether a thing is decidable or not."

These instances of an aporia between grammar and rhetoric occur in statements that are in one way or another self-reflexive, statements that are themselves included in the class of things to which they refer. A simple example of such a self-including statement would be the sentence "All statements containing seven words are false." Precisely because the sentence is itself a statement made up of seven words, we are faced with a paradox: if this statement is true, it is false, and if it is false, it is true. Similarly, in an aporia between grammar and rhetoric we are faced, as de Man notes, with a single grammatical pattern that engenders two mutually exclusive meanings. By very reason of the fact that they include themselves in the class of things to which they refer, these statements double back upon themselves and exhibit that uncanny reversal-into-the-opposite inherent in doubling. One thinks in this connection of Russell's paradox. Distinguishing between two kinds of classes (those which do not include themselves as members and those which do), Russell calls the first class "normal" and the second "non-normal" and he then doubles back upon itself this distinction between nonself-including and self-including classes by asking whether *the class of all normal classes* is a normal or a non-normal class. By definition *the class of all normal classes* includes within itself all normal classes. Consequently, if it is itself a normal class, it must be included in itself. But self-inclusion is the distinguishing characteristic of a non-normal class. *The class of all "normal classes"* is, then, a concept whose form and content are at odds: the concept involves, on the one hand, a formal notion of *class* as absolutely inclusive, which is to say, as ultimately self-inclusive, that is contradicted, on the other hand, by the content, by the specific definition of the *"classes"* which the former is to include completely within itself. As a result the class of all normal classes is normal only if it is non-normal, and non-normal only if it is normal. Part of the infinite fascination of paradoxes of self-inclusion is, of course, that they seem to reflect in the facing mirrors of language and logic the mysterious nature of self-consciousness as that which seeks to include wholly within itself an exact representation of that which by its very essence cannot wholly include itself.

At the very start of her essay Johnson sets the tone for all the self-including statements that are to follow when she remarks that in Poe's tale, Lacan's reading, and Derrida's critique, "it is the *act of analysis* which seems to occupy the center of the discursive stage, and the *act of analysis of the act of analysis* which in some way disrupts that centrality. In the resulting asymmetrical, abyssal structure, no analysis—including this one—can intervene without transforming and repeating other elements in the sequence, which is thus not a stable sequence, but which nevertheless produces certain regular effects" (p. 110). The key phrase, of course, is "no analysis—including this one." It has about it the brisk American quality of Mark Twain's "No general statement is worth a damn—including this one"—a general statement worth a damn only if general statements aren't worth a damn. The very fact that Johnson makes an analytic statement that includes itself, which is to say, an analysis of her own analysis, in the sentence immediately following her statement that it is the act of analysis of the act of analysis that skews analysis in Poe, Lacan, and Derrida is her way of announcing her strategy at the start. It is not that Johnson will do anything different in her essay from what Lacan and Derrida have done in theirs. Indeed, it is not clear that she thinks that anything different can be done at this point inasmuch as Lacan and Derrida have already replayed the structure of the tale in a critical register by acting out the game of even and odd in their opposing positions. What will be different in her version is that these positions will be repeated with a complete awareness of their implications, a total critical self-consciousness that aims to create an insight without a blind spot; for what is at

issue here is not so much whether one's critical argument is logically true or false, or one's reading of the tale perceptive or dull, but whether one's interpretive stance is methodologically self-aware or methodologically naive. In its translation from fiction to criticism, the project of analyzing the act of analysis becomes in effect the program of being infinitely self-conscious about self-consciousness. Or put another way, if the structure that we find in **"The Purloined Letter"** involves doubling an opponent's thought processes in order to turn his own methods against him, then the only defense against having the same strategy repeated against oneself by the next player is to produce an insight or take a position that is already self-consciously doubled back upon itself, as is the case with the type of self-including statement that says one thing grammatically but conveys its opposite rhetorically. For a position that knowingly includes itself and its opposite seems to leave no ground on which it can be undermined.

III

The commitment to an increasingly self-conscious analytic posture that animates this cumulative series of interpretations produces at last a kind of intellectual vertigo, a not uncharacteristic side-effect of thought about thought—the rational animal turning in circles to catch itself by a tale it doesn't have. And certainly no one enjoyed creating this vertiginous effect more than did Poe, an effect that he imaged as dizziness at the edge of a vortex or on the brink of a precipice. That the giddy, self-dissolving effect of thought about thought—what Johnson calls the "asymmetrical, abyssal structure" of analyzing the act of analysis—forms the continuing theme of the Dupin stories is announced in the opening sentence of the first tale, **"The Murders in the Rue Morgue."** The story begins with the narrator's lengthy prefatory remarks on the nature of the analytical power, remarks that conclude by presenting the detective story as a "commentary upon the propositions just advanced" (2: 531). But those prefatory remarks start with this curious proposition: "The mental features discoursed of as the analytical are, in themselves, but little susceptible of analysis" (2: 527). Now inasmuch as this statement initiates the narrator's own brief analysis of the analytical power, it is self-reflexive: as an analytic statement about the non-susceptibility of analysis to being analyzed, the statement is included in the class of things to which it refers, but what the statement says in effect is that analytic statements cannot wholly include themselves. In analyzing the act of analysis, self-conscious thought doubles back upon itself to discover that it cannot absolutely coincide with itself. This insight about the nature of thought is, of course, at least as old in our tradition as the philosophies of Zeno and Parmenides and as new as Gödel's proof and Borges's (and Carroll's and Royce's) map of natural size. It is the paradoxical insight that if one considers the act of thinking and the content of thought as two distinguishable things—as it seems one must in dealing with self-consciousness, with thought that is able to represent itself to itself, able to take itself as its own object—, then the attempt to analyze the act of analysis, to include wholly the act of thinking within the context of thought, will be a progression of the order n + 1 to infinity. Which is to say that there will always be one more step needed in order to make the act of thinking coincide with the content of thought.

Since the self-including gesture of analyzing the act of analysis involves a doubling back in which self-consciousness, attempting to be absolutely even with itself, finds that it is originally and essentially at odds with itself, it is not surprising that Dupin, in illustrating the way that one doubles the thought processes of an opponent, gives as an example "the game of 'even and odd'" (3: 984). In this game "one player holds in his hand a number" of marbles "and demands of another whether that number is even or odd. If the guess is right, the guesser wins one; if wrong, he loses one" (3: 984). Dupin then tells the story of an eight-year-old boy who was so good at this guessing game that he won all the marbles at his school. The boy's "mode of reasoning" involved "an identification of the reasoner's intellect with that of his opponent" (3: 984), and this doubling of the opponent's thought processes was achieved by a physical doubling of his appearance. The boy explained to Dupin: "I fashion the expression of my face, as accurately as possible, in accordance with the expression" of the opponent "and then wait to see what thoughts or sentiments arise in my mind or heart, as if to match or correspond with the expression" (3: 984-85). The narrator comments that "the identification of the reasoner's intellect with that of his opponent, depends, . . . upon the accuracy with which the opponent's intellect is admeasured" (3: 985); and Dupin, agreeing with this observation, adds that "the Prefect and his cohort fail so frequently, first, by default of this identification, and, secondly, by ill-admeasurement, or rather through non-admeasurement, of the intellect with which they are engaged. They consider only their *own* ideas of ingenuity; and, in searching for anything hidden, advert only to the modes in which *they* would have hidden it . . . but when the cunning of the individual felon is diverse in character from their own, the felon foils them, of course. This always happens when it is above their own, and very usually when it is below. They have no variation of principle in their investigations" (3: 985).

Now what is going on here? Dupin cannot be the close reasoner that he is reputed to be and not realize that

what he has just said undermines his use of the game of even and odd as an illustration of the way one doubles the thought processes of an opponent in order to be one up on him. First of all, if "the identification of the reasoner's intellect with that of his opponent, depends, . . . upon the accuracy with which the opponent's intellect is admeasured," then it cannot be that the Prefect and his men fail, "first, by default of this identification, and, secondly, by ill-admeasurement, or . . . non-admeasurement," for if the identification follows from admeasurement, the Prefect's first failure would have to be in admeasuring the opponent's intellect. And if the reason that the Prefect and his men fail so frequently in this admeasurement is that "they consider only their *own* ideas of ingenuity," that they are unable to imagine or conceive of the workings of a mind "diverse in character from their own" (always the case when the level of the mind is above their own and usually the case when it is below), then is there anything that occurs in the rest of Poe's tale that would lead us to believe this observation of Dupin's about the reason for the Prefect's failure? Which is to say, if the Prefect and his men can only catch felons whose minds are similar to their own and if what they need in this case is the ability to imagine the workings of a mind radically different from their own, then does Dupin's method of outwitting the Minister provide us with any evidence that this ability to imagine a mind radically different from one's own really exists? In fact, isn't all of the tale's emphasis on the resemblance between Dupin and the Minister, on their possessing the same dual creative/resolvent power, part of a plot line in which Dupin outwits the Minister only because their minds are so much alike? Isn't it precisely because the Minister has hidden the letter at his residence in the same way that the Queen hid it in the royal boudoir—by turning it over and leaving it out in the open—that Dupin already knows where to look for the letter when he visits the Minister? And doesn't Dupin recover the letter by replaying the same scenario by which the Minister originally stole it?

Isn't all this simply a device to make us realize that it is impossible to imagine or conceive of a mind whose workings are radically different from one's own? We don't have any direct access to another's thoughts. Our ideas of the workings of another person's mind may be derived from what that person says or does or tells us he is thinking, but our ideas of another's mind are still *our* ideas, a projection that we make of another mind's otherness to one's own based on the only immediate experience that one's mind has of psychic otherness, the self's original otherness to itself, that difference that constitutes personal identity. In his story **"Morella"** (1835) Poe quotes Locke's definition of personal identity as "the sameness of a rational being" (2: 226). But one immediately thinks, "Sameness as opposed to what?" For in differential terms, it makes no sense to speak of the rational being's continuing sameness with itself unless there is also a sense in which the rational being is continually different from itself. In **"Morella"** Poe says, "Since by person we understand an intelligent essence having reason, and since there is a consciousness which always accompanies thinking, it is this consciousness which makes every one to be that which he calls 'himself'—thereby distinguishing him from other beings that think, and giving him his personal identity" (2: 226). It is this difference of thought from itself—which Poe evokes here as the difference between thinking and "a consciousness which always accompanies thinking"—that enables the rational being to recognize its sameness with itself and thus recognize its difference from others, distinguish itself "from other beings that think." It is precisely because the self's thought of another mind's otherness to it reflects the otherness of thought to itself that the effort to imagine the thought processes of an opponent produces a specular, antithetical double of the self, the self's own projection of psychic difference. And consequently, for all that **"The Purloined Letter"** purports to be about the way in which one effects "an identification of the reasoner's intellect with that of his opponent," it is in fact about that psychic difference which permits thought to be identified with itself, that difference which constitutes self-identity but which prevents thought from ever absolutely coinciding with itself, indeed, which constitutes self-identity precisely *because* it prevents thought from being absolutely even with itself. And it is this difference, this condition of self-conscious thought's being originally and essentially at odds with itself, that Poe evokes at the very start of the Dupin stories when he says that the "mental features discoursed of as the analytical are, in themselves, but little susceptible of analysis."

As is often the case in his fiction, Poe, using the picture language of radicals, emblematizes this latent meaning on the level of etymology, a level to which he explicitly directs our attention in **"The Purloined Letter"** when he has Dupin, in arguing against those who equate analysis with algebra, remark, "If a term is of any importance—if words derive any value from applicability—then 'analysis' conveys 'algebra' about as much as, in Latin, 'ambitus' implies 'ambition,' 'religio,' 'religion,' or 'homines honesti,' a set of *honorable* men" (3: 987). Since in each of these examples an English word has a meaning different from that of its Latin root, the inference seems clear: in **"The Purloined Letter"** "if a term is of any importance," we should submit that term to philological analysis to see

if the root from which it derives has different or additional meanings compared to its English form, meanings that might alter, reverse, or deepen the significance of the passages in which these words appear.

Let me apply this principle suggested by Dupin's remark to two interlocking pairs of words in the tale. On his first visit, the Prefect introduces the affair of the letter like this: "The fact is, the business is *very* simple indeed, and I make no doubt that we can manage it sufficiently well ourselves; but then I thought Dupin would like to hear the details of it, because it is so excessively *odd.*" To which Dupin replies, "Simple and odd" (3: 975). Dupin's emphatic repetition of the words is meant to fix them in our minds so that later when he describes the game of even and odd, we hear the echo and link the pairs. And to make sure that we don't miss the connection, Dupin, immediately after mentioning the game of even and odd, says, "This game is simple" (3: 984).

Simple, even, odd—what are their roots? The word "simple" comes from the Latin *simplex,* meaning "single," "unmixed," "uncompounded."[7] The word "even" derives from the Anglo-Saxon *efne,* meaning "flat," "level," and ultimately from the Indo-European base ★*im-nos-*, meaning "what is the same," and containing the adverbial base ★*im-*, meaning "just like" (p. 503). The word "odd" derives from the Old Norse *oddi,* meaning a "point of land, triangle, hence (from the third angle) odd number" (p. 1017). Three words and at the root of each a number—simple, single, *one*; even, things just alike, *two*; odd, a triangular point of land, *three*. And these three words are grouped into two pairs—simple/odd, even/odd—that contain, as it were, four syntactic places between them which the three words fill by having one of the words repeated. The doubling of the word "odd" links the two pairs; it gives them their element of sameness, evoking that condition of being at odds with itself, that difference with itself, which constitutes the sameness of a rational being (a condition of being at odds with itself that is most clearly perceived when thought tries to be absolutely even with itself). The three words—both through their meanings and through the way that they are paired and linked—are an emblem of the numerical structure that governs the tale, which is to say, of the numerical steps or geometrical patterns that self-consciousness goes through in trying to analyze itself.

Dupin says that the game of even and odd is simple, and throughout the Dupin stories Poe associates simplicity with the highest, purest form of ratiocination. It is in this vein that Dupin suggests to the Prefect on his first visit that "the very simplicity" of the affair of the letter constitutes its oddness: "Perhaps the mystery is a little *too* plain . . . A little *too* self-evident" (3:

975). And later Dupin says that the Minister, in hiding the letter, "would be driven, as a matter of course, to *simplicity,* if not deliberately induced to it as a matter of choice" (3: 989). As in that "game of puzzles . . . played upon a map" (3: 989), the Minister would choose a hiding place that would "escape observation by dint of being excessively obvious," relying on the fact that "the intellect suffers to pass unnoticed those considerations which are too obtrusively and too palpably self-evident" (3: 990). But what is that simple thing whose very simplicity makes it so odd, that thing which is so mysterious because so obvious, hiding out in the open "immediately beneath the nose of the whole world" (3: 990)? What but self-consciousness, that condition of being at odds with itself that constitutes the sameness, the singleness, the simplicity of a rational being?

By definition a number is odd if when the number is divided by two, there is a remainder of one. And by that definition the first odd number is three. In that simple game of even and odd in which self-consciousness analyzes itself, the question inevitably arises as to whether, when the mind's desire to be absolutely even with itself is divided into the mind's essential condition of being at odds with itself, the one that is always left over is the same as the number one that precedes two, that is, the same as that mythic, original, undivided unity prior to all paring/pairing. Or put another way, when the mind tries to make the act of thinking coincide absolutely with the content of thought only to find that there is always one more step needed to achieve this coincidence, is the infinite progression that results simply the mirror image, the antithetical double, of a Zenonian infinite regression which, by dividing a quantity in half, then dividing the half in half, then dividing the quarter in half and so on to infinity, seeks a lower limit, a part that cannot be halved again, a thing so small that, being indivisible, it represents an undivided unity, an original one? Poe is too good both as philosopher and philologist not to know that the simple thing that is self-consciousness could never be as simple as that. Indeed, if the mind were ever able to make the act of thinking and the content of thought coincide absolutely so that there was no difference between them, then self-consciousness, that self-identity constituted by thought's difference from itself, would simply go out like a light. Such an undifferentiated one would be indistinguishable from zero. Though the root of the word "simple," the Latin *simplex,* means "single," "unmixed," "un-compounded," the roots of the word *simplex*—the Latin words *semel,* meaning "once," "a single time," and *plico,* meaning "to fold, fold together"[8]—make it clear that to be unmixed or uncompounded does not mean to be undifferentiated. For in

the picture language of these radicals we can see that a thing which is single-fold is something—like a sheet of paper, a letter—that in being folded a single time is doubled back upon itself. That the image of self-consciousness as a *simple* fold doubling an inscribed surface back on itself was in Poe's mind when he plotted the folding/re-folding of the purloined letter can be inferred from an 1845 poem on folding money called "Epigram For Wall Street" attributed to him:

> I'll tell you a plan for gaining wealth,
>   Better than banking, trade or leases—
> Take a bank note and fold it up,
>   And then you will find your money in *creases*!
> This wonderful plan, without danger or loss,
>   Keeps your cash in your hands, where nothing can trouble it;
> And every time that you fold it across,
>   'Tis as plain as the light of the day that you *double* it!

(1: 378)

The infinite progression implicit in the analysis of the act of analysis is evoked at the end of **"The Purloined Letter"** with the revelation of Dupin's revenge on the Minister, for this attempt by a mastermind to get even with his specular double clearly serves as a figure of the analytic mind's attempt at mastery, its attempt to be absolutely even with itself. Knowing that the Minister "would feel some curiosity in regard to the identity of the person who had outwitted him" (3: 993), Dupin leaves him a clue by substituting for the purloined letter one containing a quotation from Crébillon's *Atrée* copied out in Dupin's own handwriting, a hand with which the Minister "is well acquainted" (3: 993). In signing his deed, Dupin marks it as revenge, which is to say, he insures that the Minister will interpret his actions not simply as the paid intervention of a gifted amateur sleuth or a duel of wits between two of the cleverest men in Paris, but as a repayment for the evil turn which the Minister did Dupin at Vienna. For I take it that the satisfaction of revenge requires—except in those cases where it is carried out on a substitute—a moment of revelation in which the object of revenge learns by whom, and for what, he is being paid back, a point that Poe underlines by having Dupin choose his quotation-signature from just such a revelatory moment in an eighteenth-century revenger's tragedy. And yet from what we know of the Minister it is inconceivable that once he learned of Dupin's revenge he would let the matter rest there—and equally inconceivable that his double would not know this. For though it might seem that with Dupin's revenge the score between them is even at one apiece (one bad turn at Vienna repaid by one bad turn at Paris), if the Minister allows Dupin's trick to go unanswered, then Dupin will have had the last turn; and as proverbial wisdom assures us, the last word or the last laugh is not just one word or one laugh like any other. The power to say the last word or have the last laugh, the power to bring a series of reciprocal actions to an end, like the power to originate, involves the notion of a one that is simultaneously more than one. Consequently, we are left with the paradoxical situation in which Dupin's outwitting of the Minister will constitute an evening of the score between them at one apiece only if the Minister *does not* allow Dupin's trick to end the series, does not allow it to be that one last turn which in its finality is always more than one. It is not so much that one bad turn deserves another as that one bad turn demands another if it is to be experienced as simply one turn. All of which emphasizes the mutually constitutive contradictoriness of seeking *to get even* with a specular double *by being one up on him.*

In using the affair of the letter to even an old score, Dupin gives up his "objective," fourth position as an apparently disinterested observer of the triangular structure of King, Queen, and Minister described by the Prefect in order to insert himself for personal reasons into the third position of an analogous triangle in which the police and the Minister occupy respectively the first and second positions. Similarly, in describing this triangular structure in which Dupin shifts the Minister from the third to the second position, Lacan would himself appear to occupy an "objective," fourth position as a disinterested observer outside the triangle. Yet to a supposedly more objective observer of Lacan's position such as Derrida, Lacan's description is not disinterested at all, but simply a psychoanalyst's imposition of the structure of the Oedipal triangle on a double story, an imposition that, though it seems to be made from an objective fourth position outside the triangle, has the effect of inserting Lacan into the third position of a triangle in which the psychoanalyst's "objective" unmasking of the personal motive that lies behind Dupin's "disinterested" involvement in the affair of the letter shifts Dupin into the second position and his double the Minister into the first. Or so says Derrida from a fourth position outside Lacan's triangle, a fourth position that will itself be shifted in turn. This mechanism by which the shifting from the third to the second position within the triangle is extended (as a supposedly more objective point of view is assumed from which to observe the subjective triangle), and thus becomes the shifting from a fourth position outside the triangle to the third position within it, evokes the infinite regression that, in this quest for absolute self-consciousness, accompanies infinite progression as its shadow image. For while the progressive series moves in one direction in its flight from subjective involvement, in its termless search for an absolutely objective point of view from which to ex-

amine the self, it only exists *as a series* because of the regressive movement of consciousness, because of the retrospective gaze that keeps all the earlier terms of the series in view so that they are perceived as related, as serial in character. Thus the mental step that one takes in order to separate the self from itself, to distinguish absolutely the observer from the observed, is always a backward step, a step in the opposite direction from the one in which we are looking.

Notes

A shorter version of this essay was delivered at the annual meeting of the Poe Studies Association in 1981 at the kind invitation of Kent Ljungquist and Ben Fisher. The essay is part of a book entitled *The Mystery to a Solution: Poe, Borges, and the Analytic Detective Story* presently being completed.

1. Raymond Chandler, "The Simple Art of Murder," in *Detective Fiction: Crime and Compromise,* eds. Dick Allen and David Chacko (New York: Harcourt Brace Jovanovich, 1974), p. 398.

2. Edgar Allan Poe, *Collected Works of Edgar Allan Poe,* ed. Thomas Ollive Mabbott, 3 vols. (Cambridge, Mass.: Harvard University Press, 1969-78), 2: 521n. All subsequent quotations from Poe are taken from this edition.

3. Jorge Luis Borges, "Ibn Hakkan al-Bokhari, Dead in His Labyrinth," in *The Aleph and Other Stories, 1933-1969,* trans. Norman Thomas di Giovanni (New York: E. P. Dutton, 1978), p. 123. All subsequent quotations from Borges's fiction are taken from this edition.

4. Jacques Lacan, "Seminar on 'The Purloined Letter'," trans. Jeffrey Mehlman, *Yale French Studies* 48 (1972), p. 41. Unless otherwise noted, all subsequent quotations from the "Seminar on 'The Purloined Letter'" are taken from this edition.

5. Barbara Johnson, "The Frame of Reference: Poe, Lacan, Derrida," in *The Critical Difference* (Baltimore: The Johns Hopkins University Press, 1980), p. 118. All subsequent quotations from Johnson are taken from this edition.

6. Jacques Derrida, "The Purveyor of Truth," trans. W. Domingo, J. Hulbert, M. Ron, and M. -R. Logan, *Yale French Studies* 52 (1975), p. 100. All subsequent quotations from Derrida are taken from this edition.

7. *Webster's New World Dictionary of the American Language,* College Edition (Cleveland and New York: World Publishing Co., 1964), p. 1359, "simple." The etymologies of "even" and "odd" are also taken from this edition.

8. D. P. Simpson, *Cassell's Latin Dictionary* (New York: Macmillan, 1978), p. 556, "simplex."

Dennis Porter (essay date spring 1988)

SOURCE: Porter, Dennis. "Of Poets, Politicians, Policemen, and the Power of Analysis." *New Literary History* 19, no. 3 (spring 1988): 501-19.

[*In the following essay, Porter surveys the psychological power structures uncovered in psychoanalysis and the subtext of patriarchal power in Poe's tale.*]

Although they disagree energetically on so much else, few contemporary commentators are likely to deny the consensus that has emerged concerning Poe's third and final Dupin story, a consensus that finds there the fascinating tale of loins, letters, and pur- or partial blindness announced in its title.[1] If **"The Purloined Letter"** is a locus classicus of the new literary history—or, what amounts to the same thing, a terrain on which to exercise the differences between current theories—it is because it manages to conjoin those questions of sexuality and of language, of seeing and of the retreat from meaning, which for some time now have preoccupied contemporary critics of certain persuasions.[2] To judge by its effects, this knowing text was also already aware of the unconscious, even if it declined to name it.

Exploring the implications of Lacan's reading of **"The Purloined Letter"** for any future consideration of the relationship between psychoanalysis and literature, Shoshana Felman offers a number of decisive formulations of what the Poe and the Lacan texts do for each other.[3] By way of summarizing her arguments, she refers in no less than three places to the allegorical character of the Poe tale. She speaks of it as "an allegory of psychoanalysis" (138), as "an allegory of psychoanalytic reading" (140), and, finally, as "not just an allegory of psychoanalysis but also, at the same time, an allegory of poetic writing" (144). To this triple affirmation of the tale's allegorical status, I would like to add a fourth. This reading of **"The Purloined Letter"** will focus on Poe's text as an allegory of relations of power insofar as they are manifested in what the author himself calls "analysis." I will then go on to draw out some of the implications of Poe's thinking on that subject for psychoanalysis before and after Lacan. The purpose is to contextualize the story differently, to reframe it yet again, but in such a way that my reading places itself athwart (if that is ever really possible) and not in continuity with recent psychoanalytic or deconstructive readings.

Relations of power are, on the whole, what previous commentators on **"The Purloined Letter"** overlook[4]—overlooking being that which, as we all now know, any interpretive project always does in the construction of its interpretation. Every act of reading is, I take it, both an act of looking and overlooking, of seeing and failing to see; this is a condition of its efficacy. And it is precisely this which is thematized by Poe, first, in the failure of the second "exalted personage"—the story does not call him "king" anymore than it calls the queen "a queen"—to "see" the first "illustrious personage's" letter; second, in the Prefect's blindness to what is most apparent; and, third, in the Minister D—'s sudden myopia in relation to Dupin. It is, in fact, such an overlooking—as structurally determined for at least two of the positions in the analytical situation—that is the main theme of Lacan's seminar on the work.

What my own look will attempt to bring into focus are those elements in **"The Purloined Letter"** that, taken together, raise the possibility that Poe was, so to speak, a genealogist *avant la lettre*. Following Nietzsche, Foucault defined the genealogist as someone who historicizes everything, including categories, beliefs, and morals. The genealogist is alert to the vicissitudes of history in general, as well as to its "systems of subjections" and its "hazardous play of dominations" in particular.[5] Not the least interest of this tale of the early 1840s, therefore, lies in that it puts into play those apparently separate and heterogeneous entities that are poetry, politics, and the police in connection with its master concept of "analysis." And it does so in such a way as to break down the old entities in order to disclose unsuspected affinities between them. In other words, it turns out that in its complexity, Poe's story invites a reading that sees it as both a manifestation of the discourse of power of the new disciplinary society, about which Foucault wrote so illuminatingly, and a text that puts the discursive practices of that society on display.

* * *

That in all three Dupin stories questions of relations of power are thematized in a variety of ways is not difficult to demonstrate. In the first and probably most popular of the stories—in the tale that is generally assumed to have furnished the prototype for the detective story genre, **"The Murders in the Rue Morgue"**—the relationship between analysis and power is emphasized from the beginning. Power, in the form of an "analytical power"[6] exercised by superior minds over others, is celebrated there by the narrator from the opening lines. Therefore, because I believe, after Jacques Derrida, that it is important to remember there are three Dupin stories, three variations on a scene of crime or scenario of power with significant structural repetitions, I will look first at the familiar opening pages of **"The Murders in the Rue**

Morgue" before turning to **"The Purloined Letter."** In what amounts to a preface to the trilogy, the language which Poe's narrator employs in celebration of "the analyst" is of particular interest because, as always, it tells us more than it knows.

"The mental features discoursed of as the analytical are, in themselves, but little susceptible of analysis. We appreciate them only in their effects. We know of them, among other things, that they are always to their possessor, when inordinately possessed, a source of the liveliest enjoyment. As the strong man exults in his physical ability, delighting in such exercises as call his muscles into action, so glories the analyst in that moral activity which *disentangles*" (397, Poe's emphasis). What is established from the third sentence on is a relationship between "analysis" (as a faculty of mind), "possession" ("when inordinately possessed"), and pleasure ("the liveliest enjoyment") that can only be described as autoerotic.[7] The following sentence goes on to evoke the category of "the analyst" in order to reinforce the sense that what is most apparent in the activity of analysis is a form of narcissistic play by a "strong man" of the mind (who "exults," "glories"). It is worth noting that in his comparison, the narrator has recourse to a visual image in which the tenor of the metaphor is less significant than its vehicle, the "strong man" and his "muscles." Thus Poe's analyst is *visualized* in terms of that self-contemplating perfect wholeness which characterizes the imaginary register. Moreover, in this opening image, it is male narcissism that is invoked and a male body/mind that is on display.

Further, analysis is defined as "that moral activity which *disentangles*." From the context, it seems that "moral" is to be understood as a cognate of *moraliste* in the French sense, that is, belonging to that familiar tradition of peculiarly French writers or worldly philosophers, admired by Nietzsche, who from Montaigne to Stendhal tended to use skeptical aphorisms in their commentary on human conduct.[8]

Disentangling, in any case, has no necessary connection with the idea of "the moral" in its more usual sense, both because it is associated with the sadistic sport of taking apart[9] and because it exercises itself just as readily on unimportant as on important things with no goal beyond the putting of itself into play: "He [the analyst] derives pleasure from even the most trivial occupations bringing his talent into play. He is fond of enigmas, of conundrums, of hieroglyphics; exhibiting in his solutions of each a degree of *acumen* which appears to the ordinary apprehension praeternatural" (397). The word I would highlight here (alongside Poe's) is "exhibiting," both because it repeats the powerful element of narcissism referred to

above and because it suggests the desire to underline the distance between the "analyst" and "ordinary apprehension," which can only remain in awe of such ascendancy. Even before the narrator goes on to discuss draughts and whist as the games which best exercise the analytical faculty in the art of establishing power over others, it is clear that the pleasures of potency, of possession, and of self-possession are all engaged.

Beyond this, the first four pages of **"The Murders in the Rue Morgue"** proceed to confirm that the analyst's narcissism needs to be continually reaffirmed in the look of defeated opponents. Analysis is a form of power which, in order to know and take pleasure in itself, must be continually exercised in a variety of agonistic encounters. As defined by the story, analysis is a kind of reasoning that always involves an outreasoning, of wit that is outwitting. It is thus no accident that the higher powers of the "reflective intellect" are more adequately tested by "the unostentatious game of draughts than by all the elaborate frivolity of chess" (397). It is in draughts rather than chess that the analyst's technique of insight through identification with an opponent is shown to best advantage.

If whist is also given prominence, it is because it shows in simplified form power/knowledge in action. The traditional card game offers a scene of confrontation in which are reenacted "the endlessly repeated play of dominations."[10] For the genealogist, it is such a play that characterizes the relations between individuals and groups at all levels of life and in all situations: "proficiency in whist implies capacity for success *in all those more important undertakings where mind struggles with mind*" (398, my emphasis). The narrator's choice of words here underlines the sheer worldliness of that "reflective intellect" which romantic thought had sought to assimilate to the otherworldly and the spiritual—or, in a word, the poetical. It is, in other terms, a view of analysis that already connects it to the public as well as to the private life, to politics and to policing as well as to poetry—and, in our time, to psychoanalysis itself.

In this connection, it is significant that Poe's successful player of whist is well-practiced in the art of surveillance. In the dialogic encounter of a game, everything is subsumed to the law of signification; nothing is assumed to be irrelevant or external to the purpose of overpowering an opponent. As a result, he scrutinizes the countenances, expressions, minute gestures of partner and opponent alike, and is attentive not only to their acts and acting but, like a good psychoanalyst, also to their accidents: "He recognizes what is played through feint, by the air with which it is thrown upon the table. A casual or inadvertent word; the accidental dropping or turning of a card, with the accompanying anxiety or carelessness in regard to its concealment; the counting of the tricks, with the order of their arrangement; embarrassment, hesitation, eagerness or trepidation—all afford, to his apparently intuitive perception, indications of the true state of affairs" (399).

For Poe's ideal player of whist, then, as for Freud, all behavior is motivated behavior. But it would be a mistake to read into Poe's celebration of the player/analyst a psychopathology of the whist table. The "mind analysis" described in the opening "propositions" of **"The Murders in the Rue Morgue"**—as opposed, perhaps, to the tale that is the narrative "commentary" on them—is not psychoanalysis.[11] Poe's player/analyst, who will receive a fuller characterization in the *chevalier* C. Auguste Dupin himself, seems rather to be the intextualization of a fantasy of omnipotence as clairvoyance, of a mind that reads minds—"The true state of affairs." If Dupin was produced fully formed as the prototype of the Great Detective, it is chiefly because he embodies the myth of the potential transparency of the human world, its openness to surveillance. To that extent at least, Poe's Dupin stories are not external to the discourse of disciplinary power in his time but implicated in it.

If such already seems to be the case with **"The Murders in the Rue Morgue,"** it is more patently so with **"The Purloined Letter."** In the opening chapter of *Story and Situation*, Ross Chambers suggests that a study like his should eventually open "onto ideological and cultural analysis of those enabling agreements, that is, onto what Clifford Geertz might call 'thick description.' *Sarrasine* is as embedded in the male-female relationships of Paris in the 1830s as **'The Purloined Letter'** is in a certain American mercantilism."[12]

In the case of the Dupin stories, such "thick description" would also need to emphasize the emergence in Western Europe as well as in the United States of modern urban and industrialized life, of mass living and of that disciplinary society buttressed by newly centralized agencies of state power, including increasingly professionalized and scientific policing. The role of those "human sciences" that arose during the Enlightenment in the establishment of the disciplines is, of course, crucial to Foucault's argument. It was precisely the "human sciences" that took human bodies and human minds as their object. By means of a disciplinary anatomo-politics and a regulatory bio-politics, they transformed those bodies and minds into productive citizens and self-regulated subjects. It was the "human sciences" that made possible the fixing and surveillance of populations in the complex, new urban

spaces of barracks, prisons, clinics, factories, schools, city neighborhoods, and even homes. It is, in fact, the populous and dangerous city—"polluted Paris"—whose crimes already constituted a staple of the new mass circulation press, which especially informs the criminal investigation of **"The Mystery of Marie Roget."**

A valid "thick description" of Poe's tales would also require a consideration of the place of poetry and of the poet in the new order which emerged after the eclipse of the *ancien régime*. Whereas in courtly and aristocratic society the poet had the kind of connection to political power evoked by Raymond Williams in *The Country and the City*[13]—a connection through various forms of patronage—in post-revolutionary French society or in the United States, his place came increasingly to be redefined as that of exile in his own land. Thus it is no accident if Poe's supreme analyst is represented as a man of letters with a poet's imagination, as a decadent, and, before Baudelaire, as a nocturnal *flâneur* in the streets of the modern city, streets that he shared with the criminal underclass and with the police that map its movements. Modernism in literature was born with the emergence of the poet as a social outcast or *poète maudit*.

The chief interest of **"The Purloined Letter"** from the point of view of the present essay is that, more clearly than in either **"The Murders in the Rue Morgue"** or **"The Mystery of Marie Roget,"** the political question is brought out into the open and connected to the questions of poetry and policing. Where in **"The Rue Morgue"** [**"The Murders in the Rue Morgue"**] Dupin as poet is confronted with the Prefect of police, that is, with the head of the state apparatus responsible for imposing order, in **"Marie Roget"** [**"The Mystery of Marie Roget"**] it is above all the editors of the mass circulation newspapers who prove unequal to the challenge of Dupin's poetic imagination—in the mythology of Romanticism, the newspaperman figures alongside the policeman and the businessman as a type of antipoet.

In **"The Purloined Letter"** the case is then explicitly political. Dupin's principal adversary there is not the Prefect—he had proven himself inadequate in the earlier stories—but a leading politician; a minister, no less. Thus Dupin's victory over him signifies the victory of a man with nothing more valuable than the discredited *ancien régime* title of *chevalier* over the power of the police and that of a contemporary political officeholder. *Chevalier* (Knight) is not only an archaic title that signified in the 1830s loss of status and of power; it also implies continuity with the chivalric code that tested male self-worth through combat and service to womankind—a chivalric code that was also at the time enjoying a revival in Poe's own lost South among Southern gentlemen. It is in any case the *chevalier* who in the story proves to be not only the most "poetical" but also the most "political," and he does so, in effect, by collapsing those categories.

"Marie Roget" had already developed the fantasy of the poet/analyst as a powerful and admired figure, as someone in the public eye: "It may readily be supposed that the part played by my friend, in the drama at the Rue Morgue, had not failed of its impression upon the fancies of the Parisian police. With its emissaries, the name of Dupin had grown into a household word" (507-8). **"The Purloined Letter"** is even more obviously a tale of policing in which, the narrator informs us, the political stakes are especially high. In the Prefect's first account of the theft in that story, he is at pains to emphasize the national political significance of the theft and the stature of the figures involved. Both the loss and the gain of power here concern politics in the narrowest sense of that word. It is "an affair demanding the greatest secrecy": possession of the letter gives "its holder a certain power in a certain quarter where such power is immensely valuable," gives, in fact, "an ascendency over the illustrious personage"; it is a question of "a personage of most exalted station." Finally, the Prefect acknowledges, "the power thus attained has, for some months past, been wielded, for political purposes, to a very dangerous extent" (681-83). Yet what these purposes were and the nature of the danger involved are not disclosed, any more than the contents of the stolen letter are disclosed, because they are, in fact, irrelevant to the structure of Poe's allegory.

The anecdote in the tale that best illustrates the practice of analysis and its connection with power concerns once again a game, but this time the game is even simpler than draughts or whist and has even more the character of a paradigmatic confrontation between minds—namely, the schoolboy game of "even and odd." Like Dupin himself, the eight-year-old boy he describes excited in his sphere "universal admiration" for his prowess at "outguessing" his opponents and, as a consequence, won all the marbles in his school. Dupin's example is significant because it once again combines the motifs of potency, possession, and, indirectly, of self-display. It also emphasizes that unlike the outmoded investigative techniques of the Prefect, Dupin's "art of policing" is methodologically self-conscious in addressing the criminal as individual subject: "Of course he had some principle of guessing; and this lay in mere observation and admeasurement of the astuteness of his opponents" (689).

From such descriptions, it is possible to see that what Poe calls "analysis" is analogous to one of Foucault's "dubious sciences." It is a form of will to knowledge

that is buttressed by a body of theory and a concomitant microtechnique for the purpose of exercising power and of obtaining the rewards of power. Bentham's Panopticon seems to be once again an appropriate model for what Poe is thinking about. If Dupin was to become the prototype of the Great Detective of popular fiction, it is precisely because he functions in the social body as an unseen seer who can look right into men's souls: "He boasted to me, with a low chuckling laugh, that most men, in respect to himself, wore windows in their bosoms" (401). If the site of power in disciplinary society is a place from which one sees without being seen, then within the terms of Poe's narrative, Dupin occupies such a site even as he moves about the city of Paris. He prefers a dark room when he engages in analysis, he surrounds himself with a veil of smoke, he plays roles and dons disguises (the "green spectacles") in order to conceal his observations.

The performance of the schoolboy analyst seen alongside that of Dupin suggests in yet another respect—a further effect of repetition—that **"The Purloined Letter"** can be read as an allegory of relations of power. For a boy in a nineteenth-century schoolyard to end up with all the marbles is to achieve a degree of domination for which it is difficult to find an equivalent in adult life. Those of us who can still remember the thrill of a pocket swollen with marbles will recognize there a signifier of potency and of self-possession calculated to excite an unusual quantity of pleasure in Dupin's young reasoner. Yet it is a very similar kind of pleasure that Dupin procures for himself when he by no means disdains to accept the reward of the Prefect's check: "[The Prefect] *finally filled up* [not *out* but *up*] and signed a check for fifty thousand francs, and handed it across the table to Dupin. The latter *examined it carefully* and deposited it in his pocket-book" (688, my emphasis). For a nineteenth-century gentleman, a "pocket-book" was, I take it, as good as a pocket for a schoolboy.

Moreover, the significance of the schoolyard is that, unlike home and family, it is a place without fathers. Relations of power there are not between generations but between peers; consequently, the mythic model which presides over the tale is not that of Oedipus but precisely the one invoked by Dupin himself in the quotation from the *Atrée* of Crébillon *fils*—namely, that of two brothers, Atreus and Thyestes. Like Crébillon's tragedy, **"The Purloined Letter"** is also a tale of two brothers. As previous commentators have noted, various clues in Poe's text invite a reading that views the rivalry of Dupin and the Minister as fraternal, even before Dupin's final citation yokes their names to a mythic destiny. Do not both their names begin with "D"? Have they not known each other for some time? Are they not both poets in their way? "'But is this really the poet?' I asked. 'There are two brothers, I know; and both have attained reputation in letters'" (691).

It is then difficult to avoid acknowledging that at one level Poe's story concerns a deadly serious political game. Just as **"The Purloined Letter"** opens with references to a given political situation, it ends in the same way. Even if Dupin does not disclose "the content" of his politics, any more than he reveals the content of the Queen's letter, as opposed to his own flagrant substitution (another conundrum), he does admit he is at least *aussi royaliste que la reine*: "'You know my political prepossessions. In this matter, I act as a partisan of the lady concerned. For eighteen months the Minister has had her in his power. She has now him in hers; since, being unaware that the letter is not in his possession, he will proceed with his exactions as if it was. Thus will he inevitably commit himself, at once, to his political destruction'" (697).

The difference here is between two styles of political behavior, that of a Minister and that of a *chevalier*, but the frequent harshness of Dupin's language leaves no doubt that relations of power are involved for both parties. Whereas a politician of the first kind is shown to be a *"monstrum horrendum*, an unprincipled man of genius," a politician who is also a *chevalier* hides his political will behind the mask of chivalry or of loyal service to a Queen's cause. However, isn't "the partisan of the lady" the one who in the end has "her in his power"? In the complicated agonistic game of possession of the Queen's letter—pre-possession, dispossession, re-possession—the two men of letters or brother poets turn out to be fratricidal politicians, such that it is impossible to tell which is the more dangerous.

It is also impossible to tell—and it is here in Poe's text that one recognizes the subtlety of the genealogist—where the poet ends and the politician begins. Dupin proves himself indeed, with his final theatrical flourish, the Minister's double, a *poetician*. Who can tell, given the ambiguities of the tale's political "content"—the text's own "diplomatic cant"—which of the two is on the side of the right? Which the morally upright or politically "correct" brother? All we learn is that an "evil turn" done in the imperial city of Vienna is repaid with interest by a destructive deed perpetrated in another capital of imperial power, Paris.[14]

In fact, the tale also permits us—but how could it deny a master discourse that comes after?—to read the difference between the two D—s as a difference in relation to the castration complex. Doesn't the Minister

reanimate the fraternal rivalry by exposing through his theft—that purr-loining, pussy-raid—the fact of castration on the site of the maternal body itself? A close reading of the passage that I do not have the space to develop here confirms, in fact, how overdetermined Poe's text is in this respect.

I would simply note that the Minister's theft of the Queen's letter—he "fathoms her secret" (682)—is in context tantamount to exposing the fact of castration. Doesn't the *chevalier*, on the other hand, through his act of restoration of the letter to its "rightful place," manage in the end to make the female "exalted personage" (Queen/Mother) whole again? Moreover, can't we interpret his act as motivated by the will to deny sexual difference, with its threat of castration, and to preserve his imaginary relationship to her? In which case Dupin's monarchism is no more than the effect of a fetishism that strives to keep intact the (maternal) body politic (*la* patrie, *la* nation). Poe's tale of two sons would then have to be read as the story of a good son and a bad or, shall we say, of a split son, who simultaneously affirms and denies the fact of female castration. Perhaps the most fascinating consequence of such a reading is that it identifies Poe's hero as a fetishist who denies culturally affirmed sexual difference—a possibility that opens up a whole new approach both to the political question of "restoration" and to the mass appeal of the detective story genre, which the Dupin stories inaugurated in modern times.

Furthermore, the denouement of **"The Purloined Letter"** is of particular significance because it harks back to the opening of **"The Murders in the Rue Morgue."** If in the beginning there is a narcissistically perfect male body, at the end there is a female one restored to wholeness. In one sense at least, one could argue that if, as Lacan suggested, Dupin is "feminized" at the end, the Queen is also "masculinized." With her repossession of the letter she may once again sit firmly on her throne. In all three Dupin stories the crime involved concerns an assault on, mutilation, and/or murder of women, but it is only in the last of the three that the power of Dupin's analysis is such that he not only wins out over his rivals, but also restores the female body to a fantasized wholeness.

But it is time to return to a line of thought that is more germane to the central argument of this paper: namely, the question of analysis and relations of force, of poetry and power, as raised by Poe's text. Paradoxically, the denouement of **"The Purloined Letter"** that I have just described also manages to demythify the poet whose triumphant revenge it also celebrates. Whereas Romantic thought in general discovered in the poet's social marginality the source of his spiritual strength and the proof of his political innocence, his externality to all relations of power, Poe's tale thinks genealogically and, as a consequence, suggests that such poetic "virtue" is no more than a strategy for countering force with force. Just as "the literary" emerged during the Romantic period as a category of written texts different in kind from other more obviously purposeful forms of writing, so did "poetry" come to mean that which was peculiarly ineffable within "the literary." Yet it is to Poe's great credit—and this in spite of that posthumous adulation in France itself that celebrated in him *le Poète, "tel qu'en Lui-même enfin l'éternité le change"* (changed by eternity into himself)—that he saw, however unsteadily, what elsewhere in his time and ours has gone largely overlooked.

"The Purloined Letter" demonstrates in its own peculiar way that like the schoolboy, the policeman, and the politician—each in his different sphere—the poet, too, is an analyst equally caught up in "the endlessly repeated play of dominations." Poetry itself is a discursive practice in the Foucauldian sense with its norms and its regularities, its inclusions and exclusions—a discursive practice, moreover, that is subject to periodic breaks and supported by a whole network of nondiscursive practices and worldly institutions.

Poe's tale does not, of course, enter into a discussion of the specificities of "poetic power," but the variety of connections it suggests between poetic writing and what is still widely assumed to be external to it, if not its monstrous Other, leaves the categories of "poet," "politician," "policeman" all looking disturbingly different. It was not difficult, after Baudelaire and Mallarmé, to find Poe in *poe-etry*; but it required perhaps the intervention of a Foucault for us to discover what was always already there on the surface, "a little too evident," had we only had the eyes or "green spectacles" to see it—namely, that *poe-liceman* and *poe-litician* are rebuses that contain the same proper name.

* * *

"The Purloined Letter" leaves us with three words that will never seem quite the same again. And therein lies its *poe-etic,* which is at the same time its genealogical power. The implied insertion of that extra "e" has modified forever a stable semantic field that is also, self-evidently, a political field. By grouping the three categories together under the rubric of "analysis," Poe rethinks the relations between them. Happily for us, that word in that context—and here I come to the second and more controversial part of this article—also reaches out to touch psychoanalysis itself, which until recently at least had seemed capable of containing it easily. One of the most important problems that

the changed semantic field bequeaths us, in fact, concerns that body of psychoanalytic theory and practice which has been so influential and so controversial in our time.

Since the problem posed by Poe's story is preeminently one of "analysis" and its relations of power, I will simply follow its trajectory and make a few tentative remarks about relations of power "in psychoanalysis." Not in order to bring out possible connections between psychoanalysis, as a body of thought and as therapeutic method, and some monolithic state apparatus—although the psychiatric practices of the Gulag do not allow us to reject that out of hand as a useful avenue of inquiry—but merely to call attention to its specificity as discursive and nondiscursive practice. Perhaps Foucault's greatest lesson has been that the study of power is most illuminating when conducted from the bottom up in its multiple and overlapping local forms. We now recognize that politics, like charity, begins at home. There is a politics of the schoolyard and of the street, of the workplace and of "the health professions," as well as of presidents and parties.[15]

What, in brief, do the Dupin stories as a whole and **"The Purloined Letter"** in particular, with their various scenarios of relations of power, tell us about psychoanalysis—as well as about Lacan's contribution to the development of psychoanalytic thought?

It is, I assume, no longer possible to adopt the once familiar and heroic view of psychoanalysis as a scientifically grounded, normative, and developmental model of psychic behavior from birth to the grave.[16] It was, of course, such a body of theory together with its institutionalized practices, training methods, and therapeutic goals that was systematically castigated by Lacan, especially in the form of American ego psychology. The effect of Lacan's teaching has been to illuminate the ideology of a normative practice that managed to repress its own political unconscious. In the notorious return to Freud, in any case, it is possible to identify a politics of psychoanalysis that, as Stuart Schneiderman among others has suggested, is on one level a resistance to the geopolitical reality that made the United States after the Second World War the preeminent world power.[17]

Moreover, the fury expended over the last few decades in the French psychoanalytic movement, largely as a consequence of Lacan's interventions, has forced the issue of relations of power in previously unsuspected ways. The history of the splits and schisms, the banishments and usurpations and founding of counter-schools there, has all the virulence of those Greek myths which, both within psychoanalysis and outside it, our culture still raids for its narrative models. One might even suspect that Foucault was thinking of the postwar history of the French psychoanalytic movement, in fact, when he summarized Nietzsche on "the passion of scholars"[18]—were it not for the many other examples at hand of bitter scholarly and intellectual infighting in the French capital.

To descend to a level that is more appropriate to the dimensions of this paper and the particular problematic opened up by **"The Purloined Letter,"** I suggest that the effect of Lacanian thought has been, on the one hand, to demythify the authority of the analyst and, on the other, to remythify him differently. Lacan divested the analyst of the authority of a "subject supposed to know" and of a master through discourse of the analysand's fate. Instead of a relation between analyst and analysand of subject to object, Lacan reaffirmed the analyst's place within the dialogic structure of the analytical situation. And he did this in part by positing, in the place of countertransference, the crucial concept of the analyst's desire. As a result, he set himself in opposition to psychoanalysis as a discourse of power whose problematic prehistory is to be found in the dubious scientificity of Charcot's theater of hysteria—a theater that involved the production, before an audience, of the disorder in female patients through the application of pressure by male subjects at hysterogenic points, including the ovaries. It is no wonder hysteria has come to be regarded in certain feminist circles as a patriarchal political diagnosis.[19]

Moreover, some of the hostility that has been visited on such dubious interventionist practices—whom did they serve?—has inevitably attached itself to the early association of psychoanalysis itself with studies in hysteria.[20] To read Freud's early case histories is indeed to be struck by the continuity as well as the breaks with both Charcot and Bernheim. All the talk of massaging the patient—not yet an analysand—of the laying on of hands, of hydrotherapy, and of the application of electric charges, situates Freud's thought in a problematic that in retrospect seems not merely alien to a modern psychoanalytic sensibility, but precisely the stuff of the most dubious of "dubious sciences." Such methods from the prehistory of psychoanalysis also include hypnosis, which was obviously crucial to Breuer's "talking cure." Hypnosis required of the patient not a putting of herself into male hands but a submission to the controlling (male) look. And even after the abandonment of hypnosis, the suspicion remains that the psychoanalytic encounter has not fully divested itself of its suspect beginnings.

As in different ways both Poe and Foucault tell us, the site of maximum power, in a society that is committed to the disciplining of bodies and the normalizing of populations, is a place where one sees without being seen. It is also a place where one hears without being heard,[21] which is to say not unlike the traditional place of the analyst—behind the analysand's prone body and out of her line of sight, a place from which to listen even more than to observe. Thus the analytical space is not unlike the enclosed space of the confessional. Both are materially constructed, as Foucault implies in his history of the confession as a political technology, to promote "confidences," to induce the subject/object to speak the truth of herself in the interrupted dialogue with the disembodied voice of the interlocutor.

Further, the "talking cure" implies an orgy of listening and a master listener, who is the director of a theatrical encounter that requires him to divest himself of personhood and play a prescribed role. He is no more, in theory, than a mere vis-à-vis who, via transference, is to be sexed and aged by the analysand. What the analyst does not control, any more than does the analysand, is the script. And once again it has been Lacan's insistence that has made us more acutely aware of this. The movements of the transference in the analytic situation dictate those unforeseeable adventures in language of two desires brought into a close proximity that, under other circumstances, connotes intimacy. The Lacanian algebra of the four discourses—those of The Master, The Hysteric, The University, and The Analyst—conveniently suggests, in the shifting positions of agent and other, how radical is Lacan's problematization of the traditional subject/object relation of medicalized therapies.

Nevertheless, the suspicion remains among skeptical laymen that the analyst is also a listening post by means of which "society" may overhear and correct the pathologies produced within it at the level of individual subjects. Psychoanalysis, like all forms of psychotherapy, is more labor-intensive than Bentham's Panoptic prison, since the relation of observer to observed is one to one; but it is potentially no less effective as a form of social control.

If Lacan demythified the analyst, however, he also remythified him, possibly in spite of himself. And he did this most clearly in the analyst's function as "teacher" and "author." I would like, in fact, to suggest that Lacan devised for each of these functions a new "theatrics" and a new "poetics" which would be more consistently psychoanalytic than anything seen before, and in which the discourses of the Master and of the University are subverted respectively by the discourses of the Hysteric and the Analyst. Both the new "theatrics" and the new "poetics" involve an acting out and an acting up, a foregrounding of language production as a writing (the *Écrits*) and as a speaking (the

Séminaires), such that theory always remains embodied and subject to re-vision at the moment of its articulation. The threat of slippage is always there. The result is, of course, the notoriously knotted and allusive style of his writing and of his speaking. "La communication," Lacan commented in a lecture at the University of Louvain, "ça fait rire."

It is apparent that for Lacan the lesson of psychoanalysis—and the meaning of the return to Freud—was that the only "true discourse" is one that is self-subversive, one that enacts the precariousness of its control. Lacan's is, therefore, a form of writing that demands to be read differently from traditional expository writing. It strives to be the practice of its own theory. Through the attention it pays to the dance of its own signifiers and to the patterns they are seen to trace *après coup,* it is analyst and analysand at the same time. Yet it is in large measure because of the resulting complexity of his prose that Lacan maintains his hold over his readers, in ways that are discussed by Ross Chambers in his accounts of narrative seduction. The force of Lacan's texts persists so long as their difficulty continues to fascinate the reader. Their riddling invests them with the power of the shaman or the Zen master.[22]

As for the seminars of the later decades of his career, they have, of course, become legendary. Clearly, a form of public spectacle was involved that recalls the theater of hysteria of Charcot. Yet unlike the latter's nineteenth-century bourgeois theater of illusion, Lacan's was, if anything, Brechtian. The "teaching style" of the Seminars was what might be called *hysterionic*; its effect was to hystericize the space of the lecture hall in the same way that his analytic technique, particularly the notorious short sessions, effectively hystericized the analytical space. It was a way of teaching that combined a form of narcissistic self-production with psychoanalytic doublespeak, a speaking from two places at once—that of Charcot and of the patient, of the University and of the Hysteric. The effect of Lacan's calculated theatricality, however, unlike Dupin's ostentatious *coups de théâtre,* was to put self-display itself on display, to reflect the narcissism of power in a magnifying mirror. Such performances, it seems to me, give charlatanism a good name.[23] As in Brecht's theory of epic theater, the actor is distanced from his role in order to break the illusionist spell over the audience, which for Lacan meant the hold of the imaginary.

Yet it is easier to assert the need for such breaks than to achieve them; harder, too, to shatter the wand which signifies awesome power than the example of Prospero suggests. *The Tempest* is after all a romance. As far as Lacan is concerned, in any case, who can tell

the dancer from the dance, the actor from his role? However one interprets Lacan's *hysterionics* finally, he certainly demonstrated that it is much more difficult to divest oneself of one's power than (to shift to tragedy) the fate of King Lear would have us believe. Unlike Shakespeare's foolish king, Lacan did not find himself, in spite of schisms and banishments, naked on a heath with his sole Fool for company, but in spite of defections, surrounded by courtiers to the end. One can pass on one's kingdom but one cannot will away power because power, as Lacan's own reading of **"The Purloined Letter"** acknowledges, is a place in a system. Yet for all its insights into the structure of mastery, the *Séminaire* declines to elaborate on Poe's story as an allegory of those very relations of power that are constantly reenacted at all levels, both within the psychoanalytic enterprise and outside it. And this despite the fact that unlike Poe's games—from "even and odd," draughts, and whist to "political detection" and Politics with a capital "P"—psychoanalysis affords not just another model scenario of relations of power but also something of a theory of such relations.

As was suggested above, the structure which is narrativized in **"The Purloined Letter"** is that of a competition between male protagonists in which a woman and her body are themselves the game by means of which they compete in narcissistic play. It is a body over which psychoanalysts have always competed—in "Studies in Hysteria," "Was will das Weib?", "Encore," and so on—although the male adversaries have now been joined by others who call themselves female. And the same structure of relations is to be found among those "analysts" who have taken up the challenge of Poe's story, including this one. Whatever our sex, in our role as commentators are we not all "brothers" in relation to the game or maternal body that is the text, claiming to restore to it the purloined "thing"—one remembers the unabashed fetishism of New Criticism's insistence on "organic wholeness"—and ready to repay "the evil turn" of those who previously dispossessed it?

If I had to compress the lesson of Poe's narrative into a sentence or two—a lesson that one can only read there in our current situation, that is, after Foucault—it would be once again that power is indeed everywhere and structures all relations between human subjects. Moreover, it turns out that in the end the poet is equally as implicated as the policeman or the politician. Yet if Poe's tale obliges us to acknowledge, with Foucault, that poetry, too, is a discourse in the sense defined above, it also forces the recognition, with psychoanalysis, that a discourse never assures the mastery it implicitly claims. On the contrary: it is in the nature of language as employed by human subjects to tell always more and less than it affirms. All of which leads to two propositions that need to be asserted side by side: that current psychoanalytic thought which affirms there is no metalanguage needs to be balanced by the Foucauldian notion that there is also no innocence in language—no "poetry," in the discredited Romantic sense, which is external to relations of power.

On the other hand, there is and always has been a "poetry" of the post-Jakobsonian kind, that is, a use of language as play among signifiers which escapes the intentionalities of individual consciousness and of collective discursive practices alike—something that goes largely unacknowledged in Foucault. Moreover, our life in language is situated somewhere between the polarities of "discourse" and "poetry" in this second sense; it is always, in short, inhabited by power but never power-full, never able to realize in reality that fantasy of omnipotence that the Great Detective embodies.

Poe and Lacan, Dupin and the Minister D—, are to different degrees simultaneously poets, politicians, policemen; but the two legendary authors have, as authors, the advantage over the fictional characters. Poe's *poe-etic* tale knows more than Dupin, knows that the power of analysis as expounded by him is a metalanguage and, therefore, fantastic. Thus Dupin's discourse is contained by the narrative and not vice versa. To this extent, Poe's supreme analyst is not a psychoanalyst; he makes a claim, based on a method, to clairvoyance, to the power to read minds, that psychoanalysis should properly reject as fantasm. "Analysis" is what psychoanalysis always risks becoming and what it never quite ceases to be. Analysis is psychoanalysis's authoritarian Other. Thus whereas Dupin's kind of analysis is merely a discourse of power—a how-to for those with the will to it—psychoanalysis, in the hands of its subtlest practitioners at least, is a form of poetry, which, however, as we now know, is by no means innocent of power. Psychoanalysis is indeed a "dubious science" like the other *sciences humaines* but, unlike the others, it is at its best *theoretically* aware of its dubiousness, conscious of its unconscious.

Therefore, in a manner similar to Poe's story, Lacan's writings and pedagogical theatrics reenact scenarios of mastery and of authority that they simultaneously subvert. Like Poe himself, Lacan was, one might say, a *poe-etician.* And his posthumous career in the world enables us to perceive in retrospect the extent to which Freud himself was a *poe-etician,* too. In spite of his pose of powerlessness—as detached man of science and as a Jew in the anti-Semitic capital of the Austro-Hungarian Empire—hasn't Freud through his texts also had the last word? If we remember Vienna at all nowadays, it is chiefly for its music and for its psychoanalysis. The "evil turn" done Freud in that capital over fifty years ago has been more than repaid in Paris during the last few decades.

Notes

A shorter version of this paper was given at the conference held at the University of Massachusetts, Amherst, in June 1985: *Lacan's Legacy: Lessons of the Transference.*

1. The most significant contributions to the debate include: Jacques Lacan, "Séminaire sur 'La Lettre Volée,'" in *Écrits* (Paris, 1966), partially translated by Jeffrey Mehlman as "The Seminar on 'The Purloined Letter,'" in *Yale French Studies: French Freud,* No. 48 (1972), 39-72; Jacques Derrida, "The Purveyor of Truth," in *Yale French Studies,* No. 52 (1975), 31-113; Barbara Johnson, "The Frame of Reference: Poe, Lacan, Derrida," in *The Critical Difference: Essays on the Contemporary Rhetoric of Reading* (Baltimore, 1980), pp. 110-46; and Shoshana Felman, "On Reading Poetry: Reflections on the Limits and Possibilities of Psychoanalytic Approaches," in *The Literary Freud: Mechanisms of Defense and the Poetic Will,* ed. Joseph H. Smith, Vol. 4 of *Psychiatry and the Humanities* (New Haven, 1980), pp. 119-48.

2. For a convenient recent discussion of these issues, see *Desire* (London, 1984).

3. Felman, "On Reading Poetry"; hereafter cited in text.

4. Ross Chambers is obviously concerned with some of the issues I raise in his valuable new study of "narrative as transaction." See his "Narrational Authority and 'The Purloined Letter,'" in his *Story and Situation: Narrative Seduction and the Power of Fiction* (Minneapolis, 1984). As the title of his Poe chapter suggests, however, he chiefly limits himself to the establishment and maintenance of authority at the level of the exchange between text and reader, of "the exercise of authority through discourse" (p. 54).

5. As Michel Foucault remarks in "Nietzsche, Genealogy, History," in *Language, Counter-memory, Practice,* ed. Donald F. Bouchard (Ithaca, 1977), p. 148, "Genealogy . . . seeks to reestablish the various systems of subjection: not the anticipatory power of meaning, but the hazardous play of dominations."

6. Edgar Allan Poe, *Poetry and Tales,* ed. Patrick F. Quinn (New York, 1984), p. 399; hereafter cited in text.

7. The narrator goes on to remark on Dupin's analytical power a few pages later: "He seemed to

take an eager delight in its exercise—if not exactly in its display—and did not hesitate to confess the pleasure thus derived" (401).

8. The Seneca whose epigraph stands at the beginning of the story is just such a worldly philosopher as, in their different ways, are the four writers whose "spurious profundity" is said to have its source in an analytical practice similar to that of Dupin's schoolboy. It is also of significance that one of the names involved is that of not just a political theorist, but the author of *The Prince.*

9. "Disentangling" here has a similar force to the kind of historical sense implied in Nietzsche's notion of "effective history" (*wirkliche Historie*): "it corresponds to the acuity of a glance that distinguishes, separates, and disperses." See Foucault, p. 153.

10. Foucault, p. 150.

11. It is interesting that Poe's choice of words here reverses our usual assumptions about the relationship between critical theory and creative practice. It is the narrative that is the "commentary" on a set of abstract "propositions" and not vice versa.

12. Chambers, p. 9.

13. Raymond Williams, *The Country and the City* (New York, 1973).

14. Dupin's memory of the "evil turn" has, in fact, something of the character of a screen memory. Both in the intensity of its affect and in its nondisclosure of the event concerned, it points to an even earlier and more powerful memory long repressed.

15. In response to a question concerning the meaning he gave to the word "political" in speaking of sexuality as a "political apparatus," Foucault commented: "The political is not something which determines in the last analysis (or over-determines) relations that are elementary and by nature 'neutral.' Every relation of force implies at each moment a relation of power (which is in a sense its momentary expression) and every power relation makes a reference, as its effect but also as its condition of possibility, to a political field of which it forms a part. To say that 'everything is political,' is to affirm this ubiquity of relations of force and their immanence in a political field." See "The History of Sexuality," in *Power/Knowledge: Selected Interviews and Other Writings,* ed. Colin Gordon (New York, 1980), p. 189.

16. Stuart Schneiderman, in his *Jacques Lacan: The Death of an Intellectual Hero* (Cambridge, Mass., 1983), p. 47, has remarked that "the flaw in psychoanalysis derives from its base in medicine, from the idea that it ought to be a curative enterprise."

17. See Schneiderman, ch. 8.

18. See Foucault, "Nietzsche, Genealogy, History," p. 142: "a devotion to truth and the precision of scientific methods arose from the passion of scholars, their reciprocal hatred, their fanatical and unending discussions, and their spirit of competition—the personal conflicts that slowly forged the weapons of reason."

19. For a recent discussion of nineteenth-century medical opinion on the neuroses and their treatment, see George Frank Drinka, *The Birth of Neurosis: Myth, Malady and the Victorians* (New York, 1984).

20. The Great Dora Debate is perhaps the site on which these political questions have been most thoroughly aired by feminist theorists. See *The Unopened Gift/Interpreting Psychoanalysis,* ed. Claire Kahane and Charles Bernheimer (New York, 1984).

21. If technologies of observation and surveillance of a visual kind are the primary concern of Foucault's *Discipline and Punish: The Birth of the Prison,* tr. Alan Sheridan (New York, 1977), the incitement to speech and the practice of listening dominate his work in *The History of Sexuality,* tr. Robert Hurley (New York, 1978).

22. Ross Chambers, in "Narrational Authority," p. 58, refers to "the art of maintaining (narrative) authority through non-disclosure."

23. "There was," comments the narrator of "The Murders in the Rue Morgue" in a symptomatic gesture of disavowal, "not a particle of *charlatanerie* about Dupin" (403).

Da'an Pan (essay date June 1996)

SOURCE: Pan, Da'an. "The Purloined Letter and the 'Purblind' Lacan: The Intertextual Semiotics of Poe and Lacan." *Studies in the Humanities* 23, no. 1 (June 1996): 53-69.

[*In the following essay, Pan applies the psychoanalytic theories of Sigmund Freud and the semiotics of Jacques Lacan to "The Purloined Letter" and Honoré de Balzac's "Adieu."*]

REREADING AND "INTERIMPLICATION"

In the "Proteus" episode of James Joyce's *Ulysses,* Stephen Dedalus's monologue reveals a protean world both inside and outside his mind: ". . . thought through my eyes. Signatures of all things I am here to read . . ." (37). Such a world is essentially a world of signs, in which all phenomena including psychological ones fit into a sign system and therefore can be defined as sign operations. In the field of psychoanalysis *terrae incognitae* remain, as the semiotics of human consciousness has not yet been thoroughly explored. Despite that, various types of mental activity and disorder can still be interpreted or in some cases better understood in terms of sign theory. Writing about the boundary between semiotics and psychoanalysis, Daniel Laferriere points out, "A more important reason for bringing semiotics and psychoanalysis together is a remarkable parallel between the function of the sign and the function of the signifying subject" (12). In a sense, psychoanalysis is semiotics dealing specifically with the sign language of the unconscious, or, in Lacanian terms, with the discourse of the Other. As Laferriere explains, "If the signifying subject feels an affect such as pain at the absence of what is signified, then both the psychologist and the semiotitian should have something to say about the semiosis" (14).

This paper demonstrates the advantage of integrating semiotics with psychoanalysis as an interpretive strategy for reading literary texts while problematizing such practice in the process. It does so by juxtaposing two literary texts—Poe's **"The Purloined Letter"** (hereafter, **"Letter"** [**"The Purloined Letter"**]) and Balzac's "Adieu" (otherwise titled "Farewell" in English translation)—for a comparative reading in the context of two psychosemiotic discourses—Lacan's "Seminar on 'The Purloined Letter'" (hereafter, "Seminar")[1] and Freud's *Beyond the Pleasure Principle* (hereafter *Principle*). **"Letter"** and "Adieu" each structure their plot on the repetition of a scene that is essentially the repetition of semiosis; a comparative reading of such a repetition sheds new light on the semiotics of consciousness. The repetition of semiosis in **"Letter"** is turned into an allegory of psychosemiotics through Lacan's ingenious but arguably reductive reading in his "Seminar."[2] In "Adieu" the repetition of semiosis is used as a semiotic "shock therapy" for a mental patient (though the efficacy of such a "therapy" is yet to be clinically tested), which aptly illustrates the principle of repetition compulsion even before it is theorized by Freud. Commenting on Lacan's approach to the literary text, Shoshana Felman points out:

> Lacan's importance . . . does not . . . lie specifically in any new dogma his 'school' may propose, but in his outstanding demonstration that there is more than one way to implicate psychoanalysis in literature; that how to implicate psychoanalysis in literature is itself a question for interpretation, a challenge to the ingenuity and insight of the interpreter. . . .
>
> (49)

In other words, Lacan's reading of **"Letter"** is to be appreciated mainly in terms of his attempt to reread this literary text into a psychosemiotic discourse by first implicating semiotics in psychoanalysis and then implicating psychosemiotics in literature. Emulating Lacan's modus operandi, this paper rereads Poe's and Balzac's texts by implicating in them Lacan's and Freud's psychosemiotic discourses and then exploring the intertextuality or "interimplication" between semiotics and psychoanalysis and between literature and psychosemiotics. It is hoped that such an endeavor will not only provoke further rereading of Poe, Balzac, Lacan, and Freud but also help develop protocols of rereading towards interdisciplinary and intercultural implication. As Jacques Derrida explains, "Reading is transformational. . . . But this transformation cannot be executed however one wishes. It requires protocols of reading" (63).

"Blank Mail" and "Blackmail"

In his "Seminar" Lacan allegorizes Poe's **"Letter"** to develop his psychosemiotic premise that "it is the symbolic order which is constitutive for the subject" (29). He does so "by demonstrating . . . the decisive orientation which the subject receives from the itinerary of a signifier" and by defining the itinerary of the twice-purloined letter as a signifying chain which is associated with the symbolic order (29). According to him, within the symbolic order the letter-signifier dominates over the subjects and transforms them by its effects; "the subjects . . . grasped in their intersubjectivity, who line up, . . . model their very being on the moment of the signifying chain which traverses them" and "the displacement of the signifier determines the subjects in their acts, in their destiny . . ." (43). Lacan traces an analogy between the letter in **"Letter"** and what he terms the "pure signifier," which, travelling from the imaginary to the symbolic order, "is destined by nature to signify the annulment of what it signifies" (46). Such an analogy, however, is based on a reductive logic which makes Lacan "purblind" to the letter.

In **"Letter"** the two letter-purloining scenes each feature a semiosis in which the displacement and replacement of the letter-signifier take place. As a "pure signifier" the letter signifies independently of its signified, i.e., its contents, which exist only in the form of absence-as-presence. It is true that in the first scene the letter is a signifier but equally true is that the Queen herself as its reader is also a signifier. The Queen is interrupted by the unexpected entrance of the King while perusing the letter, the very presence of which poses an immediate threat to her queenship and even her life. After a vain attempt to conceal the letter, the Queen is forced to leave it open on a table, which escapes the King's notice despite the fact that both its address and contents lie exposed within His Majesty's vision. At this juncture, however, enters Minister D—, the sign-reader, who quickly determines the semiotic implications of the letter and its political potential. As the story goes, "His lynx eye immediately perceives the paper, recognizes the handwriting of the address, observes the confusion of the personage addressed, and fathoms her secret" (919). After the four steps of his sign-reading: perceiving, recognizing, observing, and fathoming, his letter-purloining ensues. Such being the case, Lacan, by claiming in his "Seminar" that **"Letter"** "tells us nothing of the message it conveys" (41), seems to have lost sight of the fact that the letter cannot signify without telegraphing the message it conveys. Strictly speaking, it is the Queen's confusion as the signifier, along with the letter's telltale handwriting as a collateral signifier, that tells her "tale" as well as the "tale" of the letter. Exposed as it is, the letter appears to be a "blank mail" in the eyes of the sign-blind King and therefore passes unnoticed. In Minister D—'s semiotic "lynx eye," however, it lies temptingly open as a sign of empowerment that would make him politically one up on the Queen. In this sense, Minister D—, the Queen (along with the letter), and her secret fathomed by D— form a semiotic triangle; and what happens within this triangle indicates the occurrence of a semiosis. During the semiosis not only does Minister D— see the Queen's telltale confusion along with the letter's telltale handwriting but also fathoms "her secret," i.e., the compromising contents of the letter and hence the Queen's unbecoming conduct. This secret, which remains hypothetical throughout the story, is taken for granted. It is such a foregone conclusion that serves as the signified and prompts Minister D—'s to commit the audacious theft, thus turning the "blank mail" into a "blackmail." If, according to Lacan, the letter as a "pure signifier" is destined to signify the annulment of what it signifies, it would necessarily signify the annulment of the motivation of the theft, and this virtually subjects Lacan's argument to the risk of self-deconstruction.

THE PRIMAL SCENE AND SEMIOTIC LITERACY

In Poe's **"Letter"** the second scene is also a scene of semiosis in which, while the act of letter-purloining is repeated, the participating parties are different from those in the previous scene. As the letter now lies camouflaged, Dupin, the sign-hunter, tries to decode Minister D—'s mind, body, and apartment, hunting for the signifiers that would reveal the hideout of the letter. Earlier, the police's failure in their hair-splitting and microscopic house search (for they actually enlist the microscope in their search) and body frisk suggests that Minister D—'s modus operandi of letter-hiding may well have copied the Queen's, i.e., making the letter appear absent by its very conspicuousness. Based on his knowledge of Minister D—'s normal

pattern of behavior, Dupin sees the minister's behavioral aberration as behavioral camouflage, which signifies the possibility of his camouflaging the letter. The semiosis taking place in this scene is more complex than that in the first scene, for it is actually composed of a series of sub-semiosis involving a group of sub-signifiers which form a composite signifier: the police's failure in their search, the minister's nocturnal absences and faked ennui, the "radicalness of the differences" of the camouflaged letter from its true self, the inconsistency between the feigned bad condition of the letter and the "true methodical habits of D—," and the "hyperobtrusive situation" of the letter.

The second scene witnesses a semiotic duel of wits, first between Minister D— and Prefect G. and then between Minister D— and Dupin. In order to foil the police's effort to reclaim the letter, the minister resorts to semiotic "red herrings": His nightly absence is meant to signify, or rather mis-signify that the letter is not hidden on the premises of his dwelling. His feigned ennui is meant to mis-signify his lack of vigilance, which would be necessary for him to safeguard the letter. The letter's radical difference from its original is meant to belie its true self. Its "hyperobtrusive situation" is meant to "delude the beholder into an idea of the worthlessness of the document" (Poe 931). These "red herrings" as signifiers, or mis-signifiers, carry paradoxical signifieds: To Prefect G, they signify what is exactly intended by Minister D—, which makes him fall into the latter's semiotic trap. To Dupin, however, they signify what the minister tries to hide, he knowing full well that "these things . . . were strongly corroborative of suspicion, in one who came with the intention to suspect" (Poe 931). Strictly speaking, the letter lying camouflaged in the second scene cannot be considered a signifier since Dupin's sign-hunt is targeted at what would signify its hideout rather than itself, and the semiosis in this scene does not involve its direct participation. Viewed in this light, Lacan's allegorization of Poe's **"Letter,"** especially his designation of the letter as a "pure signifier," follows a reductive logic, which makes his reading "anti-Poe-etic." As Poe says through the mouth of Dupin, "The material world . . . abounds with *very strict* analogies to the immaterial; and thus some color of truth has been given to the rhetorical dogma, that metaphor, or simile, may be made to strengthen an argument, as well as to embellish a description" (929; my emphasis). Owing to its lack of factual and logical strictness Lacan's letter-signifier analogy actually handicaps his argument about the relationship between the symbolic order and the subject.

In analyzing the signifying economy of Poe's **"Letter"** Lacan defines the similarity between the two letter-purloining scenes in terms of two types of repetition: the repetition of an "inter-subjective complex" formed of three subjects—the loser, the robber, and the third party, and the repetition of the primal scene. As he argues, "There are two scenes, the first of which we shall straightway designate the primal scene, and by no means inadvertently, since the second may be considered its repetition in the very sense we are considering today" (30). In Freudian terms, the primal scene, which is essentially a scene of semiosis, features the child as the sign-reader who observes parental sex but is too innocent to read it in a correct context.[3] To him, the parental bed scene appears uncanny; and he draws an analogy between his parents' sexual relationship and his own relationship to his younger brother whom he used to ill-treat and then subsumes what has happened between his parents under the rubric of violence and struggling (*The Interpretation of Dreams* 624). Interpreted in Lacanian terms, the experience gained by the child sign-reader in the primal scene belongs to the imaginary order as he is innocent of the adult language as a prerequisite for decoding parental sex. With his emphasis on the notion of repetition, Lacan invokes the primal scene in an attempt to tackle the Freudian problematics of repetition compulsion in relation to the insistence of the signifying chain.

In analogizing the first theft scene in **"Letter"** as the primal scene and the second one as a repetition Lacan again falls into the trap of reductionism. The fact is that what can be allegorized legitimately to represent the imaginary experience and the symbolic order respectively, or the primal scene and the Oedipal phase, are not the two actual theft scenes but the experience or behavior of individual subjects in relation to one another and to the letter. Semiotically speaking, the first scene hardly fits Freud's definition of the primal scene, for neither are there any sex-like signs to puzzle the "child" nor any "child"-like sign-readers to be puzzled; nor is there any imaginary experience gained by any party to be linked to the symbolic order at a later stage. The primal scene, if any, that does bear analogy to the Freudian model, should be defined in terms of the subject's experience in the semiosis. In this sense, the "primal scene" occurs to Prefect G twice: first at Minister D—'s apartment, where he is baffled by the enigmatic concealment of the letter, and then at Dupin's apartment, where he is astounded at the miraculous recovery of the letter. His reaction on the latter occasion is described in Poe's story as follows: "The Prefect appeared absolutely thunder-stricken. For some minutes he remained *speechless* [italics mine] and motionless, looking incredulously at my friend with open mouth and eyes that seemed starting from their sockets . . ." (924).

Significantly, G's bafflement and astonishment suggest his "child"-like experience which belongs only to the imaginary order. His *speechlessness,* allegorized in Lacanian terms, refers to his lack of language that is typical of the imaginary experience and his lack of access to the symbolic order or the Oedipal phase, both of which are identified with language. Since the letter-signifier travels exclusively within the symbolic order in which the purloining is repeated and yet to which G is an outsider due to his semiotic illiteracy, his failure to recover the letter is foredoomed. As a signifier the letter can only be decoded, purloined, concealed, and recovered within the symbolic order wherein all the subjects involved change their identities as the letter itself changes its identity from a "blank mail" to a "blackmail." These subjects fall into two opposed categories, definable in terms of the seer versus the blind person. The seer, being capable of seeing the letter (the Queen sees its potential threat to herself; Minister D— sees its potential power over the Queen; Dupin sees its hideout), belongs to the symbolic order, which, as Kaja Silverman interprets from a Lacanian perspective, "introduces the subject to language and Oedipal triangulation" (Silverman 157). The blind person, being blind to either the letter or the robber (the King and Prefect G are blind to the letter; the Queen and Minister D— are blind to the respective robbers of the letter), belongs to the imaginary order, which is "most classically exemplified by the mirror stage" (Silverman 157). By the same token, Minister D— and the Queen each can also be defined as "purblind": he sees the incriminating nature of the letter as well as the Queen's guilty conscience but is blind to Dupin's stratagem for outwitting him; she sees the King's entrance but is blind to the minister's attempt to purloin the letter. Their "purblindness" makes them straddle the imaginary and the symbolic order; and their paradoxical identity as the seer and the blind person incarnates the inseparability and coexistence of the imaginary and the symbolic order. As Silverman explains, ". . . the imaginary order—the order of equations and identifications—and the symbolic order—the order of language, discourse, narrative—are so closely imbricated as to be virtually inseparable" (162). According to her, within the Lacanian scheme the imaginary order "not only precedes the symbolic order" but "continues to coexist with it afterward" (157). In Poe's **"Letter"** these two orders, which correspond respectively to the two types of subjective experience, coexist despite the temporal sequence of the two scenes.

In the Lacanian paradigm both the seer and the blind person can be defined in terms of language and literacy, as both theft scenes are scenes of reading. In the first scene, Minister D— reads the Queen's body and mind and subsequently succeeds in purloining the letter. In the second scene whereas the minister fails to read Dupin's mind his own mind and body are correctly read by Dupin. In the same scene Prefect G fails to read Minister D—'s mind and therefore inevitably fails to recover the letter. Semiotically speaking, the primal scene is a scene of misreading, in which the child sign-reader is confronted with the task of reading his parents' bodies and minds, a task which, unfortunately but unavoidably, ends up in misreading. In the "primal scene" in Poe's **"Letter"** Prefect G and Minister D— (in relation to Dupin) each play a "child"-like role, who are incapable of reading their adversaries' "mind language" and "body language" and consequently are denied entry into the symbolic order or the Oedipal phase. Both "children" read the "parental" minds in terms of their own as if reading from the mirror and therefore are lost in the imaginary experience or the mirror stage. As Barbara Johnson observes in critiquing the reading of Poe's **"Letter"** by Lacan and Derrida, "The 'primal scene' is not a scene but an interpretive infelicity whose result was to situate the interpreter in an intolerable position" (142).

REPETITION COMPULSION AND THE REPETITION OF "ADIEU"

For all his reductionism in allegorization and analogization due to his "purblindness" to the overall signifying economy of Poe's **"Letter,"** Lacan shows his insights into the relationship between the subject and the symbolic order. He interprets the Freudian notion of repetition compulsion (or, repetition automatism, as he himself terms it) in terms of the insistence of the signifying chain within the symbolic order which he considers to be constitutive for the subject (Lacan 29). As he writes in his "Seminar,"

> Given the intersubjective modulus of the repetitive action, it remains to recognize in it a repetition automatism in the sense that interests us in Freud's text. . . . What interests us today is the manner in which the subjects relay each other in their displacement during the intersubjective repetition. We shall see that their displacement is determined by the place which a pure signifier—the purloined letter—comes to occupy in their trio. And that is what will confirm for us its status as repetition automatism.
>
> (32)

As he further explains,

> This is indeed what happens in the repetition automatism. What Freud teaches us in the text we are commenting on is that the subject must pass through the channels of the symbolic, but what is illustrated here is more gripping still: it is not only the subject, but the subjects, grasped in their intersubjectivity, who line up . . . and . . . model their very being on the moment of the signifying chain which traverse them.
>
> (43)

The significance of Lacan's "Seminar" to psychoanalysis and semiotics is twofold. On the one hand, through an allegorical reading of Poe's **"Letter"** in a psycho-semiotic context Lacan theorizes the psychoanalytic situation in which the patient's unconscious repressed as embodied by the letter can be "purloined," i.e., put far off, or concealed by the patient. As Bice Benvenuto and Roger Kennedy point out, "The basic analytic task is to locate and find the letter, or at least trace its track, and to do this entails an understanding of the Symbolic Order" (101). On the other, in his attempt to demonstrate the letter's insistence in the signifying chain through its repetitive displacement and replacement, Lacan reveals "the way in which the story's plot, its sequence of events (as, for Freud, the sequence of events in a life-story), is contingent on, overdetermined by, a principle of repetition that governs it . . ." (Felman 40). According to him, "Unconscious desire, once repressed, survives in displaced symbolic media that govern the subject's life and actions without his ever being aware of their meaning or of the repetitive pattern they structure" (Felman 42).

Strictly speaking, Lacan's analogy between repetition compulsion, which symbolically repeats unpleasant experiences by overriding the pleasure principle, and the insistence of the signifying chain, in which the subject is determined by the signifier and transformed by the latter's effects, again follows a reductive logic when it is drawn through the reading of Poe's **"Letter"** in which the letter's status as the signifier proves to be ambiguous and problematic. As a matter of fact, such an analogy can be better illustrated by Balzac's short story "Adieu" included in the *Philosophical Studies* of his *Comedie humaine,* which combines a tragic love story with a pseudo-scientific experiment on psychotherapy and which, more significantly, can be allegorized to demonstrate the repetition of the primal scene. In "Adieu" the heroine, Countess Stephanie de Vandieres, is traumatized and driven mad in the passage of the Beresina during the French army's retreat from Moscow in the winter of 1812. Later, she regains sanity through the effects of a déja vu scene of river-crossing that is theatrically induced under the "remote control" of her former lover Colonel Philippe.

Balzac's story, its pseudo-scientific elements notwithstanding, provides a clue to the cause of traumatic psychoneurosis in which the blocked impulse seeks expression in a disguised form, to the mechanism of repetition compulsion, and to the possible therapeutic effects of activating this mechanism in psychoanalysis to make the patient re-experience unwanted situations and painful emotions. In "Adieu" Stephanie's madness is caused by the trauma she experiences during the chaotic and perilous river-crossing. In his *Principle,* Freud defines as "traumatic" "any excitations from outside which are powerful enough to break through the protective shield" (23). He thus explains the consequence of external trauma:

> Such an event . . . is bound to provoke a disturbance on a large scale in the functioning of the organism's energy and to set in motion every possible defensive measure. At the same time, the pleasure principle is for the moment put out of action. There is no longer any possibility of preventing the mental apparatus from being flooded with large amounts of stimulus. . . .
>
> (23)

Then, he introduces the element of fright in effecting the trauma:

> It is caused by lack of any preparedness for anxiety, including lack of hypercathexis of the systems that would be the first to receive the stimulus. Owing to their low cathexis those systems are not in a good position for binding the inflowing amounts of excitation and the consequences of the breach in the protective shield follow all the more easily.
>
> (25)

According to him, the strategic importance of the preparedness for anxiety and the hypercathexis of the receptive systems lies in that both "constitute the last line of defence of the shield against stimuli" (25).

Freud's theory provides a plausible explanation to the cause of Stephanie's loss of sanity: the lack of preparedness for anxiety and the lack of hypercathexis in the receptive systems of her mental apparatus, as she receives the fatal shock in a state of total lethargy that causes her fright. His theory also helps explain why Philippe is able to recover his senses after having received the violent shock upon recognizing the mad Stephanie. On the one hand, the uncanny aura about the old monastery and his close observation of both the deaf-mute peasant woman Genevieve and the bestialized Stephanie have prepared him for the shock to some extent. This means that there is a certain amount of anxiety in him at the moment of recognition. On the other, as Freud suggests, sometimes "a gross physical injury caused simultaneously by the trauma diminishes the chances that a neurosis will develop," for "the simultaneous physical injury, by recalling for a narcissistic hypercathexis of the injured organ, would bind the excess of excitation" (27). According to the story, before his encounter with Stephanie Philippe has endured prolonged hunger the effect of which amounts to that of physical injury. No wonder his doctor would say: "If Monsiuer le Colonel had not been fasting, the shock must have killed him" (333).

Philippe's therapy for his former mistress, which works a miracle in the story, is yet to be tested and rationalized by modern psychoanalysis and psychiatry.

Still, it can be used to illustrate Freud's theory of repetition compulsion. In his *Principle* Freud suggests that while dreams as wish fulfillment are usually under the dominance of the pleasure principle, in the case of patients of traumatic neuroses, their dreams are not in the service of that principle but always evoke traumatic situations. Such dreams, arising in obedience to the principle of repetition compulsion, may help carry out the unusual task of mastering the stimulus retrospectively by developing the anxiety whose omission is the cause of traumatic neurosis (26). Viewed from this perspective, the simulated scene of river-crossing in "Adieu" seems to function as a dream, a live dream, as it were, performing the same task postulated by Freud; and the retrospective mastery of the stimulus may have helped Stephanie regain sanity. Such a dream produces a powerful shock, which is essentially a semiotic shock, that rudely awakens Stephanie from madness in the middle of the horror drama as if she wakes up in a nightmare.

In his *Principle* Freud also points out:

> The patient [in analysis] cannot remember the whole of what is repressed in him, and what he cannot remember may be precisely the essential part of it. . . . He is obliged to *repeat* the repressed material as a contemporary experience instead of, as the physician would prefer to see, *remembering* it as something belonging to the past. These reproductions . . . emerge with . . . unwished-for *exactitude*. . . .
>
> (12)

According to him:

> The physician cannot as a rule spare his patient this phase of the treatment. He must get him to re-experience some portion of his forgotten life, but must see to it, on the other hand, that the patient retains some degree of *aloofness* [italics mine], which will enable him, in spite of everything, to recognize that what appears to be reality is in fact only a reflection of a forgotten past. If this can be successfully achieved, the patient's sense of conviction is won, together with the therapeutic success that is dependent on it.
>
> (12-13)

Freud's theory serves as an etiology for Stephanie's sudden death right after she regains sanity. According to the story, in preparing his scheme Philippe omits "no device that could reproduce that most hideous of all scenes" (363) and makes sure that "no detail might be lacking to recall the scene in all its horror" (364). While the unwished-for *exactitude* of the horror scene successfully induces a déja vu in Stephanie, it leaves no room for *aloofness* which would otherwise absorb part of the shock that proves to be fatal to the patient.

In terms of its traumatic effect on the subject, the scene of river-crossing is a primal scene for Stephanie. Philippe's scheme, which helps Stephanie regain sanity, is analogous to the analyst's intervention, which brings about a symbolic repetition of the trauma through transference, thus relieving the patient of the symptom. As Freud explains, the activation of the primal scene has "the same effect as though it were a recent experience" (*From the History of an Infantile Neurosis* 44). In "Adieu" the magic word "adieu" is the key to restoring Stephanie's sanity. It is the only human sound accompanying her madness. It is both the last word she utters before losing sanity and the first word she utters after regaining sanity. Interpreted in Freudian terms, Stephanie's frequent utterance of "adieu" in her madness signifies that "when conscious purposive ideas are abandoned, concealed purposive ideas assume control of the current of ideas," insisting on being expressed and heard beyond any adherence to the pleasure principle (*The Interpretation of Dreams* 570). Such utterance is a symbolic repetition of unpleasant experience repressed in the unconscious that works upon the principle of repetition compulsion.

As a signifier "adieu" sends off a spark of hope in Philippe, who comes to realize that his poor darling is not totally beyond cure. This also seems to explain why Stephanie would run toward him upon hearing the air he whistles: *Partant pour la Syrie,* which is evocative of the memories of their love. Interpreted in Lacanian terms, "adieu," like the purloined letter, also travels in a signifying chain associated with the symbolic order, along whose route and by whose effects the heroine-subject, though being the same person, changes her psychic identity from the besieged countess to the bestialized madwoman and then back to the dying Stephanie with regained sanity. The relationship formed within the symbolic order between "adieu" as the determining signifier and Stephanie as the subject being determined illustrates more plausibly than does Poe's story that the symbolic order is constitutive for the subject.

As a signifier "adieu" is associated with Stephanie's traumatic experience of river-crossing and her loss of a beloved object—Colonel Philippe. Combined, the scene of river-crossing and its reenactment are analogous to the "*fort*"/"*da*" game played by Freud's grandson, as both cases involve objects lost and found. In the "*fort*"/"*da*" game, "*fort*," when uttered alone, serves as what Lacan calls the "unary" signifier, which lacks any paradigmatic or syntagmatic "company" (Silverman 170). "*Da*," on the other hand, refers back to "*fort*" both paradigmatically and syntagmatically as what Lacan calls the "binary" signifier, which, when added to "*fort*," becomes the latter's signifier (Silverman 171). The significance of the "*fort*"/"*da*" game in the Freudian and Lacanian context of psychosemiotics lies in that its complete version must be seen as "the child's first signifying chain and hence

his entry into language" (Silverman 170). By analogy, the repressed memory of the absence of Stephanie's beloved Philippe, as signified by the word "adieu," insists on expressing itself in symbolic repetition; and the déja vu scene of river-crossing is a symbolic repetition of Stephanie's losing Philippe. In her swan song "Adieu, Philippe! . . . I love you . . ." "adieu" is no longer uttered alone but is linked to "Philippe," which becomes the latter's signifier when added to "adieu" in a fashion analogous to the Freudian "*da*." The linkage between "adieu" and "Philippe," similar to that between "*fort*" and "*da*," can also be interpreted as a signifying chain whose formation signifies Stephanie's entry into the lucid zone, which is analogous to the child's entry into language and the symbolic order. Such an analogy could have well served Lacan's purpose of reinterpreting the Freudian principle of repetition compulsion. As Samuel Weber observes, "For Lacan, *Beyond the Pleasure Principle* is above all the text that describes the entry of the subject into the realm of the Symbolic, that is, of language structured by the Signifier" (96). But that analogy is hard to draw from the experience of Poe's letter without jeopardizing itself to reductionism.

Another advantage the word "adieu" has over Poe's letter in illustrating Lacan's theory lies in its being a speech sound. Commenting on the shortcoming of Lacan's "Seminar," Bevenuto and Kennedy write:

> Still one reasonable objection to the whole programme of the essay can be made concerning the letter itself. Lacan was supposed to be emphasizing the power of speech in psychoanalysis, yet he used a written letter as a metaphor of the signifier, and in the Poe essay made relatively little reference to the nature of speech.
>
> (101-102)

Such being the case, it seems that Balzac's story, which uses the speech sound "adieu" as a metaphor of the signifier, provides Lacan with a more appropriate text that would illustrate his notion of the nature and power of speech. Bevenuto and Kennedy also point out that in Lacan's "Seminar" a series of questions concerning the nature of the symbolic order remain unanswered. According to them, Lacan does not give clear boundaries for his concept of the symbolic order since he refuses to acknowledge that the signifier can be permanently bound to the signified; and the lack of conceptual boundaries exposes Lacan's theory to the risk of being incoherent (102). For all his "lynx's eye" view of the subjects' minds Lacan virtually turns a "purblind" eye to the overall semiotic situation of letter-purloining in Poe's **"Letter,"** thus leading his analysis astray onto a reductive path. What is more ironic is that as Balzac's compatriot Lacan seems "purblind" to the significance of "Adieu" to his own psychosemiotic cause as a better case than Poe's **"Letter"** for his argument.

THE PURLOINED LETTER AND THE LOST PEARL

While Poe's **"Letter"** along with Lacan's **"Letter"**-reading has been read, reread, and even overread Balzac's "Adieu" has not yet been read much in a Freudian or Lacanian context.[4] Balzac's story "Sarrasine," however, does become a test model of semiotic *explication de texte* in Roland Barthes's *S/Z,* in which Barthes develops the binary oppositions of the writerly text versus the readerly text. According to Barthes, the writerly text makes the reader "no longer a consumer, but a producer of the text" (4); the readerly text is the "countervalue" of the writerly text—"its negative, reactive value: what can be read, but not written" (4). The former is "infinitely plural and open to the free play of signifiers and of differences, unconstrained by representative considerations, and transgressive of any desire for decidable, unified, totalized meaning" (Johnson 6); the latter, "constrained by considerations of representation," is by contrast "irreversible, 'natural,' decidable, continuous, totalizable, and unified into a coherent whole based on the signified" (Johnson 5-6). For a text to acquire the status of the writerly text entails the Barthesian mode of rereading, which is "an operation contrary to the commercial and ideological habits of our society, which would have us 'throw away' the story once it has been consumed," and from which the writerly text derives itself (*S/Z* 15-16).[5] In this sense, Lacan's "Seminar" virtually transforms Poe's **"Letter"** into a model of the writerly text. In so doing he not only implicates both semiotics and psychoanalysis in literature but also implicates semiotics and psychoanalysis in each other, thus providing the semiotician and the psychologist with a critical *lingua franca* in which to read "the discourse of the Other." It is here that Lacan's reading of Poe's **"Letter"** becomes most insightful, though such reading also exposes his "purblindness" in the process.

In fairness to Lacan, he is not alone in being at once insightful and purblind in his reading, for such a paradoxical vision is symptomatic of almost all readers whose insights often blind them from the textual truth. In the world of reading no one is endowed with Dupin's detective clairvoyance; everyone is either a Prefect G or a Minister D—. A case in point is that while attempting to deconstruct Lacan, Derrida himself is targeted for deconstruction by Johnson. But is Johnson deconstruction-proof, then? Deconstructing as she does in a language which itself originates in the Logos, as Derrida always argues, Johnson cannot escape the blinding impact of logocentrism any more than do her two predecessors.[6]

Significantly, Poe's **"Letter,"** as a modern allegory about the "pure signifier" lost and found, acquires a level of crosscultural comparability with the ancient Chinese Taoist allegory about the Yellow Emperor's Dark Pearl (a metaphor for the Tao) lost and found. This allegory appears in the chapter "Heaven and Earth" in the *Zhuangzi* reputedly authored by Zhuangzi (*ca.* 369-286 B.C.), the cofounder of Taoist philosophy: The Yellow Emperor lost his Dark Pearl during his trip. He sent Knowledge, Insight, and Eloquence respectively to look for it, but none of them was able to find it. At last, he sent Imageless (who incarnates the Taoist notion of *zi-ran-wu-wei* or, literally, naturalness and inaction) to look for it, and Imageless found it. The Yellow Emperor was astonished, saying: "How odd! How come Imageless was able to find it in the end?" (Yang 216). Interpreted in Taoist theory, the first three imperial detectives' respective failures to recover the Dark Pearl are due to the fact that the Tao is both intangible and ineffable and therefore cannot be found through the exercise of conventional knowledge, insight, or eloquence. Laozi (ND, an older contemporary of Confucius [551-479 B.C.]), the founder of Taoist philosophy, begins his discourse on the Tao in the *Dao de jing* (*Classic of the Tao and Virtues*) with the premise that "(T)he Tao that can be spoken of is not the true Tao" (Chen 53). The Tao, as he describes, is "shadowy and shapeless" (Chen 148). The Yellow Emperor's three unsuccessful detectives each are blinded by their stereotyped intelligence which lacks the naturalness of the Tao. By contrast, Imageless, endowed with Taoist naturalness, is unencumbered with any "artificial intelligence" that does not conform to the Tao. The Yellow Emperor's astonishment at Imageless's ability to find the Dark Pearl betrays his ignorance of the truth of the Tao, which explains why he would lose the pearl-Tao. By analogy, the reason behind Prefect G's failure to recover the purloined letter is that he relies too much on his dogmatic expertise for lack of a "Taoist" approach to his investigation. In other words, his ill-fated search is too "readerly" and "logocentric" to locate the letter.[7] As Dupin explains in **"Letter"** with the following hindsight in diagnosing the police's failure:

> They consider only their *own* ideas of ingenuity; and, in searching for anything hidden, advert only to the modes in which *they* would have hidden it. . . . They have no variation of principle in their investigations; at best, when urged by some unusual emergency—by some extraordinary reward—they extend or exaggerate their old modes of *practice,* without touching their principles.
>
> (926)

For all our insights into the blindness of Lacan, Derrida, Minister D—, Prefect G, and the Yellow Emperor's three detectives, we as readers and re-readers are no better-off than these figures in pursuit of textual or intertextual truth. The truth of a text or between texts is either like the purloined letter lying in disguise or like the Tao, shadowy and shapeless; and what makes us blind or purblind to that truth and prevents us from becoming "the purveyor of truth" (to borrow Derrida's term) is more often than not our own "insights." Isn't this the paradox, or the truth in disguise, of reading and rereading? Let it be not purloined.

Notes

1. Lacan's "Seminar on 'The Purloined Letter,'" translated by Jeffrey Mehlman, is included in Muller and Richardson, *The Purloined Poe: Lacan, Derrida, and Psychoanalytic Reading,* 28-54. This book contains a variety of readings of Poe's "Letter" and Lacan's "Seminar."

2. In his essay "The Purveyor of Truth" (trans. Alan Bass; retitled *The Postcard* in its newly translated version) Derrida deconstructs Lacan's "Seminar" on grounds of metaphysical reduction and logo-centrism. Derrida's essay itself is subjected to deconstruction by Barbara Johnson in her essay "The Frame of Reference." Earlier versions of both essays appeared in *Yale French Studies*: Derrida in no. 52 (1975) and Johnson in nos. 55-56 (1977).

3. For a narratological definition of the primal scene in literary criticism, see Peter Brooks, "Fictions of the Wolf Man: Freud and Narrative Understanding" in *Reading for the Plot: Design and Invention in Narrative* (New York: Knopf, 1984), 264-85. Also see Ned Lukacher's comments on Brooks in *Primal Scenes: Literature, Philosophy, Psychoanalysis* (Ithaca: Cornell University Press, 1986), 37-38.

4. For a feminist reading of "Adieu," see Shoshana Felman's "Woman and Madness: The Critical Phallacy" in *Diacritics* (Winter 1975), 2-10.

5. A similar point is made by Barthes in his "Textual Analysis of a Tale of Poe" (in Marshall Blonsky, ed., *On Signs.* Baltimore: The Johns Hopkins University Press, 1985, pp. 84-97) when he writes: "Our goal is not to discover *the* meaning, or even *a* meaning for the text, and our work is not akin to a hermeneutic type of literary criticism (whose aim is to interpret the text according to the truth it believes is hidden within). . . . Our goal is ultimately to conceive, to imagine, to live the plurality of the text, the open-endedness of its significance" (84). Barthes read Poe's tale "The Facts in the Case of M. Valdemar" in Baudelaire's translation: *La vérité sur le cas de M. Valdemar.*

6. For an ingenious comparative reading of Lacan's "Seminar," Derrida's "The Purveyor of Truth," and Johnson's "The Frame of Reference: Poe, Lacan, Derrida," see John T. Irwin, *The Mystery to a Solution: Poe, Borges, and the Analytic De-*

tective Story (Baltimore: The Johns Hopkins University Press, 1994), 3-9. Irwin reads these three readings by "isolating a thread that runs through all three, a clue to conduct us through labyrinthine passages" (3). According to him, that thread is "the position that each essay takes on what we might call the numerical/geometrical structure of the story" (3).

7. There is an interesting discussion on the analogy between the Tao and the Logos in terms of the dichotomy of thought and speech and of inner reality and outward expression in Longxi Zhang, *The Tao and the Logos: Literary Hermeneutics, East and West* (Durham: Duke University Press, 1992), 22-33. According to the author, ". . . the metaphysical hierarchy of thinking, speech, and writing exists not only in the West but in the East as well, and logocentrism does not just inhabit the Western way of thinking but constitutes the very way of thinking itself" (30). His argument serves as a critical provocateur to incite further crosscultural comparisons of the nature and mode of reading.

Works Cited

Balzac, Honore de. "Adieu," *The Works of Honore de Balzac.* New York: John D. Avil, 1901.

Barthes, Roland. *S/Z.* Trans. Richard Miller. New York: Hill and Wang, 1974.

Benvenuto, Bice, and Kennedy, Roger. *The Works of Jacques Lacan.* New York: St. Martin's P, 1986.

Chen, Guying, ed. *Laozi zhu-yi ji ping-jie (An Annotation, Translation, and Critique of the Laozi).* Beijing: Chinese P, 1984.

Derrida, Jacques. *Positions.* Trans. Alan Bass. Chicago: U of Chicago P, 1981.

Felman, Shoshana. *Jacques Lacan and the Adventure of Insight.* Cambridge: Harvard UP, 1987.

Freud, Sigmund. *Beyond the Pleasure Principle.* Trans. and ed. James Strachey. New York: W. W. Norton, 1961.

———. *The Interpretation of Dreams.* Trans. and ed. James Strachey. New York: Avon Books, 1965.

———. "From the History of an Infantile Neurosis," *The Standard Edition of the Complete Psychological Works of Sigmund Freud,* Vol. 17. London: The Hogarth P, 1955.

Johnson, Barbara. "The Frame of Reference: Poe, Lacan, Derrida," *The Critical Difference: Essays in the Contemporary Rhetoric of Reading.* Baltimore: The Johns Hopkins UP, 1980.

Joyce, James. *Ulysses.* New York: Vintage, 1966.

Lacan, Jacques. "Seminar on 'The Purloined Letter,'" trans. Jeffrey Mehlman. In Muller, *The Purloined Poe*, 28-54.

Laferriere, Daniel. *Sign and Subject*. Lisse: The Peter De Ridder P, 1978.

Muller, John, and William Richardson, eds. *The Purloined Poe: Lacan, Derrida, and Psychoanalytic Reading*. Baltimore: The Johns Hopkins UP, 1988.

Poe, Edgar Allan. *The Unabridged Edgar Allan Poe*. Philadelphia: Running P, 1983.

Silverman, Kaja. *The Subject of Semiotics*. Oxford: Oxford UP, 1983.

Weber, Samuel. *The Legend of Freud*. Minneapolis: U of Minnesota P, 1982.

Yang, Liuqiao, ed. *Zhuangzi yi-gu* (*A Translation and Annotation of the Zhuangzi*). Shanghai: Shanghai Classics P, 1991.

Louis A. Renza (essay date summer 2000)

SOURCE: Renza, Louis A. "Edgar Allan Poe, Henry James, and Jack London: A Private Correspondence." *Boundary 2* 27, no. 2 (summer 2000): 83-111.

[*In the following essay, Renza suggests that "The Purloined Letter," Henry James's "The Private Life," and the works of Jack London all attempt to retain hidden meaning while operating in the realm of public expression. Renza views this literary strategy as a means of resisting the invasiveness of the capitalist marketplace.*]

> We can scarcely imagine a time when there did not exist a necessity, or at least a desire, of transmitting information from one individual to another, in such manner as to elude general comprehension.
>
> —Edgar Allan Poe, "A Few Words on Secret Writing"

1

Everywhere one turns today in academic journals, it is politics as usual: All texts are subject to political short-arm inspections. Not, as Jerry Seinfeld might say, that there's anything wrong with that. Who wants to return to the closet silences and claustrophobias enforced by prejudices of race, gender, class, ethnicity, and/or sexual orientation(s)? Who wants to discourage those still in the grip of oppressive, dominant discourses and their endorsements of ignoble forms of behavior from breaking silence; from joining enclaves to air old and present social wounds; in short, from going public and thereby introducing discursive cacophony into what passes for the prevailing public sphere of the "humanities" profession? If no consensus exists about its

particulars, this politicization—for example, of literary studies—surely stands for one in general. To be sure, I may choose not to regard literary works in terms of their political emissions or the cultural work they purportedly do, but in the present academic environment, this choice, too, will perforce appear political. The fact that this observation has itself become a cliché simply proves the point.

So it is no surprise that a familiar type of critical practice opts for more exposé, more "outings," when it comes to, among other things, the culturally influential issue of canon formation: for example, debunking Edgar Allan Poe for his alleged racist sentiments (albeit based on scattered evidence) or his oft-proclaimed aesthetic ideology; Nathaniel Hawthorne for his misogyny or literary politicking regarding *The Scarlet Letter*; or Mark Twain for his use of the word *nigger* in *Huckleberry Finn*.[1] Other critics, conversely, focus on recovering works and writers excluded for political reasons from the recommended, American literary canon, if only to show the political reasons why they should now be included. No doubt some of these critics underplay inconvenient facts—Harriet Beecher Stowe's notion of Liberian colonization for freed slaves, for example. But few expect such facts or canonical configurations to go uncontested. Indeed, these contestations help fuel more political conversation,[2] leaving uncontested only the issue of canonical thinking itself.

Strangely enough, however, from one perspective, this critical zeitgeist, or foregrounding of criticism as a performative activity, exists in the historical mainstream of American social practices, the effect of which has been to dilute private considerations of all things, including literary texts. Notwithstanding the value accorded the privatization of everything from business enterprises to personal life, the public-private binary in U.S. culture has almost always meant the obeisance of the private to the public life. This was so for early Republican leaders, who felt that public duty superseded inclinations toward the private life, as well as for those whose socio-geographical circumstances lent privacy the negative connotation it had assumed in Western antiquity, specifically the sense of "isolation, deprivation, and separation."[3] And so it was for many nineteenth-century, American middle-class women, relegated as they were to domestic households, which arguably comprised a reactionary refuge from a dominant and increasingly more impersonal, competitive marketplace.

One need not agree, then, with Richard Hixson's contention that because of geo-demographic options, especially the frontier, Americans throughout much of the nineteenth century could take privacy "for granted" or feel it "was not seriously threatened."[4] On the contrary, the infrastructural linkages of cities and rural communities, sponsored by the U.S. government during this period, already posed such a threat: "The process of building public thruways, bridges, wharfs, and even parks involved the public expropriation and extinguishment of preexisting rights, usages, and expectations. The invention of public space was contested terrain in the early nineteenth century, requiring a full deployment of the rhetorics and techniques of the well-regulated society."[5] In this context, the notion of domestic privacy could exist only as an imaginary refuge from, or, in revisionary feminist terms, a latent protest against, both the civic and commercial pressures defining the American public sphere. Moreover, as Nancy Dunlap Bercaw notes, "by the 1850s the household had become an extrusion of the state, not only involved in the institutionalization of charity, health, and child-care." Indeed, as Tamara K. Hareven points out, it was also "an institution of industrial capitalism, with its characteristic equipment, organization, management, and cast of characters."[6]

Nor could liberal defenses of privacy stem the expanding public tide. Among other reasons, defending privacy against an "impersonal" public sphere that makes privacy valuable in the first place patently seems contradictory. For example, most contemporary legal defenses and definitions of privacy take their cue from, even as they attempt to revise, Samuel Warren and Louis Brandeis's article "The Right to Privacy," published in the *Harvard Law Review* (1890). Warren and Brandeis sought to limit the threats to a person's "right to be let alone" posed by "recent inventions and business methods," especially those employed by a publicity-rapacious mass media.[7] Based on the liberal-individualist principle of one's "inviolate personality,"[8] this article amounts to a rear-guard defense against the trend in U.S. culture, evident in the late nineteenth century, toward the de facto extinction of personal privacy. But the article also committed itself to the centrality of a bureaucratic public realm, which these "inventions and business methods" were enlisted to facilitate. Hence it and the liberal ideology based on it ended up effectively endorsing the elimination of the private life that it ostensibly desired to salvage through legal-political means.

Moreover, this defense of privacy argues only for a qualified and politically unthreatening kind of privacy. What Warren and Brandeis characterize as the right to be "let alone" appears already circumscribed by a specifically definable and dominant public sphere. The public, in short, here assumes final authority in determining at what point privacy becomes a refuge of antisocial (including antiegalitarian) self-interest.[9] Summarizing the views of certain critics on this issue,

Patricia Boling notes that while this liberal construction of privacy "protects us from scrutiny and interference," it "sometimes . . . shuts off parts of our lives from public debate and prevents us from taking political action to improve those parts of our lives."[10] At bottom, in fact, liberal arguments for privacy hinge on the rationale that its recovery would effect a more civic-minded public sphere. But this rationale can only succumb to more defensive views of privacy in light of the expanding commercialism, technological progress, and political reforms that such arguments also advance. This is the dilemma Rochelle Gurstein repeats in staging a turn-of-the-century social "reticence" and its "far richer appreciation of the public realm" giving way to the victorious onslaught of public "exposure" that resulted from "mass-circulation newspapers, photographs, and advertising," along with literary-realistic exposés of "the trials and tribulations of everyday domestic life."[11]

In our time, of course, the manifest threats to privacy cited by liberals have become conspicuously exacerbated, thanks to the surge of a pervasive, late-capitalist commodity culture and revolutionary technological advances most evident in the area of communications. Whatever the public sphere once meant, it now means "publicity," an amplified social space in which hyper-attention can be trained on persons or events, with its most visible aspect consisting precisely in the commercial exploitation of celebrities' private lives by the mass media—the trials and travails of the president's penis, for instance. If formerly the public took precedence over or threatened the private realm, it nevertheless assumed the appearance of an external, impersonal agency in relation to a separate or "other" sphere of existence. Now, however, one is additionally encouraged to regard the private as always already public. For what can privacy mean in an era of publicly accessible, user-friendly, and electronically facilitated reproductions of what were formerly regarded as utterly private events: the videotaping of weddings, funerals, scenes of sex, deaths, and births, for instance? In effect, we ourselves internalize (and thus regard our experiences in terms of) this electronic public sphere and its instantaneous amplifications of such events. Arguably less a matter of social control than the impulse to witness and objectify (in other words, represent) private affairs as secrets, these internalized tools of perception realize Michel Foucault's famous version of Jeremy Bentham's Panopticon with a vengeance.

This panoptic invasion, however, ostensibly concerns traditional tropes of privacy, such as physical solitude, intimacy, control over access to our bodies and information, and even domestic privacy. These devolve on discernible activities or relations with others. But what of more subjective private affairs, such as thinking or feeling? Here, too, however, twentieth-century thought, hardly in any mood to inhabit investigations into mental phenomena and the rapid dissemination of its findings, in effect propagates a "tell-all" ethos in accord with runaway, technological constructions of the public realm. For one can easily cite a host of modern and postmodern theories that themselves contribute to the wholesale evacuation of privacy. Ludwig Wittgenstein eviscerates the possibility of private languages; recent philosophers of mind, among them Thomas Nagel (not to mention their cybernetic antagonists, for example, Daniel Dennett), question the possibility of private experience; psychoanalysts "assume that it is possible to access and examine the motivations of others," thus placing "an agent's [subjective] intimacy claims" within "the reach of others."[12] Cultural critique today perforce regards privacy as a sociopolitical construction. Even deploying postmodern, guerrilla-like strategies against panoptic disciplinary methods and concepts—for example, Oedipal paradigms and the like—inversely legitimates the political cachet of their respective deconstructions.[13]

In brief, phenomenological convictions about privacy can't pass critical muster. Privacy, here denoting whatever (including privacy itself) I feel, perceive, think, imagine, do (or feel, perceive, think, imagine I am doing), beyond, but not necessarily excluding, the actual presence of others, turns out to be refracted by a host of mediations—linguistic, cultural, political, gendered, familial, geographical, even architectural. On reflection, whatever I feel, perceive, think, imagine, or do is *not,* strictly speaking, private at all. In this sense, occupied by a public that happens to dominate my living and thinking environment at any given moment, privacy does not exist. The personal is indeed political, and not just as a political credo. So today's critical practitioners of "going public," whatever their different social agendas—egalitarian, antihegemonic, or, perchance, even reactionary—are right on, so it seems, for the social good they want to do. Who would want it otherwise? What for?

2

Still, and beyond the fact that many of these same critics remain closet liberals regarding *certain* private matters, the public, from a literary-critical perspective, depends on the private as much as vice versa, if only not to implode into a realm of utter, aesthetic disinterest. This recognition motivates, for example, Poe's "imp of the perverse," which, in the public terms of his time, signifies a motiveless and thus, for him, radically private *imp*ulse.[14] It also accounts for his interest in cryptography and his rhetorical dalliance with submerged puns, anagrams, or, more thematically, unread-

able figures, such as both the narrator and the ostensible protagonist of **"The Old Man of the Crowd."**[15] Or, witness the lines from Crébillon's play that Dupin, at the end of **"The Purloined Letter,"** inscribes in "my MS" on the otherwise blank facsimile letter he intends Minister D— to discover (***CW*** [***Collected Works of Edgar Allan Poe***], 3: 993). Besides revealing Dupin as their author, thus avenging (since D— will no longer be able to exploit the letter's political, that is, public, value) an "'evil turn'" D— once did him, these lines allude to, but leave unspecified, the actual content of this "turn," which is thus left conspicuously private.

Like the minister and Dupin, Poe, in effect, here claims privacy *in public*: He all *but* represents his/their motivations in stealing the tale's letter and the tale itself from a medium (literature/letter writing) through which private, personal matters are quintessentially made public to others. **"The Purloined Letter,"** that is, makes public only the fact of its own withholding of information. Moreover, Poe's contemporary readers, encouraged by the tale's narrator, and here surrogate reader, would likely overlook this particular occurrence in following the tale's plot, which is to say the representational "how" of the letter's recovery. In short, one could argue that this emplotted scene of reading manifests a wish to go private.

Or does it? For what I call Poe's private rhetorical moves could just as easily comprise one of his notorious, Dupin-like mind games. Might they not reflect, for example, a *qualified* private ruse, intended to mock or, simply for the sheer superior feeling elicited, hoodwink the mass-cultural public to whom he often disparagingly referred as the mob? It seems equally feasible that, given his economic circumstances and feeling of entrapment in the magazine prison-house, Poe seeks to attract public attention for his work—to succeed somehow, some way, in the literary marketplace—by exploiting this public's interest in things secret. Conversely, his private moves instead possibly disclose his resistance to the commodification of his work in this mass-cultural milieu.[16] Yet the sophistication required simply to recognize such moves may also confess Poe's investment in a more serious literary game. Averring this in various places, he wants his art, after all, to strike readers with "a suggestive indefiniteness of meaning, with the view of bringing about a definitiveness of vague and therefore of spiritual *effect*" ("Marginalia," *Essays,* 1331). Here the "private," synonymous with this desired effect, comes down to a shareable aesthetic, whatever its antisocial formalism might imply for Poe's present-day political detractors. At the very least, this "vague" aesthetic principle allows for the possibility of his having designed tales to seduce any suspicious, hypercritical reader into appreciating the prolonged—a French connotation for "purloined"—semiotic status of his literary letter beyond first impressions.

These are all public-oriented, if not exactly public-spirited, motivations. For that matter, not even the latter is out of the question, for one can always align Poe's private inscriptions with the previously remarked American privacy concerns raised during this period. Milette Shamir, for example, argues that such concerns set the precedent for what was to become the legal "right to privacy" and did so "precisely in order to counter the problem of the alienability of personhood that emerged with modern capitalism, in order to keep stories about the self from circulating in the market and hence to resist the risk of appropriation by the market."[17] In effect, Poe's encrypted rhetorical shenanigans work to frustrate such circulation. This is the position Jonathan Auerbach assumes in stating that Poe fears "fad[ing] into obscurity as soon as his work enters the public domain." As a writer and editor of magazine journals, Poe understands that "once the published word becomes a commodity to be proliferated endlessly, the journalist loses control over his creations and finds the identity he has invested in the writing dispersed and dislocated among the masses." Poe therefore stages the fictionality of his tales by allegorically emplotting their readers, the better to control their reception and "verify his identity for the reader."[18]

The privacy concerns of the period primarily centered on the issue of domestic privacy and were expressed by other antebellum writers, most notably Hawthorne, whose *Twice-Told Tales* Poe favorably reviewed more than once. For instance, Shamir maintains that in Hawthorne's story "The Minister's Black Veil," the protagonist's terminal refusal to take off his veil—the reason for which Poe thinks the "rabble" will not apprehend but that he intuits as a crime of passion ("Nathaniel Hawthorne," *Essays*, 574-75)—protests his "absolute privacy" as household head from "the intrusions of official authorities . . . [,] from the inquisitive gossip of the congregation (the 'multitudes'), and even from the sympathetic queries of his fiancée" (Shamir, 752). In *The House of the Seven Gables,* Hawthorne specifically shuns surveillance by the masses over household affairs as facilitated by such new technologies as the daguerreotype and such psychologically invasive, scientific practices as mesmerism, both of which the character Holgrave represents in this romance novel. To Hawthorne, such devices were "expanding the private sphere indefinitely" and thereby "threaten[ing] to eliminate privacy altogether" (Shamir, 766). Hawthorne himself evinces guilt as a novelist for disclosing the secrets and private goings-on of his fictional "house," and so has Holgrave learn

"that the power of the seer needs to be used for the protection and even for the construction of domestic privacy, rather than for its violation and destruction. He learns, that is, to be a romancer rather than a reforming novelist" (Shamir, 771).

From this viewpoint, Hawthorne adopts what I earlier termed a contradictory, liberal-ideological stance toward privacy. At bottom, he believes communal sociality can harmoniously coexist with self-autonomy (*Romance*, 72). This belief, however, includes an important qualification. On the one hand, it marks, for example, his ambivalent relation to the minister's radical stance in "The Minister's Black Veil," the historical setting of which poses the negotiable problem of face-to-face, social surveillance versus anyone's right to privacy. Assuming personal privacy is one thing; insisting on it radically within the minister's communally concrete situation amounts to *sin.* On the other hand, Hawthorne's nineteenth-century public, the American market-inflected and anonymous readership he presupposes in writing, lacks such immediate, human definition. For this reason, it makes more sense to claim that his ministerial tale at best expresses his *desire* to believe in self-other relations.

Thus, as Auerbach suggests, when Hawthorne comes to write *The Blithedale Romance,* the last of his extended, first-person romances, he can neither identify with his narrator, Miles Coverdale, nor imagine his other characters with full, fictional identities (*Romance,* 91, 98). Put another way, in writing this work, Hawthorne continually finds himself caught in a web of fiction making per se, or in the very public theatricality that he attributes to these characters and to which he, as a mid-nineteenth-century American, is equally drawn. Consequently, "from one romance to the next, relations among persons become more and more an artificial function of plot for Hawthorne because he finds more immediate forms of intimacy increasingly threatening," specifically to his liberal notion of a society based on autonomous selves (*Romance,* 111). Such "intimacy," in fact, assumes the threatening guise of radical privacy—a privacy reminiscent of his earlier minister—as much as an ever tempting publicity.

But at least Hawthorne attempts to balance the claims these two separating spheres make on him and his writing. For instance, he had earlier tried to go public with his own private proclivities in *The Scarlet Letter,* in which, in "The Custom-House" preface, he famously states his desire to write from "a neutral territory, somewhere between the real world and fairyland, where the Actual and the Imaginary may meet."[19] Indeed, Hester and Dimmesdale's tryst in effect occurs offstage—in private[20]—during Hawthorne's quasi-private autobiographical chat with the novel's readers, in which, significantly, he asserts his intention to seek a wider public for his work. The casual tone of his preface here belies the anxious standoff of the "Actual" public consequences of this "Imaginary" private act. The two never quite come to coexist harmoniously. For at the end of *The Scarlet Letter*, Hester lives alone, an aid to, but not full participant in, her community. Her wish as a woman to go public—voluntarily wearing the scarlet letter to represent feminine desires forcibly made private by patriarchal communities in America's past and, thanks to their enforced association with domestic privacy, also in Hawthorne's present—is deferred to some better liberal future. Neither can Hawthorne the writer here resolve his wish to write both romance, the infiltration of private wish into public idiom, and novel, the public translation of this wish that would nullify its "Imaginary" aura.

Shamir analogously sees *The House of the Seven Gables* "filled with tension that arises from the desire to stress the writer's inclusive vision"—Hawthorne's novelistic inclination to expose private affairs, not unlike Holgrave's initial intention to publish his findings in the press, in contrast with "his self-proclaimed responsibility to participate in the production of privacy" (Shamir, 774). Auerbach sees only Hawthorne's final failure in *The Blithedale Romance* to sustain the tension of his liberal romance. But in either case, his writing both in theme and method reflects a socially representative struggle to adjudicate while keeping separate the private and public realms. For different reasons, one might invoke this liberal-individualist struggle to account for Poe's private "I" tales as well. By emplotting reader-surrogates in his tales, Poe arguably wants to control, as Auerbach suggests, his literary presentation of self before others. He therefore resorts to literary stratagems that will fend off readers and the mass-public marketplace he associates with them. But his desire for literary recognition leads him simultaneously to bank on others desiring the same control, which in turn qualifies his putative privacy claims: "The author accustomed to seclusion, and mingling for the first time with those who have been associated with him only through their [*sic*] works, is astonished and delighted at finding common to all whom he meets conclusions which he had blindly fancied were attained by himself alone" ("Literati," *Essays*, 1120).

But this liberal-individualist apologia for Poe's privacy concerns never quite rings true. For one thing, the emplotted readers in his tales comprise foils that confirm only by misreading Poe's literary identity. They resemble, for example, those mass-public figures in **"The Murders in the Rue Morgue"** (1841), who, as reported by the public press, translate the sounds of the murdering ape into their different linguistic codes—islands of cultural privacy, so to speak. In short, they miss identifying the ape altogether, which of course conceals Poe's own inscribed anagram (E.A.P.). Moreover, as his very name suggests, Dupin, as he will again do in **"The Purloined Letter,"** also dupes the putatively trusted and would-be privy reader; that is, he withholds his solution of the crime until the last moment from the narrator, who lives with him in a private abode, where they indulge in "reading, writing, or conversing": "Our seclusion was perfect. We admitted no visitors. Indeed the locality of our retirement had been carefully kept a secret from my own former associates; and it had been many years since Dupin had ceased to know or be known in Paris. We existed within ourselves alone" (*CW*, 2: 533, 532). Like the actual reader of Poe's tale, the narrator remains entirely subject to Dupin's narrative. Moreover, Dupin, as in the famous street scene, in which he duplicates the narrator's "meditations" (*CW*, 2: 534), can read the narrator's mind without the reverse being also true.

Poe, I would argue, thus inscribes in his fiction a more radical sense of literary privacy than does Hawthorne in his romances. Envisioned in a series of metamorphosing versions, the reader is stripped of otherness, or at least made to serve Poe's pursuit of such privacy. This is not to say that he lacks the capacity to imagine the other *as* other, which Auerbach asserts in claiming Poe's "inability to conceive of human relationships altogether" (*Romance*, 25). Auerbach makes this claim based on evidence from the tale **"William Wilson,"** in which the narrator Wilson never recognizes himself in the other Wilson figure, or double, a relationship that itself doubles Poe's with his first-person narrator. But this double also doubles as Poe's reader, a figure for the intrusive public he writes to baffle, here exemplified by the tale's ambiguous ending. If Wilson has indeed killed his conscience, that is, the mandates of Poe's literary public, why does he write this narrative? Out of guilt, which otherwise implies the resurrection of public determinations of self? Or from the wish to insist on his perverse because unshareable originality precisely in the face of this public?[21]

Dupin's return to the scene of a publicity-amplified crime after his voluntary withdrawal from public affairs to pursue private, literary ones suggests that Poe never denies the eternal recurrence of the public's attractive pull on his art. He, too, simply as a writer, exists in the force field of such attraction. Indeed, like Dupin in **"The Purloined Letter,"** Poe, here unlike Hawthorne, himself has little compunction about invading the privacy of others: "'I confess, however, that I should like very well to know the precise character of [Minister D—'s] thoughts, when . . . he is reduced to opening the letter which I left for him in the card-rack'" (*CW,* 3: 993). But as this scene from the tale already indicates, Dupin's voyeurism, which itself conflates public with private, effectively aims to secure its author's privacy at the expense of D—'s. Dupin, that is, steals back the letter by first entering the minister's private residence and then distracting him by a staged commotion in the street. Moreover, Dupin places the facsimile of this letter on the minister's card-rack, an early Victorian site customarily used for receiving visitors' messages and mail—in other words, an intersection precisely of public-private correspondence. And as if all this were insufficiently invasive, Dupin further entertains the wish to witness undetected the minister's private scene of reading the facsimile's Crébillon or "literary" message, the fictional-autobiographical significance of which remains accessible only to Dupin.

So conspicuous as to go unnoticed, like the letter and its facsimile in the tale, **"The Purloined Letter"** thus figures privacy in the mode of an ersatz endless becoming. The tale itself expresses the specified absence of Poe's semiotic motivation in writing it and uses precisely its public exteriority *as* a written (and later published) letter to do so. In effect, Poe himself steals back this letter from his imagined public: from language, the public medium par excellence, and from language's own most public stage, literature. And he purloins it not simply from the mass reader, who is intent on narrative thrills and imaginary public spectacles like those in the street and therefore bound to miss these redundant stratagems, but even from a critical reader, who, like Poe himself, with his notorious suspicions and putative detections of other writers' plagiarisms, suspects the tale's self-referential rumblings or privately encoded thematic. Deploying a variety of provocative narrative maneuvers that at once invite and disable any one proper decodification of his tale (for instance, D— as the double of *D*upin, and Dupin as Poe's pronominal surrogate in the tale), Poe himself, on a par with Dupin's reading of the minister's reading of the facsimile's literary allusion, emplots the reader's reading of his tale so as to witness such reading(s) as if from an undetected, private position.

In **"The Murders in the Rue Morgue,"** Dupin's return to a highly publicized crime similarly suggests that Poe uses this public to pursue his wish to realize a sense of literary originality unmitigated by the lurking judgments or conscience he associates with others. At bottom, this wish is what Poe's tales at once concern and stage. They would position themselves as if always one step ahead of their inevitable manifestation in the variously inflected idioms of language or what he elsewhere calls "the power of words" (*CW,* 3: 822-25). In this sense, Poe's private performatives, not un-

like Dupin's apparent, public return in **"The Murders in the Rue Morgue"** and ancillary, voyeuristic wish in **"The Purloined Letter,"** come after, not before—hence do not preclude—the tale's apprehension by an imagined reading public. It is as if he were continually constructing escape clauses in his tales for no other reason than that they might allow him to hedge his de facto commitment as a writer to one or another prevailing socioliterary contract, which is to say that they ought to possess at least *some* recoverable public or manifest social value.

Poe, in short, pushes the envelope of literary privacy. His parasitic vision of privacy—making the public private rather than vice versa—means that he not only invents the detective or "private-eye" genre. He also raises the "private I" in American writing to a level beyond its subsumption into ideological concepts such as private property, commodity, domestic relations, liberal individualism—anything that might resolve itself into a public datum. As the police amply demonstrate in **"The Purloined Letter,"** Poe's purloined tales can never be found in publicly defined private spaces. They elude even as they invite critical inspection, and they do so precisely by not resisting the public, which for him is the only way to indite literary privacy or send private letters without conceding to public determinations.

3

The foregoing discussion surely leads one to ask, What critical sense does it make not only to examine but to valorize literary fiction in terms of its discernible wishes to go private? As Poe intuited, the public "What for?" can never be far behind such efforts. More explicitly than fiction, criticism does sociocultural work and, at least in today's critical climate, requires that fiction do the same: either reinforce or criticize the social values by which its readers live. But what happens when a literary work resists precisely this charge, not because it privileges some antisocial, aesthetic privatism but because it seeks a privacy that, if only in imaginary terms and as the primary condition of its very writing, would reconfigure the social minus the public abstractions to which it is always heir? And yet doing so would also mean not setting out to do so.

More than Poe's, certain works by Henry James, Poe's otherwise unlikely literary descendant, go private in this manner. James's fiction internalizes its own critical responses the better to extrude a private surplus. It determines this surplus, in other words, by, in effect, staging the inability of its criticisms to penetrate the literary privacy of the text. James, of course, has received critical attention before for notably thematizing the American privacy crisis near the time of Warren and Brandeis's article, particularly in such works as *The Bostonians, The Reverberator, The Aspern Papers, The Sacred Fount,* and such short stories as "The Private Life" and "The Figure in the Carpet."[22] One way or another, these works clearly expose the egregious aspects of an intrusive, postbellum press, the prurient curiosity of a modern public to know intimate details of others' personal lives, and the critical attempts to determine artistic intention in works of art. To say the least, James hardly embraces the "growing mass of increasingly heterogeneous, potentially intrusive readers."[23] His private view of such publicity seems quite decisive, as when, in his *Notebooks,* he inveighs against "the shamelessness of the newspaper and the interviewer, the devouring publicity of life, the extinction of all sense between public and private."[24]

Yet one could argue that, at least in his fiction, James represents this public threat ambiguously and in this sense affiliates his vision not with Poe's pursuit of radical privacy but instead with Hawthorne's liberal attempt to preserve the distinction between public and private realms in matters of writing as well as domestic life. Even his well-known position about the autonomy of art perpetuates this distinction. For instance, his use of such self-effacing, publicity-minded, voyeuristic narrators as those in *The Aspern Papers* and "The Figure in the Carpet" is presented with elusive motivations that, as Auerbach notices, leave James's own authorial self "outside his text" (*Romance,* 171). His works, that is, *practice* authorial privacy, in effect warding off what he regards as a rapaciously curious, abstract public that treats writers and their texts like appropriable commodities in the American marketplace.[25]

At the same time, however, this practice imagines an alternative public wherein not only readers interact with artistic works but, here answering Hawthorne's worry about his own artistic intrusiveness, writers do the same with their living models. According to Brook Thomas, James's art never strives to appropriate "the real. It is instead an act that allows for more exchanges. Those exchanges depend on the existence of a space between a work and the very life that it would appropriate, for if a work's act of appropriation were complete it would lose its status as art."[26] The public, that is, can appropriate only private objects and intrude only on private scenes; but for James, this publicity-vulnerable privacy, synonymous, say, with the poet Aspern's letters or portrait, merely comprises the residue of a simultaneously appearing, more recessive privacy determined by elusive exchanges among reader, writer, and work.

Literary privacy is a *given* for James, reinforced by an imaginary critical public that amounts to a liberal fantasy of a premodern, less impersonal American public

sphere. Barbara Hochman suggests that this vision of public-private harmony even carries over into the way James later dictated his letters for the typewriter, with "the depersonalization associated with the production of type . . . partially balanced by the quiet interpolation of the live secretary."[27] In the same way, one could claim that his fiction sooner or later imagines the accommodation rather than the opposition of private and public realms. In "The Private Life" (1892), to take one instance, the writer Clare Vawdrey, tabbed a "genius" by the English literary world, shows none of this talent in his conversations with the story's anonymous narrator or with the other four high-society characters vacationing at a Swiss hotel. In public, "'I never found him anything but loud and liberal and cheerful, and I never heard him utter a paradox or express a shade or play with an idea.'"[28] Perplexed by this discrepancy between the writer's banal public self and the genius manifested in his works, the narrator eventually testifies to Vawdrey's having a private "'double'" (*CW,* 2: 533), the two indivisibly linked, "'for after all they're members of a firm, and one of them would never be able to carry on the business without the other'" (James, 218).

If nothing else, this theme of doubling puts one in mind of Poe, as if he—or rather, his pursuit of radical literary privacy—were James's own private double in writing this story. And it turns out that such privacy pervades the entire narrative. For one thing, the narrator's testimony of Vawdrey's possessing what Poe's narrator in **"The Murders in the Rue Morgue"** dubs a "Bi-Part Soul" (*CW,* 3: 402) occurs in a whirl of possible motivations that cast doubt on whether the narrator actually witnesses Vawdrey's private scene of writing. As if he were conning even his most intimate public, Vawdrey is asked to but cannot show the manuscript for a play he claims to be writing. Blanche Adney, a still beautiful, middle-aged actress, who wants a part to justify her career, a part that even her own husband, a musical composer, cannot give her, desires to see this manuscript. At first skeptical about its existence, the narrator is impelled to supply such evidence for Adney, with whom he, along with the other male characters, appears to desire some form of intimacy. Himself acting the prying, public voyeur (James's bête noire), the narrator, assuming Vawdrey is downstairs, one evening opens his darkened room hoping to find the manuscript. Instead, he comes upon Vawdrey himself—so he thinks—a "figure seated at a table near one of the windows" and "whom an instant before I had to the best of my belief left below in conversation with Mrs. Adney. His back was half-turned to me and he bent over the table in the attitude of writing, but I took in at every pore his identity" (James, 207-8). The narrator, who purports to be a literary critic a notch above "reviewers" with whom he faults Vawdrey for concerning himself (James, 228), only *possibly* witnesses him as writer ("his identity") in the "attitude" of composing a work. The narrator thus calls our attention to his own present act of writing, in which *his* "attitude" (here referring to his disposition to believe he has found out Vawdrey) is thus as much and as little exposed to us.

In fact, far from balancing public and private selves, let alone salvaging a socially beleaguered privacy, "The Private Life" stages the public everywhere as imploding into the private. This occurs even with the story's other central figure, Lord Mellifont, the handsome host of the social occasion as well as an amateur sketch artist. Because he leads the group's conversations—"what he contributed above all to English public life" (James, 199)—the narrator associates him with the public man par excellence: "He was all public and had no corresponding private life, just as Clare Vawdrey was all private and had no corresponding public" (James, 215). Mellifont's identity devolves entirely on the presence of others; otherwise, it doesn't seem to exist at all. He appears before Adney when she has been looking for him in the mountainous area around the hotel, disappears when she leaves, and appears yet again when she returns:

> "He lost *me*—that appears the way of it. He supposed me gone."
>
> "You did find him, however," I said. . . .
>
> "It was he who found *me*. . . . He's there from the moment he knows somebody else is."
>
> (James, 221; James's emphases)

If Vawdrey has two selves, then, "'there isn't so much as one, all told, of Lord Mellifont,'" according to Adney (James, 214). In this sense, Mellifont functions as Vawdrey's double in the story as much as does Vawdrey's own "'other self,'" the designation by which she revises the narrator's more technical reference to Vawdrey's "'alternate identity'" (James, 217).

But the narrator, a busybody gossip committed to disclosures of private intimacies and so a figure of modern publicity, also exists as Mellifont's more intrusive public double. Mellifont's old-style public identity, that is, retains a dimension of privacy every bit as resistant to such disclosures as Vawdrey's private scene of writing. Mellifont, the narrator surmises, "represented to his wife and was a hero to his servants, and what one wanted to arrive at was what really became of him when no eye could see—and *a fortiori* no soul admire. . . . [H]ow intense an *entr'acte* to make possible more such performances!" (James, 216). The narrator ostensibly regards these private moments as

mere "'intermissions'" (James, 221) to Mellifont's public "performances." But it becomes clear that Mellifont's "'private life'" (James, 219) constantly piques the narrator's curiosity throughout his narrative, as with his pressing Adney to tell him about her private contretemps with Mellifont on their walk. She informs the narrator that to witness this life, he must come upon Mellifont unawares in his room. But such witnessing will hardly resolve this issue, at least not for Adney. Resorting to a double entendre, she suggests that if the narrator indeed follows her advice, he will find that Mellifont lacks any private life, or else that his private life is more private than the narrator can grasp: "'You won't see anything'" (James, 214).

This disclosure, that others cannot ever perceive the private life of others, defines the story's theme and symbolic action. On the pretext of gaining Lord Mellifont's signature for a watercolor sketch presented to Adney, the narrator indeed attempts to open Mellifont's room and witness him offstage, as it were, but he is intercepted by Lady Mellifont at the last moment. Adney has previously suggested to the narrator that Lady Mellifont also wants to catch her husband in his room alone, for she, too, apparently suspects and is afraid that she will find nothing there (James, 223). Prompted by this suggestion, the narrator reads in "her frightened face a still deeper betrayal—a possibility of disappointment if I should give way" and *not* enter the room (James, 227). But as is often the case in James's fiction, the narrator has perhaps overread the situation. For after Lady Mellifont deposits the sketch in her separate room to have her husband sign it later, she responds to the narrator's noting a "change of weather" by claiming that she and Mellifont will have to "'go immediately.'" He reads this statement as a wish to "escape with her threatened secret" yet feels "the more surprised therefore when, as I was turning away, she put out her hand to take mine." The narrator remains adamant in his rationale, thinking that what her friendly gesture of farewell "really conveyed was . . . 'If I should know, who would help me then?'" (James, 228); but this exchange inevitably insinuates that she is making the best of an embarrassing public situation—and privately protecting her and her husband's private life.

Like the story, this entire scene abounds with analogues that all point to private goings-on which the narrator further misreads and thus never penetrates, himself forced into his own private perspective. For we never know his motives in trying to penetrate Vawdrey's and Lord Mellifont's privacy. Does he do it from natural curiosity, from a pathological voyeurism, or, for that matter, from a wish to purchase some sublimated form of sexual intimacy with Adney, which even she thinks possibly makes him "'jealous'" at least of Vawdrey (James, 210)? Moreover, it is never clear if Adney coyly kindles his intimate overtures in order to conceal her sexual liaison with Mellifont, about which we, too, remain uncertain. Meaning it differently, the narrator even asks her if "'he [made] love to you on the glacier'" (James, 204). And this liaison may be what Adney thinks Lady Mellifont suspects about her husband, since she admits to being "nervous . . . if my husband's away from me for any time" and fears "'the general sense that he'll never come back'" (James, 196).

After all, Adney's remarks to the narrator, rich throughout with double entendres, often slide into sexual innuendos. For example, when discussing her encounter with Mellifont on the first day's walk, the analogue of unsatisfactory intercourse abounds everywhere:

> "He was too absent, too utterly gone, as gone as a candle blown out; for some reason best known to himself. It was probably some moment of fatigue. . . ."
>
> "Couldn't he [the narrator asks] have been somewhere else?"
>
> "He couldn't have been, in the time, anywhere but just where I had left him. Yet the place was utterly empty—as empty as this stretch of valley in front of us. . . ."
>
> "And where did the sun rise?"
>
> "Just where it ought to—just where he would have been and where I should have seen him had he been like other people."
>
> ". . . . How long a time elapsed between the moment you were sure of his absence and the moment you called?"
>
> "Oh but a few seconds. I don't pretend it was long."
>
> (James, 222)

In contrast, Adney's claim, near the story's end, to have sighted Vawdrey's private self—"'He was there—you saw him?'" the narrator asks her—alludes to a more successful sexual experience:

> "He saw *me*. It was the hour of my life!"
>
> "It must have been the hour of his, if you were half as lovely as you are at this moment."
>
> "He's splendid," she pursued as if she didn't hear me. "He *is* the one who does it." I listened, immensely impressed, and she added: "We understood each other."
>
> "By flashes of lightning?"
>
> "Oh I didn't see the lightning then!"
>
> (James, 230; James's emphases)

Adney also plays on and even mocks the narrator's sexual naïveté, turning him into an unwitting panderer. For example, his "sensual" obsession to make private

lives public (James, 217) initially stokes her own sexual interest in Vawdrey over Mellifont: "'. . . but that was before I fell in love. You blotted [Mellifont] out with *your* story'" about Vawdrey's private double (James, 219; James's emphasis). Likewise, she preps the narrator for "go-between" service by at once flattering his romantic sensitivity and deflecting its sexual postscript; she calls him, that is, "'a searcher of hearts—that frivolous thing an observer,'" in other words, someone who, since she knows his attraction to her, will "'go and get [Vawdrey's] papers'" in his room and thus "'expose'" him (James, 204, 205).

But is sex the primary issue with Adney, or even with James's story? For it could just as easily serve the Poesque function of a "suggested meaning run[ning] through the obvious one in a *very* profound undercurrent" ("Nathaniel Hawthorne," *Essays,* 582). After her "suggested" ecstatic, sexual experience with the private Vawdrey ("'I adore him'" [James, 230]), she shuts him out the next day. He asks the narrator "what was the matter with her—she suddenly appeared to dislike him" (James, 231). She abruptly leaves for England with her husband, whose lack of passion is, as she has told the narrator earlier, "'exactly why I adore him. Doesn't a woman with my history know the passions of others for insupportable?'" (James, 218). Sex or sexual conquest thus seems secondary to Adney's "obvious" goal, namely her expressed ambition to get a dramatic "part" that will consummate her artistic career, which she has apparently realized by visiting Vawdrey's private room: "'I shall have my part—I shall have my part!'" (James, 230). Yet her sudden coldness to Vawdrey equally insinuates the inadequacy of this explanation, too.

"The Private Life," in short, stages the desire and failure to penetrate privacy at all levels of public understanding. The narrator never gains access to Mellifont's private self, which probably remains as much a private vacuum to himself as it does to Lady Mellifont and Adney, even supposing that the latter's sexual dalliance with him occurred. The narrator also seeks and fails to gain sexual intimacy with Adney, which he never acknowledges to himself as such so that it, too, remains private. He clearly desires a literary intimacy with Vawdrey, for when Vawdrey utters his concern about the reviewers, the narrator acknowledges, "I suppose I wanted him to make an exception for *me*—for me all alone" (James, 229; James's emphasis). But sexual, artistic, or critical intimacy fails to capture the private writer. In the end, both the narrator and Adney witness firsthand Vawdrey's scene of writing, which leaves unresolved the conundrum of his public banality and private genius.

The same situation affects readers of "The Private Life" as well. At the literal level, it keeps withholding definitive information about the characters, each of whom—and not merely the narrator, Mellifont, and Vawdrey—gains aesthetic interest precisely because we are not fully privy to their motivations. Why, for instance, does Adney's husband put up with her sexual dalliances? Adney herself gains public interest as an actress because "people thought she told them the secrets of the pictorial [public] nature"; for the narrator and the reader, however, she is of interest because she has "told them nothing" (James, 202). Even Lady Mellifont "had a secret, and if you didn't find it out as you knew her better"—which, again, neither the narrator nor readers come to do—"you at least felt sure she was gentle[,] unaffected and limited, as well as rather submissively sad" (James, 195).

Not least, given its "suggested," sexual "undercurrent," the story teases us into apprehending its own less literal or *relatively* private codification. But this reading proves to be only another hermeneutic detour that confronts us all the more with the story's semiotically blank, literary privacy. For one thing, the narrative's sexual scenarios not only appear ambiguous or allusive, but, as with Adney's cold and abrupt withdrawals from Mellifont, Vawdrey, and the narrator—she presumably has gotten what she wanted from them—in the end prove ancillary to its thematization of privacy per se: the fact that one cannot know the other's private life without drifting back into an uninteresting, public life. Thus Adney eventually produces Vawdrey's play, but she "is still nevertheless in want of the great part" (James, 231). This is why "The Private Life" passionately pursues its own private scene of writing, which, rather than consisting of a determinable secret known by James—that the story really concerns, say, the covert, late-Victorian labyrinths of sexual desire—instead traduces its reader to focus on the contentless privacy of, precisely, what this secret might be. The story refers, in short, to the secret code generating its very narrative, in other words, to its own "private life."

Of course, the story tempts readers to persist in trying to expose this code, but they can do so only at the cost of converting the text into a dissatisfying tease primarily aimed at public performance. If nothing else, by intimating withheld "secrets," Adney's hollow and ultimately unfulfilling, artistic seductions of London audiences testify to the necessity that the story's author must do otherwise. Anonymity thus characterizes its internalized image of the author: of the writer who himself is always turning into the reader of his own text and, therefore, becoming unknown to himself, can, like Vawdrey, never articulate how it got done. Only by this metamorphosis can James, well-known writer and, like the narrator, would-be playwright, avoid deploying dramatic and representational ambi-

guities as if constructing a puzzle for his readers to solve. Neither does James use them to signify nothing, to indulge, that is, an aesthetic mystification akin to an intimate, sensual scene, the actual representation or witnessing of which remains perpetually deferred or left up in the air. "'I wish you'd let an observer write you a play!'" says the narrator to Adney or, in effect, James to his stimulating, muse-like public audience:

> "People don't care for what you write: you'd break any run of luck."
>
> "Well, I see plays all around me, . . . the air is full of them tonight."
>
> "The air? Thank you for nothing! I only wish my table-drawers were."
>
> (James, 204)

So, in another switch, James, in his verbal sketch of "The Private Life," dons the all-public mask of Lord Mellifont, the artist who doesn't sign *his* watercolor sketch and who remains anonymous even to the critically inquisitive reader—the narrator who never manages to procure Mellifont's personal signature. This anonymity allows James, like Vawdrey, to go private, to use these literary "private parts" to supply the vital principle for an otherwise imaginatively bankrupt public sphere. For by going private, James, at the same time, leaves in public his strangely still unexposed fictional papers.

4

Poe and James shift the terms of the nineteenth-century American privacy issue by posing the question that the narrator of "The Private Life" asks *en scène*: "Why was he writing in the dark and why hadn't he answered me?" (James, 208). Both writers configure privacy in ways that would slip its contemporary, public formations, which nevertheless help instigate such private pursuits to begin with. For example, like Vawdrey, neither writer mystifies privacy as an assumed bastion of bourgeois privilege or a threatened self-autonomy. Privacy here means more than a defensive reaction to an American-democratic ethos that sponsors "the public's right to know" as well as to an impersonal, American *Gesellschaft* composed of newly invasive marketplace, political, and/or media practices.

Nor does either writer purvey the domestic realm, the most notable social trope of nineteenth-century American privacy, to counter this increasingly pervasive public sphere. With their Usher-like perversities, what alternative private solace do Poe's fictional households provide in relation to his abject position in the American marketplace? In James, the household already comprises a mini-public stage that promulgates elliptical miscommunications between characters and intractable ambiguities for readers. In this sense, Poe's and James's pursuits of a scriptural "private life" also skirt both the century's "separate-spheres" ideology and, in effect, its recent criticism. Some feminist critics maintain, for example, that this dichotomy and its very conceptual use oversimplify the "complicated ways" that contemporary men and women of different racial, regional, and class backgrounds interacted among themselves and wrote literary works.[29] Like reactionary defenses of privacy, this critique frames the private as just minutes away from becoming public—the gist of Cathy Davidson's plea for "no more separate spheres."

Poe and James instead attempt to radicalize the boundaries defining the public-private dichotomy such that the private, if it possesses any public value at all, forces the public to question its multidisciplinary constructions of the private.[30] And such constructions include notions of Emersonian self-reliance or of romantic inwardness generally, which may at first appear particularly to define the private both writers seek. But Poe pitches notions of romantic self-consciousness on the brink of self-delusion and disaster everywhere in his tales. James scripts his surrogate author in the grips of writing a text, the translation of which to a public stage (like the play Adney wants a part in) remains disjoined for himself as well as his prying observers from its singularly "dark" genesis. In this context, intimacy, a frequent psychological trope for privacy, also fails to account for what Poe and James pursue in their "write to privacy." Poe stymies would-be reader doubles with tales that cannot be read; James stages surrogate readers that spin their literary prying to no avail. In and of their respective texts, both writers emplot misreaders of all stripes and to such an extent that, no matter how historical circumstances pose different conventional and critical reading publics, these emplotments in principle obstruct future readers as well.

It is as if public formations of the private were never private enough for either writer. At the same time, this configuration presupposes an always prior engagement with—by no means a literal abstention from—activities and concerns of a public sphere or any marked social space in which one seeks recognition for one's (literary) labor and authorial identity ("personality"). Poe and James give ample play to these attractions of the public. They not only ply various literary conventions and presuppose audience responses; they also unavoidably trace topics and issues of public moment, such as the American privacy issue itself. But they do so all the while pushing to an extreme one aspect of writing per se. Historically, Ferdinand Schoeman has argued, literacy by itself "provided people with a new kind of private experience for discovering and consid-

ering ideas without confronting direct social pressure."[31] Poe and James exploit the fact that this ineradicable private experience, devoid of content, coterminously haunts the public trajectory of writing. To readjust Warren and Brandeis's formulation, both writers indeed pursue an inviolate privacy, but not that of one's social persona and not before staging the multiple, public means of the very violation of this privacy.

In this latter formulation, Poe and James may just give voice to an unconscious desideratum of radical privacy tugging at its apparently less rigorous pursuit in the work of other mid-nineteenth- through turn-of-the-century U.S. writers. Bastardized by coerced or defensive forms of social privacy, this desideratum in effect generates a cabala of American-Constitutional Writ, a poetic maximization, as it were, of checks and balances. On the one hand, counterindicating imaginary responses and even efforts to redress one or another "bad" or alienated public, such defenses inversely manifest frustrated or restoratively motivated communitarian longings. This is one way to read not only Hawthorne's private literary reflexes but also, for example, Henry David Thoreau's going to Walden Pond (and writing *Walden*) to "transact some private business," Herman Melville's Bartleby's disaffection from social volition, or perhaps even Emily Dickinson's self-sequestered scenes of writing her cryptically elliptical poems.

On the other hand, the privacy Poe and James pursue leaves such private, literary gestures intact without altogether dismissing their public justifications. This privacy occurs precisely in excess of the otherwise totalizing attractions of major and minor publics—bad *and* good—for self-recognition. In Aristotelian terms, the private here converts the public from final to efficient cause, whether as a negative spur or an engaging, *Gemeinschaft* ideal suddenly confronted with its finitude by a private other: mine, yours, anyone's, singly, but only in and as the process of pursuing it. Before becoming annexed by a different public idealism, this situation equally obtains, after all, in sociocultural situations where, for instance, a minority culture's praxis, construed as private from the viewpoint of a dominant culture, spoils the latter's ambition to determine what the public consists of.

In the privacy-unplugged mode of Poe and James, literary representation transforms the infinite, cusplike cultural occurrences of such public-private dichotomies into pro-tem tropes. Literature comes down to a public, linguistic space, in which the writer awaits the arrival or mourns the imaginary *jouissance* of an effervescent, because always figuratively impermanent, private experience. Such loss, for example, marks the massive public topos and photorealistic exposé of the Civil War comprising Stephen Crane's *Red Badge of Courage*.[32] Even Jack London, I would suggest, belongs in this already strange mix of private literary bedfellows. At first glance, of course, his works openly proselytize a populist stew of autodidactic socialism, Spencerian Darwinism, and Nietzschean superior-race theories. In short, his literary ideological agendas have little to do with privacy and, in fact, would deny it; instead, they are fashioned to overcome the market-driven, class-oppressive social system and bourgeois values that generally identify the dominant, U.S. public sphere of his time.

Nor does London's writing simply focus on public matters. In *Male Call*, Auerbach, extending his earlier argument about Poe and James in *The Romance of Failure*, makes a good case for London's further channeling these matters into the issue of his own literary publicity as a writer. He contends that in works written between 1893 and 1904 (roughly *The Call of the Wild* through *The Sea-Wolf*), London allegorically traces his ambition to become a public, literary persona. That is, he here inscribes his own ambition to "gain public recognition and power" as a man of letters and, in this way, dispel "the threat of anonymity" induced by the exchange marketplace of literary commodities and "the national public sphere" for which such commodities signify entry in imaginary terms.[33] In short, these works express his desire to make his name a "trademark," to become a commodified authorial self, thereby literally capitalizing on his name and his legendary reputation for adventure writing (*Male Call*, 26-27, 72).

Yet the private tracks both London's ambition to become an entirely public literary man and Auerbach's critical discussion of it. These earlier works record London's ambivalence toward—akin to a budding defense of authorial privacy against—his capitulation to such ambition. For example, in *The Call of the Wild*, his first publicly acclaimed novel, London notably converts literary *work,* as defined by the capitalist, literary market, into accomplished *literary* work. Here, the protagonist, London's "alter ego," is a wolf-dog, thus, in effect, "an illiterate mail carrier," or "postman," who will indeed first deliver London's literary "mail" to the public at large (*Male Call*, 84, 85). He reinforces this identification by representing Buck actually "toiling in the [frozen white wilderness] to deliver letters," so that both animal and author "leave their own marks on the white landscape" and "fulfill their calling" (*Male Call,* 98). London's instinctive impulse is to resist the established, capitalist ideology of his American public and, especially, this ideology's metamorphosis into publicity. But this ideology constantly tempts him to let down his critical guard and

shamelessly use his writing to promote himself *as a* writer. London's works thus always bespeak his inability to sustain such resistance in the end. The fulfillment of his "calling" finally refers to the sheer circulation of his name in public, just as the actual content of the letters the wolf-dog carries doesn't matter.

This argument, too, however, struggles with and eventually capitulates to public demands, although of a late-twentieth-century, American-academic sort. Using London as his example, Auerbach wants to expose the totalitarian reach of capitalist ideology, especially as coupled with a heterosexual norm in the case of *The Sea-Wolf*. If he sees London testing his ideological complex in the novel's first narrative section, Auerbach also sees him becoming an unwitting victim of it in the second section. In short, London abandons any effort to resist submerging himself into the mass public sphere and in fact becomes compulsively unable to "stop publishing—himself as well as his writing" (*Male Call*, 232).

Yet how can London entirely eliminate his private life of writing when, given Auerbach's astute observation (and methodological tack) that "from reading Poe London learned how to autobiographically encode his person in his fiction to protect himself from a largely anonymous mass market of readers" (*Male Call*, 190)?[34] Notwithstanding its public content, this allegorized encoding itself purveys the privacy of London's scene of writing. Auerbach's critical disclosures, not London's writing per se, "can't stop publishing" this scene, whereas this allegorized substratum remains constitutively private for London himself, either in the sense of his not knowing it, or, like Poe, in London's deliberate effort to disguise his metaliterary tracks from public inspection.

Neither London's works nor their criticism can quite suppress the privacy subtending their writing. Even the post-1904 London occasionally leaves behind a private postscript to his public literary "mail" that tells a version of his fall from private man different from Auerbach's. In the novel *Martin Eden* (1909), the protagonist commits suicide precisely at the moment he achieves literary success. One might regard such success as London's ironic critique of the alienated public sphere dominated by market capitalism. Or perhaps Eden's fate represents London's sense of futility in having tried to overcome this public by his populist amalgam of socialist and Nietzschean *self*-centered ideals.[35] Yet the novel equally accounts for Eden's fate in terms more akin to the loss of vocational privacy, traced in particular by Eden's having failed to heed the poet Brissenden's Poesque advice: "'It is not what you succeed in doing that you get your joy, but in the doing of it. . . . Beauty hurts you. Why should you palter with magazines? Let beauty be your end.'"[36] Eden can no longer recover this primal or "Edenic" scene of writing. But, as his first name suggests—his namesake is the fourth-century St. Martin, who was coerced into leaving his monastic retreat to become a church bishop—this earlier scene once fostered a private mode of work that Eden/London need never have relinquished to public suasions.

Notes

I wish to thank Mark Bauerlein for his careful readings of this essay and his excellent editorial recommendations for its subsequent revisions.

1. John Carlos Rowe makes a recent polemical case against Poe's alleged racism and modern critical tendencies to deny or elide this issue. See *At Emerson's Tomb: The Politics of Classic American Literature* (New York: Columbia University Press, 1997), 42-62. For a sound interrogation of the evidence for Poe's racism, see Terence Whalen, *Edgar Allan Poe and the Masses: The Political Economy of Literature in Antebellum America* (Princeton, N.J.: Princeton University Press, 1999), 111-46. Poe's "aesthetic ideology" appears in his critical remarks throughout his career. See, for example, Edgar Allan Poe, "Letter to B—," in *Essays and Reviews,* ed. G. R. Thompson (New York: Library of America, 1984), 11: "A poem, in my opinion, is opposed to a work of science by having, for its *immediate* object, pleasure, not truth" (Poe's emphasis). Hereafter, essays from this work are cited parenthetically. Jane Tompkins discusses Hawthorne's literary politicking in her *Sensational Designs: The Cultural Work of American Fiction, 1790-1860* (New York: Oxford University Press, 1985), claiming that his literary "canonization was the result of a network of common interests—familial, social, professional, commercial, and national" (32). The political problems attached to Twain's use of the word *nigger* in *The Adventures of Huckleberry Finn* are well known, but see Jonathan Arac, *Huckleberry Finn as Idol and Target: The Functions of Criticism in Our Time* (Madison: University of Wisconsin Press, 1997), esp. chap. 1.

2. See Seyla Benhabib's representative statement of this position in "Models of Public Space: Hannah Arendt, the Liberal Tradition, and Jürgen Habermas," in *Habermas and the Public Sphere,* ed. Craig Calhoun (Cambridge: MIT Press, 1992), esp. 84: "All struggles against oppression in the modern world begin by redefining what had previously been considered private, nonpublic, and nonpolitical issues as matters of public concern . . . that need discursive legitimation."

3. Julie C. Inness, *Privacy, Intimacy, and Isolation* (New York: Oxford University Press, 1992), 6.

4. Richard F. Hixson, *Privacy in a Public Society: Human Rights in Conflict* (New York: Oxford University Press, 1987), 18.

5. William J. Novak, *The People's Welfare: Law and Regulation in Nineteenth-Century America* (Chapel Hill: University of North Carolina Press, 1996), 117.

6. Nancy Dunlap Bercaw, "Solid Objects/Mutable Meanings: Fancywork and the Construction of Bourgeois Culture, 1840-1880," *Winterthur Portfolio* 26 (1991): 238-39; and Tamara K. Hareven, "The Home and the Family in Historical Perspective," in *Home: A Place in the World,* ed. Arien Mack (New York: New York University Press, 1993), 239.

7. Samuel Warren and Louis Brandeis, "The Right to Privacy," in *Killing the Messenger: One Hundred Years of Media Criticism,* ed. Tom Goldstein (New York: Columbia University Press, 1989), 8.

8. Warren and Brandeis, "Right to Privacy," 13.

9. Carl D. Schneider, *Shame, Exposure, and Privacy* (New York: W. W. Norton, 1992), succinctly depicts this charge against privacy, particularly its being "a recent historical phenomenon, a luxury available only to bourgeois capitalism. The private is seen as a form of false consciousness in which communal life is sacrificed for personal possession and property claims" (152).

10. Patricia Ann Boling, *Privacy and the Politics of Intimate Life* (Ithaca, N.Y.: Cornell University Press, 1996), xi. Nancy Fraser, "Rethinking the Public Sphere: A Contribution to the Critique of Actually Existing Democracy," in *Habermas and the Public Sphere,* echoes this feminist complaint in arguing that liberal conceptions of privacy tend to stifle any radical critique of abusive publics and conversely inhibit the force of "multivalent" publics like the domestic realm (142).

11. Rochelle Gurstein, *The Repeal of Reticence: A History of America's Cultural and Legal Struggles over Free Speech, Obscenity, Sexual Liberation, and Modern Art* (New York: Hill and Wang, 1996), 47, 32.

12. Inness, *Privacy, Intimacy, and Isolation,* 89.

13. See Jean-François Lyotard, *The Postmodern Condition: A Report on Knowledge,* trans. Geoff Bennington and Brian Massumi (Minneapolis: University of Minnesota Press, 1984). Lyotard contests the possibility of a single, dominant public sphere in the postmodern world, even one like Haber-

mas's well-known ideal of a consensual public. Postmodern publics "search for dissent" (66) instead of those founded on consensus-oriented language-games.

14. "The Purloined Letter," in *Tales and Sketches, 1843-1849,* vol. 3 of *Collected Works of Edgar Allan Poe,* ed. Thomas Ollive Mabbott (Cambridge: Belknap Press, 1978), 827. Hereafter, references to Poe's tales are from this volume or from vol. 2, *Tales and Sketches: 1831-1842,* and are cited as *CW.*

15. I discuss Poe's punning, use of anagrams, and allegorization of writer-reader roles in my essay, "Poe's Secret Autobiography," in *The American Renaissance Reconsidered,* ed. Walter Benn Michaels and Donald E. Pease, Selected Papers from the English Institute, 1982-83 (Baltimore, Md.: Johns Hopkins University Press, 1985), 58-89. Also see Michael J. S. Williams, *A World of Words: Language and Displacement in the Fiction of Edgar Allan Poe* (Durham, N.C.: Duke University Press, 1988).

16. In *Beneath the American Renaissance: The Subversive Imagination in the Age of Emerson and Melville* (New York: Alfred A. Knopf, 1988), David Reynolds takes the high road on this issue, arguing that Poe, "disturbed by the cruelty and venality of the literary marketplace," exposed in his works "the grim realities of popular publishing" and its raising to "spurious celebrity" status sentimentalist and sensationalist fiction writers alike (229). In contrast, Jonathan Elmer, in *Reading at the Social Limit: Affect, Mass Culture, and Edgar Allan Poe* (Stanford, Calif.: Stanford University Press, 1995), maintains that for all of Poe's literary efforts to escape "the prescriptive right of the mob," he succumbs to a mass-cultural "undoing" (92).

17. Milette Shamir, "Hawthorne's Romance and the Right to Privacy," *American Quarterly* 49, no. 4 (December 1997): 748. Hereafter, this work is cited parenthetically as Shamir.

18. Jonathan Auerbach, *The Romance of Failure: First-Person Fictions of Poe, Hawthorne, and James* (New York: Oxford University Press, 1989), 52, 56, 71. Hereafter, this work is cited parenthetically as *Romance.*

19. Nathaniel Hawthorne, *The Scarlet Letter,* ed. Sculley Bradley, Richard Croom Beatty, and E. Hudson Long (New York: Norton, 1961), 31.

20. James M. Cox notes this offstage aspect in *"The Scarlet Letter*: Through the Old Manse and the Custom House," *Virginia Quarterly Review* 51 (1975): 432-47.

21. Auerbach also situates Poe in the liberal-individualist fold by arguing that Poe, like Wilson with his commonplace name, not only fears loss of self in the anonymous public—for instance, the modern, urban "crowd" explicitly staged in "The Man of the Crowd" (1840)—but that he equally experiences anxiety in desiring an original self (*Romance,* 33). But Donald E. Pease argues, in *Visionary Compacts: American Renaissance Writings in Cultural Context* (Madison: University of Wisconsin Press, 1987), that Poe resists his American individualistic environment by inscribing in his tales a wish for a pre-nineteenth-century aristocratic community, an imaginary public sphere not beset by such individualism (186-91).

22. See, for example, Janna Malamud Smith, *Private Matters: In Defense of the Personal Life* (Reading, Mass.: Addison-Wesley Publishing Company, 1997), esp. 145-72; Rochelle Gurstein, *Repeal of Reticence*; Brook Thomas, *American Literary Realism and the Failed Promise of Contract* (Berkeley: University of California Press, 1997), esp. chap. 3; and Barbara Hochman, "Disappearing Authors and Resentful Readers in Late Nineteenth-Century American Fiction: The Case of Henry James," *English Literary History* 63 (1996): 177-201.

23. Hochman, "Disappearing Authors," 181.

24. Quoted in Gurstein, *Repeal of Reticence,* 35.

25. Hochman, "Disappearing Authors," 193.

26. Thomas, *American Literary Realism,* 78.

27. Hochman, "Disappearing Authors," 194.

28. Henry James, "The Private Life," in *The Figure in the Carpet and Other Stories,* ed. Frank Kermode (New York: Penguin Books, 1986), 994. Hereafter, this work is cited parenthetically as James.

29. See, for example, the forum of essays collected in *American Literature* 70 (September 1988), in which Cathy Davidson makes this observation in "Preface: No More Separate Spheres!" 445. See also Nancy Walker, "'Wider than the Sky': Public Presence and Private Self in Dickinson, James, and Woolf," in *The Private Self: Theory and Practice of Women's Autobiographical Writings,* ed. Shari Benstock (Chapel Hill: University of North Carolina Press, 1988), 275; and Kathy Peiss, "Going Public: Women in Nineteenth-Century Cultural History," *American Literary History* 3 (winter 1991): 817-28. Feminist criticism on domesticity tends to valorize the public by framing the private as a de facto counterpublic sphere, but, like Peiss, can worry whether "the blurring of boundaries between public and private erase meaningful distinctions between the two terms" (826).

30. Such radicalization may be another way besides Paul Bové's suggestive use of Peircean "abduction"—"thinking" that "requir[es] never accepting the common sense of the already known, never yielding to the temptation of recognition"—for "speaking against power" (always a public matter) without slipping back into consensus, academic "forms of knowing" that become subject to "the political police of left and right." See "Policing Thought: On Learning How to Read Henry Adams," *Critical Inquiry* 23 (summer 1997): 944.

31. Ferdinand David Schoeman, *Privacy and Social Freedom* (New York: Cambridge University Press, 1992), 132-33.

32. I briefly discuss this aspect of the novel in "Crane's *Red Badge of Courage*," *Explicator* 56 (winter 1998): 82-83.

33. Jonathan Auerbach, *Male Call: Becoming Jack London* (Durham, N.C.: Duke University Press, 1996), 33, 18, 14, 50. Hereafter, this work is cited parenthetically as *Male Call*. Auerbach argues, for instance, that London eschews organizing his early Northland stories in terms of "a unifying principle [of a single character that] too closely resembled earlier dime novel, mass-market methods of production that allowed the author to be subsumed and rendered anonymous by standardized, generic fictional protagonists" (52).

34. Auerbach connects Poe and London in terms of their analogous desires for popular literary success. In particular, he sees London himself explicitly drawing this connection in a retrospective essay, written around the time of *The Sea-Wolf*, concerning one of his first published stories, "A Thousand Deaths." Auerbach claims that the essay not only credits the story "with saving his (literary) life" (188) but that it also suggests London's identification with Poe on the basis of how their writing helped them both overcome early rejections by "mass-market" publics. Originally published in a journal called *The Black Cat*—the title of one of Poe's most famous tales—London's story, as his essay retells its occurrence, here in effect gets rescued by Poe, just as its Poesque first-person narrator gets rescued from drowning *in* the story.

35. To take one example from the novel: "When he starved, his thoughts had dwelt often upon the thousands he knew were starving the world over; but now that he was feasted full . . . [h]e forgot about them, and, being in love, remembered the countless lovers in the world. Without deliberately thinking about it, *motifs* for love-lyrics began to agitate his brain." See Jack London, *Martin Eden*, in *Novels and Social Writings,* ed. Donald Pizer (New York: Library of America, 1982), 766.

36. London, *Martin Eden*, 814.

Kay Stockholder (essay date fall 2000)

SOURCE: Stockholder, Kay. "Is Anybody at Home in the Text? Psychoanalysis and the Question of Poe." *American Imago* 57, no. 3 (fall 2000): 299-334.

[*In the following essay, Stockholder argues against the Lacanian analysis of "The Purloined Letter," claiming that the short story (along with the other two Dupin stories) can be read as a dream of the narrator in which psychosexual aggression toward women is brought to the fore.*]

Like all detective fiction written since Poe's Dupin trilogy, each of Poe's famous tales is composed of two stories. One story has occurred in a time defined as the past of the tale and is uncovered in the process of narration. The other story is of the manner in which the first was discovered. This two-story construction is definitive of the detective story, and Poe could be said to have invented it, were it not for the fact that Sophocles did so before him in *Oedipus Rex*. However, *Oedipus Rex* is rendered unusual among detective fiction by the interested nature of the detective, so that there is little difference between the high passion of the process of discovery and the high passions involved in the story that is discovered. Most detective fiction follows the lead Poe established by building the first two of the Dupin stories on a contrast between a story of discovery whose protagonist is cool and disinterested, and the high passions that characterize the discovered story. However, it is hard to think of a detective who is as coolly detached from the stories that he uncovers as Poe's Dupin, and it is also hard to think of a work of detective fiction that creates a greater divide between the scientifically cool tenor of the story of discovery and the passions that are implicit in the barely described action of the discovered story in the **"The Murders in the Rue Morgue"** and **"The Mystery of Marie Rogêt."** In the first of these the story of discovery consists of the narrator's musing on the superior talent needed to play draughts over the merely calculative abilities needed for chess, an account of his own meeting with Dupin, and of the latter's almost uncanny expertise in understanding what goes on in the minds of other people, including the narrator's own. The contrast between these emotional levels comes into play during the prolonged account of the newspaper descriptions of the puzzling details of the room, locked from the inside, in which Madame L'Espanaye and her daughter were murdered, the older women, almost decapitated, being found below an apparently locked window, and the daughter's body found jammed up a fireplace chimney. Dupin examines the room, and on the basis of various clues places an ad addressed to a sailor about a lost ourang-outang. He surprises the narrator and astounds the prefect when the sailor turns up with the discovered story that Dupin had anticipated of how the escaped ourang-outang killed the women. The second story also begins with a discourse on Dupin's combination of poetic and mathematical abilities. This time the prefect asks him for help in solving the mysterious murder of Marie Roget, and once again the story of discovery consists of Dupin's method of reasoning, while the discovered story, again reduced to a bit at the end, consists in the account of how Marie had gone to meet her secret sailor lover, and was murdered by him.

"The Purloined Letter" differs from the previous two tales, however, and is not as clearly a predecessor of the detective genre. There is less of a divide between the tone of the two stories in this tale because both are almost equally cool, and the story of discovery divides in two. First, the narrator's reminiscences about Dupin's previous successes are interrupted when the Prefect suddenly enters to appeal to Dupin for help in earning the reward he will receive for recovering a letter that the Minister has stolen from the Queen by which he is able to blackmail her; second, after a month the Prefect returns, and is duly astonished when Dupin, in return for half of the now doubled reward, hands him the letter. After the Prefect has left in stunned silence, Dupin explains to the narrator his strategy in outsmarting the Minister, and the discovered story is reduced to a description of the way in which the latter had foiled the Prefect by leaving the letter open, turned inside out, stuffed in a letter rack that hangs from the mantle in plain view. Unlike the previous tales, the discovered story involves no death or mayhem to contrast to Dupin's coolness. Until the last paragraph, therefore, the entire story is remarkably distant, with the emotional drama limited to contests for status between Dupin and the Prefect, and Dupin and the Minister. However, the last paragraph changes everything; suddenly it is revealed that Dupin's passionate investment is greater than that of the characters in the discovered story. They are merely seeking one kind or another of profit, while Dupin's desire, nurtured over many years, to avenge himself for the "evil turn" done him (appropriately enough) in Vienna is associated with one of the bloodiest and most grotesque tales of violent passion in western literature, that of Atreus and Thyestes as rendered by Crébillon in *Atrée*. The passions suggested by this reference reveal Dupin as one who uses his superior and cool intelligence not only as a mask for intense passion, but as a tool in its service. Furthermore, when one takes into account the connections among the three tales, the final reference also suggests a hidden link between the three tales of discovery and their discovered stories; it reveals that the violence that Dupin finds is that which he, in some sense, has sought, and that the elaboration

of the story of discovery and the minimal presentation of the discovered story constitutes, in psychoanalytic terms, a strategy of concealment.

But whose strategy is it, who has something to hide, and for whom is the text meaningful? The problems generated by various critical attempts that assume that meaning lies in authorial intention and by those for whom the author is irrelevant are conveniently visible in the volume of essays devoted to analyses of **"The Purloined Letter"** that was generated by the chain of commentaries upon each other initiated by Lacan's discussion of the tale. In this paper I will discuss the various ways in which these essays deal with the question of intentionality, and the related question of what constitutes meaning in fiction, and show how the assumptions of these critics doom them to a partial understanding of the work. I will then show how an oneiric reading that assumes the work to be the dream of one of its characters combines what is powerful in the different approaches and gives a more comprehensive account that accommodates the text's intellectual, emotional, and literary force.

These essays encapsulate the paradoxical configuration that has been created for literary studies by recent critical theory. On the one hand, almost all contemporary varieties of critical theory, derived as they are from different branches of structuralist, marxist, or post-Freudian psychological theory, tell us that we are in error to look in a work of literature for a center of consciousness. A work of literature, these theories tell us, should be seen either as a model of the building blocks of which human societies are composed, as a manifestation of the reigning political hegemony, as expressing a struggle between the hegemony and attempts to subvert it, or as revealing and manifesting the psychic fragments of which we are composed, despite our illusion of being a unified self or ego. All of these approaches to literature can generate understandings of texts that have force and cogency in that they bring into focus aspects of fiction that were not previously perceived as centrally significant. Their abstraction is satisfying in that eliminating a consciousness as the organizing force of a fictional work shifts attention onto the formal attributes, the discourse rather than the story, more than did traditional criticism, or even New Criticism. However, the claim implicit in these critical approaches to a more objective overview of texts than can be had by those who limit their interest to the representation of action or the communication of ideas is vitiated by their implicit assumption that texts are allegorical of some truth of the human situation.[1] A text necessarily reveals a truth, whether or not the author knows it, because it is the nature of fictional texts, or even all texts, to reveal some truth of the human situation. They do so either as a consequence of the truth speaking through them, or, in a slightly different version, because something in an author's act of writing makes writing itself exemplary of a principle at work in human affairs.

On the other hand, readings that honour the sense of human intentionality with which literature is imbued must locate meaning in authorial intention, characters' intentions, or readers' responses. This approach replaces interest in the work with interest in the author, despite the fact that it is only the work that makes the author of interest. If one locates the experiencing consciousness in a character, one is likely to be treating literary characters as though they were real persons. This criticism is not so telling, because in speaking about characters' intentions, one is in reality hypothesizing kinds of living persons that the literary portraits resemble. But the difficulty is that locating meaning in characters omits the aesthetic and formal characteristics of literature. When one discusses a character's intentions, in a psychoanalytic or any other mode, it makes no difference whether one is speaking of a novel, a comedy, a poem, or a tragedy, and all structural and formal characteristics of the work that constitute the character's world are consequently ignored. To include such aesthetic and formal concerns, one must necessarily step back from the character to consider the author's intention in his or her creation and disposition of the character. The meaning of the work, then, cannot be identical with the meaning of the character, and we are back with the problem of the author, with which we started.

The third possibility is to resign ourselves to the author's death, and to locate meaning in the audience or reader. But this option either leads away from interest in literary interpretation altogether, replacing it with interest in our own psychological processes, or it is involved in a contradiction. The contradiction is that any psychoanalytic statement about how a reader responds is predicated on his responding to something, and that something can only be in the text. As soon as that is acknowledged, then one is free to talk about fuller and less full responses, more or less adequate responses. In order to avoid a return to conventional psychoanalytic concern with characters or authors this question raises, reader response theory tends to adapt deconstructive ways of speaking about the text to its more emotional concerns. In doing so it locates meaning in a kind of intending unconsciousness hovering in an imaginary space somewhere between author, character, and audience, and it tends to define meaning as what fiction does to readers. In this view works do not mean but they do; they act on the reader in such a way as to encourage certain attitudes or effects, and their meaning lies in those effects and/or in the way in which they are produced. This assumption allows for more discussion of formal aspects than did other modes of psychoanalytic criticism, but it entails the logical problems of talking about what texts consciously or unconsciously intend. As well, because it emphasizes readers' emotional responses rather than their cognition, it implicitly or explicitly equates meaning with emotional response rather than with the fruits of analytic skills, which it tends to see merely as a means by which readers legitimize their idiosyncratic responses.

In this discussion I will point out the different ways in which these issues appear in the commentaries that comprise *The Purloined Poe.* I will then present a reading of **"The Purloined Letter"** that assumes the narrator to be the dreamer of this, as well as of the previous two Dupin tales. Finally, I will discuss the ways an oneiric reading that assumes the narrator to be the dreamer of the configuration of which he is a part integrates the formal and abstract issues that characterize post-modernist approaches, with a discussion of the tales' affective force and their relevance to immediate and specific human experience that are the concern of both conventional and of the reader-response varieties of psychoanalytic criticism.

The Purloined Poe is for the most part organized around Lacan's seminar on **"The Purloined Letter"** and Derrida's response to it. Though Derrida and Lacan differ in the aspects of the story they emphasize and in its final significance, they agree about the source of consciousness in the story and the nature of literary meaning. Unlike his Freudian predecessors who assume that literature expresses the unique psychological constitution of its author, Lacan's discussion assumes that literature tells us the truth about our place in the cosmos. In using **"The Purloined Letter"** to illustrate a general truth about the role of language in human life, Lacan assumes not that Poe has set out to communicate this truth, though he hints that Poe, as a poet, might known it, but that poetry itself is the veiled way by which the Universe reveals its veiled (Heideggerian) Truth. The meaning of fiction consists in its truth, for it is pervaded by a kind of universal consciousness. For Lacan **"The Purloined Letter"** is an allegory of man's relation to the linguistic signifier and thereby to language. Language, by alienating us forever from the biological being that we share with animals, has confronted us with the knowledge of our own death that alone renders us human.

Because the story is about a letter, the exact contents of which we do not know, this represents for Lacan the fundamental divorce between signifier and signified upon which language depends. Because signifiers have no determinate meaning, and because man has his humanity only in language, man is doomed to yearn for a stable plenitude of meaning which he can achieve only by confronting the void, analogous to castration and to death, upon which his human life is based. The letter, therefore, as pure signifier, represents castration, or the phallus that is possessed by no one. It marks the absence of the phallus that makes its presence significant, and it thereby initiates the system of differences that constitutes the realm of language and social forms entirely. Just as one's place in the social order determines one's innermost being, and awaits one's entry into it, so the relationship of the various figures in Poe's story to the letter determines the nature of their being, even their gender. Refusal of submission to this truth condemns one endlessly to repeat one's habitual pattern of denial, and this psychological mechanism is demonstrated in the repetition of the configuration of the first scene by the second. Each scene is constructed of three positions, occupied in turn by different persons. In the first, the Queen, to avoid arousing the King's suspicions, casually leaves the compromising letter in full view; the King who sees nothing is in the first position. In the second place, called the feminine position by Lacan, is the Queen who thinks herself unseen, but is seen by the Minister who purloins her letter and leaves a counterfeit. He is in the third position, equated with the Symbolic and with Language, because he has an overview of the others. In what Lacan, collapsing two distinct timeframes, calls the second scene, the prefect is ignorant like the king; the Minister, like the Queen, thinks he has escaped detection by leaving the disguised letter in open view, but is himself overseen by another: and Dupin replaces the Minister as the one who sees all. In reading this as an allegory of the repetition compulsion Lacan converts Freud's conception of a personal repetition of traumatic events into an intersubjective event in which subjects "more docile than sheep, model their very being on the moment of the signifying chain which traverses them" (43). Possession of the letter promises to empower the possessor. Yet because the phallus belongs to no one, being a signifier and thereby a function of language, such illusory empowerment makes one subject to others' power, and thereby renders one feminine in relation to them. To think one can possess the Phallus is, for Lacan, to deny one's powerlessness in the face of death; therefore the time during which Dupin holds the letter constitutes a third scene in which Dupin has the woman's part. That is, Dupin thinks he has the overview of others, but doesn't know himself as seen, now by Lacan, or the therapist whose vision partakes of the symbolic because he alone knows his place in it. That is, Lacan claims that Dupin forgoes his overview when it is revealed that he has acted from a desire for wealth and for revenge. This doesn't quite make sense, for the Queen's motives remain same during the time that she

does and does not have the letter, Dupin was so motivated before his motivations are revealed, and the prefect also is motivated by the desire for the reward.[2]

Whatever the contradictions are in Lacan's analysis, and there are many, his interpretation, unlike much allegorizing criticism, is based on the formal structure of the work, rather than on character or specific language or plot, because he attends primarily to the repetition of a configuration. Yet because this repetition does not affect any single character, the story becomes one of emotional forms in general, emptied of specific import. In a version of reader response theory in which meaning is located in what a work does rather than what it says, Lacan claims that the **"The Purloined Letter"** activates in its readers the sense of their enslavement to the signifier just as the purloined letter does to the characters inside the story. However, on this level too, he empties the form of specific emotional content. Therefore, in bringing the story's structure into psychoanalytic significance, Lacan empties of significance all detail of character portrayal and of language. Furthermore, he implies that literature embodies an ideal of impartial truth, to which the poet and the therapist have particular access, when he says that Dupin falls from the Symbolic into the dyadic relations of the imaginary in revealing his personal motivations.

It is against Lacan's assertion of a Truth that Derrida launches his analysis of the story and critique of Lacan. He argues that Lacan's claim to reveal the story's truth, to exhibit "the primary content beneath the secondary revision" contradicts his Heideggerian belief that the Truth can be shown only as veiled. If he is right about the truth, then in unveiling the story he destroys its truth, and his enterprise is invalid. Furthermore, Lacan's argument not only fails, but it results in a misreading of the story that, correctly read, supports Derrida's anti-logocentric philosophy rather than Lacan's phallogocentric one. He bases his argument on three major points. First, Lacan's ignoring the general narrator, and, as he puts it, the scene of narration, reveals his commitment to the logocentric primacy of the spoken over the written upon which western culture supposedly is based, whereas Poe's inclusion of the general narrator renders the story a manifestation of the underlying primacy of the written. Second, there is the issue of the indivisibility of the signifier. By this Lacan means that while the signifier is embodied in the material realm, either the letter, or the physical organs that articulate words, it nevertheless exists independently of that material medium. It therefore cannot be destroyed, even if the material letter is. **"The Purloined Letter"** illustrates this truth because the letter's significance is independent of any specific content. Derrida rightly argues that this is simply false because we do know that the letter reveals either an adulterous relationship or a subversive political liaison, or both. For Derrida the story illustrates the dependence of meaning on the shifting sands of the material world by the fact that the letter is stolen. Third, Lacan insists that the letter must inevitably return to its sender because individuals must finally submit to the Symbolic discourse within which they have their being, while Derrida claims that in this view the signifier becomes purely ideal, rather than a manifestation of an ultimate contingency. Given Derrida's assumptions, all tales must mean the same thing. And because that is so, he focuses on only one aspect of the links between this story and those that precede it, despite having criticized Lacan for ignoring them, and he ignores as well the affective center and the discovered story. Though, more than Lacan, he attends to the manner of the story's telling, he also disregards the discovered story because for him all tales can tell finally only of their own undoing. Therefore for Derrida, as for Lacan, the meaning of a text lies in its rendering of a truth that derives not from the intention or consciousness of an author, but in a rather mysterious way from "the text" as a reflection of a transhistorical kind of non-consciousness.

Most of the commentators, whether they defend Lacan from Derrida or use Lacanian terms to expand on Lacan's reading, share Derrida's and Lacan's assumption that the story's meaning resides in one or another kind of allegorical presentation of a general truth about the human condition or of human cognition. Barbara Johnson, in "The Frame of Reference: Poe, Lacan, and Derrida" (1988), who notes that Derrida relies on a truth claim as much as does Lacan, for the most part argues against Derrida's accusation that Lacan contradicts his argument that the letter is a pure signifier by treating it as the story's signified. While defending Lacan, she also develops her own view that the letter, as signifier, is "a *knot* in a structure where words, things, and organs can neither be definably separated nor compatibly combined" (245) and that therefore the story illustrates the undecidability of such questions as whether life is contingent or fated. A similar assumption underlies François Peraldi's "Time in 'The Purloined Letter'" (1988), which also locates meaning in the story's reflection of a general truth of human affairs, as described by Lacan. Peraldi extends Lacan's application of Lacanian theory by arguing that in **"The Purloined Letter"** the perception of time as continuous is a symbolic activity, that loss of that sense when engaged in reverie or when intensely preoccupied is imaginary, and that a sudden eruption, like the Prefect's appearance, connotes the real.

There are three contributors to the volume whose commentary introduces some sense of human drama. They rely on a combination of a traditional location of meaning in mimetic and thematic aspects of texts, not entirely identified with authorial intention, but not excluding it either. In "Narrational Authority" (1988), Ross Chambers distinguishes narratorial authority from narrative authority as the authority gained by a self-conscious narrator of a work of fiction that thematizes narration. The story's meaning resides in "the substitution of text for absence . . . and from the production of a relationship between narrator and narratee" (292) that duplicates the competitive relationship between Dupin and the Minister. In asserting that the contents of the letter are unknown, Chambers, like Lacan and others, equates meaning with an allegory of a truth that writes itself, in this case a cosmic truth about the mediation of human relations by signs that depend for their presence on possible absence. However, he also asserts a more conventional definition of meaning as representation of particular human acts, in this case those between competitive males. As a consequence of dwelling on this emotionally charged theme, Chambers highlights some of the subtleties of the tale's language. However, his commitment to Lacan's values appears when he is fooled by Dupin's denial that he cares for the money that he pockets and ignores the first tale in which Dupin has been characterized as an impoverished aristocrat. Therefore he falls for aristocratic duplicity when he reads the story as revealing the universal truth that Dupin's haughty pretense of indifference shows how competition for money and status involve a "fool's exchange" (302).

John Muller, in "Negation in 'The Purloined Letter': Hegel, Poe, and Lacan" (1988), also assumes authorial intention in his argument that other commentators on Lacan wrongly emphasize the structure of his three positions, rather than explaining the circulation of figures. He argues that both Lacan and Poe were drawing on Hegel, whose dialectic based on negation explains why subjects must displace each other. Having elaborated his Hegelian reading of Lacan's three positions, Muller argues that Lacan's Hegelian reading is a correct reading of Poe, in that it places the story in the context from which it was initially written, and that the story is about the role of negation in human affairs. However, he implies a source of meaning other than authorial intention in asserting that the process of negation illustrated by the story and observed by Lacan repeats itself in the commentaries of Johnson, Derrida, and Harvey, perhaps because of the "dynamic character of the letter as the 'pure signifier' of negation" (365). After discussing negation as characteristically human, and an essential feature of non-psychotic dialogue, Muller concludes that Hegel, Poe, and Lacan each in his different way communicates this truth. Muller seems to assume that this truth derives from Poe's intention, rather than from the nature of fiction, though he does not emphasize this distinction.

Without calling attention to it, Muller assumes that the meaning of the story can be located only in its relation to its context, despite Derrida's assertion that there is no way to stabilize what counts as a margin between a text and its context. Barbara Johnson takes Derrida to task for assuming that the Dupin trilogy constitutes the correct frame, when what is in question for her is the adequacy of any frame to constitute a frame of reference. However, she goes on to demonstrate the relevance of some other standard and nicely appropriate scholarly frames, these being *Sketches of Conspicuous Living Characters in France* in which Poe, a great reader like Dupin, found Dupin; a fuller reading of the relation between Crébillon's play, the plot of which turns on a purloined letter; and *Macbeth,* in which the protagonist sends his wife a letter, and whose assertion that he "dares do all that becomes a man, / Who dares do more is none," shows him tinged with the femininity that Lacan claims takes possession of all who possess the letter. For Irene Harvey in "Structures of Exemplarity in Poe, Freud, Lacan and Derrida," (1988) context dependency becomes theme when she argues that **"The Purloined Letter"** reveals the exemplary function of all texts, both literary and expository. In order to defend Lacan against Derrida's accusation of reducing the signifier to a signified and of ignoring the narrator, she argues, in a somewhat confusing way, that the narrator of the tales, whom she calls "Poe," uses **"The Murders in the Rue Morgue"** to exemplify the character of Dupin, and uses the case of Marie Rogêt to illustrate the means by which the actual crime on which he based his story might have been solved.[3] On this basis she claims that Poe's tales, rather than illustrating that "fiction necessarily forms the framework or context in which the truth is found and must necessarily be situated" (259-60), are "*illustrating* exactly what Derrida is arguing for and arguing against with respect to Lacan. That is, fiction and Truth relate reciprocally as example/exemplified in such a way that neither can be deciphered as the origin or source of the other" (262). Having found that Poe, Lacan, and Derrida all rely on the concept of exemplification, she calls for the deconstruction of the concept, presumably in order to discover what we already know, that most often examples are imperfect for our purposes, or to invoke a pseudo-Kantian morality to render all texts ends in themselves.

The third critical location of meaning invoked by these articles is in the reader's response, though several merge a reader response theory with a deconstructive textual approach. Barbara Johnson invokes a kind of cognitive reader response theory in asserting that critical argument such as that between Lacan and Derrida must repeat the relations of the figures inside the story, further undermining the frame of reference that Derrida assumes when he criticizes Lacan for ignoring the previous stories. **"The Purloined Letter"** tricks the reader into looking for meaning in the non-message of the letter, and so educates her about the nature of the signifier. However, in arguing that the story makes such reproduction inevitable, Johnson fails to account for Lacan's having avoided falling into the story's trap. This notion of reader response merges with the concept that a text tells a truth, for in Johnson's conception all readers are assumed to respond in the same way. Therefore whether a story delivers its message by means of expressing or of enacting a cosmic or existential truth, the implication remains that the story reveals the truth, in this case the truth about the relations of readers to texts. A similar combination of cognitive reader response theory and an idea of the text as containing or performing an embodied truth is found in Jane Gallop's "The American Other" (1988). She argues that the "neutral, homogeneous, transparent element of the tale" is analogous to the "pure mirror of an unruffled surface" that the true analyst presents to his analysand (280).

At the opposite pole from these readings of the tales as renderings of the formal conditions for cognition or experience are the two psychoanalytic accounts of the work. As an example of early psychobiographical literary criticism, Marie Bonaparte's work is dismissed as naive and reductive. Lacan makes a snide reference to her, Derrida disparages Lacan by accusing him of repeating Bonaparte's interpretation of the letter, while concealing his indebtedness to her work, and Johnson insults Derrida by saying that he accuses Lacan of what he himself is guilty. There is some justice in the disparaging attitudes taken towards Bonaparte. She is naive about literary meaning in her unwavering confidence that she has uncovered the work's deepest significance when she has found its source in Poe's early biography, as when she says, "Nevertheless, this simple displacement served to keep Poe ignorant, as for almost a century his readers, that these ailing sylphs were but forms of Elizabeth Arnold" (643), and that such ratiocinations as appear in the Dupin stories are "not to be taken at face value" (660), because they express infantile curiosity about sex.[4] Her discussions depend upon familiar static equations, so that all the characters in **"The Murders in the Rue Morgue"** represent specific figures in Poe's past or specific aspects of Poe's own desire. In **"The Purloined Letter,"** the letter represents the maternal penis of the preOedipal mother, and the fire-place, like the chimney in the first story, her "cloaca." The Minister represents John Allan, as well as his mother's lover, with whom Poe also identifies.

On the other hand, some of Bonaparte's general comments on literature have the potential to incorporate formal concerns into a psychoanalytic approach, though she makes no specific use of them. For example, she makes a scale of types of literature, from realistic to dream-like. On what she calls the objective end of this scale the author's psyche manifests itself in the choice and manner of elaboration of the theme. On the subjective end, authors more nearly approach the feeling of dream or nightmare, and these touch more immediately on the infantile emotional level (639-40). As well, formal concerns are implicit in her discussion of the role in literature of splitting, condensation, displacement, and doubling, the emotional significance of which can be discussed apart from the author. She goes beyond the reductiveness of finding behind every bush a version of Poe's mother, or, like Lacan, of the phallus of the pre-phallic mother, and opens a way for more subtle readings when she makes a distinction between infantile and more mature modes of symbolization. Saying that "the son's yearning for these symbolic mothers is revealed in the passion with which Poe's various heroes seek to explore and win the earth, the sky, the seas," and that in Poe's three sea tales, "the sea yawns into vast funnels down which the son precipitously returns to the place wherefrom he issued" (106), she opens a way to discuss the significance of emotional resonance and of movement between different emotional levels apart from the specific figures in an author's biography.

Bonaparte, like Freud, assumes a universal reader response in arguing that the exaggerated drives that composed what she calls Poe's sadonecrophilia shaped his tales in ways that appeal to readers' less extreme versions of these unconscious drives. Though the tales are generated by Poe's particular forms, in her conception all readers bring to the tales the same psyche, just as they do for Lacan or Johnson. Norman Holland develops a more sophisticated and individualized version of reader response theory in his transactive model of literary commentary. He finds access to the text by analogizing to his own particular experience, and in turn uses that recovered personal experience as a ground from which to look for further analogues in the text. In this way he establishes a feed-back loop between reader and text. In "Recovering 'The Purloined Letter'" (1988) Holland imports some of his semiotic and deconstructive opponents' strategies into a reader-response mode by beginning with reminiscences of the volume in which he first read Poe, and the meaning for him, as well as meditations on the etymology of the word "purloined." Though Holland is not averse to assuming that meanings have something to do with authors, as when he says that "his" Poe "is the child who must know by mind alone the Other he should have held in his mouth and heart" (315), he emphasizes the transaction between the text and the reader as he associates the letter being turned inside out with the Prefect ransacking the room and to Dupin's penetration of the narrator's mind in **"The**

Murders in the Rue Morgue." He relates this motif to his own adolescent guilt and pleasure in having dirty little secrets, as well as to many bits of omitted information about various characters and places. Objecting to the bloodless abstraction of Derrida and Lacan, as well as to the formulaic and safe terminology of Bonaparte, he teases from the story its "human truth," its concern for the "royal sex and power" (310). Holland's strategy provides an emotionally rich reading that attends to many different levels as well as to the dynamic relations among them.

Both Holland and Bonaparte focus on particular and emotional aspects of depicted individual lives and their generalizing resonance, and in this respect both are at odds with the other commentators, who emphasize the literary representation of people's relation to language and thought rather than their relation to erotic drives. Holland distances himself from Bonaparte in positing a more active text, and he engages the specific psychological dynamic of readers. In basing his readings on readers' associations he draws more on preconscious than on unconscious forms. However, Holland falls more than he knows into the camp of his enemies because he erodes the distinction between text and commentary and that between emotion and rational analysis. In making no distinction between personal associations and rational cognition, he replaces Lacan's private intellectual associations with his private emotional associations, and his theory erodes the line between text and commentary and relies on private associative responses. Thus without intending to, he aligns himself with Lacanian and Derridean critics, despite decrying their replacement of the emotional richness of literature with abstract issues.

The approach I propose overcomes this problem by limiting associations to those within a text, conceived as a dream and therefore distinct from waking experience. Two commentators in the volume touch on this oneiric level within which one can integrate the various abstract, emotional, and formal concerns that we have discussed. Though Liahna Klenman Babner, in "The Shadow's Shadow" (1988), assumes that the author has mimetic and thematic intentions, her interpretation of Dupin and the Minister as not only fraternal figures, but as two aspects of a single psyche, glances at the kind of intrapsychic dynamic that is central to my study. In making the anachronistic argument that Poe doubles Dupin and the Minister, thereby equating them morally, in order to "call into question the customary ethical norms of the detective tale," she draws out the somewhat dream-like nature of the narration suggested by the emphasis on darkness and the smoky atmosphere. Babner concludes that the story's ultimate significance lies in its exploration of "the composition of the self, and the double becomes a metaphor for the variant phases—hunter and hunted-of the human mind" (333). Poe's doubled figures render the story paradigmatic of less overtly dream-like (she doesn't use the term) relations between figures in other detective stories. Logically her argument would extend to any paired figures in fiction, as well as to relations between figures not so obviously paired. In this way her approach rests on assumptions in common with mine, but she does not apply them in a systematic way.

Shoshana Felman can be seen to touch upon this oneiric area if one assumes that what she calls Poe's "poetic effect" relates to the obvious presence in Poe's work of the dream dimension of the mind. She argues that Lacan opens new ground for psychological criticism in looking not for "the *readable,* but the *unreadable,* and the *effect* of the unreadable. What calls for analysis is the insistence of the unreadable in the text" (italics hers, 1988, 149), and Poe anticipated Lacan in saying in **"The Purloined Letter"** that the analytical itself goes unanalyzed. Equating the omissions and puzzles in Poe's work with the gaps in an analysand's narrative, she argues for an identity between the poetic effect and the unconscious effect. Felman implies a connection between the poetic effect and poetic genius in saying that Lacan, as poet therapist, has entered into the possibility of understanding genius that Freud, in his introduction to Bonaparte's book on Poe, declared beyond analysis. The literal-minded Prefect, like ordinary analysts, is condemned to the blindness of his own psychological predilection; but, like Lacan, the poet Dupin looks for truth in a signifier's place in a signifying chain. For Lacan to realize the emptiness of the signifier is to confront one's own death, and for Felman the gaps and puzzles suggested by the text are the source of the "poetic effect." Therefore the implication is that the source, or impact, of the poetic effect and of genius lies in the evocation of death. Though Felman doesn't quite put it in this way, the difference between a Lacanian and a conventional analysis of a dream in which a letter like that in Poe's story appeared would be that the latter would try to recover associations that would, in essence, supply the missing contents, while the former would in some way make the absence itself the focus of analysis. While for Felman the limitation of the first principle when applied to literature is that it omits the significance of the gap in information, the limitation of the second is that it can not take into account the ideational or emotional content. It can only be formal in that it can only render all literature an allegory of Lacan's psychoanalytic spiritual therapy. The consequence of interpreting dreams or reading literature as the dream of its protagonist or narrator is to recover the drama of conflicting desires and fears, of which the Lacanian fear of death is but one, by bringing together both of these approaches. Particularly in the absence of associations external to the literary construct, one does not look so much for an original repressed, but rather for signs of stress within the web of interlocking ideas and feelings that constitute the dreamer's compromise resolution.

In arguing that textual omissions and gaps constitute the poetic effect, Felman forgets the by now common wisdom that the art of literary realism lies in the rhetorical effects that its artistry is meant to conceal. The most realistic novel retains a poetic effect because a principle of selection, in part conscious and in part not, controls everything in it, from its largest plot structure to the smallest detail of language. To interpret any fiction, or any dream, is to discover that principle of selection. Felman is wrong in thinking that the poetic effect or, in my terms, the dream-like, cannot be analyzed, for as Bonaparte says, the kind of symbolization is itself a factor in analysis. And were it not so that the analytical mind can be sufficiently free from what it studies to avoid being absorbed into it, there would be no possibility of psychoanalysis. The interpretation of dreams rests on the assumption that one can bring unconscious thoughts and feelings to the light of a shared rationality in order to discover what the dream means to the dreamer. In psychoanalysis one needs the dreamer's associations because the dream utilizes more private associations than public. My mode of interpretation takes advantage of the fact that literature necessarily relies largely on public forms and that it contains within itself the associations that are needed to render private references intelligible. The consequence is that fiction can open to view the joining places of the unconscious parts of the mind that produce dreams and the conscious mind that produces worlds.

Despite Johnson's assertion that "any attempt to do 'justice' to three such complex texts as the Dupin stories is obviously out of the question" (214), one can, without the benefit of the dreamer's presence, track the relationship between the conscious and public realm of experience, and the unconscious or dream layer by assuming that a figure inside the fiction is the dreamer. In this way one does justice to the tales by assuming that the meaning of literary works is what it means to the dreamer, who is analogous not to us dreaming, but rather to the figure inside our dream that we identify as ourselves. Her thoughts, feelings, and actions constitute her self-definition, while the figures with which she peoples her world express either alternate self-images or the kinds of encounters she needs to find in the world in order to play out, to concretize, her emotional drama. The thought and feeling with which she responds to the ideas and values these figures embody constitute the chains of associations that structure her world and bind the public and abstract to the personal and emotional. The way in which other figures are placed in relation to her own figure indicates the relative availability of their emotional significance to her consciousness, while changing circumstances constitute her strategy for dealing with the conflicted emotions and ideas that have generated the entire configuration. Her intentions and feelings, conscious and unconscious, determine every aspect of the construction; its mysteries are her mystifications, its atmosphere expresses the background colouring of her being; its genre form expresses her characteristic stance towards herself; and the degree of its coherence, comprehensibility, or probability gives a measure of the proximity of her emotional life to ordinary reality.

Rather than say more about the principles of such a mode of analysis, I will exemplify it by taking the narrator of the three Dupin stories as dreamer.[5] I will show their interrelations, and then will indicate the ways in which this mode of analysis comprehends the cognitive levels of **"The Purloined Letter"** that are the concern of post-modern commentators, and the affective levels that are the concern of more traditional commentary, while taking full account of the text without sacrificing human meaning.[6]

THE OBSERVANT DREAMER

In defining himself as the narrator, the dreamer of **"The Purloined Letter"** adopts a role of passive observer; in that posture he identifies himself with Dupin, who is also an observer of others. The narrator, therefore, as an observer of an observer both identifies with and distances himself from Dupin. In this configuration Dupin becomes his front man, whose prying curiosity expresses his own unacknowledged desire to pry into secret things. The close parallels between himself and Dupin show that this sense of himself is close to the surface. He uses this identification to justify his curiosity by defining it as serving the Queen. However, his hostility towards this distanced maternal figure appears in the Minister's enmity to her, and he flirts with espousing his hostility in the brief time that Dupin retains the letter that could ensure his domination over her and, by implication, over the entire political structure that constitutes the background of the story. In the Inspector the dreamer expresses his self disgust for the curiosity that he both manifests and disguises in the elegant insouciance of both Dupin and, to a lesser extent, in the Minister. In his meticulous but fruitless physical examination of the Minister's room the Narrator disespouses a crude version of the desire to ferret out secrets and transforms it into an ego ideal constituted by intelligence and detachment.

All of these male figures function in a filial relation to the King, who constitutes a remote paternal authority. All these figures collude in setting him aside in order to take his place in relation to the Queen, who, again in a removed way, constitutes a maternal figure. The specific emotional components of this basic Oedipal configuration are obscured by the great distance and coolness the dreamer puts between himself and the main action, both of the story of discovery and of the discovered story. Yet the intense passions that are in this way concealed finally burst onto the scene when Dupin, with studied casualness, tells the narrator that he had written in the letter he substituted for the original, after he had stolen it from the Minister's room, a quotation from Crébillon's dramatic version of the Atreus and Thyestes myth, perhaps the most horrendously violent story in western literature.

The stark contrast between the level of passion suggested by that reference and the general tenor of the tale suggests the level of emotional intensity from which the dreamer so distances himself. The tale by itself provides little to help explain the discrepancy, but placing it in relation to the two previous tales in which there is a more obvious divide between the story of discovery and the discovered stories brings forward the obscured emotional correlates. This third tale lacks the overt violence of the others, but various parallels suggest that hidden in the greater remoteness of this tale are keys to the significance of both the violent murders of the previous tales and the elaborate devices by which the narrator distances his own figure in all three tales. That this tale is to be understood in relation to the previous tales is indicated when the narrator tells of how the Prefect of Police burst into his dark room just as he was "mentally discussing" topics that had arisen from a conversation with Dupin about the murder in the Rue Morgue and the murder of Marie Rogêt. These images of the murders, secreted within the dark interior of the narrator's head, link the coolly undramatic events of this tale to the violent murders of the previous tales.

Both the Rue Morgue murder and that of Marie Rogêt are narrated in so matter of fact and scientific a way as to drain affect away from these grotesque acts and to transfer it to the circumstances of their narration. In this way their import is at once obvious and hidden, just as is the letter in the final tale. It is obvious in that the murders constitute the central matter of the stories, and hidden in that attention is diverted from them by the emphasis placed on the cleverness of Dupin's method of solution and the contrasting ineptness of the Prefect. The overall strategy of the narrator exemplifies Dupin's principle that the solution to mysteries lies in looking for the obvious. In the first of the tales, **"The Murders in the Rue Morgue,"** a link between the detached narrative manner and the gory detail of the murders calls into question the stance of detachment by the brief, but repeated and detailed, descriptions of the bloody hairs torn from Madame L'Espanaye's nearly severed head, and of the marks upon her daughter's neck and body. The repetitions suggest a denied but obsessive fascination with the "*grotesquerie* in horror absolutely alien from humanity," and reveals the obsessive interest in the details of mutilated female bodies that the matter-of-fact tone conceals. At the core of the story, therefore, are those mutilated figures in a room that is apparently impossible to enter. Gaining entrance to the mystery of the sealed room is the story's *raison d'être* and every aspect of it is devoted to disown the horrendous desires that are secreted within it.

However, strategies of denial cannot but constitute chains of association. Therefore, the various devices by which the core action is distanced from the narrator will reveal aspects of the emotions and related ideas that make it necessary for this distancing to occur. In the initial association the narrator defines himself as a connoisseur of analytic power, such as is demonstrated a skillful whist player, whose detached apprehension of the subtlest movements and expressions of his partners not only ensures his victory, but also conceals his desire for it:

> The first two or three rounds having been played, he is in full possession of the contents of each hand, and thence forward puts down his cards with as absolute a precision of purpose as if the rest of the party had turned outward the faces of their own.
>
> (143)

The narrator demurs from making such claims for himself by introducing Dupin, who will incarnate what he calls the creative talents of the whist player, and who, like him, will have his own game to play. We know, therefore, that the narrator espouses Dupin's talents, and flirts with acknowledging his psychic use of this double when he says that he amuses himself with the "fancy of a double Dupin—the creative and the resolvent" (144). But he distances himself from both Dupin's active use of his powers, as well as from his motives.

The reasons for his doing so appear in his account of their relationship. While appearing to give himself the paternal role by providing domicile for his impoverished friend, the narrator subordinates himself socially to this scion "of an illustrious family" (143). He also subordinates himself intellectually when he tells of Dupin's capacity to read the minds of others. While the two have been walking in silence, the narrator has been thinking silently about a young cobbler of small

stature named Chantilly, who exposed himself to ridicule by playing the heroic title role in Crébillon's play *Xerxes*. He is startled when Dupin, as though responding to his unspoken thought, says, "'He is a very little fellow, that's true, and would do better for the *Théâtre des Variétés*'" (145). After Dupin has reconstructed the associative chain by which the narrator had come to reflect upon the diminutive actor, the narrator, in saying that he felt "even more startled than [he] would have been willing to express" (145), reveals both his emotional investment in and intense shame at having the privacy of his mind open to Dupin's gaze. In the configuration he casts himself in a passive posture to be penetrated by Dupin's mind in a way that both gratifies and humiliates him. The configuration also expresses the narrator's identification with Chantilly when Dupin observes that "You thought of the poor cobbler's immolation. So far, you had been stooping in your gait; but now I saw you draw yourself up to your full height. I was then sure that you reflected upon the diminutive figure of Chantilly" (147). The narrator not only fears that he, like Chantilly, might be exposed to ridicule by aspiring to a part that he feels too small to play, but also associates his inferiority with a low social status, like that of the aspiring cobbler, which places him at a disadvantage to the aristocratic Dupin. He chooses Dupin, then, as a front man to carry out his dream project, the responsibility for which he declines. However, this compromise strategy leaves the narrator vulnerable to the figure whom he has endowed with the powers he himself is afraid to claim.

A second aspect of the narrator's relationship with Dupin conflates this underlying competitiveness with an identification in which the two cooperatively enjoy their maleness in relation to women. Women appear first in a remote way in the setting of the "time eaten and grotesque mansion" (144) the narrator chooses as their domicile; they appear more explicitly in the image of the night, "the sable divinity [who] would not herself dwell with us always" (144), but whose presence they "counterfeit" during the day by drawing the shades. As though uneasy about this way of life, he attributes it to Dupin, who was "enamored of the night for her own sake," and he again hints at being in a female posture relative to Dupin in adding that he gave himself "up to [Dupin's] wild whims with a perfect *abandon*" (144, Poe's italics). The ambivalence about his own unstable emotional life that occasions this doubling of himself appears in subtly expressed ambivalence about Dupin. On the one hand, he says that Dupin's behavior might be "the result of an excited, or perhaps of a diseased, intelligence" (144-45). On the other hand, he says that with Dupin his soul felt "enkindled . . . by a wild fervor" and that he valued

Dupin's society as a "treasure beyond price" (143). This erotic suggestiveness, together with female images of the night within which it flowers, reveals that the narrator, with Dupin as both his excuse and his partner, lives inside a maternal envelope, one that contracts during the day to the house, and expands at night to the entire city. With the loneliness of his stance relieved by this doubling that affords an aura of homoerotic gratification, the maternal protective womb provides a haven in which he can cast himself as superior observer of, rather than inferior actor in, the drama of human passions.

The reasons for his having dispersed the female presence into a nocturnal atmosphere, and the other side of his emotional coin in relation to women, appears in the story of the murders, which reveals that he has retreated from ordinary life in order to avoid the fear and horror inspired by his perverse sexual form in which his desires are aroused by images of mutilated women, and perhaps by images of mutilating them. This avoidance is expressed as well in the absence in all three Dupin stories of any sense of the physical substantiality of the male figures that contrasts to the sharply etched physical description of mutilated female bodies. In effect, the narrator has disembodied himself and all male figures whose identity with himself he might acknowledge, with the exception of the ourang-outang. The bestiality attributed to this figure keeps him at a sufficient distance from the narrator's self-definition to make it safe for him to allow the animal's physicality to come into focus.

However, the narrator deviously satisfies his abhorrent desires by setting up a series of observers being observed: himself most distant from the action watching Dupin, Dupin watching the sailor, who owns the ourang-outang, which he watches as it mutilates and kills the women. The narrator expresses his identification with the sailor both as one who observes, and as one who by virtue of his occupation is also alienated from ordinary life. In this figure he accepts some responsibility, both for having allowed the beast to escape and for the voyeurism implicit in the observer's stance. Furthermore, it was only after his owner appeared at the window that the ourang-outang, in a frenzy of fear of being punished, becomes violent. The animal itself, though exonerated of moral responsibility by virtue of being a beast, is nonetheless associated with the human by the descriptions of its hands, by the human emotions attributed to it, but most of all when its cries are taken by all the multi-national witnesses to be a language, albeit one of which each supposes him- or her-self to be ignorant. In this way the dreamer acknowledges his kinship with the desires that are so appalling to his conscious self-image, and reveals a psychic configuration in which his ego-ideal

under the guise of restraining and punishing the bestial desires that are embodied in the ourang-outang in fact whips them to a frenzy in which they find their satisfaction. The value the narrator places on his repudiated desires is suggested when the valuable animal is put in a zoo rather than being killed, as well as by the sailor's exclamations, repeated by each of the witnesses, "sacré, diable," and "mon Dieu." This perverse sexuality links the discovered story to the story of discovery when Dupin says of the Prefect, who in his chagrin at his failure makes sarcastic remarks about people who don't mind their own business,

> Let him discourse; it will ease his conscience. I am satisfied with having defeated him in his own castle. Nevertheless, that he failed in the solution of this mystery, is by no means that matter for wonder which he supposes it; for, in truth, our friend the Prefect is somewhat too cunning to be profound. In his wisdom there is no *stamen*. It is all head and no body, like the pictures of the Goddess Laverna—or at best, all head and shoulders, like a codfish.
>
> (168)

In thus suggesting that in Dupin's insight there is a stamen, that is, the sexual organ of a flower, the narrator brings closer to consciousness the link between sexual gratification and the acumen that permits Dupin to see, as through a window, the hidden recesses of other's bosoms, and thereby to solve murder mysteries.

The narrator approaches more closely to the emotional and sexual core in **"The Mystery of Marie Rogêt,"** in which there is an actual murderer, and there is a sexual relation between the murderer and his victim. The discovered story is a simple one in which Marie Rogêt, a charming girl who works in a perfume shop, twice goes to meet her secret lover, and the second time is murdered by him. The story provides no motive for her lover to murder Marie, but in the omission the dreamer implies that he killed her because she came to him, and because the killing itself constitutes sexual fulfillment. That is, the conjunction of a sexual approach of a beautiful woman who carries the tantalizing aromas of perfume, and a murderous response associates the two with each other, rendering violence a perverse sexual fulfillment. As in the first story, the dreamer remains remote from this event, first by keeping the core story well in the background of the story of discovery, and, second, by not allowing any description of the murder itself to surface as Dupin narrates only the murderer's frantic efforts to dispose of the body. The murder falls into a kind of textual void, from which emerges an obsessive interest, more intense even than in the first story, in the details that are repeated with great clarity with each new speculation of how the body ended up in the river.

This evasion of a direct representation of the sexual characterizes the entire tale. In the first disappearance of Marie Rogêt the narrator makes an approach to envisioning a sexual encounter with a woman.[7] But he cannot disentangle sexuality from its terrifying association with violence that forces him to maintain his lonely life, so that the second effort to generate such an encounter results in the murder. The murder, committed in an unknown place, both constitutes a sexual fulfillment, and punishes the woman for daring to break into the isolation, represented in his murky rooms, that protects the dreamer from his sexual form. In the description of the way in which the murderer trussed up the body to drag it to the river, she becomes a piece of baggage, and in the suicide of her would-be lover the dreamer expresses his sense of the extensive range of violence and death that ensues from contact with women. This aura of violence is deepened by the images embedded in what Dupin proves to be the false account of the murder. In the newspaper accounts marauding hordes of young hoodlums infest the banks of the river Seine, killing and raping other women. A more humanized version of the ourang-outang of the previous story, these generalized images of violence constitute the circumference of a circular dream structure at the centre of which will be found the act of perverted sexuality committed this time by a naval officer, a version of the observing sailor of the previous story.

As the narrator more closely approaches envisioning the human act of sexual violence, he compensates by keeping his voice at an even greater distance than in the previous tale from the central action. He denies any significance to the discovered story by casting all the emphasis on the story of discovery, stressing that his sole purpose is to "depict some very remarkable features in the mental character of my friend, the Chevalier C. Auguste Dupin" (170). Dupin and the narrator remain in their domicile throughout the whole tale, whereas in the previous tale they examined the site of the murders; and an even larger percentage is taken up with lengthy beginning and ending cogitations about the mathematical "Calculus of Probabilities," and Dupin's discourse on the faulty logic of the newspaper accounts. However, in a countermove the dreamer brings himself into greater immediacy with his dream configuration by means of the links made between the fictional account of Marie Rogêt and the actual New York newspaper accounts of the murder of Mary Rogers on which it is based. By linking the two levels, the narrator, now difficult to distinguish from his author, insists on the reality of the event even as he fictionalizes it in a way that barely allows it to be visualized.

This vagueness, together with the way in which the narrator withholds information about the amount of the reward, allows the aura of mystery to remain after the solution of the crime. In this it is similar to the previous tale in which the sense of mystery that surrounds Dupin and that hovers in the general atmosphere remains after the murders are solved. This savouring of mystery for its own sake gives the tales their characteristic atmosphere, and hints at the hidden presence of emotional layers to which the details will not by themselves provide clues.[8] This gratuitous sense of mystery is nowhere so evident as in **"The Purloined Letter,"** in which the omission of the letter's specific contents teases the curiosity, while one in fact knows the general nature of the contents sufficiently to understand the story. However, since the plot associates the original letter with the one Dupin substitutes for it, the letter's full meaning must have to do with the quotation from Crébillon's *Antrée* that Dupin inscribes in it. Just as the previous stories cast light forward onto the last one, so the end of **"The Purloined Letter"** will cast light back, not only on its beginning, but on the previous two as well.

This story, like the others, centers on violence done to a woman. Though the Queen appears only in the prefect's account of the letter's theft, she is the centre around which the story circles, and the link made by the narrator between the story about to unfold and the previous two suggests that the violence of those two is to be found here as well. By substituting the stolen letter for the Queen, the narrator deflects attention from her body to the violation of her privacy and threat to her reputation. The physical violence that is done to women in the previous stories here is done to the letter. The dark silence of the letter suggests the obscured but intense emotion related to the Queen's infidelity to the King. The narrator's fear of acknowledging his own sexual appetite appears, once again, in his remoteness from the action, while the unacknowledged hate and rage appear in action surrounding the letter instead. The covert violence appears first in the methods by which the despised and stupid Prefect searches the Minister's rooms, which as Lacan says, become an image writ large of the female body. His is a methodical version of the violence with which the ourang-outang tore up Madame L'Espanaye's room, a room the animal would not have entered had the women had the light on in order to read old letters.[9] The detail with which his search is described has the same obsessive intensity disguised as scientific inquiry as that used in the previous stories to describe the murdered bodies. But in defining the Prefect as stupid, the narrator repudiates his crassness in favor of the Minister's more elegant violence, while the improbability that Holland notes of the letter escaping the Prefect's notice indicates the emotional import of the contrast. In wandering the night streets, like Dupin and the narrator earlier, the Minister is associated with a generalized sexuality as well as with the prefect's lascivious attention to the room that his absence from it permits.

However, the most ferocious attack on the female body is implied in the description of how the Minister hides the purloined letter. In **"The Purloined Letter"** the discovered story consists only of the description of the letter on the mantle piece. This description replaces and is analogous to the more obviously violent discovered stories of the previous works. Just as there is a sharp contrast between the bodilessness of the male figures and the corporality of the murdered women, so here there is an analogous contrast between the vague description of the Minister's apartment and the specific detail of the fireplace, mantle, knob, and the letter stuffed in a compartment of "a trumpery filigree card-rack of pasteboard, that hung dangling by a dirty blue ribbon, from a little brass knob just beneath the middle of the mantel piece" (220). Under cover of the substitution of the letter for the body, the violated maternal body receives its fullest representation in the description of the camouflaged letter: like the body of Madame L'Espanaye it is torn nearly in two and dirty; like the body of her daughter stuffed in the chimney, it is stuffed in a compartment of the tawdry card rack.[10] The fire place source of warmth aptly represents the maternal body, and the mantle the maternal breasts, but the card rack with its dirty ribbon has no particular force in the domain of public symbols; it contributes nothing to the narration, and it is manifestly out of place in the apartments of the elegant Minister. It therefore calls attention to itself as the locus of secrets. Redolent of desire and disgust, it functions as a combined image of the maternal womb and mutilated female genitals that expresses the narrator's desire to expose the mysteries of and do violence to the maternal womb. Finally, Dupin describes the letter as stamped with the Minister's seal. In the improbability of the Minister's putting his own seal on a letter addressed to himself the narrator expresses his fierce possessiveness.

Using his capacity simultaneously to read minds and solve mysteries, Dupin penetrates the Minister's mind, realizes he has found the letter, and arranges to steal it. By directly involving Dupin in the action, the narrator diminishes the distance between himself from the dirty violence of the discovered stories. He counters this approach to involvement by contrasting Dupin to the Minister as making restitution to the Queen whom the former has violated. The narrator heightens this contrast between the Minister and Dupin by the strong parallels in their attributes and actions. Both Dupin

and the Minister combine mathematical skills with poetic talent that is associated with the ability to penetrate the mysteries of others' minds, the Minister that of the Queen and the Prefect, and Dupin that of the Minister and the Prefect. In possessing the letter both have power over the Queen; only where the Minister makes use of his to blackmail her, Dupin defines himself as her protector by restoring the letter, thereby putting the Minister in her power. In this devious way the narrator both gratifies his eroticized hatred of woman in the figure of the Minister, while in Dupin's simultaneously declaring himself as "a partisan of the lady concerned" he protects her image from the former's destructiveness. Thus the narrator maintains a self-image as woman's protector, and punishes himself for his contrary desires when Dupin ensures the Minister's political destruction.

Finally, the narrator's ambivalent relation to women, mothers, and female sexuality merges with his ambivalent relation to male figures in connection with the letter that Dupin substitutes for the original in the Minister's hotel. That letter contains a quotation from Crébillon's *Atrée* in which Atrée says of his plan to murder the young man who was brought up believing himself to be his son, but was in fact the product of the adulterous relationship between Thyeste and Atrée's wife, that it is "Un dessein si funeste, / S'il n'est digme d'Atrée, est digne de Thyeste" (222). The fatal plot that is unworthy of Atrée's dignity, but that is justified by the heinousness of Thyeste's seduction of Atrée's wife, is not only the murder, but also the succeeding action in which Atrée, under the guise of presenting Thyeste with a cup of wine to symbolize their reconciliation, presents him instead with a cup of his son's blood. As he envisions accomplishing this long delayed revenge, he savours the pleasures of knowing that Thyeste knows the identity of his tormentor and of watching his pain while he toys with it as a cat does a mouse. Intuiting that the blood is that of his son before he drinks it, Thyeste throws it away, and his worst fears are confirmed when his daughter, who had fallen in love with the son before she knew that they were siblings, reports his death. When the agonized Thyeste asks Atrée why he did not kill him, Atrée responds that the pleasures of watching his agony far surpass those he would get by murdering him.

The sudden way in which the quotation leaps at us as the last line of an otherwise apparently passionless text both invites us to look for its significance to the story we have just been told and frustrates our attempts to do so. The story of the two brothers of Crébillon's play encourages us retrospectively to see significance in the common first initial of Dupin and the otherwise unnamed Minister, in the information that the Minister has a brother who is a poet, and in the similar ways in which the two men are described. Both men are associated with high or aristocratic families, and both men are described as poets. On the one hand, therefore, we are encouraged to think that Dupin is actually brother to the Minister and that we are to take literally the identification with Atrée suggested by his letter. On the other hand, the likelihood of their being so is diminished by the reference to Vienna, rather than *somewhere in* France, as the place in which the evil turn was done and by the likelihood that the Prefect, or at least the narrator, would have mentioned this fraternal relation. In this flurry of confusion the narrator comes close to showing his own presence behind all of the figures, as the poet who in writing the tale outdoes both of the poets he writes about. As with the letter, one can construct a realistic account of a quasi-fraternal relationship, perhaps a friendship such as that between the narrator and Dupin, in which the Minister in Vienna stole a woman from Dupin, by so doing wrecked Dupin's career and left him in the impoverished state in which he is introduced to us in the first tale. This would explain the cat and mouse pleasure Dupin, like Atrée, takes in toying with the Minister and in imagining the latter's now misplaced confidence in the power having the letter gives him, and his agony of horror when he realizes that he does not have the letter. Just as an important part of Atrée's revenge is that Thyeste should know him as the cause of his suffering, so an important part of Dupin's revenge is that the Minister should know that it was he who retrieved the letter. However, in a characteristic way, and unlike Atrée, Dupin's self-image demands of him the stance of indifferent casualness with which he tells of writing the quotation in the duplicate letter. The clashing irony between his saying that, knowing the Minister would be curious, he "thought it a pity not to give him a clue," and the nature of the clue that is given, reveals the hatred and rage that have been concealed in the stance of detached observer throughout the three tales. At the same time, the elusive silence and final undecidability about Dupin's own story generate a new sense of mystery around Dupin that washes back over all the tales in the process of resolving the old one, showing Dupin, as the poet, as the narrator hinted at the beginning of **"The Murders in the Rue Morgue,"** as both resolving and creating mysteries. It also firmly links Dupin's mystery to the violence and grotesquerie of the mysteries that he solves, and it both deepens and intensifies the emotional significance of that violence by linking it to familial betrayal and outrage.

In this complex narrative structure the narrator expresses a basically straightforward emotional underlying configuration, surrounded by a complex system of mediation and denial. On the one hand he thinks of woman as unfaithful, but his emotions are separated from his cognition, so that he simultaneously defends the image of the actual woman while expressing his fear and detestation of the generalized feminine in images of mutilation and horror that also gratify perverse sexual desire. He denies and manages these feelings by evoking mythically empowered images of the woman as Night, and casting himself through Dupin as her protector. But his deeper feelings emerge in the final parallel between the Minister and Thyeste, and Dupin and Atrée. Insofar as he identifies with the guilty Minister and Thyeste he reveals his fear of male reprisal should he claim the woman, and insofar as he identifies with Dupin and Atrée, he reveals his rage at and desire to avenge himself upon the rival paternal male. Whether this turmoil of horrifying desires in themselves generate the self-image of one who feels inadequate and frightened of the world, or whether the sense of inadequacy functions as a defense against the need for action, he expresses his sense of being too small for the kind of action he would like to take in the image of Chantilly, who is too small for the role of Xerxes, the conqueror, and who, by extension, is also too small for the role of Atrée, the avenger. He covers this self-image in turn with that of the man of superior and intellectual detachment, and expresses the aggressive and potentially violent aspects of that intellectual acuity through Dupin. But using Dupin as his psychological front man also renders this man whom he has empowered with such penetrating acuity dangerous to his own fragile self image. And so the relation between the two men at the end of the last story dissolves into the renewed aura of mystery about Dupin's past. Finally it is by means of savouring the poetry of mystery that the narrator keeps the components of his fiercely conflicted psyche in a perpetually unstable balance.

This analysis has united concern for form and content. It has taken account of the different narrative levels; it has attended to the configuration of character and event at the same time as it comprehends the characters' feelings and intentions; it has accounted for the sense of mystery surrounding the letter, even when logically there is none; it relates the conscious concerns and ideas about analysis and poetic thought processes to the emotional content, to the genre form, and to atmospheric effects. The sense of intentionality that pervades the experience of reading is accommodated without making unnecessary claims about authors' conscious or unconscious intentions, or assumptions about a cosmos that expresses itself mysteriously through literature. Meaning becomes what the tales mean for a figure inside the work, and because human beings generally are interested in each other, their meaning for us lies in their rendering of a consciousness constructing meaningful worlds from his contending psychic drives. One can be precise about the tale's meaning for the narrator without making unwarranted claims about the author or about readers in general. While undoubtedly the selection of what to emphasize and what to omit reflects my own psychic forms, limiting associations either to what most obviously lies within the general culture or to the associative links in the tales makes a reasonable margin between this commentary and that on which it comments.

Milan Kundera concludes his article on Kafka, "In Saint Garta's Shadow" with the assertion that Kafka was the first to make the breach in the closed novel with its boring psychology that for André Breton excluded it from the realm of dream. Quoting him as saying that "'I believe that in future there will be a resolution of these two states, dream and reality, apparently so contradictory, into a kind of absolute reality, or surreality, if we can so put it'" (1991, 4). Kundera sees Kafka's merger of dream form with ordinary reality as a precursor and enabler of worlds of mixed realities that compose the fiction of Márquez, Fuentes, Rushdie, and, one might add, Poe's and Kundera's. When such literature is approached as the dream of a character or of its narrator, the dream-like quality itself becomes part of the experience being rendered. Such fiction lifts to the surface the dream dimension that the art of realistic fiction conceals, but that remains in the structuring principle and appears as the sense of aesthetic inevitability. However, to regard realistic fictional worlds as the dream configurations of a narrator or protagonist is to recover and expose to scrutiny the dream dimension hidden in the most realistic of fiction.

Notes

1. Roger Seamon discusses the way in which the claims to a scientific criticism conceal new interpretative strategies, or rather the uncovering of an unfamiliar set of themes, in "Poetics Against Itself: On the Self-Destruction of Modern Scientific Criticism," *PHLA* (May, 1989) 294-305.

2. Lacan claims that Dupin's victory is empty, for by the time the letter is returned to the queen it becomes a signifier without signification, and the minister, Lacan opines, will lay down his cards and "leave the table in time to avoid disgrace." But in the story Dupin's revenge has been accomplished in the interval between the time he stole the letter and the time he gives it to the prefect, for in that time the Minister, supposing that he still had the letter, will have taken irreversible steps that will bring ruin upon him once it is known to the Queen that he does not have the let-

ter. Therefore Dupin's revenge, whether or not his rage is "manifestly feminine," has already been accomplished.

3. This might seem a trivial cavil, but Poe uses vastly different narrators in his stories, in one even a woman. He clearly was experimenting with the narrative voice, and calls its veracity into question in "The System of Doctor Tarr and Doctor Fether." Though the Dupin stories that involve an American narrator in France invite one to conflate the narrator with his author, Poe was fully as capable as Philip Roth in riding the edge of the fictional presentation of the authorial voice.

4. Bonaparte's assertion that the image of the phallic mother and the horror introduced by her castration, goes back to the earliest oral psychic layers simply ignores the fact that a nursing boy knows nothing about his penis or his mother's having or not having one. If such a notion acquires psychological importance, it could do so only at a later stage of development.

5. For a full account of and rationale for this critical mode see Kay Stockholder, *Dream Works: Lovers and Families in Shakespeare's Plays.* Toronto: University of Toronto Press, 1987.

6. I have chosen the narrator as dreamer of these stories, but one could choose also Dupin. While the basic configuration would remain the same, it would be more awkward to account for the tale's narrative structure. Dupin would be one who evades responsibility for his actions by defining himself as being determined by another, that is, by the narrator. If one chooses a minor character, one would be talking about someone more like the narrator, that is, a person who defines himself as at the margins of life, and sees his own psychological drama enacted by others. Generally speaking, I believe things work out best if in narrative fiction one chooses the narrator as dreamer if he or she has a dramatic presence. In serious dramatic literature one generally would choose the protagonist, whereas in comedy one would choose the character who is most central to the plot structure.

7. Bonaparte comments that this is the only story that mentions actual sex. She connects it to Poe's relation to Mary Deveraux, whom he visited at the time of his wife's illness and hemorrhaging, which recalled memories of his mother's dying and activated his sadism.

8. It is this atmosphere of mystery, this aura of the unsaid, that creates what Felman calls the poetic effect.

9. Marie Bonaparte in her discussion of "The Murders in the Rue Morgue" notices that the iron box

found in the murdered women's room contained letters. The light required to read them was what attracted the Ourang-outang to the room, so that the women were, in a sense, murdered for reading them. Bonaparte associates these letters to love letters Poe's natural mother received from her lover, who Bonaparte believes to have been the father of Poe's sister. Noticing also the discrepancy between the first description, in which the letters are scattered on the floor, and the second, given by the sailor, in which they are inside the chest, Bonaparte comments that Poe's mother's secrets are sealed with her death. Whether or not one credits Bonaparte's specific story (it isn't a bad one), as dreamer the narrator associates the purloined letter of the later story with the letters that occasioned the death of the women in the earlier story, and so indicates that the letter signifies violent impulses towards women.

10. Interestingly, all of the commentaries omit mention of the card rack, even the detailed reading of Marie Bonaparte, whom Holland mocks for taking account even of the brass knob as a representation of the mother's clitoris.

References

Babener, Liahna Klenman. 1988. "The Motif of the Double in Edgar Allan Poe's 'The Purloined Letter.'" In *The Purloined Poe.* Edited by John P. Muller and William J. Richardson. Baltimore: Johns Hopkins University Press.

Bonaparte, Marie. 1949. Selections from *The Life and Works of Edgar Allan Poe: A Psychoanalytic Interpretation.* London: Imago Publishing Co. Ltd.

Chambers, Ross. 1988. "Narratorial Authority and 'The Purloined Letter.'" In *The Purloined Poe.* Baltimore: Johns Hopkins University Press.

Derrida, Jacques. 1977. "The Purveyor of Truth." Translated by Allan Bass.

Felman, Shoshana. 1988. "On Reading Poetry: Reflections on the Limits and Possibilities of Psychoanalytic Approaches." In *The Purloined Poe.* Baltimore: Johns Hopkins University Press.

Gallop, Jane. 1988. "The American Other." In *The Purloined Poe.* Baltimore: Johns Hopkins University Press.

Harvey, Irene. 1988. "Structures of Exemplarity in Poe, Freud, Lacan and Derrida." In *The Purloined Poe.* Baltimore: Johns Hopkins University Press.

Holland, Norman. 1980. "Re-covering 'The Purloined Letter': Reading as a Personal Transaction." Princeton: Princeton University Press.

Johnson, Barbara. 1988. "The Frame of Reference: Poe, Lacan, and Derrida." In *The Purloined Poe.* Baltimore: Johns Hopkins University Press.

Kundera, Milan. 1991. "In Saint Garta's Shadow." *Times Literary Supplement,* May 24, 1991.

Lacan, Jacques. 1972. "Seminar on 'The Purloined Letter.'" *Yale French Studies* 48: 38-72.

Muller, John. 1988. "Negation in 'The Purloined Letter': Hegel, Poe, and Lacan." In *The Purloined Poe.* Baltimore: Johns Hopkins University Press.

Peraldi, Françis. 1988. "Time in 'The Purloined Letter.'" In *The Purloined Poe.* Baltimore: Johns Hopkins University Press.

Seamon, Roger. 1989. "Poetics Against Itself: On the Self-Destruction of Modern Scientific Criticism." PMLA, May, 1989.

Stockholder, Kay. 1987. *Dream Works: Lovers and Families in Shakespeare's Plays.* Toronto: University of Toronto Press.

James V. Werner (essay date March 2001)

SOURCE: Werner, James V. "The Detective Gaze: Edgar A. Poe, the *Flaneur,* and the Physiognomy of Crime." *ATQ* n.s. 15, no. 1 (March 2001): 5-21.

[*In the following essay, Werner draws on the essays of Walter Benjamin to investigate the role of the* flaneur— *or detached interpreter of the urban milieu—in Poe's tale.*]

Among the many achievements in the short and difficult life of Edgar A. Poe was the creation of the detective tale as a popular literary genre. The extraordinary feats of ratiocination performed by C. Auguste Dupin in **"The Murders in the Rue Morgue," "The Purloined Letter,"** and **"The Mystery of Marie Rogêt"** have entertained countless young readers in the past 150 years, and attracted enormous critical attention. Some of that attention, most notably Dana Brand's *The Spectator and the City in Nineteenth-Century American Literature,* has focused on the relationship between Poe's detective and the flaneur, the solitary strolling metropolitan observer theorized by Walter Benjamin in "Paris: Capital of the Nineteenth Century," in his essay "The Flaneur," and in its revised version "On some motifs in Baudelaire." Within the context of these discussions, Benjamin points briefly to Poe's connection to the flaneur who, Benjamin argues, enjoyed his heyday in Paris during the 1830s, just when Poe was launching his literary career.[1] Benjamin's references, typically aphoristic, deserve to be more fully unpacked; and Brand's analysis of this connection, while extremely useful, tends to downplay the significance of the flaneur for Poe. In fact, the flaneur represents a pivotal influence on Poe's philosophical perspective and fictional aims and strategies overall, perhaps nowhere more evidently than in his detective tales.

WALTER BENJAMIN, THE FLANEUR, AND THE DETECTIVE

There is considerable disagreement among scholars as to the nature and origins of the flaneur. As Keith Tester indicates, "definitions are at best difficult and, at worst, a contradiction of what the flaneur means. In himself, the flaneur is, in fact, a very obscure thing" (7). Yet certain features recur in most if not all delineations of this figure. The ancient "pseudo-science" of physiognomy, of reading a person's facial features and external characteristics for evidence of inner qualities, plays a central role in flanerie.[2] Another critical element is the flaneur's apparently detached, aimless, and desultory (but in reality, highly present and focused) observation. The flaneur's methodology is intuitive; he bases his conclusions solely on observation and inference. According to an 1806 French pamphlet titled *Le Flaneur au Salon,* he was an outsider within the metropolis, walking "through the streets at random and alone . . . suspended from social obligation, disengaged, disinterested, dispassionate"; his leisurely manner and his ties to aristocratic privilege make him appear to be a "loafer" or "lazybones" (qtd. in Ferguson 26, 24). The flaneur must preserve this liminal perspective to interpret the city. He must be immersed in the crowd, and yet must remain aloof from it; part of the marketplace, he must still keep his distance from it and its commodities.

For a while, Benjamin argues, the flaneur remained "still on the threshold, of the city as of the bourgeois class. Neither has engulfed him; in neither is he at home" ("Paris" 156). However, for Benjamin, the flaneur was constantly in danger of being reduced to the status of passive window-shopper or consumer, a transformation that, as Priscilla Parkhurst Ferguson suggests, "effectively ends the flaneur's connection with creativity" (35). Also, the flaneur quickly became a literary figure, generating "a panorama literature" of "physiologies" which "investigated types that might be encountered by a person taking a look at the marketplace" ("Flaneur" 36). Ultimately, then, the flaneur became gainfully employed, and his written observations became commodities within the market. For Rob Shields, the "ambiguous process of consumption and self-implication" inherent in flanerie poses a fundamental question: "How to gain knowledge yet remain unchanged; how to witness, yet remain unmoved?" (75-76).

The triumph of societal forces, Benjamin argues, was putting the flaneur to use as a detective. As the "physiologies" waned in popularity, perhaps reflecting doubts as to the flaneur's ability to give order to the metropolis and its masses, "the flaneur is . . . turned into an unwilling detective" ("Paris" 40). Benjamin argues that the flaneur's newfound employment "does him a lot of good socially, for it accredits his idleness" (40), but it also clearly signals the demise of the flaneur in his "pure" state. The now productive flaneur-turned-detective was assimilated into the utilitarian society that he had formerly resisted. If Baudelaire's flaneur was "a prince who everywhere rejoices in his incognito" (9-10), the rise of the detective reflects society's uneasiness about the flaneur and its pressures to mitigate his elusiveness: "the detective story came into being when this most decisive of all conquests of a person's incognito had been accomplished. Since then the end of efforts to capture a man in his speech and actions has not been in sight" ("Paris" 48).

Such attempts to "conquer the incognito" reflect the continuing tension between public and private in the social contract. For Benjamin, the fragmentation of the worker's psyche is mirrored in the spatial split between "public" places of business and "private" interiors that become shrines to the art of collection.

> For the private person, living space becomes, for the first time, antithetical to the place of work. The former is constituted by the interior; the office is its complement. The private person who squares his accounts with reality in his office demands that the interior be maintained in his illusions. . . . From this spring the phantasmagorias of the interior. For the private individual the private environment represents the universe. In it he gathers remote places and the past. His drawing room is a box in the world theater.
>
> ("Paris" 154)

Paradoxically, the bifurcation of public and private, of "inner" and "outer" space that Benjamin illustrates, tends to invert itself. In adorning his private interior with his collection, the bourgeois collector establishes a trail by which he may be traced, by none other than the public sphere's latest recruit: the flaneur-turned-detective, who now performs a "physiognomy of the interior." The specific reasons for bourgeois culture's peculiar "adoption" of the flaneur, the particular ways in which the flaneur was commodified, and the implications of his relationship to nineteenth-century culture are intriguing matters to be explored in a future article. The focus of the study at hand is Poe's innovative use of flanerie at the very heart of his detection tales.

THE CASE OF POE: FLANERIE OR DETECTION?

It is as "physiognomist of the interior" that Benjamin discusses Poe as a progenitor of the detective tale:

> The interior is not only the universe but also the etui of the private person. To live means to leave traces. In the interior these are emphasized. An abundance of covers

and protectors, [of] liners and cases[,] is devised, on which the traces of objects of everyday use are imprinted. The traces of the occupant also leave their impression on the interior. The detective story that follows these traces comes into being. His "philosophy of furniture," along with his detective novellas, shows Poe to be the first physiognomist of the interior.

(155-56)

Benjamin mentions Poe again in "One Way Street," suggesting the appropriateness, even the inevitability of murder "in a certain type of detective novel at the dynamic center of which stands the horror of apartments" (64). "That this kind of detective novel begins with Poe—at a time when such accommodations hardly yet existed—is no counter argument," Benjamin argues. "For without exception the great writers perform their combinations in a world that comes after them" (64).

Poe's connection to the detective is readily apparent, of course, in his tales about C. Auguste Dupin: **"The Murders in the Rue Morgue," "The Purloined Letter,"** and **"The Mystery of Marie Rogêt."** Poe's connection to the flaneur is perhaps less obvious but equally important, and more pervasive than has been acknowledged to date. Having lived in various metropolitan centers on the Eastern seaboard (Richmond, Baltimore, Philadelphia, New York), Poe was certainly sensitive to the practice of flanerie. Hans Bergmann's *God in the Street* clearly illustrates the extent to which literary flanerie was practiced in ante-bellum American periodicals, and Dana Brand has illustrated how Poe was thoroughly familiar with the conventional literary flaneur. Catherine Quoyeser notes that Poe's "Doings of Gotham" series emulated the work of Nathaniel Parker Willis, whom she views as a prime example of the nineteenth-century American literary "salaried flaneur" (158). And Poe's interest in phrenology and autography suggests his fascination with physiognomical observation and interpretation. But Poe applied the principles of flanerie in ways far more interesting and subtle, employing its methods even as he subverted its fantasies of control, capitalizing on its inversions of public and private space, of "inner" and "outer."

Probably the most famous instance of flanerie in Poe's works may be found in his story **"The Man of the Crowd,"** which Benjamin calls Poe's early contribution to a "physiognomics of the crowd" ("Paris" 156). The tale's narrator relates how as a "convalescent" he sat in a London coffeehouse, observing the crowds passing by his window on the busy street. He begins to regard "with minute interest the innumerable varieties of figure, dress, air, gait, visage, and expression of countenance" (389). He distinguishes between people

of different classes by means of their physiognomy. The "tribe of clerks" is "obvious" because of their "tight coats, bright boots, well-oiled hair, and supercilious lips," their "dapperness of carriage," and the "cast-off graces of the gentry" (389-90). The "upper clerks" are especially notable in that they uniformly have "slightly bald heads, from which the right ears, long used to pen-holding, [have] an odd habit of standing off on end" (390). The "swell pickpockets" are recognizable from their "voluminous wristband" and their "air of excessive frankness." The gamblers are "distinguished by a certain sodden swarthiness of complexion, a filmy dimness of eye, and pallor and compression of lip," not to mention a "guarded lowness of tone in conversation, and a more than ordinary extension of the thumb at right angles with the fingers" (390).

As Poe's narrator proceeds with his detection and classification of the crowd, however, he is confronted by a face that baffles his method by virtue of "the absolute idiosyncrasy of its expression": he can muster no more than "confused" and "paradoxical" ideas of "vast mental power, of caution, of penuriousness, of avarice, of coolness, of malice, of blood-thirstiness, of triumph, of merriment, of excessive terror, of intense—of supreme despair" (392). He follows this mysterious stranger, who compulsively immerses himself in the crowd, but ultimately abandons his scrutiny, saying, "This old man is the type and the genius of deep crime. He refuses to be alone. He is the man of the crowd. It will be in vain to follow; for I shall learn no more of him, nor of his deeds. The worst heart of the world is a grosser book than the 'Hortulus Animae,' and perhaps it is but one of the great mercies of God that 'er lasst sich nicht lesen'" ("it does not permit itself to be read") (396).

Dana Brand, one of the few scholars to have addressed Poe's connection to the flaneur in detail, offers a rich discussion of this topic in *The Spectator and the City in Nineteenth-Century American Literature.* However, I find Brand's analysis of the relation between the flaneur and the detective in Poe somewhat confusing, and overly dismissive of the flaneur's importance for Poe. Brand argues early on that the presence of the illegible face of the wanderer in **"The Man of the Crowd"** represents Poe's "critique of the interpretive strategies of the flaneur" (89), that "ultimately, **'The Man of the Crowd'** suggests that the urban crowd cannot be reduced to comfortable transparency" (88). For Brand, Poe's tale "implies that an urban observer is needed who can read and in some sense master what the flaneur cannot" (89). Brand maintains that in Poe's detective Dupin, the author created that "urban interpreter . . . who could provide a more credible and complex assurance of urban legibility than could be found in the literature of the flaneur" (90).

The implication here is that the detective represents a figure distinctly different from the flaneur, and is therefore more capable to observe and interpret modern urban phenomena. Brand's emphasis on the differences between the two types and his assessment of the flaneur's effectiveness are misleading, though. In the end, after forging an argument to distinguish the detective from the flaneur, Brand ultimately suggests that Dupin "shares . . . many of the objectives and functions of his predecessor" (102); he argues that "in spite of their differences, the detective is not a contradiction of the flaneur so much as a dialectical adaptation of him," an adaptation better suited to "the changing intellectual and aesthetic expectations of his audience" (105). Though somewhat contradictory, the case Brand makes for the affinities between the flaneur and the detective seems much more compelling. In Poe's formulation the flaneur and detective are closely aligned in characteristics and methodology. The narrator in **"The Man of the Crowd"** and Dupin are of one spirit, and in Poe's detective tales one finds some of his most successful instances of flanerie.

For example, the flaneur/detective, whom Poe refers to as the "analyst" in **"Rue Morgue"** [**"The Murders in the Rue Morgue"**], pays minute attention to details regarding facial features, expressions, and body language. Poe's Dupin also shares the flaneur's association with wealth and aristocracy: "This young gentleman was of an excellent—indeed of an illustrious family, but, by a variety of untoward events, had been reduced to such poverty that the energy of his character succumbed beneath it, and he ceased to bestir himself in the world, or to care for the retrieval of his fortunes" (400). This association allows Dupin time and resources to observe the city and its inhabitants at his leisure, despite the fact that his is an aristocracy in decline; his indolence as regards "productive" and "socially valuable" labor is also evident. Dupin also exhibits the flaneur's traditional isolation and detachment from society, though he consents to the narrator's unobtrusive accompaniment:

> I was permitted to be at the expense of renting, and furnishing in a style which suited the rather fantastic gloom of our common temper, a time-eaten and grotesque mansion, long deserted through superstitions into which we did not inquire, and tottering to its fall in a retired and desolate portion of the Faubourg St. Germain. . . . Our seclusion was perfect. We admitted no visitors. . . . We existed within ourselves alone.
>
> (400-01)

Dupin and the narrator also engage in the flaneur's traditional behavior of sauntering, after the "advent of true Darkness," when they "sallied forth into the streets, arm in arm, continuing the topics of the day, or roaming far and wide until a late hour, seeking, amid the wild lights and shadows of the populous city, that infinity of mental excitement which quiet observation can afford" (401). Indeed, that observation, Dupin admits, "has become with me, of late, a species of necessity" (403), and he boasts to the narrator of his flaneuristic skills, saying that "most men, in respect to himself, wore windows in their bosoms" (402).

Dupin's flanerie also dramatizes the importance of intuition, one of the main ideas Poe would later raise in his speculative cosmogony, *Eureka: A Prose Poem.* Dupin claims that while his technique of observation may seem to be more intuitive than "scientific," it is in fact more methodical (and on a higher plane) than the "mere method" of the police. The analyst exhibits "in his solutions of each a degree of *acumen* which appears to the ordinary apprehension praeternatural. His results, brought about by the very soul and essence of method, have, in truth, the whole air of intuition" (397). Dupin's dialectic of close analytical scrutiny and disengaged, casual theorization is developed at greater length in *Eureka,* where Poe asserts that the "intuition" of "theorists" like Kepler is actually *"the conviction arising from those inductions or deductions of which the processes are so shadowy as to escape our consciousness, elude our reason, or defy our capacity of expression"* (1276). In his detective tales, Poe seems unwilling to argue (as he later would in *Eureka*) for the scientific validity of such "guesses" outright. Dupin concedes, "I will not pursue these guesses—for I have no right to call them more—since the shades of reflection upon which they are based are scarcely of sufficient depth to be appreciable by my own intellect, and since I could not pretend to make them intelligible to the understanding of another. We will call them guesses then, and speak of them as such" (425). But clearly such guesses are crucial to solve the mystery in the detective tales, just as in *Eureka* they identify the "cloud" behind which *must* lie the answer to questions about the universe (1293-94).

READING THE CRIMINAL INTERIOR

Perhaps most intriguing are the ways in which the methods of Poe's detective reveal and play on the flaneur's liminality, his ability to remain "in" the scene yet "removed" from it, "neither in nor out," as Poe phrased it in his sub-title for an early tale called **"Loss of Breath."** One way this ability is manifested is in Dupin's capacity for "reading" the hidden thoughts of other characters. To do so, he must be fully present, alive to sensory stimuli. In fact, he must be more than "in" the moment; he must identify and empathize completely with his opponent, to get "inside" his mind.

"The analyst," we are told, "throws himself into the spirit of his opponent, identifies himself therewith, and not unfrequently sees thus, at a glance, the sole methods (sometimes indeed absurdly simple ones) by which he may seduce into error or hurry into miscalculation" (398). This may be accomplished in a simple fashion, according to Dupin in **"The Purloined Letter,"** by approximating the opponent's face to read his thoughts, as one schoolboy did particularly well in the game of "even and odd":

> This game is simple, and is played with marbles. One player holds in his hand a number of these toys, and demands of another whether that number is even or odd. . . . The boy to whom I allude won all the marbles of the school. Of course he had some principle of guessing; and this lay in mere observation and ad-measurement of the astuteness of his opponents. . . . [U]pon inquiring of the boy by what means he effected the thorough identification in which his success consisted, I received answer as follows: 'When I wish to find out how wise, or how stupid, or how good, or how wicked is any one, or what are his thoughts at the moment, I fashion the expression of my face, as accurately as possible, in accordance with the expression of his, and then wait to see what thoughts or sentiments arise in my mind or heart, as if to match or correspond with the expression'. . . .
>
> (689-90)

However, Dupin achieves his masterly reading of individuals not simply by seeing "deeper into" their hidden souls, but by moving at will "into" their psyches and "out" to get a distanced perspective on them. In **"Rue Morgue,"** Dupin illustrates how the analyst employs the flaneur's detached physiognomic scrutiny to become "proficient" at the game of whist. That proficiency includes "a comprehension of *all* the sources whence legitimate advantage may be derived," which are "not only manifold but multiform, and lie frequently among the recesses of thought altogether inaccessible to the ordinary understanding" (398). The analyst must consider but also transcend the "limits of mere rule," making "a host of observations and inferences" and "deductions from things external to the game" (398):

> He examines the countenance of his partner, comparing it carefully with that of each of his opponents. He considers the mode of assorting the cards in each hand; often counting trump by trump, and honor by honor, through the glances bestowed by their holders upon each. He notes every variation of face as the play progresses, gathering a fund of thought from the differences in the expression of certainty, of surprise, of triumph, or of chagrin. From the manner of gathering up a trick he judges whether the person taking it can make another in the suit. He recognises what is played through feint, by the air with which it is thrown upon the table. A casual or inadvertent word; the accidental dropping or turning of a card, with the accompanying

anxiety or carelessness in regard to its concealment; the counting of the tricks, with the order of their arrangement; embarrassment, hesitation, eagerness or trepidation—all afford, to his apparently intuitive perception, indications of the true state of affairs.

> (398-99)

The analyst's success in reading his opponents' physiognomy and behavior for their "hidden" thoughts is revealed—and mirrored—in his complete knowledge of their cards, "as if the rest of the party had turned outward the faces" of those cards (399).

In both cases, the flaneur employs a method that incorporates close physiognomic scrutiny with an ability to detach himself from the game itself. He must, as Benjamin notes, remain "on the threshold," existing "neither in nor out" of the situation at hand. The consideration of physiognomic details that are ostensibly "external" to the game enables the analyst to rise "above," to see "past" the mere "rules" and proscribed "method" of play. The knowledge of an opponent's behavior represents an advantage that can be gained without any extraordinary understanding of the game's more intricate strategies, if there are any. Indeed, to focus too much on the play itself is to neglect this "external" information, and to obscure the "necessary knowledge . . . of *what* to observe" (398). Dupin's claim that such advantages are only found in "recesses" of thought "altogether inaccessible to the ordinary understanding" is somewhat misleading, as this data is emphatically available on the "surface" of the situation. But to one too thoroughly engaged in the complexity of play and unable to distance himself, the most obviously superficial reality becomes a "hidden recess." The most effective route to perceive a person's "inner" secrets is not a direct or linear trajectory "inward," but an oscillating zig-zag, an in-and-out movement that tends to problematize the traditional opposition of "inner" to "outer."

The detective must consider this flexible relation between interiority and exteriority when reading the physiognomy of a room's interior to solve a crime. Both of Poe's most famous Dupin mysteries, **"The Murders in the Rue Morgue"** and **"The Purloined Letter,"** are based upon apparent violations of fundamental principles of the interior. As John T. Irwin has pointed out in *The Mystery to a Solution,* **"The Murders in the Rue Morgue"** is a "locked-room" mystery: a substantial part of the mystery is how the murderers gain ingress and egress from the seemingly locked apartment. **"The Purloined Letter,"** on the other hand, is a "hidden-object" mystery; here the detective/flaneur must "read" an interior in order to locate the document that the Minister has stolen:

> A locked-room mystery asks how a solid body got out of (or into) an internally sealed space without violating

the space's appearance of closure, while a hidden-object mystery asks how a solid object remains present within a finite physical space without, as it were, making an appearance. In one case we are certain that what we seek is not inside a given space, in the other that what we seek cannot possibly be outside it.

(181)

Conventions such as "locked-room" or "hidden-object" mysteries suggest that the genre inherently questions concepts of "interiority" and "exteriority." Poe's tales are prototypical in this regard. The orangutan in **"Rue Morgue"** escapes from the "locked" interior of the sailor's closet, proceeds out onto the urban street, obtains access into another "locked" interior, that of the apartment in the Rue Morgue, only to escape again. In **"The Purloined Letter,"** the Minister's apartment, though locked, is easily permeated by the Prefect's agents; ostensibly open in this way, it nevertheless conserves its secret "enclosed" within its walls. The artificial boundaries created through interiors are defied throughout Poe's detective tales, reinforcing the ambiguous and problematic relationship between "inner" and "outer" upon which Benjamin's flaneur would capitalize, turning the street into an interior, as much at home in that street as he would be in his study. And Dupin defies these boundaries in the same way he gains access to other characters' "inner minds"; as Shawn James Rosenheim points out in *The Cryptographic Imagination: Secret Writing from Edgar Poe to the Internet*, "Dupin's ability to enter and leave [these] space[s], like his ability to identify the murderer from the evidence at the crime scene, is an attenuated form of his ability to read minds" (67).

The flaneur's ability to abstract himself from the deceptive complexity of his immediate surroundings also applies to these interiors. In both stories, while considerable attention is paid to the actual interiors in question and their peculiar details (i.e., the grisly crime scene in **"Rue Morgue"** and the microscopic examination of the Prefect in **"Purloined Letter"**), Poe devotes much more care to the articulation of Dupin's method of reading these interiors "at one remove" (Ferguson 28), and how it surpasses the plodding method of the Prefect and the Parisian police. The initial analysis of the crime scene by the police in **"Rue Morgue"** lacks the flaneur's simultaneous engagement and detachment, according to Dupin:

> The Parisian police, so much extolled for *acumen,* are cunning, but no more. There is no method in their proceedings, beyond the method of the moment. . . . The results attained by them are brought about by simple diligence and activity. When these qualities are unavailing, their schemes fail. . . . [T]here is such a thing as being too profound. Truth is not always in a well. In fact, as regards the more important knowledge, I do believe that she is invariably superficial.

(411-12)

The police have made the error of "getting too close," of losing themselves in the complexity of the "game," as Dupin points out in the following passage:

> The wild disorder of the room; the corpse thrust, with the head downward, up the chimney; the frightful mutilation of the body of the old lady; these considerations, with those just mentioned, and others which I need not mention, have sufficed to paralyze the powers, by putting completely at fault the boasted *acumen,* of the government agents. They have fallen into the gross but common error of confounding the unusual with the abstruse.

(414)

The Prefect, Dupin maintains, "perpetually errs by being too deep or too shallow, for the matter in hand" (689). When viewing an object of complexity, to hold it too close to the eye is to become bedazzled, immersed, and literally "a-mazed" in its labyrinths. The Prefect thus represents a prefiguration of the inductive "ground-moles" Poe lampoons in *Eureka,* full of painstaking yet short-sighted and ultimately ineffective method; Dupin is the truly analytical "theorist," without specialized training, but endowed with naturally superior vision and reason (1264-70). It is necessary to pay attention to details, but it is also important to gain a detached distance, so as to identify which details are crucial, and which are simply contributing to the confusing complexity of the situation.[3]

If, as Dupin points out, truth is not always found "in a well," but is frequently discovered on the "surface" of a situation, then the ability *only* to plumb the "profound" and "deep" detail of an event's intricate "recesses" amounts to blindness, no matter how adept the viewer is at this type of scrutiny. The detective must detach himself and become a "meta-reader" of not only the "game" but the psychology of its players. If not, he will (like the Prefect) commit fatal errors of assumption, as Dupin suggests:

> Do you not see he has taken it for granted that *all* men proceed to conceal a letter,—not exactly in a gimlet-hole bored in a chair-leg—but, at least, in *some* out-of-the-way hole or corner suggested by the same tenor of thought which would urge a man to secrete a letter in a gimlet-hole bored in a chair-leg? And do you not see also, that such *recherchés* nooks for concealment are adapted only for ordinary occasions, and would be adopted only by ordinary intellects; for in all cases of concealment, a disposal of the article concealed—a disposal of it in this *recherché* manner—is, in the very first instance, presumable and presumed; and thus its discovery depends, not at all upon the acumen, but altogether upon the mere care, patience, and determination of the seekers. . . .

(690-91)

Dupin, on the other hand, recognizes that the Minister, as "both poet and mathematician," would be sufficiently "analytic" to anticipate the Prefect's highly thorough, microscopic, yet essentially simplistic and misguided procedures. The Minister would perceive that "the most intricate and remote recess of his hotel would be as open as his commonest closets to the eyes, to the probes, to the gimlets, and to the microscopes of the Prefect," which in turn would "imperatively" cause the Minister "to despise all the ordinary *nooks* of concealment" (693-94).

PHYSIOGNOMIES OF LANDSCAPE AND LANGUAGE

Adopting the detective/flaneur's perspective thus involves a curious inversion (or, to use one of Poe's favorite words, a *"bouleversement"*) regarding traditional concepts of "inner" and "outer." If the "recess" of an event or an interior, with its devious complexities, becomes the focus of methodical and diligent scrutiny, its conventionally "hidden" objects will eventually be plain to see, but the surface becomes obscure. Thus, "deep" complexity becomes simple and "ordinary," and "*simplicity*" or superficiality becomes the more sophisticated and complex strategy. All that is concealed on the "inside" of the mystery is revealed, whereas all that is practically advertised on its "external" surface, though readily visible, becomes unseeable. This is why, Dupin tells the Prefect, "it is the very simplicity of the thing which puts you at fault. . . . Perhaps the mystery is a little *too* plain. . . . A little *too* self-evident" (681). Appropriately enough, Dupin explains the matter to the narrator first in terms of the urban street, home of the flaneur, and then of the map, which projects the intricacies of the street onto a global and even cosmic scale, though this time with words rather than topography:

> [H]ave you ever noticed which of the street signs, over the shop-doors, are the most attractive of attention? . . . There is a game of puzzles . . . which is played upon a map. One party playing requires another to find a given word—the name of a town, river, state, or empire—any word, in short, upon the motley and perplexed surface of the chart. A novice in the game generally seeks to embarrass his opponents by giving them the most minutely lettered names; but the adept selects such words as stretch, in large characters, from one end of the chart to the other. These, like the over-largely lettered signs and placards of the street, escape observation by dint of being excessively obvious; and here the physical oversight is precisely analogous with the moral inapprehension by which the intellect suffers to pass unnoticed those considerations which are too obtrusively and too palpably self-evident.
>
> (694)

Language and letters, designed to identify, locate and thereby control the physical terrain, become invisible when they are magnified or made "excessively obvious" to heighten their "readability." In effect, what was intended to be a verbal label "outside" of the to-pography becomes part of the landscape itself, and contributes to its complexity rather than clarifying it. The problematic nature of language, its deceptive promise of analytic distance from what it describes, is an important issue for the detective/flaneur. He reads ephemeral periodicals and listens analytically to accounts of eye-witnesses, as part of an already complex physiognomic landscape. For Poe, all external reality constitutes a "surface" that is to be read, by means of its phrenological "bumps," its topography: "it is by these deviations from the plane of the ordinary, that reason feels its way, if at all, in the search for the true" (414). Language is part of that topography; in two of the detective tales (**"Rue Morgue"** and **"Marie Rogêt"** [**"The Mystery of Marie Rogêt"**]), Dupin arrives at a clearer understanding of the situation by "removing" himself from the crime scene and focusing on newspaper accounts of the crime. Such accounts do not guarantee genuine detachment, though. Certainly, by "reading" the crime through the mediation of the news media, Dupin distances himself from the immediacy of the crime's overwhelmingly violent, complex, and sensational reality. He reiterates the importance of such abstraction implicitly in **"The Purloined Letter"**: "If it is any point requiring reflection," he observes, "we shall examine it to better purpose in the dark" (680). But in dealing with such topics, periodicals at this time often heightened their sensationalism; as David Reynolds illustrates in *Beneath the American Renaissance,* "the antebellum public was fed an increasingly spicy diet of horror, gore, and perversity" in the ephemeral press (171). Such accounts must therefore be read at yet another level of remove, as a flaneur would; they provide fragments only the flaneur can piece together, as he reads them at a meta-level.

Dupin brings such superior observational skills to bear on the interior of the Minister's apartment, searching not its "recesses" or "*recherchés*" nooks for concealment" but its "surface." It is intriguing to note further that he must present a deceptive and unreadable "surface" of his own face: "I prepared myself with a pair of green spectacles, and called one fine morning . . . at the Ministerial hotel. . . . I complained of my weak eyes, and lamented the necessity of the spectacles, under cover of which I cautiously and thoroughly surveyed the apartment, while seemingly intent only upon the conversation of my host . . ." (695). The reader imagines Dupin must keep his face turned towards the Minister even while scanning the interior, thus completing the union between the flaneur's oblique glance and the attentive gaze of the detective:[4]

> [W]hile I maintained a most animated discussion with the Minister, on a topic which I knew had never failed to interest and excite him, I kept my attention really riveted upon the letter. In this examination, I commit-

ted to memory its external appearance and arrangement in the rack; and also fell, at length, upon a discovery which set at rest whatever trivial doubt I might have entertained. In scrutinizing the edges of the paper, I observed them to be more chafed than seemed necessary. They presented the broken appearance which is manifested when a stiff paper, having been once folded and pressed with a folder, is refolded in a reversed direction, in the same creases or edges which had formed the original fold. This discovery was sufficient. It was clear to me that the letter had been turned, as glove, inside out, re-directed, and re-sealed. . . .

(696)

The symbolic value and problematic nature of the purloined letter itself has been the subject of considerable recent scholarly attention. In his seminar on the story, Jacques Lacan argues that the letter represents an empty signifier, important not for its contents, but for its function within the story as the (un)observed object of Oedipal triangulations of characters. Irwin argues in *The Mystery to a Solution* that the purloined letter illustrates

> that the most accurate physical representation of the link between body and mind is the reversal or interchangeability of dimensional oppositions considered as the sign of the metaphysical's transcendence of the bodily. The turning of the purloined letter inside out symbolically depicts the relationship between the physicality of writing and the metaphysicality of thought as a continuous container/contained oscillation.

(126)

This symbolism functions on a more literal level as well, to questions of interiority and exteriority rather than to thought and writing, to philosophical ends rather than psychoanalytic ones. The letter itself, its inside turned out, becomes Poe's final reminder of the flexible nature of seemingly fixed relations between inner and outer, precisely the kind of inversion between surface and depth Dupin points to in his analogy of the map, or the city street. Irwin describes this convertibility nicely in the following passage:

> The letter is concealed in plain sight on the surface, on the outside of this inside (the house), a concealment accomplished by, and symbolized in, the turning of the letter itself inside out. Thus everted, its outside—the part of the letter whose appearance is known to the prefect and Dupin from the queen's description, the part that usually serves to conceal, to envelop, the letter's contents—now becomes the content to be concealed from the eyes of the police; while the inside—the reality that gives this letter its special significance, the part of it that is not known to the prefect and Dupin—becomes a new outside that gives the letter a different appearance.

(181-82)[5]

The flaneur, who can move mentally within and without his observed subject, is uniquely (perhaps solely) qualified to perceive such physical fluidity.

Numerous scholars have pointed out that Dupin achieves his impossible mastery of crime without discovering or disclosing its deeper roots, settling in the end for a detached position "outside" these interiors, removed from the events occurring within them. As Thomas Joswick suggests, this represents an important limitation of Dupin's "mastery":

> [B]y translating brutal events into a discursive order, Dupin can remain unperturbed by what most unsettles the narrator and readers: the horrifying violence of an 'Ourang-Outang' that uncannily resembles the violence of human mastery. With a 'mood of mind' detached because triumphant over senseless events, Dupin returns to the sanctuary of his own thought once the horror is explained. The world of sensational shocks and murderous impulses is left for the reader to wonder and tremble at.

(241)

And, as Rosenheim suggests, this "translation" of events into a "discursive order" involves a reductionism that may be the price for Dupin's ultimate disengagement: "Objects and events in the world must be deprived of their polyvalent materiality, since the semiotic schema, as conceived by Poe, requires the replacement of contingency and indeterminacy with the detective's single, verifiable meaning. Just as in theory a deciphered code ought to be completely intelligible, so Dupin believes in a corresponding transparency of events in the world . . ." (25).

But if Dupin's mastery represents a comforting fantasy of control, what remains in opposition to that fantasy are disturbing messages regarding the stability of architectural and conceptual boundaries. The persistence of such an unsettling porosity undercuts whatever comfort Dupin's ratiocination provides, by subverting the most basic reduction at the heart of the detective tale, perhaps even all human experience: the division of inner and outer. The fluidity of that division is at the heart of both the flaneur's approach to urban landscapes and the detective's scrutiny of people and crime scenes. Its ambiguity in Poe's detective tales, along with Dupin's striking affinities with the flaneur, points to the intimate connection between the flaneur and the detective, and the central importance of the former in Poe's creation of the latter. Despite the scholarly rumors of his demise, in Poe's detective tales the flaneur (like so many of Poe's own fictional characters) has refused to stay buried.

Notes

1. The male possessive is used here because, with few exceptions, the flaneur has been described as an explicitly male figure; however, scholars such as Deborah Parsons and Janet Wolff have pointed to the problems women face[d] in attempting to

"stroll" urban streets as leisurely observers. Cf. Deborah Parsons' *Streetwalking the Metropolis: Women, the City, and Modernity,* and Janet Wolff, "The Invisible Flaneuse: Women and the Literature of Modernity," and "The Artist and the Flaneur: Rodin, Rilke, and Gwen John in Paris" in *The Flaneur,* ed. Keith Tester, 111-37.

2. No one is so consistently associated with physiognomy as Johann Caspar Lavater (1741-1801), whose essays on physiognomy were astoundingly popular; between its original publication in 1770 and 1810, his *Physiognomische Fragmente,* or *Physiognomical Fragments,* went through "no fewer than sixteen German, fifteen French, two American, two Russian, one Dutch, and twenty English editions" (Shookman 2). John Graham notes a passage from *The Gentlemen's Magazine* of 1801 on Lavater's principles: "In the enthusiasm with which they were studied and admired, they were thought as necessary in every family as even the Bible itself. A servant would, at one time, scarcely be hired till the descriptions and engravings of Lavater had been consulted, in *careful* comparison with the lines and features of the young man's or woman's countenance" (61).

3. This inability to "pull back" from one's interior becomes a major element in scenes from Poe's "tales of sensation," such as "The Pit and the Pendulum" and *The Narrative of Arthur Gordon Pym,* wherein narrators are forced to "grope" their way blindly through dark and complex (or apparently complex) interiors.

4. This passage also brings to mind Christopher Benfey's discussion of the "twin fantasies of utter exposure and complete secrecy" in Poe's work, which are united in the incomplete reading of the flaneur's gaze. Benfey implies a causal relation between the two, particularly in "The Tell-Tale Heart," in which the narrator, "for all his secrecy . . . claims to have access to the mind of the old man. His very privacy, his enclosedness, seems to allow him to see into the minds of other people" (33).

5. Irwin also addresses this convertibility in *American Hieroglyphics,* in reference to the narrator's ruminations in "Morella" on the fluidity of identity:

> The paradox here involves the way in which a mutually constitutive opposition simultaneously depends upon and dissolves the notion of a limit, whether that limit be internal or external. Like a Möbius strip in which a two-sided surface is turned into a one-sided surface but is still experienced as if it had two sides, a mutually constitutive opposition involves the same bewildering interpenetration of one and two.
>
> (122)

If we substitute "inner and outer" for "one and two," we can perceive the same disorienting "effect."

Works Cited

Baudelaire, Charles. *The Painter of Modern Life and Other Essays.* London: Phaedon, 1964.

Benfey, Christopher. "Poe and the Unreadable: 'The Black Cat' and 'The Tell-Tale Heart.'" *New Essays on Poe's Major Tales.* Ed. Silverman, Kenneth. Cambridge: Cambridge UP, 1993.

Benjamin, Walter. "The Flaneur." *Charles Baudelaire: A Lyric Poet in the Era of High Capitalism.* London: Verso, 1983.

———. "One Way Street." Demetz, 61-97.

———. "On Some Motifs in Baudelaire." *Illuminations: Essays and Reflections.* Ed. Hannah Arendt. New York: Schocken Books, 1968.

———. "Paris: Capital of the Nineteenth Century." Demetz, 146-63.

Bergmann, Hans. *God in the Street: New York Writing from the Penny Press to Melville.* Philadelphia: Temple UP, 1995.

Brand, Dana. *The Spectator and the City in Nineteenth-Century American Literature.* Cambridge and New York: Cambridge UP, 1991.

Demetz, Peter, ed. *Reflections: Essays, Aphorisms, Autobiographical Writings.* By Walter Benjamin. New York: Schocken Books, 1978.

Ferguson, Priscilla Parkhurst. "The flâneur on and off the streets of Paris." Tester, 22-43.

Graham, John. *Lavater's Essays on Physiognomy: A Study in the History of Ideas.* Bern and Las Vegas: Lang, 1979.

Irwin, John. *American Hieroglyphics: The Symbol of the Egyptian Hieroglyphics in the American Renaissance.* Baltimore and London: Johns Hopkins UP, 1980.

———. *The Mystery to a Solution: Poe, Borges, and the Analytic Detective Story.* Baltimore and London: Johns Hopkins UP, 1994.

Johnson, Barbara. "The Frame of Reference: Poe, Lacan, Derrida." *The Purloined Poe: Lacan, Derrida & Psychoanalytic Reading.* Eds. John P. Muller and William J. Richardson. Baltimore and London: Johns Hopkins UP, 1988.

Joswick, Thomas. "Moods of Mind: The Tales of Detection, Crime, and Punishment." *A Companion to Poe Studies.* Ed. Eric W. Carlson. Westport, CT, and London: Greenwood P, 1996.

Lavater, Johan Caspar. *Essays on Physiognomy: For the Promotion of the Knowledge and the Love of Mankind.* London: C. Whittingham for H. D. Symonds, 1804.

Parsons, Deborah. *Streetwalking the Metropolis: Women, the City, and Modernity.* Oxford: Oxford UP, 2000.

Poe, Edgar Allan. *Essays and Reviews.* Library of America, 1984.

———. *Poetry and Tales.* Library of America, 1984.

Quoyeser, Catherine Jean. "'Fugitives' and 'standards': Journalism and the Commodification of Literature in Antebellum America." Diss. Stanford University, 1990.

Reynolds, David S. *Beneath the American Renaissance: The Subversive Imagination in the Age of Emerson and Melville.* Cambridge and London: Harvard UP, 1988.

Rosenheim, Shawn James. *The Cryptographic Imagination: Secret Writing from Edgar Poe to the Internet.* Baltimore and London: Johns Hopkins UP, 1997.

Rosenheim, Shawn, and Stephen Rachman, eds. *The American Face of Edgar Allan Poe.* Baltimore and London: Johns Hopkins UP, 1995.

Shields, Rob. "Fancy footwork: Walter Benjamin's notes on flânerie." Tester, 61-81.

Shookman, Ellis, ed. *The Faces of Physiognomy: Interdisciplinary Approaches to Johann Caspar Lavater.* Columbia, S.C.: Camden House, 1993.

Tester, Keith. *The Flâneur.* London and New York: Routledge, 1994.

Wolff, Janet. "The Invisible Flaneuse: Women and the Literature of Modernity." *The Problems of Modernity: Adorno and Benjamin.* Ed. Andrew Benjamin. London: Routledge, 1989: 141-56.

———. "The Artist and the Flaneur: Rodin, Rilke, and Gwen John in Paris." Tester, 111-37.

James R. Guthrie (essay date fall 2002)

SOURCE: Guthrie, James R. "Broken Codes, Broken Seals, and Stolen Poems in 'The Purloined Letter.'" *Edgar Allan Poe Review* 3, no. 2 (fall 2002): 92-102.

[*In the following essay, Guthrie interprets the purloined letter as an encrypted poem that is being unlocked by the rivalry between Dupin and the Minister.*]

In *The Cryptographic Imagination: Secret Writing From Edgar Poe to the Internet,* Shawn Rosenheim enumerates some of the many techniques Poe used to promote secrecy in his writing: "private ciphers, acrostics, allusions, hidden signatures, chiasmal framing, etymological reference, and plagiarism; purloined writing and disappearing inks; . . . anonymity [and] doubling."[1] A notable omission from this list is Poe's poems, which occasionally seem designed not so much to be read as *solved.* In "A Valentine," for example, successive letters spell out the name Francis Sargent Osgood, while "An Enigma," a rather cleverly rhymed Spenserian sonnet, contains an anagram of the name Sarah Anna Lewis ("Stella"). Poe alternately taunts and tantalizes readers in these poems, hinting at the presence of encrypted information while simultaneously declaring that all attempts to decipher it will prove futile. In "A Valentine," he begins by promising diligent readers a veritable pirate's chest of meaning, exhorting them to "Search narrowly the lines!—they hold a treasure / Divine—a talisman—an amulet," but soon after, he says "Cease trying! / You will not read the riddle, though you do the best you *can* do."[2] Such poems resemble both the cryptographic brainteasers Poe printed in his popular newspaper column as well as the encrypted map Legrand uses to find Captain Kidd's treasure in **"The Gold-Bug."** Indeed, as Rosenheim points out, a treatment of language itself as a kind of code is a hallmark of Poe's literary style.[3] While it lacks a cryptogram *per se,* **"The Purloined Letter,"** the best of Poe's three detective stories, is also premised upon an occult relationship of poetry to cryptography. This essay will treat C. Auguste Dupin's battle of wits with the "Minister D____" in that story as a rivalry between secretive, larcenous poets, and the eponymous letter itself as an encrypted poem.

As conceived by Poe, the detective story genre is firmly grounded, like his anagrammatic poems and cryptographic puzzles, in play. This quality serves simultaneously to remove the detective story from the domain of realism (thereby distinguishing it from the later, grittier *policier*), and to magnify the importance of the text itself, as a source of clues. But the unreality of **"The Purloined Letter"** in particular is heightened by a virtually complete temporal and spatial stasis, the action in the story being compressed first into a description of the mystery and then into an explanation of the solution. Within the claustrophobic confines of his private library, detective Dupin tells the astonished narrator how he had managed to retrieve the stolen letter from its hiding place in a similarly restricted space, the hotel room of "Minister D____." Various deconstructionist interpretations have pointed out that the world portrayed in **"The Purloined Letter"** is as flat as the missing letter itself, whose two-dimensionality resists the Parisian police's three-dimensional, volumetrically determined search techniques.[4] Moreover, because, as Rosenheim points out, the detective story is a "completely textual world," the dominant activity for all involved parties, readers and characters alike, is interpretation. Dupin's highly developed "resolvent" skill as a detective is based only secondarily upon his touted skills at induction; in the sense that he can discover the significant detail among a welter of obscuring information, he is actually an especially perceptive *reader*. Jacques Lacan, in his famous "Seminar," sees the character of Dupin as prefiguring that of the psychoanalyst, who, in determining the reasons underlying a patient's behavior, traces the "itinerary of a signifier,"[5] but I think the figure of the detective may be interpreted just as validly as a projection of the reader's interpolated consciousness, which must unravel a complex fabric of meanings symbolized, here at the inauguration of an entire genre, by the ostensibly insoluble crime itself.

In keeping with the spirit of gaming, Dupin is pitted against an opponent of comparable mettle. What makes the Minister so formidable is the peculiarly binary quality of his mind, for he is both mathematician and poet. Skill in mathematics, insofar as it is presented to us by the story, consists largely of an ability to perceive sequences, while the poetic imagination is presented as the capability to transcend sequential patterns by innovating radically, often spontaneously. We will recall that, according to Dupin, had the Minister been *only* a mathematician, the excessively methodical Parisian police would have been able to frustrate his scheme easily, while if he had been *only* a poet, no one could foil him, for his imagination would circumvent every strategy. This rare combination of skills places the Minister beyond the reach of the conventional police while rendering him especially vulnerable to the detective, who is also both mathematician and poet. Dupin's identity as the former is proved (at least for the sake of attempting to convince the reader) by a long, convoluted monologue about algebra and probability. Dupin's identity as poet, however, remains almost unacknowledged in the tale, save for two significant references near its beginning and end. Early in the narrative Dupin implicitly refutes the Prefect's blockheaded observation that poets are only "one remove from a fool" by admitting that he has been "guilty of certain doggerel" himself. Dupin's self-deprecation here must be taken with a grain of salt, for, in all likelihood, so literate a man would probably be an accomplished versifier rather a writer of mere "doggerel." Later in the narrative, Dupin openly ridicules the Prefect for having based his generalization about poets upon faulty logic, specifically an undistributed middle term in a syllogism, yet the whole

point of Dupin's demonstration would seem to be that some poets are anything but fools. Finally, at the story's dénouement, Dupin leaves behind for his adversary, as if from one poet to another, an especially appropriate quotation from Crébillon's poem *Atrée*.

But the resemblance between detective and criminal goes well beyond a shared interest in mathematics and verse. As several critics have observed, an emphasis upon fraternal ties pervades the story.[6] The Minister is said at one point to have a brother who also has "attained [a] reputation in letters" (the word "letters" generating, in a story about "purloined letters," a wonderfully complex frame of reference) whom we never encounter, and this elided fraternal bond is displaced by the story's structure onto Dupin and the Minister, who are also implicitly compared in the story's culminating quotation to the antagonistic brothers Atreus and Thyestes. In addition to being intellectually ambidextrous, the Minister and the detective resemble each other in being erudite, in being good actors, and in possessing last names beginning with the letter "D." But a possible provenance for Poe's resolvent hero and his wily opponent presents us with still another reason for thinking of them as unacknowledged brothers, even twins. Barbara Johnson points out that Poe probably patterned both characters upon a single historic personage, André-Marie-Jean-Jacques Dupin, a statesman renowned for having an encyclopedic memory and for being a polyglot.[7] Indeed, in *Marginalia*, Poe says the actual Dupin was fluent in so many tongues that according to one contemporary, he could speak "as nobody else, the language of every body" (except, perhaps, the nearly impenetrable transcendentalist jargon spouted by the New England "frogpondians," Poe suggests).[8] That the original Dupin was a governmental minister provides an important basis, in fact, for Liahna Klenmer Babener's observation that Dupin and the Minister D____ resemble two halves of the same personality.[9] Poe evidently divided the real Dupin's talents between the two fictional characters, so that the detective Dupin possesses the vaster knowledge, while the Minister is a skilled statesman, courtier, and politician.

Someone who can speak the language of "every body" might also be, we may conjecture, adept at translating or deciphering simple substitution codes, and Johnson's historical provenance for the composite Dupin/Minister D____ figure suggests that Poe did, in fact, associate diplomacy with cryptography. In his essay "A Few Words On Secret Writing," Poe asserts that the devising and unraveling of secret codes has always been an essential tool of statecraft. He says that cryptography "is still commonly practiced" by governments in order to conceal politically sensitive material, and he supports his claim with a virtually contemporary example. The Duchess de Berri, who had fled Paris to escape the Jacobins, sent an encrypted letter to some of her fellow royalists, but the key to her cipher was lost in transit. Berryer, her governmental ally, was able to decipher the message nonetheless by using frequency curves for vowels and consonants. Poe culled this anecdote about a political use of code from the same book in which he had read about the diplomat Dupin, "Sketches of Conspicuous Living Characters in France." Thus the fused figure of detective/diplomat in **"The Purloined Letter"** may be thought of as possessing—in addition to encyclopedic knowledge, fluency in several languages, and a flair for intrigue—a knack for making and breaking secret codes, based upon a statistical approach to language. Poe observes in his essay that good cryptographers, if only because they must be competent statisticians *and* linguists, are "rare indeed."[10]

As mathematicians and poets, Dupin and the Minister D____ are both quite capable of encrypting information by turning letters inside out, by lying or acting (so that their behavior and appearance are themselves encrypted), and by concealing taunts inside lines of quoted poetry. Yet the Minister's critical shortcoming would seem to be that he would rather imitate than innovate. Although he does think creatively when he commits the original theft, improvising brilliantly on the spot by substituting a letter he happens to have on hand for the one addressed to the Queen, afterward he lapses into a pattern of mimicry. Instead of altering the letter completely, so that it would no longer be even recognizable *as* a letter, the Minister is fatally content to let the document remain what it was, a *billet doux*. Then too, when he had first encountered the letter, it had been left lying unconcealed in the Queen's chamber, and his strategy for hiding it from the police is to replicate the original situation by leaving it in plain view in his own rooms.

Like the Minister, Dupin too is an excellent mimic, and he even claims that by re-fashioning his face to resemble an adversary's, he can anticipate what his opponent will do next. He calls the narrator's attention to the child's game of odds and evens, in which the winner will be whoever is the first to detect a pattern. Through "an identification of the reasoner's intellect with that of his opponent," the narrator agrees, one player will be able to predict the other's next move. For Poe, this feat of gamesmanship is attributable to an exercise of the poetic imagination, which permits the poet to enter briefly into an alternate state of existence. Then, the imitator assimilates not only what his opponent does or says, but also a portion of his being or identity, and by "becoming" him, learns what he will do next. Dupin's reference to games is foregrounded in the narrative, and indeed, the conflict between the detective and the Minister may remind us more of boys at play rather than of a battle between good and evil. Despite Dupin's labeling of the Minister as "that *monstrum horrendum,* an unprincipled man of genius," the detective resembles his antagonist so closely that the accusation rings somewhat hollow. The Minister "loses" in the competition between them not because he is unprincipled, but because he has been simply *outplayed.* Dupin "wins" by reconceiving the Minister's non-concealment of the letter as being systematic in its own right, that is, as being expressly designed to escape the notice of the exclusively "mathematical" police. Alternatively, we might say that Dupin re-perceives the Minister's activities as a kind of code, a sequence that is internally consistent and which can therefore be "read." Once Dupin understands that the Minister has hidden the letter in plain sight, he moves his opponent, in a displacement resembling the triadic shifts Lacan traces in this story, out of his initial position as poet-thief into that of methodical mathematician, so that the Minister is compelled to substitute, in his turn, for the originally "clueless" Prefect.

The contest Dupin and the Minister wage over who shall be the better, or at least the *last,* poet turns upon possession of the purloined letter itself, which becomes a sort of trophy, or rather, a disputed trophy poem. Poe's perhaps unconscious equating of the letter with a poem is responsible, I think, for the presence of a glaring error in the story, that is, the Minister's addition of his own wax seal to the letter. We will recall that, according to the narrative, the Minister attempts to represent the stolen letter as an almost discarded letter sent to him by an almost rejected mistress. He has turned the letter inside out, refolded it, had it re-addressed to himself in a feminine hand, and placed it in a card rack hanging from the fireplace mantel, the most prominent location in the room. Of course, if the letter had been sent to the Minister by a woman, it would bear *her* seal, not his; the Minister could hardly be expected to have sent a letter to himself. Yet Dupin says of the letter, "Here the seal was large and black, with the D____ cipher; there [that is, on the letter as it had originally appeared] it was small and red, with the ducal arms of the S____ family." Lacan, for one, wonders how such a mistake in the story's plot could have been made: "Whether that omission be intentional or involuntary, it will surprise in the economy of a work whose meticulous rigor is evident."[11] It does seem doubtful that the Minister, who is as fastidious a criminal as Lacan perceives Poe to be as a writer, would make such an obvious error. So whose mistake is it—the Minister's, or Poe's?

On one level, the seal's appearance merely conforms to the story's thematic emphasis upon the detection of similarities and oppositions. A reader must be able to distinguish among several paired sets of people, events, and objects. The stolen letter turns out not to have been hidden in some obscure cranny, but rather in an "opposite" location, that is, in plain sight. Further, the solution to the mystery depends upon Dupin's realization that the stolen letter and the letter in the Minister's apartments are one and the same. Moreover, the letter has been disguised as the gendered antithesis of itself. Accordingly, the handwriting of the address has been altered: previously "bold and decided," it is changed to being "diminutive and feminine." The original seal on the letter was "small and red"; on the disguised one it is the "large and black" seal of the Minister's own family. The very "radicalness" of the differences between the genuine letter and the impostor, Dupin says, is what initially arouses his suspicions, for they are more pronounced than they would be between two randomly selected and compared letters.

Yet the counterfeit wax seal, in being so drastically different from the original, proves to be the undoing of the Minister, and perhaps of Poe, too. If the mistake is the Minister's, he has been, at the very least, unforgivably careless, for in seeking to present the letter as its antithesis, he has altered the "gender" of the seal incongruously. The original red seal had been applied, presumably, by a man; therefore, the seal on the disguised letter should be a woman's. And yet the gendered language used to characterize the original letter could understandably lead to such confusion. The purloined letter is described as bearing the "small and red" seal of the "S_____" family, to which the Queen's lover, we may assume, belongs, but this description is itself incongruous, for stereotypically, the adjective "small" connotes femininity. The quality of "smallness," on the Minister's disguised letter, applies only to the handwritten address, which is written in a "diminutive female hand." Thus the property of feminine "smallness" would seem to have been transferred, in looking at the original letter and the impostor, from the medium of wax to that of handwriting. Moreover, the logic of the story's symbolism equates the original purloined letter, with its "small" and "red" seal, with the Queen, the letter's recipient, rather than with its sender, so that the letter comes to represent, somewhat illogically, the Queen herself. Poe may have reversed the gender of the original letter as a means of intensifying his tale's dramatic impact. If the purloined letter is construed as being "feminine," the Minister's seizure of it acquires overtones of rape and kidnaping, for, figuratively speaking, the Minister subsequently "imprisons" the Queen in his hotel room.[12] Similarly, the Minister's imposition of his conventionally masculine seal upon the disguised "captured" letter may be seen

as further confirmation of his domination over the Queen's person, the symbolic equivalent of his use of blackmail to curtail her actual freedom of movement and speech.

Still, I think Poe was motivated to affix the wrong seal twice to a letter by psychological factors having to do with poetry's complex relation, for him, to cryptography. Within the story's symbolic structure, the purloined letter stands not only for the Queen's abstracted body, but also, as I have said, for a disputed poem, a free-floating artifact which, once it has been stolen, loses its provenance, and therefore, its authorship. That Poe might conceive of poems as seals stamped into wax is suggested by a comment in his lecture "The Poetic Principle," in which he cautions poets, while still maintaining that poems must be brief to be effective, against being *too* brief, saying, "A very short poem, while now and then producing a brilliant or vivid, never produces a profound or enduring, effect. There must be the steady pressing down of the stamp upon the wax."[13] As forms of insignia, wax seals intrinsically denote authorship, and the Minister's application of his seal to the letter asserts his identity as its creator, as much as any signature would, following a poem's final line. Yet it is not the love letter to the Queen itself for which the Minister makes an implicit claim of authorship, but rather for his original theft, conceived in a moment of inspiration. In altering the letter, and in affixing his seal to it, he simply supplies a physical confirmation of his crime's transformation into a work of art.

Yet the "D" in the seal could just as reasonably be seen as standing for "Dupin," and, in an inspired moment of his own, the detective takes advantage of the coincidence. He, too, commits a theft, by taking the letter from the Minister's rooms and substituting a facsimile for it, just as the Minister had done in the Queen's chambers. The document Dupin leaves behind as a placeholder is not truly a letter, but rather a poem, or at least a quotation from one. Again, however, the questions of "authorship" and "ownership" are permitted to remain ambiguous, for although Dupin *says* to the narrator that the lines are drawn from Crébillon's *Atrée,* his letter contains no attribution. This omission may be explained away by assuming that the quotation is so widely known, and that the Minister himself is so literate, that an explicit attribution would be superfluous, yet in the story's compact and highly reciprocal symbolic economy, the poetic excerpt is effectually presented as having been written by Dupin. Thus the detective vanquishes the Minister not just by discerning an underlying pattern in his behavior, but also by committing two crimes to his one: Dupin steals the stolen letter and he cribs Crébillon. In leaving behind his own poem-letter, Dupin only seems to be requiting the Minister, symbolically, for having stolen his beautiful crime, whereas he is really cheating him by ensuring that the document he exchanges for the real one has been plagiarized, so that it is doubly false.

Poe, an adept plagiarist during his career as well as detector of plagiarisms, was always peculiarly sensitive to the issue of authorial authenticity, and neither of the main characters in **"The Purloined Letter"** is indeed the bona fide author of the two texts involved. Dupin's plagiarism, which is really just another form of acting, transcends the Minister's theft by encompassing his entire identity. In replacing the purloined letter with his counterfeit, Dupin also replicates the sign that stands for the Minister's presence, that is, his seal. Dupin says, "I stepped to the card-rack, took the letter, put it in my pocket, and replaced it by a *facsimile,* (so far as regards externals) which I had carefully prepared at my lodgings—imitating the D_____ cipher, very readily, by means of a seal formed of bread." It is important to notice that Dupin would not have had such an opportunity to substitute himself, symbolically, for the Minister, had the purloined letter not improperly displayed a "large" and "black" seal. Yet it is also significant, I think, that the word Dupin uses here to designate the wax seal is "cipher." A "cipher" is a zero; it is also, of course, a code. While a cipher remains encrypted, its opaqueness rests intact, and the message it conceals remains literally unreadable. Once a message has been "deciphered," however, it loses its signifying value of zero—instead, it becomes an integer, something countable, and therefore comprehensible. By fashioning a duplicate of the Minister's seal out of bread, Dupin succeeds in "deciphering" the letter. Or rather, it may have de-ciphered itself before Dupin even saw it, stuck into the card rack, for the "cipher" on the letter, that is, the "large" and "black" seal on it, had already been broken. It *must* have been broken, if we are to assume the Minister has disguised the note to the Queen as an already perused letter sent to him by his mistress. The breaching of his mistakenly applied seal renders the Minister an ineligible claimant for the letter, effectively permitting Dupin to step in and seize it after he has "deciphered" its true identity.

Writing that is encrypted conceals not only its meaning, but also the author's identity, and in **"The Purloined Letter,"** decryption depends primarily upon a correct attribution of authorship. Dupin brings this truth home forcefully at the end of the story by neglecting to cite Crébillon, an act of plagiarism that shows the Minister, by example, how mis- or unattributed writings may be rendered worthless. In this sense, Dupin's claim upon the letter is both authentic and inauthentic. So long as the purloined letter-poem duplicitously bears the Minister's seal or cipher, anyone else, including the detective, may step in and claim it. Dupin says at the story's conclusion that the Minister will have no trouble determining who has defeated him because he is familiar with Dupin's "M.S.," or his handwriting, yet "m.s." is also, of course, the abbreviation for manuscript. "He is well acquainted with my MS.," says Dupin, "and I just copied into the middle of the blank sheet the words." Poe's phraseology here could be construed again as implying that the poem by Crébillon is his own work, secured, paradoxically, through his "copying" of it.

Thus we may see that in the years succeeding Poe's invention of the detective story, as exemplified in **"The Purloined Letter,"** we have gotten a few things right about the genre, and a few wrong. Yes, the detective and the criminal are estranged brothers, both of whom operate along morality's shadowy margins. Yes, the detective story is a sort of game in which the reader is compelled to participate by the text's insistent materiality. But what we have forgotten is that the detective was also originally a kind of thieving poet who, in solving crimes, somewhat hypocritically asserted the necessity of returning pilfered property to its rightful owner, even while he is engaged in appropriating other people's creative endeavors. As Kenneth Silverman says, the story is "about the theft of language,"[14] and the disputed poem/letter/crime is passed around from hand to hand as if in a contest to discover who its rightful owner might be. Yet the genre also perturbs and problematizes the question of identity itself. Through his facility as a poet, Poe's detective assumes other people's identities, his imperialistic imagination swelling to include not only their accomplishments, but them as well. Correspondingly, the Minister's mistaken application of his own seal to the letter associates him powerfully with Poe, and yet Poe simultaneously redeems himself through his creation of the twinned, "virtuous" plagiarist Dupin, who exercises his mimetic talents for the public's welfare. Significantly, however, Dupin turns out not to be motivated solely by altruism. The reward for solving the puzzle and returning the letter to the Queen, like the "treasure" to be gained by deciphering Captain Kidd's map, is substantial.

Poe's detective story genre, rooted in both cryptography and poetry, also seems especially well suited for inviting readers to become players in this game of shifting identities. Brought in through the mediating consciousness of the Watson-like narrator, enticed by the implied promise of information to be divulged, a treasure to be unearthed or a solution to be found, readers willingly enter into the game by trying to imitate the detective and unravel clues themselves. Yet when they help decode a text, readers necessarily also become stewards of information that is potentially socially disruptive, perhaps even politically destabilizing, as in the case of diplomats who must code their dispatches. The successful reading of text "encrypted" overtly in code, or covertly in clues or in poetic figures, implies a simultaneous assumption of the perspective of a consciousness that evidently had its reasons for wishing to remain concealed. Thus Poe uses the detective genre to spread around the "guilt" of writing and reading "doggerel," or any other kind of secretive text, and in so doing, he seems to anticipate Baudelaire's later famous phrase, half accusation and half invitation: "*Hypocrite lecteur,—mon semblable,— mon frère!*"

Notes

1. Shawn James Rosenheim, *The Cryptographic Imagination: Secret Writing From Edgar Poe to the Internet* (Baltimore: Johns Hopkins UP, 1997), 2.

2. The version of the poem I quote from here is Griswold's, reprinted in T. O. Mabbott's *Collected Works of Edgar Allan Poe* (Cambridge: The Belknap P., 1969), vol. 1, 389-90. Lines 5-6, 19-20.

3. See Rosenheim, 3.

4. See, for example, Barbara Johnson, "The Frame of Reference: Poe, Lacan, Derrida": "[I]ndeed, the question of the fallacies inherent in a Euclidean model of intelligibility . . . is central to the very plot of 'The Purloined Letter' itself. For it is precisely the notion of space as finite and homogeneous that underlies the Prefect's method of investigation." *Yale French Studies*, 1977; reprinted in *The Purloined Poe: Lacan, Derrida & Psychoanalytic Reading*, ed. John P. Muller and William J. Richardson (Baltimore: The Johns Hopkins UP, 1988), 231-2.

5. "Seminar on 'The Purloined Letter,'" trans. Jeffrey Mehlman. *Yale French Studies*, 1972. Reprinted in *The Purloined Poe*, 29.

6. See, for example, Kenneth Silverman, *Mournful and Never-ending Remembrance* (New York: Harper Perennial edition; originally printed by Harper Collins Publishers, 1991), 229.

7. Johnson, 245.

8. *Marginalia*. Ed. John Carl Miller (Charlottesville: UP of Virginia, 1981), 207.

9. "The Shadow's Shadow: The Motif of the Double in Edgar Allan Poe's 'The Purloined Letter,'" reprinted in Muller and Richardson, *The Purloined Poe*, 323.

10. On p. 1284. Perhaps somewhat wistfully, Poe also says that cryptographers employed by governmental agencies are invariably well paid for their services.

11. Lacan, "Seminar," 48.

12. Lacan characterizes the presence of the purloined letter in the Minister's room as "an immense female body," 48.

13. *Poe: Essays and Reviews* (New York: The Library of America, 1984), 73.

14. Silverman, 229.

Warren Hill Kelly (essay date fall 2003)

SOURCE: Kelly, Warren Hill. "Detecting the Critic: The Presence of Poe's Critical Voice in His Stories of Dupin." *Edgar Allan Poe Review* 4, no. 2 (fall 2003): 77-86.

[*In the following essay, Kelly maintains that Dupin acts as a mouthpiece for Poe's critical evaluation of his readers' inability to fully understand the meaning of his work.*]

Within the large body of literary criticism, relatively little considers the relationship between the critical output of the great creative writers who have also commented on other writers' creative efforts and the creative output of those writer-critics. The enterprise seems a logical undertaking because potentially enlightening points of intersection may connect an author's attitudes as a reviewer and his or her practices as a creative writer, and those attitudes evident in the author's critical work may appear in his creative practices at levels of technique and content. The intersection I consider here in regard to Poe is the writer-critic's awareness of readers' reading—which may be the most significant (and obvious) juncture between the different activities of the writer-critic, because the creative writer desires to fashion art worthy of an audience's reading and the critic aims to discern the value of literature as the object of that audience's reading.

Some scholars have preceded me in the consideration of Poe's awareness of his readers in his fiction and in his Dupin stories in particular. Burton R. Pollin suggests that in **"The Murders in the Rue Morgue,"** Poe attempts to dupe his readers into accepting the impossible;[1] Benjamin F. Fisher IV argues that the three Dupin stories display a "false start" in supernatural Gothicism, which functions as a literary hoax;[2] and, Dennis Eddings asserts that, in the Dupin stories, "the reader's position to the text [is] analogous to Dupin's position to the crime he solves."[3] I propose the additional possibility that Poe places his own critical voice within Dupin's. More specifically, I contend first that Poe constructs his readers, or appropriates his readers' process of reading, within his Dupin stories, through his creation of a first-person narrator who reports the speech of the stories' focal character, Dupin, whom Poe invests with his own critical voice, and second that Poe's attempt to produce his audience's reception in its reading those stories parallels his work as a critic. That mirroring of Poe's critical ideas on readership within the voice of Dupin finds substantiation in the manner in which both Poe's literary technique and content reflect his attitudes toward the readers of his day.[4]

In order to recognize Poe's incorporation of his contemporary readership, according to his estimation of them, into the very narrative framework of the Dupin stories, as well as into the subject matter of those stories, we should be grounded in Poe's evaluation of those readers. One basis for arriving at that knowledge resides in Poe's particular use of the terms "mob," "herd," and "mass"—that is, terms of uninquisitive, trend-abiding collectives.[5] Poe's linkage of the first of those terms, "mob," with his contemporary readers occurs, among other places, in *Marginalia* 27. There, Poe endorses the "helluo liborum," or the "book worm," or literally the "devourer of books," because the "helluo" can winnow "the matter of which the typo mumbled both the seeds and the chaff."[6] That voracious reading and its accompanying discernment may, with the proper encouragement to students from educators, become "a common thing," according to Poe, or "may become the method of the mob" in a future generation (134). Poe's use of "mob" in that last quotation is, of course, ironic. His restriction of a prevalence of the "helluo liborum" and its sense of appreciation to only a future time implies that the average reader in Poe's own day and his or her literary tastes were of a lower caliber than those of Poe's vision—than those of "the mob" of a future time. With that word "mob," Poe acknowledges the reading community of his time not only as being less sophisticated than his model "helluo liborum," but also as possessing specifically the negative traits of any mob, those of mindless adherence to trends.

Further evidence that Poe generally regarded his contemporary readers as "mobish" appears elsewhere in *Marginalia*. In *Marginalia* 56, where Poe condemns the moralizing literati's practice of devaluing the best novels of his day, he writes: "now, the fashionable novels are just the books which most do circulate among the class unfashionable (166)." As a corollary, he adds: "With the herd, to admire and to attempt imitation are the same thing." With those statements, Poe, again, suggests that the tendency among his readership was mindless adherence to prevailing fashions in literature, regardless of that literature's quality. And in rendering that evaluation, he identifies his contemporary readership with a term for an uninquisitive collective; this time, he uses "herd," but he could have as easily used "mob" or "mass."

The identification of an unquestioning collective with fashionable readers appears frequently enough in Poe's writing that we would not be irresponsible to assume that even the occurrences of those terms that are unaccompanied by a context of readers' reading come to bear on that matter. Accordingly, the uncontextualized references to the "mob" in *Marginalia* may contribute to the understanding that Poe had of the average early nineteenth-century reader of English as an uninquisitive follower of trends. That characterization appears in part in Poe's definition of a "mob" in *Marginalia* 232: "In drawing a line of distinction between a people and a mob, we shall find that a people aroused to action are a mob; and that a mob trying to think, subside into a people" (380). That thinking transforms a mob into a people, implies that a mob is disinclined in the first place to question a trend, and because Poe attributes such a trait to a mob, he extends ownership of that same quality to his contemporary readership elsewhere in his writing, where he associates the terms "mob" and "readership."

To his readership's and a mob's possession of an uninquisitive nature, Poe adds the property of gullibility, as we read in *Marginalia* 226: "The nose of a mob is its imagination. By this at any time, it may be quietly led" (337). Because a mob cannot imagine beyond whatever is immediately in front of it, it will adopt the most obvious solution to a problem at hand. Fans of Poe's Dupin fictions may recognize that criticism, directed at a mob, as similar to those Dupin directs at the Parisian police—and indirectly at the narrator, for his initial participation in the same course of reasoning as the police's, and again indirectly at us, for being so easily guided by the first-person narrator, or in effect, for allowing Poe to "read" for us.

In my argument regarding the relationship between Poe's critical work and his narrative technique in his Dupin stories, I propose that the first-person narrator stands for us, Poe's readers, receiving the facts regarding each crime, responding predictably to them, and then absorbing the corrections Dupin makes to the restricted logic. In a way, the narrator does all of the reading for us and anticipates all of our responses. Aware that Poe perceived his reading public as an unquestioning, trend-abiding collective, we can now surmise the point he may be seeking to illustrate most vividly (if not too vividly) through his narrative technique, as I have defined it, in the Dupin stories: perhaps Poe concluded that the most poignant manner of demonstrating to readers their own insensitivity in reading and their own susceptibility to being led by the nose in interpretation would be to guide them through their own process of reading by means of a particular narrative arrangement.

A foundation for my argument appears in Poe's letter of August 9, 1846 to Philip Pendelton Cooke, in which Poe, commenting on the positive reception of his detective fiction, states: "Where is the ingenuity of unravelling a web which you yourself (the author) have woven for the purpose of unravelling? The reader is made to confound the ingenuity of the suppositious Dupin with that of the writer of the story."[7] Converting the passive voice of that last sentence into the active reveals an agency that Poe might have wished to draw attention away from: "The author makes the reader to confound." With that, we should ask how the author confounds the reader, or creates the confounded reader. If the author's voice is actually most closely identified with Dupin's, we might assume that the first-person narrator not only is Dupin's audience but also represents (in effect) Poe's audience, because he accepts Dupin's reasoning and then invites us to join him in accepting it. All the while, that first-person narrator, who might be more accurately regarded as a substitute reader, gives the impression of possessing the author's voice.

The "displacement" of the authorial voice and its mediation through a seemingly unbiased narrator results in a storytelling that often reads like a report (not to mention the inclusion of reports within the stories). Like news reports, the stories tend to enforce a particular manner of reading a situation, while they seem to present facts. In the Dupin stories, the enforcement results from the first-person narrator's "posing" as us, the readers, and eventually accepting Dupin's reasoning for us, while it might seem to us that we are reading the narrator's "neutral" account of Dupin. Poe's appropriation of his readership's reading in the Dupin stories perhaps should not surprise us, because Poe often assumed the role of a critic and thereby attempted to shape reader's attitudes—or to cite errors in their attitudes.

The schema that I just described along with the purpose I have attributed to it would be difficult, if not impossible, to prove conclusively. All the same, the evidence that contributes the most to its substantiation comes not from a close examination of the workings of the narrative technique, which are fairly straightforward, but rather from a consideration of the extent to which the content of the stories comments on the proposed purpose of the narrative technique, that of exposing readers' insensitivity. The narrative technique and thematic content should echo each other in as much as they both echo Poe's critical voice, if the Dupin tales indeed reflect his critical ideas on the mis-

direction of readers in reading. If Poe adhered to laws of decorum, the Dupin stories may be calculated exercises in meta-reading, in which the content alerts readers to the experiment being conducted upon them during their reading. In making a case for that understanding, I examine situations in **"The Murders in the Rue Morgue"** and **"The Purloined Letter,"** and propose examples of Poe's planted suggestions from the stories' content that expose the Dupin-narrator relationship as a commentary on the Poe-reader relationship—a commentary that relies upon the equivalence of Dupin and Poe-the-critic and of the narrator (and of the police) and Poe's readers.[8]

We have already heard Poe's own equation of himself as the author with Dupin, in his letter to Cooke. The Dupin stories themselves, however, contain additional clues that Dupin possesses Poe's authorial voice. In **"The Murders in the Rue Morgue,"** we can hear Poe, by means of Dupin, instructing the uninquisitive, trend-abiding readers in the proper way in which to "read," if you will, a crime situation. For example, after Dupin and the narrator have read the *Gazette des Tribunaux*'s long report of the murders, including accounts given by auditory witnesses—and it may be quite telling that Dupin and the narrator spend much of the story in the act of "reading" the report—Dupin criticizes the Parisian police, the trend-setting and would-be authoritative readers of the crime, by saying, "There is no method in their proceedings, beyond the method of the moment."[9] Poe might have made a similar comment about his contemporary readers' following conventional expectations in interpreting literature and their not inquiring beyond those expectations. In the fiction, Poe places additional emphasis upon the importance of original inquiry, after Dupin has rejected the police's predictable interpretation of the murders, because at that point Dupin instructs the narrator in the proper method of reading a crime, a method which begins with a reader's questioning according to his or her own terms. That particular instruction appears in the story as Dupin tells the narrator: "As for these murders, let us enter into some examination for ourselves, before we make up an opinion respecting them," adding: "We will go and see the premises [of the crime] with our own eyes" (TOM 546). Poe might have wished his contemporary readers to read through their own eyes, in a sense, rather than through those eyes that fashion imposed upon them.

During their visit to the Rue Morgue, Dupin asks the narrator repeatedly whether or not he has seen anything "peculiar"—with Poe adding special emphasis to that word "peculiar." The narrator says, "no, nothing peculiar," and then says, "nothing more, at least, than we both saw in the paper" (TOM 547). With that response, the narrator may reveal himself as a figure corresponding to the uninquisitive and uninsightful readers whom Poe describes in his *Marginalia,* readers who had learned to look only for the ordinary details that an establishment, such as the press, prescribed to them, and not for peculiar details. Likewise, Dupin's frequent use of that word "peculiar" resonates with Poe-the-critic's railings against his readers' confinement to expectation. In the voice of Dupin, Poe may be teaching his own readers to adopt individuality in reading. Such a message would be entirely in keeping with Poe's critical ideology on the matter; we should recall that, concerning fashionable readers, Poe remarks: "With the herd, to admire and to attempt imitation are the same thing" (166). Poe speaks out against the perpetuation of sameness in meanings and the methods in arriving at those meanings, and he does so with the purpose of educating his audience, in both his criticism and his Dupin stories.

The assertion that Poe's goal in these stories is in part instructional finds a degree of verification in some telling comments by Dupin to the narrator, such as: "I know not what impression I may have made, so far, upon your understanding" (TOM 550). That remark and others like it usually do not follow Dupin's detailed explanation of the mystery's solution; instead, they follow his guiding the narrator through a re-examination and a rethinking of the case. The skills of re-examination and re-thinking may be Dupin's greatest lesson to the narrator. Moreover, it may not be too far-fetched for us to hear Poe, in the voice of Dupin, directing that last quotation and the lesson that preceded it in the story, beyond the non-descript narrator, to us, his readers.

A strong suggestion that Dupin's (or Poe's) lessons in re-examination and rethinking pertain particularly to the matter of reading comes appropriately at the moment in the story when the narrator grasps the solution to the crime. After the narrator has just realized that the handprint on the throat of Mademoiselle L'Espanaye "is the mark of no human hand," Dupin states, "Read now this passage from Cuvier," a technical description of an orangutan, and upon having read it, the narrator recounts: "I understood the full horrors of the murder at once" (TOM 559). It was specifically the act of reading—and reading out of fashion—that provided Dupin and in turn the narrator the background knowledge to solve, or to interpret properly, the crime requiring their reading. As we would expect, a wide range of reading experience ranks among Poe's top criteria for an ability to interpret and appreciate literature beyond fashion's expectations. We need to look no further than Poe's elevation of the "helluo liborum" for evidence of his endorsement of reading widely.

Identifying the textual self-reflexive interplay between Poe's content and narrative technique may be even more of a straightforward enterprise in **"The Purloined Letter"** than it is in **"The Murders in the Rue Morgue,"** because the crime in the former is, of course, misappropriation of a piece of writing—and we should note that the letter might represent "lettres" of the literary variety. In the search for that hidden letter, the narrow-minded, would-be authoritative readers of the crime, the Parisian police and the narrator, too, in as much as he participates in the police's line of reasoning and outside of Dupin's, employ inappropriate methods in attempting to solve the crime; that is, they "read" situations too much according to the expectations and practices they have learned according to fashion. That appraisal of the Parisian police dominates the substance of the following commentary, which Dupin renders to the narrator:

> They consider only their own ideas of ingenuity; and in searching for anything hidden, advert only to the modes in which they would have hidden it. They are right in this much—that their own ingenuity is a faithful representation of that of the mass—but when the cunning of the individual felon is diverse in character from their own, the felon foils them, of course.
>
> (TOM 985)

The connection between Dupin's critique of the Parisian police and Poe's estimation of his contemporary readership is somewhat suggested by Dupin's (or Poe's) use of the word "mass" in the forgoing quotation; it functions as another one of Poe's terms for an unquestioning collective, a flawed readership. Further evidence for a veiled equivalence of the Parisian police to poor readers of literature takes the form of similarity in their activities: the mob possesses an imagination that reaches as far as the end of its members' noses. Accordingly, mobish readers have a great limitation in their ability to identify a meaning hidden within a text beyond a meaning they might have encoded there themselves; in much the same way, the Parisian police cannot envision an ingenuity beyond their own in concealing a letter.

That pattern of being confined to expectations of thought resembles that in **"The Murders in the Rue Morgue,"** but in **"The Purloined Letter"** it has an added dimension, one that contributes even further to the linking of Poe's creative voice in his Dupin stories with his critical voice. I refer to Poe's referencing the particular (or peculiar) genius of an author—that is, at the fictional level, the author of a crime, and at the literal level, the author of a literary work. Poe's articulation of the author figure appears in the previous quotation in the form of the "individual felon," who "is diverse in character" from those people who are attempting to discover the object he has hidden, but who are unprepared to find it because they have not taken particular account of the felon's ingenuity. It may not be too much of a stretch for us to translate the relationship between the felon figure and the people opposing him, into that of an author and his readers reading his work: the author "is diverse in character" from his readers who are trying to uncover the meaning he has hidden, but they are unprepared to interpret the author's text because they have not taken proper account of the author's peculiar genius in his literary methods. Poe's identification of the root of the problem in his readers' failure to interpret his meaning—their dismissal of the author—is suggested, again, when Dupin evaluates the Parisian police's investigative techniques: "The measures [of the police] then were good in their kind, and well executed; their defect lay in their being inapplicable to the case, and to the man" (TOM 983). The "man" is the masterful felon, who represents the ingenious author, whose literary designs, situated outside the parameters of his readers' realm of familiarity, elude them, just as the felon's unfamiliar methods escape the police.

Poe's identification of one of his readers' errors in reading—and quite possibly their major error in reading, in his view—within the symbolic language of **"The Purloined Letter"** furthers the case for the presence of Poe's critical voice in the Dupin tales, especially because Poe stresses "authorial originality" in "The Philosophy of Composition" and elsewhere in his criticism and reviews. For Poe-the-critic, a good writer is an original writer, and a good reader recognizes the importance of that originality. Average readers' failure to recognize that importance was certainly one of Poe's greatest frustrations as an artist. And a self-referencing art—one, for example, in which the author, in the guise of Dupin, attempts to explain his own actions, those of Minister D—Dupin's symbolic double—might have seemed a means toward hope.[10]

Notes

I would like to thank Dennis Eddings, Ben Fisher, and Richard Fusco for suggestions they have made toward this paper.

1. Burton R. Pollin, "Poe's 'Murders in the Rue Morgue': The Ingenious Web Unravelled," *Studies in the American Renaissance* (1977): 235-59.

2. Benjamin F. Fisher IV, "Blackwood Article a la Poe: How to Make a False Start Pay," *RLV [Revue de Langues Vivantes]* 39 (1973): 432.

3. Dennis W. Eddings, "Poe, Dupin, and the Reader," *The University of Mississippi Studies in English* 3 (1982): 128-35.

4. Poe's awareness of his readership, as it is visible in his overall literary output, has been addressed significantly in at least two book-length studies: Michael Allan's *Poe and the British Magazine Tradition* (New York: Oxford UP, 1969) and Michael J. S. Williams' *A World of Words: Language and Displacement in the Fiction of Edgar Allan Poe* (Durham: Duke UP, 1988).

5. Readers interested particularly in Poe's stance against trend-abiding readers, should consult Terence Whalen's *Edgar Allan Poe and the Masses* (Princeton: Princeton UP, 1999), where the author demonstrates that Poe attempted to divest information produced for mass consumption of its cultural power and to invest that power in individualized intellectual efforts.

6. Edgar Allan Poe, "The Brevities," in *Collected Writings of Edgar Allan Poe*, ed. Burton R. Pollin (New York: Gordian P., 1985), 134. Further references to this text will appear in parentheses.

7. Edgar Allan Poe, *The Letters of Edgar Allan Poe*, ed. John Ward Ostrom (New York: Gordian P., 1966).

8. I leave "The Mystery of Marie Roget" out of my discussion for reasons of concision and of personal preference: I regard it in some ways as the least artistic of the three Dupin stories. Nonetheless, I should note that it readily sustains the same type of interpretive work I perform on the other two stories, in part because it, like "The Murders in the Rue Morgue," involves the reading and critique of newspapers. For a reading that presents this tale in a more favorable light, see Richard Benton's "'The Mystery of Marie Roget'—A Defense," *Studies in Short Fiction* 6 (1969): 144-51.

9. Edgar Allan Poe, *Collected Works of Edgar Allan Poe: Tales and Sketches, 1831-1842*, ed. Thomas Ollive Mabbott (Cambridge: Belknap P., 1978), 545. Further references to Poe's tales will be from this edition and indicated in parentheses.

10. The concept of the symbolic double in "The Purloined Letter" is well articulated in Liahna Babener's "The Shadow's Shadow: The Motif of the Double in Edgar Allan Poe's 'The Purloined Letter,'" *Mystery and Detection Annual*, ed. Donald Adams (Pasadena: Castle P., 1972), 21-32.

Dennis R. Perry (essay date 2003)

SOURCE: Perry, Dennis R. "Ratiocination: Original Unity." In *Hitchcock and Poe: The Legacy of Delight and Terror*, pp. 17-43. Lanham, Md.: The Scarecrow Press, Inc., 2003.

[*In the following essay, Perry outlines the thematic treatment of theatricality, duality, and appearance ver-*

sus reality in Poe's tale and in Alfred Hitchcock's films Dial M for Murder *and* Murder!.]

Hitchcock's relationship to the detective genre that Poe is credited with inventing has always been ambiguous. On the one hand he is blatantly against the whole idea:

> For seventeen years I have been making pictures described alternately as thrillers, dark mysteries, and chillers, yet I have never actually directed a whodunit or puzzler. Off hand this may sound like debunking, but I do not believe that puzzling the audience is the essence of suspense.[1]

On the other hand, he admits that his films have a "touch of murder and an air of mystery" about them (114). Interestingly, Hitchcock mentions the **"Murders in the Rue Morgue"** as particularly important in his own development, learning that fear can be fun when you know you are safe. Hitchcock synthesized both Poe and his successors in the field of mystery thrillers to create an original approach focused on suspense rather than on intellectual crime puzzles. Hitchcock never set aside important lessons he learned from Poe; as Herb says in *Shadow of a Doubt* about detective heroes as a whole, "You can say what you like about Sherlock Holmes, but that Frenchman beats them all."[2]

Among its many phases of development, the universe in *Eureka* begins in harmonious order, though embedded with attractive and diffusive forces. These forces are in balance until, inexplicably, the diffusive force strikes an uneven balance which causes apocalyptic fragmentation that increases separation and diffusion of the fragments. Within this overarching Eurekan narrative framework, the detective tale functioned as Poe's fantasy of arresting the irrational forces of diffusion through reason. But, as J. Gerald Kennedy notes, all of Poe's fiction comes back to concern over reason versus irrational feeling.[3] In the detective story, however, reason triumphs most convincingly. With his new genre Poe exercised his fascination with puzzle solving, cryptograms, and conundrums by applying it to narrative, indulging in the pleasing dream, so untrue in his own experience, that order could rein in chaos. His detective stories exist in the Eurekan interstices between the end of harmony and the beginning of fragmentation.

As the widely recognized creator of the detective story, Edgar Allan Poe has directly or indirectly influenced virtually every detective, mystery, sensation, and thriller writer since his time. This applies, of course, to Alfred Hitchcock, whose films are also both directly and indirectly influenced by several of Poe's narrative formulas. Like Charles Dickens, who knew of Poe and

his innovations but developed his crime fiction in his own original directions, Hitchcock added his own touches of pure cinema to the genre. Despite the continuous modifications to Poe's detective story, many of which profoundly influenced him, Hitchcock continued to look back toward Poe's approach in terms of the doubleness of the sublime, maintaining a link between the detective and the gothic-horror tale. Poe and Hitchcock approached the challenge of creating sublimity within the limits of an essentially intellectual genre by exploring (1) the ambiguity between reason and intuition in a world where the line between reality and illusion is blurred, (2) the doubleness of characters, and (3) theatricality. Because questions of the ambiguity of reality and identity are characteristic of the theater, these become a central thematic and narrative undercurrent of the detective stories of Poe and Hitchcock. Violence and eccentric characters, suspense and interest are developed as characters slip in and out of various roles, stage theatrical traps, and thus manipulate reality and illusion. This chapter will examine these overlapping concerns by comparing the Dupin tales mainly with Hitchcock's *Murder!* (1930), *Dial M for Murder* (1954), and *Spellbound* (1946).

While Poe synthesized several source texts to develop the detective story, the result in terms of genre has been the most ubiquitous constant in popular literature since his time.[4] In his five tales of detection and mystery (**"The Murders in the Rue Morgue"** [1841], **"The Mystery of Marie Roget"** [1842-1843], **"The Gold Bug"** [1843], **"Thou Art the Man"** [1844], and **"The Purloined Letter"** [1845]), amazingly, Poe touched on most of the approaches to follow: the sensational thriller, analytical exercise, classic detective story, puzzle/code-based story, and small town murder mystery. Poe was also a pioneer in making the least likely suspect the guilty one, having the crime's perpetrator plant false clues, and employing ballistics evidence. Despite these dazzling innovations, the single most influential element Poe created was the character of C. Auguste Dupin, the analytic genius who became the prototype for Sherlock Holmes and most subsequent puzzle solvers of detective fiction.[5] Dupin, a fallen aristocrat who resides with the unnamed narrator of his adventures in "a time-eaten and grotesque mansion, long deserted . . . and tottering to its fall in a retired and desolate portion of the Faubourg St. Germain," becomes the first detective hero of literature and the first series hero in literature.[6] As a man of imaginative intuition—the key to his analytical genius—Dupin and his narrator friend are recluses who live in artificial darkness each day because it "suited the rather fantastic gloom of [their] common temper" (532). In these circumstances they meditate, read, and speak away their time in analytical fancies. The narrator's descriptions of Dupin's analytical acumen, including his capacity to read minds through inspired observation, becomes what Leroy Panek names in these stories a "general thesis on genius."[7] In fact, two of the three Dupin stories are introduced with lengthy explanations of the superior type of analysis the hero engages in.

Dupin's analytical method involves careful and creative scrutiny that simplifies elements of a problem and uncovers information that, though hidden, is observably on the surface. Growing out of romantic philosophy, Poe distinguishes between ingenuity and analysis, associating the former with the fancy, the latter with imagination. In the process of explaining his methods to his friend, Dupin identifies his reasoning with poetry, claiming it as the source of his analytical powers. However, Poe embodies this method differently in each of the three Dupin tales. In **"Murders in the Rue Morgue,"** in which a mother and a daughter are inexplicably and horribly murdered, Dupin makes observations at the scene of the crime that contradict police observations, makes deductions about who could have entered, escaped, and handled the bodies in the peculiarly violent way displayed, and finally stages a theatrical mousetrap to affirm his conclusions that the murderer was none other than an orangutan. In **"The Mystery of Marie Roget,"** Dupin engages in literary interpretation by closely reading various newspaper accounts in order to sort through correct and incorrect assumptions.[8] **"The Purloined Letter"** offers a third application of imaginative analysis as Dupin identifies himself psychologically with his criminal counterpart. By accurately measuring the intelligence of his adversary, who stole and hid a letter, Dupin, without leaving his apartment, is able to intuit how the "hidden" letter is actually in plain sight.

Born in 1899, Hitchcock was fascinated, like the rest of England at the time, with true crime as well as crime fiction. Like Dickens, Hitchcock attended the Old Bailey, watching trials and storing up materials. He went to the Black Museum at Scotland Yard, a sort of police chamber of horrors, and read accounts of crime in the Sunday papers. He eventually amassed a large library of criminal cases and never tired of such famously gruesome murderers as Christie, who strangled eight women for sexual satisfaction and then buried them under the floor-boards (reminiscent of Hitchcock's *Frenzy* and Poe's **"The Tell-Tale Heart"**). Although, as we have seen, Hitchcock reveals elements in his films from many of the detective writers noted above, he always claimed that "fear in the cinema is my special field" (118). Despite these various influences, Hitchcock never forgot the Poe thrillers that so affected him in his youth. Significantly, in Hitchcock's homage to Poe he explicitly mentions

"Murders in the Rue Morgue" and **"The Gold Bug,"** tales of crime and mystery that continued to resonate for him. When Hitchcock said that he "can't help but compare what I try to put in my films with what Poe put in his stories" (143), among the things he meant certainly included Poe's doubleness of vision. Ketterer notes that for Poe everyday reality is deception, that the limits of seeing reality were "basic to Poe."[9] This certainly describes many scenes in Hitchcock's films, where people (Uncle Charlie, Eve Kendall, the Draytons) or situations (Armstrong's defection, the saboteur's wealthy charity ball, Mr. Memory's performance) are not what they seem. Hitchcock's double vision, like Poe's, led him to create a slippery world in which reality and dream, guilt and innocence, art and life, and the creative and resolvent are often indistinguishable. Such doubleness creates a suspenseful atmosphere that reflects the delight and terror of the sublime, the literature of unsettling schizophrenia in which one's worst fears become perversely exhilarating.[10] Like Poe, Hitchcock provides his audiences with enjoyable terror and safe horror. He has a therapeutic view of fear: "Our nature is such that we must have these 'shake-ups,' or we grow sluggish and jellified" (109). But he also notes that this approach has its limitations: "You want them to get off the switchback railway [roller coaster] giggling with pleasure: like the woman who comes out of a sentimental movie and says, 'It was lovely. I had a good cry.'"[11]

Elements from Poe's *Eureka,* his manifesto of the sublime consciousness, link the detective story back to his horror stories. Note the pattern Poe established, as described by Magistrale and Poger: "in both horror and detection individuals and the human community itself are threatened by a destructive agency. To counterbalance its influence, reason and ratiocination are employed to discover the identity of the murderer. The murderer is then banished, and order is restored."[12]

Poe's detective tales fit this pattern as Dupin's analytical prowess disentangles ambiguous clues to vanquish the various threats to order. But, as John Irwin notes, **"Murders in the Rue Morgue"** includes elements from Poe's horror tales. For example, "the irrational assault on a mother and daughter by a male animal within a locked room was a continuation of that violence against the female double by a male figure trapped within the symbolic womb of the family/home in the dying women stories."[13] Like the horror tales, the detective tales represent a threat to reason itself—without Dupin crimes become insoluble and the forces of chaos dominate. Herein is the crux of the difference between Poe's detective stories and his tales of terror.

While *Eureka* describes a fragmentation and final re-unification of the original unity of the universe, only the detective stories in Poe's canon consistently restore order.[14]

Sounding as if he were discussing *Eureka,* Irwin calls this restoration of order the "figuration of the womb fantasy across the three Dupin stories [in which] one can detect a clear trajectory running from a physical sense of return to origin to a mental one" (319). Through Dupin's god-like mind, the powers of perverse self-destruction are held at bay, chaos is checked, and harmony is restored. In that sense, embodied within the story itself is the sense of safety that Hitchcock says is the pleasure of the horror tales, perhaps accounting for their popularity. In his horror tales Poe supplies the terror while the reader must sometimes work hard to supply a sense of well-being. With his detective story, however, Poe supplies both the "horror" of chaos unleashed and the well-being of containing it.

The central character of Poe's tales of ratiocination, C. Auguste Dupin, with his sublime double vision, provides the link between the Poe and Hitchcock mysteries. The double nature of the detective, which is associated closely with the double nature of reason itself ("the creative and the resolvent"), is introduced by Poe's narrator as he describes how Dupin seems to go into a trance during the analytic process. The creative side of Dupin seems to be the analytical process of inspired observation; the resolvent side is the transcendence achieved when solving a puzzle. The resolvent is the result of Dupin's meditating in the dark, busying his soul "in dreams" (533), enabling him, free of distractions, to reduce a puzzle's terms to its lowest forms until he is finally free from the bonds of earthly reason, associated here with standard investigative methods—the initial steps in Dupin's analytic process. Thus the resolvent Dupin uses facts to transcend rationality; he becomes frigid, his eyes vacant, and his voice rising. In an interesting tie-in with the horror tales, the narrator suggests that perhaps these symptoms are the product of "a diseased intelligence" (533). Because analysis is associated with madness, we, like the narrator, are awed by Dupin. This is partly because Dupin's mind renders ambiguous all theories of the rational, leaving, as Ketterer observes, "the difference between order and chaos . . . merely a 'perspective anomaly'" (xiv). While one admires his superior ratiocinative abilities, they are so unusual that delight is tempered with a measure of terror—not unlike watching a magician saw a woman in half. Hoffman notes that since Dupin's reasoning partakes of the irrational, it is higher, tapping into a preconscious dream mind of associativeness.[15] In returning from this strange state triumphant and unscathed, Dupin's analytical process

somewhat mirrors the *Eureka* cycle by beginning in one state, moving into another, and finally returning again. He leaves his secure and orderly state, enters into the chaos and fragmentation of a seemingly insoluble case, and returns having imagined and enacted a reordering of the world. In fact, Dupin is like *Eureka*'s god who created the universe and at whose inscrutable will its fragmented and diffused parts return together.

Because even Dupin can't rely on his ratiocinative powers alone to solve his cases (though he tries to in **"The Mystery of Marie Roget"**), theatricality becomes part and parcel of the ratiocinative process and of the narrative pleasure in recounting his analytical steps. Loisa Nygaard has noted that detectives like Dupin and his successors, because they are detached from life to a significant degree, make ratiocination a game.[16] She might more accurately have suggested that they make ratiocination like a stage play. True to his double nature, Dupin resorts to theatrical methods to complete his cases in **"Rue Morgue"** [**"The Murders in the Rue Morgue"**] and **"Purloined Letter."** In the former, he places an ad concerning the orangutan, luring its owner into an apartment where he confronts him. He pretends to have discovered and captured the creature, drawing the sailor into admitting his ownership. For the sailor this bit of theater becomes a slippery business, as Dupin and the narrator shift from his innocent helpers to dangerous, armed antagonists who force a confession from him. In another example of theatrical surprise from **"Thou Art the Man,"** a grand guignol-like mousetrap is created when the narrator sends a wine cask to murderer Charles Goodfellow. When he opens the cask, the corpse rises and seems to say, "Thou art the man," inducing the murderer's instant confession.

In the **"Purloined Letter"** Dupin's stagecraft is most thoroughly displayed. Early on, he pretends to go along with the prefect in criticizing poets as fools. Later, upon the prefect's second visit to discuss the location of the stolen letter, Dupin pretends not to have it. After he lets the prefect express his frustration, Dupin begins asking about the promised reward and then chides the prefect that he has not exerted himself "to the utmost in this matter" (982). He continues to forestall the conclusion by telling a parable of the need to seek advice, finally reducing the prefect to declare, "I am *perfectly* willing to take advice, and to pay for it." Dupin then brings his little drama to a climax by drawing a checkbook from his drawer, stating that "you may as well fill me up a check for the amount mentioned. When you have signed it, I will hand you the letter" (983). After a long, suspenseful pause, the prefect signs the check and Dupin produces the letter. Having kept back his discoveries, letting the mystery of the stolen letter remain incomprehensible, Dupin uses theatricality to punctuate his cleverness by perfectly manipulating his audience. Dupin not only solves incomprehensible mysteries but creates them in the process, an interesting double movement that gives further dimension to the two sides of Dupin's nature. As when he seems to read the narrator's mind in **"Rue Morgue,"** Dupin uses the unexpected to create for the narrator, and for us, a world where magic things can happen. The rational equivalent of Israfel, he is himself an artist of the highest caliber, in essence embodying the narrative structure of surprise that is characteristic of the detective story.

Dupin's final theatrical wizardry in **"Purloined Letter"** is no less dazzling when he visits Minister D— wearing dark glasses and pretending to have weak eyes so that he can scan the room unnoticed and detect the whereabouts of the stolen and openly disguised letter. He returns later and stages a ruckus on the street outside to draw D— to the window, allowing Dupin to replace the stolen letter with a facsimile. Again he punctuates the effect of his drama with a climax by enclosing in the facsimile a verse from *Atree et Thyeste* that will remind D— that Dupin had promised to be avenged for a wrong D— had done him previously. The incredible feat in fathoming D—'s hiding place is his utter accuracy in pinpointing the coordinates between D—'s dual nature as both mathematician and poet and then predicting exactly where such a person would hide a letter of the type stolen in order to evade police scrutiny and yet keep it handy.

Thus, in his ratiocination tales, Dupin has a dual nature, and his theatrical special effects make the world a double realm between reality and theater, linking the intellectual with the sublime (even the genre itself is slippery, hovering between sketch and tale). This sense of uncertainty about the state of the world and its potential slipperiness, as well as Dupin's double nature and ratiocinative genius, provide sublime elements of surprise, suspense, and wonder in the tales, yet Poe always concludes with the comforting assurance that justice triumphs.

Murder!

While Rohmer and Chabrol call *Murder!* (1930) an "absolutely classic detective plot," Thomas Leitch points out that little attention is focused on the investigative process.[17] Nevertheless, Hitchcock's hero in the film, Sir John, utilizes Dupin's methods, especially his theatricality, in solving crimes. Other themes and situations from Poe's tales of ratiocination also emerge, such as the doubleness of individuals and situations that makes appearance and reality ambiguous. These issues are subsumed in the film under the running mo-

tif of acting and the theater. As in Poe's **"Rue Morgue"** and **"Purloined Letter,"** a female victim, Diana Baring, is at the center of the case. The investigations are conducted using intuition, imagination, and theatrics. In addition, the "detective," Sir John Menier, like Dupin, is an amateur, a prominent actor/playwright whose imagination surpasses the routine analytical methods of the unimaginative police. As in **"Rue Morgue"** analyzing how a high window could be accessed by the murderer becomes a key clue in the mystery, and like **"Purloined Letter"** the answer—in this case the murderer—is in plain sight all along, since the murderer, Handel Fane, is clearly seen but disguised as a policeman. Like Dupin, Sir John meditates, reads people, sees the significance of evidence overlooked by the police, and uses a dramatic mousetrap to elicit a confession from the murderer. In addition to these parallels, the sublime slipperiness of reality is suggested through the double aspects of Sir John, the ambiguity between reason and intuition, and the fine line between reality and drama. In this film set in the world of the theater, all the world is indeed a stage and practically "all the men and women merely players."

Like Dupin, Sir John is presented as a unique character set apart by his wealth, breeding, and, importantly, artistic talent as actor, playwright, and producer. Dupin too is an aristocrat (though a poor one), which, with his extraordinary talents, sets him apart. The theatricality of his character is echoed by the camera's presentation of him. Sir John's appearance in the film is coyly delayed, he being the last juror in the Baring murder trial to be noticed by the camera, which has been slowly circling the jury. When the camera finally reveals him, we discover that he is the eccentric one, the only juror who is not in a hurry and who has concluded that Diana Baring is innocent. When attention is drawn to him, he states that he is not a businessman, theatrically announcing himself as "a poor actor," a title suggesting that he makes a career out of being a double of himself. Though he does all he can to defend Diana Baring, he is ultimately unable to move the jury/audience to reconsider and is bullied into going along with a guilty verdict. He is next introduced, like Dupin, in his "cloistered intimacy,"[18] through a series of shots that takes us from outside his home in Berkeley Square to the outer doors, doorbell, elevator, front door, living room, and finally into his bathroom. These images serve as curtains opening the next act in Sir John's passion.

These shots also suggest our deeper approach into Sir John's mind as we are led into his meditations about the jury trial, as he looks at himself in the mirror while shaving. Punctuating the doubleness suggested by this scene, Hitchcock shows Sir John's mirror reflection and the back of his head and shoulders in the foreground, giving the impression of two people talking together. While this scene, like the later mouse-trap scene, has roots in Shakespearean soliloquies, it also links Sir John to Dupin's meditative side. In some sense Sir John's tryst with his other self in the mirror is like the trance Dupin enters during his "Bi-Part" "resolvent" phases. Sir John also seems in another world as he ponders the details of the case. The case in *Murder!* like those of Dupin's, presents Sir John with difficulty in the sublime sense of a seemingly insurmountable problem. The case has been heard and judged, and the sentence of death pronounced, and all Sir John has are intuitions that fall flat with the rest of the jury. While shaving, Sir John hears a flawed and incomplete radio report of Diana's case. Like the newspaper reports in **"Murders in the Rue Morgue"** and **"Mystery of Marie Roget,"** such reports suggest the mundane analytical powers of the masses and the press establishment. Wagner's overture to *Tristan and Isolde,* which follows the news, reflects Sir John's awareness of growing feelings for Diana, and its crescendos punctuate his intuitive revelations about the overlooked significance of the brandy at the crime scene and the fact that someone else must have been in the room to commit the murder. In essence, Sir John's entranced mind is guided by the intuitive logic of Wagner's music. In his trancelike state at the mirror Sir John experiences a change, separating his passive and active, his perplexed and purposive selves, discovering an inner resolve to rescue Diana Baring because an SOS radio story inspires him. Additionally, he is moved by his love for the imprisoned actress, a side of himself he only finally acknowledges during his self-interview at the mirror. Love becomes a transcendent spur behind his investigation, empowering his intuition and guiding his thought. In his trance, Sir John resembles the "resolvent Dupin." Sir John's intuition also feeds on mundane facts and is based on the fact that he, like Dupin, identifies with the crime victims, in this case fellow thespian Diana Baring.

Throughout *Murder!* Hitchcock incorporates other doubles to emphasize the dream world of the theater. Even the trial itself is presented as a play, a fanfare accompanying the title, "Rex vs. Diana Baring." Sir John's own double nature as actor and playwright is confirmed as he adds "detective" to his list of theatrical selves. This role is part of his "new play," which he equates with his investigation. It requires him to do things a wealthy man like him wouldn't normally do, including consorting intimately with the lower-class Markhams. As theatrical managers, they can grant Sir John access to people and places associated with the murder. The idea that Mr. Markham is actually one of his doubles is visually reinforced with the cut from Sir John's living room to Markham's home, revealing them both wearing similarly striped robes. Here Hitchcock foreshadows the striped circus tent at the end of the film, reinforcing a further doubling of the circus and the theater, and also suggests the "acts" all are called on to perform in this film. Sir John's association with the Markhams often becomes humorous as he brings the Markhams up to his level ("we artists") and purposely uses the wrong spoon during lunch to avoid embarrassing Mrs. Doucie Markham, who uses a teaspoon to eat her soup. Tania Modleski accurately points out that in addition to writing his play about the murder case, his acting in a way to include the Markhams is applying techniques of his art to life.[19] In an amusing early scene in which the police are questioning Diana's acting troupe from backstage during the performance (fittingly, of a farce), we see many costume changes, which suggest the slipperiness of identity in the world of this film. Among these changes is Handel Fane taking off a policeman's uniform while another actor dons an identical police costume (which, while we don't yet realize it, reveals the murderer's disguise). Fane himself, who we later learn is the murderer, is repeatedly doubled in his various guises—actor, trapeze artist, pure Caucasian, and female impersonator.

Fane is also the most significant of Sir John's doubles; they are reminiscent of Dupin and Minister D—. Among other similarities to Sir John, Fane loves Diana. Even their behavior reflects each other, both moving and speaking slowly and deliberately, suggesting both real and "feigned" good breeding. Their doubleness is tested with Sir John's suggestion that they collaborate on his play, *The Inner History of the Baring Case,* which of course Fane also does in the note he leaves behind after committing suicide. During the mousetrap scene, Fane proves to be a worthy adversary. He avoids giving himself away and plays off of Sir John's trap by insisting he needs a poker to get into the part for which he is reading. Like Sir John, he is an actor, slipping in and out of various roles as needed. Finally, Sir John's circus-striped robe links him to Fane, in another reflection of the theater. As in **"Purloined Letter,"** the doubling of detective and criminal introduces moral ambiguities, particularly the transfer of guilt. In this case, Sir John is unable to convince the jury of his intuition about Diana's innocence, making him partly responsible for her predicament, reflecting Fane's deeper guilt at not rescuing Diana by confessing his crime.

The ambiguity between reason and intuition that underlies Poe's Dupin stories is highlighted in the jury scene. For example, one woman agrees with the psychoanalytic defense that Diana was in a "fugue state" and acted without knowing what she did. Another woman juror suggests that if that were true and Diana were released, then the jury would be responsible for other possible murders she might commit due to her "dual personality." While the jury accepts this reasoning, obviously it is based on pure speculation. Other jurors also confuse the issue, one feeling there is too much responsibility placed on them and another finding Diana so "perfectly ripping" that he can't imagine a "girl of that sort" murdering anybody. Such opinions are soundly put in their place as the foreman notes that the world can't be run on sentiment and that how "the young lady" appeals to one is irrelevant to the "case at hand." The foreman becomes a foil for Sir John. Like Sir John, he is well-spoken and intelligent, a natural leader. But unlike Sir John, he is a practical, not particularly sensitive businessman who is quick to reject anything that is not based on apparent facts. He is solid, respectable, and seemingly wiser than most of the others.

The early proceedings of the jury, and how they are framed by Hitchcock, make Sir John's hesitancy to vote guilty suspect: his reasons, in the context of the other weak ones, seem equally unimpressive. He claims, for example, that he is "convinced" Diana is telling the truth, that he has been "impressed" with her behavior. He offers no evidence for these statements; they rely on his intuitive sense of what she could and couldn't do based on his feelings alone. Sir John claims that his intuitions are deeper than those of the earlier juror who found Diana "ripping," but they don't necessarily seem so. In fact, when told that Fane's testimony was of no use since "he was so obviously in love with the prisoner," Sir John looks up quickly with the shock of self-recognition, suggesting to us that he too has tender feelings for the prisoner. This certainly throws his intuition into doubt as we are immediately reminded that the one juror who likes Diana was told that an ugly woman would likely have little chance with him. We are not certain that Sir John himself would be hesitant to condemn Diana were she less attractive. Even worse, Sir John justifies his perspective on his experience as an actor and playwright:

> My time on the stage would be shortened if I had not for years trained myself to . . . apply the techniques of life to the problems of my art. But today, ladies and gentlemen, that process is reversed. I find myself applying the techniques of my art to a problem of real life, and my art is not satisfied.

As in **"Rue Morgue"** and **"Purloined Letter,"** which emphasizes poetry over mathematics, the analytic imagination is here identified with art.[20] These unscientific remarks bring the jurors to their feet to surround Sir John and bombard him with questions of facts that he cannot satisfactorily answer. As the jurors in unison repeatedly asks him, "Any answer to that,

Sir John?" they become a Greek chorus praising the fact-based method of analysis shared by the public, the court, and the press. Sir John, like Poe's Dupin, has challenged assumptions, except that he is not yet prepared to prove his impressions. In these scenes Hitchcock raises the issue of what is acceptable evidence and, specifically, if and when intuitive impressions are justified.

Although Sir John's investigation proceeds to demonstrate the uncertainty of impressions, it increasingly confirms that his are correct. The uncertainty of impressions, as in **"Rue Morgue,"** is demonstrated in hearing voices and making assumptions about them. Diana's landlady says that she had heard none but women's voices on the night of the murder, but when Sir John leaves the room and imitates a woman's voice, the landlady is fooled (as are we), obviously demonstrating the unreliability of such assumptions. His case is based on the idea that apparent facts are often built on assumptions, their value depending on how imaginatively read. For example, that Diana smelled of alcohol convinced the jury that she had drunk the brandy. However, Sir John raises the question that perhaps she merely smelled of dinner wine. Also, since no other person was known to be in the room when the murder took place, it is assumed by the court and jury that no one was there. Sir John suggests that another person may have been there, but *who* remains unknown. In each case, facts prove less reliable than intuition. Finally, when Sir John realizes that the policeman seen disappearing after the crime was an impersonator, he proves once and for all the unreliability of appearances. If we had any doubts about Sir John's approach, we certainly are given pause about the certainty with which we process things we see—especially in Hitchcock's film.

Finally, the images of the theater further suggest the ambiguity of reality and illusion. With so many doublings, actors, and costume changes, *Murder!* is a veritable house of mirrors in a carnival where images only seem real. As in Poe's Dupin tales, Hitchcock puts an emphasis on the gaze, which, as Modleski notes, is related inherently to detective stories (31). Not surprisingly, the film begins and ends with deceptive images. The opening scenes show a clock tower chiming from the end of the street, followed by a scream and a series of windows opening and people trying to see what the ruckus is all about. These people suggest spectators at a play trying to get a better look at the stage from an obscure balcony seat. As it will turn out, since the first policeman seen is the murderer in disguise, the entire scene becomes a bit of theater and the people are quite rightly assuming the role of audience. In fact, with the film's "audience," we are deceived early in the scene as Hitchcock's shooting script arranges the shot of a woman's silhouette changing: "a glimpse of a silhouette of a beautiful figure and profile on blind. As the latter goes up we find to our disappointment that it is the angry face of an unattractive woman."[21] Hitchcock maintains this perspective as the murder investigation and Sir John's mousetrap play become synonymous. The film's ending also proves to be something other than it seems as the camera retreats from what appears to be the last scene of the film, but is actually the end of a play starring Sir John and Diana Baring. Thus the concluding scene is both the end of the film and the end of Sir John's play, which had been one all along. The deceptions at the end and the beginning of the film thrust the audience into the position of the reader of the Dupin stories—a state of sublime uncertainty about the nature of reality. As Modleski states of the film, "at the heart of the film is the fear that theater may so infuse and confuse reality that proper distinctions and boundaries by which make sense of life no longer hold true" (32).

Many of the sequences in *Murder!* are mounted theatrically. During the opening scenes, once the neighbors get inside the scene of the crime, Hitchcock shows us a theatrical tableau: Diana sits entranced with the murdered Edna Druce at her feet with silent spectators looking on. The camera accommodates our curiosity by making a circular tour of the scene, moving from the policeman down Diana's body to her limp hand, fire poker on the floor, prostrate body of Edna, and back up to the policeman. Ironically, the policeman is pointing a light on Diana as if the appearances in the room and their meaning were reliably clear. In effect, it becomes a stage light that merely clarifies appearances. Such use of circular camera work is common to the film, circumscribing space like a stage and linking various elements of the film together, suggesting again the slippery nature of the identity of things. For example, Hitchcock's circular pan around the jury table suggests the problem of pinpointing truth, going around and around the jury as the jury does the truth of the case. Just as in the circular camera movement at the crime scene noted above, circularity avoids truth by going around it. Sir John is attempting to get at the center itself, based on his faith that truth involves more than hovering around seemingly obvious facts. The image of circularity leads to the circus climax with its rings. It is here, when first at the circus, that Sir John conceives, or at least reveals, his mousetrap scheme to trap Fane.

Before the mousetrap scene is introduced, Hitchcock combines a melodramatically suspenseful series of shots in cyclical repetition, telescoping time, as Sir John searches for Fane and his investigation begins to enclose the culprit. The round of shots moves sequentially from a weather vane (William Rothman suggests

the vane is an emblem of Fane [or feign])[22] to a high-angle shot of Diana's circular pacing, to the shadow of a circular noose that is slowly rising up a wall.[23] In addition, the spinning vane itself reinforces the circular imagery. Diana's pacing reminds us how she has been stepping around Fane throughout the case. If he isn't found, her neck, instead of his, will fill that circular hangman's noose. Hitchcock accelerates the pace of the shot series, as well as our suspense, until a voice-over reveals that Fane has been found working at the circus. We then see Sir John and Markham at the circus watching Fane's trapeze act, which is illuminated by searchlights that surround him in circular light. In essence, Fane has stepped out of the closet into center ring to be scrutinized. The full-circle plot of detective tales, bringing things back into order in the end, reflects the reuniting of the diffused fragments of Poe's universe. The quickening pace of the ending of this montage cycle reflects the increased rotary speed of the vortical gathering of universal fragments in God's Eurekan plot.

Sir John is led to Fane because of Diana's slip that he was half-caste. Realizing instantly that trying to maintain his secret motivated Fane's murdering Edna, Sir John's shock of recognition becomes a similar emotional high point for the film to the horrified narrator in **"Rue Morgue"** learning from Dupin that the hair specimen found at the L'Espanaye room isn't human. Both moments create a sense of strangeness and otherness, further amplified in the film by Fane's cross-dressing. In addition to this plot movement connecting Fane and the ape, they are also connected through their incredible athleticism. Dupin realizes early on, based on the window latch and locked door, that nothing human could have accessed the room. Similarly, on finding the sink in Fane's dressing room damaged, Sir John realizes that someone with the extraordinary strength of a trapeze artist could climb out the window and do the seemingly impossible trick of accessing Diana's house without touching the ground. Like Poe's tale, the film resolves its case with a spectacularly weird and unguessable circumstance that is at once surprising and uncanny.

The major theatrical event in the film comes as Sir John brings Fane in supposedly to read for his new play, *The Inner History of the Baring Case,* but really intends to force a confession. As Sir John suggests to Markham, this mousetrap scheme comes from Hamlet's attempt to prove his uncle's guilt in a play within a play. This is a third level of play within play, since Sir John's investigation/play is also a play within Hitchcock's film. Here Hitchcock is harking back to Poe as well as to Shakespeare, since in both **"Rue Morgue"** and **"Purloined Letter"** Dupin traps his prey with customized theatrical scenes that reveal the truth of his analyses. While Hitchcock begins the film as a whodunit, these last twenty minutes become a suspense thriller. This is a pattern he will follow in films like *Rebecca* (1940) and *Vertigo* (1958), which start out as one thing and become another.[24]

In the important play scene in *Murder!*, the line dividing appearance and reality becomes very fuzzy. The mousetrap takes place in Sir John's office, which is decorated with massive columns that fittingly remind us of the classical frame of a proscenium arch—the perfect setting for the little drama he has set up for Fane. The room also features a polar bear rug that suggests Sir John's predatory role as cat to Fane's mouse. As Fane theatrically enters and Sir John explains that he has written a play about the Diana Baring murder case, their conversation is filmed without cuts, the camera moving back and forth between the two. This important image, like the circle, has appeared several times already, particularly at Sir John's interview with Diana in prison and in Fane's trapeze act. In this instance, the back-and-forth camera suggests the life-and-death struggle between these competitive actors, both pretending to be something they are not, with the added complication of Sir John's triple role as playwright, actor, and spectator of Fane's reactions to being cast as Edna Druce's murderer. Sir John attempts to cause Fane to break down psychologically and emotionally by equating him with the murderer in his play ("*You* make *your* entrance"). In other words Sir John is trying to get Fane to cross the line from play to reality. Reality becomes hard to distinguish from "imagination," a word used often and conspicuously during the scene: the brandy was not "exploited with sufficient imagination"; and instead of using a real poker for the reading, Fane is told he must "use [his] imagination." Sir John's statement that the police have little sense of drama, not exploiting the brandy angle better, alerts Fane that Sir John *has* sufficient imagination to have figured out the case. Fane's request for a real poker to play the scene, as Rothman has pointed out, would give him some chance to escape the office by force (86). Like Minister D— in **"Purloined Letter,"** whom Dupin knows to be "desperate" and capable of killing him, Fane is dangerous and willing to kill to protect himself and his secret. Ironically, at this point, Sir John, rather than a poker, offers Fane a pencil, the weapon he has used to write this mousetrap.

Play and reality—and Hitchcock's thriller—converge at the climactic moment when Sir John reads from the script Edna's unfortunate line, "he's a half . . ." Hitchcock jump-cuts to a high-angle view of the two looking at their scripts in an unbearably shocking and silent moment that seems to reenact the moment of the murder, which left Diana Baring in shocked silence.

Quickly the script is turned to a blank page, and with Sir John we are held in suspension, awaiting a climactic turn of events.

Later, back at the circus, Sir John's forestalled denouement finally plays out. Ending the film at the circus is appropriate, since it is the place for exotic extremes in performance, reflecting Fane's roles as both woman and murderer. As he goes back and forth on the trapeze bar, his shadow centers in the circular searchlights that illuminate his act. The back-and-forth of the trapeze act emphasizes the trap Fane finds himself in. Just as he can go in only those two directions, no matter where he goes, Sir John will be there—not only to accuse him of murder but to reveal his half-caste secret. Fane is also caught between two ambiguities: his desire to flaunt himself as actor, circus performer, female impersonator, and his need to hide himself and keep his secret from others. His need to expose himself is reinforced by the circular imagery of the circus, its rings, lights, and the circular headdress of Fane's costume. His need to hide is shown most clearly as he swings back and forth and sees in his mind's eye Sir John and Diana staring at him—the two people who know his secret. Fane has the last word in his defeat, however. He creates a surprise ending to Sir John's play by hanging himself during his act and leaving a confession note behind that will save Diana Baring from the noose. While circus fans enjoy safe thrills, suicide is too much and sends them into hysteria (as Hitchcock's killing of the boy in *Sabotage* a couple of years later will also do). Thus Fane adds taboo entertainment to his violations (murder, cross-dressing, sexuality, and race). The tensions Fane experiences in living with all of his dualities—white and black, man and woman, actor and circus performer—embodies the psychomachia described by Poe in *Eureka,* causing fragmentation, diffusion, and finally psychological breakdown. His various roles finally defy categorization, as Modleski notes, making Sir John a restorer of social boundaries in solving the case.[25]

The case is thus solved, giving Sir John, finally, a response to the jury's repeated question, "Any answer for that, Sir John?" Like Dupin, Sir John has solved a case in a way that differs from the one taken by the public, courts, and press. He sees deeper by applying the techniques of his art to a problem of life. His "sense of drama," a knowledge of character and correct casting, consistent motivation, and a playwright's knowledge that all which appears to be is not, enables him to use peculiar analytic tools imaginatively exploiting possibilities that routine police and jury methods overlook or dismiss ("We are the experts of highbrow shockers, Markham"). Likewise, his dramatic orientation enables him to set the crucial mousetrap to solve the case. Like Sir George, Sir John has heroically slain the dragon that threatens the fair maiden and everyone else, pulling order and reality out from the brink of racial, sexual, and theatrical chaos.

The film's many circular images take us back to the cyclical development of the universe in Poe's *Eureka*. There reality slips in and out in endless cycles between harmony and reason, fragmentation and madness. The world, like the circus, is a place of jeopardy, full of death-defying feats that supply sublime thrills. As in the theater and in the circus, with its "acts," little in the film is stable or reliable. Even more than the theater, circus "acts" effectively reflect the fragmentation of the universe, in which no continuous narrative is attempted.

Dial M for Murder

Another Hitchcock film having characteristics of the detective tale is *Dial M for Murder* (1954), which harks back to issues in Poe's ratiocinative tales but turns some of them on their head. The interest here isn't on finding out who committed a crime, since that is shown clearly, but in watching would-be murderer Tony Wendice as he reacts and adapts to the police investigation. Adapted by Frederick Knott from his popular stage play, the film offered a ready-made and sure-fire property to recoup Warner Bros. losses from *Under Capricorn* (1949) and to promote Warner's 3-D experiments. However, these practical reasons were not the only ones attracting Hitchcock to the play. Elements similar to his own style—such as the claustrophobic setting (*Lifeboat* and *Rope*), doubles (*Shadow of a Doubt* and *Strangers on a Train*), a horrifically graphic death scene (*Spellbound* and *Rope*), object-centered plot (a key in *Notorious* and a rope in *Rope*), and the mousetrap motif (*Murder!* and *Stage Fright*)—made it even more enticing. As Rohmer and Chabrol correctly comment, despite being an adaptation, *Dial M* is "quite Hitchcockian."[26] Of course, these Hitchcockian elements are also Poe-esque, and the numerous adaptations of Poe's detective elements in the play undoubtedly attracted Hitchcock as well. For example, *Dial M* is centered around a female victim of violence and blackmail, reminiscent of the brutalized females in **"Rue Morgue"** and the blackmailed queen in **"Purloined Letter."** Inspector Hubbard's switching keys under Tony Wendice's nose to set up his mousetrap resolution to the case is also like **"Purloined Letter."** In addition, Tony and Hubbard both electrify others with their surprise revelations in the manner of Poe's Dupin. Although it was commercially attractive, Hitchcock chose to film *Dial M* for much the same reason he did *Vertigo*—it was tailor-made for him. Finally, beyond the fact that *Dial M* came with Poe and Hitchcock elements firmly in place, Hitchcock made important modifications to the play, enabling him to bring in his own thematic concerns.[27]

The plot of *Dial M* is interesting because it goes beyond Poe's one-on-one confrontation between Dupin and a single antagonist. Hitchcock exploits a three-way battle for analytical wit and theatrical dominance between Inspector Hubbard, mystery writer Mark Halliday, and would-be murderer Tony Wendice. They are pitted against each other not only mentally but artfully as playwrights who, like Sir John and Fane, concoct competing scenarios of the murder case before them.

Hitchcock's twist on Poe is that he makes the police inspector—the establishment figure with his old, proven methods—the genius who ultimately outwits the clever would-be murderer and the writer to solve the crime. (Hitchcock reverts to his usual Poe-esque denunciation of the police in his next film, *Rear Window*.) *Dial M* opens and closes with the protective image of the ever vigilant bobby standing guard on the streets of London. However, knowing that Hitchcock has little affinity for authority figures—especially the police who supposedly locked him up as little boy for five minutes at his father's behest—we can't take these images at face value. The rank-and-file police are generally not presented in a positive light, even in *Dial M*. First, they are easily duped by Tony, who plants evidence against his wife that they accept without question. Later, Inspector Hubbard has to prevent one policeman from foppishly carrying Margot's purse on his wrist: "You clot! You can't go out in the street like that. You'll be arrested." In fact, Inspector Hubbard is portrayed as quite apart from the ordinary policeman. He has intelligence, taste, breeding, and a tremendous ego: on recognizing an oversight of his, for example, he comments that "even I didn't guess that at once. Extraordinary!" Also like Dupin, he thoughtfully smokes a pipe. Hence, the images of the protective bobby that open and close the film are more ironic than sincere, highlighting the fact that only an especially brilliant and civilized detective like Hubbard can match wits with Wendice. The regular policemen would have let him kill his wife right under their noses—since it seems to be in front of the Wendices' flat that we see the vigilant neighborhood bobby (booby?) stationed.

Hubbard is also pitted against mystery writer Mark Halliday. This becomes ironic in the context of Poe's detective tales, in which Dupin extols the poet's imagination as the superior means of analysis (though Halliday is a pulp writer and not a poet). While Halliday comes close to figuring out how Tony planned the crime, he leaves out some crucial details and fails to note Tony's suspicious behavior. In an obvious allusion to discussion in **"The Purloined Letter"** of analytically playing draughts—a game that requires keen observation of opposing players—Halliday admits that he is a "lousy bridge player." In the context of Poe's correlation of game playing and analysis, it is clear that Mark is one-dimensional, understanding the mechanics of crime but not the motivations of real people. While Mark claims as a writer to put himself "in the criminal's shoes" (one of Dupin's crucial talents), in real life he is blinded by assumptions. Inspector Hubbard proves the superior analyst in two ways: (1) he worries about the details more deeply and (2) he suspects everybody, including Tony. Mark's oversight of Tony's potential guilt creates a tense scene that is reminiscent of the mousetrap scene in *Murder!* between Sir John and Fane. As Mark explains to Tony that he should confess to plotting Margot's murder, he actually figures out nearly every detail of Tony's plan. However, his failure to imagine Tony's guilt makes the potential mousetrap ineffective. Indeed, as Inspector Hubbard later states, "They talk about flat-footed policeman. May the saints protect us from the gifted amateur."

Ultimately, Hubbard, Halliday, and Tony all use Dupin's technique of anticipating the thinking of others, although differently and with varied results. In designing the crime Tony anticipates the reactions of Swann very accurately, as well as those of the police. When Swann suggests that Tony is smart, he replies that "I've just had time to think things out, put myself in your position." When the police come to investigate Swann's death, Tony plants clues that not only anticipate, but manipulate police thinking. Making himself a criminal designing a crime, Mark uses the method in his writing. Of course, he also uses this method effectively in imagining what Tony might confess to free Margot. Finally, Inspector Hubbard traps Tony by anticipating his thinking: "He will put two and two together and use the key under the stair carpet." The use of anticipating others' thoughts is also part of the theme of appearance and reality. Each character becomes an actor in a play within a play of his own composition. Tony's play is the murder plot in which Swann is cast as star. In his own play Tony acts the part of the faithful and innocent husband. With Swann, he pretends at first to want to be shopping, then walks Swann through the part of murderer, and then while he is on the phone Swann walks through a rehearsal himself. For his part, Halliday acts as Margot's platonic friend, when he is actually her illicit lover. And Detective Hubbard acts as if he were uninterested in the facts of the case, often looking up distractedly to say "hmm?" when given seemingly important information. Like Dupin with Minister D—, Hubbard knows the value of pretending to know nothing. This later enables him to prepare the final theatrical he concocts to test Margot and Tony and thus solve the crime.

The parallel roles of Hubbard and Tony to Dupin and Minister D— are remarkable. In addition to the likeness Hubbard bears Dupin, Tony is quite like Minister D— in being a cunning and ruthless sophisticate who outwits the average policeman with only half trying. And like D—, he steals his wife's love letter and uses it to blackmail her. Later, just as Dupin had stolen D—'s stolen letter and replaced it with another, Hubbard steals Tony's key. He does so by sending Tony to the window to check on Halliday, reminiscent of the distraction Dupin created to take D— to the window while he exchanged his facsimile for the real letter.

All of this suggests how difficult it could be to distinguish appearance from reality in the world of this film. But the deeper theatrical ambitions of Hubbard, Tony, and Mark make reality even more slippery and the film's suspense all the more gripping. In fact, the film can be divided into a series of plays that continually collide with each other. The first is by Mark and Margot; following their adulterous affair, they pretend to be mere friends for Tony's sake. Unfortunately for them, Tony skips a tennis tournament to follow them and watches their backstage performance through a window as they are cooking spaghetti. This, as well as Mark's love letter purloined from Margot's purse, leads him to create his own scenario and recast their parts. Luring Swann to his flat under false pretenses, Tony begins his play by casting the crooked Swann in the role of murderer in his play by blackmailing him.[28] After giving appropriate background to the story behind the play, Tony blocks out the action in his flat. Hitchcock's overhead shot follows Tony as the entire murder is laid out. Later, when Margot spoils the murder by killing Swann, Tony enters into another playwriting phase revision. Having failed to murder his wife, he arranges details so that she will be convicted of murdering her blackmailer. To this point, Tony seems in firm control of the police and of his own destiny.

Mark, however, offers a competing version of things on the eve of Margot's execution. Having figured out that Margot can be saved if Tony will essentially own up to what he has in fact done (though Mark doesn't know that he has done it), he attempts to recast Tony's play with him as the murderer. Visually, the scene closely parallels Tony's blocking out the murder for Swann as Mark walks Tony through the plan. When Inspector Hubbard arrives, with the opening scene of his own play, he seemingly supports Tony's contempt for Mark's rewrite. Hubbard's first act, but the film's last, ostensibly involves details of money Tony is spending, but in reality is about getting into the flat and switching keys with him and getting him to pick up Margot's things at the police station. The complexity of three simultaneous scenarios colliding in these scenes is dizzying: Tony pretending he is sympathetic with Mark despite having evidence of Margo's guilt; Mark now knowing Tony is the murderer (after finding the briefcase full of money) but being unable to prove it; Hubbard pretending to be there on some routine police matter while actually feeling Mark is right.

The real contest involves who can improvise a revision the most effectively. Mark came to the apartment with his rescuing scheme but realizes Tony's guilt on finding the money he hid for paying Swann. Tony, when confronted with this new evidence against him, turns it all on Margot, that the money was there because she was to pay off Swann. The quick-wittedness is dazzling—like having three Dupins trying to outwit each other. This battle of wits becomes consciously competitive as Tony challenges, "Go on Mark, make your move."

Hubbard, of course, proves to be the real Dupin of the story since his mousetrap prevails in the end. This trap is so cleverly set that Tony himself uses the key and walks right into it. Even he becomes confused by the unending twists in the world he himself made slippery by turning it into an ever complicating mystery. Hubbard, like Dupin, disentangles the chaos Tony starts and returns the fragments back into the whole. Notwithstanding, a strange note is sounded in the film, which seems ultimately positive. Before the murder, Mark warns Tony that perfect murders are only perfect on paper; in real life things never turn out as you think they will. And in the end, Tony explicitly concedes the point ("As you said Mark, it might have worked on paper . . ."). But this actually raises the question about whether the world is as unpredictable and slippery as the shifting fictional ones our three antagonists create. Thus the sublime is created not only in the murder scene or in the intellectual prowess of the antagonists, but in the implications about life itself poised on the edge of chaos, creating the need for ineffective bobbies to stand guard. Had not Tony made the mistake of spreading all of that money around his neighborhood, the forces of chaos, in the form of Margot's extinction and Mark's sorrow, certainly would have prevailed. Another aspect of the sublime in *Dial M* is our ambiguous connection to Tony, whom Hitchcock makes somewhat sympathetic. After all, he is charming and his wife has been unfaithful (Hitchcock certainly punishes her in the film). Typical of many Hitchcock films, *Dial M* makes the audience uncomfortable identifying with characters.

With the detective tale, both Poe and Hitchcock dip our big toes into the icy waters of chaos and terror, drawing them out again before we fall all the way in. The forces of violence, crime, and confusion are presented only to be disentangled and rendered ultimately harmless by reason. Interestingly, the forces of chaos are overcome as detectives employ their own illusions of ambiguity, theatricality, and doubleness. Most importantly, intuition, rather than purely scientific reason, becomes the means to discerning the irrational impulses that lay behind criminal behavior. As Dupin explains about discovering where Minister D— had hidden the letter: "I knew him, however, as both mathematician and poet, and my measures were adapted to his capacity, with reference to the circumstances by which he was surrounded. I knew him as a courtier, too, and as a bold *intriguant*. Such a man, I considered, could not fail to be aware of the ordinary political modes of action" (988). Whatever poetic genius provided D— with his concept for hiding the letter in plain sight also provided Dupin with the means of discovering his secret. Hence we have two sides of the same impulse, reflecting the doubleness of the Eurekan universe itself with its attractive and diffusive impulses in tension.

In addition to theatricality, doubleness, appearance versus reality, and analytical methods, Hitchcock, like Poe, layers his stories with much more than meets the eye. John T. Irwin writes of Poe: "In **'The Gold Bug,'** for example, Poe uses the cryptographic writing of Captain Kidd's note (a physical writing that is literally invisible until heat is applied to the scrap of parchment) to evoke the invisibility of a text's meaning compared to the visibility of its writing."[29] Similarly Hitchcock layers his films with details that critics have yet to exhaust the significance of, suggesting his complicated vision of reality. It took French critics to peel away the apparent limits of Hitchcock's "mere" commercial product from his more complex art. The same process has developed around Poe's writings. It is these layers, these more complex stories, that lead to the darker affinities between Poe and Hitchcock beyond the detective story.

Notes

1. Sidney Gottlieb, ed., *Hitchcock on Hitchcock: Selected Writings and Interviews* (Berkeley: University of California Press, 1995), 113. Unless otherwise noted, all Hitchcock quotations throughout this volume are taken from Gottlieb's book.

2. The "Frenchman" could mean Dupin, the most famous of French detectives. The other obvious choice is Hercules Poirot, though this would be ambiguous since he is Belgian. Joe's subsequent comment that "bubbles don't necessarily kill a person" seems a non sequitur, referring to Dorothy Sayer's *Unnatural Death* (1927).

3. J. Gerald Kennedy, "The Limits of Reason: Poe's Deluded Detectives," in *On Poe: The Best from American Literature,* eds. Louis J. Budd and Edwin H. Cady (Durham, N.C.: Duke University Press, 1993), 172-73.

4. Voltaire, Vidoq, Shakespeare, and Sophocles' *Oedipus Rex* are all cited as contributors to the development of the detective story.

5. While Doyle made his own contributions, he openly acknowledged his debt to Poe: "Where was the detective story until Poe breathed the breath of life into it?" (A. E. Murch, *The Development of the Detective Novel* [New York: Greenwood, 1968], 83). He further said that "Poe's masterful detective, M. Dupin, had from my childhood been one of my heroes" (Leroy Lad Panek, *An Introduction to the Detective Story* [Bowling Green, Ohio: Bowling Green University Press, 1987], 77).

6. "The Murders in the Rue Morgue," in *Edgar Allan Poe: Tales and Sketches,* vol. 1, ed. Thomas Ollive Mabbott (Urbana: University of Illinois Press, 1978), 532. All subsequent references to works by Poe will refer to this edition unless otherwise specified.

7. Leroy Lad Panek, *An Introduction to the Detective Story* (Bowling Green, Ohio: Bowling Green University Press, 1987), 277.

8. Poe is trying to become Dupin himself, as the case is based closely on the actual murder of Mary Rogers in New York City.

9. David Ketterer, *The Rationale of Deception in Poe* (Baton Rouge: Louisiana State University Press, 1979), xii, 1.

10. On Hitchcock's doubleness, see Leslie Brill, *The Hitchcock Romance: Love and Irony in Hitchcock's Films* (Princeton: Princeton University Press, 1988), 73-74. He sees both irony and romance in Hitchcock's vision in tension—at once opposite and identical. Richard Allen, "Hitchcock, or the Pleasures of Metaskepticism," in *Alfred Hitchcock: Centenary Essays,* eds. Richard Allen and S. Ishi Gonzales (London: BFI, 1999), 222, responds to Brill, claiming that he privileges romance, which reduces the tension Brill claims. Allen defines Hitchcock's doubleness as a mixture of irony and romance; Hitchcock "at once affirms the reality of appearances and affirms the 'fiction' or romance appearances serve to sustain, yet, at the same time, calls into question the reality of appearances, and by doing so undermines the 'fiction' or romance of exposing its fictiveness."

11. Alfred Hitchcock, BBC interview by Huw Wheldon in "Monitor," *The Listener,* August 6, 1964, 190.

12. Tony Magistrale and Sidney Poger, *Poe's Children: Connections between Tales of Terror and Detection* (New York: Peter Lang, 1999), 4.

13. John T. Irwin, *The Mystery to a Solution: Poe, Borges, and the Analytic Detective Story* (Baltimore: Johns Hopkins University Press, 1994), 318.

14. Two exceptions in Poe are "The Pit and the Pendulum," in which order is restored deus ex machina in the end, and "Descent into the Maelstrom," which like a detective tale restores order through the careful observation and analysis of the protagonist in getting out of the whirlpool.

15. Daniel Hoffmann, *Poe, Poe, Poe, Poe, Poe, Poe, Poe* (New York: Avon, 1972), 107-8.

16. Loisa Nygaard, "Winning the Game: Inductive Reasoning in Poe's 'Murders in the Rue Morgue,'" *Studies in Romanticism,* 33 (1994): 225.

17. Eric Rohmer and Claude Chabrol, *Hitchcock: The First Forty-Four Films,* trans. Stanley Hochman (New York: Frederick Unger, 1957), 27; Thomas Leitch, *Find the Director, and Other Hitchcock Games* (Athens: University of Georgia Press, 1991), 66-67. Maurice Yacowar claims that *Stage Fright* (1950) and *Trouble with Harry* (1957) are the only other whodunits Hitchcock made (*Hitchcock's British Films* [Hamden, Conn.: Archon, 1977], 123).

18. David Halliburton, *Edgar Allan Poe: A Phenomenological View* (Princeton: Princeton University Press, 1973), 237.

19. Tonia Modleski, *The Women Who Knew Too Much: Hitchcock and Feminist Theory* (New York: Methuen, 1988), 32.

20. Ketterer, *Rationale of Deception,* 242.

21. Page 3 of shooting script, quoted in Yacowar, 130.

22. See William Rothman, *Hitchcock: The Murderous Gaze* (Cambridge: Harvard University Press, 1982), 84.

23. This sequence echoes the earlier shot series in the jury room when Sir John is surrounded and the following dialogue is essentially repeated a number of times: (1) Sir John is told a fact that condemns Diana, (2) at which another juror says "That's right," (3) followed by the jury in unison chanting, "Any answer for that, Sir John?" (4) to which Sir John answers wearily, "Not at the moment."

24. See Susan Smith, *Hitchcock: Suspense, Humor, and Tone* (London: BFI, 2000), 17, 35-36.

25. Modleski, *Women Who Knew Too Much,* 26, 36.

26. Rohmer and Chabrol, *Hitchcock,* 120.

27. See Peter Bordonaro, "*Dial M for Murder*: A Play by Frederick Knott/A Film by Alfred Hitchcock," *Sight and Sound* 45, no. 3 (1976), for a thorough

examination of how Hitchcock makes Tony more sympathetic while adding emphasis to Margot's adulterous guilt. The result complicates the play and problematizes audience response to the characters.

28. Leitch points out that the flat becomes a series of traps: for Swann, then Margot, and finally for Tony himself (163).

29. Irwin, *Mystery*, 320.

Terry Fairchild (essay date December 2004)

SOURCE: Fairchild, Terry. "Maharishi Vedic Science and Literary Theory." *Consciousness, Literature, and the Arts* 5, no. 3 (December 2004): http://blackboard.lincoln.ac.uk/bbcswebdav/users/dmeyerdinkgrafe/archive/fairchild2.html.

[*In the following essay, Fairchild uses the principles of Maharishi Vedic Science, an application of ancient Hindu scripture, to reveal the trifold development of human consciousness represented by the minister, the prefect, and Dupin in "The Purloined Letter."*]

PART I: EVOLUTION OF A CRITICAL METHOD

TEXTUALITY AND CONTEMPORARY THEORY

Literary theory has *always* existed. There have always been those who read and interpreted literary texts. Both Plato and Aristotle were literary critics. Plato read the poets, found them wanting, and banned them from his *Utopia*. Aristotle critiqued Sophocles' *Oedipus Rex* and in doing so founded the western tradition of literary theory. Even the Prince of Peace, Jesus Christ, can be viewed as a literary critic. Interpreting the law of Jehovah, he tossed the Pharisees from the temple. As the custodian of the ten commandments, Moses too must have been a critic. Even the mythical Adam and Eve operate as critics when they interpreted the original covenant between man and God. Every philosopher, every artist, every sage critiques the textual artifacts that precede them. This is the operative explanation of literary criticism today. Everything in existence is a text; every text is inter-related with every other text, past, present, and future, and every person is, thus, involved in textual analysis by continuously "reading" the world we are involved in.

Following this line, Maharishi Mahesh Yogi is arguably the greatest literary critic of the age. He has completely reinterpreted the body of Vedic literature and restored its effectiveness to its original enlightened value. Maharishi accomplishes this elevation of Vedic literature by founding it on Consciousness, the source of all creation that gives rise to and governs every aspect of existence. In the introduction to his translation and commentary on the Bhagavad-Gita, Maharishi justifies adding one more explanation to a scripture that has been critiqued more that any other literary text:

> Wise commentators, in their attempt to fulfill the need of their times, have revealed the truth of the teaching as they found it. By so doing they have secured a place in the history of human thought. They stand out as torchbearers on the long corridor of time. They have fathomed great depths of the ocean of wisdom. Yet with all their glorious achievements they have not brought out the central point of the *Bhagavad-Gita*. It is unfortunate that the very essence of this ancient wisdom should have been missed.[1]

Maharishi's rationale for applying another commentary to a text that has been analyzed more than any other reveals the essential need for literary theory. It isn't enough for a text to just say whatever the author intended it to say. A text "read" well enough, Maharishi has explained, can transform the life of a reader. If the consciousness of the reader is sufficiently developed, the reader can discover in any text the finest level of creation, the most subtle laws of nature, the absolute, transcendental, source of life itself. The act of reading, the experience of critical practice, has the potential to be for the reader the vehicle for Self-regeneration. This is the value of literary texts, and taken in this sense, literary criticism emerges as one of the noblest and most indispensable professions.

Although literary theory can be demonstrated to have always existed, it has existed as a profession for a little more than a century. The rise of literary theory coincided with the change of the university. The old university that predated the twentieth century was a system of privilege dominated by class and gender. Its ostensible purpose was to refine the sons of the socially and economic elite, shaping them to be the rulers of nations. The curriculum was heavily weighted in the arts, sciences, and philosophy, and its aim was broad-based in scope. But by the late nineteenth century, democracy had reared its inexorable head, and institutions throughout the globe were under siege to change. Universities, at the instigation of a much more inclusive society, began to transform themselves from dispensers of a general education into institutions that prepared students for specific occupations. Literature, a product of the old guard, found itself in the position of having to reinvent itself or parish altogether. One of its first endeavors was to increase its importance in the university. Enter F. R. Leavis.

DEVELOPMENT OF A PROFESSIONAL PRACTICE

Leavis, his future wife Q. D. Roth, I. A. Richards, and other members of the Cambridge movement in the early twentieth century redefined the role of the literary critic. Their predecessors, symbolized and vilified by Terry Eagleton in the guise of Sir Arthur Quiller Couch, were privileged aristocrats who created the literary canon out of social preference. Their reading of literary works has come to be known as the "common sense" approach, which consisted of little more than agreeing with the author and stating the obvious. Leavis fashioned a professional method of analyzing literature that emphasized closely adhering to the "words on the page." This form of *close reading* eliminated much of the opinionated analysis that had passed for literary criticism. This new criticism was guided by rigid standards that held both the critic and the work itself accountable for the meanings they produced. Even more important than its methodology of reading, however, was the enormous value Leavis and his followers attributed to English literature:

> In the early 1920's it was desperately unclear why English was worth studying at all; by the early 1930's it had become a question of why it was worth wasting your time on anything else. English was not only a subject worth studying, but also *the* supremely civilizing pursuit, the spiritual essence of the social formation.[2]

Concurrent with the movement spearheaded by the Leavises, in their journal *Scrutiny,* was a sympathetic form of literary analysis led by T. S. Eliot now known as *New Criticism.* At the basis of New Criticism was a belief in the hierarchical supremacy of great literature. Certain literature could be proved to be universal, to have a spiritual unity, that existed separately from its author and the circumstances of its creation. New Critics, influenced by Asian theology, shared the method of the Scrutineers in reading the words on the page. They were further motivated, however, to resolve a work's tensions by closely examining its techniques and ultimately searching for an overall textual unity (*logocentric*). Because great literature was timeless, the New Critics argued, it must be judged on its own merits, free from the time-bound context of author, history, and environment (*ahistorical*). This removal from its historical conditions was seen by a new set of literary theorists, a group raised on Marxist socialism and Freudian relativism, as artificial, false, and self-serving.

Marxist sociological critics were in particular put off by New Criticism since its universalism flew in the face of their most cherished beliefs. Karl Marx preached a form of social evolution based on and demonstrated by historical process. Prior to the Renaissance, a small, economically privileged, landed-aristocracy dominated Europe into the twentieth century. However, by the end of the Medieval period, a rising middle-class had already begun to challenge the political and economic power of the aristocrats.

This social and economic revolution had excluded any similar alteration among the working classes, but it set a precedence, according to Marx, for a later proletarian revolution. Marx saw as the ideal conditions for such a revolution in the Nineteenth century with the abuses of the Industrial Revolution. Literary criticism in the twentieth century eventually picked up Marx's ideas, as it does with all significant theories of life, and began to analyze literary texts as the products of their social context and historical change.

Later during the "revolutionary 60's" another major socio-political movement emerged. A second wave of feminism began examining every kind of gender interaction, including those found in literature. A huge field, feminism and its methods vary even more widely than those of Marxism. An early form of feminist literary criticism protested against male constructed images of women—the *femme fatale,* the goddess, the shrew, the domestic, etc. Such images, feminists argued, were facile stereotypes that conformed to male perceptions. Moreover, they propagated the dominant position men have exploited in gender relationships throughout history. As feminist literary criticism gained momentum, it began to engage in more sophisticated tactics. It urged women, for example, to "read against the grain," to "read as a woman," to find in literature not the obvious, but a portrait of women that adhered to a woman's own experiences and needs. Eventually, women began to seek a "literature of their own." They began a moral reshaping of the literary canon, constructed from an academic old boy's network, into a more balanced reflection of gender perspectives.

The examples of Marxist and Feminist criticism demonstrate that literature in the twentieth century was becoming at least in analogy as complicated as life itself. It therefore demanded multitudinous ways to examine it. Readers in the twentieth century were no longer content to simply find in a work of literature those meanings intended by the author (*intentional fallacy*). Literature had become more like a prism that reflected different colors depending on the angle from which it was examined. Disciplines that had developed with no thought of literature were now being applied to literary texts copiously. Freudian psychology is an apt example. Critics somewhere along the line began to realize that characters in stories behaved like people in life. Armed with this assumption, critics could now make the simple jump in logic that it would be possible to psychoanalyze characters as a way of coming to grips with a work of literature. As a result, such familiar Freudian ideas as the *Oedipus Complex,* repression, the unconsciousness, and the Id-Ego-Superego relationship, began showing up regularly in the examination of literary characters. Hamlet, in one famous essay, was Freudianly critiqued for his obsessive relationship with his mother, the operative factor in his inability to act. A further development of Freudian criticism was that not only could characters be subjected to the psychoanalytic method but so could the literary texts that contained them. For example, feminist critics argued that male writers repressed the idea of patriarchy (male dominance). Feminists argued that the idea of chivalry, for instance, emerged as a way of hiding and repressing the male need to maintain control of women.

The Scrutineers, New Criticism, Marxism and Feminism were all movements that developed as attempts to assess literature's content—plot, character, theme, symbols, sound devices, tropes and so forth, along with its moral, ethical, spiritual, political, economic, social, and psychological characteristics. A second strand of literary criticism that parallels (and often superimposes) the one we have been considering targets a literary work's formal properties as a way of knowing it. As scientific analysis gained steam in the previous century, the humanities began to look for ways of incorporating science into what had been previously inhospitable realms. But science's suitability as a vehicle for criticism can again be taken from the rationale that literature is an expression of life. And if life can stand up to scientific scrutiny so should literature. One form scientific inquiry took was the search for fundamental patterns that transcend racial and cultural boundaries. Myth critics, inspired by Carl Jung's study of archetypes, looked beyond the more superficial qualities of a work to find those essences that were not only universal but also essential. Examples of universal forms in literature include unconditional love, the passage from youth into adulthood, and the quest for ultimate meaning. The details of such *archetypes* varied greatly from work to work and culture to culture, but the pattern, the deeper less material form, would be virtually the same. Among the most renown myth critics are Northrop Frye and Joseph Campbell.

STRUCTURALISM AND POST-STRUCTURALISM

Paralleling myth criticism was a form of anthropology that examined the creation and structure of words and other fundamental elements of language. Vladimir Propp, for example, examined a work of literature not for its narrative sequence but rather for functional aspects that existed from work to work. In an analysis of fairy tales he found such typical elements as the following:

• A difficult task is proposed to the hero.

• The task is resolved.

• The hero is recognized.

• The false hero is villain exposed.

• The false hero is given a new appearance.

• The villain is punished.

• The hero is married and ascends the throne.[3]

Claude Lévi-Strauss does something similar to Propp in his analysis of *Oedipus Rex,* locating its elementary units in what he calls *mythemes.* Such turning away from content to an emphasis on form led to the greatest paradigm shift in literary theory to date, and one that continues to foster academic antagonism. The result of this shift was the development of *Structuralism.* At its foundation is the pioneering work of Swiss linguist Ferdinand de Saussure[4] whose *Course in General Linguistics* (1915), published posthumously, was the catalyst of what was tantamount to a theoretical and linguistic mutiny.

Saussure's most significant component is his division of the word into component parts, *signifier* (the sound image) and *signified* (concept), defining language as "a system of differences with no positive terms."[5] Unlike the Vedic Literature which at the *Pashyanti* level of language unifies a word form with its meaning, the relevance of this division is that it introduces enormous arbitrariness into life. Following the train of logic of Saussure's disciples, because language is the basis of human thought and utterance, a divided language intrinsically introduces randomness into all human experience. Human beings are thus trapped in their language systems.[6] They cannot act without thinking, and thinking is determined by language. Every thought, according to Structuralist ideology, is determined by the social biases of a given place and time, leaving us one and all at the mercy of an ever shifting maze of language. This is a sobering notion if we consider the limitations of a language-generated thought as essential for the dual processes of interpretation and communication. Gustave Flaubert once pointed out the limitations of language:

> It "is like a cracked kettle on which we hammer out tunes to make bears dance,
>
> when what we long for is the compassion of the stars."[7]

The second pillar of linguistic literary criticism, built upon its predecessor, is Post-Structuralism. The birth child of the most commanding critical figure of the twentieth century—Jacques Derrida—Post-Structuralism is as ingenious as it is disturbing. Derrida was concerned with the continuous attempt of history to establish an authoritative center (being, presence), be it Allah, Jehovah, Indra, Marx, science, etc. The consequences of such *logocentrism* is the establishment of tyrannies throughout time and the abuses that have accompanied them. Derrida, through his concept of *deconstruction,* discovered a way to at least theoretically undermine logocentrism and establish a foundational democracy inherent in nature. Derrida's position is that all "violent hierarchies" are social constructs with the first term in the hierarchy privileged over the second: Adam/Eve, good/bad, man/woman, white/black, conscious/unconscious, speech/writing, and so forth. Derrida demonstrates that through deconstruction hierarchies can be analyzed and reversed and then done away with by resisting creating a new hierarchy out of the reversal.

Along with deconstruction, Derrida's most important theoretical brainchild is *différancé*. Derrida's coinage is a combination of two different but related terms: to differ, a spatial concept derived from the difference located in the two halves of the sign (signifier and signified), and to defer, a temporal quality suggesting that meaning is always deferred over time. Expanding on Saussure, Derrida holds that not only is a sign (word) divided in form and meaning, but it's signified (concept) is actually just another signifier (mark) looking for another signified. He argues his position by pointing out that when we look up a word's definition in the dictionary what we find is not closure, but just more words (signifiers) also in need of definitions (signifieds), *ad infinitum*. Hence, the profound implications of *différancé* for Derrida, are that meaning can never be absolutely achieved. In fact, his hypothesis suggests that all understanding and all communication are fragmented, spread out over an infinite chain of elusive signifiers. This means we can never fully know what we think and never completely say what we believe. Even more disturbing is that since the self is discovered through language, according to post-structuralists, the self can never really be known. To put it simply, we are condemned to live a form of controlled anarchy. Derrida is not completely incorrect, but his ideas are only applicable at a grosser experience of the world. It is possible to go beyond such troublesome assumptions and erect a more palatable literary theory founded on an absolute basis that is universally accessible. This theory exists as Maharishi Vedic Science, a comprehensive body of knowledge that acknowledges the ability to transcend differences to a field of absolute consciousness through the practice of the Transcendental Meditation technique.

MAHARISHI VEDIC SCIENCE AS LITERARY THEORY

Maharishi didn't develop Vedic Science to be literary theory, but neither were most of the critical practices we have encountered. Nevertheless, each provides fresh insights into the nature of literature and an access to a literary work's subtext not previously available. Maharishi Vedic Science similarly expands the meaning of literature but advances it far beyond other literary theories. The goal of Maharishi Vedic Science is to take a human being from ignorance and suffering to a state of eternal bliss in unity consciousness. This aim, so far beyond lesser ideological systems, makes calling it literary theory almost demeaning. However, because Maharishi Vedic Science is so inclusive, it can simultaneously wear the hats of smaller but important disciplines; it can be science, economics, an approach to health, a theory of management, a theory of architecture, and also literary theory.

The mistake of those who have had little familiarity with critical practice is to believe that literary theory's purpose is simply to make texts clearer and to reveal some of their "artistic" features. If these were ever the legitimate aims of literary theory, such meager aspirations have long been surpassed. To look at literature as something that can be reduced to a few cogent observations, is to see it as simply entertainment, hardly more than fashionable indulgence. If literary works were no more than a fascinating but complex story, a pleasant but ingenious poem, then Plato would have been right to toss the poets from his Utopia, and he may as well add the readers who revere literature as well. But for many, not unlike the rosy-eyed devotees of F. R. Leavis, literature is eminently vital and of essential worth, a worth routinely overlooked by pragmatists. And it is this need to illustrate literature's value, to bring it to the public as well as the academic eye, that has given rise to the corollary discipline of literary theory.

Literature, like music and painting, like architecture, like gardening, like any aesthetic endeavor that has constantly evolved, says more than I am the product of a culturally advanced time and place. It is an artifact alive with those commonly overlooked expressions of inherent nature, of cosmic beauty, of divine truth and justice, of God in whatever form, by a society engaged in the mundane pursuit of material existence. It is the link to our higher selves, the lost cord to our glorious pre-historical past. Maharishi says that literature contains the consciousness of the artist structured within it. If the consciousness is high enough, the depth of what can be discovered in literature is enormous. And Literary Theory in its various forms is the means we use to mine the treasures of literature. If we are merely satisfied in knowing whether a plot is closed or open-ended, a character is static or dynamic, a poem is an Italian rather than an English sonnet, then any old literary theory will suffice. However, if we expect from literature the promise of a more refined existence, a life that is better because we have read, then the choice of literary theory is significant. Maharishi, as literary theorist, says that literature seen through the lens of Vedic Science can take one to unity consciousness. A total transformation of one's being is undoubtedly the most audacious promise of literature, of literary theory, and of the reader. It is what makes Maharishi Vedic Science not just a literary theory but a theory that can bring all other theories to fulfillment.

Maharishi Vedic Science is a body of knowledge based upon the Veda—*Total Knowledge*⁸ see Appendix for a full treatise on Total Knowledge] and Vedic literature. The field of Total Knowledge underlies, gives rise to, and supports all manifest creation. The Vedic literature are those literary texts, not composed by men but divinely cognized by enlightened sages. They embody the Laws of Nature—the first expressions of the Veda—and the techniques for individual beings to rise to complete freedom and bliss in *Brahma Chetna*—unity consciousness. Maharishi Vedic Science deals with universal qualities found in the Vedic literature belonging to enlightened societies and enlightened beings. These qualities found throughout creation are generally overlooked because time has withered away our capacity to see our natural status (created in the image of God) and our means to rise to a full valuation of our lives.

Maharishi has stated that one way of understanding enlightenment is as a re-identification with pure consciousness—the field of Total Knowledge—that is, a realization that the unbounded, eternal, non-material field of transcendental consciousness lying beyond one's physical existence is one's true, fundamental Self. The most direct route to such an identification Maharishi states is through the Transcendental Meditation and TM-Sidhi Program that allow the mind to transcend the world of change and destruction and know the field of non-changing immortality and, then, to function from this level of mistake-free life. A way one might enhance this process of Self development is to gravitate towards and identify with the most refined and most universal elements in life, including works of literature. Hence, when Maharishi Vedic Science is used to critique a literary text it is employed to do more than just comprehend what an author has written, it is used to actually aid a person's evolution. This is a value that no other literary theory can assert.

In 1968 Roland Barthes stunned the literary world with his now famous essay "The Death of the Author."⁹ Barthes' position is that "individual utterances are the product of impersonal language systems." His outlandish statement is meant to indicate that different modes and different levels of meaning exist unknown to a text's composer. Maharishi willingly acknowledges a writer's contribution when he says a literary work contains the consciousness of the writer. He also recognizes a range of linguistic significance beyond

the knowledge of most writers, beginning with *Baikhari*, spoken speech, language experienced by the senses; to *Madhyama*, mental or intellectual speech; to *Pashyanti*, the finest impulse of speech; to *Para*, the vibrant, silent, preverbal source of language. Through the practice of Maharishi's Transcendental Meditation and TM-Sidhi program this range of language can be experienced and known. Maharishi also, not unlike *reader-response* critics, acknowledges the reader's role in creating meaning apart from the author. As readers' consciousness expand, by means of Maharishi Vedic Science, they discover an ever-increasing profundity in a text. So complete is a literary text, that Maharishi once said a single word known in its entirety is enough to fully transform an individual from ignorance to enlightenment. This is the immense scope and profundity of Maharishi Vedic Science as a literary theory.

PART II: LITERARY THEORY IN PRACTICE

UNVEILING "THE PURLOINED LETTER"

Edgar Allan Poe's **"The Purloined Letter"** is a charming tale that along with **"The Murders in the Rue Morgue"** has historical significance for helping to establish the mystery story. But beyond that there is little in it that immediately accounts for its being the object of intense criticism by some of the most celebrated critics of our time. Barbara Johnson, one of those critics, gives an explanation for its importance. She says, all works of literature beg the reader to re-read them. Poe's story does so more than most:

> A literary text that both analyzes itself and shows that it actually has neither a self nor any neutral metalanguage with which to do the analyzing calls out irresistibly for analysis.¹⁰

If we ignore, for a moment, the self-reflexive quality of Poe's story that Johnson alludes to, its repressed plot, and its hydra-headed meaning, what we first experience is a simple exercise in deduction. The Prefect of the Parisian police, a somewhat pompous and facile man, is frustrated by his department's failure to locate an incriminating letter "purloined from the royal apartments." As the affair is both simple and baffling, it is beyond the Prefect. In dejection he turns to the famous detective Dupin to bail him out. He lays before Dupin the facts of the case: An incriminating letter has been taken from the Queen placing her honor in peril if revealed. "The individual who purloined it is known; this beyond a doubt; he was seen to take it. It is known, also, that it still remains in his possession" (p. 209). Minister D—, the Prefect explains, undoubtedly has the letter in his apartment. This is a certainty, because in order to perpetuate his blackmail he must be able to produce it at a moment's notice. Armed with this knowledge, the Parisian police, using the most advanced methods of detection, have more than once sifted every corner of D—'s apartment and each time failed to procure the letter. From this summary, Dupin makes an immediate deduction. If the police have looked *everywhere* the letter might be hidden, the Minister must, therefore, have placed it in plain sight. Dupin, being an acquaintance and a member of the thief's social class, contrives to visit the Minister. To the utter astonishment of the Prefect, Dupin miraculously retrieves the letter and returns it to its proper owner.

What intrigues contemporary critics most about **"The Purloined Letter"** is not its ingenious plot, but rather the manner in which the letter, at the center of the story, functions as a text within the frame of a larger text, the story itself. The letter as text has meaning beyond any designs Poe may have had for it, meaning that will vary from reader to reader and from context to context.

Jacques Lacan's essay, "Seminar on 'The Purloined Letter,'" illustrates the dominant direction of critical theory since the middle of the past century. His purpose is not simply to offer another analysis of Poe's mystery story; it is meant to provide a new way of looking at texts in general and even a "new way to read ourselves."[11] Modern critical theorists, as stated above, have set out to extend the range of both critical analysis and literary relevance. From a wide variety of philosophical perspectives, they have demonstrated that literary texts have far greater significance than is usually understood. Literary texts are, if read correctly, maps of the human condition. Lacan, a postmodern psychoanalytic critic, has married Freudian psychology to Saussurean linguistics to form his own unique brand of textual criticism. He interprets **"The Purloined Letter"** in a manner not dissimilar to Freud's interpretation of *Oedipus Rex,* but with the added dimension supplied by Ferdinand de Saussure's boundary-breaking discussion of language as symbol system.[12]

Lacan begins his dissection of **"The Purloined Letter"** by adopting Saussure's position on the function of language. Lacan takes his cue from a pun on the word *letter,* meaning both a literary epistle and the most basic element of language. Let's review Saussure's primary thesis: he begins by postulating that a word is not the stable unit we imagine, with an inherent relationship between meaning and form. A word is actually a symbol, the product of socialization. Its shifting meaning depends upon context: time, place, and set of speakers or writers. Saussure also sees the word as divided into two component parts: a *signifier,* the mark on the page, and a *signified,* the concept the writer is thinking when making the mark. The rela-

tionship between the two elements of the sign is an arbitrary one; therefore, meaning is not imminent. Hence, language is no more than a system of *difference.*

In **"The Purloined Letter,"** according to Lacan, the reader assumes the letter is "real." That is how we, like the Prefect and his gendarmes, are duped. The police are materialists who conceive of the letter as physical, so that is what they look for. But for Lacan it is not the piece of paper that is important, nor even the letter's contents; rather it is simply the control of the letter that is significant. Whoever controls the letter controls its meaning. With this reduction in the import of the letter's actual substance, we are left with a form of *displacement.* This the postmodernists have found in their reading of texts from a reexamination of Saussure. Following Saussure's lead the post-structuralists too see language as a system of differences. But even more disconcerting is their view of meaning, which they contend can never be located because by its relative nature it will always be deferred over time. As we have seen, signifiers (symbols) are always searching for signifieds (meanings), but every time a signified is located it turns out to be just another signifier looking for its own signified. Because the post-structuralist sees human life as language based, it is impossible in this system to ever get to the bottom of who we are. We too are deferred over time. Our lives are also displaced.

Lacan says that language is always absent. Hence, the Prefect looking for an object will never find the letter; it is already gone. What is it, after all, Lacan asks? We are never told the letter's contents, nor are we ever told who wrote it. This prompts Lacan to ask to whom the letter belongs. Is its owner the original composer or its intended recipient? Lacan's conclusion is that "the responsibility of the author of the letter takes second place to that of its holder."[13] This is the position of modern critical theory. A literary text cannot be controlled by its author. It will mean whatever its reader believes it to mean. The queen, since the letter was sent to her, has reason to claim ownership, but she cannot because in so doing she would be compromised. It is thus apparent that the letter—its physical nature and its contents—have been reduced to the level of the abstract and symbolic. The letter, once out of the hands of the author or its recipient, no longer belongs to either. We can say the same for Poe's story. Once it is in the hands of Lacan, or anyone else, the text no longer belongs to Poe.

In Poe's telling of his story, we are led by Dupin as narrator to see the Prefect as a dunce and his attempt to discover the letter simplistic. He is the foil to Minister D—, concocted as a worthy adversary to Dupin of the superior intellect. This, however, is only one form of the story, and textuality has its own way of writing a text. As we have seen, meaning is constantly being deferred. It cannot be *arrested,* but that is exactly what the Minister attempts to do. He wishes to control the queen by controlling the text. However, like Icarus who could not control Apollo's chariot, D— has no more power over the letter than does her royal highness. In fact, he uses the same format of nakedly concealing the text as she had, leaving himself just as vulnerable. Just as she tried to hide it in the open but was exposed to the Minister's eyes, so the Minister attempts to hide the letter in plain site but is exposed to Dupin's eyes.

But if the Minister cannot arrest the text, he can alter it. He does this by literally and symbolically turning the letter inside out. He smudges and tears it, and he adds an address to himself and his own large black D— seal. This is analogous to the act of reading. All readers alter texts when they come into their possession. Even when the letter is no longer in D—'s possession, it will in his mind remain the same exact text until he realizes there has been a switch. Again this demonstrates that a text has value (or meaning) beyond its contents. With the letter no longer in the Minister's possession, Lacan asks, "what remains of a signifier when, it has no more signification?"[14] The answer in **"The Purloined Letter"** is that it will continue to have signification (meaning) as long as anyone still considers it important. The signified just changes as it always does. At the story's end, instead of existing as the form of blackmail against the queen, the letter will cause the downfall of Minister D—.

Much of the significance Lacan derives from **"The Purloined Letter"** has to do with two scenes that contain a triadic structure. The first takes place in the queen's boudoir. In this scene, the "blind" king thinks he knows but does not. Lacan views the king as symbolic of the pure objective. The queen sees that the king does not see, but does not see that the Minister does see. She is for Lacan pure subjectivity. The Minister sees both what the king does not and what the queen does. He, therefore, represents the balance of subjectivity and objectivity. The same triad exists between the Prefect who is blind, the Minister who does not see what Dupin sees, and Dupin who sees what both the Prefect and the Minister do not. Elizabeth Wright has suggested that this relationship to the text between these two groups can stand for the superego (objectivity), the ego (subjectivity), and the linguistic Id (repressed unconsciousness)—the three aspects of human consciousness according to Freud.[15] What Lacan demonstrates is that "reading," which involves the making sense of all human experience (textuality), is intimately a form of self-fashioning.

Jacques Derrida's "The Purveyor of Truth," his response to Lacan, is an example of how *inter-textuality* works. Lacan parasitically creates a text by grafting his essay to Poe's **"The Purloined Letter."** Derrida does the same when he attaches his text to Lacan's as does Barbara Johnson when she grafts hers to Poe, Lacan, and Derrida, and now this text to Poe, Lacan, Derrida, and Johnson. We have seen that a text according to modern theory, rather than having a material existence, is an opportunity for *pluralistic* meanings. There are no original meanings; there is just a reconstitution of meanings. Everything draws upon everything else, and the writer is reduced to a kind of reorganizer. This is what the post-modern Roland Barthes meant when he declared *the death of the author.*

Derrida takes exception to Lacan's reading of **"The Purloined Letter"** as he takes exception to psychoanalytic readings in general. As in the most famous literary, psychoanalytic readings, Freud's analysis of *Oedipus Rex,* Lacan sees literary texts as having a symbolic order analogous to the human unconscious. Uncovering a work's symbolic significance is tantamount to locating its truth. For most *post-structuralists,* texts by their very nature are constructed out of *difference.* They are, therefore, immune to absolute truths. Because meaning is always being deferred, truth can never be contained. Meaning is always in the midst of change, so there is no place to locate truth. At best there is the *trace,* the sense of being able to locate a meaning that has already passed. Acknowledging that truth can be obtained from the reading of a work of literature is acknowledging the existence of authorial supremacy. For Derrida this constitutes *logocentricism,* the recognition of a single, dominant authority for both the text of literature and the text of life. In other words, hegemony.

Textuality works against logocentricism, and Derrida argues that for all of his discussion of signifier and signified, Lacan ignores the actual self-production of the text and reverts instead to a slightly disguised classical interpretation of **"The Purloined Letter."** Moreover, he implicitly accuses Lacan of making himself the author of the text by rewriting it, that is by ignoring the story as a whole and building his case for its "truth" derived from two scenes he has isolated from the rest. Finally, Lacan, according to Derrida, has closed the text in his final statement, "a letter always arrives at its destination."[16] This is a form of "circularity" or unity that the psychoanalyst, a kind of detective like Dupin himself, achieves through an analysis of the text. Derrida, furthermore, accuses Lacan's reading of not only being reductive but also being inaccurate. By ignoring the narrator, Lacan is fixated on the plot, more to the point, a small part of the plot. But because the story is narrated by Dupin's confidante, the story is reflection of the narrator's consciousness. By ignoring the narrator's shaping of the story is to misread the entire story. This is what Derrida accuses psychoanalysis of always doing. It does not read the text as it exists; it reads a text as psychoanalysis, as itself.

Derrida's criticism of Lacan is not what it first appears. Derrida seems to be deriding Lacan for his faulty reading of literature. To some extent this is true. More true is that Derrida is using Lacan as an occasion to put forth his own ideas. Consciously or unconsciously, this is the nature of all textual interactions. We reinvent a text to satisfy our own view of the world. Barbara Johnson says that no analysis "can intervene without transforming and repeating other elements in a sequence" (p. 410). When we read, she explains, we both fill in the gaps that we feel are missing and misread when we feel it is convenient to do so, something she demonstrates in both Lacan's reading of **"The Purloined Letter"** and Derrida's reading of both Poe and Lacan: "since Lacan's text is read as if it said what Derrida says it says" (p. 415).

By now it should be apparent that neither Lacan, Derrida, nor Johnson are interested in examining a work of literature in the classical sense, that is, simply to make sense of it and pointing out some of its *artistic* features. It should also be clear that they do not regard a work of literature purely as a creative endeavor. They see literary works as texts in a way that all forms of communication are texts. And because everything in existence communicates, everything arguably is a text. They have thus used literary criticism as a means to enter into a dialogue about the meaning of life. Lacan, who sees a literary text as a form of consciousness, believes it can be psychoanalyzed in a similar way to human beings with similar results. Derrida sees a text as a single moment already passed in an infinite chain of texts always in flux. And Barbara Johnson sees the reading of texts as a form of transformation that is continuously altering what a text is.

All of these approaches to analyzing literature have discovered something fundamental about the nature of texts and the nature of reading, although Derrida would object to the word fundamental. However, because of the fragmented way in which they perceive, none of these critics ever approach a text's fullest possibilities. A text may be read in an almost infinite variety of ways, but to know its essence it must be understood from a position of unshakeable truth. This is possible through Maharishi's techniques that raise the consciousness of both the writer and the reader of texts. And these are supplemented by his development of

Maharishi Vedic Science, a system of knowledge whose range of consideration is all inclusive, from "the smallest of the smallest to the largest of the largest."

READING AS A MAHARISHI VEDIC SCIENTIST

A "Maharishi Vedic Scientist," one who adheres to Maharishi's exposition on evolution and the Vedas, reads literature with certain firm precepts. Like the physical scientist who begins an investigation with a comprehension that sub-atomic particles exist, the Vedic Scientist enters into any inquiry with an understanding of the existence of Total Knowledge. But what separates Vedic Scientists from other literary theorists is that the knowledge that makes up their critical practice is not simply speculative. It is based upon the empirical evidence from having regularly experienced the state of pure consciousness, the field of Total Knowledge, along with confirmations from the various fields of modern science. Hence we begin with the affirmation that not only does Total Knowledge— the eternal Veda—exist, it has always existed, and it is knowledge supremely worth knowing. It is the source, course, and goal of all knowledge. At certain times in history, the reality of Total Knowledge is more apparent than at others. But it never ceases to be because it is the most fundamental field of life that gives birth to everything in creation. It is the nature of Total Knowledge to make itself known, but because the structure of phenomenal existence is cyclical, there will be times when Total Knowledge is well known and times when it is little known. And yet there will always be those who know of its existence and how to access it. Such individuals we call seers.

There are an almost infinite number of ways a text can be approached from the perspective of Maharishi Vedic Science because as the field of Consciousness its possibilities are infinite. But I am going to progress with this idea that Total Knowledge exists and its existence can be known. Moreover, understanding that Total Knowledge exists changes fundamentally how any text is understood. This introduction of Total Knowledge into any intellectual consideration is similar to suddenly discovering your house has a whole other wing, one that is more magnificent than the house you have been occupying all your life. Once known, the house can never be looked upon in the same limited way.

"THE PURLOINED LETTER" THROUGH THE EYE OF MAHARISHI VEDIC SCIENCE

Derrida, Lacan, and Johnson are correct that the epistle is the key to **"The Purloined Letter."** However, the letter is more than simply an opportunity to exert power, the way Lacan symbolically sees it. If we look carefully how the letter functions, in an all inclusive way, changing with each circumstance and each character, we can say it exists as the representative of Total Knowledge—the field of all possibilities. The reason the letter functions as Total Knowledge is due in part to its non-material character. As we have seen, its contents are never known. Secondly, its physical existence undergoes continuous transformation, not unlike Derrida's signified, so that its existence can never be fully arrested. The Prefect can not see it because physically it has a specific shape to him that is already absent. The Minister changes its shape with the idea of capturing it and making it his own. And Dupin changes it again to the point of completely replacing it, while to the Minister it remains the same letter. In this respect, the protean letter imitates the non-physical, attributeless, field of Total Knowledge. But more important than its lack of permanent physical characteristics, is its self-referral nature. Maharishi most prominently identifies Total Knowledge with the quality of self-referral [see Appendix]. Completely self-contained, it manifests without manifesting, creates without effort, and causes the inconceivable universe without diminishment. As a person comes to know the field of Total Knowledge through the Transcendental Meditation technique, the experience is also one of self-referral. One experiences what one always has been. Self-referral is also the experience of the seeker of knowledge who evolves from one state of Higher Consciousness. The letter functions like this in Poe's story. As each character comes in contact with the letter, what each sees is his or her self. Theoretically, this is the way all texts work. Ironically, Derrida accuses Lacan of looking at the letter and seeing himself, but this is what we all do. In Poe's story, the text of the letter just allows that self-referral experience to happen more easily. It can do that because the letter operates more as a self-referral opportunity than an ordinary epistle. Finally, because of its abstract nature, the letter behaves as a primary characteristic of Total Knowledge—total potential. The letter exists for each character either as the fulfillment of desire or moral retribution.

Let's examine the relationship of the letter to each of the story's major characters. The Prefect's connection to the letter is the simplest. He is a materialist steeped in ignorance who only knows how to operate from the most sensual and obvious approaches to knowledge. He cannot see what is directly in front of him because he possesses a restricted consciousness. Total Knowledge is beyond his grasp because he possesses neither the imagination nor the techniques to acquire it. He can only act in a sensual and rational manner. The letter on the Minister's bulletin board symbolizes the multiple possibilities of Total Knowledge which is both stable and dynamic. It changes with time and circumstance while remaining ever the same. It is always the letter, but it is simultaneously a different letter for everyone it touches. This is the nature of Total Knowledge. It is the field that expresses itself as infinite creation while remaining eternally unchanged. The Prefect, deceived by his senses, can only perceive things that are static. The letter to him is the letter the queen described. That letter no longer exists. It is the nature of the field of change to hide. What cannot be hidden, to those who see, is that value of life that never changes. To a person fully enlightened, nothing is hidden. Such a person sees Total Knowledge in everything in creation. But for all his ignorance, the Prefect does the best thing he can. He seeks the assistance of someone with greater awareness than himself, that is Dupin. In all traditions, this is the pattern of the seeker of knowledge surrendering to the knower of knowledge. Until the seeker actually asks, help cannot be given.

Dupin is the seer in the story. Maharishi has pointed out that a person with expanded awareness not only sees what others do not, that person sees what is lacking in someone else's sight. Dupin *immediately* sees the fallacy in the Prefect's thinking. This is an essential point. It demonstrates that there are no boundaries to Dupin's vision. He may on one level of the story be a cunning logician; he also functions as one from whom truth cannot be hidden. Once the Prefect confesses that the case of the purloined letter is both simple and baffling, Dupin observes that "Perhaps it is the very simplicity of the thing which puts you at fault . . . perhaps the mystery is a little *too* plain" (p. 209). Again, this statement indicates Dupin's status. Not only are there no boundaries to his vision, there are no boundaries to his success. Total Knowledge is the simplest state of awareness. For those who function on the level of Total Knowledge, achievement is both simple and easy. For the ignorant, life is complex and difficult. The Prefect with all of his resources cannot discover the letter. On the other hand, he no sooner gives the details of the case, and already Dupin sees the answer. If all possible complexities are eliminated then simplicity is the only possibility.

Poe sets Dupin up to be a kind of detective genius, the precursor of Sherlock Holmes and Hercule Poirot, but he possesses much more than genius. History is crammed full of superior intellects with myopic vision. Dupin's intellect is supplemented by a developed consciousness. He judges less on a case's facts and more on his insights into an opponent's character. He deduces that the Parisian police, including the Prefect, see only what is like themselves; "they consider only their own ideas of ingenuity" (p. 216). The Prefect regards Minister D— a fool because he writes poetry. Anything that lies outside the Prefect's range of consciousness is beyond him. Maharishi explains this concept in the keystone verse of the Rk Veda, the essence of Total Knowledge. One part of the verse asks the question, yStNn vedÖ ikm>>ûc; kijr,,yitÖ (yastanna veda kim richa karisyati) "he whose awareness is not open to this field [Total Knowledge] what can the verses accomplish for him?" (Maharishi (1996) p. 138)[17] The RK Veda is the eternal scripture of absolute truth. It describes the means to rise from ignorance into enlightenment. But the verses can do nothing for the person who is not awake to them. The Prefect can only imagine the world as he perceives it. The possibility that the letter could be hidden in plain site just does not exist for the Prefect; just as the field of Transcendental Consciousness—Total Knowledge—will not exist for the complete materialist. To convince one otherwise, one might as well be speaking in a different language. The Prefect's lack of awareness accounts for his utter amazement (that leaves him speechless) when Dupin produces the letter. He walks away in a befuddled fog because he cannot fathom that Dupin has accomplished what to him was impossible.

Dupin also possesses an awareness expanded enough to comprehend a consciousness completely different than the Prefect's—the mind of Minister D—. Where the Prefect longs for knowledge, D— desires power. A complete egoist, the Minister is an opportunist alert to possibilities for self-gratification and control. One such opportunity presents itself as the Queen's compromising letter. Because he is an egoist, D— is unmoved by the pain he causes others. In fact, suffering is the means for him to wield power which he perceives as the ultimate good. Insensitivity to another's pain is an indication of his severe limitations. Consciousness is all compassionate. It is that element of existence that promotes unity rather than diversity. It unites life rather than seeks out differences. In *Brahma Chetna,* when an individual rises to unity consciousness, differences remain on the superficial level of life, but simultaneously one realizes that all of creation, every single person, is none other than one's own unbounded Self. It is why the enlightened engage in the activity of *ahimsa,* causing no harm to anyone. The reality of life—on the level of Total Knowledge—is that everything is the same undifferentiated, eternal Consciousness. Acting from this level, the thought does not even arise to cause pain to another. Conversely, that the Minister can distribute pain indiscriminately is an indication of just how unbalanced he is in life.

Augmenting D—'s need for power is his exceptional intellect. For Poe it is the intellect that constitutes the battlefield between D— and Dupin. To demonstrate that Dupin is a formidable opponent, Poe contrasts his intellectual powers with the ordinary minds of the narrator (a predecessor of Watson) and the Prefect. Moreover, Poe digresses from the plot for several pages to let us witness Dupin's extraordinary intelligence at work. But intellect is only one factor in the equation that allows Dupin to out maneuver the Minister. If victory were dependent solely upon intelligence, D— would never have been bested.

The Minister of **"The Purloined Letter"** possesses an almost unequalled mind. He, first of all, in the presence of the king understands that the Queen is attempting to hide a letter from her husband. She proves successful with her spouse but not the Minister. Secondly, D— immediately calculates the letter's value for him, how he can turn it to devious advantage. Once he comprehends its worth, he on the spot devises a plan to purloin it right before the queen's eyes. His superior intellect, moreover, gives him the boldness and audacity to engage in personal conflict with a royal personage. He also reasons with what desperation the queen will attempt to retrieve the letter. Moreover, he conceptualizes the police's limitations and capabilities and the action they will take. Finally, it is his intellect that leads him to an impudent display of the purloined letter in plain view, only slightly disguised. What Minister D— does not see is the backlash his actions will produce. Acting only out of indulgence for his own small self, he violates not only the queen, but as the people's royal representative, the whole national populace. Acting solely within the confines of his unbridled intellect, his actions are cruel and harmful, gross violations of Natural Law.

The queen also violates Natural Law, and it is the cause of the difficult spot she finds herself. We may not know exactly what the letter contains, and Poe was perceptive enough to leave it intentionally vague, but we realize she has committed a serious indiscretion that has left her vulnerable. She has, furthermore, allowed herself to be placed under the power of the unmerciful D—. Again we see the function of the letter as Total Knowledge. For the Prefect, it could do nothing for him because he could not see it. For the queen and the Minister who, are on one level opposites since he is blackmailing her, are on another parallel characters. Each has transgressed, and each has paid or will pay for that transgression. Each has violated Natural Law. Maharishi explains that the Laws of Nature are responsible for the creation and maintenance of all life. Those in tune with the Laws of Nature are supported by them, so that their desires are easily fulfilled. This is action in the direction of enlightenment that upholds the needs of both the individual and society. However, those who act out of a blind egoism, who put their own selfish desires, their own evolution at risk, run counter to the Laws of Nature, the way one might swim against an immense wave. The result is that Nature produces a pinch as a signal to correct one's actions. The impropriety of the queen, the wife of the head of state, exceeds that of an ordinary person because her territory of influence is greater, and thus the potential for disaster is greater. If she falls, the ramifications will vibrate throughout France and beyond. But the queen who possesses a conscience is susceptible to the moral influence of Nature. The Minister is not.

Dupin it is obviously superior to Minister D—. Not only does he possess an equal intellect, and not only does he act for what we might call the moral good, but he acts in a way that is guided by Consciousness. He is not constrained by the demands of his own small ego as is D—. If, for example, he were to use the letter the way D— has, for personal power, he would actually be placing himself at the mercy of the letter. He would create enmity in those he attempted to negatively influence, and he would open himself up to revenge. But Dupin, as we have witnessed, sees. That is, he sees the wholeness of the situation. He sees what is hidden, even if what is hidden is in plain site. And just as he had seen through the Prefect's limitations, he also sees through those of the Minister, who believes himself safe because he has outwitted the Parisian police. But D—'s lack of awareness does not allow him to account for Dupin, a person with the awareness, sense of justice, compassion, courage, duty, and yes intellect needed to overcome the Minister's efforts.

Dupin's earlier comments on the Prefect's opacity, that the affair for him was "a little *too* plain," applies to his dealings with D— as well. Consciousness works like this. It contains no barriers to either sight or achievement because it is transcendental, beyond all barriers. As a result, someone with an elevated consciousness like Dupin perceives the truth as simply as "a black spot of ink in a pan of white milk."[18] In his expanded consciousness, Dupin sees not only exactly where the Minister has hidden the letter, he envisions precisely what is necessary to retrieve it. Visiting D—, Dupin wears a pair of green glasses, symbolic of the vision he uses to discover the letter's hiding place.

Dupin's thinking and actions are holistic. By recovering the letter, he reestablishes social and political equilibrium. Because it is the nature of consciousness always to be restoring balance to life, Dupin harmoniously acts within the design of Nature, a possibility that exists only for someone whose consciousness is situated at the very depths of Natural Law. In returning the letter, Dupin compassionately relieves the queen of personal suffering while simultaneously removing the potential for national disaster as long as the Minister controls the letter. Dupin's awareness

even extends further. Not satisfied to just make off with the letter, he also weakens D—'s power. He does this by allowing him to continue operating as if he still possessed the letter. When he next attempts to force policy based on the power of blackmail, D— will cause his own destruction. Finally, Dupin must act with impunity (one of Poe's favorite words). Hence, he leaves a duplicate of the Minister's letter in place of the original; in essence using the Minister's exact ruse against him. Maharishi explains that superior action is that which brings support of Nature to the doer but also no harm. In the Bhagavad-Gita, Lord Krishna leads Arjuna to an understanding that only established in Pure Consciousness, Total Knowledge, will his action be totally right, bringing no harm to himself, his loved ones, and even his enemies for whom he saves from committing further wrong action. In **"The Purloined Letter,"** Dupin's Consciousness and his actions approaches this quality of wholeness.

Elizabeth Wright saw the relationship of the Minister, the Prefect, and Dupin as symbolic of the Id (unbridled desire), the Superego (social convention), and the Ego (the individual self). It is just as easy to see this trio representing the stages of developing consciousness. The Prefect symbolizes what we might call the juvenile. In this stage the knower looks outward, sees only objective, cause-and-effect relationships. In this state the inner Self, the foundation of Total Knowledge, the potential for full development, the unity between the individual and all creation simply does not exist. This person's thoughts and actions are based upon a severely limited assessment of life, and as a result failure and suffering cannot be avoided. The Minister represents a growing awareness. He is aware of greater possibilities in life and subtler laws of Nature. His mind isn't limited to what the undependable senses provide. His actions are more powerful and his influence is greater. However, he is still driven by a selfish gratification of the small ego. As long as his consciousness cannot transcend what will bring him pleasure, it cannot expand beyond his own small needs. He too is restricted, and he too, unable to place himself in the stream of all mighty Nature, the force of evolution, cannot escape suffering as well. Dupin represents action in accord with Natural Law. He succeeds with the least amount of effort, and he is amply rewarded for his efforts. His actions uphold the needs of society, promote harmony, and restore order. It is for the most part the action of the Self-actualized man.

Dupin is not an enlightened human being, a person permanently established in the field of Total Knowledge beyond the restrictions and limitations of the ever changing world, a person living an eternal state of contentment. There is no indication that such a full transformation has taken place in his life, the kind of transformation that can be augmented by Maharishi's Transcendental Meditation and TM-Sidhi Program. But in a relative setting, confined by ever destabilizing circumstances, Dupin suggests the possibilities of living a life of fulfillment, free of mistakes, in accord with the Divine Plan. Maharishi Vedic Science, as Literary Theory, allows us to see both the potential in the content and structure of texts, as well as a text's deepest nature. It can do this, because Maharishi Vedic Science is based upon a set of knowledge that is not man-made. It is taken from Maharishi's commentaries on the eternal, imperishable truths of life found in the Vedic Literature and cognized (not imagined or analyzed) by enlightened sages who saw the totality of life found in individual expressions. Because all of ever-changing existence, including literary texts, are the manifestations of the deeper truths of life, Maharishi Vedic Science, the science of life is the most suitable form critical analysis for the understanding of all texts.

APPENDIX

TOTAL KNOWLEDGE

Maharishi begins his elucidation of Total Knowledge with the understanding that all intellectual disciplines in pursuit of complete knowledge can ultimately acquire only partial knowledge. This is an intellectual certainty. The reason is that Total Knowledge consists of both the field of change and the unified field[19] of non-change which produces the field of change. Moreover, Maharishi explains that complete knowledge is not limited to intellectual knowledge; it is knowledge directly experienced and verified by intellectual understanding derived not by human thought but through the direct cognition of sages whose intellects are already established in the field of Total Knowledge. The cognitions of these rishis include the nature of the source of life, the mechanics of the Laws of Nature, and the corresponding application of those laws in the phenomenal world. Because of the enormity of such knowledge, only a person in the highest level of consciousness—*Brahmin Consciousness*—is capable of fully grasping Total Knowledge. Nevertheless, it can be subjectively verified through regular experiences of the field of Total Knowledge, the transcendental field of pure consciousness. And it can be verified scientifically through changes in human physiology, such as increases in the orderly functioning of brain waves. This is demonstrated during EEG studies as individuals subjectively confirm their experiences of the field of Total Knowledge. Other scientific studies corroborate the effect of regularly experiencing the field of Total Knowledge in the growth, happiness, and evolution of regular practitioners of the Transcendental Meditation and TM-Sidhi Program.

Maharishi says the vision of Total Knowledge emerges from

> [t]he discovery of the Unified Field of all the Laws of Nature as the self-referral reality, having a three-in-one structure, completely corresponds with the Unified Field of Vedic Science (Saṃhitā of Rishi, Devatā, Chhandas). It is interesting to observe that the <u>objective</u> approach of modern science has revealed the self-referral field of <u>intelligence</u>, or consciousness, at the basis of all objective material creation, the complete knowledge of which is available in the Veda and Vedic literature.

> (Maharishi (1977), p. 6)

In the field of Total Knowledge, knowledge is self-referral; it knows only itself. Knowledge in this field is always unified—always Saṃhitā. Nevertheless, without ever losing its unified structure, its qualities of Rishi, Devatā, Chhandas (knower, process of knowing, and known) that make up the characteristics of knowledge are eternally interacting, and out of their various combinations creation in its almost infinite variety emerges.

Knowledge without the knowledge of the source of knowledge, the field of Total Knowledge, is ignorance. Anything less than Total Knowledge is partial knowledge. Attempting to acquire knowledge (i.e. full knowledge) of anything in the phenomenal field is both enormous and ultimately impossible. The reality of this statement is true because of the changeability of knowledge, and more importantly, because the essential nature of knowledge is transcendental and lies outside the domain of the phenomenal world. Fortunately, attaining the knowledge of the field of Total Knowledge is both possible, and as human beings, our birthright. We need only a reliable technique that will allow us to experience this field regularly. This Maharishi has provided as the Transcendental Meditation technique. Having gained the field of Total Knowledge, through this practice, one gains the essence of all knowledge. This is possible because this fundamental field is not only the source of all knowledge, it is the deepest most profound level of every aspect of knowledge, of every point in creation.

Notes

1. Maharishi (1969), pp. 19-20.

2. Eagleton, pp. 30-32.

3. Selden, pp. 72-73.

4. Saussure is the founder of *semiotics,* the study of sign systems that underlie human life, including language.

5. Belsey, pp. 38-42.

6. This belief is fostered by and ignorance of the Transcendental Meditation Program that allows the mind to transcend the finest level of language and reach the source of thought, the field of Total Knowledge.

7. Kennedy, p. 301.

8. Maharishi 1997, Total Knowledge, the Unified Field of all the Laws of Nature, the Samhita of Rishi, Devata, and Chhandas.

9. Barthes, pp. 142-148.

10. Johnson, p. 457.

11. Staton, p. 320.

12. See Saussure's *Course in General Linguistics.*

13. Lacan, p. 58.

14. Lacan, p. 70.

15. Stanton, p. 322.

16. Lacan, p. 72.

17. Rk Veda 1.164.39. The Verses of the Veda exist in the collapse of fullness (the kshara of "A") in the transcendental field, in which reside the Devas, the impulses of Creative Intelligence, the Laws of Nature responsible for the whole manifest universe. He whose awareness is not open to this field what can the verses accomplish for him? Those who know this level of reality are established in evenness, wholeness of life.

18. Maharishi used this analogy to indicate how obvious it is for a person with a high consciousness to perceive the mistakes of those acting in ignorance.

19. Maharishi (1997), p. 2.

Bibliography

Barthes, Roland. (1977). *Image-music-text.* New York: Hill and Wang.

Belsey, Catherine. (1980). *Critical practice.* New York: Methuen.

Connor, Steven. (1989). *Postmodernist culture: An introduction to theories of the contemporary.* Cambridge: Basil Blackwell.

Derrida, Jacques. (1975). "The Purveyor of Truth." *Yale French studies,* no. 52, pp. 31-113.

Eagleton, Terry. (1983). *Literary theory: An introduction.* Minneapolis: University of Minnesota Press.

Johnson, Barbara. (1977). "The frame of reference: Poe, Lacan, Derrida." *Yale French Studies,* no. 55-56, pp. 409-423.

Kennedy, E. J. and Dana Gioia. (1994). *An introduction to Poetry,* eighth edition. New York: Harper Collins.

Lacan, Jacques. (1972). "Seminar on 'The Purloined Letter.'" *Yale French studies,* no. 48, pp. 39-72.

Lovejoy, Margot. (1997). *Postmodern currents: Art and artists in the age of electronic media.* Upper saddle river, N.J.: Prentice Hall.

Maharishi Mahesh Yogi. (1969). *Maharishi Mahesh Yogi on the Bhagavad-Gita: A new translation and commentary,* chapters 1-6. Baltimore: Penguin Books.

Maharishi Mahesh Yogi. (1994). *Maharishi Vedic university: Introduction.* Holland: Maharishi Vedic University Press.

Maharishi Mahesh Yogi. (1996). *Inaugurating Maharishi Vedic university.* India: Age of enlightenment publications.

Maharishi Mahesh Yogi. (1997). *Celebrating perfection in education: Dawn of Total Knowledge.* India: Maharishi Vedic university press.

Poe, Edgar Allen. (1938). "The purloined letter." *The complete tales and poems of Edgar Allen Poe.* New York: The Modern Library, pp. 208-222.

Sarup, Madan. (1993). *Post-structuralism and postmodernism.* Athens: The university of Georgia press.

Selden, Raman, Peter Widdowson, and Peter Brooker. (1985). *A reader's guide to contemporary literary theory,* fourth edition. New York: Prentice Hall.

Staton, Shirley F. (1987). *Literary Theory in Praxis.* Philadelphia: University of Pennsylvania Press.

A. Samuel Kimball (essay date spring 2005)

SOURCE: Kimball, A. Samuel. "D-Ciphering Dupin's Fac-Simile Signature: The Infanticidal Implications of a 'Dessein si Funeste.'" *Edgar Allan Poe Review* 6, no. 1 (spring 2005): 20-36.

[*In the following essay, Kimball discusses Poe's short story as an illustration of the connection between vengeful desire and the rationalized violence of the economic marketplace.*]

I: INTRODUCTION

In **"The Purloined Letter,"** Edgar Allan Poe's famous "tale of ratiocination," Dupin nurses a powerful emotional need behind his persona of the detached intellectual. Unwilling or unable to name this want, he nevertheless hints at it when he twice uses the imagery of infanticide in the course of explaining how he accomplished his revenge against his political rival and enemy double, Minister D_____. Embedding his vengeance within a discourse of intellection, he thereby distracts attention away from what he hides in the open—that is, in the imagery of infanticide—about the affective intensity and implications of his desire. Thus, Dupin describes his vengeance as a "good-humored" effort to even the score over an unspecified "evil turn" the Minister has done to him years before.[1] To this end Dupin characterizes his vengeance as a clever move in a game of wits—much like the game of "even and odd"—thereby masking what I will show to be his murderous, specifically infanticidal, rage. Dupin stipulates the cognitive principle but not the emotional payoff for playing this game when he explains the Prefect's inability to imagine that someone else thinks differently from the way he does. The Prefect is like the schoolboy who is outwitted by the superior "mode of reasoning" of his classmate, who always wins the guessing game and whose apparently dispassionate triumph others cannot explain except in terms of "luck" (3: 984).

As Dupin claims and the story's narrator affirms, this person's "luck" is not a matter of chance but of an epistemological labor involving an "identification of the reasoner's intellect with that of his opponent," which is superficially free of emotion and which allows him to know the mind of the other better than the other knows his own mind (3: 984). Clearly, Poe constructs **"The Purloined Letter"** as a series of moves in an extended version of this game, moves which enable Dupin to engage in an "identification" with the Minister D_____ that is not merely sympathy-free but pitiless, and which therefore allow him to defeat his nemesis in a manner that satisfies both his personal and political reasons for seeking revenge.[2]

Why, however, does Dupin pursue his revenge in the way that he does? What is the satisfaction that the infanticidal terms of his vengeance give him? Since Dupin openly alludes to the specific danger of infanticide in much the same way that Minister D_____ hides the letter in his apartment in plain view, why has this motif gone unnoticed? What does this inattention suggest about the emotional significance of the vengeful desire that Dupin makes light of as he asserts his ratiocinative mastery over the Minister? What, in other words, is the logic by which **"The Purloined Letter"** associates vengeance, infanticide, and the knowledge of another's mind? Finally, what links these themes to the political economy of the world depicted in the story, a world centered on monarchial authority compromised by the king's unfaithful wife, a suborned police force, and a black market?

II: DUPIN'S INFANTICIDAL DESIGN

On two occasions, Dupin alludes to infanticide in the course of explaining how he has outwitted his adversary. The Minister has purloined a letter from the "royal *boudoir*" of "an illustrious personage" of "exalted station," evidently the queen (3: 977). He blackmails her with a letter that apparently implicates her in an adulterous affair, which she wishes to keep from her husband, the king. Dupin is a "partisan of the lady" and an opponent of the Minister, whom he considers to be nothing less than a "*monstrum horrendum,* an unprincipled man of genius." This malefic individual, Dupin declares, once "did me an evil turn, which I told him quite good-humoredly, that I should remember" (3: 993). Dupin's efforts to help the queen escape Minister D_____'s political control over her also allows him to pursue an additional payoff in the form of his personal revenge, which he effects when he resteals the letter and replaces it with a "fac-simile" designed to delay Minister D_____'s recognition that he no longer holds the real letter—the source of his present political influence—and also from realizing that he has been duped (3: 992).

To accomplish this two-fold aim, Dupin hires "a man in my own pay" to pretend to be "a lunatic or a drunkard" and to create a disturbance in the streets, which Dupin anticipates will distract the Minister. The plan proceeds without a hitch. Engaging in seemingly "frantic behavior," Dupin's confederate fires a "musket among a crowd of women and children" (3: 992). When the Minister goes to a window to see what is happening, Dupin switches the original letter with his facsimile.

The crowd's reaction to the musket shot reveals what Dupin hides in the open about his motivation. Although the gun "proved [. . .] to have been without ball," the crowd of women and children does not know this. The musket's "report," therefore, creates an instant panic and elicits "a series of fearful screams, and the shoutings of a [terrified] mob" (3: 992). Clearly, Dupin is willing to sacrifice the public peace, even to touch off a riot that endangers the lives of children and the women caring for them, in order to re-purloin the letter and protect the "honor and peace" of the adulterous queen (3: 976).[3] In other words, by staging a scene of insurrection, one with potentially infanticidal consequences, Dupin flouts the law in a manner that metonymically expands the political threat implicit in the queen's adultery; that is, he makes explicit the social chaos and the reproductive costs of this chaos, which result when the paternity of the king is in doubt and the authority of the king's law is disregarded or deliberately violated. Through this deeply problematic ruse, Dupin reveals how readily desire shifts from being conceptive and reproductive to being potentially infanticidal.

Dupin's charade is an intensified, adult form of the childhood game in which the stakes are no longer a trivial object of little value—marbles—but the lives of those in whom society's future is vested. When Dupin orchestrates public pandemonium, then, he hints at the profound ambiguity of the nexus between production and reproduction that is the basis of all political economy, a point to which I shall return later. More immediately, he underscores the reproductive politics contained in the letter the woman conceals from her husband. If this man is the monarch, as the story hints, then she is engaging in behavior that is transgressive not merely of her marital relation but of her position as subject of the king. Insofar as the letter could prove her adultery, it is a metonymy of her affair, which, by upsetting the reproductive basis of the line of royal succession, imperils the paternal basis of the king's authority and thus of the law itself.[4] If the king is rendered impotent by his vulnerability to raising an illegitimate heir, then the unstated possibility of the queen's pregnancy poses a radical challenge to the king's own legitimacy and to his governmental authority. She is, therefore, in danger not only of being discovered but also of arousing his rage and inciting him to take revenge, perhaps by destroying her illegitimate child. In this instance, infanticide would be an effort to protect the law from possible sabotage—specifically, from a sexual and reproductive transgression.

No discourse can master the transgressive force of this desire. Indeed, the Prefect, smug in his knowledge of his procedural expertise, and Dupin, utterly confident of his superior intellection, both remain captive to and repeat the queen's desire. Suborned by the queen, the Prefect directs his police to do her bidding; he thereby uses the power of the state against the very person, the king, who is the source of the Prefect's sworn duty to enforce the state's laws. The Prefect, in other words, supports the queen in her efforts to cover up her illicit affair.

So, too, does Dupin, whom the Prefect entices with the prospect of a large reward. In agreeing to regain the compromising letter for the queen, Dupin tacitly facilitates both her cuckolding of the king and her cover up of her infidelity and its political consequences. What is more, Dupin abets the queen's effort to decouple her desire from her reproductive and other political obligations to the king, and hence to the state. When Dupin orchestrates the riotous street scene, he publicly rehearses the infanticidal threat implicit in the queen's transgression and the ability of the Minister to "produce" the letter that would confirm that behavior (3: 977). Not surprisingly, Dupin saves the queen not

merely by purloining the letter again but by substituting for it a simulacrum—that is, a *reproduction* of the letter. This forged document—a false or illegitimate reproduction of an apparently illicit intimacy that itself entails the possibility of an illegal conception—gives the lie to the paternal basis of the law and to the social order it underwrites.

The queen, the Prefect, and Dupin thus play the law against itself. Each undermines the king while simultaneously upholding the appearance of his authority, upon which they all attempt to capitalize. In this way, each seeks to maintain the seeming legitimacy of the law and the social order it guards while mocking the law's impotence. The result is twofold. On the one hand, as a paternal force the law is without the foundation and legitimacy traditionally attributed to it. On the other hand, desire, including its reproductive outcome, can subvert the state and its law. Infanticide is the trope Poe employs to figure this turning of the law's authority against itself.

Between the lines of the purloined letter, the narrative joins the themes of illicit sexual congress, reproductive politics, and revenge. These motifs reveal one of the tale's central ironies: the intersubjective relations among the characters take shape as triangular Oedipal contests (King, Queen, and the Minister D_____; then the Prefect, Minister D_____, and Dupin). The potentially illegitimate outcome must be checked or even destroyed, at least figuratively, in order for Dupin to save the queen's "honor" and consign his foe to "political destruction" (3: 976, 993).[5]

To this double end Dupin makes his second allusion to infanticide when he gives the Minister a "clue" regarding "the identity of the person who had outwitted him." He "just copied into the middle of the blank sheet" a quotation he has cited before in a manuscript with which the Minister "is well acquainted [. . .] 'Un dessein si funeste, / S'il n'est digne d'Atrée, est digne de Thyeste'" (3: 993). The citation—"So deadly a scheme, if not worthy of Atreus, is worthy of Thyestes"—is from a 1707 tragedy by Prosper-Jolyot de Crébillon, *Atrée et Thyeste*. Crébillon was an official censor of the French Academy and thus another player in a politically motivated game of linguistic hide and seek. His work retells the story of how Atreus takes infanticidal revenge against his brother Thyestes. When he learns that his wife has been seduced by Thyestes, Atreus slaughters his brother's three sons and serves them as a cannibalistic meal to the unsuspecting father. Thus, when Dupin—unmarried and childless, hence doomed to a reproductive dead end—invokes the cross-generational consequences attending Atreus and Thyestes' war, he insures that the Minister D_____ will understand the fratricidal-cum-infanticidal implications of his defeat.

Dupin's allusion underscores his own hunger for revenge. He clearly relishes the thought not only of the Minister's "downfall" but of the moment when the Minister will recognize the author of his destruction. With the distaste of the Minister's treachery in mind, Dupin all but smacks his lips over the letter he has "carefully prepared at my lodgings," as if he were preparing a textual version of the horrific meal Crébillon describes. No wonder, then, that he "imitat[es] the 'D' cipher, very readily, by means of a seal formed of bread" (3: 992). As Servanne Woodward notes, it is a seal formed *du pain* or *Dupin*; it is, I would add, a seal formed of the pain that Dupin has suffered from the Minister's "evil turn."[6]

The result is that Dupin performs a profane Eucharist—bloodless, denatured, and inverted—whereby he sacrifices the other to himself in the name of an economizing pitilessness when he returns the letter for a large reward: "I have no sympathy—at least no pity—for him who descends" (3: 993). Dupin here repudiates the salvific force of the ritual he invokes: Jesus inaugurates the Eucharist in order to commemorate the way he sacrifices himself to the other in the name of unreserved love; Dupin "prepares" his meal in order to commemorate his enemy's political death if not literal execution in the name of a hatred from which he will profit enormously.

Dupin's desire for revenge is as psychologically inflationary as it is monetarily so. On one hand, he waits until the reward has doubled before he produces the letter; on the other, he does not return the Minister's earlier evil for a like evil in a tit-for-tat response. That would be too "simple," too mimetic of the Prefect's lack of poetic imagination. "The business is *very* simple indeed," the Prefect claims; Dupin, however, knows better. He recognizes that what makes the "business" both "simple and odd" is the chance not of evening the score with the Minister but of exposing him as politically impotent, of crushing him (3: 975). For this reason, Dupin escalates the evil the Minister has "turned" against him.[7] In consequence, he becomes indistinguishable from his enemy double: he takes on the "dessein si funeste" that he sees in the Minister, he assumes the baneful design that is worthy of both Atreus and Thyestes, neither of whom got the last word.

The infanticidal consequences of the enmity between the two brothers in the myth preclude the possibility of a victor. As the myth unfolds, Atreus avenges the betrayal of his brother only to have his descendants retaliated against in turn. In seeking revenge, Atreus repeats the infanticide of his grandfather Tantalus and subjects his future descendants to the very reproductive curse by which he would obliterate his brother's

lineage. Tantalus invites the gods to a banquet, kills his son Pelops, and prepares a stew from the dismembered body, which he then serves to the gods, ostensibly to test their omniscience. Resurrected by Hephaestus, Pelops eventually sires Atreus and Thyestes.[8] After Atreus destroys his sons, Thyestes incestuously begets an heir with his daughter, Pelopia. This child, Aegisthus, grows up, kills his uncle, and repeats his father's adultery by sleeping with Clytemnestra, wife of his cousin Agamemnon (son of Atreus and Aerope), whom he and Clytemnestra slaughter when the king returns home from Troy.[9] Clytemnestra conspires against her husband, of course, because he had sacrificed their daughter Iphigeneia. Over and again, the myth of the house of Atreus turns on the spectacle of infanticide.

The trope of infanticide in Poe's story—unnamed as such but readable in Dupin's facsimile signature to the letter that accomplishes his revenge—encapsulates Dupin's unspoken, infantile, murderous rage. The trope encrypts the fury that no words or intellectual formulations can "admeasure," a fury that compels Dupin to attempt just such an admeasurement of his enemy (3: 985). "I reflected," he says, on the Minister's "daring, dashing, and discriminating ingenuity" so as to imitate those very qualities of mind in carrying out his own infanticidal vengeance (3: 990). By the trope of infanticide, Dupin both accuses the Minister of a life-negating aggression and confesses that a similar aggression fuels his own "dessein si funeste" against his antagonist. Thus, the citation from Crébillon, in which the perfidy is worthy of either brother, applies as much to Dupin as to the Minister.

The fates of both Atreus and Thyestes bespeak not just the ratiocinator's victory over the Minister but Dupin's symbolic self-destruction. Thus, Atreus wins only for the moment; when Thyestes discovers his brother's savagery, he invokes a fatal curse against the house of Atreus, one that condemns his brother's lineage to infanticidal self-destruction. But it is also a curse that ironically consumes Thyestes' own lineage. So, too, does Dupin put himself in the position of triumphing—but only for the moment and with no recognition of its temporariness or the way it might elicit the Minister's retaliation.

Whether or not Dupin achieves a final triumph over the Minister, it is telling that he thinks he does and even more telling that he imagines his victory in terms of infanticide, a violence that marks not his ratiocinative generativity but his viciousness and lethality of mind. The result reveals the economy of **"The Purloined Letter"** to be predicated not on a conceptive epistemological principle of exchange but on a primitive, contraceptive emotionality. The trope of infanticide signals the dispossession of reason by this irrational passion to destroy the other.[10]

III: False Belief, the Poverty of Consciousness, and the Nihilism of Revenge

Paradoxically, the irrationality of this passion is rooted in the rationality it upsets. In *The Mystery to a Solution,* John T. Irwin examines the astonishing subtlety and condensation of allusion by which Poe plays the rationality of mathematics against itself to discern an irreducible irrationality at its algebraic roots. Irwin does so in order to elucidate how Poe figures "the mysterious nature of self-consciousness."[11] This mystery can be formulated in logical terms as the set of all paradoxes that result from the mind's ability to represent itself—including its representations of its representations of itself, its representations of its representations of its representations of itself, and so on—in theory, for infinity, without ever attaining a final, all-encompassing, meta-level of representation that would provide an escape from this self-referential cognitive abyss.

According to contemporary cognitive scientists, the ability to represent the other's representations—specifically, the recognition that another can have a different point of view from one's own—marks the accession of a child to a rudimentary theory of mind that enables the child to pass what is called the "false belief test." In one version of this test, an experimenter introduces the young child to two dolls, Sally and Ann. In the imaginary theater that follows, Sally places some candy under a pillow on a chair and then leaves the room, whereupon Ann takes the candy and puts it in her pocket. When Sally returns, the experimenter asks, "Where does Sally think the sweets are?" Before the age of four, the child says they are "in Ann's pocket." By the age of four-and-a-half, most children know otherwise: "Under the pillow," the child says, often "adding with a conspiratorial glee, 'but they aren't there!'"[12] The child here has achieved the ability to engage in a second-order representation of another's representation—specifically, to project how a situation appears to someone else who does not know that some feature central to the initial situation has altered. The child now understands that someone else can have a false belief.

More generally, the child has begun to understand that individuals experience themselves as having an unmediated, private, and privileged access to their own self-consciousness but only a mediated, public, and secondary access to the self-consciousness of others. Individuals seem to be able to know themselves directly—by an immediate, self-present intuition of themselves—but only to know about another's self-perception. The result is a knowledge barrier in the form of an epistemological asymmetry that prevents individuals from knowing others or being known by them in the way that each individual knows (or thinks he knows) himself.

Initially, the child represents the other's belief not as different per se but as false. That is, the child privileges its own perspective. Eventually, however, all children discover that they themselves can entertain a false belief. Moreover, at the very moment of thinking they knew "the truth" (the moment they believed that they knew what they knew), they were in fact wrong.

This discovery can be restated in terms of the Cartesian illusion of self-certainty: if I mistakingly believe a falsity to be true, I cannot simultaneously know that I am in error. The present tense is crucial: I can recognize that a belief I once held is false, and thus I can have had such mistaken knowledge. But only others can know in the present moment that I am mistaken. They can also know that because I believe what I believe, I do not and cannot presently experience the falsity of my belief. Indeed, the other is able to occupy an epistemological position that is denied me: the other can recognize that I am wrong, that I do not recognize that I am wrong, that I am unaware that someone else might be able to see what I do not, and that I am not merely ignorant but abyssally self-ignorant at precisely the moment I am convinced I know.[13]

The other's consciousness of me, in short, is in principle superior to my consciousness of myself; the other is more capable than I am of an accurate "admeasurement" of my seeming mental presence to myself. Thus, insofar as the object of its knowing is subject to an indeterminate future falsifiability, the epistemological basis of self-consciousness is radically provisional. Indeed, it is a source of epistemological self-impoverishment. The mystery of self-consciousness is not its capacity for infinite regress via a series of self-inclusive self-representations but the fact that it can only represent the error of its representations belatedly.[14]

The moral dilemma posed by this incapacity, which structures consciousness around a secret it keeps from itself, is that one can never know, until some future moment, whether or not one's present beliefs reflect anything other than self-interest.[15] The moral challenge is to recognize that one can achieve certain knowledge only after one's sense of certainty has proven to be false—for example, one can realize one has made the wrong decision only after one is committed to a course of action. Confronted with this conundrum, Dupin ruthlessly capitalizes on his knowledge of his enemy's ignorance concerning the limits of his own capitalizing calculations (of the Minister's ignorance that his threat of blackmail has been rendered impotent and that Dupin now has the queen in his debt). At the end, then, knowing that the Minister does not know that the letter has been recovered, knowing that the Minister does not know that he does not know, Dupin anticipates and takes on the nihilism of the modern market: he makes a symbolically infanticidal *killing.* Thus, he delivers his enemy a political coup de grâce by means of a psychologically murderous performative signature. In effect, he signs his substitute letter, "You are as if an infanticide. C. Auguste Dupin."

Near the end of *The Mystery to a Solution,* Irwin writes that "Poe's aesthetic task [. . .] was to find mysteries that would serve as dramatic correlatives for the central mystery of the human condition, and the fact that the mysteries he created were ones associated with the commission of crimes simply evokes the ancient sense that the structure of self-consciousness [. . .] is basically transgressive" (416). I would qualify this characterization of Poe's own artistic labor: to give oneself over to the transgression, as the Minister D_____ and Dupin do, is to capitulate to a despairing rage over the poverty of self-consciousness, a reaction evident in the infanticidal imagery by which Dupin indicates the affective violence at the heart of his intellection. This violence is a lethal aggressivity that will politically isolate the other, reducing him to the same condition to which Dupin had been "reduced" in **"The Murders in the Rue Morgue"** by "such poverty that the energy of his character succumbed beneath it" and by which "he ceased to bestir himself in the world."[16] In **"The Purloined Letter,"** Dupin comes back from the dead, as it were; but if he is reanimated, it is to engage the living (his narrator friend, the Prefect, the Minister, and the confederate) so as to haunt the Minister, whose downfall provides Dupin with the monetary resources for a new life. The cost, however, is that Dupin damns himself in sentencing the other to a fratricidal revenge that is either impotent, contraceptive, or anti-reproductive. He thus surrenders himself and his enemy to an ontologically self-evacuating, infanticidal aggression.

IV: THE VIOLENCE OF THE MARKET

This aggression links the story's insight about the poverty of consciousness to its implicit criticism of, and perhaps Poe's ambivalence toward, the market economy that stimulates such violence. Writing at a time when the literary marketplace was rapidly expanding and the literary text was becoming increasingly commoditized, Poe might seem to let Dupin, the narrator, and the reader have their cake and eat it too—by permitting Dupin to cash in on his vengeance, and by extending Dupin's payoff both to the narrator, who acquires the material for his story, and to the reader, who receives the opportunity to experience

vengeance as a highly profitable and aesthetically rich motivation. In this view **"The Purloined Letter"** capitalizes on the way the marketplace transforms primitive desires—here the violence of escalating revenge—into a contractual service and a literary commodity.

Such an interpretation implies that the market functions psychoanalytically to relieve the participant of the aggression and hatred that would otherwise disrupt a peaceable, culturally stabilizing process of commercial exchange. To this end Jeffrey Mehlman argues that by exchanging the letter for money, Dupin escapes the intersubjective blindness that initially overtakes him as it has the others who have possessed the letter. Mehlman reads the "devastating quotation" with which Dupin signs the substitute letter as an "expression of [the] *blind* rage" that accompanies the narcissistic false belief that he sees without being seen. Because Dupin is alert to this emotional and cognitive trap, however, he quickly gets rid of the letter by selling it to the Prefect. Mehlman concludes that this exchange frees Dupin of the "venom" which "the counterfeit letter betrays."[17] The market accomplishes this end presumably by associating the individual's furious emotionality, and the absolute value it has for the infuriated individual, with some good or service, the value of which is relative to what the market will bear. The result is to convert charged affect into an object the symbolic value of which must be negotiated by entering into an exchange process in which one realizes one's own point of view is subject to the inspection and differential valuation of the other. The appeal of this interpretation is the psychic relief it provides Dupin, the narrator, and any reader who identifies with the narrator's tale of Dupin's success.

In fact, however, the fictional market of **"The Purloined Letter"** ironizes such a putative Aristotelian catharsis. Rather than purging Dupin of his aggression, the market rationalizes it. When Dupin sells the letter to the Prefect, he deepens his collaboration in the queen's betrayal of the king. The market then legitimizes his and everyone else's role in the political conspiracy by inscribing the covert exchanges among the colluders in a system of overt, rationally self-interested exchanges. In this way the market substitutes a public, legal tender for a private, illegal letter. The story's marketplace thereby hides desire in the open—in the neutral monetary signs that substitute for the signs of the socially problematic, appropriative desire that motivates the circuit of exchange. For his part the narrator reproduces the market's reappropriation when he converts Dupin's vengeful motivation and self-congratulatory account of his intellectual superiority over Minister D_____ into an aesthetic good. Readers, too, risk buying into this process, especially if they neglect the rationalized aggression that underwrites the story's transactions.

Poe is critical of, if ambivalent about, the relation between monetary exchange, psychic economy, and violence. Indeed, in **"The Purloined Letter"** the productivity of the market enacts the paradox that underlies *Eureka*: *"In the Original Unity of the First Thing lies the Secondary Cause of All Things, with the Germ of their Inevitable Annihilation."*[18] The aboriginal productivity of the world undoes itself in an oxymoronic movement of "germinal" self-destruction. Daniel A. Underwood and Paul G. King have articulated a modern version of this insight concerning the limits of human economy, which inevitably "increase[s] the entropy of the universe and diminish[es] the future productive potential of the biosphere."[19] The physical laws of universe imply its eventual and inevitable death.

In the infanticidal—that is, anti-generative, unbegetting, future-destroying—imagery Dupin employs to secure his revenge and to make a symbolic killing on the black market, **"The Purloined Letter"** provides an encrypted glimpse of what remains all but inconceivable to those who have yet to accept the epistemological blindness that blocks them from recognizing their own infanticidal self-interestedness. Such blindness becomes manifest whenever individuals or groups think they see a truth their opponents do not and, in seeking to take advantage of their opponents' blindness, fail to see they share a common fate. In that moment is born the denial of the infanticidal "germ" Poe intuits.

Notes

I am grateful to Peter Norberg and Richard Fusco for their astute suggestions, editorial care, and considerateness as they shepherded this work into print.

1. "The Purloined Letter," *Edgar Allan Poe: Tales and Sketches,* Vol. 3: 1843-1849, ed. Thomas Olive Mabbott (Cambridge: Belknap/Harvard UP, 1978), 993. Subsequent references to this edition of the story will be included in the text.

2. Commenting on Dupin's desire to answer the Minister's "evil turn," John T. Irwin notes that Dupin's answer to the Minister's earlier "evil turn" "will constitute an evening of the score between them at one apiece only if the Minister does not allow Dupin's trick to end the series," for the last "trick" turns the gesture of "trying to *get even*" into the paradoxical act of "being *one up*." See *The Mystery to a Solution: Poe, Borges, and the Analytic Detective Story* (Baltimore: Johns Hopkins UP, 1994), 29.

3. In *The Narrative of A. Gordon Pym* (1838), published seven years before "The Purloined Letter" (1845), the only time Pym uses the word "purloin" is in the course of describing an infanticidal scene of predation among the penguins and albatrosses, the cooperative nesting behavior that he describes at length. Having evoked the mathematical arrangement of the "rookery" shared by the two species of bird, between whom "the most singular friendship exists," Pym then notes that the eggs of either bird "are never left uncovered at all—while one bird leaves the nest, the other nestling is by its side. This precaution is rendered necessary by the thievish propensities prevalent in the rookery, the inhabitants making no scruple to purloin each other's eggs at every good opportunity." See *Poetry and Tales of Edgar Allan Poe,* ed. Patrick F. Quinn (New York: Library of America, 1984), 1119. In a forthcoming article, I examine the larger pattern of infanticidal implication in *Pym* as well as in *Moby-Dick.* See "Travel, Travail, and the Biblical Itinerary of the Word: The Contrasting Examples of Poe and Melville," *Les écrivain en voyage: Nouveaux mondes, nouvelles idées (Writers and Their Travels: New Worlds, New Ideas),* ed. Sharon Fuller and Roy Fuller, forthcoming 2006.

4. Dennis Porter points out that the story is, among other things, a "fascinating tale of loins." See "Of Poets, Politicians, Policemen, and the Power of Analysis," *New Literary History* 19.3 (Spring 1988), 501. As Irwin notes, "In the final Dupin story, of course, the queen is the victim not of physical but of psychological violence (blackmail); and once again the violence has a sexual dimension, for the letter the Minister holds over her head apparently implicates her in an adulterous affair." See *The Mystery to a Solution,* 237-38. And yet, as Ross Chambers observes, the letter's contents "are unknown to the reader; they are a secret that is never disclosed. (Is it a love letter? Does it contain evidence of a political plot?)." See "Narratorial Authority and 'The Purloined Letter,'" in John P. Muller and William J. Richardson, eds., *The Purloined Poe: Lacan, Derrida and Psychoanalytic Reading* (Baltimore: Johns Hopkins UP, 1988), 290.

5. In his "Seminar" on Poe, Jacques Lacan traces the transit of desire back to the story's reenactment of the Freudian "primal scene," in which the child sees or imagines the parents engaged in intercourse. The primal scene stimulates the child's "instinct for knowledge" by raising two questions: what is the nature of sexual difference, and where do babies come from. The primal scene provides an initial—terrifying—answer insofar as children experience the event, Freud believes, as aggres-

sive, violent, and destructive and as the source of a potentially life-shaping anxiety. See *Three Essays on the Theory of Sexuality,* trans. and ed. James Strachey (New York: Basic Books, 1975), 62. Freud links the child's dread to two threats, which he all but describes as infanticidal threats: the mutilating threat of castration and "the threat to the bases of [his or her] existence offered by the discovery or the suspicion of the arrival of a new baby and the fear that he may, as a result of it, *cease to be cared for and loved*" (60-61). The phallic power of the father and the birthing capacity of the mother deliver the child to a fearful self-consciousness of its vulnerability to castration and infanticidal replacement. The primal scene, in other words, stages the advent both of life and of the child's initial consciousness of itself in terms of a life-subtracting, life-revoking peril.

Lacan, like Freud, has trouble explicitly naming as infanticidal the implications of the primal scene because of the way he conceives the Symbolic Order. Lacan locates the primal scene in Poe's story in the "intersubjective" triad of the queen, the king, and Minister D_____, which is then displaced onto a second triad constituted by the Minister, the Prefect, and Dupin. Lacan discerns in this repetition nothing less than a force that "impregnates our acts" and "delivers" us to our identities within the Symbolic Order. That is, Lacan himself conceives of the letter in terms that transfer reproductivity from the body to language, within which all birthing is shown to be linguistically circumscribed. See Jacques Lacan, "Seminar on 'The Purloined Letter,'" in Muller and Richardson, eds., *The Purloined Poe,* 41 and 39.

In criticizing Lacan, Derrida examines the disseminating rather than inseminating character of language. He thus refuses the metaphor of conception as an adequate means of apprehending the inscription of the human subject within a field of forces that are simultaneously erotic *and* thanatotic, life-producing *and* death-producing. See "Le Facteur de la Vérité," in *The Post Card: From Socrates to Freud and Beyond,* trans. Alan Bass (Chicago: U of Chicago P, 1987), 413-96.

6. "Dupin's intellectual feat is mainly motivated by an unintellectual common denominator for humanity, a need for bread (*du pain* if one adds an 'a' to Dupin's name.) This pun is made by Dupin himself when he makes his 'D-cipher' out of bread in order to sign his *fac-simile*." See "Lacan and Derrida on 'The Purloined Letter,'" *Comparative Literature Studies* 26.1 (1989), 42. Lawrence Howe also discusses Dupin's "signature pun which

signs off the detective series," in "Poe and the Critical Pun; or The Revenge of the Detective Tales," *LIT/Literature, Interpretation, Theory* 3.3 (1992), 200.

7. The motif of intensification is a fundamental aesthetic feature of Poe's work. Here it takes the form of an escalating violence, as it does in "The Cask of Amontillado," where it develops according to the psychodynamic sequence René Girard has outlined: admiration leads to emulation, envy, and eventually a hatred that, sufficiently intensified, erupts into murderous aggression. See, for example, *Violence and the Sacred,* trans. Patrick Gregory (Baltimore: Johns Hopkins UP, 1977). In other works—for example, "Descent into the Maelström," "The Fall of the House of Usher," and "The Tell-Tale Heart"—the intensification takes the form of increasingly lurid, sensational, and harrowing experiences or increasingly acute and even psychotic perceptions.

8. In the meantime, his sister Niobe, wife of the legendary cofounder of Thebes, boasts of her superior reproductivity to Leto and, consequently, twelve of her fourteen children are killed by Apollo and Artemis.

9. Believing Aegisthus to be his son by Pelopia, Atreus summons him to destroy Thyestes. When Aegisthus learns from Pelopia that Thyestes is his real father, however, he turns on Atreus and stabs him from behind. See Barry B. Powell, *Classical Myth,* 3rd ed. (New Jersey: Prentice Hall, 2001), 513. The theme of false paternity in the myth of Atreus and Thyestes adds to the suggestion that the lady of "The Purloined Letter" may be pregnant and that the issue of paternity is in question. Whether or not her adultery led to conception, the theme of dubious paternity converges with the issue of delivering the letter back into the hands of the woman.

10. It is overdetermined, then, that he will take his revenge against the Minister by symbolically "screwing" him: "Dupin does not use his acumen merely to grasp the Minister's maneuvers (as his friend understands his arguments); he uses it also to penetrate the Minister's duplicity and to reveal the fraudulence of his techniques." See Chambers, "Narratorial Authority and 'The Purloined Letter,'" 295-96.

11. See Irwin, *The Mystery to a Solution,* 10.

12. See Robin Dunbar, *Grooming, Gossip, and the Evolution of Language* (Cambridge: Harvard UP), 86. Dunbar continues: "Having a Theory of mind means being able to understand what another individual is thinking, to ascribe beliefs, desires, fears

and hopes to someone else, and to believe that they really do experience these feelings as mental states. We can conceive of a kind of natural hierarchy: you can have a mental state (a belief about something) and I can have a mental state about your mental state (a belief about a belief). [. . .] These are now usually referred to as orders of 'intensionality.' [. . .] There is good reason to believe that humans are capable of keeping track of, at most, six orders of intensionality, and after that they probably have to see it written down" (83-84). Daniel C. Dennett provides an extended discussion of intensionality in *Kinds of Mind: Toward an Understanding of Consciousness* (New York: Basic Books/HarperCollins, 1996).

13. R. D. Laing translates the intersubjective binds (the "knots" of his title) that can arise in the course of representing representation—one's own and that of the other—into a series of logically contradictory statements and dialogic exchanges. See *Knots* (New York: Pantheon/Random House, 1970).

14. This incapacity is intrinsic to the experience of one's own consciousness. As Jacques Derrida has explained, consciousness, especially as conscience, seems to occur as an unmediated self-voicing in which one's thought is available to oneself as a signified that is seemingly independent of any signifier and that therefore has a completely non-material being, a non-material presence to the subject who hears itself thinking. "This experience of the effacement of the signifier in the voice is not merely one illusion among many—since it is the condition of the very idea of truth. [. . .] This illusion is the history of truth." See *Of Grammatology,* trans. Gayatri Chakravorty Spivak (Baltimore: Johns Hopkins UP, 1974), 20. For this reason the truth of the truth—the truth that the experience of truth derives from an illusory experience of seeming self-presence—is not able to be introjected, not able to become the non-illusory basis of the experience of one's self-consciousness.

15. In his exposition of Poe's story, Lacan frames the problem of intersubjectivity in terms of the epistemological asymmetry between (1) "a glance that sees nothing: the King and the police," (2) "a glance which sees that the first sees nothing and deludes itself as to the secrecy of what it hides: the Queen, then the Minister," and (3) a glance that "sees that the first two glances leave what should be hidden exposed to whomever would seize it: the Minister and finally Dupin." See "Seminar," 32. What the third glance for its part does not see is that the self-limitations of the first

two glances traverse the entire intersubjective hierarchy such that the third glance is as vulnerable as the others to the destructiveness of its desire.

16. See *Collected Works of Edgar Allan Poe,* Vol. 2, *Tales and Sketches: 1831-1842,* ed. Thomas Olive Mabbott (Cambridge: Belknap/Harvard UP, 1978), 531.

17. See "Poe Pourri: Lacan's Purloined Letter," *Boundary 2* (1974), 55.

18. See *Poetry and Tales of Edgar Allan Poe,* 1261.

19. See "On the Ideological Foundations of Environmental Policy," *Ecological Economics* 1 (1989), 322. Underwood and King explain that "the more society relies on an increase in material flows to satisfy an increasing demand for production, the greater will be the level of pollution and the disamenities associated with it; the greater will be the demand placed on the assimilative capacity of the biosphere; and finally, the smaller will be the productive potential of the biosphere in the future" (323 n10). The consequences are inevitable: "a global society with an endlessly increasing thirst for material production dependent upon a coinciding flow of resources is doomed to extinction," for the laws of thermodynamics and conservation impose an absolute energy limit in the form of "absolute scarcity" (322). Quite simply, the carrying capacity of the earth is not inexhaustible but thermodynamically bounded. "The fact that there are no known exceptions to the laws of thermodynamics should be incorporated into the axiomatic foundations of economics" (329).

Dana Medoro (essay date fall 2007)

SOURCE: Medoro, Dana. "So Very Self-Evident: Adultery and Abortion in 'The Purloined Letter.'" *Literature and Medicine* 26, no. 2 (fall 2007): 342-63.

[*In the following essay, Medoro focuses on sexual double-entendres in "The Purloined Letter," theorizing that this suggestiveness points to concerns about female reproductive control in the nineteenth century.*]

The cushions we probed with the fine long needles you have seen me employ.

Edgar Allan Poe, **"The Purloined Letter,"** 1845

In 1846, the sixteenth edition of William A. Alcott's *The Young Man's Guide* hit the American streets, maintaining its cautionary message that the world was an awfully smutty place, "abound[ing] in impure publications [and] licentious paintings and engravings, which circulate in various ways."[1] According to Alcott, not only was it crucial for a young man's moral development to avoid such objects, but it was also necessary for him to know their subtle traps: the obscene picture "under cover of a watch case," the seemingly innocuous book steeped in double entendres (334). To make sure that his readership understood what he meant by "double entendres," Alcott included both a phonetic key to it—"pronounced *entaunders*"—and a definition:

> By this is meant *decent speeches, with double meanings.* I mention these because they prevail, in some parts of the country, to a most alarming degree. . . . Now no serious observer of human life and conduct can doubt that by every species of impure language, whether in the form of hints, innuendos, double entendres, or plainer speech, impure thoughts are awakened, a licentious imagination inflamed, and licentious purposes formed, which would otherwise never have existed.
>
> (311)

For Alcott, as for many of his concerned medical and moral contemporaries, the lure of these vices ("not only *social* but also *solitary*") dangerously illuminated the way "to disease and premature death" (314). Such pronouncements formed, of course, an increasingly common refrain of nineteenth-century sexual advice literature directed at both men and women; to take up Michel Foucault's paradigmatic formulation, they were part of the social mechanisms that turned sex into "*the* secret" in an "endlessly proliferating economy" of biopolitical discourses and regulations.[2] But what is so interesting about Alcott's account here lies less with its anxieties about human erotic activity than it does with Alcott's sense of having to wage an almost losing battle against a kind of print culture that promoted, in increasingly cunning and indefatigable ways, the very activity he sought to restrict. If, as historian Ronald Walters shows, we can trace an intensification of concern with the sexual behavior of the young American population to the proliferation of advice literature in the 1830s and 40s, then we must also see this concern as a motivated response, at least in part, to the creative flair of a certain kind of text passing itself off as something very different from its surface appearance—as something that slips across a guarded threshold, narrowly eluding the vigilant eyes of America's reputable establishment, rather like a purloined letter, the secret contents of which threaten to bring down the entire house.[3]

This is how the nineteenth-century market in reproductive control and sexual education operated. Although Alcott does not directly mention it, perhaps for fear of appearing lewd, the publishers of pamphlets, advertisements, and tracts publicly disseminating racy information drew upon a vibrant realm of double entendres and euphemisms, particularly in the wake of state laws passed against the sale of contraceptives and the practice of abortion in the two decades before the Civil War.[4] According to Janet Farrell Brodie in her extraordinary *Contraception and Abortion in Nineteenth-Century America,* antebellum Americans quickly learned that "[d]omestic manuals" and "private medical guides for ladies" carried contraceptive advice and ways of incurring miscarriage and that condoms and douching syringes could be purchased where "voluntary-motherhood" products were sold.[5] Throughout the 1840s, gynecological surgeons couched surgical abortions in terms of "unblocking" uterine obstructions; regular physicians sometimes added tiny postscripts to advertisements noting that their wives served female patients for "ailments" related to "suppressed" or arrested menstruation.[6] And like many of their colleagues in the medical profession, popular lecturers on health and physiology imparted details about reproduction in, as Brodie puts it, a "far from unique . . . mix of information and innuendo" (109). Moreover, printed warnings about such insidious materials, by critics like Alcott for instance, inadvertently effected a broader awareness of the availability of birth-control information and erotic materials; in the process of denouncing fornication or abortion, they often disseminated crucial information about it. In some cases, the denouncement itself was just a cover for an announcement, a kind of deft double entendre governing the appearance of outrage. For example, the July 21, 1839, edition of New York's *Sunday Morning News* carried an article proclaiming that the famous abortionist Mrs. Restell "persevered in her nefarious traffic" of pills for "married women who had been indiscreet." Following a statement about New York City's "wise statute" against abortion, as well as a warning that Mrs. Restell euphemistically called herself a "midwife and professor of diseases of women," the author of the article astonishingly reproduces Mrs. Restell's ad in its entirety: "Mme Restell's Sure Remedies— Price $5 and $10; can only be procured at her office, No 1 East 52nd Street." Within this mixture of admonition and exposition, the extent to which the article actually opposed the distribution of Mrs. Restell's product is sufficiently obscured.[7]

Such diverse and circuitous routes around genteel morality and state laws did not proceed entirely unnoticed, however, and several states went so far as to draft legislation against the use of any ambiguous language in reports, pamphlets, and advertisements concerning ailments particular to women. Yet, throughout the 19th century, the laws against it notwithstanding, ambiguous, euphemistic wording continued to frame the sale of products and procedures: the "Female Regulator," the "Woman's Friend," the "Samaritan's

Gift for Females." In the words of one New York gynecologist, "every schoolgirl knows the meaning of these terms."[8] According to Helen Lefkowitz Horowitz, many purveyors of abortion and contraception also figured out how to blur "the boundary between commerce in contraceptives and works of physiology. . . . Given the way that many works of physiology were advertised, it seemed possible that some authors were using the cover of science to print racy material" (284). In fact, in a fairly early American printing of *Aristotle's Masterpiece* (1817), the publisher seems to have attempted to head off exactly this accusation, avowing in the preface that the book was not intended to "stir up bestial appetites" of "unclean" readers but that it was made for women whose "modesty" precluded them from asking for help "in matters of the womb."[9]

In the medical schools themselves, the number of publications on the anatomy of female fertility—particularly the mysteries of ovulation and menstruation—also grew at an extraordinary rate. As historian of gynecology, James Ricci, puts it: "The gynaecological literature of the first half of the nineteenth century is immense; of the latter half, gigantic."[10] By mid-century, American gynecologists were divided in their support of abortion, and those who opposed it began actively seeking the support of church and state. With the promotion of the theory that life began at conception, abortion became linked to the "characteristic privilege of sovereign power . . . the right to decide life and death" (to quote Foucault on the state's surveillance of sex), and as an increasing number of gynecologists began to equate it with infanticide, abortion came under a new slate of statutory regulations.[11] Abortion also became tied to fears of adultery and promiscuity, to a prevailing belief that the procedure literally erased evidence of sexual misconduct and therefore licensed it. For one mid-century gynecologist, anxious about the direction of American civilization, it seemed that "the old-fashioned womb [would] cease to exist, except in history."[12]

It is within this remarkably public world of advertisements, books, newspaper articles, and laws on the subject of reproductive control that I wish to place **"The Purloined Letter."** Published in 1845, at the high point of what Walters calls the "public discourse about sex and related matters" in nineteenth-century America, Poe's tale engages with the controversies these discourses generated and revealed, and it does so by means of the very same indirection and innuendo that suffuse many of them.[13] As a result, it illuminates, even as it attempts to screen, the secrets contained within the purloined letter, pushing us to ask what exactly is so pressing about the "affair" of a letter stolen from a woman's "boudoir":

'Perhaps it is the very simplicity of the thing which puts you at fault,' said [Dupin].

'What nonsense you *do* talk!' replied the Prefect, laughing heartily.

'Perhaps the mystery is a little *too* plain,' said Dupin.

'Oh, good heavens! who ever heard of such an idea?'

'A little *too* self-evident.'

'Ha! ha! ha!—ha! ha! ha!—ho! ho! ho!'—roared our visiter, profoundly amused.

(331)

If we're the kind of readers who are in the know, those familiar with the trials of famous abortionists (such as Madame Restell) printed throughout the New England papers in the 1840s, with the trade in erotic materials (as well as with the arrests of the tradesmen), and with the contraception ads that seemed to have been slipped into every possible magazine, then we can begin to hear the subject of reproductive control being spoken in **"The Purloined Letter."** As Jacques Lacan notes about Poe's tale, the "dialogue may be more fertile than it seems."[14] It is only by inferring the matter and magnitude of the letter's contents, moreover, that we can then fathom both the depth of the urgency it repeatedly communicates and the questions the letter raises about adultery and abortion in mid-nineteenth-century America.

In this essay, I argue that Poe's **"The Purloined Letter"** is immersed in the kind of double entendres that Alcott discerns in every corner of his mid-nineteenth-century world—from euphemistic advertisements for abortions to slyly erotic medical guidebooks—and that the tale's "decent speeches with double meanings" underscore its exploration of the decoys surrounding sex in 1840s America. Through its layers of innuendo and its metaphors, **"The Purloined Letter"** also explores the theme of passing (as white, as faithful, as legitimate, as something other than what you are), binding the notion of a counterfeit self or appearance to cultural tensions about the sexual freedom of white women. It is this particular anxiety about women, captured in the maneuvers of Poe's "exalted royal personage," that the tale's most famous critics, Jacques Lacan, Jacques Derrida, and Barbara Johnson, at once detect and overlook in their discussions of its hidden and surface narratives. Contrary to their shared conviction that the contents of the letter are never revealed, that the letter's significance does not lie with this revelation but with the actions its absence precipitates, I will demonstrate that the contents of the letter are almost entirely divulged and necessarily so; we just have to identify the context within which the tale's innuendo resonates. Like the light-fingered and "lynx-eye[d]" Minister, who assembles a series of interconnected hints, manages to decipher the overturned letter and thus "fathom[s] [the woman's] secret," Poe's reader can follow the same trail toward the peculiar and perilous nature of an open secret.[15]

A key hint arises in the tale's attention to the cleverness of the characters who can decode what another character's body tries to disguise or suppress. Thus, although the Minister cannot read an "unexposed" letter, he discerns its significance by tracing its appearance on the table first to the "confusion of the personage" and then to her sudden composure in relation to the "personage who stood at her elbow" (332-333). Dupin adopts the same strategy, reading the Minister's body language—his "yawning, lounging, and dawdling"—as an elaborate performance designed to mask an intensity of energy at the same time that Dupin himself conceals the movement of his own eyes behind dark glasses (346). If two can play at that game, then so can three. Because the woman in the tale, who also uses the strategy, does not overtly react when the Minister steals her letter, she quickly obscures her despair, splitting her bodily appearance from what she hides beneath its surface or within it. To the man at her elbow, nothing changes. He sees her for what she is: completely visible and above suspicion, like the letter on the table. He does not presume any contradictory meaning to her composure, nor the fact that something on display might also be out of sight.

In such ways, Poe's narrative immediately connects the physical existence of the woman with the letter, placing their shared and material manifestations into a framework of congruency. In fact, the kinetic shift through which the Minister "perceives the paper" and then "fathoms her secret" effectively merges the woman with the letter, as the one entity encloses the secret of the other. The word "fathom" is telling, too, because its etymological affinity with nautical exploration suggests the sense of literally plumbing something deep and dark. What I want to stress in this discussion, or to return to the surface of the tale, is the contextual legibility not only of the letter but also of the woman's body. She may never directly appear to the narrator, may never come forward for a complete description, but she sets all of the events in motion; she contacts the police, devises a reward, and describes the letter to the Prefect, whose own detailed description of it to Dupin and the narrator is not duplicated, only recounted. This sly, second-hand representation on the part of Poe's narrator once again aligns the woman's body with her letter, generating the idea that what she wants back is precisely that alignment, that ability to decide how to represent—and perhaps whether to deliver—something in her keeping. As she works behind the scenes to regain this control, Poe indicates that the potential danger to her body is very

real, for his narrator opens **"The Purloined Letter"** with reference to "the affair of the Rue Morgue and the mystery attending the murder of Marie Rogêt," and therefore casts **"The Purloined Letter"** as part of a trilogy in which the women compelling the other two investigations are mutilated cadavers (330). Their wretched fate frames her story, and she seems to know it.

The tale abruptly shifts from the narrator's recollection of the murdered women to the intrusion into his study of the Prefect, an action he casts as a coincidence in light of his present musings.

> [T]o any casual observer, [Dupin and the narrator] might have seemed intently and exclusively occupied with the curling eddies of smoke that oppressed the atmosphere of the chamber. For myself, however, I was mentally discussing certain topics which had formed matter for conversation between us at an earlier period of the evening; I mean the affair of the Rue Morgue, and the mystery attending the murder of Marie Rogêt. I looked upon it, therefore, as something of a coincidence, when the door of our apartment was thrown open and admitted our old acquaintance, Monsieur G—, the Prefect of the Parisian police.
>
> (330)

This is a significant narrative move because it indicates another behind-the-scenes design: a prompting to bear in mind that the narrator is not omniscient but present in the tale, making decisions about what to include and suppress, about what to cast as coincidental or interconnected. As an ally and admirer of Dupin, who is himself a "partisan of the lady concerned," the narrator finds himself treading carefully around the particulars of the purloined letter (348). Too much is at stake. But he is also a story-teller, and his impulse is to urge his reader through artful suggestions and juxtapositions toward the secrets opening up around him. His hinting is rich, and things are laid out with a seeming innocence and frankness—and the double entendres and sexual innuendo cover their own tracks. Thus, if he had to, he could protest that his inclusion of the description of the musket that shoots blanks is just a description of an empty musket and not an allusion to anyone's penis (347-348); that the reference to an "unusual gaping in the joints" or to a "secret drawer" simply describes furniture and not a woman's pelvis (335, 336); that Paris is Paris and America, America.

No discussion of Poe's tale can proceed without taking into account the fact that Poe's cagey language compelled extended deliberations from, as Barbara Johnson puts it, "two eminent French thinkers whose readings emit their own . . . call-to-analysis."[16] For it seems that the debate between Jacques Lacan and

Jacques Derrida over **"The Purloined Letter,"** coupled with Johnson's own dazzling intervention into it, has come to frame Poe's text with a definitive, if not final, word on it. Getting past this circumference in order to offer anything new necessitates, I think, keeping in clear view the levels of complexity and the textual detail that each of these thinkers brings to bear upon and unearths from **"The Purloined Letter."** We cannot, in other words, simply acknowledge the Lacan-Derrida-Johnson context for reading **"The Purloined Letter"** and then set it aside. Again in Johnson's words: "The urgency of these undertakings [Derrida's, Lacan's] cannot . . . be overestimated, since the logic of metaphysics, of politics, of belief, and of knowledge itself is based on the imposition of definable objective frontiers and outlines whose possibility and/or justifiability are here [in **"The Purloined Letter"**] being put into question" (231). Between them, Lacan and Derrida entirely overturn the impression that "much is made of nothing" in Poe's tale, as an early reviewer described it in 1845.[17] And, following them, Johnson elucidates the link Poe forges between language and power, clarifying what it means for subjectivity to be formed within a structure and "by a letter" (248).

Because all three analyses take up questions surrounding being, legitimacy, and femininity, all three inadvertently point to the same issues surrounding abortion in the 1840s, issues that become legible in **"The Purloined Letter"** once a historical frame of reference is set around it. When this frame is set, the lines of inquiry in Lacan and Derrida through Poe's text to questions concerning why "the law holds the woman in position as a signifier," as Lacan puts it, can then be directed to concerns that reproductive control liberated women in unpredictable social and symbolic ways.[18] To clarify: if Lacan sees at work in **"The Purloined Letter"** the law of language as it forces the subject into a system of sexual difference, a law he understands as a paternal claim to and redirection of maternal production and identification, then the question of the subject's origin within the maternal body becomes another level of that claim. The phallus (understood as patriarchal discourse and injunction) shores up the immense anxiety of non-existence and of existence's contingency upon the mother's prerogative, bringing the physiological origin of an embryo in line with the symbolic origin of an embryonic subject. The vulnerability of the entire system rests on the possibility that the mother can violate the law and suspend this teleological narrative of subjectivity; if careful and quiet, only she knows if a fetus truly exists and what its name really might be—bastard or heir—regardless of paternal entitlement. The criminalization of abortion in Poe's time developed out of that existential vulnerability and through a medical-philosophical narrative that pulled the fetus into view and obscured the woman attached to it. Thus, it is at precisely the places where Lacan and Derrida work out such concepts as sign and origin in Poe's tale that the allusive themes of pregnancy and termination also unfold, and **"The Purloined Letter"** aligns the question of a woman's reproductive choice with the broader questions of framing and truth, contingencies and contracts.[19] The medical archives of nineteenth-century gynecology permit us to recognize what Poe's innuendo intimates on a very specific level: "a personage of most exalted station" is pregnant by a man other than her husband, "the other exalted personage," and she possesses the option of abortion, a procedure by which she can erase the only material evidence, apart from the letter, of her affair (332).

Given the presence of arguments in 1840s America that abortion and adultery went hand in hand—that reproductive control could license women to cuckold men—it is significant that Lacan calls the woman in Poe's tale the guardian of legitimacy and notes that "we are assured of but one thing: the Queen cannot bring [the letter] to the knowledge of her lord and master" (42). In fact, it's as though Lacan assumes **"The Purloined Letter"** is about an affair, that it is of course a love letter connected in some way to betrayal and to "the ceremony of returning letters [at] the extinction of the fires of love's feasts" activating the plot (40). For Lacan, that people in high places commit adultery is a matter not really worth discussing; the exalted rank of the protagonists in **"The Purloined Letter"** simply saves their escapades "from vaudeville" (33). Yet, the more pressing issue in his analysis involves the way in which the tale functions as an allegory of psychoanalysis and the letter a signifier that possesses its subjects. As a result, he at once raises and evades the very questions he poses about legitimacy and about the role that a woman (or "woman") plays as its "guardian" within a structure of paternal inheritance and naming. What, for instance, is indicated about this structure if the words of a woman function as the only confirmation of both the presence of a fetus and the identity of its father? Lacan traces instead the path by which the letter, associated as it is with absence and femininity, arrives at the place of sexual difference. In a way, my argument follows his route, back to the female body and to a scene of symbolic castration in which the phallus is cut off from the certainty of paternity.[20]

According to Lacan, even if Dupin were to rip up the letter, we would still have a kind of metaphysical language, still be subjected to it; Dupin's guarantee of the letter's return to its protector demonstrates the fulfillment of his duty to communicate the sign's conflict with being: its split nature in relation to, as Derrida puts it, the symbolic absence "between the legs of woman," "the place of castration."[21] But the woman is more than the letter's guardian or protector; she is also its source, and the condition of its theft points to an identifiable relocation and not necessarily to a timeless law. For Derrida, Lacan's interpretation not only establishes the phallus as a privileged signifier "depend-[ing] neither on the signified, nor on the subject," but also erects a kind of "authentic life" for it, one that somehow persists in a realm beyond its material contingencies (423). "Materiality," says Derrida, "the sensory and repetitive side of the recording, the paper letter, drawings in ink, can be divided or multiplied, destroyed or set adrift. . . . If by some misfortune the phallus were divisible or reduced to the status of a part object, the entire edifice would collapse, and this must be [he adds with irony] avoided at all costs" (472-73, 478-79). The system of the symbolic, as Lacan thus formulates it, keeps the phallus in its proper place as, Derrida says, a "symbol only of an absence" and in the custody of (though not represented by) the woman (424). Derrida argues that, as a consequence, Lacan invests his interpretation in the "truth" of castration and in a theory of the signifier's "destiny as destination" (436). "What is called man and what is called woman might be subject to [phallogocentrism]," Derrida concedes, but "[a]ll of phallogocentrism is articulated on the basis of a determined *situation, . . .* An (individual, perceptual, local, cultural, historical, etc.) situation on the basis of which what is called a 'sexual theory' is elaborated . . ." (480-481).

From Derrida's perspective, the woman in **"The Purloined Letter"** is a figure who both sustains and threatens the system which contains her; everything about her leaks its divisions. The power of her letter resides in the writing itself, not in some original essence, for as Poe's tale indicates, the contracts, cast as both fiat and blackmail, bind one figure to another within a structure of fiction and narration. Poe's narrator is deeply invested in writing, Derrida reminds us, and how it transmits history and inheritance through a network of narrated frames.[22] In this network, and in the absence of any other proof, one could add that a child is the King's if the Queen says it is. Derrida's insistence upon the importance of the *parergon,* or the narrative frames, in fact creates an analogy with the woman's corporeal existence: like the story's enclosure within other stories, which gets repeatedly overlooked, her pregnant body becomes rendered as similarly supplemental, derivative, and ornamental material in relation to the paternal narrative of birthright that is generated through it. Yet, like Lacan, Derrida does not elaborate upon this analogy, nor upon the pun repeatedly produced around the issue of the woman "deliv-

ering" the letter. Though similarly rich in double entendres that open up the structure of sexual difference to the problem of its reproduction, Derrida's essay stops short of exploring how the threat of femininity, as Poe's tale indicates, is located between her words and her body—a body that threatens to split not in half but into two (438).

In her essay on the dizzying triptych of Poe, Lacan, and Derrida, Barbara Johnson draws attention to the rivalry between Dupin and the Minister within **"The Purloined Letter"** and to the rivalry between Derrida and Lacan over it. Pointing out where their theories tend to overlap and illuminate each other, Johnson notes Derrida's failure to acknowledge his debt to Lacan's *Écrits* and Lacan's refusal to credit Derrida's grammatology. In her own reading of Poe's tale, she folds their points together in order to address a third rivalry: that of Atreus and Thyestes, the story Dupin refers to in the letter he leaves for the Minister in place of the stolen one. Thus, enclosed within **"The Purloined Letter"** is an allusion to a tale involving adultery, infanticide, and debts recovered by ruthless violence. In fact, the Atreus-Thyestes reference functions as much more than a literary allusion and becomes a powerful echo, sounding a message down through Poe's tale and into the letters (Dupin's, the woman's) themselves. In Johnson's words, the "story is framed by its own content" (236). Moreover, in the version of the myth to which Dupin refers, it's a purloined letter that informs King Atreus of his wife's betrayal with his brother Thyestes; the Queen's own handwriting names Thyestes, not Atreus, as the father of her child. Brilliantly taking all of these debts and rivalries together, Johnson asserts that "the questions [raised by these texts] are legion: What is a man? Who is the child's father? What is the relation between incest, murder, and the death of a child? What is a king? How can we read the letter of our destiny? What is seeing?" (236).

Although Johnson does not track these questions back into **"The Purloined Letter,"** preferring to leave them as latent implications about the contingent nature of power, the tale itself follows them through to prospective answers. It binds the mythological account of adultery to the events at hand and artfully implies that, like Atreus's wife, this "exalted personage" is also pregnant. And although Johnson contends that the "letter's message is never revealed" (113), we are permitted to read all of the other words in **"The Purloined Letter"** and to consider what we select for detection—to go wide instead of deep. Without disputing the far-reaching, philosophical ideas that Johnson uncovers in or addresses through the tale, I remain unsure about her point that Poe offers "no possibility of a position of analytic mastery" (214). For, as a potential victim of the fierce retribution steadily referenced across the tale, the woman must assume this position and influence the interpretative direction of her letter. It is she who must master the events in an attempt to secure the letter's return to her, and her perspective exists in relation to the narrator's dispersed and repeated references to death and mutilation. She not only faces the prospect of being killed but of being killed in the kind of frenzy of violence that engulfs the women in the Rue Morgue and Marie Rogêt, as well as the cadavers served up for dinner in the myth of Atreus and Thyestes.

Ostensibly describing a "game of puzzles," Dupin's words here hint at the text's method of disclosing how the woman's hidden letter reflects her "excessively obvious" embodied perspective:

> A novice in the game generally seeks to embarrass his opponents by giving them the most minutely lettered names; but the adept selects such words as stretch, in large characters, from one end of the chart to the other. These, like the over-largely lettered signs and placards in the street, escape observation by dint of being excessively obvious; and here the physical oversight is precisely analogous with the moral inapprehension by which the intellect suffers to pass unnoticed those considerations which are too obtrusively and too palpably self-evident.
>
> (345)

The letter's content may not be directly presented to us but its message is disseminated throughout (or "stretched" across) the tale and beyond it, in the Atreus-Thyestes myth and in the texts circulating in Poe's 19th-century America. These signifiers indicate a signified and even a referent: a fetus, one that the "exalted royal personage" may or may not bring to term.

We are told at the outset, for example, that the woman's urgent concern rests on 'the non-appearance of certain results'—evasive wording that slyly imparts how the suspicion of pregnancy begins with the non-appearance of a certain monthly event (332). The Prefect later divulges that "[t]he personage robbed is more thoroughly convinced, every day, of the necessity of reclaiming her letter" (333). And again later: "[t]he fact is, it is becoming of more and more importance every day; and the reward has been lately doubled" (337). The passage of time, a pivotal element in the woman's distress, becomes bound up with the growing size of the reward, and because the latter does not remain fixed as the former progresses, this implication follows: that as the days and months pass, the reward is not the only thing growing in size. Mirroring or duplicating (in financial terms) another expanding entity in the woman's keeping, the reward has both a meta-phorical and literal purpose in the text. This purpose becomes especially legible when it is considered in relation to the words "conceal" and "concealment," which occur no fewer than seven times in the tale and which resonate with a lengthy (at least two-centuries) legal and public perception of hidden, clandestine pregnancies and suspicious infant deaths. Poe's nineteenth-century audience would have known that the word "concealment," accompanied by any hint of a missing newborn, denoted a very serious crime. In Dupin's words, "in all cases of concealment, a disposal of the article concealed—a disposal of it in this *recherché* manner—is in the very first instance, presumable and presumed" (341).

If a child is in fact born in the eighteen-month time frame of the tale, then he or she bears only the appearance of legitimacy and presents a surface behind which something else is hidden, a surface the letter threatens to break, a lineage it can set off course. "'Well, I may venture so far as to say,' the Prefect hints, 'that the paper gives its holder a certain power in a certain quarter where such power is immensely valuable'" (332). The implicit question as to why lineage is traced through paternity thus also resonates throughout the tale, for paternal naming and inheritance involve the sovereignty of the conceptual over the material and a severing of the link to the mother's body. In the tale's "economy of justice," to borrow Johnson's terminology—**"The Purloined Letter"** is after all a *"crime* story," she emphatically reminds us (214)—the redirection (or theft) of legitimacy from a maternal connection to a paternal claim underscores all of the male rivalries over the letter. The purloining of what belongs to a woman, moreover, takes place in front of her eyes: "Its rightful owner saw, but, of course, dared not call attention to the act, in the presence of the third personage who stood at her elbow" (Poe 333). That is, she comprehends the system of which she is a part, she perfectly sees how it works, and she maneuvers for latitude within it. As John Muller and William Richardson suggest in their interpretation of Lacan's essay on the tale, "The position of woman as signifier recalls Lévi-Strauss's thesis . . . : that the origin of language and culture involved establishing pacts by means of the exchange of women between groups (for whom the women then symbolized the pacts)."[23] A suggestive pun quickly emerges in the word "letter": if we consider that a woman's body lets blood monthly, makes her a blood letter, then this letter's circulation within a male system founds her value upon a process of exchange. The patrilineal direction of kinship, in other words, equates the meaning of the female body with a sealed envelope, one that contains a contract formulated in relation to a restricted economy. As Derrida muses, what if the letter were the property of no one, if its writing were set "adrift," "graft[ed] onto other writings" (484)? Or, in the words of one of the 1840s' most popular physicians and lecturers on sex and reproduction, Frederick Hollick, "No mater how obtained, by purchase, force, or strategem, a woman, as a wife, has always been considered . . . as a mere possession, like an animal. [The idea] crops up in many of our laws, customs, and ways of thinking and speaking. The term, 'my wife,' is still used by many with the same intent and meaning as my dog, or my horse."[24]

In **"The Purloined Letter,"** we are told that the Minister who takes the letter fixes a "large black" seal on it, a seal bearing the D— cipher or the Minister's initial. The seal, originally "small and red, with the ducal arms of the S— family," is obscured and the woman's "diminutive and feminine" handwriting is marked over in a "bold and decided" way (346). These seals determine the worth and authenticity of the letter and its contents, a letter that, now protruding from a cheap card-rack, gives the appearance of "worthlessness" (347). By virtue of the tale's metaphorical dexterity, the image of the letter's placement (the careless thrusting of it, no less) among "five or six visiting cards" insinuates the idea of promiscuity and illuminates the idea that the Minister can take the same entity (the woman, her letter, her fetus) and cast it within an entirely different frame (346). He possesses the story that can turn something pure into something prostituted. Suspended in this narrative, the woman risks the loss of her whiteness; the "soiled and torn condition of the letter" reflects back upon her and her offspring. Should the letter's contents be revealed, the possible child would be written off as worthless and illegitimate, a dead-end in the line of descent. He or she may look like the real thing, but would fall into the same category as a "trumpery fillagree card-rack of pasteboard," hanging from an umbilical-like "dirty blue ribbon" (346).

The play of color, of black against blue and red, furthermore, draws definitions of race and blood quantum into the crisis. Given that antebellum white women, especially the "exalted" or blueblood ones, were invested with the safekeeping of blood purity against any kind of amalgamation, it is possible that the tale's resolutely unnamed matter of blackmail generates the homophonic double of "black male" and thus adds another level of possible transgression to the secrets of the letter.[25] Although any kind of promiscuity threatened to sidetrack a line of descent from its so-called uncorrupted origin, it was the potential for contamination of white by black that lent the threat such urgency. As Joan Dayan writes in "Poe, Persons, and Property":

> Poe moves us back to a time when a myth of blood conferred an unpolluted, legitimate pedigree (**"The Fall of the House of Usher"** or **"William Wilson,"** both 1839) and forward to an analytics of blood that ushered in a complex of color: the ineradicable stain, the drop that could not be seen but must be feared (**"Ligeia," "The Masque of the Red Death,"** or *The Narrative of Arthur Gordon Pym* [1838]). . . . An innate quality (the unseen blood stain) could result in the conversion of a person into property. . . .[26]

The transformation through blood did not work the other way around, of course, for a white man's seal on a black woman's body conferred nothing in antebellum America, and descent remained traced through her.

Like the tales mentioned by Dayan, **"The Purloined Letter"** captures, in similarly allusive language, the possibility of an imperceptible stain upon a family of a "most exalted station" (Poe 332). And, at the same time that it explores the ways in which adultery in the 1840s was not just a matter of infidelity but a crime against the blood, an opening up of blood-lines to uncontrolled circulation, it gestures toward the accompanying development of proto-eugenic gynecological treatises on racial degeneration through bad breeding.[27] As physician Thomas Burgeland rhetorically asks in his 1837 study *Physiological Observations,* "would [the abolitionist] feel any objection for his daughter to enter into a matrimonial connexion with one of those beings whose cause he so impetuously advocated?" (35). Or as Hester Pendleton exclaims in a similar vein, a woman must choose her mate wisely; it is not by chance that "one child is born a fool, another a prodigy."[28] In an oblique reference to Madame Restell, the "infamous lady physician," Pendleton warns her readers to avoid the services she advertises "in the daily papers"; a woman should not do what she wants and then allow herself to "be probed with a whalebone." All of these kinds of perils crowd upon and into the purloined letter, a document that is, as we are told, "much soiled and crumpled" as it passes from the woman's boudoir to the Minister's apartment (Poe 346).

In such a degraded condition, the letter's description yields a subtle pattern of double entendres, especially when it is combined with that of the Minister's apartment. Noting these echoes, Derrida raises the possibility that "'the purloined letter, like an immense female body, stretch[es] out across the Minister's office when Dupin enters,'" adding that Dupin ultimately locates it "between the 'legs' of the fireplace" (440). In the context of nineteenth-century gynecology, the letter's position on the fireplace becomes a tongue-in-cheek reference to popular theories of a wayward woman's over-heated womb, the *furor uterinus,* resulting from thwarted and illicit love.[29] Moreover, if we can read the woman's body as metaphorically "stretched across" the room, then the very medical-like instruments used to probe it should not be tossed aside as irrelevant information, even if they're considered ineffective procedure on the tale's literal level of narration. Because these instruments tend only to be noted in the tale's scholarship as evidence of the police's failed detective work, the woman's body once more recedes to the background and the obvious "protrusion" of her letter fails to designate what is happening with her belly. Putting this stretched and splayed body back in the picture brings into focus the subject of nineteenth-century reproductive control, spotlighting in particular the trademark utensils of gynecology's abortion procedures: the uterine sound and curette, two long and needle-like utensils used to probe the uterus for different types of growths.

In *One Hundred Years of Gynaecology, 1800-1900,* James Ricci discusses how the development of gynecology into the nineteenth century's largest field of medical specialization was accompanied by countless new procedures and instruments. As he puts it, "The female genital organs were subjected to minute analysis and [different] areas were described in detail" (5). Gynecologists created four-hundred different kinds of specula and used them, along with the sound and the curette, to boldly "explore the cavity of the uterus" (25). Although Ricci does not mention it, the spectacular expansion of gynecology in the 1830s and 40s—as well as the controversies he notes over women's submission to hazardous treatments involving sounds and curettes—must be understood in terms of women's quest for reproductive control. A curette, for instance, was not in all cases used to tap benign uterine cysts. Many nineteenth-century American women would have learned how to read the secondary meanings of gynecological procedures and advertisements. Making something illegal or illicit does not repress it, as Foucault reminds us, but rather multiplies ways of saying and not saying it:

> 'Suppose you detail,' said [the narrator of **"The Purloined Letter"**], 'the particulars of your search.'
>
> 'Why the fact is,' [replied the Prefect] . . . 'we searched *every where.* . . . We opened every possible drawer; and I presume you know that, to a properly trained police agent, such a thing as a *secret* drawer is impossible. Any man is a dolt who permits a "secret" drawer to escape him in a search of this kind. The thing is *so* plain. There is a certain amount of bulk—of space—to be accounted for in every cabinet. . . . After the cabinets we took the chairs. The cushions we probed with the fine long needles you have seen me employ. From the tables we removed the tops.'
>
> 'Why so?' [asked the narrator] . . . 'Couldn't the cavity be detected by sounding?' . . .

> 'By no means, if, when the article is deposited, a sufficient wadding of cotton be placed around it.'
>
> . . . . .
>
> 'But you could not have removed—you could not have taken to pieces *all* the articles of furniture in which it would have been possible to make a deposit in the manner you mention. A letter may be compressed into a thin spiral roll, not differing much in shape or bulk from a large knitting-needle, and in this form it might be inserted into the rung of a chair, for example. . . . I presume . . . you probed the beds and bed-clothes'
>
> . . . . .
>
> 'Certainly: we opened every package and parcel. . . . We also measured the thickness of every book-*cover,* with the most accurate admeasurement, and applied to each the most jealous scrutiny of the microscope. Had any of the bindings been recently meddled with it would have been utterly impossible that the fact should have escaped observation. Some five or six volumes, just from the hands of the binder, we carefully probed, longitudinally, with the needles.'
>
> . . . . .
>
> 'You looked into the cellars?'
>
> 'We did.'
>
> (335-337)

With trenchant echoes of gynecological instruments and procedures, and through droll metaphors for the dark interiority of the female anatomy (cabinets, cavities, cellars), this dialogue represents the unrepresentable: the secret of abortion contained within the purloined letter.[30] "What is all this boring, and probing, and sounding, and scrutinizing with the microscope . . . ?," asks Dupin in both a condensed recapitulation of the telling verbs and an almost verbatim duplication of the language of surgical gynecology (341). Like everything else in the tale, that which is private, secret, and unspoken is at the same time public, clear, and apparent—at least when approached through a particular frame of reference.

As a result, gestures and words meant to disguise information may in fact divulge it. This is Dupin's advantage. Behind his dark glasses and ironic statements, he reads both linguistic and corporeal signs: the Minister's sham laziness, the Prefect's vocal hesitations. The question of the body's production of signs also occurs in the tale's attention to handwriting; it seems that handwriting is something unique, inherently recognizable, something that ties, like an umbilical cord, the production of the words to the producer of them. It's because the letter is in the woman's distinctive handwriting that she is in such trouble. Furthermore, Dupin remarks that the Minister will know who fooled him with a new letter because Dupin's own handwriting will be familiar to him. We also observe the Prefect write and sign the reward check for Dupin. In each case, the handwriting at once materializes a source and a destination.

But, twice the word *"fac-simile"* occurs in the tale, thus collapsing any guarantee or endorsement of authenticity (347, 348). **"The Purloined Letter"** here opens onto the issue of passing that follows from its exploration of adultery and abortion. In other words, if bodies give something away or express something authentic, it is because a conceptual framework of surface and depth, of the feigned and the *bona fide,* is already in place. What is counterfeit in one context is sterling in another. Though the body may be a source of signifying innovations, there is nothing inherent in the blood, nothing that yields a timeless secret or value. Even a maternal body, with its pronounced dilation, can be concealed or circumvented, and the question of paternity can certainly be covered up.

Dupin returns exactly this possibility to the woman in **"The Purloined Letter."** If there is a child born (after all that probing), then Dupin permits it to pass as legitimate, realizing that passing is all there is. If an abortion took place, he leaves it out of his scheme's equation; his goal is not to see the woman punished as an adulteress who tried to get rid of the evidence.[31] Though motivated by his own desire to outwit the Minister and to cash in on the reward, Dupin's remarks about the success of his reasoning resonate with significance about blood quantum, legitimacy, and morality. He states:

> [M]athematical reasoning is merely logic applied to observation upon form and quantity. The great error lies in supposing that even the truths of what is called *pure* algebra, are abstract or general truths. . . . What is true of relation—of form and quantity—is often grossly false in regard to morals, for example. . . . There are numerous other mathematical truths which are only truths within the limits of *relation.* . . . [O]ccasions may occur where x^2+px is *not* altogether equal to q.
>
> (342-43)

His words here seem to directly quote and disparage the kind of racial "science" circulating in early nineteenth-century America and evident in this 1815 algebraist's theorem:

> . . . [T]he algebraical notation is the most convenient and intelligible. Let us express the pure blood of the white in the capital letters of the printed alphabet, the pure blood of the negro in the small letters of the printed alphabet, and any given mixture of either, by way of abridgment in MS. letters.
>
> Let the first crossing be of *a,* a pure negro, with A, pure white. The unit of blood of the issue being composed of the half of that of each parent, will be $a/2+A/2$. Call it, for abbreviation b (half-blood).
>
> Let the second crossing be that of b and B, the blood of the issue will be $b/2+B/2$, or substituting $b/2$ its equivalent, it will be $a/4+A/4+B/2$, call it q (quarteroon) being ¼ negro blood.[32]

The algebraist then continues through several more mathematical formulas, concluding with "e": "But if e be emancipated, he becomes a free white man, and a citizen of the United States to all intents and purposes" (114). For Dupin, the world cannot be so neatly ordered; it is a place of metaphors and combinations and not of rigid categories. Repudiating the kind of black-and-white notions which dictate, for instance, that no one man can be both "mathematician and . . . poet," he refuses to allow the purloined letter to be put in the service of taxonomies of blood and legitimacy (Poe 344). In the end, his thinking averts the kind of fratricidal violence implied in the myth of Atreus and Thyestes, which, in 1845, amounts to a foreboding message about the escalating rhetoric surrounding racial identity, white motherhood, and the future of the nation.

Notes

1. 330. Alcott's italics.

2. *The History of Sexuality,* 35, 48. Foucault's italics.

3. See Walters' Introduction to *Primers for Prudery: Sexual Advice to Victorian Americans,* in which he analyzes the market for the literature in terms of a complex "web of personal and social considerations" (15).

4. In the 1830s and 1840s, every major New England newspaper carried advertisements for abortion drugs, condoms, and surgical abortion procedures; in some cities, advertisements for these products and procedures were also left in hotel lobbies and in railroad depots. In response to the emerging legislation, the number of ads remained high, but their wording became increasingly veiled. See also Horowitz, *Rereading Sex,* 70-122.

5. See Janet Farrell Brodie's chapter titled "The Antebellum Public Audience," 136-80. See also Nancy Theriot's *Mothers and Daughters in Nineteenth-Century America,* in which she demonstrates that the term "voluntary motherhood" was in circulation well before the late nineteenth-century feminist movement of the same name came into being (Theriot, 41-2).

6. For example, the January 7, 1843, issue of *The New York Lancet,* which carried an advertisement by a Mr. J. H. Ross, "Cupper and Leecher," who publicized in barely readable text that "Mrs. R. applies Leeches to the Os Uteri"—one way to cure the problem of a woman's so-called arrested monthly bleeding.

7. New York *Sunday Morning News,* July 21, 1835.

8. Quoted in Brodie, *Contraception and Abortion,* 225. See also her chapter titled "Criminalizing

Reproductive Control" for the progression of state laws against contraception and abortion in the second half of the nineteenth century.

9. Pseudo-Aristotle, v.

10. *One Hundred Years,* vii.

11. Foucault, 147. See the last chapter of *The History of Sexuality, Vol. I,* in which Foucault analyzes how definitions of sex and life came under state power. The "thorough medicalization of women's bodies," Foucault asserts, was carried out "in the name of the responsibility [women] owed to the health of their children, the solidity of the family institution, and the safeguarding of society" (146). See also Brodie on the rise of restrictive legislation in her chapter "Criminalizing Reproductive Control," which opens with her argument that the second half of the nineteenth century saw a new effort to "restore American 'social purity'" through the restriction of sexuality and the "control of reproduction" (254).

12. Quoted in Ricci, *One Hundred Years,* 37.

13. Walters, *Primers for Prudery,* 2.

14. "Seminar," 34.

15. Edgar Allan Poe, "The Purloined Letter." *The Fall of the House of Usher and Other Writings* (London: Penguin, 1986), 332. All quotations from the tale are from this text. All italics are Poe's.

16. "The Frame of Reference," 213.

17. "There is much made of nothing in 'The Purloined Letter,'" writes the reviewer in 1845, "the story of which is simple. . . ." Quoted in Mabbott, "The Text," 5.

18. "Seminar," 81.

19. If anything breaks the contract binding women to a notion of instinctive motherhood, it's abortion. According to Helen Lefkowitz Horowitz's findings, any news in the 1840s that a married woman had paid a visit to Madame Restell threatened the foundations of "male control" (206).

20. For example, on the front page of *Madame Restell,* by a physician of New York, the author included the epigraph, "Thou shalt not commit adultery."

21. *The Post Card,* 444, 439. Derrida's italics.

22. The Dupin trilogy repeatedly calls our attention to written material: the reward check, the letter, and the Prefect's notes in "The Purloined Letter"; the books, newspaper articles, and the reward notice for the orangutan in "The Murders in the Rue Morgue"; the quoted newspaper articles that make up the majority of "The Mystery of Marie Rogêt."

23. *The Purloined Poe,* 95.

24. *The Origin of Life,* 723.

25. The word "blackmail" had entered the language about a half-century before Poe's time. For a great discussion of blackmail and its link to the policing of sexual standards, see McLaren, *Sexual Blackmail.*

26. 119.

27. To offer just three examples here: Burgeland, *Physiological Observations,* which asserts that *"the Negro Race nearly approaches the monkey"* (36, Burgeland's italics); Walker, *Intermarriage; or the Mode in Which, and the Causes Why, Beauty, Health and Intellect Result from Certain Unions, and Deformity, Disease and Insanity, from Others,* which establishes criteria for mate selection; and Lugol, *Why Will You Die, or Researches on Scrofula,* with reference to the propagation of disease by inheritance and intermarriage, which imagines great families becoming "extinct" because of "defects" produced by "cross[ing] the races" (106, 233).

28. *The Parents Guide,* 1, 209.

29. See Dixon, *Perilous Chastity: Women and Illness in Pre-Enlightenment Art and Medicine* for an in-depth discussion of this condition. Dixon's study of numerous paintings of seventeenth- and eighteenth-century lovesick women highlights the repeated depiction of a woman with open legs before a firepot or a fireplace. See, in particular, her chapter titled "The Womb Occupied, Restored, and Satiated: Corporeal Cures" for the references to *furor uterinus* in medical treatises, proverbs, emblem books, and dictionaries of the time. Though Dixon does not mention it, many of the paintings she reproduces for discussion also depict the spread-legged woman holding a letter, the contents of which we cannot see, as she swoons before a doctor.

30. This notion of the obscured representation of abortion is also asserted by Laura Saltz in her essay on "The Mystery of Marie Rogêt." Demonstrating that Poe knew that a botched abortion was the probable cause of Mary Rogêt's death and drawing on the newspaper accounts of Madame Restell's trials, Saltz argues that "The Mystery" is a tale that buries an abortion within its elliptical, layered narrative. Saltz also discusses "The Murders in the Rue Morgue," the other tale in the trilogy that includes "The Purloined Letter," but she only once refers to "The Purloined Letter." In a provocative assertion, she states: "Like the purloined letter, her [Marie's] corpse is visible, but the undisclosed crime against her is held in sufferance" (242).

31. I don't necessarily mean to turn Dupin into a reproductive-rights hero here; it's implied, for instance, that he holds onto the letter until the reward exponentially increases. In other words, by waiting for things to get bigger and bigger, he prolongs the woman's anxiety and possibly waylays her option of seeking an abortion. What Dupin seems most invested in—other than the money—is the permission for something or someone to be two things at once.

32. Quoted in Sellers, *Neither Black nor White*, 113-14.

Bibliography

Alcott, William A. *The Young Man's Guide.* 16th ed. Boston: T. R. Marvin, 1846.

Brodie, Janet F. *Contraception and Abortion in Nineteenth-Century America.* Ithaca: Cornell University Press, 1994.

Burgeland, Thomas. *Physiological Observations.* London: W. Day, 1837.

Dayan, Joan. "Poe, Persons, and Property." In *Romancing the Shadow: Poe and Race.* Edited by J. Gerald Kennedy and Liliane Weissberg, 106-26. Oxford: Oxford University Press, 2001.

Derrida, Jacques. *The Post Card: From Socrates to Freud and Beyond.* Translated by Alan Bass. Chicago: University of Chicago Press, 1987.

Dixon, Laurinda. *Perilous Chastity: Women and Illness in Pre-Enlightenment Art and Medicine.* Ithaca: Cornell University Press, 1995.

Foucault, Michel. *The History of Sexuality: An Introduction.* Vol. 1, *The History of Sexuality.* New York: Vintage, 1990.

Hollick, Frederick. *The Origin of Life.* New York: The American News Company, 1845.

Johnson, Barbara. "The Frame of Reference: Poe, Lacan, Derrida." In *The Purloined Poe: Lacan, Derrida, and Psychoanalytic Reading.* Edited by John P. Muller and William J. Richardson, 213-51. Baltimore: Johns Hopkins University Press, 1988.

Lacan, Jacques. "Seminar on 'The Purloined Letter.'" *The Purloined Poe: Lacan, Derrida, and Psychoanalytic Reading.* Edited by John P. Muller and William J. Richardson, 28-54. Baltimore: Johns Hopkins University Press, 1988.

Lefkowitz, Helen H. *Rereading Sex: Battles over Sexual Knowledge and Suppression in Nineteenth-Century America.* New York: Alfred A. Knopf, 2002.

Lugol, J. G. *Why Will You Die, or Researches of Scrofula.* New York: Fowler and Wells, 1847.

Mabbott, Thomas O. "The Text of 'The Purloined Letter,' with Notes." In *The Purloined Poe: Lacan, Derrida, and Psychoanalytic Reading.* Edited by John P. Muller and William J. Richardson, 3-27. Baltimore: Johns Hopkins University Press, 1988.

McLaren, Angus. *Sexual Blackmail: A Modern History.* Cambridge: Harvard University Press, 2002.

Muller, John and William Richardson, ed. *The Purloined Poe: Lacan, Derrida, and Psychoanalytic Reading.* Baltimore: Johns Hopkins University Press, 1988.

New York *Sunday Morning News.* July 21, 1835.

Pendleton, Hester. *The Parents Guide for the Transmission of Desired Qualities to Offspring.* New York: Fowler and Wells, 1848.

Physician of New York. *Madame Restell: An Account of Her Life and Horrible Practices.* New York: 1847.

Poe, Edgar Allan. "The Purloined Letter." In *The Fall of the House of Usher and Other Writings.* London: Penguin, 1986.

Pseudo-Aristotle. *Aristotle's Master-piece.* New York: 1817.

Ricci, James. *One Hundred Years of Gynaecology, 1800-1900.* Philadelphia: Blakiston, 1945.

Ross, J. H. "Cupper and Leecher." *The New York Lancet.* January 7, 1843.

Saltz, Laura. "(Horrible to Relate!) Recovering the Body of Marie Rogêt." In *The American Face of Edgar Allan Poe.* Edited by Shawn Rosenheim and Stephen Rachman, 237-70. Baltimore: Johns Hopkins University Press, 1995.

Sellers, Werner. *Neither Black nor White Yet Both: Thematic Explorations of Interracial Literature.* Oxford: Oxford University Press, 1997.

Theriot, Nancy. *Mothers and Daughters in Nineteenth-Century America: The Biosocial Construction of Femininity.* Lexington: University Press of Kentucky, 1996.

Walker, Alexander. *Intermarriage; or the Mode in Which, and the Causes Why, Beauty, Health and Intellect Result from Certain Unions, and Deformity, Disease and Insanity, from Others.* London: John Churchill, 1838.

Walters, Ronald. *Primers for Prudery: Sexual Advice to Victorian Americans.* Baltimore: Johns Hopkins University Press, 2000.

Alexander Schlutz (essay date summer 2008)

SOURCE: Schlutz, Alexander. "Purloined Voices: Edgar Allan Poe Reading Samuel Taylor Coleridge." *Studies in Romanticism* 47, no. 2 (summer 2008): 195-224.

[*In the following essay, Schlutz traces the influence of Samuel Taylor Coleridge's philosophical views on Poe's work from the early essay "Letter to B——" to the long poem* Eureka. *Schlutz asserts that "The Purloined Letter" emphasizes the superiority of the power of poetic imagination alone over the union of poetry, philosophy, and faith posited by Coleridge.*]

The pervasive influence of Samuel Taylor Coleridge's work on the writings of Edgar Allan Poe is well documented. As early as 1930, in his article "Poe's Debt to Coleridge," Floyd Stovall maintained that Coleridge was "the guiding genius of Poe's entire intellectual life."[1] Daniel Hoffman's contention from 1972 that "the philosophical breadth of Coleridge underlies Poe's acute narrowness as the pyramid on the Great Seal of the United States at its summit supports one assured and unblinking eye" is equally far-reaching.[2] Yet, as undeniable as the influential presence of Coleridge's thought in Poe's texts might be, the insinuation of seamless continuity that underpins these and similar assessments needs to be called into question. Poe is in fact far from completing the philosophical structure that Coleridge had attempted to build, and if he inhabits it, he does so not as a headstone in its supporting arch, but rather as a threat to its desired foundations.

Poe felt without a doubt that he had discovered the voice of a kindred spirit in Coleridge's early poetry, a voice that would continue to reverberate in Poe's prose, where elements of Coleridge's *Rime of the Ancyent Marinere* resurface with the persistence of those subconscious depths of guilt and speechless dread that fascinated both writers equally. It is also an open secret that Poe the reviewer and literary critic freely borrowed from Coleridge's poetological reflections to suit his needs, unabashedly presenting Coleridge's aesthetic principles, specifically those developed in the *Biographia Literaria,* as his own critical insights. Even Poe's famous "tales of ratiocination," which institute the modern genre of detective fiction, owe, as Christopher Kearns has rightfully pointed out, a debt to Coleridge that is just as heavy as it is unacknowledged.[3] Despite their pervasiveness, such "effects" of literary influence would not have greatly troubled Coleridge, for whom Poe, who ultimately no more than adopts Coleridge's own strategies of textual appropriation, obviously presented no direct literary competition. What would have been of some concern for Coleridge, however—had Poe, like the "Frogpondian" Emerson, been able to make the pilgrimage to Highgate for a hypothetical table talk with the sage of British Romantic letters—is the fact that the philosophical and religious convictions that underpin Coleridge's thought ceased to have any purchase on Poe's thought and prose. If Emerson's Unitarianism no longer seemed a tenable religious position for the ex-Unitarian Coleridge, deeply immersed in Trinitarian belief in the

last years of his life, the differences in religious, philosophical, and aesthetic sensibility between Coleridge and Poe ultimately run far deeper than such doctrinal conflicts.

Coleridge's desire for an all-encompassing philosophical system based on, and reconcilable with, Christian religious belief is firmly rooted in the philosophical discussion of the European Romantic period, in which the products and processes of the poetic imagination, a "faculty divine" for Coleridge, could be seen to mediate between the only seemingly irreconcilable realms of the empirical and the transcendent. Only a few decades later this very desire would appear as no less than unpoetic for Poe, who had already embarked on the vessel of an aesthetics that would mark the end of the nineteenth century, and for which the work of art is no longer proof of the connection between the human and the divine, but rather an autonomous aesthetic creation that derives its specific dignity from the moment of poetic eternity it upholds in the face of the inevitability of human death. Poe's appropriation of Coleridge's philosophical voice, which cannot entail the casting of an even wider analytical net, is, as I will attempt to demonstrate on the following pages, rather part of a narrative strategy that represents the systematic urge of the philosopher as the desire of the storyteller to weave together the various strands of his narrative in a satisfactory fashion. Where Coleridge speaks of philosophical method, Poe sees the workings of a plot, and it will be the task of this essay to delineate the intricate intertextual movement from one perspective to the other. This endeavor will then indeed span Poe's entire intellectual career, as it leads from his earliest poetological text, "Letter to B—," via one of his best-known tales, **"The Purloined Letter,"** to *Eureka,* the rarely discussed final work of Poe's life. Each of these texts, while relying on Coleridgean ideas outlined in the *Biographia Literaria* and *The Friend,* thoroughly remakes its unacknowledged sources, hiding a dependency that is ultimately a springboard to something new.

1. LETTER TO B—

To properly unravel the process of transformation and appropriation that constitutes Edgar Allan Poe's reading of Samuel Taylor Coleridge it seems advisable to begin at the beginning and to turn our attention to Poe's earliest poetological text, "Letter to Mr.—," the preface to an 1831 collection of Poe's poems that would be published separately and with only slight alterations in the *Southern Literary Messenger* in 1836 as "Letter to B—." Here one can find the following, typically ambivalent, passage with regard to Coleridge:

> Of Coleridge I cannot speak but with reverence. His towering intellect! his gigantic power! He is one more evidence of the fact "que la plupart des sectes ont rai-

son dans une bonne partie de ce qu'elles avancent, mais non pas en ce qu'elles nient." He has imprisoned his own conceptions by the barrier he has erected against those of others. It is lamentable to think that such a mind should be buried in metaphysics, and, like the Nyctanthes, waste its perfume upon the night alone.[4]

These words present neither the unquestioning acceptance of a "guiding genius" or of a philosophical foundation for Poe's own work, nor do they simply express the common combination of admiration and regret with regard to Coleridge's philosophical endeavors that is usually founded on a mere refusal to actually come to terms with Coleridge the philosopher and metaphysician. There is more at stake in "Letter to B—" than is apparent at a merely superficial glance. In its original form, the text is designed as a defense of Poe's own poetry, which he fears will be judged by his American reviewers according to the positions of the "Lake school." In Poe's rendition, a conception of poetry as a philosophical and metaphysical practice of instruction is foremost among these positions, a tenet against which he upholds the view of poetry as solely a means for the production of beauty and pleasure: "Against the subtleties which would make poetry a study—not a passion—it becomes the metaphysician to reason—but the poet to protest" (*Essays* 8).

In his protest, Poe devotes lengthy passages to ridicule Wordsworth, but it is quite obvious that the true object and the only real threat against which he prepares his defense is Coleridge. Poe had in fact sufficient reason for such a strategy of distraction, for when he claims at the end of his text, that "A poem, in my opinion, is opposed to a work of science by having for its *immediate* object, pleasure, not truth . . ." he is lifting his opinion directly from Chapter 14 of the *Biographia Literaria*[5] (*Essays* 11). Poe, who must have known how obvious the unacknowledged source for the central poetological claim of his own text would be for anybody familiar with Coleridge—who was after all no stranger on the American intellectual and literary scene of the 1830s—had compared Wordsworth's genius to that of a pickpocket only a few pages earlier. Given Poe's adeptness at the literary "picking of pockets" in the same text, such allusions seem less the product of a guilty conscience than the indulgences of a trickster who enjoys the game of hiding his purloined letters in plain sight, more or less taunting the reader to discover them. In this respect, the closing lines of "Letter to B—" are difficult to surpass in their thinly veiled irony. Summing up "this long rigmarole," which attempts to carve out a position of originality for his own poetry, Poe once more expresses his open disdain "for the metaphysical poets," for whom "*as* poets" he has "the most *sovereign* contempt" (*Essays* 11, second emphasis mine). The fact that these metaphysically inclined poets have a large following, Poe

then attests, cannot be adduced as proof of the superior quality of their poetry, a claim he himself will "prove" with the following quoted lines: "No Indian prince has to his palace / More followers than a thief to the gallows." After openly appropriating Coleridge's very words in order to argue for his own superiority over Coleridge and the poets of the "Lake School," Poe can only have added these closing lines of the text in the "spirit of perversity" he would later immortalize in his short stories, and which inexorably forces the criminal to divulge his perfect crime to the police.

At the same time, the best audience for Poe's ingenuity as a pickpocket might in fact be Coleridge himself, since Poe, who had closely read the *Biographia*, does not merely purloin Coleridge but does so quite consciously in truly Coleridgean fashion. In a calculated rhetorical move, not only Poe's own position, but also his preceding critique of Coleridge is presented in words—French and English—that are taken verbatim from Chapter 12 of the *Biographia*, where Coleridge himself had written the following:

> The spirit of sectarianism has been hitherto our fault and the cause of our failures. We have imprisoned our conceptions by the lines which we have drawn, in order to exclude the conceptions of others. J'ai trouvé que la plupart des sectes ont raison dans une bonne partie de ce qu'elles avancent, mais non pas tant en ce qu'elles nient.[6]

While Poe was unaware that the French just as much as the English in Coleridge's passage is derived from the writings of Leibniz, the French clearly indicated to him that he was quoting a quote. In what Jonathan Bate has described as a true act of homage to Coleridge, Poe hence repeats almost uncannily Coleridge's own pastiche-like practice of creating his text out of a network of quotes.[7] He thus ironically undermines Coleridge's authority by a repetition of the latter's very own textual practice: he usurps his voice and makes it his own. The first version of Poe's text, "Letter to Mr—," as Bate points out, in fact still acknowledges the quote and reads as follows: "To use an author quoted by himself [i.e., Coleridge], 'J'ai trouvé que la plupart des sectes ont raison dans une bonne partie de ce qu'elles avancent, mais non pas en ce qu'elles nient.' . . ." Using the quote against Coleridge, Poe then continues: "and, to employ his own language, he has imprisoned his own conceptions by the barrier he has erected against those of others" (Bate 256). The fact that in "Letter to B—" Poe removes all indications that the French quote is derived from the *Biographia* only heightens the effect of a conscious usurpation of Coleridge's voice, which, however, is even less Coleridge's "own" than Poe expected. Whether such acts of appropriation can be seen as acts of homage, as Bate suggests, or whether they are, as Christopher Kearns puts it, "symptomatic of an attitude hovering uneasily between admiration and an almost Bloomian anxiety of influence," they are ultimately indicative of more than the either uneasy or almost flippant relationship of a young American writer to an elder statesman of English Romantic letters (Kearns 4).

For Poe also seizes this quote from one of the most central passages in the *Biographia Literaria,* where it appears at the end of what is in fact an extended direct translation from Leibniz via Jacobi, in which the latter outlines the concern that is also situated at the heart of Coleridge's own philosophical project. Coleridge claims in Leibniz's doubly translated words that if all philosophical systems known so far were considered in their fundamental and only seemingly contradictory truths, they would be found "united in one perspective central point, which shows regularity and coincidence of all the parts in the very object, which from every other point of view must appear confused and distorted" (*BL* 1: 247). This promise, which immediately precedes the passage quoted by Poe, is none other than the ultimate philosophical goal Coleridge had set himself for his still to be written "magnum opus," where in the system of all systems every possible philosophical perspective could ultimately be reduced to the same underlying principles.

From which position, then, is it possible for Poe at this very moment to appropriate Coleridge's own, albeit borrowed words, turn them inside out and present precisely this all-inclusive philosophical position as Coleridge's own "imprisonment"? Obviously, Poe could not pretend to present a more inclusive philosophical position than that of Coleridge himself. It is not after all the metaphysician who reasons here, but rather the poet, who protests. Part of the answer is again, as Christopher Kearns has demonstrated, a premeditated alteration in Poe's text of Coleridge's Leibnizean quotation: Whereas Leibniz and thus Coleridge had claimed that most philosophical "sects" could be found to be correct in what they claimed "but *not so much* in what they deny"—"mais non pas tant en ce qu'elles nient"—Poe, whose excellent knowledge of French makes it quite probably more than a simple oversight, drops the "tant" to alter the sentence to "mais non pas en ce qu'elles nient"—"but *not* in what they deny." Poe thus attributes to Coleridge precisely the kind of exclusionary perspective against which Coleridge had originally used the quote, a strategy which in turn gives Poe, who actively "imprisons" Coleridge, as Kearns remarks, by way of a mistranscription, the necessary space to take up a contrary perspective (Kearns 12). Coleridge's desired philosophical position, under which all others could be subsumed without harm or distortion, must be actively made to deny the right of entry to at least one: Poe's own poetic protest against the paternal gesture of such all-inclusiveness itself.

Ultimately more important, however, than the textual sleight of hand that makes room for it, is the precise nature of the perspective that Poe feels he needs to free for himself in "Letter to B—." For Poe is of course aware that he misrepresents Coleridge's position when he insinuates that the latter's view of poetry would turn the aesthetic text into a mere vehicle for philosophical instruction. Borrowing Coleridge's very words to present his own aesthetic perspective makes that more than obvious, and Poe, an avid reader of Coleridge's poetry, would have had no doubts that his categorical assertions were far from the truth. What Poe ultimately does object to in "Letter to B—" is not Coleridge's championing of philosophy over poetry, clearly no more than a rhetorical straw man to present Poe's argument more forcefully, but rather the ultimate *union* of poetry and philosophy that was so essential for Coleridge. For the latter had written after all—in a passage of the *Biographia Literaria* with which Poe was certainly familiar, and which functions there, in another twist of textual irony, to disqualify the poetic authority of Wordsworth—that "No man was ever yet a great poet, without being at the same time a profound philosopher" (*BL* 2: 25f.). This assertion presents a claim Poe is no longer willing to make, and while his position may in part reflect the unwillingness of the American writer to burden himself with the bulky British ballast of a Coleridgean erudition, it mainly derives from an aesthetic perspective that demands complete autonomy for art and poetry, aesthetic discourses which should no longer rely for their justification on fulfilling a mediatory function in the establishment of a philosophical system. And this, I would hold, is precisely the rift which needs to be located in the intertextual relation of these two writers, marked by an intricate simultaneity of sameness and difference, where the same words take on different meanings as they make their way from Coleridge's page to Poe's pen. While Coleridge strove to maintain the delicate balance of poetry and philosophy, Poe, who could no longer believe in a basis of their union, read Coleridge's words solely with the eyes of the writer. What embodied a philosophical desire for the latter becomes an aesthetic construct for the former, and the "Letter to B—" is emblematic of the loss of faith in the explanatory power of philosophical systems that informs Poe's reading of Coleridge.

Poe in fact brilliantly institutes this very reversal in the following paragraph in "Letter to B—," which makes a rather despairing claim about Coleridge's "philosophical breadth" in the *Biographia Literaria*:

He goes wrong by reason of his very profundity, and of his error we have a natural type in the contemplation of a star. He who regards it directly and intensely sees, it is true, the star, but it is the star without a ray—while he who surveys it less inquisitively is conscious of all for which the star is useful to us below—its brilliancy and its beauty.

(*Essays* 8)

The analogy Poe uses here to illustrate Coleridge's "error" is of course by no means as "natural" as he would lead the reader to believe. Poe has undoubtedly lifted it from Plato's "Phaedo," where the fatal effects for the eye of a direct gaze into the sun had already been connected to the problems of philosophical investigation. But Poe, in by now familiar fashion not only hides the textual origin of a "natural type," he also (mis)uses it quite consciously to undermine the authority of his unacknowledged sources. This kind of textual borrowing might in fact be Poe's very own version of "that moral mechanism by which the simplicity of a child may overbalance the wisdom of a man," which he had advocated in the previous paragraph. Not only must we assume that Poe here in not quite serious presumptuousness chides Coleridge for not having understood his Plato, Poe also employs the Phaedo's imagery in order to replace the Platonic philosopher-king with the exiled poet as the most adept at judging what is "useful to us" in the sublunar world.

In one short paragraph Poe reverses and ultimately severs the connection between the noumenal and the phenomenal world, as well as the union of the True, the Good, and the Beautiful so essential for both Plato and Coleridge. In the "Phaedo," Plato's Socrates had after all denounced the philosophical focus on *empirical* phenomena as a possible source of epistemological blindness, a danger against which he recommends the use of theories and thus of abstract vision in the endeavor to understand the causes of the empirical world. A reliance on *aisthesis,* on the eyes and the bodily senses, threatens to be blinding in the "Phaedo," while the truth about the empirical world can only be revealed through the "indirect" way of mental vision that is philosophical theory. This "second voyage" of deduction, as is well known, ultimately leads to the affirmation of the noumenal realm of forms as the truly real, an abstract truth of which the world of empirical objects is only a reflection. Poe, however, denounces precisely the metaphysical reflections of the philosopher as the gaze into the sun that would blind him, and thus urges a greater attention to the things "here below," while recommending only the occasional and less inquisitive glance in the direction of the stars above. Yet even though a nod to Francis Bacon in the preceding paragraph might suggest such a conclusion, Poe does not advocate here an exclusive preference

for the empirical over the ideal. What the quoted paragraph praises are rather the *aesthetic effects* of the star, "its brilliancy and its beauty." These effects prove ultimately more essential than the star itself, which becomes negligible and even detrimental in the search for truth Poe delineates. To contemplate the essence of the star will reveal only empty words and concepts— "it is true, the star"—, which have no discernible meaning for the human observer. Such empty talk— the metaphysical cant of popularized Transcendentalism Poe so passionately disdained—is equivalent to mere darkness, "the star without a ray," and the investigation of a solar eclipse, which had served Plato as the vehicle for his philosophical metaphor, has more than lost its interest in Poe's aesthetic argument. Beauty and aesthetic brilliancy in turn, rather than having their causes in the ideal form of Beauty from which they partake and derive their *quidditas* according to the Socrates of the Phaedo, now become the only truth available, and the only one of any moral use to those living below. Art thus replaces philosophy as the *deuteros plous* and the practice best-suited to afford some much-needed light to human affairs.

From such a perspective it must necessarily seem "lamentable" that Coleridge's mind should be "buried in metaphysics," and that he, like the Nyctanthes, the "sad tree" of India, which flowers brilliantly at night but drops its blossoms at dawn, should "waste[s] his perfume upon the night alone." And who better predisposed than Poe, master of literary ventriloquism and expert in channeling narrative voices from the grave and the cells of the condemned, to free Coleridge from such ostensibly self-imposed imprisonment, bringing the perfume of his brightest nightly flowers to the dark light of day? To observe more closely how Poe picks the locks of Coleridge's metaphysical chains, we now need to skip fourteen years ahead, to 1845, the date of publication of that tale of Poe which is most overtly concerned with the problem of imprisoned perspectives and the possibility of a privileged point of observation from which they could all be united.

PURLOINED LETTERS AND ESSAYS ON METHOD

"The Purloined Letter" is not only one of Poe's best-known and probably the most-discussed of his stories, but also a tale that attests to the lasting influence of Coleridge's ideas on Poe's thought and prose. Indeed, the very Coleridgean predicament that Poe takes up in the "Letter to B—" also constitutes the central problem and determines the narrative structure of **"The Purloined Letter,"** which juxtaposes two modes of reasoning, an "imprisoned," mechanical and a "liberated," imaginative one in the characters' struggle for the enigmatic piece of writing. In his effort to retrieve the mysterious letter that the cunning Minister D. is using to blackmail a "certain royal personage," the Parisian Prefect G is quite unsuccessful, even though his search of the Minister's hotel is certainly rigorous beyond reproach. "The remote source of his defeat," as the protagonist of Poe's story, Auguste Dupin, puts it, lies in the fact that the Prefect is quite thoroughly imprisoned in his own perspective, excluding that of others. Unable to imagine an approach other than his own, it is impossible for him to reflect back on the principles of his search and hence to assume a position that would allow him to see beyond their limits. What lies outside the Prefect's comprehension is precisely the fact that our principles of observation constrain what we are able to observe, since no matter how much one might refine a certain model, it will only yield results which confirm to its presuppositions.

The Prefect, to borrow from a distinction that Poe's narrator develops in another tale of ratiocination, **"The Murders in the Rue Morgue,"** is merely "ingenious" and far from being "analytic." While ingenuity as defined by Poe's narrator is a mere mechanical skill of correctly combining the facts, obeying the law of cause and effect, analysis is a truly creative power, not determined in its outcome by a strict adherence to such external rules. The close relation of this distinction to Coleridge's differentiation in the *Biographia Literaria* between "fancy" and "imagination" need not even be deduced, it is openly suggested in Poe's text. In a telling aside, the narrator of **"The Murders in the Rue Morgue"** remarks that "Between ingenuity and the analytic ability there exists a difference far greater, indeed, than that between the fancy and the imagination, but of a character very strictly analogous. It will be found, in fact, that the ingenious are always fanciful, and the *truly* imaginative never otherwise than analytic."[8] Dupin himself is a true example of the analyst: not confined to a single perspective, his observations are not limited to a specific set of presuppositions. Rather, through an act of imaginary identification, he is able to put himself in the mind of the Minister, which allows him to recreate the latter's thoughts and hence to "intuit" his strategy.

The crux of the problem is the question of how one is to arrive at the principles that will make this analytical "leap of the imagination" possible in the first place. What is the position from which all other perspectives become accessible and how does one reach it?[9]—The narrator of **"The Murders in the Rue Morgue"** has no trouble admitting that there is in fact no way to reach such a position by means of analysis itself, as the method that allows us to perceive the rules and laws according to which we decide to frame our observations, cannot itself rely on a set of analyzable principles. Hence the results of the analyst's performance, "brought about by the very soul and essence

of method, have, in truth, the whole air of intuition" (*Poetry* 397). This reference to the "essence of method" again openly alludes to Coleridge, whose "Essays on the Principles of Method," a central part of the 1818 edition of Coleridge's *The Friend,* Poe would have read in James Marsh's American edition from 1831.[10] It is here that Poe found the philosophical model for the two modes of reasoning described in **"The Murders in the Rue Morgue"** and narrativized in **"The Purloined Letter."** We thus need to turn to *The Friend* to develop a clearer understanding of what is at stake when the "essence of method" is transferred from Coleridge's text to Poe's tales.

The "science of Method," as Coleridge describes it in *The Friend,* will enable its practitioners to satisfactorily construct a system, be it scientific, aesthetic, philosophical, or otherwise. Method thus constitutes a science that does not treat specific classes of objects, but rather the *relations* between the objects of knowledge as its primary material. Method, in other words, has thought and reflection itself as its objects:

> METHOD, therefore, becomes natural to the mind which has been accustomed to contemplate not *things* only, or for their sake alone, but likewise and chiefly the *relations* of things, either their relations to each other, or to the observer, or to the state and apprehension of the hearers.[11]

The relations that can form the material for Method are of two kinds, Coleridge explains. The second and lesser type of relation stems from the observation of empirical facts and will thus always suggest a systematical arrangement governed by the mechanical laws of cause and effect. Coleridge labels this mode of classification "theory" and defines it as a relation "in which the existing forms and qualities of objects, discovered by observation or experiment, suggest a given arrangement of many under one point of view: and this not merely or principally in order to facilitate the remembrance, recollection, or communication of the same; but for the purposes of understanding, and in most instances of controlling, them" (*The Friend* 464).

Such is the systematic approach of the Prefect in Poe's story, whose attempts at theoretical control of the given facts are described by Dupin as "a sort of Procrustean bed, to which he forcibly adapts his designs" (*Poetry* 689). This approach is doomed to failure because the Prefect, unlike Dupin, has not the motivations of the Minister D. in view, but rather a set of external circumstances, which he believes to be thoroughly in his control. It does not occur to him to examine the hypothesis underlying his theoretical approach, which, as the product of an abstraction from empirical data, necessarily remains arbitrary as Coleridge explains:

> For what shall determine the mind to abstract and generalize one common point rather than another? and

within what limits, from what number of individual objects, shall the generalization be made? The theory must still require a prior theory for its own legitimate construction.

(*The Friend* 476)

If this were all, however, the science of Method would be caught in an infinite regress. Every meta-theory would be as groundless as the theory it was designed to explain, and its generalizations would hence be in need of yet another theory for their justification. Dupin, to put it in the terms of Poe's story, would be yet another Prefect, simply on a superior level, different in degree, but not in kind.[12]

For Coleridge, the central problem of "theory," no matter how abstract its principles, is its reliance on observation and empirical data. Built on such an insecure basis ("observation, though aided by experiment, is necessarily limited and imperfect" [*The Friend* 477]), a merely theoretical system could never provide any insight that goes beyond these empirical limitations. For this reason, only mathematics could qualify as a perfect science, since it operates unconcerned with empirical reality and deals exclusively with intellectual entities that are the synthetic products of prior definitions.[13] Following the model of mathematics, true philosophical insight can thus only be achieved if the relations that are the material of Method originate not in empirical observation, but in the mind of the observer. This superior kind of relation, which Coleridge terms "Law," occupies the foremost place in the science of Method.

> . . . in whatever science the relations of the parts to each other and to the whole is predetermined by a truth originating in the *mind*, and not abstracted or generalized from observation of the parts, there we affirm the presence of a *law*.
>
> (*The Friend* 459)

Unlike the definitions of mathematics, however, the principles of Law are not only intellectual principles but also account for the relations between and for the very existence of the objects of empirical reality. They can do so because they are the divine causes of empirical phenomena that can never be derived from the latter through the deductive processes of theory. The science of Method, which has ultimately little to do with Poe's purloined principles of analysis, is firmly grounded in religious faith.

> . . . we contemplate it [Law] as exclusively an attribute of the Supreme Being, inseparable from the idea of God: adding, however, that from the contemplation of law in this, its only perfect form, must be derived all true insight into all other grounds and principles necessary to Method, as the science common to all sciences. . . .
>
> (*The Friend* 459f)

The "essence of method," which has "the whole air of intuition," is hence for Coleridge an act of faith, while the mere ingenuity of theory is due to the lack of a religious principle:

> Alienated from this (intuition shall we call it? or steadfast faith?) ingenious men may produce schemes, conducive to the peculiar purposes of particular sciences, but no scientific system.
>
> (*The Friend* 460)

Coleridge's science of Method, much like Johann Gottlieb Fichte's *Theory of Scientific Knowledge,* is a science of science, a propaedeutical discipline which is to supply in Coleridge's words "A Principle of Unity with Progression" that would provide the foundation, unity, and first principle of a truly comprehensive philosophical system, capable of continuous development[14] (*The Friend* 476). Based on the principle of Law, this scientific philosophical method thus extols religion as the ultimate goal and unifying element of any systematic endeavor:

> Religion therefore is the ultimate aim of philosophy, in consequence of which philosophy itself becomes the supplement of the sciences, both as the convergence of all to the common end, namely, wisdom; and as supplying the copula, which modified in each in the comprehension of its parts to one whole, is in its principles common to all, as integral parts of one system. And this is METHOD, itself a distinct science, the immediate offspring of philosophy, and the link or *mordant* by which philosophy becomes scientific and the sciences philosophical.
>
> (*The Friend* 463)

This religious principle uniting philosophy and the sciences needs to be recognized, according to Coleridge, if one aims to construct a satisfactory philosophical system. Coleridge's philosopher is ultimately a philosopher *only* because he has access to the source of divine reason which provides him with the vantage point from which to truly perceive the *necessary* relations of things, which form the primary material of the science of Method. It is this capacity which distinguishes theory from Method and a mere mechanical arrangement of facts from an organic system. It *demands* of the philosopher an act of faith.

FAITH, IMAGINATION, AND THE SUBJECT

Neither Dupin nor the Minister D. are given to overt professions of faith, nor are these the rule in Poe's œuvre as a whole. Poe's death-bound tales after all provide ample proof for the conviction that it is impossible for the human mind to come to know itself, let alone its divine origin.[15] If there is any higher power involved in the telling of **"The Purloined Letter,"** it is that of a good plot. Poe's story is entirely the product of literary machinations: It begins in the dark of a library and it ends with a quotation. One can wonder, after all, if the mysteriously incriminating letter has ever existed to begin with. And the reason why Dupin is so perfectly able to intuit the actions of the Minister D., is, like the letter purloined by both of them, almost too obvious to see: Twin brothers in physical appearance and mental capacity, they mirror each other as the figments of the imagination of one and the same creator, who claims no divine inspiration for his aesthetic constructs.

In this narrative transformation of Coleridge's Method, it is once again not the metaphysician who reasons but rather the poet who protests. For poetry, not philosophy, let alone religion, is what makes Dupin and the Minister D. superior thinkers in Poe's story. While both of them are, quite in Coleridge's sense, mathematicians and not empirical scientists, they neither combine philosophy nor faith with their mathematical reasoning, but rather their experience as poets. Only because of their imaginative poetic faculties are both able to outwit the merely ingenious and fanciful Prefect, who is trapped in his conviction that an insurmountable difference separates the realm of poetic imagination from effective methods of rational calculation. As Dupin argues, the Prefect's blindness to the shortcomings of his approach ultimately "lies in the supposition that the Minister is a fool, because he has acquired renown as a poet" (*Poetry* 691). When the narrator of **"The Purloined Letter"** contends that to his knowledge the Minister was no poet, but a mathematician who had received acclaim for his writings on differential calculus, Dupin reinforces the necessity to see these two professions as united:

> You are mistaken; I know him well; he is both. As poet *and* mathematician, he would reason well; as mere mathematician, he could not have reasoned at all, and thus would have been at the mercy of the Prefect.
>
> (*Poetry* 691)

Poetic imagination thus replaces religious faith as the key element of systematic thought in Poe's narrative. In performing this shift, Poe severs the union of poetry and philosophy that was essential for Coleridge. And in an irony he may have privately enjoyed, Poe himself could thus be seen as "that *monstrum horrendum*" as Dupin ultimately comes to describe the Minister—"an unprincipled man of genius," Poe's version of what Coleridge would have called "a man of method without faith."[16]

It will prove illuminating to return once more to the *Biographia Literaria* in order to examine the unity of poetry, philosophy, and faith in the Coleridgean text from which Poe purloins the other distinction that is central to his tales of ratiocination, that between fancy and imagination. For this purpose we can in fact return to the very page where the quotation from the "Letter to B—" that I discussed at the beginning of this essay had left off: Coleridge, immediately after he introduced the goal of completing an all-inclusive philosophical system, now addresses the question of where the first principle of such a system might be found. For the same reason that theory was discarded as a means to provide it in the "Essays on the Principles of Method," Coleridge here excludes the possibility that this principle could be located in memory, the mechanical part of the human intelligence. Such an approach would immediately lead to the familiar problem of infinite regress, as this part of the human mind after all constitutes part of what the system as a whole should be able to explain:

> A system, which aims to deduce the memory with all the other functions of intelligence, must of course place its first position from beyond the memory, and anterior to it, otherwise the principle of solution would be itself a part of the problem to be solved. Such a position therefore must, in the first instance be demanded, and the first question will be, by what right is it demanded?
>
> (*BL* 1: 247)

This question complicates the central assumption of the "Essays on the Principles of Method," where Coleridge asserted the existence of the divine relations of Law as a necessity that only had to be reinforced by the shortcomings of theory. In his attempt to demonstrate the right to *demand* such a first principle located outside the confines of mere mechanical ingenuity, Coleridge now moves to the writings of Friedrich Wilhelm Joseph Schelling and continues his text with an embellished translation from the latter's "Über Postulate in der Philosophie" [On Postulates in Philosophy]. In this text, which is an appendix to Schelling's "Abhandlungen zur Erläuterung des Idealismus der Wissenschaftslehre," written in 1796 and 1797, Schelling uses the postulation of first principles in geometry as an analogy which "supplies philosophy with the example of a primary intuition, from which every science that lays claim to *evidence* must take its commencement," and Coleridge thus returns to the example of mathematics he had also given in *The Friend* (*BL* 1: 250).[17] Geometry's first principle, expands Coleridge translating Schelling, an undetermined line, or rather an undetermined point in motion, is in fact a mere postulate. It needs to be inferred from the two observable types of movement: straight lines and circles. Ultimately, the possibility of an externally undetermined line, "undetermined through any point without, and determined through itself," which cannot be demonstrated, must be *intuited* as the middle ground of the two movements. "The mathematician," like Poe's analyst, hence "does not begin with a demonstrable proposition, but with an intuition, a practical idea" (*BL* 1: 250).

Coleridge, via Schelling, uses the mathematical discipline of geometry as an analogy for philosophical activity. Just as much as the mathematician needs to intuit the first principle of geometry, the philosopher needs to discover the first principle and postulate of philosophy by means of a "most original construction."[18] In Schelling's early text, which still operates within the terminological framework of Fichte's *Wissenschaftslehre,* this "most original construction," which provides the first principle of philosophy, is the self-reflexive construction of the "I" in consciousness. This original activity, in which the "I" creates itself simultaneously as subject and object, is the philosophical equivalent of the mathematical postulate. Since this postulate, as a purely internal act, can never be empirically demonstrated, it will only be evident to those who possess the "philosophical organ" that will allow them to recreate the same moment of construction within themselves. This activity has to be *demanded* to make the philosophical position communicable and comprehensible.

> . . . it [philosophy] is evident for anyone who possesses the organ for it (who does not lack the inner capacity for construction), just like mathematics, which is also not made comprehensible by means of figures, stenciled in copper, or through mere contemplation, but by means of an inner organ (the imagination).[19]
>
> (Schelling 447)

The central postulate of transcendental philosophy, which Schelling here renders as the command "become conscious of yourself in your original activity!"[20] is thus a product of imagination. As the "philosophical organ," this faculty constitutes the irreplaceable element that alone can differentiate a merely mechanical set of presuppositions from the living whole of an organic system. Without access to this self-reflexive inner organ, every thinker remains a mere Prefect in Coleridge's translation of Schelling's text:

> So is there many a one among us, yes, and some who think themselves philosophers, too, to whom the philosophical organ is entirely wanting. To such a man, philosophy is a mere play of words and notions, like a theory of music to the deaf, or like the geometry of light to the blind. The connection of the parts and their logical dependencies may be seen and remembered; but the whole is groundless and hollow, unsustained by living contact, unaccompanied with any realizing intuition which exists by and in the fact that affirms its existence, which is known, because it is, and is, because it is known.[21]
>
> (*BL* 1: 251)

This absolute ground of reality in which the activity of thinking or knowing and being are one and the same, however, has different connotations for Schelling and Coleridge. Ultimately, Coleridge proves to be purloining Schelling's concepts just as much as Poe would later purloin his own. For Coleridge, the absolute identity of knowing and being, epistemology and ontology, which the passage in the *Biographia Literaria* professes as the outcome of "living contact" and "realizing intuition," is a property of the living God and can as such, like the principles of Law, only be attributed to a supreme being. What had been for Schelling the recognition of the original activity that constitutes the "I," which creates itself in absolute causality in the act of thinking itself, is rendered by Coleridge as a gift from heaven: "The postulate of philosophy and at the same time the test of philosophic capacity, is no other than the heaven-descended KNOW THYSELF" (*BL* 1: 252).

In the *Biographia Literaria,* just as much as in *The Friend,* the act of self-knowledge that underlies transcendental philosophy has thus for Coleridge its true foundation in divine reason. This conviction is reinforced throughout the remainder of Chapter 12 where Coleridge continues to unfold the necessary prerogatives of a complete philosophical system by creating his own text out of a series of translated quotes from Schelling. Coleridge now mainly draws and translates from Schelling's *System of Transcendental Idealism,* which presents a decisively less Fichtean position than the earlier texts Coleridge also used. In Schelling's system, transcendental philosophy, which has the "I" or self-consciousness as its object, now forms only one part of a comprehensive philosophy and needs to be complemented by natural philosophy, the science which treats of the objective activity of nature. It is the task of Schelling's system to show that these two poles of human knowledge are ultimately identical and simply two different expressions of one and the same absolute activity, an absolute which is now no longer located within the "I," but constitutes a higher sphere that comprises both the subject and nature. While Coleridge reproduces Schelling's argument in broad stretches of his own text, he continues to significantly alter these Schellingian passages. Schelling had described the highest goal of natural philosophy as showing the identity of nature and self-consciousness. Coleridge, however, presents this identity as an affirmation of the creative presence of the Judeo-Christian God.

> The theory of natural philosophy would then be completed, when all nature was demonstrated to be identical in essence with that, which in its highest known power exists in man as intelligence and self-consciousness; when the heavens and the earth shall declare not only the power of their maker, but the glory and the presence of their God, even as he appeared to the great prophet during the vision of the mount in the skirts of his divinity.
>
> (*BL* 1: 256)

Coleridge's religious transformation of Schelling's Absolute is most clearly visible when Coleridge describes his own expectations of the "equatorial point" of both natural and transcendental philosophy that "would be the principle of a total and undivided philosophy" (*BL* 1: 282). In a description that recalls Coleridge's assertion from *The Friend,* religion and philosophy would be seen as interchangeable in this point of absolute identity:

> In other words, philosophy would pass into religion, and religion become philosophy. We begin with the I KNOW MYSELF, in order to end with the absolute I AM. We proceed from the SELF, in order to lose and find all self in GOD.

> (*BL* 1: 283)

Coleridge's text here foreshadows his definition of imagination, which will be presented in Chapter 13 of the *Biographia* as a substitute for an extensive deduction of the "equatorial point" of philosophy, which Coleridge, using the ploy of a cautionary letter from a friend, had postponed for a later work on "constructive philosophy" (*BL* 1: 302). Imagination, as central for Coleridge as it is for Schelling, provides the possibility of an actual connection of the self and God and thus the unity of philosophy and religion in the medium of artistic activity. It is after all precisely the unity of the finite and the infinite that defines primary imagination in Coleridge's well-known formulation that describes it as "a repetition in the finite mind of the eternal act of creation in the infinite I AM" (*BL* 1: 304). What the self grasps in the act of imagination envisioned by Coleridge is its connection to the divine. This divine relation differentiates the "living contact" of imagination from the "mere play of words and notions" that is the product of the recollective faculty of fancy, which remains bound by the mechanical law of association. With this vital connection of imagination and the divine first principle of Coleridge's desired philosophical system in mind, we can now return to Edgar Allan Poe, who purloins Coleridge's conceptions for his own aesthetic purposes.

Eureka

Coleridge never completed his oft-promised *opus magnum,* in which the desired all-inclusive Christian philosophical system through which all others could be shown to be "united in one perspective central point" would have been exhaustively developed.[22] Poe on the other hand *did* publish what he considered the crowning effort of his life's work, the tour-de-force prose-poem *Eureka,* his *Essay on the Material and Spiritual Universe.* "I have no desire to live since I have done 'Eureka.' I could accomplish nothing more," Poe wrote with rhetorical flourish to his mother-in-law, Maria

Clemm, three months before his death, suggesting that what his efforts as a writer ultimately tended towards was his very own peculiar version of an all-inclusive philosophico-literary utterance.[23] For *Eureka* presents itself precisely as what in "Letter to B—" Poe had deemed Coleridge's *Biographia Literaria* to be: "a treatise *de omni scibili et quibusdam aliis*" (*Essays* 8). There, as will be recalled, Poe had accused Coleridge of having made a grave mistake in pursuing precisely such an endeavor, of going wrong "by reason of his very profundity," wasting his precious poetic powers on the lonely metaphysical night.

It is thus unlikely that Poe was entirely serious when he first presented *Eureka,* Coleridge-style, as a public lecture at the New York Society Library on February 3, 1848. Yet, it is equally unlikely that Poe would have designed the most extensive work of his writing career, which attempts to synthesize contemporary astronomical theories from Simon de Laplace to Alexander von Humboldt in an effort to present a coherent theory able to explain no less than "the essence, origin, creation, present condition and destiny of the universe," *entirely* as a hoax. If that were the case, Susan Manning has rightfully remarked, the joke is ultimately on Poe, since the effort he must have invested in its execution far outweighs its possible effect on any audience, including that of Poe scholars, who only rarely pay the text extended critical attention.[24] It is thus, as Joan Dayan has argued, precisely the fundamental and self-conscious ambiguity of Poe's text, the undecidability of *Eureka*'s ultimate rhetorical stance that needs to be seen as Poe's literary achievement and as one that is undoubtedly aligned with the underlying thrust of Poe's œuvre as a whole.[25] The undecidable status of Poe's literary cosmology *as a text* can ultimately be seen to match the undecidability of the epistemological problem it depicts in all its outrageous digressions. If Coleridge had attempted to restore philosophical certainty to the epistemological process by grounding human consciousness in the divine, Poe would be unwilling to disregard the possibility, worthy of Descartes' *genius malignus,* that the universe might be no more than an elaborate joke at the expense of humanity's desire for knowledge. If the latter were true, the artist might be better equipped than the philosopher to retaliate by writing a text of ambiguous purpose, indicating simultaneously that the writer had fallen into the trap of believing to actually have unraveled the secrets of the universe, and that he had embarked on a satirical project, ridiculing precisely such a belief and the naïve trust in both the human conceptual apparatus and human language it betrays, or else that he might have done both, thus equally exposing the inescapable shortcomings of human cognition *and* reveling in the possibility of literary language to create a self-conscious universe all its own. In *Eureka*'s all-inclusive rhetorical posture—"and it may be as well here to mention that by the term 'universe,' wherever employed without qualification in this essay, I mean to designate *the utmost conceivable expanse of space, with all things, spiritual and material, that can be imagined to exist within the compass of that expanse*"—that Poe both goes farthest in usurping Coleridge's philosophical voice, and in which simultaneously the crucial difference in approach between those two writers comes into clearest focus (*Poetry* 1262).

The underlying cosmological plot developed in *Eureka* can be roughly summarized as follows: The divine volition creates a first particle, characterized by oneness and simplicity. By a primal divine act, this particle is then forced to diffuse itself completely by means of radiation. The ensuing atoms, once completely diffused, interact while governed by the two forces of attraction and repulsion which account for all the successive states of the universe. By attraction, the atoms strive to regain their primal unity in a common center, while repulsion ensures that the divine goal of utmost relation between the atoms is reached, precluding them from uniting until that point in time when the force of attraction will eventually be stronger than the force of repulsion, allowing the universe to coalesce again into one common center. Upon completion of this cosmological cycle, the process promptly begins anew. Poe himself condenses his "general proposition" in the style of the idealist philosophical theses he would have found in Chapter 12 of Coleridge's *Biographia Literaria* as follows: "*In the original unity of the first thing lies the secondary cause of all things, with the germ of their inevitable annihilation*" (*Poetry* 1261). And Poe's two contrary and complementary forces of contraction and expansion, attraction and repulsion, which make this process possible, equally lead us back to the *Biographia*, now to the beginning of Chapter 13, where Coleridge, again presenting what is essentially a direct quote from Schelling's *System of Transcendental Idealism* had written:

> DesCartes, speaking as a naturalist, and in imitation of Archimedes, said give me matter and motion and I will construct you the universe. We must of course understand him to have meant; I will render the construction of the universe intelligible. In the same sense the transcendental philosopher says; grant me a nature having two contrary forces, the one of which tends to expand infinitely, while the other strives to apprehend or *find* itself in this infinity, and I will cause the world of intelligences with the whole system of their representations to rise up before you.[26]
>
> (*BL* 1: 297)

While Poe claims to have achieved no less than precisely that in *Eureka*, a text which thus seems to fulfill

the idealist project both in spirit and to the letter, Poe's two material and spiritual forces ultimately construct a poetic universe that is fundamentally different from that of an idealist system. The difference between the two approaches becomes almost instantly apparent in the opening pages of *Eureka*, when Poe locates his version of Coleridge's "equatorial" and thus Archimedean point from which the universe could be perceived in its oneness on the top of mount Ætna:

> He who from the top of Ætna casts his eyes leisurely around, is affected chiefly by the *extent* and *diversity* of the scene. Only by a rapid whirling of the heel could he hope to comprehend the panorama in the sublimity of its *oneness*.
>
> (*Poetry* 1261)

Mount Ætna, however, of course has no top, and there is thus no position from which to make such an observation, except that of a free fall into the mouth of a volcano. Like the legendary Empedokles, to whom this passage alludes, Poe's fictional observer has to embrace death in order to experience the universe in its oneness.[27] The ideal unity and the perfect relations of Law, which for Coleridge could be intuited through the divine faculties of reason and imagination, constitute for Poe the object of an aesthetic desire, which can be sought in the process of writing, but—like the bottom of the Maelström in Poe's short story **"A Descent into the Maelström"**—could only be attained in the moment of self-annihilation. The Archimedian point of autonomous subjectivity from which the philosopher might attempt to move the world is thus a mere surface effect in Poe's text. It is constantly revealed—for anyone who cares to look and read—as an aesthetic illusion of the written word, an impossible "mental gyration" in the void (*Poetry* 1262). Clearly, nobody could even contemplate such a performance on the empirically existing or rather non-existing "summit of Ætna," and the "prospect" the ensuing view would afford can thus only be envisioned by means of an aesthetic simulacrum of death in the literary text. Poe can thus claim a Cartesian originality for the considerations developed in *Eureka*:

> But as, on the summit of Ætna, no man has thought of whirling on his heel, so no man has ever taken into his brain the full uniqueness of the prospect; and so, again, whatever considerations lie involved in this uniqueness have as yet no practical existence for mankind.
>
> (*Poetry* 1261)

If Poe was indeed the first to contemplate such a precarious philosophical position, he voiced it for the first time not in *Eureka* but rather in "Letter to B—," where he wrote the following with regard to Coleridge: "In reading his poetry, I tremble, like one who stands upon a volcano, conscious, from the very darkness bursting from the crater, of the fire and the light that are weltering below" (*Essays* 11). Once again it is Coleridge, who gives Poe the cue for a vision of the self decidedly unlike the former himself would advocate in his philosophical texts. But even if Poe must have recognized the threats to the rational conception of the self at the basis of Coleridge's philosophical voice, threats that ultimately engulf it in the poetic utterance of texts like "The Rime of the Ancyent Marinere," the metaphor Poe utilizes to depict the relation of these two differing conceptions of subjectivity could not be further from Coleridge's own desires. Coleridge wrote his philosophical texts after all as a means of protection against precisely such an onslaught of the irrational. Poe, on the other hand, once again reverses the relation Coleridge had sought to establish, when he locates the true source of light and fire *below* the rational surface of the *cogito,* in those subconscious volcanic depths that deny the self any firm ground or stable first principle to stand on.

Consequently, the method Poe uses to structure this free-fall into the volcano is once again the same he had already propounded and executed in his stories of ratiocination. In *Eureka,* this method surfaces as a message in a bottle found floating on the *Mare Tenebrarum.* Poe's narrator presents the bottle's content, a curious letter written in the year 2848, as a methodological prelude, meant to prepare the reader for the actual project on which he is about to embark.[28] The fictitious letter writer, whose voice the narrator now impersonates, is looking back on intellectual history and shows himself surprised that in earlier years only two roads to truth had been accepted by mankind: those of deduction and induction, of a priori and a posteriori philosophy. After thoroughly ridiculing both paths of reasoning, he finally relates what in his day is conceived as the most direct road to absolute truth:

> . . . none of them [earlier philosophers] fell, even by accident, into what we now so distinctly perceive to be the broadest, the straightest and most available of all mere roads—the great thoroughfare—the majestic highway of the *Consistent*[.] Is it not wonderful that they should have failed to deduce from the works of God the vitally momentous consideration that *a perfect consistency can be nothing but an absolute truth*? . . . By its means, investigation has been taken out of the hands of the ground-moles, and given as a duty, rather than a task, to the true—to the *only* true thinkers—to the generally-educated men of ardent imagination.
>
> (*Poetry* 1269)

The difference to Coleridge's approach is striking. While Coleridge, both in *The Friend* and the *Biographia Literaria,* had argued for a common principle in which both induction and deduction, as well as materialist and idealist philosophies could be seen

as united, Poe no longer bases his road to truth on correspondence to an essence, but on formal consistency. In other words, the theory developed in *Eureka,* as the product of an "ardent imagination," is judged for its aesthetic value. As an aesthetic construct it no longer reflects a fundamental principle of unity, but creates its own coherent system. The discovery of the rationally consistent structure of the universe thus requires a leap of imagination that is, however closely related to Coleridge's principles of Method, no longer grounded in divine Law.

The scientific spokesperson chosen in *Eureka* to represent this imaginative method of reasoning and who is extolled by Poe's letter writer as one of the first to have grasped this route to truth, is the German seventeenth-century astronomer and mystic Johannes Kepler. Without the "vital laws" discovered by Kepler, claims Poe's letter writer, Newton, confined to the dead ends of inductive and deductive reasoning, would have been unable to postulate anything of true import. Kepler's planetary laws, which made the discovery of the Newtonian laws of gravitation possible, were arrived at neither inductively nor deductively, but rather by means of imaginative guess-work:

> Yes!—these vital laws Kepler *guessed*—that is to say, he *imagined* them. Had he been asked to point out either the *deductive* or *inductive* route by which he attained them, his reply might have been—I know nothing about *routes*—but I *do* know the machinery of the Universe. Here it is. I grasped it with *my soul*—I reached it through mere dint of intuition.[29]
>
> (*Poetry* 1270)

In this capacity, as Joan Dayan has suggested, Kepler may very well ultimately be a stand-in for Poe himself, who might thus glorify himself in *Eureka* when the fictitious letter-writer proclaims about the words of Kepler that "I glow with a sacred fire when I even think of them, and I feel that I shall never grow weary of their repetition" (*Poetry* 1270). Those words, which the former has the "real pleasure of transcribing," and which bring his equally transcribed letter to a close, are the following:

> I care not whether my work be read now or by posterity. I can afford to wait a century for readers when God himself has waited six thousand years for an observer. I triumph. I have stolen the golden secret of the Egyptians. I will indulge my sacred fury.
>
> (*Poetry* 1270)

Both Thomas Ollive Mabbot and Joan Dayan have pointed out that Poe here indeed quite faithfully transcribes Kepler's own words written in a letter of 1618 upon the discovery of the third of his planetary laws.[30] Poe's sources for Kepler's own triumphal *Eureka!*

may have been either Sir David Brewster's *The Martyr's of Science, or, the Lives of Galileo, Tycho Brahe, and Kepler* (London, 1841), or John Elliot Drinkwater Bethune's *Life of Kepler* (1830). The reverence for Kepler as such, however, who was not uncommon as a hero of pre-enlightenment science for the Romantics, also once more leads us back to Coleridge's *The Friend*, where Poe would have found Kepler praised as a true man of method. In his "Essays on the Principles of Method," Coleridge had written the following about Kepler:

> But Kepler seemed born to prove that true genius can overpower all obstacles. If he gives an account of his modes of proceeding, and of the views under which they first occurred to his mind, how unostentatiously and *in transitu,* as it were, does he introduce himself to our notice: and yet never fails to present the living germ out of which the genuine method, as the inner form of the tree of science, springs up![31]

(*The Friend* 485)

That "living germ" and "inner form of the tree of science" however, was for Kepler, as it would be again for Coleridge, based on a *correspondence* between the divine and the human mind, a correspondence which allowed for the "inner" discovery of the "outer" laws of the universe in a moment of anamnesis. In Poe's text, on the other hand, the Keplerian moment of intuition, despite the insight it produces, is not the revelation of correspondence to an essence. Like the top of mount Ætna and the absent letter that allows the story of Dupin and the Minister D. to circulate in perpetuity, the imaginative grasping in Poe's text reveals no origin. Here, rather than discovering the principle of unity behind its distinctions, which would secure its correspondence to the world it observes, the mind has to be satisfied with the consistency of its constructs. Thus, Kepler's astronomical laws and Coleridge's philosophical principles of Method are significantly altered in Poe's transcription. In a striking reversal that turns the Coleridgean relation of artistic creation and the divine on its head, the "golden secret" of Poe's own text, his particular and as such original *Eureka* emerges as the narrative principle of plot:

> In the construction of *plot,* for example, in fictitious literature, we should aim at so arranging the incidents that we shall not be able to determine, of any one of them, whether it depends from any one other or upholds it. In this sense, of course, *perfection* of plot is really, or practically, unattainable—but only because it is a finite intelligence that constructs. The plots of God are perfect. The Universe is a plot of God.

(*Poetry* 1342)

Method has thus turned into plot, and the principle of Law, which according to Coleridge "in its absolute perfection is conceivable only of the Supreme Being,"

is now the creative principle of a divine narrator. Where Coleridge's divine Law "not only appoints to each thing its *position,* but in that position and in consequence of that position, gives it its qualities, yea, it gives its very existence as *that particular* thing," Poe's God does so in a universe that has turned into fiction (*BL* 1: 459).

But Poe not only defines the universe as a piece of fiction, he also fulfills this definition in the written performance of his own text. *Eureka* is based on a set of fundamental paradoxes and ambiguities, constantly undercutting the principle of cause and effect, which leave the task of unraveling the text's self-referential plot to the reader. Consider for example Poe's rendition of the prospective apocalyptic ending of the universe, which finds close parallels in the rushes to destruction of **"A Descent into the Maelström"** and **"MS. Found in a Bottle,"** as well as in Arthur Gordon Pym's enigmatic journey to the south pole:

> . . . and now, with a million-fold electric velocity, commensurate only with their material grandeur and with their spiritual passion for oneness, the majestic remnants of the tribe of Stars flash, at length, into a common embrace. The inevitable catastrophe is at hand.

(Poe, *Poetry* 1353)

This final catastrophe will reinstate the universe's lost unity by a complete annihilation of all matter, leaving God once again to remain all in all. Such an ending, however, did not appeal to Poe's notion of a denouement:

> But are we here to pause? Not so. On the Universal agglomeration and dissolution, we can readily conceive that a new and perhaps totally different series of conditions may ensue—another creation and radiation, returning into itself—another action and reaction of the Divine Will. Guiding our imaginations by that omniprevalent law of laws, the law of periodicity, are we not, indeed, more than justified in entertaining a belief—let us say, rather, in indulging a hope—that the processes we have here ventured to contemplate will be renewed forever, and forever; a novel Universe swelling into existence, and then subsiding into nothingness, at every throb of the Heart Divine?

(*Poetry* 1356)

While this periodic throbbing of the Heart Divine, reminiscent of the cosmogonies of classical antiquity in its cyclical pattern of creation and destruction, may very well be modeled on Empedocles' rhythm of the cosmic breath, as David Ketterer has suggested, Poe's "Heart Divine" also clearly has the qualities of the **"Tell-Tale Heart"** in Poe's famous story, for it now forces the perpetrator to divulge the literary machinations of his cosmological crime:

> And now—this Heart Divine—what is it? *It is our own.* / Let not the merely seeming irreverence of this idea frighten our souls from that cool exercise of conscious-

ness—from that deep tranquility of self-inspection—
through which alone we can hope to attain the presence
of this, the most sublime of truths, and look it leisurely
in the face.

(Poetry 1356)

More reminiscent of a Nietzschean proclamation of
the death of God than of a mode of religious contemplation, this self-avowedly irreverent moment of introspection turns the Coleridgean notion of self-
knowledge completely upside down. It is not the
intuition of a universal reason, governing our conscious mind by the same principles which account for
the existence of the universe and which provide the
key for self-knowledge as well as for a comprehension
of the Absolute. Poe's sublime moment, leisurely presented as a "cool exercise of consciousness" is not
akin to that of the British Romantics and certainly not
to the version of sublimity advocated by Coleridge. In
Poe's narration, *Eureka*'s plot does not "proceed from
the SELF in order to lose and find all self in GOD,"
and it is decidedly not the experience of "a repetition
in the finite mind of the eternal act of creation in the
infinite I AM" (*BL* 1: 304). Quite on the contrary, in
Poe's account, the "eternal I AM" is ultimately a product of the mind's own workings. It only subsists as a
remnant in each individual's desire for unity:

> each soul is, in part, its own God—its own Creator:—in
> a word, that God—the material *and* spiritual God—
> *now* exists solely in the diffused Matter and Spirit of
> the Universe; and that the regathering of this diffused
> Matter and Spirit will be but the re-constitution of the
> *purely Spiritual* and Individual God.

(Poetry 1357)

Not only would the pantheistic position espoused here
have been anathema to Coleridge, what should serve
as the unifying concept of Poe's treatise also presents
itself as an unresolved ambiguity in which cause and
effect cannot be told apart. It remains undecidable
whether the former existence of a unity causes the desire for its re-constitution in the individuals' minds, or
if it is simply an effect of this same desire which has
predicated Poe's poetical account of the mind's divine
origins. Poe himself has introduced this suspicion into
his text in the form of a quotation from Alexander von
Humboldt, to whom *Eureka* is dedicated. Refuting in
his *Kosmos* of 1845 Johann Heinrich von Mädler's
hypothesis of a gigantic celestial body in the gravita-
tional center of the universe von Humboldt had
claimed that: "It is but Man's longing for a fundamental First Cause, that impels both his intellect and his
fancy to the adoption of such an hypothesis"[32] (*Poetry*
1357).

Poe's *Eureka* thus does not offer itself as a revelation
about the true nature of the universe, but rather attempts to reproduce the universe's structure *as a plot*—

that is, as an autonomous creation of the mind which
owes its consistency to its creator's concerted effort of
reason and imagination. Its unity is solely produced by
the impossible gyration around a lost center which is
performed in the work of art. The process of ratiocination thus produces a consistent whole, yet one which
no longer reflects the first principle of a comprehensive philosophy but rather the self-reflexive unity of
an autonomous aesthetic system.

It is tempting to construe the relationship of Samuel
Taylor Coleridge and Edgar Allan Poe within the
framework of **"The Purloined Letter,"** as one sees
Poe purloining and ventriloquizing Coleridge, who
was already a philosophical ventriloquist himself, repeating his words but altering his voice. It is obvious,
however, that Poe, if he plays Dupin to Coleridge's
Minister D., does not find the letter that Coleridge had
hidden, but rather one that could not have been written by the author from whom its words would seem to
be stolen. Thus, even Poe's definition of plot itself, the
central aesthetic device of his tales that thwarts the
Coleridgean desire for first principles, is ironically a
direct quote from Coleridge. Here is Poe's definition
of plot in a book review of 1841: ". . . plot . . . properly defined, is *that in which no part can be displaced
without ruin to the whole.* It may be described as a
building so dependently constructed, that to change
the position of a single brick is to overthrow the entire
fabric" (*Essays* 149)—The purloined Coleridge, who
in turn had echoed Aristotle, had made the very same
assertions about the poetry of Shakespeare and Milton
in Chapter 1 of the *Biographia Literaria*. It is thus
with a gesture of appropriation, continuation, repetition and disillusion that the voice of the Modern makes
itself heard from within the Romantic, overthrowing
the entire fabric in order to constitute a new whole.

Notes

1. Floyd Stovall, "Poe's Debt to Coleridge," *University of Texas Studies in English* 10 (1930): 70-127
   (71).

2. Daniel Hoffman, *Poe Poe Poe Poe Poe Poe Poe*
   (Garden City: Doubleday, 1972) 87.

3. Christopher Kearns, "Rehearsing Dupin: Poe's
   Duplicitous Confrontation with Coleridge," *The
   Edgar Allan Poe Review* 3.1 (Spring 2002): 3-17.

4. Edgar Allan Poe, *Essays and Reviews,* ed. G. R.
   Thompson (New York: Library of America, 1984)
   10f. Hereafter cited as *Essays* in the text.

5. Coleridge's text reads as follows: "A poem is that
   species of composition, which is opposed to works
   of science, by proposing for its immediate object
   pleasure, not truth. . . ." Samuel Taylor Col-

eridge, *Biographia Literaria* 2, ed. James Engell and W. Jackson Bate, *The Collected Works of Samuel Taylor Coleridge,* 16 vols. (Princeton: Princeton UP, 1983) 7.2: 13. Hereafter cited as *BL 2* in the text.

6. Samuel Taylor Coleridge, *Biographia Literaria* 1, ed. James Engell and W. Jackson Bate, *The Collected Works of Samuel Taylor Coleridge,* 16 vols. (Princeton: Princeton UP, 1983) 7.1: 247. Hereafter cited as *BL 1* in the text.

7. Jonathan Bate, "Edgar Allan Poe: A Debt Repaid," *The Coleridge Connection—Essays for Thomas McFarland,* ed. Richard Gravil and Molly Lefebure (London: McMillan, 1990) 254-73 (258). As already James Engell and Walter Jackson Bate point out in their annotations to Coleridge's *Biographia Literaria,* Coleridge's immediate source here is in fact not Leibniz, but rather F. H. Jacobi's German translation of passages from Leibniz in *Über die Lehre des Spinoza* (1789). While Coleridge's English is a translation of Jacobi's German, the French is indeed Leibniz' own, as also Jacobi had preserved this sentence in the original. Coleridge, as Bate remarks, is ultimately no less disingenuous than Poe, who "found in the *Biographia* exactly what Coleridge found in Jacobi: a depository of wise quotations" (258).

8. Edgar Allan Poe, *Poetry and Tales,* ed. Patrick F. Quinn (New York: Library of America, 1984) 399f. Hereafter cited as *Poetry* in the text.

9. Or, to put it in the words of Jacques Lacan in his "Seminar on 'The Purloined Letter,'" how does one put oneself in the imaginary position of "absolute master"? How does one fulfill the desire that Jacques Derrida in "The Purveyor of Truth," his subsequent critique of Lacan's reading, would describe as inherently deluded? While it is not my goal in this essay to engage the Lacan-Derrida debate about Poe's story directly or in detail, I do think that a shift in frame, as Derrida would put it, emphasizing the text's close relation to the work of Coleridge, who thus becomes another duped possessor as well as addressee of the purloined letter, presents a useful addition to the discussion between psychoanalytic and deconstructionist criticism. For Lacan's and Derrida's essays in English translation and a good source of information about the debate and its subsequent continuation, see John P. Muller and William J. Richardson, eds, *The Purloined Poe—Lacan, Derrida & Psychoanalytic Reading* (Baltimore: Johns Hopkins UP, 1988). For an extensive analysis of "The Purloined Letter" as a response to the work of Samuel Taylor Coleridge, see Daniel Burgoyne, "The Colloquy of Edgar Allan Poe and Samuel Taylor Coleridge," diss., University of Washington, 1998.

10. Marsh also published an edition of Coleridge's *Aids to Reflection* in 1829. These two editions and in particular Marsh's foreword to the *Aids to Reflection* were instrumental for Coleridge's impact on American intellectual life. See also Anthony Harding, "Coleridge and Transcendentalism," *The Coleridge Connection—Essays for Thomas McFarland* 233-54.

11. Samuel Taylor Coleridge, *The Friend* 1, ed. Barbara Rooke, *The Collected Works of Samuel Taylor Coleridge,* 16 vols. (Princeton: Princeton UP, 1969) 4.1: 451. Hereafter cited as *The Friend* in the text. Coleridge's formulation cannot but ring odd to the contemporary ear, which is acquainted with "scientific method" but seems to balk at the suggestion of a "science *of* Method." Coleridge's attempt to philosophically describe the process of arriving at scientific hypothesis itself, it seems, must of necessity produce a terminology that encapsulates contradictions. Poe, as we will see, will find a different solution to the problem in *Eureka.*

12. The status of Dupin, and by extension that of the psychoanalyst, once he has gained possession of the letter from the Minister D., is of course also at the heart of the debate between Lacan and Derrida. Coleridge, as we will see in the following, has no reservations about a source of truth that makes an absolute difference in kind possible for the place occupied by Poe's detective. For Coleridge, there decidedly *is* a place outside the Lacanian chain of signification and the Derridean process of dissemination, allowing for a law that is free of the "blindness" of the "law of castration."

13. "With the mathematician the definition *makes* the object, and pre-establishes the terms which, and which alone, can occur in the after reasoning," writes Coleridge, echoing Kant's assessment of the mathematician's synthetic *a priori* judgments in the *Critique of Pure Reason.* While Kant is never directly referred to in the "Essays on Method," nor in *The Friend* as a whole, the influence of Kantian philosophy on Coleridge's systematic approach developed here is undeniable. The distinction, so essential for Coleridge, between theory and law and understanding and reason is clearly derived from his study of Kant (*The Friend* 476).

14. Ultimately, Coleridge's science of Method, in its effort to provide the "supersensual essence, which being at once the *ideal* of reason and the cause of the material world, is the pre-establisher of the harmony in and between both" is closer to the transcendental idealism of Friedrich Wilhelm Joseph von Schelling, as we shall see in the discussion of Coleridge's *Biographia Literaria* (*The Friend* 463). Nevertheless, the systematic impulse

to truly transform philosophy into an exact science has its roots in Fichte's *Wissenschaftslehre*. Neither of the two German idealists' systems, however, proved sufficient for Coleridge's aspiration to firmly ground a comprehensive philosophical system in his religious beliefs.

15. This sobering fear had in fact already been Coleridge's as well. Had Poe been able to read Coleridge's notebooks, he would have discovered that Coleridge's thought could be even closer to his own than the admirer of the *Ancient Mariner* already suspected. For in the private pages of his notebooks, particularly in his entries concerning the workings of imagination in nightmares, Coleridge sketches out a view of the self to which even the darkest of Poe's stories have ultimately little to add. Cut off from its most desired connection to the divine reason, Coleridge's nightmare self is rather the helpless prey of irrational and demonic mental forces, originating from the frailties of the body, in face of which the rational self finds itself a powerless observer of its own destruction. The notebooks thus illustrate what Coleridge had already admitted in Chapter 9 of the *Biographia*, the fact that the philosophical convictions he develops here are not the admonitions of a righteous believer, but rather the "necessary beliefs" of a mind often lost in the "sandy deserts of utter unbelief" (*BL* 1: 152). Poe for his part, would ultimately simply probe the depths of this abyss much more openly than Coleridge, who still thought to build a philosophical bridge across it.

16. Derrida is thus almost uncannily doubly correct when he points to Lacan's deliberate misquotation of Poe's and Dupin's quote from Crébillon's *Atrée* at the end of "The Purloined Letter," for what is at stake in Poe's text is certainly poetic *dessein* rather than tragic *destin*. And Lacan, in thus continuing the practice of appropriating quotes, joining the chain that had already linked Coleridge and Poe, seems unconsciously to fall prey to the same "Wiederholungszwang" that the seminar had set out to discuss (see Muller and Richardson 206).

17. The quotation is Coleridge's direct translation from Schelling in Chapter 12 of the *Biographia Literaria*. Here is Schelling's German original from his *On Postulates in Philosophy*: "Die Mathematik gibt also der Philosophie das Beispiel einer ursprünglichen Anschauung, von der jede Wissenschaft ausgehen muß, welche auf Evidenz Anspruch machen will," F. W. J. von Schelling, "Über Postulate in der Philosophie," *Sämtliche Werke*, 14 vols., ed. K. F. A. Schelling (Stuttgart: Cotta, 1856-1964) 1: 444-52 (444).

18. Coleridge's translation: "Nevertheless philosophy, if it is to arrive at evidence, must proceed from the most original construction . . ." (*BL* 1: 250). Schelling's original: "Nun muß aber die Philosophie, wenn sie evident werden soll, von der ursprünglichsten Construction ausgehen . . ." (445).

19. ". . . sie ist evident für jeden, der das Organ dazu hat (dem das innere Constructionsvermögen nicht abgeht), gerade so wie die Mathematik, die auch nicht durch die Figuren, in Kupfer gestochen, oder durch das Ansehen allein, sondern durch ein inneres Organ (die Einbildungskraft) verständlich wird." The English translation here is mine; this part of Schelling's text is not incorporated by Coleridge in Chapter 12 of the *Biographia Literaria*.

20. ". . . werde deiner selbst in deiner ursprünglichen Thätigkeit bewußt!" (Schelling 448).

21. The last three lines of this quotation are no longer a translation from "Über Postulate in der Philosophie," but are derived from another of Schelling's early texts which Coleridge uses throughout the remainder of Chapter 12 of the *Biographia*: "Vom Ich als Princip der Philosophie oder über das Unbedingte im menschlichen Wissen" [About the I as the Principle of Philosophy or about the Absolute in Human Knowledge]. Here Schelling had written: "For the ultimate ground of all reality is a something that is only thinkable through itself, i.e., through its being, which is only thought insofar as it is, in short, in which the principle of being and thinking fall in one" ["Der letzte Grund aller Realität nämlich ist ein Etwas, das nur durch sich selbst, d.h. durch sein Seyn denkbar ist, das nur insofern gedacht wird, als es ist, kurz, bei dem das Princip des Seyns und des Denkens zusammenfällt"]. F. W. J. von Schelling, "Vom Ich als Princip der Philosophie oder über das Unbedingte im menschlichen Wissen," *Sämtliche Werke*, 1: 149-245 (163); my translation.

22. Even though Coleridge's "Great Work" was never completed, parts and fragments of it do nevertheless exist. Presented and collected by Thomas McFarland with the assistance of Nick Halmi they make up *Opus Maximum*, vol. 15 of Coleridge's collected works.

23. Edgar Allan Poe, *The Letters of Edgar Allan Poe*, 2 vols., ed. John Orstrom (Cambridge: Harvard UP, 1948) 2: 452.

24. Susan Manning, "'The plots of God are perfect': Poe's *Eureka* and American Creative Nihilism," *Journal of American Studies* 23.2 (August 1989): 235-51 (236).

25. See Joan Dayan, *Fables of Mind—An Inquiry into Poe's Fiction* (Oxford: Oxford UP, 1987).

26. Only the second sentence and the mentioning of Archimedes are originally Coleridge's. For Schell-

ing's original German see Engell's and Bate's footnote to the passage in *BL 1.*

27. For a discussion of Empedocles' pre-socratic philosophy as a possible source for the cosmogony developed in *Eureka,* see Peter C. Page, "Poe, Empedocles, and Intuition in *Eureka*," *Poe Studies* 11.2 (December 1978): 21-26; and, with a different position with regard to the ultimate seriousness of Poe's project, David Ketterer, "Empedocles in *Eureka*: Addenda," *Poe Studies* 18.2 (December 1985): 24-25.

28. Another version of the same letter appears in Poe's *Mellonta Tauta,* where it is read by Pundita, aboard the balloon "skylark" on April 1, 2848, and thus doubly framed as a lark *and* an April Fools prank.

29. Just as much as Poe arguably develops a consistence theory of truth *avant la lettre* in *Eureka,* the leap of imagination that is part and parcel of Poe's processes of ratiocination is akin to and may even have influenced Charles Saunders Peirce's principle of "abduction." Poe would certainly have agreed with Peirce's following definition of the term: "Abduction is the process of forming an explanatory hypothesis. It is the only logical operation which introduces a new idea; for induction does nothing but determine a value, and deduction merely evolves the necessary consequences of a pure hypothesis." See Nancy Horrovitz, "The Body of the Detective Novel: Charles S. Peirce and Edgar Allan Poe," *The Sign of the Three. Dupin, Holmes, Peirce,* ed. Umberto Eco and Thomas A. Sebeok (Bloomington: Indiana UP, 1983) 179-97 (181).

30. *Collected Works of Edgar Allan Poe,* ed. Thomas Ollive Mabbott (Cambridge, MA: Belknap P at Harvard UP, 1978) 3: 1319. See also Dayan 34f.

31. It should at this point no longer come as a surprise that Coleridge's contention that Kepler proves "that true genius can overpower all obstacles," is, as Nick Halmi points out, a direct plagiarism from Goethe, taken from the latter's chapter on Kepler in his *Farbenlehre.* I am grateful to Nick Halmi for sharing with me the manuscript of a talk, "What Kepler taught the Romantics about Nature," presented at the 1994 NASSR conference at Duke University. His analysis of the relation between Kepler's positions with regard to the mind's connection to nature and those of the Romantics has been most helpful in writing this section of the present essay.

32. Poe presents von Humboldts' original German in a footnote as follows: "Das Streben nach den letzten und höchsten Grundursachen macht freilich

die reflectierende Thätigkeit des Menschen, wie seine Phantasie, zu einer solchen Annahme geneigt."

Stavros Theodorakis (essay date winter 2009)

SOURCE: Theodorakis, Stavros. "The Motto in Edgar Allan Poe's 'The Purloined Letter.'" *ANQ* 22, no. 1 (winter 2009): 25-7.

[*In the following essay, Theodorakis argues that Poe took the epigram of "The Purloined Letter" from Petrarch, by way of novelist Samuel G. Warren, and not from Seneca, as Poe claimed.*]

"Nil sapientiae odiosius acumine nimio" ("Nothing is more hateful to wisdom than excessive cunning"). Edgar Allan Poe used this Latin phrase in 1845 as the motto of the second edition of his tale **"The Purloined Letter"** (*Tales and Sketches* 2: 974), attributing it to Seneca. He had also previously used it near the end of the 1843 version of **"The Murders in the Rue Morgue,"** but omitted it in later texts. In that particular version the precise text reads:

> *Nil sapientiae odiosius acumine nimio,* is, perhaps, the only line in the puerile and feeble Seneca not absolutely unmeaning; and, in truth, our friend the Prefect is somewhat too cunning to be profound.
>
> (*Tales and Sketches* 1: 568)

However, the phrase is not attributable to Seneca. In fact, it does not appear in any of Seneca's works (*Tales and Sketches* 2: 993).

This expression was authored by the humanist Francesco Petrarca (1304-74), commonly known as Petrarch. It appears in *De ingenio* (*On cleverness*), the seventh dialogue of the first book of his work *De remediis utriusque fortunae* (*Remedies for Fortune Fair and Foul*), a collection of Latin dialogues.[1] The context for this statement is as follows:

Gaudium:

> Acutissimum ingenium est mihi.

Ratio:

> Nihil sapientiae odiosius acumine nimio. Nihil vero philosophanti molestius quam sophista: ideo invisam Palladi finxere veteres araneam, cuius subtile opus, ac tenues telae sunt, sed fragiles, nullique usui. Ut mucronis ergo, sic ingenii acies sit, non penetret modo, sed subsistat.
>
> (Petrarch 1.7.56)

The English translation of this text reads:

JOY:

> My mind is the sharpest.

REASON:

> Nothing is more hateful to wisdom than too much sharpness, nothing more bothersome to the serious thinker than a sophist, and, for that reason, the ancients invented the spider "hated by Pallas" whose work is delicate, with fine webs, but fragile and useless. A sharp mind should be like a sword, which pierces but comes to a stop at the hilt and goes no farther.

(Rawski 24)

Sir Walter Raleigh uses the phrase in the first chapter of the first book of his *History of the World* (*Works* 17), but without mentioning the source. "Nihil sapientiae odiosius acumine nimio" also appeared in *The Harleian Miscellany* in 1810, where it was anonymously considered an "observation of judicious Raleigh" (*Harleian Miscellany* 59). Poe may have read the 1829 edition of *The Works of Sir Walter Raleigh*; in the 1831 edition of his poems, he cites a portion of Raleigh's poem "The Lie" that strongly reminds us of his **"Purloined Letter"** motto: "Tell wit how much it wrangles in fickle points of niceness—Tell wisdom it entangles itself in overwiseness" (*Complete Poems* 155). Note that there is no mention of Seneca's name in Raleigh's use of the Latin phrase.

It is therefore more likely that Poe discovered this quotation in another source. In addition to its appearances in the works of Petrarch and Raleigh, "Nihil sapientiae odiosius acumine nimio" also surfaced in July 1840 in the ninth part of Samuel G. Warren's novel *Ten Thousand a Year*, printed in *Blackwood's Edinburgh Magazine*:

> On the contrary, a thoughtful observer of what goes on in any of our courts, will believe that our judges have considered the truth of that saying of Seneca—*Nil sapientiae odiosius* ACUMINE NIMIO; and modelled themselves after the great portraiture of the judicial office drawn by the most illustrious of philosophers.

(109)

The second edition of Warren's novel was printed in six volumes in 1840-41 by Carey and Hart in Philadelphia and was one of the most popular novels of its time. Poe reviewed *Ten Thousand a Year* in the November 1841 issue of *Graham's Magazine*, calling it "shamefully ill-written" (*Essays and Reviews* 349). It is therefore likely that Warren's novel is the source for the quotation in question.

This assertion is supported by the fact that both Warren and Poe use the word *Nil*, whereas Raleigh and Petrarch use the equivalent form *Nihil*. Further, Raleigh does not attribute the quotation to anyone, while Warren erroneously attributes it to Seneca.

It should be noted that the work *De remediis fortuitorum*, once believed to have been written by Seneca, was the inspiration for Petrarch's *De remediis utriusque fortunae*. Petrarch has often been called "the modern Seneca." His writings are filled with allusions to that philosopher (Ullman 27). This may explain why Warren, and probably others, ascribed "Nihil sapientiae odiosius acumine nimio" to Seneca.

Note

1. An electronic version of this text can be found at <http://books.google.com/books?id=A3APAAAA QAAJ&printsec=frontcover&dq%22De+remediis+ utriusque+fortunae%22&hl=el.>. See also Nicholas Mann (87).

Works Cited

The Harleian Miscellany. Vol. 9. London: Printed for Robert Dutton, 1810.

Mann, Nicholas. "Arnold Geilhoven: An Early Disciple of Petrarch in the Low Countries." *Journal of the Warburg and Courtauld Institutes* 32 (1969): 73-108.

Petrarch. *De remediis utriusque fortunae*. 2 books. 5th ed. Geneva: Esaiam le Preux, 1613.

Poe, Edgar Allan. *Complete Poems*. Ed. Thomas Ollive Mabbott. Urbana: U of Illinois P, 2000.

———. *Essays and Reviews*. Ed. G. R. Thompson. New York: The Library of America, 1984.

———. *Tales and Sketches*. Ed. Thomas Ollive Mabbott. 2 vols. Urbana: U of Illinois P, 2000.

Raleigh, Walter. *The Works of Sir Walter Raleigh* (sic). Vol. 2. Oxford: Oxford UP, 1829.

Rawski, Conrad H. *Petrarch's Remedies for Fortune Fair and Foul: A Modern English Translation of De Remediis Utriusque Fortunae*. Bloomington: Indiana UP, 1991.

Ullman, B. L. "Petrarch's Favorite Books." *Proceedings of the American Philological Association*. Baltimore: Johns Hopkins UP, 1923. 21-38.

Warren, Samuel G. *Ten Thousand a Year*. *Blackwood's Edinburgh Magazine* 48 (1840): 109.

———. *Ten Thousand a Year*. 6 vols. Philadelphia: Carey and Hart, 1840-41.

Alexandra Urakova (essay date December 2009)

SOURCE: Urakova, Alexandra. "'The Purloined Letter' in the Gift Book: Reading Poe in a Contemporary Context." *Nineteenth-Century Literature* 64, no. 3 (December 2009): 323-46.

[*In the following essay, Urakova places Poe's story in the sociological and historical context of its original publication and addresses Poe's masculine inversion of the tenets of the gift-book format.*]

Framing Edgar Allan Poe's **"The Purloined Letter"** (1844) was a fashionable intellectual practice in the 1970s and 1980s, inspired mostly by Jacques Lacan's "Le Séminaire sur 'La lettre volée'" (1956).[1] In 1975 Jacques Derrida, accusing Lacan of having excluded the textual fiction from its frame, accordingly "replaced" the tale in Poe's detective trilogy **"The Murders in the Rue Morgue"** (1841), **"The Mystery of Marie Rogêt"** (1842-43), and **"The Purloined Letter."**[2] Barbara Johnson reconstructed a broader frame of reference, reading the tale together with Prosper-Jolyet de Crebillon's *Atrée et Thyeste* (1707) overtly and Shakespeare's *Macbeth* covertly alluded to in Poe's tale.[3] John T. Irwin pushed the frame forward by rereading Jorge Luis Borges rereading **"The Purloined Letter."**[4] And finally, Joseph N. Riddel made Poe's tale both a metonymical and an allegorical figure of nineteenth-century American literary practice.[5] While suggesting yet another possible "frame of reference," I do not intend to reanimate or follow the famous poststructuralist debate, nor to build on a new interpretation of the tale's logical structure. By returning Poe's tale to *The Gift: A Christmas, New Year, and Birthday Present, 1845* (1844), the gift book where it was first printed, I explore in this essay the relation of the story to its apparently arbitrary periodical framing. Further, I discuss the connection of **"The Purloined Letter"** to the economy of the gift book, showing how the heterosexual commerce of commodified seduction implied by the mainstream stories in gift books finally leads up to the homosocial erotics in Poe's tale.[6]

"The Purloined Letter" was published in *The Gift,* a popular Philadelphia annual or gift book, in September 1844.[7] Later it was revised by Poe for the 1845 Wiley and Putnam edition of the *Tales,* and Poe made additional changes to the text in his own copy of the *Tales,* known as the J. Lorimer Graham copy, in 1849. This final revision has become a now-canonical version of the tale included in works and anthologies of Poe's fiction.[8] **"The Purloined Letter"** was also immediately reprinted from *The Gift* in *Chambers' Edinburgh Journal* in 1844, but the *Chambers'* reprint, copied in turn by a number of American periodicals, was excessively abridged and unauthorized.[9] The publication in *The Gift* thus is not just the first but also the only authorized periodical version of the tale.

Poe's story appears in *The Gift* volume together with two tales contributed by well-published authors, Caroline Kirkland and Nathaniel Parker Willis. Kirkland's "The Schoolmaster's Progress" is a story about love letters being stolen, concealed, and finally discovered; in Willis's "The Power of an 'Injured Look'" a letter ruins, although temporarily, a politician's career.[10] It is not hard to recognize the storylines corresponding with Poe's tale—a purloined letter, a letter as an in-

strument of political manipulation. Thematically organizing the annual's materials was not an uncommon editorial practice in *The Gift*. At the same time, these two tales, while forming a rather spontaneous, accidental trilogy with **"The Purloined Letter,"** were different in their style and genre. Kirkland's tale is a humorous "frontier" story and a love story with a happy ending, and "The Power of an 'Injured Look'" is a political satire, while Poe's **"The Purloined Letter"** is an early sample of detective genre and is itself a sequel to the two Dupin tales.[11] Yet the very fact that these tales with a common subject matter appear under the cover of the same annual makes it tempting to examine their possible interrelations.

"The Schoolmaster's Progress" is a story about fake correspondence. Miss Harriet Bangle, a snobbish Easterner visiting a small western village, decides to punish Master William Horner for his indifference to her. She starts sending him love letters on behalf of his beautiful student Ellen Kingsbury, whom he is secretly attached to. The idea of tricking the teacher occurs to Miss Bangle at the public spelling-school, where Horner himself is trying "by tricks to put down those [students] whom he cannot overcome in fair fight" ("The Schoolmaster's Progress," p. 16). The trick that originated from the spelling exam in turn resembles a spelling exercise. The seriousness of Horner's attachment to the imaginary correspondent improves his style, giving "both grace and dignity to his once awkward diction" (p. 19). As Miss Bangle perceives, she "herself had turned schoolmistress," and Master Horner, "instead of being merely her dupe, had become her pupil too" (p. 19). When the poor teacher attempts to talk with Ellen about their secret correspondence, he causes a scandal with her father and other villagers involved. His only testimony, the letters kept in a "precious parcel" (p. 24) and locked in his desk, disappear. As it turns out, Miss Bangle and her mate unlocked the desk with the help of a crooked nail and purloined the parcel. But Miss Bangle is finally herself betrayed by her mate, who steals the letters for his own purposes. At the end of the story the letters are accidentally discovered during a school performance, the deceiver is exposed, and Horner is justified and rewarded by Miss Kingsbury's benevolence.

It is not hard to see that a similar role-exchange structure, inherited from classical rhetorical tradition, is perfected in the famous "round robin" plot in Poe's **"The Purloined Letter"**: the Queen duping the King is duped by the Minister D——, who is in turn duped by Dupin. What distinguishes Poe's plot, though, is its merely functional appropriation free from didactic overtones, not to mention the symmetrical character of the plot based on repetition. The motif of fake correspondence is also implied in Poe's tale, as the letter found in D——'s apartment is "addressed, in a diminutive female hand, to D——, the minister, himself" (**"The Purloined Letter,"** p. 58). Concealing the letter, D—— readdresses and reseals it, forging a correspondence of an obviously intimate nature between himself and a fabricated female addressee. What betrays the Minister among other things is the soiled and torn condition of the paper, "so inconsistent with the *true* methodical habits of D——" (p. 59), as Dupin observes, and with a customary way of keeping love correspondence, as one might guess (as in the "precious parcel" where Master Horner keeps his letters locked in "The Schoolmaster's Progress"). In Poe's tale the letter's disposition is by no means evident, but it is evident just enough for Dupin to figure it out. A man such as D—— would not hide the document of extreme importance inside a chair or under the carpet as the Prefect expects, but neither would he keep a love letter, even unimportant and worthless, in such a suggestively careless way.

The plot of "The Power of an 'Injured Look'" corresponds with another aspect of Poe's tale: a letter as a vehicle of political destruction. Willis's tale is not as much about the letter(s) as Kirkland's and Poe's tales are. It is plotted around the heroine's natural gift of exciting popular sympathy and pity (her "injured look"), which the narrator reads "in the lowering pupil of her eye" ("Power of an 'Injured Look,'" p. 33) and which remains unnoticed by her fiancé and then a husband, McRueit, who claims to be a connoisseur of human nature. The narrator shares this secret with McRueit's political enemy, Mr. Develin, and also tells him about a widow named "Wanmaker," whose courtship cost the politician a place in Saratoga because his wife's "look" turned public opinion against him. Develin, having checked the spelling of the widow's last name, sends Mrs. McRueit a letter the very day her husband is making his electoral speech. We can only guess what the fatal letter is about, but its message, translated by Mrs. McRueit's injured look, leaves no doubt to the whole electorate that the husband is guilty of treason. The attention of the audience is drawn from the speaker's lips to his wife's eyes and to a large placard with the words "injured wife," "unfaithful husband," and "Widow W-n-k-r" written in capital letters (p. 36).[12] McRueit loses at the election but learns a lesson. He understands that "he felt overmastered by the key she [Mrs. McRueit] had to popular sympathy" and manages "to make it turn in his favour" ("Power of an 'Injured Look'" p. 37). "Readdressing" the message of her eloquent look, McRueit eventually becomes a very powerful person in the government.

In Poe's tale the facsimile of the purloined letter left to the Minister by Dupin also foreshadows Dupin's future downfall. D——'s political destruction appears somehow more menacing and disturbing than McRueit's fate, not the least because the political exposure itself is suspended, put off. And still the similar structure is reenacted in **"The Purloined Letter"**: the letter passing from the Queen to D——, from D—— to Dupin, and finally from Dupin back to the Queen is in turn empowering and disempowering its holders.

The type of relations between the tales can best be explained by the term "artistic ensemble," suggested by Yuri Lotman, where texts in the same periodical, though different in style, design, and school, form "a kind of unity in the consciousness of the contemporaries hard for us to understand today."[13] Undoubtedly the same subject matter can be found in many other periodical pieces of the time. Still, semantic patterns repeated in each of the three tales in *The Gift* give an idea of the basic expectations of the annual's reader. Deceiver is duped, untruthful husband punished though not destroyed. A fake correspondent is unmasked, as happens in "The Schoolmaster's Progress," but it also occurs in **"The Purloined Letter,"** where the Minister's readdressing and resealing the letter, his invention of a nonexistent addressee, serves as a clue to the mystery. In each tale the reader's attention is focused not so much on the content of the letter as on its displacements, which eventually constitute the plot. A letter becomes a public message metonymically displaced by Mrs. McRueit's injured look. A missing "parcel" or a "glove" turned inside out, the letters figure as material items, objects of loss and desire. Poe brings the letter's materiality to its logical extreme, as its content is a semantic gap playing no significant role in the power structure of the tale. The itinerary of the letter or letters keeping the reader's interest throughout the narrative is again predictable. The schoolmaster not only gets his letters back but also gains Ellen's heart, the tale thus following the triumph-of-love pattern. Mrs. McRueit teaches her husband a lesson, and his final repossession of her secret "power" ironically reaffirms matrimonial values. It is not surprising in this context that Dupin, "a partisan of the lady" as he calls himself (**"The Purloined Letter,"** p. 60), eventually returns the letter to the Queen, restores her power, and saves her reputation. Poe's tale seems to be perfectly fitted in its gift book framing.

The typical gift book reader I am referring to is a (usually) middle- or upper-class female well read in the sentimental, entertaining, and didactic fiction of contemporary periodicals. Yet the relation of Poe's tale to its "frame" cannot be explained without considering the specifics of the annual itself, a medium that was defining both editorial politics and reading practices to no lesser degree than the literary market in general. Therefore, I find it important for my purposes to mark some of the distinguishing features of the gift book.

* * *

The Gift: A Christmas and New Year's Present was one of the numerous literary annuals that burst into the American print market in the 1830s and 1840s under such names as *Souvenir, Offering, Token of Affection, Forget Me Not, Violet, Snow-Drops,* and the like. According to Ralph Thompson, *The Gift* was the "most ambitious undertaking" of the Carey and Hart publishing house "in the gift book field."[14] There were eight volumes in total issued from 1833 to 1845, which included works by Poe, Washington Irving, Ralph Waldo Emerson, Henry Wadsworth Longfellow, Willis, Kirkland, Harriet Beecher Stowe, Catherine Maria Sedgwick, Lydia Sigourney, and William Burton, not to mention illustrations by Thomas Sully. The often high quality of literary materials and engravings notwithstanding, *The Gift* was still representative of the literary annuals of its type.

To begin with, a gift book was not just a periodical: it was also an expensive present and object of luxury, an exquisite artifact. Engravings played an even more important role in gift books than in other periodical editions. As one of the leading engravers of the time, John Sartain, stated in 1849: "*Now* an annual is bought to look at. No one ever thinks of reading them."[15] One might suggest that the plates were not as often cut out from annuals as, say, famous fashion plates were cut from *Godey's Lady's Book.* The relevance of the gift book's integrity is suggested by the evidences of the way in which it was usually kept. Thompson writes: "For nearly a generation the resplendent gift book was among the most treasured of personal belongings. Unlike other volumes, it was not, once read, forgotten. Thruout the year it lay upon the parlor table, an ornament awaiting reexamination in an idle hour" (*American Literary Annuals and Gift Books,* pp. 1-2). In her tale "The Souvenir," itself published in *Affection's Gift* in 1832, Eliza Leslie describes her heroine receiving "the elegant souvenir" of a gift book as a present:

> She spread a clean handkerchief over her lap before she drew the book from its case, that it might not be soiled in the slightest degree, and she removed to a distance from the fire lest the cover should be warped by the heat. After she had eagerly looked all through it, she commenced again, and examined the plates with the most minute attention. She then showed them to her little brother and sister.[16]

This fragment emphasizes two important aspects: first, reading is eventually replaced by looking and showing; and second, the exaggerated care stresses the souvenir's economic and symbolic value. While lady's magazines were bought mostly with a purpose to clip and collect fashion plates, gift books were purchased to be given as presents to keep.[17]

The practice of giving gift books as presents defined "the asymmetrical conditions of gift book circulation," which situated them "at a pivot point between economic and affective systems of exchange," in the words of Meredith L. McGill.[18] According to McGill, "As they pass from purchaser to receiver, suitor to woman sought, gift books also need to be transformed from mass-produced commodities into another kind of currency, 'tokens of affection' that will be rewarded by a return of the same" (*American Literature and the Culture of Reprinting,* p. 34). The gift book's role in the courtship process was, indeed, significant.[19] A book was one of the very few presents (along with "a bouquet," "one or two autographs of distinguished persons," and "a few relics or momentos of memorable places") that were acceptable for a lady to receive from a gentleman, as Eliza Leslie's *Behaviour Book: A Guide and Manual for Ladies* of 1851 insists.[20] Leslie was herself editor of a number of gift books, including the first four volumes of *The Gift.*

It is not surprising, then, that a gift book more or less explicitly reminded the reader of its functional, gift-related character. In *The Gift* volume for 1837 (issued in 1836) we find a poem of the same name by N. C. Brooks, the editor of the gift book *Amethyst.* The poet speaks rather loosely of his name inscribed on "the tablet of a female heart," as the token of faith and friendship emphasizes the word "Gift."[21] An even better example is from another of Miss Leslie's annuals, *The Violet: A Christmas and New Year's Gift, or Birthday Present.* The volume of *The Violet* published in 1838 opens with a poem called "The Blossom Spirit" by Mrs. C. E. Goosh, praising a violet, which is baptized as "Forget-me-not" by the King of flowers:

> I give—the name Forget-me-not
> Be thine,—and henceforth thou shalt be
> The symbol dear to memory.[22]

"Forget-me-not" is not just a symbol of memory but, more important, the name of a famous and fashionable British gift book (the gift book vogue came to the United States from Great Britain, where it was in its zenith in the 1810s and 1820s). The poem, indeed, assumes illocutionary, initiating power. Further, nearly every tale in the volume has something to do with either flowers or holidays, as the titles "The Rose Bud in Autumn," "Drops of Water and Prisms," "The Holiday," "The Birth-day Ball," "The New-Year Gifts," and the like suggest.[23] The annual does not let a reader forget for a moment that she is holding a birthday or

New Year's present, or at least a token of affection, a souvenir and forget-me-not.[24]

The above-mentioned distinguishing features of a gift book—its integrity, ornamental character, and currency in the libidinal exchange—more or less explicitly acknowledged, indeed defined, the way in which certain gift book tales were meant to be read. One would think of holiday tales, tales with a gift-giving motif, and stories about the exchange of affection tokens in general. Poe's **"The Purloined Letter"** obviously does not fit any of these categories, yet in order to specify its place in *The Gift* and its relation to the annual's economy, I find it relevant to read Poe's tale against the background of the works expressing the gift book's underlying ideology. Thus, I propose to "broaden" our frame of reference and to discuss two other tales of *The Gift* that I see as representative of the annual's politics.

One of these tales, "The Old Valentine," in *The Gift* for 1839 (published in 1838), was contributed by Maria Griffith, a popular gift book author.[25] The title gives it away as a "holiday" tale, and there is little doubt that "The Old Valentine" was written especially for the annual. The tale's heroine, Sophia Lee, receives a valentine that she believes was written by Mr. Samuel Day, her aunt's accountant. But Mr. Day is a serious "man of business" who would not very likely send a valentine to express his feelings and who besides looks too calm and self-conscious for a secret admirer. Sophia carefully examines the letter, musing: "there is some mystery about this—pray, when did he write it? it must have been lately, for here is 1837, and yet—stay—I declare there has been an erasure, for I see the top part of a 6 or 5 above the 7, and look here, too, *Gift* is in paler ink: a word has been scratched out there. It never struck me before, but the paper is not as white as the envelope" ("The Old Valentine," p. 50). The word that is scratched out is, one would guess, the name of the addressee. As it finally turns out, Mr. Day wrote this valentine at the request of their mutual friend, who had bad handwriting. Thus, he was writing it "mechanically, without considering the import of the words at all" (p. 57). But this fact does not seem to matter. "We do not care for the rhyme nor for the design, you know, it is the pleasant feeling that these little bits of paper give one," Sophia tells her girlfriends (p. 45), who got the valentines which she herself cut, painted, and wrote, doing a favor for the same friend. Thanks to the "dear little paper" (p. 57), Mr. Day and Sophia reveal their feelings to each other, not accidentally on Sophia's birthday.

The letter thus assumes meaning and value only when it becomes a token of true affection, a sign of secret attachment. "The Old Valentine" is indeed emblem-atic. The valentine serves as a perfect substitute for *The Gift* as a volume, as a valentine is already itself something in-between a love letter and a present. *The Gift,* very much like the valentine, is compiled and designed for nobody in particular. The name that is left blank in *The Gift,* like the one scratched out in Sophia's letter, needs to be filled in, in each individual case. The true addressee of the valentine—true of course in a supreme, symbolic sense—is finally discovered. *The Gift,* indeed, functions in very much the same way, converting depersonalized economic relations of seller-buyer into personalized affective bonds of sender-receiver.

The other tale that I will discuss in the same context is "The Unpresuming Mr. Hudson" by Catherine Maria Sedgwick, printed in *The Gift* for 1836 (issued in 1835).[26] Sedgwick, according to Thompson, was "one of the most admired of gift book writers" (*American Literary Annuals and Gift Books,* p. 22); she published also in Philadelphia's *Atlantic Souvenir* and Boston's *The Token,* among others. Her tale opens this volume of *The Gift,* its place thus indicating the tale's and the author's significance. Sedgwick's tale, unlike the happy-ending narrative of Maria Griffith, is rather a didactic story with a moral, "meditating upon the trials of a pretty young girl who is chaperoned to watering-places by a silly, expecting, and credulous mother" ("The Unpresuming Mr. Hudson," p. 38).

The story's heroine, Louise Campbell, traveling with her mother in a stagecoach to the Springs, is courted by the gentlemen who accompany them—with the exception of one Mr. Hudson. He is the only member of the group who does not give the flowers he has collected to Louise. Louise's mother is more willing to "read" Hudson's indifference as the sign of his shyness concealing a secret attachment. Hudson remains equally "unpresuming" during the whole time they spend together on a steamboat. And yet on the day of departure Louise, going to her cabin in search of something she has left behind, finds there "a book neatly enveloped in white paper, on which was written in pencil, '*To L. C. from C. H.*' and under it the trite of quotation from the text-book of lovers, 'The world is divided into two parts—that where she is, and that where she is not'" ("The Unpresuming Mr. Hudson," p. 35). The heroine unbinds the envelope's blue ribbon "with a fluttering hand": "It was a blank album, with flowers pressed between its leaves, the very flowers that the 'unpresuming Mr. Hudson' had not the courage to offer to Louise on the first day of their acquaintance. Here they were embalmed by love and poetry; for on each page was pencilled a quoted stanza from some popular amorous poet" (p. 35). Yet Louise misreads both the flower language and the envelope's address. The initials "C. H." are correctly deciphered as

"Charles Hudson." But "L. C." is not Louise Campbell, it is her former schoolmate Laura Clay, who has just arrived at the same cabin and who presents herself as Hudson's fiancée. When the real addressee is found out, the narrator, Louise's elderly female companion, secretly restores the album "to its right place" (p. 38). Louise's imagination stirred up by her mother's ambitions therefore betrays her. She does not guess that the address written on the envelope may be the wrong one, assuming that "L. C." can have only one signified, that is herself. "L. C." instead could ideally make an infinite number of combinations and be nearly anybody at all, in the same way that earlier, in the conversation with Louise's mother, it turns out that Hudson does not belong to the Hudsons of Boston or of Baltimore or of New York.

The album in "The Unpresuming Mr. Hudson," like the valentine in the story by Maria Griffith, functions as a gift book's double. Many familial, handwritten albums were bound in the gift book style and were even entitled "Casket of Thoughts" or "Token of Affection" (see Thompson, _American Literary Annuals and Gift Books,_ p. 20). Like gift books, as Kevin J. Hayes reminds us, "albums were often given as holiday presents."[27] Thompson counts "at least fifty" annuals "dealing with flowers and flower-language," "appropriately named 'Flora's Album,' 'Flora's Dial,' 'Flora's Interpreter,' 'Floral Keepsake,' 'Poetry of Flowers,' or 'Flower Garden'" (_American Literary Annuals and Gift Books,_ p. 17). As in "The Old Valentine," the addressee's name in "The Unpresuming Mr. Hudson" remains unknown (and misleading) until the end; it is not scratched out but ciphered in the initials, a common way of signing love messages as well as poems in the periodicals, including _The Gift._ The flowers in the album have a special meaning for Louise (_those_ flowers that were collected by Hudson on the day of their acquaintance). Yet they are not _the_ flowers but just flowers speaking a universal language of love, like the quotation on the envelope labeled as "trite." And still, what causes disappointment to Louise Campbell gives "a pleasant feeling" to her substitute, Laura Clay, proving to Laura as well as to the readers the love and truthfulness of her fiancé. Louise was determined that "the flowers should not fail to their destination" ("The Unpresuming Mr. Hudson," p. 24), and they did not. Sedgwick's didactic tale restages the same plot pattern as does Griffith's valentine story: the itinerary of the flower album corresponds to the libidinal nature of a gift book circulation.

* * *

Returning to Poe's tale, we can see that _The Gift's_ reader would, indeed, expect Dupin to scrutinize the letter, noting the minute details with almost feminine attentiveness, and to decipher correctly the letter's address. Indeed, Sophia's examination of the valentine strikingly resembles Dupin's detection of the purloined letter's material form. The color of the paper proves to Sophia that the valentine was written much earlier than it was sent; "the soiled and torn condition of the paper" makes Dupin suspect D——'s intentional "design to delude the beholder into an idea of the worthlessness of the document" (**"The Purloined Letter,"** p. 59). The Prefect, instead, very much like Louise, reads the clues too straightforwardly, expecting the signifier to coincide with the signified and thus looking for the letter "with the ducal arms of S—— family" (p. 59). The excessive materiality of the letter in Poe's story is again explicable in the context of the annual, which overemphasizes the value of its ornaments and plates and where the literary works often refer back to the book's physical form. At the same time, the letter like the gift book is not only the _thing_ but a _sign,_ in the words of Ora Avni, functioning in the text as a pure signifier and a variable object of exchange.[28] As mentioned earlier, the final arrival of the letter to the Queen, its real addressee and owner, seems to be a matter of fact. Yet the tale's plot, apparently in tune with the symbolic itinerary of _The Gift's_ letters and parcels, does not fit so easily in the annual's ideological pattern.

Dupin does return the letter to the Queen via the Prefect. But he does not _give_ the letter, he asks the Prefect to write him a check. Before that, he rather cynically tells the Prefect "the story . . . of Abernethy": a rich miser wants to get a medical opinion of a famous physician for free, and the physician, Abernethy, not willing to be duped, advises him to "take _advice_" (**"The Purloined Letter,"** p. 50). The Prefect understands the hint and offers fifty thousand francs. In _The Gift's_ version this is even stressed: "I would _really_ give fifty thousand francs, every _centime_ of it, to any one who would aid me in the matter!" (p. 50) (in later revisions "every _centime_ of it," with the word centime emphasized, is omitted).[29] "'In that case,' replied Dupin, opening a drawer, and producing a check-book, 'you may as well fill me up a check for the amount mentioned. When you have signed it, I will hand you the letter'" (**"The Purloined Letter,"** p. 50). The checkbook thus comes before the letter.

The giving-a-letter-(a book)-as-a-gift motif in the tales, as discussed earlier, is indeed a disguise of the real economic relations between the annual and its readers. Gift books circulated in the market as commercial projects, and it was part of this project to make their readers forget that fact. The discrepancy between a book, with its average price of three and a half dollars, and a gift of affective nature was noticeable. Exchanging the letter for the check in Poe's story disrupts its ideal itinerary, which would be expected in *The Gift's* tale. Though excluded from affective relations altogether, the returned letter could have still been a token of Dupin's partisanship and loyalty, his admiration or respect. Dupin, indeed, does become a sender of the letter, entrusting the Prefect to deliver it to the Queen. Yet he prefers simply to be paid for his service, choosing to remain anonymous.

Poe was certainly well aware of the entirely commercial nature of *The Gift* and similar annuals. The Carey and Hart project was the opposite of Poe's own project of *The Stylus,* an ideal magazine aiming to improve the general taste and quality of American periodicals. Poe planned to sell *The Stylus* for the price of a gift book (three dollars per volume), and yet at the same time he insisted on the subsidiary function of the ornaments, for example: "Engravings, when used, will be in the highest style of Art, but are promised only in obvious illustration of the text, and in strict keeping with the Magazine character."[30] "The Prospectus of The Stylus," written the same year as **"The Purloined Letter,"** juxtaposes the "TRUTH" of its editor's *"iron pen"* and the general dishonesty of contemporary periodicals. Poe's reluctance to disguise the true, commercial nature of exchange relations could therefore be viewed as a tongue-in-cheek attempt to smuggle the "TRUTH" in the conventional format of a sellable story. The fifty thousand francs that Dupin earns is a considerable sum of money, but it is still part of "a *very* liberal reward" that the Prefect is going to get for the letter. Although Poe believed that the tale's effect could "be estimated better by the circulation of the Magazine,"[31] the overall profit from the circulation was often beyond estimation and always beyond the reach of the individual contributor. The author, as the detective, has only a share in the reward.

And yet thinking more broadly of Poe's "economic imagination,"[32] a more likely suggestion is that the idea of gift giving was incompatible for Poe with the idea of intellectual property. A good example is his gift-book-mediated correspondence with Washington Irving related to Poe's tale **"William Wilson"** (1839). In the essay "The Unwritten Drama of Lord Byron" published in *The Gift* for 1836 (published in 1835), Irving generously offered an allegedly Byronic plot "to a poet or a dramatist of the Byron school."[33] Poe took the challenge and realized the idea in **"William Wilson,"** issued in *The Gift* four years later.[34] No matter how tempting it could be to think of Irving-Poe relations in the terms of a gift-exchange, Poe himself considered Irving a shareholder rather than a donor. Sending a copy of his tale to Irving, Poe wrote: "I have hoped that, having thus a right of ownership in my **'William Wilson',** you will be induced to read it—and I also hope that, reading it, you will find in it

something to approe [approve]."[35] A request of a public letter in favor of **"William Wilson"** was an attempt to charge Irving with responsibility for the plot he had given away. Unlike a gift-giver, a shareholder should take interest in investment, even if the expected profit from the share is symbolic. Equally, the letter's itinerary in **"The Purloined Letter"** lies entirely within the sphere of economic relations between the agents, excluded from any sort of affectionate gift-giving (the presumed love-correspondence between the Queen and S—— is pushed to the narrative's margin).

A different type of relation manifests itself near the tale's closure when Dupin leaves the facsimile of the purloined letter to D—— and signs it, breaking his anonymity. His signature is itself a cipher, a quotation, but Dupin has no doubts that D——, well acquainted with his signature, will recognize it. The facsimile is thus not a facsimile in the strict sense: when signed and readdressed, it becomes an independent message. This is emphasized in the tale's narrative structure: the story of Dupin's and D——'s past relations has, indeed, nothing to do with the purloined-letter plot. Dupin says at the end: "To be sure, D——, at Vienna once, did me an evil turn, which I told him, quite good-humouredly, that I should remember. So, as I knew he would feel some curiosity in regard to the identity of the person who had outwitted him, I thought it a pity not to give him a clue" (**"The Purloined Letter,"** p. 61). The replaced letter becomes a token of hatred, an instrument of revenge; further, the allusion to the myth about Atreus and Thyestes in the quotation left by Dupin ("Un dessein si funeste, / S'il n'est digne d'Atrée, est digne de Thyeste" [p. 61]) suggests the motif of blood feud between him and D——, his antipode and double.[36] The homological structure of gift exchange and blood feud is a commonplace in social anthropology, potlatch being one of its best illustrations. Dupin, like his creator, the "literary Mohawk" Edgar Allan Poe, mediating revenge with a letter, replaces a violent gesture by a literary quotation.[37] The gift motif thus reappears at the very end of **"The Purloined Letter,"** but, indeed, "turned . . . inside out" (**"The Purloined Letter,"** p. 59).[38]

There has been a long tradition of reading **"The Purloined Letter"** as an autobiographical tale, and of reading this particular final scene as an allusion to Poe's own literary battles. The rivalries, thefts, invasions of privacy, and personal assaults that Poe witnessed during his magazinist career, are, indeed, looming behind the plot.[39] In January 1845 he notoriously attacked *The Waif,* a gift book compiled by Longfellow. Like Dupin, who identifies an apparently worthless piece of paper (a real waif, indeed!) as a purloined letter, Poe found a purloined poem in the book:

"Having fairly transcribed the two poems (about the respective dates of which we knew nothing) we have only to remark, as quietly as we can, that *somebody is a thief*."[40] Accusing Longfellow himself of imitating American poems deliberately omitted from the selection, Poe initiated a famous debate with "Outis," presumably his self-created fictional opponent. The literary theft "in the open day" was one of the points at issue in their polemics.

But placing **"The Purloined Letter"** in the gift book framework, we can see that Poe does not simply register literary practices of the time. He rather mediates the conventional gift book narrative of a heterosexual intrigue by a homosocial one, and thus engages the typical gender economy of the annual. The letter exchange takes place not between a lady and her admirer (a reader and her loving friend and/or a caring publisher) but "between men," as it were. The reader's attention is violently redirected from the itinerary of a love message to the dynamics of power; a female's personal secret is but a "use-value" object in the men's struggle. The "asymmetrical conditions of gift-book circulation" are replaced by the striking symmetry of the tale's "round robin" plot.

Paradoxically, Poe understands the male world of power as a grotesque inversion of the female literary world, the one of gift books, lady's books, and literary annuals. In Letter 6 (18 June 1844) of his "Doings of Gotham" series Poe speaks of the "masculine energy and ability" of the editor of the gift book *Opal,* Sarah Hale.[41] But his "androgynous" Dupin[42] is, indeed, Achilles, who "hid himself among women," as the famous motto to **"The Murders in the Rue Morgue"** from Thomas Browne might well suggest ("What song the Syrens sang, or what name Achilles assumed when he hid himself among women, although puzzling questions, are not beyond *all* conjecture").[43] **"The Purloined Letter,"** framed by female or female-addressed writing, seems to combine analytic powers of detection, commonly attributed to men, with feminine attenuated apprehension of material data. And still Dupin not so much recovers "the second story—'the woman's story'—which has previously gone untold," as Cynthia Jordan contends ("Poe's Re-Vision," p. 5), but purloins it instead. The homosocial erotics of **"The Purloined Letter"** strikingly reveals itself when put against the background of the gift book tradition more or less openly commodifying heterosexual conventions.

Jacques Lacan's insightful reading was needed in order to discover the "feminine nature" of Dupin's hostility to D——.[44] The gift book framework seems to support Lacan's idea about the materiality of the signifier as well as his observation concerning "the odd-

est *odor di femina*" passing from one purloiner to the other ("Seminar on 'The Purloined Letter,'" p. 48). His famous statement that "a letter always arrives at its destination" (p. 58) works beautifully if we read Poe's tale together with "The Schoolmaster's Progress," "The Old Valentine," "The Unpresuming Mr. Hudson," or even "The Power of an 'Injured Look.'" But at the same time, in the "high theory" self-reflexive interpretations of **"The Purloined Letter,"** Poe's own tale begins to play the same function as the letter does in the story: it becomes an object of hatred and revenge, an instrument of insult.

As is well known, Jacques Derrida in "The Purveyor of Truth," attempting to undermine Lacan's authoritative position, stressed Lacan's "disdainful nervousness" ("The Purveyor of Truth," p. 189) toward Marie Bonaparte, the author of a psychobiographical study on Poe and a loyal disciple of Sigmund Freud (Lacan called her a "cook" in a footnote referring to the "grilling" nature of her analysis).[45] Barbara Johnson further demonstrated Derrida's involvement in the "feud" with Lacan as she step-by-step deconstructed Derrida's deconstruction of "The Seminar" and brought in the issue of the personal offense.[46] Johnson's own relation to the story of rivalry was neutralized by the chosen "undecidability" of her position, as John Irwin pointed out.[47] But more recently, Kay Stockholder has accused Johnson of *insulting* Derrida "by saying that he accuses Lacan of what he himself is guilty."[48]

The odd turn of Poe's plot becomes reenacted in its critical readings and gets similar implications. The "contagious" logic of the purloined letter, to borrow Johnson's term ("Frame of Reference," p. 214), maps out relations between the agents of a new literary milieu according to the same fictional pattern. Further, new details being added flesh out the story of rivalry between Lacan and Bonaparte, Lacan and Derrida. The word "cook" in Lacan's footnote, one critic suggests, is a hint at Bonaparte's "unsuccessful surgical interventions and cauterizing (grilling) of her clitoris in a vain attempt to regain her sexual sensitivity"; she was (as we learn) "obsessed by the belief that frigidity was due to a malfunction or a misplacement of the clitoris, to which she compared the little brass knob in her comment on Poe's tale."[49] The violent attack on Bonaparte attributed to Lacan initiates wordplay around her name. Another critic speaks of Lacan's insult as of "the murder of Marie," bringing together **"The Mystery of Marie Rogêt"** (the middle story in Poe's trilogy) and "maternal Marie," Lacan's own middle name.[50] The royal name of Mme Bonaparte eventually turns her into a "psychoanalytic Marie Antoinette" (Bretzius, "The Figure-Power Dialectic," p. 683), the "murder" therefore becomes symbolic regicide. The violated body of a woman, present in Poe's first two detective tales and missing in **"The Purloined Letter,"** returns to the thus expanded plot in the course of its reenactment and (re)narration. The body of Marie, she of the cauterized clitoris or she of the decapitated head, reinforces the homosocial nature of the tale's intrigue as it gets a new turn in its critical interpretations.

Dynamics of writing, reading, and power in and around **"The Purloined Letter"** had therefore a direct impact on the famous debate, revealing the hidden potential of the plot. The endurance of Poe's storyline and its forceful erotic implications reinforce the fact that his tale (to use the terms of Pierre Bourdieu) rather than being a "pure product of a milieu," contributed to "transforming" the milieu, "which is accomplished, in part, through the objectification of that milieu."[51] This objectification can best be explained as a purloining and inverting of what represented, more or less overtly, the existing ideology of emerging literary culture. The affinities between *The Gift* and **"The Purloined Letter"** as well as their discrepancies are spontaneous and accidental. But the fact that Poe's tale fits in the ideological framework of the nineteenth-century periodical and resists it at the same time, both matching and disrupting its reader's expectations, is symptomatic.[52]

In Sedgwick's story the album, a gift book substitute, is neatly enveloped in white paper bound with a blue ribbon. The card-rack of pasteboard where Dupin discovers the purloined letter hangs under the mantelpiece, "dangling by a dirty blue riband" (**"The Purloined Letter,"** p. 58; "ribbon" in the revision of 1845), its paper being soiled and torn. The only line written on the envelope beneath the initials is a "quotation from the text-books of lovers." Dupin copies "into the middle of the blank sheet" (p. 61) of his letter a quotation from Crebillon's revenge play, and leaves it inside. While Poe's tale inverts the exemplary plot-model of *The Gift*, the purloined letter in the story strikingly resembles a gift book turned inside out.

Notes

1. See Lacan, "Seminar on 'The Purloined Letter,'" trans. Jeffrey Mehlman, in *The Purloined Poe: Lacan, Derrida and Psychoanalytic Reading*, ed. John P. Muller and William J. Richardson (Baltimore: Johns Hopkins Univ. Press, 1988), pp. 28-54 (originally published 1956). The first version of the present essay was presented as a lecture to faculty and graduate students at the English Department, University of Virginia, on 18 January 2008. I am grateful to Stephen Railton for his assistance.

2. See Derrida, "The Purveyor of Truth," trans. Alan Bass, in *The Purloined Poe*, pp. 173-212 (originally published 1975). Derrida famously stresses: "the framing of the frames, the interminable supplementary of the quotation marks, the insertion of 'The Purloined Letter' into a purloined letter beginning before it, through the narratives of narratives in 'The Murders in the Rue Morgue,' and the newspaper clippings in 'The Mystery of Marie Rogêt' (A Sequel to 'The Murders in the Rue Morgue')" ("Purveyor of Truth," p. 204).

3. See Johnson, "The Frame of Reference: Poe, Lacan, Derrida," in *The Purloined Poe*, pp. 213-51 (originally published 1977). What is more, Johnson highlights the repetition of the fatal-letter plot in both alluded works: "And what is Lady Macbeth doing when we first catch sight of her? She is reading a letter. Not a purloined letter, perhaps, but one that contains the ambiguous letter of destiny, committing Macbeth to the murder of the King, whose place Macbeth will take and whose fate he will inevitably share. Kings seem to be unable to remain unscathed in the face of a letter— Atreus betrayed by his wife's letter to his brother; Duncan betrayed by Macbeth's letter to Lady Macbeth; Macbeth himself betrayed by his own confidence in his ability to read the letter of his Fate; and of course, the King in 'The Purloined Letter,' whose power is betrayed by his not even knowing about the existence of the letter that betrays him" ("Frame of Reference," p. 236).

4. See Irwin, "Mysteries We Reread, Mysteries of Rereading: Poe, Borges, and the Analytic Detective Story; Also Lacan, Derrida, and Johnson," *MLN*, 101 (1986), 1,168-1,215.

5. See Riddel, *The Purloined Letters: Originality and Repetition in American Literature*, ed. Mark Bauerlein (Baton Rouge: Louisiana State Univ. Press, 1995).

6. In using the term "homosocial" I refer to Eve Kosofsky Sedgwick, *Between Men: English Literature and Male Homosocial Desire* (New York: Columbia Univ. Press, 1985), where it was introduced for the first time. I would like to thank H. Aram Veeser for his insightful suggestions concerning this subject. The implicit homoerotic meanings of Poe's tales are discussed in Leland S. Person, "Queer Poe: The Tell-Tale Heart of His Fiction," *Poe Studies*, 41 (2008), 7-30.

7. See Edgar A. Poe, "The Purloined Letter," in *The Gift: A Christmas, New Year, and Birth-day Present, 1845* (Philadelphia: Carey and Hart, 1844), pp. 41-61. Further references to "The Purloined Letter" are to this edition and appear in the text. Although this volume of *The Gift* was published in 1844, it was sold away for the year that followed. Further in the essay I refer to the year of issue of this and other editions of gift books. In the footnotes I indicate both dates.

8. See Thomas Ollive Mabbott, textual notes for "The Purloined Letter," in *Collected Works of Edgar Allan Poe,* ed. Mabbott, 3 vols. (Cambridge, Mass.: Belknap Press of Harvard Univ. Press, 1978), III, 973-74. Mabbott also mentions the version that appeared in *The Works of the Late Edgar Allan Poe,* ed. Rufus W. Griswold (1850-56), which he describes as "merely a reprint of an unrevised copy of the *Tales*" with "no independent authority."

9. The *Chambers'* version was copied by *Littell's Living Age,* a Bostonian magazine that specialized in unauthorized reprints from foreign periodicals (18 January 1845); by the Philadelphian *Spirit of the Times* (20 and 22 January 1845); and by the *New York Weekly News* (25 January 1845). See Mabbott's notes in *Collected Works,* III, 974.

10. See [Caroline] Kirkland, "The Schoolmaster's Progress," in *The Gift* (1845 [1844]), pp. 10-25; and N. P. Willis, "The Power of an 'Injured Look,'" in *The Gift* (1845 [1844]), pp. 28-37. The three tales are published in sequence ("The Schoolmaster's Progress," "The Power of an 'Injured Look,'" and "The Purloined Letter") intermingled with a couple of poetical pieces and a plate. While I propose to read together the "neighboring" works, there is an example of reading together the "narratives" of two neighboring authors, Poe and Frederick Douglass, who lived "only a few blocks from each other" in Baltimore in the early 1830s. See J. Gerald Kennedy, "'Trust No Man': Poe, Douglass, and the Culture of Slavery," in *Romancing the Shadow: Poe and Race,* ed. J. Gerald Kennedy and Liliane Weissberg (New York: Oxford Univ. Press, 2001), p. 225.

11. Poe mentions both "the affair of the Rue Morgue" and "the murder of Marie Roget" at the beginning of "The Purloined Letter" ("The Purloined Letter," p. 41). Further, as Amy Gilman Srebnick suggests, there could be an even closer relation of "The Purloined Letter" to "The Mystery of Marie Rogêt." According to Srebnick, Poe, by quoting Crebillon's *Atrée et Thyeste,* pointed to William Attree, the crime reporter for *The New York Herald* who had "created" the Mary Rogers story, which implies another possible set of references. See Amy Gilman Srebnick, *The Mysterious Death of Mary Rogers: Sex and Culture in Nineteenth-Century New York* (New York: Oxford Univ. Press, 1995), pp. 123-24.

12. It is fascinating to read Dupin's famous, often-quoted statement in this context: "A novice in the game [the game of puzzles] generally seeks to embarrass his opponents by giving them the most minutely lettered names; but the adept selects such words as stretch, in large characters, from one end of the chart to the other. These, like the over-largely lettered signs and placards of the street, escape observation by dint of being excessively obvious" ("The Purloined Letter," p. 57).

13. See Lotman, "Hudozhestvenni ansambl' kak bitovoe prostranstvo" [Artistic Ensemble as Domestic Space], in Yuri Lotman, *Ob iskusstve* (Sankt-Peterburg: Iskusstvo-SPB, 2005), p. 581 (originally published 1974). In his turn, Cary Nelson suggests that periodicals should be read as texts that have a unity different from but comparable to that of individual books (see Nelson, *Repression and Recovery: Modern American Poetry and the Politics of Cultural Memory, 1910-1945* [Madison: Univ. of Wisconsin Press, 1989], p. 219). On the emerging field of periodical studies, which examines magazines and newspapers as "rich, dialogic texts" creating "often surprising and even bewildering points of contact between disparate areas of human activity," see Sean Latham and Robert Scholes, "The Rise of Periodical Studies," *PMLA,* 121 (2006), 517-53, 528.

14. See Thompson, *American Literary Annuals and Gift Books, 1825-1865* (New York: H. W. Wilson Co., 1936), p. 74.

15. John Sartain, *Sartain's Magazine,* 1 (1849); quoted in Frank Luther Mott, *A History of American Magazines, 1741-1850* (New York: D. Appleton and Co., 1930), p. 421.

16. E[liza] L[eslie], "The Souvenir" (1832), quoted in Thompson, *American Literary Annuals and Gift Books,* p. 2.

17. James D. Hart, also stating that "the gift book was clearly understood to be ornament," estimates that "publishers generally spent three times as much on the so-called embellishments as on the printed matter and twice as much again on the bindings of watered silk, flamboyantly stamped gilding, embossed leather, or varnished papier-mâché with inlaid mother-of-pearl" (Hart, *The Popular Book: A History of America's Literary Taste* [New York: Oxford Univ. Press, 1950], p. 89).

18. See McGill, *American Literature and the Culture of Reprinting, 1834-1853* (Philadelphia: Univ. of Pennsylvania Press, 2003), p. 34.

19. Although of course it could have been given as a family present as well. The inscription on the blank page of the copy of *The Gift* volume for 1845 (1844) at the Small Special Collections Library, the University of Virginia, for example, reads: "Presented to Mary A. Coleman Dec. 25, 1844, by her Father."

20. See [Eliza] Leslie, *Miss Leslie's Behaviour Book: A Guide and Manual for Ladies* (1851; 1859 ed., rpt. New York: Arno Press, 1972), p. 181.

21. He writes: "How bless'd my lot! could I remain / Engraven on thy breast and brain, / And Friendship bid my memory stay, / When all beside has passed away,— / And this fair GIFT a token be / Of faith, and friendship felt for thee" (N. C. Brooks, "The Gift," in *The Gift: A Christmas and New Year's Present for 1837,* ed. [Eliza] Leslie [Philadelphia: E. L. Cary and A. Hart, 1836], p. 325).

22. C. E. Goosh, "The Blossom Spirit," in *The Violet: A Christmas and New Year's Gift, or Birth-day Present* (1839 [1838]), p. 21.

23. The violet color of the prism in the story "Drops of Water and Prisms" (*The Violet* [1839 (1838)], 72-93) by Maria Griffith bluntly refers to Eliza Leslie's "beautiful little souvenir" "called the VIOLET" (p. 76). The title of the story itself points at the gift book tradition in general (i.e., a gift book titled *Snow-Drops*).

24. Two other examples of the gift-volume's self-referential character can be taken from *The Gift* for 1836 (published in 1835) and *The Gift* for 1845 (1844). In *The Gift* for 1836 there is an engraving titled "Fanny Kemble" by J. Cheney, taken from Thomas Sully's 1834 painting (on the title facing page of the gift book), and a poem by C. W. Thomson titled "On a Female Head by Sully." The poet narrating the story of the lady painted by Sully says: "Her dreams are full of hope and love," "For he, the loved one far away, / Has sent his message sweet" (Thomson, "On a Female Head by Sully," in *The Gift: A Christmas and New Year's Present for 1836,* ed. [Eliza] Leslie [Philadelphia: E. L. Carey and A. Hart, (1835)], p. 183). The other example is even more interesting in our case. C. R. Leslie's plate, coming in *The Gift* for 1845 just before Poe's "The Purloined Letter," shows a girl looking at a necklace that she has just taken from a parcel. The plate poem by Anne C. Lynch called "The Necklace" leaves no doubt that the necklace is not a sign of vanity but a "talisman," "Love's own amulet" (Lynch, "The Necklace," in *The Gift* [1845 (1844)], p. 40).

25. See M[aria] Griffith, "The Old Valentine," in *The Gift: A Christmas and New Year's Present for 1839,* ed. [Eliza] Leslie (Philadelphia: E. L. Carey and A. Hart, 1838), pp. 44-58.

26. See [Catherine Maria] Sedgwick, "The Unpresuming Mr. Hudson," in *The Gift* (1836 [1835]), pp. 2-38.

27. Hayes, *Poe and the Printed Word* (Cambridge: Cambridge Univ. Press, 2000), p. 21.

28. See Avni, "The Semiotics of Transactions: Mauss, Lacan and *The Three Musketeers*," trans. John Rosenthal, *MLN,* 100 (1985), 728-57.

29. Mabbott compares different editions of the tale in his textual notes to "The Purloined Letter" (see *Collected Works,* III, 972-74).

30. See Edgar Allan Poe, "Prospectus of The Stylus" (1845), in his *Essays and Reviews,* ed. G. R. Thompson (New York: Literary Classics of the United States, 1984), p. 1,033.

31. See Edgar Allan Poe, letter to Thomas W. White, 30 April 1835, in *The Letters of Edgar Allan Poe,* ed. John Ward Ostrom, 2 vols. (Cambridge, Mass.: Harvard Univ. Press, 1948), I, 58.

32. See Terence Whalen, *Edgar Allan Poe and the Masses: The Political Economy of Literature in Antebellum America* (Princeton: Princeton Univ. Press, 1999), p. 52.

33. Washington Irving, "An Unwritten Drama of Lord Byron," in *The Gift* (1836 [1835]), p. 171.

34. See Edgar A. Poe, "William Wilson: A Tale," in *The Gift: A Christmas and New Year's Present for 1840,* ed. [Eliza] Leslie (Philadelphia: Carey and Hart, 1839), pp. 229-53.

35. Edgar Allan Poe, letter to Washington Irving, 12 October 1839; quoted in John Ostrom, "Supplement to *The Letters of Poe*," *American Literature,* 24 (1952), 360.

36. Derrida writes about the "rivalrous and duplicitous identification of the two brothers," Dupin and D—— (see "Purveyor of Truth," p. 203). For discussions of the Doppelganger motif in the tale, see Patrick F. Quinn, *The French Face of Edgar Poe* (Carbondale: Southern Illinois Univ. Press, 1957), pp. 223-56; Joseph J. Moldenhauer, "Murder as a Fine Art: Basic Connections between Poe's Aesthetics, Psychology, and Moral Vision," *PMLA,* 83 (1968), 284-97; and Liahna Klenman Babener, "The Shadow's Shadow: The Motif of the Double in Edgar Allan Poe's 'The Purloined Letter,'" in *The Purloined Poe,* pp. 323-34 (originally published 1972).

37. Poe was called "Our Literary Mohawk" in A. J. H. Duganne's poem "A Mirror for Authors," published in *Holden's Dollar Magazine,* 3 (1849), together with a caricature by F. O. C. Darley representing Poe as a ferocious Indian with a tomahawk in his hand. In fact, Poe's image as an Indian, "scalping, brow-beating and otherwise using-up" a "herd of poor-devil authors," "assumed almost the status of a critical cliché" in the 1840s (see Leon Jackson, "'Behold Our Literary Mohawk, Poe': Literary Nationalism and the 'Indianation' of Antebellum American Culture," *ESQ,* 48 [2002], 97. Jackson quotes from Poe's "The Literary Life of Thingum Bob, Esq." [1844]).

38. Quite a different example is the publication of "The Gold-Bug" in the *Dollar Newspaper* in 1843, which Louis A. Renza describes in terms of "dou-

bling" (rather than "inversion"): "doubled by the 'dollar' newspaper in which he published 'The Gold-Bug,' there exists the synonymy between treasure and the likely commodity-value Poe places on his tale within his literary-journalistic marketplace. For that matter, its serial mode of publication arguably redoubles the tale's narrative suspense, thereby overtly soliciting public interest to increase its market value" (Renza, *Edgar Allan Poe, Wallace Stevens, and the Poetics of American Privacy* [Baton Rouge: Louisiana State Univ. Press, 2002], p. 34).

39. See, for example, Arthur Quinn's statement in his canonical critical biography: "Both of them [Dupin and D——] have characteristics of Poe, the power of analysis and the imagination that transcends analysis. Like Dupin, Poe could long remember an injury; like D—— he could neglect to remember that he had injured a possible enemy" (Arthur Hobson Quinn, *Edgar Allan Poe: A Critical Biography* [New York: D. Appleton-Century Co., 1941], pp. 421-22).

40. See Edgar Allan Poe, "Longfellow's *Waif,* with an Exchange" (1845), in *Essays and Reviews,* p. 702. The poem discussed by Poe is Thomas Hood's "The Death-Bed" (1831). Poe gives the example of the "parallel poem" by James Aldrich from Rufus W. Griswold's *Poets and Poetry of America* (1842).

41. Hale was a famous editor of *Godey's Lady's Book.* See Edgar Allan Poe, "Doings of Gotham, Letter VI," *Columbia Spy,* 18 June 1844, p. 3; rpt. in Poe, *Doings of Gotham,* ed. Jacob E. Spannuth and Thomas Ollive Mabbott (Pottsville, Penn.: Jacob E. Spannuth, 1929), p. 68.

42. See Cynthia S. Jordan, "Poe's Re-Vision: The Recovery of the Second Story," *American Literature,* 59 (1987), 12.

43. See Edgar Allan Poe, "The Murders in the Rue Morgue" (1841), in his *Poetry and Tales,* ed. Patrick F. Quinn (New York: Literary Classics of the United States, 1984), p. 397. Jordan comments: "The epigraph to the first tale, 'The Murders in the Rue Morgue,' introduces the idea of crossing gender boundaries to recover the now 'dim-remembered story' of female experience" ("Poe's Re-Vision," p. 13).

44. See Lacan, "Seminar on 'The Purloined Letter,'" p. 51.

45. See Lacan, "Seminar on 'The Purloined Letter,'" pp. 48, 54 n. 14. Lacan refers here to Charles Baudelaire's mistranslation of the passage regarding the exact location of the letter mentioned by Bonaparte. The location—beneath the mantel piece as in Poe's tale, not above it as in the mis-

translation—was crucial for Bonaparte, who interpreted the letter as a penis hanging from a little brass knob of the mother's body. See Marie Bonaparte, *The Life and Works of Edgar Allan Poe: A Psycho-Analytic Interpretation,* trans. John Rodker (New York: Humanities Press, 1971), pp. 483-84 (originally published 1958).

46. See Johnson, "Frame of Reference," p. 219. Following Derrida, Johnson carefully examines the footnotes—now to Derrida's book *Positions* (1972). There she finds Derrida mentioning Lacan's "acts of aggression" in his address.

47. See Irwin, "Mysteries We Reread," p. 1,177.

48. See Stockholder, "Is Anybody at Home in the Text? Psychoanalysis and the Question of Poe," *American Imago,* 57 (2000), 312.

49. See François Peraldi, "A Note on Time in 'The Purloined Letter,'" in *The Purloined Poe,* p. 337.

50. See Stephen Bretzius, "The Figure-Power Dialectic: Poe's 'Purloined Letter,'" *MLN,* 110 (1995), 682-83.

51. Bourdieu, *The Rules of Art: Genesis and Structure of the Literary Field,* trans. Susan Emanuel (Oxford: Polity Press, 1992), p. 104.

52. During the discussion that followed my lecture at the University of Virginia, Stephen Railton pointed out another possible twist. Returning the letter to the Queen, Dupin sustains (presumably) adulterous relations, very much at odds with the didactical character of the annual. Indeed, Dupin is at the same time the partisan of the lady—not the least because he respects her privacy (on this topic, see Richard Hull, "'The Purloined Letter': Poe's Detective Story vs. Panoptic Foucauldian Theory," *Style,* 24 [1990], 201-14)—and an accomplice in the "crime" against the royalty and, as one might suspect, against the moral.

Lynne L. Doty (essay date spring 2010)

SOURCE: Doty, Lynne L. "Poe's Portrait of Mathematicians in 'The Purloined Letter': Some Historical Context." *Interdisciplinary Literary Studies* 11, no. 2 (spring 2010): 117-26.

[*In the following essay, Doty explains how the critique of classical mathematics in "The Purloined Letter" anticipates the greater openness of twentieth-century mathematical thinking.*]

The famous diatribe against mathematicians in **"The Purloined Letter"** is most usefully understood in the context of the history of mathematics. Students in the

Humanities are apt to seize upon Poe's scathing portrait of the mathematician with glee, interpreting it as high-class reinforcement of their own fears or antipathies. Instructors whose own mathematical background is limited may have little idea how to help such students to situate Poe's comments—or rather, those of Poe's protagonist—in a larger cultural framework. Familiarity with some key developments in the field of mathematics both before and after the story's publication in 1845 is essential, however, if readers are to appreciate the full implications of its presentation of "mathematical truths" (**"Letter"** [**"The Purloined Letter"**] 218).

Embedded in the quest to discover the whereabouts of the letter stolen by Minister D—, Auguste Dupin's detailed analysis of the flawed premises underlying "mathematical reason" appears digressive: certainly it serves no practical purpose in solving the case (**"Letter"** 217). In undertaking his analysis, the detective is defending himself, along with the thieving Minister D—, against the contemptuous opinion of poets expressed by the Prefect of the Parisian police: a poet, the Prefect contends, is "'only one remove from a fool'" (211). The Prefect is wrong in this judgment, clearly; in the course of the story he is outwitted by two poets. Minister D—, "a poet," successfully conceals stolen property from him while Dupin, who slyly admits that he, too, has been "'guilty of certain doggerel,'" swiftly discovers the solution to the problem baffling his counterpart in officialdom (211). In Dupin's comparison of poetic and mathematical applications of "reason," moreover, he suggests a resemblance between the mathematician and the inept policeman who fails at his job. Though complacent about his abilities, the Prefect is intellectually rigid. In Dupin's view, mathematicians suffer from very similar limitations. He charges them with mental inflexibilities very like those hampering the Prefect in his search for the stolen letter. Thus Dupin folds his critique of mathematicians neatly into discussion of the Prefect's intellectual handicaps and mistaken procedures.

It may seem unremarkable that a writer of fiction, working intensively in the realm of creative imagination, would allow his protagonist to praise the poetic faculty at the expense of the mathematical. Indeed, many well known writers have targeted mathematics for scornful treatment. Assuming that the mathematician lacks emotional sensitivity, one of Jane Austen's heroines assigns to this stereotypical figure "the sturdiest brain" but "the coldest heart" (*Emma* 265). A narrator created by Edith Wharton refers with a sarcastic shudder to "the hovering shadow of an algebraic problem" ("The Pelican" 59). As such examples suggest, mathematics tends to be portrayed in literary works as an enterprise inspiring fear and dread, chosen only by those who are incapable of intuition and devoid of artistic sensibilities. This stereotype is perpetuated, perhaps forgivably, by writers who lack knowledge or experience of real mathematics. But what are readers to make of an author like Poe, who distinguished himself by winning honors in mathematics at West Point (1830-31), where he studied the subject in depth? (Silverman 61). The unflattering portrait of mathematicians in **"The Purloined Letter"** can be explained neither by ignorance of the subject area on Poe's part, nor by inability to succeed in it.

The mathematics that was studied in institutions like West Point in the early eighteen hundreds was very different from the mathematics that is taught in modern colleges and universities. Even in the more advanced intellectual circles of Europe, mathematics was studied primarily in military schools in order to produce military engineers or under the patronage of rulers in order to improve civic functions (Katz 637). It was, in short, a subject in which practical results were emphasized. The development of new methods of understanding physical phenomena was not nearly as important as building a bridge, calculating the correct pitch of water drains, or producing a correct survey of a sovereign's lands. In America, a young nation committed of necessity to pragmatic expenditure of energies, applied mathematics took clear precedence over theory. In Poe's day, for example, the curriculum at West Point "consisted of descriptive geometry and fundamental algebra" (Silverman 61). Most mathematical historians list only three mathematicians of note in America before the late nineteenth century, and these three were known for their work in land surveying, astronomy, and clock-making (Katz 40-42). Although Benjamin Franklin and Thomas Jefferson both championed study in the field, they focused solely on the mathematics that would address immediate needs, that is, trigonometry, basic algebra, and some logarithms; anything beyond this was considered a "delicious luxury" by Jefferson (qtd. in Katz 642). Thus the conception of mathematics put forward by Poe's Dupin as "'merely logic applied to observation upon form and quantity'" represents, quite accurately, the very narrow view of the field that predominated in America and much of Europe through the first half of the nineteenth century (**"Letter"** 217).

The nature of mathematics through the mid-nineteenth century had been shaped by overwhelmingly successful applications of Euclidean geometry and, later, of Newtonian calculus to mechanical, astronomical, and engineering problems. The impressive usefulness of applied mathematics led, almost immediately, to the emergence of pure mathematics. Mathematical concepts and tools that proved so effective in practical arenas claimed attention in their own right as philosophical ideas. The model of abstraction and logical deduction that still characterizes mathematical thinking was established by Euclid's *Elements* in 300 B.C. It is by far the most widely known work of Greek mathematics, associated with the Pythagorean School and its successor, the Academy of Plato (Kline 40-42). From the beginning, those working with Euclidean geometry expressed awe, even reverence, for the apparently irrefutable truths it contained. The Pythagoreans not only associated mathematical investigation with the search for truth, they regarded the validity of Euclid's axioms as "unquestionable" and "absolute" (Kline 43, Grant 22). Displaying a similarly reverential attitude, Plato maintained that God himself must have made use of the five regular types of polyhedra, whose existence Euclid had proven, in shaping the cosmos (Kline 47). By emphasizing the relationship of mathematics to the eternal and the non-corporeal, and at the same time denigrating merely material applications of its concepts, Plato helped to elevate pure mathematics to the highest philosophical plane (Kline 50-51, Grant 22). As the Greek world continued to make great strides in mathematical knowledge, the tendency to associate its new insights with aesthetic, moral, and metaphysical values only increased: the circle and the sphere were associated with perfection and eternity, for instance (Kline 55).

Thus the assumption that mathematical knowledge is inherently and eternally valid is an important legacy of the Greeks (Kline 58). Well through the Enlightenment, philosophy and mathematics remained intertwined, and many renowned thinkers continued to perpetuate a reverence for mathematical truth. Descartes is perhaps the best known of the mathematician-philosophers and Locke, too, preferred mathematical knowledge to other kinds on the grounds that its insights are "certainties" (Kline 245). Kant went so far as to make mathematical ideas a "central pillar" of his philosophy, relying on the veracity of Euclidean geometry as "guaranteed" (Kline 251). The creation of the calculus in the seventeenth century, notably by Leibniz and Newton, had increased the importance of applied mathematics dramatically, with concomitant effect on the centrality of mathematics in the realm of philosophy. To a public awed by the new discoveries, "it seemed to be only a question of time before all phenomena, natural, social, and moral, would be reduced to mathematical laws" (Kline 238). Mathematical reasoning was lauded as "the embodiment of the purest, deepest, and most efficacious form of all thought," and the principles governing virtually every field of human endeavor were expected to be "recast" in short order (Kline 238, 239). The conviction prevailed, almost universally, that the world runs according to mathematically describable law (Kline 25, Grant 24). Leibniz, for one, was convinced that "truth and error" in every domain would prove to be "simply a matter of correct or erroneous calculation" (Boyer 407).

Inevitably, the prevalence of such increasingly vast claims for mathematical truth began to draw criticism—even ridicule (Grant 24). Philosophers like Voltaire, who famously satirized Leibniz in *Candide*, found expectations for mathematical solutions to all the world's problems not only exaggerated but repellent. Berkeley and Hume initially undermined faith in mathematical descriptions of reality by arguing that there is no provable relationship between the human mind and the physical world (Kline 245-49). Early in the nineteenth century, poets and aestheticians such as Wordsworth and Coleridge launched a full-scale attack on mathematically-based understandings of the universe, understandings that had come to seem mechanistic. Mathematics became "a prime target . . . of the Romantic protest against all that the Age of Reason stood for" (Grant 25). Reverence for mathematics as the highest form of human thought, which had prevailed for so many centuries, was countered by accusations of spiritual deadness, emotional obtuseness, and aesthetic barrenness. The spirit of the times is indicated by a toast proposed by a group of poets (including Lamb, Keats, Wordsworth, among others) in 1817: "Newton's health, and confusion to mathematics" (Kline 282). Concerted efforts to dethrone mathematical methods and laws from their historically elevated position, carried forward with especial gusto by literary figures, provide the context in which the denunciation of "mathematical reason" by Poe's detective-protagonist takes place.

Dupin's narrator-sidekick makes clear from the outset that the detective's portrait of mathematicians deviates from "'the well-digested ideas of centuries'" (**"Letter"** 217). "'The mathematical reason,' he protests, 'has long been regarded as *the* reason *par excellence*'" (217). Dupin responds that such admiration, however longstanding, is misplaced, a "'popular error'" (217). He argues that mathematical thinking is and must be limited because it applies only to "'form and quantity'" (217). He follows up this swift blow to the intellectual value of applied mathematics with a more detailed and excoriating critique of pure mathematics (217). "'The great error,' he announces, 'is in supposing that even the truths of what is called *pure* algebra are abstract or general truths'" (217). Here Dupin dismisses at a stroke an idea that had been gaining momentum since the time of the Greeks, namely, the idea that mathematical laws can explain every feature of the universe—physical or metaphysical, psychological or psychosocial. He pauses a moment to rail at the unaccountable "universality" with which this assumption has been accepted (217). He then offers examples, with accompanying explanation, of instances in which mathematical theories prove inaccurate when transferred to non-mathematical situations such as morality or chemistry. His chief point—that rules governing operations in geometry or algebra "are *not* axioms of general truth"—stands as a no-holds-barred rebuttal of the optimistically sweeping predictions made by philosophers and mathematicians of the preceding century (218).

Dupin follows up his central pronouncement with an unflattering comparison: literary artists may occasionally forget that "pagan fables" are not "existing realities," he acknowledges, and therefore draw erroneous inferences from them. "The algebraists," however, "who are pagans themselves," are consistently and unrepentantly guilty of believing their own fables ("**Letter**" 218). That is, they "clandestinely hold it as a point of . . . faith" that their formulae are "absolutely and unconditionally" valid (218). In consequence, the mathematician falls victim to an excessively exalted conception of his discipline. Failing to perceive that there are limits to the applicability of his knowledge, he misuses that knowledge and falls into errors of reasoning. A more realistic assessment of the scope and utility of mathematical insights, Dupin contends, would rescue the thinker in this field from many stubborn and foolish mistakes. Thus Poe's detective seeks to strip mathematics of the elevated reputation and overweening expectations associated with that discipline since the time of Pythagoras.

Dupin's sarcastic references to the mathematician's "faith" in the universal applicability of his axioms lead readers directly back to the errors committed by police searching in vain for the purloined letter. Like the mathematician deluded into thinking his axioms possess universal validity, the Prefect and his staff allow their efforts to be guided by "one principle . . . of search" ("**Letter**" 216). Guilty of "an exaggeration *of the application* of the one principle," they resemble mathematicians who err because they expect their formulae to yield truth across the board. The mental rigidity of the mathematician mirrors that of the Prefect, whose inability to vary his methods is the source of his failure. The Prefect's incompetence is rendered more culpable, as well as more ludicrous, by the smug self-satisfaction he so frequently expresses. The mockery with which he is portrayed casts a reflection, necessarily, upon the mathematician who is said to share his flaws. Those who assume the universality of local truths will remain trapped within the confines of an intellectual "Procrustean bed" of their own manufacture (215).

Dupin is allying himself, obviously, with writers and thinkers engaged in a wide-scale protest against a formidable philosophical tradition, a tradition that had placed mathematics at the center of the quest for truth. To what extent Dupin's views of mathematics—and its limits—are shared by his creator, however, is a matter not easily determined (see Moldenhauer 290-291). By assigning his critique of mathematicians to a fictional character, first of all, Poe in effect distances himself from it. Though it seems plausible to identify his astute and successful detective closely with Poe himself (Bandy 509, Garner 134, Kelly 81-83), there are reasons to suspect that this identification is not complete. Dupin's supreme self-confidence, buttressed by the worshipful attitude of his narrator-companion, may lead readers to derive occasional amusement from his unwitting egotism. In embryonic form, as twentieth-century readers have observed, he exhibits some of the traits Agatha Christie used to such advantage in creating the undoubtedly brilliant but entertainingly smug Hercule Poirot.[1] Christie's detective becomes an object of simultaneous mockery and admiration because of the immodest pleasure he displays in the workings of his own *little gray cells*. Certainly the irritation with which Dupin lambastes mathematicians, like the passion with which he announces that "these gentlemen" will "knock you down" if their "faith" in their formulae is challenged, goes far to indicate a lack of objectivity in his analysis ("**Letter**" 218). Readers are bound to infer some degree of comic exaggeration in his diatribe.

Further evidence that Poe intends to leave some narrative space between himself and Dupin's negative portrait of mathematicians is provided by the discovery that clever Minister D— is "poet *and* mathematician" ("**Letter**" 217). If mathematicians are to become the object of unadulterated criticism, why attribute mathematical knowledge to the character who is second only to the protagonist in reasoning power? The narrator explains that Minister D— is well known for his attainments in the field: "he has written learnedly on the Differential Calculus" (217). This bit of biographical trivia is in no way important to the story's plot; it simply provides the excuse for Dupin's fulminations. Given Dupin's high opinion of his opponent, D—'s impressive accomplishments in mathematics suggest that not all mathematicians are handicapped by the mental limitations of which they stand accused. Dupin, of course, argues that the minister is an able reasoner only because he is also a poet, but D—'s mathematical abilities remain susceptible to more favorable interpretation. Readers have been quick to notice, too, how much criminal and detective mirror each other in ability and in *modus operandi* (Blythe 311, 312). There are hints that Minister D— may be Dupin's brother (Ketterer 252); certainly he appears to function as an *alter ego* of some sort. In consequence, many readers tend to assume that Dupin, like his adversary, is well educated in mathematics as well as in humane letters (Buranelli 85, Dameron 160, Garner 140). "It takes one poet-mathematician to untie the plot which another has contrived" (Hoffman 121).

There is evidence from outside the story, too, that Poe's view of mathematicians does not coincide in every respect with Dupin's damning portrait. In discussing the composition of "The Raven," for example, Poe explains with obvious pride that the work of designing this famous poem "proceeded, step by step, to its completion with the precision and rigid consequence of a mathematical problem" ("Philosophy of Composition" 14-15). On several occasions his fictional characters similarly confront difficulties or solve problems by employing their knowledge of mathematics or related fields. The plot in **"Maezel's Chess-Player,"** for example, centers on the successful investigation of a fraud: the narrator-protagonist states at the outset that he will employ "a mathematic demonstration" to prove his case (424). Knowledge of the laws of physics, particularly the relationship of shape (and surface resistance) to "relative velocities" of objects caught in a whirlpool, enables the protagonist of **"A Descent into the Maelstrom"** to save his life (137). The most elaborate support for the utility of mathematical knowledge is provided by Dupin himself in the context of another story in which he pays a starring role. In **"The Murders in the Rue Morgue,"** the narrator acknowledges that "the faculty of re-solution is possibly much invigorated by mathematical study" (141). He goes on to explain that the "highest branch" of mathematics is known as "analysis," eventually insisting that "the *truly* imaginative are never otherwise than analytic" (143). This seems close to an admission that human intelligence is most effective when poetic and mathematical faculties work in tandem (see Kesting 56-59). Minister D— from **"The Purloined Letter"** commands such a combination of abilities, and the story's narrator provides support here for the assumption that Dupin is likewise doubly gifted. Seeing Dupin in problem-solving mode, his admiring companion reports, is like watching the "Bi-Part Soul" in action: "a double Dupin—the creative and the resolvent" (144).

It seems likely, on balance, that Poe intends readers to take Dupin's pronouncements about mathematicians in **"The Purloined Letter"** with a grain of salt. At the same time, nonetheless, Poe would scarcely have devoted space to opinions he found wholly objectionable, or not, at least, without subjecting them to obviously satiric treatment. Thus he appears to join his contemporaries in challenging the historically preeminent status of mathematics, but he does so with perceptible ambivalence. That ambivalence may stem, in part, from a conviction of the value of his own mathematical training. It also may reflect his generally forward-looking intellectual tendencies. Just as he seems to have anticipated Freud with the modernity of his psychological insights, Poe manifests uncanny foresight about the direction mathematics was about to take in the latter part of the nineteenth century. He has been credited, in fact, with prescience in diverse arenas of scientific and mathematical thought, having articulated embryonic understandings of modern ideas such as relativity (of time, space, and matter), atomism, and even evolution (Brown). And in Dupin's analysis of games such as checkers, Poe is said to have anticipated a modern branch of applied mathematics known as game theory (Benton 117-118).

At the very moment in time when Poe was composing Dupin's critique of mathematics in **"The Purloined Letter,"** as it happens, mathematicians themselves (led by Gauss, Bolyai, and Lobatchevsky) had just begun to question Euclidean geometry.[2] The realization, mid-nineteenth century, that *there are geometries different from Euclid's,* all equally valid, changed conceptions of mathematics as a discipline profoundly, undermining its "privileged ontological status" (Kline 417, Grant 22). Mathematics had been unique in guaranteeing the "supreme certainty" of its contributions to human knowledge (Grant 23). By offering "several contradictory geometries," each logically coherent, mathematicians now seemed to admit that truth is partial, multiple, and provisional (Kline 429). The effect of the new geometries on the history of thought was nothing short of cataclysmic, influencing future developments in areas as disparate as philosophy, religion, sociology, psychology, and political science (Kline 428). Although it is difficult to imagine that Poe had direct information about this budding revolution in the field of mathematics, the portrait he creates of the truth-seeker in the character of Dupin is entirely consistent with newly emerging ideas about the nature of knowledge. Like the new geometers, forced to recognize that no one system of thought precludes the existence or the legitimacy of other systems, Dupin seeks to understand a variety of "ideas of ingenuity" (**"Letter"** 216).

Success in solving baffling problems, Dupin argues, requires great mental agility, the capacity to grasp alien points of view. His scorn for those who claim "absolute" and "unconditional" validity for their methods and insights, like his contempt for those who confine their quest for knowledge to "one principle or set of principles" marks him as a man ahead of his times (**"Letter"** 218, 216). To solve problems that baffle others, he integrates methodologies from very different areas of study: simultaneously "creative and resolvent," he augments analytical and logical reasoning with information derived from processes of association and intuition (**"Murders"** [**"The Murders in the Rue Morgue"**] 144). Derogating old-style mathematicians, together with traditional assumptions that mathematics is a repository of unassailable truth, Dupin himself provides a credibly modern model of mathematical thinking. This detective-hero exercises the "imagination, insight, and creative ability" that are hallmarks of mathematical method in the twentieth century and beyond; an openness to external points of view enables such a thinker to recognize "possible lines of attack where others would not" (Klein 459). In creating his story, Poe does indeed challenge the historically "privileged . . . status" of mathematics, both applied and pure (Grant 22). In doing so, moreover, he looks forward to a radical shift in the field, a shift that was beginning to take place even as he wrote, and which was to alter the human search for knowledge in every conceivable branch.

Notes

1. J. Lasley Dameron and W. T. Bandy point to parallels between Dupin and Poirot, identifying Poe's detective-thinker as the literary ancestor of Christie's: see "Poe's Auguste Dupin" (159) and "Who Was Monsieur Dupin?" (509).

2. Bolyai published his ground-breaking work on "new geometries" in 1833, and Lobatchevsky's documents appeared a few years later (Kline 414). Only with the publication of posthumous writings by Gauss on the topic of non-Euclidean geometry approximately thirty years later, however, did the creation of non-Euclidean geometry begin to earn appropriate recognition (Kline 413-15). Benton suggests that "by the 1830's . . . new geometries . . . had convinced the forward-looking that truth in mathematics in terms of absolute exactitude . . . had been cast into doubt" (119), but historians in the field locate this shift in thought somewhat later. In the 1840's, when Poe was composing the three detective stories featuring Auguste Dupin, non-Euclidean geometry existed but was not yet widely discussed, even among mathematicians.

Works Cited

Austen, Jane. *Emma.* 1816. New York: NAL/Signet, 1980.

Bandy, W. T. "Who Was Monsieur Dupin?" *PMLA* 79.4 (1964): 509-10.

Benton, Richard P. "The Dupin MSS. as 'Contes A Clef,' Mathematics, an Imaginative Creation." *Perspectives on Poe.* Ed. D. Ramakrishna. New Delhi: APC Publications, 1996. 109-25.

Blythe, Hal, and Charlie Sweet. "The Reader as Poe's Ultimate Dupe in 'The Purloined Letter.'" *Studies in Short Fiction* 26.3 (1989): 311-15.

Boyer, Carl B. *A History of Mathematics.* 2nd ed. Rev. Uta C. Merzbach. New York: John Wiley, 1991.

Brown, Kevin. "The Thought of a Thought—Edgar Allan Poe." 6. Oct. 2007. *Math Pages.* 18 Jan. 2008. www.mathpages.com/homekmath522/kmath-522.

Buranelli, Sylvia E. *Edgar Allan Poe.* Boston, MA: Twayne, 1977.

Dameron, J. Lasley. "Poe's Auguste Dupin." *No Fairer Land: Southern Studies in Literature Before 1900.* Ed. J. Lasley Dameron and James W. Mathews. Troy, NY: Whitstone, 1986. 159-71.

Garner, Stanton. "Emerson, Thoreau, and Poe's 'Double Dupin.'" *Poe and His Times: The Artist and His Milieu.* Ed. Benjamin Franklin Fisher IV. Baltimore: Edgar Allan Poe Society, 1990. 130-45.

Grant, Hardy. "A Sketch of the Cultural Career of Mathematics." *Essays in Humanistic Mathematics.* Ed. Alvin M. White. Washington, DC: Mathematical Association of America, 1993. 21-28.

Hoffman, Daniel. *Poe Poe Poe Poe Poe Poe Poe.* New York: Paragon, 1990.

Katz, Victor J. *A History of Mathematics: An Introduction.* 2nd ed. Reading, MA: Addison Wesley Longman, 1998.

Kelly, Warren Hill. "Detecting the Critic: The Presence of Poe's Critical Voice in His Stories of Dupin." *Edgar Allan Poe Review* 4.2 (2003): 77-86.

Kesting, Marianne. "Auguste Dupin, der Wahrheitsfinder und sein Leser: Inwiefern Edgar Allan Poe nicht der Initator der Detektivgeschichte war." *Poetia: Zeitschrift für Sprach- und Literaturwissenschaft* 10 (1978): 53-65.

Ketterer, David. *The Rationale of Deception in Poe.* Baton Rouge: Louisiana State UP, 1979.

Kline, Morris. *Mathematics in Western Culture.* New York: Oxford UP, 1953.

Moldenhauer, Joseph J. "Murder as a Fine Art: Basic Connections between Poe's Aesthetics, Psychology, and Moral Vision." *PMLA* 83.2 (1968): 284-97.

Poe, Edgar Allan. "A Descent into the Maelstrom." 1841. *The Complete Tales and Poems of Edgar Allan Poe.* New York: Vintage, 1975. 127-40.

———. "The Philosophy of Composition." 1846. *Essays and Reviews.* New York: Library of America, 1985. 13-25.

———. "The Murders in the Rue Morgue." 1841. *The Complete Tales and Poems of Edgar Allan Poe.* 141-68.

———. "The Purloined Letter." 1845. *The Complete Tales and Poems of Edgar Allan Poe.* 208-22.

Silverman, Kenneth. *Edgar A. Poe: Mournful and Never-ending Remembrance.* New York: HarperCollins, 1991.

Wharton, Edith. "The Pelican." *The Muse's Tragedy and Other Stories.* New York: NAL/Signet, 1990. 59-78.

FURTHER READING

Criticism

Bretzius, Stephen. "The Figure-Power Dialectic: Poe's 'Purloined Letter.'" *MLN* 110, no. 4 (September 1995): 679-91.

Discusses the role of material reality in Poe's short story.

Harris, Paul A. "Poe-Tic Mathematics: Detecting Topology in 'The Purloined Letter.'" *Poe Studies* 36 (2003): 18-31.

Comments on the subtext of mathematical inquiry in Poe's short story, concluding that it anticipates contemporary interest in topology, the geometrical study of spatial properties.

———. "The Smooth Operator: Serres Prolongs Poe." In *Mapping Michel Serres,* edited by Niran Abbas, pp. 113-35. Ann Arbor: University of Michigan Press, 2005.

Compares the treatment of space in Poe's tale with that in the work of Guy de Maupassant and theorist Michel Serres.

Johnson, Barbara. "The Frame of Reference: Poe, Lacan, Derrida." *Yale French Studies,* nos. 55-6 (1977): 457-505.

Investigates the notion of psychoanalytic interpretation in Poe's short story and its importance to French thought.

Liu, Lydia H. "The Cybernetic Unconscious: Rethinking Lacan, Poe, and French Theory." *Critical Inquiry* 35, no. 2 (winter 2010): 288-320.

Explores cybernetics and game theory in Poe's story and in French literature generally.

Major, René. "The Parable of the Purloined Letter: The Direction of the Cure and Its Telling." *Stanford Literature Review* 8, nos. 1-2 (spring-fall 1991): 67-102.

Views Poe's story as a medical allegory.

Mawhinney, Heather. "'Vol du Bourbon': 'The Purloined Letter' in Perec's 'La Disparition.'" *Modern Language Review* 97, no. 1 (January 2002): 47-58.

Compares Poe's tale to works by Agatha Christie and Georges Perec.

Smith, Muriel. "Chesterton, Poe, and Others." *Chesterton Review* 21, no. 4 (November 1995): 487-503.

Comparison of Poe's detective stories with those of G. K. Chesterton.

Sucur, Slobodan. "Lacanian Poe." In *Poe, Odoyevsky, and Purloined Letters: Questions of Theory and Period Style Analysis,* pp. 21-49. Frankfurt am Main: Peter Lang, 2001.

Analyzes Lacan's response to Poe's story.

Additional coverage of Poe's life and career is contained in the following sources published by Gale: *American Writers; American Writers: The Classics,* **Vol. 1;** *American Writers Retrospective Supplement,* **Vol. 2;** *Authors and Artists for Young Adults,* **Vol. 14;** *Beacham's Encyclopedia of Popular Fiction: Biography & Resources,* **Vol. 3;** *Beacham's Guide to Literature for Young Adults,* **Vols. 5, 11;** *Concise Dictionary of American Literary Biography,* **1640-1865;** *Dictionary of Literary Biography,* **Vols. 3, 59, 73, 74, 248, 254;** *DISCovering Authors; DISCovering Authors: British Edition; DISCovering Authors: Canadian Edition; DISCovering Authors Modules: Most-studied Authors,* **and** *Poets; DISCovering Authors 3.0; Exploring Poetry; Exploring Short Stories; Gale Contextual Encyclopedia of American Literature; Gothic Literature: A Gale Critical Companion,* **Ed. 3;** *Literary Movements for Students,* **Vol. 1;** *Literature and Its Times,* **Vol. 2;** *Literature and Its Times Supplement,* **Ed. 1:1;** *Literature Resource Center; Mystery and Suspense Writers; Nineteenth-Century Literature Criticism,* **Vols. 1, 16, 55, 78, 94, 97, 117, 211;** *Poetry Criticism,* **Vols. 1, 54;** *Poetry for Students,* **Vols. 1, 3, 9;** *Poets: Americans and British; Reference Guide to American Literature,* **Ed. 4;** *Reference Guide to Short Fiction,* **Ed. 2;** *St. James Guide to Crime & Mystery Writers,* **Ed. 4;** *St. James Guide to Horror, Ghost, & Gothic Writers; St. James Guide to Science Fiction Writers,* **Ed. 4;** *Science Fiction, Fantasy, and Horror Writers; Science Fiction Writers,* **Eds. 1, 2;** *Short Stories for Students,* **Vols. 2, 4, 7, 8, 16, 26, 29;** *Short Story Criticism,* **Vols. 1, 22, 34, 35, 54, 88, 111;** *Something about the Author,* **Vol. 23;** *Supernatural Fiction Writers; Twayne's United States Authors; World Literature Criticism,* **Ed. 4;** *World Poets;* **and** *Writers for Young Adults.*

J. R. R. Tolkien
1892-1973

(Full name John Ronald Reuel Tolkien) English short story writer, novelist, essayist, and poet.

The following entry provides an overview of Tolkien's short fiction.

INTRODUCTION

Tolkien is widely regarded as the originator of modern fantasy fiction. Drawing on his extensive knowledge of mythology, traditional fairy tales, and epic literature, he created a fictional world with its own history, legends, and heroes. Although he is best known for the novels that comprise the *Lord of the Rings* cycle, he also composed a small body of short fiction that sheds light on his role as a preeminent teller of fantastic tales.

BIOGRAPHICAL INFORMATION

Tolkien was born in Bloemfontein, South Africa, where his father, Arthur Reuel Tolkien, worked as a bank manager. In 1894, however, the child's health began to fail. His mother, Mabel Suffield Tolkien, took him and his younger brother, Hilary, back to England early the next year, where they settled near Birmingham. Arthur Tolkien, who had stayed behind in Africa, planned to join his family in a year or so, but he contracted rheumatic fever and died in 1896. Mabel Tolkien introduced her eldest son to two of his strongest loves—the Catholic Church and the study of language—before her death of complications caused by diabetes in 1904. She left her orphaned sons under the guardianship of her close friend and confessor, Father Francis Xavier Morgan. Father Morgan provided Tolkien with a father figure and helped finance his studies at King Edward's School in Birmingham, and later at Oxford University. Tolkien's passion for languages expanded while he attended King Edward's School. Latin and Greek were important components of the curriculum, and Tolkien excelled at both. With the encouragement and assistance of several of his teachers, he also taught himself some Welsh, Old and Middle English, Old Norse, and Gothic. It was also while attending King Edward's that Tolkien met his future wife, Edith Bratt. Tolkien began to create the fictional world known as Middle Earth before he enlisted to fight in World War I. He served in the army throughout the war, although illness kept him out of combat most of the time. After the armistice was signed in 1918, he took a position on the *Oxford English Dictionary* project for a couple of years and then joined the staff of Leeds University. In 1925 he was elected Rawlinson and Bosworth Professor of Anglo-Saxon at Oxford University, a post he held for twenty years. While teaching at Oxford, he began to compose his first major work, *The Hobbit* (1937). The book was a great success, and Tolkien soon began work on a sequel, which eventually turned into the famous trilogy *The Lord of the Rings*. Consisting of *The Fellowship of the Ring* (1954), *The Two Towers* (1954), and *The Return of the King* (1955), the trilogy would come to be regarded as one of the most accomplished works of fantasy ever written. In the meantime, Tolkien had become Merton Professor of English Language and Literature in 1945. He retired from teaching in 1959 but continued to work on his fiction. His wife died in 1971, and he followed her soon afterward. In the last two years of his life, Tolkien was appointed a Commander of the Order of the British Empire and he received an honorary doctorate of letters from Oxford University for his contributions to philology.

MAJOR WORKS OF SHORT FICTION

Tolkien's short fiction employs familiar motifs of the fairy story to explore the nature of the genre itself. The heroic archetype is gently parodied in "Farmer Giles of Ham." The eponymous farmer is an ordinary man who drives a giant from his property. His neighbors regard him as a hero, and the King gives him a sword with which to slay a fearsome dragon. Instead, Farmer Giles spares the dragon in return for the beast's treasure. In "Leaf by Niggle," an artist (Niggle) commits himself to a grand painting that depicts the leaves of a tree in precise detail. When Niggle is sent away on a vaguely described trip, his neighbor, Parish, uses the canvas to patch a hole in his roof but preserves one of the painted leaves. Meanwhile, Niggle performs acts of menial labor until he is sent away for some "gentle treatment." The countryside to which he is sent turns out to be the location of a tree that correlates exactly to his painting. Niggle is soon joined by Parish on another ambiguous journey, and the countryside comes to be known as Niggle's Parish. The figure of Niggle can be read as a fictional surrogate for Tolkien, who labored over his fantasy fiction with a seriousness that suggested his belief in the reality of his created world. The novella *Smith of Wootton Major* (1967) deals with Tolkien's attitude toward the true power of Faery stories, as opposed to the superficial enchantment of fairy tales. The narrative concerns a cake that is served every twenty-four years at the Feast of Good Children. The baking of the cake is the supreme task of the Master Cook, Nokes. Viewing fairy stories as a superficial treat for children, Nokes places a fairy doll on the cake and orders his assistant, Alf, to fill it with various trinkets. One of these items, a fay-star, is an authentic emblem from the land of Faery, but Nokes dismisses it as mere decoration. Young Smith eats a piece of cake containing the star and subsequently begins to show unusual grace in his singing and, when he grows up, in his ironwork. He establishes a friendship with Alf and occasionally travels to Faery, where he embarks upon a number of adventures. As another Feast of Good Children draws near, Smith decides to pass on the gift of the star by putting it back into the long-awaited holiday cake. He hands over the star to Alf, now the Master Cook, only to discover that his friend is actually the King of Faery.

CRITICAL RECEPTION

Although Tolkien's short works were originally viewed as a minor aspect of his oeuvre, they have garnered increased critical attention in recent years. For example, critics have characterized "Leaf by Niggle" as a creative retelling of the fifteenth-century Christian morality play *Everyman,* as well as an allegory for Tolkien's desire to remain creative in a constraining society. Reviewers have also compared "Leaf by Niggle" to Isaac Bashevis Singer's "Menaseh's Dream," contending that both stories subtly suggest the possibility of life after death. In addition, they have deemed "Farmer Giles of Ham" a satirical look at standard fantasy narratives. According to scholar Friedhelm Schneidewind, "Tolkien describes a thoroughly 'classical' dragon and a thoroughly classical dragon slayer story which nevertheless has a parodistic spin." Furthermore, commentators have suggested that *Smith of Wootton Major* functions as both a traditionally structured allegory and a refutation of the aesthetic of fellow fantasy writer George MacDonald. They have also interpreted the novella as Tolkien's veiled treatise on the relationship between Faery, or the authentic power of fairy tales, and the reader. As critic Josh B. Long summarized, "Nokes and Smith's approaches to the star reflect two divergent attitudes; while it supplies Nokes with nothing more than a snide

snicker, Smith is changed and empowered by it. Here, Tolkien seems to be commenting on the fact that regardless of how compelling Faery might be, it is ultimately up to the individual to accept it or reject it. In other words, Faery fails the moment at which the hearer no longer takes it seriously. The literary belief is lost and the sense of wonder is forsaken."

PRINCIPAL WORKS

Short Fiction

Farmer Giles of Ham 1949
*Tree and Leaf 1964
The Tolkien Reader 1966
Smith of Wootton Major (novella) 1967
†Poems and Stories (poetry and short stories) 1980
Tales from the Perilous Realm 1997

Other Major Works

The Hobbit; or, There and back Again (novel) 1937
The Fellowship of the Ring: Being the First Part of The Lord of the Rings (novel) 1954
The Two Towers: Being the Second Part of The Lord of the Rings (novel) 1954
The Return of the King: Being the Third Part of The Lord of the Rings (novel) 1955
The Adventures of Tom Bombadil, and Other Verses from The Red Book (poetry) 1962
The Father Christmas Letters (novels) 1976
The Silmarillion (novel) 1977
Letters of J. R. R. Tolkien: A Selection (letters) 1981
The Monsters and the Critics, and Other Essays (essays) 1983
Roverandom (novel) 1998
The Tale of the Children of Húrin (novel) 2007

*Includes "On Fairy-Stories" and "Leaf by Niggle."

†Includes "The Adventures of Tom Bombadil"; "The Homecoming of Beorhtnoth, Beorhthelm's Son"; "On Fairy-Stories"; "Leaf by Niggle"; "Farmer Giles of Ham"; and "Smith of Wootton Major."

CRITICISM

Margaret Sammons (essay date autumn 1985)

SOURCE: Sammons, Margaret. "Tolkien on Fantasy in *Smith of Wootton Major.*" *Mythlore* 12, no. 1 (autumn 1985): 3-7, 37.

[*In the following essay, Sammons traces themes of innocence, creativity, and communal interaction in Tolkien's novella.*]

One of the great frustrations in studying fantasy is simply defining what it is. J. R. R. Tolkien has a quite specific and even unusual definition of fantasy, where it comes from, who receives the gift of the creative imagination, and what effects it has on the receiver. These ideas are presented in three of his lesser read yet significant works, "On Fairy Stories," **"Leaf by Niggle,"** and *Smith of Wootton Major.* The first two comprise *Tree and Leaf,* which Tolkien says is primarily about the idea of "sub-creation." The non-fiction essay "On Fairy Stories," delivered as a lecture at St. Andrews College, discusses what fairy tales are, their origin, and function, and C. S. Lewis considered it the best thing of its kind ever written. **"Leaf by Niggle"** is a brief, allegorical tale about the problems of the fantasy writer as he faces death and is really an autobiographical piece about Tolkien himself and his frustrations in bringing together his massive mythology. Finally, *Smith of Wootton Major,* published in 1967, appears on first reading to be a fairly light-hearted yet odd and perplexing little story, and it has been given very little critical attention. But through this simple and pleasant to read tale, Tolkien presents many of the same views about fantasy found in *Tree and Leaf,* as well as further insights into his own despair about writing. Clyde Kilby interprets it as "primarily about the creative process and the special problems of a fantasy writer like Tolkien."[1]

The story takes place in a little village called Wootton Major, noted for its craftsmen and especially its cooking. Although the town seems very British, the time and location are fairly vague. One of the most important events of the town around which the story centers is the Feast of Good Children, held only once every 24 years for just 24 children. For this great occasion, the Master Cook, a key figure in town, must provide the Great Cake. The Master Cook at the beginning of the story is Rider (who we learn later is Smith's grandfather). Disappearing unexpectedly for a while, he returns merrier and able to sing gay songs; he also brings back a seemingly too young apprentice named Alf. When Rider suddenly leaves again for good, the townspeople panic and appoint a plump, sly, incompetent man named Nokes as Master Cook, instead of Alf. Since Nokes knows little about cooking, he has to sneak lessons from Alf to learn how it is done.

Naturally, when the time comes for the next Feast, Nokes despairs, for he knows nothing about how to make a Great Cake. A fairylike cake, he assumes, must be iced in sugar with a pretty little fairy on top. While searching for some spices to add to the cake, he discovers a tiny, tarnished star. He decides to mix this, along with other trinkets and coins, into the Cake as

surprises for the children. But Alf sternly warns him that this is a "Fay" star—from Faerie—and thus should be treated seriously.

On the day of the feast, each child gets a slice of cake; some get trinkets, others none. A quiet boy named Smith unknowingly swallows the magic Fay star which waits quietly within him for several months. Then one spring day he is suddenly awakened to the beauty of the world, begins to sing strange and wonderful songs, and becomes a skilled craftsman. The star is affixed to his forehead. Most important, though, he begins to take several journeys to the realm of Faerie and is privileged to witness many wondrous and marvellous things. Eventually told by the Queen of Faery that the time has come for him to choose a successor to wear the star, Smith reluctantly returns it to the King of Faery, Alf (Elf) himself, who has now become the Master Cook. Smith chooses Tim, Nokes' great-grandson, as the next recipient of the star.

Such a plot seems to lend itself to neither quick allegorical interpretation nor profound insights into the nature of fantasy. Yet we can begin to understand it better by placing it in the context of Tolkien's life. Just as **"Leaf by Niggle"** was written during a period of frustration over trying to finish *Lord of the Rings,* *Smith of Wootton Major* was composed at the end of January 1965 at a time of despair over the inability to work on the *Silmarillion* and fear of approaching old age. As Tolkien explained in an unpublished letter to Professor Clyde Kilby, the story evolved quite by accident.[2] At the request of an editor, Tolkien was attempting to write a Preface to a new edition of George MacDonald's *The Golden Key,* a fairy tale for children. Tolkien said he was not "as warm an admirer of George MacDonald as C. S. Lewis was" but that he did "think well" of *The Golden Key.*[3] In the course of trying to explain the term "fantasy" to his readers, Tolkien began to illustrate what he was talking about: "This could be put into a short story like this. . . ." When the result was about ten pages of a first version of *Smith of Wootton Major,* Tolkien realized that the story "had developed a life of its own, and should be completed as a thing by itself." Apparently, Tolkien also wrote up his own list of characters and said he knew a lot more about them than he actually told about them in his final draft. The original title was **"The Great Cake,"** perhaps indicating a shift in focus from the work of fantasy to the creator himself. Tolkien said although "the title is intended to suggest an early Woodhouse [*sic*] or story in the B[oys'] O[wn] P[aper], it is of course nothing of the kind" (Ibid., p. 370). Since P. G. Wodehouse wrote humorous stories with characters with unusual names living in an escapist world where nothing serious happens, Tolkien seems to imply his serious intentions.

The very simply told and, in part, humorous story, is nevertheless grave and often mysterious in tone and meaning. Humphrey Carpenter says critics received it well but did not note the personal references or uncharacteristic use of allegory.[4] One is, as with **"Leaf by Niggle"** and *Lord of the Rings,* tempted to try to associate characters and key symbols with what they "represent." But as Tolkien emphasizes in the Introduction to the *Rings* trilogy, he detested allegory; similarly, concerning **Smith of Wootton Major,** he wrote: "There is *no* allegory in the Faery, which is conceived as having a real extramental existence. There is some trace of allegory in the Human part, which seems to me obvious though no reader or critic has yet averted to it. As usual there is no 'religion' in the story; but plainly enough the Master Cook and the Great Hall, etc. are a (somewhat satirical) allegory of the village-church, and village parson: its functions steadily decaying and losing all touch with the 'arts,' into mere eating and drinking—the last trace of anything 'other' being left in the children" (Ibid.).

Certainly the Great Cake and Fay Star are symbolic. As the story seems to suggest, the Cake is the created work of fantasy, and the Master Cook is the creative writer who must always try to provide "plentiful and rich fare" for the festival. In "On Fairy Stories" Tolkien also likens fairy story writers to Cooks. Rider, the first Master Cook, apparently travels for a while in Faery and chooses Alf, King of Faery, as his successor. A good Cake must be created by one who knows what should go *inside* it, even though a poor baker like Nokes can unwittingly produce an effective Cake. The Cake first must have various spices (devices, techniques). In "On Fairy Stories," Tolkien says that the "colouring, the atmosphere, the unclassifiable details of a story" and the "general purport" which gives life to the plot are key elements.[5] Most important, though, the "fairy" element is produced not by simply including fairies and elves in the story but Fay, the region of Faerie itself. This is represented by the seemingly small, tarnished star which not only eventually gives off its own light but is reflected in the eyes of those who have it. The Cake must also be novel, not a repetition of other cakes. And it is no bigger than needed; there is "no coming again" for the children. While some children find several trinkets, others get none, "for that is the way luck goes, whether there is a doll with a wand on the cake or not." Perhaps Tolkien is saying that people get various rewards from fantasy, but only from a true fairy tale can the chosen receive the special, magic gift of the Fay star.

Professor Kilby says Tolkien "staunchly denied" the story has any autobiographical meaning: "It was, he said, originally intended as 'just a story about cake'" (Kilby, p. 37). Yet in some points of the story, Nokes seems to be a personal reference to Tolkien himself. In his letters, Tolkien wrote that it was "not intended for children! An old man's book, already weighted with the presage of 'bereavement'" (Letters, p. 389-90). He also wrote that it was "written with deep emotion, partly drawn from the experience of the bereavement of retirement and of advancing age" because he knew he was getting old and would soon have to pass on the star to someone else.[6] In fact, **Smith** [*Smith of Wootton Major*] was the last story Tolkien ever wrote. He had experienced twelve frustrating years turning out a sequel to the popularly received children's story, *The Hobbit.* The publisher wanted another story about hobbits, yet Tolkien wanted it to be sufficiently new and allow him to include elements of his own grand mythology. At the time he wrote **Smith,** Tolkien was experiencing similar depression over trying to find time to work on *The Silmarillion.* Like Tolkien, Nokes worries about making the Great Cake for the next Feast of Good Children. For he has only been appointed Master Cook by the townspeople and knows little about cakes: "although with seven year's practice he could turn out passable cakes and pastries for ordinary occasions, he knew that his Great Cake would be eagerly awaited, and would have to satisfy severe critics. Not only the children. A smaller cake of the same materials and baking had to be provided for those who came to help at the feast. Also it was expected that the Great Cake should have something novel and surprising about it and not be a mere repetition of the one before."

Nokes, whose name appropriately is an obscure word for "ninny" or "fool," seems to "represent" the person with typical misconceptions about what a "fairy" and "fairy tale" are; he is also the bad writer. Unsure of what a "fairylike" cake should be like, he decides to coat it with sugar-icing—"That will make it pretty and fairylike." For one, he thought, never grows out of liking sweets, though everyone grows out of fairies. This notion violently contrasts Tolkien's conviction that fairy stories should not even be associated with children. In fact "if a fairy-story as a kind is worth reading at all it is worthy to be written for and read by adults" (OFS, 45).

As Professor Kilby in his book, *Tolkien and the* Silmarillion, suggests, Old Nokes may also represent George MacDonald, whom Tolkien frequently criticized and felt had written nothing worthwhile. If this is the case, Tolkien is perhaps saying that MacDonald believes Faerie is merely something sweet and funny and has little notion of what to put inside a great Tale. Nokes thought the star "funny" and therefore amusing to children, but his young apprentice, who was actually a far better cook, insisted it was *faerie* and a serious business. Nokes' idea of a "fairy" is a glittering and sparkling "little doll on a pinnacle . . . dressed all in white, with a little wand in her hand ending in a tinsel star, and *Fairy Queen* written in pink icing round her feet." Furthermore, he warns the children that she is a "tricky," whimsical little creature. These are the typical views of fairies, writes Tolkien in "On Fairy Stories." Whereas even the lexicographer defines fairies as the "fluttering species," "supernatural being of diminutive," "flower-and-butterfly minuteness," it is man who, in contrast, is diminutive. When Smith later meets the Queen of Faerie herself, he ashamedly compares her to Nokes' little fairy on the cake: "she wore no crown and had no throne. She stood there in her majesty and her glory, and all about her was a great host shimmering and glittering like the stars above; but she was taller than the points of their great spears, and upon her head there burned a white flame."

When Smith returns home he seems odd to his friends but bears a light a fairy Queen gives him. Kilby believes this may mean one of two things. One is that Tolkien is saying that though "MacDonald knows nothing about the real inside of a cake, nevertheless he may accomplish something by the saccharine figures he presents." The other meaning may be that the imitation fairy Nokes had wanted to stick on the cake inspired Smith to find the true Queen, just as Tolkien was influenced by MacDonald (Kilby, p. 39).

Naturally, Nokes is also unsure what should go *inside* a great cake—of what devices, techniques, and elements constitute a true fairy story. Finding most of the old recipes from past cooks undecipherable, Nokes hunts up some of their spices, only to find them old and musty. But in one compartment of a dusty black box filled with such things, he discovers a small, tarnished star. So he decides to throw it into the cake, along with trinkets and other "pretty little things," to make the children laugh.

But the star, warns Alf, is "Fay—from Faerie"—and it is thus the true ingredient he needs to make the Cake a true fairy story. Nokes misunderstands the true purpose and nature of Faerie even though his Cake contains the right elements: "Fantasy thus, too often, remains undeveloped; it is and has been merely for decoration: it remains merely 'fanciful'" (OFS, 48). Despite the fact that Nokes doesn't know what he is doing, he nevertheless manages to create a Cake containing the true Fay element. In his Preface to *The Golden Key,* Tolkien wrote: "Fairy is very powerful. Even the bad author cannot escape it. He probably makes up his tale out of bits of older tales, or things he half remembers, and they may be too strong for him to spoil or disenchant. Someone may meet them for the first time in his silly tale, and catch a glimpse of Fairy, and go on to better things" (Carpenter, p. 242).

Unfortunately, Nokes remains unaware of what Faerie is all his life. But like Atkins in **"Leaf by Niggle"** who cannot stop thinking about the small fragment of Niggle's painting, Nokes cannot get the strange star out of his mind: "It was the best cake I ever made . . . a good cake . . . enjoyed and praised. . . . It's the little trinket, the star. I cannot make up my mind what became of it." But he remains impervious to Alf's explanation: "Nokes," says Alf, "your knowledge is so great that I have only twice ventured to tell you anything. I told you that the star came from Faery; and I have told you that it went to the smith. You laughed at me. Now at parting I will tell you one thing more. Don't laugh again! You are a vain old fraud, fat, idle, and sly. I did most of your work. Without thanks you learned all that you could from me—except respect for Faery, and a little courtesy." (Is Tolkien again, perhaps, sadly referring to himself here?) But Nokes only sneers at Alf, half expecting some tiny fairy to wave his little wand over him in rebuke. Even after Alf reveals himself as King of Faerie and sends him such disturbing dreams that he becomes gaunt, Nokes believes it all a nonsensical, silly little dream: "Why, he hadn't no wand. And if you stop eating you grow thinner. That's natural. Stands to reason. There ain't no magic in it."

What happened to the star? It disappears, eaten unknowingly by Smith. And it "remained with him, tucked away in some place where it could not be felt, for that was what it was intended to do." Kilby says the unconscious swallowing of the star "suggests the manner in which creativity rises in seemingly accidental fashion without precedent" (Kilby, p. 38). For the gift of fantasy is not revealed until the time is right, several months later. Then one spring day, "the world seemed quiet and expectant. A little breeze, cool and fragrant, stirred the waking trees. Then the dawn came, and far away he heard the dawn-song of the birds beginning, growing as it came towards him, until it rushed over him . . . like a wave." His gift is now awakened, and with the star affixed to his forehead, Smith immediately begins to show the effects of Faerie. Like his grandfather, the first Master Cook who had returned greatly changed from Faerie, merrier and able to sing gay songs, Smith too begins to sing strange words in a high, clear voice. In fact, his voice becomes so increasingly beautiful that people, appreciative of his gift, come not only to listen to him sing but just to hear him speak. Later, Tim, the next recipient of the star, shows the same effects. With a new light in his eyes, the plump, clumsy little boy begins to laugh, become merry, and sing softly to himself. "Then he got up and began to dance all alone with an odd grace that he had never shown before."

Smith's workmanship changes, too. The useful and practical objects he makes—tools, pots and pans, horseshoes and bolts—are not only durable but graceful and pleasing to behold. Kilby believes the autobiography is "unmistakable," comparing the useful things Smith makes with Tolkien's scholarship. Smith also creates delicate and beautiful things, both light and wonderful yet strong as iron. Thus Faerie takes hold of even the most simple and practical objects and gives them a new beauty. "Fantasy," writes Tolkien, "is made out of the Primary World, but a good craftsman loves his material, and has a knowledge and feeling for clay, stone and wood which only the art of making can give. By the forging of Gram cold iron was revealed; by the making of Pegasus horses were enobled; in the Trees of the Sun and Moon root and stock, flower and fruit are manifested in glory" (OFS, 59).

Most important, Smith becomes acquainted with Faerie itself, just as Tolkien became called to the world of Middle Earth and gave up the seemingly "practical" world of scholarship for his grand vision. Tolkien's fiction was looked upon skeptically by many of his colleagues: "The beauty and terror seen by Smith on his longer journeys clearly represent . . . Tolkien's particular birth into the world of myth and his own 'calling' to the myth of Middle-earth, a calling which is intensified by visits to elfish country and the tree-bearing 'leaves and flowers and fruits uncounted'" (Ibid.). This vision is one aspect of the story, Tolkien emphasizes, which is not allegorical but has a "real extramental existence." According to Tolkien, the Faerie realm is central to a fairy story: "Faerie contains many things besides elves and fays, and besides dwarfs, witches, trolls, giants, or dragons: it holds the seas, the sun, the moon, the sky; and the earth, and all things that are in it: tree and bird, water and stone, wine and bread, and ourselves, mortal men, when we are enchanted" (OFS, 9). Smith discovers "lesser folk and the gentler creatures in the woods and meads of fair valleys," and Great Mountains in which, as in **"Leaf by Niggle,"** is the heart of Faerie.

But contrary to our expectations, Faerie is also a "Perilous Realm," containing dangers, wonders and mysteries, beauty and terror, joy and grief, "beauty that is an enchantment, and an ever-present peril; both joy and sorrow as sharp as swords" (OFS, 3). As in *Lord of the Rings,* great moral battles of which we know nothing are waged in Faerie, battles that would render weapons from our world ineffective and powerless. For the "marvels of Faery cannot be approached without danger, and . . . many of the Evils cannot be challenged without weapons of power too great for any mortal to wield." Smith sees great white ships returning from battles on the Dark Marches and the glorious

elven mariners "tall and terrible; their swords shone and their spears glinted and a piercing light was in their eyes. Suddenly they lifted up their voices in a song of triumph, and his heart was shaken with fear, and he fell upon his face." Such wonders as these are so indescribably rich and strange that they "tie the tongue of a traveller who would report them" (OFS, 3); thus Smith can neither remember much of his journeys nor report them to his friends.

Smith does return to the world with a clearer view of things and a satisfying of his desires. In "On Fairy Stories," Tolkien calls the first important effect of Faerie "Recovery." Fantasy allows a reader to see the dull, drab, and trite things in his own world without the veil of familiarity because he has seen them in Faerie in a new context. Smith's voyages through Faerie which fill him with "wonder" cleanse his perspective of ordinary things. In Faerie, for example, he is able to see the immeasurable depths of a cliff; the air there is so lucid that he can "see the red tongues of birds as they sing on the trees on the far side of the valley"; he even sees a new kind of green. When he returns from Faerie for the last time, ready to pass on the star to someone else, the Great Hall appears to him in a totally new light. Then as he removes the star from his forehead, he cries, "I cannot see clearly" anymore; yet his sight does return. Though he is no longer possessor of the creative imagination, his perspective remains affected, and he is able to gaze at the beauty of the luminous Moon and Even-star.

Another result of fantasy, says Tolkien, is fulfillment of our desire to commune with other living things. Smith is able to speak "without words" to the Queen, "learning many things in her thought." And when he dances with her, he is able to experience "swiftness" and "power" and "joy." Smith, says the Queen, was granted entrance to Faerie because he had a desire or, as C. S. Lewis calls it, *Sehnsucht,* longing for something "other." After his first taste of the new realm, Smith is unable to forsake Faerie and has a desire to "go deep into the land."

So Faerie is a very real place with real effects on one who enters it. The fantasy writer, Tolkien suggests, creates a Secondary World which your mind can enter, hopefully a self-consistent world with its own laws. He calls this artistic activity "sub-creation," the most nearly pure form of art. In his poem "Mythopoeis," Tolkien writes:

> . . . Although now long estranged,
> Man is not wholly lost nor wholly changed.
> Disgraced he may be, yet is not de-throned,
> And keeps the rags of lordship once he owned:
> Man, Sub-creator, the refracted Light

through whom is splintered from a single White
to many hues, and endlessly combined
in living shapes that move from mind to mind.
Though all the crannies of the world we filled
with Elves and Goblins, though we dared to build
Gods and their houses out of dark light,
and sowed the seed of dragons—twas our right
(used or misused). That right has not decayed:
we make still by the law in which we're made.

(OFS, 54)

Man creates because he is made in the image of the Creator and because there is a part of him which is unsatisfied by the rational, natural world. He uses materials from our world, drawing on "reality," but expresses truths that cannot be expressed or explained in any other way. According to Tolkien, the Secondary World of fantasy, perceived and created by the imagination, is the world of "fact" in space and time. In his biography of Tolkien, Humphrey Carpenter notes that Tolkien treated the ideas and events in *Lord of the Rings* and *The Silmarillion* not as his own personal story but as actual history.

Tolkien holds an almost Platonic view of reality, symbolized in **Tree and Leaf** by the Tree, but to him reality is dynamic and we can add to it. In **"Leaf by Niggle,"** Niggle's life work is a Great Painting of a tree; but because he concentrates on individual leaves, he never completes the picture. Again, Tolkien is referring to the creation of his approaching old age and his tendency as a perfectionist to rework individual stories and details within his mythology, Tolkien feared the work would never be finished. After Niggle dies, he goes to an afterworld where, to his amazement, he sees his Tree, now alive and completed: "Before him stood the Tree, his Tree, finished. . . . All the leaves he had ever laboured at were there, as he had imagined them rather than as he had made them; there were others that had only budded in his mind, and many that might have budded, if only he had had time" (**LBN** ["Leaf by Niggle"], 103-4). In "On Fairy Stories," Tolkien explains that this Tree is Truth itself, and each sub-creator can reveal parts of this Tree in his own work: "It is easy for the student to feel that with all his Labour he is collecting only a few leaves, many of them now torn or decayed, from the countless foliage of the Tree of Tales, with which the Forest of Days is carpeted. It seems vain to add to the litter. Who can design a new leaf? The patterns from bud to unfolding, and the colours from spring to autumn were all discovered by men long ago. But that is not true. . . . Each leaf, of oak and ash and thorn, is a unique embodiment of the pattern, and for some this very year may be *the* embodiment, the first ever seen and recognized, though oaks have put forth leaves for countless generations of men" (OFS, 56).

During his journeys through Faerie, Smith spends hours studying just one tree or one flower, pieces of the Pattern itself. Then one day he discovers the King's Tree, arising from a shadow: "its light was like the sun at noon; and it bore at once leaves and flowers and fruits uncounted, and not one was the same as any other that grew on the Tree." Although Smith searches for the Tree ever after with much suffering, he never sees it again. Through fantasy, then, we can gain a "sudden glimpse of the underlying reality or truth" of things (OFS, 71). Just as Niggle's painting of the Tree is only a "glimpse," the Queen of Faerie consoles Smith that even a pretty little fairy on a cake is better than no idea of Faerie: "Better a little doll, maybe, than no memory of Faery at all. For some the only glimpse. For some the awaking."

Smith is fortunate in being able, for a short while, to experience both worlds. For only a brief moment the two worlds are actually in union: "he seemed to be both in the World and in Faery, and also outside them and surveying them, so that he was at once in bereavement, and in ownership, and in peace." In what Professor Kilby feels is a very personal reference, when Smith returns home, even his son (Christopher Tolkien?) recognizes that his father has experienced Truth itself. As he stands by the fire, Smith's shadow looms up in the darkness. "You look like a giant, Dad," Ned remarks. Later, Ned perceives the significance of this symbol: "'Father,' he said, 'Do you remember the day when you came back with the Flower? And I said that you looked like a giant by your shadow. Your shadow was the truth.'" Smith can impart to his son an important kind of knowledge, even after he is forced to relinquish the star: "there is much you can teach me yet," Ned realized. "And I do not mean only the working of iron." It is thus appropriate that "Wooton" most likely means "town where one knows."[7]

Tolkien holds an almost Wordsworthian view of man— that, as children, we were still near to the eternal state of innocence from which we came but, as adults, we have lost that state, forgotten who we are. Even Nokes, in reading recipes of past cooks, finds things in them that "he had forgotten and now had no time to get." When Smith's creativity is first awakened in him, the music of the birds sweeping over him like a wave reminds him of Faery, and he begins to sing "strange words that he seemed to know by heart." During his journeys in Faery, he witnesses things of "both beauty and terror that he could not clearly remember or report to his friends, though he knew they remained in his mind as wonders and mysteries that he often recalled." He brings back delicate bells from Faery, and even his son remarks, "Dad, there is a scent in the bells: a scent that reminds me of, reminds me, well, of something I've forgotten." I think Tolkien is saying that we too can know Faery if we only remember: "There was a village once, not very long ago for those with long memories."

Only some receive the gift of creative imagination, though: "For some the only glimpse. For some the awakening." And often, the person who receives the star is not the obvious choice. Smith was quiet and slow: Tim, Smith's successor, is not only fat and clumsy, but Nokes' great-grandson! The 24 children who attend the very rarely occurring festival come almost by chance of birthday, and "some who deserved to be asked were overlooked, and some who did not were invited by mistake." Rider, Smith, Tim, Alf, and Harper are all chosen. Tolkien also makes it clear that the star is a Gift, lent only to those who truly need it. Remaining tucked away, unnoticed and unfelt in Smith, it is activated only when the time is ripe; and when the time comes, Smith must pass it on. Similarly, Smith brings back a flower from Faerie, kept in a locked casket. Although his family could open the box to gaze at this reminder of Faerie, it closed on its own, for "the time of its shutting was not theirs to choose."

It is certainly significant, then, as Paul Kocher notes, that time is carefully recorded all through the story. Smith is 57 years old when he is told that it is time for him to give up the star (two 24 year apart feasts have passed; he was nine years old when he received it). Tolkien, too, was 57 when he completed *Lord of the Rings* in 1949 and sadly notes that a Master Cook seldom lasted long enough to make a second Great Cake. Alf, too, goes away at the end of the story, but most of the townspeople are glad: "they had had him for a very long time and were not sorry to have a change." So it is not difficult to see in this haunting little story not only Tolkien's explanation of the meaning and significance of fantasy and the preciousness of the gift of the creative artist, but perhaps his own sad farewell to his art.

Notes

1. Clyde S. Kilby, *Tolkien and the* Silmarillion (Wheaton, Illinois: Harold Shaw, 1976), p. 37. I would like to acknowledge the help of Professor Kilby, who provided me with his notes on *Smith*. Professor Kilby spent several months helping Tolkien prepare *The Silmarillion* and read the then unpublished draft of *Smith*, recording his comments of the story at that time. Paul Kocher's comments on *Smith* in *Master of Middle Earth* (New York: Ballantine, 1972), pp. 184-93, are also very enlightening, especially his discussion of the Tree symbol.

2. This unpublished letter is available at the Marion Wade Collection at Wheaton College, Wheaton, Illinois.

3. Humphrey Carpenter, ed., *The Letters of J. R. R. Tolkien* (Boston: Houghton Mifflin, 1981), p. 351.

4. Humphrey Carpenter, *Tolkien* (Boston: Houghton Mifflin, 1977), p. 243.

5. "On Fairy Stories," *The Tolkien Reader* (New York: Ballantine, 1966), pp. 18-19. All future references to "On Fairy Stories" (OFS) and "Leaf by Niggle" (LBN) will be noted in the text.

6. Letter to Prof. Kilby, October 1967.

7. "Woot" is probably derived from the archaic English form of the verb "wit," or "to know," as in the Witan Council.

Millicent Lenz (essay date spring 1994)

SOURCE: Lenz, Millicent. "Archetypal Images of Otherworlds in Singer's 'Menaseh's Dream' and Tolkien's 'Leaf by Niggle.'" *Children's Literature Association Quarterly* 19, no. 1 (spring 1994): 3-7.

[*In the following essay, Lenz analyzes the metaphorical treatment of the possibility of life after death in "Leaf by Niggle" and in Isaac Bashevis Singer's "Menaseh's Dream," concluding that Tolkien's story emphasizes the timelessness of art.*]

Realistic fiction for today's children treats death candidly, with no "junk about God needing angels" (Smith 54). Such candor is laudable, yet it does not answer the need for imaginative speculation on immortality, a topic on which realistic children's literature is, by and large, silent; there exists a certain neglect by omission, as though the very thought of a possible life after death were somehow improper. Yet speculation on what lies beyond death, if anything, is one of the oldest themes in literature: it is central to *Gilgamesh* and the Book of Job, to cite just two examples.

Writers of fantasy, happily, are granted more freedom to explore the realms of "otherwhere," including a possible heaven or hell. Without stories providing images of life in other dimensions, a child's imagination is unduly impoverished; how dreary a world devoid of faerie, of elves, angels, leprechauns, Santa Claus, and imaginary beings. Moreover, stories presenting images of possible futures beyond death can help readers to structure imaginatively the fears, hopes, and dreams surrounding mortality and the longing for immortality. Literature can reassure us of the inevitability of life's eternal renewal in a way experience cannot; as

Northrop Frye remarks in his discussion of the theme of ascent in romance: "The feeling that death is inevitable comes to us from ordinary experience; the feeling that new life is inevitable comes to us from myth and fable. The latter is therefore both more true and more important" (132).

Myth, fable, and fantasy, exploring as they do the archetypal depths of human imagination, offer readers speculative stories of the afterlife. Narratives portraying the afterlife or the journey to the "otherworld" have a long and honored tradition in literature; many epic adventures incorporate a visit to the underworld: Homer's *Odyssey* or Dante's *Divine Comedy,* for instance. Bunyan's *Pilgrim's Progress,* a significant influence upon children's literature, traces the pilgrim's journey through this world and into the next. Nineteenth-century literature offers a number of examples of visits to the otherworld in narratives read to or by children, such as Charles Dickens's *A Christmas Carol,* in which Scrooge is redeemed by visions of the afterlife. Death and the future life are at the heart of another late nineteenth-century fantasy, George Mac-Donald's *At the Back of the North Wind,* an important contribution to literature addressing young readers' concerns about death, survival, and the perpetuation of individual identity. As North Wind tells Diamond, the country which lies at her back is not what it superficially seems to be: it is misconstrued as "Bad Fortune," "Evil Chance," or "Ruin" (she refuses to utter the word "Death" to him), for as Robert Lee Wolff observes, North Wind is associated with "the good, the welcome death" which MacDonald also portrays in *Phantastes* and *The Golden Key.* This death is actually "a reunion with the cosmos and mother earth," a death "not to be feared but sought" (155-56).

Madeleine L'Engle's *A Ring of Endless Light* is notable for its expression of an intuitive belief in an afterlife in the passage where Adam speaks to Vicki of "archaic understanding," the "deepest, mythic sense" which knows the immortality of the soul. Adam declares such understanding to be inherent in all children, but then "school comes along, and the pragmatic Cartesian world" takes intellectual control, denying this deep knowledge (231). In fantasy literature, there are numerous other examples of novels reflecting a belief in otherworlds (the novels of C. S. Lewis, still widely read by youngsters, spring to mind), and there exists a considerable number of other books with supernatural events, such as Richard Peck's Blossom Culp series and his *Unfinished Portrait of Jessica* (Delacorte 1991). The popularity of such books indicates that readers enjoy speculation about immortality and otherworlds.[1]

Contemporary literary criticism, oddly, rarely probes the theme of immortality in books for youngsters, despite evidence from the studies of children's concepts of death and their expressed beliefs about life after death that they need to discuss these topics with parents or professionals. In his essay, "Children's Concepts of God, Death, and Life After Death," Rabbi Stephen A. Moss, coordinator of the Jewish Chaplaincy Services at the Memorial Sloan-Kettering Cancer Center in New York City, reports the results of his research into children's thinking. He found more than forty percent of the children in his religious school expressing belief in life after death, *prior* to their having experienced the death of a significant person, and without any dogmatic teaching of concepts about death and the afterlife in the religious classroom (15-16). Admittedly the children in his survey group represent strongly religious home environments, but the concerns of youngsters of all backgrounds with ultimate, speculative, unanswerable questions, including attempts to image heaven and hell, are corroborated in Robert Coles's recent book, *The Spiritual Life of Children* (1990).

Just as Ulysses's visit to the underworld serves to strengthen him for a return to this world, a child's imaginative "visit" to the afterlife can help to form, at a tender age, a framework for what philosophers call eschatological thought, ideas about ultimate or last things. As Isaac Bashevis Singer observes, children often ask such basic questions as:

> . . . Who created the world? Who made the earth, the sky, people, animals? Children cannot imagine the beginning or end of time and space. As a child I asked all the questions I later found discussed in the works of Plato, Aristotle, Spinoza, Leibnitz, Hume, Kant and Schopenhauer. Children think about and ponder such matters as justice, the purpose of life, the why of suffering. . . . They are bewildered and frightened by death.
>
> (Singer, "Are Children" (337)

It is grownups, Singer maintains, who are "hooked on realism"; jaded by experience, they may cease to ask ultimate questions, "but the child is a philosopher and a seeker of God" (337-38). Adult motives for neglecting to speak of ultimate questions with children need scrutiny, for as Gareth B. Matthews, whose *Philosophy and the Young Child* bears out Singer's assertions, has remarked, "sometimes our effort to protect children from thinking about death simply masks an effort to protect ourselves" (87).

In view of the importance of fantasies of the afterlife or a possible otherworld to children, as well as a renewed contemporary adult interest in these concerns,[2] it seems timely to consider how two masters of the fantasy genre, Singer and J. R. R. Tolkien, treat these topics in stories accessible to young readers. These stories need not be seen as advocating any particular religious belief; rather, they can be understood as manifesting what anthropologist Cottie A. Burland has called the simple, universal "belief in survival [after death]," an "archetypal" concept, built into the human personality. For present purposes, it is not the particular details that matter, but rather the fact that "a belief in an afterlife seems to be endemic among the human race" (52-53). The stories present two different views, one hierarchically structured and traditional; the other non-hierarchical and more metaphorical. They are, moreover, for different age levels. The protagonists of the two stories differ markedly, one being middle-aged, the other a child; one visiting the afterworld briefly in a dream, the other undergoing a permanent transition. The young Menaseh in Singer's story dreams vividly of the eternal realm and awakens to his earthly life spiritually fortified. The middle-aged protagonist of Tolkien's **"Leaf by Niggle,"** on the other hand, dies prematurely and proceeds to an afterworld where he gains a new perspective on life on earth.

Tolkien's "little man called Niggle" is portrayed as a painter whose persistent preoccupation is what he calls "my real picture"—a large painting of a tree with "all of its leaves in the same style, and all of them different" (88). When his lame neighbor, Parish, needs Niggle's canvas and his help to patch his roof in order that Parish's ill wife might not suffer, Niggle does the good deed, catching a fatal cold as a result. Niggle's character is, however, as his name implies, less than imposing. The Random House dictionary meaning of the verb "to niggle" is "to criticize in a peevish or petty way; carp . . ."; "to spend too much time and effort on inconsequential detail . . ."; "to work ineffectively, trifle . . ." (2nd ed.). Niggle's very name connotes inconsequentiality or absurdity, further suggesting "niggard" and "wiggle." The narrator speaks of him as "a very ordinary and rather silly old man" (90), constantly torn between what he believes to be his true calling—finishing his painting—and somewhat grudgingly performing acts of kindness to others. Niggle's guilt over his failure to use his time productively heightens his awareness of the inevitability of death. His age is not specified, but his harried state and keen consciousness of his mortality suggest that he is of late middle age.

An allegorical reading of Tolkien's text seems irresistible, despite Tolkien's well known declaration in the preface to the Ballantine edition of *Lord of the Rings* that "I cordially dislike allegory in all of its manifestations," a position explored by Richard L. Purtill in "Heaven and Other Perilous Realms." But as Purtill perceives, Tolkien is thinking of *strict* allegory—"philosophy or fiction dressed up as story," where there is a one-to-one correspondence between each person or

event and some abstract idea. Many critics, Tolkien says, confuse *applicability* with allegory: applicability "resides in the freedom of the reader," allegory in "the proposed domination of the author" (Purtill 3). Purtill finds three levels of application in **"Leaf by Niggle"**: the *moral,* this-worldly one, whereby "Niggle is Everyman and the application is to a person's work and to the person's relation with other persons and with society"; the *aesthetic* application, wherein Niggle is Every Artist and his picture represents devotion to the arts; and the *religious* application, wherein again Niggle is Everyman but the journey represents death and the picture his life's achievement (or failure to achieve) (3-4).

Death is presented at the opening of the narrative through the metaphor of "a long journey," a distasteful but unavoidable trip Niggle faces, made doubly hard by the torment of his visions of the exact way to portray the idealized Tree against a distant mountain. Relentless Death, personified as the Driver of a carriage, turns a deaf ear to Niggle's plea for a delay. When Niggle protests that his painting is "not even finished," the Driver replies coldly, "Not finished? . . . Well, it's finished with, so far as you're concerned. . . ." Niggle manages only to grab a little bag containing his "paint-box and a small book of his own sketches" before being escorted to the railway station by the tall, black-garbed Driver; there, very tired and sleepy, he boards a train which runs "almost at once into a dark tunnel" (96). The moral lesson can hardly be missed. In Purtill's words, our "careers" or "projects" are in society's view subordinate to the demands of our relationships; social and religious values insist that Niggle give priority to helping Parish rather than indulging his artistic pursuits. The story also makes clear, however, that "the conflict between career and personal relations is often, though not always, illusory: it is our weakness and failings which lead to situations where we must neglect one obligation to fulfill another, and if we give due place to personal relations it will be better for our careers as well as ourselves" (3). Yet because few can attain to so lofty a standard of performance, Niggle, like all the rest of us, needs justice "tempered with mercy" (3).

In Singer's story, in contrast, the protagonist is an orphan boy of "about twelve, with a longish face, black eyes, sunken cheeks" (82), who lives with his uncle, a poor glazier, and is destined to be apprenticed to a bookbinder. Like many children, he is incessantly curious, pestering adults with questions such as "Why are people born?" "Why do they die?" One day he quarrels with his Aunt Dvosha and, skipping lunch, makes his way into the forest, carrying his only possession, Singer's book *Alone in the Wild Forest* (1911). Lonely and weak from hunger, Menaseh thinks,

"Maybe I'm going to die. Then I will soon be with Daddy and Mama" (85). Falling asleep in a blueberry patch, he dreams of chancing upon a beautiful castle and sees his own portrait inside, with his likeness luxuriously clothed. He has been transported to a realm where wishes become reality.

Menaseh's psychological transport to the other world by means of a dream stands in contrast to Niggle's bodily travel. Whereas Niggle's voyage to the other world is permanent and irreversible, reflecting the finality of his physical death, Menaseh's flight is temporary: he is a visitor in the eternal realm, not a permanent resident. This difference is appropriate to their different ages, for Menaseh, as a young child, belongs clearly to this world, while Niggle's demise is imminent and only hastened somewhat by his untimely illness.

Differences also appear in the otherworlds into which the two characters pass. Menaseh's otherworld involves no hierarchy of spiritual beings nor underlying theological structure. There is no intimation of a heaven/hell dichotomy in Singer's future world and no religious allegory.[3] Menaseh is greeted by an atmosphere of festivity. The castle, metaphorically paradise, is filled with familiar people, among them members of Menaseh's own family, now richly gowned and bejeweled. Separated by the window glass from the joyous gathering, Menaseh cries to be allowed in. His Grandpa Tobias lovingly tells him, "One day you will live with us here, but the time has not yet come" (87). Tobias further reveals how Menaseh's mother and father and other loved ones "know everything . . . think about you and . . . love you." They see life as "a long journey," the same metaphor used by Tolkien at the outset of Niggle's story. At Menaseh's insistence, after consulting with other family members, his grandpa allows him into the castle, "but only for a little while." The entrance to the future world is conditional. "We will show you around the castle and let you see some of our treasures, but then you must leave" (87).

Once Menaseh wins entry into this otherworld, hunger and weariness depart, to be replaced by a floating sensation. Strangely, though his parents hug and kiss him, they do not utter a single word. In this dreamworld, he travels back and forth in time. The rooms of the magical castle alternately display images from his past and future. In one room he beholds "all the toys he ever owned," and in another, "the characters in the stories his parents told him at bedtime." Among these storybook heroes and heroines are the characters of *Alone in the Wild Forest*, suggesting Singer's linking of the earthly and the eternal realms through the power of art to transcend limitations of space and time.

In the seventh room, Menaseh glimpses his future: "Men and women, animals, and many things completely strange to him" (92) appear in transparent and shrouded images. Most prominent is a golden-haired girl of Menaseh's own age. When he asks the logical question, "Where am I?" his grandfather replies, "in a castle that has many names. We like to call it the place where nothing is lost" (92). This wonderful realm turns out to be for Menaseh a "forbidden place" (95), which vanishes when his parents bid him a silent farewell.

Back in the realm of time, Menaseh awakens at night to find the girl of his dream, Channelah of the golden braids, bending over him. No longer fearful of his uncle's anger and his aunt's scolding, Menaseh now is assured of a "mysterious world" where "everything lives and nothing in time is ever lost" (96). Singer places the final emphasis where it belongs, on Menaseh's life in the here and now. The story of Menaseh's dream enables young readers to share in a marvelous realm where nothing is lost, yet they may return spiritually fortified to the present world where losses are inevitable.

In contrast to Singer's home-like, semi-familiar otherworld, Tolkien's afterworld is hierarchically structured and operates by strict theological rules. Niggle must exert great effort to make his way in the Dantean purgatory he encounters; the "Workhouse" where he is assigned is a place where the soul must be purged of its dross and earthly attachments. Reassigned to the Workhouse infirmary when he falls ill, he finds it "more like . . . a prison than a hospital" (97). There he labors hard at "digging, carpentry, and painting bare walls one plain colour. He was never allowed outside, and the windows all looked inward. They kept him in the dark for hours at a stretch, 'to do some thinking,' they said" (97). This forced labor and contemplation seem calculated to humble his artistic ambitions.

At first he worries over the past, speculating that, had he called on Parish earlier, as he had good intentions of doing, the loose roof tiles would have been no trouble to fix and both Mrs. Parish and he might have escaped illness. He then might have had the time to finish his Tree. With the passage of time, however, he forgets what it was that he had wished to accomplish in his earthly existence and feels no pleasure but rather the sensation of satiety: "a feeling of—well, satisfaction: bread rather than jam!" (98). The only time he can call his own is when he is alone in his bed-cell. Despite this recognition, he feels that he is becoming "master of his time; he began to know just what he could do with it" (98). This gives him a quiet peace within himself. Reassigned once more, this time to the back-breaking work of digging, he finally cannot manage another spadeful, and a doctor orders that he be given "complete rest—in the dark" (99).

At this point Tolkien's theological emphasis becomes strong. Niggle lies in the dark, overhearing the Voices involved in a theological debate between Justice and Mercy. Justice insists Niggle is not deserving of advancement to the next stage, for he thoughtlessly wasted time in his earthly life. The Voice of Mercy recommends "a little gentle treatment." After all, this Voice continues, Niggle was a painter "by nature"; special allowances ought therefore to be made: ". . . a leaf by Niggle has a charm of its own. He took a great deal of pains with leaves, just for their own sake. But he never thought that made him important. There is no note in the Records of his pretending, even to himself, that it excused his neglect of things ordered by law" (100). As one might expect on the basis of Tolkien's Catholicism, Mercy wins out. Niggle's attention to his neighbors' "calls," which he had seen on earth as interruptions, viewed from the perspective of eternity make him eligible to progress toward salvation. Caught listening to the Voices, Niggle is embarrassed; asked what he has to say, he inquires after Parish, even putting in a word of praise for him, mentioning his willingness to let Niggle have "excellent potatoes very cheap" (101).

Niggle passes to the next level of his spiritual education. He boards the train once more and, disembarking, finds a bicycle labeled NIGGLE. Riding over the countryside, he comes upon a familiar landscape. At the crest of a hill, he sees an astounding sight: "Before him stood the Tree, his Tree, finished. If you could say that of a Tree that was alive, its leaves opening, its branches growing and bending in the wind. . . . 'It's a gift!' he said. He was referring to his art, and also to the result; but he was using the word literally" (104). Here the aesthetic application, as Purtill calls it, is paramount, for the artist Niggle finds "salvation" in the embodiment of the beauty he had imaginatively conceived on earth. Paradise is a place where the artistic dream becomes actual; the artistic vision becomes incarnate: the word, or in this case the image, becomes flesh. The religious application is intertwined with the aesthetic, for this idealized Tree, in the context of Christian doctrine, resonates with overtones of the Cross after the Resurrection. Tolkien may well have had in mind also the tree, forest, and mountain images so important to the landscape of Dante's *Inferno*.[4]

One may compare Niggle's vision of his art's embodiment with Menaseh's vision of the fictional characters who come alive in his dream. However, only Tolkien develops the aesthetic allegory; he includes a comment on the artist's need for another kind of human being, a sort of Sancho Panza to his Don Quixote, the kind of source of "help and advice" that Niggle finds when he meets his old friend Parish in paradise. There, by example and by instinct, the two complement and instruct each other, and each takes on some of the virtues of the other. Niggle becomes more open to the fascination of the practical arts of gardening and building; Parish develops his aesthetic appreciation of the beauty of the Tree. The wondrous tonic given both, taken "in water from the Spring, before resting" (clearly the water of regeneration), invigorates them, clears their heads, and cures Parish's limp (101). Tolkien's paradise is ultimately a romantic one, a place of creative activity, where human failures of the imagination are remedied and creative capabilities are developed to the maximum.

Even more artistic satisfaction is in store for Niggle; he discovers that the landscape he now inhabits is called "Niggle's Country," and a shepherd tells him "It is Niggle's Picture, or most of it: a little of it now is Parish's Garden" (108). Parish can see Niggle in a new light, not as a foolish Dauber, but as a creative artist, and Niggle realizes Parish is something more than an Old Earthgrubber. In Tolkien's future life, people see and respond to the best in themselves and others. Tolkien leaves the next stage in paradise unilluminated. We as readers can go no farther than our last sight of Niggle, smiling and headed for the Mountains with the shepherd. In the words of the story, what the Mountains "are really like, and what lies beyond them, only those can say who have climbed them" (110). Much is left mysterious, for Tolkien as a medievalist knew how to respect "God's privetee." The parallel in Singer's story is the silence of the parents towards their son Menaseh; some things cannot be told.

Tolkien closes his story with a final brief scene on earth, relating a conversation between two men who reflect on Niggle's life. Councillor Tompkins, a crass utilitarian, sees Niggle as "a silly little man . . . worthless, in fact . . . ," and continues with a gratuitous shot at educators for failing to know their business, a shortcoming that results in their turning out "useless people" (110). Atkins, who is himself "nobody of importance, just a schoolmaster," fails to respond to Tompkins's jibe and rather weakly chimes in to call Niggle a "poor little man" who "never finished anything." Atkins nonetheless cannot forget a certain painting, a remnant of which he found in the corner of a field. It was "damaged, but legible: a mountain peak and a spray of leaves" (111). One beautiful leaf remains intact, and the sensitive Atkins frames it. On his demise, he bequeaths it to the Town Museum, "and for a long while **'Leaf by Niggle'** hung there in a recess, and was noticed by a few eyes. But eventually the Museum was burnt down, and the leaf, and Niggle, were entirely forgotten in his old country" (112). The Voices of Paradise have the last word, revealing that the region created by Niggle and Parish, now called "Niggle's Parish" (Tolkien's witty linguistic marriage of their destinies), serves in the future life as a place of holiday, refreshment, convalescence, and transition to the Mountains. Niggle and Parish, despite their earthly insignificance, are immortalized in the realm where, to borrow Singer's phrase, "nothing is lost," and where indeed, earthly deficiencies are remedied.

Tolkien's narrative emphasizes the theme of the transcendent nature of art and artistic endeavor. The timelessness of art figures as an important element in Singer's narrative as well. In another story by Singer, "Naftali the Storyteller and His Horse, Sus," this belief in the immortality of narrative art is made explicit: "Yes, individual creatures die, but this doesn't end the story of the world. The whole earth, all the stars, all the planets, all the comets represent within them one divine history, one source of life, one endless and wondrous story that only God knows in its entirety" (183). As a boy, Naftali had been told by Reb Zebulun, "When a day passes, it is no longer there. What remains of it? Nothing more than a story. If stories weren't told or books weren't written, man would live like the beasts, only for the day" (172). Singer and Tolkien alike offer young readers assurance that the eternal verities captured by art are real and immortal. Perhaps more significantly, they become aware that they can experience these truths in their own lives.[5]

Singer's narrative will be the more appealing to children, since the protagonist is closer to their own age and his activities easier to identify with; Tolkien's story is more suitable to young adults. Yet both stories serve all readers, on different levels, by giving meaning and value to life in this world. Both present images representing, in Bruno Bettelheim's words, "the metaphoric death of an old, inadequate self in order to be reborn on a higher plane of existence" (35). Mircea Eliade has spoken of the "initiatory meaning" of stories of descent into the underworld as lying in their ability to free the protagonist from the fear of death (64). Similarly the images of the future life presented by both Singer and Tolkien can give readers of any age an imaginative means of shaping and evaluating the hopes and fears that cluster around the mystery of dying. After reading them, we know no more about the ultimate destiny of the human soul than we did before. We know a great deal more, however, about the progress of the human spirit in this world. Both writers envision the future life in images derived from this

one; they could hardly do otherwise. As Singer remarks in the close of another story, "Fool's Paradise," "What paradise is really like, no one can tell" (*Zlateh* 16).

Notes

1. Apart from fantasy, some contemporary realistic books mention life after death. Kathy Piehl analyzes forty novels randomly selected from recent books written expressly for young adults. Only five books mention a possible afterlife: *Dogsong* by Gary Paulsen (Bradbury, 1985), *Center Line* by Joyce Sweeney (Delacorte, 1984), *Shadow and Light* by Katherine Jay Bacon (Macmillan/McElderry 1987), *Just One Friend* by Lynn Hall (Macmillan, 1985), and *Invincible Summer* by Jean Farris (Farrar, 1987).

2. Consider Verlyn Klinkenborg's "At the Edge of Eternity: Learning from Encounters with Death," featured in *Life*, March 1992, as well as the existence of the scholarly *Journal of Near-Death Studies*.

3. The simplicity of Singer's picture of the afterworld is in keeping with the contemporary absence of a definitive Jewish doctrine on the immortality of the soul; there is, however, according to Leo Rosten, an allowance for belief in the immortality of the soul, "an immortality whose nature is known only to God," alongside a rejection of "literal ideas of heaven and hell" (146). The central emphasis in Jewish belief is on life in this world (Hertzberg 212).

4. Some links to Dante's *Inferno* suggested by the editors are the dark wood (*selva oscura*) in which the pilgrim finds himself in the opening lines, and the mountain (*colle*) at whose foot he stands (Canto I).

5. Singer wrote a story titled "Ole & Trufa: A Story of Two Leaves" rather like "Leaf by Niggle." The personified leaves of the title discover death is not what it appears to be. Rather, it is a passage to unity with "the divine plan," the miracle of "the enormous energy" of being ("Ole & Trufa" 253).

Works Cited

Bettelheim, Bruno. *The Uses of Enchantment: The Meaning and Importance of Fairy Tales.* New York: Knopf, 1976.

Burland, Cottie A. "Primitive Societies." *Life After Death.* Ed. Arnold J. Toynbee and Arthur Koestler. New York: McGraw-Hill, 1976.

Coles, Robert. *The Spiritual Life of Children.* Boston: Houghton Mifflin, 1990.

Eliade, Mircea. *Rites and Symbols of Initiation: The Mysteries of Birth and Rebirth.* New York: Harper, 1965.

Frye, Northrop. *The Secular Scripture: A Study of the Structure of Romance.* Cambridge, MA: Harvard UP, 1976.

Hertzberg, Arthur, ed. *Judaism.* New York: Washington Square P, 1962.

Klinkenborg, Verlyn. "At the Edge of Eternity: Learning from Encounters with Death." *Life* 15 (March 1992): 64-73.

Matthews, Gareth B. *Philosophy and the Young Child.* Cambridge, MA: Harvard UP, 1980.

Moss, Steven A. "Children's Concepts of God, Death, and Life after Death." *Children and Death: Perspectives from Birth through Adolescence.* Ed. John E. Schowalter, and others. New York: Praeger, 1987. Foundation of Thanatology Series 9. 11-17.

Piehl, Kathy. "The Presence of Religion in Young Adult Novels: 1983-87." *JOYS* 4 (Spring 1991): 267-80.

Purtill, Richard L. "Heaven and Other Perilous Realms." *Mythlore* 6.4 (Fall 1979): 3-6.

Rosten, Leo, ed. *Religions of America: Ferment and Faith in an Age of Crisis.* New York: Simon and Schuster, 1975.

Singer, Isaac Bashevis. *Alone in the Wild Forest.* New York: Farrar, Straus, and Giroux, 1971.

———. "Are Children the Ultimate Literary Critics?" *Stories for Children.* New York: Farrar, Straus, and Giroux, 1984. 332-38.

———. "Menaseh's Dream." *Stories for Children.* New York: Farrar, Straus, and Giroux, 1984. 313-21.

———. "Naftali the Storyteller and His Horse, Sus." *Stories for Children.* New York: Farrar, Straus, and Giroux, 1984. 167-83.

———. "Ole & Trufa: A Story of Two Leaves." *Stories for Children.* New York: Farrar, Straus, and Giroux, 1984. 249-53.

———. "Fool's Paradise." *Zlateh the Goat and Other Stories.* New York: Harper, 1966. 5-16.

Smith, Doris Buchanan. *A Taste of Blackberries.* Ill. Charles Robinson. New York: Scholastic, 1973.

Tolkien, J. R. R. "Leaf by Niggle." *Tree and Leaf.* Boston: Houghton Mifflin, 1985.

Wolff, Robert Lee. *The Golden Key: A Study of the Fiction of George MacDonald.* New Haven: Yale UP, 1961.

Verlyn Flieger and T. A. Shippey (essay date 2001)

SOURCE: Flieger, Verlyn, and T. A. Shippey. "Allegory versus Bounce: Tolkien's 'Smith of Wootton Major.'" *Journal of the Fantastic in the Arts* 12, no. 2 (2001): 186-200.

[*In the following essay, Flieger maintains that Tolkien's tale is not meant to be read as autobiographical allegory, while Shippey argues that it carries on the tradition of English allegory set by John Bunyan and Edmund Spenser.*]

This exchange originates from two recent published analyses of Tolkien's late short story, **"Smith of Wootton Major,"** by Verlyn Flieger, in chapter 11 of *A Question of Time* (1997), and by Tom Shippey, on pp. 296-304 in *J. R. R. Tolkien: Author of the Century* (2000/2001). The two critics take quite different views of the story. Disagreement between critics is so routine as not normally to be worth comment, but in this case the two are dealing with a relatively short text, extremely clearly written, and moreover have no evidently opposed critical stances. Most important, they are prepared to write freely and candidly (which in critical discourse is by no means routine). It was felt, then, that this disagreement, if probed, might lead to an explanation of how critics come to read differently, a problem too often passed by. With this intention in mind, Drs. Flieger and Shippey presented a joint session at the ICFA conference in Florida on March 22nd, 2001, and now present their statements here more formally.

Verlyn Flieger

The issue of allegory and **"Smith of Wootton Major"** resides not so much in whether there is allegory to be found in the story (for there are at least demonstrable leftovers of an original allegorical intent) as in whether a reading on that level comes closest to Tolkien's final intent and best serves the story as a work of art. In *The Road to Middle-Earth* Professor Shippey asserts that "[**"Smith"** (**"Smith of Wootton Major"**)]'s] mode is allegorical and its subject is the author himself, especially the relations between his job and his private sources of 'inspiration'" (203). Here Shippey reads the first Cook as a "philologist-figure," the crass and materialistic Nokes as a "Critic-figure," and Smith himself as "a Tolkien-figure" (205). He is equally positive in his later *J. R. R. Tolkien: Author of the Century,* where he heads his discussion of the story "Autobiographical allegory: 2 *Smith of Wootton Major*" (296). Shippey's autobiographical allegory 1 is **"Farmer Giles of Ham,"** though he concedes that **"Farmer Giles"** [**"Farmer Giles of Ham"**] "makes too much sense in its own right to need an allegorical reading"

(289). The implication is that **"Smith"** does *not* make such sense in its own right and thus benefits from a reading as allegory.

I yield to none in my admiration for Professor Shippey as a scholar, a critic, and a fellow lover of Tolkien. Nevertheless, with regard to **"Smith,"** I must respectfully disagree on all counts.

(1). The story's mode is fairy tale, not allegory, as Tolkien himself made clear. "This short tale is not 'allegory'," he declared in his notes, "though it is capable of course of allegorical interpretation at certain points. *It is a Fairy Story* [my emphasis] of the kind in which beings that may be called 'fairies' or 'elves' play a part and are associated in action with human people, and are regarded as having a 'real' existence, that is one in their own right and independent of human imagination and invention" (*Question* 232).

(2). Its subject is the experience of a human in the Faery world, not "the author himself," though the reader is free to speculate that Tolkien may have had such experience.

(3). The characters are believable in their roles within the fiction and require no reference to philology, critics, or Tolkien's supposed conflict between art and life in order to be understood.

4). The purpose of fairy tales is not to make sense but to give the reader a glimpse of the perilous realm that Tolkien called Faery (or Faërie; his spellings of the word vary).

As he himself put it, "Faërie cannot be caught in a net of words; for it is one of its qualities to be indescribable, though not imperceptible. It has many ingredients, but analysis will not necessarily discover the secret of the whole" ("On Fairy-Stories" 114). Even more to the purpose are Tolkien's words about *Beowulf* and against its interpretation by critics as a philological, archaeological or historical document rather than, as he chose to read it, a poem. "The significance of myth is not easily to be pinned on paper by analytical reasoning. It is at its best when it is presented by a poet who feels rather than makes explicit what his theme portends" (*"Beowulf"* 14-15); for "myth is alive at once and in all its parts, and dies before it can be dissected" (*"Beowulf"* 15).

Shippey's interpretation of the story as autobiographical allegory of Tolkien's struggle with the opposing forces of fantasy and philology, or fantasy and faith, is precisely the kind of analysis Tolkien argues against. It may be plausible and persuasive if one is searching for biographical information about the author, though

Shippey produces no external evidence that Tolkien felt such a conflict. It may conceivably tell us something about Tolkien and perhaps about Professor Shippey (as my argument here will say something about me), but it tells us nothing about what happens to Smith—not Tolkien—in Faery.

As Tolkien declared of his reading of *Beowulf,* "it is the mood of the author, the essential cast of his imaginative apprehension of the world, that is my concern" (*"Beowulf"* 20), not the author's history for its own sake. Making the first Cook a philologist-figure does not improve understanding of Tolkien's imaginative apprehension of the world. However, the Cook can easily be understood in the context of the other Elf-friends in Tolkien's fiction, such as Eriol, Ælfwine, Edwin Lowdham and Bilbo Baggins, who leave Middle-earth for the Faery realm. Making Smith a Tolkien-figure takes him right out of the story and puts him in Oxford in the twentieth century. The story's association of craft with art and art with Faery is understandable without allegorizing it, and Smith as a character works better in juxtaposition to Nokes than to Tolkien. Nokes is also a craftsman, though not a very inventive one since he largely depends on old recipes, and his unimaginative cooking, especially his over-sweetening of the cake, brands him as a journeyman.[1] He is never, like Smith, the master of his craft.

Shippey's imposition of allegorical meaning on **"Smith"** does not simply devalue the story as a *story*; it is necessarily based on the presumption that Tolkien was engaged in an interior struggle of which **"Smith"** is the coded expression. There is no hard evidence for this. The fact that Tolkien spent the majority of his daily life in teaching and scholarship and wrote fantasy and mythology in his spare time (and largely at night) does not necessarily mean that he felt the two areas were at war in himself. On the contrary, they worked very well together. His poetic gift enriches the most memorable of his critical essays, *"Beowulf*: The Monsters and the Critics" and "On Fairy-Stories," while his lifetime study of Old and Middle English and his reading in Norse, Welsh, and Finnish languages and mythology add authority to his fiction.

Roger Lancelyn Green's early review of **"Smith of Wootton Major"** warned against looking too hard for a message in what was essentially a fairy tale, writing that, "To seek for the meaning is to cut open the ball in search of its bounce" (Tolkien, *Letters* 388). Green's caution has not stopped others from searching for the bounce, and in the process making some fairly bounce-deadening cuts in the fabric of the ball. Professor Shippey's extension of Green's metaphor of ball and bounce into a contention that the ball "bounces better" after it has been cut into, and that the story "makes more sense" when read as allegory is itself open to question. Balls do not bounce well after they have been cut open, if indeed they bounce at all. Moreover, the function of art is not to make "sense," but to give a glimpse of the wider realm to which art is the gateway.

Nevertheless, "Smith" is undeniably a perplexing narrative, of all Tolkien's works the most uncompromising in its presentation of the experience of mortals in the faery realm, and the opacity of the story invites interpretation. Whether it benefits from it is another issue altogether. What allegory there is in the story can be addressed and disposed of fairly easily. Tolkien has said that "Smith" began as an allegorical response to the (to him) common misconception of the word *fairy*, correlating the writer who would sweeten and prettify the notion for children to a cook baking an over-sweet cake on the assumption that all children liked sugar.

The story outgrew this concept, but the remnants can still be found in his notes although his concern had apparently moved from the meaning of fairy to the state of organized religion. The notes show that he had thought of the shabby Great Hall no longer properly tended as the village church, of the Cook Nokes with his sugary misconception of Faery as the parson, of the craft or occupation of cooking as "personal religion and prayer." However, those same notes go on to make it clear that he vacillated widely between allegory and no allegory, obviously uncertain himself of how much meaning he should impose on the reader (*Question* 229-233).

On the model of Tolkien's argument for the centrality of the "On Fairy-Stories" to *Beowulf*, I would suggest that the Faery—the actual experience of enchantment by Smith—is at the center of "Smith," while any leftover allegory is at the edges—the beginning and the end. This is all to the good. If the residual allegorical elements—the cake, the Cook, the Great Hall—comprised the major thrust of the narrative as published, "Smith" might be a good allegory but it would be a very dull story. It is not a dull story, though it is a surprisingly severe one—certainly not "sweet" in any respect. If we take Tolkien at his word that there is (or was) allegory in "Smith," we would do well also to remember his words descriptive of another story, that "the tale grew in the telling." In that process the focus moved from the cake (in draft the story was titled "The Great Cake") to the central character in the story, the smith named Smith, who while still a boy swallows a magic star embedded in his slice of cake. The star functions as his entry visa into Faery, which Tolkien called "the perilous land," and of which he wrote that, it has both beauty and "an ever-present peril" ("Monsters" 107).

The heart of "Smith of Wootton Major" lies not so much in the village machinery of Great Hall, Cook, and Parson, as in Smith's wanderings in Faery and in the reader's participation in his enchantment, bewilderment, and acceptance of that which he cannot understand. In his total lack of any key to the meaning of the phenomena to which he is witness Smith is in the position of the reader, or rather, the reader is in the position of Smith and both are in the position described by Tolkien in his opening to "On Fairy-Stories." "In that realm [Faery] a man may, perhaps, count himself fortunate to have wandered, but its very richness and strangeness tie the tongue of a traveller who would report them" (*"On Fairy-Stories"* 109). I suggest that this is precisely Tolkien's intention. To assume that Tolkien intended the Faery of the story to stand for something outside itself would subordinate that very richness and strangeness to some extra-literary agenda. One could no longer read it as itself, then, but only use it as a guide to another and presumably more important story. Readers would be subject to just what Tolkien objected to in allegory, "the purposed domination of the author" (*LOTR*, Foreword xvii), rather than being left free, like Smith, to find their own way and make their own associations.

As a wanderer in Faery, Smith is witness to scenes and events he cannot understand and that are never explained. He sees "things of both beauty and terror that he [can] not clearly remember or report to his friends." He stands beside the Sea of Windless Storm where blue waves bear "the white ships that return from battles on the Dark Marches of which men know nothing"; he sees a "great ship cast high upon the land. . . . elven mariners" who pass over him and go "away into the echoing hills" ("Smith" 28). Most mysterious of all, he comes to a lake "harder than stone and sleeker than glass." When he steps on the surface and falls, its ringing boom wakes the Wild Wind which drives him up the slopes "whirling and falling like a dead leaf" (32). He clings for safety to a young birch tree, and when the Wind has passed he sees that the birch, now stripped of all its leaves, is weeping. Setting his hands on its white bark, he asks what he can do to make amends or give thanks. The tree's answer is both unequivocal and puzzling. "Nothing," it says. "Go away. The Wind is hunting you. You do not belong here. Go away and never return" (32).

The power of this episode, its bounce, resides in its mystery. Smith does not understand the action of the Wind or the words of the birch. He is not meant to. Nor is the reader. Smith asks for no explanation, and none is forthcoming. I suggest that in reading the episode it would be well to remember Tolkien's own caution about the realm of Faërie: that while "in that realm a man may, perhaps, count himself fortunate to have wandered," nevertheless, "it is dangerous for him to ask too many questions, lest the gates be shut and the keys be lost" (*"On Fairy-Stories"* 109).

Shippey asks questions. "What is the birch that saves, the wind that threatens?" (*Road* 206). His citation of sources and analogues in Tolkien's poem "Éadig béo êu," in the Child ballad "The Wife of Usher's Well," and in Walter Scott's anecdote of the birch as protection against the wind of the world, supply his answers, but tell us nothing about Smith. His speculation that "Smith's Wind could be the world," as in Scott, "the birch its traditional opponent, scholarly study," as in "Éadig béo êu" (*Road* 207), allows him to ask more questions, now based entirely on his own interpretation.

"Did Tolkien feel he had *exploited* philology for his fiction?" "Did he feel, perhaps, that in writing his fiction he was trespassing in a 'perilous country' against some unstated law?" (*Road* 207). There is no evidence to support this, and to allow this kind of speculation to override Tolkien's own treatment is to do the story a disservice. Such a reading removes the mystery and power from the episode and replaces them with one-to-one correlations, thereby cutting open the ball and effectively removing the bounce. The mystery is not just explained—it is explained away.

In sum, the reading **"Smith of Wootton Major"** as allegory goes counter to Tolkien's own artistic principles. Granted, the story began as allegory. Granted, the remnants still lurk around the edges. But the story transcends its own beginnings and the allegorical leftovers add nothing to the reader's understanding of its particular and unexplainable magic. To illustrate the point, I will close with Tolkien's own best-known use of outright allegory, the allegory of the tower in "*Beowulf*: The Monsters and the Critics." After carefully implying one-to-one correspondences between contemporary critical interpretations of the poem and the field of old stone, the older hall, the present house, and the tower, he abandons allegory for art in his conclusion, which is that, "from that tower the man had been able to see the sea."

There is no allegorical correlative to the sea, and the vision implied cannot be tied down to a specific meaning. The same is true of **"Smith of Wootton Major."**

T. A. SHIPPEY

My comments take off from the statement made by Roger Lancelyn Green in a review of **"Smith"** shortly after its publication—a statement endorsed by Tolkien and quoted with approval by Dr. Flieger, and others.[2] Dr. Flieger's paraphrase of Green runs as follows:

Green observed that the effect of the story transcends any explicit reference and warned against looking too hard for a specific message. He wrote of it that "To seek for the meaning is to cut open the ball in search of its bounce." This may prove to be the best summation of the story's appeal. The bounce is clearly there, but to search for it is to defeat its effect; to allegorize it is to deaden the bounce completely.

(*A Question of Time* 233)

I accept Flieger's paraphrase, but I reject Green's metaphor. More important, if "the bounce" here is "whatever it is that makes reading the story pleasurable," then I can testify that as far as I am concerned Flieger's last phrase, "to allegorize it is to deaden the bounce completely," is not true of my experience at all. Much of the pleasure I take in the story comes from searching out allegory. This does not go away, but increases with re-reading, and re-searching. Green's metaphor, to use another metaphor, seems to me like saying "put that ball on the mantelpiece, and for goodness' sake don't bounce it, it will break!" But it doesn't break—or not when I bounce it.

I have no wish, accordingly, to try to confute Dr. Flieger's reading, but I do have to record that my experience is not hers. We are clearly reading the same text (and I do not believe that either of us has much patience with mystical notions that there is no such thing as "the same text"), but we are not reading it the same way. Is this the result of different initial presuppositions? Different areas of knowledge? Or perhaps we are reading it differently on a purely mechanical level, in the way our eyes move and we take in words?

I begin with a simple possibility: perhaps we have different views about allegory. What is an "allegory"? This question, like almost all matters of definition, has been put to the Four Wise Men of Oxenford,[3] and as with "blunderbuss" their answer is not especially helpful: the core of it runs "a figurative narrative . . . in which properties and circumstances attributed to the apparent subject really refer to the subject they are meant to suggest," a definition which leaves one wondering about words like "really" and "meant."[4] I find it more useful to look at Tolkien's own theory and practice, and these are on the face of it incompatible. Tolkien wrote, for instance, in the "Foreword" to the 2nd edition of *The Lord of the Rings,* "I cordially dislike allegory in all its manifestations, and always have done so since I grew old and wary enough to detect its presence."[5] I hesitate to say that this is not true (as stated above, you cannot tell people what they like or dislike), but the fact is that Tolkien was something of a serial allegorist. Much of the force of the opening of his famous lecture "*Beowulf*: The Monsters and the Critics" comes from three short allegories in sequence:

Beowulf seen as a child to whose christening one fairy (Poesis) has not been invited; the criticism of *Beowulf* viewed as a Babel of tongues; and most important and most extensive, the allegory of *Beowulf* as a tower. Tolkien explicitly identifies this long paragraph as "yet another allegory," and says at the end of it, "I hope I shall show that that allegory is just."[6]

The idea of "just-ness" seems to me important, and perhaps explains the contradiction indicated above. In Tolkien's view, allegory is essentially a set of equations. Each item in the surface narrative has to correspond to an item in the unstated meaning, and those items have to fit together in closely similar ways. It was this view that led him to reject the idea that *The Lord of the Rings* was an allegory of World War II (with the Ring implicitly as atomic power). If this had been the case, he pointed out in a scornful paragraph in the "Foreword" already cited, the Ring would not have been destroyed, it would have been used; Saruman would have been enabled to make his own Ring; and so on. Amateur allegorists of his work, Tolkien felt, did not know their own business. Their allegory was not "just."

By contrast, though, Tolkien in the *Beowulf* lecture did know his own business. Every item in the "tower" allegory makes perfect sense if translated into the world of *Beowulf*-criticism, and so (I believe) does every item in the "Babel" allegory.[7] The point of the allegories is also perfectly clear. They function as *reductio ad absurdum*: the image of the busy critics destroying the tower, then complaining what a mess it is in, and saying it was a silly idea to build it anyway, is evidently absurd, but bears a strong resemblance to what German critics of the poem actually did. They did not think what they did was absurd, but Tolkien's allegory tries to persuade one that it was. Allegory used this way, one can see, is a simplifying and argumentative mode.

This has made it unpopular in modern critical terms. Nowadays what is valued is complexity, diversity, dialogism, multiple meanings, freedom to interpret the inexhaustible text (etc.); and allegory, with its one-to-one correspondences and its strict discipline, is viewed as limited and pedantic. In the "Foreword" already mentioned, Tolkien opposes it to "applicability," notes that many confuse the two, and expresses the distinction as, "the one [applicability] resides in the freedom of the reader, and the other [allegory] in the purposed domination of the author." It would be possible for me to avoid contradicting Tolkien by saying that I seek only for "applicability" in **"Smith,"** not "allegory." But I would point out, first, that there is an extensive scale between perfect freedom and perfect domination; and second, that several major works of English litera-

ture (including ones which Tolkien respected, and ones he probably did not) are commonly taken to be allegories, which demand interpretation and will not work without it, but where the "domination of the author" has certainly not led to a final, deadened solution.

I mean works like Langland's *Piers Plowman,* Spenser's *Faerie Queene,* Bunyan's *Pilgrim's Progress,* but, perhaps most strikingly in modern times, also Orwell's *Animal Farm.* It would be an extremely unambitious and unproductive procedure to read any of the three just mentioned "just for the story," though I can imagine there are some people who do so. Children, for instance, might read the Orwell story just as a sort of joke, though even they, I think, would feel some sense of fear, some awareness that this story is not just about animals. But in such cases the story, the attractive surface narrative, is there partly though not entirely to provoke a quest for a further meaning, clearly intended and sometimes indicated by the author; and no-one suggests that this quest should be abandoned, for fear of losing a hypothetical "bounce."[8] It is in this category of allegorical work that I would put **"Smith."**

There are then two points that I would add. One is that I would put **"Leaf by Niggle"** in the same, or a similar category. I think this is quite clearly an allegory, and an autobiographical one, and one of the signs of this is the work's extreme "just-ness." Many of the details in it, just as with Tolkien's allegory of the tower, can be given one-to-one correspondences with reality (in my view, Niggle's house, garden, paintings, potatoes, shed, journey, temperament, and much else). These details (rightly interpreted) make the story both funnier and more threatening—they add to the bounce.[9] But the second point is that, obviously with *The Faerie Queene* and even with the much shorter and clearer **"Leaf by Niggle,"** no-one is ever going to catch every detail. Probably the authors themselves could not have done so. Allegories of an extended kind have a habit of getting away from their authors, as the surface narrative imposes its own logic. They are also clearly used by many authors (Langland and Bunyan prominent among them) as a way of trying to understand their own feelings and their own situation, as an investigative mode as well as an explanatory one. In only the shortest and simplest allegories does the author "dominate" the reader (as Tolkien said) or even (and this is my addition) his/her own text. The advantage of all this is that it is quite possible to read an extended allegory, like **"Smith,"** or **"Leaf by Niggle,"** or *Piers Plowman,* and find something new every time—but still something allegorical. Like tennis balls, they bounce higher the more you warm them up, and the way you warm them up is by playing with them.

To abandon metaphor and turn to reading **"Smith,"** it seems to me that my readings of the story depend on identifying details. It is amazing how easy these are to miss. Thus (and I owe the following identifications to Dr. Flieger, who has had the advantage of reading Tolkien's own commentary on his text, from which I now quote): "The Great Hall is evidently in a way an 'allegory' of the village church; the Master Cook . . . is plainly the Parson and the priesthood." Cooking meanwhile equates to "personal religion and prayer."[10] Tolkien here uses the words "evidently" and "plainly," but I do not think I made these equations on first or even later reading. What the account of the Great Hall and its festivities told me was that I was reading an allegory of some kind: social behavior in Wootton Major was too far removed from real-life behavior at any period of English history for me to accept it as just surface narrative. However, once the equations between Hall and church, etc., have been made, several other details take on meaning.

Rather late on in the tale, for instance, we are told that once Alf takes over as Master Cook from Nokes, the Hall was "re-glazed and re-painted." Some called this "new-fangled," but "some with more knowledge knew that it was a return to old custom." It is important to note that these sentences have no further narrative point. It makes no difference to the rest of the story what the Hall looks like. This rather extensive description is "narratively redundant." In an allegory, though, what is narratively redundant is likely to be allegorically especially significant. Here it seems to me that Tolkien is expressing approval of changes in church fashion in his own day, away from the careful sobriety, the "Sunday suit" style of Victorian devotion, and towards a more cheerful and more dramatic attitude to worship, seen by many as disrespectful and modernistic, but by Tolkien as a return to the medieval integration of religion with everyday life and with imaginative richness (as in the carving and painting of gargoyles, which he mentions particularly).

The Hall/church identification may make one wonder, further, about the place Smith lives, Wootton Major. Why Wootton? Why Major? Here I agree with Dr. Flieger that Wootton means, philologically, Woodtown, the town in the wood; and the wood is a highly significant image. Dr. Flieger suggests that woods are gateways to the other world, as in Dante, and this is so.[11] To it I would add that woods are for Tolkien ambiguous places.[12] He loved them as much as anyone, but he also saw them as places where travellers easily become confused, "bewildered," lose sight of the stars, lose their (physical and moral) bearings. They represent the world of reality, the mundane world, because in them it is so easy to forget that there is a world outside them, and to despair. Smith, of course, is above all the character with an available exit from Wootton, or the wood of the world, into Faerie. Meanwhile, why Major? Does the story need a Minor, and a Walton? In view of Tolkien's Catholicism, it is tempting to see the Church of Wootton Major as the Catholic Church, with Wootton Minor perhaps as its Anglican offshoot. An interesting detail here is that Nokes, not liked and not accepted as an apprentice by the previous Master Cook (so outside the "apostolic succession," so to speak) is "a solid sort of man with a wife and children." If he is "plainly" a parson, then, as Tolkien declared, he must be a Protestant one. Possibly the Major/Minor suggestion made just above is the wrong way round—as, in purely English terms, would be the case.

The question of names is especially relevant to allegory because, in normal life, names do not mean anything: surnames especially, as we all know, are not chosen but come by accident of birth; most people do not in fact know what their names "mean" (i.e., what they used to mean long ago, before they became just names). In a story, though, the author chooses the names. In realistic stories they will be chosen to sound random, as in reality. In an allegory they are likely once again to have strong suggestion. Here, and speaking entirely for myself, I cannot get over the choice of the name "Nokes." There is a Noakes in *The Lord of the Rings,* "Old Noakes of Bywater," and in his "Guide to the Names in *The Lord of the Rings*" Tolkien noted the derivation from Middle English *atten oke(s)*, "at the oak(s)," and added, for the benefit of his translators, "since this is no longer recognized, this need not be considered. The name is in the tale unimportant."[13] It is just a label, in other words, like most names; but that is in *The Lord of the Rings,* which is not an allegory, and which has hundreds of names without narrative meaning.

What I cannot forget, reading **"Smith,"** is that for Tolkien "oak" had a clear private meaning, several times recalled.[14] "Oak" in Old English is *ác*, and it is also the name for the rune representing "A". The name for "B" in the Old English runic alphabet is *beorc*, or "birch." In the syllabus Tolkien devised at Leeds University, and which he tried unsuccessfully to transplant to Oxford,[15] the "B-scheme" was the one he controlled, the language-and-medieval scheme of study, and the "A-scheme" was the one controlled by his colleague the Professor of Literature. These two schemes existed on terms of strong mutual ideological hostility, which it would take many pages to explain. I can only say here that to me (the inheritor of many of Tolkien's feuds), Alf Prentice's sharp rebuke to Nokes almost at the end has many resonances. "You are a vain old fraud," he says, "fat, idle, and sly. I did most of your work. Without thanks you learned all that you could from me—except respect for Faery, and a little courtesy." Ignoring the first sentence, which is just rude, the next two seem to me to represent reasonably well the relationship between philology (the "B-scheme") and literary studies (the "A-scheme" represented by Nokes): English departments in universities were established by philologists, who created a discipline of vernacular literary study, and were then ungratefully pushed aside by critics who, notoriously, had no time for fantasy, or Faery, whether medieval or modern. If Tolkien did not intend this equation, why choose the name "Nokes" rather than one of the many thousand neutral names available?

I have to accept, of course, that this is very largely a private symbolism, which Tolkien could not have expected more than a few of his readers to notice. Most of his readers, though, could still get the point, or most of the point: Nokes is annoying not just because he has only a feeble image of Faerie himself, but because he insists that that is the only one there is. He is indeed absolutely precisely one of those "professional persons" who "suppose their dullness and ignorance to be a human norm," and whom Tolkien picked out for special assault in his "Valedictory Address to the University of Oxford," clearly meaning in that context to indicate professors of literature.[16] And then we have the strange scene in which Smith is protected from the Wind by the weeping birch. I have said what I think about this elsewhere, and have clearly failed to convince Dr. Flieger;[17] but this perhaps brings us close to one reason for our disagreements. It seems to me, as said above, that my readings depend above all on details, and on "just-ness." I can accept that I miss details, and equations, like the very obvious Hall/church one. One reason why the "bounce" does not weaken, in my opinion, is that I hope to catch or identify a few more details on every new reading. What I do not think is that I am supposed just not to wonder about them, to accept them as part of surface narrative, as I might in a realistic novel.

Dr. Flieger, in a word, takes **"Smith"** holistically, while I take it bit by bit. There is no doubt that her way fits modern critical taste better than mine, as does a liking for dialogism, multiple meanings, freedom to interpret the inexhaustible text (etc.), as said above. Whether modern critical taste has much to do with Tolkien may, however, be doubted. I note also, in Dr. Flieger's analysis, a conviction that the whole text is somehow too fragile to be rudely disassembled. My "oak-and-birch" theory is not rejected outright, but is felt to "place a heavy burden on a story whose effect depends not a little on its lightness of touch." Elsewhere—and also in the context of rejecting autobiographical and allegorical elements—we hear of its "gossamer appeal," its "unpretentious air" and "effort-less ability to imply without stating."[18] Light, gossamer, effortless: this is an image of Faerie, but I have a feeling that this is a Shakespearean one rather than a Tolkienian one. As I have said elsewhere, Tolkien was in a technical sense one of the most "tough-minded" of authors, not a holistic person at all.[19]

One does, of course, in the end have to consider the story as a whole, the story "in its own terms," as Dr. Flieger insists, though for me one has to go through the bit-by-bit stage of considering details first: things like names are for me quite literally the story's carefully-selected "own terms." I can only say here that for me the critical facts about the story are that it is double-stranded; that it is about succession; and that Smith himself appears to fail, or to enjoy only temporary success, along both strands. The one strand is cooking. The succession of Master Cooks goes Rider / Nokes / Alf Prentice / Harper. The other is possession of the star, and its succession goes Rider / Smith / Nokes's Tim. According to Tolkien's own statement, the Hall, the Master Cooks, and cooking in general, are all to be equated with religion; while it seems obvious that the star which gives entry into Faerie stands for something like Tolkien's own inspiration, a quality essentially literary and imaginative.

This basic separation seems to me, however, hard to maintain in detail. For one thing, Nokes the Cook shows a revealingly shallow attitude to Faerie, which seems to have more to do with literature than with religion. For another, it is hard for me to see Alf, the elf-king (elves are proverbially soulless) simply as a parson, a representative of the Church. I conclude, therefore, that as one might expect these two strands are not readily separable, but relate to each other. The theme of **"Smith"** is the integration of fantasy with belief; the question it resolves is whether fantasy—the deliberate, imaginative, literary creation of myth by individuals—is compatible with belief in the myth created by God (the Christian myth). Strict views have long insisted that this is not the case. Tolkien took such strict views seriously, but he very much did not want to accept them. **"Smith"** works out that debate, and also makes the case for the autonomy of fantasy against the beef-witted, rigorously practical, "stands to reason" attitude of Nokes (so often repeated since by "modernist" critics).

Uncertainty is conveyed once more by redundancy, this time by "redundant characters." These are the characters introduced, it seems, so as to be excluded from both sequences of succession: Smith's son Ned, and his grandson Tomling. Neither becomes Cook, neither receives the star. Indeed, in one of the least expected strokes of the narrative, the star goes to a descendant of Nokes, Nokes of Townsend's Tim. These surprising introductions seem to me to be capable of interpretation, but perhaps the point to make here is that they seem to me to demand it. Surely Tolkien here is saying something at once pessimistic (no-one can control the future) and optimistic (inspiration may appear to be lost, but will return in some entirely unpredicted form): it reminds me of the debate between Legolas and Gimli in Minas Tirith, Gimli taking the pessimistic view (human works all fail), Legolas the optimistic one (but their seed does not fail).[20]

My essential point about allegory and its "bounciness" is however this: a full reading of **"Smith,"** for me, would look like a long edited text, with footnoted commentary on several score, or several hundred separate points. To name a very small selection of them, the character Rider, the Fairy Queen doll, and the contrast between it and the real Fairy Queen, the "old books of recipes" which Nokes can barely read, the strange sequence in Smith's family of Nokes-like names (Nell, Nan, Ned), the King's Tree, the Living Flower which *is* inherited by Smith's kin, the scented bell-flowers which go to Tomling, the story's forty-eight year time-span, the character Harper who "comes from your own village," the name Townsend (Nokes of Townsend is "quite different"), the word "nimble," almost the last word of the story and one marked like Ned, Nan, Nell and Nokes by the philological feature of "nunnation." What do all these mean? In some cases, I think I know, but it would take a long and separate comment to explain; in others I do not know, but am still thinking about it (which means that there is still "bounce" in reserve). But it seems to me that that is the way complex allegories work. Their life is in detail. Their texture is not "gossamer," but surprisingly tough. The fear that their charm may be destroyed by too close an analysis is misplaced. They ask for careful thought, not just emotional response, because they have something serious and complex to express. This is emphatically not to say, however, that what they have to express can be reduced to some (once decoded) much simpler meaning. It is perhaps this last mistaken belief which has created the modern reaction against the allegorical mode. But that is not the way that medieval allegorists worked, nor necessarily modern ones.

Notes

1. Nokes far more evokes the figure of Ted Sandyman than of any critic except possibly Edmund Wilson. But then Wilson, at least in his understanding of *The Lord of the Rings,* might be said to be a Sandyman-figure.

2. See Flieger *A Question of Time* 233, and Doughan 17.

3. I refer here to Tolkien's joke about the word "blunderbuss," in *Farmer Giles of Ham,* 16. To him "the Four Wise Clerks of Oxenford" were the editors of the *Oxford English Dictionary,* see Kocher 161. There are more than four of them now, of course.

4. See the *Oxford English Dictionary,* eds. J. Simpson and E. S. C. Weiner, 2nd ed. 1989, s.v. "allegory."

5. *The Lord of the Rings,* 2nd edition, London: George Allen & Unwin, 1966, and Boston: Houghton Mifflin, 1967.

6. See Tolkien, *The Monsters and the Critics and Other Essays* 8.

7. For an interpretation of the "tower" allegory, see Shippey *Road* 1982: 36-7 and *Road* 1992: 43. I regret to say that both times there is a critical misprint—the "man's own descendants" question should read, "Why did not he restore the old house?" The "Babel" allegory has never been explained in detail, though most of the evidence for such an explanation is to be found in Shippey and Haarder 1998. A full edition of the early drafts of Tolkien's lecture, with commentary, is in preparation by Michael Drout for Arizona State University Press.

8. Quite a lot of people might like to argue that the quest should be turned in some other direction. The rather obvious equations of *Animal Farm* (old Major as Marx, Snowball as Trotsky, Napoleon as Stalin, Moses the raven as the clergy) have been repeatedly denied—and it is true that one wonders what happened to Lenin.

9. For my reading of this story, see Shippey *J. R. R. Tolkien: Author of the Century* 266-77. The reading there contains significant additions of detail to the original theory as advanced in Shippey *Road* 1982: 34-5 and *Road* 1992: 40-41.

10. For these, see Flieger *A Question of Time* 232.

11. See once more Flieger *A Question of Time* 250.

12. The point has also been made by Flieger in a new article, "Taking the Part of Trees."

13. See Tolkien, "Guide to the Names," 1975: 170.

14. It is most obvious in the Old English poem called "Eadig Beo Thu!" in *Songs for the Philologists,* 13, translated Shippey *Road* 1982: 229.

15. See Tolkien "The Oxford English School," 1930.

16. See Tolkien *The Monsters and the Critics and Other Essays* 225.

17. See Shippey *Road,* 1982: 206-7, 1992: 244-6, 320, and Flieger *A Question of Time* 243-4.

18. See Flieger *A Question of Time* 244, 231, 233.

19. I have to repeat that "tough-mindedness" here has a special sense, of being concerned with details, single facts, rather than systems, see Shippey *Road* 1982: 215-6, *Road* 1992: 291-2. It is quite possible to be "tough-minded" and "tender-hearted" at once. The basic idea is William James'.

20. See *Lord of the Rings* III: 149 (start of the chapter "The Last Debate").

References

Doughan, David. "In Search of the Bounce: Tolkien seen through Smith." *Leaves from the Tree: Tolkien's Shorter Fiction.* Ed. Alex Lewis. London: The Tolkien Society. 17-22.

Flieger, Verlyn. *A Question of Time: J. R. R. Tolkien's Road to Faërie.* Kent, Ohio: Kent State University Press, 1997.

———. *A Question of Time: J. R. R. Tolkien's Road to Faerie.* Kent, Ohio: Kent State UP, 1997.

———. "Taking the Part of Trees: Eco-Conflict in Middle-earth." *J. R. R. Tolkien and his Literary Resonances: Views of Middle-earth.* Eds. George Clark and Daniel Timmons. Westport, Conn. and London: Greenwood, 2001. 147-58.

Kocher, Paul. *Master of Middle-earth: The Achievement of J. R. R. Tolkien in Fiction.* Harmondsworth: Penguin Books, 1974.

Shippey, T. A. *J. R. R. Tolkien: Author of the Century.* London: HarperCollins, 2000.

———. *J. R. R. Tolkien: Author of the Century.* London: HarperCollins 2000 and Boston: Houghton Mifflin, 2001

———. *The Road to Middle-Earth.* London: George Allen & Unwin, 1982.

———. *The Road to Middle-earth.* London: George Allen & Unwin, 1982, and Boston: Houghton Mifflin, 1983; 2nd expanded edition, London: HarperCollins, 1992.

——— and Andreas Haarder, Eds. *Beowulf: the Critical Heritage.* London and New York: Routledge, 1998.

Simpson, J. A. and E. S. C. Weiner, Eds. *Oxford English Dictionary.* 2nd ed. Oxford: Oxford UP, 1989.

Tolkien, J. R. R. "*Beowulf*: The Monsters and the Critics." *The Proceedings of the British Academy,* Volume XXII. London: Oxford University Press, 1936.

———. *Farmer Giles of Ham. The Adventures of Tom Bombadil.* London: Unwin Paperbacks, 1975.

———. "Guide to the Names in *The Lord of the Rings.*" *A Tolkien Compass.* Ed. Jared Lobdell. La Salle, Ill: Open Court Press, 1975. 153-201.

———. *The Letters of J. R. R. Tolkien.* Ed. Humphrey Carpenter with Christopher Tolkien. Boston: Houghton Mifflin, 1981.

———. *The Lord of the Rings.* 2nd edition, London: George Allen & Unwin, 1966; and Boston: Houghton Mifflin, 1967.

———. *The Lord of the Rings.* 3 vols. London: HarperCollins, 1991.

———. *The Monsters and the Critics and Other Essays.* Ed. Christopher Tolkien. London: HarperCollins, 1997.

———. "On Fairy-Stories." *Tolkien: The Monsters and the Critics and Other Essays.* Ed. Christopher Tolkien. London: George Allen & Unwin, 1983.

———. "The Oxford English School." *Oxford Magazine* 48/21 (29 May 1930): 778-82.

———. *Smith of Wootton Major.* Boston: Houghton Mifflin, 1978.

———. *Tree and Leaf. Smith of Wootton Major. The Homecoming of Beohtnoth.* London: Unwin Paperbacks, 1975.

——— and E. V. Gordon and Others. *Songs for the Philologists.* Privately printed at University College, London, 1936.

Friedhelm Schneidewind (essay date 2008)

SOURCE: Schneidewind, Friedhelm. "*Farmer Giles of Ham*: The Prototype of a Humorous Dragon Story."[1] In *Tolkien's Shorter Works: Proceedings of the 4th Seminar of the Deutsche Tolkien Gesellschaft and Walking Tree Publishers Decennial Conference,* edited by Margaret Hiley and Frank Weinreich, pp. 77-100. Zurich: Walking Tree Publishers, 2008.

[*In the following essay, Schneidewind places "Farmer Giles of Ham" within the Western tradition of dragon tales and investigates the influence of Tolkien's short story on subsequent dragon narratives.*]

"Never laugh at live dragons, Bilbo you fool!"

Bilbo in *The Hobbit* (J. R. R. Tolkien)

Draco dormiens nunquam titillandus

—Never Tickle a Sleeping Dragon!—

Hogwarts' Motto (Joanne K. Rowling)

INTRODUCTION

Tolkien took a lively interest in dragons ever since childhood[2]. While they play a rather subordinate role in the stories published in his lifetime and set in

Middle-earth in other works of Tolkien's they appear more often. To which extent he occupied himself with these creatures can be seen, for instance, in his art as in the beautiful painting "Glorund setting forth to seek Túrin"[3] (1927, Hammond and Scull 51) and in the rather amusing sketches "Untitled (Dragon and Warrior)" (1928) and "Ringborta Heorte Gefysed" (1929, both Hammond and Scull 52). In 1923, Tolkien published a first version of the poem "The Hoard" (*ATB* 107-109) which includes a very "traditional" dragon[4]. Dragons also appear in the story of "Roverandom" and in one of the five sketches belonging to it that are supposed to have been created around 1927. A dragon also plays a role in the "Letters from Father Christmas" (*FC* 1927).

The profound and humorous story **Farmer Giles of Ham** with its dragon Chrysophylax was already written in 1936, but as it was only published in 1949, the first dragon with which Tolkien became famous was Smaug from *The Hobbit* (1937). On January 1st 1938, shortly after *The Hobbit* was published, Tolkien held a Christmas lecture about dragons for children in the natural science (!) museum, during which he also showed some of his sketches. In his academic work, too, Tolkien was occupied with dragons now and then, for instance in his lecture "*Beowulf*: The Monsters and The Critics"[5], and in the essay "On Translating Beowulf"[6].

The focal point of this article is **Farmer Giles of Ham.** We begin with a short introduction to the mythology and history of dragons in Western culture, to which Tolkien refers in the first place, and a general overview of dragons in Tolkien's works. After a look at the various editions of **Farmer Giles** [**Farmer Giles of Ham**] we will take a closer look at the topics and motifs from myths, sagas and tales used therein as well as at Tolkien's humour in this story and the tradition in which he participates. After a survey of the influence which the story has had on modern dragon stories, we will conclude by showing in how many different regards **Farmer Giles** is a prototype of the dragon story, and that it is typical for Tolkien's way of storytelling and humour in more than one sense.

WESTERN TRADITION BEFORE TOLKIEN

Following the same pattern as he did in other areas, Tolkien united different myths and sagas for his dragons. For thousands of years dragons have been seen as mythological, mostly winged creatures that are usually equated with snakes. Often they are very mighty, such as the goddess Tiamat, a female dragon, that was killed by Marduk, the highest god of the Assyrians and Babylonians, god of light and life; according to the myth of creation *Enuma Elish* he formed heaven and earth

from her corpse and mankind from her blood and clay. In Hindu belief Vishnu and his spouse Lakshmi rested in the "sea of milk", carried by the male dragon (or snake) Ananta with a thousand heads, the embodiment of all cosmic energies, who was left after heaven, earth and underworld evolved from the First Ocean. At the end of all times, Ananta will spit venomous fire and destroy all creation.

The Midgard Serpent from Norse mythology, Jormungand, clasps itself around the world; Tolkien refers to it by its Norse name *Miðgarðsormr* in his Beowulf lecture (*BUK* 154); like Hel and the giant wolf Fenrir it is a child of Loki. Thor fights against it three times, and at Ragnarök they will kill each other. After Ragnarök the carrion-eating Nidhöggr (dragon of envy) will die, too; since the beginning of the world he has been gnawing at the root of the world ash Yggdrasil.

The snake in Genesis is interpreted in very different ways by the Jewish and Christian religions, and is in no way always equated with the devil. The dragons Leviatan[7] and Behemoth[8] that appear in the Hebrew Bible mostly played a role in medieval imagination and are used as metaphors in political and sociological writings since then. The story of Daniel, who killed a Babylonian dragon (idol) by feeding it with flat blobs made of pitch, grease and hair (Dan 14, 23-27), can be read as an allegory as well as a tale about a very inventive prophet.

For Christian mythology and for Tolkien's ideas about dragons the Book of Revelations is of greatest importance, in which the dragon is equated with Satan. The fight between dragon and angel shows visible parallels to the fight between Eärendil and Ancalagon, also in that respect that on both sides entire armies fought (*S* 302-303): "And there was war in heaven: Michael and his angels fought against the dragon; and the dragon fought and his angels, And prevailed not; neither was their place found any more in heaven. And the great dragon was cast out, that old serpent, called the Devil, and Satan, which deceiveth the whole world: he was cast out into the earth, and his angels were cast out with him." (Rev 12, 8-9).[9]

Apart from this early Christian tradition ideas about dragons have been marked strongly in the Occident by Greek sagas and myths. Heracles has to defeat a dragon in order to gain the Golden Apples of the Hesperides (depending on the version he does this himself or he cunningly sends someone else), and he kills the seven-headed Ladon, a version of a dragon.

Typhon, son of Gaia and Tartarus, often described as giant with a hundred dragon or snake heads; he could not be killed, but was buried by Zeus under Mount

Etna, where he spits fire even today. Perseus freed Andromeda before she was sacrificed to a dragon. Cadmus, founder and king of Thebes, killed a dragon and planted its teeth into the ground; they gave rise to the five ancestors of the Theban noble families. After his death the father of Europe is said to have been turned into a dragon.

From the early Middle Ages on, all these basic elements grew together to form different ideas and sagas, in which the dragonslayer is of higher importance than the dragon itself. One of the most famous literary versions of this in the German language is the *Nibelungenlied*[10] and in English it is the *Beowulf* epic.[11] In terms of Christian culture it is important to name the many holy dragon slayers, of whom St. George is the most outstanding example.[12] Only a few of them treat dragons in a kind way, for instance Saint Martha, who tamed the sea dragon Tarasque in the 12th century; she is still commemorated annually today in Tarascon.

According to common lore, these dragons especially like to feed on virgins, that have to be sacrificed to them; this is also the case in antiquity such as in Perseus's and Andromeda's story. In his poem "Der Taucher" ("the Diver"), the German poet Friedrich Schiller describes dragons that dwell in the deep abyss. According to some myths, dragon blood is said to make invulnerable; this is the case for Siegfried in the Nibelung saga, who took a bath in the dragon's blood. Unfortunately, a leaf on his back prevented his whole body from becoming invincible. In the *Edda,* Sigurd can understand the speech of birds after tasting the blood (the "hürnen Seyfried" has to eat the heart of the dragon to be able to do so). But on the whole it is more common that dragon blood is venomous, which is the reason why Beowulf is not so much killed by the wound that he receives by the dragon but by the venom with which it is infected. Here, Tolkien sticks very closely to the sagas, for example with Glaurung[13], also considering the dangerous, even paralyzing gaze of dragons. In this regard the dragon is a close relative of the basilisk, feared in medieval times[14].

During the Middle Ages another dragon was of importance as a symbol for the cyclical nature of the universe: the writhing Ouroborus or Uroboros, that bit itself into its tail and is related to Oceanus and the Midgard Snake. It was also the symbol of the Dragon Order[15].

Until the early 19th century it was commonly agreed upon in the Western world that dragons existed. Conrad Gessner presented them in his famous *Schlangenbuch* (Book of Snakes, 1589), as did other famous zoologists like Ulisse Aldrovandi in his *Serpentum et*

Draconum historia (1605) and the unknown author of the *Musaeum Hermeticum* (1678). The Lindwurmbrunnen (dragon well) in Klagenfurth, Austria (created around 1590) is just one example for the widespread dissemination of ideas about dragons; other examples are siege machinery formed as a dragon (around 1465) and the depiction of the "Kriegsfurie" (war fury) as a dragon on a copperplate print by Jacques Callot (around 1630). On the coat of arms of the Duke of Marlborough two dragons are shown and one can be seen on the Welsh flag. It is therefore no wonder that dragon stories were and are also common in literature. With **Farmer Giles of Ham** Tolkien became a member of a respectable tradition, to which we can, among many other stories, count the humorous dragon tales of the well-known author of children's books Edith Nesbit (1858-1924), an author of which Tolkien was fond.[16]

TOLKIEN'S DRAGONS

Let us at first take a look at the dragons beyond Middle-earth (excepting, of course, **Farmer Giles of Ham**; which will be examined more closely later on).

In the earliest published work in which a dragon plays an important role, the poem "The Hoard"[17], a very typical young dragon kills a dwarf and takes his treasure. He guards his hoard greedily until he is very old and slain by a young warrior:

> There was an old dragon under grey stone;
> his red eyes blinked as he lay alone.
> His joy was dead and his youth spent,
> he was knobbed and wrinkled, and his limbs bent
> in the long years to his gold chained;
> in his heart's furnace the fire waned.
> To his belly's slime gems stuck thick,
> silver and gold he would snuff and lick:
> he knew the place of the least ring
> beneath the shadow of his black wing.
> Of thieves he thought on his hard bed,
> and dreamed that on their flesh he fed,
> their bones crushed, and their blood drank:
> his ears drooped and his breath sank.
> Mail-rings rang. He heard them not.
> A voice echoed in his deep grot:
> a young warrior with a bright sword
> called him forth to defend his hoard.
> His teeth were knives, and of horn his hide,
> but iron tore him, and his flame died.

(ATB 108)

This poem is a wonderfully melancholic and moral ballad about greed and the loss of magic and beauty in the world; the character of the dragon is, like all other protagonists, kept deliberately stereotypical.

The white dragon in *Roverandom*[18] comes from the moon, as all white dragons do according to this story. In olden times he lived on the earth and fought in

Merlin and Arthur's time with the red dragon of Caer-dragon ("Castle of Dragons"); here Tolkien refers to an old legend, in which the red dragon of the Celts was defeated by the white dragon of the Anglo-Saxons. The white dragon from the moon is able to breathe red or green fire with which he can dye the moon red; sometimes he also darkens it with his smoke. When it comes to such a lunar eclipse, the Man in the Moon has to fix the problem with strong magic charms. After the dragon was awakened by the moon dogs Rover and Roverandom and had chased them over the moon, the Man in the Moon manages to make him crash with a charm. Because of this charm, the white dragon has now black spots on his belly and is therefore called the Mottled Monster (*R* 43-45). We notice by means of this example, as in many other situations in *Roverandom,* how much Tolkien likes to unfold stories which explain reality through myths and tales, and phenomena of the primary world through events or conditions of the secondary world. We will also see this pattern later on in *Farmer Giles of Ham.*[19]

Apart from the scholarly works on *Beowulf* and *On Fairy-Stories,* there are no other dragons outside of Middle-earth apart from the one in *Farmer Giles.* This is why we will take a brief look at the dragons in Middle-earth now. They are quite remarkable, as Tolkien developed a consistent overall concept with them. While the dragons examined previously, which were mostly thought up for children, are rather humorous and entertaining (except the dragon in "The Hoard", which fulfils a prototypical function), the ones of Middle-earth have to be taken absolutely seriously because they are thoroughly perfected in terms of mythology, biology and literature.

Tolkien developed an extended and conclusive evolutionary history for the dragons of Middle-earth. They were created by Melkor in Angband by breeding, magical manipulation and combination of different creatures, e.g. captured eagles.[20]

The first dragons in Middle-earth were the wingless Urulóki ("fire-drakes"), that looked like giant saurians. The most powerful of them was their progenitor, Glaurung the Golden. They could breathe magic fire; like in many sagas their excrement and their blood was poisonous (*S* 260, 266). They were intelligent, vain, malicious and able to talk; some of them also had magic at their disposal. Glaurung, for example, enchanted Túrin and Niënor with his gaze (*S* 255-256, 261, 267). Whether we should take his name "father of dragons" literally has to remain undecided, but it is still imaginable that the other dragons really were his descendants.[21]

Later on Melkor bred two other variations of dragons: cold-drakes, which could fly excellently but breathed no fire and the winged fire-dragons (like Smaug), which moved rather clumsily in the air and looked a bit like giant bats. The latter's fire was magical and so strong that it probably even could have destroyed the Rings of Power, except the One.[22] The mightiest Fire Dragon was Ancalagon the Black, vanquished by Earendil in the last battle of the First Age.[23] In the Second and the Third Age there were still cold-drakes[24] and fire-dragons like Smaug in existence.[25]

FARMER GILES OF HAM

The subheading of the story alone shows through its language and layout that *Farmer* [*Farmer Giles of Ham*] is a humorous story.

Aegidii Ahenobarbi Julii Agricole de Hammo
Domini de Domito
Aule Draconarie Comitis
Regni Minimi Regis
et Basilei mira facinora
et mirabilis

or in the vulgar tongue

The Rise and Wonderful Adventures
of Farmer Giles, Lord of Tame,
Count of Worminghall
and King of the Little Kingdom

Tolkien wrote this story around 1936 and offered it to Allen & Unwin in 1937; the publishing house rejected it. In 1938 he revised it for a lecture in front of a student union, and the revised version was accepted by the publishers. Because of the beginning war, the following economic lull and the shortage of paper as well as disagreements concerning the illustrations, the story was published only later on in 1949, and one year later in the US. In 1955 it was published in Germany by Reclam (in English). Several reprints and translations followed in Swedish (1961), Polish (1965), Hebrew (1968), Dutch (1971), Italian (1975), French (1975) and Japanese (1975). The first German edition was published bilingually in 1970, a licensed edition followed in 1974 by the publishing company dtv and in 1992 and 1999 new editions were made available; both had a slightly changed title. The publishing house Klett-Cotta published the story in the anthology *Fabelhafte Geschichten* (fabulous stories) in 1975.

CONTENT, TOPIC AND MOTIFS

As in "The Hoard", a dragon and a treasure are two of the main "ingredients" in this profound and humorous story. Another is the Farmer mentioned in the title, and yet there are many more subtly described protagonists. Tolkien writes this mock-heroic tale as if it were a dubious report taken from a medieval family chronicle; the bombastic subheading and the frequent use of Latin words in the tale alone plainly show this. And in a pseudo-scholarly preface he supports this:

Of the history of the Little Kingdom few fragments have survived; but by chance an account of its origin has been preserved: a legend, perhaps, rather than an account; for it is evidently a late compilation, full of marvels, derived not from sober annals, but from the popular lays to which its author frequently refers. For him the events that he records lay already in a distant past; but he seems, nonetheless, to have lived himself in the lands of the Little Kingdom. [. . .] Since Brutus came to Britain many kings and realms have come and gone. The partition under Locrin, Camber, and Albanac, was only the first of many shifting divisions. What with the love of petty independence on the one hand, and on the other the greed of kings for wider realms, the years were filled with swift alternations of war and peace, of mirth and woe, as historians of the reign of Arthur tell us: a time of unsettled frontiers, when men might rise or fall suddenly, and songwriters had abundant material and eager audiences. Somewhere in those long years, after the days of King Coel maybe, but before Arthur or the Seven Kingdoms of the English, we must place the events here related; and their scene is the valley of the Thames, with an excursion northwest to the walls of Wales.

(FGH [Farmer Giles of Ham] 3-4)

This is the place where, supposedly during the 5th century, Farmer Giles, his wife and his trusting, if also cowardly, dog Garm live a contented life in a little village until the onset of various adventures begins. Giles defeats a giant by accident and becomes a local hero. He unintentionally defeats the dragon Chrysophylax twice, and together with the dragon defends his and the people's rights against their greedy king, thus in the end he becomes king himself.

This story is one of the best that Tolkien ever wrote. It is not only full of humour and fantastical imagination, but also contains irony and sarcasm. This "fairy-story" in the Tolkienian sense (OFS)[26] is at the same time a very successful classical fantasy story (e.g. following Weinreich's definition 32-38), a political parable, a satire and a socially edifying text[27]—and, last but not least, a linguistic pun and a highly enjoyable piece of literature.

In this story Tolkien uses many popular mythological, legendary and literary topics.

First, the "hero": he is, like in many (folk) tales and sagas a "naïve fool", but stands out due to a great portion of native cunning (just think of Gulliver). Good-natured, traditional and rather cowardly, he grows cleverer during the story, even nearly wise and shows a "laudable discretion" (*FGH* 47)—an absolutely prototypical development in many tales.

Second, the magic weapon is so common in myths, tales and fantasy that it has become a true cliché and is often parodied. Thanks to their magic swords,

Arthur, Elric and many others who win numerous fights and entire kingdoms. In connection with dragons, it is especially worth mentioning the swords Gram, the sword of Sigurd (in Richard Wagner's opera version called Notung/Nothung), and Siegfried's sword Balmung.[28]

Third the enemy is, of course, also of great importance. In his lecture on *Beowulf* Tolkien pointed out how important it is to have a mighty and convincing enemy for the hero; indeed, one could almost say that the whole lecture is basically about this message (its name was not chosen without reason: *The Monsters and the Critics*). Only the right enemy lets the "average" hero become a "special" one:

> The same heroic plot can yield good and bad poems, and good and bad sagas. The recipe for the central situations of such stories, studied in the abstract, is after all as 'simple' and as 'typical' as that of folktales. There are in any case many heroes but very few good dragons. [. . .] Something more significant than a standard hero, a man faced with a foe more evil than any human enemy of house or realm, is before us, and yet incarnate in time, walking in heroic history [. . .]
>
> *(BMC 17)*

This is the case in the stories of Beren and of Túrin, of Eärendil and of Gil-galad, of Aragorn and of Frodo: Only by their enemies (which can be monsters, adverse circumstances or even a ring) and their efforts to overcome them do they become truly exceptional heroes. And this is also the case with Giles, who is cheered and applauded because he is seen as a beacon of heroism (and potential employer), when he forces the dragon into the village (*FGH* 49).

Of course, the classical dragon is the ideal enemy and at best only beaten by a deity or someone of similar quality in the myth as in the fairy story (this is also borne out in many new novels):

> He esteemed dragons, as rare as they are dire, as some do still. He liked them—as a poet, not as a sober zoologist; and he had good reason.
>
> *(BMC 12)*

> As for the dragon: as far as we know anything about these old poets, we know this: the prince of the heroes of the North [. . .] was a dragon slayer. And his most renowned deed [. . .] was the slaying of the prince of legendary worms. Although there is plainly considerable difference between the later Norse and the ancient English form of the story alluded to in *Beowulf,* already there it had these two primary features: the dragon, and the slaying of him as the chief deed of the greatest of heroes [. . .] A dragon is no idle fancy. Whatever may be his origins, in fact or invention, the dragon in legend is a potent creation of men's imagination, richer in significance than his barrow is in gold.
>
> *(BMC 16)*

And Chrysophylax, like Smaug (and created almost at the same time), is a nearly perfect prototype of a dragon: powerful, strong and brave—he kills and drives off a horde of knights—fire-breathing and winged, intelligent and cunning, experienced and clever, deceitful but also a bit cowardly. He is not really "bad", whatever that may be, and his behaviour is more a reaction to the circumstances than anything else. So at the end he becomes an ally against the incompetent bureaucratic representatives of an exploitative regime and allows the hero to preserve his moral integrity, without having to get his hands dirty in the business of civil insurrection.[29] At the end, Chrysophylax is powerful enough to drive out a young dragon from his cave and to give the giant a piece of his mind—it is a happy ending for him, too. Chrysophylax, to conclude, is the perfect enemy in a (comparatively) bloodless, but exciting story.

Other classical topics in myths and legends are, of course, the stupid, incompetent, selfish, greedy and exploitative master/politician and the cowardly, incompetent knights. The contrast between the "simple man" and the aristocracy, between the honest labour in the house and on the farm as well as the courtly fuss is pointed out. The decadence of the upper class is typical of many tales and often has a political message. However, like in many other folk tales the system itself is not questioned or exchanged. In this case the more or less enlightened monarchy and its system of aristocracy/knights remains, but the unworthy in power are replaced by (it is to be hoped) better ones. The only things that disappear are the—nicely caricatured—decadent forms of behaviour and the exaggerated bureaucracy.

Two of the characters in the story mirror classical, literary and mythological characters: the parson, who discovers the secret of the sword, is the clever advisor, well-read and familiar with foreign languages and texts. He is more than the wise and magically or scientifically educated advisor, like Nestor or Dumbledore, for as a parson he is at the same time a spiritual advisor; with that he fulfills the same two functions as Merlin, who was, at least according to the most widespread myth-making, as a druid active in the field of politics and science, as well as religion.

The male form of "Cassandra", the augur of ill, is the blacksmith, "a slow, gloomy man, vulgarly known as Sunny Sam, though his proper name was Fabricius Cunctator" (*FGH* 24). But unlike Cassandra, he is wrong with his warnings of disaster. His Latin surname can be traced back to a popular, pre-Christian Roman general, consul and dictator.[30]

The clever grey mare brings to mind numerous horses that play important roles in myths and tales, from Od-in's eight-legged steed Sleipnir to the many speaking steeds in especially Eastern European and Oriental tales. In these a seemingly old, usually forgotten or neglected mare often turns into a spirited horse for the hero. Although the grey mare does not do exactly this, she becomes braver and has many shrewd ideas.

Garm, the speaking, rather cowardly dog, is almost a parody of a companion and guardian. Named after the giant, four-eyed dog of the Norse goddess of death, Hel, who will die during Ragnarök by killing Tyr, the dog Garm, Giles's dog, is just the exact opposite of a frightening beast and a rather amusing sidekick.

HUMOUR IN "GOOD" TRADITION

Explaining real phenomena by, in the broadest sense, fantastic, and quite often transcendental ideas is possibly as old as mankind. We can find it in religions and myths—consider, for instance, the Greek stories which try to explain lightning and thunder, volcanos and echoes—as well as in philosophy. But on the literary level, too, there have been early attempts to explain reality by myths or fairy-tales, or (to use Tolkien's count of worlds) phenomena of the primary world by events or conditions in the secondary world. We can state that even the early epic of Gilgamesh belongs to this category of tales.

We now turn to the special area of humorous interpretation or explanation that can be found in *Farmer Giles of Ham*. That Tolkien is here partaking in a long and respectable tradition can be demonstrated by the following examples.

It was already Aristophanes (ca. 448-ca. 385 B.C.), one of the most important representatives of Greek comedy, who portrayed the mythological explanations of the forces of nature in a parodistic way. In the comedy *Eirene* (421 B.C., "The Peace") a wine-grower flies into the Olymp on a dung beetle to ask Zeus about the war, and he learns that thunder is caused by Zeus's breaking wind.

The Brothers Grimm sometimes also tried to explain reality in a humorous way; some of their tales have an air of parody and explain unfamiliar phenomena. In modern fantasy there is a broad range of humorous explanations of our world, and it is often hard to differentiate between an explanation of commonly accepted phenomena and descriptions "invented" by the authors themselves. Edith Nesbit and Arthur Conan Doyle have been already mentioned, newer authors are, for example, Robert Lynn Asprin and Roger Zelazny. Tolkien himself describes events in our world in *Roverandom* and in the *Father Christmas Letters,* such as the aforementioned lunar eclipses or conspicuously big Northern Lights: the polar bear Karhu, one of Father Christmas's helpers, sets all Northern Lights for the next two years off. Thus, a gigantic firework erupts, the moon splits into four parts, and the Man in the Moon falls down into the kitchen garden of Father Christmas (*FC* 1926). Tolkien provides an especially odd description of the invention of golf. In 1147, Shire reckoning (in 2747 of the Second Age), a group of orcs under their leader Golfimbul attacked the Shire and were defeated by the hobbits at the Battle of the Green Fields. The hobbit-troops were led by

> [. . .] Old Took's great-granduncle Bullroarer, who was so huge (for a hobbit) that he could ride a horse. He charged the ranks of the goblins of Mount Gram in the Battle of the Green Fields, and knocked their king Golfimbul's head clean off with a wooden club. It sailed a hundred yards through the air and went down a rabbit hole, and in this way the battle was won and the game of Golf invented at the same moment.
>
> (*H* 17)

In *Farmer Giles of Ham* we also find such a humorous explanation, where the fantastic secondary world is connected to our primary world. In this case Tolkien's professional field is concerned: philology. In the preface he explains: "An excuse for presenting a translation of this curious tale [. . .] may be found in the glimpse that it affords of life in a dark period of the history of Britain, not to mention the light that it throws on the origin of some difficult place-names" (*FGH* 3). And towards the end of the story he writes:

> Now those who live still in the lands of the Little Kingdom will observe in this history the true explanation of the names that some of its towns and villages bear in our time. For the learned in such matters inform us that Ham, being made the chief town of the new realm, by a natural confusion between the Lord of Ham and the Lord of Tame, became known by the latter name, which it retains to this day; for Thame with an h is a folly without warrant. Whereas in memory of the dragon, upon whom their fame and fortune were founded, the Draconarii built themselves a great house, four miles north-west of Tame, upon the spot where Giles and Chrysophylax first made acquaintance. That place became known throughout the kingdom as Aula Draconaria, or in the vulgar Worminghall, after the king's name and his standard.
>
> The face of the land has changed since that time, and kingdoms have come and gone; woods have fallen, and rivers have shifted, and only the hills remain, and they are worn down by the rain and the wind. But still that name endures; though men now call it Wunnle (or so I am told); for villages have fallen from their pride. But in the days of which this tale speaks Worminghall it was.
>
> (*FGH* 56)

Tolkien acknowledges in the preface that the story is also worth reading for those who have no special in-

terest in his games with language: "Some may find the character and adventures of its hero attractive in themselves." (*FGH* 3).

Tolkien's explanations of lunar eclipses, names of rivers and the game of golf are so wonderfully absurd that they can indeed compete with the things produced on this subject by other great authors in the last years. The following authors are notable for this (and their works recommended for reading): Douglas Adams with *The Hitchhiker's Guide to the Galaxy* and its fellow volumes, Eoin Colfer with his five *Artemis Fowl* novels and Joanne K. Rowling (although her funniest explanations of the world are not in her *Harry Potter* novels, but in the pseudo-school book *Quidditch Through the Ages*). These three authors demonstrate that Tolkien and his humour in *Farmer Giles* belongs to a good, long and continuing tradition.

INFLUENCE ON MODERN DRAGON STORIES

Tolkien's Chrysophylax is a prototype, and Tolkien's mastery as an author is of such import that *Farmer Giles* had a strong influence on subsequent dragon stories (the numerous homages or persiflages are not meant here).

While Nesbit described rather funny and atypical dragons in the aforementioned stories, Tolkien was the first who awarded a typical, dangerous dragon positive aspects (this was not the case in *The Hobbit!*) and described a kind of "Gentlemen's Agreement" or "peaceful coexistence" between dragon and human.

Since then numerous works have been published in which dragons are portrayed as powerful, positive, and wise, and this not only in foreign worlds where dragons have another descent, such as the *Dragon-riders of Pern* cycle by Anne McCaffrey. Some of the highlights of dragon literature are the dragon books by Barbara Hambly, which deal with the story of the black dragon Morkeleb, and the *Earthsea* novels by Ursula K. Le Guin.

Following the tradition of *Farmer Giles of Ham* are Roger Zelazny, who inverts the circumstances in "The Monster and the Maiden", and Isaac Asimov with the wonderful parody "Prince Delightful and the Flameless Dragon". Tolkien's influence with Chrysophylax and Smaug on dragon and fantasy literature cannot be measured highly enough.

CONCLUDING REMARKS

Farmer Giles of Ham is the prototype of a dragon story. Tolkien describes a thoroughly "classical" dragon and a thoroughly classical dragon slayer story which nevertheless has a parodistic spin. This story contains everything necessary for such a tale, and Tolkien uses typical literary and mythological topoi which also make him an outstanding role model for modern authors like, for instance, Rowling.

In more than one way, this story is typical for Tolkien: it shows his humour, which is also evident in *The Hobbit* and his other works, and with which he belongs in a good tradition, as well as the fun he has playing with history and language and his passion for explaining phenomenon of the real world by means of literary, invented events in a secondary world.

Thus, this story, like others of his so often underestimated "smaller works", shows Tolkien's humorous and highly entertaining side, as the master of the small form.

Notes

1. Translated by Julia Bachale (www.jbachale.de).

2. "I desired dragons with a profound desire. Of course, I in my timid body did not wish to have them in the neighbourhood, intruding into my relatively safe world, in which it was, for instance, possible to read stories in peace of mind, free from fear. But the world that contained even the imagination of Fàfnir was richer and more beautiful, at whatever cost of peril" (OFS 135).

3. Glórund is one of several early forms of Glaurung, whom I will discuss later on. Even if Glórund's story was only published posthumously in *The Silmarillion,* it was finished in its most important features around 1919 ("Turambar and the Foalóke", *CH* 9).

4. Concerning the context of the story and characteristics of the dragon described, see Part 3 of the present paper: "Tolkien's Dragons".

5. Held in 1936 before the British Academy, published in 1937 in the "Proceedings of the British Academy 22" (*MC* 5-48).

6. "Prefatory Remarks on Prose Translation of *Beowulf*" about "Beowulf and the Finnesburg Fragment: A Translation into Modern English Prose", revised edition of the Beowulf translation by John R. Clark Hall (1911 by C. L. Wrenn, 1940) (*MC* 49-71).

7. Also *Leviathan,* from the Hebrew word liwyatan (serpentine animal): dragon of the ancient oriental mythology, described in Job 40 and 41 as a terrible flame-spitting, plated monster, symbol of chaos and the world powers that are hostile to god, and it is killed by god: "In that day the LORD with his sore and great and strong sword shall punish leviathan the piercing serpent, even leviathan that crooked serpent; and he shall slay the dragon that is in the sea" (Jes 27, 1; King James Bible).

8. According to Job 40, 15-24, it is a vegetarian counterpart to Leviathan that lives on dry land, and is sometimes taken to be a hippopotamus; in the apocryphal 1st Book of Henoch (Ethiopian book of Henoch) it appears as the male counterpart to the female Leviathan, together with her sent by god as a scourge for mankind and being Lord of the Desert (1st Hen 59,7 fp.); in the Middle Ages often presented as a demon, servant of the devil and "cupbearer and cellarman of Hell".

9. There are only few biblical books that can be (and are) interpreted so diversely. In art history the Book of Revelations has a high status. "The Apocalypse had an influence on hundreds of books and films. First and foremost it is complicated to interpret the relation between the dragon and the beast, which has the number 666 and is often equated with the antichrist and which is finally defeated by the lamb" (Rev 13, 1-18).

10. Epic, written down by an unknown poet at the end of the 12th century with strong influence on modern art, for example on Richard Wagner and Tolkien.

11. As mentioned before, Tolkien has occupied himself with this work very carefully; for him as a specialist in Anglo-Saxon language the Beowulf epic as an epochal work for English literature (the title has been added to the text only in 1805, named after the main character) was a target of scholarly approach as well as a source of inspiration from early childhood on. It is seen as the most important Anglo-Saxon heroic epic, the most extensive preserved Old Germanic epic song and the first big epic in verses, which has been written and handed down in a Germanic vernacular speech. It takes place in a later time than the "Nibelungenlied", in the Swedish Götaland in the first half of the 6th century. It is possible that this combination of Scandinavian history, antique examples, pagan mythology and Christian elements was written down during the 8th or 9th century by an educated monk. In *Beowulf* one can find some roots of parts of the Siegfried saga, the "Nibelungenlied".

12. According to Markus Heitz, a German author of fantasy literature, the Austrian Museum of Folklore presented in an exhibition 83 different dragon saints, most of them men that had killed dragons; all of them were recognized as authentic by the catholic church.

13. This is similar in many other tales. In several tales of the Grimm Brothers the venom in the dragon's blood overwhelms and kills the heroes; and J. K. Rowling introduces at least 12 different forms of usage for dragon blood in her *Harry Potter* series.

14. According to Hildegard of Bingen, the "King of Snakes" (Greek: basileus = king), hatches from the egg of a snake, which is bred by a toad. Even in the ancient world there were rumours about its all-petrifying gaze and its breath of pestilence, which created the desert. The sometimes winged monster with the head of a bird and the body of a snake could only be killed by the smell of a weasel or the crowing of a rooster. According to the *Malleus maleficarum* of 1487 the basilisk hatches from the egg of a seven to nine year-old rooster that has been bred by a road, and it brings death, the plague and drought. It can only be killed by reflecting its gaze in a mirror. The monster in Terry Gilliam's film *Jabberwocky* is one kind of basilisk; the most popular basilisk nowadays is killed by Harry Potter in his second year at Hogwarts.

15. The "gesellschaft mit dem trakchen" (society with the dragon), also called "ordo draconis" and "societas draconia/draconis", was founded in 1408 by Sigismund of Luxembourg (1368-1437, Hungarian king in 1387, German king in 1411, emperor in 1433) in order to fight the Pagans (the Turks) and the "im Verborgenen wütenden Christen" (Christians that rage in secret; i.e. the Hussites); its motto was: "O quam misericors est Deus justus et pius" ("Oh, the Lord is merciful, just and devout"). Among its members were Vlad Dracul the Second and his son, Vlad Tepes Draculea the Third, that have indirectly given the vampire Dracula his name.

16. E.g. the book *The Seven Dragons* (1899) and the story *The Last Of The Dragons* (1925). The female author of over 40 children's books (1858-1924) is seen as both a classic and trailblazer of English children's literature; she influenced Tolkien (one of her characters was the base for the Psamathists, the sand sorcerors, in *Roverandom*) and besides C. S. Lewis she is the outstanding idol of Joanne K. Rowling. Nesbit, Tolkien and Rowling belong to the same tradition not only because of their use of dragons, but also because of their humour (see also footnote 31).

17. First published in 1923 in another version with the title "lúmonna Gold Galdre Bewunden" in *The Gryphon* (New Series, Vol. IV No. 4, January 1923, p. 130, Leeds University, Swan Press, Leeds), then in 1937 with the same title in *The Oxford Magazine* (Vol. LV No. 15, 4. March 1937, p. 473, Oxford, The Oxonian Press) and then in 1962 as 14th poem with the title "The Hoard" in *The Adventures of Tom Bombadil and other verses from The Red Book*; in 1970 again published with the title "The Hoard" in *The Hamish Hamilton Book of Dragons* (ed. Roger Lancelyn Green, p. 246-248, Hamish Hamilton, London).

18. Tolkien told this story to his children in 1925 intending to comfort his son Michael, who had lost his black and white toy dog at the beach during the summer holidays. It was written down in 1927 at the latest; in 1936 it was offered to George Allen & Unwin, but the publishing house rejected it. The story was finally published in 1998.

19. Of course *The Lord of the Rings* can be read in this way, too. Many other authors liked to write in a similar vein; this pattern can already be found in texts from the ancient world. Nesbit had it mastered to perfection, Arthur Conan Doyle loved it and Rowling, too, is proficient in it; see also Section 4.2. The reliance on patterns of myth is also a distinguishing feature of the *Letters from Father Christmas*. In one of them Tolkien explains how it came to a lunar eclipse in 1927: The Man in the Moon had visited Father Christmas at the North Pole, where he had eaten and drunk too much and overslept, so he had not returned to the moon in time. The dragons of the moon had dared to come out and caused the lunar eclipse by producing too much smoke (*FC* 1927).

20. "Men dwelt in darkness and were troubled by many evil things that Morgoth had devised in the days of his dominion: demons, and dragons, and misshapen beasts, and the unclean Orcs that are mockeries of the Children of Iluvatar" (*S* 310). Further information on biology and evolutionary history of dragons, is found in Schneidewind, *Biology*.

21. In *The Children of Húrin* Glaurung is introduced and described in more detail than in *The Silmarillion*, but regarding his main characteristics he stays the same.

22. "It has been said that dragon-fire could melt and consume the Rings of Power, but there is not now any dragon left on earth in which the old fire is hot enough; nor was there ever any dragon, not even Ancalagon the Black, who could have harmed the One Ring, the Ruling Ring, for that was made by Sauron himself" (*LotR* 70).

23. In his last battle against the Valar, Morgoth "loosed upon his foes the last desperate assault that he had prepared, and out of the pits of Angband there issued the winged dragons, that had not before been seen; and so sudden and ruinous was the onset of that dreadful fleet that the host of the Valar was driven back, for the coming of the

dragons was with great thunder, and lightning, and a tempest of fire" (*S* 302). As already mentioned, this battle calls to mind the Book of Revelations, chapter 12.

24. In the 21st century of the Third Age Fram of Rohan killed the dragon Scatha (*LotR* III, 246); Dáin I., King of the dwarfs, and his second son Frór were "slain by a great cold-drake" in the entrance of his palace in Ered Mithrin in the year 2589 of the same Age (*LotR* III, 353).

25. "Smaug the Golden" was the "greatest of the dragons of his day" (*LotR* III, 353). So there must have been more dragons, at least in the time of the expulsion of the dwarves from Erebor, 250 years before the Ring War. Tolkien also thought about the possibility that dragons could have survived the Third Age: "Dragons. They had not stopped; since they were active in far later times, close to our own. Have I said anything to suggest the final ending of dragons? If so it should be altered" (*L* No. 144, 177). If fire-drakes, cold-drakes and fire-dragons had survived and if there had also been surviving cross breeds, this would explain all forms of myths and legends concerning dragons—this is again an example of Tolkien's ability to explain phenomena of the real world with the fantasy world.

26. It fulfills every condition Tolkien demands of a fairy-story: "Fantasy, Recovery, Escape and Consolation", OFS 138-154). The political and social aspects are most important for the latter (see also footnote 30).

27. It speaks, among other things, about greed, power and exploitation, about cowardice and egoism, about bureaucracy and group pressure, about justice and the moral legitimation of power and finally about a nearly peaceful "bottom-up revolution"—much of this can mean "consolation" in the Tolkienian sense (OFS, pp. 153-155). Political and social aspects are no novelty in fantastic literature, just think of Swift, Mark Twain and Orwell, or more currently the *Bartimaeus*-trilogy by Jonathan Stroud and the *Harry Potter* novels by J. K. Rowling.

28. Tolkien does not parody the sword, he puts emphasis on fulfilling his own demands on a fairy story: "There is one proviso: if there is any satire present in the tale, one thing must not be made fun of, the magic itself. That must in that story be taken seriously, neither laughed at nor explained away" (OFS 114). The farmer, the king, the knights, even the dragon can be humorous, but never ever the magical sword!

29. This gives rise to some interesting questions: From what point on can we act against the regime in a justified way? When does the "popular opinion" turn into dangerous injustice on its own behalf? Tolkien gives us a lot to think about in the guise of an innocent story.

30. Quintus Fabius Maximus Verrucosus (verrusosus: lat., warty), ca. 275-203 B.C., general of the Roman Republic, five times consul and twice dictator, fought against Hannibal during the Second Punic War; because of his defensive warfare he was called *Cunctator,* the hesitator. At first, this was an abuse, but after the defeat of Cannae 216 B.C. it became a title of honour. Later on he became the stereotype of the deliberately tough Roman. Fabianism and the Fabian Society are named after him; one of their founders was Edith Nesbit (see also footnote 15). It is quite fitting with the development in the Little Kingdom since the Fabian Society, as a socialist and intellectual movement (and precursor of the Labour Party), wants to turn society in a revolutionary way into the direction of a pure and simple life.

Works Cited

Asimov, Isaac. "Prince Delightful and the Flameless Dragon" (1991). *Magic: The Final Fantasy Collection.* London: HarperCollins Publishers, 1996.

The Bible, King James Version [http://www.gutenberg.org/etext/10 and also http://www.bibleserver.com. cited 9.2.2008].

Gier, Kerstin. "Jeremy Ohneland und der Drache". *Das Vermächtnis des Rings.* Stefan Bauer (Hg.). Bergisch Gladbach: Bastei-Lübbe, 2001. 13-68.

Hammond, Wayne G. and Christina Scull. *J. R. R. Tolkien: Artist & Illustrator.* London: HarperCollins Publishers, 1995.

Nesbit, Edith. *The Last of the Dragons and Some Others.* London: Puffin Books, 1985.

———. *The Seven Dragons and Other Stories.* [no place]: Alan Rodgers Books, 2006.

Schneidewind, Friedhelm. *Lexikon von Himmel und Hölle.* Berlin: Lexikon Imprint Verlag, 2000.

———. "Biologie, Genetik und Evolution in Mittelerde". *Tolkiens Weltbild(er).* Thomas Formet-Ponse et. al. (Hg). *Hither Shore* 2. Interdisciplinary Journal on Modern Fantasy Literature. Jahrbuch der Deutschen Tolkien Gesellschaft e. V. (DTG). Düsseldorf: Scriptorium Oxoniae, 2006. 41-66.

———. *Drachen. Das Schmökerlexikon.* Saarbrücken: Verlag der Villa Fledermaus, 2008.

Tolkien, John Ronald Reuel. "*Beowulf:* The Monsters and the Critics" (first published 1937). *The Monsters and the Critics and Other Essays.* London: George Allen & Unwin, 1983. 5-48.

———. *The Hobbit or There And Back Again* (1937). Revised Edition. New York: Ballantine Books, 1982.

———. "On Translating Beowulf" (1941). *The Monsters and the Critics and Other Essays.* London: George Allen & Unwin, 1983. 49-71.

———. "On Fairy Stories" (1947). *The Monsters and the Critics and Other Essays.* London: George Allen & Unwin, 1983. 109-161.

———. "Farmer Giles of Ham" (1949). *Tales from The Perilous Realm.* London: HarperCollins Publishers, 2002. 1-57.

———. *Die Geschichte von dem Bauern Giles und dem Drachen Chrysophylax.* zweisprachige Ausgabe. Ebenhausen near München: Verlag Langewiesche-Brandt, 1970.

———. *Farmer Giles of Ham—Die Geschichte vom Bauern Giles und dem Drachen.* Bilingual edition. München: Deutscher Taschenbuch Verlag, 1974.

———. "Bauer Giles von Ham". *Fabelhafte Geschichten.* Stuttgart: Klett-Cotta, 1975.

———. *Farmer Giles of Ham—Der Bauer Giles von Ham und der Drache.* Bilingual edition. München: Deutscher Taschenbuch Verlag, 1992.

———. *Farmer Giles of Ham—Bauer Giles von Ham.* Bilingual edition. München: Deutscher Taschenbuch Verlag, 1999.

———. *The Lords of the Rings* (1954/55). London: HarperCollins, 1995.

———. "The Adventures of Tom Bombadil" (1962). *Tales from The Perilous Realm.* London: HarperCollins Publishers, 2002. 59-118.

———. *Letters from Father Christmas* (1976). Ed. Baillie Tolkien. London: HarperCollins Publishers, 1995.

———. *The Silmarillion* (1977). Ed. Christopher Tolkien. London: HarperCollins Publishers, 1999.

———. *The Letters of J. R. R. Tolkien* (1981). Ed. Humphrey Carpenter with the assistance of Christopher Tolkien. London: HarperCollins Publishers, 1995.

———. *Roverandom* (1998). Ed. Christina Scull and Wayne G. Hammond. London: HarperCollins Publishers, 1998.

———. *The Children of Hurin* (2007). Ed. Christopher Tolkien. London: HarperCollins Publishers, 2007.

Weinreich, Frank. *Fantasy. Einführung.* Essen: Oldib-Verlag, 2007.

Zelazny, Roger. "The Monster and the Maiden" (1964). *The Monster Book of Monsters.* Ed. Michael O'Shaughnessy. London: Xanadu Publications, 1988. 69-70.

Bertrand Alliot (essay date 2008)

SOURCE: Alliot, Bertrand. "The 'Meaning' of 'Leaf by Niggle.'"[1] In *Tolkien's Shorter Works: Proceedings of the 4th Seminar of the Deutsche Tolkien Gesellschaft and Walking Tree Publishers Decennial Conference,* edited by Margaret Hiley and Frank Weinreich, pp. 165-90. Zurich: Walking Tree Publishers, 2008.

[*In the following essay, Alliot interprets "Leaf by Niggle" as an allegory for Tolkien's desire to observe the rules of society while committing himself to the asocial demands of his writing.*]

The title of my paper, *The "Meaning" of Leaf, by Niggle,* may seem a bit pretentious. Nobody really knows the "meaning" of **"Leaf, by Niggle"**; there can only ever be interpretations of the text. If Tolkien were among us today he would probably tell us: "you should not talk so much about my stories but you should rather enjoy them for their own sake". In fact, it is because he wrote his stories to stimulate literary pleasure that most of them have to be appreciated for what they are: fascinating tales.

Nonetheless, if Tolkien told us this we might respond as follows: "Sorry, Professor, but **"Leaf, by Niggle"** is not a mere story and we can speak about it as much as we want since in writing it you wanted to do more than entertain us; your story is an allegory worthy of special attention". Indeed, it won't hurt for once, Tolkien used an allegorical method to write **"Leaf by Niggle,"** which is, considering his usual creative process, very uncommon. For once with Tolkien, the tale is not self-sufficient; we do not have to content ourselves with appreciating a "mere story" (*L* 144), but we can try to go beyond the words to understand a "meaning". In fact, **"Leaf, by Niggle"** gives us the opportunity to study what Tolkien "meant" whereas usually we have to be content with what his stories may mean through or even despite himself.

We will see that, throughout this little story, Tolkien presents something that worried him during his entire life: the incompatibility between the necessities of life (or the satisfaction of daily needs—in a sense almost biological needs) and artistic creation. This observation particularly affected him because he was deeply involved in the latter but, at the same time, for reasons that we will try to clarify, also quite convinced that priority must be given to the first necessity. **"Leaf by Niggle"** shows a character just as Tolkien was: tormented by this incompatibility and, no matter what, even clumsily, trying to put up with it. Despite his weakness and failures, thanks to his hopes and deep desires, he will try to find a path in a life for him made more complicated by his determination not to neglect two things driven by contradictory forces.

The "Laws" and the World Split down the Middle

First of all, **"Leaf, by Niggle"** shows the concerns the author had about what he calls the "laws". We learn at the beginning of the story that Niggle "might get a visit from an inspector" (*TL* [*Tree and Leaf*] 77) and that the latter might notice that his garden is "rather neglected" (*TL* 77). As we all know, an inspector is tasked with enforcing the law and we can already deduce that in Niggle's "world" not taking care of your garden is forbidden; it is against the law. Later, when, as expected, an inspector has arrived, we learn more about these laws. The inspector reproaches Niggle during the storm, while the Emergency Services are trying to deal with crises in the rest of the neighbourhood, for not having helped his neighbour to "make temporary repairs and prevent the damage from getting more costly to mend than necessary" (*TL* 81). The inspector even tells Niggle that he should have used the only materials available: canvas, wood and waterproof paint from his picture! Niggle seems terrified by the idea of using his picture to repair a roof but the inspector is very clear about the fact that "houses come first." As he puts it, "that is the law" (*TL* 82).

Niggle's interaction with the inspector shows us what these laws are: very basic rules to be respected under any circumstances, things that come first in order of priority. Why? Simply because not respecting them could jeopardise life itself. You first have to have a house and food; only then can you think about taking up a hobby like painting or playing football. Denis Diderot used to say, "first survive, then philosophise". This, in fact, could be the motto of Niggle's world. The laws which the inspectors have to enforce on Niggle and his fellow citizens are an allegory of what in life we cannot escape from, what was imposed on us from the very beginning of human life on earth and what we have to accept so as not to compromise our own existence in the world. In real life these laws don't need to be written down anywhere or be enforced by anyone. Still, it would be appropriate to respect them.

Two types of men make their appearance in this story, each with a very different attitude towards the laws. The first type is personified by Niggle, the second by Parish. Niggle seems to find it very difficult to comply with the laws: he is obsessed by his painting, that is to say by a creative activity, and this seems to distance him from reality and from the necessity of observing his legal duties. Parish, on the other hand, has no difficulties in adhering to the laws and we could even argue that the laws are the only things that he is aware

of. Parish does not understand the first thing about Niggle's picture but notices immediately that Niggle's garden is overrun with weeds, as is evident in the following passage:

> When Parish looked at Niggle's garden (which was often) he saw mostly weeds; and when he looked at Niggle's pictures (which was seldom) he saw only green and grey patches and black lines, which seemed to him nonsensical. He did not mind mentioning the weeds (a neighbourly duty), but he refrained from giving any opinion of the pictures.
>
> (*TL* 79)

Readers of **"Leaf by Niggle"** are given the impression that although Niggle and Parish are neighbours, they do not live on the same planet. One lives in a world where pointing out the presence of weeds is a "neighbourly duty", while the other is obsessed by his paintings. They are strangers to each other and don't see the world in the same way. Although they treat each other with respect, we still feel that they don't like each other very much.

However, to be fair, we have to mention that Niggle sometimes goes to visit Parish's planet. In fact, the story often shows Niggle trying as best he can to adhere to the laws. For instance, he abandons his picture and rides in the rain to fetch the doctor and the builder for Parish. However, importantly, he doesn't do so spontaneously but rather because he cannot escape from doing it. In a sense, the necessity of having to respect the laws catches up with him. As one of the voices says when the time comes for Niggle to be judged, "He did answer a good many Calls" (*TL* 85), mainly because he feels "things ordered by the laws" cannot be neglected. On the other hand, though, although he tries to respect the laws, he cannot help but consider them as "interruptions". This is the reason why he tries to comply with them as quickly as possible (to go back to what he likes doing most). In his haste, Niggle doesn't really fulfil his tasks to the best of his abilities. Rather, we could say that most of the time he contents himself with a "skeleton service" and this is why his case has to be considered carefully by the voices in charge of judging him. Niggle eventually does "pass the exam" but only meets minimum requirements.

It is a pity that Tolkien does not depict how Parish is judged, but we can easily imagine that he would have passed his "test" more easily than Niggle did. Considering the respect that Parish has for the laws, we can assume that he would not consider the laws as "interruptions" to the things that he would rather do, but simply as things that have to be done. In complying with the laws, he is at peace with himself. In fact, Parish seems to have quite a relaxed attitude towards life, taking things in his stride.

The particular importance Tolkien attributes to the laws in **"Leaf by Niggle"** certainly reflects a phenomenon that he seems to have been grappling with for a significant part of his life. This phenomenon can be summarised as the assumption that in everyday life the world is split in two as far as people's attitude towards the laws is concerned. In his writings, we very often find representatives of both worlds. In *The Lord of the Rings,* for instance, the Hobbits are no doubt, like Parish, very aware of the laws. They are very sensible and have both feet firmly planted on the ground. On the other hand, the Elves are "out of the world"; they are engrossed by poetry and beauty, just as Niggle is engrossed by his picture. The Elves have to force themselves when it is time for them to participate in saving Middle-earth; similarly, it takes quite some time for Niggle to finally respond to Parish's demands. But even in the small Hobbit society there are varying levels of awareness of the laws. We can imagine that what Tolkien calls a "genuine Hobbit" (*L* 105) is the type of Hobbit who has an immediate respect for the laws. Other Hobbits, like Bilbo, are more "sophisticated" in that they are haunted by the temptation to withdraw from the world and to leave their immediate surroundings for an imaginary "elsewhere". There would certainly be many other examples showing that Middle-earth's characters tend to be naturally divided into these two different camps.

It would appear that Tolkien, in terms of how he perceives the laws, falls in the Elves or Niggle rather than Hobbit or Parish camp (in **"Leaf by Niggle,"** Niggle is Tolkien himself[2]). Still, although he is perfectly aware of "belonging" to the side that attributes less importance to the laws, he nonetheless highlights the qualities of individuals "from the other side". Amongst all the races inhabiting Middle-earth, he has a clear preference for the Hobbits and amongst the Hobbits for the most law-abiding of creatures, namely Samwise Gamgee.[3] In his letters, Tolkien also shows great respect for what he calls the "dull stodges": "young men and women of sub-public school class and home backgrounds book-less and cultureless" (*L* 303-304) and of course for the common people he met in the trenches of World War I. By contrast, he distrusts those of "higher intelligence". He thinks that simple people, like Parish, are somehow superior or better than himself or others like him. Also, it is evident that during his life Tolkien tried to let himself be inspired by these simple people, forcing himself to pay more careful attention to the laws. In his letters, he often mentions the effort he is making in trying to

respect them and that his work is neither essential nor really important, that he and his correspondents should not speak too much or too seriously about it. Tolkien knew that he tended to stay shut up indoors with his only company being his "tree". To compensate for his lack of consideration for the real world he made it his duty to respond to the "calls" and to focus on the laws as much he possibly could.[4]

Why, according to Tolkien, was making so great an effort so important? Because, otherwise, we might be swept aside by life's dynamics or by the wind of history. To live, we need to eat first. Of course, we do not forget to eat because our bodies remind us to feed ourselves, but there are many other basic needs which we are not reminded of. Life within the world provides a new challenge every day, which is why we have to face reality. To remain, like Niggle, in a "tall shed" is dangerous or is a sign of obliviousness that could be fatal.

Niggle's carefree life is fragile and is only possible because others are now in charge of what Niggle previously discarded with thoughtlessness. Tolkien says Niggle "was thinking all the time about his big canvas, in the tall shed that had been built for it out in his garden (on a plot where once he had grown potatoes)" (*TL* 76). The mention of the potatoes being replaced by the tall shed is of crucial importance, because it means that there is an incompatibility between being engaged in a creative activity and responding appropriately to life's daily needs. The more time we spend painting or singing or even studying, for example, the less time we have to grow potatoes. However, what is certain is that we cannot escape from the fact that we need potatoes to survive and this is why growing potatoes should take priority. Niggle, after his course of treatment in the Workhouse, realises that Parish has been a good neighbour because he "let [him] have excellent potatoes very cheap, which saved [him] a lot of time" (*TL* 87). Niggle can devote himself to his canvas thanks to Parish's kindness, thanks to the man who does not understand anything about painting, but who is level-headed enough to deal with supplying food. In a letter to Sir Stanley Unwin, Tolkien again refers to the apparent incompatibility between art and what we could call "necessity" by saying that creative desire "seems to have no biological function, and to be apart from the satisfactions of plain ordinary biological life, with which, in our world, it is indeed usually at strife" (*L* 145).

THE LIGHT AND CONSISTENT WORLDS

This conflict or antagonism appears everywhere in Tolkien's work. It often materialises in the form of a recurring superimposition: that of the "light" world on the "consistent" world. The light world is a world where nothing really matters, where there are no consequences to one's actions, where Niggle and his canvas move for example. The consistent world, on the other hand, is where things matter. This is the world of Parish and his potatoes. In *The Lord of the Rings,* Tom Bombadil lives in the light world, while the others live in the consistent world. The moon from "The Man in the Moon" also represents the light world, whereas the earth is the consistent world. Finally, then, what is very important for Tolkien is that adventures take place in a "light world" and differ considerably from "real life" or history that are set in the "consistent world".

In *The Hobbit,* Gandalf sends Bilbo on an "adventure"; this means that the hero will not suffer any negative consequences as a result of his actions.[5] *The Lord of the Rings* begins in the same setting and the reader might think that Bilbo is about to experience another adventure. However, Frodo, the new Bilbo, is soon drawn onto a new path, that of real life. This means that his adventure has the potential to become serious and to potentially turn tragic. Here then we have the difference between adventures and history or real life. On the stairs of Cirith Ungol Sam tells Frodo the following:

> I used to think that [adventures] were things the wonderful folk of the stories went out and looked for, because they wanted them, because they were exciting and life was a bit dull, a kind of a sport, as you might say. But that's not the way of it with the tales that really mattered, or the ones that stay in the mind.
>
> (*TT* 321)

Here, we find a kind of disillusionment: the character realises that life is not a game, that it is made of "tales that really mattered", therefore of things that are not tales. As Sam is experiencing Middle-earth he progressively feels the consistency of it, and the laws (and his growing awareness of the fragility of life) are weighing more and more on his shoulders.

In *The Lord of the Rings,* Bombadil is the only character who lives in a world where nothing really matters. Firstly, he is brought into the narrative because Tolkien wanted "an adventure on the way" (*L* 192): at this stage of the story, Tolkien still thought that his new book would be intended for children, in other words, he wanted his characters to meet a new challenge that they could overcome before the next one, of course every time succeeding in being safe and sound, reaching the end victorious. Bombadil is a remnant of the country of adventures, which is why the Ring fails to affect him[6]. This is also the reason why so many people

find the character to be out of touch with the rest of the story. Secondly, Bombadil is, according to Tolkien, a "particular embodying of pure natural science" (*L* 179) which means that he "studies" natural things for no other purpose than studying itself. Like Niggle with his canvas, Bombadil is engrossed in something that is of no practical use and is therefore, by implication, locked in a type of "tall shed" of his own. Tolkien, however, does make it clear that Bombadil lives in a more consistent world: "ultimately only the victory of the West will allow Bombadil to continue, or *even to survive.* Nothing would be left for him in the world of Sauron" (*L* 179; italics added). Bombadil lives within the light world that lies within the consistent world. Tolkien's words on Bombadil highlight the fact that it would be impossible to live in a light world with an existence of its own, that would be self-sufficient with its own rules. The only rules that count are those of the consistent world that also includes the light world. There, one cannot allow oneself to be careless, the laws have to be respected and the calls have to be answered. Tolkien was most likely also tempted to stay peacefully in the shed and, like Niggle, probably also secretly dreamt of having a "public pension" that would allow him to spend more time in it. However Tolkien knew his dream to be dangerous because it would make the occasions on which he was called into the real world rarer and would result in a progressive loss of his sense of the consistent world.

Therefore, Tolkien's characters are irresistibly drawn towards the side of the consistent world: the Man in the Moon falls down to the earth, the light environment in which first Bombadil and Bilbo move (in *The Hobbit* and at the beginning of *The Lord of the Rings*) becomes progressively more consistent and "serious", adventures become history and real life, and so on. To use an image, the reader is placed with the Hobbits in a hot-air balloon that is irresistibly going down to the ground. Leaving the basket and treading land underfoot, the passengers feel themselves suddenly vulnerable because the environment has changed. This movement with which the characters are carried away, from the light to the heavy, from the air to the earth, reflects the fact that the author cannot forget the seriousness of life, this seriousness that always ends up catching up with him. He can no more free himself from the heaviness of the laws than he can escape gravity. In *The Lord of the Rings,* a poem heralds the change of tone and style and warns the reader that *terra firma* has been reached. The poem is first said by Bilbo and later by Frodo. It is almost exactly the same poem: only one word changes, a word that changes everything:

By Bilbo
The Road goes ever on and on
Down from the door where it began,
Now far ahead the Road has gone,
And I must follow, if I can,
Pursuing it with *eager* feet
Until it joins some larger way
Where many paths and errands meet.
And whither then? I cannot say.

(*LotR* 44; my emphasis)

By Frodo
The Road goes ever on and on
Down from the door where it began,
Now far ahead the Road has gone,
And I must follow, if I can,
Pursuing it with *weary* feet
Until it joins some larger way
Where many paths and errands meet.
And whither then? I cannot say.

(*LotR* 82; my emphasis)

Once 'on the ground', the atmosphere is tense because it is now filled with rules and laws that weigh on every individual, putting his or her life within impassable limits. It is precisely the presence of these limits framing life that imposes a particular discipline, that decides that not everything is possible, and that finally force the protagonist to walk hesitantly with *weary feet*. The feet are no longer *eager* because from now on, each additional step will leave on the ground a footprint, each act shall have a consequence.

By stating that the obligations and duties of every day life are in conflict with one's creative desire, Tolkien probably realised what each of us should easily be able to notice: the less one busies oneself with practical things, the less one is aware of what is important or crucial. By contrast, the more one occupies oneself with the nitty-gritty of "real" life, the more one is "in water", to borrow a Tolkienian expression'; in other words, the more one is able to face reality and to survive.

Tolkien's experience of the war probably convinced him of this and of the fact that simple people, those who naturally respond to the calls and respect the laws, are better equipped to take up the challenges we face in everyday life. Before the war, Tolkien was part of the TCBS (Tea Club and Barrovian Society): a club of four cultured and ambitious young men. According to one of them, G. B. Smith, the TCBSians wanted the members of the club "to leave the world a better place than when they found it, 'to re-establish sanity, cleanliness, and the love of real and true beauty'" (Garth 253). Tolkien himself in his early years thought the TCBSians were destined to kindle a "new light in the world at large" (*L* 10).

And how did the TCBSians think they would do that? With words: they wanted to change the world by means of poetry and art. But after his experiences in the trenches we can imagine how pretentious this appeared to Tolkien. In the trenches, those that really make a difference were not the individuals who had the pretension to change the world by writing verses but the tommy, "the plain soldier from the agricultural counties" (*L* 54). Tolkien wanted to change the world and he realised that, according to his own words, he was in the battle "inefficient and unmilitary" (*L* 54). He wanted to change the world but he couldn't efficiently participate in saving it. Therefore, he probably progressively realised the lightness of the TCBS's words and project, a project easy to formulate in the mind but reduced to nothing in the acid water of reality.

In a sense, he admired the *tommies* because they do not think too much, and instead face their challenges head on. Someone more "sophisticated", such as Niggle, Tolkien, or you and me, is too much "out of water" and out of reality. This means that if someone sophisticated sees danger coming, he/she will be thinking so much about the nature of this danger that he/she will not be able to respond to it effectively. A very intelligent individual will attentively study the situation and will soon be completely paralysed by the complexity of the problem. Intelligence or sophistication are not in keeping with courage: Rousseau already noticed that during antiquity, the less sophisticated people, those who had not been "corrupted" by *arts and sciences,* were far more courageous than the Greeks or the Romans.

REDUCING THE CONTRADICTION

Now that we know why Tolkien thought being out of real life was rather perilous and why he trusted those who were simpler than himself or Niggle, it is time to try and understand how he dealt with this apparent contradiction. We have already revealed a part of the answer. Tolkien, like Niggle, tried as much he could to respond to the calls and to respect the laws without considering them as interruptions. He also never took his creative work seriously. The voices echo that: "there are no notes in the Records of his pretending, even to himself, that [his painting activity] excused his neglect of things ordered by the laws" (*TL* 85). Tolkien thought that one should be able to make sacrifices, to give priority to the tangible rather than the abstract. The voices show leniency towards Niggle notably because he has been capable of a "genuine sacrifice"; in order to help Parish he does a "wet bicycle ride" and in so doing he "was throwing away his last chance with his picture" (*TL* 86). And what at last saves

Niggle is his sudden and almost unexpected acknowledgement: Parish "was a very good neighbour, and let me have excellent potatoes very cheap, which saved me a lot of time," Niggle says. In response, the First Voice answers, "Did he? . . . I am glad to hear it" (*TL* 87). This is exactly the kind of acknowledgement that shows the reader that the Voice is no longer sceptical about letting Niggle off. Tolkien was deeply convinced of the absolute necessity of swearing allegiance to what I, in a previous paper, have called the "simple" (Alliot).

Tolkien, despite his admiration for all things simple, did not try to become a simple man. He did not discard his creative activity because he knew that this would be impossible; the fact that he was attracted to the aesthetic was something he had to accept. "He was a painter by nature" says the Second Voice (*TL* 85), which is very true of Niggle, because in painting he simply responds to nature, thereby respecting a kind of law. To paint is not a "glamorous pose" for Niggle, but should rather be seen as a natural act. Even the voices are compelled to consider that in his favour. Another important point to consider here is that Niggle "took a great deal of pains with leaves, just for their own sake" (*TL* 85). This means that Niggle is not engrossed in a big, grandiose, complicated project and this is probably the reason why he stays humble when it comes to his work and why he is capable of fulfilling his other duties. He is not pretentious, he does not reason too much and he respects what his heart commands him to do. He focuses neither on the tree nor on the entire landscape but only on the leaves. In painting them he is only catching something that is already in the air: "It had begun with a leaf caught in the wind, and it became a tree; and the tree grew, sending out innumerable branches, and thrusting out the most fantastic roots" (*TL* 76). Everything passes through him and finally creates a painting of a greater scope that is the result of a surge, of a movement that has never stopped since the beginning of the world and that has been breathed into life by the creator himself. Tolkien's entire subcreative process is represented here. Tolkien once had an ambitious project: he planned to build a body of legend "high and purged of gross [. . .] ranging from the large and cosmogonic to the level of romantic fairy" (*L* 144) but he told Milton Waldman it was "absurd" and added:

> The mere stories were the thing. They arose in my mind as 'given' things, and as they came, separately, so too the links grew. An absorbing, though continually interrupted labour (. . .): yet always I had the sense of recording what was already 'there', somewhere: not of 'inventing'
>
> (*L* 145)

Tolkien discarded his initial complicated project to focus on the *mere stories* that are the equivalent of Niggle's leaves. This attitude reveals the subcreator's humility. The subcreator contents himself with being carried away by something that has surpassed him, something he does not need to invent but that is already there. In order to be revealed, this "something" needs to pass through somebody. Then, the subcreator has to pay attention and trust his own deep feelings: if he is attracted to fascinating stories, then he has to "follow" them and will see where they take him. The result is of course often unexpected and wonderful: *The Lord of the Rings* is the tree that emerged thanks to the confidence that Tolkien put in leaves. One can easily see that this humble attitude towards creation could prevent the widening of the gap that usually separates the creator from the world he or she is living in. The subcreator is not asked to withdraw himself from reality in inventing something that does not really exist. He or she is not engaged in a sophisticated process that could finally result in his or her isolation from real life. This attitude that characterises the creative process remains compatible with the necessary attitude that everybody has to remain plainly aware of the laws. There seems to be something like a link between having the good sense to be aware of life's challenges, while at the same time being attracted by fascinating stories. Both attitudes are a product of the same "habit of thinking".

THE 'BACK COUNTRY'

Finally, it becomes necessary to examine what it is that occupies Niggle's mind while he is working in his tall shed. Of course, he absolutely wants to finish his painting and he needs to spend time on doing that, but we also feel that this is the kind of work that cannot be finished, that is always in progress. Niggle always seems dissatisfied and spends a lot of time trying to improve his leaves. Unfortunately, he is only able to imagine the perfect leaf that he would like to paint, for example when he is riding in the rain: "now he was out of the shed, he saw exactly the way in which to treat that shining spray which framed the distant vision of the mountain" (*TL* 80). Niggle is seeking something that cannot be captured.

To better understand what Niggle's dilemma is all about, I would like to take a quick detour to look at the work of the French poet Yves Bonnefoy. In one of his loveliest prose texts, Bonnefoy tells us that his entire life he has been drawn to what he calls *l'Arrière-Pays*. *L'Arrière Pays,* also the title of this text, can be translated as *hinterland* or *back country*. During his boyhood, he mostly felt this longing when he returned to visit his parents' home in the country each summer.

Experiencing the call of the back country can be compared to looking at a precise location in the distance and having the sensation that the latter is the "vrai lieu" ("real place", my translation; Bonnefoy 16) to beas the poet would put it. The "real place" is a place where we would be able to live in contentment and fulfilment, whereas our situation as after-the-fall creatures makes us dissatisfied by nature. The back country can be interpreted as the place of the absolute, a place, in a non-modern context, that would be filled with some essence of God and with which one could fill oneself. One could compare it to a dwelling place, a brief survey of paradise. Bonnefoy gives the reader an idea of what the back country looks like by likening it to a place that is bathed in light—a tree on the other side of a valley, for example.[8] Twilight and dawn seem to be particularly good times to recognise or see such a place.

Being drawn to the back country is something that many modern human beings have experienced; it is certainly the revelation of what Bonnefoy has often called *being* ("l'être") in a world that has been deserted by being.[9]

For the medieval thinking, Bonnefoy states, God offered some of his "being"[10] to all living creatures and even to all inert things. Being could be what God, as the perfect being, spread around himself: it was a kind of warmth that one could feel if one would approach him. Therefore, for man at that time, all things and creatures were filled with such a warmth; they were filled with "being" that came directly from God. God was everywhere in the natural world, signs of his presence showed through numerous symbols and signs. The cosmos was a book full of these signs testifying His presence. The individual knew the "pourquoi du monde" (the "why of the world"). Man felt being in him and around him and if he lived in miserable conditions he, at least, had a compensation: "ontologic security" (the certainty to be accompanied by being, to be part of something bigger). In addition, Bonnefoy explains, everyone's lives were meaningful because their function in society had been determined by the supreme being. Therefore for people of that time, everything made sense and formed part of an order, an order that the artist tried to duplicate on his canvas: the paintings show a cosmos organised by God. But, Bonnefoy continues, from the 17th century onwards the scientific reading of the universe had come to progressively disqualify the inherited vision of the elders. For the modern and enlightened man the world is not a display of being: God withdrew from the world. No signs or symbols remained in the cosmos which no longer was an ordered one. Therefore, for humanity, from the advent of modern science onwards being

progressively left the world and the latter became meaningless: only remained the matter. Modern humans, because they got rid of God, ended up living in a barren environment, and found themselves lost and desperate in a silent and dry world. They discovered the world's and life's absurdity: they lost the "ontologic security" and losing that is probably what characterises modern condition.

Sometimes, though, in the middle of this lunar landscape, this meaningless world, modern man, thanks to a type of miraculous intervention, seems to be able to see or to slowly approach something like the former "being". Bonnefoy, in his lecture but also, for instance, in a preface of a new edition of a book of Gaëtan Picon[11] (and Gaëtan Picon himself) try to explain that the modern artist, almost subconsciously, is finally in the search of the lost being. The modern artist experiences something mysterious: sometimes, somewhere in the distance, being seems to appear again (in the form, for example, of an apparent "real place"), although it is only sporadically visible. The modern artist, instead of depicting an order as ancient artists did, will simply try to take advantage of such a moment and will try to capture this thing that resembles "being", or the location of the fullness, when he comes face to face with it. Painting a landscape, with which, Gaëtan Picon states, the modern painting begins,[12] is the fruit of such an attempt: a landscape is not a depiction of an order but rather a depiction of the 'visible' as it is at a precise moment, as it is "here and now"[13]. In the same way, the Impressionists tried to capture an "impression", an impression the artist was given and thanks to which he had the feeling of telling or depicting something of a truth.

My interpretation is that Bonnefoy lived the same fundamental and characteristic experience when referring to the back country. He also realised, however, that the back country (the country of being) always remains in the distance and that one is only able to see it for a short period of time: for instance, a change in the light could make it disappear. Also, the more he was approaching what he thought to be the back country, the more the latter was disappearing. Thus, he was taken in by an everlasting movement that was dragging him towards the horizon. The explicit lesson of *l'Arrière-pays* ultimately is that the back country is an illusion, that it is a point that does not exist and that cannot be reached.[14] In other words, we are condemned to see it only from a distance, we cannot enter the setting without at the same time losing what we are looking for. We will remain disunited, for ever removed from the 'full dwelling place'. Therefore, we can deduce from our interpretation of Bonnefoy and Picon, that the modern artist tries to capture this elusive Truth before it has vanished entirely and also tries to hold on to it.

I believe that Niggle, in trying constantly to improve his leaves, as well as Tolkien, who—in his own eyes—tried without fail to improve his stories, are in a way in search of this Truth. They remain dissatisfied because it is quite impossible to reach it, even for the best subcreator. The artist's work will forever stay imperfect because the perfection of the Truth cannot be matched. Truth or being are in the distance and the leaves or the stories might be headed in its direction but are unable to reach it. They are drawn, along with the author, to the back country and the horizon. Tolkien sums all that up in these few words written to his son in 1945:

> A story must be told or there'll be no story, yet it is the untold stories that are most moving. I think you are moved by Celebrimbor because it conveys a sudden sense of endless untold stories: mountains seen far away, never to be climbed, distant trees (like Niggle's) never to be approached—or if so only to become 'near trees' (unless in Paradise or Niggle's Parish).
>
> (*L* 111)

Tolkien and Niggle are in search of this place and try to reach it through their art. They are drawn to that which is shying away. Now, we can better understand what differentiates the people in the two different camps. People such as Niggle and Tolkien from the first camp are those who are much more sensitive to the call of the back country, who are more capable of catching a glimpse of it in the distance and above all who have the time to try and meet it at. On the contrary, others such as Parish are not at all haunted by the back country, they are not attracted by something moving away, but, rather, by something that is approaching them or that is already there and not likely to disappear.

But what makes an individual more sensitive than others to the call of the back country? First, as we have seen, it depends on up to which point one is kept "busy" with satisfying the demands of one's plain ordinary biological life. The more time you spend satisfying your metabolism the less you are sensitive to the other dimensions of life. It is precisely why Niggle/Tolkien dreamed of getting a "public pension". A public pension allows the person who receives it to get rid of the necessity of "earning a living", in other words of working to get the money that he or she needs to live and therefore to satisfy his or her body. With a public pension one has a tendency to become carefree because one no longer worries about the necessities of life. Then, with such assistance, Niggle or Tolkien could, without any obstacle, devote themselves entirely to their art, they could freely search for this unobtainable Truth after which they are running and that makes them dream. But, as we know now, they would also progressively lose their sense of reality, they would live in a world that does not exist and they would, as mortals, waste the little time they have been given for something lost already. Secondly, this distancing depends on up to which point one has been educated. Education allows an individual to distance himself or herself from the world he or she is living in. It allows anybody to remove the hold of reality and to perceive new things amongst which are the beauty of nature and the call of the back country. The distance also allows humans to better understand the world and to explain phenomena (but only thanks to mental representation, therefore, they still remain distant from the world); in a manner of speaking, they become more "intelligent". Unfortunately the distance makes humans less adapted to life on earth because they tend to get lost in conjecture and details rather than taking things as simply as they are and as they feel them; they become more sophisticated. This is why, when Tolkien mentioned in 1969 the "dull stodges" and "those of higher intelligence", he said the second were "corrupted and disintegrated by school, and the climate of our present days" (*L* 403-404).

Tolkien, with the ability of one who was educated and partly freed from necessities, realised that the particular location where being lies cannot be approached, and if so "distant trees become only 'near trees'". Bonnefoy and he both noticed the same thing. This search will always turn out to be fruitless and this is why it is all the more important not to stay in the tall shed but to respond to the calls and to respect the laws that are "already here". Trying to reach the back country is vanity and should be resisted. From the moment the Númenóreans decided to sail west towards the "Blessed Realm" they turned from "beneficence (. . .) to pride, desire of power and wealth" (*L* 205). In 1964 Tolkien says "One loyal to the Valar, content with the bliss and prosperity within the limits prescribed" (*L* 347).

The impossibility of reaching the "Undying Land" (*L* 194) is also the theme of the poem "The Last Ship" published in *The Adventures of Tom Bombadil*. A girl named Firiel sees an elf-boat going by and the elves invite her to join them; they are going to "Elvenhome, where the white tree is growing". "Do you hear the call, Earth-maiden?" the elves say; this call Niggle, Tolkien and Bonnefoy also received. But when Firiel dares to take one step to come on board, "deep in clay her feet sank" and "slowly the elven-ship went by". "I cannot come [. . .] I was born Earth's daughter!", cries Firiel. Inhabitants of the earth can see the boat going to the Blessed Realm but they cannot reach the ship. It is only possible to see it moving away from the river-bank, as only in the distance is it possible to see the back country. Here arises one of the biggest frustrations that can possibly be felt by modern man: being able to see heaven but being unable to be in it.

The lesson of **"Leaf, by Niggle"** is that the back country is not to be found here and while we are on earth we have to stay "within the limits prescribed". If we are meant to find it, it can only be after death: in paradise or Niggle's Parish. It is after his journey and his judgement and not before that Niggle is able to enter the landscape and move among his leaves "as he had imagined them rather than as he had made them" (**TL** 88-89).

> As he walked away, he discovered an odd thing: the forest, of course, was a distant Forest, yet he could approach it, even enter it, without its losing that particular charm. He had never before been able to walk into the distance without turning it into mere surroundings.
>
> (**TL** 89)

Niggle has finally reached his place, but he has left for good the consistent world. Now he will be able to finish his painting that is also a garden, with the help of Parish of course. Then he will go to where it had always been forbidden or impossible for him to go when he was still on earth: beyond the mountains.

> Beyond that I cannot guess what became of him. Even little Niggle in his old home could glimpse the Mountains far away, and they got into the borders of his picture; but what they are really like, and what lies beyond them only those can say who have climbed them
>
> (**TL** 93)

says the tale at the end. However, we know that Tolkien was also hoping to find a resting place, the celestial dwelling place, a place, he told his son, "called 'heaven' where the good here unfinished is completed, and where the stories unwritten, and the hopes unfulfilled are continued" (**L** 55). This Tolkien's deep desire is the same as Bilbo's at the beginning of *The Lord of the Rings* and gives an extraordinary strength to this heartfelt cry: "I want to see mountains again, (. . .)—mountains; and then find somewhere where I can rest" (I, 41).

CONCLUSION

The message conveyed by Tolkien through **"Leaf, by Niggle"** is no doubt very relevant to the present situation. In fact, on a large scale, humans tend to be more and more sophisticated. Firstly, today, humans "know" probably more than they have ever known. Thanks to science and schooling, knowledge has spread. But, for all that, it doesn't mean that we are better equipped for facing reality. In the Fifties in the Netherlands, it was perfectly well known that the country would be the victim of terrible flooding because of the fragility of the sea walls and of the fact that many people lived under the sea level. The Dutch "knew" it thanks to their thinking abilities and intelligence. Unfortunately, "to know" something is often useless, only to "live" something is really useful: the heralded catastrophe happened, thousands of people died and finally the authorities decided to improve their protections against the sea. There would be many other examples showing that the sphere of intelligence and reason does not intersect with the sphere of real life. Sometimes, one can have the impression that both are side by side unable to act on each other. Secondly, humans have been able to make their lives more comfortable. Rather than growing potatoes, we go to the supermarket to get food: it's much faster and really less tiring. With the saved time and efforts, we study, have some spare-time activities, play sport, go to cinema, write books or papers . . . ultimately, we live far from the earth, shut up indoors in a secondary reality. But, the problem is we might find ourselves in the situation of the inhabitants of Antioch in the year 256. That year, Chantal Delsol tells[15] on one occasion everyone was at the theatre and no one saw the archers from the Persian army deploying under the terraces. No longer reminded of reality and concrete things by the necessity to satisfy their biological needs and also without the earth's teaching, inhabitants of the city forgot the essential: that their city could be attacked and must be defended. This is the biggest danger which carefree man is confronted with and which, I think, Tolkien had always in mind: to forget tangible realities.

At last, we can also evoke how this story is marked by Christian morals[16]. At first glance, Christian faith might not seem to value the earthly life because it never stopped saying that the "genuine life" would be after death in the celestial dwelling place. The terrestrial sojourn is imperfect and is nothing compared to what humanity has been promised later. But something essential came and changed the deal: God himself became a human through His son. Jesus came down on earth, he came to Firiel's river bank and he too trod the clay. While he could have stayed in the perfect, he decided to descend to the imperfect. The message of the incarnation was made for the humans tending to gaze too much beyond the mountains, to remind them that the time had not come. More important and urgent things are waiting for them during their terrestrial sojourn, things not to be neglected.

Notes

1. Acknowledgments: thanks to Nikki Funke and Héléne Beaugy for having proofread this article.

2. In his letters, Tolkien clearly compares his own situation to Niggle's. *L* 199, p. 257, he says that "Leaf by Niggle" "arose from [his] own preoccupation with *The Lord of the Rings,* the knowledge that it would be finished in great detail or not at all, and the fear (near certainty) that it would be 'not at all'." *L* 241, p. 321, he tries to explain why "Leaf by Niggle" was written. Among other explanations he says "(. . .) of course, I was anxious about my own internal Tree, *The Lord of the Rings*. It was growing out of hand, and revealing endless new vistas—and I wanted to finish it, but the world was threatening." It is also true that in the same letter he tries to minimise the allegorical aspects of the story but I still think that Niggle represents Tolkien himself. He minimises this aspect because, for him, as we have already said, stories have to be appreciated as mere stories; that is to say that even if there is an allegory, the latter has no importance: the story must continue to exist without it. Tolkien encourages his interlocutors to not pay attention to this king of thinks but rather to read any story with a 'basic' manner. We think he states this clearly in the letter to his aunt, *L* 241, p. 322: "But none of that really illuminates 'Leaf by Niggle' much, does it? If it has any virtues, they remain as such, whether you know all this or not."

3. I think a preference for Hobbits is visible throughout his letters. See for example *L* 109, p. 121 ("hobbits (whom I love) . . .") or *L* 246, p. 329 ("all Hobbits at times affect me the same way, though I remain fond of them"). I try to analyse his preference for Hobbits as a love for the "simple" in a previous article "Tolkien: a simplicity between the truly earthy and the absolutely modern", published in *Tolkien and Modernity*, Vol. 1.

4. In the foreword to the first and second editions (1954 and 1966) of *The Lord of the Rings,* Tolkien insists that writing *The Lord of the Rings* took a long time because he had no spare time during the period and because he did not neglect his numerous obligations. It is as though he feels the need to justify himself for having written a big book, feeling guilty for having done so. In fact, to forestall any critics, he explains how the writing of his book did not prevent him from respecting the laws and from paying attention to things that really matter. These words are meant for some hypothetical judges in case he would have to answer for his acts.

5. Tolkien insists a lot in his letter (pp. 145, 215, 298, 346) on the fact that *The Hobbit* was destined to children. The tone and style change between *The Hobbit* and *The Lord of the Rings*. The first is not "serious", it is just an adventure made to entertain us. Tolkien says the Hobbit "can be seen to begin in what might be called a more 'whimsy' mode, and in places even more facetious" (*L* 298). In this context, nothing bad can really happen to the protagonists.

6. Moreover, a Ring such as Sauron's, with all its characteristics, could not fit in *The Hobbit* or in Bombadil's kingdom: this item is too fraught with consequences to be part of such a light world. Here, the Ring is inevitably harmless because it has to fit in with the atmosphere it is in. There is just no way a Ring such as Sauron's can exist in Bombadil's country. In the same way, it is impossible to find a piece of scorching coal in water because in entering into water the incandescence automatically vanishes. Then, there is no problem with taking it with the hands and playing with it. In penetrating water embers change nature; it is the same thing for the Ring.

7. See *L* 52, p. 64, "I imagine the fish out of water is the only fish to have an inkling of water."

8. See p. 106. Bonnefoy also says that the Massif Central of his boyhood or Toscanie, that he visited many years later, also resemble the "arrière-pays" even if these two different places cannot really provide the fullness that the back country could possibly offer.

9. *Being ("l'être")* is a word that only appears marginally in *l'Arrière-pays* but this word is essential in Bonnefoy's poetry and thought and that is why I link it to his experience of the back country. It is quite delicate to understand what being is. In order to clarify its meaning, I am referring to a lecture that Bonnefoy gave at the Bibliothèque Nationale de France in 2001 where he spoke about being. I think that would allow us to better understand l'Arrière-pays and ultimately, "Leaf by Niggle." The title of the conference was *Passants et passantes d'un Paris qui change,* 26th November 2001. Available as a enregistrement sonore at the Bibiothèque Nationale de France.

10. In this paragraph all the words or expressions in quotation marks are used by Bonnefoy in his lecture.

11. Picon: *1863, naissance de la peinture moderne.*

12. Gaëtan Picon (119) says: "L'histoire thématique de la peinture moderne commence avec le paysage, quand il est traité lui-même et directement. La tradition classique n'admet le paysage qu'intégré à une composition: comme décor d'une scène, et comme idéalisation".

13. This expression, "ici et maintenant", is used by Gaëtan Picon (101).

14. Bonnefoy acknowledges quite rapidly in his text that he has always known that the back country does not exist: "Et je dirai d'abord que si l'arrière-pays m'est resté inaccessible—et même, je le sais bien, je l'ai toujours su, n'existe pas—[. . .]" (33).

15. In *le souci contemporain,* 273. This book has been translated in English under the title *Icarus Fallen.*

16. We have to remember that the story was delivered to the *Dublin Review* after the editor of the latter asked Tolkien in 1944 "for a story which would help his magazine to be a 'effective expression of Catholic humanity'" (Shippey 266).

Works Cited

Alliot, Bertrand. Tolkien: a simplicity between the truly earthy and the absolutely modern. *Tolkien and Modernity,* Vol. 1 (ed. Frank Weinreich and Thomas Honegger). Zurich, Bern: Walking Tree Publishers, 2006.

Bonnefoy, Yves. *L'Arrière Pays* (first edition 1972). Paris: Poésie/Gallimard, 1992.

Delsol, Chantal. *Le souci contemporain.* Paris: La Table Ronde, la peteite vermillon, 2004

———. *Icarus Fallen, The Search for Meaning in an Uncertain World.* Wilmington: ISI Books, 2003

Garth, John. *Tolkien and the Great War: the Threshold of Middle Earth.* Boston, New York: Houghton Mifflin, 2003.

Picon, Gaëtan. *1863, naissance de la peinture moderne,* Paris: Gallimard, 1988.

Shippey, Tom. *J. R. R. Tolkien Author of the Century.* Boston, New York: Houghton Mifflin, 2000.

Tolkien, John Ronald Reuel. *The Fellowship of the Ring.* Boston, New York: Houghton Mifflin, 1993.

———. *The Two Towers.* 2nd ed. Boston: Houghton Mifflin, 1993.

———. *Tree and Leaf.* London: George Allen & Unwin, 1975.

———. *The Letters of J. R. R. Tolkien* (edited by Humphrey Carpenter, with the assistance of Christopher Tolkien). London: George Allen & Unwin, 1981.

———. *The Hobbit.* London: George Allen & Unwin, 1987.

———. *The Adventures of Tom Bombadil,* (first edition 1962). London: HarperCollins, 1995.

Marie Nelson (essay date spring/summer 2010)

SOURCE: Nelson, Marie. "J. R. R. Tolkien's 'Leaf by Niggle': An Allegory in Transformation." *Mythlore* 28, nos. 3/4 (spring/summer 2010): 5-19.

[*In the following essay, Nelson notes thematic similarities between "Leaf by Niggle" and the late medieval drama* Everyman, *while pointing out the autobiographical elements of Tolkien's story.*]

J. R. R. Tolkien's essay "On Fairy-Stories," with its presentation of the essential features of the fantasy genre, and his story **"Leaf by Niggle,"** which I intend to show is a re-telling of the story of the late fifteenth century play *Everyman,* were both first separately published, Tolkien explains in his "Introductory Note" to their re-publication together in **Tree and Leaf.** My primary purpose here is to present a reading of **"Leaf by Niggle"** with reference to its apparent source and to terms Tolkien defines in "On Fairy-Stories," but, since Tolkien tells the *Everyman* story in ways that can readily be related to his own life story, I will also give attention to *this* story as Humphrey Carpenter and T. A. Shippey tell it in *J. R. R. Tolkien: A Biography* and *J. R. R. Tolkien: Author of the Century*; as Wayne G. Hammond and Christina Scull tell it in *J. R. R. Tolkien: Artist and Illustrator*; and as it can be read in Carpenter and Christopher Tolkien's edition of *The Letters of J. R. R. Tolkien.*

As the following sequence of parallels shows, Tolkien re-tells the basic *Everyman* story in **"Leaf by Niggle."**

Everyman[1]	"Leaf by Niggle"[2]
God decrees that each man must face a "rekenynge" (lines 45-46).	Niggle has "a long journey to make" (87). Aware that little time remains, he nevertheless allows frequent interruptions to keep him from completing his painting of his Tree.
Death appears and says to Everyman, "thou must take a longe Iourney" (103).	An Inspector and Driver appear. They announce that Niggle must set forth (94-95).
Everyman offers Death a thousand pounds to delay his departure. He asks that Fellowship, Kindred, Cousin, and Goods be allowed to accompany him. All refuse, but Good Deeds, if he were not so "sore bounde" (487) by Everyman's sins, would be willing to help.	The Driver refuses to grant Niggle's request for delay and takes him to the train station from which he must depart (96).

Everyman[1]	"Leaf by Niggle"[2]
Knowledge leads Everyman to Confession, who gives him a "precyous Iewell [. . .] Called penaunce voyder of aduersyte" (557-58).	Niggle is transported by train through a "dark tunnel" to a place where he is put in an ambulance that takes him to a "Workhouse Infirmary" (96-97).
Everyman accepts the gift and the duty to scourge himself that accompanies it.	Niggle learns through confinement and hard work how to "take up a task the moment one bell rang, and lay it aside promptly the moment the next one went, all tidy and ready to be continued at the right time" (98).
Good Deeds and Knowledge accompany Everyman as he continues his journey.	Niggle, awakening from a "gift" of Gentle Rest, hears two Voices debating his fate. His complaints may negate their redemptive value but he has often performed good deeds, and the First Voice reluctantly agrees to let him "go on to the next stage" (102).
Beauty, Strength, Discretion, and Five Wits appear and offer support, but cannot go with Everyman as he continues his journey.	Niggle's unaccompanied journey by train continues—now through a world of bright daylight—to a place where "Before him [stands] the Tree, his Tree, finished" (103).
Everyman travels on and meets an Angel who will lead him on to heaven.	A shepherd comes who may, when Niggle is ready, guide him to the Mountains he has glimpsed between the leaves of his Tree.

As Shippey observes, "Allegorical meaning is signaled at once by the first sentence [of **"Leaf by Niggle"**]" (267). This sentence reads "There was once a little man named Niggle, who had a long journey to make" (**"Leaf"** [**"Leaf by Niggle"**] 87), and it *is* immediately evident that Niggle's story will be the story of *Everyman* retold. And if there is any doubt about this, when Tolkien, having told of Niggle's preoccupation with his life work—the painting of his Tree—and of the many interruptions to his progress, writes that "At length Niggle's time became really precious. His acquaintances in the distant town began to remember that the little man had got to make a troublesome journey, and some began to calculate how long at the latest he could put off starting" (90), we know that Niggle, like Everyman, has come very close to the end of his life.

The "acquaintances in the distant town" who anticipate Niggle's departure do not assume the status of Fellowship, Kindred, or Cousin, personified abstractions who, along with Goods and Good Deeds; Knowledge and Confession; and Beauty, Strength, Discretion, and Five Wits, make *Everyman* a clear example of the type of allegory M. H. Abrams defines as "the allegory of ideas, in which the literal characters represent abstract concepts and the plot serves to communi-

cate a doctrine or thesis" (*A Glossary of Literary Terms* 4-5), but, as we read **"Leaf by Niggle"** and see the parallels between *Everyman* and **"Leaf"** unfold, this question comes to mind: Why would J. R. R. Tolkien, who is often quoted as saying that he "cordially dislike[d] allegory in all its manifestations" (*Lord of the Rings,* Foreword xxiv), choose to re-tell the story of *Everyman*?

Before beginning to try to answer this question, I should note that Tolkien was more specific about the *kind* of allegory he couldn't stand in a letter to publisher Milton Waldman in which he wrote "I dislike Allegory—*the conscious and intentional allegory* [italics mine]" (*Letters* 145). And, judging from a statement of intention that survives in a draft of a letter to Peter Hastings, the manager of the Newman Bookshop in Oxford, in which he wrote "I tried to show allegorically how [sub-creation] might come to be taken up into Creation in some plane in my 'purgatorial' story **'Leaf by Niggle'**" (*Letters* 195), it would seem that Tolkien did find allegory that served a justifiable intention—like helping him to understand and explain his own creative process—to be acceptable.

Letters Tolkien wrote to publisher Stanley Unwin and to Caroline Everett, who was engaged in research for a thesis about his work, can, however, be read as denials that he had any purpose like this in mind when he wrote **"Leaf by Niggle."** In a letter to Unwin dated *circa* 18 March 1945, Tolkien wrote that "that story was the only thing I have ever done which cost me absolutely no pains at all." Here, contrasting the composition of **"Leaf"** with his usual "difficulty and endless rewriting," Tolkien wrote "I woke up one morning (more than 2 years ago) with that odd thing virtually complete in my head" (*Letters* 113). And years later, in his 24 June 1957 response to her request for information about other stories he might have written, he wrote to Everett, "I have not published any other short story but **'Leaf by Niggle.'** They do not arise in my mind. **'Leaf by Niggle'** arose suddenly and almost complete. It was written down almost at a sitting, and very nearly in the form in which it now appears" (*Letters* 257). But Shippey, having noted that Tolkien received a request from the editor of *The Dublin Review* on 6 September 1944 for "a story which would help his magazine to be 'an effective expression of Catholic humanity'" and that he sent **"Leaf by Niggle"** to him on 12 October, which "by Tolkien's standards [. . .] was practically by return of post" (266), expressed his doubts that Tolkien could have written the story so quickly. It seemed more likely to Shippey, taking his normal composition processes into account, that Tolkien had already written **"Leaf by Niggle"** when he received the request that led to its first publication.

Of course more was involved in its composition than the sudden appearance of **"Leaf by Niggle"** on the page. If in fact he had not already written it when he received the *Dublin Review* editor's request, the basic *Everyman* story would nevertheless have been stored in Tolkien's mind, ready to be retold. By this time, Paul H. Kocher notes, Tolkien had a deep and comprehensive understanding of medieval literature; and, referring to his glossary for Kenneth Sisam's *Fourteenth Century Verse and Prose,* adds that Tolkien "obviously knew medieval drama well" (234). So more than a "sudden appearance" must have been involved. Tolkien did not just write **"Leaf by Niggle"** as an almost immediate response to a request from its first publisher. His groundwork preparation included years of careful, dedicated scholarship.

And another source—Tolkien's own life experience—merits consideration as well. The "Kindred" of *Everyman* may or may not be the ancestor of Councillor Tomp*kins,* Per*kins,* and At*kins,* who briefly appear in **"Leaf,"** but the name "Niggle," Shippey points out, is derived from a verb defined in the *Oxford English Dictionary* as "'To work . . . in a trifling, fiddling, or ineffective way . . . to work or spend time unnecessarily on petty details, to be over-elaborate in minor points,'" and he adds that "This was certainly a vice of which Tolkien could be accused" (267). Tolkien's personal "vice," then, becomes an element that helps to define the central figure of his retelling of the *Everyman* story. And this is just one aspect of his own experience that Tolkien incorporates in his *Everyman* transformation.

But let us, for the moment, turn back to *Everyman.* The opening lines of Tolkien's source are considerably more dramatic than the opening lines of **"Leaf by Niggle."** The first speaker is a Messenger who issues a command to members of his audience to listen with reverence to a "morall playe [called] The somonȳge of eueryman" (*Everyman* lines 3-4) that will show how transitory the lives of men on earth are, and how fellowship and jollity, strength, pleasure, and beauty will fade as quickly "as floure in maye" (16-18). The stern voice of an angry God determined to "Haue a rekenynge of euery mannes persone" (46) is the next to be heard, and then Death appears, ready to obey God's command to summon Everyman for his day of reckoning. Fellowship, Kindred, Cousin, and Goods communicate a single message: They will not accompany Everyman when he is required to set forth on his journey. Good Deeds *would* accompany him if he were not so strongly held back by Everyman's sins, but at this early point in the sequence of events there is little that he can do to help. But Knowledge leads Everyman to Confession, who gives him a "precyous Iewell [. . .] called penaunce voyder of aduersyte" (557-58),

a gift Everyman gratefully accepts along with the duty to scourge himself that comes with it. Knowledge and Good Deeds now accompany Everyman as he continues his journey. Beauty, Strength, Discretion, and Five Wits appear briefly, but they do not join Everyman as he travels on to a place where he meets an Angel who will lead him on to heaven.

And now, turning to Tolkien's Everyman story, we find that no Messenger calls for our attention here. Generations after the play was regularly performed by traveling actors, we simply open to the printed page of *The Tolkien Reader.* We may, however, hear echoes of the ominous voice of Death when the Inspector and Driver appear, and it is possible, borrowing a word Shippey uses to refer to the process Tolkien, who was both a writer and a visual artist, called upon to create the painter Niggle, to see a "bifurcation" of Death in the "Niggle" Inspector and Driver. Death, whose part was performed by a single actor in *Everyman,* becomes two characters in **"Leaf by Niggle."**

The Inspector presents Niggle with his summons. Supporting his authority as "Inspector of Houses" by holding up his "appointment card," he reprimands him for not having helped his neighbor properly repair the damage to his home caused by a recent storm. "That is the law," the Inspector says, and he says it twice (95). The Driver, who appears almost immediately after the Inspector's knock on his door interrupts Niggle's work, then takes on the role of Death with this announcement, "You start today on your journey, you know" (96). The two-word ending of the Driver's speech may slightly undercut the seriousness of his summons, but, though his utterance hardly equals the stern command of Death to Everyman, a man *he* sees as one who pays little heed to his [Death's] "cummynge" and whose "mynde is on flesshely lustes and his treasure" (81-82), the Driver's assertion nevertheless functions as a command Niggle must hear and, whether or not his bag is packed, obey. He *should* have packed, the Driver tells Niggle (heeded the lesson *Everyman* spectators were obligated to learn?), but the "little bag" in the hall that Niggle grabs as he is ushered out contains "only a paint-box and a small book of his own sketches" (96).

This last minute act may be an unspoken, unintended further expression of his verbal response to the Driver's announcement that it is time for him to go. The weeping Niggle's words at this point are "Oh dear! [. . .] And it's not, not even finished!" (96). The "it" of this sentence is Niggle's life work, his painting of a Tree that began with just "a leaf caught in the wind" and became a tree that "[sent] out innumerable branches" that grew into a vision that required a canvas to continue its creation and a tall shed to shelter the work in progress (88). But in any case the tired, sleepy Niggle, suffering from a cold presumably caused by his grudging venture into a driving storm to summon a doctor for his neighbor Parish's ailing wife and a builder to patch his roof, is forced to abandon his painting. And his little bag is lost, along with his ability to move of his own volition, when Niggle is bundled into a compartment on a train that takes him through a long dark tunnel to his first stop, a railway station from which he is immediately sent to "the Workhouse Infirmary," where he is sentenced to what can be read as a parallel to the "penaunce voyder of aduersytye" of *Everyman* ll. 557-58. Niggle's penance is "digging, carpentry, and painting bare boards all one plain colour" (97). Hard labor for an artist!

I hesitate to equate the two voices Niggle hears when he awakens from the Gentle Treatment rest he is allowed after his time in the Workhouse Infirmary (Purgatory) with the voices of God the Father and God the Son, as Paul Nolan Hyde reads them in his essay "Leaf and Key" (29); as an update of a Dante's *Purgatorio* debate between the four daughters of God, with Righteousness and Truth opposed to Mercy and Peace, as Paul H. Kocher reads them in *Master of Middle-earth* (164); or as the voices of Justice and Mercy, *two* of the daughters of God, as Tom Shippey suggests in *J. R. R. Tolkien: Author of the Century* (276), but it seems clear that Tolkien is again making use of bifurcation to tell his story. This time the splitting in two is not the creative process that enabled Tolkien the writer to tell a story of another side of himself as Tolkien the visual artist, but a separation of the single voice of the sternly judgmental God of *Everyman* into two voices. And this results in a debate that can almost be heard as a trial scene involving two Judges who are not seen, but only heard by Niggle as he awakens.

The First Voice is severely judgmental and the Second Voice speaks in Niggle's defense. Careful not to overstate his case, the Second Voice says that Niggle has, albeit unwillingly, helped his neighbor Parish a number of times with his problems with property maintenance and with his own health concerns and those of his wife; and his assertion that Niggle never expected any gratitude for this makes a positive impression on the First Voice. But Niggle is not helped simply by the good deeds he himself has performed during his time on earth. He is also helped by his attribution of generosity to his neighbor Parish. And it is the Second Voice's report of Niggle's concern for Parish, who, he says, was "a very good neighbor, and let me have excellent potatoes very cheap, which saved me a lot of time" that leads to the First Voice's "Did he? [. . .] I am glad to hear it" (101). And as we later see, Parish

believes that Niggle's report of his generosity was a good deed that helped him when *his* turn to set forth came. The Good Deeds character of Tolkien's source may survive, then, not as a personified abstraction, but in the grudging help Niggle provides for his neighbor, in Parish's down-to-earth generosity, and in Niggle's willingness to speak well of Parish and his inquiry about his neighbor's well being. And these can be seen not precisely as a sequence of transformations perhaps, but as traces of a primary virtue members of the *Everyman* audience were, as a "Doctour" who delivered the final message of the play told them, obligated to remember. They were to forsake "pryde" and remember that "beaute," "[five] wyttes," and "strength" all finally forsake "euery man," and that they can take only their "good dedes" with them to heaven (904-7).

So—Tolkien said he hated allegory, but he retold the *Everyman* story. In a number of letters Tolkien, the apparently constant writer, also responded in negative terms to questions that seemed intended to lead to interpretation of his fiction in terms of events in his own life. He may have written in his **Tree and Leaf** "Introductory Note" that one of the sources of **"Leaf by Niggle"** was "a great-limbed poplar tree that [. . .] was suddenly lopped and mutilated by its owner" (2), and Hammond and Scull provide abundant evidence of Tolkien the visual artist's dedication to capturing the essence of individual trees and forests, but in an October 1971 draft of a letter to Peter Szabo Szentmihalyi he declared, "One of my strongest opinions is that investigation of an author's biography (or such glimpses of his 'personality' as can be gleaned by the curious) is an entirely vain and false approach to his works—and especially to a *work of narrative art,* of which the object aimed at by the author was to be *enjoyed* as such" (*Letters* 414, italics original). But, as the following sequence of parallels from Shippey's *J. R. R. Tolkien: Author of the Century* suggests, it is difficult *not* to make connections between **"Leaf by Niggle"** and Tolkien's life story. Tolkien may have opposed efforts to read an author's life into his fiction, but **"Leaf by Niggle"** can be read not just as a transformation of an allegory from an earlier time, but as Shippey reads it, as a story of Tolkien's own life.

"Leaf by Niggle"	Life of Tolkien
"Niggle" (proper noun): name of central character.	"'To niggle,' according to the *OED*, means 'To work . . . in a trifling fiddling, or ineffective way . . . to work or spend time unnecessarily on petty details; to be over-elaborate in minor points'" (267).
The "long journey" Niggle must take (87).	No doubt about what "journey" means—the long journey is death (267).

"Leaf by Niggle"	Life of Tolkien
Artist—Niggle was a painter.	Writer and Artist—Tolkien was "pre-eminently" a writer, but he was also an artist (268).
Primary concern: finishing the Tree (88).	Primary concern: completing the whole history from the creation of Arda told in *The Silmarillion* to the end of the Third Age (269).
Townsmen's question about whether Niggle's garden would be better kept by the next property owner (90).	Colleagues' criticism, conjectures about who would get Tolkien's Oxford University Chair when he retired (269-73).
Time—autumn, "very wet and windy" (90).	Tolkien in his late forties (273).
Distractions: Parish's requests for help (91-94).	Distractions: multiple duties of Oxford Professor: tutorials, lectures, scholarly publication, etc. (272).

Shippey first gives attention to the verb-proper noun connection between Tolkien's apparently almost compulsive re-writing and the name he gives to Niggle. He then shows how Tolkien "bifurcates," or calls upon two different sides of his own creative life. Tolkien, Shippey writes, was "preeminently" a writer, and this is what enables him to tell Niggle's story, but in telling his story he focuses on Niggle's skills of visual representation.

Tolkien consistently downplayed his own skills as a visual artist in letters to publishers, but Humphrey Carpenter gives attention to early demonstrations of his drawing skill in the "Birmingham" sequence of "Part II, 1892-1916" of his *Tolkien* biography, noting that the young Tolkien was especially good at drawing trees and that "he liked most of all to be *with* trees" (22). And Wayne G. Hammond and Christina Scull, having begun "Early Work," Chapter I of *J. R. R. Tolkien: Artist and Illustrator,* with a reference to Tolkien's description of Niggle as a painter, "but not a very successful one, partly because he had many other things to do," provide representations (none of which are larger than the drawings and paintings themselves, which never exceeded twelve inches in height or width), along with descriptions of his work in support of their assertion that though Tolkien "was by no means a professional artist [. . .] he was no dilettante" (9). Hammond and Scull observe, as Carpenter does, that trees were one of Tolkien's central passions, and trees can be seen to play a major role in the topographical drawings they present in their opening chapter. And here they also write that Tolkien "would struggle through several versions of a picture, if needed, to capture his inner vision" (9). And thus we have a double connection between Tolkien the visual artist and the painter of **"Leaf by Niggle"**: his love of trees and his Niggle-like willingness to spend the time and effort required to give form to his thoughts.

As for Shippey's "autumn" connection to Tolkien's age at the time he wrote his story, "the autumn of our years," with its suggestion that we may not have much time left, is a commonly used metaphor, and Tolkien frequently expressed his concern that he might not be able to complete and achieve publication of *The Lord of the Rings* in his letters. As for the criticism of his colleagues, just as Niggle knew that neighboring townsmen were critical of the way he kept his garden, Tolkien knew that, despite the fact that (as Shippey points out) he had published about a dozen scholarly articles before 1939, some of his colleagues talked about his failure to continue to publish at this rate (272). (The fact that a single *Beowulf* article is cited as *"One Essential Essay"* and "The most influential literary criticism of the poem ever published" in Bruce Mitchell and Fred C. Robinson's *Beowulf: An Edition* [235-6] would not seem likely to have impressed them.) All these connections, then, can be seen as results of what Shippey calls the "bifurcation" of Tolkien the writer and Tolkien the artist.

And Tolkien was also a gardener. He provided this short self-description in a letter to Deborah Webster dated 28 October 1958: "I am in fact a *Hobbit* (in all but size). I like *gardens* [emphasis mine], trees, and unmechanized farmlands" (*Letters* 288), and he refers in a number of letters to family members to work he has done in his garden. In an 11 May 1944 airgram to his son Christopher Tolkien, for example, he gives attention to *LotR* progress and writes of "time filled with lectures, house, garden (very exigent just now: lawns, hedges, marrow-beds, weeding)" (*Letters* 79), and writes again on 21 May to report "I have taken advantage of a bitter cold grey week (in which the lawns have not grown in spite of a little rain) to write" (81). Maintenance of his garden may not have been a matter of comparable concern to Niggle, but Tolkien nevertheless includes gardening in his *Everyman* transformation. He assigns this aspect of his own complex personality to Parish, Niggle's neighbor.

And bicycling was also part of Tolkien's everyday life.[3] An October 1944 letter to Christopher Tolkien suggests the role that riding his bicycle played in the creative process that led to the publication of **"Leaf by Niggle"**:

> I was riding along on a bicycle one day, not so long ago, past the Radcliffe Infirmary, when I had one of those sudden clarities which sometimes come in dreams (even anaesthetic-produced ones). I remember saying aloud with absolute conviction: 'But of course! Of course that's how things really do work.' But I could not reproduce any argument that had led to this, though the sensation was the same as having been convinced by *reason* (if without reasoning).

> (*Letters* 101)

Niggle relied on his bicycle for errands like contacting a builder to repair his neighbor's roof and summoning a doctor for Parish's wife. And, turning to the time when he awakens after completing his "penance" and receives permission to go to the railway station and embark on the next stage of his journey, we learn that the train takes Niggle to a place that seems familiar. Here he sees a bicycle that seems to be his and in fact has a yellow label with NIGGLE written on it. He swiftly rides downhill, falls off his bicycle, and a green shadow falls upon him. He looks up and sees "the Tree, his Tree, finished" (103).

Tolkien's October 1944 letter to Christopher tells of a sudden "Aha!" moment that I, since I have been bicycling to school to teach my classes for more years than I wish to recall, can relate to. I don't know how many times I have had a sudden insight when, after hours of floundering, I finally took time to go out doors and get on my bike. But what is relevant here, as far as the **"Leaf"**/Life connection is concerned, is that Niggle has just been released from the Workhouse Infirmary and Tolkien was riding past the *Radcliffe Infirmary*. And what is more significant, as far as Tolkien's transformation of the *Everyman* story is concerned, is what Niggle sees when he looks at the Tree. All its leaves are beautiful, but the most beautiful are the ones he knows were "produced in collaboration with Mr. Parish" (104).

Niggle (a representation of Tolkien's visual artist side) and his neighbor Parish (a representation of his down-to-earth gardening side) are able, once they have emerged from their Purgatory experience, to work together to create an ideal setting that will serve, in the Second Voice's later words, as "a holiday, and a refreshment [. . .] splendid for convalescence, and not only for that, for many it is the best introduction to the Mountains" (**"Leaf"** 112). But this is getting ahead of the story. I should note before continuing that it is at this point that Parish, who has now gained an ability to see beauty that he did not have before, says to Niggle, "This is grand! [. . .] I oughtn't to be here, really. Thank you for putting in a good word for me" (**"Leaf"** 106). Niggle refuses to take credit for what Parish sees as the good deed that got him out of the purgatory phase of his journey sooner than he would otherwise have been able to emerge. He gives credit instead to the Second Voice for their opportunity to work together to create an ideal world, an appropriate setting for Niggle's completed Tree, with "a house in the hollow, the garden, the grass, the forest, and all the country [. . .] nearly complete, in its own proper fashion" (107-8).

This of course is not a precise equivalent to an appearance of Good Deeds any more than the shepherd (who will appear when Niggle and Parish have completed their garden and Niggle is almost ready to go on while Parish chooses to remain and wait for his wife) is a reincarnation of the Angel who guides Everyman on to heaven. But Tolkien does, even as he tells the *Everyman* story his own way, continue to include the essential features of his source.

In a letter to his son Michael dated 9 June 1941 Tolkien wrote, "There is a place called 'heaven' where the good here unfinished is completed; and where the stories unwritten, and the hopes unfulfilled, are continued" (*Letters* 55). This, it would seem, is a statement of belief that can be directly related to Shippey's presentation in "*The Silmarillion*: The Work of His Heart" (*J. R. R. Tolkien: Author of the Century*, 226-263) of Tolkien's commitment to tell the whole story that began with *The Silmarillion* and the creation of Arda, and it leads to yet another **"Leaf"**/Life connection.

So far I have focused on ways that Tolkien said he did *not* want his stories to be read. He did not like allegory of the *Everyman* type, allegory intended to force a message upon the reader; and he did not want readers to read his fiction with the intention of deducing what in his personal life caused him to write it—even though, I might add, he sometimes pointed to the connections himself. I will turn now to consideration of what his essay "On Fairy-Stories" suggests about how he *would* like his story to be read.

Both the essay "On Fairy-Stories" and the story **"Leaf by Niggle,"** Tolkien writes, develop the symbolism of tree and leaf, and both accomplish this through "sub-creation,"[4] a word he found useful for reference to human endeavor that relies upon the gift of imagination.

Tolkien defines the more familiar word "imagination" upon which the meaning of "sub-creation" depends as the capability of the human mind to form "mental images of things not actually present" ("On Fairy-Stories" [OFS] 46). This "gift" enables Niggle to see a vision of what his Tree can become in just "a leaf caught in the wind" (**"Leaf"** 88), and it can enable readers to see "the little man Niggle" as he continues to look beyond his everyday life obligations. Tolkien's definition of "Imagination," then, is directly related to the way he enables *us* to see the single wind-blown leaf with which Niggle's vision of his Tree begins, and then to see *him* when he sees the completed Tree and looks forward to the Mountains and what lies beyond.

As Tolkien continues his definition of the genre in which he chose to write he finds "Escape" to be one of the main functions of fairy-stories (60), and sees no fault in this (there were things in his own world like electric street lamps that he would be happy to escape from). He then turns to "the oldest and deepest desire, the Great Escape: the Escape from Death" (67). Niggle of course cannot escape from death. The Inspector of Houses and the Driver come to his door and he knows that it is time. But the "consolation of the happy ending," or the "good catastrophe, the sudden joyous 'turn'" (68-69) is also an element of Fantasy as Tolkien defines it, and this "eucatastrophe" is what Niggle experiences when he emerges from the Workhouse and is transported to the wondrous place where he sees his Tree, completed.

In **"Leaf by Niggle,"** Niggle's skill as a painter is a manifestation of his "sub-creative art," the "operative link" between "Imagination" and "Sub-creation," the making that human beings are capable of. And the "hard recognition" of "creative fantasy" would seem to relate to an acknowledgement that life in this world has certain requirements: gardens that provide sustenance require care, shelters from storms require maintenance, and everyone has a responsibility to respond to the need of his neighbor. But Tolkien, willing to accept its realities, is also determined to see beyond the everyday world. "We should look at green again," he writes in "On Fairy-Stories," "and be startled anew (but not blinded) by blue and yellow and red" (57), and, since Niggle is a sub-creation of Tolkien, he can be granted a "Recovery," a renewed capability to see, when he experiences his vision of the completed Tree and the beauties of the world that surround it; and Parish, also a sub-creation, is able to see beauty that he could not see before.

Tolkien gives attention to two more critical terms in the "Fairy-Story" sequence that bears the title "Recovery, Escape, Consolation." Here, having first distanced himself from the "tone of scorn or pity with which 'Escape' is now so often used" (60), he turns to consideration of "the oldest and deepest desire, the Great Escape: the Escape from Death" (67). Niggle is no more able to escape death than Everyman was. He is a mortal man and he must die. But this is not the end. After his purgatorial experience he is allowed a "Great Escape," and his story ends with the "consolation of the happy ending," or "Eucatastrophe," which, as Tolkien, the constant philologist, explains, is a word "that does not deny the existence of *dyscatastrophe,* of sorrow and failure" (68). Both possibilities are present in the story of Niggle. He *could* have accepted the scorn of the townsmen, but he does not do this. He persists in his great ambition, his intention to complete the task to which he has dedicated himself. And this leads him to "a fleeting glimpse of Joy, Joy beyond the walls of the world, poignant as grief" (OFS 68).

The "primary world," as Tolkien defines it, is the world created by God, and here he acknowledges the debt of human beings to their Creator just as the creator of

Everyman acknowledged it. Tolkien's "secondary world" is a world created by the writer of fantasy, who thus becomes a "sub-creator." The sub-creator is a human being, himself a creation of God, who wishes in some measure to be a real maker, or hopes that he is drawing on reality. In **"Leaf by Niggle"** Tolkien enables us to enter a "real world" in which townsmen—with one exception, a man named Atkins who finds a fragment from the canvas on which Niggle was painting his tree, gives it the title **"Leaf by Niggle,"** and has it framed and placed on display—see Niggle as a "little man who never amounted to much." And he leads us to a place where Niggle and his neighbor Parish recognize each other's strengths and take great pleasure in working together to create, or sub-create, another world.

As Tolkien ends the story in which he extends his own abilities to sub-create to Niggle and his neighbor (and this is a radical difference from his source—Everyman had no choice but to obey Death's command), the two are said to hear the Second Voice (who from the time he first appears takes on a role as Niggle's defender) tell what the place Niggle and Parish have made is now called. The artist and the gardener learn that the Driver of the train who takes travelers to this place where they can find respite calls it "Niggle's Parish," and we, as we come to the end of **"Leaf by Niggle,"** hear the Porter's report of their response: "They both laughed. Laughed—the Mountains rang with it!" (112).

And if we can take pleasure in their laughter Tolkien has accomplished his story-telling purpose. What is remarkable, or one of the things that is remarkable, in Tolkien's transformation of a fifteenth century play intended for oral performance to a twentieth-century text to be silently read is the fact that the reader—if she listens as she reads—can hear the authority in the voice of the Inspector as he identifies himself. This is not the voice of the Messenger who serves the Creator of *Everyman,* Who announces that He, in His majesty, perceives that the creatures to whom He has given life are so drowned in sin that they do not know Him as their God, but the Inspector leaves no doubt that he strongly disapproves of Niggle's failure to use the "canvas, wood, waterproof paint" (95) he has on hand—and he points to Niggle's painting in process to show what he means when he says this—to repair damages from a recent storm sustained by his neighbor's home, and the Driver's two word order, "Come along!" resonates with a no-nonsense brevity as well (96).

Niggle hears the First and Second Voice debate his fate as he lies in the dark, and his hearing, though Tolkien does not say this, may be sharpened by his dependence on this sense alone. He cannot see the two speakers, and he does not know what is happening. All he can tell is that "There seemed to be a Medical Board, or perhaps a Court of Inquiry, going on close at hand, in an adjoining room with the door open, possibly, though he could not see any light" (99). And *our* hearing is enhanced by what almost seem to be stage directions. The first voice is "a severe voice," while the second is "a voice that you might have called gentle, though it was not soft—it was a voice of authority, and sounded at once hopeful and sad" (99).

When Niggle sees his Tree completed this is what Tolkien enables *us* to see: "He gazed at the Tree, and slowly he lifted his arms and opened them wide" (104), and, though we may silently read Niggle's words from the page, when he says "It's a gift!" (104) we can almost *hear* the joy in his voice. The pleasure Niggle and Parish take in working together when Parish arrives at the stopping place that suddenly materialized when Niggle was freed from the Workhouse Infirmary becomes both visible and audible, and it would be remarkable, I think, if we could *not* hear their laughter when they later learn that their sub-creation has been named "Niggle's Parish." We may have been long conditioned to read words silently from the page on which they are written, but this is a joyous laughter that we can hear in our minds.

Hammond and Scull's closing reproduction of Tolkien's pencil and watercolour "The Misty Mountains" (*J. R. R. Tolkien: Artist & Illustrator,* 208) provides us with an opportunity to see a result of Tolkien the visual artist's own persistent effort to give visible form to what he envisioned as a life beyond the world in which we live. We may not have the ability to see that Tolkien's Niggle had acquired by the time he was able to look beyond his completed Tree and see the mountains of a further distance; and the men who live on in the world from which Niggle and Parish have been transported (and this world of course is also a product of sub-creation) have certainly not acquired that ability. Returning briefly to that world we hear Perkins say that he never knew that Niggle painted and Councillor Tompkins dismiss the man whose house he has taken over as "a silly little man [. . .] Worthless in fact, no use to Society at all" (110). But we can take some small comfort in learning that Atkins at least, despite the fact that Tompkins dismisses *his* usefulness—Atkins is just a schoolmaster, a member of a group the Chancellor feels might be better put to work "washing dishes in a communal kitchen or something" (110)—valued Niggle's life work enough to save a leaf, or fragment, from his Tree and have it framed and placed in the Town Museum. That Museum may have burned to the ground, taking with it the "leaf" that Atkins rescued, but Tolkien's story, with its lesson of persistence rewarded, lives on.

Notes

1. *Everyman,* reprinted by W. W. Greg from the edition by John Skot, will be the source for line citations to the play.

2. Page citations are to *The Tolkien Reader.* "Leaf by Niggle" was first published in *The Dublin Review,* January 1945, while the essay "On Fairy-Stories" was originally composed as an Andrew Lang lecture delivered at the University of St. Andrews in 1938 and "eventually published" by Oxford University Press in 1947 in *Essays Presented to Charles Williams.* The story and essay then appeared together under the title *Tree and Leaf* "when the *Lord of the Rings* was beginning to unroll itself," Tolkien writes, and were republished in *The Tolkien Reader* when *Tree and Leaf* had become "no longer easy to obtain" (2).

3. It is apparent from a reproduction Hammond and Scull include in their "Early Life" chapter that in addition to seeing himself as a writer and an artist, Tolkien also saw himself as a bicycle rider. In "High Life at Gipsy Green," a pencil and coloured pencil drawing that presents different aspects of the Tolkiens' daily life in the early years of their marriage, Tolkien shows his wife Edith playing the piano and engaging in other activities, his young son John in his cot, and himself, in two very small representations, riding a bicycle (27).

4. *The Oxford English Dictionary,* citing the publication of "On Fairy-Stories" in *Essays Presented to Charles Williams,* gives credit to Tolkien for introducing this word to the language with the following definition of *sub-creation*: "J. R. R. Tolkien's word for the process of inventing an imaginary or secondary world, different from the primary world but internally consistent."

Works Cited

Abrams, M. H. *A Glossary of Literary Terms.* 3rd ed. New York: Holt, Rinehart and Winston, 1971.

Beowulf: An Edition. Ed. Bruce Mitchell and Fred C. Robinson. Oxford, UK and Malden, Massachusetts: Blackwell, 1988.

Carpenter, Humphrey. *J. R. R. Tolkien: A Biography.* Boston: Houghton Mifflin, 1977.

Everyman. Ed. John Skot. Rpt. W. W. Greg. London: David Nutt, 1909.

Hammond, Wayne G. and Christina Scull. *J. R. R. Tolkien: Artist & Illustrator.* Boston: Houghton Mifflin, 1995.

Hyde, Paul Nolan. "Leaf and Key." *Mythlore* 12.4, no. 46 (Summer 1986): 27-29, 36.

Kocher, Paul H. *Master of Middle-earth: The Fiction of J. R. R. Tolkien.* Boston: Houghton Mifflin, 1972.

The Oxford English Dictionary. Oxford, England, and New York: Clarendon Press and Oxford University Press.

Shippey, T. A. *J. R. R. Tolkien: Author of the Century.* Boston: Houghton Mifflin, 2001.

Sisam, Kenneth. *Fourteenth Century Verse and Prose.* London: Oxford University Press, 1921.

Tolkien, J. R. R. "*Beowulf*: The Monsters and the Critics." *Proceedings of the British Academy* 22 (1936): 245-95.

————. "Leaf by Niggle." *The Dublin Review,* Jan. 1945: 46-61. Rpt. in *Tree and Leaf* and *The Tolkien Reader.*

————. *The Letters of J. R. R. Tolkien.* Ed. Humphrey Carpenter. Boston: Houghton Mifflin, 1981.

————. "On Fairy-Stories." *Essays Presented to Charles Williams.* London, New York, Oxford: Oxford University Press, 1947. Rpt. in *Tree and Leaf* and *The Tolkien Reader.*

————. *The Lord of the Rings.* Boston: Houghton Mifflin, 1994.

————. *The Silmarillion.* Ed. Christopher Tolkien. Boston: Houghton Mifflin, 1977.

————. *The Tolkien Reader.* New York: Ballantine, 1966.

————. *Tree and Leaf.* Boston and Cambridge: Houghton Mifflin and Riverside Press, 1965. Rpt. in *The Tolkien Reader.*

Josh B. Long (essay date 2011)

SOURCE: Long, Josh B. "Two Views of Faërie in *Smith of Wootton Major*: Nokes and His Cake, Smith and His Star." *Mythlore* 26, nos. 3/4 (spring/summer 2008): 89-100.

[*In the following essay, revised by the author in 2011, Long contends that Nokes embodies an incorrect, superficial understanding of the meaning of fairy tales, while Smith embodies an appreciation of their potential power, terror, and wonder.*]

Smith of Wootton Major, like many of Tolkien's other works, is a fairy tale.[1] It is about both Faërie (the region) and fairies (the fantastical creatures); though in Tolkien's own understanding of the word, the latter is not a qualification of the genre. What is most remarkable about **Smith** [**Smith of Wootton Major**] is

how it reveals Tolkien's comprehension of the world of Faërie; in other words, it tells us how he specifically wanted his stories to be read and how he generally wanted fairy tales to be written. One might say **Smith** is a handbook on how to write a well-written Tolkienian story. In this respect, it is perhaps best viewed as an epilogue or addendum to "On Fairy-stories."[2] The richness of the text is due to the fact that the story functions at two levels. At the narrative level, Tolkien is simply presenting a story that embodies the literary aesthetics of what he believes to be necessary for a good fairy tale. However, at a deeper level, he uses the story as a framework to explore the theory of "On Fairy-stories." To do so, he positions the characters of Nokes and Smith as antithetical counterparts in order to show the writer and reader alike what Faërie should and shouldn't look like.[3]

One does not have to look far to see that the characters of Nokes and Smith are readily comparable; the thrust of the story largely rests on these two characters's differing attitudes towards Faërie. In order to distinguish between their points of view, Tolkien deliberately employs two variant spellings of the word— Nokes uses the modern spelling *fairy,* while Smith employs the more archaic form *Faery.*[4] In an endnote to her edition of **Smith,** Verlyn Flieger observes, "It is worth noticing that the word is consistently spelled 'Fairy' when used by old Nokes, while the preferred spelling, 'Faery', is standard usage for the story's narrator as well as for Smith, the Queen, and Alf" (143n86).[5] Tolkien did not include different spellings for mere variety; his purpose was to present two contrasting views of the word—the proper historical understanding and the modern mistaken notion.[6]

"Fairy," with its conventional spelling, carries with it the modern misconceptions that fairies are diminutive and only suitable for children. This is plainly how Nokes understands the word. In **Smith,** the narrator explains,

> Fairies and sweets were two of the very few notions [Nokes] had about the *tastes of children. Fairies he thought one grew out of;* but of sweets he remained very fond. 'Ah! fairylike', he said, 'that gives me an idea'; and so it came into his head that he would stick a *little* doll on a pinnacle in the middle of the Cake, dressed all in white, with a *little* wand in her hand ending in a tinsel star.
>
> (11, emphasis added)

From Tolkien's perspective, Nokes's ignorance is two-fold—he both misunderstands what Faery is and who it is intended for. In "On Fairy-stories," Tolkien writes, "Among those who still have enough wisdom not to think fairy-stories pernicious, the common opinion seems to be that there is a natural connection between the minds of children and fairy-stories, of the same order as the connection between children's bodies and milk. I think this is an error; at best an error of false sentiment" (*MC* 130). Nokes inevitably maintains this perspective. He makes his cake "fairylike" because he supposes that fairies are synonymous with childhood. But as Tolkien would be quick to point out, "Children as a class [. . .] neither like fairy-stories more, nor understand them better than adults do; and no more than they like many other things" (130).

Nokes's "little doll" view of fairies is also wrongheaded. In "On Fairy-stories," Tolkien notes, "Of old there were indeed some inhabitants of Faërie that were small (though hardly diminutive), but smallness was not characteristic of that people as a whole" (*MC* 110-1). In Tolkien's view, modern writers had undermined Faery by making fairies small and sweet; as it was, Tolkien was determined to redeem the word from the modern world. Flieger writes, "He chose the older spellings to dissociate the word from its modern connotations of prettiness, delicacy, and diminutive stature, and return it to the older, considerably darker meanings it once had had" (*Smith* 143).

Though Tolkien rejected fairy littleness, he allowed Nokes to hold this view in order to show the shortness of his mental and imaginative capacities.[7] According to the *OED, nokes* is an obsolete word for ninny or fool.[8] It is not simply that he is ignorant, but that he obstinately, even arrogantly, subscribes to his misbelief. He is guilty of both undervaluing and overlooking Faery. He does not and will not take it seriously. When he first discovers the fay-star, he exclaims, "That's funny!" (*Smith* 12). After Alf corrects him and explains that "it is *fay*"[9] and that "it comes from Faery," he replies, "It means much the same; but call it that if you like. You'll grow up some day. Now you can get on with stoning the raisins. If you notice any funny fairy ones, tell me" (13, emphasis in original). In light of the rest of the story, Nokes's pronouncement, "You'll grow up some day," is absurdly ironic. Alf, who is the King of Faery, is actually older and wiser than Nokes.

Alf again tries to correct him, "But this isn't a trinket, Master, it's a fay-star" (*Smith* 13). To which Nokes replies, "So you've said already. Very well, I'll tell the children. *It'll make them laugh*" (14, emphasis added). Alf's admonitions are in vain because Nokes is hubristic; he does not even try to understand the true nature of Faery.[10] Flieger points out that, for Nokes, "Faery is at best a mere children's fable and at worst a joke" (60). He doesn't grasp that "an ever-present peril" exists in it (*MC* 109).

If Nokes is indicative of how one should *not* view fairy, Smith is plainly a portrait of how one should.

Smith's "Faery" carries with it the wonder, enchantment, and terror of that Perilous Realm—the place where he journeys, which is home to both the fay-star and the Faery Queen. In truth, Nokes and Smith's approaches to the star reflect two divergent attitudes; while it supplies Nokes with nothing more than a snide snicker, Smith is changed and empowered by it. Here, Tolkien seems to be commenting on the fact that regardless of how compelling Faery might be, it is ultimately up to the individual to accept it or reject it. In other words, Faery fails the moment at which the hearer no longer takes it seriously. The literary belief is lost and the sense of wonder is forsaken.

Though Smith swallows the star at the Twenty-four Feast in the winter, it is not until June that the star reveals its true Faërian wonder. It is interesting to note the effect the fay-star has on Smith (as a child) as opposed to the impression Nokes's cake leaves on the children. At first glance, the children seem to take to the cake; a couple even clap and shout, reiterating Nokes's own words that the cake is "pretty and fairylike" (*Smith* 11, 15). However, it must be remembered that there are twenty-four children at the feast and only two (at the most) are vocally excited about the cake. That is not to say that the cake is necessarily bad; it is simply satisfactory. The narrator observes, "It was a good cake, and no one had any fault to find with it, except that it was no bigger than was needed. When it was all cut up there was a large slice for each of the children, but nothing left over: no coming again" (18). The cake may not be a good depiction of fairy, but it is fair. It is eaten and enjoyed but soon after forgotten. Towards the end of the story, we learn, "[Nokes] just made his century: the only memorable thing he ever achieved" (59).[11] If making his century was his only noteworthy accomplishment, the assumption is that his cake was not very memorable.[12] Tolkien believed that Faery should both move you and change you; Nokes's cake fails to do either; it remains inadequate because it cannot and does not offer the revision of recovery or the overwhelming joy of eucatastrophe.

While Nokes's cake remains acceptable but forgettable, Smith's first encounter with the star is life-changing and transformational. It is appropriate that on his tenth birthday, Smith is essentially reborn by the star. "A little breeze, cool and fragrant" begins the morning (*Smith* 19). Traditionally, the breeze and wind are associated with inspiration. The breeze "stir[s] the waking trees" and the "dawn-song of the birds" begins (19). Smith is so moved by the music that he begins to sing: "Then he began to sing, high and clear, in strange words that he seemed to know by heart; and in that moment the star fell out of his mouth and he caught it on his open hand" (20).[13] He clapped the star to his head, where "he wore it for many years" (20).

Unlike Nokes's cake, the star significantly affects Smith—he is given new sight, and his voice is awakened.[14] "Some of [the star's] light passed into his eyes" (*Smith* 20). Evidently, his vision has been transformed; Faery has changed how he sees the world at large. Tolkien is, of course, alluding to what he calls "recovery," which he argues is an important function of fairy tales. "Recovery (which includes return and renewal of health) is a re-gaining—regaining of a clear view. I do not say 'seeing things as they are' and involve myself with the philosophers, though I might venture to say 'seeing things as we are (or were) meant to see them'—as things apart from ourselves" (*MC* 146).[15]

This is essentially what happens to Smith; the light from the fay-star enters his eyes and gives him a clear view. The fantastic of Faery brings to life his own world. Tolkien explains it this way, "We should look at green again, and be startled anew (but not blinded) by blue and yellow and red. We should meet the centaur and the dragon, and then perhaps suddenly behold, like the ancient shepherds, sheep, and dogs, and horses—and wolves. This recovery fairy-stories help us to make" (*MC* 146). It is this quality that allows Smith to excel in his own craft and become "the best smith between Far Easton and the Westwood" (*Smith* 21). Though he mostly creates "things of iron" that are "meant for daily needs," they "had a grace about them" (21). In addition, we are told that when he made things for "delight," "they were beautiful, for he could work iron into wonderful forms" (21). He has the ability to see the world in a fresh, new way—this is a gift that Faery has given him.

The other immediate transformation that takes place is in Smith's voice. "His voice, which had begun to grow beautiful as soon as the star came to him, became ever more beautiful as he grew up. People liked to hear him speak, even if it was no more than a 'good morning'" (*Smith* 20).[16] There is a sense that the more Smith experiences Faery, the lovelier his voice becomes. It is not the words themselves that are remarkable but the tone of his voice. Smith has been changed and the way he speaks and how he sees will never be the same.

Another way that Smith differs strikingly from Nokes is he comes to understand Faery and grows to respect it. The narrator states, "For Smith became acquainted with Faery, and some regions of it he knew as well as any mortal can" (*Smith* 22). The narrator adds, "For he soon became wise and understood that the marvels

of Faery cannot be approached without danger" (24). Certainly Tolkien is juxtaposing Smith's wisdom to Nokes's foolishness. Nokes does not realize that "Faërie is a perilous land" (*MC* 109); he neither comprehends that it is dangerous, nor understands that it is a place.

While Nokes does not grasp the severity of Faery, Smith "had seen things of both beauty and terror that he could not clearly remember nor report to his friends" (*Smith* 26). Here, Tolkien is alluding to a passage from "On Fairy-stories":

> The realm of fairy-story is wide and deep and high and filled with many things: all manner of beasts and birds are found there; shoreless seas and stars uncounted; *beauty* that is an enchantment, and an ever-present *peril*; *both joy and sorrow* as sharp as swords. In that realm a man may, perhaps, count himself fortunate to have wandered, but its very richness and strangeness tie the tongue of a traveller who would *report* them.
>
> (*MC* 109, emphasis added)

The two passages are related semantically as well as syntactically. In both passages, Tolkien emphasizes that Faery contains both light and dark—"beauty and terror" he writes in *Smith,* and "beauty" and "peril" and "joy and sorrow" he points out in his essay. In addition, each passage identifies that the wanderer is unable to "report" the wonders he has seen. Syntactically, "both beauty and terror" is similar to "both joy and sorrow."

This notion, that Faery is dichotomous, was an important one for Tolkien, and Smith's four Faery visions best exemplify this. The first vision of the elven mariners exhibits terror. "His heart was shaken with fear" (*Smith* 26). The next one of the King's Tree displays beauty. "Its light was like the sun at noon; and it bore at once leaves and flowers and fruits uncounted" (28). The third vision of the birch tree elicits sorrow. "His heart was saddened as he went on his long road" (30). The following vision when he dances with the elven maiden produces joy. "He knew what it was to have [. . .] the joy to accompany her" (33). These scenes are not meant to be allegorized but to be experienced by Smith and the reader alike. The same strangeness that astounds Smith should fill the reader with the same awe and perplexity. As we read, we journey with Smith as visitors and wanderers in that enchanted realm. Perhaps one of the reasons Tolkien left these visions of Faery so enigmatically strange was so the reader might simply enjoy them without trying to discover some underlying meaning.

Smith's final venture into Faery, however, definitely "means" something. That is not to say that it is allegorical, but it is rich with applicability. The scene, when Smith comes to meet the Faery Queen, is interesting for two reasons—for the Faery Queen's contrast to Nokes's fairy queen and for what she says. Perhaps the only commonality the Queen shares with Nokes's queen is they are both queens; there the similarities end. The narrator provides this apt description of her, "She wore no crown and had no throne. She stood there in her majesty and her glory, and all about her was a great host shimmering and glittering like the stars above; but she was taller than the points of their great spears, and upon her head there burned a white flame" (*Smith* 36-7). Unlike Nokes's queen, she is someone to be reckoned with. The same terrible beauty that Galadriel exemplifies in *The Lord of the Rings* resurfaces here in the Queen. Tolkien recognized that ugliness and evil had become so inextricably tied together that it was difficult for the modern mind to perceive of something that was both beautiful and terrifying. He writes in "On Fairy-stories," "The fear of the beautiful fay that ran through the elder ages almost eludes our grasp" (*MC* 151). He was bent on restoring the origins of not only the word Faery but also the world of Faery; he was trying to recreate the greatness of a past that had been forgotten and lost.[17]

Nokes's queen pales in comparison to the real one, and Smith comes to realize this: "Suddenly he saw again the little dancing figure with its wand, and in shame he lowered his eyes from the Queen's beauty" (*Smith* 37). The Queen is regal yet she responds graciously to Smith, "Do not be grieved for me, Starbrow. Nor too much ashamed of your own folk. Better a little doll, maybe, than no memory of Faery at all. For some the only glimpse. For some the awaking" (37-8). Her words are telling; they are, to some extent, Tolkien's own. Speaking of the "bad author" in his abandoned introduction to *The Golden Key*, Tolkien writes, "Someone may meet them [marvels of Fairy] for the first time in his silly tale, and catch a glimpse of Fairy, and go on to better things" (61). Although Tolkien is referring to the bad writer in general, he definitely has George MacDonald at the back of his mind, when he wrote both of these passages. He is essentially saying (through the Queen) that although some may not possess, in his view, a proper understanding of Faery, their mistaken notions and flawed depictions are *perhaps* better than no Faery at all.[18]

If Nokes's fairy was so unsuccessful with the children and he is depicted as misguided throughout the story, why all of a sudden is this concession made? Tolkien is not negating his criticism of Nokes but is simply recognizing the fact that for many the only glimpse of fairy they will ever encounter is this one. Clearly, Nokes's fairy had, for the most part, failed, but there were a couple of children that had been excited by his cake. It is Tolkien's hope that those children discover Faery through Nokes's *fairy*; that they "go on to better things." It is as if Tolkien is reluctantly willing to accept something he reviles in order to ensure that the world of Faery is not lost. Even so, the Queen specifically says, "Better a little doll, *maybe*" (emphasis added), as if the Queen and Tolkien are in agreement that they are not quite sure that Nokes's view is in fact better than no Faery at all.

Though we are introduced to Nokes at the beginning of the story, he does not reappear until the end. What is most interesting about him is how much he has *not* changed. He is now approaching ninety, yet he remains largely the same—certainly he is no wiser than he was before. He still erroneously calls the star a "trinket" (*Smith* 54). If he has changed at all, he has simply become more stubborn, more set in his ways. After Alf comes to visit him, Nokes inquires about who swallowed the star. However, before Alf has a chance to tell him, Nokes starts guessing names. To no avail, he finally exclaims, "Then I give up. Who was it?" (55). Alf tells him Smith, to which Nokes characteristically laughs (55). Just as he ignorantly laughs at the fay-star, he does the same thing to the King of Faery.

After Nokes accuses him of stealing the star out of the cake, Alf loses his patience and rebukes him,

> Nokes, your knowledge is so great that I have only twice ventured to tell you anything. I told you that the star came from Faery; and I have told you that it went to the smith. You laughed at me. Now at parting I will tell you one thing more. Don't laugh again! You are a vain old fraud, fat, idle and sly. I did most of your work. Without thanks you learned all that you could from me—except respect for Faery, and a little courtesy.
>
> (*Smith* 57)

Tolkien reminds us, "[Alf's] last conversation with Nokes as a very old man must not be taken as baiting or gloating over a stupid and defeated opponent" (98). It is perhaps best to understand Alf's words as a final caveat. He is correcting someone that is in desperate need of it. Rather than accept Alf's harsh reproof, Nokes resorts to insulting him in return. He knows precisely where Alf is most vulnerable. He once again laughs, "If you've got one of your fairy friends hidden in the Kitchen, send him to me and I'll have a look at him. If he waves his little wand and makes me thin again, I'll think better of him" (57-8). Ironically, he is granted his wish. For all his vanity and lack of generosity, he is paid back accordingly.

Alf, who has been "hidden in the Kitchen" for years, reveals himself as the King of Faery. "To Nokes' dismay [Alf] grew taller as he spoke. He threw back his cloak. He was dressed like a Master Cook at a Feast, but his white garments shimmered and glinted, and on his forehead was a great jewel like a radiant star. His face was young but stern" (***Smith*** 58). Alf's advance towards Nokes is evocative of Gandalf when he insists that Bilbo give up his ring in *The Lord of the Rings*.[19] "[Gandalf] took a step towards the hobbit, and he seemed to grow *tall* and *menacing*; his shadow filled the little room" (*LotR* 33, emphasis added). In both instances, the wiser, more powerful individual is forced to demonstrate his authority to an unrelenting, stubborn subordinate. The responses by Bilbo and Nokes are equally analogous. "[Alf] stepped forward, and Nokes shrank from him, *trembling*" (***Smith*** 58, emphasis added). "Gandalf's eyes remained bent on the hobbit. Slowly his hands relaxed, and he began to *tremble*" (*LotR*, emphasis added). Though Nokes receives what he wants (to be thin), Bilbo surrenders what he desires (the ring). The former, however, faces the harsher end. Nokes becomes so thinly decrepit that the children christen him "old Rag-and-Bones" (***Smith*** 59).

Just as Nokes's physical appearance becomes feeble, his understanding of Faery takes on a similar form. In addition to all his misconceptions and stereotypes, he now foolishly associates Faery with dreaming. "Ugh! What a dream!" he says about his encounter with the Faery King (***Smith*** 59). He later adds, "Alarming, you might call it; but a silly dream, when you come to think of it" (59). Evidently, Nokes is one of those people that Tolkien speaks of in "On Fairy-stories" who "stupidly and even maliciously confound Fantasy with Dreaming" (*MC* 139).[20]

Arriving at the conclusion of ***Smith***, it seems strange that Tolkien's fairy story should end on such a melancholic note—Smith is left bereaved, and Nokes remains oblivious. Where is the eucatastrophe—the happy ending, the good turning that Tolkien calls the "highest function" of a fairy tale? (*MC* 153). I believe it comes in one of the final scenes when the star is passed on. It is important and appropriate which child is chosen to receive it—Tim, Nokes's great-grandson. The turn occurs in two ways. Though Smith is saddened by his own loss, he finds contentment in the fact that the star will be put to good use. "All is *well* then. So you are my heir. I wonder what strange places the star will lead you to?" he thinks (***Smith*** 61, emphasis added). The second and perhaps more powerful effect of the eucatastrophe is the fact that although Nokes never comes to understand the true nature of Faery, his great-grandson will come to value and appreciate it. As Smith notes, "Poor old Nokes. Still I suppose he will never know what a shocking thing has happened in his family" (61). Hope is found in neither Smith nor Nokes but in Tim; it is the next generation

that holds the key to Faery. Tolkien notes that the story "includes sacrifice, and the handing on, with trust and without keeping a hand on things, of power and vision to the next generation" (81).

Notes

1. Tolkien once wrote, "*The Lord of the Rings* was a deliberate attempt to write a large-scale adult fairy-story" (qtd. in Manlove 158). This quotation is taken from a letter dated 8 February 1967 to C. N. Manlove.

2. "On Fairy-stories" was fresh in Tolkien's mind as he began writing *Smith*. Prior to the composition of *Smith*, he had been revising this essay for inclusion in *Tree and Leaf*. Evidence in Hammond and Anderson's bibliography suggests that the bulk of Tolkien's work for *Tree and Leaf* was done between July 1963 and September 1963 (183). *Tree and Leaf* was published on 28 May 1964. Shortly after, Tolkien began work on *Smith* in late 1964 (Scull and Hammond, *Chronology* 625; *Smith* 59).

3. Verlyn Flieger suggests, "Smith as a character works better in juxtaposition to Nokes than to Tolkien" ("Allegory versus Bounce" 188).

4. As early as 1915, Tolkien used this variant spelling in his poem "The Shores of Faëry" (*The Book of Lost Tales II* 271-2).

5. This appears to be a slight but important emendation to her original assessment made in *A Question of Time*, where she writes, "In any case, his use of the simpler form [Faery] is consistent throughout the story" (228). Here, she makes no mention of "Fairy." In an earlier version of this chapter, published in *Saga: Best New Writings on Mythology* as an independent article, she points out in a footnote, "The spelling of this important word in Tolkien's lexicon is as elusive as the bounce. It appears in his writing variously as Faery (as above), Fairy (see quote below), Faérie, and Fayery. However changable [sic] the spelling, the meaning remained constant, it was 'the Perilous Realm itself and the air that blows in that country'" (158n1).

6. For a further discussion of "Faery" and "Fairy," see *The Ring of Words: Tolkien and the* Oxford English Dictionary (124-127).

7. It should be noted, however, that in Tolkien's early work he often depicted fairies as small. Scull and Hammond observe, "Some of his earliest writings, such as the poems *Goblin Feet* and *The Princess Ní*, portray similar diminutive beings, and it was his intention in *The Book of Lost Tales* that in the future the Elves would actually fade and diminish and become transparent, and so become

the 'fairies' as commonly conceived" (*Reader's Guide* 280). John D. Rateliff references "Goblin Feet," "The Princess Ní," and "Tinfang Warble" as early examples of poetry in which Tolkien depicts little fairies (120). He writes, "Tolkien later came to disavow the idea of elves as cute little fairies and moved his own elves firmly in the direction of medieval elf-lore" (120).

8. Jane Chance first noted this in her 1979 book *Tolkien's Art: A Mythology for England* (70); Margaret Sammons identified this in her 1985 article "Tolkien on Fantasy in *Smith of Wootton Major*" *Mythlore* 43, 12.1 (4); Eric S. Graff again pointed this out in his 1992 article "The Three Faces of Faërie in Tolkien's Shorter Fiction: Niggle, Smith and Giles," *Mythlore* 69, 18.3 (17); Perry C. Bramlett briefly referenced this in his 2003 book *I Am in Fact a Hobbit: An Introduction to the Life and Work of J. R. R. Tolkien* (44); and most recently, Flieger cited it in her edition of *Smith*. She writes, "While etymologically it does indeed mean 'living by the oak', it is also, as Tolkien knew, a type-name for a fool or ninny, an ignorant person" (144).

9. "*Fay*, 'magic, possessing magical powers'" (Flieger, *Smith* 134).

10. The extent of Nokes's vanity is best seen in this narcissistic description: "He used to put on the tall white hat and look at himself in a polished frying pan and say: 'How do you do, Master. That hat suits you properly, might have been made for you. I hope things go well with you'" (*Smith* 10). In addition, at the end of the story, Alf calls Nokes "a vain old fraud" (*Smith* 57). Tolkien is using the word in two senses. Though Nokes is vain in the sense that he is overly conceited, Tolkien would have also been aware of the word's archaic denotation, meaning foolish.

11. The pagination of Flieger's Extended Edition of *Smith* is a bit skewed. The actual story of *Smith* ends on p. 62, while Flieger's "Afterword" begins on p. 59. Therefore, there are two pages numbered 59, two pages numbered 60, and so forth, up to 62.

12. Smith does, however, ashamedly remember Nokes's fairy queen when he visits the real Queen. In addition, Alf tells Nokes in their final meeting, "I remember it very well. . . . It was a good cake, and it was enjoyed and praised" (*Smith* 54). These are not inconsistencies. Smith does not remember the cake because it is memorable but because it is regrettable. The fact that Alf remembers the cake does not mean much. As the Faery King, he probably remembers many things "very well." In addition, his kind words towards Nokes do not necessarily reflect the truth but illustrate his generosity. There are many indicators that Alf, in fact, did not think too well of Nokes's cake. For instance, he tells Nokes, "I'll do it [make the fairy queen] if you are too busy. But it was your idea and not mine" (*Smith* 14). See also Alf's demeanor at the feast (*Smith* 15-18).

13. Music and song play a prominent role in Tolkien's fiction. Songs are scattered throughout *The Hobbit* and *The Lord of the Rings*. One of his most successful uses of music can be found in his creation story "Ainulindalë" in *The Silmarillion*. Ilúvatar, with the assistance of the Ainur, sings creation into existence. "Ainulindalë" is arguably Tolkien's greatest and most perfect piece of prose. Robert Murray suggests, "In all literatures since the formation of the sacred books of humankind, surely there is hardly a creation myth to equal, in beauty and imaginative power, the one with which *The Silmarillion* begins" ("Sermon at Thanksgiving Service" 19).

14. Interestingly, the idea that Elvishness affects a mortal's sight and voice was also suggested in *The Lord of the Rings*. Goldberry tells Frodo, "I see you are an elf-friend; the light in your eyes and the ring in your voice tells it" (*LotR* 122).

15. It is apparent that the star provides its wearer with recovery because immediately after Smith gives it up, he explains, "I cannot see clearly" (*Smith* 47). In addition, after the star is passed on to Tim, the narrator notes that "a light began to shine in his eyes" (*Smith* 61).

16. It is noteworthy that Tolkien's own idiolect was known to be muddled or difficult to comprehend. If one were to apply a psychoanalytical reading to this text, one might suggest that Tolkien desired this same clarity in his own speech. Did most of Tolkien's students and colleagues "like to hear him speak"? To hear some audio clips of Tolkien, see *J. R. R. Tolkien: An Audio Portrait* or *A Film Portrait of J. R. R. Tolkien*. It is also interesting how clear his speech was when he was reading rather than conversing.

17. It is interesting to note that Nokes's response to Alf when he reveals himself as the King of Faery is also trembling. If there is one point that Tolkien is trying to make, it is that fairies or elves are not cute but awe-inspiring and terrifying.

18. Kilby was the first to identify this connection. He rhetorically asks, "Does Tolkien mean that though MacDonald knows nothing about the real inside of a cake, nevertheless he may accomplish something by the saccharine figures he presents?" (*Tolkien* 39).

19. There are other notable parallels between *Smith* and *The Lord of the Rings*. Flieger observes, "In three years [Rider] disappears again, saying farewell only to his Apprentice in a speech that strikingly recalls Bilbo's farewell to Gandalf at the end of the first chapter of *The Lord of the Rings*" ("The Footsteps of Ælfwine" 195). I would add that the scene when Alf urges Smith to surrender his star is analogous to the one when Gandalf advises Bilbo to give up his ring. Smith asks, "Isn't it mine?" just as Bilbo asserts, "It is mine" (*Smith* 41; *LotR* 33). David Bratman also pointed out to me that "greed and the possession of jewels is a constant theme in Tolkien, everywhere from the Silmarils to the dwarves' gold-lust in *The Hobbit*" (Private Correspondence). Evidently, Tolkien chose to return to this theme in *Smith*.

20. Lest we think too badly of Nokes, Tolkien reminds us, "Nokes had however a virtue, or the remains of one. He seems to have been generally fond of children, in his way" (*Smith* 97). As Tolkien's children and grandchildren can attest, this was certainly true of Tolkien as well. See for instance *The Tolkien Family Album*.

Works Cited

Bramlett, Perry C. *I Am in Fact a Hobbit: An Introduction to the Life and Work of J. R. R. Tolkien*. Macon: Mercer University Press, 2003.

Bratman, David. Email to the author. 24 July 2007.

Chance, Jane. *Tolkien's Art: A Mythology for England*. New York: St. Martin's Press, 1979.

A Film Portrait of J. R. R. Tolkien. Dir. Derek Bailey. Narr. Judi Dench. Visual Corporation, 1992.

Flieger, Verlyn. "The Footsteps of Ælfwine." *Tolkien's Legendarium: Essays on The History of Middle-earth*. Eds. Verlyn Flieger and Carl F. Hostetter. Westport: Greenwood Press, 2000. 183-198.

———. "Pitfalls in Faërie." *Saga: Best New Writings on Mythology*. Ed. Jonathan Young. Vol. 1. Ashland: White Cloud Press, 1996. 157-171.

———. *A Question of Time: J. R. R. Tolkien's Road to Faërie*. Kent: The Kent State University Press, 1997.

Flieger, Verlyn, and T. A. Shippey. "Allegory versus Bounce: Tolkien's *Smith of Wootton Major*." *Journal of the Fantastic in the Arts*. 46, 12.2 (2001): 186-200.

Gilliver, Peter, Jeremy Marshall, and Edmund Weiner. *The Ring of Words: Tolkien and the Oxford English Dictionary*. Oxford: Oxford University Press, 2006.

Graff, Eric S. "The Three Faces of Faërie in Tolkien's Shorter Fiction: Niggle, Smith and Giles." *Mythlore*. 18.3 (1992): 15-19.

Hammond, Wayne G., and Douglas A. Anderson. *J. R. R. Tolkien: A Descriptive Bibliography*. Winchester Bibliographies of 20th Century Writers. New Castle: Oak Knoll Books, 1993.

Kilby, Clyde. *Tolkien and* The Silmarillion. Wheaton: Harold Shaw, 1976.

Manlove, C. N. *Modern Fantasy: Five Studies*. Cambridge: Cambridge University Press, 1978.

Murray, Robert. "Sermon at Thanksgiving Service, Keble College Chapel, 23rd August 1922." *Proceedings of the J. R. R. Tolkien Centenary Conference 1992*. Eds. Patricia Reynolds and Glen H. GoodKnight. Altadena: Tolkien Society, Mythopoeic Press. 17-20.

Rateliff, John D. *The History of* The Hobbit *Part One: Mr. Baggins*. London: HarperCollins, 2007.

Sammons, Margaret. "Tolkien on Fantasy in *Smith of Wootton Major*." *Mythlore*. 12.1 (1985): 3-7, 37.

Scull, Christina, and Wayne G. Hammond. *The J. R. R. Tolkien Companion & Guide: Chronology*. Boston: Houghton Mifflin, 2006.

———. *The J. R. R. Tolkien Companion & Guide: Reader's Guide*. Boston: Houghton Mifflin, 2006.

Sibley, Brian. *J. R. R. Tolkien: An Audio Portrait*. BBC Worldwide Ltd. 2001.

Tolkien, John, and Priscilla Tolkien. *The Tolkien Family Album*. Boston: Houghton Mifflin, 1992.

Tolkien, J. R. R. *The Book of Lost Tales, Part II*. Ed. Christopher Tolkien. Boston: Houghton Mifflin, 1984.

———. *The Lord of the Rings*. Boston: Houghton Mifflin, 1994.

———. *The Monsters and the Critics and Other Essays*. Ed. Christopher Tolkien. London: HarperCollins, 1990.

———. *Smith of Wootton Major*. Extended Edition. Ed. Verlyn Flieger. London: HarperCollins, 2005.

Josh B. Long (essay date 2011)

SOURCE: Long, Josh B. "Clinamen, Tessera, and the Anxiety of Influence: Swerving from and Completing George MacDonald." *Tolkien Studies* 6 (2009): 127-50.

[*In the following essay, revised by the author in 2011, Long applies critic Harold Bloom's concept of "the anxiety of influence" to* Smith of Wootton Major, *claiming that Tolkien's text functions as a critical response to and correction of George MacDonald's* The Golden Key.]

In 1973, the year J. R. R. Tolkien passed away, Harold Bloom released his seminal work *The Anxiety of Influence: A Theory of Poetry.* Although Bloom's book has had a profound effect on the topic of literary influence, his theory has received minimal attention within the field of Tolkien studies. Faye Ringel takes a Bloomian approach in her article "Women Fantasists: In the Shadow of the Ring," though, ultimately, her article focuses primarily on those whom Tolkien influenced. Diana Glyer also considers *The Anxiety of Influence* in the final chapter of her book length study *The Company They Keep: C. S. Lewis and J. R. R. Tolkien as Writers in Community*; however, she is more interested in expanding the notion of literary influence rather than evaluating how Tolkien's fiction fits into Bloom's paradigm. This article serves to demonstrate that Bloom's theory is relevant to both Tolkien's creative journey in general and **Smith of Wootton Major** in particular.

In *The Anxiety of Influence,* Bloom develops six revisionary ratios—ways in which one poet influences another. I am only interested in the first two—*clinamen* and *tessera*. The former might be best described as a corrective swerve, a turning away from a precursor poet in attempt to correct what he did wrong; the latter is antithetical completion, which occurs when a poet retains a precursor's terms but means them in a different way (Bloom 14).

These revisionary ratios are performed by a poet as a means "to clear imaginative space for" himself (Bloom 5). As the modern writer (post-Enlightenment) seeks to achieve literary greatness, he inevitably becomes anxious over influence and, consequently, reacts to his literary precursor. Through a revisionary movement in his own text, the writer is able to create something original and thus pacify his fear of indebtedness. At the heart of Bloom's theory is this idea: "*The history of fruitful poetic influence, which is to say the main tradition of Western poetry since the Renaissance, is a history of anxiety and self-saving caricature, of distortion, of perverse, wilful revisionism without which modern poetry as such could not exist*" (30, emphasis in original). In **Smith** [**Smith of Wootton Major**], Tolkien sought to correctively swerve from and antithetically complete MacDonald's *The Golden Key.*

THE UNFINISHED PREFACE TO *THE GOLDEN KEY*

When Tolkien began **Smith** in late 1964, he was not intending to write a story about Faërie. In fact, he was not even initially trying to tell a tale; the story arose almost accidentally.[1] It began with a simple request from a publisher. Pantheon Books of New York inquired on 2 September 1964 whether Tolkien would write a preface to a new edition of George Mac-

Donald's *The Golden Key.* Tolkien responded to their query on 7 September: "I should like to write a short preface to a separate edition of *The Golden Key.* I am not as warm an admirer of George MacDonald as C. S. Lewis was; but I do think well of this story of his" (*Letters* 351). Though Tolkien had supervised a B.Litt. thesis on MacDonald in 1934 and may have reread him in 1938 or 1939 while working on "On Fairy-stories," he had almost certainly not read MacDonald for nearly three decades.[2] Therefore, when he accepted the request from Pantheon books to write a preface to *The Golden Key,* he was basing his decision largely on the fact that he had praised the story in "On Fairy-stories." In actuality, he only had vague memories of what it was really like.

After rereading *The Golden Key,* Tolkien discovered that he did not like it at all. According to Humphrey Carpenter, Tolkien claimed that it was "illwritten, incoherent, and bad, in spite of a few memorable passages" (qtd. in *Biography* 244). Elsewhere, he stated that "rereading G[eorge] M[acdonald] critically filled me with distaste" (*Smith* 69).[3] In spite of these misgivings, he persisted in trying to write a preface:

> A fairy tale is a tale about that world, a glimpse of it; if you read it, you enter Fairy with the author as your guide. He may be a bad guide or a good one: bad if he does not take the adventure seriously, and is just 'spinning a yarn' which he thinks is good enough 'for children'; good, if he knows something about Fairy, and has himself caught some glimpses of it which he is trying to put into words. But Fairy is very powerful. Even the bad guide cannot escape it. He probably makes up his tale out of bits of older tales, or things he half remembers, and they may be too strong for him to spoil or disenchant.
>
> (*Smith* 74-5)

Tolkien's tone is slightly cynical, if not critical. He was struggling to write a preface for a book and an author he now disliked; his contempt seeps into his prose. Surely, Tolkien considered MacDonald a "bad guide"; however, this view would not be made plain until the actual story of **Smith.**

THE NEGATIVE INFLUENCE OF MACDONALD

[4]Understandably, Tolkien never completed his preface to *The Golden Key.* He abandoned it because he had lost interest in MacDonald and found a story of his own beginning to unfold. Tolkien notes, "If I had gone on [writing the preface] I should only have written a severely critical or 'anti' essay on G[eorge] M[acDonald]—unnecessary, and a pity since G[eorge] M[acDonald] has performed great services for other minds—such as Jack's" (*Smith* 69).[5] Although the 'anti' essay was never written, **Smith** undoubtedly be-

came charged with Tolkien's feelings of deep resentment and discontent over MacDonald's stories—particularly *The Golden Key.*

On at least two separate occasions, Tolkien acknowledged MacDonald's negative influence on **Smith.** On 26 October 1966, Tolkien read **Smith** aloud at Blackfriars, the Dominican house of studies in St. Giles, Oxford. In his prefatory comments, he remarked, "The story was (as often happens) the result of an *irritant.* And since the irritant will in some degree affect the presentation of the movement in the mind that it sets going I will just say what the *irritant* was in this case. George MacDonald. A writer for whom I have a sincere and humble—dislike" (qtd. in Scull and Hammond, *Reader's Guide* 945). Additionally, in writing to Clyde S. Kilby, Tolkien called **Smith** "an anti-G[eorge] M[acDonald] tract" (**Smith** 70). Inevitably, Tolkien was so dissatisfied with MacDonald that he felt compelled to write a reactionary story to *The Golden Key.*

What was it that bothered him so much about MacDonald's writing? First, Tolkien was dissatisfied with the *The Golden Key*'s tone; he felt that fairy tales shouldn't be written with children in mind. MacDonald had succumbed to this "error of false sentiment" (*MC* 130). In a note he sent to Kilby, he observes, "I had of course, never thought of *The G[olden] K[ey]* as a story for children," but then adds this parenthetical jab, "(though apparently G[eorge] McD[onald] did)" (**Smith** 69).[6] Tolkien's attitude is further emphasized by the fact that on 2 March 1966, he told Henry Resnik: "I didn't write [*The Lord of the Rings*] for children. That's why I don't like George MacDonald very much; he's a horrible old grandmother" (41).[7] Second, he felt MacDonald had a tendency to ruin his fairy tales by being overly didactic—they came off more as sermons than stories. Kilby recalls, "He called him an 'old grandmother' who preached instead of writing" (*Tolkien* 31). Tolkien mentioned this less hostilely in his unfinished preface to *The Golden Key,* "All the same I must warn you that [MacDonald] is a preacher, not only on the platform or in the pulpit; in all his many books he preaches" (**Smith** 71). Finally, Tolkien was also displeased that MacDonald wrote allegories—a form he inherently disliked. Tolkien explains, "But [C. S. Lewis] was evidently born loving (moral) allegory, and I was born with an instinctive distaste for it. 'Phantastes' [by MacDonald] wakened him, and afflicted me with profound dislike" (**Smith** 69).[8]

CLINAMEN: THE CORRECTIVE SWERVE

Despite Tolkien's praise of *The Golden Key,* he now saw MacDonald's story as a flawed and ineffective

work, and as it was, he was determined to rewrite it the way he felt it should have been written. In part, this is what he tried to accomplish through **Smith.** Bloom notes,

> A poet swerves away from his precursor, by so reading his precursor's poem as to execute a *clinamen* in relation to it. This appears as a corrective movement in his own poem, which implies that the precursor poem went accurately up to a certain point, but then should have swerved, precisely in the direction that the new poem moves.
>
> (14)

This is an accurate description of the process of writing **Smith.** Tolkien believed MacDonald's story "went accurately up to a certain point," but when MacDonald should have been concerned with the integrity of Faërie, he fell to "juvenilizing," moralizing, and allegorizing it.

What MacDonald did right, however, was that he attempted stories about the fantastical. Regardless of how distasteful Tolkien now found his approach to Faërie, he valued the basic structure of *The Golden Key.* After all, **Smith** and *The Golden Key* contain very similar plots—a character or characters journey throughout an enchanted Otherworld. Consequently, MacDonald was the immediate influence that prompted Tolkien to write a fairy tale in which a human comes into contact with Faërie.

CORRECTING THE JUVENILITY

Tolkien was not necessarily opposed to what MacDonald was doing but *how* he was doing it. He was bothered by the superfluous asides found in *The Golden Key* that were intended to help children follow the storyline, keep them engaged, or teach them. We know that **Smith** was not written with children in mind. Tolkien made this plain: "But the little tale was (of course) *not* intended for children!" (*Letters* 388-9). This conviction about fairy tales—that they "should not be *specially* associated with children"—was an idea he first proposed in "On Fairy-stories" (*MC* 135), and it greatly affected his approach in *The Lord of the Rings.*[9] It was, however, in **Smith** that Tolkien made his most adamant pronouncement that the fairy tale is really an adult genre.

The first indication of Tolkien's *clinamen* can be found in the opening sentence of the story. Like *The Golden Key,* **Smith** begins quite traditionally, yet it establishes a very different tone than MacDonald's story.

> **Smith**: "There was a village once, not very long ago for those with long memories, nor very far away for those with long legs."
>
> (5)

The Golden Key: "There was a boy who used to sit in the twilight and listen to his great aunt's stories."

(1)

At first glance, the two sentences appear alike; however, each author has a different audience in mind. In *The Golden Key*, Mossy listens to his aunt's storytelling just as many children first hear *The Golden Key* read aloud. In this way, MacDonald is able to establish sympathy between his juvenile audience and the protagonist of the story. In addition, MacDonald assumes that his audience has little patience for an opening setting because he advances directly into the story.

Tolkien's approach is wholly different and intended for a more mature reader. His narrative begins with wordplay; the word *long* is used to refer to a duration of time, extended mental capacities, and height. Though an inexperienced reader might grow confused, to an adult, the sentence is intriguing and engaging. Moreover, the parallelism makes the sentence syntactically lucid, and the alliteration and consonance makes it dictionally graceful. "There was a village once, not very long ago for those with long memories, nor very far away for those with long legs" (5). What is more, unlike MacDonald, Tolkien develops an opening setting; in typical Tolkienian fashion, he spends three paragraphs discussing the workings of Wootton Major before he even mentions the first character (5-7). *Smith* and *The Golden Key* are initially distinct. As we move through both narratives, the differences between the two texts become even more pronounced.

Whether *The Golden Key* was originally written for children is less important than the fact that it appears to be. MacDonald assists the child by indicating that he is shifting scenes. "And now I will go back to the borders of the forest" (10). Such an interpolation is unnecessary. An adult could figure this out for himself, but such a shift would be more difficult for a young reader to make. *The Golden Key* also contains childish questions. After Mossy finds the golden key, the narrator asks, "Where was the lock to which the key belonged? It must be somewhere, for how could anybody be so silly as make a key for which there was no lock? Where should he go to look for it?" (9). MacDonald is obviously trying to draw in the young reader, but to an adult, such questions are patronizing.

The intrusive narrator also takes on more of a didactic approach. He is decidedly concerned with Mossy and Tangle's hygienic practices. The morning after Tangle is first cleansed by Grandmother, he observes, "For having once been in her grandmother's pond, [Tangle] must be clean and tidy ever after; and, having put on

her green dress, felt like a lady" (28). As if the narrator's emphasis on routine bathing is not enough, he takes it one step further by teaching his readers a lesson on altruism. "But the wearer of Grandmother's clothes never thinks about how he or she looks, but thinks always how handsome other people are" (33). We begin to see why Tolkien referred to MacDonald as a grandmother.

Tolkien, unlike MacDonald, is not interested in the child as reader, and this can be seen most clearly in his visions of Faery. They are baffling for an adult, let alone a child. Verlyn Flieger provides an accurate assessment of the enigmatic nature of these visions: "Wandering in myth he does not understand, Smith of Wootton Major witnesses a whole world to which he does not have the key; nor, in consequence, does the reader. [. . .] The questions are not just unanswered, they are unasked" ("Footsteps" 196). Indeed, Tolkien's portrayal of Faery remains so mysterious that when Tolkien swerved from MacDonald, he turned around rather than to the side. While MacDonald is condescending, Tolkien falls on the opposite end—he neither explains nor instructs; and although his descriptions of the Faerian world remain discernible, the intentions or motives of its inhabitants remain unclear.

Tolkien's Faery is most interesting for what it does not say. We meet the elven mariners *in medias res*. They appear to be returning from battle and have evidently won (*Smith* 26), but whom they defeated or where they are headed cannot be determined. Next, we behold the King's Tree in all its glory, but know nothing about its purpose (28). It exists and its beauty requires no explanation. Finally, Smith is responsible for awakening the Wind, but what offence he has committed cannot be discerned—if he has, in fact, done anything wrong (29-30). We are just as perplexed as Smith as we experience a world we do not fully understand—a world we are not meant to fully understand. After all, the text makes it plain that there are things in Faery "which men know nothing" about (26). And by saying nothing, not explaining these matters, Tolkien is at once saying something—he is defending the world of Faery. In reaction to MacDonald, who inundated *The Golden Key* with too much meaning and elucidation, Tolkien creates an Otherworld full of uncertainty. If there is one thing he is trying to get across, it is that Faery exists as a thing in its own right and needs no other purpose than to delight and excite, which it does for the reader and Smith alike.[10]

The imagery altogether overshadows the action of these scenes, giving the text more of a poetic feel. Tolkien's paratactic style, use of alliteration, and rhythmic repetition of the word "and" further heightens the poetic element. Such stylistic preferences align these passages with *Beowulf,* which relies heavily on both alliterative meter and parataxis. My point is not that Tolkien had *Beowulf* in mind or that he was even consciously imitating the poem, but that Tolkien's style contains both a heroic seriousness and poetic eloquence that harkens back to Old English verse. Syntactic parallelisms add to the overall rhythm and flow of these scenes (identified below with brackets). And finally, Tolkien even employs internal rhyme, such as "down to the ground" and "sun at noon" (consonantal rhyme).

Elven Mariners Episode

Suddenly they lifted up their voices in a song of triumph, [*and* his heart was shaken with fear], [*and* he fell upon his face], [*and* they passed over him] [*and* went away into the echoing hills.]

(*Smith* 26)

King's Tree Episode

He saw the King's Tree springing up, tower upon tower, into the sky, *and* its light was like the sun at noon; *and* it bore at once leaves *and* flowers *and* fruits uncounted, *and* not one was the same as any other that grew on the Tree.

(*Smith* 28)

Wind and Birch Episode

At once the breeze rose to a wild Wind, [roaring like a great beast], [*and* it swept him up] [*and* flung him on] the shore, [*and* it drove him up] the slopes whirling *and* [falling like a dead leaf].

(*Smith* 29)

Even when it seems that Tolkien has succumbed to triteness with such similes as "like the sun at noon" and "like a dead leaf," there is artistic intention in his selection. If understood within the context, the similes are not just appropriate but powerful. Leading up to the sun simile is a description of the tree towering up into the sky; thus, it only makes sense that the tree should be compared to the sun. The sun simile does not detract from our visual image but adds to it. The tree is so overwhelming in both size and radiance that it appears, if only for a moment, that it is not merely like the sun but it is the sun. I think this is the image the passage is trying to evoke.

The leaf simile functions similarly. The wind is so strong that Smith is not like a leaf as much as he is a leaf. This picture invokes reverse personification, where the human takes on characteristics of an inanimate object. Therefore, it is fitting that we find Smith clinging to the stem of a birch; he metaphorically be-

comes a leaf. What is more, the parallel simile used to describe the wind as "a great beast" is not just syntactically analogous; it is important to the scene; the wind is personified in the same instance that Smith undergoes reverse personification.

In addition to these visions of Faery that give the story more of an adult feel, Tolkien incorporated thematic elements that were geared towards adults. Just as MacDonald sought to establish a connection between children and his characters, Tolkien did likewise with adults by imbuing his text with a profound sense of bereavement—that inexplicable and inescapable feeling of loss that comes with old age.

Tolkien frequently made reference to this element of **Smith.** In writing to Roger Lancelyn Green, he referred to the story as "an old man's book, already weighted with the presage of 'bereavement'" (*Letters* 389).[11] The story begins and ends with bereavement. After twenty-four years of service as Master Cook, Rider retires unexpectedly (*Smith* 9). Nevertheless, Rider is not the one left bereaved; he is almost too willing to give up his position in order to return to Faery.[12] The townspeople are the ones most affected by his sudden disappearance, which is, in a sense, a death because he is never heard from or seen of again. The main difference, however, is that the townspeople carp rather than mourn their loss (*Smith* 9).

In addition, we soon discover that this is not the whole story and that the history of Wootton Major goes all the way back to the birth of Rider. In Tolkien's essay on **Smith,** he devotes a large portion of it to recounting the events of Rider's life, and from it, we learn that Rider was one well acquainted with loss. Tolkien writes, "[Rider's] sadness and 'air of having his mind elsewhere' [while he was Master Cook] was due no doubt not only to his bereavement but also to this deprivation" (*Smith* 96). Rider's bereavement is a result of the untimely death of his wife Rose, who died while giving birth to their daughter Ella, Smith's mother. To make matters worse, Rider's position as Master Cook prevents him from visiting Faery, which is what Tolkien means by "this deprivation." Though none of these events take place in the published text, they assist in giving us a fuller understanding of the bereavement that surrounds the narrative.

Though the loss that begins the story (and back-story) is rich and complex, the bereavement that Smith endures at the end of the tale is most profound. After meeting the Faery Queen and experiencing some type of transcendence, Smith comes to the realization "that his way now led back to bereavement" (*Smith* 39). The next paragraph begins, "That meeting-place was now far behind him, and here he was, walking among the fallen leaves, pondering all that he had seen and learned" (39). This moment of solitude, before he meets up with the Faery King and relinquishes his star, is remarkable for its subtlety—it says much without saying a lot. The outward setting becomes indicative of Smith's inward struggle; the barrenness of his surroundings parallels his own internal landscape. Though he has not given up his star yet, he reflects on his past experiences and realizes that he does not have much time remaining. His encounter with the Faery Queen might very well be his final venture into Faery.

Smith reluctantly gives up the star. After he returns home, the full extent of his bereavement sets in: "His son lit candles, and for a while they sat by the fire without speaking; for a great weariness and bereavement was on the smith" (*Smith* 49). In "Suggestions for the ending of the story," Tolkien explains Smith's loss, which is to some extent his own, when he writes, "A time comes for writers and artists, when invention and 'vision' cease and they can only reflect on what they have seen and learned" (*Smith* 81). This quality of bereavement reemphasizes the adult nature of *Smith*. As a corrective swerve to MacDonald, Tolkien made his story adult-like not only tonally and stylistically, but also thematically.

CORRECTING THE ALLEGORY

The question of allegory has been an important issue in *Smith* criticism. In fact, two of the top Tolkien scholars take almost opposite positions on this matter—Tom Shippey finds the text to be rich with allegorical meaning, while Verlyn Flieger argues that the work is better read as a fairy tale and valued as a thing in its own right (Shippey and Flieger 186-200). Part of the problem lies in Tolkien's own comments on the story. In his *Smith* essay, he notes that it "is not an 'allegory', though it is capable of allegorical interpretations at certain points" (*Smith* 84). He explains this in greater detail in a letter sent to Kilby: "[*Smith* is] *not* an allegory (however applicable to this or that) in intention: certainly not in the 'Fay' parts, and only fleetingly in the Human, where evidently The Cook and the Great Hall etc. represent The Parson and Church and their decay" (qtd. in Scull and Hammond, *Reader's Guide* 40).[13] At face value, Tolkien's explanations seem incongruous, but his understanding of the "allegory" in *Smith* is reconcilable.

It is important to begin by defining Tolkien's terms. In his *Smith* essay, he makes a distinction between allegory and allegorical interpretations. What do these terms mean and how do they differ? Tolkien's clearest definition of allegory can be found in his comments on *Pearl* in the Introduction to his translation of the poem. He writes, "To be an 'allegory' a poem must *as a whole*, and with fair consistency, describe in other terms some event or process; its entire narrative and all its significant details should cohere and work together to this end" (18). Ultimately, *Smith* is not an allegory because the entire narrative does not work together to produce a fair and complete secondary meaning. For instance, the Faery King and Queen are not symbols of anything else, just as the elven mariners are elves and the King's Tree is a tree. The sustained one-to-one correspondences are simply not there.

On the other hand, *Smith* "is capable of allegorical interpretations at certain points." But what does Tolkien mean by this? He explains the term in a letter to Milton Waldman by distinguishing it from allegory: "[T]he more 'life' a story has the more readily will it be susceptible of allegorical interpretations: while the better a deliberate allegory is made the more nearly will it be acceptable just as a story" (*Letters* 145).

Although allegory and allegorical interpretations appear similar, Tolkien makes it clear that they start out from opposite ends. Allegory is a deliberate attempt on the part of the author to dominate the story and reader's mind; the secondary meaning is infused within the narrative framework. Allegorical interpretations, in contrast, arise as a reader comes into contact with a text. A story is imbued with so much life that it begins to exhibit allegorical qualities, and the reader soon discovers a number of symbolic elements.

Tolkien makes a distinction between not only allegory and allegorical interpretations, but also the Faery and Human parts of *Smith*. He was concerned that the Faery would be interpreted allegorically and the literary belief would be lost or stifled. In his essay on *Sir Gawain*, he speaks of "los[ing] Faerie only to gain a formalized allegory" (*MC* 79). I think this is what he feared with *Smith*—that readers would merely hunt for secondary meaning rather than endeavor to appreciate the story as a story. It seems to me that if you are going to trust what Tolkien says about his work, you cannot feasibly interpret the Faery allegorically.

Taken as a whole, *Smith* functions as a corrective swerve because *The Golden Key* is an allegory and *Smith* is not. Furthermore, while Tolkien insisted that his story's Faery remain free of allegorical interpretations, *The Golden Key*'s Fairyland exists primarily to sustain its secondary meaning.

The allegory in *The Golden Key* is plain; it is the story of Mossy and Tangle's journey to heaven. Mossy is an everyman just as John Bunyan's Christian is one; the same is true of Tangle. Even the names of the two children hint at the depravity of humanity—that we are grimy and mixed-up. The golden key may be taken to be salvation; after all, it is what allows Mossy and Tangle to enter heaven. MacDonald's fairies appear to represent angels, especially the aëranthes, who act as guardian angels for the two children—protecting, directing and guiding them along their journey (13-14, 27, 45).

Grandmother is a Christ-figure; she welcomes both children openly and without reserve (14, 31). She emanates warmth and humility, and is responsible for washing both Mossy and Tangle clean. She teaches and instructs the children on various matters. In fact, at one point, her speech strongly recalls Christ's own words in the gospel of Matthew.

> Grandmother: "You must look for the keyhole. That is your work. I cannot help you. I can only tell you that if you look for it you will find it."
>
> (31)
>
> Matthew 7:7: "Seek and you will find; knock and the door will be opened to you."

Both passages not only emphasize seeking and finding but also contain door imagery.

Despite these allegorical parallels, the clearest indication that *The Golden Key* is an allegory comes in the Platonic vision the children encounter when they enter the Valley of Shadows. MacDonald transforms Plato's *Allegory of the Cave* into a profoundly Christian model. Heaven becomes the ultimate reality, while this world and its shadows are a mere glimpse of eternity. It is only after seeing the world for what it truly is that the children experience a moment of epiphany. "After sitting for a while, each, looking up, saw the other in tears: they were each longing after the country whence the shadows fell" (41). For the rest of the story, the two children seek to find this place.

Shortly after this, Mossy and Tangle are separated—which suggests that death has cut them off from one another (42). We follow Tangle for most of the remaining portion of the story as she journeys through a purgatorial realm, encountering the Old Man of the Sea, the Old Man of the Earth, and the Old Man of the Fire (45-65). Each Old Man represents a process of cleansing, purging, and refining that Tangle must undergo to attain eternal life. Mossy only has to face the Old Man of the Earth before he is directed to

heaven. The story ends with Mossy and Tangle reuniting, opening a door with the golden key, ascending a staircase, and then entering into a rainbow, which is obviously heaven (73-78).

Unlike *The Golden Key*, *Smith*'s allegorical content is positioned in the Human part of the story. Though Tolkien's own allegorical interpretation of the Master Cook and the Great Hall can be found in the text, this reading is ineffective because it is too subtle—besides the author, no one else was able to detect its presence. The most obvious allegorical interpretation of *Smith* relates to the cake, fairy queen, and Nokes, which seems to me to be a commentary on MacDonald and his art.

Before I develop this allegorical interpretation, I would like to make several prefatory comments. Firstly, as Tom Shippey has pointed out in regard to his own allegorical reading of *Smith*: "[A]t the more advanced stages of reading an allegory, it is not essential to come up with the one single correct solution. [. . .] A suggestive or a provocative one will do" (*Author* 298).

Secondly, it cannot be overstated just how much Tolkien came to dislike MacDonald towards the end of his life. His own statements confirm this, but even more compelling is the first-hand account we get from Kilby: "[Tolkien] said he had found MacDonald terrible and his broadside criticism of him implied that nothing he had written was worthwhile" (*Tolkien* 36-7).

Finally, it should be noted that I am not the first commentator to view Nokes as a MacDonald-figure. Kilby suggests that Nokes "may represent MacDonald" because he could make a cake that was appealing on the outside, but had no idea of what went into making a Great one (*Tolkien* 37). Margaret Sammons also finds Nokes to be a MacDonald-figure. She observes, "Tolkien is perhaps saying that MacDonald believes Faerie is merely something sweet and funny and has little notion of what to put inside a great Tale" (4).

It is no mere accident that Nokes is the antagonist of the story, nor is it by chance that his name means fool. Also, he is the only character who uses the modern form *fairy*—the very spelling MacDonald uses in *The Golden Key*. Though this spelling is not unique to MacDonald, there are other passages in *Smith* that clearly tie Nokes to him. Nokes' description of the fairy queen as "a tricky little creature" (*Smith* 15) strongly recalls MacDonald's portrayal of the "little creatures" who "play [the maids] all manner of uncomfortable tricks" (*Golden* 10-11). In addition, after the children finish eating their cake, Nokes exclaims, "Bless me! Then [the star] can't have been made of silver after all; it must have melted. Or perhaps Mr. Prentice was right and it was really magical, and it's just vanished and gone back to Fairyland. Not a nice trick to play, I don't think" (*Smith* 18). Nokes is the only character to use the term "Fairyland," which is the term MacDonald uses throughout *The Golden Key*. Moreover, in this passage, Nokes reemphasizes the tricky nature of fairies. Even the fact that Nokes insists that fairy is funny is an idea put forth in *The Golden Key*—MacDonald's fairies accidentally make Tangle laugh (*Golden* 12). Clearly, Nokes is a somewhat satirical portrait of MacDonald.

Just as Nokes is analogous to MacDonald, his fairy queen is modeled after MacDonald's fairies—the aëranth. MacDonald's aëranth is described as "a lovely little creature in human shape, with large white wings" (*Golden* 26), and "a beautiful little creature with wings" (45). Nokes' fairy queen is depicted quite similarly as "a little doll . . . dressed all in white, with a little wand in her hand" (*Smith* 11) and "a tiny white figure on one foot like a snow-maiden dancing" (14). Both are diminutive, white, and pretty. Moreover, each contains a traditional characteristic of the little fairy—wings and a wand respectively. Nokes' fairy is plainly an exaggerated caricature of MacDonald's aëranth.

Tolkien was so opposed to the idea of fairy littleness that he satirized it by having Nokes fill his cake with an excessive number of small artifacts. It is not just the queen and her wand that are small, but little trinkets and coins are mixed into the batter, and little trees and a small mountain are placed on the outside. Nokes includes all of these because he assumes that "it amuses the children" (*Smith* 13). Tolkien is commenting on MacDonald's art; he felt MacDonald had geared his "Great Cake" to what he perceived was the reach of children's tastes, and by doing so, he had produced a work that was overly sweet, petty, and inadequate. It is no wonder that only two of the twenty-four children at the feast are vocally excited about the cake, and after it is passed out, there is "nothing left over: no coming again" (18). Moreover, Nokes' cake does not go down in history. "Indeed it is said that [Nokes] just made his century: the *only* memorable thing he ever achieved" (59, emphasis added).

Although most commentators have identified Smith as a Tolkien-figure, few have discussed Smith as a child. This portion of the story fits, if with more work, into my reading. Tolkien "grew up on" MacDonald, as Lewis puts it (*Collected Letters* 2: 96). In other words,

MacDonald was one of Tolkien's first encounters with Fairy. My allegorical interpretation suddenly takes on autobiographical implications. Although Nokes' cake had mostly failed, it did contain a "glimpse" of Faery (i.e. the star) as the Queen alludes to later. It was this inspiration that eventually led Tolkien to true Faery. When Tolkien writes in his abandoned Introduction to *The Golden Key*, "Some one may meet them [the marvels of Fairy] for the first time in his silly tale, and catch a glimpse of Fairy and go on to better things" (*Smith* 74), he is likely recounting his own history with MacDonald.

TESSERA: REDEEMING THE WORD THROUGH ANTITHETICAL COMPLETION

Tolkien's *clinamen* affected the larger elements of *Smith*—the story's tone and themes, and the positioning and use of allegory, but Tolkien's *tessera* shaped the smaller elements of the story—the words. Bloom describes this revisionary ratio thus: "A poet antithetically 'completes' his precursor, by so reading the parent-poem as to retain its terms but to mean them in another sense, as though the precursor had failed to go far enough" (14). This ratio, even more so than *clinamen*, works well with Tolkien because of the nature of his profession. As a philologist and wordsmith, he was naturally concerned with words and their meanings. If there is one word that Tolkien was trying to redeem from MacDonald, it was certainly the word *fairy*.[14]

In *Smith,* the first indication that Tolkien was attempting a *tessera* is seen in the fact that he includes a different spelling of the word. Flieger observes,

> He felt that the word *fairy* as conventionally used in modern English had been debased, and divorced from its original complex and powerful meaning. He chose the older spellings [Faërie, Fayery, and Faery] to dissociate the word from its modern connotations of prettiness, delicacy, and diminutive stature, and return it to the older, considerably darker meanings it once had had.
>
> (*Smith* 143)

In *Smith,* Tolkien settled on *Faery*; all of the characters use this form except Nokes (*Smith* 143). This was by no means the first time that Tolkien employed this spelling. As early as 1915, he used it in his poem "The Shores of Faëry" (*Lost Tales II* 271-2). Nevertheless, this does not minimize or lessen his *tessera*. He included this spelling in *Smith* primarily to juxtapose it to MacDonald's *fairy*.

Although Tolkien retained MacDonald's word, his understanding of the term was antithetically different. This is seen most clearly in both authors' depictions of fairies. In *The Golden Key,* MacDonald's fairies do not play a major role. Nonetheless, they are described and do serve a purpose in inadvertently prompting Tangle towards Fairyland. In addition, they also serve as guides once the children are there. MacDonald introduces them in this fashion: "Now it is well known that *the little creatures commonly called fairies,* though there are many different kinds of fairies in Fairyland, have an exceeding dislike to untidiness. Indeed, they are quite spiteful to slovenly people" (10-11, emphasis added). In contrast, Tolkien describes the Faery Queen: "She wore no crown and had no throne. She stood there in her majesty and her glory, and all about her was a great host shimmering and glittering like the stars above; but *she was taller than the points of their great spears,* and upon her head there burned a white flame" (*Smith* 36-7, emphasis added). The most apparent difference between the two is physical size; however, I think Tolkien's understanding of Faeries is distinct in other ways as well. The Faery Queen's splendor causes humanity (Smith) to tremble in her presence—one might say she is just short of divinity. MacDonald's fairies pale in comparison—they are mischievous at best. Leaving the maids with bruises, they are just short of hilarity. In fact, his fairies are so incompetent that the first time they try to make Tangle run away from home they actually cause her to laugh (12).

In addition, it is also worth noting how both authors approach their fairies. Typical of MacDonald, he utilizes them as an instrument for instruction. Clearly appealing to his Victorian sensibilities, he stresses the need for cleanliness and tidiness. In a way, his juvenile audience is being frightened into keeping their rooms and/or appearances clean because the assumption is if they do not, bad fairies will come and harass them. In keeping with the tone of the rest of the story, this passage reemphasizes MacDonald's didactic proclivity, which often carries to the point of condescension. In this way, his fairies are not just inferior to Tolkien's; they are insignificant in and of themselves; they exist as mere children's props and contain none of the terror or beauty that Tolkien believed was a necessary part of their tradition.

Tolkien, on the other hand, uses the Faery Queen to exemplify and re-establish the concept of terrifying beauty—something he believed had been lost in modern times. In "On Fairy-stories," he writes, "The fear of the beautiful fay that ran through the elder ages almost eludes our grasp" (*MC* 151). Furthermore, the seriousness of the situation is apparent; unlike MacDonald, Tolkien values his Faeries and suggests that they should be feared, not laughed at. In fact, the same awe-inspiring trepidation that the Faery Queen instills in Smith can also be seen in the elven mariners, when Smith first encounters them (*Smith* 26-27), and Alf, when he reveals himself as the King of Faery (58). Moreover, both the elven mariners and Alf are described as tall (26, 39, 58). Tolkien was determined to antithetically complete MacDonald's word by making his Faeries tall and terrifying.

The final difference between the two fairies is that Tolkien's Faeries radically affect the primary world—they improve it. MacDonald's fairies may be concerned with keeping the primary world tidy, but they are not very good at it, and ultimately, their contribution is of no real significance. In contrast, Alf transforms the town of Wootton Major. Towards the end of the story, we learn that "the Hall had been re-glazed and re-painted" (*Smith* 46). This renovation—the decoration of the Great Hall—is surely something Alf is responsible for. Just as Smith's life was enriched by the fay-star, the town of Wootton Major is forever changed by Alf's presence. Though his Faerian adornment appears to some as new, it is actually a return to a forgotten but important tradition—which allows more than just the smith to come into contact with Faery.

In juxtaposition to Nokes's cake at the beginning of the tale, which leaves only a couple of children outwardly excited, the story closes with Alf's Great Cake. It is important and appropriate that this cake enthuses all the children. "The children all laughed and clapped" (*Smith* 61). Tolkien is again commenting on the superiority of his own art and the inferiority of MacDonald's, but the real point is that the children have now caught a glimpse of *Faery.* After Alf departs, the narrator notes that the town "kept the Hall gilded and painted in memory of Alf" (62). Alf has left a lasting impression on the children and adults alike—this is something Nokes could never do.

In the end, Tolkien's *tessera* was not so much a turning away as a returning to; like Alf's renovation of the Hall, Tolkien was looking to the past to restore the present. He expressed this most poignantly in an interview he gave to William Cater on the 2 August 1966. "By writing about elves as tall as men I am restoring tradition, trying to rescue the word from the nursery" (10).[15] For him, the world of Faery and the word *Faery* were so intricately and inextricably connected that in order to do justice to the former, one first had to have a proper understanding of the latter. For Tolkien, MacDonald had failed in his depiction of fairies because he did not have an accurate conception of them—he was misusing them for children and misrepresenting them as small—in size as well as significance.

THE ANXIETY OF MACDONALD

Tolkien's relationship with MacDonald is complex because although he read him as a child and praised his stories as an adult, he grew to despise him later in life. Even so, he recognized that MacDonald did affect his imagination. In a rejected beginning to "On Fairy-stories," he asserts, "For me at any rate fairy-stories are especially associated with Scotland [. . .] by reason of the names of Andrew Lang and George MacDonald. To them in different ways I owe the books which most affected the background of my imagination since childhood" (Tolkien, "On Fairy-stories" 207).[16]

Undoubtedly, MacDonald exerted some influence on him as a writer. In a 1954 letter to Naomi Mitchison, he explained, "[Orcs] are not based on direct experience of mine; but owe, I suppose, a good deal to the goblin tradition [. . .] especially as it appears in George MacDonald" (*Letters* 178).[17] In 1958, he acknowledged in a letter to Mrs. L. M. Cutts that his Ents contained "perhaps some remote influence from George MacDonald's *Phantastes* (a work I do not actually much like)" (qtd. in Hammond and Scull, *Companion* 382). Although he recognized that he owed some minor influence to MacDonald, there is a hesitancy about his admission, as if he wasn't quite willing to acknowledge his debt. Carpenter tells another story that confirms much the same,

> I did once suggest to [Tolkien], one of the few conversations I remember having with him myself, that *The Princess and the Goblin* [by MacDonald] has certain resemblances to *The Hobbit*. Beneath the mountain in both books there are goblins mining, and he was, I think, momentarily disconcerted by his suggestion and did admit that there might have been some very slight influence there, a memory from childhood, but no conscious influences.
>
> (Carpenter, Sayer and Kilby 17)

What this reveals is that although Tolkien was willing to admit to trivial influences, deep down inside he was anxious about MacDonald. Bloom writes,

> The poet *in every reader* does not experience the same disjunction from what he reads that the critic in every reader necessarily feels. What gives pleasure to the critic in a reader may give anxiety to the poet in him, an anxiety we have learned, as readers, to neglect, to our own loss and peril. This anxiety, this mode of melancholy, is the anxiety of influence.
>
> (25)

That Tolkien was plagued by this type of anxiety is quite evident. George Sayer recalls, "On the whole, Tolkien was, even then, not inclined to admit to the influence on him of any other writers at all" (Carpenter, Sayer and Kilby 15). Carpenter more specifically observes, "Tolkien, like Lewis, knew MacDonald's children's stories during his own childhood. He later repudiated any influence of MacDonald's along with repudiating the influence of practically everybody else" (Carpenter, Sayer and Kilby 17). Kilby asserts, "It looked to me as if he had used MacDonald and very much didn't want to confess it—it was a strange thing. It wouldn't have made any difference if he did" (Carpenter, Sayer and Kilby 17).

Yet it would have made *all* the difference according to Bloom. He suggests, "Poets as poets cannot accept substitutions, and fight to the end to have their initial chance alone" (8).[18] Tolkien's insistent denial of influence was a defense mechanism, a way of maintaining his own poetic vision; his very existence as a writer depended on it. In fact, for him to admit to the influence of MacDonald essentially meant he was a lesser writer. "Where generosity is involved," proposes Bloom, "the poets influenced are minor or weaker; the more generosity, and the more mutual it is, the poorer the poets involved" (30). This is a relatively modern view of literature, which has not always been prevalent. Kilby provides a good account of our contemporary understanding: "Today we feature the 'star' and tend to become more enamored of a name than of an accomplishment. We also worship utter originality to the point of eccentricity and regard literary indebtedness as shameful. These things were not always so" ("Tolkien as Scholar" 9). In fact, the meaning of "original" as new or without imitation did not emerge until midway through the neoclassical period. The *OED* records that Joseph Warton was the first to use this word in this sense. In his 1757 work *Essay on the Genius and Writings of Pope,* he writes of the "new and original images" of Thomson (42), praises Dante's "sublime and original poem" (190), and acknowledges that while Pope was "a most excellent improver," he was "no great original inventor" (298).

For the medieval writer, the word carried an entirely different meaning—it was much more connected with its root word "origin." When Gower alludes to "the lawe original" (*Confessio Amantis*), he is talking about the first and most perfect law. In *The Legend of Good Women,* when Chaucer writes, "Ye gete no more of me, but ye wil rede / Thoriginal [the original], that telleth al the cas," he is referring back to an earlier work, most likely Ovid's *Heroides* (Skeat 171). "Original" had nothing to do with novelty, and in terms of literature, it actually consisted of *using* a precursor's material. In her book *Absent Narratives, Manuscript Textuality, and Literary Structure in Late Medieval England,* Elizabeth Scala observes, "A medieval definition of 'originality,' then, would call attention to the origins from which a story comes. Originality in the Middle Ages points toward tradition rather than innovation, even as its literary productions begin approaching such novelty" (3).[19]

Although Tolkien was a medievalist, he did not subscribe to the medieval understanding of "original." Like most of his contemporaries, he fought to preserve his own creative enterprise—a vision that was uniquely and wholly his own. According to Bloom, in a poet's attempt to pursue his own artistic ends, he inevitably becomes engrossed in his own creation. Bloom posits, "Poets, by the time they have grown strong, do not read the poetry of X, for really strong poets can read only themselves. For them, to be judicious is to be weak, and to compare, exactly and fairly, is to be not elect" (19). Such a self-focused approach is indicative of the strong poet. In his pursuit after greatness, he becomes solely devoted to and completely consumed by his own work.

Tolkien faced such a poetic dilemma. In writing to C. S. Lewis in January 1948, he admitted, "I have something that I deeply desire to *make,* and which it is the (largely frustrated) bent of my nature to make. Without any vanity or exaggerated notion of the universal importance of this, it remains a fact that other things are to *me* less important" (*Letters* 126-7). Tolkien is, of course, referring to *The Lord of the Rings,* or more generally, his mythology as whole. He began *The Lord of the Rings* in December 1937, "The Silmarillion" about two decades earlier; at this point in his life, both remained unpublished and unfinished. Surely, Tolkien had grown preoccupied with his own poetic aim. Other things were to him far less important than his own making. About two decades later, he would reaffirm himself as a strong poet in an interview.

> I think I was born with what you might call an inventive mind, and the books that have remained in my mind remain as those things which I acquired and don't really seem much like the book itself. For instance, I now find that I can't stand George McDonald's books at any price at all. I find that now I can't take him. *The same with most books that I've read.*
>
> (qtd. in Resnik 40, emphasis added)

Tolkien reiterated this in yet another interview: "In any case, I don't read much now, not even fairy-stories. And then I'm always looking for something I can't find. Something like what I wrote myself" (qtd. in Plimmer 35). In his mind, all other books paled in comparison to his own. He did "not read the poetry of X" because he could "read only" himself (Bloom 19).

Much of Tolkien's denial of influence stems from his anxiety over it. Like many writers before him, he believed that originality was a natural byproduct of literary greatness. He offers up this very notion in *Smith*: "It was expected that the Great Cake should have something novel and surprising about it and not be a mere repetition of the one before" (11). This is as much a comment about his own art as it is MacDonald's. Tolkien had indubitably been influenced by MacDonald, but he could not accept this. He had poured himself into his fiction—it was rightfully his, and he did not want to have his own poetic vision confused with that of MacDonald's. Bloom rhetorically asks, "For what strong maker desires the realization that he has failed to create himself?" (5). Tolkien definitely felt this tension. His hostility toward MacDonald was as much a result of anxiety as disgust; he feared that others would associate him with a writer he now considered inferior.

In fact, some of the very criticisms Tolkien made about MacDonald can be found in Tolkien's own early work. *The Hobbit,* for example, contains the same kind of patronizing tone that Tolkien accused MacDonald of using. He told Philip Norman on 9 August 1966,

> *The Hobbit* was written in what I should now regard as bad style, as if one were talking to children. There's nothing my children loathed more. They taught me a lesson. Anything that in any way marked out 'The Hobbit' as for children instead of just for people, they disliked—instinctively. I did too, now that I think about it. All this 'I won't tell you any more, you think about it' stuff. Oh no, they loathe it; it's awful.
>
> (100)

In addition, "Goblin Feet," one of Tolkien's earliest published poems, is swarming with little fairy-creatures.[20] In 1971, he denounced the piece altogether when he insisted, "I wish the unhappy little thing, representing all that I came (so soon after) to fervently dislike, could be buried for ever" (qtd. in *Lost Tales I* 32). Clearly, Tolkien had derived his initial ideas about fairies and fairy tales from MacDonald and his contemporaries. As he told W. H. Auden in a 1955 letter: "[*The Hobbit*] has some of the sillinesses of manner caught unthinkingly from the kind of stuff I had had served to me" (*Letters* 215). Another reason Tolkien was so disparaging towards MacDonald was because he had exhibited an influence on Tolkien that had tarnished his own early writing.

It was through *The Lord of the Rings* that Tolkien first broke away from his "Poetic Father" (Bloom 42), but Tolkien's corrective movement and turning were not fully actualized until **Smith.** As a reactionary piece, **Smith** allowed Tolkien "to clear imaginative space" for himself (Bloom 5); it provided him with a chance at "something novel" (**Smith** 11). MacDonald had failed to live up to Tolkien's staunch standards and pedantic expectations. There is an obvious air of superiority in Tolkien's swerve and completion—it is that MacDonald was wrong and would have done better had he been more like Tolkien. Bloom suggests, "The stronger the man, the larger his resentments, and the more brazen his *clinamen*" (43). Evidently, Tolkien must have contained a considerable amount of strength.

Epilogue: A Brief Defense of MacDonald

It must be remembered that Tolkien was "a man of limited sympathies" and that his "taste [was] not normal" (*Letters* 349, 34). We should be slow to adopt his dislikes, especially those he acquired late in life when his opinions on various matters changed substantially. Despite Tolkien's many severe criticisms of *The Golden Key*, it remains an extremely moving story. Like Lewis's Narnian Chronicles, *The Golden Key*'s greatest strength lies in its ability to speak to children while at the same time, comment on deeper spiritual truths. All the same, the story's Fairy is fantastical enough that it can be read and reread without ever taking any notice of its allegorical content. It captures the imagination and raptures the reader into an Otherworld full of beauty and mystery.

The most profound scene occurs when Mossy and Tangle enter the Valley of Shadows. This passage is attractive in a number of ways. First, the description of the barren landscape teeming with shadows is captivating; as a reader, you are drawn in, yet you hesitantly fear the strangeness. Such vivid description recalls some of Smith's own poignant adventures. MacDonald is at his best when he simply describes rather than explains. Second, the children's sorrowful realization that they are longing for a far off country speaks powerfully to the human condition because we all have at one time or another longed for something beyond ourselves or situation. Third, MacDonald places himself in a larger intellectual context by combining Plato's metaphysics with Christian theology. In short, the allegory satisfies the literary critics; the Platonism satisfies the philosophers; and the Christian theology satisfies the theologians.

Notes

1. Sammons notes, "As Tolkien explained in an unpublished letter to Professor Clyde Kilby, the story evolved quite by accident" (4).

2. The thesis is entitled *The Fairy Tales and Fantasies of George MacDonald* by Mary M. McEldowney (Scull and Hammond, *Chronology* 174).

3. See also Scull and Hammond (*Chronology* 625).

4. Glyer defines negative influence as "a situation where one work is created in deliberate opposition to another" (37).

5. C. S. Lewis was known to his close friends and family as "Jack."

6. It is true that in Tolkien's original assessment of *The Golden Key* he did not perceive that it was a children's story. In a note to "On Fairy-stories," he writes that it "is not for children but children do read it for pleasure" (Tolkien, "On Fairy-stories" 250).

7. See also Scull and Hammond (*Reader's Guide* 570).

8. Although in this quote Tolkien mentions *Phantastes* rather than *The Golden Key,* he plainly understood the latter to be an allegory as well. In his notes to "On Fairy-stories," he specifies that it was "*constructed* with consc[ious] alleg[ory]" (qtd. in Scull and Hammond, *Reader's Guide* 570).

9. Tolkien once wrote, "*The Lord of the Rings* was a deliberate attempt to write a large-scale adult fairy-story" (qtd. in Manlove 158). This quotation is taken from a letter dated 8 February 1967 to C. N. Manlove.

10. Many of the ideas presented in this section owe a great deal to Flieger's discussion of *Smith* in her article "The Footsteps of Ælfwine" (196).

11. See also Carpenter (244).

12. Though it can be inferred from the narrative that Rider returns to Faery after he leaves Wootton Major, Tolkien makes it plain in his essay that Rider "went back to Walton, where by the 'entrance' long familiar to him, he could enter Faery, but live and end his days among his wife's kin" (*Smith* 99).

13. See also *Smith* (70, 99-100) and Scull and Hammond (*Reader's Guide* 945).

14. Bloom asserts, "The *tessera* represents any later poet's attempt to persuade himself (and us) that the precursor's Word would be worn out if not redeemed as a newly fulfilled and enlarged Word of the ephebe" (67).

15. John D. Rateliff notes, "The usage in *The Book of Lost Tales* establishes 'fairy' as a synonym for 'elf'" (59). I have found this to be the case in "On Fairy-stories" as well, where Tolkien writes, "*Fairy*, as a noun more or less equivalent to *elf*, is a relatively modern word" (*MC* 112). Moreover, the fact that he gives the Faery King the name Alf (Elf) reaffirms this interpretation.

16. See also Scull and Hammond (*Reader's Guide* 277).

17. See also *Letters* (185). For a more detailed discussion of MacDonald's influence on Tolkien's Orcs, see Rateliff (140-141) and Green (69-71).

18. Later, Bloom adds, "A poet's stance, his Word, his imaginative identity, his whole being, *must* be unique to him, and remain unique, or he will perish, as a poet" (71).

19. C. S. Lewis observes, "One is tempted to say that almost the typical activity of the medieval author consists in touching up something that was already there; as Chaucer touched up Boccaccio, as Malory touched up French prose romances which themselves touched up earlier romances in verse, as La amon works over Wace, who works over Geoffrey, who works over no one knows what. We are inclined to wonder how men could be at once so original that they handled no predecessor without pouring new life into him, and so unoriginal that they seldom did anything completely new" (*Discarded* 209). A couple pages later, he concludes, "The originality which we regard as a sign of wealth might have seemed to them a confession of poverty" (211).

20. Scull and Hammond write, "Some of [Tolkien's] earliest writings, such as the poems "Goblin Feet" and "The Princess Ní," portray similar diminutive beings, and it was his intention in *The Book of Lost Tales* that in the future the Elves would actually fade and diminish and become transparent, and so become the 'fairies' as commonly conceived" (*Reader's Guide* 280). Rateliff references "Goblin Feet," "The Princess Ní," and "Tinfang Warble" as early examples of poetry in which Tolkien depicts little fairies. He claims, "Tolkien later came to disavow the idea of elves as cute little fairies and moved his own elves firmly in the direction of medieval elf-lore; the Rivendell episodes in *The Hobbit* mark virtually its last appearance in the 'main line' of his legendarium" (120).

Works Cited

Bloom, Harold. *The Anxiety of Influence: A Theory of Poetry.* London: Oxford University Press, 1975.

Carpenter, Humphrey. *Tolkien: A Biography.* Boston: Houghton Mifflin, 2000.

———, George Sayer, and Clyde Kilby. "A Dialogue." *Minas Tirith Evening-Star,* 9 no. 2 (January 1980): 14-18.

Cater, William. "Lord of the Hobbits." *Daily Express,* 22 November 1966: 10.

Flieger, Verlyn. "The Footsteps of Ælfwine." In *Tolkien's Legendarium: Essays on The History of Middle-earth,* ed. Verlyn Flieger and Carl F. Hostetter. Westport, CT: Greenwood Press, 2000: 183-198.

Glyer, Diana Pavlac. *The Company They Keep: C. S. Lewis and J. R. R. Tolkien as Writers in Community.* Kent, OH: Kent State University Press, 2007.

Green, William H. *The Hobbit: A Journey into Maturity.* New York: Twayne Publishers, 1995.

Hammond, Wayne G., and Christina Scull. *The Lord of the Rings: A Reader's Companion.* Boston: Houghton Mifflin, 2005.

Kilby, Clyde S. *Tolkien and* The Silmarillion. Wheaton, IL: Harold Shaw, 1976.

———. "Tolkien as a Scholar and Artist." *Tolkien Journal,* 3, no. 1 (1967): 9-11.

Lewis, C. S. *The Collected Letters of C. S. Lewis.* Ed. Walter Hooper. 3 vols. London: HarperCollins, 2000-07.

———. *The Discarded Image: An Introduction to Medieval and Renaissance Literature.* Cambridge: Cambridge University Press, 1964.

MacDonald, George. *The Golden Key.* New York: Farrar, Straus, and Giroux, 1967.

Manlove, C. N. *Modern Fantasy: Five Studies.* Cambridge: Cambridge University Press, 1975.

Norman, Philip. "The Prevalence of Hobbits." *New York Times Magazine,* 15 January 1967: 30-31, 97, 100, 102. http://www.nytimes.com/1967/01/15/books/tolkien-interview.html [Accessed 12 February 2005].

Plimmer, Charlotte, and Denis Plimmer. "The Man Who Understands Hobbits." *The Daily Telegraph Magazine,* 22 March 1968: 31-32, 35.

Rateliff, John D. *The History of* The Hobbit *Part One: Mr. Baggins.* London: HarperCollins, 2007.

Resnik, Henry. "An Interview with Tolkien." *Niekas* 18 (Spring 1967): 37-47.

Ringel, Faye. "Women Fantasists: In the Shadow of the Ring." In *J. R. R. Tolkien and His Literary Resonances: Views of Middle-earth,* ed. George Clark and Daniel Timmons. Westport, CT: Greenwood Press, 2000: 159-171.

Sammons, Margaret. "Tolkien on Fantasy in *Smith of Wootton Major.*" *Mythlore* 12, no. 1 (whole no. 43; Autumn 1985): 3-7, 37.

Scala, Elizabeth. *Absent Narratives, Manuscript Textuality, and Literary Structure in Late Medieval England.* New York: Palgrave Macmillan, 2002.

Scull, Christina, and Wayne G. Hammond. *The J. R. R. Tolkien Companion & Guide: Chronology.* Boston: Houghton Mifflin, 2006.

———. *The J. R. R. Tolkien Companion & Guide: Reader's Guide.* Boston: Houghton Mifflin, 2006.

Shippey, Tom. *J. R. R. Tolkien: Author of the Century.* Boston: Houghton Mifflin, 2002.

———, and Verlyn Flieger. "Allegory versus Bounce: Tolkien's *Smith of Wootton Major.*" *Journal of the Fantastic in the Arts* 12, no. 2 (whole no. 46; 2001): 186-200.

Skeat, Walter W., ed. *Chaucer: The Legend of Good Women.* By Geoffrey Chaucer. Whitefish, MT: Kessinger Publishing, 2006.

FURTHER READING

Criticism

Chance, Jane. "Subversive Fantasist: Tolkien on Class Difference." In *The Lord of the Rings, 1954-2004: Scholarship in Honor of Richard E. Blackwelder,* edited by Wayne G. Hammond and Christina Scull, pp. 153-68. Milwaukee: Marquette University Press, 2006.

Provides a sociological reading of "Farmer Giles of Ham."

Segura, Eduardo. "'Leaf by Niggle' and the Aesthetics of Gift: Towards a Definition of J. R. R. Tolkien's Notion of Art." In *Myth and Magic: Art According to the Inklings,* edited by Eduardo Segura and Thomas Honegger, pp. 315-37. Zollikofen, Switzerland: Walking Tree Publishers, 2007.

Treats themes of art and redemption in "Leaf by Niggle" and in the poem "Mythopoeia."

Additional coverage of Tolkien's life and career is contained in the following sources published by Gale: *Authors and Artists for Young Adults,* Vol. 10; *Authors in the News,* Vol. 1; *Beacham's Encyclopedia of Popular Fiction: Biography & Resources,* Vol. 3; *British Writers: The Classics,* Vol. 2; *British Writers Supplement,* Vol. 2; *Children's Literature Review,* Vols. 56, 152; *Concise Dictionary of British Literary Biography,* 1914-1945; *Contemporary Authors,* Vols. 17-18, 45-48; *Contemporary Authors New Revision Series,* Vols. 36, 134; *Contemporary Authors Permanent Series,* Vol. 2; *Contemporary Literary Criticism,* Vols. 1, 2, 3, 8, 12, 38; *Contemporary Novelists,* Ed. 1; *Contemporary Popular Writers,* Ed. 1; *Dictionary of Literary Biography,* Vols. 15, 160, 255; *DISCovering Authors; DISCovering Authors: British Edition; DISCovering Authors: Canadian Edition; DISCovering Authors Modules: Most-Studied Authors, Novelists,* and *Popular Fiction and Genre Authors; DISCovering Authors 3.0; Encyclopedia of World Literature in the 20th Century,* Ed. 3; *Epics for Students,* Vols. 1:2, 2:1; *Gale Contextual Encyclopedia of World Literature; Junior DISCovering Authors; Literary Movements for Students* Vol. 2; *Literature and Its Times,* Vol. 1; *Literature and Its Times Supplement,* Vol. 1:2; *Literature Resource Center; Major Authors and Illustrators for Children and Young Adults,* Eds. 1, 2; *Major 20th-Century Writers,* Eds. 1, 2; *Major 21st-Century Writers,* eBook 2005; *Modern British Literature,* Ed. 2; *Novels for Students,* Vols. 8, 26; *Reference Guide to English Literature,* Ed. 2; *St. James Guide to Children's Writers,* Ed. 5; *St. James Guide to Fantasy Writers; St. James Guide to Science Fiction Writers,* Ed. 4; *St. James Guide to Young Adult Writers; Science Fiction, Fantasy, and Horror Writers; Something about the Author,* Vols. 2, 24, 32, 100; *Supernatural Fiction Writers; Twayne's English Authors; Twentieth-Century Literary Criticism,* Vol. 137; *World Literature Criticism,* Ed. 6; *Writers for Children;* and *Writers for Young Adults.*

How to Use This Index

The main references

> **Calvino, Italo**
> 1923-1985 .... CLC **5, 8, 11, 22, 33, 39,**
> **73**; SSC **3, 48**

list all author entries in the following Gale Literary Criticism series:

AAL = *Asian American Literature*
BG = *The Beat Generation: A Gale Critical Companion*
BLC = *Black Literature Criticism*
BLCS = *Black Literature Criticism Supplement*
CLC = *Contemporary Literary Criticism*
CLR = *Children's Literature Review*
CMLC = *Classical and Medieval Literature Criticism*
DC = *Drama Criticism*
FL = *Feminism in Literature: A Gale Critical Companion*
GL = *Gothic Literature: A Gale Critical Companion*
HLC = *Hispanic Literature Criticism*
HLCS = *Hispanic Literature Criticism Supplement*
HR = *Harlem Renaissance: A Gale Critical Companion*
LC = *Literature Criticism from 1400 to 1800*
NCLC = *Nineteenth-Century Literature Criticism*
NNAL = *Native North American Literature*
PC = *Poetry Criticism*
SSC = *Short Story Criticism*
TCLC = *Twentieth-Century Literary Criticism*
WLC = *World Literature Criticism, 1500 to the Present*
WLCS = *World Literature Criticism Supplement*

The cross-references

> See also CA 85-88, 116; CANR 23, 61;
> DAM NOV; DLB 196; EW 13; MTCW 1, 2;
> RGSF 2; RGWL 2; SFW 4; SSFS 12

list all author entries in the following Gale biographical and literary sources:

AAYA = *Authors & Artists for Young Adults*
AFAW = *African American Writers*
AFW = *African Writers*
AITN = *Authors in the News*
AMW = *American Writers*
AMWR = *American Writers Retrospective Supplement*
AMWS = *American Writers Supplement*
ANW = *American Nature Writers*
AW = *Ancient Writers*
BEST = *Bestsellers*
BPFB = *Beacham's Encyclopedia of Popular Fiction: Biography and Resources*
BRW = *British Writers*
BRWS = *British Writers Supplement*
BW = *Black Writers*
BYA = *Beacham's Guide to Literature for Young Adults*
CA = *Contemporary Authors*
CAAS = *Contemporary Authors Autobiography Series*
CABS = *Contemporary Authors Bibliographical Series*
CAD = *Contemporary American Dramatists*
CANR = *Contemporary Authors New Revision Series*
CAP = *Contemporary Authors Permanent Series*
CBD = *Contemporary British Dramatists*
CCA = *Contemporary Canadian Authors*
CD = *Contemporary Dramatists*
CDALB = *Concise Dictionary of American Literary Biography*

CDALBS = *Concise Dictionary of American Literary Biography Supplement*
CDBLB = *Concise Dictionary of British Literary Biography*
CMW = *St. James Guide to Crime & Mystery Writers*
CN = *Contemporary Novelists*
CP = *Contemporary Poets*
CPW = *Contemporary Popular Writers*
CSW = *Contemporary Southern Writers*
CWD = *Contemporary Women Dramatists*
CWP = *Contemporary Women Poets*
CWRI = *St. James Guide to Children's Writers*
CWW = *Contemporary World Writers*
DA = *DISCovering Authors*
DA3 = *DISCovering Authors 3.0*
DAB = *DISCovering Authors: British Edition*
DAC = *DISCovering Authors: Canadian Edition*
DAM = *DISCovering Authors: Modules*
   DRAM: *Dramatists Module;* **MST:** *Most-studied Authors Module;*
   MULT: *Multicultural Authors Module;* **NOV:** *Novelists Module;*
   POET: *Poets Module;* **POP:** *Popular Fiction and Genre Authors Module*
DFS = *Drama for Students*
DLB = *Dictionary of Literary Biography*
DLBD = *Dictionary of Literary Biography Documentary Series*
DLBY = *Dictionary of Literary Biography Yearbook*
DNFS = *Literature of Developing Nations for Students*
EFS = *Epics for Students*
EW = *European Writers*
EWL = *Encyclopedia of World Literature in the 20th Century*
EXPN = *Exploring Novels*
EXPP = *Exploring Poetry*
EXPS = *Exploring Short Stories*
FANT = *St. James Guide to Fantasy Writers*
FW = *Feminist Writers*
GFL = *Guide to French Literature,* Beginnings to 1789, 1798 to the Present
GLL = *Gay and Lesbian Literature*
HGG = *St. James Guide to Horror, Ghost & Gothic Writers*
HW = *Hispanic Writers*
IDFW = *International Dictionary of Films and Filmmakers: Writers and Production Artists*
IDTP = *International Dictionary of Theatre: Playwrights*
LAIT = *Literature and Its Times*
LAW = *Latin American Writers*
JRDA = *Junior DISCovering Authors*
MAICYA = *Major Authors and Illustrators for Children and Young Adults*
MAICYAS = *Major Authors and Illustrators for Children and Young Adults Supplement*
MAWW = *Modern American Women Writers*
MJW = *Modern Japanese Writers*
MTCW = *Major 20th-Century Writers*
NCFS = *Nonfiction Classics for Students*
NFS = *Novels for Students*
PAB = *Poets: American and British*
PFS = *Poetry for Students*
RGAL = *Reference Guide to American Literature*
RGEL = *Reference Guide to English Literature*
RGSF = *Reference Guide to Short Fiction*
RGWL = *Reference Guide to World Literature*
RHW = *Twentieth-Century Romance and Historical Writers*
SAAS = *Something about the Author Autobiography Series*
SATA = *Something about the Author*
SFW = *St. James Guide to Science Fiction Writers*
SSFS = *Short Stories for Students*
TCWW = *Twentieth-Century Western Writers*
WLIT = *World Literature and Its Times*
WP = *World Poets*
YABC = *Yesterday's Authors of Books for Children*
YAW = *St. James Guide to Young Adult Writers*

Literary Criticism Series
Cumulative Author Index

Aldrich, Bess Streeter
1881-1954 .... **TCLC 125**
See also CLR 70; TCWW 2

Alegria, Claribel
See Alegria, Claribel

Alegria, Claribel 1924- .... **CLC 75; HLCS 1; PC 26**
See also CA 131; CAAS 15; CANR 66, 94, 134; CWW 2; DAM MULT; DLB 145, 283; EWL 3; HW 1; MTCW 2; MTFW 2005; PFS 21

Alegria, Claribel Joy
See Alegria, Claribel

Alegria, Fernando 1918-2005 .... **CLC 57**
See also CA 9-12R; CANR 5, 32, 72; EWL 3; HW 1, 2

Aleixandre, Vicente 1898-1984 .... **HLCS 1; TCLC 113**
See also CANR 81; DLB 108, 329; EWL 3; HW 2; MTCW 1, 2; RGWL 2, 3

Alekseev, Konstantin Sergeivich
See Stanislavsky, Constantin

Alekseyer, Konstantin Sergeyevich
See Stanislavsky, Constantin

Aleman, Mateo 1547-1615(?) .... **LC 81**

Alencar, Jose de 1829-1877 .... **NCLC 157**
See also DLB 307; LAW; WLIT 1

Alencon, Marguerite d'
See de Navarre, Marguerite

Alepoudelis, Odysseus
See Elytis, Odysseus

Aleshkovsky, Joseph 1929- .... **CLC 44**
See also CA 121; 128; DLB 317

Aleshkovsky, Yuz
See Aleshkovsky, Joseph

Alexander, Barbara
See Ehrenreich, Barbara

Alexander, Lloyd 1924-2007 .... **CLC 35**
See also AAYA 1, 27; BPFB 1; BYA 5, 6, 7, 9, 10, 11; CA 1-4R; 260; CANR 1, 24, 38, 55, 113; CLR 1, 5, 48; CWRI 5; DLB 52; FANT; JRDA; MAICYA 1, 2; MAIC-YAS 1; MTCW 1; SAAS 19; SATA 3, 49, 81, 129, 135; SATA-Obit 182; SUFW; TUS; WYA; YAW

Alexander, Lloyd Chudley
See Alexander, Lloyd

Alexander, Meena 1951- .... **CLC 121**
See also CA 115; CANR 38, 70, 146; CP 5, 6, 7; CWP; DLB 323; FW

Alexander, Rae Pace
See Alexander, Raymond Pace

Alexander, Raymond Pace
1898-1974 .... **SSC 62**
See also CA 97-100; SATA 22; SSFS 4

Alexander, Samuel 1859-1938 .... **TCLC 77**

Alexander of Hales c.
1185-1245 .... **CMLC 128**

Alexeiev, Konstantin
See Stanislavsky, Constantin

Alexeyev, Constantin Sergeivich
See Stanislavsky, Constantin

Alexeyev, Konstantin Sergeyevich
See Stanislavsky, Constantin

Alexie, Sherman 1966- .... **CLC 96, 154; NNAL; PC 53; SSC 107**
See also AAYA 28, 85; BYA 15; CA 138; CANR 65, 95, 133, 174; CN 7; DA3; DAM MULT; DLB 175, 206, 278; LATS 1:2; MTCW 2; MTFW 2005; NFS 17, 31; SSFS 18

Alexie, Sherman Joseph, Jr.
See Alexie, Sherman

al-Farabi 870(?)-950 .... **CMLC 58**
See also DLB 115

Alfau, Felipe 1902-1999 .... **CLC 66**
See also CA 137

Alfieri, Vittorio 1749-1803 .... **NCLC 101**
See also EW 4; RGWL 2, 3; WLIT 7

Alfonso X 1221-1284 .... **CMLC 78**

Alfred, Jean Gaston
See Ponge, Francis

Alger, Horatio, Jr. 1832-1899 .... **NCLC 8, 83**
See also CLR 87; DLB 42; LAIT 2; RGAL 4; SATA 16; TUS

Al-Ghazali, Muhammad ibn Muhammad
1058-1111 .... **CMLC 50**
See also DLB 115

Algren, Nelson 1909-1981 ..... **CLC 4, 10, 33; SSC 33**
See also AMWS 9; BPFB 1; CA 13-16R; 103; CANR 20, 61; CDALB 1941-1968; CN 1, 2; DLB 9; DLBY 1981, 1982, 2000; EWL 3; MAL 5; MTCW 1, 2; MTFW 2005; RGAL 4; RGSF 2

al-Hamadhani 967-1007 .... **CMLC 93**
See also WLIT 6

al-Hariri, al-Qasim ibn 'Ali Abu Muhammad al-Basri
1054-1122 .... **CMLC 63**
See also RGWL 3

Ali, Ahmed 1908-1998 .... **CLC 69**
See also CA 25-28R; CANR 15, 34; CN 1, 2, 3, 4, 5; DLB 323; EWL 3

Ali, Monica 1967- .... **CLC 304**
See also AAYA 67; BRWS 13; CA 219; CANR 158, 205; DLB 323

Ali, Tariq 1943- .... **CLC 173**
See also CA 25-28R; CANR 10, 99, 161, 196

Alighieri, Dante
See Dante

al-Kindi, Abu Yusuf Ya'qub ibn Ishaq c.
801-c. 873 .... **CMLC 80**

Allan, John B.
See Westlake, Donald E.

Allan, Sidney
See Hartmann, Sadakichi

Allan, Sydney
See Hartmann, Sadakichi

Allard, Janet .... **CLC 59**

Allen, Betsy
See Harrison, Elizabeth (Allen) Cavanna

Allen, Edward 1948- .... **CLC 59**

Allen, Fred 1894-1956 .... **TCLC 87**

Allen, Paula Gunn 1939-2008 . **CLC 84, 202, 280; NNAL**
See also AMWS 4; CA 112; 143; 272; CANR 63, 130; CWP; DA3; DAM MULT; DLB 175; FW; MTCW 2; MTFW 2005; RGAL 4; TCWW 2

Allen, Roland
See Ayckbourn, Alan

Allen, Sarah A.
See Hopkins, Pauline Elizabeth

Allen, Sidney H.
See Hartmann, Sadakichi

Allen, Woody 1935- ..... **CLC 16, 52, 195, 288**
See also AAYA 10, 51; AMWS 15; CA 33-36R; CANR 27, 38, 63, 128, 172; DAM POP; DLB 44; MTCW 1; SSFS 21

Allende, Isabel 1942- ... **CLC 39, 57, 97, 170, 264; HLC 1; SSC 65; WLCS**
See also AAYA 18, 70; CA 125; 130; CANR 51, 74, 129, 165, 208; CDWLB 3; CLR 99; CWW 2; DA3; DAM MULT, NOV; DLB 145; DNFS 1; EWL 3; FL 1:5; FW; HW 1, 2; INT CA-130; LAIT 5; LAWS 1; LMFS 2; MTCW 1, 2; MTFW 2005; NCFS 1; NFS 6, 18, 29; RGSF 2; RGWL 3; SATA 163; SSFS 11, 16; WLIT 1

Alleyn, Ellen
See Rossetti, Christina

Alleyne, Carla D. .... **CLC 65**

Allingham, Margery (Louise)
1904-1966 .... **CLC 19**
See also CA 5-8R; 25-28R; CANR 4, 58; CMW 4; DLB 77; MSW; MTCW 1, 2

Allingham, William 1824-1889 ...... **NCLC 25**
See also DLB 35; RGEL 2

Allison, Dorothy E. 1949- . **CLC 78, 153, 290**
See also AAYA 53; CA 140; CANR 66, 107; CN 7; CSW; DA3; DLB 350; FW; MTCW 2; MTFW 2005; NFS 11; RGAL 4

Alloula, Malek .... **CLC 65**

Allston, Washington 1779-1843 .... **NCLC 2**
See also DLB 1, 235

Almedingen, E. M.
See Almedingen, Martha Edith von

Almedingen, Martha Edith von
1898-1971 .... **CLC 12**
See also CA 1-4R; CANR 1; SATA 3

Almodovar, Pedro 1949(?)- .... **CLC 114, 229; HLCS 1**
See also CA 133; CANR 72, 151; HW 2

Almqvist, Carl Jonas Love
1793-1866 .... **NCLC 42**

al-Mutanabbi, Ahmad ibn al-Husayn Abu al-Tayyib al-Jufi al-Kindi
915-965 .... **CMLC 66**
See also RGWL 3; WLIT 6

Alonso, Damaso 1898-1990 . **CLC 14; TCLC 245**
See also CA 110; 131; 130; CANR 72; DLB 108; EWL 3; HW 1, 2

Alov
See Gogol, Nikolai

al'Sadaawi, Nawal
See El Saadawi, Nawal

al-Shaykh, Hanan 1945- .... **CLC 218**
See also CA 135; CANR 111; CWW 2; DLB 346; EWL 3; WLIT 6

Al Siddik
See Rolfe, Frederick (William Serafino Austin Lewis Mary)

Alta 1942- .... **CLC 19**
See also CA 57-60

Alter, Robert B. 1935- .... **CLC 34**
See also CA 49-52; CANR 1, 47, 100, 160, 201

Alter, Robert Bernard
See Alter, Robert B.

Alther, Lisa 1944- .... **CLC 7, 41**
See also BPFB 1; CA 65-68; CAAS 30; CANR 12, 30, 51, 180; CN 4, 5, 6, 7; CSW; GLL 2; MTCW 1

Althusser, L.
See Althusser, Louis

Althusser, Louis 1918-1990 .... **CLC 106**
See also CA 131; 132; CANR 102; DLB 242

Altman, Robert 1925-2006 .... **CLC 16, 116, 242**
See also CA 73-76; 254; CANR 43

Alurista
See Urista, Alberto

Alvarez, A. 1929- .... **CLC 5, 13**
See also CA 1-4R; CANR 3, 33, 63, 101, 134; CN 3, 4, 5, 6; CP 1, 2, 3, 4, 5, 6, 7; DLB 14, 40; MTFW 2005

Alvarez, Alejandro Rodriguez
1903-1965 . **CLC 49; DC 32; TCLC 199**
See also CA 131; 93-96; EWL 3; HW 1

Alvarez, Julia 1950- .. **CLC 93, 274; HLCS 1**
See also AAYA 25, 85; AMWS 7; CA 147; CANR 69, 101, 133, 166; DA3; DLB 282; LATS 1:2; LLW; MTCW 2; MTFW 2005; NFS 5, 9; SATA 129; SSFS 27, 31; WLIT 1

Alvaro, Corrado 1896-1956 .... **TCLC 60**
See also CA 163; DLB 264; EWL 3

Amado, Jorge 1912-2001 ... **CLC 13, 40, 106, 232; HLC 1**
See also CA 77-80; 201; CANR 35, 74, 135; CWW 2; DAM MULT, NOV; DLB 113, 307; EWL 3; HW 2; LAW; LAWS 1; MTCW 1, 2; MTFW 2005; RGWL 2, 3; TWA; WLIT 1

Ambler, Eric 1909-1998 .... **CLC 4, 6, 9**
See also BRWS 4; CA 9-12R; 171; CANR 7, 38, 74; CMW 4; CN 1, 2, 3, 4, 5, 6; DLB 77; MSW; MTCW 1, 2; TEA

Ambrose c. 339-c. 397 .... **CMLC 103**

Ambrose, Stephen E. 1936-2002 .... **CLC 145**
See also AAYA 44; CA 1-4R; 209; CANR 3, 43, 57, 83, 105; MTFW 2005; NCFS 2; SATA 40, 138

Amichai, Yehuda 1924-2000 .. **CLC 9, 22, 57, 116; PC 38**
See also CA 85-88; 189; CANR 46, 60, 99, 132; CWW 2; EWL 3; MTCW 1, 2; MTFW 2005; PFS 24; RGHL; WLIT 6

Amichai, Yehudah
See Amichai, Yehuda

Amiel, Henri Frederic 1821-1881 .... **NCLC 4**
See also DLB 217

Amis, Kingsley 1922-1995 . **CLC 1, 2, 3, 5, 8, 13, 40, 44, 129**
See also AAYA 77; AITN 2; BPFB 1; BRWS 2; CA 9-12R; 150; CANR 8, 28, 54; CDBLB 1945-1960; CN 1, 2, 3, 4, 5, 6; CP 1, 2, 3, 4; DA; DA3; DAB; DAC; DAM MST, NOV; DLB 15, 27, 100, 139, 326, 352; DLBY 1996; EWL 3; HGG; INT CANR-8; MTCW 1, 2; MTFW 2005; RGEL 2; RGSF 2; SFW 4

Amis, Martin 1949- ... **CLC 4, 9, 38, 62, 101, 213; SSC 112**
See also BEST 90:3; BRWS 4; CA 65-68; CANR 8, 27, 54, 73, 95, 132, 166, 208; CN 5, 6, 7; DA3; DLB 14, 194; EWL 3; INT CANR-27; MTCW 2; MTFW 2005

Amis, Martin Louis
See Amis, Martin

Ammianus Marcellinus c. 330-c. 395 .... **CMLC 60**
See also AW 2; DLB 211

Ammons, A.R. 1926-2001 .. **CLC 2, 3, 5, 8, 9, 25, 57, 108; PC 16**
See also AITN 1; AMWS 7; CA 9-12R; 193; CANR 6, 36, 51, 73, 107, 156; CP 1, 2, 3, 4, 5, 6, 7; CSW; DAM POET; DLB 5, 165, 342; EWL 3; MAL 5; MTCW 1, 2; PFS 19; RGAL 4; TCLE 1:1

Ammons, Archie Randolph
See Ammons, A.R.

Amo, Tauraatua i
See Adams, Henry

Amory, Thomas 1691(?)-1788 .... **LC 48**
See also DLB 39

Anand, Mulk Raj 1905-2004 ..... **CLC 23, 93, 237**
See also CA 65-68; 231; CANR 32, 64; CN 1, 2, 3, 4, 5, 6, 7; DAM NOV; DLB 323; EWL 3; MTCW 1, 2; MTFW 2005; RGSF 2

Anatol
See Schnitzler, Arthur

Anaximander c. 611B.C.-c. 546B.C. .... **CMLC 22**

Anaya, Rudolfo 1937- ...... **CLC 23, 148, 255; HLC 1**
See also AAYA 20; BYA 13; CA 45-48; CAAS 4; CANR 1, 32, 51, 124, 169; CLR 129; CN 4, 5, 6, 7; DAM MULT, NOV; DLB 82, 206, 278; HW 1; LAIT 4; LLW; MAL 5; MTCW 1, 2; MTFW 2005; NFS 12; RGAL 4; RGSF 2; TCWW 2; WLIT 1

Anaya, Rudolfo A.
See Anaya, Rudolfo

Anaya, Rudolpho Alfonso
See Anaya, Rudolfo

Andersen, Hans Christian 1805-1875 ...... **NCLC 7, 79, 214; SSC 6, 56; WLC 1**
See also AAYA 57; CLR 6, 113; DA; DA3; DAB; DAC; DAM MST, POP; EW 6; MAICYA 1, 2; RGSF 2; RGWL 2, 3; SATA 100; TWA; WCH; YABC 1

Anderson, C. Farley
See Mencken, H. L.; Nathan, George Jean

Anderson, Jessica (Margaret) Queale 1916- .... **CLC 37**
See also CA 9-12R; CANR 4, 62; CN 4, 5, 6, 7; DLB 325

Anderson, Jon (Victor) 1940- .... **CLC 9**
See also CA 25-28R; CANR 20; CP 1, 3, 4, 5; DAM POET

Anderson, Lindsay (Gordon) 1923-1994 .... **CLC 20**
See also CA 125; 128; 146; CANR 77

Anderson, Maxwell 1888-1959 .... **DC 43; TCLC 2, 144**
See also CA 105; 152; DAM DRAM; DFS 16, 20; DLB 7, 228; MAL 5; MTCW 2; MTFW 2005; RGAL 4

Anderson, Poul 1926-2001 .... **CLC 15**
See also AAYA 5, 34; BPFB 1; BYA 6, 8, 9; CA 1-4R; 181; 199; CAAE 181; CAAS 2; CANR 2, 15, 34, 64, 110; CLR 58; DLB 8; FANT; INT CANR-15; MTCW 1, 2; MTFW 2005; SATA 90; SATA-Brief 39; SATA-Essay 106; SCFW 1, 2; SFW 4; SUFW 1, 2

Anderson, R. W.
See Anderson, Robert

Anderson, Robert 1917-2009 .... **CLC 23**
See also AITN 1; CA 21-24R; 283; CANR 32; CD 6; DAM DRAM; DLB 7; LAIT 5

Anderson, Robert W.
See Anderson, Robert

Anderson, Robert Woodruff
See Anderson, Robert

Anderson, Roberta Joan
See Mitchell, Joni

Anderson, Sherwood 1876-1941 ... **SSC 1, 46, 91, 142; TCLC 1, 10, 24, 123; WLC 1**
See also AAYA 30; AMW; AMWC 2; BPFB 1; CA 104; 121; CANR 61; CDALB 1917-1929; DA; DA3; DAB; DAC; DAM MST, NOV; DLB 4, 9, 86; DLBD 1; EWL 3; EXPS; GLL 2; MAL 5; MTCW 1, 2; MTFW 2005; NFS 4; RGAL 4; RGSF 2; SSFS 4, 10, 11; TUS

Anderson, Wes 1969- .... **CLC 227**
See also CA 214

Andier, Pierre
See Desnos, Robert

Andouard
See Giraudoux, Jean

Andrade, Carlos Drummond de
See Drummond de Andrade, Carlos

Andrade, Mario de
See de Andrade, Mario

Andreae, Johann V(alentin) 1586-1654 .... **LC 32**
See also DLB 164

Andreas Capellanus fl. c. 1185- .... **CMLC 45**
See also DLB 208

Andreas-Salome, Lou 1861-1937 ... **TCLC 56**
See also CA 178; DLB 66

Andreev, Leonid
See Andreyev, Leonid

Andress, Lesley
See Sanders, Lawrence

Andrew, Joseph Maree
See Occomy, Marita (Odette) Bonner

Andrewes, Lancelot 1555-1626 .... **LC 5**
See also DLB 151, 172

Andrews, Cicily Fairfield
See West, Rebecca

Andrews, Elton V.
See Pohl, Frederik

Andrews, Peter
See Soderbergh, Steven

Andrews, Raymond 1934-1991 .... **BLC 2:1**
See also BW 2; CA 81-84; 136; CANR 15, 42

Andreyev, Leonid 1871-1919 ... **TCLC 3, 221**
See also CA 104; 185; DLB 295; EWL 3

Andreyev, Leonid Nikolaevich
See Andreyev, Leonid

Andrezel, Pierre
See Blixen, Karen

Andric, Ivo 1892-1975 .... **CLC 8; SSC 36; TCLC 135**
See also CA 81-84; 57-60; CANR 43, 60; CDWLB 4; DLB 147, 329; EW 11; EWL 3; MTCW 1; RGSF 2; RGWL 2, 3

Androvar
See Prado (Calvo), Pedro

Angela of Foligno 1248(?)-1309 .... **CMLC 76**

Angelique, Pierre
See Bataille, Georges

Angell, Judie
See Angell, Judie

Angell, Judie 1937- .... **CLC 30**
See also AAYA 11, 71; BYA 6; CA 77-80; CANR 49; CLR 33; JRDA; SATA 22, 78; WYA; YAW

Angell, Roger 1920- .... **CLC 26**
See also CA 57-60; CANR 13, 44, 70, 144; DLB 171, 185

Angelou, Maya 1928- ...... **BLC 1:1; CLC 12, 35, 64, 77, 155; PC 32; WLCS**
See also AAYA 7, 20; AMWS 4; BPFB 1; BW 2, 3; BYA 2; CA 65-68; CANR 19, 42, 65, 111, 133, 204; CDALBS; CLR 53; CP 4, 5, 6, 7; CPW; CSW; CWP; DA; DA3; DAB; DAC; DAM MST, MULT, POET, POP; DLB 38; EWL 3; EXPN; EXPP; FL 1:5; LAIT 4; MAICYA 2; MAICYAS 1; MAL 5; MBL; MTCW 1, 2; MTFW 2005; NCFS 2; NFS 2; PFS 2, 3, 33, 38; RGAL 4; SATA 49, 136; TCLE 1:1; WYA; YAW

Angouleme, Marguerite d'
See de Navarre, Marguerite

Anna Comnena 1083-1153 .... **CMLC 25**

Annensky, Innokentii Fedorovich
See Annensky, Innokenty (Fyodorovich)

Annensky, Innokenty (Fyodorovich) 1856-1909 .... **TCLC 14**
See also CA 110; 155; DLB 295; EWL 3

Annunzio, Gabriele d'
See D'Annunzio, Gabriele

Anodos
See Coleridge, Mary E(lizabeth)

Anon, Charles Robert
See Pessoa, Fernando

Anouilh, Jean 1910-1987 ..... **CLC 1, 3, 8, 13, 40, 50; DC 8, 21; TCLC 195**
See also AAYA 67; CA 17-20R; 123; CANR 32; DAM DRAM; DFS 9, 10, 19; DLB 321; EW 13; EWL 3; GFL 1789 to the Present; MTCW 1, 2; MTFW 2005; RGWL 2, 3; TWA

Anouilh, Jean Marie Lucien Pierre
See Anouilh, Jean

Ansa, Tina McElroy 1949- .... **BLC 2:1**
See also BW 2; CA 142; CANR 143; CSW

Anselm of Canterbury 1033(?)-1109 .... **CMLC 67**
See also DLB 115

Anthony, Florence
See Ai

Anthony, John
See Ciardi, John (Anthony)

Anthony, Peter
See Shaffer, Anthony; Shaffer, Peter
Anthony, Piers 1934- .... **CLC 35**
See also AAYA 11, 48; BYA 7; CA 200;
CAAE 200; CANR 28, 56, 73, 102, 133,
202; CLR 118; CPW; DAM POP; DLB 8;
FANT; MAICYA 2; MAICYAS 1; MTCW
1, 2; MTFW 2005; SAAS 22; SATA 84,
129; SATA-Essay 129; SFW 4; SUFW 1,
2; YAW
Anthony, Susan B(rownell)
1820-1906 .... **TCLC 84**
See also CA 211; FW
Antin, Mary 1881-1949 .... **TCLC 247**
See also AMWS 20; CA 118; 181; DLB
221; DLBY 1984
Antiphon c. 480B.C.-c. 411B.C. .... **CMLC 55**
Antoine, Marc
See Proust, Marcel
Antoninus, Brother
See Everson, William
Antonioni, Michelangelo
1912-2007 .... **CLC 20, 144, 259**
See also CA 73-76; 262; CANR 45, 77
Antschel, Paul
See Celan, Paul
Anwar, Chairil 1922-1949 .... **TCLC 22**
See also CA 121; 219; EWL 3; RGWL 3
Anyidoho, Kofi 1947- .... **BLC 2:1**
See also BW 3; CA 178; CP 5, 6, 7; DLB
157; EWL 3
Anzaldua, Gloria (Evanjelina)
1942-2004 .... **CLC 200; HLCS 1**
See also CA 175; 227; CSW; CWP; DLB
122; FW; LLW; RGAL 4; SATA-Obit 154
Apess, William 1798-1839(?) .... **NCLC 73;
NNAL**
See also DAM MULT; DLB 175, 243
Apollinaire, Guillaume 1880-1918 .... **PC 7;
TCLC 3, 8, 51**
See also CA 104; 152; DAM POET; DLB
258, 321; EW 9; EWL 3; GFL 1789 to
the Present; MTCW 2; PFS 24; RGWL 2,
3; TWA; WP
Apollonius of Rhodes
See Apollonius Rhodius
Apollonius Rhodius c. 300B.C.-c.
220B.C. .... **CMLC 28**
See also AW 1; DLB 176; RGWL 2, 3
Appelfeld, Aharon 1932- ... **CLC 23, 47; SSC
42**
See also CA 112; 133; CANR 86, 160, 207;
CWW 2; DLB 299; EWL 3; RGHL;
RGSF 2; WLIT 6
Appelfeld, Aron
See Appelfeld, Aharon
Apple, Max 1941- .... **CLC 9, 33; SSC 50**
See also AMWS 17; CA 81-84; CANR 19,
54, 214; DLB 130
Apple, Max Isaac
See Apple, Max
Appleman, Philip (Dean) 1926- .... **CLC 51**
See also CA 13-16R; CAAS 18; CANR 6,
29, 56
Appleton, Lawrence
See Lovecraft, H. P.
Apteryx
See Eliot, T. S.
Apuleius, (Lucius Madaurensis) c. 125-c.
164 .... **CMLC 1, 84**
See also AW 2; CDWLB 1; DLB 211;
RGWL 2, 3; SUFW; WLIT 8
Aquin, Hubert 1929-1977 .... **CLC 15**
See also CA 105; DLB 53; EWL 3
Aquinas, Thomas 1224(?)-1274 ..... **CMLC 33**
See also DLB 115; EW 1; TWA

Aragon, Louis 1897-1982 .... **CLC 3, 22;
TCLC 123**
See also CA 69-72; 108; CANR 28, 71;
DAM NOV, POET; DLB 72, 258; EW 11;
EWL 3; GFL 1789 to the Present; GLL 2;
LMFS 2; MTCW 1, 2; RGWL 2, 3
Arany, Janos 1817-1882 .... **NCLC 34**
Aranyos, Kakay 1847-1910
See Mikszath, Kalman
Aratus of Soli c. 315B.C.-c.
240B.C. .... **CMLC 64, 114**
See also DLB 176
Arbuthnot, John 1667-1735 .... **LC 1**
See also BRWS 16; DLB 101
Archer, Herbert Winslow
See Mencken, H. L.
Archer, Jeffrey 1940- .... **CLC 28**
See also AAYA 16; BEST 89:3; BPFB 1;
CA 77-80; CANR 22, 52, 95, 136, 209;
CPW; DA3; DAM POP; INT CANR-22;
MTFW 2005
Archer, Jeffrey Howard
See Archer, Jeffrey
Archer, Jules 1915- .... **CLC 12**
See also CA 9-12R; CANR 6, 69; SAAS 5;
SATA 4, 85
Archer, Lee
See Ellison, Harlan
Archilochus c. 7th cent. B.C.- .... **CMLC 44**
See also DLB 176
Ard, William
See Jakes, John
Arden, John 1930- .... **CLC 6, 13, 15**
See also BRWS 2; CA 13-16R; CAAS 4;
CANR 31, 65, 67, 124; CBD; CD 5, 6;
DAM DRAM; DFS 9; DLB 13, 245;
EWL 3; MTCW 1
Arenas, Reinaldo 1943-1990 .. **CLC 41; HLC
1; TCLC 191**
See also CA 124; 128; 133; CANR 73, 106;
DAM MULT; DLB 145; EWL 3; GLL 2;
HW 1; LAW; LAWS 1; MTCW 2; MTFW
2005; RGSF 2; RGWL 3; WLIT 1
Arendt, Hannah 1906-1975 .... **CLC 66, 98;
TCLC 193**
See also CA 17-20R; 61-64; CANR 26, 60,
172; DLB 242; MTCW 1, 2
Aretino, Pietro 1492-1556 .... **LC 12, 165**
See also RGWL 2, 3
Arghezi, Tudor
See Theodorescu, Ion N.
Arguedas, Jose Maria 1911-1969 .... **CLC 10,
18; HLCS 1; TCLC 147**
See also CA 89-92; CANR 73; DLB 113;
EWL 3; HW 1; LAW; RGWL 2, 3; WLIT
1
Argueta, Manlio 1936- .... **CLC 31**
See also CA 131; CANR 73; CWW 2; DLB
145; EWL 3; HW 1; RGWL 3
Arias, Ron 1941- .... **HLC 1**
See also CA 131; CANR 81, 136; DAM
MULT; DLB 82; HW 1, 2; MTCW 2;
MTFW 2005
Ariosto, Lodovico
See Ariosto, Ludovico
Ariosto, Ludovico 1474-1533 ... **LC 6, 87; PC
42**
See also EW 2; RGWL 2, 3; WLIT 7
Aristides
See Epstein, Joseph
Aristides Quintilianus fl. c. 100-fl. c.
400 .... **CMLC 122**
Aristophanes 450B.C.-385B.C. .... **CMLC 4,
51; DC 2; WLCS**
See also AW 1; CDWLB 1; DA; DA3;
DAB; DAC; DAM DRAM, MST; DFS
10; DLB 176; LMFS 1; RGWL 2, 3;
TWA; WLIT 8

Aristotle 384B.C.-322B.C. .... **CMLC 31, 123;
WLCS**
See also AW 1; CDWLB 1; DA; DA3;
DAB; DAC; DAM MST; DLB 176;
RGWL 2, 3; TWA; WLIT 8
Arlt, Roberto 1900-1942 . **HLC 1; TCLC 29,
255**
See also CA 123; 131; CANR 67; DAM
MULT; DLB 305; EWL 3; HW 1, 2;
IDTP; LAW
Arlt, Roberto Godofredo Christophersen
See Arlt, Roberto
Armah, Ayi Kwei 1939- . **BLC 1:1, 2:1; CLC
5, 33, 136**
See also AFW; BRWS 10; BW 1; CA 61-
64; CANR 21, 64; CDWLB 3; CN 1, 2,
3, 4, 5, 6, 7; DAM MULT, POET; DLB
117; EWL 3; MTCW 1; WLIT 2
Armatrading, Joan 1950- .... **CLC 17**
See also CA 114; 186
Armin, Robert 1568(?)-1615(?) .... **LC 120**
Armitage, Frank
See Carpenter, John
Armstrong, Jeannette (C.) 1948- .... **NNAL**
See also CA 149; CCA 1; CN 6, 7; DAC;
DLB 334; SATA 102
Armytage, R.
See Watson, Rosamund Marriott
Arnauld, Antoine 1612-1694 .... **LC 169**
See also DLB 268
Arnette, Robert
See Silverberg, Robert
**Arnim, Achim von (Ludwig Joachim von
Arnim)** 1781-1831 .. **NCLC 5, 159; SSC
29**
See also DLB 90
Arnim, Bettina von 1785-1859 ...... **NCLC 38,
123**
See also DLB 90; RGWL 2, 3
Arnold, Matthew 1822-1888 ..... **NCLC 6, 29,
89, 126, 218; PC 5, 94; WLC 1**
See also BRW 5; CDBLB 1832-1890; DA;
DAB; DAC; DAM MST, POET; DLB 32,
57; EXPP; PAB; PFS 2; TEA; WP
Arnold, Thomas 1795-1842 .... **NCLC 18**
See also DLB 55
Arnow, Harriette (Louisa) Simpson
1908-1986 ...... **CLC 2, 7, 18; TCLC 196**
See also BPFB 1; CA 9-12R; 118; CANR
14; CN 2, 3, 4; DLB 6; FW; MTCW 1, 2;
RHW; SATA 42; SATA-Obit 47
Arouet, Francois-Marie
See Voltaire
Arp, Hans
See Arp, Jean
Arp, Jean 1887-1966 .... **CLC 5; TCLC 115**
See also CA 81-84; 25-28R; CANR 42, 77;
EW 10
Arrabal
See Arrabal, Fernando
Arrabal, Fernando 1932- .. **CLC 2, 9, 18, 58;
DC 35**
See also CA 9-12R; CANR 15; CWW 2;
DLB 321; EWL 3; LMFS 2
Arrabal Teran, Fernando
See Arrabal, Fernando
Arreola, Juan Jose 1918-2001 .... **CLC 147;
HLC 1; SSC 38**
See also CA 113; 131; 200; CANR 81;
CWW 2; DAM MULT; DLB 113; DNFS
2; EWL 3; HW 1, 2; LAW; RGSF 2
Arrian c. 89(?)-c. 155(?) .... **CMLC 43**
See also DLB 176
Arrick, Fran
See Angell, Judie
Arrley, Richmond
See Delany, Samuel R., Jr.

Ayme, Marcel (Andre) 1902-1967 ... **CLC 11; SSC 41**
See also CA 89-92; CANR 67, 137; CLR 25; DLB 72; EW 12; EWL 3; GFL 1789 to the Present; RGSF 2; RGWL 2, 3; SATA 91

Ayrton, Michael 1921-1975 .... **CLC 7**
See also CA 5-8R; 61-64; CANR 9, 21

Aytmatov, Chingiz
See Aitmatov, Chingiz

Azorin
See Martinez Ruiz, Jose

Azuela, Mariano 1873-1952 .. **HLC 1; TCLC 3, 145, 217**
See also CA 104; 131; CANR 81; DAM MULT; EWL 3; HW 1, 2; LAW; MTCW 1, 2; MTFW 2005

Ba, Mariama 1929-1981 ...... **BLC 2:1; BLCS**
See also AFW; BW 2; CA 141; CANR 87; DLB 360; DNFS 2; WLIT 2

Baastad, Babbis Friis
See Friis-Baastad, Babbis Ellinor

Bab
See Gilbert, W(illiam) S(chwenck)

Babbis, Eleanor
See Friis-Baastad, Babbis Ellinor

Babel, Isaac
See Babel, Isaak (Emmanuilovich)

Babel, Isaak (Emmanuilovich) 1894-1941(?) . **SSC 16, 78; TCLC 2, 13, 171**
See also CA 104; 155; CANR 113; DLB 272; EW 11; EWL 3; MTCW 2; MTFW 2005; RGSF 2; RGWL 2, 3; SSFS 10; TWA

Babits, Mihaly 1883-1941 .... **TCLC 14**
See also CA 114; CDWLB 4; DLB 215; EWL 3

Babur 1483-1530 .... **LC 18**

Babylas
See Ghelderode, Michel de

Baca, Jimmy Santiago 1952- . **HLC 1; PC 41**
See also CA 131; CANR 81, 90, 146; CP 6, 7; DAM MULT; DLB 122; HW 1, 2; LLW; MAL 5

Baca, Jose Santiago
See Baca, Jimmy Santiago

Bacchelli, Riccardo 1891-1985 .... **CLC 19**
See also CA 29-32R; 117; DLB 264; EWL 3

Bacchylides c. 520B.C.-c. 452B.C. .... **CMLC 119**

Bach, Richard 1936- .... **CLC 14**
See also AITN 1; BEST 89:2; BPFB 1; BYA 5; CA 9-12R; CANR 18, 93, 151; CPW; DAM NOV, POP; FANT; MTCW 1; SATA 13

Bach, Richard David
See Bach, Richard

Bache, Benjamin Franklin 1769-1798 .... **LC 74**
See also DLB 43

Bachelard, Gaston 1884-1962 ...... **TCLC 128**
See also CA 97-100; 89-92; DLB 296; GFL 1789 to the Present

Bachman, Richard
See King, Stephen

Bachmann, Ingeborg 1926-1973 ..... **CLC 69; TCLC 192**
See also CA 93-96; 45-48; CANR 69; DLB 85; EWL 3; RGHL; RGWL 2, 3

Bacigalupi, Paolo 1973- .... **CLC 309**

Bacon, Francis 1561-1626 ..... **LC 18, 32, 131**
See also BRW 1; CDBLB Before 1660; DLB 151, 236, 252; RGEL 2; TEA

Bacon, Roger 1214(?)-1294 ... **CMLC 14, 108**
See also DLB 115

Bacovia, G.
See Bacovia, George

Bacovia, George 1881-1957 .... **TCLC 24**
See Bacovia, George
See also CA 123; 189; CDWLB 4; DLB 220; EWL 3

Badanes, Jerome 1937-1995 .... **CLC 59**
See also CA 234

Bage, Robert 1728-1801 .... **NCLC 182**
See also DLB 39; RGEL 2

Bagehot, Walter 1826-1877 .... **NCLC 10**
See also DLB 55

Bagnold, Enid 1889-1981 .... **CLC 25**
See also AAYA 75; BYA 2; CA 5-8R; 103; CANR 5, 40; CBD; CN 2; CWD; CWRI 5; DAM DRAM; DLB 13, 160, 191, 245; FW; MAICYA 1, 2; RGEL 2; SATA 1, 25

Bagritsky, Eduard
See Dzyubin, Eduard Georgievich

Bagritsky, Edvard
See Dzyubin, Eduard Georgievich

Bagrjana, Elisaveta
See Belcheva, Elisaveta Lyubomirova

Bagryana, Elisaveta
See Belcheva, Elisaveta Lyubomirova

Bailey, Paul 1937- .... **CLC 45**
See also CA 21-24R; CANR 16, 62, 124; CN 1, 2, 3, 4, 5, 6, 7; DLB 14, 271; GLL 2

Baillie, Joanna 1762-1851 ...... **NCLC 71, 151**
See also DLB 93, 344; GL 2; RGEL 2

Bainbridge, Beryl 1934-2010 ..... **CLC 4, 5, 8, 10, 14, 18, 22, 62, 130, 292**
See also BRWS 6; CA 21-24R; CANR 24, 55, 75, 88, 128; CN 2, 3, 4, 5, 6, 7; DAM NOV; DLB 14, 231; EWL 3; MTCW 1, 2; MTFW 2005

Baker, Carlos (Heard) 1909-1987 .... **TCLC 119**
See also CA 5-8R; 122; CANR 3, 63; DLB 103

Baker, Elliott 1922-2007 .... **CLC 8**
See also CA 45-48; 257; CANR 2, 63; CN 1, 2, 3, 4, 5, 6, 7

Baker, Elliott Joseph
See Baker, Elliott

Baker, Jean H.
See Russell, George William

Baker, Nicholson 1957- .... **CLC 61, 165**
See also AMWS 13; CA 135; CANR 63, 120, 138, 190; CN 6; CPW; DA3; DAM POP; DLB 227; MTFW 2005

Baker, Ray Stannard 1870-1946 .... **TCLC 47**
See also CA 118; DLB 345

Baker, Russell 1925- .... **CLC 31**
See also BEST 89:4; CA 57-60; CANR 11, 41, 59, 137; MTCW 1, 2; MTFW 2005

Baker, Russell Wayne
See Baker, Russell

Bakhtin, M.
See Bakhtin, Mikhail Mikhailovich

Bakhtin, M. M.
See Bakhtin, Mikhail Mikhailovich

Bakhtin, Mikhail
See Bakhtin, Mikhail Mikhailovich

Bakhtin, Mikhail Mikhailovich 1895-1975 .... **CLC 83; TCLC 160**
See Bakhtin, Mikhail Mikhailovich
See also CA 128; 113; DLB 242; EWL 3

Bakshi, Ralph 1938(?)- .... **CLC 26**
See also CA 112; 138; IDFW 3

Bakunin, Mikhail (Alexandrovich) 1814-1876 .... **NCLC 25, 58**
See also DLB 277

Bal, Mieke 1946- .... **CLC 252**
See also CA 156; CANR 99

Bal, Mieke Maria Gertrudis
See Bal, Mieke

Baldwin, James 1924-1987 ...... **BLC 1:1, 2:1; CLC 1, 2, 3, 4, 5, 8, 13, 15, 17, 42, 50, 67, 90, 127; DC 1; SSC 10, 33, 98, 134; TCLC 229; WLC 1**
See also AAYA 4, 34; AFAW 1, 2; AMWR 2; AMWS 1; BPFB 1; BW 1; CA 1-4R; 124; CABS 1; CAD; CANR 3, 24; CDALB 1941-1968; CN 1, 2, 3, 4; CPW; DA; DA3; DAB; DAC; DAM MST, MULT, NOV, POP; DFS 11, 15; DLB 2, 7, 33, 249, 278; DLBY 1987; EWL 3; EXPS; LAIT 5; MAL 5; MTCW 1, 2; MTFW 2005; NCFS 4; NFS 4; RGAL 4; RGSF 2; SATA 9; SATA-Obit 54; SSFS 2, 18; TUS

Baldwin, William c. 1515-1563 .... **LC 113**
See also DLB 132

Bale, John 1495-1563 .... **LC 62**
See also DLB 132; RGEL 2; TEA

Ball, Hugo 1886-1927 .... **TCLC 104**

Ballard, James G.
See Ballard, J.G.

Ballard, James Graham
See Ballard, J.G.

Ballard, J.G. 1930-2009 ..... **CLC 3, 6, 14, 36, 137, 299; SSC 1, 53, 146**
See also AAYA 3, 52; BRWS 5; CA 5-8R; 285; CANR 15, 39, 65, 107, 133, 198; CN 1, 2, 3, 4, 5, 6, 7; DA3; DAM NOV, POP; DLB 14, 207, 261, 319; EWL 3; HGG; MTCW 1, 2; MTFW 2005; NFS 8; RGEL 2; RGSF 2; SATA 93; SATA-Obit 203; SCFW 1, 2; SFW 4

Ballard, Jim G.
See Ballard, J.G.

Balmont, Konstantin (Dmitriyevich) 1867-1943 .... **TCLC 11**
See also CA 109; 155; DLB 295; EWL 3

Baltausis, Vincas 1847-1910
See Mikszath, Kalman

Balzac, Guez de (?)-
See Balzac, Jean-Louis Guez de

Balzac, Honore de 1799-1850 ... **NCLC 5, 35, 53, 153; SSC 5, 59, 102, 153; WLC 1**
See also DA; DA3; DAB; DAC; DAM MST, NOV; DLB 119; EW 5; GFL 1789 to the Present; LMFS 1; NFS 33; RGSF 2; RGWL 2, 3; SSFS 10; SUFW; TWA

Balzac, Jean-Louis Guez de 1597-1654 .... **LC 162**
See also DLB 268; GFL Beginnings to 1789

Bambara, Toni Cade 1939-1995 ..... **BLC 1:1, 2:1; CLC 19, 88; SSC 35, 107; TCLC 116; WLCS**
See also AAYA 5, 49; AFAW 2; AMWS 11; BW 2, 3; BYA 12, 14; CA 29-32R; 150; CANR 24, 49, 81; CDALBS; DA; DA3; DAC; DAM MST, MULT; DLB 38, 218; EXPS; MAL 5; MTCW 1, 2; MTFW 2005; RGAL 4; RGSF 2; SATA 112; SSFS 4, 7, 12, 21

Bamdad, A.
See Shamlu, Ahmad

Bamdad, Alef
See Shamlu, Ahmad

Banat, D. R.
See Bradbury, Ray

Bancroft, Laura
See Baum, L. Frank

Bandello, Matteo 1485-1561 .... **SSC 143**

Banim, John 1798-1842 .... **NCLC 13**
See also DLB 116, 158, 159; RGEL 2

Banim, Michael 1796-1874 .... **NCLC 13**
See also DLB 158, 159

Banjo, The
See Paterson, A(ndrew) B(arton)

Bentley, Eric 1916- .... **CLC 24**
  See also CA 5-8R; CAD; CANR 6, 67;
  CBD; CD 5, 6; INT CANR-6
Bentley, Eric Russell
  See Bentley, Eric
ben Uzair, Salem
  See Horne, Richard Henry Hengist
Beolco, Angelo 1496-1542 .... **LC 139**
Beranger, Pierre Jean de
  1780-1857 .... **NCLC 34; PC 112**
Berdyaev, Nicolas
  See Berdyaev, Nikolai (Aleksandrovich)
Berdyaev, Nikolai (Aleksandrovich)
  1874-1948 .... **TCLC 67**
  See also CA 120; 157
Berdyayev, Nikolai (Aleksandrovich)
  See Berdyaev, Nikolai (Aleksandrovich)
Berendt, John 1939- .... **CLC 86**
  See also CA 146; CANR 75, 83, 151
Berendt, John Lawrence
  See Berendt, John
Berengar of Tours c. 1000-1088 .. **CMLC 124**
Beresford, J(ohn) D(avys)
  1873-1947 .... **TCLC 81**
  See also CA 112; 155; DLB 162, 178, 197;
  SFW 4; SUFW 1
Bergelson, David (Rafailovich)
  1884-1952 .... **TCLC 81**
  See also CA 220; DLB 333; EWL 3
Bergelson, Dovid
  See Bergelson, David (Rafailovich)
Berger, Colonel
  See Malraux, Andre
Berger, John 1926- .... **CLC 2, 19**
  See also BRWS 4; CA 81-84; CANR 51,
  78, 117, 163, 200; CN 1, 2, 3, 4, 5, 6, 7;
  DLB 14, 207, 319, 326
Berger, John Peter
  See Berger, John
Berger, Melvin H. 1927- .... **CLC 12**
  See also CA 5-8R; CANR 4, 142; CLR 32;
  SAAS 2; SATA 5, 88, 158; SATA-Essay
  124
Berger, Thomas 1924- .... **CLC 3, 5, 8, 11, 18,
  38, 259**
  See also BPFB 1; CA 1-4R; CANR 5, 28,
  51, 128; CN 1, 2, 3, 4, 5, 6, 7; DAM
  NOV; DLB 2; DLBY 1980; EWL 3;
  FANT; INT CANR-28; MAL 5; MTCW
  1, 2; MTFW 2005; RHW; TCLE 1:1;
  TCWW 1, 2
Bergman, Ernst Ingmar
  See Bergman, Ingmar
Bergman, Ingmar 1918-2007 ..... **CLC 16, 72,
  210**
  See also AAYA 61; CA 81-84; 262; CANR
  33, 70; CWW 2; DLB 257; MTCW 2;
  MTFW 2005
Bergson, Henri(-Louis) 1859-1941 . **TCLC 32**
  See also CA 164; DLB 329; EW 8; EWL 3;
  GFL 1789 to the Present
Bergstein, Eleanor 1938- .... **CLC 4**
  See also CA 53-56; CANR 5
Berkeley, George 1685-1753 .... **LC 65**
  See also DLB 31, 101, 252
Berkoff, Steven 1937- .... **CLC 56**
  See also CA 104; CANR 72; CBD; CD 5, 6
Berlin, Isaiah 1909-1997 .... **TCLC 105**
  See also CA 85-88; 162
Bermant, Chaim (Icyk) 1929-1998 ... **CLC 40**
  See also CA 57-60; CANR 6, 31, 57, 105;
  CN 2, 3, 4, 5, 6
Bern, Victoria
  See Fisher, M(ary) F(rances) K(ennedy)
Bernanos, (Paul Louis) Georges
  1888-1948 .... **TCLC 3**
  See also CA 104; 130; CANR 94; DLB 72;
  EWL 3; GFL 1789 to the Present; RGWL
  2, 3

Bernard, April 1956- .... **CLC 59**
  See also CA 131; CANR 144
Bernard, Mary Ann
  See Soderbergh, Steven
Bernard of Clairvaux 1090-1153 .. **CMLC 71**
  See also DLB 208
Bernard Silvestris fl. c. 1130-fl. c.
  1160 .... **CMLC 87**
  See also DLB 208
Bernart de Ventadorn c. 1130-c.
  1190 .... **CMLC 98**
Berne, Victoria
  See Fisher, M(ary) F(rances) K(ennedy)
Bernhard, Thomas 1931-1989 ..... **CLC 3, 32,
  61; DC 14; TCLC 165**
  See also CA 85-88; 127; CANR 32, 57; CD-
  WLB 2; DLB 85, 124; EWL 3; MTCW 1;
  RGHL; RGWL 2, 3
Bernhardt, Sarah (Henriette Rosine)
  1844-1923 .... **TCLC 75**
  See also CA 157
Bernstein, Charles 1950- .... **CLC 142,**
  See also CA 129; CAAS 24; CANR 90; CP
  4, 5, 6, 7; DLB 169
Bernstein, Ingrid
  See Kirsch, Sarah
Beroul fl. c. 12th cent. - .... **CMLC 75**
Berriault, Gina 1926-1999 .... **CLC 54, 109;
  SSC 30**
  See also CA 116; 129; 185; CANR 66; DLB
  130; SSFS 7,11
Berrigan, Daniel 1921- .... **CLC 4**
  See also CA 33-36R, 187; CAAE 187;
  CAAS 1; CANR 11, 43, 78, 219; CP 1, 2,
  3, 4, 5, 6, 7; DLB 5
Berrigan, Edmund Joseph Michael, Jr.
  1934-1983 .... **CLC 37; PC 103**
  See also CA 61-64; 110; CANR 14, 102;
  CP 1, 2, 3; DLB 5, 169; WP
Berrigan, Ted
  See Berrigan, Edmund Joseph Michael, Jr.
Berry, Charles Edward Anderson
  1931- .... **CLC 17**
  See also CA 115
Berry, Chuck
  See Berry, Charles Edward Anderson
Berry, Jonas
  See Ashbery, John
Berry, Wendell 1934- ..... **CLC 4, 6, 8, 27, 46,
  279; PC 28**
  See also AITN 1; AMWS 10; ANW; CA
  73-76; CANR 50, 73, 101, 132, 174; CP
  1, 2, 3, 4, 5, 6, 7; CSW; DAM POET;
  DLB 5, 6, 234, 275, 342; MTCW 2;
  MTFW 2005; PFS 30; TCLE 1:1
Berry, Wendell Erdman
  See Berry, Wendell
Berryman, John 1914-1972 ... **CLC 1, 2, 3, 4,
  6, 8, 10, 13, 25, 62; PC 64**
  See also AMW; CA 13-16; 33-36R; CABS
  2; CANR 35; CAP 1; CDALB 1941-1968;
  CP 1; DAM POET; DLB 48; EWL 3;
  MAL 5; MTCW 1, 2; MTFW 2005; PAB;
  PFS 27; RGAL 4; WP
Berssenbrugge, Mei-mei 1947- .... **PC 115**
  See also CA 104; DLB 312
Bertolucci, Bernardo 1940- ...... **CLC 16, 157**
  See also CA 106; CANR 125
Berton, Pierre (Francis de Marigny)
  1920-2004 .... **CLC 104**
  See also CA 1-4R; 233; CANR 2, 56, 144;
  CPW; DLB 68; SATA 99; SATA-Obit 158
Bertrand, Aloysius 1807-1841 .... **NCLC 31**
  See also DLB 217
Bertrand, Louis oAloysiusc
  See Bertrand, Aloysius
Bertran de Born c. 1140-1215 .... **CMLC 5**
Besant, Annie (Wood) 1847-1933 ..... **TCLC 9**
  See also CA 105; 185

Bessie, Alvah 1904-1985 .... **CLC 23**
  See also CA 5-8R; 116; CANR 2, 80; DLB
  26
Bestuzhev, Aleksandr Aleksandrovich
  1797-1837 .... **NCLC 131**
  See also DLB 198
Bethlen, T.D.
  See Silverberg, Robert
Beti, Mongo 1932-2001 .... **BLC 1:1; CLC 27**
  See also AFW; BW 1, 3; CA 114; 124;
  CANR 81; DA3; DAM MULT; DLB 360;
  EWL 3; MTCW 1, 2
Betjeman, John 1906-1984 ...... **CLC 2, 6, 10,
  34, 43; PC 75**
  See also BRW 7; CA 9-12R; 112; CANR
  33, 56; CDBLB 1945-1960; CP 1, 2, 3;
  DA3; DAB; DAM MST, POET; DLB 20;
  DLBY 1984; EWL 3; MTCW 1, 2
Bettelheim, Bruno 1903-1990 .... **CLC 79;
  TCLC 143**
  See also CA 81-84; 131; CANR 23, 61;
  DA3; MTCW 1, 2; RGHL
Betti, Ugo 1892-1953 .... **TCLC 5**
  See also CA 104; 155; EWL 3; RGWL 2, 3
Betts, Doris (Waugh) 1932- ..... **CLC 3, 6, 28,
  275; SSC 45**
  See also CA 13-16R; CANR 9, 66, 77; CN
  6, 7; CSW; DLB 218; DLBY 1982; INT
  CANR-9; RGAL 4
Bevan, Alistair
  See Roberts, Keith (John Kingston)
Bey, Pilaff
  See Douglas, (George) Norman
Beyala, Calixthe 1961- .... **BLC 2:1**
  See also EWL 3
Beynon, John
  See Harris, John (Wyndham Parkes Lucas)
  Beynon
Bhabha, Homi K. 1949- .... **CLC 285**
Bialik, Chaim Nachman
  1873-1934 .... **TCLC 25, 201**
  See also CA 170; EWL 3; WLIT 6
Bialik, Hayyim Nahman
  See Bialik, Chaim Nachman
Bickerstaff, Isaac
  See Swift, Jonathan
Bidart, Frank 1939- .... **CLC 33**
  See also AMWS 15; CA 140; CANR 106,
  215; CP 5, 6, 7; PFS 26
Bienek, Horst 1930- .... **CLC 7, 11**
  See also CA 73-76; DLB 75
Bierce, Ambrose 1842-1914(?) ...... **SSC 9, 72,
  124; TCLC 1, 7, 44; WLC 1**
  See also AAYA 55; AMW; BYA 11; CA
  104; 139; CANR 78; CDALB 1865-1917;
  DA; DA3; DAC; DAM MST; DLB 11,
  12, 23, 71, 74, 186; EWL 3; EXPS; HGG;
  LAIT 2; MAL 5; RGAL 4; RGSF 2; SSFS
  9, 27; SUFW 1
Bierce, Ambrose Gwinett
  See Bierce, Ambrose
Biggers, Earl Derr 1884-1933 .... **TCLC 65**
  See also CA 108; 153; DLB 306
Bilek, Anton F. 1919-
  See Rankin, Ian
  See also CA 304
Billiken, Bud
  See Motley, Willard (Francis)
Billings, Josh
  See Shaw, Henry Wheeler
Billington, Lady Rachel Mary
  See Billington, Rachel
Billington, Rachel 1942- .... **CLC 43**
  See also AITN 2; CA 33-36R; CANR 44,
  196; CN 4, 5, 6, 7

Bly, Robert 1926- ..... CLC 1, 2, 5, 10, 15, 38, 128; PC 39
See also AMWS 4; CA 5-8R; CANR 41, 73, 125; CP 1, 2, 3, 4, 5, 6, 7; DA3; DAM POET; DLB 5, 342; EWL 3; MAL 5; MTCW 1, 2; MTFW 2005; PFS 6, 17; RGAL 4

Bly, Robert Elwood
See Bly, Robert

Boas, Franz 1858-1942 .... TCLC 56
See also CA 115; 181

Bobette
See Simenon, Georges

Boccaccio, Giovanni 1313-1375 ... CMLC 13, 57; SSC 10, 87
See also EW 2; RGSF 2; RGWL 2, 3; SSFS 28; TWA; WLIT 7

Bochco, Steven 1943- .... CLC 35
See also AAYA 11, 71; CA 124; 138

Bock, Charles 1970- .... CLC 299
See also CA 274

Bode, Sigmund
See O'Doherty, Brian

Bodel, Jean 1167(?)-1210 .... CMLC 28

Bodenheim, Maxwell 1892-1954 .... TCLC 44
See also CA 110; 187; DLB 9, 45; MAL 5; RGAL 4

Bodenheimer, Maxwell
See Bodenheim, Maxwell

Bodker, Cecil
See Bodker, Cecil

Bodker, Cecil 1927- .... CLC 21
See also CA 73-76; CANR 13, 44, 111; CLR 23; MAICYA 1, 2; SATA 14, 133

Boell, Heinrich 1917-1985 ..... CLC 2, 3, 6, 9, 11, 15, 27, 32, 72; SSC 23; TCLC 185; WLC 1
See also BPFB 1; CA 21-24R; 116; CANR 24; CDWLB 2; DA; DA3; DAB; DAC; DAM MST, NOV; DLB 69, 329; DLBY 1985; EW 13; EWL 3; MTCW 1, 2; MTFW 2005; RGHL; RGSF 2; RGWL 2, 3; SSFS 20; TWA

Boell, Heinrich Theodor
See Boell, Heinrich

Boerne, Alfred
See Doeblin, Alfred

Boethius c. 480-c. 524 .... CMLC 15
See also DLB 115; RGWL 2, 3; WLIT 8

Boff, Leonardo (Genezio Darci) 1938- .... CLC 70; HLC 1
See also CA 150; DAM MULT; HW 2

Bogan, Louise 1897-1970 .... CLC 4, 39, 46, 93; PC 12
See also AMWS 3; CA 73-76; 25-28R; CANR 33, 82; CP 1; DAM POET; DLB 45, 169; EWL 3; MAL 5; MBL; MTCW 1, 2; PFS 21; RGAL 4

Bogarde, Dirk
See Van Den Bogarde, Derek Jules Gaspard Ulric Niven

Bogat, Shatan
See Kacew, Romain

Bogomolny, Robert L. 1938- .... SSC 41; TCLC 11
See also CA 121, 164; DLB 182; EWL 3; MJW; RGSF 2; RGWL 2, 3; TWA

Bogomolny, Robert Lee
See Bogomolny, Robert L.

Bogosian, Eric 1953- .... CLC 45, 141
See also CA 138; CAD; CANR 102, 148, 217; CD 5, 6; DLB 341

Bograd, Larry 1953- .... CLC 35
See also CA 93-96; CANR 57; SAAS 21; SATA 33, 89; WYA

Bohme, Jakob 1575-1624 .... LC 178
See also DLB 164

Boiardo, Matteo Maria 1441-1494 .... LC 6, 168

Boileau-Despreaux, Nicolas 1636-1711 .... LC 3, 164
See also DLB 268; EW 3; GFL Beginnings to 1789; RGWL 2, 3

Boissard, Maurice
See Leautaud, Paul

Bojer, Johan 1872-1959 .... TCLC 64
See also CA 189; EWL 3

Bok, Edward W(illiam) 1863-1930 .... TCLC 101
See also CA 217; DLB 91; DLBD 16

Boker, George Henry 1823-1890 . NCLC 125
See also RGAL 4

Boland, Eavan 1944- ... CLC 40, 67, 113; PC 58
See also BRWS 5; CA 143, 207; CAAE 207; CANR 61, 180; CP 1, 6, 7; CWP; DAM POET; DLB 40; FW; MTCW 2; MTFW 2005; PFS 12, 22, 31

Boland, Eavan Aisling
See Boland, Eavan

Bolano, Roberto 1953-2003 .... CLC 294
See also CA 229; CANR 175

Bolingbroke, Viscount
See St. John, Henry

Boll, Heinrich
See Boell, Heinrich

Bolt, Lee
See Faust, Frederick

Bolt, Robert (Oxton) 1924-1995 ...... CLC 14; TCLC 175
See also CA 17-20R; 147; CANR 35, 67; CBD; DAM DRAM; DFS 2; DLB 13, 233; EWL 3; LAIT 1; MTCW 1

Bombal, Maria Luisa 1910-1980 .... HLCS 1; SSC 37
See also CA 127; CANR 72; EWL 3; HW 1; LAW; RGSF 2

Bombet, Louis-Alexandre-Cesar
See Stendhal

Bomkauf
See Kaufman, Bob (Garnell)

Bonaventura .... NCLC 35
See also DLB 90

Bonaventure 1217(?)-1274 .... CMLC 79
See also DLB 115; LMFS 1

Bond, Edward 1934- .... CLC 4, 6, 13, 23
See also AAYA 50; BRWS 1; CA 25-28R; CANR 38, 67, 106; CBD; CD 5, 6; DAM DRAM; DFS 3, 8; DLB 13, 310; EWL 3; MTCW 1

Bonham, Frank 1914-1989 .... CLC 12
See also AAYA 1, 70; BYA 1, 3; CA 9-12R; CANR 4, 36; JRDA; MAICYA 1, 2; SAAS 3; SATA 1, 49; SATA-Obit 62; TCWW 1, 2; YAW

Bonnefoy, Yves 1923- . CLC 9, 15, 58; PC 58
See also CA 85-88; CANR 33, 75, 97, 136; CWW 2; DAM MST, POET; DLB 258; EWL 3; GFL 1789 to the Present; MTCW 1, 2; MTFW 2005

Bonner, Marita
See Occomy, Marita (Odette) Bonner

Bonnin, Gertrude 1876-1938 .... NNAL
See also CA 150; DAM MULT; DLB 175

Bontemps, Arna 1902-1973 ... BLC 1:1; CLC 1, 18; HR 1:2
See also BW 1; CA 1-4R; 41-44R; CANR 4, 35; CLR 6; CP 1; CWRI 5; DA3; DAM MULT, NOV, POET; DLB 48, 51; JRDA; MAICYA 1, 2; MAL 5; MTCW 1, 2; PFS 32; SATA 2, 44; SATA-Obit 24; WCH; WP

Bontemps, Arnaud Wendell
See Bontemps, Arna

Boot, William
See Stoppard, Tom

Booth, Irwin
See Hoch, Edward D.

Booth, Martin 1944-2004 .... CLC 13
See also CA 93-96, 188; 223; CAAE 188; CAAS 2; CANR 92; CP 1, 2, 3, 4

Booth, Philip 1925-2007 .... CLC 23
See also CA 5-8R; 262; CANR 5, 88; CP 1, 2, 3, 4, 5, 6, 7; DLBY 1982

Booth, Philip Edmund
See Booth, Philip

Booth, Wayne C. 1921-2005 .... CLC 24
See also CA 1-4R; 244; CAAS 5; CANR 3, 43, 117; DLB 67

Booth, Wayne Clayson
See Booth, Wayne C.

Borchert, Wolfgang 1921-1947 .... DC 42; TCLC 5
See also CA 104; 188; DLB 69, 124; EWL 3

Borel, Petrus 1809-1859 .... NCLC 41
See also DLB 119; GFL 1789 to the Present

Borges, Jorge Luis 1899-1986 ... CLC 1, 2, 3, 4, 6, 8, 9, 10, 13, 19, 44, 48, 83; HLC 1; PC 22, 32; SSC 4, 41, 100; TCLC 109; WLC 1
See also AAYA 26; BPFB 1; CA 21-24R; CANR 19, 33, 75, 105, 133; CDWLB 3; DA; DA3; DAB; DAC; DAM MST, MULT; DLB 113, 283; DLBY 1986; DNFS 1, 2; EWL 3; HW 1, 2; LAW; LMFS 2; MSW; MTCW 1, 2; MTFW 2005; PFS 27; RGHL; RGSF 2; RGWL 2, 3; SFW 4; SSFS 17; TWA; WLIT 1

Borne, Ludwig 1786-1837 .... NCLC 193
See also DLB 90

Borowski, Tadeusz 1922-1951 .... SSC 48; TCLC 9
See also CA 106; 154; CDWLB 4; DLB 215; EWL 3; RGHL; RGSF 2; RGWL 3; SSFS 13

Borrow, George (Henry) 1803-1881 .... NCLC 9
See also BRWS 12; DLB 21, 55, 166

Bosch (Gavino), Juan 1909-2001 ..... HLCS 1
See also CA 151; 204; DAM MST, MULT; DLB 145; HW 1, 2

Bosman, Herman Charles 1905-1951 .... TCLC 49
See also CA 160; DLB 225; RGSF 2

Bosschere, Jean de 1878(?)-1953 ... TCLC 19
See also CA 115; 186

Boswell, James 1740-1795 ...... LC 4, 50, 182; WLC 1
See also BRW 3; CDBLB 1660-1789; DA; DAB; DAC; DAM MST; DLB 104, 142; TEA; WLIT 3

Boto, Eza
See Beti, Mongo

Bottomley, Gordon 1874-1948 ..... TCLC 107
See also CA 120; 192; DLB 10

Bottoms, David 1949- .... CLC 53
See also CA 105; CANR 22; CSW; DLB 120; DLBY 1983

Boucicault, Dion 1820-1890 .... NCLC 41
See also DLB 344

Boucolon, Maryse
See Conde, Maryse

Bourcicault, Dion
See Boucicault, Dion

Bourdieu, Pierre 1930-2002 .... CLC 198, 296
See also CA 130; 204

Bourget, Paul (Charles Joseph) 1852-1935 .... TCLC 12
See also CA 107; 196; DLB 123; GFL 1789 to the Present

Bourjaily, Vance 1922-2010 .... CLC 8, 62
See also CA 1-4R; CAAS 1; CANR 2, 72; CN 1, 2, 3, 4, 5, 6, 7; DLB 2, 143; MAL 5

Brautigan, Richard 1935-1984 .. CLC 1, 3, 5, 9, 12, 34, 42; PC 94; TCLC 133
See also BPFB 1; CA 53-56; 113; CANR 34; CN 1, 2, 3; CP 1, 2, 3, 4; DA3; DAM NOV; DLB 2, 5, 206; DLBY 1980, 1984; FANT; MAL 5; MTCW 1; RGAL 4; SATA 56

Brautigan, Richard Gary
See Brautigan, Richard

Brave Bird, Mary
See Crow Dog, Mary

Braverman, Kate 1950- .... CLC 67
See also CA 89-92; CANR 141; DLB 335

Brecht, Bertolt 1898-1956 .... DC 3; TCLC 1, 6, 13, 35, 169; WLC 1
See also CA 104; 133; CANR 62; CDWLB 2; DA; DA3; DAB; DAC; DAM DRAM, MST; DFS 4, 5, 9; DLB 56, 124; EW 11; EWL 3; IDTP; MTCW 1, 2; MTFW 2005; RGHL; RGWL 2, 3; TWA

Brecht, Eugen Berthold Friedrich
See Brecht, Bertolt

Brecht, Eugen Bertolt Friedrich
See Brecht, Bertolt

Bremer, Fredrika 1801-1865 .... NCLC 11
See also DLB 254

Brennan, Christopher John
1870-1932 .... TCLC 17
See also CA 117; 188; DLB 230; EWL 3

Brennan, Maeve 1917-1993 ... CLC 5; TCLC 124
See also CA 81-84; CANR 72, 100

Brenner, Jozef 1887-1919 .... TCLC 13
See also CA 111; 240

Brent, Linda
See Jacobs, Harriet A.

Brentano, Clemens (Maria)
1778-1842 .... NCLC 1, 191; SSC 115
See also DLB 90; RGWL 2, 3

Brent of Bin Bin
See Franklin, (Stella Maria Sarah) Miles (Lampe)

Brenton, Howard 1942- .... CLC 31
See also CA 69-72; CANR 33, 67; CBD; CD 5, 6; DLB 13; MTCW 1

Breslin, James
See Breslin, Jimmy

Breslin, Jimmy 1930- .... CLC 4, 43
See also CA 73-76; CANR 31, 75, 139, 187; DAM NOV; DLB 185; MTCW 2; MTFW 2005

Bresson, Robert 1901(?)-1999 .... CLC 16
See also CA 110; 187; CANR 49

Breton, Andre 1896-1966 .. CLC 2, 9, 15, 54; PC 15; TCLC 247
See also CA 19-20; 25-28R; CANR 40, 60; CAP 2; DLB 65, 258; EW 11; EWL 3; GFL 1789 to the Present; LMFS 2; MTCW 1, 2; MTFW 2005; RGWL 2, 3; TWA; WP

Breton, Nicholas c. 1554-c. 1626 .... LC 133
See also DLB 136

Breytenbach, Breyten 1939(?)- .. CLC 23, 37, 126
See also CA 113; 129; CANR 61, 122, 202; CWW 2; DAM POET; DLB 225; EWL 3

Bridgers, Sue Ellen 1942- .... CLC 26
See also AAYA 8, 49; BYA 7, 8; CA 65-68; CANR 11, 36; CLR 18; DLB 52; JRDA; MAICYA 1, 2; SAAS 1; SATA 22, 90; SATA-Essay 109; WYA; YAW

Bridges, Robert (Seymour)
1844-1930 .... PC 28; TCLC 1
See also BRW 6; CA 104; 152; CDBLB 1890-1914; DAM POET; DLB 19, 98

Bridie, James
See Mavor, Osborne Henry

Brin, David 1950- .... CLC 34
See also AAYA 21; CA 102; CANR 24, 70, 125, 127; INT CANR-24; SATA 65; SCFW 2; SFW 4

Brink, Andre 1935- .... CLC 18, 36, 106
See also AFW; BRWS 6; CA 104; CANR 39, 62, 109, 133, 182; CN 4, 5, 6, 7; DLB 225; EWL 3; INT CA-103; LATS 1:2; MTCW 1, 2; MTFW 2005; WLIT 2

Brink, Andre Philippus
See Brink, Andre

Brinsmead, H. F(ay)
See Brinsmead, H(esba) F(ay)

Brinsmead, H. F.
See Brinsmead, H(esba) F(ay)

Brinsmead, H(esba) F(ay) 1922- ...... CLC 21
See also CA 21-24R; CANR 10; CLR 47; CWRI 5; MAICYA 1, 2; SAAS 5; SATA 18, 78

Brittain, Vera (Mary)
1893(?)-1970 .... CLC 23; TCLC 228
See also BRWS 10; CA 13-16; 25-28R; CANR 58; CAP 1; DLB 191; FW; MTCW 1, 2

Broch, Hermann 1886-1951 ... TCLC 20, 204
See also CA 117; 211; CDWLB 2; DLB 85, 124; EW 10; EWL 3; RGWL 2, 3

Brock, Rose
See Hansen, Joseph

Brod, Max 1884-1968 .... TCLC 115
See also CA 5-8R; 25-28R; CANR 7; DLB 81; EWL 3

Brodkey, Harold (Roy) 1930-1996 .. CLC 56; TCLC 123
See also CA 111; 151; CANR 71; CN 4, 5, 6; DLB 130

Brodskii, Iosif
See Brodsky, Joseph

Brodskii, Iosif Alexandrovich
See Brodsky, Joseph

Brodsky, Iosif Alexandrovich
See Brodsky, Joseph

Brodsky, Joseph 1940-1996 ..... CLC 4, 6, 13, 36, 100; PC 9; TCLC 219
See also AAYA 71; AITN 1; AMWS 8; CA 41-44R; 151; CANR 37, 106; CWW 2; DA3; DAM POET; DLB 285, 329; EWL 3; MTCW 1, 2; MTFW 2005; PFS 35; RGWL 2, 3

Brodsky, Michael 1948- .... CLC 19
See also CA 102; CANR 18, 41, 58, 147; DLB 244

Brodsky, Michael Mark
See Brodsky, Michael

Brodzki, Bella .... CLC 65

Brome, Richard 1590(?)-1652 .... LC 61
See also BRWS 10; DLB 58

Bromell, Henry 1947- .... CLC 5
See also CA 53-56; CANR 9, 115, 116

Bromfield, Louis (Brucker)
1896-1956 .... TCLC 11
See also CA 107; 155; DLB 4, 9, 86; RGAL 4; RHW

Broner, E. M. 1930- .... CLC 19
See also CA 17-20R; CANR 8, 25, 72, 216; CN 4, 5, 6; DLB 28

Broner, Esther Masserman
See Broner, E. M.

Bronk, William 1918-1999 .... CLC 10
See also AMWS 21; CA 89-92; 177; CANR 23; CP 3, 4, 5, 6, 7; DLB 165

Bronstein, Lev Davidovich
See Trotsky, Leon

Bronte, Anne 1820-1849 .... NCLC 4, 71, 102, 235
See also BRW 5; BRWR 1; DA3; DLB 21, 199, 340; NFS 26; TEA

Bronte, (Patrick) Branwell
1817-1848 .... NCLC 109
See also DLB 340

Bronte, Charlotte 1816-1855 ...... NCLC 3, 8, 33, 58, 105, 155, 217, 229; WLC 1
See also AAYA 17; BRW 5; BRWC 2; BRWR 1; BYA 2; CDBLB 1832-1890; DA; DA3; DAB; DAC; DAM MST, NOV; DLB 21, 159, 199, 340; EXPN; FL 1:2; GL 2; LAIT 2; NFS 4, 36; TEA; WLIT 4

Bronte, Emily 1818-1848 ... NCLC 16, 35, 165, 244; PC 8; WLC 1
See also AAYA 17; BPFB 1; BRW 5; BRWC 1; BRWR 1; BYA 3; CDBLB 1832-1890; DA; DA3; DAB; DAC; DAM MST, NOV, POET; DLB 21, 32, 199, 340; EXPN; FL 1:2; GL 2; LAIT 1; NFS 2; PFS 33; TEA; WLIT 3

Bronte, Emily Jane
See Bronte, Emily

Brontes
See Bronte, Anne; Bronte, (Patrick) Branwell; Bronte, Charlotte; Bronte, Emily

Brooke, Frances 1724-1789 .... LC 6, 48
See also DLB 39, 99

Brooke, Henry 1703(?)-1783 .... LC 1
See also DLB 39

Brooke, Rupert 1887-1915 . PC 24; TCLC 2, 7; WLC 1
See also BRWS 3; CA 104; 132; CANR 61; CDBLB 1914-1945; DA; DAB; DAC; DAM MST, POET; DLB 19, 216; EXPP; GLL 2; MTCW 1, 2; MTFW 2005; PFS 7; TEA

Brooke, Rupert Chawner
See Brooke, Rupert

Brooke-Haven, P.
See Wodehouse, P. G.

Brooke-Rose, Christine 1923(?)- ..... CLC 40, 184
See also BRWS 4; CA 13-16R; CANR 58, 118, 183; CN 1, 2, 3, 4, 5, 6, 7; DLB 14, 231; EWL 3; SFW 4

Brookner, Anita 1928- . CLC 32, 34, 51, 136, 237
See also BRWS 4; CA 114; 120; CANR 37, 56, 87, 130, 212; CN 4, 5, 6, 7; CPW; DA3; DAB; DAM POP; DLB 194, 326; DLBY 1987; EWL 3; MTCW 1, 2; MTFW 2005; NFS 23; TEA

Brooks, Cleanth 1906-1994 . CLC 24, 86, 110
See also AMWS 14; CA 17-20R; 145; CANR 33, 35; CSW; DLB 63; DLBY 1994; EWL 3; INT CANR-35; MAL 5; MTCW 1, 2; MTFW 2005

Brooks, George
See Baum, L. Frank

Brooks, Gwendolyn 1917-2000 .... BLC 1:1, 2:1; CLC 1, 2, 4, 5, 15, 49, 125; PC 7; WLC 1
See also AAYA 20; AFAW 1, 2; AITN 1; AMWS 3; BW 2, 3; CA 1-4R; 190; CANR 1, 27, 52, 75, 132; CDALB 1941-1968; CLR 27; CP 1, 2, 3, 4, 5, 6, 7; CWP; DA; DA3; DAC; DAM MST, MULT, POET; DLB 5, 76, 165; EWL 3; EXPP; FL 1:5; MAL 5; MBL; MTCW 1, 2; MTFW 2005; PFS 1, 2, 4, 6, 32; RGAL 4; SATA 6; SATA-Obit 123; TUS; WP

Brooks, Gwendolyn Elizabeth
See Brooks, Gwendolyn

Brooks, Mel 1926- .... CLC 12, 217
See also AAYA 13, 48; CA 65-68; CANR 16; DFS 21; DLB 26

Brooks, Peter 1938- .... CLC 34
See also CA 45-48; CANR 1, 107, 182

Brooks, Peter Preston
See Brooks, Peter

Brooks, Van Wyck 1886-1963 .... **CLC 29**
See also AMW; CA 1-4R; CANR 6; DLB 45, 63, 103; MAL 5; TUS

Brophy, Brigid 1929-1995 ...... **CLC 6, 11, 29, 105**
See also CA 5-8R; 149; CAAS 4; CANR 25, 53; CBD; CN 1, 2, 3, 4, 5, 6; CWD; DA3; DLB 14, 271; EWL 3; MTCW 1, 2

Brophy, Brigid Antonia
See Brophy, Brigid

Brosman, Catharine Savage 1934- ..... **CLC 9**
See also CA 61-64; CANR 21, 46, 149

Brossard, Nicole 1943- .... **CLC 115, 169; PC 80**
See also CA 122; CAAS 16; CANR 140; CCA 1; CWP; CWW 2; DLB 53; EWL 3; FW; GLL 2; RGWL 3

Brother Antoninus
See Everson, William

Brothers Grimm
See Grimm, Jacob Ludwig Karl; Grimm, Wilhelm Karl

The Brothers Quay
See Quay, Stephen; Quay, Timothy

Broughton, T(homas) Alan 1936- ..... **CLC 19**
See also CA 45-48; CANR 2, 23, 48, 111

Broumas, Olga 1949- .... **CLC 10, 73**
See also CA 85-88; CANR 20, 69, 110; CP 5, 6, 7; CWP; GLL 2

Broun, Heywood 1888-1939 .... **TCLC 104**
See also DLB 29, 171

Brown, Alan 1950- .... **CLC 99**
See also CA 156

Brown, Charles Brockden 1771-1810 .... **NCLC 22, 74, 122**
See also AMWS 1; CDALB 1640-1865; DLB 37, 59, 73; FW; GL 2; HGG; LMFS 1; RGAL 4; TUS

Brown, Christy 1932-1981 .... **CLC 63**
See also BYA 13; CA 105; 104; CANR 72; DLB 14

Brown, Claude 1937-2002 ..... **BLC 1:1; CLC 30**
See also AAYA 7; BW 1, 3; CA 73-76; 205; CANR 81; DAM MULT

Brown, Dan 1964- .... **CLC 209**
See also AAYA 55; CA 217; LNFS 1; MTFW 2005

Brown, Dee 1908-2002 .... **CLC 18, 47**
See also AAYA 30; CA 13-16R; 212; CAAS 6; CANR 11, 45, 60, 150; CPW; CSW; DA3; DAM POP; DLBY 1980; LAIT 2; MTCW 1, 2; MTFW 2005; NCFS 5; SATA 5, 110; SATA-Obit 141; TCWW 1, 2

Brown, Dee Alexander
See Brown, Dee

Brown, George
See Wertmueller, Lina

Brown, George Douglas 1869-1902 .... **TCLC 28**
See also CA 162; RGEL 2

Brown, George Mackay 1921-1996 ... **CLC 5, 48, 100**
See also BRWS 6; CA 21-24R; 151; CAAS 6; CANR 12, 37, 67; CN 1, 2, 3, 4, 5, 6; CP 1, 2, 3, 4, 5, 6; DLB 14, 27, 139, 271; MTCW 1; RGSF 2; SATA 35

Brown, James Willie
See Komunyakaa, Yusef

Brown, James Willie, Jr.
See Komunyakaa, Yusef

Brown, Larry 1951-2004 .... **CLC 73, 289**
See also AMWS 21; CA 130; 134; 233; CANR 117, 145; CSW; DLB 234; INT CA-134

Brown, Moses
See Barrett, William (Christopher)

Brown, Rita Mae 1944- .... **CLC 18, 43, 79, 259**
See also BPFB 1; CA 45-48; CANR 2, 11, 35, 62, 95, 138, 183; CN 5, 6, 7; CPW; CSW; DA3; DAM NOV, POP; FW; INT CANR-11; MAL 5; MTCW 1, 2; MTFW 2005; NFS 9; RGAL 4; TUS

Brown, Roderick (Langmere) Haig-
See Haig-Brown, Roderick (Langmere)

Brown, Rosellen 1939- .... **CLC 32, 170**
See also CA 77-80; CAAS 10; CANR 14, 44, 98; CN 6, 7

Brown, Sterling Allen 1901-1989 ...... **BLC 1; CLC 1, 23, 59; HR 1:2; PC 55**
See also AFAW 1, 2; BW 1, 3; CA 85-88; 127; CANR 26; CP 3, 4; DA3; DAM MULT, POET; DLB 48, 51, 63; MAL 5; MTCW 1, 2; MTFW 2005; RGAL 4; WP

Brown, Will
See Ainsworth, William Harrison

Brown, William Hill 1765-1793 .... **LC 93**
See also DLB 37

Brown, William Larry
See Brown, Larry

Brown, William Wells 1815-1884 ... **BLC 1:1; DC 1; NCLC 2, 89**
See also DAM MULT; DLB 3, 50, 183, 248; RGAL 4

Browne, Clyde Jackson
See Browne, Jackson

Browne, Jackson 1948(?)- .... **CLC 21**
See also CA 120

Browne, Sir Thomas 1605-1682 .... **LC 111**
See also BRW 2; DLB 151

Browne of Tavistock, William 1590-1645 .... **LC 192**
See also DLB 121

Browning, Robert 1812-1889 . **NCLC 19, 79; PC 2, 61, 97; WLCS**
See also BRW 4; BRWC 2; BRWR 3; CD-BLB 1832-1890; CLR 97; DA; DA3; DAB; DAC; DAM MST, POET; DLB 32, 163; EXPP; LATS 1:1; PAB; PFS 1, 15; RGEL 2; TEA; WLIT 4; WP; YABC 1

Browning, Tod 1882-1962 .... **CLC 16**
See also CA 141; 117

Brownmiller, Susan 1935- .... **CLC 159**
See also CA 103; CANR 35, 75, 137; DAM NOV; FW; MTCW 1, 2; MTFW 2005

Brownson, Orestes Augustus 1803-1876 .... **NCLC 50**
See also DLB 1, 59, 73, 243

Bruccoli, Matthew J. 1931-2008 .... **CLC 34**
See also CA 9-12R; 274; CANR 7, 87; DLB 103

Bruccoli, Matthew Joseph
See Bruccoli, Matthew J.

Bruce, Lenny
See Schneider, Leonard Alfred

Bruchac, Joseph 1942- .... **NNAL**
See also AAYA 19; CA 33-36R; 256; CAAE 256; CANR 13, 47, 75, 94, 137, 161, 204; CLR 46; CWRI 5; DAM MULT; DLB 342; JRDA; MAICYA 2; MAICYAS 1; MTCW 2; MTFW 2005; PFS 36; SATA 42, 89, 131, 176; SATA-Essay 176

Bruin, John
See Brutus, Dennis

Brulard, Henri
See Stendhal

Brulls, Christian
See Simenon, Georges

Brunetto Latini c. 1220-1294 .... **CMLC 73**

Brunner, John (Kilian Houston) 1934-1995 .... **CLC 8, 10**
See also CA 1-4R; 149; CAAS 8; CANR 2, 37; CPW; DAM POP; DLB 261; MTCW 1, 2; SCFW 1, 2; SFW 4

Bruno, Giordano 1548-1600 .... **LC 27, 167**
See also RGWL 2, 3

Brutus, Dennis 1924-2009 ..... **BLC 1:1; CLC 43; PC 24**
See also AFW; BW 2, 3; CA 49-52; CAAS 14; CANR 2, 27, 42, 81; CDWLB 3; CP 1, 2, 3, 4, 5, 6, 7; DAM MULT, POET; DLB 117, 225; EWL 3

Bryan, C.D.B. 1936-2009 .... **CLC 29**
See also CA 73-76; CANR 13, 68; DLB 185; INT CANR-13

Bryan, Courtlandt Dixon Barnes
See Bryan, C.D.B.

Bryan, Michael
See Moore, Brian

Bryan, William Jennings 1860-1925 .... **TCLC 99**
See also DLB 303

Bryant, William Cullen 1794-1878 . **NCLC 6, 46; PC 20**
See also AMWS 1; CDALB 1640-1865; DA; DAB; DAC; DAM MST, POET; DLB 3, 43, 59, 189, 250; EXPP; PAB; PFS 30; RGAL 4; TUS

Bryusov, Valery Yakovlevich 1873-1924 .... **TCLC 10**
See also CA 107; 155; EWL 3; SFW 4

Buchan, John 1875-1940 .... **TCLC 41**
See also CA 108; 145; CMW 4; DAB; DAM POP; DLB 34, 70, 156; HGG; MSW; MTCW 2; RGEL 2; RHW; YABC 2

Buchanan, George 1506-1582 .... **LC 4, 179**
See also DLB 132

Buchanan, Robert 1841-1901 .... **TCLC 107**
See also CA 179; DLB 18, 35

Buchheim, Lothar-Guenther 1918-2007 .... **CLC 6**
See also CA 85-88; 257

Buchner, (Karl) Georg 1813-1837 ..... **DC 35; NCLC 26, 146; SSC 131**
See also CDWLB 2; DLB 133; EW 6; RGSF 2; RGWL 2, 3; TWA

Buchwald, Art 1925-2007 .... **CLC 33**
See also AITN 1; CA 5-8R; 256; CANR 21, 67, 107; MTCW 1, 2; SATA 10

Buchwald, Arthur
See Buchwald, Art

Buck, Pearl S. 1892-1973 .... **CLC 7, 11, 18, 127**
See also AAYA 42; AITN 1; AMWS 2; BPFB 1; CA 1-4R; 41-44R; CANR 1, 34; CDALBS; CN 1; DA; DA3; DAB; DAC; DAM MST, NOV; DLB 9, 102, 329; EWL 3; LAIT 3; MAL 5; MTCW 1, 2; MTFW 2005; NFS 25; RGAL 4; RHW; SATA 1, 25; SSFS 33; TUS

Buck, Pearl Sydenstricker
See Buck, Pearl S.

Buckler, Ernest 1908-1984 .... **CLC 13**
See also CA 11-12; 114; CAP 1; CCA 1; CN 1, 2, 3; DAC; DAM MST; DLB 68; SATA 47

Buckley, Christopher 1952- .... **CLC 165**
See also CA 139; CANR 119, 180

Buckley, Christopher Taylor
See Buckley, Christopher

Buckley, Vincent (Thomas) 1925-1988 .... **CLC 57**
See also CA 101; CP 1, 2, 3, 4; DLB 289

Buckley, William F., Jr.
See Buckley, William F.

Buckley, William F. 1925-2008 .... **CLC 7, 18, 37**
See also AITN 1; BPFB 1; CA 1-4R; 269; CANR 1, 24, 53, 93, 133, 185; CMW 4; CPW; DA3; DAM POP; DLB 137; DLBY 1980; INT CANR-24; MTCW 1, 2; MTFW 2005; TUS

Buckley, William Frank
See Buckley, William F.
Buckley, William Frank, Jr.
See Buckley, William F.
Buechner, Frederick 1926- ..... **CLC 2, 4, 6, 9**
See also AMWS 12; BPFB 1; CA 13-16R;
CANR 11, 39, 64, 114, 138, 213; CN 1,
2, 3, 4, 5, 6, 7; DAM NOV; DLBY 1980;
INT CANR-11; MAL 5; MTCW 1, 2;
MTFW 2005; TCLE 1:1
Buell, John (Edward) 1927- .... **CLC 10**
See also CA 1-4R; CANR 71; DLB 53
Buero Vallejo, Antonio 1916-2000 ... **CLC 15, 46, 139, 226; DC 18**
See also CA 106; 189; CANR 24, 49, 75;
CWW 2; DFS 11; EWL 3; HW 1; MTCW
1, 2
Bufalino, Gesualdo 1920-1996 .... **CLC 74**
See also CA 209; CWW 2; DLB 196
Buffon, Georges-Louis Leclerc
1707-1788 .... **LC 186**
See also DLB 313; GFL Beginnings to 1789
Bugayev, Boris Nikolayevich
1880-1934 .... **PC 11; TCLC 7**
See also CA 104; 165; DLB 295; EW 9;
EWL 3; MTCW 2; MTFW 2005; RGWL
2, 3
Bukowski, Charles 1920-1994 ... **CLC 2, 5, 9, 41, 82, 108; PC 18; SSC 45**
See also CA 17-20R; 144; CANR 40, 62,
105, 180; CN 4, 5; CP 1, 2, 3, 4, 5; CPW;
DA3; DAM NOV, POET; DLB 5, 130,
169; EWL 3; MAL 5; MTCW 1, 2;
MTFW 2005; PFS 28
Bulgakov, Mikhail 1891-1940 .... **SSC 18; TCLC 2, 16, 159**
See also AAYA 74; BPFB 1; CA 105; 152;
DAM DRAM, NOV; DLB 272; EWL 3;
MTCW 2; MTFW 2005; NFS 8; RGSF 2;
RGWL 2, 3; SFW 4; TWA
Bulgakov, Mikhail Afanasevich
See Bulgakov, Mikhail
Bulgya, Alexander Alexandrovich
1901-1956 .... **TCLC 53**
See also CA 117; 181; DLB 272; EWL 3
Bullins, Ed 1935- ...... **BLC 1:1; CLC 1, 5, 7; DC 6**
See also BW 2, 3; CA 49-52; CAAS 16;
CAD; CANR 24, 46, 73, 134; CD 5, 6;
DAM DRAM, MULT; DLB 7, 38, 249;
EWL 3; MAL 5; MTCW 1, 2; MTFW
2005; RGAL 4
Bulosan, Carlos 1911-1956 .... **AAL**
See also CA 216; DLB 312; RGAL 4
Bulwer-Lytton, Edward
1803-1873 .... **NCLC 1, 45, 238**
See also DLB 21; RGEL 2; SATA 23; SFW
4; SUFW 1; TEA
**Bulwer-Lytton, Edward George Earle
Lytton**
See Bulwer-Lytton, Edward
Bunin, Ivan
See Bunin, Ivan Alexeyevich
Bunin, Ivan Alekseevich
See Bunin, Ivan Alexeyevich
Bunin, Ivan Alexeyevich 1870-1953 ... **SSC 5; TCLC 6, 253**
See also CA 104; DLB 317, 329; EWL 3;
RGSF 2; RGWL 2, 3; TWA
Bunting, Basil 1900-1985 ..... **CLC 10, 39, 47; PC 120**
See also BRWS 7; CA 53-56; 115; CANR
7; CP 1, 2, 3, 4; DAM POET; DLB 20;
EWL 3; RGEL 2
Bunuel, Luis 1900-1983 ... **CLC 16, 80; HLC 1**
See also CA 101; 110; CANR 32, 77; DAM
MULT; HW 1

Bunyan, John 1628-1688 .... **LC 4, 69, 180; WLC 1**
See also BRW 2; BYA 5; CDBLB 1660-
1789; CLR 124; DA; DAB; DAC; DAM
MST; DLB 39; NFS 32; RGEL 2; TEA;
WCH; WLIT 3
Buonarroti, Michelangelo
1568-1646 .... **PC 103**
See also DLB 339
Buravsky, Alexandr .... **CLC 59**
Burchill, Julie 1959- .... **CLC 238**
See also CA 135; CANR 115, 116, 207
Burckhardt, Jacob (Christoph)
1818-1897 .... **NCLC 49**
See also EW 6
Burford, Eleanor
See Hibbert, Eleanor Alice Burford
Burgess, Anthony 1917-1993 . **CLC 1, 2, 4, 5, 8, 10, 13, 15, 22, 40, 62, 81, 94**
See also AAYA 25; AITN 1; BRWS 1; CA
1-4R; 143; CANR 2, 46; CDBLB 1960 to
Present; CN 1, 2, 3, 4, 5; DA3; DAB;
DAC; DAM NOV; DLB 14, 194, 261;
DLBY 1998; EWL 3; MTCW 1, 2; MTFW
2005; NFS 15; RGEL 2; RHW; SFW 4;
TEA; YAW
Buridan, John c. 1295-c. 1358 ...... **CMLC 97**
Burke, Edmund 1729(?)-1797 .... **LC 7, 36, 146; WLC 1**
See also BRW 3; DA; DA3; DAB; DAC;
DAM MST; DLB 104, 252, 336; RGEL
2; TEA
Burke, Kenneth (Duva) 1897-1993 ... **CLC 2, 24**
See also AMW; CA 5-8R; 143; CANR 39,
74, 136; CN 1, 2; CP 1, 2, 3, 4, 5; DLB
45, 63; EWL 3; MAL 5; MTCW 1, 2;
MTFW 2005; RGAL 4
Burke, Leda
See Garnett, David
Burke, Ralph
See Silverberg, Robert
Burke, Thomas 1886-1945 .... **TCLC 63**
See also CA 113; 155; CMW 4; DLB 197
Burke, Valenza Pauline
See Marshall, Paule
Burney, Fanny 1752-1840 .... **NCLC 12, 54, 107**
See also BRWS 3; DLB 39; FL 1:2; NFS
16; RGEL 2; TEA
Burney, Frances
See Burney, Fanny
Burns, Robert 1759-1796 . **LC 3, 29, 40, 190; PC 6, 114; WLC 1**
See also AAYA 51; BRW 3; CDBLB 1789-
1832; DA; DA3; DAB; DAC; DAM MST,
POET; DLB 109; EXPP; PAB; RGEL 2;
TEA; WP
Burns, Tex
See L'Amour, Louis
Burnshaw, Stanley 1906-2005 ..... **CLC 3, 13, 44**
See also CA 9-12R; 243; CP 1, 2, 3, 4, 5, 6,
7; DLB 48; DLBY 1997
Burr, Anne 1937- .... **CLC 6**
See also CA 25-28R
Burroughs, Augusten 1965- .... **CLC 277**
See also AAYA 73; CA 214; CANR 168,
218
Burroughs, Augusten Xon
See Burroughs, Augusten
Burroughs, Edgar Rice 1875-1950 . **TCLC 2, 32**
See also AAYA 11; BPFB 1; BYA 4, 9; CA
104; 132; CANR 131; CLR 157; DA3;
DAM NOV; DLB 8; FANT; MTCW 1, 2;
MTFW 2005; RGAL 4; SATA 41; SCFW
1, 2; SFW 4; TCWW 1, 2; TUS; YAW

Burroughs, William S. 1914-1997 . **CLC 1, 2, 5, 15, 22, 42, 75, 109; TCLC 121; WLC 1**
See also AAYA 60; AITN 2; AMWS 3; BG
1:2; BPFB 1; CA 9-12R; 160; CANR 20,
52, 104; CN 1, 2, 3, 4, 5, 6; CPW; DA;
DA3; DAB; DAC; DAM MST, NOV,
POP; DLB 2, 8, 16, 152, 237; DLBY
1981, 1997; EWL 3; GLL 1; HGG; LMFS
2; MAL 5; MTCW 1, 2; MTFW 2005;
RGAL 4; SFW 4
Burroughs, William Seward
See Burroughs, William S.
Burton, Sir Richard F(rancis)
1821-1890 .... **NCLC 42**
See also DLB 55, 166, 184; SSFS 21
Burton, Robert 1577-1640 .... **LC 74**
See also DLB 151; RGEL 2
Buruma, Ian 1951- .... **CLC 163**
See also CA 128; CANR 65, 141, 195
Bury, Stephen
See Stephenson, Neal
Busch, Frederick 1941-2006 .. **CLC 7, 10, 18, 47, 166**
See also CA 33-36R; 248; CAAS 1; CANR
45, 73, 92, 157; CN 1, 2, 3, 4, 5, 6, 7;
DLB 6, 218
Busch, Frederick Matthew
See Busch, Frederick
Bush, Barney (Furman) 1946- .... **NNAL**
See also CA 145
Bush, Ronald 1946- .... **CLC 34**
See also CA 136
Busia, Abena, P. A. 1953- .... **BLC 2:1**
Bustos, Francisco
See Borges, Jorge Luis
Bustos Domecq, Honorio
See Bioy Casares, Adolfo; Borges, Jorge
Luis
Butler, Octavia 1947-2006 . **BLC 2:1; BLCS; CLC 38, 121, 230, 240**
See also AAYA 18, 48; AFAW 2; AMWS
13; BPFB 1; BW 2, 3; CA 73-76; 248;
CANR 12, 24, 38, 73, 145, 240; CLR 65;
CN 7; CPW; DA3; DAM MULT, POP;
DLB 33; LATS 1:2; MTCW 1, 2; MTFW
2005; NFS 8, 21, 34; SATA 84; SCFW 2;
SFW 4; SSFS 6; TCLE 1:1; YAW
Butler, Octavia E.
See Butler, Octavia
Butler, Octavia Estelle
See Butler, Octavia
Butler, Robert Olen, Jr.
See Butler, Robert Olen
Butler, Robert Olen 1945- .... **CLC 81, 162; SSC 117**
See also AMWS 12; BPFB 1; CA 112;
CANR 66, 138, 194; CN 7; CSW; DAM
POP; DLB 173, 335; INT CA-112; MAL
5; MTCW 2; MTFW 2005; SSFS 11, 22
Butler, Samuel 1612-1680 .... **LC 16, 43, 173; PC 94**
See also DLB 101, 126; RGEL 2
Butler, Samuel 1835-1902 .... **TCLC 1, 33; WLC 1**
See also BRWS 2; CA 143; CDBLB 1890-
1914; DA; DA3; DAB; DAC; DAM MST,
NOV; DLB 18, 57, 174; RGEL 2; SFW 4;
TEA
Butler, Walter C.
See Faust, Frederick
Butor, Michel (Marie Francois)
1926- .... **CLC 1, 3, 8, 11, 15, 161**
See also CA 9-12R; CANR 33, 66; CWW
2; DLB 83; EW 13; EWL 3; GFL 1789 to
the Present; MTCW 1, 2; MTFW 2005
Butts, Mary 1890(?)-1937 ... **SSC 124; TCLC 77**
See also CA 148; DLB 240

Chabon, Michael 1963- ... **CLC 55, 149, 265; SSC 59**
See also AAYA 45; AMWS 11; CA 139; CANR 57, 96, 127, 138, 196; DLB 278; MAL 5; MTFW 2005; NFS 25; SATA 145

Chabrol, Claude 1930-2010 .... **CLC 16**
See also CA 110

Chairil Anwar
See Anwar, Chairil

Challans, Mary
See Renault, Mary

Challis, George
See Faust, Frederick

Chambers, Aidan 1934- .... **CLC 35**
See also AAYA 27; CA 25-28R; CANR 12, 31, 58, 116; CLR 151; JRDA; MAICYA 1, 2; SAAS 12; SATA 1, 69, 108, 171; WYA; YAW

Chambers, James .... **CLC 21**
See also CA 124; 199

Chambers, Jessie
See Lawrence, D. H.

Chambers, Robert W(illiam)
1865-1933 .... **SSC 92; TCLC 41**
See also CA 165; DLB 202; HGG; SATA 107; SUFW 1

Chambers, (David) Whittaker
1901-1961 .... **TCLC 129**
See also CA 89-92; DLB 303

Chamisso, Adelbert von
1781-1838 .... **NCLC 82; SSC 140**
See also DLB 90; RGWL 2, 3; SUFW 1

Chamoiseau, Patrick 1953- ..... **CLC 268, 276**
See also CA 162; CANR 88; EWL 3; RGWL 3

Chance, James T.
See Carpenter, John

Chance, John T.
See Carpenter, John

Chand, Munshi Prem
See Srivastava, Dhanpat Rai

Chand, Prem
See Srivastava, Dhanpat Rai

Chandler, Raymond 1888-1959 .... **SSC 23; TCLC 1, 7, 179**
See also AAYA 25; AMWC 2; AMWS 4; BPFB 1; CA 104; 129; CANR 60, 107; CDALB 1929-1941; CMW 4; DA3; DLB 226, 253; DLBD 6; EWL 3; MAL 5; MSW; MTCW 1, 2; MTFW 2005; NFS 17; RGAL 4; TUS

Chandler, Raymond Thornton
See Chandler, Raymond

Chandra, Vikram 1961- .... **CLC 302**
See also CA 149; CANR 97, 214; SSFS 16

Chang, Diana 1934-2009 .... **AAL**
See also CA 228; CWP; DLB 312; EXPP; PFS 37

Chang, Eileen 1920-1995 .... **AAL; SSC 28; TCLC 184**
See also CA 166; CANR 168; CWW 2; DLB 328; EWL 3; RGSF 2

Chang, Jung 1952- .... **CLC 71**
See also CA 142

Chang Ai-Ling
See Chang, Eileen

Channing, William Ellery
1780-1842 .... **NCLC 17**
See also DLB 1, 59, 235; RGAL 4

Chao, Patricia 1955- .... **CLC 119**
See also CA 163; CANR 155

Chaplin, Charles Spencer
1889-1977 .... **CLC 16**
See also AAYA 61; CA 81-84; 73-76; DLB 44

Chaplin, Charlie
See Chaplin, Charles Spencer

Chapman, George 1559(?)-1634 . **DC 19; LC 22, 116; PC 96**
See also BRW 1; DAM DRAM; DLB 62, 121; LMFS 1; RGEL 2

Chapman, Graham 1941-1989 .... **CLC 21**
See also AAYA 7; CA 116; 129; CANR 35, 95

Chapman, John Jay 1862-1933 .... **TCLC 7**
See also AMWS 14; CA 104; 191

Chapman, Lee
See Bradley, Marion Zimmer

Chapman, Walker
See Silverberg, Robert

Chappell, Fred 1936- . **CLC 40, 78, 162, 293; PC 105**
See also CA 5-8R, 198; CAAE 198; CAAS 4; CANR 8, 33, 67, 110, 215; CN 6; CP 6, 7; CSW; DLB 6, 105; HGG

Chappell, Fred Davis
See Chappell, Fred

Char, Rene 1907-1988 ..... **CLC 9, 11, 14, 55; PC 56**
See also CA 13-16R; 124; CANR 32; DAM POET; DLB 258; EWL 3; GFL 1789 to the Present; MTCW 1, 2; RGWL 2, 3

Char, Rene-Emile
See Char, Rene

Charby, Jay
See Ellison, Harlan

Chardin, Pierre Teilhard de
See Teilhard de Chardin, (Marie Joseph) Pierre

Chariton fl. 1st cent. (?)- .... **CMLC 49**

Charlemagne 742-814 .... **CMLC 37**

Charles I 1600-1649 .... **LC 13, 194**

Charriere, Isabelle de 1740-1805 .. **NCLC 66**
See also DLB 313

Charron, Pierre 1541-1603 .... **LC 174**
See also GFL Beginnings to 1789

Chartier, Alain c. 1392-1430 .... **LC 94**
See also DLB 208

Chartier, Emile-Auguste
See Alain

Charyn, Jerome 1937- .... **CLC 5, 8, 18**
See also CA 5-8R; CAAS 1; CANR 7, 61, 101, 158, 199; CMW 4; CN 1, 2, 3, 4, 5, 6, 7; DLBY 1983; MTCW 1

Chase, Adam
See Marlowe, Stephen

Chase, Mary (Coyle) 1907-1981 .... **DC 1**
See also CA 77-80; 105; CAD; CWD; DFS 11; DLB 228; SATA 17; SATA-Obit 29

Chase, Mary Ellen 1887-1973 .... **CLC 2; TCLC 124**
See also CA 13-16; 41-44R; CAP 1; SATA 10

Chase, Nicholas
See Hyde, Anthony

Chase-Riboud, Barbara (Dewayne Tosi)
1939- .... **BLC 2:1**
See also BW 2; CA 113; CANR 76; DAM MULT; DLB 33; MTCW 2

Chateaubriand, Francois Rene de
1768-1848 .... **NCLC 3, 134**
See also DLB 119; EW 5; GFL 1789 to the Present; RGWL 2, 3; TWA

Chatelet, Gabrielle-Emilie Du
See du Chatelet, Emilie

Chatterje, Saratchandra -(?)
See Chatterji, Sarat Chandra

Chatterji, Bankim Chandra
1838-1894 .... **NCLC 19**

Chatterji, Sarat Chandra
1876-1936 .... **TCLC 13**
See also CA 109; 186; EWL 3

Chatterton, Thomas 1752-1770 ..... **LC 3, 54; PC 104**
See also DAM POET; DLB 109; RGEL 2

Chatwin, (Charles) Bruce
1940-1989 .... **CLC 28, 57, 59**
See also AAYA 4; BEST 90:1; BRWS 4; CA 85-88; 127; CPW; DAM POP; DLB 194, 204; EWL 3; MTFW 2005

Chaucer, Daniel
See Ford, Ford Madox

Chaucer, Geoffrey 1340(?)-1400 ... **LC 17, 56, 173; PC 19, 58; WLCS**
See also BRW 1; BRWC 1; BRWR 2; CD-BLB Before 1660; DA; DA3; DAB; DAC; DAM MST, POET; DLB 146; LAIT 1; PAB; PFS 14; RGEL 2; TEA; WLIT 3; WP

Chaudhuri, Nirad C(handra)
1897-1999 .... **TCLC 224**
See also CA 128; 183; DLB 323

Chavez, Denise 1948- .... **HLC 1**
See also CA 131; CANR 56, 81, 137; DAM MULT; DLB 122; FW; HW 1, 2; LLW; MAL 5; MTCW 2; MTFW 2005

Chaviaras, Strates 1935- .... **CLC 33**
See also CA 105

Chayefsky, Paddy 1923-1981 .... **CLC 23**
See also CA 9-12R; 104; CAD; CANR 18; DAM DRAM; DFS 26; DLB 23; DLBY 7, 44; RGAL 4

Chayefsky, Sidney
See Chayefsky, Paddy

Chedid, Andree 1920-2011 .... **CLC 47**
See also CA 145; CANR 95; EWL 3

Cheever, John 1912-1982 ..... **CLC 3, 7, 8, 11, 15, 25, 64; SSC 1, 38, 57, 120; WLC 2**
See also AAYA 65; AMWS 1; BPFB 1; CA 5-8R; 106; CABS 1; CANR 5, 27, 76; CDALB 1941-1968; CN 1, 2, 3; CPW; DA; DA3; DAB; DAC; DAM MST, NOV, POP; DLB 2, 102, 227; DLBY 1980, 1982; EWL 3; EXPS; INT CANR-5; MAL 5; MTCW 1, 2; MTFW 2005; RGAL 4; RGSF 2; SSFS 2, 14; TUS

Cheever, Susan 1943- .... **CLC 18, 48**
See also CA 103; CANR 27, 51, 92, 157, 198; DLBY 1982; INT CANR-27

Chekhonte, Antosha
See Chekhov, Anton

Chekhov, Anton 1860-1904 ...... **DC 9; SSC 2, 28, 41, 51, 85, 102, 155; TCLC 3, 10, 31, 55, 96, 163; WLC 2**
See also AAYA 68; BYA 14; CA 104; 124; DA; DA3; DAB; DAC; DAM DRAM, MST; DFS 1, 5, 10, 12, 26; DLB 277; EW 7; EWL 3; EXPS; LAIT 3; LATS 1:1; RGSF 2; RGWL 2, 3; SATA 90; SSFS 5, 13, 14, 26, 29, 33; TWA

Chekhov, Anton Pavlovich
See Chekhov, Anton

Cheney, Lynne V. 1941- .... **CLC 70**
See also CA 89-92; CANR 58, 117, 193; SATA 152

Cheney, Lynne Vincent
See Cheney, Lynne V.

Chenier, Andre-Marie de 1762-1794 . **LC 174**
See also EW 4; GFL Beginnings to 1789; TWA

Chernyshevsky, Nikolai Gavrilovich
See Chernyshevsky, Nikolay Gavrilovich

Chernyshevsky, Nikolay Gavrilovich
1828-1889 .... **NCLC 1**
See also DLB 238

Cherry, Carolyn Janice
See Cherryh, C.J.

Cherryh, C.J. 1942- .... **CLC 35**
See also AAYA 24; BPFB 1; CA 65-68; CANR 10, 147, 179; DLBY 1980; FANT; SATA 93, 172; SCFW 2; YAW

Chesler, Phyllis 1940- .... **CLC 247**
See also CA 49-52; CANR 4, 59, 140, 189; FW

Clark, M. R.
See Clark, Mavis Thorpe

Clark, Mavis Thorpe 1909-1999 ...... **CLC 12**
See also CA 57-60; CANR 8, 37, 107; CLR 30; CWRI 5; MAICYA 1, 2; SAAS 5; SATA 8, 74

Clark, Walter Van Tilburg
1909-1971 .... **CLC 28**
See also CA 9-12R; 33-36R; CANR 63, 113; CN 1; DLB 9, 206; LAIT 2; MAL 5; RGAL 4; SATA 8; TCWW 1, 2

Clark-Bekederemo, J. P. 1935- ...... **BLC 1:1; CLC 38; DC 5**
See also AAYA 79; AFW; BW 1; CA 65-68; CANR 16, 72; CD 5, 6; CDWLB 3; CP 1, 2, 3, 4, 5, 6, 7; DAM DRAM, MULT; DFS 13; DLB 117; EWL 3; MTCW 2; MTFW 2005; RGEL 2

Clark-Bekederemo, John Pepper
See Clark-Bekederemo, J. P.

Clark Bekederemo, Johnson Pepper
See Clark-Bekederemo, J. P.

Clarke, Arthur
See Clarke, Arthur C.

Clarke, Arthur C. 1917-2008 .. **CLC 1, 4, 13, 18, 35, 136; SSC 3**
See also AAYA 4, 33; BPFB 1; BYA 13; CA 1-4R; 270; CANR 2, 28, 55, 74, 130, 196; CLR 119; CN 1, 2, 3, 4, 5, 6, 7; CPW; DA3; DAM POP; DLB 261; JRDA; LAIT 5; MAICYA 1, 2; MTCW 1, 2; MTFW 2005; SATA 13, 70, 115; SATA-Obit 191; SCFW 1, 2; SFW 4; SSFS 4, 18, 29; TCLE 1:1; YAW

Clarke, Arthur Charles
See Clarke, Arthur C.

Clarke, Austin 1896-1974 .... **CLC 6, 9; PC 112**
See also BRWS 15; CA 29-32; 49-52; CAP 2; CP 1, 2; DAM POET; DLB 10, 20; EWL 3; RGEL 2

Clarke, Austin C. 1934- .... **BLC 1:1; CLC 8, 53; SSC 45, 116**
See also BW 1; CA 25-28R; CAAS 16; CANR 14, 32, 68, 140; CN 1, 2, 3, 4, 5, 6, 7; DAC; DAM MULT; DLB 53, 125; DNFS 2; MTCW 2; MTFW 2005; RGSF 2

Clarke, Gillian 1937- .... **CLC 61**
See also CA 106; CP 3, 4, 5, 6, 7; CWP; DLB 40

Clarke, Marcus (Andrew Hislop)
1846-1881 .... **NCLC 19; SSC 94**
See also DLB 230; RGEL 2; RGSF 2

Clarke, Shirley 1925-1997 .... **CLC 16**
See also CA 189

Clash, The
See Headon, (Nicky) Topper; Jones, Mick; Simonon, Paul; Strummer, Joe

Claudel, Paul (Louis Charles Marie)
1868-1955 .... **TCLC 2, 10**
See also CA 104; 165; DLB 192, 258, 321; EW 8; EWL 3; GFL 1789 to the Present; RGWL 2, 3; TWA

Claudian 370(?)-404(?) .... **CMLC 46**
See also RGWL 2, 3

Claudius, Matthias 1740-1815 .... **NCLC 75**
See also DLB 97

Clavell, James 1925-1994 .... **CLC 6, 25, 87**
See also BPFB 1; CA 25-28R; 146; CANR 26, 48; CN 5; CPW; DA3; DAM NOV, POP; MTCW 1, 2; MTFW 2005; NFS 10; RHW

Clayman, Gregory .... **CLC 65**

Cleage, Pearl 1948- .... **DC 32**
See also BW 2; CA 41-44R; CANR 27, 148, 177; DFS 14, 16; DLB 228; NFS 17

Cleage, Pearl Michelle
See Cleage, Pearl

Cleaver, (Leroy) Eldridge
1935-1998 .... **BLC 1:1; CLC 30, 119**
See also BW 1, 3; CA 21-24R; 167; CANR 16, 75; DA3; DAM MULT; MTCW 2; YAW

Cleese, John (Marwood) 1939- .... **CLC 21**
See also CA 112; 116; CANR 35; MTCW 1

Cleishbotham, Jebediah
See Scott, Sir Walter

Cleland, John 1710-1789 .... **LC 2, 48**
See also DLB 39; RGEL 2

Clemens, Samuel
See Twain, Mark

Clemens, Samuel Langhorne
See Twain, Mark

Clement of Alexandria
150(?)-215(?) .... **CMLC 41**

Cleophil
See Congreve, William

Clerihew, E.
See Bentley, E(dmund) C(lerihew)

Clerk, N. W.
See Lewis, C. S.

Cleveland, John 1613-1658 .... **LC 106**
See also DLB 126; RGEL 2

Cliff, Jimmy
See Chambers, James

Cliff, Michelle 1946- .... **BLCS; CLC 120**
See also BW 2; CA 116; CANR 39, 72; CD-WLB 3; DLB 157; FW; GLL 2

Clifford, Lady Anne 1590-1676 .... **LC 76**
See also DLB 151

Clifton, Lucille 1936-2010 .... **BLC 1:1, 2:1; CLC 19, 66, 162, 283; PC 17**
See also AFAW 2; BW 2, 3; CA 49-52; CANR 2, 24, 42, 76, 97, 138; CLR 5; CP 2, 3, 4, 5, 6, 7; CSW; CWP; CWRI 5; DA3; DAM MULT, POET; DLB 5, 41; EXPP; MAICYA 1, 2; MTCW 1, 2; MTFW 2005; PFS 1, 14, 29; SATA 20, 69, 128; WP

Clifton, Thelma Lucille
See Clifton, Lucille

Clinton, Dirk
See Silverberg, Robert

Clough, Arthur Hugh 1819-1861 .. **NCLC 27, 163; PC 103**
See also BRW 5; DLB 32; RGEL 2

Clutha, Janet
See Frame, Janet

Clutha, Janet Paterson Frame
See Frame, Janet

Clyne, Terence
See Blatty, William Peter

Cobalt, Martin
See Mayne, William

Cobb, Irvin S(hrewsbury)
1876-1944 .... **TCLC 77**
See also CA 175; DLB 11, 25, 86

Cobbett, William 1763-1835 .... **NCLC 49**
See also DLB 43, 107, 158; RGEL 2

Coben, Harlan 1962- .... **CLC 269**
See also AAYA 83; CA 164; CANR 162, 199

Coburn, D(onald) L(ee) 1938- .... **CLC 10**
See also CA 89-92; DFS 23

Cockburn, Catharine Trotter
See Trotter, Catharine

Cocteau, Jean 1889-1963 ... **CLC 1, 8, 15, 16, 43; DC 17; TCLC 119; WLC 2**
See also AAYA 74; CA 25-28; CANR 40; CAP 2; DA; DA3; DAB; DAC; DAM DRAM, MST, NOV; DFS 24; DLB 65, 258, 321; EW 10; EWL 3; GFL 1789 to the Present; MTCW 1, 2; RGWL 2, 3; TWA

Cocteau, Jean Maurice Eugene Clement
See Cocteau, Jean

Codrescu, Andrei 1946- .... **CLC 46, 121**
See also CA 33-36R; CAAS 19; CANR 13, 34, 53, 76, 125; CN 7; DA3; DAM POET; MAL 5; MTCW 2; MTFW 2005

Coe, Max
See Bourne, Randolph S(illiman)

Coe, Tucker
See Westlake, Donald E.

Coelho, Paulo 1947- .... **CLC 258**
See also CA 152; CANR 80, 93, 155, 194; NFS 29

Coen, Ethan 1957- .... **CLC 108, 267**
See also AAYA 54; CA 126; CANR 85

Coen, Joel 1954- .... **CLC 108, 267**
See also AAYA 54; CA 126; CANR 119

The Coen Brothers
See Coen, Ethan; Coen, Joel

Coetzee, J. M. 1940- ..... **CLC 23, 33, 66, 117, 161, 162, 305**
See also AAYA 37; AFW; BRWS 6; CA 77-80; CANR 41, 54, 74, 114, 133, 180; CN 4, 5, 6, 7; DA3; DAM NOV; DLB 225, 326, 329; EWL 3; LMFS 2; MTCW 1, 2; MTFW 2005; NFS 21; WLIT 2; WWE 1

Coetzee, John Maxwell
See Coetzee, J. M.

Coffey, Brian
See Koontz, Dean

Coffin, Robert P. Tristram
1892-1955 .... **TCLC 95**
See also CA 123; 169; DLB 45

Coffin, Robert Peter Tristram
See Coffin, Robert P. Tristram

Cohan, George M. 1878-1942 .... **TCLC 60**
See also CA 157; DLB 249; RGAL 4

Cohan, George Michael
See Cohan, George M.

Cohen, Arthur A(llen) 1928-1986 ...... **CLC 7, 31**
See also CA 1-4R; 120; CANR 1, 17, 42; DLB 28; RGHL

Cohen, Leonard 1934- .. **CLC 3, 38, 260; PC 109**
See also CA 21-24R; CANR 14, 69; CN 1, 2, 3, 4, 5, 6; CP 1, 2, 3, 4, 5, 6, 7; DAC; DAM MST; DLB 53; EWL 3; MTCW 1

Cohen, Leonard Norman
See Cohen, Leonard

Cohen, Matt(hew) 1942-1999 .... **CLC 19**
See also CA 61-64; 187; CAAS 18; CANR 40; CN 1, 2, 3, 4, 5, 6; DAC; DLB 53

Cohen-Solal, Annie 1948- .... **CLC 50**
See also CA 239

Colegate, Isabel 1931- .... **CLC 36**
See also CA 17-20R; CANR 8, 22, 74; CN 4, 5, 6, 7; DLB 14, 231; INT CANR-22; MTCW 1

Coleman, Emmett
See Reed, Ishmael

Coleridge, Hartley 1796-1849 .... **NCLC 90**
See also DLB 96

Coleridge, M. E.
See Coleridge, Mary E(lizabeth)

Coleridge, Mary E(lizabeth)
1861-1907 .... **TCLC 73**
See also CA 116; 166; DLB 19, 98

Coleridge, Samuel Taylor
1772-1834 ..... **NCLC 9, 54, 99, 111, 177, 197, 231; PC 11, 39, 67, 100; WLC 2**
See also AAYA 66; BRW 4; BRWR 2; BYA 4; CDBLB 1789-1832; DA; DA3; DAB; DAC; DAM MST, POET; DLB 93, 107; EXPP; LATS 1:1; PAB; PFS 4, 5; RGEL 2; TEA; WLIT 3; WP

Coleridge, Sara 1802-1852 .... **NCLC 31**
See also DLB 199

Coles, Don 1928- .... **CLC 46**
See also CA 115; CANR 38; CP 5, 6, 7

Crane, R(onald) S(almon)
1886-1967 .... **CLC 27**
See also CA 85-88; DLB 63

Crane, Stephen 1871-1900 ..... **PC 80; SSC 7, 56, 70, 129; TCLC 11, 17, 32, 216; WLC 2**
See also AAYA 21; AMW; AMWC 1; BPFB 1; BYA 3; CA 109; 140; CANR 84; CDALB 1865-1917; CLR 132; DA; DA3; DAB; DAC; DAM MST, NOV, POET; DLB 12, 54, 78, 357; EXPN; EXPS; LAIT 2; LMFS 2; MAL 5; NFS 4, 20; PFS 9; RGAL 4; RGSF 2; SSFS 4, 28; TUS; WYA; YABC 2

Crane, Stephen Townley
See Crane, Stephen

Cranmer, Thomas 1489-1556 .... **LC 95**
See also DLB 132, 213

Cranshaw, Stanley
See Fisher, Dorothy (Frances) Canfield

Crase, Douglas 1944- .... **CLC 58**
See also CA 106; CANR 204

Crashaw, Richard 1612(?)-1649 .. **LC 24; PC 84**
See also BRW 2; DLB 126; PAB; RGEL 2

Cratinus c. 519B.C.-c. 422B.C. ..... **CMLC 54**
See also LMFS 1

Craven, Margaret 1901-1980 .... **CLC 17**
See also BYA 2; CA 103; CCA 1; DAC; LAIT 5

Crawford, F(rancis) Marion
1854-1909 .... **TCLC 10**
See also CA 107; 168; DLB 71; HGG; RGAL 4; SUFW 1

Crawford, Isabella Valancy
1850-1887 .... **NCLC 12, 127**
See also DLB 92; RGEL 2

Crayon, Geoffrey
See Irving, Washington

Creasey, John 1908-1973 .... **CLC 11**
See also CA 5-8R; 41-44R; CANR 8, 59; CMW 4; DLB 77; MTCW 1

Crebillon, Claude Prosper Jolyot de (fils)
1707-1777 .... **LC 1, 28**
See also DLB 313; GFL Beginnings to 1789

Credo
See Creasey, John

Credo, Alvaro J. de
See Prado (Calvo), Pedro

Creeley, Robert 1926-2005 .... **CLC 1, 2, 4, 8, 11, 15, 36, 78, 266; PC 73**
See also AMWS 4; CA 1-4R; 237; CAAS 10; CANR 23, 43, 89, 137; CP 1, 2, 3, 4, 5, 6, 7; DA3; DAM POET; DLB 5, 16, 169; DLBD 17; EWL 3; MAL 5; MTCW 1, 2; MTFW 2005; PFS 21; RGAL 4; WP

Creeley, Robert White
See Creeley, Robert

Crenne, Helisenne de 1510-1560 .... **LC 113**
See also DLB 327

Crevecoeur, J. Hector St. John de
1735-1813 .... **NCLC 105**
See also AMWS 1; ANW; DLB 37

Crevecoeur, Michel Guillaume Jean de
See Crevecoeur, J. Hector St. John de

Crevel, Rene 1900-1935 .... **TCLC 112**
See also GLL 2

Crews, Harry 1935- .... **CLC 6, 23, 49, 277**
See also AITN 1; AMWS 11; BPFB 1; CA 25-28R; CANR 20, 57; CN 3, 4, 5, 6, 7; CSW; DA3; DLB 6, 143, 185; MTCW 1, 2; MTFW 2005; RGAL 4

Crichton, John Michael
See Crichton, Michael

Crichton, Michael 1942-2008 .. **CLC 2, 6, 54, 90, 242**
See also AAYA 10, 49; AITN 2; BPFB 1; CA 25-28R; 279; CANR 13, 40, 54, 76, 127, 179; CMW 4; CN 2, 3, 6, 7; CPW;

DA3; DAM NOV, POP; DLB 292; DLBY 1981; INT CANR-13; JRDA; LNFS 1; MTCW 1, 2; MTFW 2005; NFS 34; SATA 9, 88; SATA-Obit 199; SFW 4; YAW

Crispin, Edmund
See Montgomery, Bruce

Cristina of Sweden 1626-1689 .... **LC 124**

Cristofer, Michael 1945(?)- .... **CLC 28**
See also CA 110; 152; CAD; CANR 150; CD 5, 6; DAM DRAM; DFS 15; DLB 7

Cristofer, Michael Ivan
See Cristofer, Michael

Criton
See Alain

Croce, Benedetto 1866-1952 .... **TCLC 37**
See also CA 120; 155; EW 8; EWL 3; WLIT 7

Crockett, David
See Crockett, Davy

Crockett, Davy 1786-1836 .... **NCLC 8**
See also DLB 3, 11, 183, 248

Crofts, Freeman Wills 1879-1957 .. **TCLC 55**
See also CA 115; 195; CMW 4; DLB 77; MSW

Croker, John Wilson 1780-1857 .... **NCLC 10**
See also DLB 110

Crommelynck, Fernand 1885-1970 .. **CLC 75**
See also CA 189; 89-92; EWL 3

Cromwell, Oliver 1599-1658 .... **LC 43**

Cronenberg, David 1943- .... **CLC 143**
See also CA 138; CCA 1

Cronin, A(rchibald) J(oseph)
1896-1981 .... **CLC 32**
See also BPFB 1; CA 1-4R; 102; CANR 5; CN 2; DLB 191; SATA 47; SATA-Obit 25

Cross, Amanda
See Heilbrun, Carolyn G.

Crothers, Rachel 1878-1958 .... **TCLC 19**
See also CA 113; 194; CAD; CWD; DLB 7, 266; RGAL 4

Croves, Hal
See Traven, B.

Crow Dog, Mary (?)- .... **CLC 93; NNAL**
See also CA 154

Crowfield, Christopher
See Stowe, Harriet Beecher

Crowley, Aleister
See Crowley, Edward Alexander

Crowley, Edward Alexander
1875-1947 .... **TCLC 7**
See also CA 104; GLL 1; HGG

Crowley, John 1942- .... **CLC 57**
See also AAYA 57; BPFB 1; CA 61-64; CANR 43, 98, 138, 177; DLBY 1982; FANT; MTFW 2005; SATA 65, 140; SFW 4; SUFW 2

Crowne, John 1641-1712 .... **LC 104**
See also DLB 80; RGEL 2

Crud
See Crumb, R.

Crumarums
See Crumb, R.

Crumb, R. 1943- .... **CLC 17**
See also CA 106; CANR 107, 150, 218

Crumb, Robert
See Crumb, R.

Crumbum
See Crumb, R.

Crumski
See Crumb, R.

Crum the Bum
See Crumb, R.

Crunk
See Crumb, R.

Crustt
See Crumb, R.

Crutchfield, Les
See Trumbo, Dalton

Cruz, Victor Hernandez 1949- ... **HLC 1; PC 37**
See also BW 2; CA 65-68, 271; CAAE 271; CAAS 17; CANR 14, 32, 74, 132; CP 1, 2, 3, 4, 5, 6, 7; DAM MULT, POET; DLB 41; DNFS 1; EXPP; HW 1, 2; LLW; MTCW 2; MTFW 2005; PFS 16; WP

Cryer, Gretchen (Kiger) 1935- .... **CLC 21**
See also CA 114; 123

Csath, Geza
See Brenner, Jozef

Cudlip, David R(ockwell) 1933- .... **CLC 34**
See also CA 177

Cuervo, Talia
See Vega, Ana Lydia

Cullen, Countee 1903-1946 ..... **BLC 1:1; HR 1:2; PC 20; TCLC 4, 37, 220; WLCS**
See also AAYA 78; AFAW 2; AMWS 4; BW 1; CA 108; 124; CDALB 1917-1929; DA; DA3; DAC; DAM MST, MULT, POET; DLB 4, 48, 51; EWL 3; EXPP; LMFS 2; MAL 5; MTCW 1, 2; MTFW 2005; PFS 3; RGAL 4; SATA 18; WP

Culleton, Beatrice 1949- .... **NNAL**
See also CA 120; CANR 83; DAC

Culver, Timothy J.
See Westlake, Donald E.

Cum, R.
See Crumb, R.

Cumberland, Richard
1732-1811 .... **NCLC 167**
See also DLB 89; RGEL 2

Cummings, Bruce F. 1889-1919 ..... **TCLC 24**
See also CA 123

Cummings, Bruce Frederick
See Cummings, Bruce F.

Cummings, E. E. 1894-1962 ...... **CLC 1, 3, 8, 12, 15, 68; PC 5; TCLC 137; WLC 2**
See also AAYA 41; AMW; CA 73-76; CANR 31; CDALB 1929-1941; DA; DA3; DAB; DAC; DAM MST, POET; DLB 4, 48; EWL 3; EXPP; MAL 5; MTCW 1, 2; MTFW 2005; PAB; PFS 1, 3, 12, 13, 19, 30, 34; RGAL 4; TUS; WP

Cummings, Edward Estlin
See Cummings, E. E.

Cummins, Maria Susanna
1827-1866 .... **NCLC 139**
See also DLB 42; YABC 1

Cunha, Euclides (Rodrigues Pimenta) da
1866-1909 .... **TCLC 24**
See also CA 123; 219; DLB 307; LAW; WLIT 1

Cunningham, E. V.
See Fast, Howard

Cunningham, J. Morgan
See Westlake, Donald E.

Cunningham, J(ames) V(incent)
1911-1985 .... **CLC 3, 31; PC 92**
See also CA 1-4R; 115; CANR 1, 72; CP 1, 2, 3, 4; DLB 5

Cunningham, Julia (Woolfolk)
1916- .... **CLC 12**
See also CA 9-12R; CANR 4, 19, 36; CWRI 5; JRDA; MAICYA 1, 2; SAAS 2; SATA 1, 26, 132

Cunningham, Michael 1952- .... **CLC 34, 243**
See also AMWS 15; CA 136; CANR 96, 160; CN 7; DLB 292; GLL 2; MTFW 2005; NFS 23

Cunninghame Graham, R. B.
See Cunninghame Graham, Robert Bontine

Cunninghame Graham, Robert Bontine
1852-1936 .... **TCLC 19**
See also CA 119; 184; DLB 98, 135, 174; RGEL 2; RGSF 2

Cunninghame Graham, Robert Gallnigad Bontine
See Cunninghame Graham, Robert Bontine
Curnow, (Thomas) Allen (Monro)
1911-2001 .... **PC 48**
See also CA 69-72; 202; CANR 48, 99; CP 1, 2, 3, 4, 5, 6, 7; EWL 3; RGEL 2
Currie, Ellen 19(?)- .... **CLC 44**
Curtin, Philip
See Lowndes, Marie Adelaide (Belloc)
Curtin, Phillip
See Lowndes, Marie Adelaide (Belloc)
Curtis, Price
See Ellison, Harlan
Cusanus, Nicolaus 1401-1464
See Nicholas of Cusa
Cutrate, Joe
See Spiegelman, Art
Cynewulf fl. 9th cent. - .... **CMLC 23, 117**
See also DLB 146; RGEL 2
Cyprian, St. c. 200-258 .... **CMLC 127**
Cyrano de Bergerac, Savinien de
1619-1655 .... **LC 65**
See also DLB 268; GFL Beginnings to 1789; RGWL 2, 3
Cyril of Alexandria c. 375-c. 430 . **CMLC 59**
Czaczkes, Shmuel Yosef Halevi
See Agnon, S. Y.
Dabrowska, Maria (Szumska)
1889-1965 .... **CLC 15**
See also CA 106; CDWLB 4; DLB 215; EWL 3
Dabydeen, David 1955- .... **CLC 34**
See also BW 1; CA 125; CANR 56, 92; CN 6, 7; CP 5, 6, 7; DLB 347
Dacey, Philip 1939- .... **CLC 51**
See also CA 37-40R, 231; CAAE 231; CAAS 17; CANR 14, 32, 64; CP 4, 5, 6, 7; DLB 105
Dacre, Charlotte c. 1772-1825(?) . **NCLC 151**
Dafydd ap Gwilym c. 1320-c. 1380 ..... **PC 56**
Dagerman, Stig (Halvard)
1923-1954 .... **TCLC 17**
See also CA 117; 155; DLB 259; EWL 3
D'Aguiar, Fred 1960- ..... **BLC 2:1; CLC 145**
See also CA 148; CANR 83, 101; CN 7; CP 5, 6, 7; DLB 157; EWL 3
Dahl, Roald 1916-1990 ...... **CLC 1, 6, 18, 79; TCLC 173**
See also AAYA 15; BPFB 1; BRWS 4; BYA 5; CA 1-4R; 133; CANR 6, 32, 37, 62; CLR 1, 7, 41, 111; CN 1, 2, 3, 4; CPW; DA3; DAB; DAC; DAM NOV, POP; DLB 139, 255; HGG; JRDA; MAICYA 1, 2; MTCW 1, 2; MTFW 2005; RGSF 2; SATA 1, 26, 73; SATA-Obit 65; SSFS 4, 30; TEA; YAW
Dahlberg, Edward 1900-1977 . **CLC 1, 7, 14; TCLC 208**
See also CA 9-12R; 69-72; CANR 31, 62; CN 1, 2; DLB 48; MAL 5; MTCW 1; RGAL 4
Dahlie, Michael 1970(?)- .... **CLC 299**
See also CA 283
Daitch, Susan 1954- .... **CLC 103**
See also CA 161
Dale, Colin
See Lawrence, T. E.
Dale, George E.
See Asimov, Isaac
d'Alembert, Jean Le Rond
1717-1783 .... **LC 126**
Dalton, Roque 1935-1975(?) ..... **HLCS 1; PC 36**
See also CA 176; DLB 283; HW 2
Daly, Elizabeth 1878-1967 .... **CLC 52**
See also CA 23-24; 25-28R; CANR 60; CAP 2; CMW 4

Daly, Mary 1928-2010 .... **CLC 173**
See also CA 25-28R; CANR 30, 62, 166; FW; GLL 1; MTCW 1
Daly, Maureen 1921-2006 .... **CLC 17**
See also AAYA 5, 58; BYA 6; CA 253; CANR 37, 83, 108; CLR 96; JRDA; MAICYA 1, 2; SAAS 1; SATA 2, 129; SATA-Obit 176; WYA; YAW
Damas, Leon-Gontran 1912-1978 ... **CLC 84; TCLC 204**
See also BW 1; CA 125; 73-76; EWL 3
Damocles
See Benedetti, Mario
Dana, Richard Henry Sr.
1787-1879 .... **NCLC 53**
Dangarembga, Tsitsi 1959- .... **BLC 2:1**
See also BW 3; CA 163; DLB 360; NFS 28; WLIT 2
Daniel, Samuel 1562(?)-1619 .... **LC 24, 171**
See also DLB 62; RGEL 2
Daniels, Brett
See Adler, Renata
Dannay, Frederic 1905-1982 .... **CLC 3, 11**
See also BPFB 3; CA 1-4R; 107; CANR 1, 39; CMW 4; DAM POP; DLB 137; MSW; MTCW 1; RGAL 4
D'Annunzio, Gabriele 1863-1938 ... **TCLC 6, 40, 215**
See also CA 104; 155; EW 8; EWL 3; RGWL 2, 3; TWA; WLIT 7
Danois, N. le
See Gourmont, Remy(-Marie-Charles) de
Dante 1265-1321 .... **CMLC 3, 18, 39, 70; PC 21, 108; WLCS**
See also DA; DA3; DAB; DAC; DAM MST, POET; EFS 1:1, 2:1; EW 1; LAIT 1; RGWL 2, 3; TWA; WLIT 7; WP
d'Antibes, Germain
See Simenon, Georges
Danticat, Edwidge 1969- . **BLC 2:1; CLC 94, 139, 228; SSC 100**
See also AAYA 29, 85; CA 152, 192; CAAE 192; CANR 73, 129, 179; CN 7; DLB 350; DNFS 1; EXPS; LATS 1:2; LNFS 3; MTCW 2; MTFW 2005; NFS 28, 37; SSFS 1, 25; YAW
Danvers, Dennis 1947- .... **CLC 70**
Danziger, Paula 1944-2004 .... **CLC 21**
See also AAYA 4, 36; BYA 6, 7, 14; CA 112; 115; 229; CANR 37, 132; CLR 20; JRDA; MAICYA 1, 2; MTFW 2005; SATA 36, 63, 102, 149; SATA-Brief 30; SATA-Obit 155; WYA; YAW
Da Ponte, Lorenzo 1749-1838 .... **NCLC 50**
d'Aragona, Tullia 1510(?)-1556 .... **LC 121**
Dario, Ruben 1867-1916 .... **HLC 1; PC 15; TCLC 4**
See also CA 131; CANR 81; DAM MULT; DLB 290; EWL 3; HW 1, 2; LAW; MTCW 1, 2; MTFW 2005; RGWL 2, 3
Darko, Amma 1956- .... **BLC 2:1**
Darley, George 1795-1846 .... **NCLC 2**
See also DLB 96; RGEL 2
Darrow, Clarence (Seward)
1857-1938 .... **TCLC 81**
See also CA 164; DLB 303
Darwin, Charles 1809-1882 .... **NCLC 57**
See also BRWS 7; DLB 57, 166; LATS 1:1; RGEL 2; TEA; WLIT 4
Darwin, Erasmus 1731-1802 .... **NCLC 106**
See also BRWS 16; DLB 93; RGEL 2
Darwish, Mahmoud 1941-2008 .... **PC 86**
See also CA 164; CANR 133; CWW 2; EWL 3; MTCW 2; MTFW 2005
Darwish, Mahmud -2008
See Darwish, Mahmoud
Daryush, Elizabeth 1887-1977 ...... **CLC 6, 19**
See also CA 49-52; CANR 3, 81; DLB 20

Das, Kamala 1934-2009 ..... **CLC 191; PC 43**
See also CA 101; 287; CANR 27, 59; CP 1, 2, 3, 4, 5, 6, 7; CWP; DLB 323; FW
Dasgupta, Surendranath
1887-1952 .... **TCLC 81**
See also CA 157
Dashwood, Edmee Elizabeth Monica de la Pasture 1890-1943 .... **TCLC 61**
See also CA 119; 154; DLB 34; RHW
da Silva, Antonio Jose
1705-1739 .... **NCLC 114**
Daudet, (Louis Marie) Alphonse
1840-1897 .... **NCLC 1**
See also DLB 123; GFL 1789 to the Present; RGSF 2
Daudet, Alphonse Marie Leon
1867-1942 .... **SSC 94**
See also CA 217
d'Aulnoy, Marie-Catherine c.
1650-1705 .... **LC 100**
Daumal, Rene 1908-1944 .... **TCLC 14**
See also CA 114; 247; EWL 3
Davenant, William 1606-1668 .... **LC 13, 166; PC 99**
See also DLB 58, 126; RGEL 2
Davenport, Guy (Mattison, Jr.)
1927-2005 . **CLC 6, 14, 38, 241; SSC 16**
See also CA 33-36R; 235; CANR 23, 73; CN 3, 4, 5, 6; CSW; DLB 130
David, Robert
See Nezval, Vitezslav
Davidson, Donald (Grady)
1893-1968 .... **CLC 2, 13, 19**
See also CA 5-8R; 25-28R; CANR 4, 84; DLB 45
Davidson, Hugh
See Hamilton, Edmond
Davidson, John 1857-1909 .... **TCLC 24**
See also CA 118; 217; DLB 19; RGEL 2
Davidson, Sara 1943- .... **CLC 9**
See also CA 81-84; CANR 44, 68; DLB 185
Davie, Donald (Alfred) 1922-1995 .... **CLC 5, 8, 10, 31; PC 29**
See also BRWS 6; CA 1-4R; 149; CAAS 3; CANR 1, 44; CP 1, 2, 3, 4, 5, 6; DLB 27; MTCW 1; RGEL 2
Davie, Elspeth 1918-1995 .... **SSC 52**
See also CA 120; 126; 150; CANR 141; DLB 139
Davies, Ray 1944- .... **CLC 21**
See also CA 116; 146; CANR 92
Davies, Raymond Douglas
See Davies, Ray
Davies, Rhys 1901-1978 .... **CLC 23**
See also CA 9-12R; 81-84; CANR 4; CN 1, 2; DLB 139, 191
Davies, Robertson 1913-1995 .. **CLC 2, 7, 13, 25, 42, 75, 91; WLC 2**
See also BEST 89:2; BPFB 1; CA 1, 33-36R; 150; CANR 17, 42, 103; CN 1, 2, 3, 4, 5, 6; CPW; DA; DA3; DAB; DAC; DAM MST, NOV, POP; DLB 68; EWL 3; HGG; INT CANR-17; MTCW 1, 2; MTFW 2005; RGEL 2; TWA
Davies, Sir John 1569-1626 .... **LC 85**
See also DLB 172
Davies, Walter C.
See Kornbluth, C(yril) M.
Davies, William Henry 1871-1940 ... **TCLC 5**
See also BRWS 11; CA 104; 179; DLB 19, 174; EWL 3; RGEL 2
Davies, William Robertson
See Davies, Robertson
Da Vinci, Leonardo 1452-1519 ..... **LC 12, 57, 60**
See also AAYA 40
Daviot, Gordon
See Mackintosh, Elizabeth

Deloney, Thomas 1543(?)-1600 .... **LC 41; PC 79**
 See also DLB 167; RGEL 2

Deloria, Ella (Cara) 1889-1971(?) ..... **NNAL**
 See also CA 152; DAM MULT; DLB 175

Deloria, Vine, Jr. 1933-2005 .... **CLC 21, 122; NNAL**
 See also CA 53-56; 245; CANR 5, 20, 48, 98; DAM MULT; DLB 175; MTCW 1; SATA 21; SATA-Obit 171

Deloria, Vine Victor, Jr.
 See Deloria, Vine, Jr.

del Valle-Inclan, Ramon
 See Valle-Inclan, Ramon del

Del Vecchio, John M(ichael) 1947- .. **CLC 29**
 See also CA 110; DLBD 9

de Man, Paul (Adolph Michel)
 1919-1983 .... **CLC 55**
 See also CA 128; 111; CANR 61; DLB 67; MTCW 1, 2

de Mandiargues, Andre Pieyre
 See Pieyre de Mandiargues, Andre

DeMarinis, Rick 1934- .... **CLC 54**
 See also CA 57-60, 184; CAAE 184; CAAS 24; CANR 9, 25, 50, 160; DLB 218; TCWW 2

de Maupassant, Guy
 See Maupassant, Guy de

Dembry, R. Emmet
 See Murfree, Mary Noailles

Demby, William 1922- ...... **BLC 1:1; CLC 53**
 See also BW 1, 3; CA 81-84; CANR 81; DAM MULT; DLB 33

de Menton, Francisco
 See Chin, Frank

Demetrius of Phalerum c.
 307B.C.- .... **CMLC 34**

Demijohn, Thom
 See Disch, Thomas M.

De Mille, James 1833-1880 .... **NCLC 123**
 See also DLB 99, 251

Democritus c. 460B.C.-c. 370B.C. . **CMLC 47**

de Montaigne, Michel
 See Montaigne, Michel de

de Montherlant, Henry
 See Montherlant, Henry de

Demosthenes 384B.C.-322B.C. ...... **CMLC 13**
 See also AW 1; DLB 176; RGWL 2, 3; WLIT 8

de Musset, (Louis Charles) Alfred
 See Musset, Alfred de

de Natale, Francine
 See Malzberg, Barry N(athaniel)

de Navarre, Marguerite 1492-1549 .... **LC 61, 167; SSC 85**
 See also DLB 327; GFL Beginnings to 1789; RGWL 2, 3

Denby, Edwin (Orr) 1903-1983 .... **CLC 48**
 See also CA 138; 110; CP 1

de Nerval, Gerard
 See Nerval, Gerard de

Denham, John 1615-1669 .... **LC 73**
 See also DLB 58, 126; RGEL 2

Denis, Claire 1948- .... **CLC 286**
 See also CA 249

Denis, Julio
 See Cortazar, Julio

Denmark, Harrison
 See Zelazny, Roger

Dennis, John 1658-1734 .... **LC 11, 154**
 See also DLB 101; RGEL 2

Dennis, Nigel (Forbes) 1912-1989 ...... **CLC 8**
 See also CA 25-28R; 129; CN 1, 2, 3, 4; DLB 13, 15, 233; EWL 3; MTCW 1

Dent, Lester 1904-1959 .... **TCLC 72**
 See also CA 112; 161; CMW 4; DLB 306; SFW 4

Dentinger, Stephen
 See Hoch, Edward D.

De Palma, Brian 1940- .... **CLC 20, 247**
 See also CA 109

De Palma, Brian Russell
 See De Palma, Brian

de Pizan, Christine
 See Christine de Pizan

De Quincey, Thomas 1785-1859 ..... **NCLC 4, 87, 198**
 See also BRW 4; CDBLB 1789-1832; DLB 110, 144; RGEL 2

De Ray, Jill
 See Moore, Alan

Deren, Eleanora 1908(?)-1961 .. **CLC 16, 102**
 See also CA 192; 111

Deren, Maya
 See Deren, Eleanora

Derleth, August (William)
 1909-1971 .... **CLC 31**
 See also BPFB 1; BYA 9, 10; CA 1-4R; 29-32R; CANR 4; CMW 4; CN 1; DLB 9; DLBD 17; HGG; SATA 5; SUFW 1

Der Nister 1884-1950 .... **TCLC 56**
 See also DLB 333; EWL 3

de Routisie, Albert
 See Aragon, Louis

Derrida, Jacques 1930-2004 ...... **CLC 24, 87, 225**
 See also CA 124; 127; 232; CANR 76, 98, 133; DLB 242; EWL 3; LMFS 2; MTCW 2; TWA

Derry Down Derry
 See Lear, Edward

Dershowitz, Alan M. 1938- .... **CLC 298**
 See also CA 25-28R; CANR 11, 44, 79, 159

Dershowitz, Alan Morton
 See Dershowitz, Alan M.

Dersonnes, Jacques
 See Simenon, Georges

Der Stricker c. 1190-c. 1250 .... **CMLC 75**
 See also DLB 138

Derzhavin, Gavriil Romanovich
 1743-1816 .... **NCLC 215**
 See also DLB 150

Desai, Anita 1937- . **CLC 19, 37, 97, 175, 271**
 See also AAYA 85; BRWS 5; CA 81-84; CANR 33, 53, 95, 133; CN 1, 2, 3, 4, 5, 6, 7; CWRI 5; DA3; DAB; DAM NOV; DLB 271, 323; DNFS 2; EWL 3; FW; MTCW 1, 2; MTFW 2005; SATA 63, 126; SSFS 28, 31

Desai, Kiran 1971- .... **CLC 119**
 See also BRWS 15; BYA 16; CA 171; CANR 127; NFS 28

de Saint-Luc, Jean
 See Glassco, John

de Saint Roman, Arnaud
 See Aragon, Louis

Desbordes-Valmore, Marceline
 1786-1859 .... **NCLC 97**
 See also DLB 217

Descartes, Rene 1596-1650 .... **LC 20, 35, 150**
 See also DLB 268; EW 3; GFL Beginnings to 1789

Deschamps, Eustache 1340(?)-1404 .. **LC 103**
 See also DLB 208

De Sica, Vittorio 1901(?)-1974 .... **CLC 20**
 See also CA 117

Desnos, Robert 1900-1945 ...... **TCLC 22, 241**
 See also CA 121; 151; CANR 107; DLB 258; EWL 3; LMFS 2

Destouches, Louis-Ferdinand
 See Celine, Louis-Ferdinand

De Teran, Lisa St. Aubin
 See St. Aubin de Teran, Lisa

de Teran, Lisa St. Aubin
 See St. Aubin de Teran, Lisa

de Tolignac, Gaston
 See Griffith, D.W.

Deutsch, Babette 1895-1982 .... **CLC 18**
 See also BYA 3; CA 1-4R; 108; CANR 4, 79; CP 1, 2, 3; DLB 45; SATA 1; SATA-Obit 33

de Vere, Edward 1550-1604 .... **LC 193**
 See also DLB 172

Devi, Mahasweta 1926- .... **CLC 290**

Deville, Rene
 See Kacew, Romain

Devkota, Laxmiprasad 1909-1959 . **TCLC 23**
 See also CA 123

De Voto, Bernard (Augustine)
 1897-1955 .... **TCLC 29**
 See also CA 113; 160; DLB 9, 256; MAL 5; TCWW 1, 2

De Vries, Peter 1910-1993 ..... **CLC 1, 2, 3, 7, 10, 28, 46**
 See also CA 17-20R; 142; CANR 41; CN 1, 2, 3, 4, 5; DAM NOV; DLB 6; DLBY 1982; MAL 5; MTCW 1, 2; MTFW 2005

Dewey, John 1859-1952 .... **TCLC 95**
 See also CA 114; 170; CANR 144; DLB 246, 270; RGAL 4

Dexter, John
 See Bradley, Marion Zimmer

Dexter, Martin
 See Faust, Frederick

Dexter, Pete 1943- .... **CLC 34, 55**
 See also BEST 89:2; CA 127; 131; CANR 129, 219; CPW; DAM POP; INT CA-131; MAL 5; MTCW 1; MTFW 2005

Diamano, Silmang
 See Senghor, Leopold Sedar

Diamant, Anita 1951- .... **CLC 239**
 See also CA 145; CANR 126, 219; NFS 36

Diamond, Neil 1941- .... **CLC 30**
 See also CA 108

Diaz, Junot 1968- .... **CLC 258; SSC 144**
 See also AAYA 83; BYA 12; CA 161; CANR 119, 183; LLW; NFS 36; SSFS 20

Diaz del Castillo, Bernal c.
 1496-1584 .... **HLCS 1; LC 31**
 See also DLB 318; LAW

di Bassetto, Corno
 See Shaw, George Bernard

Dick, Philip K. 1928-1982 ... **CLC 10, 30, 72; SSC 57**
 See also AAYA 24; BPFB 1; BYA 11; CA 49-52; 106; CANR 2, 16, 132; CN 2, 3; CPW; DA3; DAM NOV, POP; DLB 8; MTCW 1, 2; MTFW 2005; NFS 5, 26; SCFW 1, 2; SFW 4

Dick, Philip Kindred
 See Dick, Philip K.

Dickens, Charles 1812-1870 . **NCLC 3, 8, 18, 26, 37, 50, 86, 105, 113, 161, 187, 203, 206, 211, 217, 219, 230, 231, 239; SSC 17, 49, 88; WLC 2**
 See also AAYA 23; BRW 5; BRWC 1, 2; BYA 1, 2, 3, 13, 14; CDBLB 1832-1890; CLR 95, 162; CMW 4; DA; DA3; DAB; DAC; DAM MST, NOV; DLB 21, 55, 70, 159, 166; EXPN; GL 2; HGG; JRDA; LAIT 1, 2; LATS 1:1; LMFS 1; MAICYA 1, 2; NFS 4, 5, 10, 14, 20, 25, 30, 33; RGEL 2; RGSF 2; SATA 15; SUFW 1; TEA; WCH; WLIT 4; WYA

Dickens, Charles John Huffam
 See Dickens, Charles

Dickey, James 1923-1997 .... **CLC 1, 2, 4, 7, 10, 15, 47, 109; PC 40; TCLC 151**
 See also AAYA 50; AITN 1, 2; AMWS 4; BPFB 1; CA 9-12R; 156; CABS 2; CANR 10, 48, 61, 105; CDALB 1968-1988; CP 1, 2, 3, 4, 5, 6; CPW; CSW; DA3; DAM NOV, POET, POP; DLB 5, 193, 342;

DLBD 7; DLBY 1982, 1993, 1996, 1997, 1998; EWL 3; INT CANR-10; MAL 5; MTCW 1, 2; NFS 9; PFS 6, 11; RGAL 4; TUS

Dickey, James Lafayette
See Dickey, James

Dickey, William 1928-1994 .... **CLC 3, 28**
See also CA 9-12R; 145; CANR 24, 79; CP 1, 2, 3, 4; DLB 5

Dickinson, Charles 1951- .... **CLC 49**
See also CA 128; CANR 141

Dickinson, Emily 1830-1886 ... **NCLC 21, 77, 171; PC 1; WLC 2**
See also AAYA 22; AMW; AMWR 1; CDALB 1865-1917; DA; DA3; DAB; DAC; DAM MST, POET; DLB 1, 243; EXPP; FL 1:3; MBL; PAB; PFS 1, 2, 3, 4, 5, 6, 8, 10, 11, 13, 16, 28, 32, 35; RGAL 4; SATA 29; TUS; WP; WYA

Dickinson, Emily Elizabeth
See Dickinson, Emily

Dickinson, Mrs. Herbert Ward
See Phelps, Elizabeth Stuart

Dickinson, Peter 1927- .... **CLC 12, 35**
See also AAYA 9, 49; BYA 5; CA 41-44R; CANR 31, 58, 88, 134, 195; CLR 29, 125; CMW 4; DLB 87, 161, 276; JRDA; MAICYA 1, 2; SATA 5, 62, 95, 150; SFW 4; WYA; YAW

Dickinson, Peter Malcolm de Brissac
See Dickinson, Peter

Dickson, Carr
See Carr, John Dickson

Dickson, Carter
See Carr, John Dickson

Diderot, Denis 1713-1784 .... **LC 26, 126**
See also DLB 313; EW 4; GFL Beginnings to 1789; LMFS 1; RGWL 2, 3

Didion, Joan 1934- . **CLC 1, 3, 8, 14, 32, 129**
See also AITN 1; AMWS 4; CA 5-8R; CANR 14, 52, 76, 125, 174; CDALB 1968-1988; CN 2, 3, 4, 5, 6, 7; DA3; DAM NOV; DLB 2, 173, 185; DLBY 1981, 1986; EWL 3; MAL 5; MBL; MTCW 1, 2; MTFW 2005; NFS 3; RGAL 4; TCLE 1:1; TCWW 2; TUS

di Donato, Pietro 1911-1992 .... **TCLC 159**
See also AMWS 20; CA 101; 136; DLB 9

Dietrich, Robert
See Hunt, E. Howard

Difusa, Pati
See Almodovar, Pedro

di Lampedusa, Giuseppe Tomasi
See Lampedusa, Giuseppe di

Dillard, Annie 1945- ...... **CLC 9, 60, 115, 216**
See also AAYA 6, 43; ANW; AMWS 6; CA 49-52; CANR 3, 43, 62, 90, 125, 214; DA3; DAM NOV; DLB 275, 278; DLBY 1980; LAIT 4, 5; MAL 5; MTCW 1, 2; MTFW 2005; NCFS 1; RGAL 4; SATA 10, 140; TCLE 1:1; TUS

Dillard, R(ichard) H(enry) W(ilde) 1937- .... **CLC 5**
See also CA 21-24R; CAAS 7; CANR 10; CP 2, 3, 4, 5, 6, 7; CSW; DLB 5, 244

Dillon, Eilis 1920-1994 .... **CLC 17**
See also CA 9-12R, 182; 147; CAAE 182; CAAS 3; CANR 4, 38, 78; CLR 26; MAICYA 1, 2; MAICYAS 1; SATA 2, 74; SATA-Essay 105; SATA-Obit 83; YAW

Dimont, Penelope
See Mortimer, Penelope (Ruth)

Dinesen, Isak
See Blixen, Karen

Ding Ling
See Chiang, Pin-chin

Diodorus Siculus c. 90B.C.-c. 31B.C. .... **CMLC 88**
Dionysius of Halicarnassus c. 60B.C.-c. 7B.C. .... **CMLC 126**
Diphusa, Patty
See Almodovar, Pedro

Disch, Thomas M. 1940-2008 .... **CLC 7, 36**
See also AAYA 17; BPFB 1; CA 21-24R; 274; CAAS 4; CANR 17, 36, 54, 89; CLR 18; CP 5, 6, 7; DA3; DLB 8, 282; HGG; MAICYA 1, 2; MTCW 1, 2; MTFW 2005; SAAS 15; SATA 92; SATA-Obit 195; SCFW 1, 2; SFW 4; SUFW 2

Disch, Thomas Michael
See Disch, Thomas M.

Disch, Tom
See Disch, Thomas M.

d'Isly, Georges
See Simenon, Georges

Disraeli, Benjamin 1804-1881 ... **NCLC 2, 39, 79**
See also BRW 4; DLB 21, 55; RGEL 2

D'Israeli, Isaac 1766-1848 .... **NCLC 217**
See also DLB 107

Ditcum, Steve
See Crumb, R.

Dixon, Paige
See Corcoran, Barbara (Asenath)

Dixon, Stephen 1936- .... **CLC 52; SSC 16**
See also AMWS 12; CA 89-92; CANR 17, 40, 54, 91, 175; CN 4, 5, 6, 7; DLB 130; MAL 5

Dixon, Thomas, Jr. 1864-1946 ..... **TCLC 163**
See also RHW

Djebar, Assia 1936- .... **BLC 2:1; CLC 182, 296; SSC 114**
See also CA 188; CANR 169; DLB 346; EWL 3; RGWL 3; WLIT 2

Doak, Annie
See Dillard, Annie

Dobell, Sydney Thompson 1824-1874 .... **NCLC 43; PC 100**
See also DLB 32; RGEL 2

Doblin, Alfred
See Doeblin, Alfred

Dobroliubov, Nikolai Aleksandrovich
See Dobrolyubov, Nikolai Alexandrovich

Dobrolyubov, Nikolai Alexandrovich 1836-1861 .... **NCLC 5**
See also DLB 277

Dobson, Austin 1840-1921 .... **TCLC 79**
See also DLB 35, 144

Dobyns, Stephen 1941- .... **CLC 37, 233**
See also AMWS 13; CA 45-48; CANR 2, 18, 99; CMW 4; CP 4, 5, 6, 7; PFS 23

Doctorow, Cory 1971- .... **CLC 273**
See also AAYA 84; CA 221; CANR 203

Doctorow, E. L. 1931- ...... **CLC 6, 11, 15, 18, 37, 44, 65, 113, 214**
See also AAYA 22; AITN 2; AMWS 4; BEST 89:3; BPFB 1; CA 45-48; CANR 2, 33, 51, 76, 97, 133, 170, 218; CDALB 1968-1988; CN 3, 4, 5, 6, 7; CPW; DA3; DAM NOV, POP; DLB 2, 28, 173; DLBY 1980; EWL 3; LAIT 3; MAL 5; MTCW 1, 2; MTFW 2005; NFS 6; RGAL 4; RGHL; RHW; SSFS 27; TCLE 1:1; TCWW 1, 2; TUS

Doctorow, Edgar Lawrence
See Doctorow, E. L.

Dodgson, Charles Lutwidge
See Carroll, Lewis

Dodsley, Robert 1703-1764 .... **LC 97**
See also DLB 95, 154; RGEL 2

Dodson, Owen (Vincent) 1914-1983 .... **BLC 1:1; CLC 79**
See also BW 1; CA 65-68; 110; CANR 24; DAM MULT; DLB 76

Doeblin, Alfred 1878-1957 .... **TCLC 13**
See also CA 110; 141; CDWLB 2; DLB 66; EWL 3; RGWL 2, 3

Doerr, Harriet 1910-2002 .... **CLC 34**
See also CA 117; 122; 213; CANR 47; INT CA-122; LATS 1:2

Domecq, Honorio Bustos
See Bioy Casares, Adolfo; Borges, Jorge Luis

Domini, Rey
See Lorde, Audre

Dominic, R. B.
See Hennissart, Martha

Dominique
See Proust, Marcel

Don, A
See Stephen, Sir Leslie

Donaldson, Stephen R. 1947- ... **CLC 46, 138**
See also AAYA 36; BPFB 1; CA 89-92; CANR 13, 55, 99; CPW; DAM POP; FANT; INT CANR-13; SATA 121; SFW 4; SUFW 1, 2

Donleavy, J(ames) P(atrick) 1926- .... **CLC 1, 4, 6, 10, 45**
See also AITN 2; BPFB 1; CA 9-12R; CANR 24, 49, 62, 80, 124; CBD; CD 5, 6; CN 1, 2, 3, 4, 5, 6, 7; DLB 6, 173; INT CANR-24; MAL 5; MTCW 1, 2; MTFW 2005; RGAL 4

Donnadieu, Marguerite
See Duras, Marguerite

Donne, John 1572-1631 ... **LC 10, 24, 91; PC 1, 43; WLC 2**
See also AAYA 67; BRW 1; BRWC 1; BRWR 2; CDBLB Before 1660; DA; DAB; DAC; DAM MST, POET; DLB 121, 151; EXPP; PAB; PFS 2, 11, 35; RGEL 3; TEA; WLIT 3; WP

Donnell, David 1939(?)- .... **CLC 34**
See also CA 197

Donoghue, Denis 1928- .... **CLC 209**
See also CA 17-20R; CANR 16, 102, 206

Donoghue, Emma 1969- .... **CLC 239**
See also CA 155; CANR 103, 152, 196; DLB 267; GLL 2; SATA 101

Donoghue, P.S.
See Hunt, E. Howard

Donoso, Jose 1924-1996 ..... **CLC 4, 8, 11, 32, 99; HLC 1; SSC 34; TCLC 133**
See also CA 81-84; 155; CANR 32, 73; CDWLB 3; CWW 2; DAM MULT; DLB 113; EWL 3; HW 1, 2; LAW; LAWS 1; MTCW 1, 2; MTFW 2005; RGSF 2; WLIT 1

Donoso Yanez, Jose
See Donoso, Jose

Donovan, John 1928-1992 .... **CLC 35**
See also AAYA 20; CA 97-100; 137; CLR 3; MAICYA 1, 2; SATA 72; SATA-Brief 29; YAW

Don Roberto
See Cunninghame Graham, Robert Bontine

Doolittle, Hilda 1886-1961 . **CLC 3, 8, 14, 31, 34, 73; PC 5; WLC 3**
See also AAYA 66; AMWS 1; CA 97-100; CANR 35, 131; DA; DAC; DAM MST, POET; DLB 4, 45; EWL 3; FL 1:5; FW; GLL 1; LMFS 2; MAL 5; MBL; MTCW 1, 2; MTFW 2005; PFS 6, 28; RGAL 4

Doppo
See Kunikida Doppo

Doppo, Kunikida
See Kunikida Doppo

Dorfman, Ariel 1942- .... **CLC 48, 77, 189; HLC 1**
See also CA 124; 130; CANR 67, 70, 135; CWW 2; DAM MULT; DFS 4; EWL 3; HW 1, 2; INT CA-130; WLIT 1

Dorn, Edward 1929-1999 .... **CLC 10, 18; PC 115**
See also CA 93-96; 187; CANR 42, 79; CP 1, 2, 3, 4, 5, 6, 7; DLB 5; INT CA-93-96; WP

Dorn, Edward Merton
See Dorn, Edward

Dor-Ner, Zvi .... **CLC 70**

Dorris, Michael 1945-1997 .... **CLC 109; NNAL**
See also AAYA 20; BEST 90:1; BYA 12; CA 102; 157; CANR 19, 46, 75; CLR 58; DA3; DAM MULT, NOV; DLB 175; LAIT 5; MTCW 2; MTFW 2005; NFS 3; RGAL 4; SATA 75; SATA-Obit 94; TCWW 2; YAW

Dorris, Michael A.
See Dorris, Michael

Dorris, Michael Anthony
See Dorris, Michael

Dorsan, Luc
See Simenon, Georges

Dorsange, Jean
See Simenon, Georges

Dorset
See Sackville, Thomas

Dos Passos, John 1896-1970 ...... **CLC 1, 4, 8, 11, 15, 25, 34, 82; WLC 2**
See also AMW; BPFB 1; CA 1-4R; 29-32R; CANR 3; CDALB 1929-1941; DA; DA3; DAB; DAC; DAM MST, NOV; DLB 4, 9, 274, 316; DLBD 1, 15; DLBY 1996; EWL 3; MAL 5; MTCW 1, 2; MTFW 2005; NFS 14; RGAL 4; TUS

Dos Passos, John Roderigo
See Dos Passos, John

Dossage, Jean
See Simenon, Georges

Dostoevsky, Fedor
See Dostoevsky, Fyodor

Dostoevsky, Fedor Mikhailovich
See Dostoevsky, Fyodor

Dostoevsky, Fyodor 1821-1881 ... **NCLC 2, 7, 21, 33, 43, 119, 167, 202, 238; SSC 2, 33, 44, 134; WLC 2**
See also AAYA 40; DA; DA3; DAB; DAC; DAM MST, NOV; DLB 238; EW 7; EXPN; LATS 1:1; LMFS 1, 2; NFS 28; RGSF 2; RGWL 2, 3; SSFS 8, 30; TWA

Doty, Mark 1953(?)- .... **CLC 176; PC 53**
See also AMWS 11; CA 161, 183; CAAE 183; CANR 110, 173; CP 7; PFS 28

Doty, Mark A.
See Doty, Mark

Doty, Mark Alan
See Doty, Mark

Doty, M.R.
See Doty, Mark

Doughty, Charles M(ontagu) 1843-1926 .... **TCLC 27**
See also CA 115; 178; DLB 19, 57, 174

Douglas, Ellen 1921- .... **CLC 73**
See also CA 115; CANR 41, 83; CN 5, 6, 7; CSW; DLB 292

Douglas, Gavin 1475(?)-1522 .... **LC 20**
See also DLB 132; RGEL 2

Douglas, George
See Brown, George Douglas

Douglas, Keith (Castellain) 1920-1944 .... **PC 106; TCLC 40**
See also BRW 7; CA 160; DLB 27; EWL 3; PAB; RGEL 2

Douglas, Leonard
See Bradbury, Ray

Douglas, Michael
See Crichton, Michael

Douglas, (George) Norman 1868-1952 .... **TCLC 68**
See also BRW 6; CA 119; 157; DLB 34, 195; RGEL 2

Douglas, William
See Brown, George Douglas

Douglass, Frederick 1817(?)-1895 .. **BLC 1:1; NCLC 7, 55, 141, 235; WLC 2**
See also AAYA 48; AFAW 1, 2; AMWC 1; AMWS 3; CDALB 1640-1865; DA; DA3; DAC; DAM MST, MULT; DLB 1, 43, 50, 79, 243; FW; LAIT 2; NCFS 2; RGAL 4; SATA 29

Dourado, (Waldomiro Freitas) Autran 1926- .... **CLC 23, 60**
See also CA 25-28R, 179; CANR 34, 81; DLB 145, 307; HW 2

Dourado, Waldomiro Freitas Autran
See Dourado, (Waldomiro Freitas) Autran

Dove, Rita 1952- . **BLC 2:1; BLCS; CLC 50, 81; PC 6**
See also AAYA 46; AMWS 4; BW 2; CA 109; CAAS 19; CANR 27, 42, 68, 76, 97, 132, 217; CDALBS; CP 5, 6, 7; CSW; CWP; DA3; DAM MULT, POET; DLB 120; EWL 3; EXPP; MAL 5; MTCW 2; MTFW 2005; PFS 1, 15, 37; RGAL 4

Dove, Rita Frances
See Dove, Rita

Doveglion
See Villa, Jose Garcia

Dowell, Coleman 1925-1985 .... **CLC 60**
See also CA 25-28R; 117; CANR 10; DLB 130; GLL 2

Downing, Major Jack
See Smith, Seba

Dowson, Ernest (Christopher) 1867-1900 .... **TCLC 4**
See also CA 105; 150; DLB 19, 135; RGEL 2

Doyle, A. Conan
See Doyle, Sir Arthur Conan

Doyle, Sir Arthur Conan 1859-1930 ..... **SSC 12, 83, 95; TCLC 7; WLC 2**
See also AAYA 14; BPFB 1; BRWS 2; BYA 4, 5, 11; CA 104; 122; CANR 131; CDBLB 1890-1914; CLR 106; CMW 4; DA; DA3; DAB; DAC; DAM MST, NOV; DLB 18, 70, 156, 178; EXPS; HGG; LAIT 2; MSW; MTCW 1, 2; MTFW 2005; NFS 28; RGEL 2; RGSF 2; RHW; SATA 24; SCFW 1, 2; SFW 4; SSFS 2; TEA; WCH; WLIT 4; WYA; YAW

Doyle, Conan
See Doyle, Sir Arthur Conan

Doyle, John
See Graves, Robert

Doyle, Roddy 1958- .... **CLC 81, 178**
See also AAYA 14; BRWS 5; CA 143; CANR 73, 128, 168, 200; CN 6, 7; DA3; DLB 194, 326; MTCW 2; MTFW 2005

Doyle, Sir A. Conan
See Doyle, Sir Arthur Conan

Dr. A
See Asimov, Isaac; Silverstein, Alvin; Silverstein, Virginia B.

Drabble, Margaret 1939- ...... **CLC 2, 3, 5, 8, 10, 22, 53, 129**
See also BRWS 4; CA 13-16R; CANR 18, 35, 63, 112, 131, 174, 218; CDBLB 1960 to Present; CN 1, 2, 3, 4, 5, 6, 7; CPW; DA3; DAB; DAC; DAM MST, NOV, POP; DLB 14, 155, 231; EWL 3; FW; MTCW 1, 2; MTFW 2005; RGEL 2; SATA 48; TEA

Drakulic, Slavenka
See Drakulic, Slavenka

Drakulic, Slavenka 1949- .... **CLC 173**
See also CA 144; CANR 92, 198; DLB 353

Drakulic-Ilic, Slavenka
See Drakulic, Slavenka

Drakulic-Ilic, Slavenka
See Drakulic, Slavenka

Drapier, M. B.
See Swift, Jonathan

Drayham, James
See Mencken, H. L.

Drayton, Michael 1563-1631 . **LC 8, 161; PC 98**
See also DAM POET; DLB 121; RGEL 2

Dreadstone, Carl
See Campbell, Ramsey

Dreiser, Theodore 1871-1945 .... **SSC 30, 114; TCLC 10, 18, 35, 83; WLC 2**
See also AMW; AMWC 2; AMWR 2; BYA 15, 16; CA 106; 132; CDALB 1865-1917; DA; DA3; DAC; DAM MST, NOV; DLB 9, 12, 102, 137, 361; DLBD 1; EWL 3; LAIT 2; LMFS 2; MAL 5; MTCW 1, 2; MTFW 2005; NFS 8, 17; RGAL 4; TUS

Dreiser, Theodore Herman Albert
See Dreiser, Theodore

Drexler, Rosalyn 1926- .... **CLC 2, 6**
See also CA 81-84; CAD; CANR 68, 124; CD 5, 6; CWD; MAL 5

Dreyer, Carl Theodor 1889-1968 ...... **CLC 16**
See also CA 116

Drieu la Rochelle, Pierre 1893-1945 .... **TCLC 21**
See also CA 117; 250; DLB 72; EWL 3; GFL 1789 to the Present

Drieu la Rochelle, Pierre-Eugene 1893-1945
See Drieu la Rochelle, Pierre

Drinkwater, John 1882-1937 .... **TCLC 57**
See also CA 109; 149; DLB 10, 19, 149; RGEL 2

Drop Shot
See Cable, George Washington

Droste-Hulshoff, Annette Freiin von 1797-1848 .... **NCLC 3, 133**
See also CDWLB 2; DLB 133; RGSF 2; RGWL 2, 3

Drummond, Walter
See Silverberg, Robert

Drummond, William Henry 1854-1907 .... **TCLC 25**
See also CA 160; DLB 92

Drummond de Andrade, Carlos 1902-1987 .... **CLC 18; TCLC 139**
See also CA 132; 123; DLB 307; EWL 3; LAW; RGWL 2, 3

Drummond of Hawthornden, William 1585-1649 .... **LC 83**
See also DLB 121, 213; RGEL 2

Drury, Allen (Stuart) 1918-1998 .... **CLC 37**
See also CA 57-60; 170; CANR 18, 52; CN 1, 2, 3, 4, 5, 6; INT CANR-18

Druse, Eleanor
See King, Stephen

Dryden, John 1631-1700 ..... **DC 3; LC 3, 21, 115, 188; PC 25; WLC 2**
See also BRW 2; BRWR 3; CDBLB 1660-1789; DA; DAB; DAC; DAM DRAM, MST, POET; DLB 80, 101, 131; EXPP; IDTP; LMFS 1; RGEL 2; TEA; WLIT 3

du Aime, Albert
See Wharton, William

du Aime, Albert William
See Wharton, William

du Bellay, Joachim 1524-1560 .... **LC 92**
See also DLB 327; GFL Beginnings to 1789; RGWL 2, 3

Duberman, Martin 1930- .... **CLC 8**
See also CA 1-4R; CAD; CANR 2, 63, 137, 174; CD 5, 6

Dubie, Norman (Evans) 1945- .... **CLC 36**
See also CA 69-72; CANR 12, 115; CP 3, 4, 5, 6, 7; DLB 120; PFS 12

Dybek, Stuart 1942- .... **CLC 114; SSC 55**
See also CA 97-100; CANR 39; DLB 130;
SSFS 23
Dye, Richard
See De Voto, Bernard (Augustine)
Dyer, Geoff 1958- .... **CLC 149**
See also CA 125; CANR 88, 209
Dyer, George 1755-1841 .... **NCLC 129**
See also DLB 93
Dylan, Bob 1941- ... **CLC 3, 4, 6, 12, 77, 308;
PC 37**
See also AMWS 18; CA 41-44R; CANR
108; CP 1, 2, 3, 4, 5, 6, 7; DLB 16
Dyson, John 1943- .... **CLC 70**
See also CA 144
Dzyubin, Eduard Georgievich
1895-1934 .... **TCLC 60**
See also CA 170; DLB 359; EWL 3
E. V. L.
See Lucas, E(dward) V(errall)
Eagleton, Terence
See Eagleton, Terry
Eagleton, Terence Francis
See Eagleton, Terry
Eagleton, Terry 1943- .... **CLC 63, 132**
See also CA 57-60; CANR 7, 23, 68, 115,
198; DLB 242; LMFS 2; MTCW 1, 2;
MTFW 2005
Early, Jack
See Scoppettone, Sandra
Early, Tom
See Kelton, Elmer
East, Michael
See West, Morris L(anglo)
Eastaway, Edward
See Thomas, (Philip) Edward
Eastlake, William (Derry)
1917-1997 .... **CLC 8**
See also CA 5-8R; 158; CAAS 1; CANR 5,
63; CN 1, 2, 3, 4, 5, 6; DLB 6, 206; INT
CANR-5; MAL 5; TCWW 1, 2
Eastman, Charles A(lexander)
1858-1939 .... **NNAL; TCLC 55**
See also CA 179; CANR 91; DAM MULT;
DLB 175; YABC 1
Eaton, Edith Maude
1865-1914 .... **AAL; TCLC 232**
See also CA 154; DLB 221, 312; FW
Eaton, (Lillie) Winnifred 1875-1954 .... **AAL**
See also CA 217; DLB 221, 312; RGAL 4
Eberhart, Richard 1904-2005 ...... **CLC 3, 11,
19, 56; PC 76**
See also AMW; CA 1-4R; 240; CANR 2,
125; CDALB 1941-1968; CP 1, 2, 3, 4, 5,
6, 7; DAM POET; DLB 48; MAL 5;
MTCW 1; RGAL 4
Eberhart, Richard Ghormley
See Eberhart, Richard
Eberstadt, Fernanda 1960- .... **CLC 39**
See also CA 136; CANR 69, 128
Ebner, Margaret c. 1291-1351 ...... **CMLC 98**
**Echegaray (y Eizaguirre), Jose (Maria
Waldo)** 1832-1916 .... **HLCS 1; TCLC 4**
See also CA 104; CANR 32; DLB 329;
EWL 3; HW 1; MTCW 1
Echeverria, (Jose) Esteban (Antonino)
1805-1851 .... **NCLC 18**
See also LAW
Echo
See Proust, Marcel
Eckert, Allan W. 1931- .... **CLC 17**
See also AAYA 18; BYA 2; CA 13-16R;
CANR 14, 45; INT CANR-14; MAICYA
2; MAICYAS 1; SAAS 21; SATA 29, 91;
SATA-Brief 27
Eckhart, Meister 1260(?)-1327(?) .. **CMLC 9,
80, 131**
See also DLB 115; LMFS 1

Eckmar, F. R.
See de Hartog, Jan
Eco, Umberto 1932- .... **CLC 28, 60, 142, 248**
See also BEST 90:1; BPFB 1; CA 77-80;
CANR 12, 33, 55, 110, 131, 195; CPW;
CWW 2; DA3; DAM NOV, POP; DLB
196, 242; EWL 3; MSW; MTCW 1, 2;
MTFW 2005; NFS 22; RGWL 3; WLIT 7
Eddison, E(ric) R(ucker)
1882-1945 .... **TCLC 15**
See also CA 109; 156; DLB 255; FANT;
SFW 4; SUFW 1
Eddy, Mary (Ann Morse) Baker
1821-1910 .... **TCLC 71**
See also CA 113; 174
Edel, (Joseph) Leon 1907-1997 .. **CLC 29, 34**
See also CA 1-4R; 161; CANR 1, 22, 112;
DLB 103; INT CANR-22
Eden, Emily 1797-1869 .... **NCLC 10**
Edgar, David 1948- .... **CLC 42**
See also CA 57-60; CANR 12, 61, 112;
CBD; CD 5, 6; DAM DRAM; DFS 15;
DLB 13, 233; MTCW 1
Edgerton, Clyde 1944- .... **CLC 39**
See also AAYA 17; CA 118; 134; CANR
64, 125, 195; CN 7; CSW; DLB 278; INT
CA-134; TCLE 1:1; YAW
Edgerton, Clyde Carlyle
See Edgerton, Clyde
Edgeworth, Maria 1768-1849 ... **NCLC 1, 51,
158; SSC 86**
See also BRWS 3; CLR 153; DLB 116, 159,
163; FL 1:3; FW; RGEL 2; SATA 21;
TEA; WLIT 3
Edmonds, Paul
See Kuttner, Henry
Edmonds, Walter D(umaux)
1903-1998 .... **CLC 35**
See also BYA 2; CA 5-8R; CANR 2; CWRI
5; DLB 9; LAIT 1; MAICYA 1, 2; MAL
5; RHW; SAAS 4; SATA 1, 27; SATA-
Obit 99
Edmondson, Wallace
See Ellison, Harlan
Edson, Margaret 1961- ...... **CLC 199; DC 24**
See also AMWS 18; CA 190; DFS 13; DLB
266
Edson, Russell 1935- .... **CLC 13**
See also CA 33-36R; CANR 115; CP 2, 3,
4, 5, 6, 7; DLB 244; WP
Edwards, Bronwen Elizabeth
See Rose, Wendy
Edwards, Eli
See McKay, Claude
Edwards, G(erald) B(asil)
1899-1976 .... **CLC 25**
See also CA 201; 110
Edwards, Gus 1939- .... **CLC 43**
See also CA 108; INT CA-108
Edwards, Jonathan 1703-1758 .... **LC 7, 54**
See also AMW; DA; DAC; DAM MST;
DLB 24, 270; RGAL 4; TUS
Edwards, Marilyn
See French, Marilyn
Edwards, Sarah Pierpont 1710-1758 .. **LC 87**
See also DLB 200
Efron, Marina Ivanovna Tsvetaeva
See Tsvetaeva, Marina
Egeria fl. 4th cent. - .... **CMLC 70**
Eggers, Dave 1970- .... **CLC 241**
See also AAYA 56; CA 198; CANR 138;
MTFW 2005
Egoyan, Atom 1960- .... **CLC 151, 291**
See also AAYA 63; CA 157; CANR 151
Ehle, John (Marsden, Jr.) 1925- ...... **CLC 27**
See also CA 9-12R; CSW
Ehrenbourg, Ilya
See Ehrenburg, Ilya

Ehrenbourg, Ilya Grigoryevich
See Ehrenburg, Ilya
Ehrenburg, Ilya 1891-1967 ... **CLC 18, 34, 62**
See also CA 102; 25-28R; DLB 272; EWL
3
Ehrenburg, Ilya Grigoryevich
See Ehrenburg, Ilya
Ehrenburg, Ilyo
See Ehrenburg, Ilya
Ehrenburg, Ilyo Grigoryevich
See Ehrenburg, Ilya
Ehrenreich, Barbara 1941- ..... **CLC 110, 267**
See also BEST 90:4; CA 73-76; CANR 16,
37, 62, 117, 167, 208; DLB 246; FW;
LNFS 1; MTCW 1, 2; MTFW 2005
Ehrlich, Gretel 1946- .... **CLC 249**
See also ANW; CA 140; CANR 74, 146;
DLB 212, 275; TCWW 2
Eich, Gunter
See Eich, Gunter
Eich, Gunter 1907-1972 .... **CLC 15**
See also CA 111; 93-96; DLB 69, 124;
EWL 3; RGWL 2, 3
Eichendorff, Joseph 1788-1857 .... **NCLC 8,
225**
See also DLB 90; RGWL 2, 3
Eigner, Larry
See Eigner, Laurence (Joel)
Eigner, Laurence (Joel) 1927-1996 ..... **CLC 9**
See also CA 9-12R; 151; CAAS 23; CANR
6, 84; CP 1, 2, 3, 4, 5, 6, 7; DLB 5; WP
Eilhart von Oberge c. 1140-c.
1195 .... **CMLC 67**
See also DLB 148
Einhard c. 770-840 .... **CMLC 50**
See also DLB 148
Einstein, Albert 1879-1955 .... **TCLC 65**
See also CA 121; 133; MTCW 1, 2
Eiseley, Loren
See Eiseley, Loren Corey
Eiseley, Loren Corey 1907-1977 .... **CLC 7**
See also AAYA 5; ANW; CA 1-4R; 73-76;
CANR 6; DLB 275; DLBD 17
Eisenstadt, Jill 1963- .... **CLC 50**
See also CA 140
Eisenstein, Sergei (Mikhailovich)
1898-1948 .... **TCLC 57**
See also CA 114; 149
Eisler, Steve
See Holdstock, Robert
Eisner, Simon
See Kornbluth, C(yril) M.
Eisner, Will 1917-2005 .... **CLC 237**
See also AAYA 52; CA 108; 235; CANR
114, 140, 179; MTFW 2005; SATA 31,
165
Eisner, William Erwin
See Eisner, Will
Ekeloef, Bengt Gunnar
See Ekelof, Gunnar
Ekeloef, Gunnar
See Ekelof, Gunnar
Ekelof, Gunnar 1907-1968 ... **CLC 27; PC 23**
See also CA 123; 25-28R; DAM POET;
DLB 259; EW 12; EWL 3
Ekelund, Vilhelm 1880-1949 .... **TCLC 75**
See also CA 189; EWL 3
Ekman, Kerstin 1933- .... **CLC 279**
See also CA 154; CANR 124, 214; DLB
257; EWL 3
Ekman, Kerstin Lillemor
See Ekman, Kerstin
Ekwensi, C. O. D.
See Ekwensi, Cyprian

Ensler, Eve 1953- .... **CLC 212**
See also CA 172; CANR 126, 163; DFS 23

Enzensberger, Hans Magnus
1929- .... **CLC 43; PC 28**
See also CA 116; 119; CANR 103; CWW
2; EWL 3

Ephron, Nora 1941- .... **CLC 17, 31**
See also AAYA 35; AITN 2; CA 65-68;
CANR 12, 39, 83, 161; DFS 22

Epictetus c. 55-c. 135 .... **CMLC 126**
See also AW 2; DLB 176

Epicurus 341B.C.-270B.C. .... **CMLC 21**
See also DLB 176

Epinay, Louise d' 1726-1783 .... **LC 138**
See also DLB 313

Epsilon
See Betjeman, John

Epstein, Daniel Mark 1948- .... **CLC 7**
See also CA 49-52; CANR 2, 53, 90, 193

Epstein, Jacob 1956- .... **CLC 19**
See also CA 114

Epstein, Jean 1897-1953 .... **TCLC 92**

Epstein, Joseph 1937- .... **CLC 39, 204**
See also AMWS 14; CA 112; 119; CANR
50, 65, 117, 164, 190

Epstein, Leslie 1938- .... **CLC 27**
See also AMWS 12; CA 73-76, 215; CAAE
215; CAAS 12; CANR 23, 69, 162; DLB
299; RGHL

Equiano, Olaudah 1745(?)-1797 ..... **BLC 1:2;
LC 16, 143**
See also AFAW 1, 2; AMWS 17; CDWLB
3; DAM MULT; DLB 37, 50; WLIT 2

Erasmus, Desiderius 1469(?)-1536 ..... **LC 16,
93**
See also DLB 136; EW 2; LMFS 1; RGWL
2, 3; TWA

Ercilla y Zuniga, Don Alonso de
1533-1594 .... **LC 190**
See also LAW

Erdman, Paul E. 1932-2007 .... **CLC 25**
See also AITN 1; CA 61-64; 259; CANR
13, 43, 84

Erdman, Paul Emil
See Erdman, Paul E.

Erdrich, Karen Louise
See Erdrich, Louise

Erdrich, Louise 1954- .... **CLC 39, 54, 120,
176; NNAL; PC 52; SSC 121**
See also AAYA 10, 47; AMWS 4; BEST
89:1; BPFB 1; CA 114; CANR 41, 62,
118, 138, 190; CDALBS; DA3; DAM MULT,
NOV, POP; DLB 152, 175, 206; EWL 3;
EXPP; FL 1:5; LAIT 5; LATS 1:2; MAL
5; MTCW 1, 2; MTFW 2005; NFS 5, 37;
PFS 14; RGAL 4; SATA 94, 141; SSFS
14, 22, 30; TCWW 2

Erenburg, Ilya
See Ehrenburg, Ilya

Erenburg, Ilya Grigoryevich
See Ehrenburg, Ilya

Erickson, Stephen Michael
See Erickson, Steve

Erickson, Steve 1950- .... **CLC 64**
See also CA 129; CANR 60, 68, 136, 195;
MTFW 2005; SFW 4; SUFW 2

Erickson, Walter
See Fast, Howard

Ericson, Walter
See Fast, Howard

Eriksson, Buntel
See Bergman, Ingmar

Eriugena, John Scottus c.
810-877 .... **CMLC 65**
See also DLB 115

Ernaux, Annie 1940- .... **CLC 88, 184**
See also CA 147; CANR 93, 208; MTFW
2005; NCFS 3, 5

Erskine, John 1879-1951 .... **TCLC 84**
See also CA 112; 159; DLB 9, 102; FANT

Erwin, Will
See Eisner, Will

Eschenbach, Wolfram von
See von Eschenbach, Wolfram

Eseki, Bruno
See Mphahlele, Es'kia

Esekie, Bruno
See Mphahlele, Es'kia

Esenin, S.A.
See Esenin, Sergei

Esenin, Sergei 1895-1925 .... **TCLC 4**
See also CA 104; EWL 3; RGWL 2, 3

Esenin, Sergei Aleksandrovich
See Esenin, Sergei

Eshleman, Clayton 1935- .... **CLC 7**
See also CA 33-36R, 212; CAAE 212;
CAAS 6; CANR 93; CP 1, 2, 3, 4, 5, 6,
7; DLB 5

Espada, Martin 1957- .... **PC 74**
See also CA 159; CANR 80; CP 7; EXPP;
LLW; MAL 5; PFS 13, 16

Espriella, Don Manuel Alvarez
See Southey, Robert

Espriu, Salvador 1913-1985 .... **CLC 9**
See also CA 154; 115; DLB 134; EWL 3

Espronceda, Jose de 1808-1842 ..... **NCLC 39**

Esquivel, Laura 1950- ..... **CLC 141; HLCS 1**
See also AAYA 29; CA 143; CANR 68, 113,
161; DA3; DNFS 2; LAIT 3; LMFS 2;
MTCW 2; MTFW 2005; NFS 5; WLIT 1

Esse, James
See Stephens, James

Esterbrook, Tom
See Hubbard, L. Ron

Esterhazy, Peter 1950- .... **CLC 251**
See also CA 140; CANR 137; CDWLB 4;
CWW 2; DLB 232; EWL 3; RGWL 3

Estleman, Loren D. 1952- .... **CLC 48**
See also AAYA 27; CA 85-88; CANR 27,
74, 139, 177; CMW 4; CPW; DA3; DAM
NOV, POP; DLB 226; INT CANR-27;
MTCW 1, 2; MTFW 2005; TCWW 1, 2

Etherege, Sir George 1636-1692 . **DC 23; LC
78**
See also BRW 2; DAM DRAM; DLB 80;
PAB; RGEL 2

Euclid 306B.C.-283B.C. .... **CMLC 25**

Eugenides, Jeffrey 1960- .... **CLC 81, 212**
See also AAYA 51; CA 144; CANR 120;
DLB 350; MTFW 2005; NFS 24

Euripides c. 484B.C.-406B.C. .... **CMLC 23,
51; DC 4; WLCS**
See also AW 1; CDWLB 1; DA; DA3;
DAB; DAC; DAM DRAM, MST; DFS 1,
4, 6, 25, 27; DLB 176; LAIT 1; LMFS 1;
RGWL 2, 3; WLIT 8

Eusebius c. 263-c. 339 .... **CMLC 103**

Evan, Evin
See Faust, Frederick

Evans, Caradoc 1878-1945 ... **SSC 43; TCLC
85**
See also DLB 162

Evans, Evan
See Faust, Frederick

Evans, Marian
See Eliot, George

Evans, Mary Ann
See Eliot, George

Evarts, Esther
See Benson, Sally

Evelyn, John 1620-1706 .... **LC 144**
See also BRW 2; RGEL 2

Everett, Percival 1956- .... **CLC 57, 304**
See also AMWS 18; BW 2; CA 129; CANR
94, 134, 179, 219; CN 7; CSW; DLB 350;
MTFW 2005

Everett, Percival L.
See Everett, Percival

Everson, R(onald) G(ilmour)
1903-1992 .... **CLC 27**
See also CA 17-20R; CP 1, 2, 3, 4; DLB 88

Everson, William 1912-1994 .... **CLC 1, 5, 14**
See also BG 1:2; CA 9-12R; 145; CANR
20; CP 1; DLB 5, 16, 212; MTCW 1

Everson, William Oliver
See Everson, William

Evtushenko, Evgenii Aleksandrovich
See Yevtushenko, Yevgenyn

Ewart, Gavin (Buchanan)
1916-1995 .... **CLC 13, 46**
See also BRWS 7; CA 89-92; 150; CANR
17, 46; CP 1, 2, 3, 4, 5, 6; DLB 40;
MTCW 1

Ewers, Hanns Heinz 1871-1943 ..... **TCLC 12**
See also CA 109; 149

Ewing, Frederick R.
See Sturgeon, Theodore (Hamilton)

Exley, Frederick (Earl) 1929-1992 .... **CLC 6,
11**
See also AITN 2; BPFB 1; CA 81-84; 138;
CANR 117; DLB 143; DLBY 1981

Eynhardt, Guillermo
See Quiroga, Horacio (Sylvestre)

Ezekiel, Nissim (Moses) 1924-2004 .. **CLC 61**
See also CA 61-64; 223; CP 1, 2, 3, 4, 5, 6,
7; DLB 323; EWL 3

Ezekiel, Tish O'Dowd 1943- .... **CLC 34**
See also CA 129

Fadeev, Aleksandr Aleksandrovich
See Bulgya, Alexander Alexandrovich

Fadeev, Alexandr Alexandrovich
See Bulgya, Alexander Alexandrovich

Fadeyev, A.
See Bulgya, Alexander Alexandrovich

Fadeyev, Alexander
See Bulgya, Alexander Alexandrovich

Fagen, Donald 1948- .... **CLC 26**

Fainzil'berg, Il'ia Arnol'dovich
See Fainzilberg, Ilya Arnoldovich

Fainzilberg, Ilya Arnoldovich
1897-1937 .... **TCLC 21**
See also CA 120; 165; DLB 272; EWL 3

Fair, Ronald L. 1932- .... **CLC 18**
See also BW 1; CA 69-72; CANR 25; DLB
33

Fairbairn, Roger
See Carr, John Dickson

Fairbairns, Zoe (Ann) 1948- .... **CLC 32**
See also CA 103; CANR 21, 85; CN 4, 5,
6, 7

Fairfield, Flora
See Alcott, Louisa May

Falco, Gian
See Papini, Giovanni

Falconer, James
See Kirkup, James

Falconer, Kenneth
See Kornbluth, C(yril) M.

Falkland, Samuel
See Heijermans, Herman

Fallaci, Oriana 1930-2006 .... **CLC 11, 110**
See also CA 77-80; 253; CANR 15, 58, 134;
FW; MTCW 1

Faludi, Susan 1959- .... **CLC 140**
See also CA 138; CANR 126, 194; FW;
MTCW 2; MTFW 2005; NCFS 3

Faludy, George 1913- .... **CLC 42**
See also CA 21-24R

Faludy, Gyoergy
See Faludy, George

Fanon, Frantz 1925-1961 ...... **BLC 1:2; CLC
74; TCLC 188**
See also BW 1; CA 116; 89-92; DAM
MULT; DLB 296; LMFS 2; WLIT 2

Francis, Paula Marie
See Allen, Paula Gunn
Francis, Richard Stanley
See Francis, Dick
Francis, Robert (Churchill)
1901-1987 .... **CLC 15; PC 34**
See also AMWS 9; CA 1-4R; 123; CANR 1; CP 1, 2, 3, 4; EXPP; PFS 12; TCLE 1:1
Francis, Lord Jeffrey
See Jeffrey, Francis
Franco, Veronica 1546-1591 .... **LC 171**
See also WLIT 7
Frank, Anne 1929-1945 ... **TCLC 17; WLC 2**
See also AAYA 12; BYA 1; CA 113; 133; CANR 68; CLR 101; DA; DA3; DAB; DAC; DAM MST; LAIT 4; MAICYA 2; MAICYAS 1; MTCW 1, 2; MTFW 2005; NCFS 2; RGHL; SATA 87; SATA-Brief 42; WYA; YAW
Frank, Annelies Marie
See Frank, Anne
Frank, Bruno 1887-1945 .... **TCLC 81**
See also CA 189; DLB 118; EWL 3
Frank, Elizabeth 1945- .... **CLC 39**
See also CA 121; 126; CANR 78, 150; INT CA-126
Frankl, Viktor E(mil) 1905-1997 ...... **CLC 93**
See also CA 65-68; 161; RGHL
Franklin, Benjamin
See Hasek, Jaroslav
Franklin, Benjamin 1706-1790 .. **LC 25, 134; WLCS**
See also AMW; CDALB 1640-1865; DA; DA3; DAB; DAC; DAM MST; DLB 24, 43, 73, 183; LAIT 1; RGAL 4; TUS
Franklin, Madeleine
See L'Engle, Madeleine
Franklin, Madeleine L'Engle
See L'Engle, Madeleine
Franklin, Madeleine L'Engle Camp
See L'Engle, Madeleine
Franklin, (Stella Maria Sarah) Miles (Lampe) 1879-1954 .... **TCLC 7**
See also CA 104; 164; DLB 230; FW; MTCW 2; RGEL 2; TWA
Franzen, Jonathan 1959- .... **CLC 202, 309**
See also AAYA 65; AMWS 20; CA 129; CANR 105, 166, 219
Fraser, Antonia 1932- .... **CLC 32, 107**
See also AAYA 57; CA 85-88; CANR 44, 65, 119, 164; CMW; DLB 276; MTCW 1, 2; MTFW 2005; SATA-Brief 32
Fraser, George MacDonald
1925-2008 .... **CLC 7**
See also AAYA 48; CA 45-48; 180; 268; CAAE 180; CANR 2, 48, 74, 192; DLB 352; MTCW 2; RHW
Fraser, Sylvia 1935- .... **CLC 64**
See also CA 45-48; CANR 1, 16, 60; CCA 1
Frater Perdurabo
See Crowley, Edward Alexander
Frayn, Michael 1933- .... **CLC 3, 7, 31, 47, 176; DC 27**
See also AAYA 69; BRWC 2; BRWS 7; CA 5-8R; CANR 30, 69, 114, 133, 166; CBD; CD 5, 6; CN 1, 2, 3, 4, 5, 6, 7; DAM DRAM, NOV; DFS 22, 28; DLB 13, 14, 194, 245; FANT; MTCW 1, 2; MTFW 2005; SFW 4
Fraze, Candida 1945- .... **CLC 50**
See also CA 126
Fraze, Candida Merrill
See Fraze, Candida
Frazer, Andrew
See Marlowe, Stephen

Frazer, J(ames) G(eorge)
1854-1941 .... **TCLC 32**
See also BRWS 3; CA 118; NCFS 5
Frazer, Robert Caine
See Creasey, John
Frazer, Sir James George
See Frazer, J(ames) G(eorge)
Frazier, Charles 1950- .... **CLC 109, 224**
See also AAYA 34; CA 161; CANR 126, 170; CSW; DLB 292; MTFW 2005; NFS 25
Frazier, Charles R.
See Frazier, Charles
Frazier, Charles Robinson
See Frazier, Charles
Frazier, Ian 1951- .... **CLC 46**
See also CA 130; CANR 54, 93, 193
Frederic, Harold 1856-1898 ... **NCLC 10, 175**
See also AMW; DLB 12, 23; DLBD 13; MAL 5; NFS 22; RGAL 4
Frederick, John
See Faust, Frederick
Frederick the Great 1712-1786 .... **LC 14**
Fredro, Aleksander 1793-1876 .... **NCLC 8**
Freeling, Nicolas 1927-2003 .... **CLC 38**
See also CA 49-52; 218; CAAS 12; CANR 1, 17, 50, 84; CMW 4; CN 1, 2, 3, 4, 5, 6; DLB 87
Freeman, Douglas Southall
1886-1953 .... **TCLC 11**
See also CA 109; 195; DLB 17; DLBD 17
Freeman, Judith 1946- .... **CLC 55**
See also CA 148; CANR 120, 179; DLB 256
Freeman, Mary E(leanor) Wilkins
1852-1930 .... **SSC 1, 47, 113; TCLC 9**
See also CA 106; 177; DLB 12, 78, 221; EXPS; FW; HGG; MBL; RGAL 4; RGSF 2; SSFS 4, 8, 26; SUFW 1; TUS
Freeman, R(ichard) Austin
1862-1943 .... **TCLC 21**
See also CA 113; CANR 84; CMW 4; DLB 70
French, Albert 1943- .... **CLC 86**
See also BW 3; CA 167
French, Antonia
See Kureishi, Hanif
French, Marilyn 1929-2009 . **CLC 10, 18, 60, 177**
See also BPFB 1; CA 69-72; 286; CANR 3, 31, 134, 163; CN 5, 6, 7; CPW; DAM DRAM, NOV, POP; FL 1:5; FW; INT CANR-31; MTCW 1, 2; MTFW 2005
French, Paul
See Asimov, Isaac
Freneau, Philip Morin 1752-1832 .. **NCLC 1, 111**
See also AMWS 2; DLB 37, 43; RGAL 4
Freud, Sigmund 1856-1939 .... **TCLC 52**
See also CA 115; 133; CANR 69; DLB 296; EW 8; EWL 3; LATS 1:1; MTCW 1, 2; MTFW 2005; NCFS 3; TWA
Freytag, Gustav 1816-1895 .... **NCLC 109**
See also DLB 129
Friedan, Betty 1921-2006 .... **CLC 74**
See also CA 65-68; 248; CANR 18, 45, 74; DLB 246; FW; MTCW 1, 2; MTFW 2005; NCFS 5
Friedan, Betty Naomi
See Friedan, Betty
Friedlander, Saul
See Friedlander, Saul
Friedlander, Saul 1932- .... **CLC 90**
See also CA 117; 130; CANR 72, 214; RGHL
Friedman, Bernard Harper
See Friedman, B.H.
Friedman, B.H. 1926-2011 .... **CLC 7**
See also CA 1-4R; CANR 3, 48

Friedman, Bruce Jay 1930- ...... **CLC 3, 5, 56**
See also CA 9-12R; CAD; CANR 25, 52, 101, 212; CD 5, 6; CN 1, 2, 3, 4, 5, 6, 7; DLB 2, 28, 244; INT CANR-25; MAL 5; SSFS 18
Friel, Brian 1929- .. **CLC 5, 42, 59, 115, 253; DC 8; SSC 76**
See also BRWS 5; CA 21-24R; CANR 33, 69, 131; CBD; CD 5, 6; DFS 11; DLB 13, 319; EWL 3; MTCW 1; RGEL 2; TEA
Friis-Baastad, Babbis Ellinor
1921-1970 .... **CLC 12**
See also CA 17-20R; 134; SATA 7
Frisch, Max 1911-1991 ...... **CLC 3, 9, 14, 18, 32, 44; TCLC 121**
See also CA 85-88; 134; CANR 32, 74; CD-WLB 2; DAM DRAM, NOV; DFS 25; DLB 69, 124; EW 13; EWL 3; MTCW 1, 2; MTFW 2005; RGHL; RGWL 2, 3
Froehlich, Peter
See Gay, Peter
Fromentin, Eugene (Samuel Auguste)
1820-1876 .... **NCLC 10, 125**
See also DLB 123; GFL 1789 to the Present
Frost, Frederick
See Faust, Frederick
Frost, Robert 1874-1963 . **CLC 1, 3, 4, 9, 10, 13, 15, 26, 34, 44; PC 1, 39, 71; TCLC 236; WLC 2**
See also AAYA 21; AMW; AMWR 1; CA 89-92; CANR 33; CDALB 1917-1929; CLR 67; DA; DA3; DAB; DAC; DAM MST, POET; DLB 54, 284, 342; DLBD 7; EWL 3; EXPP; MAL 5; MTCW 1, 2; MTFW 2005; PAB; PFS 1, 2, 3, 4, 5, 6, 7, 10, 13, 32, 35; RGAL 4; SATA 14; TUS; WP; WYA
Frost, Robert Lee
See Frost, Robert
Froude, James Anthony
1818-1894 .... **NCLC 43**
See also DLB 18, 57, 144
Froy, Herald
See Waterhouse, Keith
Fry, Christopher 1907-2005 .. **CLC 2, 10, 14; DC 36**
See also BRWS 3; CA 17-20R; 240; CAAS 23; CANR 9, 30, 74, 132; CBD; CD 5, 6; CP 1, 2, 3, 4, 5, 6, 7; DAM DRAM; DLB 13; EWL 3; MTCW 1, 2; MTFW 2005; RGEL 2; SATA 66; TEA
Frye, (Herman) Northrop
1912-1991 .... **CLC 24, 70; TCLC 165**
See also CA 5-8R; 133; CANR 8, 37; DLB 67, 68, 246; EWL 3; MTCW 1, 2; MTFW 2005; RGAL 4; TWA
Fuchs, Daniel 1909-1993 .... **CLC 8, 22**
See also CA 81-84; 142; CAAS 5; CANR 40; CN 1, 2, 3, 4, 5; DLB 9, 26, 28; DLBY 1993; MAL 5
Fuchs, Daniel 1934- .... **CLC 34**
See also CA 37-40R; CANR 14, 48
Fuentes, Carlos 1928- .. **CLC 3, 8, 10, 13, 22, 41, 60, 113, 288; HLC 1; SSC 24, 125; WLC 2**
See also AAYA 4, 45; AITN 2; BPFB 1; CA 69-72; CANR 10, 32, 68, 104, 138, 197; CDWLB 3; CWW 2; DA; DA3; DAB; DAC; DAM MST, MULT, NOV; DLB 113; DNFS 2; EWL 3; HW 1, 2; LAIT 3; LATS 1:2; LAW; LAWS 1; LMFS 2; MTCW 1, 2; MTFW 2005; NFS 8; RGSF 2; RGWL 2, 3; TWA; WLIT 1
Fuentes, Gregorio Lopez y
See Lopez y Fuentes, Gregorio
Fuentes Macias, Carlos Manuel
See Fuentes, Carlos
Fuertes, Gloria 1918-1998 .... **PC 27**
See also CA 178; 180; DLB 108; HW 2; SATA 115

Glasgow, Ellen 1873-1945 .... SSC **34**, **130**; TCLC **2**, **7**, **239**
See also AMW; CA 104; 164; DLB 9, 12; MAL 5; MBL; MTCW 2; MTFW 2005; RGAL 4; RHW; SSFS 9; TUS

Glasgow, Ellen Anderson Gholson
See Glasgow, Ellen

Glaspell, Susan 1882(?)-1948 ..... DC **10**; SSC **41**, **132**; TCLC **55**, **175**
See also AMWS 3; CA 110; 154; DFS 8, 18, 24; DLB 7, 9, 78, 228; MBL; RGAL 4; SSFS 3; TCWW 2; TUS; YABC 2

Glassco, John 1909-1981 .... CLC **9**
See also CA 13-16R; 102; CANR 15; CN 1, 2; CP 1, 2, 3; DLB 68

Glasscock, Amnesia
See Steinbeck, John

Glasser, Ronald J. 1940(?)- .... CLC **37**
See also CA 209

Glassman, Joyce
See Johnson, Joyce

Gleick, James 1954- .... CLC **147**
See also CA 131; 137; CANR 97; INT CA-137

Gleick, James W.
See Gleick, James

Glendinning, Victoria 1937- .... CLC **50**
See also CA 120; 127; CANR 59, 89, 166; DLB 155

Glissant, Edouard 1928-2011 ..... CLC **10**, **68**
See also CA 153; CANR 111; CWW 2; DAM MULT; EWL 3; RGWL 3

Glissant, Edouard Mathieu
See Glissant, Edouard

Gloag, Julian 1930- .... CLC **40**
See also AITN 1; CA 65-68; CANR 10, 70; CN 1, 2, 3, 4, 5, 6

Glowacki, Aleksander
See Prus, Boleslaw

Gluck, Louise 1943- . CLC **7**, **22**, **44**, **81**, **160**, **280**; PC **16**
See also AMWS 5; CA 33-36R; CANR 40, 69, 108, 133, 182; CP 1, 2, 3, 4, 5, 6, 7; CWP; DA3; DAM POET; DLB 5; MAL 5; MTCW 2; MTFW 2005; PFS 5, 15; RGAL 4; TCLE 1:1

Gluck, Louise Elisabeth
See Gluck, Louise

Glyn, Elinor 1864-1943 .... TCLC **72**
See also DLB 153; RHW

Gobineau, Joseph-Arthur 1816-1882 .... NCLC **17**
See also DLB 123; GFL 1789 to the Present

Godard, Jean-Luc 1930- .... CLC **20**
See also CA 93-96

Godden, (Margaret) Rumer 1907-1998 .... CLC **53**
See also AAYA 6; BPFB 2; BYA 2, 5; CA 5-8R; 172; CANR 4, 27, 36, 55, 80; CLR 20; CN 1, 2, 3, 4, 5, 6; CWRI 5; DLB 161; MAICYA 1, 2; RHW; SAAS 12; SATA 3, 36; SATA-Obit 109; TEA

Godoy Alcayaga, Lucila
See Mistral, Gabriela

Godwin, Gail 1937- ...... CLC **5**, **8**, **22**, **31**, **69**, **125**
See also BPFB 2; CA 29-32R; CANR 15, 43, 69, 132, 218; CN 3, 4, 5, 6, 7; CPW; CSW; DA3; DAM POP; DLB 6, 234, 350; INT CANR-15; MAL 5; MTCW 1, 2; MTFW 2005

Godwin, Gail Kathleen
See Godwin, Gail

Godwin, William 1756-1836 .. NCLC **14**, **130**
See also BRWS 15; CDBLB 1789-1832; CMW 4; DLB 39, 104, 142, 158, 163, 262, 336; GL 2; HGG; RGEL 2

Goebbels, Josef
See Goebbels, (Paul) Joseph

Goebbels, (Paul) Joseph 1897-1945 .... TCLC **68**
See also CA 115; 148

Goebbels, Joseph Paul
See Goebbels, (Paul) Joseph

Goethe, Johann Wolfgang von 1749-1832 . DC **20**; NCLC **4**, **22**, **34**, **90**, **154**; PC **5**; SSC **38**, **141**; WLC **3**
See also CDWLB 2; DA; DA3; DAB; DAC; DAM DRAM, MST, POET; DLB 94; EW 5; GL 2; LATS 1; LMFS 1:1; RGWL 2, 3; TWA

Gogarty, Oliver St. John 1878-1957 .... TCLC **15**; PC **121**
See also CA 109; 150; DLB 15, 19; RGEL 2

Gogol, Nikolai 1809-1852 .... DC **1**; NCLC **5**, **15**, **31**, **162**; SSC **4**, **29**, **52**, **145**; WLC **3**
See also DA; DAB; DAC; DAM DRAM, MST; DFS 12; DLB 198; EW 6; EXPS; RGSF 2; RGWL 2, 3; SSFS 7, 32; TWA

Gogol, Nikolai Vasilyevich
See Gogol, Nikolai

Goines, Donald 1937(?)-1974 .... BLC **1:2**; CLC **80**
See also AITN 1; BW 1, 3; CA 124; 114; CANR 82; CMW 4; DA3; DAM MULT, POP; DLB 33

Gold, Herbert 1924- ... CLC **4**, **7**, **14**, **42**, **152**
See also CA 9-12R; CANR 17, 45, 125, 194; CN 1, 2, 3, 4, 5, 6, 7; DLB 2; DLBY 1981; MAL 5

Goldbarth, Albert 1948- .... CLC **5**, **38**
See also AMWS 12; CA 53-56; CANR 6, 40, 206; CP 3, 4, 5, 6, 7; DLB 120

Goldberg, Anatol 1910-1982 .... CLC **34**
See also CA 131; 117

Goldemberg, Isaac 1945- .... CLC **52**
See also CA 69-72; CAAS 12; CANR 11, 32; EWL 3; HW 1; WLIT 1

Golding, Arthur 1536-1606 .... LC **101**
See also DLB 136

Golding, William 1911-1993 . CLC **1**, **2**, **3**, **8**, **10**, **17**, **27**, **58**, **81**; WLC **3**
See also AAYA 5, 44; BPFB 2; BRWR 1; BRWS 1; BYA 2; CA 5-8R; 141; CANR 13, 33, 54; CD 5; CDBLB 1945-1960; CLR 94, 130; CN 1, 2, 3, 4; DA; DA3; DAB; DAC; DAM MST, NOV; DLB 15, 100, 255, 326, 330; EWL 3; EXPN; HGG; LAIT 4; MTCW 1, 2; MTFW 2005; NFS 2, 36; RGEL 2; RHW; SFW 4; TEA; WLIT 4; YAW

Golding, William Gerald
See Golding, William

Goldman, Emma 1869-1940 .... TCLC **13**
See also CA 110; 150; DLB 221; FW; RGAL 4; TUS

Goldman, Francisco 1954- .... CLC **76**, **298**
See also CA 162; CANR 185

Goldman, William 1931- .... CLC **1**, **48**
See also BPFB 2; CA 9-12R; CANR 29, 69, 106; CN 1, 2, 3, 4, 5, 6, 7; DLB 44; FANT; IDFW 3, 4; NFS 31

Goldman, William W.
See Goldman, William

Goldmann, Lucien 1913-1970 .... CLC **24**
See also CA 25-28; CAP 2

Goldoni, Carlo 1707-1793 .... LC **4**, **152**
See also DAM DRAM; DFS 27; EW 4; RGWL 2, 3; WLIT 7

Goldsberry, Steven 1949- .... CLC **34**
See also CA 131

Goldsmith, Oliver 1730(?)-1774 .... DC **8**; LC **2**, **48**, **122**; PC **77**; WLC **3**
See also BRW 3; CDBLB 1660-1789; DA; DAB; DAC; DAM DRAM, MST, NOV, POET; DFS 1; DLB 39, 89, 104, 109, 142, 336; IDTP; RGEL 2; SATA 26; TEA; WLIT 3

Goldsmith, Peter
See Priestley, J(ohn) B(oynton)

Goldstein, Rebecca 1950- .... CLC **239**
See also CA 144; CANR 99, 165, 214; TCLE 1:1

Goldstein, Rebecca Newberger
See Goldstein, Rebecca

Gombrowicz, Witold 1904-1969 .... CLC **4**, **7**, **11**, **49**; TCLC **247**
See also CA 19-20; 25-28R; CANR 105; CAP 2; CDWLB 4; DAM DRAM; DLB 215; EW 12; EWL 3; RGWL 2, 3; TWA

Gomez de Avellaneda, Gertrudis 1814-1873 .... NCLC **111**
See also LAW

Gomez de la Serna, Ramon 1888-1963 .... CLC **9**
See also CA 153; 116; CANR 79; EWL 3; HW 1, 2

Gomez-Pena, Guillermo 1955- .... CLC **310**
See also CA 147; CANR 117

Goncharov, Ivan Alexandrovich 1812-1891 .... NCLC **1**, **63**
See also DLB 238; EW 6; RGWL 2, 3

Goncourt, Edmond de 1822-1896 ... NCLC **7**
See also DLB 123; EW 7; GFL 1789 to the Present; RGWL 2, 3

Goncourt, Edmond Louis Antoine Huot de
See Goncourt, Edmond de

Goncourt, Jules Alfred Huot de
See Goncourt, Jules de

Goncourt, Jules de 1830-1870 .... NCLC **7**
See Goncourt, Jules de
See also DLB 123; EW 7; GFL 1789 to the Present; RGWL 2, 3

Gongora (y Argote), Luis de 1561-1627 .... LC **72**
See also RGWL 2, 3

Gontier, Fernande 19(?)- .... CLC **50**

Gonzalez Martinez, Enrique
See Gonzalez Martinez, Enrique

Gonzalez Martinez, Enrique 1871-1952 .... TCLC **72**
See also CA 166; CANR 81; DLB 290; EWL 3; HW 1, 2

Goodison, Lorna 1947- .... BLC **2:2**; PC **36**
See also CA 142; CANR 88, 189; CP 5, 6, 7; CWP; DLB 157; EWL 3; PFS 25

Goodman, Allegra 1967- .... CLC **241**
See also CA 204; CANR 162, 204; DLB 244, 350

Goodman, Paul 1911-1972 ..... CLC **1**, **2**, **4**, **7**
See also CA 19-20; 37-40R; CAD; CANR 34; CAP 2; CN 1; DLB 130, 246; MAL 5; MTCW 1; RGAL 4

Goodweather, Hartley
See King, Thomas

GoodWeather, Hartley
See King, Thomas

Googe, Barnabe 1540-1594 .... LC **94**
See also DLB 132; RGEL 2

Gordimer, Nadine 1923- ...... CLC **3**, **5**, **7**, **10**, **18**, **33**, **51**, **70**, **123**, **160**, **161**, **263**; SSC **17**, **80**, **154**; WLCS
See also AAYA 39; AFW; BRWS 2; CA 5-8R; CANR 3, 28, 56, 88, 131, 195, 219; CN 1, 2, 3, 4, 5, 6, 7; DA; DA3; DAB; DAC; DAM MST, NOV; DLB 225, 326, 330; EWL 3; EXPS; INT CANR-28; LATS 1:2; MTCW 1, 2; MTFW 2005; NFS 4; RGEL 2; RGSF 2; SSFS 2, 14, 19, 28, 31; TWA; WLIT 2; YAW

Gordon, Adam Lindsay 1833-1870 .... NCLC **21**
See also DLB 230

Gray, Spalding 1941-2004 .... **CLC 49, 112; DC 7**
See also AAYA 62; CA 128; 225; CAD; CANR 74, 138; CD 5, 6; CPW; DAM POP; MTCW 2; MTFW 2005

Gray, Thomas 1716-1771 . **LC 4, 40, 178; PC 2, 80; WLC 3**
See also BRW 3; CDBLB 1660-1789; DA; DA3; DAB; DAC; DAM MST; DLB 109; EXPP; PAB; PFS 9; RGEL 2; TEA; WP

Grayson, David
See Baker, Ray Stannard

Grayson, Richard (A.) 1951- .... **CLC 38**
See also CA 85-88, 210; CAAE 210; CANR 14, 31, 57; DLB 234

Greeley, Andrew M. 1928- .... **CLC 28**
See also BPFB 2; CA 5-8R; CAAS 7; CANR 7, 43, 69, 104, 136, 184; CMW 4; CPW; DA3; DAM POP; MTCW 1, 2; MTFW 2005

Green, Anna Katharine
1846-1935 .... **TCLC 63**
See also CA 112; 159; CMW 4; DLB 202, 221; MSW

Green, Brian
See Card, Orson Scott

Green, Hannah
See Greenberg, Joanne (Goldenberg)

Green, Hannah 1927(?)-1996 .... **CLC 3**
See also CA 73-76; CANR 59, 93; NFS 10

Green, Henry
See Yorke, Henry Vincent

Green, Julian
See Green, Julien

Green, Julien 1900-1998 .... **CLC 3, 11, 77**
See also CA 21-24R; 169; CANR 33, 87; CWW 2; DLB 4, 72; EWL 3; GFL 1789 to the Present; MTCW 2; MTFW 2005

Green, Julien Hartridge
See Green, Julien

Green, Paul (Eliot) 1894-1981 .. **CLC 25; DC 37**
See also AITN 1; CA 5-8R; 103; CAD; CANR 3; DAM DRAM; DLB 7, 9, 249; DLBY 1981; MAL 5; RGAL 4

Greenaway, Peter 1942- .... **CLC 159**
See also CA 127

Greenberg, Ivan 1908-1973 .... **CLC 24**
See also CA 85-88; DLB 137; MAL 5

Greenberg, Joanne (Goldenberg)
1932- .... **CLC 7, 30**
See also AAYA 12, 67; CA 5-8R; CANR 14, 32, 69; CN 6, 7; DLB 335; NFS 23; SATA 25; YAW

Greenberg, Richard 1959(?)- .... **CLC 57**
See also CA 138; CAD; CD 5, 6; DFS 24

Greenblatt, Stephen J(ay) 1943- ...... **CLC 70**
See also CA 49-52; CANR 115; LNFS 1

Greene, Bette 1934- .... **CLC 30**
See also AAYA 7, 69; BYA 3; CA 53-56; CANR 4, 146; CLR 2, 140; CWRI 5; JRDA; LAIT 4; MAICYA 1, 2; NFS 10; SAAS 16; SATA 8, 102, 161; WYA; YAW

Greene, Gael .... **CLC 8**
See also CA 13-16R; CANR 10, 166

Greene, Graham 1904-1991 .. **CLC 1, 3, 6, 9, 14, 18, 27, 37, 70, 72, 125; DC 41; SSC 29, 121; WLC 3**
See also AAYA 61; AITN 2; BPFB 2; BRWR 2; BRWS 1; BYA 3; CA 13-16R; 133; CANR 35, 61, 131; CBD; CDBLB 1945-1960; CMW 4; CN 1, 2, 3, 4; DA; DA3; DAB; DAC; DAM MST, NOV; DLB 13, 15, 77, 100, 162, 201, 204; DLBY 1991; EWL 3; MSW; MTCW 1, 2; MTFW 2005; NFS 16, 31, 36; RGEL 2; SATA 20; SSFS 14; TEA; WLIT 4

Greene, Graham Henry
See Greene, Graham

Greene, Robert 1558-1592 .... **LC 41, 185**
See also BRWS 8; DLB 62, 167; IDTP; RGEL 2; TEA

Greer, Germaine 1939- .... **CLC 131**
See also AITN 1; CA 81-84; CANR 33, 70, 115, 133, 190; FW; MTCW 1, 2; MTFW 2005

Greer, Richard
See Silverberg, Robert

Gregor, Arthur 1923- .... **CLC 9**
See also CA 25-28R; CAAS 10; CANR 11; CP 1, 2, 3, 4, 5, 6, 7; SATA 36

Gregor, Lee
See Pohl, Frederik

Gregory, Lady Isabella Augusta (Persse)
1852-1932 .... **TCLC 1, 176**
See also BRW 6; CA 104; 184; DLB 10; IDTP; RGEL 2

Gregory, J. Dennis
See Williams, John A(lfred)

Gregory of Nazianzus, St.
329-389 .... **CMLC 82**

Gregory of Nyssa c. 335-c. 394 ... **CMLC 126**

Gregory of Rimini 1300(?)-1358 . **CMLC 109**
See also DLB 115

Gregory the Great c. 540-604 ..... **CMLC 124**

Grekova, I.
See Ventsel, Elena Sergeevna

Grekova, Irina
See Ventsel, Elena Sergeevna

Grendon, Stephen
See Derleth, August (William)

Grenville, Kate 1950- .... **CLC 61**
See also CA 118; CANR 53, 93, 156; CN 7; DLB 325

Grenville, Pelham
See Wodehouse, P. G.

Greve, Felix Paul (Berthold Friedrich)
1879-1948 .... **TCLC 4, 248**
See also CA 104; 141, 175; CANR 79; DAC; DAM MST; DLB 92; RGEL 2; TCWW 1, 2

Greville, Fulke 1554-1628 .... **LC 79**
See also BRWS 11; DLB 62, 172; RGEL 2

Grey, Lady Jane 1537-1554 .... **LC 93**
See also DLB 132

Grey, Zane 1872-1939 .... **TCLC 6**
See also BPFB 2; CA 104; 132; CANR 210; DA3; DAM POP; DLB 9, 212; MTCW 1, 2; MTFW 2005; RGAL 4; TCWW 1, 2; TUS

Griboedov, Aleksandr Sergeevich
1795(?)-1829 .... **NCLC 129**
See also DLB 205; RGWL 2, 3

Grieg, (Johan) Nordahl (Brun)
1902-1943 .... **TCLC 10**
See also CA 107; 189; EWL 3

Grieve, C. M. 1892-1978 ... **CLC 2, 4, 11, 19, 63; PC 9**
See also BRWS 12; CA 5-8R; 85-88; CANR 33, 107; CDBLB 1945-1960; CP 1, 2; DAM POET; DLB 20; EWL 3; MTCW 1; RGEL 2

Grieve, Christopher Murray
See Grieve, C. M.

Griffin, Gerald 1803-1840 .... **NCLC 7**
See also DLB 159; RGEL 2

Griffin, John Howard 1920-1980 ..... **CLC 68**
See also AITN 1; CA 1-4R; 101; CANR 2

Griffin, Peter 1942- .... **CLC 39**
See also CA 136

Griffith, David Lewelyn Wark
See Griffith, D.W.

Griffith, D.W. 1875(?)-1948 .... **TCLC 68**
See also AAYA 78; CA 119; 150; CANR 80

Griffith, Lawrence
See Griffith, D.W.

Griffiths, Trevor 1935- .... **CLC 13, 52**
See also CA 97-100; CANR 45; CBD; CD 5, 6; DLB 13, 245

Griggs, Sutton (Elbert)
1872-1930 .... **TCLC 77**
See also CA 123; 186; DLB 50

Grigson, Geoffrey (Edward Harvey)
1905-1985 .... **CLC 7, 39**
See also CA 25-28R; 118; CANR 20, 33; CP 1, 2, 3, 4; DLB 27; MTCW 1, 2

Grile, Dod
See Bierce, Ambrose

Grillparzer, Franz 1791-1872 .... **DC 14; NCLC 1, 102, 245; SSC 37**
See also CDWLB 2; DLB 133; EW 5; RGWL 2, 3; TWA

Grimble, Reverend Charles James
See Eliot, T. S.

Grimke, Angelina Emily Weld
See Grimke, Angelina Weld

Grimke, Angelina Weld 1880-1958 ... **DC 38; HR 1:2**
See also BW 1; CA 124; DAM POET; DLB 50, 54; FW

Grimke, Charlotte L. Forten
1837(?)-1914 .... **BLC 1:2; TCLC 16**
See also BW 1; CA 117; 124; DAM MULT, POET; DLB 50, 239

Grimke, Charlotte Lottie Forten
See Grimke, Charlotte L. Forten

Grimm, Jacob Ludwig Karl
1785-1863 .... **NCLC 3, 77; SSC 36, 88**
See also CLR 112; DLB 90; MAICYA 1, 2; RGSF 2; RGWL 2, 3; SATA 22; WCH

Grimm, Wilhelm Karl 1786-1859 .. **NCLC 3, 77; SSC 36**
See also CDWLB 2; CLR 112; DLB 90; MAICYA 1, 2; RGSF 2; RGWL 2, 3; SATA 22; WCH

Grimm and Grim
See Grimm, Jacob Ludwig Karl; Grimm, Wilhelm Karl

Grimm Brothers
See Grimm, Jacob Ludwig Karl; Grimm, Wilhelm Karl

Grimmelshausen, Hans Jakob Christoffel von
See Grimmelshausen, Johann Jakob Christoffel von

Grimmelshausen, Johann Jakob Christoffel von 1621-1676 .... **LC 6**
See also CDWLB 2; DLB 168; RGWL 2, 3

Grindel, Eugene 1895-1952 .... **PC 38; TCLC 7, 41**
See also CA 104; 193; EWL 3; GFL 1789 to the Present; LMFS 2; RGWL 2, 3

Grisham, John 1955- .... **CLC 84, 273**
See also AAYA 14, 47; BPFB 2; CA 138; CANR 47, 69, 114, 133; CMW 4; CN 6, 7; CPW; CSW; DA3; DAM POP; LNFS 1; MSW; MTCW 2; MTFW 2005

Grosseteste, Robert 1175(?)-1253 . **CMLC 62**
See also DLB 115

Grossman, David 1954- .... **CLC 67, 231**
See also CA 138; CANR 114, 175; CWW 2; DLB 299; EWL 3; RGHL; WLIT 6

Grossman, Vasilii Semenovich
See Grossman, Vasily

Grossman, Vasily 1905-1964 .... **CLC 41**
See also CA 124; 130; DLB 272; MTCW 1; RGHL

Grossman, Vasily Semenovich
See Grossman, Vasily

Grove, Frederick Philip
See Greve, Felix Paul (Berthold Friedrich)

Grubb
See Crumb, R.

Hailey, Arthur 1920-2004 .... **CLC 5**
See also AITN 2; BEST 90:3; BPFB 2; CA 1-4R; 233; CANR 2, 36, 75; CCA 1; CN 1, 2, 3, 4, 5, 6, 7; CPW; DAM NOV, POP; DLB 88; DLBY 1982; MTCW 1, 2; MTFW 2005

Hailey, Elizabeth Forsythe 1938- ..... **CLC 40**
See also CA 93-96, 188; CAAE 188; CAAS 1; CANR 15, 48; INT CANR-15

Haines, John 1924-2011 .... **CLC 58**
See also AMWS 12; CA 17-20R; CANR 13, 34; CP 1, 2, 3, 4, 5; CSW; DLB 5, 212; TCLE 1:1

Haines, John Meade
See Haines, John

Hakluyt, Richard 1552-1616 .... **LC 31**
See also DLB 136; RGEL 2

Haldeman, Joe 1943- .... **CLC 61**
See also AAYA 38; CA 53-56, 179; CAAE 179; CAAS 25; CANR 6, 70, 72, 130, 171; DLB 8; INT CANR-6; SCFW 2; SFW 4

Haldeman, Joe William
See Haldeman, Joe

Hale, Janet Campbell 1947- .... **NNAL**
See also CA 49-52; CANR 45, 75; DAM MULT; DLB 175; MTCW 2; MTFW 2005

Hale, Sarah Josepha (Buell) 1788-1879 .... **NCLC 75**
See also DLB 1, 42, 73, 243

Halevy, Elie 1870-1937 .... **TCLC 104**

Haley, Alex 1921-1992 . **BLC 1:2; CLC 8, 12, 76; TCLC 147**
See also AAYA 26; BPFB 2; BW 2, 3; CA 77-80; 136; CANR 61; CDALBS; CPW; CSW; DA; DA3; DAB; DAC; DAM MST, MULT, POP; DLB 38; LAIT 5; MTCW 1, 2; NFS 9

Haley, Alexander Murray Palmer
See Haley, Alex

Haliburton, Thomas Chandler 1796-1865 .... **NCLC 15, 149**
See also DLB 11, 99; RGEL 2; RGSF 2

Hall, Donald 1928- ... **CLC 1, 13, 37, 59, 151, 240; PC 70**
See also AAYA 63; CA 5-8R; CAAS 7; CANR 2, 44, 64, 106, 133, 196; CP 1, 2, 3, 4, 5, 6, 7; DAM POET; DLB 5, 342; MAL 5; MTCW 2; MTFW 2005; RGAL 4; SATA 23, 97

Hall, Donald Andrew, Jr.
See Hall, Donald

Hall, Frederic Sauser
See Sauser-Hall, Frederic

Hall, James
See Kuttner, Henry

Hall, James Norman 1887-1951 ..... **TCLC 23**
See also CA 123; 173; LAIT 1; RHW 1; SATA 21

Hall, Joseph 1574-1656 .... **LC 91**
See also DLB 121, 151; RGEL 2

Hall, Marguerite Radclyffe
See Hall, Radclyffe

Hall, Radclyffe 1880-1943 ...... **TCLC 12, 215**
See also BRWS 6; CA 110; 150; CANR 83; DLB 191; MTCW 2; MTFW 2005; RGEL 2; RHW

Hall, Rodney 1935- .... **CLC 51**
See also CA 109; CANR 69; CN 6, 7; CP 1, 2, 3, 4, 5, 6, 7; DLB 289

Hallam, Arthur Henry 1811-1833 .... **NCLC 110**
See also DLB 32

Halldor Laxness
See Gudjonsson, Halldor Kiljan

Halleck, Fitz-Greene 1790-1867 .... **NCLC 47**
See also DLB 3, 250; RGAL 4

Halliday, Michael
See Creasey, John

Halpern, Daniel 1945- .... **CLC 14**
See also CA 33-36R; CANR 93, 174; CP 3, 4, 5, 6, 7

Hamburger, Michael 1924-2007 ... **CLC 5, 14**
See also CA 5-8R, 196; 261; CAAE 196; CAAS 4; CANR 2, 47; CP 1, 2, 3, 4, 5, 6, 7; DLB 27

Hamburger, Michael Peter Leopold
See Hamburger, Michael

Hamill, Pete 1935- .... **CLC 10, 261**
See also CA 25-28R; CANR 18, 71, 127, 180

Hamill, William Peter
See Hamill, Pete

Hamilton, Alexander 1712-1756 .... **LC 150**
See also DLB 31

Hamilton, Alexander 1755(?)-1804 .... **NCLC 49**
See also DLB 37

Hamilton, Clive
See Lewis, C. S.

Hamilton, Edmond 1904-1977 .... **CLC 1**
See also CA 1-4R; CANR 3, 84; DLB 8; SATA 118; SFW 4

Hamilton, Elizabeth 1758-1816 ... **NCLC 153**
See also DLB 116, 158

Hamilton, Eugene (Jacob) Lee
See Lee-Hamilton, Eugene (Jacob)

Hamilton, Franklin
See Silverberg, Robert

Hamilton, Gail
See Corcoran, Barbara (Asenath)

Hamilton, (Robert) Ian 1938-2001 . **CLC 191**
See also CA 106; 203; CANR 41, 67; CP 1, 2, 3, 4, 5, 6, 7; DLB 40, 155

Hamilton, Jane 1957- .... **CLC 179**
See also CA 147; CANR 85, 128, 214; CN 7; DLB 350; MTFW 2005

Hamilton, Mollie
See Kaye, M.M.

Hamilton, Patrick 1904-1962 .... **CLC 51**
See also BRWS 16; CA 176; 113; DLB 10, 191

Hamilton, Virginia 1936-2002 .... **CLC 26**
See also AAYA 2, 21; BW 2, 3; BYA 1, 2, 8; CA 25-28R; 206; CANR 20, 37, 73, 126; CLR 1, 11, 40, 127; DAM MULT; DLB 33, 52; DLBY 2001; INT CANR-20; JRDA; LAIT 5; MAICYA 1, 2; MAI-CYAS 1; MTCW 1, 2; MTFW 2005; SATA 4, 56, 79, 123; SATA-Obit 132; WYA; YAW

Hamilton, Virginia Esther
See Hamilton, Virginia

Hammett, Dashiell 1894-1961 . **CLC 3, 5, 10, 19, 47; SSC 17; TCLC 187**
See also AAYA 59; AITN 1; AMWS 4; BPFB 2; CA 81-84; CANR 42; CDALB 1929-1941; CMW 4; DA3; DLB 226, 280; DLBD 6; DLBY 1996; EWL 3; LAIT 3; MAL 5; MSW; MTCW 1, 2; MTFW 2005; NFS 21; RGAL 4; RGSF 2; TUS

Hammett, Samuel Dashiell
See Hammett, Dashiell

Hammon, Jupiter 1720(?)-1800(?) . **BLC 1:2; NCLC 5; PC 16**
See also DAM MULT, POET; DLB 31, 50

Hammond, Keith
See Kuttner, Henry

Hamner, Earl (Henry), Jr. 1923- ...... **CLC 12**
See also AITN 2; CA 73-76; DLB 6

Hampton, Christopher 1946- .... **CLC 4**
See also CA 25-28R; CD 5, 6; DLB 13; MTCW 1

Hampton, Christopher James
See Hampton, Christopher

Hamsun, Knut
See Pedersen, Knut

Hamsund, Knut Pedersen
See Pedersen, Knut

Handke, Peter 1942- .... **CLC 5, 8, 10, 15, 38, 134; DC 17**
See also CA 77-80; CANR 33, 75, 104, 133, 180; CWW 2; DAM DRAM, NOV; DLB 85, 124; EWL 3; MTCW 1, 2; MTFW 2005; TWA

Handler, Chelsea 1976(?)- .... **CLC 269**
See also CA 243

Handy, W(illiam) C(hristopher) 1873-1958 .... **TCLC 97**
See also BW 3; CA 121; 167

Haneke, Michael 1942- .... **CLC 283**

Hanif, Mohammed 1965- .... **CLC 299**
See also CA 283

Hanley, James 1901-1985 ..... **CLC 3, 5, 8, 13**
See also CA 73-76; 117; CANR 36; CBD; CN 1, 2, 3; DLB 191; EWL 3; MTCW 1; RGEL 2

Hannah, Barry 1942-2010 ... **CLC 23, 38, 90, 270; SSC 94**
See also BPFB 2; CA 108; 110; CANR 43, 68, 113; CN 4, 5, 6, 7; CSW; DLB 6, 234; INT CA-110; MTCW 1; RGSF 2

Hannon, Ezra
See Hunter, Evan

Hanrahan, Barbara 1939-1991 .... **TCLC 219**
See also CA 121; 127; CN 4, 5; DLB 289

Hansberry, Lorraine 1930-1965 ..... **BLC 1:2, 2:2; CLC 17, 62; DC 2; TCLC 192**
See also AAYA 25; AFAW 1, 2; AMWS 4; BW 1, 3; CA 109; 25-28R; CABS 3; CAD; CANR 58; CDALB 1941-1968; CWD; DA; DA3; DAB; DAC; DAM DRAM, MST, MULT; DFS 2; DLB 7, 38; EWL 3; FL 1:6; FW; LAIT 4; MAL 5; MTCW 1, 2; MTFW 2005; RGAL 4; TUS

Hansberry, Lorraine Vivian
See Hansberry, Lorraine

Hansen, Joseph 1923-2004 .... **CLC 38**
See also BPFB 2; CA 29-32R; 233; CAAS 17; CANR 16, 44, 66, 125; CMW 4; DLB 226; GLL 1; INT CANR-16

Hansen, Karen V. 1955- .... **CLC 65**
See also CA 149; CANR 102

Hansen, Martin A(lfred) 1909-1955 .... **TCLC 32**
See also CA 167; DLB 214; EWL 3

Hanson, Kenneth O. 1922- .... **CLC 13**
See also CA 53-56; CANR 7; CP 1, 2, 3, 4, 5

Hanson, Kenneth Ostlin
See Hanson, Kenneth O.

Han Yu 768-824 .... **CMLC 122**

Hardwick, Elizabeth 1916-2007 .... **CLC 13**
See also AMWS 3; CA 5-8R; 267; CANR 3, 32, 70, 100, 139; CN 4, 5, 6; CSW; DA3; DAM NOV; DLB 6; MBL; MTCW 1, 2; MTFW 2005; TCLE 1:1

Hardwick, Elizabeth Bruce
See Hardwick, Elizabeth

Hardy, Thomas 1840-1928 . **PC 8, 92; SSC 2, 60, 113; TCLC 4, 10, 18, 32, 48, 53, 72, 143, 153, 229; WLC 3**
See also AAYA 69; BRW 6; BRWC 1, 2; BRWR 1; CA 104; 123; CDBLB 1890-1914; DA; DA3; DAB; DAC; DAM MST, NOV, POET; DLB 18, 19, 135, 284; EWL 3; EXPN; EXPP; LAIT 2; MTCW 1, 2; MTFW 2005; NFS 3, 11, 15, 19, 30; PFS 3, 4, 18; RGEL 2; RGSF 2; TEA; WLIT 4

Hare, David 1947- . **CLC 29, 58, 136; DC 26**
See also BRWS 4; CA 97-100; CANR 39, 91; CBD; CD 5, 6; DFS 4, 7, 16; DLB 13, 310; MTCW 1; TEA

Harewood, John
See Van Druten, John (William)

Harford, Henry
　　See Hudson, W(illiam) H(enry)

Hargrave, Leonie
　　See Disch, Thomas M.

Hariri, Al- al-Qasim ibn 'Ali Abu Muhammad al-Basri
　　See al-Hariri, al-Qasim ibn 'Ali Abu Muhammad al-Basri

Harjo, Joy 1951- ..... **CLC 83; NNAL; PC 27**
　　See also AMWS 12; CA 114; CANR 35, 67, 91, 129; CP 6, 7; CWP; DAM MULT; DLB 120, 175, 342; EWL 3; MTCW 2; MTFW 2005; PFS 15, 32; RGAL 4

Harlan, Louis R. 1922-2010 .... **CLC 34**
　　See also CA 21-24R; CANR 25, 55, 80

Harlan, Louis Rudolph
　　See Harlan, Louis R.

Harlan, Louis Rudolph
　　See Harlan, Louis R.

Harling, Robert 1951(?)- .... **CLC 53**
　　See also CA 147

Harmon, William (Ruth) 1938- .... **CLC 38**
　　See also CA 33-36R; CANR 14, 32, 35; SATA 65

Harper, Edith Alice Mary
　　See Wickham, Anna

Harper, F. E. W.
　　See Harper, Frances Ellen Watkins

Harper, Frances E. W.
　　See Harper, Frances Ellen Watkins

Harper, Frances E. Watkins
　　See Harper, Frances Ellen Watkins

Harper, Frances Ellen
　　See Harper, Frances Ellen Watkins

Harper, Frances Ellen Watkins
　　1825-1911 . **BLC 1:2; PC 21; TCLC 14, 217**
　　See also AFAW 1, 2; BW 1, 3; CA 111; 125; CANR 79; DAM MULT, POET; DLB 50, 221; MBL; RGAL 4

Harper, Michael S. 1938- .. **BLC 2:2; CLC 7, 22**
　　See also AFAW 2; BW 1; CA 33-36R, 224; CAAE 224; CANR 24, 108, 212; CP 2, 3, 4, 5, 6, 7; DLB 41; RGAL 4; TCLE 1:1

Harper, Michael Steven
　　See Harper, Michael S.

Harper, Mrs. F. E. W.
　　See Harper, Frances Ellen Watkins

Harpur, Charles 1813-1868 .... **NCLC 114**
　　See also DLB 230; RGEL 2

Harris, Christie
　　See Harris, Christie (Lucy) Irwin

Harris, Christie (Lucy) Irwin
　　1907-2002 .... **CLC 12**
　　See also CA 5-8R; CANR 6, 83; CLR 47; DLB 88; JRDA; MAICYA 1, 2; SAAS 10; SATA 6, 74; SATA-Essay 116

Harris, E. Lynn 1955-2009 .... **CLC 299**
　　See also CA 164; 288; CANR 111, 163, 206; MTFW 2005

Harris, Everett Lynn
　　See Harris, E. Lynn

Harris, Everette Lynn
　　See Harris, E. Lynn

Harris, Frank 1856-1931 .... **TCLC 24**
　　See also CA 109; 150; CANR 80; DLB 156, 197; RGEL 2

Harris, George Washington
　　1814-1869 .... **NCLC 23, 165**
　　See also DLB 3, 11, 248; RGAL 4

Harris, Joel Chandler 1848-1908 ..... **SSC 19, 103; TCLC 2**
　　See also CA 104; 137; CANR 80; CLR 49, 128; DLB 11, 23, 42, 78, 91; LAIT 2; MAICYA 1, 2; RGSF 2; SATA 100; WCH; YABC 1

Harris, John (Wyndham Parkes Lucas) Beynon 1903-1969 .... **CLC 19**
　　See also BRWS 13; CA 102; 89-92; CANR 84; DLB 255; SATA 118; SCFW 1, 2; SFW 4

Harris, MacDonald
　　See Heiney, Donald (William)

Harris, Mark 1922-2007 .... **CLC 19**
　　See also CA 5-8R; 260; CANR 2, 55, 83; CN 1, 2, 3, 4, 5, 6, 7; DLB 2; DLBY 1980

Harris, Norman .... **CLC 65**

Harris, (Theodore) Wilson 1921- ... **BLC 2:2; CLC 25, 159, 297**
　　See also BRWS 5; BW 2, 3; CA 65-68; CAAS 16; CANR 11, 27, 69, 114; CD-WLB 3; CN 1, 2, 3, 4, 5, 6, 7; CP 1, 2, 3, 4, 5, 6, 7; DLB 117; EWL 3; MTCW 1; RGEL 2

Harrison, Barbara Grizzuti
　　1934-2002 .... **CLC 144**
　　See also CA 77-80; 205; CANR 15, 48; INT CANR-15

Harrison, Elizabeth (Allen) Cavanna
　　1909-2001 .... **CLC 12**
　　See also CA 9-12R; 200; CANR 6, 27, 85, 104, 121; JRDA; MAICYA 1; SAAS 4; SATA 1, 30; YAW

Harrison, Harry 1925- .... **CLC 42**
　　See also CA 1-4R; CANR 5, 21, 84; DLB 8; SATA 4; SCFW 2; SFW 4

Harrison, Harry Max
　　See Harrison, Harry

Harrison, James
　　See Harrison, Jim

Harrison, James Thomas
　　See Harrison, Jim

Harrison, Jim 1937- .... **CLC 6, 14, 33, 66, 143; SSC 19**
　　See also AMWS 8; CA 13-16R; CANR 8, 51, 79, 142, 198; CN 5, 6; CP 1, 2, 3, 4, 5, 6; DLBY 1982; INT CANR-8; RGAL 4; TCWW 2; TUS

Harrison, Kathryn 1961- .... **CLC 70, 151**
　　See also CA 144; CANR 68, 122, 194

Harrison, Tony 1937- .... **CLC 43, 129**
　　See also BRWS 5; CA 65-68; CANR 44, 98; CBD; CD 5, 6; CP 2, 3, 4, 5, 6, 7; DLB 40, 245; MTCW 1; RGEL 2

Harriss, Will(ard Irvin) 1922- .... **CLC 34**
　　See also CA 111

Hart, Ellis
　　See Ellison, Harlan

Hart, Josephine 1942(?)- .... **CLC 70**
　　See also CA 138; CANR 70, 149; CPW; DAM POP

Hart, Moss 1904-1961 .... **CLC 66**
　　See also CA 109; 89-92; CANR 84; DAM DRAM; DFS 1; DLB 7, 266; RGAL 4

Harte, Bret 1836(?)-1902 .. **SSC 8, 59; TCLC 1, 25; WLC 3**
　　See also AMWS 2; CA 104; 140; CANR 80; CDALB 1865-1917; DA; DA3; DAC; DAM MST; DLB 12, 64, 74, 79, 186; EXPS; LAIT 2; RGAL 4; RGSF 2; SATA 26; SSFS 3; TUS

Harte, Francis Brett
　　See Harte, Bret

Hartley, L(eslie) P(oles) 1895-1972 ... **CLC 2, 22; SSC 125**
　　See also BRWS 7; CA 45-48; 37-40R; CANR 33; CN 1; DLB 15, 139; EWL 3; HGG; MTCW 1, 2; MTFW 2005; RGEL 2; RGSF 2; SUFW 1

Hartman, Geoffrey H. 1929- .... **CLC 27**
　　See also CA 117; 125; CANR 79, 214; DLB 67

Hartmann, Sadakichi 1869-1944 ... **TCLC 73**
　　See also CA 157; DLB 54

Hartmann von Aue c. 1170-c. 1210 .... **CMLC 15, 131**
　　See also CDWLB 2; DLB 138; RGWL 2, 3

Hartog, Jan de
　　See de Hartog, Jan

Haruf, Kent 1943- .... **CLC 34**
　　See also AAYA 44; CA 149; CANR 91, 131

Harvey, Caroline
　　See Trollope, Joanna

Harvey, Gabriel 1550(?)-1631 .... **LC 88**
　　See also DLB 167, 213, 281

Harvey, Jack
　　See Rankin, Ian

Harwood, Ronald 1934- .... **CLC 32**
　　See also CA 1-4R; CANR 4, 55, 150; CBD; CD 5, 6; DAM DRAM, MST; DLB 13

Hasegawa Tatsunosuke
　　See Futabatei, Shimei

Hasek, Jaroslav 1883-1923 ... **SSC 69; TCLC 4**
　　See also CA 104; 129; CDWLB 4; DLB 215; EW 9; EWL 3; MTCW 1, 2; RGSF 2; RGWL 2, 3

Hasek, Jaroslav Matej Frantisek
　　See Hasek, Jaroslav

Hass, Robert 1941- ...... **CLC 18, 39, 99, 287; PC 16**
　　See also AMWS 6; CA 111; CANR 30, 50, 71, 187; CP 3, 4, 5, 6, 7; DLB 105, 206; EWL 3; MAL 5; MTFW 2005; PFS 37; RGAL 4; SATA 94; TCLE 1:1

Hassler, Jon 1933-2008 .... **CLC 263**
　　See also CA 73-76; 270; CANR 21, 80, 161; CN 6, 7; INT CANR-21; SATA 19; SATA-Obit 191

Hassler, Jon Francis
　　See Hassler, Jon

Hastings, Hudson
　　See Kuttner, Henry

Hastings, Selina .... **CLC 44**
　　See also CA 257

Hastings, Selina Shirley
　　See Hastings, Selina

Hastings, Victor
　　See Disch, Thomas M.

Hathorne, John 1641-1717 .... **LC 38**

Hatteras, Amelia
　　See Mencken, H. L.

Hatteras, Owen
　　See Mencken, H. L.; Nathan, George Jean

Hauff, Wilhelm 1802-1827 .... **NCLC 185**
　　See also CLR 155; DLB 90; SUFW 1

Hauptmann, Gerhart 1862-1946 .... **DC 34; SSC 37; TCLC 4**
　　See also CA 104; 153; CDWLB 2; DAM DRAM; DLB 66, 118, 330; EW 8; EWL 3; RGSF 2; RGWL 2, 3; TWA

Hauptmann, Gerhart Johann Robert
　　See Hauptmann, Gerhart

Havel, Vaclav 1936- ..... **CLC 25, 58, 65, 123; DC 6**
　　See also CA 104; CANR 36, 63, 124, 175; CDWLB 4; CWW 2; DA3; DAM DRAM; DFS 10; EWL 3; LMFS 2; MTCW 1, 2; MTFW 2005; RGWL 3

Haviaras, Stratis
　　See Chaviaras, Strates

Hawes, Stephen 1475(?)-1529(?) .... **LC 17**
　　See also DLB 132; RGEL 2

Hawk, Alex
　　See Kelton, Elmer

Hawkes, John 1925-1998 .. **CLC 1, 2, 3, 4, 7, 9, 14, 15, 27, 49**
　　See also BPFB 2; CA 1-4R; 167; CANR 2, 47, 64; CN 1, 2, 3, 4, 5, 6; DLB 2, 7, 227; DLBY 1980, 1998; EWL 3; MAL 5; MTCW 1, 2; MTFW 2005; RGAL 4

Hawking, S. W.
　　See Hawking, Stephen W.

Hemingway, Ernest 1899-1961 .. **CLC 1, 3, 6, 8, 10, 13, 19, 30, 34, 39, 41, 44, 50, 61, 80; SSC 1, 25, 36, 40, 63, 117, 137; TCLC 115, 203; WLC 3**
See also AAYA 19; AMW; AMWC 1; AMWR 1; BPFB 2; BYA 2, 3, 13, 15; CA 77-80; CANR 34; CDALB 1917-1929; DA; DA3; DAB; DAC; DAM MST, NOV; DLB 4, 9, 102, 210, 308, 316, 330; DLBD 1, 15, 16; DLBY 1981, 1987, 1996, 1998; EWL 3; EXPN; EXPS; LAIT 3, 4; LATS 1:1; MAL 5; MTCW 1, 2; MTFW 2005; NFS 1, 5, 6, 14; RGAL 4; RGSF 2; SSFS 17; TUS; WYA

Hemingway, Ernest Miller
See Hemingway, Ernest

Hempel, Amy 1951- .... **CLC 39**
See also AMWS 21; CA 118; 137; CANR 70, 166; DA3; DLB 218; EXPS; MTCW 2; MTFW 2005; SSFS 2

Henderson, F. C.
See Mencken, H. L.

Henderson, Mary
See Mavor, Osborne Henry

Henderson, Sylvia
See Ashton-Warner, Sylvia (Constance)

Henderson, Zenna (Chlarson) 1917-1983 .... **SSC 29**
See also CA 1-4R; 133; CANR 1, 84; DLB 8; SATA 5; SFW 4

Henkin, Joshua 1964- .... **CLC 119**
See also CA 161; CANR 186; DLB 350

Henley, Beth 1952- ... **CLC 23, 255; DC 6, 14**
See also AAYA 70; CA 107; CABS 3; CAD; CANR 32, 73, 140; CD 5, 6; CSW; CWD; DA3; DAM DRAM, MST; DFS 2, 21, 26; DLBY 1986; FW; MTCW 1, 2; MTFW 2005

Henley, Elizabeth Becker
See Henley, Beth

Henley, William Ernest 1849-1903 .. **TCLC 8**
See also CA 105; 234; DLB 19; RGEL 2

Hennissart, Martha 1929- .... **CLC 2**
See also BPFB 2; CA 85-88; CANR 64; CMW 4; DLB 306

Henry VIII 1491-1547 .... **LC 10**
See also DLB 132

Henry, O. 1862-1910 . **SSC 5, 49, 117; TCLC 1, 19; WLC 3**
See also AAYA 41; AMWS 2; CA 104; 131; CDALB 1865-1917; DA; DA3; DAB; DAC; DAM MST; DLB 12, 78, 79; EXPS; MAL 5; MTCW 1, 2; MTFW 2005; RGAL 4; RGSF 2; SSFS 2, 18, 27, 31; TCWW 1, 2; TUS; YABC 2

Henry, Oliver
See Henry, O.

Henry, Patrick 1736-1799 .... **LC 25**
See also LAIT 1

Henryson, Robert 1430(?)-1506(?) ..... **LC 20, 110; PC 65**
See also BRWS 7; DLB 146; RGEL 2

Henschke, Alfred
See Klabund

Henson, Lance 1944- .... **NNAL**
See also CA 146; DLB 175

Hentoff, Nat(han Irving) 1925- .... **CLC 26**
See also AAYA 4, 42; BYA 6; CA 1-4R; CAAS 6; CANR 5, 25, 77, 114; CLR 1, 52; DLB 345; INT CANR-25; JRDA; MAICYA 1, 2; SATA 42, 69, 133; SATA-Brief 27; WYA; YAW

Heppenstall, (John) Rayner 1911-1981 .... **CLC 10**
See also CA 1-4R; 103; CANR 29; CN 1, 2; CP 1, 2, 3; EWL 3

Heraclitus c. 540B.C.-c. 450B.C. ... **CMLC 22**
See also DLB 176

Herbert, Edward 1583-1648 .... **LC 177**
See also DLB 121, 151, 252; RGEL 2

Herbert, Frank 1920-1986 ... **CLC 12, 23, 35, 44, 85**
See also AAYA 21; BPFB 2; BYA 4, 14; CA 53-56; 118; CANR 5, 43; CDALBS; CPW; DAM POP; DLB 8; INT CANR-5; LAIT 5; MTCW 1, 2; MTFW 2005; NFS 17, 31; SATA 9, 37; SATA-Obit 47; SCFW 1, 2; SFW 4; YAW

Herbert, George 1593-1633 . **LC 24, 121; PC 4**
See also BRW 2; BRWR 2; CDBLB Before 1660; DAB; DAM POET; DLB 126; EXPP; PFS 25; RGEL 2; TEA; WP

Herbert, Zbigniew 1924-1998 ..... **CLC 9, 43; PC 50; TCLC 168**
See also CA 89-92; 169; CANR 36, 74, 177; CDWLB 4; CWW 2; DAM POET; DLB 232; EWL 3; MTCW 1; PFS 22

Herbert of Cherbury, Lord
See Herbert, Edward

Herbst, Josephine (Frey) 1897-1969 .... **CLC 34; TCLC 243**
See also CA 5-8R; 25-28R; DLB 9

Herder, Johann Gottfried von 1744-1803 .... **NCLC 8, 186**
See also DLB 97; EW 4; TWA

Heredia, Jose Maria 1803-1839 ...... **HLCS 2; NCLC 209**
See also LAW

Hergesheimer, Joseph 1880-1954 ... **TCLC 11**
See also CA 109; 194; DLB 102, 9; RGAL 4

Herlihy, James Leo 1927-1993 .... **CLC 6**
See also CA 1-4R; 143; CAD; CANR 2; CN 1, 2, 3, 4, 5

Herman, William
See Bierce, Ambrose

Hermogenes fl. c. 175- .... **CMLC 6**

Hernandez, Felisberto 1902-1964 .... **SSC 152**
See also CA 213; EWL 3; LAWS 1

Hernandez, Jose 1834-1886 .... **NCLC 17**
See also LAW; RGWL 2, 3; WLIT 1

Herodotus c. 484B.C.-c. 420B.C. .. **CMLC 17**
See also AW 1; CDWLB 1; DLB 176; RGWL 2, 3; TWA; WLIT 8

Herr, Michael 1940(?)- .... **CLC 231**
See also CA 89-92; CANR 68, 142; DLB 185; MTCW 1

Herrick, Robert 1591-1674 .. **LC 13, 145; PC 9**
See also BRW 2; BRWC 2; DA; DAB; DAC; DAM MST, POP; DLB 126; EXPP; PFS 13, 29; RGAL 4; RGEL 2; TEA; WP

Herring, Guilles
See Somerville, Edith Oenone

Herriot, James 1916-1995 .... **CLC 12**
See also AAYA 1, 54; BPFB 2; CA 77-80; 148; CANR 40; CLR 80; CPW; DAM POP; LAIT 3; MAICYA 2; MAICYAS 1; MTCW 2; SATA 86, 135; SATA-Brief 44; TEA; YAW

Herris, Violet
See Hunt, Violet

Herrmann, Dorothy 1941- .... **CLC 44**
See also CA 107

Herrmann, Taffy
See Herrmann, Dorothy

Hersey, John 1914-1993 .. **CLC 1, 2, 7, 9, 40, 81, 97**
See also AAYA 29; BPFB 2; CA 17-20R; 140; CANR 33; CDALBS; CN 1, 2, 3, 4, 5; CPW; DAM POP; DLB 6, 185, 278, 299; MAL 5; MTCW 1, 2; MTFW 2005; RGHL; SATA 25; SATA-Obit 76; TUS

Hersey, John Richard
See Hersey, John

Hervent, Maurice
See Grindel, Eugene

Herzen, Aleksandr Ivanovich 1812-1870 .... **NCLC 10, 61**
See also DLB 277

Herzen, Alexander
See Herzen, Aleksandr Ivanovich

Herzl, Theodor 1860-1904 .... **TCLC 36**
See also CA 168

Herzog, Werner 1942- .... **CLC 16, 236**
See also AAYA 85; CA 89-92; CANR 215

Hesiod fl. 8th cent. B.C.- .... **CMLC 5, 102**
See also AW 1; DLB 176; RGWL 2, 3; WLIT 8

Hesse, Hermann 1877-1962 ... **CLC 1, 2, 3, 6, 11, 17, 25, 69; SSC 9, 49; TCLC 148, 196; WLC 3**
See also AAYA 43; BPFB 2; CA 17-18; CAP 2; CDWLB 2; DA; DA3; DAB; DAC; DAM MST, NOV; DLB 66, 330; EW 9; EWL 3; EXPN; LAIT 1; MTCW 1, 2; MTFW 2005; NFS 6, 15, 24; RGWL 2, 3; SATA 50; TWA

Hewes, Cady
See De Voto, Bernard (Augustine)

Heyen, William 1940- .... **CLC 13, 18**
See also CA 33-36R; 220; CAAE 220; CAAS 9; CANR 98, 188; CP 3, 4, 5, 6, 7; DLB 5; RGHL

Heyerdahl, Thor 1914-2002 .... **CLC 26**
See also CA 5-8R; 207; CANR 5, 22, 66, 73; LAIT 4; MTCW 1, 2; MTFW 2005; SATA 2, 52

Heym, Georg (Theodor Franz Arthur) 1887-1912 .... **TCLC 9**
See also CA 106; 181

Heym, Stefan 1913-2001 .... **CLC 41**
See also CA 9-12R; 203; CANR 4; CWW 2; DLB 69; EWL 3

Heyse, Paul (Johann Ludwig von) 1830-1914 .... **TCLC 8**
See also CA 104; 209; DLB 129, 330

Heyward, (Edwin) DuBose 1885-1940 .... **HR 1:2; TCLC 59**
See also CA 108; 157; DLB 7, 9, 45, 249; MAL 5; SATA 21

Heywood, John 1497(?)-1580(?) .... **LC 65**
See also DLB 136; RGEL 2

Heywood, Thomas 1573(?)-1641 . **DC 29; LC 111**
See also DAM DRAM; DLB 62; LMFS 1; RGEL 2; TEA

Hiaasen, Carl 1953- .... **CLC 238**
See also CA 105; CANR 22, 45, 65, 113, 133, 168; CMW 4; CPW; CSW; DA3; DLB 292; LNFS 1, 2, 3; MTCW 2; MTFW 2005; SATA 208

Hibbert, Eleanor Alice Burford 1906-1993 .... **CLC 7**
See also BEST 90:4; BPFB 2; CA 17-20R; 140; CANR 9, 28, 59; CMW 4; CPW; DAM POP; MTCW 2; MTFW 2005; RHW; SATA 2; SATA-Obit 74

Hichens, Robert (Smythe) 1864-1950 .... **TCLC 64**
See also CA 162; DLB 153; HGG; RHW; SUFW

Higgins, Aidan 1927- .... **SSC 68**
See also CA 9-12R; CANR 70, 115, 148; CN 1, 2, 3, 4, 5, 6, 7; DLB 14

Higgins, George V(incent) 1939-1999 .... **CLC 4, 7, 10, 18**
See also BPFB 2; CA 77-80; 186; CAAS 5; CANR 17, 51, 89, 96; CMW 4; CN 2, 3, 4, 5, 6; DLB 2; DLBY 1981, 1998; INT CANR-17; MSW; MTCW 1

Higginson, Thomas Wentworth 1823-1911 .... **TCLC 36**
See also CA 162; DLB 1, 64, 243

Higgonet, Margaret .... CLC 65

Highet, Helen
    See MacInnes, Helen (Clark)

Highsmith, Mary Patricia
    See Highsmith, Patricia

Highsmith, Patricia 1921-1995 ...... CLC 2, 4,
        14, 42, 102
    See also AAYA 48; BRWS 5; CA 1-4R; 147;
        CANR 1, 20, 48, 62, 108; CMW 4; CN 1,
        2, 3, 4, 5; CPW; DA3; DAM NOV, POP;
        DLB 306; GLL 1; MSW; MTCW 1, 2;
        MTFW 2005; NFS 27; SSFS 25

Highwater, Jamake (Mamake)
        1942(?)-2001 .... CLC 12
    See also AAYA 7, 69; BPFB 2; BYA 4; CA
        65-68; 199; CAAS 7; CANR 10, 34, 84;
        CLR 17; CWRI 5; DLB 52; DLBY 1985;
        JRDA; MAICYA 1, 2; SATA 32, 69;
        SATA-Brief 30

Highway, Tomson 1951- ..... CLC 92; DC 33;
        NNAL
    See also CA 151; CANR 75; CCA 1; CD 5,
        6; CN 7; DAC; DAM MULT; DFS 2;
        DLB 334; MTCW 2

Hijuelos, Oscar 1951- .... CLC 65; HLC 1
    See also AAYA 25; AMWS 8; BEST 90:1;
        CA 123; CANR 50, 75, 125, 205; CPW;
        DA3; DAM MULT, POP; DLB 145; HW
        1, 2; LLW; MAL 5; MTCW 2; MTFW
        2005; NFS 17; RGAL 4; WLIT 1

Hikmet, Nazim 1902-1963 .... CLC 40
    See also CA 141; 93-96; EWL 3; PFS 38;
        WLIT 6

Hildegard von Bingen
        1098-1179 .... CMLC 20, 118
    See also DLB 148

Hildesheimer, Wolfgang 1916-1991 .. CLC 49
    See also CA 101; 135; DLB 69, 124; EWL
        3; RGHL

Hill, Aaron 1685-1750 .... LC 148
    See also DLB 84; RGEL 2

Hill, Geoffrey 1932- .... CLC 5, 8, 18, 45, 251
    See also BRWR 3; BRWS 5; CA 81-84;
        CANR 21, 89; CDBLB 1960 to Present;
        CP 1, 2, 3, 4, 5, 6, 7; DAM POET; DLB
        40; EWL 3; MTCW 1; RGEL 2; RGHL

Hill, George Roy 1921-2002 .... CLC 26
    See also CA 110; 122; 213

Hill, John
    See Koontz, Dean

Hill, Susan 1942- .... CLC 4, 113
    See also BRWS 14; CA 33-36R; CANR 29,
        69, 129, 172, 201; CN 2, 3, 4, 5, 6, 7;
        DAB; DAM MST, NOV; DLB 14, 139;
        HGG; MTCW 1; RHW; SATA 183

Hill, Susan Elizabeth
    See Hill, Susan

Hillard, Asa G. III .... CLC 70

Hillerman, Anthony Grove
    See Hillerman, Tony

Hillerman, Tony 1925-2008 ...... CLC 62, 170
    See also AAYA 40; BEST 89:1; BPFB 2;
        CA 29-32R; 278; CANR 21, 42, 65, 97,
        134; CMW 4; CPW; DA3; DAM POP;
        DLB 206, 306; MAL 5; MSW; MTCW 2;
        MTFW 2005; RGAL 4; SATA 6; SATA-
        Obit 198; TCWW 2; YAW

Hillesum, Etty 1914-1943 .... TCLC 49
    See also CA 137; RGHL

Hilliard, Noel (Harvey) 1929-1996 ... CLC 15
    See also CA 9-12R; CANR 7, 69; CN 1, 2,
        3, 4, 5, 6

Hillis, Rick 1956- .... CLC 66
    See also CA 134

Hilton, James 1900-1954 .... TCLC 21
    See also AAYA 76; CA 108; 169; DLB 34,
        77; FANT; SATA 34

Hilton, Walter (?)-1396 .... CMLC 58
    See also DLB 146; RGEL 2

Himes, Chester (Bomar)
        1909-1984 .... BLC 1:2; CLC 2, 4, 7, 18,
        58, 108; TCLC 139
    See also AFAW 2; AMWS 16; BPFB 2; BW
        2; CA 25-28R; 114; CANR 22, 89; CMW
        4; CN 1, 2, 3; DAM MULT; DLB 2, 76,
        143, 226; EWL 3; MAL 5; MSW; MTCW
        1, 2; MTFW 2005; RGAL 4

Himmelfarb, Gertrude 1922- .... CLC 202
    See also CA 49-52; CANR 28, 66, 102, 166

Hinde, Thomas 1926- .... CLC 6, 11
    See also CA 5-8R; CN 1, 2, 3, 4, 5, 6; EWL
        3

Hine, (William) Daryl 1936- .... CLC 15
    See also CA 1-4R; CAAS 15; CANR 1, 20;
        CP 1, 2, 3, 4, 5, 6, 7; DLB 60

Hinkson, Katharine Tynan
    See Tynan, Katharine

Hinojosa, Rolando 1929- .... HLC 1
    See also CA 131; CAAS 16; CANR 62;
        DAM MULT; DLB 82; EWL 3; HW 1, 2;
        LLW; MTCW 2; MTFW 2005; RGAL 4

Hinton, S. E. 1950- .... CLC 30, 111
    See also AAYA 2, 33; BPFB 2; BYA 2, 3;
        CA 81-84; CANR 32, 62, 92, 133;
        CDALBS; CLR 3, 23; CPW; DA; DA3;
        DAB; DAC; DAM MST, NOV; JRDA;
        LAIT 5; MAICYA 1, 2; MTCW 1, 2;
        MTFW 2005; NFS 5, 9, 15, 16, 35; SATA
        19, 58, 115, 160; WYA; YAW

Hinton, Susan Eloise
    See Hinton, S. E.

Hippius, Zinaida
    See Gippius, Zinaida

Hiraoka, Kimitake 1925-1970 ... CLC 2, 4, 6,
        9, 27; DC 1; SSC 4; TCLC 161; WLC
        4
    See also AAYA 50; BPFB 2; CA 97-100;
        29-32R; DA3; DAM DRAM; DLB 182;
        EWL 3; GLL 1; MJW; MTCW 1, 2;
        RGSF 2; RGWL 2, 3; SSFS 5, 12

Hirsch, E.D., Jr. 1928- .... CLC 79
    See also CA 25-28R; CANR 27, 51, 146,
        181; DLB 67; INT CANR-27; MTCW 1

Hirsch, Edward 1950- .... CLC 31, 50
    See also CA 104; CANR 20, 42, 102, 167;
        CP 6, 7; DLB 120; PFS 22

Hirsch, Eric Donald, Jr.
    See Hirsch, E.D., Jr.

Hitchcock, Alfred (Joseph)
        1899-1980 .... CLC 16
    See also AAYA 22; CA 159; 97-100; SATA
        27; SATA-Obit 24

Hitchens, Christopher 1949- .... CLC 157
    See also CA 152; CANR 89, 155, 191

Hitchens, Christopher Eric
    See Hitchens, Christopher

Hitler, Adolf 1889-1945 .... TCLC 53
    See also CA 117; 147

Hoagland, Edward (Morley) 1932- .. CLC 28
    See also ANW; CA 1-4R; CANR 2, 31, 57,
        107; CN 1, 2, 3, 4, 5, 6, 7; DLB 6; SATA
        51; TCWW 2

Hoban, Russell 1925- .... CLC 7, 25
    See also BPFB 2; CA 5-8R; CANR 23, 37,
        66, 114, 138, 218; CLR 3, 69, 139; CN 4,
        5, 6, 7; CWRI 5; DAM NOV; DLB 52;
        FANT; MAICYA 1, 2; MTCW 1, 2;
        MTFW 2005; SATA 1, 40, 78, 136; SFW
        4; SUFW 2; TCLE 1:1

Hoban, Russell Conwell
    See Hoban, Russell

Hobbes, Thomas 1588-1679 .... LC 36, 142
    See also DLB 151, 252, 281; RGEL 2

Hobbs, Perry
    See Blackmur, R(ichard) P(almer)

Hobson, Laura Z(ametkin)
        1900-1986 .... CLC 7, 25
    See also BPFB 2; CA 17-20R; 118; CANR
        55; CN 1, 2, 3, 4; DLB 28; SATA 52

Hoccleve, Thomas c. 1368-c. 1437 ...... LC 75
    See also DLB 146; RGEL 2

Hoch, Edward D. 1930-2008 .... SSC 119
    See also CA 29-32R; CANR 11, 27, 51, 97;
        CMW 4; DLB 306; SFW 4

Hoch, Edward Dentinger
    See Hoch, Edward D.

Hochhuth, Rolf 1931- .... CLC 4, 11, 18
    See also CA 5-8R; CANR 33, 75, 136;
        CWW 2; DAM DRAM; DLB 124; EWL
        3; MTCW 1, 2; MTFW 2005; RGHL

Hochman, Sandra 1936- .... CLC 3, 8
    See also CA 5-8R; CP 1, 2, 3, 4, 5; DLB 5

Hochwaelder, Fritz 1911-1986 .... CLC 36
    See also CA 29-32R; 120; CANR 42; DAM
        DRAM; EWL 3; MTCW 1; RGWL 2, 3

Hochwalder, Fritz
    See Hochwaelder, Fritz

Hocking, Mary 1921- .... CLC 13
    See also CA 101; CANR 18, 40

Hocking, Mary Eunice
    See Hocking, Mary

Hodge, Merle 1944- .... BLC 2:2
    See also EWL 3

Hodgins, Jack 1938- .... CLC 23; SSC 132
    See also CA 93-96; CN 4, 5, 6, 7; DLB 60

Hodgson, William Hope
        1877(?)-1918 .... TCLC 13
    See also CA 111; 164; CMW 4; DLB 70,
        153, 156, 178; HGG; MTCW 2; SFW 4;
        SUFW 1

Hoeg, Peter
    See Hoeg, Peter

Hoeg, Peter 1957- .... CLC 95, 156
    See also CA 151; CANR 75, 202; CMW 4;
        DA3; DLB 214; EWL 3; MTCW 2;
        MTFW 2005; NFS 17; RGWL 3; SSFS
        18

Hoffman, Alice 1952- .... CLC 51
    See also AAYA 37; AMWS 10; CA 77-80;
        CANR 34, 66, 100, 138, 170; CN 4, 5, 6,
        7; CPW; DAM NOV; DLB 292; MAL 5;
        MTCW 1, 2; MTFW 2005; TCLE 1:1

Hoffman, Daniel (Gerard) 1923- . CLC 6, 13,
        23
    See also CA 1-4R; CANR 4, 142; CP 1, 2,
        3, 4, 5, 6, 7; DLB 5; TCLE 1:1

Hoffman, Eva 1945- .... CLC 182
    See also AMWS 16; CA 132; CANR 146,
        209

Hoffman, Stanley 1944- .... CLC 5
    See also CA 77-80

Hoffman, William 1925-2009 .... CLC 141
    See also AMWS 18; CA 21-24R; CANR 9,
        103; CSW; DLB 234; TCLE 1:1

Hoffman, William M.
    See Hoffman, William M(oses)

Hoffman, William M(oses) 1939- ..... CLC 40
    See also CA 57-60; CAD; CANR 11, 71;
        CD 5, 6

Hoffmann, E(rnst) T(heodor) A(madeus)
        1776-1822 ..... NCLC 2, 183; SSC 13, 92
    See also CDWLB 2; CLR 133; DLB 90;
        EW 5; GL 2; RGSF 2; RGWL 2, 3; SATA
        27; SUFW 1; WCH

Hofmann, Gert 1931-1993 .... CLC 54
    See also CA 128; CANR 145; EWL 3;
        RGHL

Hofmannsthal, Hugo von 1874-1929 ... DC 4;
        TCLC 11
    See also CA 106; 153; CDWLB 2; DAM
        DRAM; DFS 17; DLB 81, 118; EW 9;
        EWL 3; RGWL 2, 3

Hostos (y Bonilla), Eugenio Maria de
1839-1903 .... **TCLC 24**
See also CA 123; 131; HW 1

Houdini
See Lovecraft, H. P.

Houellebecq, Michel 1958- .... **CLC 179**
See also CA 185; CANR 140; MTFW 2005

Hougan, Carolyn 1943-2007 .... **CLC 34**
See also CA 139; 257

Household, Geoffrey 1900-1988 .... **CLC 11**
See also BRWS 17; CA 77-80; 126; CANR
58; CMW 4; CN 1, 2, 3, 4; DLB 87;
SATA 14; SATA-Obit 59

Housman, A. E. 1859-1936 . **PC 2, 43; TCLC
1, 10; WLCS**
See also AAYA 66; BRW 6; CA 104; 125;
DA; DA3; DAB; DAC; DAM MST,
POET; DLB 19, 284; EWL 3; EXPP;
MTCW 1, 2; MTFW 2005; PAB; PFS 4,
7; RGEL 2; TEA; WP

Housman, Alfred Edward
See Housman, A. E.

Housman, Laurence 1865-1959 .... **TCLC 7**
See also CA 106; 155; DLB 10; FANT;
RGEL 2; SATA 25

Houston, Jeanne Wakatsuki 1934- .... **AAL**
See also AAYA 49; CA 103, 232; CAAE
232; CAAS 16; CANR 29, 123, 167;
LAIT 4; SATA 78, 168; SATA-Essay 168

Hove, Chenjerai 1956- .... **BLC 2:2**
See also CP 7; DLB 360

Howard, E. J.
See Howard, Elizabeth Jane

Howard, Elizabeth Jane 1923- ..... **CLC 7, 29**
See also BRWS 11; CA 5-8R; CANR 8, 62,
146, 210; CN 1, 2, 3, 4, 5, 6, 7

Howard, Maureen 1930- .... **CLC 5, 14, 46,
151**
See also CA 53-56; CANR 31, 75, 140; CN
4, 5, 6, 7; DLBY 1983; INT CANR-31;
MTCW 1, 2; MTFW 2005

Howard, Richard 1929- .... **CLC 7, 10, 47**
See also AITN 1; CA 85-88; CANR 25, 80,
154, 217; CP 1, 2, 3, 4, 5, 6, 7; DLB 5;
INT CANR-25; MAL 5

Howard, Robert E 1906-1936 .... **TCLC 8**
See also AAYA 80; BPFB 2; BYA 5; CA
105; 157; CANR 155; FANT; SUFW 1;
TCWW 1, 2

Howard, Robert Ervin
See Howard, Robert E

Howard, Sidney (Coe) 1891-1939 .... **DC 42**
See also CA 198; DLB 7, 26, 249; IDFW 3,
4; MAL 5; RGAL 4

Howard, Warren F.
See Pohl, Frederik

Howe, Fanny 1940- .... **CLC 47**
See also CA 117, 187; CAAE 187; CAAS
27; CANR 70, 116, 184; CP 6, 7; CWP;
SATA-Brief 52

Howe, Fanny Quincy
See Howe, Fanny

Howe, Irving 1920-1993 .... **CLC 85**
See also AMWS 6; CA 9-12R; 141; CANR
21, 50; DLB 67; EWL 3; MAL 5; MTCW
1, 2; MTFW 2005

Howe, Julia Ward 1819-1910 . **PC 81; TCLC
21**
See also CA 117; 191; DLB 1, 189, 235;
FW

Howe, Susan 1937- .... **CLC 72, 152; PC 54**
See also AMWS 4; CA 160; CANR 209;
CP 5, 6, 7; CWP; DLB 120; FW; RGAL
4

Howe, Tina 1937- .... **CLC 48; DC 43**
See also CA 109; CAD; CANR 125; CD 5,
6; CWD; DLB 341

Howell, James 1594(?)-1666 .... **LC 13**
See also DLB 151

Howells, W. D.
See Howells, William Dean

Howells, William D.
See Howells, William Dean

Howells, William Dean 1837-1920 ... **SSC 36;
TCLC 7, 17, 41**
See also AMW; CA 104; 134; CDALB
1865-1917; DLB 12, 64, 74, 79, 189;
LMFS 1; MAL 5; MTCW 2; RGAL 4;
TUS

Howes, Barbara 1914-1996 .... **CLC 15**
See also CA 9-12R; 151; CAAS 3; CANR
53; CP 1, 2, 3, 4, 5, 6; SATA 5; TCLE 1:1

Hrabal, Bohumil 1914-1997 ...... **CLC 13, 67;
TCLC 155**
See also CA 106; 156; CAAS 12; CANR
57; CWW 2; DLB 232; EWL 3; RGSF 2

Hrabanus Maurus 776(?)-856 .... **CMLC 78**
See also DLB 148

Hroswitha of Gandersheim
See Hrotsvit of Gandersheim

Hrotsvit of Gandersheim c. 935-c.
1000 .... **CMLC 29, 123**
See also DLB 148

Hsi, Chu 1130-1200 .... **CMLC 42**

Hsun, Lu
See Shu-Jen, Chou

Hubbard, L. Ron 1911-1986 .... **CLC 43**
See also AAYA 64; CA 77-80; 118; CANR
52; CPW; DA3; DAM POP; FANT;
MTCW 2; MTFW 2005; SFW 4

Hubbard, Lafayette Ronald
See Hubbard, L. Ron

Huch, Ricarda (Octavia)
1864-1947 .... **TCLC 13**
See also CA 111; 189; DLB 66; EWL 3

Huddle, David 1942- .... **CLC 49**
See also CA 57-60, 261; CAAS 20; CANR
89; DLB 130

Hudson, Jeffery
See Crichton, Michael

Hudson, Jeffrey
See Crichton, Michael

Hudson, W(illiam) H(enry)
1841-1922 .... **TCLC 29**
See also CA 115; 190; DLB 98, 153, 174;
RGEL 2; SATA 35

Hueffer, Ford Madox
See Ford, Ford Madox

Hughart, Barry 1934- .... **CLC 39**
See also CA 137; FANT; SFW 4; SUFW 2

Hughes, Colin
See Creasey, John

Hughes, David (John) 1930-2005 ..... **CLC 48**
See also CA 116; 129; 238; CN 4, 5, 6, 7;
DLB 14

Hughes, Edward James
See Hughes, Ted

Hughes, James Langston
See Hughes, Langston

Hughes, Langston 1902-1967 .... **BLC 1:2;
CLC 1, 5, 10, 15, 35, 44, 108; DC 3;
HR 1:2; PC 1, 53; SSC 6, 90; WLC 3**
See also AAYA 12; AFAW 1, 2; AMWR 1;
AMWS 1; BW 1, 3; CA 1-4R; 25-28R;
CANR 1, 34, 82; CDALB 1929-1941;
CLR 17; DA; DA3; DAB; DAC; DAM
DRAM, MST, MULT, POET; DFS 6, 18;
DLB 4, 7, 48, 51, 86, 228, 315; EWL 3;
EXPP; EXPS; JRDA; LAIT 3; LMFS 2;
MAICYA 1, 2; MAL 5; MTCW 1, 2;
MTFW 2005; NFS 21; PAB; PFS 1, 3, 6,
10, 15, 30, 38; RGAL 4; RGSF 2; SATA
4, 33; SSFS 4, 7, 29; TUS; WCH; WP;
YAW

Hughes, Richard (Arthur Warren)
1900-1976 .... **CLC 1, 11; TCLC 204**
See also CA 5-8R; 65-68; CANR 4; CN 1,
2; DAM NOV; DLB 15, 161; EWL 3;
MTCW 1; RGEL 2; SATA 8; SATA-Obit
25

Hughes, Ted 1930-1998 . **CLC 2, 4, 9, 14, 37,
119; PC 7, 89**
See also BRWC 2; BRWR 2; BRWS 1; CA
1-4R; 171; CANR 1, 33, 66, 108; CLR 3,
131; CP 1, 2, 3, 4, 5, 6; DA3; DAB; DAC;
DAM MST, POET; DLB 40, 161; EWL
3; EXPP; MAICYA 1, 2; MTCW 1, 2;
MTFW 2005; PAB; PFS 4, 19, 32; RGEL
2; SATA 49; SATA-Brief 27; SATA-Obit
107; TEA; YAW

Hughes, Thomas 1822-1896 .... **NCLC 207**
See also BYA 3; CLR 160; DLB 18, 163;
LAIT 2; RGEL 2; SATA 31

Hugo, Richard
See Huch, Ricarda (Octavia)

Hugo, Richard F(ranklin)
1923-1982 .... **CLC 6, 18, 32; PC 68**
See also AMWS 6; CA 49-52; 108; CANR
3; CP 1, 2, 3; DAM POET; DLB 5, 206;
EWL 3; MAL 5; PFS 17; RGAL 4

Hugo, Victor 1802-1885 ..... **DC 38; NCLC 3,
10, 21, 161, 189; PC 17; WLC 3**
See also AAYA 28; DA; DA3; DAB; DAC;
DAM DRAM, MST, NOV, POET; DLB
119, 192, 217; EFS 1:2, 2:1; EW 6;
EXPN; GFL 1789 to the Present; LAIT 1,
2; NFS 5, 20; RGWL 2, 3; SATA 47;
TWA

Hugo, Victor Marie
See Hugo, Victor

Huidobro, Vicente
See Huidobro Fernandez, Vicente Garcia

Huidobro Fernandez, Vicente Garcia
1893-1948 .... **TCLC 31**
See also CA 131; DLB 283; EWL 3; HW 1;
LAW

Hulme, Keri 1947- .... **CLC 39, 130**
See also CA 125; CANR 69; CN 4, 5, 6, 7;
CP 6, 7; CWP; DLB 326; EWL 3; FW;
INT CA-125; NFS 24

Hulme, T(homas) E(rnest)
1883-1917 .... **TCLC 21**
See also BRWS 6; CA 117; 203; DLB 19

Humboldt, Alexander von
1769-1859 .... **NCLC 170**
See also DLB 90

Humboldt, Wilhelm von
1767-1835 .... **NCLC 134**
See also DLB 90

Hume, David 1711-1776 .. **LC 7, 56, 156, 157**
See also BRWS 3; DLB 104, 252, 336;
LMFS 1; TEA

Humphrey, William 1924-1997 .... **CLC 45**
See also AMWS 9; CA 77-80; 160; CANR
68; CN 1, 2, 3, 4, 5, 6; CSW; DLB 6, 212,
234, 278; TCWW 1, 2

Humphreys, Emyr Owen 1919- .... **CLC 47**
See also CA 5-8R; CANR 3, 24; CN 1, 2,
3, 4, 5, 6, 7; DLB 15

Humphreys, Josephine 1945- ..... **CLC 34, 57**
See also CA 121; 127; CANR 97; CSW;
DLB 292; INT CA-127

Huneker, James Gibbons
1860-1921 .... **TCLC 65**
See also CA 193; DLB 71; RGAL 4

Hungerford, Hesba Fay
See Brinsmead, H(esba) F(ay)

Hungerford, Pixie
See Brinsmead, H(esba) F(ay)

Hunt, E. Howard 1918-2007 .... **CLC 3**
See also AITN 1; CA 45-48; 256; CANR 2,
47, 103, 160; CMW 4

Irving, John 1942- . CLC 13, 23, 38, 112, 175
See also AAYA 8, 62; AMWS 6; BEST
89:3; BPFB 2; CA 25-28R; CANR 28, 73,
112, 133; CN 3, 4, 5, 6, 7; CPW; DA3;
DAM NOV, POP; DLB 6, 278; DLBY
1982; EWL 3; MAL 5; MTCW 1, 2;
MTFW 2005; NFS 12, 14; RGAL 4; TUS
Irving, John Winslow
See Irving, John
Irving, Washington 1783-1859 . NCLC 2, 19,
95, 242; SSC 2, 37, 104; WLC 3
See also AAYA 56; AMW; CDALB 1640-
1865; CLR 97; DA; DA3; DAB; DAC;
DAM MST; DLB 3, 11, 30, 59, 73, 74,
183, 186, 250, 254; EXPS; GL 2; LAIT
1; RGAL 4; RGSF 2; SSFS 1, 8, 16;
SUFW 1; TUS; WCH; YABC 2
Irwin, P. K.
See Page, P.K.
Isaacs, Jorge Ricardo 1837-1895 ... NCLC 70
See also LAW
Isaacs, Susan 1943- .... CLC 32
See also BEST 89:1; BPFB 2; CA 89-92;
CANR 20, 41, 65, 112, 134, 165; CPW;
DA3; DAM POP; INT CANR-20; MTCW
1, 2; MTFW 2005
Isherwood, Christopher 1904-1986 ... CLC 1,
9, 11, 14, 44; SSC 56; TCLC 227
See also AMWS 14; BRW 7; CA 13-16R;
117; CANR 35, 97, 133; CN 1, 2, 3; DA3;
DAM DRAM, NOV; DLB 15, 195; DLBY
1986; EWL 3; IDTP; MTCW 1, 2; MTFW
2005; RGAL 4; RGEL 2; TUS; WLIT 4
Isherwood, Christopher William Bradshaw
See Isherwood, Christopher
Ishiguro, Kazuo 1954- . CLC 27, 56, 59, 110,
219
See also AAYA 58; BEST 90:2; BPFB 2;
BRWR 3; BRWS 4; CA 120; CANR 49,
95, 133; CN 5, 6, 7; DA3; DAM NOV;
DLB 194, 326; EWL 3; MTCW 1, 2;
MTFW 2005; NFS 13, 35; WLIT 4; WWE
1
Ishikawa, Hakuhin
See Ishikawa, Takuboku
Ishikawa, Takuboku 1886(?)-1912 ..... PC 10;
TCLC 15
See Ishikawa Takuboku
See also CA 113; 153; DAM POET
Isidore of Seville c. 560-636 .... CMLC 101
Iskander, Fazil (Abdulovich) 1929- .. CLC 47
See also CA 102; DLB 302; EWL 3
Iskander, Fazil' Abdulevich
See Iskander, Fazil (Abdulovich)
Isler, Alan (David) 1934- .... CLC 91
See also CA 156; CANR 105
Ivan IV 1530-1584 .... LC 17
Ivanov, V.I.
See Ivanov, Vyacheslav
Ivanov, Vyacheslav 1866-1949 .... TCLC 33
See also CA 122; EWL 3
Ivanov, Vyacheslav Ivanovich
See Ivanov, Vyacheslav
Ivask, Ivar Vidrik 1927-1992 .... CLC 14
See also CA 37-40R; 139; CANR 24
Ives, Morgan
See Bradley, Marion Zimmer
Ivo of Chartres c. 1040-1115 .... CMLC 116
Izumi Shikibu c. 973-c. 1034 .... CMLC 33
J. R. S.
See Gogarty, Oliver St. John
Jabran, Kahlil
See Gibran, Kahlil
Jabran, Khalil
See Gibran, Kahlil
Jaccottet, Philippe 1925- .... PC 98
See also CA 116; 129; CWW 2; GFL 1789
to the Present

Jackson, Daniel
See Wingrove, David
Jackson, Helen Hunt 1830-1885 .... NCLC 90
See also DLB 42, 47, 186, 189; RGAL 4
Jackson, Jesse 1908-1983 .... CLC 12
See also BW 1; CA 25-28R; 109; CANR
27; CLR 28; CWRI 5; MAICYA 1, 2;
SATA 2, 29; SATA-Obit 48
Jackson, Laura 1901-1991 ...... CLC 3, 7; PC
44; TCLC 240
See also CA 65-68; 135; CANR 28, 89; CP
1, 2, 3, 4, 5; DLB 48; RGAL 4
Jackson, Laura Riding
See Jackson, Laura
Jackson, Sam
See Trumbo, Dalton
Jackson, Sara
See Wingrove, David
Jackson, Shirley 1919-1965 . CLC 11, 60, 87;
SSC 9, 39; TCLC 187; WLC 3
See also AAYA 9; AMWS 9; BPFB 2; CA
1-4R; 25-28R; CANR 4, 52; CDALB
1941-1968; DA; DA3; DAC; DAM MST;
DLB 6, 234; EXPS; HGG; LAIT 4; MAL
5; MTCW 2; MTFW 2005; NFS 37;
RGAL 4; RGSF 2; SATA 2; SSFS 1, 27,
30; SUFW 1, 2
Jacob, (Cyprien-)Max 1876-1944 .... TCLC 6
See also CA 104; 193; DLB 258; EWL 3;
GFL 1789 to the Present; GLL 2; RGWL
2, 3
Jacobs, Harriet A. 1813(?)-1897 ... NCLC 67,
162
See also AFAW 1, 2; DLB 239; FL 1:3; FW;
LAIT 2; RGAL 4
Jacobs, Harriet Ann
See Jacobs, Harriet A.
Jacobs, Jim 1942- .... CLC 12
See also CA 97-100; INT CA-97-100
Jacobs, W(illiam) W(ymark)
1863-1943 .... SSC 73; TCLC 22
See also CA 121; 167; DLB 135; EXPS;
HGG; RGEL 2; RGSF 2; SSFS 2; SUFW
1
Jacobsen, Jens Peter 1847-1885 ... NCLC 34,
237
Jacobsen, Josephine (Winder)
1908-2003 .... CLC 48, 102; PC 62
See also CA 33-36R; 218; CAAS 18; CANR
23, 48; CCA 1; CP 2, 3, 4, 5, 6, 7; DLB
244; PFS 23; TCLE 1:1
Jacobson, Dan 1929- ...... CLC 4, 14; SSC 91
See also AFW; CA 1-4R; CANR 2, 25, 66,
170; CN 1, 2, 3, 4, 5, 6, 7; DLB 14, 207,
225, 319; EWL 3; MTCW 1; RGSF 2
Jacopone da Todi 1236-1306 .... CMLC 95
Jacqueline
See Carpentier, Alejo
Jacques de Vitry c. 1160-1240 ...... CMLC 63
See also DLB 208
Jagger, Michael Philip
See Jagger, Mick
Jagger, Mick 1943- .... CLC 17
See also CA 239
Jahiz, al- c. 780-c. 869 .... CMLC 25
See also DLB 311
Jakes, John 1932- .... CLC 29
See also AAYA 32; BEST 89:4; BPFB 2;
CA 57-60, 214; CAAE 214; CANR 10,
43, 66, 111, 142, 171; CPW; CSW; DA3;
DAM NOV, POP; DLB 278; DLBY 1983;
FANT; INT CANR-10; MTCW 1, 2;
MTFW 2005; RHW; SATA 62; SFW 4;
TCWW 1, 2
Jakes, John William
See Jakes, John
James I 1394-1437 .... LC 20
See also RGEL 2

James, Alice 1848-1892 .... NCLC 206
See also DLB 221
James, Andrew
See Kirkup, James
James, C.L.R. 1901-1989 ...... BLCS; CLC 33
See also AMWS 21; BW 2; CA 117; 125;
128; CANR 62; CN 1, 2, 3, 4; DLB 125;
MTCW 1
James, Daniel (Lewis) 1911-1988 ..... CLC 33
See also CA 174; 125; DLB 122
James, Dynely
See Mayne, William
James, Henry Sr. 1811-1882 .... NCLC 53
James, Henry 1843-1916 . DC 41; SSC 8, 32,
47, 108, 150; TCLC 2, 11, 24, 40, 47,
64, 171; WLC 3
See also AAYA 84; AMW; AMWC 1;
AMWR 1; BPFB 2; BRW 6; CA 104; 132;
CDALB 1865-1917; DA; DA3; DAB;
DAC; DAM MST, NOV; DLB 12, 71, 74,
189; DLBD 13; EWL 3; EXPS; GL 2;
HGG; LAIT 2; MAL 5; MTCW 1, 2;
MTFW 2005; NFS 12, 16, 19, 32, 37;
RGAL 4; RGEL 2; RGSF 2; SSFS 9;
SUFW 1; TUS
James, M. R.
See James, Montague
James, Mary
See Meaker, Marijane
James, Montague 1862-1936 ...... SSC 16, 93;
TCLC 6
See also CA 104; 203; DLB 156, 201;
HGG; RGEL 2; RGSF 2; SUFW 1
James, Montague Rhodes
See James, Montague
James, P. D. 1920- .... CLC 18, 46, 122, 226
See also BEST 90:2; BPFB 2; BRWS 4;
CA 21-24R; CANR 17, 43, 65, 112, 201;
CDBLB 1960 to Present; CMW 4; CN 4,
5, 6, 7; CPW; DA3; DAM POP; DLB 87,
276; DLBD 17; MSW; MTCW 1, 2;
MTFW 2005; TEA
James, Philip
See Moorcock, Michael
James, Samuel
See Stephens, James
James, Seumas
See Stephens, James
James, Stephen
See Stephens, James
James, T. F.
See Fleming, Thomas
James, William 1842-1910 .... TCLC 15, 32
See also AMW; CA 109; 193; DLB 270,
284; MAL 5; NCFS 5; RGAL 4
Jameson, Anna 1794-1860 .... NCLC 43
See also DLB 99, 166
Jameson, Fredric 1934- .... CLC 142
See also CA 196; CANR 169; DLB 67;
LMFS 2
Jameson, Fredric R.
See Jameson, Fredric
James VI of Scotland 1566-1625 .... LC 109
See also DLB 151, 172
Jami, Nur al-Din 'Abd al-Rahman
1414-1492 .... LC 9
Jammes, Francis 1868-1938 .... TCLC 75
See also CA 198; EWL 3; GFL 1789 to the
Present
Jandl, Ernst 1925-2000 .... CLC 34
See also CA 200; EWL 3
Janowitz, Tama 1957- .... CLC 43, 145
See also CA 106; CANR 52, 89, 129; CN
5, 6, 7; CPW; DAM POP; DLB 292;
MTFW 2005
Jansson, Tove (Marika) 1914-2001 ... SSC 96
See also CA 17-20R; 196; CANR 38, 118;
CLR 2, 125; CWW 2; DLB 257; EWL 3;
MAICYA 1, 2; RGSF 2; SATA 3, 41

Japrisot, Sebastien 1931-
See Rossi, Jean-Baptiste
Jarrell, Randall 1914-1965 .... **CLC 1, 2, 6, 9, 13, 49; PC 41; TCLC 177**
See also AMW; BYA 5; CA 5-8R; 25-28R; CABS 2; CANR 6, 34; CDALB 1941-1968; CLR 6, 111; CWRI 5; DAM POET; DLB 48, 52; EWL 3; EXPP; MAICYA 1, 2; MAL 5; MTCW 1, 2; PAB; PFS 2, 31; RGAL 4; SATA 7
Jarry, Alfred 1873-1907 .... **SSC 20; TCLC 2, 14, 147**
See also CA 104; 153; DA3; DAM DRAM; DFS 8; DLB 192, 258; EW 9; EWL 3; GFL 1789 to the Present; RGWL 2, 3; TWA
Jarvis, E.K.
See Ellison, Harlan; Silverberg, Robert
Jawien, Andrzej
See John Paul II, Pope
Jaynes, Roderick
See Coen, Ethan
Jeake, Samuel, Jr.
See Aiken, Conrad
Jean-Louis
See Kerouac, Jack
Jean Paul 1763-1825 .... **NCLC 7**
Jefferies, (John) Richard
1848-1887 .... **NCLC 47**
See also BRWS 15; DLB 98, 141; RGEL 2; SATA 16; SFW 4
Jeffers, John Robinson
See Jeffers, Robinson
Jeffers, Robinson 1887-1962 .... **CLC 2, 3, 11, 15, 54; PC 17; WLC 3**
See also AMWS 2; CA 85-88; CANR 35; CDALB 1917-1929; DA; DAC; DAM MST, POET; DLB 45, 212, 342; EWL 3; MAL 5; MTCW 1, 2; MTFW 2005; PAB; PFS 3, 4; RGAL 4
Jefferson, Janet
See Mencken, H. L.
Jefferson, Thomas 1743-1826 . **NCLC 11, 103**
See also AAYA 54; ANW; CDALB 1640-1865; DA3; DLB 31, 183; LAIT 1; RGAL 4
Jeffrey, Francis 1773-1850 .... **NCLC 33**
See also DLB 107
Jelakowitch, Ivan
See Heijermans, Herman
Jelinek, Elfriede 1946- .... **CLC 169, 303**
See also AAYA 68; CA 154; CANR 169; DLB 85, 330; FW
Jellicoe, (Patricia) Ann 1927- .... **CLC 27**
See also CA 85-88; CBD; CD 5, 6; CWD; CWRI 5; DLB 13, 233; FW
Jelloun, Tahar ben
See Ben Jelloun, Tahar
Jemyma
See Holley, Marietta
Jen, Gish 1955- .... **AAL; CLC 70, 198, 260**
See also AAYA 85; AMWC 2; CA 135; CANR 89, 130; CN 7; DLB 312; NFS 30
Jen, Lillian
See Jen, Gish
Jenkins, (John) Robin 1912- .... **CLC 52**
See also CA 1-4R; CANR 1, 135; CN 1, 2, 3, 4, 5, 6, 7; DLB 14, 271
Jennings, Elizabeth (Joan)
1926-2001 .... **CLC 5, 14, 131**
See also BRWS 5; CA 61-64; 200; CAAS 5; CANR 8, 39, 66, 127; CP 1, 2, 3, 4, 5, 6, 7; CWP; DLB 27; EWL 3; MTCW 1; SATA 66
Jennings, Waylon 1937-2002 .... **CLC 21**
Jensen, Johannes V(ilhelm)
1873-1950 .... **TCLC 41**
See also CA 170; DLB 214, 330; EWL 3; RGWL 3

Jensen, Laura 1948- .... **CLC 37**
See also CA 103
Jensen, Laura Linnea
See Jensen, Laura
Jensen, Wilhelm 1837-1911 .... **SSC 140**
Jerome, Saint 345-420 .... **CMLC 30**
See also RGWL 3
Jerome, Jerome K(lapka)
1859-1927 .... **TCLC 23**
See also CA 119; 177; DLB 10, 34, 135; RGEL 2
Jerrold, Douglas William
1803-1857 .... **NCLC 2**
See also DLB 158, 159, 344; RGEL 2
Jewett, Sarah Orne 1849-1909 ..... **SSC 6, 44, 110, 138; TCLC 1, 22, 253**
See also AAYA 76; AMW; AMWC 2; AMWR 2; CA 108; 127; CANR 71; DLB 12, 74, 221; EXPS; FL 1:3; FW; MAL 5; MBL; NFS 15; RGAL 4; RGSF 2; SATA 15; SSFS 4
Jewett, Theodora Sarah Orne
See Jewett, Sarah Orne
Jewsbury, Geraldine (Endsor)
1812-1880 .... **NCLC 22**
See also DLB 21
Jhabvala, Ruth Prawer 1927- . **CLC 4, 8, 29, 94, 138, 284; SSC 91**
See also BRWS 5; CA 1-4R; CANR 2, 29, 51, 74, 91, 128; CN 1, 2, 3, 4, 5, 6, 7; DAB; DAM NOV; DLB 139, 194, 323, 326; EWL 3; IDFW 3, 4; INT CANR-29; MTCW 1, 2; MTFW 2005; RGSF 2; RGWL 2; RHW; TEA
Jibran, Kahlil
See Gibran, Kahlil
Jibran, Khalil
See Gibran, Kahlil
Jiles, Paulette 1943- .... **CLC 13, 58**
See also CA 101; CANR 70, 124, 170; CP 5; CWP
Jimenez, Juan Ramon 1881-1958 ..... **HLC 1; PC 7; TCLC 4, 183**
See also CA 104; 131; CANR 74; DAM MULT, POET; DLB 134, 330; EW 9; EWL 3; HW 1; MTCW 1, 2; MTFW 2005; NFS 36; RGWL 2, 3
Jimenez, Ramon
See Jimenez, Juan Ramon
Jimenez Mantecon, Juan
See Jimenez, Juan Ramon
Jimenez Mantecon, Juan Ramon
See Jimenez, Juan Ramon
Jin, Ba 1904-2005 .... **CLC 18**
See Cantu, Robert Clark
See also CA 105; 244; CWW 2; DLB 328; EWL 3
Jin, Ha
See Jin, Xuefei
Jin, Xuefei 1956- .... **CLC 109, 262**
See also AMWS 18; CA 152; CANR 91, 130, 184; DLB 244, 292; MTFW 2005; NFS 25; SSFS 17, 32
Jin Ha
See Jin, Xuefei
Jodelle, Etienne 1532-1573 .... **LC 119**
See also DLB 327; GFL Beginnings to 1789
Joel, Billy
See Joel, William Martin
Joel, William Martin 1949- .... **CLC 26**
See also CA 108
John, St.
See John of Damascus, St.
John of Damascus, St. c.
675-749 .... **CMLC 27, 95**
John of Salisbury c. 1120-1180 .... **CMLC 63, 128**
John of the Cross, St. 1542-1591 .... **LC 18, 146**
See also RGWL 2, 3

John Paul II, Pope 1920-2005 .... **CLC 128**
See also CA 106; 133; 238
Johnson, B(ryan) S(tanley William)
1933-1973 .... **CLC 6, 9**
See also CA 9-12R; 53-56; CANR 9; CN 1; CP 1, 2; DLB 14, 40; EWL 3; RGEL 2
Johnson, Benjamin F., of Boone
See Riley, James Whitcomb
Johnson, Charles (Richard) 1948- . **BLC 1:2, 2:2; CLC 7, 51, 65, 163**
See also AFAW 2; AMWS 6; BW 2, 3; CA 116; CAAS 18; CANR 42, 66, 82, 129; CN 5, 6, 7; DAM MULT; DLB 33, 278; MAL 5; MTCW 2; MTFW 2005; RGAL 4; SSFS 16
Johnson, Charles S(purgeon)
1893-1956 .... **HR 1:3**
See also BW 1, 3; CA 125; CANR 82; DLB 51, 91
Johnson, Denis 1949- . **CLC 52, 160; SSC 56**
See also CA 117; 121; CANR 71, 99, 178; CN 4, 5, 6, 7; DLB 120
Johnson, Diane 1934- ...... **CLC 5, 13, 48, 244**
See also BPFB 2; CA 41-44R; CANR 17, 40, 62, 95, 155, 198; CN 4, 5, 6, 7; DLB 350; DLBY 1980; INT CANR-17; MTCW 1
Johnson, E(mily) Pauline 1861-1913 . **NNAL**
See also CA 150; CCA 1; DAC; DAM MULT; DLB 92, 175; TCWW 2
Johnson, Eyvind (Olof Verner)
1900-1976 .... **CLC 14**
See also CA 73-76; 69-72; CANR 34, 101; DLB 259, 330; EW 12; EWL 3
Johnson, Fenton 1888-1958 .... **BLC 1:2**
See also BW 1; CA 118; 124; DAM MULT; DLB 45, 50
Johnson, Georgia Douglas (Camp)
1880-1966 .... **HR 1:3**
See also BW 1; CA 125; DLB 51, 249; WP
Johnson, Helene 1907-1995 .... **HR 1:3**
See also CA 181; DLB 51; WP
Johnson, J. R.
See James, C.L.R.
Johnson, James Weldon
1871-1938 .... **BLC 1:2; HR 1:3; PC 24; TCLC 3, 19, 175**
See also AAYA 73; AFAW 1, 2; BW 1, 3; CA 104; 125; CANR 82; CDALB 1917-1929; CLR 32; DA3; DAM MULT, POET; DLB 51; EWL 3; EXPP; LMFS 2; MAL 5; MTCW 1, 2; MTFW 2005; NFS 22; PFS 1; RGAL 4; SATA 31; TUS
Johnson, Joyce 1935- .... **CLC 58**
See also BG 1:3; CA 125; 129; CANR 102
Johnson, Judith 1936- .... **CLC 7, 15**
See also CA 25-28R; 153; CANR 34, 85; CP 2, 3, 4, 5, 6, 7; CWP
Johnson, Judith Emlyn
See Johnson, Judith
Johnson, Lionel (Pigot)
1867-1902 .... **TCLC 19**
See also CA 117; 209; DLB 19; RGEL 2
Johnson, Marguerite Annie
See Angelou, Maya
Johnson, Mel
See Malzberg, Barry N(athaniel)
Johnson, Pamela Hansford
1912-1981 .... **CLC 1, 7, 27**
See also CA 1-4R; 104; CANR 2, 28; CN 1, 2, 3; DLB 15; MTCW 1, 2; MTFW 2005; RGEL 2
Johnson, Paul 1928- .... **CLC 147**
See also BEST 89:4; CA 17-20R; CANR 34, 62, 100, 155, 197
Johnson, Paul Bede
See Johnson, Paul

Kierkegaard, Soren 1813-1855 ..... **NCLC 34, 78, 125**
See also DLB 300; EW 6; LMFS 2; RGWL 3; TWA

Kieslowski, Krzysztof 1941-1996 .... **CLC 120**
See also CA 147; 151

Killens, John Oliver 1916-1987 ...... **BLC 2:2; CLC 10**
See also BW 2; CA 77-80; 123; CAAS 2; CANR 26; CN 1, 2, 3, 4; DLB 33; EWL 3

Killigrew, Anne 1660-1685 .... **LC 4, 73**
See also DLB 131

Killigrew, Thomas 1612-1683 .... **LC 57**
See also DLB 58; RGEL 2

Kim
See Simenon, Georges

Kincaid, Jamaica 1949- . **BLC 1:2, 2:2; CLC 43, 68, 137, 234; SSC 72**
See also AAYA 13, 56; AFAW 2; AMWS 7; BRWS 7; BW 2, 3; CA 125; CANR 47, 59, 95, 133; CDALBS; CDWLB 3; CLR 63; CN 4, 5, 6, 7; DA3; DAM MULT, NOV; DLB 157, 227; DNFS 1; EWL 3; EXPS; FW; LATS 1:2; LMFS 2; MAL 5; MTCW 2; MTFW 2005; NCFS 1; NFS 3; SSFS 5, 7; TUS; WWE 1; YAW

King, Francis (Henry) 1923- .... **CLC 8, 53, 145**
See also CA 1-4R; CANR 1, 33, 86; CN 1, 2, 3, 4, 5, 6, 7; DAM NOV; DLB 15, 139; MTCW 1

King, Kennedy
See Brown, George Douglas

King, Martin Luther, Jr.
1929-1968 ... **BLC 1:2; CLC 83; WLCS**
See also BW 2, 3; CA 25-28; CANR 27, 44; CAP 2; DA; DA3; DAB; DAC; DAM MST, MULT; DLB 143; LAIT 5; LATS 1:2; MTCW 1, 2; MTFW 2005; SATA 14

King, Stephen 1947- .... **CLC 12, 26, 37, 61, 113, 228, 244; SSC 17, 55**
See also AAYA 1, 17, 82; AMWS 5; BEST 90:1; BPFB 2; CA 61-64; CANR 1, 30, 52, 76, 119, 134, 168; CLR 124; CN 7; CPW; DA3; DAM NOV, POP; DLB 143, 350; DLBY 1980; HGG; JRDA; LAIT 5; LNFS 1; MTCW 1, 2; MTFW 2005; RGAL 4; SATA 9, 55, 161; SSFS 30; SUFW 1, 2; WYAS 1; YAW

King, Stephen Edwin
See King, Stephen

King, Steve
See King, Stephen

King, Thomas 1943- .... **CLC 89, 171, 276; NNAL**
See also CA 144; CANR 95, 175; CCA 1; CN 6, 7; DAC; DAM MULT; DLB 175, 334; SATA 96

King, Thomas Hunt
See King, Thomas

Kingman, Lee
See Natti, Lee

Kingsley, Charles 1819-1875 .... **NCLC 35**
See also BRWS 16; CLR 77; DLB 21, 32, 163, 178, 190; FANT; MAICYA 2; MAICYAS 1; RGEL 2; WCH; YABC 2

Kingsley, Henry 1830-1876 .... **NCLC 107**
See also DLB 21, 230; RGEL 2

Kingsley, Sidney 1906-1995 .... **CLC 44**
See also CA 85-88; 147; CAD; DFS 14, 19; DLB 7; MAL 5; RGAL 4

Kingsolver, Barbara 1955- .... **CLC 55, 81, 130, 216, 269**
See also AAYA 15; AMWS 7; CA 129; 134; CANR 60, 96, 133, 179; CDALBS; CN 7; CPW; CSW; DA3; DAM POP; DLB 206; INT CA-134; LAIT 5; MTCW 2; MTFW 2005; NFS 5, 10, 12, 24; RGAL 4; TCLE 1:1

Kingston, Maxine Hong 1940- .... **AAL; CLC 12, 19, 58, 121, 271; SSC 136; WLCS**
See also AAYA 8, 55; AMWS 5; BPFB 2; CA 69-72; CANR 13, 38, 74, 87, 128; CDALBS; CN 6, 7; DA3; DAM MULT, NOV; DLB 173, 212, 312; DLBY 1980; EWL 3; FL 1:6; FW; INT CANR-13; LAIT 5; MAL 5; MBL; MTCW 1, 2; MTFW 2005; NFS 6; RGAL 4; SATA 53; SSFS 3; TCWW 2

Kingston, Maxine Ting Ting Hong
See Kingston, Maxine Hong

Kinnell, Galway 1927- ..... **CLC 1, 2, 3, 5, 13, 29, 129; PC 26**
See also AMWS 3; CA 9-12R; CANR 10, 34, 66, 116, 138, 175; CP 1, 2, 3, 4, 5, 6, 7; DLB 5, 342; DLBY 1987; EWL 3; INT CANR-34; MAL 5; MTCW 1, 2; MTFW 2005; PAB; PFS 9, 26, 35; RGAL 4; TCLE 1:1; WP

Kinsella, Thomas 1928- .... **CLC 4, 19, 138, 274; PC 69**
See also BRWS 5; CA 17-20R; CANR 15, 122; CP 1, 2, 3, 4, 5, 6, 7; DLB 27; EWL 3; MTCW 1, 2; MTFW 2005; RGEL 2; TEA

Kinsella, William Patrick
See Kinsella, W.P.

Kinsella, W.P. 1935- .... **CLC 27, 43, 166**
See also AAYA 7, 60; BPFB 2; BYA 7; CA 97-100, 222; CAAE 222; CAAS 7; CANR 21, 35, 66, 75, 129; CN 4, 5, 6, 7; CPW; DAC; DAM NOV, POP; DLB 362; FANT; INT CANR-21; LAIT 5; MTCW 1, 2; MTFW 2005; NFS 15; RGSF 2; SSFS 30

Kinsey, Alfred C(harles)
1894-1956 .... **TCLC 91**
See also CA 115; 170; MTCW 2

Kipling, Joseph Rudyard
See Kipling, Rudyard

Kipling, Rudyard 1865-1936 . **PC 3, 91; SSC 5, 54, 110; TCLC 8, 17, 167; WLC 3**
See also AAYA 32; BRW 6; BRWC 1, 2; BRWR 3; BYA 4; CA 105; 120; CANR 33; CDBLB 1890-1914; CLR 39, 65; CWRI 5; DA; DA3; DAB; DAC; DAM MST, POET; DLB 19, 34, 141, 156, 330; EWL 3; EXPS; FANT; LAIT 3; LMFS 1; MAICYA 1, 2; MTCW 1, 2; MTFW 2005; NFS 21; PFS 22; RGEL 2; RGSF 2; SATA 100; SFW 4; SSFS 8, 21, 22, 32; SUFW 1; TEA; WCH; WLIT 4; YABC 2

Kircher, Athanasius 1602-1680 .... **LC 121**
See also DLB 164

Kirk, Richard
See Holdstock, Robert

Kirk, Russell (Amos) 1918-1994 .. **TCLC 119**
See also AITN 1; CA 1-4R; 145; CAAS 9; CANR 1, 20, 60; HGG; INT CANR-20; MTCW 1, 2

Kirkham, Dinah
See Card, Orson Scott

Kirkland, Caroline M. 1801-1864 . **NCLC 85**
See also DLB 3, 73, 74, 250, 254; DLBD 13

Kirkup, James 1918-2009 .... **CLC 1**
See also CA 1-4R; CAAS 4; CANR 2; CP 1, 2, 3, 4, 5, 6, 7; DLB 27; SATA 12

Kirkwood, James 1930(?)-1989 .... **CLC 9**
See also AITN 2; CA 1-4R; 128; CANR 6, 40; GLL 2

Kirsch, Sarah 1935- .... **CLC 176**
See also CA 178; CWW 2; DLB 75; EWL 3

Kirshner, Sidney
See Kingsley, Sidney

Kis, Danilo 1935-1989 .... **CLC 57**
See also CA 109; 118; 129; CANR 61; CD-WLB 4; DLB 181; EWL 3; MTCW 1; RGSF 2; RGWL 2, 3

Kissinger, Henry A(lfred) 1923- ..... **CLC 137**
See also CA 1-4R; CANR 2, 33, 66, 109; MTCW 1

Kittel, Frederick August
See Wilson, August

Kivi, Aleksis 1834-1872 .... **NCLC 30**

Kizer, Carolyn 1925- ..... **CLC 15, 39, 80; PC 66**
See also CA 65-68; CAAS 5; CANR 24, 70, 134; CP 1, 2, 3, 4, 5, 6, 7; CWP; DAM POET; DLB 5, 169; EWL 3; MAL 5; MTCW 2; MTFW 2005; PFS 18; TCLE 1:1

Klabund 1890-1928 .... **TCLC 44**
See also CA 162; DLB 66

Klappert, Peter 1942- .... **CLC 57**
See also CA 33-36R; CSW; DLB 5

Klausner, Amos
See Oz, Amos

Klein, A. M. 1909-1972 .... **CLC 19**
See also CA 101; 37-40R; CP 1; DAB; DAC; DAM MST; DLB 68; EWL 3; RGEL 2; RGHL

Klein, Abraham Moses
See Klein, A. M.

Klein, Joe
See Klein, Joseph

Klein, Joseph 1946- .... **CLC 154**
See also CA 85-88; CANR 55, 164

Klein, Norma 1938-1989 .... **CLC 30**
See also AAYA 2, 35; BPFB 2; BYA 6, 7, 8; CA 41-44R; 128; CANR 15, 37; CLR 2, 19, 162; INT CANR-15; JRDA; MAICYA 1, 2; SAAS 1; SATA 7, 57; WYA; YAW

Klein, T.E.D. 1947- .... **CLC 34**
See also CA 119; CANR 44, 75, 167; HGG

Klein, Theodore Eibon Donald
See Klein, T.E.D.

Kleist, Heinrich von 1777-1811 .... **DC 29; NCLC 2, 37, 222; SSC 22**
See also CDWLB 2; DAM DRAM; DLB 90; EW 5; RGSF 2; RGWL 2, 3

Klima, Ivan 1931- .... **CLC 56, 172**
See also CA 25-28R; CANR 17, 50, 91; CDWLB 4; CWW 2; DAM NOV; DLB 232; EWL 3; RGWL 3

Klimentev, Andrei Platonovich
See Klimentov, Andrei Platonovich

Klimentov, Andrei Platonovich
1899-1951 .... **SSC 42; TCLC 14**
See also CA 108; 232; DLB 272; EWL 3

Klinger, Friedrich Maximilian von
1752-1831 .... **NCLC 1**
See also DLB 94

Klingsor the Magician
See Hartmann, Sadakichi

Klopstock, Friedrich Gottlieb
1724-1803 .... **NCLC 11, 225**
See also DLB 97; EW 4; RGWL 2, 3

Kluge, Alexander 1932- .... **SSC 61**
See also CA 81-84; CANR 163; DLB 75

Knapp, Caroline 1959-2002 ...... **CLC 99, 309**
See also CA 154; 207

Knebel, Fletcher 1911-1993 .... **CLC 14**
See also AITN 1; CA 1-4R; 140; CAAS 3; CANR 1, 36; CN 1, 2, 3, 4, 5; SATA 36; SATA-Obit 75

Knickerbocker, Diedrich
See Irving, Washington

Knight, Etheridge 1931-1991 .... **BLC 1:2; CLC 40; PC 14**
See also BW 1, 3; CA 21-24R; 133; CANR 23, 82; CP 1, 2, 3, 4, 5; DAM POET; DLB 41; MTCW 1, 2; MTFW 2005; PFS 36; RGAL 4; TCLE 1:1

Knight, Sarah Kemble 1666-1727 .... **LC 7**
See also DLB 24, 200

Knister, Raymond 1899-1932 .... **TCLC 56**
See also CA 186; DLB 68; RGEL 2
Knowles, John 1926-2001 ... **CLC 1, 4, 10, 26**
See also AAYA 10, 72; AMWS 12; BPFB
2; BYA 3; CA 17-20R; 203; CANR 40,
74, 76, 132; CDALB 1968-1988; CLR 98;
CN 1, 2, 3, 4, 5, 6, 7; DA; DAC; DAM
MST, NOV; DLB 6; EXPN; MTCW 1, 2;
MTFW 2005; NFS 2; RGAL 4; SATA 8,
89; SATA-Obit 134; YAW
Knox, Calvin M.
See Silverberg, Robert
Knox, John c. 1505-1572 .... **LC 37**
See also DLB 132
Knye, Cassandra
See Disch, Thomas M.
Koch, C(hristopher) J(ohn) 1932- .... **CLC 42**
See also CA 127; CANR 84; CN 3, 4, 5, 6,
7; DLB 289
Koch, Christopher
See Koch, C(hristopher) J(ohn)
Koch, Kenneth 1925-2002 .... **CLC 5, 8, 44;**
PC 80
See also AMWS 15; CA 1-4R; 207; CAD;
CANR 6, 36, 57, 97, 131; CD 5, 6; CP 1,
2, 3, 4, 5, 6, 7; DAM POET; DLB 5; INT
CANR-36; MAL 5; MTCW 2; MTFW
2005; PFS 20; SATA 65; WP
Kochanowski, Jan 1530-1584 .... **LC 10**
See also RGWL 2, 3
Kock, Charles Paul de 1794-1871 . **NCLC 16**
Koda Rohan
See Koda Shigeyuki
Koda Rohan
See Koda Shigeyuki
Koda Shigeyuki 1867-1947 .... **TCLC 22**
See also CA 121; 183; DLB 180
Koestler, Arthur 1905-1983 ... **CLC 1, 3, 6, 8,**
15, 33
See also BRWS 1; CA 1-4R; 109; CANR 1,
33; CDBLB 1945-1960; CN 1, 2, 3;
DLBY 1983; EWL 3; MTCW 1, 2; MTFW
2005; NFS 19; RGEL 2
Kogawa, Joy 1935- .... **CLC 78, 129, 262, 268**
See also AAYA 47; CA 101; CANR 19, 62,
126; CN 6, 7; CP 1; CWP; DAC; DAM
MST, MULT; DLB 334; FW; MTCW 2;
MTFW 2005; NFS 3; SATA 99
Kogawa, Joy Nozomi
See Kogawa, Joy
Kohout, Pavel 1928- .... **CLC 13**
See also CA 45-48; CANR 3
Koizumi, Yakumo
See Hearn, Lafcadio
Kolmar, Gertrud 1894-1943 .... **TCLC 40**
See also CA 167; EWL 3; RGHL
Komunyakaa, Yusef 1947- . **BLC 2:2; BLCS;**
CLC 86, 94, 207, 299; PC 51
See also AFAW 2; AMWS 13; CA 147;
CANR 83, 164, 211; CP 6, 7; CSW; DLB
120; EWL 3; PFS 5, 20, 30, 37; RGAL 4
Konigsberg, Alan Stewart
See Allen, Woody
Konrad, George
See Konrad, Gyorgy
Konrad, George
See Konrad, Gyorgy
Konrad, Gyorgy 1933- .... **CLC 4, 10, 73**
See also CA 85-88; CANR 97, 171; CD-
WLB 4; CWW 2; DLB 232; EWL 3
Konwicki, Tadeusz 1926- .... **CLC 8, 28, 54,**
117
See also CA 101; CAAS 9; CANR 39, 59;
CWW 2; DLB 232; EWL 3; IDFW 3;
MTCW 1

Koontz, Dean 1945- .... **CLC 78, 206**
See also Koontz, Dean R.
See also AAYA 9, 31; BEST 89:3, 90:2; CA
108; CANR 19, 36, 52, 95, 138, 176;
CMW 4; CPW; DA3; DAM NOV, POP;
DLB 292; HGG; MTCW 1; MTFW 2005;
SATA 92, 165; SFW 4; SUFW 2; YAW
Koontz, Dean R.
See Koontz, Dean
See also SATA 225
Koontz, Dean Ray
See Koontz, Dean
Kopernik, Mikolaj
See Copernicus, Nicolaus
Kopit, Arthur 1937- ... **CLC 1, 18, 33; DC 37**
See also AITN 1; CA 81-84; CABS 3;
CAD; CD 5, 6; DAM DRAM; DFS 7, 14,
24; DLB 7; MAL 5; MTCW 1; RGAL 4
Kopit, Arthur Lee
See Kopit, Arthur
Kopitar, Jernej (Bartholomaus)
1780-1844 .... **NCLC 117**
Kops, Bernard 1926- .... **CLC 4**
See also CA 5-8R; CANR 84, 159; CBD;
CN 1, 2, 3, 4, 5, 6, 7; CP 1, 2, 3, 4, 5, 6,
7; DLB 13; RGHL
Kornbluth, C(yril) M. 1923-1958 .... **TCLC 8**
See also CA 105; 160; DLB 8; SCFW 1, 2;
SFW 4
Korolenko, V.G.
See Korolenko, Vladimir G.
Korolenko, Vladimir
See Korolenko, Vladimir G.
Korolenko, Vladimir G.
1853-1921 .... **TCLC 22**
See also CA 121; DLB 277
Korolenko, Vladimir Galaktionovich
See Korolenko, Vladimir G.
Korzybski, Alfred (Habdank Skarbek)
1879-1950 .... **TCLC 61**
See also CA 123; 160
Kosinski, Jerzy 1933-1991 ..... **CLC 1, 2, 3, 6,**
10, 15, 53, 70
See also AMWS 7; BPFB 2; CA 17-20R;
134; CANR 9, 46; CN 1, 2, 3, 4; DA3;
DAM NOV; DLB 2, 299; DLBY 1982;
EWL 3; HGG; MAL 5; MTCW 1, 2;
MTFW 2005; NFS 12; RGAL 4; RGHL;
TUS
Kostelanetz, Richard 1940- .... **CLC 28**
See also CA 13-16R; CAAS 8; CANR 38,
77; CN 4, 5, 6; CP 2, 3, 4, 5, 6, 7
Kostelanetz, Richard Cory
See Kostelanetz, Richard
Kostrowitzki, Wilhelm Apollinaris de
1880-1918
See Apollinaire, Guillaume
Kotlowitz, Robert 1924- .... **CLC 4**
See also CA 33-36R; CANR 36
Kotzebue, August (Friedrich Ferdinand) von
1761-1819 .... **NCLC 25**
See also DLB 94
Kotzwinkle, William 1938- ..... **CLC 5, 14, 35**
See also BPFB 2; CA 45-48; CANR 3, 44,
84, 129; CLR 6; CN 7; DLB 173; FANT;
MAICYA 1, 2; SATA 24, 70, 146; SFW
4; SUFW 2; YAW
Kowna, Stancy
See Szymborska, Wislawa
Kozol, Jonathan 1936- .... **CLC 17**
See also AAYA 46; CA 61-64; CANR 16,
45, 96, 178; MTFW 2005
Kozoll, Michael 1940(?)- .... **CLC 35**
Krakauer, Jon 1954- .... **CLC 248**
See also AAYA 24; AMWS 18; BYA 9; CA
153; CANR 131, 212; MTFW 2005;
SATA 108

Kramer, Kathryn 19(?)- .... **CLC 34**
Kramer, Larry 1935- .... **CLC 42; DC 8**
See also CA 124; 126; CANR 60, 132;
DAM POP; DLB 249; GLL 1
Krasicki, Ignacy 1735-1801 .... **NCLC 8**
Krasinski, Zygmunt 1812-1859 .... **NCLC 4**
See also RGWL 2, 3
Kraus, Karl 1874-1936 .... **TCLC 5**
See also CA 104; 216; DLB 118; EWL 3
Kraynay, Anton
See Gippius, Zinaida
Kreve (Mickevicius), Vincas
1882-1954 .... **TCLC 27**
See also CA 170; DLB 220; EWL 3
Kristeva, Julia 1941- .... **CLC 77, 140**
See also CA 154; CANR 99, 173; DLB 242;
EWL 3; FW; LMFS 2
Kristofferson, Kris 1936- .... **CLC 26**
See also CA 104
Krizanc, John 1956- .... **CLC 57**
See also CA 187
Krleza, Miroslav 1893-1981 .... **CLC 8, 114**
See also CA 97-100; 105; CANR 50; CD-
WLB 4; DLB 147; EW 11; RGWL 2, 3
Kroetsch, Robert (Paul) 1927- .... **CLC 5, 23,**
57, 132, 286
See also CA 17-20R; CANR 8, 38; CCA 1;
CN 2, 3, 4, 5, 6, 7; CP 6, 7; DAC; DAM
POET; DLB 53; MTCW 1
Kroetz, Franz
See Kroetz, Franz Xaver
Kroetz, Franz Xaver 1946- .... **CLC 41**
See also CA 130; CANR 142; CWW 2;
EWL 3
Kroker, Arthur (W.) 1945- .... **CLC 77**
See also CA 161
Kroniuk, Lisa
See Berton, Pierre (Francis de Marigny)
Kropotkin, Peter 1842-1921 .... **TCLC 36**
See also CA 119; 219; DLB 277
Kropotkin, Peter Alekseieevich
See Kropotkin, Peter
Kropotkin, Petr Alekseevich
See Kropotkin, Peter
Krotkov, Yuri 1917-1981 .... **CLC 19**
See also CA 102
Krumb
See Crumb, R.
Krumgold, Joseph (Quincy)
1908-1980 .... **CLC 12**
See also BYA 1, 2; CA 9-12R; 101; CANR
7; MAICYA 1, 2; SATA 1, 48; SATA-Obit
23; YAW
Krumwitz
See Crumb, R.
Krutch, Joseph Wood 1893-1970 ..... **CLC 24**
See also ANW; CA 1-4R; 25-28R; CANR
4; DLB 63, 206, 275
Krutzch, Gus
See Eliot, T. S.
Krylov, Ivan Andreevich
1768(?)-1844 .... **NCLC 1**
See also DLB 150
Kubin, Alfred (Leopold Isidor)
1877-1959 .... **TCLC 23**
See also CA 112; 149; CANR 104; DLB 81
Kubrick, Stanley 1928-1999 .... **CLC 16;**
TCLC 112
See also AAYA 30; CA 81-84; 177; CANR
33; DLB 26
Kueng, Hans
See Kung, Hans
Kumin, Maxine 1925- .... **CLC 5, 13, 28, 164;**
PC 15
See also AITN 2; AMWS 4; ANW; CA
1-4R, 271; CAAE 271; CAAS 8; CANR
1, 21, 69, 115, 140; CP 2, 3, 4, 5, 6, 7;

CWP; DA3; DAM POET; DLB 5; EWL
3; EXPP; MTCW 1, 2; MTFW 2005;
PAB; PFS 18, 38; SATA 12

Kumin, Maxine Winokur
See Kumin, Maxine

Kundera, Milan 1929- . CLC 4, 9, 19, 32, 68,
115, 135, 234; SSC 24
See also AAYA 2, 62; BPFB 2; CA 85-88;
CANR 19, 52, 74, 144; CDWLB 4; CWW
2; DA3; DAM NOV; DLB 232; EW 13;
EWL 3; MTCW 1, 2; MTFW 2005; NFS
18, 27; RGSF 2; RGWL 3; SSFS 10

Kunene, Mazisi 1930-2006 .... CLC 85
See also BW 1, 3; CA 125; 252; CANR 81;
CP 1, 6, 7; DLB 117

Kunene, Mazisi Raymond
See Kunene, Mazisi

Kunene, Mazisi Raymond Fakazi Mngoni
See Kunene, Mazisi

Kung, Hans
See Kung, Hans

Kung, Hans 1928- .... CLC 130
See also CA 53-56; CANR 66, 134; MTCW
1, 2; MTFW 2005

Kunikida, Tetsuo
See Kunikida Doppo

Kunikida Doppo 1869(?)-1908 .... TCLC 99
See also DLB 180; EWL 3

Kunikida Tetsuo
See Kunikida Doppo

Kunitz, Stanley 1905-2006 ..... CLC 6, 11, 14,
148, 293; PC 19
See also AMWS 3; CA 41-44R; 250; CANR
26, 57, 98; CP 1, 2, 3, 4, 5, 6, 7; DA3;
DLB 48; INT CANR-26; MAL 5; MTCW
1, 2; MTFW 2005; PFS 11; RGAL 4

Kunitz, Stanley Jasspon
See Kunitz, Stanley

Kunt, Klerk
See Copeland, Stewart

Kunze, Reiner 1933- .... CLC 10
See also CA 93-96; CWW 2; DLB 75; EWL
3

Kuprin, Aleksander Ivanovich
1870-1938 .... TCLC 5
See also CA 104; 182; DLB 295; EWL 3

Kuprin, Aleksandr Ivanovich
See Kuprin, Aleksander Ivanovich

Kuprin, Alexandr Ivanovich
See Kuprin, Aleksander Ivanovich

Kureishi, Hanif 1954- ...... CLC 64, 135, 284;
DC 26
See also BRWS 11; CA 139; CANR 113,
197; CBD; CD 5, 6; CN 6, 7; DLB 194,
245, 352; GLL 2; IDFW 4; WLIT 4;
WWE 1

Kurosawa, Akira 1910-1998 ..... CLC 16, 119
See also AAYA 11, 64; CA 101; 170; CANR
46; DAM MULT

Kushner, Tony 1956- . CLC 81, 203, 297; DC
10
See also AAYA 61; AMWS 9; CA 144;
CAD; CANR 74, 130; CD 5, 6; DA3;
DAM DRAM; DFS 5; DLB 228; EWL 3;
GLL 1; LAIT 5; MAL 5; MTCW 2;
MTFW 2005; RGAL 4; RGHL; SATA 160

Kuttner, Henry 1915-1958 .... TCLC 10
See also CA 107; 157; DLB 8; FANT;
SCFW 1, 2; SFW 4

Kutty, Madhavi
See Das, Kamala

Kuzma, Greg 1944- .... CLC 7
See also CA 33-36R; CANR 70

Kuzmin, Mikhail (Alekseevich)
1872(?)-1936 .... TCLC 40
See also CA 170; DLB 295; EWL 3

Kyd, Thomas 1558-1594 .. DC 3; LC 22, 125
See also BRW 1; DAM DRAM; DFS 21;
DLB 62; IDTP; LMFS 1; RGEL 2; TEA;
WLIT 3

Kyprianos, Iossif
See Samarakis, Antonis

L. S.
See Stephen, Sir Leslie

Labe, Louise 1521-1566 .... LC 120
See also DLB 327

Labrunie, Gerard
See Nerval, Gerard de

La Bruyere, Jean de 1645-1696 .. LC 17, 168
See also DLB 268; EW 3; GFL Beginnings
to 1789

LaBute, Neil 1963- .... CLC 225
See also CA 240

Lacan, Jacques (Marie Emile)
1901-1981 .... CLC 75
See also CA 121; 104; DLB 296; EWL 3;
TWA

Laclos, Pierre-Ambroise Francois
1741-1803 .... NCLC 4, 87, 239
See also DLB 313; EW 4; GFL Beginnings
to 1789; RGWL 2, 3

Lacolere, Francois
See Aragon, Louis

La Colere, Francois
See Aragon, Louis

Lactantius c. 250-c. 325 .... CMLC 118

La Deshabilleuse
See Simenon, Georges

Lady Gregory
See Gregory, Lady Isabella Augusta (Persse)

Lady of Quality, A
See Bagnold, Enid

**La Fayette, Marie-(Madelaine Pioche de la
Vergne)** 1634-1693 .... LC 2, 144
See also DLB 268; GFL Beginnings to
1789; RGWL 2, 3

Lafayette, Marie-Madeleine
See La Fayette, Marie-(Madelaine Pioche
de la Vergne)

Lafayette, Rene
See Hubbard, L. Ron

La Flesche, Francis 1857(?)-1932 ...... NNAL
See also CA 144; CANR 83; DLB 175

La Fontaine, Jean de 1621-1695 . LC 50, 184
See also DLB 268; EW 3; GFL Beginnings
to 1789; MAICYA 1, 2; RGWL 2, 3;
SATA 18

LaForet, Carmen 1921-2004 .... CLC 219
See also CA 246; CWW 2; DLB 322; EWL
3

LaForet Diaz, Carmen
See LaForet, Carmen

Laforgue, Jules 1860-1887 .... NCLC 5, 53,
221; PC 14; SSC 20
See also DLB 217; EW 7; GFL 1789 to the
Present; RGWL 2, 3

Lagerkvist, Paer 1891-1974 ... CLC 7, 10, 13,
54; SSC 12; TCLC 144
See also CA 85-88; 49-52; DA3; DAM
DRAM, NOV; DLB 259, 331; EW 10;
EWL 3; MTCW 1, 2; MTFW 2005; RGSF
2; RGWL 2, 3; SSFS 33; TWA

Lagerkvist, Paer Fabian
See Lagerkvist, Paer

Lagerkvist, Par
See Lagerkvist, Paer

Lagerloef, Selma
See Lagerlof, Selma

Lagerloef, Selma Ottiliana Lovisa
See Lagerlof, Selma

Lagerlof, Selma 1858-1940 .... TCLC 4, 36
See also CA 108; 188; CLR 7; DLB 259,
331; MTCW 2; RGWL 2, 3; SATA 15;
SSFS 18

Lagerlof, Selma Ottiliana Lovisa
See Lagerlof, Selma

La Guma, Alex 1925-1985 .. BLCS; CLC 19;
TCLC 140
See also AFW; BW 1, 3; CA 49-52; 118;
CANR 25, 81; CDWLB 3; CN 1, 2, 3;
CP 1; DAM NOV; DLB 117, 225; EWL
3; MTCW 1, 2; MTFW 2005; WLIT 2;
WWE 1

La Guma, Justin Alexander
See La Guma, Alex

Lahiri, Jhumpa 1967- .... CLC 282; SSC 96
See also AAYA 56; AMWS 21; CA 193;
CANR 134, 184; DLB 323; MTFW 2005;
NFS 31; SSFS 19, 27

Laidlaw, A. K.
See Grieve, C. M.

Lainez, Manuel Mujica
See Mujica Lainez, Manuel

Laing, R(onald) D(avid) 1927-1989 . CLC 95
See also CA 107; 129; CANR 34; MTCW 1

Laishley, Alex
See Booth, Martin

Lamartine, Alphonse de
1790-1869 .... NCLC 11, 190; PC 16
See also DAM POET; DLB 217; GFL 1789
to the Present; RGWL 2, 3

Lamartine, Alphonse Marie Louis Prat de
See Lamartine, Alphonse de

Lamb, Charles 1775-1834 ..... NCLC 10, 113;
SSC 112; WLC 3
See also BRW 4; CDBLB 1789-1832; DA;
DAB; DAC; DAM MST; DLB 93, 107,
163; RGEL 2; SATA 17; TEA

Lamb, Lady Caroline 1785-1828 ... NCLC 38
See also DLB 116

Lamb, Mary Ann 1764-1847 ...... NCLC 125;
SSC 112
See also DLB 163; SATA 17

Lame Deer 1903(?)-1976 .... NNAL
See also CA 69-72

Lamming, George 1927- .... BLC 1:2, 2:2;
CLC 2, 4, 66, 144
See also BW 2, 3; CA 85-88; CANR 26,
76; CDWLB 3; CN 1, 2, 3, 4, 5, 6, 7; CP
1; DAM MULT; DLB 125; EWL 3;
MTCW 1, 2; MTFW 2005; NFS 15;
RGEL 2

Lamming, George William
See Lamming, George

L'Amour, Louis 1908-1988 .... CLC 25, 55
See also AAYA 16; AITN 2; BEST 89:2;
BPFB 2; CA 1-4R; 125; CANR 3, 25, 40;
CPW; DA3; DAM NOV, POP; DLB 206;
DLBY 1980; MTCW 1, 2; MTFW 2005;
RGAL 4; TCWW 1, 2

Lampedusa, Giuseppe di
1896-1957 .... TCLC 13
See also CA 111; 164; DLB 177; EW 11;
EWL 3; MTCW 2; MTFW 2005; RGWL
2, 3; WLIT 7

Lampman, Archibald 1861-1899 .. NCLC 25,
194
See also DLB 92; RGEL 2; TWA

Lancaster, Bruce 1896-1963 .... CLC 36
See also CA 9-10; CANR 70; CAP 1; SATA
9

Lanchester, John 1962- .... CLC 99, 280
See also CA 194; DLB 267

Landau, Mark Alexandrovich
See Aldanov, Mark (Alexandrovich)

Landau-Aldanov, Mark Alexandrovich
See Aldanov, Mark (Alexandrovich)

Landis, Jerry
See Simon, Paul

Landis, John 1950- .... CLC 26
See also CA 112; 122; CANR 128

Landolfi, Tommaso 1908-1979 .... CLC 11, 49
See also CA 127; 117; DLB 177; EWL 3

Lenin 1870-1924 .... **TCLC 67**
See also CA 121; 168
Lenin, N.
See Lenin
Lenin, Nikolai
See Lenin
Lenin, V. I.
See Lenin
Lenin, Vladimir I.
See Lenin
Lenin, Vladimir Ilyich
See Lenin
Lennon, John 1940-1980 .... **CLC 12, 35**
See also CA 102; SATA 114
Lennon, John Ono
See Lennon, John
Lennox, Charlotte 1729(?)-1804 ... **NCLC 23, 134**
See also BRWS 17; DLB 39; RGEL 2
Lentricchia, Frank, Jr.
See Lentricchia, Frank
Lentricchia, Frank 1940- .... **CLC 34**
See also CA 25-28R; CANR 19, 106, 148; DLB 246
Lenz, Gunter .... **CLC 65**
Lenz, Jakob Michael Reinhold 1751-1792 .... **LC 100**
See also DLB 94; RGWL 2, 3
Lenz, Siegfried 1926- .... **CLC 27; SSC 33**
See also CA 89-92; CANR 80, 149; CWW 2; DLB 75; EWL 3; RGSF 2; RGWL 2, 3
Leon, David
See Jacob, (Cyprien-)Max
Leon, Luis de 1527-1591 .... **LC 182**
See also DLB 318
Leonard, Dutch
See Leonard, Elmore
Leonard, Elmore 1925- .... **CLC 28, 34, 71, 120, 222**
See also AAYA 22, 59; AITN 1; BEST 89:1, 90:4; BPFB 2; CA 81-84; CANR 12, 28, 53, 76, 96, 133, 176, 219; CMW 4; CN 5, 6, 7; CPW; DA3; DAM POP; DLB 173, 226; INT CANR-28; MSW; MTCW 1, 2; MTFW 2005; RGAL 4; SATA 163; TCWW 1, 2
Leonard, Elmore John, Jr.
See Leonard, Elmore
Leonard, Hugh 1926-2009 .... **CLC 19**
See also CA 102; 283; CANR 78, 140; CBD; CD 5, 6; DFS 13, 24; DLB 13; INT CA-102
Leonard, Tom 1944- .... **CLC 289**
See also CA 77-80; CANR 13, 31; CP 2, 3, 4, 5, 6, 7
Leonov, Leonid 1899-1994 .... **CLC 92**
See also CA 129; CANR 76; DAM NOV; DLB 272; EWL 3; MTCW 1, 2; MTFW 2005
Leonov, Leonid Maksimovich
See Leonov, Leonid
Leonov, Leonid Maximovich
See Leonov, Leonid
Leopardi, (Conte) Giacomo 1798-1837 .... **NCLC 22, 129; PC 37**
See also EW 5; RGWL 2, 3; WLIT 7; WP
Le Reveler
See Artaud, Antonin
Lerman, Eleanor 1952- .... **CLC 9**
See also CA 85-88; CANR 69, 124, 184
Lerman, Rhoda 1936- .... **CLC 56**
See also CA 49-52; CANR 70
Lermontov, Mikhail Iur'evich
See Lermontov, Mikhail Yuryevich
Lermontov, Mikhail Yuryevich 1814-1841 .... **NCLC 5, 47, 126; PC 18**
See also DLB 205; EW 6; RGWL 2, 3; TWA

Leroux, Gaston 1868-1927 .... **TCLC 25**
See also CA 108; 136; CANR 69; CMW 4; MTFW 2005; NFS 20; SATA 65
Lesage, Alain-Rene 1668-1747 .... **LC 2, 28**
See also DLB 313; EW 3; GFL Beginnings to 1789; RGWL 2, 3
Leskov, N(ikolai) S(emenovich) 1831-1895
See Leskov, Nikolai (Semyonovich)
Leskov, Nikolai (Semyonovich) 1831-1895 ... **NCLC 25, 174; SSC 34, 96**
See also DLB 238
Leskov, Nikolai Semenovich
See Leskov, Nikolai (Semyonovich)
Lesser, Milton
See Marlowe, Stephen
Lessing, Doris 1919- .. **CLC 1, 2, 3, 6, 10, 15, 22, 40, 94, 170, 254; SSC 6, 61; WLCS**
See also AAYA 57; AFW; BRWS 1; CA 9-12R; CAAS 14; CANR 33, 54, 76, 122, 179; CBD; CD 5, 6; CDBLB 1960 to Present; CN 1, 2, 3, 4, 5, 6, 7; CWD; DA; DA3; DAB; DAC; DAM MST, NOV; DFS 20; DLB 15, 139; DLBY 1985; EWL 3; EXPS; FL 1:6; FW; LAIT 4; MTCW 1, 2; MTFW 2005; NFS 27; RGEL 2; RGSF 2; SFW 4; SSFS 1, 12, 20, 26, 30; TEA; WLIT 2, 4
Lessing, Doris May
See Lessing, Doris
Lessing, Gotthold Ephraim 1729-1781 .... **DC 26; LC 8, 124, 162**
See also CDWLB 2; DLB 97; EW 4; RGWL 2, 3
Lester, Julius 1939- .... **BLC 2:2**
See also AAYA 12, 51; BW 2; BYA 3, 9, 11, 12; CA 17-20R; CANR 8, 23, 43, 129, 174; CLR 2, 41, 143; JRDA; MAICYA 1, 2; MAICYAS 1; MTFW 2005; SATA 12, 74, 112, 157; YAW
Lester, Richard 1932- .... **CLC 20**
Lethem, Jonathan 1964- .... **CLC 295**
See also AAYA 43; AMWS 18; CA 150; CANR 80, 138, 165; CN 7; MTFW 2005; SFW 4
Lethem, Jonathan Allen
See Lethem, Jonathan
Letts, Tracy 1965- .... **CLC 280**
See also CA 223; CANR 209
Levenson, Jay .... **CLC 70**
Lever, Charles (James) 1806-1872 .... **NCLC 23**
See also DLB 21; RGEL 2
Leverson, Ada Esther 1862(?)-1933(?) .... **TCLC 18**
See also CA 117; 202; DLB 153; RGEL 2
Levertov, Denise 1923-1997 .. **CLC 1, 2, 3, 5, 8, 15, 28, 66; PC 11**
See also AMWS 3; CA 1-4R, 178; 163; CAAE 178; CAAS 19; CANR 3, 29, 50, 108; CDALBS; CP 1, 2, 3, 4, 5, 6; CWP; DAM POET; DLB 5, 165, 342; EWL 3; EXPP; FW; INT CANR-29; MAL 5; MTCW 1, 2; PAB; PFS 7, 17, 31; RGAL 4; RGHL; TUS; WP
Levi, Carlo 1902-1975 .... **TCLC 125**
See also CA 65-68; 53-56; CANR 10; EWL 3; RGWL 2, 3
Levi, Jonathan .... **CLC 76**
See also CA 197
Levi, Peter (Chad Tigar) 1931-2000 .... **CLC 41**
See also CA 5-8R; 187; CANR 34, 80; CP 1, 2, 3, 4, 5, 6, 7; DLB 40
Levi, Primo 1919-1987 ...... **CLC 37, 50; SSC 12, 122; TCLC 109**
See also CA 13-16R; 122; CANR 12, 33, 61, 70, 132, 171; DLB 177, 299; EWL 3; MTCW 1, 2; MTFW 2005; RGHL; RGWL 2, 3; WLIT 7

Levin, Ira 1929-2007 .... **CLC 3, 6**
See also CA 21-24R; 266; CANR 17, 44, 74, 139; CMW 4; CN 1, 2, 3, 4, 5, 6, 7; CPW; DA3; DAM POP; HGG; MTCW 1, 2; MTFW 2005; SATA 66; SATA-Obit 187; SFW 4
Levin, Ira Marvin
See Levin, Ira
Levin, Meyer 1905-1981 .... **CLC 7**
See also AITN 1; CA 9-12R; 104; CANR 15; CN 1, 2, 3; DAM POP; DLB 9, 28; DLBY 1981; MAL 5; RGHL; SATA 21; SATA-Obit 27
Levine, Albert Norman
See Levine, Norman
Levine, Norman 1923-2005 .... **CLC 54**
See also CA 73-76; 240; CAAS 23; CANR 14, 70; CN 1, 2, 3, 4, 5, 6, 7; CP 1; DLB 88
Levine, Norman Albert
See Levine, Norman
Levine, Philip 1928- .. **CLC 2, 4, 5, 9, 14, 33, 118; PC 22**
See also AMWS 5; CA 9-12R; CANR 9, 37, 52, 116, 156; CP 1, 2, 3, 4, 5, 6, 7; DAM POET; DLB 5; EWL 3; MAL 5; PFS 8
Levinson, Deirdre 1931- .... **CLC 49**
See also CA 73-76; CANR 70
Levi-Strauss, Claude 1908-2008 ...... **CLC 38, 302**
See also CA 1-4R; CANR 6, 32, 57; DLB 242; EWL 3; GFL 1789 to the Present; MTCW 1, 2; TWA
Levitin, Sonia 1934- .... **CLC 17**
See also AAYA 13, 48; CA 29-32R; CANR 14, 32, 79, 182; CLR 53; JRDA; MAICYA 1, 2; SAAS 2; SATA 4, 68, 119, 131, 192; SATA-Essay 131; YAW
Levon, O. U.
See Kesey, Ken
Levy, Amy 1861-1889 .... **NCLC 59, 203**
See also DLB 156, 240
Lewees, John
See Stockton, Francis Richard
Lewes, George Henry 1817-1878 .. **NCLC 25, 215**
See also DLB 55, 144
Lewis, Alun 1915-1944 .... **SSC 40; TCLC 3**
See also BRW 7; CA 104; 188; DLB 20, 162; PAB; RGEL 2
Lewis, C. Day
See Day Lewis, C.
Lewis, C. S. 1898-1963 .. **CLC 1, 3, 6, 14, 27, 124; WLC 4**
See also AAYA 3, 39; BPFB 2; BRWS 3; BYA 15, 16; CA 81-84; CANR 33, 71, 132; CDBLB 1945-1960; CLR 3, 27, 109; CWRI 5; DA; DA3; DAB; DAC; DAM MST, NOV, POP; DLB 15, 100, 160, 255; EWL 3; FANT; JRDA; LMFS 2; MAICYA 1, 2; MTCW 1, 2; MTFW 2005; NFS 24; RGEL 2; SATA 13, 100; SCFW 1, 2; SFW 4; SUFW 1; TEA; WCH; WYA; YAW
Lewis, Cecil Day
See Day Lewis, C.
Lewis, Clive Staples
See Lewis, C. S.
Lewis, Harry Sinclair
See Lewis, Sinclair
Lewis, Janet 1899-1998 .... **CLC 41**
See also CA 9-12R; 172; CANR 29, 63; CAP 1; CN 1, 2, 3, 4, 5, 6; DLBY 1987; RHW; TCWW 2
Lewis, Matthew Gregory 1775-1818 .... **NCLC 11, 62**
See also DLB 39, 158, 178; GL 3; HGG; LMFS 1; RGEL 2; SUFW

Lewis, Sinclair 1885-1951 ... **TCLC 4, 13, 23, 39, 215; WLC 4**
See also AMW; AMWC 1; BPFB 2; CA 104; 133; CANR 132; CDALB 1917-1929; DA; DA3; DAB; DAC; DAM MST, NOV; DLB 9, 102, 284, 331; DLBD 1; EWL 3; LAIT 3; MAL 5; MTCW 1, 2; MTFW 2005; NFS 15, 19, 22, 34; RGAL 4; TUS

Lewis, (Percy) Wyndham 1884(?)-1957 . **SSC 34; TCLC 2, 9, 104, 216**
See also AAYA 77; BRW 7; CA 104; 157; DLB 15; EWL 3; FANT; MTCW 2; MTFW 2005; RGEL 2

Lewisohn, Ludwig 1883-1955 .... **TCLC 19**
See also CA 107; 203; DLB 4, 9, 28, 102; MAL 5

Lewton, Val 1904-1951 .... **TCLC 76**
See also CA 199; IDFW 3, 4

Leyner, Mark 1956- .... **CLC 92**
See also CA 110; CANR 28, 53; DA3; DLB 292; MTCW 2; MTFW 2005

Leyton, E.K.
See Campbell, Ramsey

Lezama Lima, Jose 1910-1976 .... **CLC 4, 10, 101; HLCS 2**
See also CA 77-80; CANR 71; DAM MULT; DLB 113, 283; EWL 3; HW 1, 2; LAW; RGWL 2, 3

L'Heureux, John (Clarke) 1934- ...... **CLC 52**
See also CA 13-16R; CANR 23, 45, 88; CP 1, 2, 3, 4; DLB 244

Li, Fei-kan
See Jin, Ba

Li Ch'ing-chao 1081(?)-1141(?) .... **CMLC 71**

Lichtenberg, Georg Christoph 1742-1799 .... **LC 162**
See also DLB 94

Liddell, C. H.
See Kuttner, Henry

Lie, Jonas (Lauritz Idemil) 1833-1908(?) .... **TCLC 5**
See also CA 115

Lieber, Joel 1937-1971 .... **CLC 6**
See also CA 73-76; 29-32R

Lieber, Stanley Martin
See Lee, Stan

Lieberman, Laurence (James) 1935- .... **CLC 4, 36**
See also CA 17-20R; CANR 8, 36, 89; CP 1, 2, 3, 4, 5, 6, 7

Lieh Tzu fl. 7th cent. B.C.-5th cent. B.C. .... **CMLC 27**

Lieksman, Anders
See Haavikko, Paavo Juhani

Lifton, Robert Jay 1926- .... **CLC 67**
See also CA 17-20R; CANR 27, 78, 161; INT CANR-27; SATA 66

Lightfoot, Gordon 1938- .... **CLC 26**
See also CA 109; 242

Lightfoot, Gordon Meredith
See Lightfoot, Gordon

Lightman, Alan P. 1948- .... **CLC 81**
See also CA 141; CANR 63, 105, 138, 178; MTFW 2005; NFS 29

Lightman, Alan Paige
See Lightman, Alan P.

Ligotti, Thomas 1953- .... **CLC 44; SSC 16**
See also CA 123; CANR 49, 135; HGG; SUFW 2

Ligotti, Thomas Robert
See Ligotti, Thomas

Li Ho 791-817 .... **PC 13**

Li Ju-chen c. 1763-c. 1830 .... **NCLC 137**

Liking, Werewere 1950- .... **BLC 2:2**
See also CA 293; DLB 360; EWL 3

Lilar, Francoise
See Mallet-Joris, Francoise

Liliencron, Detlev
See Liliencron, Detlev von

Liliencron, Detlev von 1844-1909 .. **TCLC 18**
See also CA 117

Liliencron, Friedrich Adolf Axel Detlev von
See Liliencron, Detlev von

Liliencron, Friedrich Detlev von
See Liliencron, Detlev von

Lille, Alain de
See Alain de Lille

Lillo, George 1691-1739 .... **LC 131**
See also DLB 84; RGEL 2

Lilly, William 1602-1681 .... **LC 27**

Lima, Jose Lezama
See Lezama Lima, Jose

Lima Barreto, Afonso Henrique de 1881-1922 .... **TCLC 23**
See also CA 117; 181; DLB 307; LAW

Lima Barreto, Afonso Henriques de
See Lima Barreto, Afonso Henrique de

Limonov, Eduard
See Limonov, Edward

Limonov, Edward 1944- .... **CLC 67**
See also CA 137; DLB 317

Lin, Frank
See Atherton, Gertrude (Franklin Horn)

Lin, Yutang 1895-1976 .... **TCLC 149**
See also CA 45-48; 65-68; CANR 2; RGAL 4

Lincoln, Abraham 1809-1865 .... **NCLC 18, 201**
See also LAIT 2

Lincoln, Geoffrey
See Mortimer, John

Lind, Jakov 1927-2007 ... **CLC 1, 2, 4, 27, 82**
See also CA 9-12R; 257; CAAS 4; CANR 7; DLB 299; EWL 3; RGHL

Lindbergh, Anne Morrow 1906-2001 .... **CLC 82**
See also BPFB 2; CA 17-20R; 193; CANR 16, 73; DAM NOV; MTCW 1, 2; MTFW 2005; SATA 33; SATA-Obit 125; TUS

Lindbergh, Anne Spencer Morrow
See Lindbergh, Anne Morrow

Lindholm, Anna Margaret
See Haycraft, Anna

Lindsay, David 1878(?)-1945 .... **TCLC 15**
See also CA 113; 187; DLB 255; FANT; SFW 4; SUFW 1

Lindsay, Nicholas Vachel
See Lindsay, Vachel

Lindsay, Vachel 1879-1931 ..... **PC 23; TCLC 17; WLC 4**
See also AMWS 1; CA 114; 135; CANR 79; CDALB 1865-1917; DA; DA3; DAC; DAM MST, POET; DLB 54; EWL 3; EXPP; MAL 5; RGAL 4; SATA 40; WP

Linke-Poot
See Doeblin, Alfred

Linney, Romulus 1930-2011 .... **CLC 51**
See also CA 1-4R; CAD; CANR 40, 44, 79; CD 5, 6; CSW; RGAL 4

Linton, Eliza Lynn 1822-1898 .... **NCLC 41**
See also DLB 18

Li Po 701-763 .... **CMLC 2, 86; PC 29**
See also PFS 20; WP

Lippard, George 1822-1854 .... **NCLC 198**
See also DLB 202

Lipsius, Justus 1547-1606 .... **LC 16**

Lipsyte, Robert 1938- .... **CLC 21**
See also AAYA 7, 45; CA 17-20R; CANR 8, 57, 146, 189; CLR 23, 76; DA; DAC; DAM MST, NOV; JRDA; LAIT 5; MAICYA 1, 2; NFS 35; SATA 5, 68, 113, 161, 198; WYA; YAW

Lipsyte, Robert Michael
See Lipsyte, Robert

Lish, Gordon 1934- .... **CLC 45; SSC 18**
See also CA 113; 117; CANR 79, 151; DLB 130; INT CA-117

Lish, Gordon Jay
See Lish, Gordon

Lispector, Clarice 1925(?)-1977 .... **CLC 43; HLCS 2; SSC 34, 96**
See also CA 139; 116; CANR 71; CDWLB 3; DLB 113, 307; DNFS 1; EWL 3; FW; HW 2; LAW; RGSF 2; RGWL 2, 3; WLIT 1

Liszt, Franz 1811-1886 .... **NCLC 199**

Littell, Robert 1935(?)- .... **CLC 42**
See also CA 109; 112; CANR 64, 115, 162, 217; CMW 4

Little, Malcolm
See Malcolm X

Littlewit, Humphrey Gent.
See Lovecraft, H. P.

Litwos
See Sienkiewicz, Henryk (Adam Alexander Pius)

Liu, E. 1857-1909 .... **TCLC 15**
See also CA 115; 190; DLB 328

Lively, Penelope 1933- .... **CLC 32, 50, 306**
See also BPFB 2; CA 41-44R; CANR 29, 67, 79, 131, 172; CLR 7, 159; CN 5, 6, 7; CWRI 5; DAM NOV; DLB 14, 161, 207, 326; FANT; JRDA; MAICYA 1, 2; MTCW 1, 2; MTFW 2005; SATA 7, 60, 101, 164; TEA

Lively, Penelope Margaret
See Lively, Penelope

Livesay, Dorothy (Kathleen) 1909-1996 .... **CLC 4, 15, 79**
See also AITN 2; CA 25-28R; CAAS 8; CANR 36, 67; CP 1, 2, 3, 4, 5; DAC; DAM MST, POET; DLB 68; FW; MTCW 1; RGEL 2; TWA

Livius Andronicus c. 284B.C.-c. 204B.C. .... **CMLC 102**

Livy c. 59B.C.-c. 12 .... **CMLC 11**
See also AW 2; CDWLB 1; DLB 211; RGWL 2, 3; WLIT 8

Li Yaotang
See Jin, Ba

Li-Young, Lee
See Lee, Li-Young

Lizardi, Jose Joaquin Fernandez de 1776-1827 .... **NCLC 30**
See also LAW

Llewellyn, Richard
See Llewellyn Lloyd, Richard Dafydd Vivian

Llewellyn Lloyd, Richard Dafydd Vivian 1906-1983 .... **CLC 7, 80**
See also CA 53-56; 111; CANR 7, 71; DLB 15; NFS 30; SATA 11; SATA-Obit 37

Llosa, Jorge Mario Pedro Vargas
See Vargas Llosa, Mario

Llosa, Mario Vargas
See Vargas Llosa, Mario

Lloyd, Manda
See Mander, (Mary) Jane

Lloyd Webber, Andrew 1948- .... **CLC 21**
See also AAYA 1, 38; CA 116; 149; DAM DRAM; DFS 7; SATA 56

Llull, Ramon c. 1235-c. 1316 .... **CMLC 12, 114**

Lobb, Ebenezer
See Upward, Allen

Lochhead, Liz 1947- .... **CLC 286**
See also BRWS 17; CA 81-84; CANR 79; CBD; CD 5, 6; CP 2, 3, 4, 5, 6, 7; CWD; CWP; DLB 310

Mackey, Nathaniel Ernest
See Mackey, Nathaniel

MacKinnon, Catharine
See MacKinnon, Catharine A.

MacKinnon, Catharine A. 1946- .... **CLC 181**
See also CA 128; 132; CANR 73, 140, 189;
FW; MTCW 2; MTFW 2005

Mackintosh, Elizabeth
1896(?)-1952 .... **TCLC 14**
See also CA 110; CMW 4; DLB 10, 77;
MSW

Macklin, Charles 1699-1797 .... **LC 132**
See also DLB 89; RGEL 2

MacLaren, James
See Grieve, C. M.

MacLaverty, Bernard 1942- ..... **CLC 31, 243**
See also CA 116; 118; CANR 43, 88, 168;
CN 5, 6, 7; DLB 267; INT CA-118; RGSF
2

MacLean, Alistair 1922(?)-1987 .. **CLC 3, 13, 50, 63**
See also CA 57-60; 121; CANR 28, 61;
CMW 4; CP 2, 3, 4, 5, 6, 7; CPW; DAM
POP; DLB 276; MTCW 1; SATA 23;
SATA-Obit 50; TCWW 2

MacLean, Alistair Stuart
See MacLean, Alistair

Maclean, Norman (Fitzroy)
1902-1990 .... **CLC 78; SSC 13, 136**
See also AMWS 14; CA 102; 132; CANR
49; CPW; DAM POP; DLB 206; TCWW
2

MacLeish, Archibald 1892-1982 ... **CLC 3, 8, 14, 68; DC 43; PC 47**
See also AMW; CA 9-12R; 106; CAD;
CANR 33, 63; CDALBS; CP 1, 2; DAM
POET; DFS 15; DLB 4, 7, 45; DLBY
1982; EWL 3; EXPP; MAL 5; MTCW 1,
2; MTFW 2005; PAB; PFS 5; RGAL 4;
TUS

MacLennan, (John) Hugh
1907-1990 .... **CLC 2, 14, 92**
See also CA 5-8R; 142; CANR 33; CN 1,
2, 3, 4; DAC; DAM MST; DLB 68; EWL
3; MTCW 1, 2; MTFW 2005; RGEL 2;
TWA

MacLeod, Alistair 1936- .. **CLC 56, 165; SSC 90**
See also CA 123; CCA 1; DAC; DAM
MST; DLB 60; MTCW 2; MTFW 2005;
RGSF 2; TCLE 1:2

Macleod, Fiona
See Sharp, William

MacNeice, (Frederick) Louis
1907-1963 .... **CLC 1, 4, 10, 53; PC 61**
See also BRW 7; CA 85-88; CANR 61;
DAB; DAM POET; DLB 10, 20; EWL 3;
MTCW 1, 2; MTFW 2005; RGEL 2

MacNeill, Dand
See Fraser, George MacDonald

Macpherson, James 1736-1796 .... **CMLC 28; LC 29; PC 97**
See also BRWS 8; DLB 109, 336; RGEL 2

Macpherson, (Jean) Jay 1931- .... **CLC 14**
See also CA 5-8R; CANR 90; CP 1, 2, 3, 4,
6, 7; CWP; DLB 53

Macrobius fl. 430- .... **CMLC 48**

MacShane, Frank 1927-1999 .... **CLC 39**
See also CA 9-12R; 186; CANR 3, 33; DLB
111

Macumber, Mari
See Sandoz, Mari(e Susette)

Madach, Imre 1823-1864 .... **NCLC 19**

Madden, (Jerry) David 1933- .... **CLC 5, 15**
See also CA 1-4R; CAAS 3; CANR 4, 45;
CN 3, 4, 5, 6, 7; CSW; DLB 6; MTCW 1

Maddern, Al(an)
See Ellison, Harlan

Madhubuti, Haki R. 1942- .... **BLC 1:2; CLC 2; PC 5**
See also BW 2, 3; CA 73-76; CANR 24,
51, 73, 139; CP 2, 3, 4, 5, 6, 7; CSW;
DAM MULT, POET; DLB 5, 41; DLBD
8; EWL 3; MAL 5; MTCW 2; MTFW
2005; RGAL 4

Madison, James 1751-1836 .... **NCLC 126**
See also DLB 37

Maepenn, Hugh
See Kuttner, Henry

Maepenn, K. H.
See Kuttner, Henry

Maeterlinck, Maurice 1862-1949 .... **DC 32; TCLC 3, 251**
See also CA 104; 136; CANR 80; DAM
DRAM; DLB 192, 331; EW 8; EWL 3;
GFL 1789 to the Present; LMFS 2; RGWL
2, 3; SATA 66; TWA

Maginn, William 1794-1842 .... **NCLC 8**
See also DLB 110, 159

Mahapatra, Jayanta 1928- .... **CLC 33**
See also CA 73-76; CAAS 9; CANR 15,
33, 66, 87; CP 4, 5, 6, 7; DAM MULT;
DLB 323

Mahfouz, Nagib
See Mahfouz, Naguib

Mahfouz, Naguib 1911(?)-2006 . **CLC 52, 55, 153; SSC 66**
See also AAYA 49; AFW; BEST 89:2; CA
128; 253; CANR 55, 101; DA3; DAM
NOV; DLB 346; DLBY 1988; MTCW 1,
2; MTFW 2005; RGSF 2; RGWL 2, 3;
SSFS 9, 33; WLIT 2

Mahfouz, Naguib Abdel Aziz Al-Sabilgi
See Mahfouz, Naguib

Mahfouz, Najib
See Mahfouz, Naguib

Mahfuz, Najib
See Mahfouz, Naguib

Mahon, Derek 1941- .... **CLC 27; PC 60**
See also BRWS 6; CA 113; 128; CANR 88;
CP 1, 2, 3, 4, 5, 6, 7; DLB 40; EWL 3

Maiakovskii, Vladimir
See Mayakovski, Vladimir

Mailer, Norman 1923-2007 ... **CLC 1, 2, 3, 4, 5, 8, 11, 14, 28, 39, 74, 111, 234**
See also AAYA 31; AITN 2; AMW; AMWC
2; AMWR 2; BPFB 2; CA 9-12R; 266;
CABS 1; CANR 28, 74, 77, 130, 196;
CDALB 1968-1988; CN 1, 2, 3, 4, 5, 6,
7; CPW; DA; DA3; DAB; DAC; DAM
MST, NOV, POP; DLB 2, 16, 28, 185,
278; DLBD 3; DLBY 1980, 1983; EWL
3; MAL 5; MTCW 1, 2; MTFW 2005;
NFS 10; RGAL 4; TUS

Mailer, Norman Kingsley
See Mailer, Norman

Maillet, Antonine 1929- .... **CLC 54, 118**
See also CA 115; 120; CANR 46, 74, 77,
134; CCA 1; CWW 2; DAC; DLB 60;
INT CA-120; MTCW 2; MTFW 2005

Maimonides, Moses 1135-1204 ..... **CMLC 76**
See also DLB 115

Mais, Roger 1905-1955 .... **TCLC 8**
See also BW 1, 3; CA 105; 124; CANR 82;
CDWLB 3; DLB 125; EWL 3; MTCW 1;
RGEL 2

Maistre, Joseph 1753-1821 .... **NCLC 37**
See also GFL 1789 to the Present

Maitland, Frederic William
1850-1906 .... **TCLC 65**

Maitland, Sara (Louise) 1950- .... **CLC 49**
See also BRWS 11; CA 69-72; CANR 13,
59; DLB 271; FW

Major, Clarence 1936- ...... **BLC 1:2; CLC 3, 19, 48**
See also AFAW 2; BW 2, 3; CA 21-24R;
CAAS 6; CANR 13, 25, 53, 82; CN 3, 4,
5, 6, 7; CP 2, 3, 4, 5, 6, 7; CSW; DAM
MULT; DLB 33; EWL 3; MAL 5; MSW

Major, Kevin (Gerald) 1949- .... **CLC 26**
See also AAYA 16; CA 97-100; CANR 21,
38, 112; CLR 11; DAC; DLB 60; INT
CANR-21; JRDA; MAICYA 1, 2; MAIC-
YAS 1; SATA 32, 82, 134; WYA; YAW

Maki, James
See Ozu, Yasujiro

Makin, Bathsua 1600-1675(?) .... **LC 137**

Makine, Andrei
See Makine, Andrei

Makine, Andrei 1957- .... **CLC 198**
See also CA 176; CANR 103, 162; MTFW
2005

Malabaila, Damiano
See Levi, Primo

Malamud, Bernard 1914-1986 .. **CLC 1, 2, 3, 5, 8, 9, 11, 18, 27, 44, 78, 85; SSC 15, 147; TCLC 129, 184; WLC 4**
See also AAYA 16; AMWS 1; BPFB 2;
BYA 15; CA 5-8R; 118; CABS 1; CANR
28, 62, 114; CDALB 1941-1968; CN 1, 2,
3, 4; CPW; DA; DA3; DAB; DAC; DAM
MST, NOV, POP; DLB 2, 28, 152; DLBY
1980, 1986; EWL 3; EXPS; LAIT 4;
LATS 1:1; MAL 5; MTCW 1, 2; MTFW
2005; NFS 27; RGAL 4; RGHL; RGSF 2;
SSFS 8, 13, 16; TUS

Malan, Herman
See Bosman, Herman Charles; Bosman,
Herman Charles

Malaparte, Curzio 1898-1957 .... **TCLC 52**
See also DLB 264

Malcolm, Dan
See Silverberg, Robert

Malcolm, Janet 1934- .... **CLC 201**
See also CA 123; CANR 89, 199; NCFS 1

Malcolm X 1925-1965 ..... **BLC 1:2; CLC 82, 117; WLCS**
See also BW 1, 3; CA 125; 111; CANR 82;
DA; DA3; DAB; DAC; DAM MST,
MULT; LAIT 5; MTCW 1, 2; MTFW
2005; NCFS 3

Malebranche, Nicolas 1638-1715 .... **LC 133**
See also GFL Beginnings to 1789

Malherbe, Francois de 1555-1628 .... **LC 5**
See also DLB 327; GFL Beginnings to 1789

Mallarme, Stephane 1842-1898 ...... **NCLC 4, 41, 210; PC 4, 102**
See also DAM POET; DLB 217; EW 7;
GFL 1789 to the Present; LMFS 2; RGWL
2, 3; TWA

Mallet-Joris, Francoise 1930- .... **CLC 11**
See also CA 65-68; CANR 17; CWW 2;
DLB 83; EWL 3; GFL 1789 to the Present

Malley, Ern
See McAuley, James Phillip

Mallon, Thomas 1951- .... **CLC 172**
See also CA 110; CANR 29, 57, 92, 196;
DLB 350

Mallowan, Agatha Christie
See Christie, Agatha

Maloff, Saul 1922- .... **CLC 5**
See also CA 33-36R

Malone, Louis
See MacNeice, (Frederick) Louis

Malone, Michael 1942- .... **CLC 43**
See also CA 77-80; CANR 14, 32, 57, 114,
214

Malone, Michael Christopher
See Malone, Michael

Malory, Sir Thomas 1410(?)-1471(?) . **LC 11, 88; WLCS**
See also BRW 1; BRWR 2; CDBLB Before 1660; DA; DAB; DAC; DAM MST; DLB 146; EFS 1:2, 2:2; RGEL 2; SATA 59; SATA-Brief 33; TEA; WLIT 3

Malouf, David 1934- .... **CLC 28, 86, 245**
See also BRWS 12; CA 124; CANR 50, 76, 180; CN 3, 4, 5, 6, 7; CP 1, 3, 4, 5, 6, 7; DLB 289; EWL 3; MTCW 2; MTFW 2005; SSFS 24

Malouf, George Joseph David
See Malouf, David

Malraux, Andre 1901-1976 . **CLC 1, 4, 9, 13, 15, 57; TCLC 209**
See also BPFB 2; CA 21-22; 69-72; CANR 34, 58; CAP 2; DA3; DAM NOV; DLB 72; EW 12; EWL 3; GFL 1789 to the Present; MTCW 1, 2; MTFW 2005; RGWL 2, 3; TWA

Malraux, Georges-Andre
See Malraux, Andre

Malthus, Thomas Robert 1766-1834 .... **NCLC 145**
See also DLB 107, 158; RGEL 2

Malzberg, Barry N(athaniel) 1939- ... **CLC 7**
See also CA 61-64; CAAS 4; CANR 16; CMW 4; DLB 8; SFW 4

Mamet, David 1947- .. **CLC 9, 15, 34, 46, 91, 166; DC 4, 24**
See also AAYA 3, 60; AMWS 14; CA 81-84; CABS 3; CAD; CANR 15, 41, 67, 72, 129, 172; CD 5, 6; DA3; DAM DRAM; DFS 2, 3, 6, 12, 15; DLB 7; EWL 3; IDFW 4; MAL 5; MTCW 1, 2; MTFW 2005; RGAL 4

Mamet, David Alan
See Mamet, David

Mamoulian, Rouben (Zachary) 1897-1987 .... **CLC 16**
See also CA 25-28R; 124; CANR 85

Mandelshtam, Osip
See Mandelstam, Osip

Mandel'shtam, Osip Emil'evich
See Mandelstam, Osip

Mandelstam, Osip 1891(?)-1943(?) .... **PC 14; TCLC 2, 6, 225**
See also CA 104; 150; DLB 295; EW 10; EWL 3; MTCW 2; RGWL 2, 3; TWA

Mandelstam, Osip Emilievich
See Mandelstam, Osip

Mander, (Mary) Jane 1877-1949 ... **TCLC 31**
See also CA 162; RGEL 2

Mandeville, Bernard 1670-1733 .... **LC 82**
See also DLB 101

Mandeville, Sir John fl. 1350- ...... **CMLC 19**
See also DLB 146

Mandiargues, Andre Pieyre de
See Pieyre de Mandiargues, Andre

Mandrake, Ethel Belle
See Thurman, Wallace (Henry)

Mangan, James Clarence 1803-1849 .... **NCLC 27**
See also BRWS 13; RGEL 2

Maniere, J. E.
See Giraudoux, Jean

Mankell, Henning 1948- .... **CLC 292**
See also CA 187; CANR 163, 200

Mankiewicz, Herman (Jacob) 1897-1953 .... **TCLC 85**
See also CA 120; 169; DLB 26; IDFW 3, 4

Manley, (Mary) Delariviere 1672(?)-1724 .... **LC 1, 42**
See also DLB 39, 80; RGEL 2

Mann, Abel
See Creasey, John

Mann, Emily 1952- .... **DC 7**
See also CA 130; CAD; CANR 55; CD 5, 6; CWD; DFS 28; DLB 266

Mann, Erica
See Jong, Erica

Mann, (Luiz) Heinrich 1871-1950 ... **TCLC 9**
See also CA 106; 164, 181; DLB 66, 118; EW 8; EWL 3; RGWL 2, 3

Mann, Paul Thomas
See Mann, Thomas

Mann, Thomas 1875-1955 ...... **SSC 5, 80, 82; TCLC 2, 8, 14, 21, 35, 44, 60, 168, 236; WLC 4**
See also BPFB 2; CA 104; 128; CANR 133; CDWLB 2; DA; DA3; DAB; DAC; DAM MST, NOV; DLB 66, 331; EW 9; EWL 3; GLL 1; LATS 1:1; LMFS 1; MTCW 1, 2; MTFW 2005; NFS 17; RGSF 2; RGWL 2, 3; SSFS 4, 9; TWA

Mannheim, Karl 1893-1947 .... **TCLC 65**
See also CA 204

Manning, David
See Faust, Frederick

Manning, Frederic 1882-1935 .... **TCLC 25**
See also CA 124; 216; DLB 260

Manning, Olivia 1915-1980 .... **CLC 5, 19**
See also CA 5-8R; 101; CANR 29; CN 1, 2; EWL 3; FW; MTCW 1; RGEL 2

Mannyng, Robert c. 1264-c. 1340 .... **CMLC 83**
See also DLB 146

Mano, D. Keith 1942- .... **CLC 2, 10**
See also CA 25-28R; CAAS 6; CANR 26, 57; DLB 6

Mansfield, Katherine 1888-1923 .. **SSC 9, 23, 38, 81; TCLC 2, 8, 39, 164; WLC 4**
See also BPFB 2; BRW 7; CA 104; 134; DA; DA3; DAB; DAC; DAM MST; DLB 162; EWL 3; EXPS; FW; GLL 1; MTCW 2; RGEL 2; RGSF 2; SSFS 2, 8, 10, 11, 29; TEA; WWE 1

Mansfield, Kathleen
See Mansfield, Katherine

Manso, Peter 1940- .... **CLC 39**
See also CA 29-32R; CANR 44, 156

Mantecon, Juan Jimenez
See Jimenez, Juan Ramon

Mantel, Hilary 1952- .... **CLC 144, 309**
See also CA 125; CANR 54, 101, 161, 207; CN 5, 6, 7; DLB 271; RHW

Mantel, Hilary Mary
See Mantel, Hilary

Manton, Peter
See Creasey, John

Man Without a Spleen, A
See Chekhov, Anton

Manzano, Juan Francisco 1797(?)-1854 .... **NCLC 155**

Manzoni, Alessandro 1785-1873 ... **NCLC 29, 98**
See also EW 5; RGWL 2, 3; TWA; WLIT 7

Map, Walter 1140-1209 .... **CMLC 32**

Mapu, Abraham (ben Jekutiel) 1808-1867 .... **NCLC 18**

Mara, Sally
See Queneau, Raymond

Maracle, Lee 1950- .... **NNAL**
See also CA 149

Marat, Jean Paul 1743-1793 .... **LC 10**

Marcel, Gabriel Honore 1889-1973 . **CLC 15**
See also CA 102; 45-48; EWL 3; MTCW 1, 2

March, William 1893-1954 .... **TCLC 96**
See also CA 108; 216; DLB 9, 86, 316; MAL 5

Marchbanks, Samuel
See Davies, Robertson

Marchi, Giacomo
See Bassani, Giorgio

Marcus Aurelius
See Aurelius, Marcus

Marcuse, Herbert 1898-1979 .... **TCLC 207**
See also CA 188; 89-92; DLB 242

Marguerite
See de Navarre, Marguerite

Marguerite d'Angouleme
See de Navarre, Marguerite

Marguerite de Navarre
See de Navarre, Marguerite

Margulies, Donald 1954- .... **CLC 76**
See also AAYA 57; CA 200; CD 6; DFS 13; DLB 228

Marias, Javier 1951- .... **CLC 239**
See also CA 167; CANR 109, 139; DLB 322; HW 2; MTFW 2005

Marie de France c. 12th cent. - ...... **CMLC 8, 111; PC 22**
See also DLB 208; FW; RGWL 2, 3

Marie de l'Incarnation 1599-1672 ..... **LC 10, 168**

Marier, Captain Victor
See Griffith, D.W.

Mariner, Scott
See Pohl, Frederik

Marinetti, Filippo Tommaso 1876-1944 .... **TCLC 10**
See also CA 107; DLB 114, 264; EW 9; EWL 3; WLIT 7

Marino, Giambattista 1569-1625 ...... **LC 181**
See also DLB 339; WLIT 7

Marivaux, Pierre Carlet de Chamblain de 1688-1763 .... **DC 7; LC 4, 123**
See also DLB 314; GFL Beginnings to 1789; RGWL 2, 3; TWA

Markandaya, Kamala 1924-2004 ...... **CLC 8, 38, 290**
See also BYA 13; CA 77-80; 227; CN 1, 2, 3, 4, 5, 6, 7; DLB 323; EWL 3; MTFW 2005; NFS 13

Markfield, Wallace (Arthur) 1926-2002 .... **CLC 8**
See also CA 69-72; 208; CAAS 3; CN 1, 2, 3, 4, 5, 6, 7; DLB 2, 28; DLBY 2002

Markham, Edwin 1852-1940 .... **TCLC 47**
See also CA 160; DLB 54, 186; MAL 5; RGAL 4

Markham, Robert
See Amis, Kingsley

Marks, J.
See Highwater, Jamake (Mamake)

Marks-Highwater, J.
See Highwater, Jamake (Mamake)

Markson, David M. 1927-2010 .... **CLC 67**
See also AMWS 17; CA 49-52; CANR 1, 91, 158; CN 5, 6

Markson, David Merrill
See Markson, David M.

Marlatt, Daphne (Buckle) 1942- .... **CLC 168**
See also CA 25-28R; CANR 17, 39; CN 6, 7; CP 4, 5, 6, 7; CWP; DLB 60; FW

Marley, Bob
See Marley, Robert Nesta

Marley, Robert Nesta 1945-1981 ...... **CLC 17**
See also CA 107; 103

Marlowe, Christopher 1564-1593 . **DC 1; LC 22, 47, 117; PC 57; WLC 4**
See also BRW 1; BRWR 1; CDBLB Before 1660; DA; DA3; DAB; DAC; DAM DRAM, MST; DFS 1, 5, 13, 21; DLB 62; EXPP; LMFS 1; PFS 22; RGEL 2; TEA; WLIT 3

Marlowe, Stephen 1928-2008 .... **CLC 70**
See also CA 13-16R; 269; CANR 6, 55; CMW 4; SFW 4

Marmion, Shakerley 1603-1639 .... **LC 89**
See also DLB 58; RGEL 2

Marmontel, Jean-Francois 1723-1799 .. **LC 2**
See also DLB 314

Maron, Monika 1941- .... **CLC 165**
See also CA 201

Marot, Clement c. 1496-1544 .... **LC 133**
See also DLB 327; GFL Beginnings to 1789
Marquand, John P(hillips)
1893-1960 .... **CLC 2, 10**
See also AMW; BPFB 2; CA 85-88; CANR
73; CMW 4; DLB 9, 102; EWL 3; MAL
5; MTCW 2; RGAL 4
Marques, Rene 1919-1979 .. **CLC 96; HLC 2**
See also CA 97-100; 85-88; CANR 78;
DAM MULT; DLB 305; EWL 3; HW 1,
2; LAW; RGSF 2
Marquez, Gabriel Garcia
See Garcia Marquez, Gabriel
Marquez, Gabriel Garcia
See Garcia Marquez, Gabriel
Marquis, Don(ald Robert Perry)
1878-1937 .... **TCLC 7**
See also CA 104; 166; DLB 11, 25; MAL
5; RGAL 4
Marquis de Sade
See Sade, Donatien Alphonse Francois
Marric, J. J.
See Creasey, John
Marryat, Frederick 1792-1848 .... **NCLC 3**
See also DLB 21, 163; RGEL 2; WCH
Marsden, James
See Creasey, John
Marse, Juan 1933- .... **CLC 302**
See also CA 254; DLB 322
Marsh, Edith Ngaio
See Marsh, Ngaio
Marsh, Edward 1872-1953 .... **TCLC 99**
Marsh, Ngaio 1895-1982 .... **CLC 7, 53**
See also CA 9-12R; CANR 6, 58; CMW 4;
CN 1, 2, 3; CPW; DAM POP; DLB 77;
MSW; MTCW 1, 2; RGEL 2; TEA
Marshall, Alan
See Westlake, Donald E.
Marshall, Allen
See Westlake, Donald E.
Marshall, Garry 1934- .... **CLC 17**
See also AAYA 3; CA 111; SATA 60
Marshall, Paule 1929- .... **BLC 1:3, 2:3; CLC
27, 72, 253; SSC 3**
See also AFAW 1, 2; AMWS 11; BPFB 2;
BW 2, 3; CA 77-80; CANR 25, 73, 129,
209; CN 1, 2, 3, 4, 5, 6, 7; DA3; DAM
MULT; DLB 33, 157, 227; EWL 3; LATS
1:2; MAL 5; MTCW 1, 2; MTFW 2005;
NFS 36; RGAL 4; SSFS 15
Marshallik
See Zangwill, Israel
Marsilius of Inghen c.
1340-1396 .... **CMLC 106**
Marsten, Richard
See Hunter, Evan
Marston, John 1576-1634 ...... **DC 37; LC 33,
172**
See also BRW 2; DAM DRAM; DLB 58,
172; RGEL 2
Martel, Yann 1963- .... **CLC 192**
See also AAYA 67; CA 146; CANR 114;
DLB 326, 334; LNFS 1; MTFW 2005;
NFS 27
Martens, Adolphe-Adhemar
See Ghelderode, Michel de
Martha, Henry
See Harris, Mark
Marti, Jose 1853-1895 ..... **HLC 2; NCLC 63;
PC 76**
See also DAM MULT; DLB 290; HW 2;
LAW; RGWL 2, 3; WLIT 1
Martial c. 40-c. 104 .... **CMLC 35; PC 10**
See also AW 2; CDWLB 1; DLB 211;
RGWL 2, 3
Martin, Ken
See Hubbard, L. Ron
Martin, Richard
See Creasey, John

Martin, Steve 1945- .... **CLC 30, 217**
See also AAYA 53; CA 97-100; CANR 30,
100, 140, 195; DFS 19; MTCW 1; MTFW
2005
Martin, Valerie 1948- .... **CLC 89**
See also BEST 90:2; CA 85-88; CANR 49,
89, 165, 200
Martin, Violet Florence 1862-1915 .. **SSC 56;
TCLC 51**
Martin, Webber
See Silverberg, Robert
Martindale, Patrick Victor
See White, Patrick
Martin du Gard, Roger
1881-1958 .... **TCLC 24**
See also CA 118; CANR 94; DLB 65, 331;
EWL 3; GFL 1789 to the Present; RGWL
2, 3
Martineau, Harriet 1802-1876 ...... **NCLC 26,
137**
See also BRWS 15; DLB 21, 55, 159, 163,
166, 190; FW; RGEL 2; YABC 2
Martines, Julia
See O'Faolain, Julia
Martinez, Enrique Gonzalez
See Gonzalez Martinez, Enrique
Martinez, Jacinto Benavente y
See Benavente, Jacinto
Martinez de la Rosa, Francisco de Paula
1787-1862 .... **NCLC 102**
See also TWA
Martinez Ruiz, Jose 1873-1967 .... **CLC 11**
See also CA 93-96; DLB 322; EW 3; EWL
3; HW 1
Martinez Sierra, Gregorio
See Martinez Sierra, Maria
Martinez Sierra, Gregorio
1881-1947 .... **TCLC 6**
See also CA 115; EWL 3
Martinez Sierra, Maria 1874-1974 .. **TCLC 6**
See also CA 250; 115; EWL 3
Martinez Sierra, Maria de la O'LeJarraga
See Martinez Sierra, Maria
Martinsen, Martin
See Follett, Ken
Martinson, Harry (Edmund)
1904-1978 .... **CLC 14**
See also CA 77-80; CANR 34, 130; DLB
259, 331; EWL 3
Marti y Perez, Jose Julian
See Marti, Jose
Martyn, Edward 1859-1923 .... **TCLC 131**
See also CA 179; DLB 10; RGEL 2
Marut, Ret
See Traven, B.
Marut, Robert
See Traven, B.
Marvell, Andrew 1621-1678 ... **LC 4, 43, 179;
PC 10, 86; WLC 4**
See also BRW 2; BRWR 2; CDBLB 1660-
1789; DA; DAB; DAC; DAM MST,
POET; DLB 131; EXPP; PFS 5; RGEL 2;
TEA; WP
Marx, Karl 1818-1883 .... **NCLC 17, 114**
See also DLB 129; LATS 1:1; TWA
Marx, Karl Heinrich
See Marx, Karl
Masaoka, Shiki -1902
See Masaoka, Tsunenori
Masaoka, Tsunenori 1867-1902 ..... **TCLC 18**
See also CA 117; 191; EWL 3; RGWL 3;
TWA
Masaoka Shiki
See Masaoka, Tsunenori

Masefield, John (Edward)
1878-1967 .... **CLC 11, 47; PC 78**
See also CA 19-20; 25-28R; CANR 33;
CAP 2; CDBLB 1890-1914; CLR 164;
DAM POET; DLB 10, 19, 153, 160; EWL
3; EXPP; FANT; MTCW 1, 2; PFS 5;
RGEL 2; SATA 19
Maso, Carole 1955(?)- .... **CLC 44**
See also CA 170; CANR 148; CN 7; GLL
2; RGAL 4
Mason, Bobbie Ann 1940- ... **CLC 28, 43, 82,
154, 303; SSC 4, 101**
See also AAYA 5, 42; AMWS 8; BPFB 2;
CA 53-56; CANR 11, 31, 58, 83, 125,
169; CDALBS; CN 5, 6, 7; CSW; DA3;
DLB 173; DLBY 1987; EWL 3; EXPS;
INT CANR-31; MAL 5; MTCW 1, 2;
MTFW 2005; NFS 4; RGAL 4; RGSF 2;
SSFS 3, 8, 20; TCLE 1:2; YAW
Mason, Ernst
See Pohl, Frederik
Mason, Hunni B.
See Sternheim, (William Adolf) Carl
Mason, Lee W.
See Malzberg, Barry N(athaniel)
Mason, Nick 1945- .... **CLC 35**
Mason, Tally
See Derleth, August (William)
Mass, Anna .... **CLC 59**
Mass, William
See Gibson, William
Massinger, Philip 1583-1640 .. **DC 39; LC 70**
See also BRWS 11; DLB 58; RGEL 2
Master Lao
See Lao Tzu
Masters, Edgar Lee 1868-1950 ...... **PC 1, 36;
TCLC 2, 25; WLCS**
See also AMWS 1; CA 104; 133; CDALB
1865-1917; DA; DAC; DAM MST,
POET; DLB 54; EWL 3; EXPP; MAL 5;
MTCW 1, 2; MTFW 2005; PFS 37;
RGAL 4; TUS; WP
Masters, Hilary 1928- .... **CLC 48**
See also CA 25-28R, 217; CAAE 217;
CANR 13, 47, 97, 171; CN 6, 7; DLB
244
Masters, Hilary Thomas
See Masters, Hilary
Mastrosimone, William 1947- .... **CLC 36**
See also CA 186; CAD; CD 5, 6
Mathe, Albert
See Camus, Albert
Mather, Cotton 1663-1728 .... **LC 38**
See also AMWS 2; CDALB 1640-1865;
DLB 24, 30, 140; RGAL 4; TUS
Mather, Increase 1639-1723 .... **LC 38, 161**
See also DLB 24
Mathers, Marshall
See Eminem
Mathers, Marshall Bruce
See Eminem
Matheson, Richard 1926- .... **CLC 37, 267**
See also AAYA 31; CA 97-100; CANR 88,
99; DLB 8, 44; HGG; INT CA-97-100;
SCFW 1, 2; SFW 4; SUFW 2
Matheson, Richard Burton
See Matheson, Richard
Mathews, Harry 1930- .... **CLC 6, 52**
See also CA 21-24R; CAAS 6; CANR 18,
40, 98, 160; CN 5, 6, 7
Mathews, John Joseph 1894-1979 .. **CLC 84;
NNAL**
See also CA 19-20; 142; CANR 45; CAP 2;
DAM MULT; DLB 175; TCWW 1, 2
Mathias, Roland 1915-2007 .... **CLC 45**
See also CA 97-100; 263; CANR 19, 41;
CP 1, 2, 3, 4, 5, 6, 7; DLB 27
Mathias, Roland Glyn
See Mathias, Roland

Matsuo Basho 1644(?)-1694 ...... **LC 62; PC 3**
See also DAM POET; PFS 2, 7, 18; RGWL
2, 3; WP

Mattheson, Rodney
See Creasey, John

Matthew, James
See Barrie, J. M.

Matthew of Vendome c. 1130-c.
1200 .... **CMLC 99**
See also DLB 208

Matthews, (James) Brander
1852-1929 .... **TCLC 95**
See also CA 181; DLB 71, 78; DLBD 13

Matthews, Greg 1949- .... **CLC 45**
See also CA 135

Matthews, William (Procter III)
1942-1997 .... **CLC 40**
See also AMWS 9; CA 29-32R; 162; CAAS
18; CANR 12, 57; CP 2, 3, 4, 5, 6; DLB
5

Matthias, John (Edward) 1941- .... **CLC 9**
See also CA 33-36R; CANR 56; CP 4, 5, 6,
7

Matthiessen, F(rancis) O(tto)
1902-1950 .... **TCLC 100**
See also CA 185; DLB 63; MAL 5

Matthiessen, Francis Otto
See Matthiessen, F(rancis) O(tto)

Matthiessen, Peter 1927- ... **CLC 5, 7, 11, 32,
64, 245**
See also AAYA 6, 40; AMWS 5; ANW;
BEST 90:4; BPFB 2; CA 9-12R; CANR
21, 50, 73, 100, 138; CN 1, 2, 3, 4, 5, 6,
7; DA3; DAM NOV; DLB 6, 173, 275;
MAL 5; MTCW 1, 2; MTFW 2005; SATA
27

Maturin, Charles Robert
1780(?)-1824 .... **NCLC 6, 169**
See also BRWS 8; DLB 178; GL 3; HGG;
LMFS 1; RGEL 2; SUFW

Matute (Ausejo), Ana Maria 1925- .. **CLC 11**
See also CA 89-92; CANR 129; CWW 2;
DLB 322; EWL 3; MTCW 1; RGSF 2

Maugham, W. S.
See Maugham, W. Somerset

Maugham, W. Somerset 1874-1965 ... **CLC 1,
11, 15, 67, 93; SSC 8, 94; TCLC 208;
WLC 4**
See also AAYA 55; BPFB 2; BRW 6; CA
5-8R; 25-28R; CANR 40, 127; CDBLB
1914-1945; CMW 4; DA; DA3; DAB;
DAC; DAM DRAM, MST, NOV; DFS
22; DLB 10, 36, 77, 100, 162, 195; EWL
3; LAIT 3; MTCW 1, 2; MTFW 2005;
NFS 23, 35; RGEL 2; RGSF 2; SATA 54;
SSFS 17

Maugham, William S.
See Maugham, W. Somerset

Maugham, William Somerset
See Maugham, W. Somerset

Maupassant, Guy de 1850-1893 ..... **NCLC 1,
42, 83, 234; SSC 1, 64, 132; WLC 4**
See also BYA 14; DA; DA3; DAB; DAC;
DAM MST; DLB 123; EW 7; EXPS; GFL
1789 to the Present; LAIT 2; LMFS 1;
RGSF 2; RGWL 2, 3; SSFS 4, 21, 28, 31;
SUFW; TWA

Maupassant, Henri Rene Albert Guy de
See Maupassant, Guy de

Maupin, Armistead 1944- .... **CLC 95**
See also CA 125; 130; CANR 58, 101, 183;
CPW; DA3; DAM POP; DLB 278; GLL
1; INT CA-130; MTCW 2; MTFW 2005

Maupin, Armistead Jones, Jr.
See Maupin, Armistead

Maurhut, Richard
See Traven, B.

Mauriac, Claude 1914-1996 .... **CLC 9**
See also CA 89-92; 152; CWW 2; DLB 83;
EWL 3; GFL 1789 to the Present

Mauriac, Francois (Charles)
1885-1970 .... **CLC 4, 9, 56; SSC 24**
See also CA 25-28; CAP 2; DLB 65, 331;
EW 10; EWL 3; GFL 1789 to the Present;
MTCW 1, 2; MTFW 2005; RGWL 2, 3;
TWA

Mavor, Osborne Henry 1888-1951 .. **TCLC 3**
See also CA 104; DLB 10; EWL 3

Maxwell, Glyn 1962- .... **CLC 238**
See also CA 154; CANR 88, 183; CP 6, 7;
PFS 23

Maxwell, William (Keepers, Jr.)
1908-2000 .... **CLC 19**
See also AMWS 8; CA 93-96; 189; CANR
54, 95; CN 1, 2, 3, 4, 5, 6, 7; DLB 218,
278; DLBY 1980; INT CA-93-96; MAL
5; SATA-Obit 128

May, Elaine 1932- .... **CLC 16**
See also CA 124; 142; CAD; CWD; DLB
44

Mayakovski, Vladimir 1893-1930 ... **TCLC 4,
18**
See also CA 104; 158; EW 11; EWL 3;
IDTP; MTCW 2; MTFW 2005; RGWL 2,
3; SFW 4; TWA; WP

Mayakovski, Vladimir Vladimirovich
See Mayakovski, Vladimir

Mayakovsky, Vladimir
See Mayakovski, Vladimir

Mayhew, Henry 1812-1887 .... **NCLC 31**
See also BRWS 16; DLB 18, 55, 190

Mayle, Peter 1939(?)- .... **CLC 89**
See also CA 139; CANR 64, 109, 168, 218

Maynard, Joyce 1953- .... **CLC 23**
See also CA 111; 129; CANR 64, 169

Mayne, William 1928-2010 .... **CLC 12**
See also AAYA 20; CA 9-12R; CANR 37,
80, 100; CLR 25, 123; FANT; JRDA;
MAICYA 1, 2; MAICYAS 1; SAAS 11;
SATA 6, 68, 122; SUFW 2; YAW

Mayne, William James Carter
See Mayne, William

Mayo, Jim
See L'Amour, Louis

Maysles, Albert 1926- .... **CLC 16**
See also CA 29-32R

Maysles, David 1932-1987 .... **CLC 16**
See also CA 191

Mazer, Norma Fox 1931-2009 .... **CLC 26**
See also AAYA 5, 36; BYA 1, 8; CA 69-72;
292; CANR 12, 32, 66, 129, 189; CLR
23; JRDA; MAICYA 1, 2; SAAS 1; SATA
24, 67, 105, 168, 198; WYA; YAW

Mazzini, Guiseppe 1805-1872 .... **NCLC 34**

McAlmon, Robert (Menzies)
1895-1956 .... **TCLC 97**
See also CA 107; 168; DLB 4, 45; DLBD
15; GLL 1

McAuley, James Phillip 1917-1976 .. **CLC 45**
See also CA 97-100; CP 1, 2; DLB 260;
RGEL 2

McBain, Ed
See Hunter, Evan

McBrien, William 1930- .... **CLC 44**
See also CA 107; CANR 90

McBrien, William Augustine
See McBrien, William

McCabe, Pat
See McCabe, Patrick

McCabe, Patrick 1955- .... **CLC 133**
See also BRWS 9; CA 130; CANR 50, 90,
168, 202; CN 6, 7; DLB 194

McCaffrey, Anne 1926- .... **CLC 17**
See also AAYA 6, 34; AITN 2; BEST 89:2;
BPFB 2; BYA 5; CA 25-28R, 227; CAAE
227; CANR 15, 35, 55, 96, 169; CLR 49,

130; CPW; DA3; DAM NOV, POP; DLB
8; JRDA; MAICYA 1, 2; MTCW 1, 2;
MTFW 2005; SAAS 11; SATA 8, 70, 116,
152; SATA-Essay 152; SFW 4; SUFW 2;
WYA; YAW

McCaffrey, Anne Inez
See McCaffrey, Anne

McCall, Nathan 1955(?)- .... **CLC 86**
See also AAYA 59; BW 3; CA 146; CANR
88, 186

McCall Smith, Alexander
See Smith, Alexander McCall

McCann, Arthur
See Campbell, John W(ood, Jr.)

McCann, Colum 1965- .... **CLC 299**
See also CA 152; CANR 99, 149; DLB 267

McCann, Edson
See Pohl, Frederik

McCarthy, Charles
See McCarthy, Cormac

McCarthy, Charles, Jr.
See McCarthy, Cormac

McCarthy, Cormac 1933- .... **CLC 4, 57, 101,
204, 295, 310**
See also AAYA 41; AMWS 8; BPFB 2; CA
13-16R; CANR 10, 42, 69, 101, 161, 171;
CN 6, 7; CPW; CSW; DA3; DAM POP;
DLB 6, 143, 256; EWL 3; LATS 1:2;
LNFS 3; MAL 5; MTCW 2; MTFW 2005;
NFS 36; TCLE 1:2; TCWW 2

McCarthy, Mary 1912-1989 ...... **CLC 1, 3, 5,
14, 24, 39, 59; SSC 24**
See also AMW; BPFB 2; CA 5-8R; 129;
CANR 16, 50, 64; CN 1, 2, 3, 4; DA3;
DLB 2; DLBY 1981; EWL 3; FW; INT
CANR-16; MAL 5; MBL; MTCW 1, 2;
MTFW 2005; RGAL 4; TUS

McCarthy, Mary Therese
See McCarthy, Mary

McCartney, James Paul
See McCartney, Paul

McCartney, Paul 1942- .... **CLC 12, 35**
See also CA 146; CANR 111

McCauley, Stephen 1955- .... **CLC 50**
See also CA 141

McClaren, Peter .... **CLC 70**

McClure, Michael (Thomas) 1932- ... **CLC 6,
10**
See also BG 1:3; CA 21-24R; CAD; CANR
17, 46, 77, 131; CD 5, 6; CP 1, 2, 3, 4, 5,
6, 7; DLB 16; WP

McCorkle, Jill 1958- .... **CLC 51**
See also CA 121; CANR 113, 218; CSW;
DLB 234; DLBY 1987; SSFS 24

McCorkle, Jill Collins
See McCorkle, Jill

McCourt, Francis
See McCourt, Frank

McCourt, Frank 1930-2009 .... **CLC 109, 299**
See also AAYA 61; AMWS 12; CA 157;
288; CANR 97, 138; MTFW 2005; NCFS
1

McCourt, James 1941- .... **CLC 5**
See also CA 57-60; CANR 98, 152, 186

McCourt, Malachy 1931- .... **CLC 119**
See also SATA 126

McCoy, Edmund
See Gardner, John

McCoy, Horace (Stanley)
1897-1955 .... **TCLC 28**
See also AMWS 13; CA 108; 155; CMW 4;
DLB 9

McCrae, John 1872-1918 .... **TCLC 12**
See also CA 109; DLB 92; PFS 5

McCreigh, James
See Pohl, Frederik

McCullers, Carson 1917-1967 . CLC 1, 4, 10,
12, 48, 100; DC 35; SSC 9, 24, 99;
TCLC 155; WLC 4
See also AAYA 21; AMW; AMWC 2; BPFB
2; CA 5-8R; 25-28R; CABS 1, 3; CANR
18, 132; CDALB 1941-1968; DA; DA3;
DAB; DAC; DAM MST, NOV; DFS 5,
18; DLB 2, 7, 173, 228; EWL 3; EXPS;
FW; GLL 1; LAIT 3, 4; MAL 5; MBL;
MTCW 1, 2; MTFW 2005; NFS 6, 13;
RGAL 4; RGSF 2; SATA 27; SSFS 5, 32;
TUS; YAW

McCullers, Lula Carson Smith
See McCullers, Carson

McCulloch, John Tyler
See Burroughs, Edgar Rice

McCullough, Colleen 1937- ...... CLC 27, 107
See also AAYA 36; BPFB 2; CA 81-84;
CANR 17, 46, 67, 98, 139, 203; CPW;
DA3; DAM NOV, POP; MTCW 1, 2;
MTFW 2005; RHW

McCunn, Ruthanne Lum 1946- .... AAL
See also CA 119; CANR 43, 96; DLB 312;
LAIT 2; SATA 63

McDermott, Alice 1953- .... CLC 90
See also AMWS 18; CA 109; CANR 40,
90, 126, 181; CN 7; DLB 292; MTFW
2005; NFS 23

McDonagh, Martin 1970(?)- .... CLC 304
See also AAYA 71; BRWS 12; CA 171;
CANR 141; CD 6

McElroy, Joseph 1930- .... CLC 5, 47
See also CA 17-20R; CANR 149; CN 3, 4,
5, 6, 7

McElroy, Joseph Prince
See McElroy, Joseph

McElroy, Lee
See Kelton, Elmer

McEwan, Ian 1948- ... CLC 13, 66, 169, 269;
SSC 106
See also AAYA 84; BEST 90:4; BRWS 4;
CA 61-64; CANR 14, 41, 69, 87, 132,
179; CN 3, 4, 5, 6, 7; DAM NOV; DLB
14, 194, 319, 326; HGG; MTCW 1, 2;
MTFW 2005; NFS 32; RGSF 2; SUFW
2; TEA

McEwan, Ian Russell
See McEwan, Ian

McFadden, David 1940- .... CLC 48
See also CA 104; CP 1, 2, 3, 4, 5, 6, 7; DLB
60; INT CA-104

McFarland, Dennis 1950- .... CLC 65
See also CA 165; CANR 110, 179

McGahern, John 1934-2006 .... CLC 5, 9, 48,
156; SSC 17
See also CA 17-20R; 249; CANR 29, 68,
113, 204; CN 1, 2, 3, 4, 5, 6, 7; DLB 14,
231, 319; MTCW 1

McGinley, Patrick (Anthony) 1937- . CLC 41
See also CA 120; 127; CANR 56; INT CA-
127

McGinley, Phyllis 1905-1978 .... CLC 14
See also CA 9-12R; 77-80; CANR 19; CP
1, 2; CWRI 5; DLB 11, 48; MAL 5; PFS
9, 13; SATA 2, 44; SATA-Obit 24

McGinniss, Joe 1942- .... CLC 32
See also AITN 2; BEST 89:2; CA 25-28R;
CANR 26, 70, 152; CPW; DLB 185; INT
CANR-26

McGivern, Maureen Daly
See Daly, Maureen

McGivern, Maureen Patricia Daly
See Daly, Maureen

McGrath, Patrick 1950- .... CLC 55
See also CA 136; CANR 65, 148, 190; CN
5, 6, 7; DLB 231; HGG; SUFW 2

McGrath, Thomas (Matthew)
1916-1990 .... CLC 28, 59
See also AMWS 10; CA 9-12R; 132; CANR
6, 33, 95; CP 1, 2, 3, 4, 5; DAM POET;
MAL 5; MTCW 1; SATA 41; SATA-Obit
66

McGuane, Thomas 1939- .. CLC 3, 7, 18, 45,
127
See also AITN 2; BPFB 2; CA 49-52;
CANR 5, 24, 49, 94, 164; CN 2, 3, 4, 5,
6, 7; DLB 2, 212; DLBY 1980; EWL 3;
INT CANR-24; MAL 5; MTCW 1;
MTFW 2005; TCWW 1, 2

McGuane, Thomas Francis III
See McGuane, Thomas

McGuckian, Medbh 1950- .... CLC 48, 174;
PC 27
See also BRWS 5; CA 143; CANR 206; CP
4, 5, 6, 7; CWP; DAM POET; DLB 40

McHale, Tom 1942(?)-1982 .... CLC 3, 5
See also AITN 1; CA 77-80; 106; CN 1, 2,
3

McHugh, Heather 1948- .... PC 61
See also CA 69-72; CANR 11, 28, 55, 92;
CP 4, 5, 6, 7; CWP; PFS 24

McIlvanney, William 1936- .... CLC 42
See also CA 25-28R; CANR 61; CMW 4;
DLB 14, 207

McIlwraith, Maureen Mollie Hunter
See Hunter, Mollie

McInerney, Jay 1955- .... CLC 34, 112
See also AAYA 18; BPFB 2; CA 116; 123;
CANR 45, 68, 116, 176, 219; CN 5, 6, 7;
CPW; DA3; DAM POP; DLB 292; INT
CA-123; MAL 5; MTCW 2; MTFW 2005

McIntyre, Vonda N. 1948- .... CLC 18
See also CA 81-84; CANR 17, 34, 69;
MTCW 1; SFW 4; YAW

McIntyre, Vonda Neel
See McIntyre, Vonda N.

McKay, Claude 1889-1948 ...... BLC 1:3; HR
1:3; PC 2; TCLC 7, 41; WLC 4
See also AFAW 1, 2; AMWS 10; BW 1, 3;
CA 104; 124; CANR 73; DA; DAB;
DAC; DAM MST, MULT, NOV, POET;
DLB 4, 45, 51, 117; EWL 3; EXPP; GLL
2; LAIT 3; LMFS 2; MAL 5; MTCW 1,
2; MTFW 2005; PAB; PFS 4; RGAL 4;
TUS; WP

McKay, Festus Claudius
See McKay, Claude

McKuen, Rod 1933- .... CLC 1, 3
See also AITN 1; CA 41-44R; CANR 40;
CP 1

McLoughlin, R. B.
See Mencken, H. L.

McLuhan, (Herbert) Marshall
1911-1980 .... CLC 37, 83
See also CA 9-12R; 102; CANR 12, 34, 61;
DLB 88; INT CANR-12; MTCW 1, 2;
MTFW 2005

McMahon, Pat
See Hoch, Edward D.

McManus, Declan Patrick Aloysius
See Costello, Elvis

McMillan, Terry 1951- .. BLCS; CLC 50, 61,
112
See also AAYA 21; AMWS 13; BPFB 2;
BW 2, 3; CA 140; CANR 60, 104, 131;
CN 7; CPW; DA3; DAM MULT, NOV,
POP; MAL 5; MTCW 2; MTFW 2005;
RGAL 4; YAW

McMillan, Terry L.
See McMillan, Terry

McMurtry, Larry 1936- .... CLC 2, 3, 7, 11,
27, 44, 127, 250
See also AAYA 83; AITN 2; AMWS 5;
BEST 89:2; BPFB 2; CA 5-8R; CANR
19, 43, 64, 103, 170, 206; CDALB 1968-
1988; CN 2, 3, 4, 5, 6, 7; CPW; CSW;

DA3; DAM NOV, POP; DLB 2, 143, 256;
DLBY 1980, 1987; EWL 3; MAL 5;
MTCW 1, 2; MTFW 2005; RGAL 4;
TCWW 1, 2

McMurtry, Larry Jeff
See McMurtry, Larry

McNally, Terrence 1939- ... CLC 4, 7, 41, 91,
252; DC 27
See also AAYA 62; AMWS 13; CA 45-48;
CAD; CANR 2, 56, 116; CD 5, 6; DA3;
DAM DRAM; DFS 16, 19; DLB 7, 249;
EWL 3; GLL 1; MTCW 2; MTFW 2005

McNally, Thomas Michael
See McNally, T.M.

McNally, T.M. 1961- .... CLC 82
See also CA 246

McNamer, Deirdre 1950- .... CLC 70
See also CA 188; CANR 163, 200

McNeal, Tom .... CLC 119
See also CA 252; CANR 185; SATA 194

McNeile, Herman Cyril
1888-1937 .... TCLC 44
See also CA 184; CMW 4; DLB 77

McNickle, D'Arcy 1904-1977 .... CLC 89;
NNAL
See also CA 9-12R; 85-88; CANR 5, 45;
DAM MULT; DLB 175, 212; RGAL 4;
SATA-Obit 22; TCWW 1, 2

McNickle, William D'Arcy
See McNickle, D'Arcy

McPhee, John 1931- .... CLC 36
See also AAYA 61; AMWS 3; ANW; BEST
90:1; CA 65-68; CANR 20, 46, 64, 69,
121, 165; CPW; DLB 185, 275; MTCW
1, 2; MTFW 2005; TUS

McPhee, John Angus
See McPhee, John

McPherson, James Alan, Jr.
See McPherson, James Alan

McPherson, James Alan 1943- . BLCS; CLC
19, 77; SSC 95
See also BW 1, 3; CA 25-28R; 273; CAAE
273; CAAS 17; CANR 24, 74, 140; CN
3, 4, 5, 6; CSW; DLB 38, 244; EWL 3;
MTCW 1, 2; MTFW 2005; RGAL 4;
RGSF 2; SSFS 23

McPherson, William (Alexander)
1933- .... CLC 34
See also CA 69-72; CANR 28; INT
CANR-28

McTaggart, J. McT. Ellis
See McTaggart, John McTaggart Ellis

McTaggart, John McTaggart Ellis
1866-1925 .... TCLC 105
See also CA 120; DLB 262

Mda, Zakes 1948- .... BLC 2:3; CLC 262
See also BRWS 15; CA 205; CANR 151,
185; CD 5, 6; DLB 225

Mda, Zanemvula
See Mda, Zakes

Mda, Zanemvula Kizito Gatyeni
See Mda, Zakes

Mead, George Herbert 1863-1931 . TCLC 89
See also CA 212; DLB 270

Mead, Margaret 1901-1978 .... CLC 37
See also AITN 1; CA 1-4R; 81-84; CANR
4; DA3; FW; MTCW 1, 2; SATA-Obit 20

Meaker, M. J.
See Meaker, Marijane

Meaker, Marijane 1927- .... CLC 12, 35
See also AAYA 2, 23, 82; BYA 1, 7, 8; CA
107; CANR 37, 63, 145, 180; CLR 29;
GLL 2; INT CA-107; JRDA; MAICYA 1,
2; MAICYAS 1; MTCW 1; SAAS 1;
SATA 20, 61, 99, 160; SATA-Essay 111;
WYA; YAW

Meaker, Marijane Agnes
See Meaker, Marijane

Mo, Timothy (Peter) 1950- .... **CLC 46, 134**
See also CA 117; CANR 128; CN 5, 6, 7; DLB 194; MTCW 1; WLIT 4; WWE 1

Mo, Yan
See Yan, Mo

Moberg, Carl Arthur
See Moberg, Vilhelm

Moberg, Vilhelm 1898-1973 .... **TCLC 224**
See also CA 97-100; 45-48; CANR 135; DLB 259; EW 11; EWL 3

Modarressi, Taghi (M.) 1931-1997 ... **CLC 44**
See also CA 121; 134; INT CA-134

Modiano, Patrick (Jean) 1945- .... **CLC 18, 218**
See also CA 85-88; CANR 17, 40, 115; CWW 2; DLB 83, 299; EWL 3; RGHL

Mofolo, Thomas 1875(?)-1948 .... **BLC 1:3; TCLC 22**
See also AFW; CA 121; 153; CANR 83; DAM MULT; DLB 225; EWL 3; MTCW 2; MTFW 2005; WLIT 2

Mofolo, Thomas Mokopu
See Mofolo, Thomas

Mohr, Nicholasa 1938- .... **CLC 12; HLC 2**
See also AAYA 8, 46; CA 49-52; CANR 1, 32, 64; CLR 22; DAM MULT; DLB 145; HW 1, 2; JRDA; LAIT 5; LLW; MAICYA 2; MAICYAS 1; RGAL 4; SAAS 8; SATA 8, 97; SATA-Essay 113; WYA; YAW

Moi, Toril 1953- .... **CLC 172**
See also CA 154; CANR 102; FW

Mojtabai, A(nn) G(race) 1938- ..... **CLC 5, 9, 15, 29**
See also CA 85-88; CANR 88

Moliere 1622-1673 ..... **DC 13; LC 10, 28, 64, 125, 127; WLC 4**
See also DA; DA3; DAB; DAC; DAM DRAM, MST; DFS 13, 18, 20; DLB 268; EW 3; GFL Beginnings to 1789; LATS 1:1; RGWL 2, 3; TWA

Molin, Charles
See Mayne, William

Molina, Antonio Munoz 1956- .... **CLC 289**
See also DLB 322

Molnar, Ferenc 1878-1952 .... **TCLC 20**
See also CA 109; 153; CANR 83; CDWLB 4; DAM DRAM; DLB 215; EWL 3; RGWL 2, 3

Momaday, N. Scott 1934- ...... **CLC 2, 19, 85, 95, 160; NNAL; PC 25; WLCS**
See also AAYA 11, 64; AMWS 4; ANW; BPFB 2; BYA 12; CA 25-28R; CANR 14, 34, 68, 134; CDALBS; CN 2, 3, 4, 5, 6, 7; CPW; DA; DA3; DAB; DAC; DAM MST, MULT, NOV, POP; DLB 143, 175, 256; EWL 3; EXPP; INT CANR-14; LAIT 4; LATS 1:2; MAL 5; MTCW 1, 2; MTFW 2005; NFS 10; PFS 2, 11, 37; RGAL 4; SATA 48; SATA-Brief 30; TCWW 1, 2; WP; YAW

Momaday, Navarre Scott
See Momaday, N. Scott

Momala, Ville i
See Moberg, Vilhelm

Monette, Paul 1945-1995 .... **CLC 82**
See also AMWS 10; CA 139; 147; CN 6; DLB 350; GLL 1

Monroe, Harriet 1860-1936 .... **TCLC 12**
See also CA 109; 204; DLB 54, 91

Monroe, Lyle
See Heinlein, Robert A.

Montagu, Elizabeth 1720-1800 .... **NCLC 7, 117**
See also DLB 356; FW

Montagu, Mary (Pierrepont) Wortley 1689-1762 .... **LC 9, 57; PC 16**
See also DLB 95, 101; FL 1:1; RGEL 2

Montagu, W. H.
See Coleridge, Samuel Taylor

Montague, John (Patrick) 1929- ..... **CLC 13, 46; PC 106**
See also BRWS 15; CA 9-12R; CANR 9, 69, 121; CP 1, 2, 3, 4, 5, 6, 7; DLB 40; EWL 3; MTCW 1; PFS 12; RGEL 2; TCLE 1:2

Montaigne, Michel de 1533-1592 . **LC 8, 105, 194; WLC 4**
See also DA; DAB; DAC; DAM MST; DLB 327; EW 2; EWL Beginnings to 1789; LMFS 1; RGWL 2, 3; TWA

Montaigne, Michel Eyquem de
See Montaigne, Michel de

Montale, Eugenio 1896-1981 ... **CLC 7, 9, 18; PC 13**
See also CA 17-20R; 104; CANR 30; DLB 114, 331; EW 11; EWL 3; MTCW 1; PFS 22; RGWL 2, 3; TWA; WLIT 7

Montemayor, Jorge de 1521(?)-1561(?) .... **LC 185**
See also DLB 318

Montesquieu, Charles-Louis de Secondat 1689-1755 .... **LC 7, 69, 189**
See also DLB 314; EW 3; GFL Beginnings to 1789; TWA

Montessori, Maria 1870-1952 ...... **TCLC 103**
See also CA 115; 147

Montgomery, Bruce 1921(?)-1978 .... **CLC 22**
See also CA 179; 104; CMW 4; DLB 87; MSW

Montgomery, L. M. 1874-1942 ..... **TCLC 51, 140**
See also AAYA 12; BYA 1; CA 108; 137; CLR 8, 91, 145; DA3; DAC; DAM MST; DLB 92, 362; DLBD 14; JRDA; MAICYA 1, 2; MTCW 2; MTFW 2005; RGEL 2; SATA 100; TWA; WCH; WYA; YABC 1

Montgomery, Lucy Maud
See Montgomery, L. M.

Montgomery, Marion, Jr. 1925- .... **CLC 7**
See also AITN 1; CA 1-4R; CANR 3, 48, 162; CSW; DLB 6

Montgomery, Marion H. 1925-
See Montgomery, Marion, Jr.

Montgomery, Max
See Davenport, Guy (Mattison, Jr.)

Montgomery, Robert Bruce
See Montgomery, Bruce

Montherlant, Henry de 1896-1972 .... **CLC 8, 19**
See also CA 85-88; 37-40R; DAM DRAM; DLB 72, 321; EW 11; EWL 3; GFL 1789 to the Present; MTCW 1

Montherlant, Henry Milon de
See Montherlant, Henry de

Monty Python
See Chapman, Graham; Cleese, John (Marwood); Gilliam, Terry; Idle, Eric; Jones, Terence Graham Parry; Palin, Michael

Moodie, Susanna (Strickland) 1803-1885 .... **NCLC 14, 113**
See also DLB 99

Moody, Hiram
See Moody, Rick

Moody, Hiram F. III
See Moody, Rick

Moody, Minerva
See Alcott, Louisa May

Moody, Rick 1961- .... **CLC 147**
See also CA 138; CANR 64, 112, 179; MTFW 2005

Moody, William Vaughan 1869-1910 .... **TCLC 105**
See also CA 110; 178; DLB 7, 54; MAL 5; RGAL 4

Mooney, Edward 1951- .... **CLC 25**
See also CA 130

Mooney, Ted
See Mooney, Edward

Moorcock, Michael 1939- ...... **CLC 5, 27, 58, 236**
See also AAYA 26; CA 45-48; CAAS 5; CANR 2, 17, 38, 64, 122, 203; CN 5, 6, 7; DLB 14, 231, 261, 319; FANT; MTCW 1, 2; MTFW 2005; SATA 93, 166; SCFW 1, 2; SFW 4; SUFW 1, 2

Moorcock, Michael John
See Moorcock, Michael

Moorcock, Michael John
See Moorcock, Michael

Moore, Al
See Moore, Alan

Moore, Alan 1953- .... **CLC 230**
See also AAYA 51; CA 204; CANR 138, 184; DLB 261; MTFW 2005; SFW 4

Moore, Alice Ruth
See Nelson, Alice Ruth Moore Dunbar

Moore, Brian 1921-1999 ... **CLC 1, 3, 5, 7, 8, 19, 32, 90**
See also BRWS 9; CA 1-4R; 174; CANR 1, 25, 42, 63; CCA 1; CN 1, 2, 3, 4, 5, 6; DAB; DAC; DAM MST; DLB 251; EWL 3; FANT; MTCW 1, 2; MTFW 2005; RGEL 2

Moore, Edward
See Muir, Edwin

Moore, G. E. 1873-1958 .... **TCLC 89**
See also DLB 262

Moore, George Augustus 1852-1933 .... **SSC 19, 134; TCLC 7**
See also BRW 6; CA 104; 177; DLB 10, 18, 57, 135; EWL 3; RGEL 2; RGSF 2

Moore, Lorrie 1957- .... **CLC 39, 45, 68, 165; SSC 147**
See also AMWS 10; CA 116; CANR 39, 83, 139; CN 5, 6, 7; DLB 234; MTFW 2005; SSFS 19

Moore, Marianne 1887-1972 . **CLC 1, 2, 4, 8, 10, 13, 19, 47; PC 4, 49; WLCS**
See also AMW; CA 1-4R; 33-36R; CANR 3, 61; CDALB 1929-1941; CP 1; DA; DA3; DAB; DAC; DAM MST, POET; DLB 45; DLBD 7; EWL 3; EXPP; FL 1:6; MAL 5; MBL; MTCW 1, 2; MTFW 2005; PAB; PFS 14, 17, 38; RGAL 4; SATA 20; TUS; WP

Moore, Marianne Craig
See Moore, Marianne

Moore, Marie Lorena
See Moore, Lorrie

Moore, Michael 1954- .... **CLC 218**
See also AAYA 53; CA 166; CANR 150

Moore, Thomas 1779-1852 .... **NCLC 6, 110**
See also BRWS 17; DLB 96, 144; RGEL 2

Moorhouse, Frank 1938- .... **SSC 40**
See also CA 118; CANR 92; CN 3, 4, 5, 6, 7; DLB 289; RGSF 2

Mootoo, Shani 1958(?)- .... **CLC 294**
See also CA 174; CANR 156

Mora, Pat 1942- .... **HLC 2**
See also AMWS 13; CA 129; CANR 57, 81, 112, 171; CLR 58; DAM MULT; DLB 209; HW 1, 2; LLW; MAICYA 2; MTFW 2005; PFS 33, 35; SATA 92, 134, 186

Moraga, Cherrie 1952- ... **CLC 126, 250; DC 22**
See also CA 131; CANR 66, 154; DAM MULT; DLB 82, 249; FW; GLL 1; HW 1, 2; LLW

Moran, J.L.
See Whitaker, Rod

Morand, Paul 1888-1976 .... **CLC 41; SSC 22**
See also CA 184; 69-72; DLB 65; EWL 3

Morante, Elsa 1918-1985 .... **CLC 8, 47**
See also CA 85-88; 117; CANR 35; DLB
177; EWL 3; MTCW 1, 2; MTFW 2005;
RGHL; RGWL 2, 3; WLIT 7

Moravia, Alberto
See Pincherle, Alberto

Morck, Paul
See Rolvaag, O.E.

More, Hannah 1745-1833 ...... **NCLC 27, 141**
See also DLB 107, 109, 116, 158; RGEL 2

More, Henry 1614-1687 .... **LC 9**
See also DLB 126, 252

More, Sir Thomas 1478(?)-1535 ... **LC 10, 32,
140**
See also BRWC 1; BRWS 7; DLB 136, 281;
LMFS 1; NFS 29; RGEL 2; TEA

Moreas, Jean
See Papadiamantopoulos, Johannes

Moreton, Andrew Esq.
See Defoe, Daniel

Moreton, Lee
See Boucicault, Dion

Morgan, Berry 1919-2002 .... **CLC 6**
See also CA 49-52; 208; DLB 6

Morgan, Claire
See Highsmith, Patricia

Morgan, Edwin 1920-2010 .... **CLC 31**
See also BRWS 9; CA 5-8R; CANR 3, 43,
90; CP 1, 2, 3, 4, 5, 6, 7; DLB 27

Morgan, Edwin George
See Morgan, Edwin

Morgan, (George) Frederick
1922-2004 .... **CLC 23**
See also CA 17-20R; 224; CANR 21, 144;
CP 2, 3, 4, 5, 6, 7

Morgan, Harriet
See Mencken, H. L.

Morgan, Jane
See Cooper, James Fenimore

Morgan, Janet 1945- .... **CLC 39**
See also CA 65-68

Morgan, Lady 1776(?)-1859 .... **NCLC 29**
See also DLB 116, 158; RGEL 2

Morgan, Robin (Evonne) 1941- .... **CLC 2**
See also CA 69-72; CANR 29, 68; FW;
GLL 2; MTCW 1; SATA 80

Morgan, Scott
See Kuttner, Henry

Morgan, Seth 1949(?)-1990 .... **CLC 65**
See also CA 185; 132

Morgenstern, Christian (Otto Josef
Wolfgang) 1871-1914 .... **TCLC 8**
See also CA 105; 191; EWL 3

Morgenstern, S.
See Goldman, William

Mori, Rintaro
See Mori Ogai

Mori, Toshio 1910-1980 ... **AAL; SSC 83, 123**
See also CA 116; 244; DLB 312; RGSF 2

Moricz, Zsigmond 1879-1942 .... **TCLC 33**
See also CA 165; DLB 215; EWL 3

Morike, Eduard (Friedrich)
1804-1875 .... **NCLC 10, 201**
See also DLB 133; RGWL 2, 3

Morin, Jean-Paul
See Whitaker, Rod

Mori Ogai 1862-1922 .... **TCLC 14**
See also CA 110; 164; DLB 180; EWL 3;
MJW; RGWL 3; TWA

Moritz, Karl Philipp 1756-1793 .... **LC 2, 162**
See also DLB 94

Morland, Peter Henry
See Faust, Frederick

Morley, Christopher (Darlington)
1890-1957 .... **TCLC 87**
See also CA 112; 213; DLB 9; MAL 5;
RGAL 4

Morren, Theophil
See Hofmannsthal, Hugo von

Morris, Bill 1952- .... **CLC 76**
See also CA 225

Morris, Julian
See West, Morris L(anglo)

Morris, Steveland Judkins (?)-
See Wonder, Stevie

Morris, William 1834-1896 ..... **NCLC 4, 233;
PC 55**
See also BRW 5; CDBLB 1832-1890; DLB
18, 35, 57, 156, 178, 184; FANT; RGEL
2; SFW 4; SUFW

Morris, Wright (Marion) 1910-1998 . **CLC 1,
3, 7, 18, 37; TCLC 107**
See also AMW; CA 9-12R; 167; CANR 21,
81; CN 1, 2, 3, 4, 5, 6; DLB 2, 206, 218;
DLBY 1981; EWL 3; MAL 5; MTCW 1,
2; MTFW 2005; RGAL 4; TCWW 1, 2

Morrison, Arthur 1863-1945 .... **SSC 40;
TCLC 72**
See also CA 120; 157; CMW 4; DLB 70,
135, 197; RGEL 2

Morrison, Chloe Anthony Wofford
See Morrison, Toni

Morrison, James Douglas
1943-1971 .... **CLC 17**
See also CA 73-76; CANR 40

Morrison, Jim
See Morrison, James Douglas

Morrison, John Gordon 1904-1998 ... **SSC 93**
See also CA 103; CANR 92; DLB 260

Morrison, Toni 1931- . **BLC 1:3, 2:3; CLC 4,
10, 22, 55, 81, 87, 173, 194; SSC 126;
WLC 4**
See also AAYA 1, 22, 61; AFAW 1, 2;
AMWC 1; AMWS 3; BPFB 2; BW 2, 3;
CA 29-32R; CANR 27, 42, 67, 113, 124,
204; CDALB 1968-1988; CLR 99; CN 3,
4, 5, 6, 7; CPW; DA; DA3; DAB; DAC;
DAM MST, MULT, NOV, POP; DLB 6,
33, 143, 331; DLBY 1981; EWL 3;
EXPN; FL 1:6; FW; GL 3; LAIT 2, 4;
LATS 1:2; LMFS 2; MAL 5; MBL;
MTCW 1, 2; MTFW 2005; NFS 1, 6, 8,
14, 37; RGAL 4; RHW; SATA 57, 144;
SSFS 5; TCLE 1:2; TUS; YAW

Morrison, Van 1945- .... **CLC 21**
See also CA 116; 168

Morrissy, Mary 1957- .... **CLC 99**
See also CA 205; DLB 267

Mortimer, John 1923-2009 .... **CLC 28, 43**
See Morton, Kate
See also CA 13-16R; 282; CANR 21, 69,
109, 172; CBD; CD 5, 6; CDBLB 1960
to Present; CMW 4; CN 5, 6, 7; CPW;
DA3; DAM DRAM, POP; DLB 13, 245,
271; INT CANR-21; MSW; MTCW 1, 2;
MTFW 2005; RGEL 2

Mortimer, John C.
See Mortimer, John

Mortimer, John Clifford
See Mortimer, John

Mortimer, Penelope (Ruth)
1918-1999 .... **CLC 5**
See also CA 57-60; 187; CANR 45, 88; CN
1, 2, 3, 4, 5, 6

Mortimer, Sir John
See Mortimer, John

Morton, Anthony
See Creasey, John

Morton, Thomas 1579(?)-1647(?) .... **LC 72**
See also DLB 24; RGEL 2

Mosca, Gaetano 1858-1941 .... **TCLC 75**

Moses, Daniel David 1952- .... **NNAL**
See also CA 186; CANR 160; DLB 334

Mosher, Howard Frank 1943- .... **CLC 62**
See also CA 139; CANR 65, 115, 181

Mosley, Nicholas 1923- .... **CLC 43, 70**
See also CA 69-72; CANR 41, 60, 108, 158;
CN 1, 2, 3, 4, 5, 6, 7; DLB 14, 207

Mosley, Walter 1952- ... **BLCS; CLC 97, 184,
278**
See also AAYA 57; AMWS 13; BPFB 2;
BW 2; CA 142; CANR 57, 92, 136, 172,
201; CMW 4; CN 7; CPW; DA3; DAM
MULT, POP; DLB 306; MSW; MTCW 2;
MTFW 2005

Moss, Howard 1922-1987 . **CLC 7, 14, 45, 50**
See also CA 1-4R; 123; CANR 1, 44; CP 1,
2, 3, 4; DAM POET; DLB 5

Mossgiel, Rab
See Burns, Robert

Motion, Andrew 1952- .... **CLC 47**
See also BRWS 7; CA 146; CANR 90, 142;
CP 4, 5, 6, 7; DLB 40; MTFW 2005

Motion, Andrew Peter
See Motion, Andrew

Motley, Willard (Francis)
1909-1965 .... **CLC 18**
See also AMWS 17; BW 1; CA 117; 106;
CANR 88; DLB 76, 143

Motoori, Norinaga 1730-1801 .... **NCLC 45**

Mott, Michael (Charles Alston)
1930- .... **CLC 15, 34**
See also CA 5-8R; CAAS 7; CANR 7, 29

Moulsworth, Martha 1577-1646 .... **LC 168**

Mountain Wolf Woman 1884-1960 . **CLC 92;
NNAL**
See also CA 144; CANR 90

Moure, Erin 1955- .... **CLC 88**
See also CA 113; CP 5, 6, 7; CWP; DLB
60

Mourning Dove 1885(?)-1936 .... **NNAL**
See also CA 144; CANR 90; DAM MULT;
DLB 175, 221

Mowat, Farley 1921- .... **CLC 26**
See also AAYA 1, 50; BYA 2; CA 1-4R;
CANR 4, 24, 42, 68, 108; CLR 20; CPW;
DAC; DAM MST; DLB 68; INT CANR-
24; JRDA; MAICYA 1, 2; MTCW 1, 2;
MTFW 2005; SATA 3, 55; YAW

Mowat, Farley McGill
See Mowat, Farley

Mowatt, Anna Cora 1819-1870 ..... **NCLC 74**
See also RGAL 4

Moye, Guan
See Yan, Mo

Mo Yen
See Yan, Mo

Moyers, Bill 1934- .... **CLC 74**
See also AITN 2; CA 61-64; CANR 31, 52,
148

Mphahlele, Es'kia 1919-2008 .... **BLC 1:3;
CLC 25, 133, 280**
See also AFW; BW 2, 3; CA 81-84; 278;
CANR 26, 76; CDWLB 3; CN 4, 5, 6;
DA3; DAM MULT; DLB 125, 225; EWL
3; MTCW 2; MTFW 2005; RGSF 2;
SATA 119; SATA-Obit 198; SSFS 11

Mphahlele, Ezekiel
See Mphahlele, Es'kia

Mphahlele, Zeke
See Mphahlele, Es'kia

Mqhayi, S(amuel) E(dward) K(rune Loliwe)
1875-1945 .... **BLC 1:3; TCLC 25**
See also CA 153; CANR 87; DAM MULT

Mrozek, Slawomir 1930- .... **CLC 3, 13**
See also CA 13-16R; CAAS 10; CANR 29;
CDWLB 4; CWW 2; DLB 232; EWL 3;
MTCW 1

Mrs. Belloc-Lowndes
See Lowndes, Marie Adelaide (Belloc)

Mrs. Fairstar
See Horne, Richard Henry Hengist

M'Taggart, John M'Taggart Ellis
See McTaggart, John McTaggart Ellis

Naipaul, Shivadhar Srinivasa
See Naipaul, Shiva
Naipaul, V. S. 1932- . **CLC 4, 7, 9, 13, 18, 37, 105, 199; SSC 38, 121**
See also BPFB 2; BRWS 1; CA 1-4R; CANR 1, 33, 51, 91, 126, 191; CDBLB 1960 to Present; CDWLB 3; CN 1, 2, 3, 4, 5, 6, 7; DA3; DAB; DAC; DAM MST, NOV; DLB 125, 204, 207, 326, 331; DLBY 1985, 2001; EWL 3; LATS 1:2; MTCW 1, 2; MTFW 2005; NFS 37; RGEL 2; RGSF 2; SSFS 29; TWA; WLIT 4; WWE 1

Naipaul, Vidiahar Surajprasad
See Naipaul, V. S.
Nair, Kamala
See Das, Kamala
Nakos, Lilika 1903-1989 .... **CLC 29**
See also CA 217
Nalapat, Kamala
See Das, Kamala
Napoleon
See Yamamoto, Hisaye
Narayan, R. K. 1906-2001 ..... **CLC 7, 28, 47, 121, 211; SSC 25, 154**
See also BPFB 2; CA 81-84; 196; CANR 33, 61, 112; CN 1, 2, 3, 4, 5, 6, 7; DA3; DAM NOV; DLB 323; DNFS 1; EWL 3; MTCW 1, 2; MTFW 2005; RGEL 2; RGSF 2; SATA 62; SSFS 5, 29; WWE 1

Narayan, Rasipuram Krishnaswami
See Narayan, R. K.
Nash, Frediric Ogden
See Nash, Ogden
Nash, Ogden 1902-1971 ...... **CLC 23; PC 21; TCLC 109**
See also CA 13-14; 29-32R; CANR 34, 61, 185; CAP 1; CP 1; DAM POET; DLB 11; MAICYA 1, 2; MAL 5; MTCW 1, 2; PFS 31; RGAL 4; SATA 2, 46; WP

Nashe, Thomas 1567-1601(?) .... **LC 41, 89, 184; PC 82**
See also DLB 167; RGEL 2
Nathan, Daniel
See Dannay, Frederic
Nathan, George Jean 1882-1958 .... **TCLC 18**
See also CA 114; 169; DLB 137; MAL 5
Natsume, Kinnosuke
See Natsume, Soseki
Natsume, Soseki 1867-1916 .... **TCLC 2, 10**
See also CA 104; 195; DLB 180; EWL 3; MJW; RGWL 2, 3; TWA

Natsume Soseki
See Natsume, Soseki
Natti, Lee 1919- .... **CLC 17**
See also CA 5-8R; CANR 2; CWRI 5; SAAS 3; SATA 1, 67
Natti, Mary Lee
See Natti, Lee
Navarre, Marguerite de
See de Navarre, Marguerite
Naylor, Gloria 1950- . **BLC 1:3; CLC 28, 52, 156, 261; WLCS**
See also AAYA 6, 39; AFAW 1, 2; AMWS 8; BW 2, 3; CA 107; CANR 27, 51, 74, 130; CN 4, 5, 6, 7; CPW; DA; DA3; DAC; DAM MST, MULT, NOV, POP; DLB 173; EWL 3; FW; MAL 5; MTCW 1, 2; MTFW 2005; NFS 4, 7; RGAL 4; TCLE 1:2; TUS

Ndebele, Njabulo (Simakahle)
1948- .... **SSC 135**
See also CA 184; DLB 157, 225; EWL 3
Neal, John 1793-1876 .... **NCLC 161**
See also DLB 1, 59, 243; FW; RGAL 4

Neff, Debra .... **CLC 59**
Neihardt, John Gneisenau
1881-1973 .... **CLC 32**
See also CA 13-14; CANR 65; CAP 1; DLB 9, 54, 256; LAIT 2; TCWW 1, 2
Nekrasov, Nikolai Alekseevich
1821-1878 .... **NCLC 11**
See also DLB 277
Nelligan, Emile 1879-1941 .... **TCLC 14**
See also CA 114; 204; DLB 92; EWL 3
Nelson, Alice Ruth Moore Dunbar
1875-1935 .... **HR 1:2; SSC 132**
See also BW 1, 3; CA 122; 124; CANR 82; DLB 50; FW; MTCW 1
Nelson, Willie 1933- .... **CLC 17**
See also CA 107; CANR 114, 178
Nemerov, Howard 1920-1991 .... **CLC 2, 6, 9, 36; PC 24; TCLC 124**
See also AMW; CA 1-4R; 134; CABS 2; CANR 1, 27, 53; CN 1, 2, 3; CP 1, 2, 3, 4, 5; DAM POET; DLB 5, 6; DLBY 1983; EWL 3; INT CANR-27; MAL 5; MTCW 1, 2; MTFW 2005; PFS 10, 14; RGAL 4

Nemerov, Howard Stanley
See Nemerov, Howard
Nepos, Cornelius c. 99B.C.-c.
24B.C. .... **CMLC 89**
See also DLB 211
Neruda, Pablo 1904-1973 .. **CLC 1, 2, 5, 7, 9, 28, 62; HLC 2; PC 4, 64; WLC 4**
See also CA 19-20; 45-48; CANR 131; CAP 2; DA; DA3; DAB; DAC; DAM MST, MULT, POET; DLB 283, 331; DNFS 2; EWL 3; HW 1; LAW; MTCW 1, 2; MTFW 2005; PFS 11, 28, 33, 35; RGWL 2, 3; TWA; WLIT 1; WP

Nerval, Gerard de 1808-1855 ... **NCLC 1, 67; PC 13; SSC 18**
See also DLB 217; EW 6; GFL 1789 to the Present; RGSF 2; RGWL 2, 3
Nervo, (Jose) Amado (Ruiz de)
1870-1919 .... **HLCS 2; TCLC 11**
See also CA 109; 131; DLB 290; EWL 3; HW 1; LAW
Nesbit, Malcolm
See Chester, Alfred
Nessi, Pio Baroja y
See Baroja, Pio
Nestroy, Johann 1801-1862 .... **NCLC 42**
See also DLB 133; RGWL 2, 3
Netterville, Luke
See O'Grady, Standish (James)
Neufeld, John (Arthur) 1938- .... **CLC 17**
See also AAYA 11; CA 25-28R; CANR 11, 37, 56; CLR 52; MAICYA 1, 2; SAAS 3; SATA 6, 81, 131; SATA-Essay 131; YAW
Neumann, Alfred 1895-1952 .... **TCLC 100**
See also CA 183; DLB 56
Neumann, Ferenc
See Molnar, Ferenc
Neville, Emily Cheney 1919- .... **CLC 12**
See also BYA 2; CA 5-8R; CANR 3, 37, 85; JRDA; MAICYA 1, 2; SAAS 2; SATA 1; YAW
Newbound, Bernard Slade 1930- .... **CLC 11, 46**
See also CA 81-84; CAAS 9; CANR 49; CCA 1; CD 5, 6; DAM DRAM; DLB 53
Newby, P(ercy) H(oward)
1918-1997 .... **CLC 2, 13**
See also CA 5-8R; 161; CANR 32, 67; CN 1, 2, 3, 4, 5, 6; DAM NOV; DLB 15, 326; MTCW 1; RGEL 2
Newcastle
See Cavendish, Margaret
Newlove, Donald 1928- .... **CLC 6**
See also CA 29-32R; CANR 25

Newlove, John (Herbert) 1938- .... **CLC 14**
See also CA 21-24R; CANR 9, 25; CP 1, 2, 3, 4, 5, 6, 7
Newman, Charles 1938-2006 .... **CLC 2, 8**
See also CA 21-24R; 249; CANR 84; CN 3, 4, 5, 6
Newman, Charles Hamilton
See Newman, Charles
Newman, Edwin 1919-2010 .... **CLC 14**
See also AITN 1; CA 69-72; CANR 5
Newman, Edwin Harold
See Newman, Edwin
Newman, John Henry 1801-1890 . **NCLC 38, 99**
See also BRWS 7; DLB 18, 32, 55; RGEL 2
Newton, (Sir) Isaac 1642-1727 ...... **LC 35, 53**
See also DLB 252
Newton, Suzanne 1936- .... **CLC 35**
See also BYA 7; CA 41-44R; CANR 14; JRDA; SATA 5, 77
New York Dept. of Ed. .... **CLC 70**
Nexo, Martin Andersen
1869-1954 .... **TCLC 43**
See also CA 202; DLB 214; EWL 3; NFS 34
Nezval, Vitezslav 1900-1958 .... **TCLC 44**
See also CA 123; CDWLB 4; DLB 215; EWL 3
Ng, Fae Myenne 1956- .... **CLC 81**
See also BYA 11; CA 146; CANR 191; NFS 37
Ngcobo, Lauretta 1931- .... **BLC 2:3**
See also CA 165
Ngema, Mbongeni 1955- .... **CLC 57**
See also BW 2; CA 143; CANR 84; CD 5, 6
Ngugi, James T.
See Ngugi wa Thiong'o
Ngugi, James Thiong'o
See Ngugi wa Thiong'o
Ngugi wa Thiong'o 1938- .... **BLC 1:3, 2:3; CLC 3, 7, 13, 36, 182, 275**
See also AFW; BRWS 8; BW 2; CA 81-84; CANR 27, 58, 164, 213; CD 3, 4, 5, 6, 7; CDWLB 3; CN 1; DAM MULT, NOV; DLB 125; DNFS 2; EWL 3; MTCW 1, 2; MTFW 2005; RGEL 2; WWE 1
Niatum, Duane 1938- .... **NNAL**
See also CA 41-44R; CANR 21, 45, 83; DLB 175
Nichol, B(arrie) P(hillip) 1944-1988 . **CLC 18**
See also CA 53-56; CP 1, 2, 3, 4; DLB 53; SATA 66
Nicholas of Autrecourt c.
1298-1369 .... **CMLC 108**
Nicholas of Cusa 1401-1464 .... **LC 80**
See also DLB 115
Nichols, John 1940- .... **CLC 38**
See also AMWS 13; CA 9-12R, 190; CAAE 190; CAAS 2; CANR 6, 70, 121, 185; DLBY 1982; LATS 1:2; MTFW 2005; TCWW 1, 2
Nichols, Leigh
See Koontz, Dean
Nichols, Peter (Richard) 1927- .... **CLC 5, 36, 65**
See also CA 104; CANR 33, 86; CBD; CD 5, 6; DLB 13, 245; MTCW 1
Nicholson, Linda .... **CLC 65**
Ni Chuilleanain, Eilean 1942- .... **PC 34**
See also CA 126; CANR 53, 83; CP 5, 6, 7; CWP; DLB 40
Nicolas, F. R. E.
See Freeling, Nicolas
Niedecker, Lorine 1903-1970 ..... **CLC 10, 42; PC 42**
See also CA 25-28; CAP 2; DAM POET; DLB 48

O'Casey, Brenda
See Haycraft, Anna

O'Casey, Sean 1880-1964 .... **CLC 1, 5, 9, 11, 15, 88; DC 12; WLCS**
See also BRW 7; CA 89-92; CANR 62; CBD; CDBLB 1914-1945; DA3; DAB; DAC; DAM DRAM, MST; DFS 19; DLB 10; EWL 3; MTCW 1, 2; MTFW 2005; RGEL 2; TEA; WLIT 4

O'Cathasaigh, Sean
See O'Casey, Sean

Occom, Samson 1723-1792 .... **LC 60; NNAL**
See also DLB 175

Occomy, Marita (Odette) Bonner 1899(?)-1971 ..... **HR 1:2; PC 72; TCLC 179**
See also BW 2; CA 142; DFS 13; DLB 51, 228

Ochs, Phil(ip David) 1940-1976 .... **CLC 17**
See also CA 185; 65-68

O'Connor, Edwin (Greene) 1918-1968 .... **CLC 14**
See also CA 93-96; 25-28R; MAL 5

O'Connor, Flannery 1925-1964 ..... **CLC 1, 2, 3, 6, 10, 13, 15, 21, 66, 104; SSC 1, 23, 61, 82, 111; TCLC 132; WLC 4**
See also AAYA 7; AMW; AMWR 2; BPFB 3; BYA 16; CA 1-4R; CANR 3, 41; CDALB 1941-1968; DA; DA3; DAB; DAC; DAM MST, NOV; DLB 2, 152; DLBD 12; DLBY 1980; EWL 3; EXPS; LAIT 5; MAL 5; MBL; MTCW 1, 2; MTFW 2005; NFS 3, 21; RGAL 4; RGSF 2; SSFS 2, 7, 10, 19; TUS

O'Connor, Frank 1903-1966
See O'Donovan, Michael Francis

O'Connor, Mary Flannery
See O'Connor, Flannery

O'Dell, Scott 1898-1989 .... **CLC 30**
See also AAYA 3, 44; BPFB 3; BYA 1, 2, 3, 5; CA 61-64; 129; CANR 12, 30, 112; CLR 1, 16, 126; DLB 52; JRDA; MAICYA 1, 2; SATA 12, 60, 134; WYA; YAW

Odets, Clifford 1906-1963 ..... **CLC 2, 28, 98; DC 6; TCLC 244**
See also AMWS 2; CA 85-88; CAD; CANR 62; DAM DRAM; DFS 3, 17, 20; DLB 7, 26, 341; EWL 3; MAL 5; MTCW 1, 2; MTFW 2005; RGAL 4; TUS

O'Doherty, Brian 1928- .... **CLC 76**
See also CA 105; CANR 108

O'Donnell, K. M.
See Malzberg, Barry N(athaniel)

O'Donnell, Lawrence
See Kuttner, Henry

O'Donovan, Michael Francis 1903-1966 .... **CLC 14, 23; SSC 5, 109**
See also BRWS 14; CA 93-96; CANR 84; DLB 162; EWL 3; RGSF 2; SSFS 5

Oe, Kenzaburo 1935- ... **CLC 10, 36, 86, 187, 303; SSC 20**
See also CA 97-100; CANR 36, 50, 74, 126; CWW 2; DA3; DAM NOV; DLB 182, 331; DLBY 1994; EWL 3; LATS 1:2; MJW; MTCW 1, 2; MTFW 2005; RGSF 2; RGWL 2, 3

Oe Kenzaburo
See Oe, Kenzaburo

O'Faolain, Julia 1932- .... **CLC 6, 19, 47, 108**
See also CA 81-84; CAAS 2; CANR 12, 61; CN 2, 3, 4, 5, 6, 7; DLB 14, 231, 319; FW; MTCW 1; RHW

O'Faolain, Sean 1900-1991 ...... **CLC 1, 7, 14, 32, 70; SSC 13; TCLC 143**
See also CA 61-64; 134; CANR 12, 66; CN 1, 2, 3, 4; DLB 15, 162; MTCW 1, 2; MTFW 2005; RGEL 2; RGSF 2

O'Flaherty, Liam 1896-1984 .... **CLC 5, 34; SSC 6, 116**
See also CA 101; 113; CANR 35; CN 1, 2, 3; DLB 36, 162; DLBY 1984; MTCW 1, 2; MTFW 2005; RGEL 2; RGSF 2; SSFS 5, 20

Ogai
See Mori Ogai

Ogilvy, Gavin
See Barrie, J. M.

O'Grady, Standish (James) 1846-1928 .... **TCLC 5**
See also CA 104; 157

O'Grady, Timothy 1951- .... **CLC 59**
See also CA 138

O'Hara, Frank 1926-1966 .... **CLC 2, 5, 13, 78; PC 45**
See also CA 9-12R; 25-28R; CANR 33; DA3; DAM POET; DLB 5, 16, 193; EWL 3; MAL 5; MTCW 1, 2; MTFW 2005; PFS 8, 12, 34, 38; RGAL 4; WP

O'Hara, John 1905-1970 . **CLC 1, 2, 3, 6, 11, 42; SSC 15**
See also AMW; BPFB 3; CA 5-8R; 25-28R; CANR 31, 60; CDALB 1929-1941; DAM NOV; DLB 9, 86, 324; DLBD 2; EWL 3; MAL 5; MTCW 1, 2; MTFW 2005; NFS 11; RGAL 4; RGSF 2

O'Hara, John Henry
See O'Hara, John

O'Hehir, Diana 1929- .... **CLC 41**
See also CA 245; CANR 177

O'Hehir, Diana F.
See O'Hehir, Diana

Ohiyesa
See Eastman, Charles A(lexander)

Okada, John 1923-1971 .... **AAL**
See also BYA 14; CA 212; DLB 312; NFS 25

O'Kelly, Seamus 1881(?)-1918 .... **SSC 136**

Okigbo, Christopher 1930-1967 ..... **BLC 1:3; CLC 25, 84; PC 7; TCLC 171**
See also AFW; BW 1, 3; CA 77-80; CANR 74; CDWLB 3; DAM MULT, POET; DLB 125; EWL 3; MTCW 1, 2; MTFW 2005; RGEL 2

Okigbo, Christopher Ifenayichukwu
See Okigbo, Christopher

Okri, Ben 1959- .... **BLC 2:3; CLC 87, 223; SSC 127**
See also AFW; BRWS 5; BW 2, 3; CA 130; 138; CANR 65, 128; CN 5, 6, 7; DLB 157, 231, 319, 326; EWL 3; INT CA-138; MTCW 2; MTFW 2005; RGSF 2; SSFS 20; WLIT 2; WWE 1

Old Boy
See Hughes, Thomas

Olds, Sharon 1942- .. **CLC 32, 39, 85; PC 22**
See also AMWS 10; CA 101; CANR 18, 41, 66, 98, 135, 211; CP 5, 6, 7; CPW; CWP; DAM POET; DLB 120; MAL 5; MTCW 2; PFS 17

Oldstyle, Jonathan
See Irving, Washington

Olesha, Iurii
See Olesha, Yuri (Karlovich)

Olesha, Iurii Karlovich
See Olesha, Yuri (Karlovich)

Olesha, Yuri (Karlovich) 1899-1960 . **CLC 8; SSC 69; TCLC 136**
See also CA 85-88; DLB 272; EW 11; EWL 3; RGWL 2, 3

Olesha, Yury Karlovich
See Olesha, Yuri (Karlovich)

Oliphant, Mrs.
See Oliphant, Margaret (Oliphant Wilson)

Oliphant, Laurence 1829(?)-1888 .. **NCLC 47**
See also DLB 18, 166

Oliphant, Margaret (Oliphant Wilson) 1828-1897 ... **NCLC 11, 61, 221; SSC 25**
See also BRWS 10; DLB 18, 159, 190; HGG; RGEL 2; RGSF 2; SUFW

Oliver, Mary 1935- ... **CLC 19, 34, 98; PC 75**
See also AMWS 7; CA 21-24R; CANR 9, 43, 84, 92, 138, 217; CP 4, 5, 6, 7; CWP; DLB 5, 193, 342; EWL 3; MTFW 2005; PFS 15, 31

Olivi, Peter 1248-1298 .... **CMLC 114**

Olivier, Laurence (Kerr) 1907-1989 . **CLC 20**
See also CA 111; 150; 129

O.L.S.
See Russell, George William

Olsen, Tillie 1912-2007 .... **CLC 4, 13, 114; SSC 11, 103**
See also AAYA 51; AMWS 13; BYA 11; CA 1-4R; 256; CANR 1, 43, 74, 132; CDALBS; CN 2, 3, 4, 5, 6, 7; DA; DA3; DAB; DAC; DAM MST; DLB 28, 206; DLBY 1980; EWL 3; EXPS; FW; MAL 5; MTCW 1, 2; MTFW 2005; RGAL 4; RGSF 2; SSFS 1, 32; TCLE 1:2; TCWW 2; TUS

Olson, Charles 1910-1970 . **CLC 1, 2, 5, 6, 9, 11, 29; PC 19**
See also AMWS 2; CA 13-16; 25-28R; CABS 2; CANR 35, 61; CP 1; DAM POET; DLB 5, 16, 193; EWL 3; MAL 5; MTCW 1, 2; RGAL 4; WP

Olson, Charles John
See Olson, Charles

Olson, Merle Theodore
See Olson, Toby

Olson, Toby 1937- .... **CLC 28**
See also CA 65-68; CAAS 11; CANR 9, 31, 84, 175; CP 3, 4, 5, 6, 7

Olyesha, Yuri
See Olesha, Yuri (Karlovich)

Olympiodorus of Thebes c. 375-c. 430 .... **CMLC 59**

Omar Khayyam
See Khayyam, Omar

Ondaatje, Michael 1943- ..... **CLC 14, 29, 51, 76, 180, 258; PC 28**
See also AAYA 66; CA 77-80; CANR 42, 74, 109, 133, 172; CN 5, 6, 7; CP 1, 2, 3, 4, 5, 6, 7; DA3; DAB; DAC; DAM MST; DLB 60, 323, 326; EWL 3; LATS 1:2; LMFS 2; MTCW 1, 2; MTFW 2005; NFS 23; PFS 8, 19; TCLE 1:2; TWA; WWE 1

Ondaatje, Philip Michael
See Ondaatje, Michael

Oneal, Elizabeth 1934- .... **CLC 30**
See also AAYA 5, 41; BYA 13; CA 106; CANR 28, 84; CLR 13; JRDA; MAICYA 1, 2; SATA 30, 82; WYA; YAW

Oneal, Zibby
See Oneal, Elizabeth

O'Neill, Eugene 1888-1953 ..... **DC 20; TCLC 1, 6, 27, 49, 225; WLC 4**
See also AAYA 54; AITN 1; AMW; AMWC 1; CA 110; 132; CAD; CANR 131; CDALB 1929-1941; DA; DA3; DAB; DAC; DAM DRAM, MST; DFS 2, 4, 5, 6, 9, 11, 12, 16, 20, 26, 27; DLB 7, 331; EWL 3; LAIT 3; LMFS 2; MAL 5; MTCW 1, 2; MTFW 2005; RGAL 4; TUS

O'Neill, Eugene Gladstone
See O'Neill, Eugene

Onetti, Juan Carlos 1909-1994 ... **CLC 7, 10; HLCS 2; SSC 23; TCLC 131**
See also CA 85-88; 145; CANR 32, 63; CD-WLB 3; CWW 2; DAM MULT, NOV; DLB 113; EWL 3; HW 1, 2; LAW; MTCW 1, 2; MTFW 2005; RGSF 2

O'Nolan, Brian
See O Nuallain, Brian

Paglia, Camille 1947- .... **CLC 68**
See also CA 140; CANR 72, 139; CPW;
FW; GLL 2; MTCW 2; MTFW 2005

Pagnol, Marcel (Paul)
1895-1974 .... **TCLC 208**
See also CA 128; 49-52; DLB 321; EWL 3;
GFL 1789 to the Present; MTCW 1;
RGWL 2, 3

Paige, Richard
See Koontz, Dean

Paine, Thomas 1737-1809 .... **NCLC 62**
See also AMWS 1; CDALB 1640-1865;
DLB 31, 43, 73, 158; LAIT 1; RGAL 4;
RGEL 2; TUS

Pakenham, Antonia
See Fraser, Antonia

Palamas, Costis
See Palamas, Kostes

Palamas, Kostes 1859-1943 .... **TCLC 5**
See also CA 105; 190; EWL 3; RGWL 2, 3

Palamas, Kostis
See Palamas, Kostes

Palazzeschi, Aldo 1885-1974 .... **CLC 11**
See also CA 89-92; 53-56; DLB 114, 264;
EWL 3

Pales Matos, Luis 1898-1959 .... **HLCS 2**
See Pales Matos, Luis
See also DLB 290; HW 1; LAW

Paley, Grace 1922-2007 ... **CLC 4, 6, 37, 140,
272; SSC 8**
See also AMWS 6; CA 25-28R; 263; CANR
13, 46, 74, 118; CN 2, 3, 4, 5, 6, 7; CPW;
DA3; DAM POP; DLB 28, 218; EWL 3;
EXPS; FW; INT CANR-13; MAL 5;
MBL; MTCW 1, 2; MTFW 2005; RGAL
4; RGSF 2; SSFS 3, 20, 27

Paley, Grace Goodside
See Paley, Grace

Palin, Michael 1943- .... **CLC 21**
See also CA 107; CANR 35, 109, 179; DLB
352; SATA 67

Palin, Michael Edward
See Palin, Michael

Palliser, Charles 1947- .... **CLC 65**
See also CA 136; CANR 76; CN 5, 6, 7

Palma, Ricardo 1833-1919 .... **TCLC 29**
See also CA 168; LAW

Pamuk, Orhan 1952- .... **CLC 185, 288**
See also AAYA 82; CA 142; CANR 75, 127,
172, 208; CWW 2; NFS 27; WLIT 6

Pancake, Breece Dexter 1952-1979 . **CLC 29;
SSC 61**
See also CA 123; 109; DLB 130

Pancake, Breece D'J
See Pancake, Breece Dexter

Panchenko, Nikolai .... **CLC 59**

Pankhurst, Emmeline (Goulden)
1858-1928 .... **TCLC 100**
See also CA 116; FW

Panko, Rudy
See Gogol, Nikolai

Papadiamantis, Alexandros
1851-1911 .... **TCLC 29**
See also CA 168; EWL 3

Papadiamantopoulos, Johannes
1856-1910 .... **TCLC 18**
See also CA 117; 242; GFL 1789 to the
Present

Papadiamantopoulos, Yannis
See Papadiamantopoulos, Johannes

Papini, Giovanni 1881-1956 .... **TCLC 22**
See also CA 121; 180; DLB 264

Paracelsus 1493-1541 .... **LC 14**
See also DLB 179

Parasol, Peter
See Stevens, Wallace

Pardo Bazan, Emilia 1851-1921 .... **SSC 30;
TCLC 189**
See also EWL 3; FW; RGSF 2; RGWL 2, 3

Paredes, Americo 1915-1999 .... **PC 83**
See also CA 37-40R; 179; DLB 209; EXPP;
HW 1

Pareto, Vilfredo 1848-1923 .... **TCLC 69**
See also CA 175

Paretsky, Sara 1947- .... **CLC 135**
See also AAYA 30; BEST 90:3; CA 125;
129; CANR 59, 95, 184, 218; CMW 4;
CPW; DA3; DAM POP; DLB 306; INT
CA-129; MSW; RGAL 4

Paretsky, Sara N.
See Paretsky, Sara

Parfenie, Maria
See Codrescu, Andrei

Parini, Jay 1948- .... **CLC 54, 133**
See also CA 97-100, 229; CAAE 229;
CAAS 16; CANR 32, 87, 198

Parini, Jay Lee
See Parini, Jay

Park, Jordan
See Kornbluth, C(yril) M.; Pohl, Frederik

Park, Robert E(zra) 1864-1944 ..... **TCLC 73**
See also CA 122; 165

Parker, Bert
See Ellison, Harlan

Parker, Dorothy 1893-1967 .... **CLC 15, 68;
DC 40; PC 28; SSC 2, 101; TCLC 143**
See also AMWS 9; CA 19-20; 25-28R; CAP
2; DA3; DAM POET; DLB 11, 45, 86;
EXPP; FW; MAL 5; MBL; MTCW 1, 2;
MTFW 2005; PFS 18; RGAL 4; RGSF 2;
TUS

Parker, Dorothy Rothschild
See Parker, Dorothy

Parker, Robert B. 1932-2010 .... **CLC 27, 283**
See also AAYA 28; BEST 89:4; BPFB 3;
CA 49-52; CANR 1, 26, 52, 89, 128, 165,
200; CMW 4; CPW; DAM NOV, POP;
DLB 306; INT CANR-26; MSW; MTCW
1; MTFW 2005

Parker, Robert Brown
See Parker, Robert B.

Parker, Theodore 1810-1860 .... **NCLC 186**
See also DLB 1, 235

Parkes, Lucas
See Harris, John (Wyndham Parkes Lucas)
Beynon

Parkin, Frank 1940- .... **CLC 43**
See also CA 147

Parkman, Francis, Jr. 1823-1893 .. **NCLC 12**
See also AMWS 2; DLB 1, 30, 183, 186,
235; RGAL 4

Parks, Gordon 1912-2006 . **BLC 1:3; CLC 1,
16**
See also AAYA 36; AITN 2; BW 2, 3; CA
41-44R; 249; CANR 26, 66, 145; DA3;
DAM MULT; DLB 33; MTCW 2; MTFW
2005; NFS 32; SATA 8, 108; SATA-Obit
175

Parks, Gordon Roger Alexander
See Parks, Gordon

Parks, Suzan-Lori 1964(?)- ... **BLC 2:3; CLC
309; DC 23**
See also AAYA 55; CA 201; CAD; CD 5,
6; CWD; DFS 22; DLB 341; RGAL 4

Parks, Tim 1954- .... **CLC 147**
See also CA 126; 131; CANR 77, 144, 202;
CN 7; DLB 231; INT CA-131

Parks, Timothy Harold
See Parks, Tim

Parmenides c. 515B.C.-c.
450B.C. .... **CMLC 22**
See also DLB 176

Parnell, Thomas 1679-1718 .... **LC 3**
See also DLB 95; RGEL 2

Parr, Catherine c. 1513(?)-1548 .... **LC 86**
See also DLB 136

Parra, Nicanor 1914- ... **CLC 2, 102; HLC 2;
PC 39**
See also CA 85-88; CANR 32; CWW 2;
DAM MULT; DLB 283; EWL 3; HW 1;
LAW; MTCW 1

Parra Sanojo, Ana Teresa de la 1890-1936
See de la Parra, Teresa

Parrish, Mary Frances
See Fisher, M(ary) F(rances) K(ennedy)

Parshchikov, Aleksei 1954- .... **CLC 59**
See also DLB 285

Parshchikov, Aleksei Maksimovich
See Parshchikov, Aleksei

Parson, Professor
See Coleridge, Samuel Taylor

Parson Lot
See Kingsley, Charles

Parton, Sara Payson Willis
1811-1872 .... **NCLC 86**
See also DLB 43, 74, 239

Partridge, Anthony
See Oppenheim, E(dward) Phillips

Pascal, Blaise 1623-1662 .... **LC 35**
See also DLB 268; EW 3; GFL Beginnings
to 1789; RGWL 2, 3; TWA

Pascoli, Giovanni 1855-1912 .... **TCLC 45**
See also CA 170; EW 7; EWL 3

Pasolini, Pier Paolo 1922-1975 .. **CLC 20, 37,
106; PC 17**
See also CA 93-96; 61-64; CANR 63; DLB
128, 177; EWL 3; MTCW 1; RGWL 2, 3

Pasquini
See Silone, Ignazio

Pastan, Linda (Olenik) 1932- .... **CLC 27**
See also CA 61-64; CANR 18, 40, 61, 113;
CP 3, 4, 5, 6, 7; CSW; CWP; DAM
POET; DLB 5; PFS 8, 25, 32

Pasternak, Boris 1890-1960 ... **CLC 7, 10, 18,
63; PC 6; SSC 31; TCLC 188; WLC 4**
See also BPFB 3; CA 127; 116; DA; DA3;
DAB; DAC; DAM MST, NOV, POET;
DLB 302, 331; EW 10; MTCW 1, 2;
MTFW 2005; NFS 26; RGSF 2; RGWL
2, 3; TWA; WP

Pasternak, Boris Leonidovich
See Pasternak, Boris

Patchen, Kenneth 1911-1972 .... **CLC 1, 2, 18**
See also BG 1:3; CA 1-4R; 33-36R; CANR
3, 35; CN 1; CP 1; DAM POET; DLB 16,
48; EWL 3; MAL 5; MTCW 1; RGAL 4

Patchett, Ann 1963- .... **CLC 244**
See also AAYA 69; AMWS 12; CA 139;
CANR 64, 110, 167, 200; DLB 350;
MTFW 2005; NFS 30

Pater, Walter (Horatio) 1839-1894 . **NCLC 7,
90, 159**
See also BRW 5; CDBLB 1832-1890; DLB
57, 156; RGEL 2; TEA

Paterson, A(ndrew) B(arton)
1864-1941 .... **TCLC 32**
See also CA 155; DLB 230; RGEL 2; SATA
97

Paterson, Banjo
See Paterson, A(ndrew) B(arton)

Paterson, Katherine 1932- .... **CLC 12, 30**
See also AAYA 1, 31; BYA 1, 2, 7; CA 21-
24R; CANR 28, 59, 111, 173, 196; CLR
7, 50, 127; CWRI 5; DLB 52; JRDA;
LAIT 4; MAICYA 1, 2; MAICYAS 1;
MTCW 1; SATA 13, 53, 92, 133, 204;
WYA; YAW

Paterson, Katherine Womeldorf
See Paterson, Katherine

Patmore, Coventry Kersey Dighton
1823-1896 .... **NCLC 9; PC 59**
See also DLB 35, 98; RGEL 2; TEA

Paton, Alan 1903-1988 ..... CLC 4, 10, 25, 55, 106; TCLC 165; WLC 4
See also AAYA 26; AFW; BPFB 3; BRWS 2; BYA 1; CA 13-16; 125; CANR 22; CAP 1; CN 1, 2, 3, 4; DA; DA3; DAB; DAC; DAM MST, NOV; DLB 225; DLBD 17; EWL 3; EXPN; LAIT 4; MTCW 1, 2; MTFW 2005; NFS 3, 12; RGEL 2; SATA 11; SATA-Obit 56; SSFS 29; TWA; WLIT 2; WWE 1

Paton, Alan Stewart
See Paton, Alan

Paton Walsh, Gillian
See Paton Walsh, Jill

Paton Walsh, Jill 1937- .... CLC 35
See also AAYA 11, 47; BYA 1, 8; CA 262; CAAE 262; CANR 38, 83, 158; CLR 2, 6, 128; DLB 161; JRDA; MAICYA 1, 2; SAAS 3; SATA 4, 72, 109, 190; SATA-Essay 190; WYA; YAW

Patsauq, Markoosie 1942- .... NNAL
See also CA 101; CLR 23; CWRI 5; DAM MULT

Patterson, (Horace) Orlando (Lloyd)
1940- .... BLCS
See also BW 1; CA 65-68; CANR 27, 84; CN 1, 2, 3, 4, 5, 6

Patton, George S(mith), Jr.
1885-1945 .... TCLC 79
See also CA 189

Paulding, James Kirke 1778-1860 ... NCLC 2
See also DLB 3, 59, 74, 250; RGAL 4

Paulin, Thomas Neilson
See Paulin, Tom

Paulin, Tom 1949- .... CLC 37, 177
See also CA 123; 128; CANR 98; CP 3, 4, 5, 6, 7; DLB 40

Pausanias c. 1st cent. - .... CMLC 36

Paustovsky, Konstantin (Georgievich)
1892-1968 .... CLC 40
See also CA 93-96; 25-28R; DLB 272; EWL 3

Pavese, Cesare 1908-1950 .... PC 13; SSC 19; TCLC 3, 240
See also CA 104; 169; DLB 128, 177; EW 12; EWL 3; PFS 20; RGSF 2; RGWL 2, 3; TWA; WLIT 7

Pavic, Milorad 1929-2009 .... CLC 60
See also CA 136; CDWLB 4; CWW 2; DLB 181; EWL 3; RGWL 3

Pavlov, Ivan Petrovich 1849-1936 . TCLC 91
See also CA 118; 180

Pavlova, Karolina Karlovna
1807-1893 .... NCLC 138
See also DLB 205

Payne, Alan
See Jakes, John

Payne, John Howard 1791-1852 .. NCLC 241
See also DLB 37; RGAL 4

Payne, Rachel Ann
See Jakes, John

Paz, Gil
See Lugones, Leopoldo

Paz, Octavio 1914-1998 . CLC 3, 4, 6, 10, 19, 51, 65, 119; HLC 2; PC 1, 48; TCLC 211; WLC 4
See also AAYA 50; CA 73-76; 165; CANR 32, 65, 104; CWW 2; DA; DA3; DAB; DAC; DAM MST, MULT, POET; DLB 290, 331; DLBY 1990, 1998; DNFS 1; EWL 3; HW 1, 2; LAW; LAWS 1; MTCW 1, 2; MTFW 2005; PFS 18, 30, 38; RGWL 2, 3; SSFS 13; TWA; WLIT 1

p'Bitek, Okot 1931-1982 . BLC 1:3; CLC 96; TCLC 149
See also AFW; BW 2, 3; CA 124; 107; CANR 82; CP 1, 2, 3; DAM MULT; DLB 125; EWL 3; MTCW 1, 2; MTFW 2005; RGEL 2; WLIT 2

Peabody, Elizabeth Palmer
1804-1894 .... NCLC 169
See also DLB 1, 223

Peacham, Henry 1578-1644(?) .... LC 119
See also DLB 151

Peacock, Molly 1947- .... CLC 60
See also CA 103, 262; CAAE 262; CAAS 21; CANR 52, 84; CP 5, 6, 7; CWP; DLB 120, 282

Peacock, Thomas Love
1785-1866 .... NCLC 22; PC 87
See also BRW 4; DLB 96, 116; RGEL 2; RGSF 2

Peake, Mervyn 1911-1968 .... CLC 7, 54
See also CA 5-8R; 25-28R; CANR 3; DLB 15, 160, 255; FANT; MTCW 1; RGEL 2; SATA 23; SFW 4

Pearce, Ann Philippa
See Pearce, Philippa

Pearce, Philippa 1920-2006 .... CLC 21
See also BYA 5; CA 5-8R; 255; CANR 4, 109; CLR 9; CWRI 5; DLB 161; FANT; MAICYA 1; SATA 1, 67, 129; SATA-Obit 179

Pearl, Eric
See Elman, Richard (Martin)

Pearson, Jean Mary
See Gardam, Jane

Pearson, Thomas Reid
See Pearson, T.R.

Pearson, T.R. 1956- .... CLC 39
See also CA 120; 130; CANR 97, 147, 185; CSW; INT CA-130

Peck, Dale 1967- .... CLC 81
See also CA 146; CANR 72, 127, 180; GLL 2

Peck, John (Frederick) 1941- .... CLC 3
See also CA 49-52; CANR 3, 100; CP 4, 5, 6, 7

Peck, Richard 1934- .... CLC 21
See also AAYA 1, 24; BYA 1, 6, 8, 11; CA 85-88; CANR 19, 38, 129, 178; CLR 15, 142; INT CANR-19; JRDA; MAICYA 1, 2; SAAS 2; SATA 18, 55, 97, 110, 158, 190; SATA-Essay 110; WYA; YAW

Peck, Richard Wayne
See Peck, Richard

Peck, Robert Newton 1928- .... CLC 17
See also AAYA 3, 43; BYA 1, 6; CA 81-84, 182; CAAE 182; CANR 31, 63, 127; CLR 45, 163; DA; DAC; DAM MST; JRDA; LAIT 3; MAICYA 1, 2; NFS 29; SAAS 1; SATA 21, 62, 111, 156; SATA-Essay 108; WYA; YAW

Peckinpah, David Samuel
See Peckinpah, Sam

Peckinpah, Sam 1925-1984 .... CLC 20
See also CA 109; 114; CANR 82

Pedersen, Knut 1859-1952 .. TCLC 2, 14, 49, 151, 203
See also AAYA 79; CA 104; 119; CANR 63; DLB 297, 330; EW 8; EWL 8; MTCW 1, 2; RGWL 2, 3

Peele, George 1556-1596 .... DC 27; LC 115
See also BRW 1; DLB 62, 167; RGEL 2

Peeslake, Gaffer
See Durrell, Lawrence

Peguy, Charles (Pierre)
1873-1914 .... TCLC 10
See also CA 107; 193; DLB 258; EWL 3; GFL 1789 to the Present

Peirce, Charles Sanders
1839-1914 .... TCLC 81
See also CA 194; DLB 270

Pelagius c. 350-c. 418 .... CMLC 118

Pelecanos, George P. 1957- .... CLC 236
See also CA 138; CANR 122, 165, 194; DLB 306

Pelevin, Victor 1962- .... CLC 238
See also CA 154; CANR 88, 159, 197; DLB 285

Pelevin, Viktor Olegovich
See Pelevin, Victor

Pellicer, Carlos 1897(?)-1977 .... HLCS 2
See also CA 153; 69-72; DLB 290; EWL 3; HW 1

Pena, Ramon del Valle y
See Valle-Inclan, Ramon del

Pendennis, Arthur Esquir
See Thackeray, William Makepeace

Penn, Arthur
See Matthews, (James) Brander

Penn, William 1644-1718 .... LC 25
See also DLB 24

Penny, Carolyn
See Chute, Carolyn

PEPECE
See Prado (Calvo), Pedro

Pepys, Samuel 1633-1703 ... LC 11, 58; WLC 4
See also BRW 2; CDBLB 1660-1789; DA; DA3; DAB; DAC; DAM MST; DLB 101, 213; NCFS 4; RGEL 2; TEA; WLIT 3

Percy, Thomas 1729-1811 .... NCLC 95
See also DLB 104

Percy, Walker 1916-1990 .... CLC 2, 3, 6, 8, 14, 18, 47, 65
See also AMWS 3; BPFB 3; CA 1-4R; 131; CANR 1, 23, 64; CN 1, 2, 3, 4; CPW; CSW; DA3; DAM NOV, POP; DLB 2; DLBY 1980, 1990; EWL 3; MAL 5; MTCW 1, 2; MTFW 2005; RGAL 4; TUS

Percy, William Alexander
1885-1942 .... TCLC 84
See also CA 163; MTCW 2

Perdurabo, Frater
See Crowley, Edward Alexander

Perec, Georges 1936-1982 .... CLC 56, 116
See also CA 141; DLB 83, 299; EWL 3; GFL 1789 to the Present; RGHL; RGWL 3

Pereda (y Sanchez de Porrua), Jose Maria
de 1833-1906 .... TCLC 16
See also CA 117

Pereda y Porrua, Jose Maria de
See Pereda (y Sanchez de Porrua), Jose Maria de

Peregoy, George Weems
See Mencken, H. L.

Perelman, S(idney) J(oseph)
1904-1979 .. CLC 3, 5, 9, 15, 23, 44, 49; SSC 32
See also AAYA 79; AITN 1, 2; BPFB 3; CA 73-76; 89-92; CANR 18; DAM DRAM; DLB 11, 44; MTCW 1, 2; MTFW 2005; RGAL 4

Peret, Benjamin 1899-1959 .... PC 33; TCLC 20
See also CA 117; 186; GFL 1789 to the Present

Perets, Yitskhok Leybush
See Peretz, Isaac Loeb

Peretz, Isaac Leib (?)-
See Peretz, Isaac Loeb

Peretz, Isaac Loeb 1851-1915 .... SSC 26; TCLC 16
See Peretz, Isaac Leib
See also CA 109; 201; DLB 333

Peretz, Yitzkhok Leibush
See Peretz, Isaac Loeb

Perez Galdos, Benito 1843-1920 ..... HLCS 2; TCLC 27
See also CA 125; 153; EW 7; EWL 3; HW 1; RGWL 2, 3

Pirandello, Luigi 1867-1936 .. **DC 5; SSC 22, 148; TCLC 4, 29, 172; WLC 4**
See also CA 104; 153; CANR 103; DA; DA3; DAB; DAC; DAM DRAM, MST; DFS 4, 9; DLB 264, 331; EW 8; EWL 3; MTCW 2; MTFW 2005; RGSF 2; RGWL 2, 3; SSFS 30, 33; WLIT 7

Pirdousi
See Ferdowsi, Abu'l Qasem

Pirdousi, Abu-l-Qasim
See Ferdowsi, Abu'l Qasem

Pirsig, Robert M(aynard) 1928- ... **CLC 4, 6, 73**
See also CA 53-56; CANR 42, 74; CPW 1; DA3; DAM POP; MTCW 1, 2; MTFW 2005; NFS 31; SATA 39

Pisan, Christine de
See Christine de Pizan

Pisarev, Dmitrii Ivanovich
See Pisarev, Dmitry Ivanovich

Pisarev, Dmitry Ivanovich 1840-1868 .... **NCLC 25**
See also DLB 277

Pix, Mary (Griffith) 1666-1709 ..... **LC 8, 149**
See also DLB 80

Pixerecourt, (Rene Charles) Guilbert de 1773-1844 .... **NCLC 39**
See also DLB 192; GFL 1789 to the Present

Plaatje, Sol(omon) T(shekisho) 1878-1932 .... **BLCS; TCLC 73**
See also BW 2, 3; CA 141; CANR 79; DLB 125, 225

Plaidy, Jean
See Hibbert, Eleanor Alice Burford

Planche, James Robinson 1796-1880 .... **NCLC 42**
See also RGEL 2

Plant, Robert 1948- .... **CLC 12**

Plante, David 1940- .... **CLC 7, 23, 38**
See also CA 37-40R; CANR 12, 36, 58, 82, 152, 191; CN 2, 3, 4, 5, 6, 7; DAM NOV; DLBY 1983; INT CANR-12; MTCW 1

Plante, David Robert
See Plante, David

Plath, Sylvia 1932-1963 ..... **CLC 1, 2, 3, 5, 9, 11, 14, 17, 50, 51, 62, 111; PC 1, 37; TCLC 252; WLC 4**
See also AAYA 13; AMWR 2; AMWS 1; BPFB 3; CA 19-20; CANR 34, 101; CAP 2; CDALB 1941-1968; DA; DA3; DAB; DAC; DAM MST, POET; DLB 5, 6, 152; EWL 3; EXPN; EXPP; FL 1:6; FW; LAIT 4; MAL 5; MBL; MTCW 1, 2; MTFW 2005; NFS 1; PAB; PFS 1, 15, 28, 33; RGAL 4; SATA 96; TUS; WP; YAW

Plato c. 428B.C.-347B.C. .... **CMLC 8, 75, 98; WLCS**
See also AW 1; CDWLB 1; DA; DA3; DAB; DAC; DAM MST; DLB 176; LAIT 1; LATS 1:1; RGWL 2, 3; WLIT 8

Platonov, Andrei
See Klimentov, Andrei Platonovich

Platonov, Andrei Platonovich
See Klimentov, Andrei Platonovich

Platonov, Andrey Platonovich
See Klimentov, Andrei Platonovich

Platt, Kin 1911- .... **CLC 26**
See also AAYA 11; CA 17-20R; CANR 11; JRDA; SAAS 17; SATA 21, 86; WYA

Plautus c. 254B.C.-c. 184B.C. .... **CMLC 24, 92; DC 6**
See also AW 1; CDWLB 1; DLB 211; RGWL 2, 3; WLIT 8

Plick et Plock
See Simenon, Georges

Plieksans, Janis
See Rainis, Janis

Plimpton, George 1927-2003 .... **CLC 36**
See also AITN 1; AMWS 16; CA 21-24R; 224; CANR 32, 70, 103, 133; DLB 185, 241; MTCW 1, 2; MTFW 2005; SATA 10; SATA-Obit 150

Plimpton, George Ames
See Plimpton, George

Pliny the Elder c. 23-79 .... **CMLC 23**
See also DLB 211

Pliny the Younger c. 61-c. 112 ...... **CMLC 62**
See also AW 2; DLB 211

Plomer, William Charles Franklin 1903-1973 .... **CLC 4, 8**
See also AFW; BRWS 11; CA 21-22; CANR 34; CAP 2; CN 1; CP 1, 2; DLB 20, 162, 191, 225; EWL 3; MTCW 1; RGEL 2; RGSF 2; SATA 24

Plotinus 204-270 .... **CMLC 46**
See also CDWLB 1; DLB 176

Plowman, Piers
See Kavanagh, Patrick (Joseph)

Plum, J.
See Wodehouse, P. G.

Plumly, Stanley 1939- .... **CLC 33**
See also CA 108; 110; CANR 97, 185; CP 3, 4, 5, 6, 7; DLB 5, 193; INT CA-110

Plumly, Stanley Ross
See Plumly, Stanley

Plumpe, Friedrich Wilhelm
See Murnau, F.W.

Plutarch c. 46-c. 120 .... **CMLC 60**
See also AW 2; CDWLB 1; DLB 176; RGWL 2, 3; TWA; WLIT 8

Po Chu-i 772-846 .... **CMLC 24**

Podhoretz, Norman 1930- .... **CLC 189**
See also AMWS 8; CA 9-12R; CANR 7, 78, 135, 179

Poe, Edgar Allan 1809-1849 ..... **NCLC 1, 16, 55, 78, 94, 97, 117, 211; PC 1, 54; SSC 1, 22, 34, 35, 54, 88, 111, 156; WLC 4**
See also AAYA 14; AMW; AMWC 1; AMWR 2; BPFB 3; BYA 5, 11; CDALB 1640-1865; CMW 4; DA; DA3; DAB; DAC; DAM MST, POET; DLB 3, 59, 73, 74, 248, 254; EXPP; EXPS; GL 3; HGG; LAIT 2; LATS 1:1; LMFS 1; MSW; PAB; PFS 1, 3, 9; RGAL 4; RGSF 2; SATA 23; SCFW 1, 2; SFW 4; SSFS 2, 4, 7, 8, 16, 26, 29; SUFW; TUS; WP; WYA

Poet of Titchfield Street, The
See Pound, Ezra

Poggio Bracciolini, Gian Francesco 1380-1459 .... **LC 125**

Pohl, Frederik 1919- .... **CLC 18; SSC 25**
See also AAYA 24; CA 61-64, 188; CAAE 188; CAAS 1; CANR 11, 37, 81, 140; CN 1, 2, 3, 4, 5, 6; DLB 8; INT CANR-11; MTCW 1, 2; MTFW 2005; SATA 24; SCFW 1, 2; SFW 4

Poirier, Louis
See Gracq, Julien

Poitier, Sidney 1927- .... **CLC 26**
See also AAYA 60; BW 1; CA 117; CANR 94

Pokagon, Simon 1830-1899 .... **NNAL**
See also DAM MULT

Polanski, Roman 1933- .... **CLC 16, 178**
See also CA 77-80

Poliakoff, Stephen 1952- .... **CLC 38**
See also CA 106; CANR 116; CBD; CD 5, 6; DLB 13

Police, The
See Copeland, Stewart; Sting; Summers, Andy

Polidori, John William 1795-1821 .... **NCLC 51; SSC 97**
See also DLB 116; HGG

Poliziano, Angelo 1454-1494 .... **LC 120**
See also WLIT 7

Pollitt, Katha 1949- .... **CLC 28, 122**
See also CA 120; 122; CANR 66, 108, 164, 200; MTCW 1, 2; MTFW 2005

Pollock, (Mary) Sharon 1936- .... **CLC 50**
See also CA 141; CANR 132; CD 5; CWD; DAC; DAM DRAM, MST; DFS 3; DLB 60; FW

Pollock, Sharon 1936- .... **DC 20**
See also CD 6

Polo, Marco 1254-1324 .... **CMLC 15**
See also WLIT 7

Polonsky, Abraham (Lincoln) 1910-1999 .... **CLC 92**
See also CA 104; 187; DLB 26; INT CA-104

Polybius c. 200B.C.-c. 118B.C. ...... **CMLC 17**
See also AW 1; DLB 176; RGWL 2, 3

Pomerance, Bernard 1940- .... **CLC 13**
See also CA 101; CAD; CANR 49, 134; CD 5, 6; DAM DRAM; DFS 9; LAIT 2

Ponge, Francis 1899-1988 ..... **CLC 6, 18; PC 107**
See also CA 85-88; 126; CANR 40, 86; DAM POET; DLBY 2002; EWL 3; GFL 1789 to the Present; RGWL 2, 3

Poniatowska, Elena 1932- . **CLC 140; HLC 2**
See also CA 101; CANR 32, 66, 107, 156; CDWLB 3; CWW 2; DAM MULT; DLB 113; EWL 3; HW 1, 2; LAWS 1; WLIT 1

Pontoppidan, Henrik 1857-1943 .... **TCLC 29**
See also CA 170; DLB 300, 331

Ponty, Maurice Merleau
See Merleau-Ponty, Maurice

Poole, Josephine
See Helyar, Jane Penelope Josephine

Poole, (Jane Penelope) Josephine
See Helyar, Jane Penelope Josephine

Popa, Vasko 1922-1991 . **CLC 19; TCLC 167**
See also CA 112; 148; CDWLB 4; DLB 181; EWL 3; RGWL 2, 3

Pope, Alexander 1688-1744 ...... **LC 3, 58, 60, 64, 164; PC 26; WLC 4**
See also BRW 3; BRWC 1; BRWR 1; CD-BLB 1660-1789; DA; DA3; DAB; DAC; DAM MST, POET; DLB 95, 101, 213; EXPP; PAB; PFS 12; RGEL 2; WLIT 3; WP

Popov, Evgenii Anatol'evich
See Popov, Yevgeny

Popov, Yevgeny .... **CLC 59**
See also DLB 285

Poquelin, Jean-Baptiste
See Moliere

Porete, Marguerite (?)-1310 .... **CMLC 73**
See also DLB 208

Porphyry c. 233-c. 305 .... **CMLC 71**

Porter, Connie (Rose) 1959(?)- .... **CLC 70**
See also AAYA 65; BW 2, 3; CA 142; CANR 90, 109; SATA 81, 129

Porter, Gene Stratton
See Stratton-Porter, Gene

Porter, Geneva Grace
See Stratton-Porter, Gene

Porter, Katherine Anne 1890-1980 ... **CLC 1, 3, 7, 10, 13, 15, 27, 101; SSC 4, 31, 43, 108; TCLC 233**
See also AAYA 42; AITN 2; AMW; BPFB 3; CA 1-4R; 101; CANR 1, 65; CDALBS; CN 1, 2; DA; DA3; DAB; DAC; DAM MST, NOV; DLB 4, 9, 102; DLBD 12; DLBY 1980; EWL 3; EXPS; LAIT 3; MAL 5; MBL; MTCW 1, 2; MTFW 2005; NFS 14; RGAL 4; RGSF 2; SATA 39; SATA-Obit 23; SSFS 1, 8, 11, 16, 23; TCWW 2; TUS

Porter, Peter 1929-2010 .... **CLC 5, 13, 33**
See also CA 85-88; CP 1, 2, 3, 4, 5, 6, 7; DLB 40, 289; WWE 1

Porter, Peter Neville Frederick
   See Porter, Peter
Porter, R. E.
   See Hoch, Edward D.
Porter, William Sydney
   See Henry, O.
Portillo (y Pacheco), Jose Lopez
   See Lopez Portillo (y Pacheco), Jose
Portillo Trambley, Estela
   1927-1998 .... HLC 2; TCLC 163
   See also CA 77-80; CANR 32; DAM
   MULT; DLB 209; HW 1; RGAL 4
Posey, Alexander (Lawrence)
   1873-1908 .... NNAL
   See also CA 144; CANR 80; DAM MULT;
   DLB 175
Posse, Abel .... CLC 70, 273
   See also CA 252
Post, Melville Davisson
   1869-1930 .... TCLC 39
   See also CA 110; 202; CMW 4
Postl, Carl
   See Sealsfield, Charles
Postman, Neil 1931(?)-2003 .... CLC 244
   See also CA 102; 221
Potocki, Jan 1761-1815 .... NCLC 229
Potok, Chaim 1929-2002 ... CLC 2, 7, 14, 26, 112
   See also AAYA 15, 50; AITN 1, 2; BPFB 3;
   BYA 1; CA 17-20R; 208; CANR 19, 35,
   64, 98; CLR 92; CN 4, 5, 6; DA3; DAM
   NOV; DLB 28, 152; EXPN; INT CANR-
   19; LAIT 4; MTCW 1, 2; MTFW 2005;
   NFS 4, 34; RGHL; SATA 33, 106; SATA-
   Obit 134; TUS; YAW
Potok, Herbert Harold
   See Potok, Chaim
Potok, Herman Harold
   See Potok, Chaim
Potter, Dennis (Christopher George)
   1935-1994 .... CLC 58, 86, 123
   See also BRWS 10; CA 107; 145; CANR
   33, 61; CBD; DLB 233; MTCW 1
Pound, Ezra 1885-1972 . CLC 1, 2, 3, 4, 5, 7,
   10, 13, 18, 34, 48, 50, 112; PC 4, 95;
   WLC 5
   See also AAYA 47; AMW; AMWR 1; CA
   5-8R; 37-40R; CANR 40; CDALB 1917-
   1929; CP 1; DA; DA3; DAB; DAC; DAM
   MST, POET; DLB 4, 45, 63; DLBD 15;
   EFS 1:2, 2:1; EWL 3; EXPP; LMFS 2;
   MAL 5; MTCW 1, 2; MTFW 2005; PAB;
   PFS 2, 8, 16; RGAL 4; TUS; WP
Pound, Ezra Weston Loomis
   See Pound, Ezra
Povod, Reinaldo 1959-1994 .... CLC 44
   See also CA 136; 146; CANR 83
Powell, Adam Clayton, Jr.
   1908-1972 .... BLC 1:3; CLC 89
   See also BW 1, 3; CA 102; 33-36R; CANR
   86; DAM MULT; DLB 345
Powell, Anthony 1905-2000 ... CLC 1, 3, 7, 9,
   10, 31
   See also BRW 7; CA 1-4R; 189; CANR 1,
   32, 62, 107; CDBLB 1945-1960; CN 1, 2,
   3, 4, 5, 6; DLB 15; EWL 3; MTCW 1, 2;
   MTFW 2005; RGEL 2; TEA
Powell, Dawn 1896(?)-1965 .... CLC 66
   See also CA 5-8R; CANR 121; DLBY 1997
Powell, Padgett 1952- .... CLC 34
   See also CA 126; CANR 63, 101, 215;
   CSW; DLB 234; DLBY 01; SSFS 25
Power, Susan 1961- .... CLC 91
   See also BYA 14; CA 160; CANR 135; NFS
   11

Powers, J(ames) F(arl) 1917-1999 ..... CLC 1,
   4, 8, 57; SSC 4
   See also CA 1-4R; 181; CANR 2, 61; CN
   1, 2, 3, 4, 5, 6; DLB 130; MTCW 1;
   RGAL 4; RGSF 2
Powers, John
   See Powers, John R.
Powers, John R. 1945- .... CLC 66
   See also CA 69-72
Powers, Richard 1957- .... CLC 93, 292
   See also AMWS 9; BPFB 3; CA 148;
   CANR 80, 180; CN 6, 7; DLB 350;
   MTFW 2005; TCLE 1:2
Powers, Richard S.
   See Powers, Richard
Pownall, David 1938- .... CLC 10
   See also CA 89-92, 180; CAAS 18; CANR
   49, 101; CBD; CD 5, 6; CN 4, 5, 6, 7;
   DLB 14
Powys, John Cowper 1872-1963 ... CLC 7, 9,
   15, 46, 125
   See also CA 85-88; CANR 106; DLB 15,
   255; EWL 3; FANT; MTCW 1, 2; MTFW
   2005; RGEL 2; SUFW
Powys, T(heodore) F(rancis)
   1875-1953 .... TCLC 9
   See also BRWS 8; CA 106; 189; DLB 36,
   162; EWL 3; FANT; RGEL 2; SUFW
Pozzo, Modesta
   See Fonte, Moderata
Prado (Calvo), Pedro 1886-1952 ... TCLC 75
   See also CA 131; DLB 283; HW 1; LAW
Prager, Emily 1952- .... CLC 56
   See also CA 204
Pratchett, Terence David John
   See Pratchett, Terry
Pratchett, Terry 1948- .... CLC 197
   See also AAYA 19, 54; BPFB 3; CA 143;
   CANR 87, 126, 170; CLR 64; CN 6, 7;
   CPW; CWRI 5; FANT; MTFW 2005;
   SATA 82, 139, 185; SFW 4; SUFW 2
Pratolini, Vasco 1913-1991 .... TCLC 124
   See also CA 211; DLB 177; EWL 3; RGWL
   2, 3
Pratt, E(dwin) J(ohn) 1883(?)-1964 . CLC 19
   See also CA 141; 93-96; CANR 77; DAC;
   DAM POET; DLB 92; EWL 3; RGEL 2;
   TWA
Premacanda
   See Srivastava, Dhanpat Rai
Premchand
   See Srivastava, Dhanpat Rai
Prem Chand, Munshi
   See Srivastava, Dhanpat Rai
Premchand, Munshi
   See Srivastava, Dhanpat Rai
Prescott, William Hickling
   1796-1859 .... NCLC 163
   See also DLB 1, 30, 59, 235
Preseren, France 1800-1849 .... NCLC 127
   See also CDWLB 4; DLB 147
Preston, Thomas 1537-1598 .... LC 189
   See also DLB 62
Preussler, Otfried 1923- .... CLC 17
   See also CA 77-80; SATA 24
Prevert, Jacques 1900-1977 .... CLC 15
   See also CA 77-80; 69-72; CANR 29, 61,
   207; DLB 258; EWL 3; GFL 1789 to the
   Present; IDFW 3, 4; MTCW 1; RGWL 2,
   3; SATA-Obit 30
Prevert, Jacques Henri Marie
   See Prevert, Jacques
Prevost, (Antoine Francois)
   1697-1763 .... LC 1, 174
   See also DLB 314; EW 4; GFL Beginnings
   to 1789; RGWL 2, 3
Price, Edward Reynolds
   See Price, Reynolds

Price, Reynolds 1933-2011 .... CLC 3, 6, 13,
   43, 50, 63, 212; SSC 22
   See also AMWS 6; CA 1-4R; CANR 1, 37,
   57, 87, 128, 177, 217; CN 1, 2, 3, 4, 5, 6,
   7; CSW; DAM NOV; DLB 2, 218, 278;
   EWL 3; INT CANR-37; MAL 5; MTFW
   2005; NFS 18
Price, Richard 1949- .... CLC 6, 12, 299
   See also CA 49-52; CANR 3, 147, 190; CN
   7; DLBY 1981
Prichard, Katharine Susannah
   1883-1969 .... CLC 46
   See also CA 11-12; CANR 33; CAP 1; DLB
   260; MTCW 1; RGEL 2; RGSF 2; SATA
   66
Priestley, J(ohn) B(oynton)
   1894-1984 .... CLC 2, 5, 9, 34
   See also BRW 7; CA 9-12R; 113; CANR
   33; CDBLB 1914-1945; CN 1, 2, 3; DA3;
   DAM DRAM, NOV; DLB 10, 34, 77,
   100, 139; DLBY 1984; EWL 3; MTCW
   1, 2; MTFW 2005; RGEL 2; SFW 4
Prince 1958- .... CLC 35
   See also CA 213
Prince, F(rank) T(empleton)
   1912-2003 .... CLC 22
   See also CA 101; 219; CANR 43, 79; CP 1,
   2, 3, 4, 5, 6, 7; DLB 20
Prince Kropotkin
   See Kropotkin, Peter
Prior, Matthew 1664-1721 ...... LC 4; PC 102
   See also DLB 95; RGEL 2
Prishvin, Mikhail 1873-1954 .... TCLC 75
   See also DLB 272; EWL 3 !**
Prishvin, Mikhail Mikhailovich
   See Prishvin, Mikhail
Pritchard, William H(arrison)
   1932- .... CLC 34
   See also CA 65-68; CANR 23, 95; DLB
   111
Pritchett, V(ictor) S(awdon)
   1900-1997 .. CLC 5, 13, 15, 41; SSC 14,
   126
   See also BPFB 3; BRWS 3; CA 61-64; 157;
   CANR 31, 63; CN 1, 2, 3, 4, 5, 6; DA3;
   DAM NOV; DLB 15, 139; EWL 3;
   MTCW 1, 2; MTFW 2005; RGEL 2;
   RGSF 2; TEA
Private 19022
   See Manning, Frederic
Probst, Mark 1925- .... CLC 59
   See also CA 130
Procaccino, Michael
   See Cristofer, Michael
Proclus c. 412-c. 485 .... CMLC 81
Prokosch, Frederic 1908-1989 .... CLC 4, 48
   See also CA 73-76; 128; CANR 82; CN 1,
   2, 3, 4; CP 1, 2, 3, 4; DLB 48; MTCW 2
Propertius, Sextus c. 50B.C.-c.
   16B.C. .... CMLC 32
   See also AW 2; CDWLB 1; DLB 211;
   RGWL 2, 3; WLIT 8
Prophet, The
   See Dreiser, Theodore
Prose, Francine 1947- .... CLC 45, 231
   See also AMWS 16; CA 109; 112; CANR
   46, 95, 132, 175, 218; DLB 234; MTFW
   2005; SATA 101, 149, 198
Protagoras c. 490B.C.-420B.C. ...... CMLC 85
   See also DLB 176
Proudhon
   See Cunha, Euclides (Rodrigues Pimenta)
   da
Proulx, Annie 1935- . CLC 81, 158, 250; SSC
   128
   See also AAYA 81; AMWS 7; BPFB 3; CA
   145; CANR 65, 110, 206; CN 6, 7; CPW
   1; DA3; DAM POP; DLB 335, 350; MAL
   5; MTCW 2; MTFW 2005; SSFS 18, 23

Rowling, Joanne Kathleen
See Rowling, J.K.
Rowson, Susanna Haswell
1762(?)-1824 .... **NCLC 5, 69, 182**
See also AMWS 15; DLB 37, 200; RGAL 4
Roy, Arundhati 1961- .... **CLC 109, 210**
See also CA 163; CANR 90, 126, 217; CN
7; DLB 323, 326; DLBY 1997; EWL 3;
LATS 1:2; MTFW 2005; NFS 22; WWE
1
Roy, Gabrielle 1909-1983 .... **CLC 10, 14;**
TCLC 256
See also CA 53-56; 110; CANR 5, 61; CCA
1; DAB; DAC; DAM MST; DLB 68;
EWL 3; MTCW 1; RGWL 2, 3; SATA
104; TCLE 1:2
Roy, Suzanna Arundhati
See Roy, Arundhati
Royko, Mike 1932-1997 .... **CLC 109**
See also CA 89-92; 157; CANR 26, 111;
CPW
Rozanov, Vasilii Vasil'evich
See Rozanov, Vassili
Rozanov, Vasily Vasilyevich
See Rozanov, Vassili
Rozanov, Vassili 1856-1919 .... **TCLC 104**
See also DLB 295; EWL 3
Rozewicz, Tadeusz 1921- ...... **CLC 9, 23, 139**
See also CA 108; CANR 36, 66; CWW 2;
DA3; DAM POET; DLB 232; EWL 3;
MTCW 1, 2; MTFW 2005; RGHL;
RGWL 3
Ruark, Gibbons 1941- .... **CLC 3**
See also CA 33-36R; CAAS 23; CANR 14,
31, 57; DLB 120
Rubens, Bernice (Ruth) 1923-2004 . **CLC 19,**
31
See also CA 25-28R; 232; CANR 33, 65,
128; CN 1, 2, 3, 4, 5, 6, 7; DLB 14, 207,
326; MTCW 1
Rubin, Harold
See Robbins, Harold
Rudkin, (James) David 1936- .... **CLC 14**
See also CA 89-92; CBD; CD 5, 6; DLB 13
Rudnik, Raphael 1933- .... **CLC 7**
See also CA 29-32R
Ruffian, M.
See Hasek, Jaroslav
Rufinus c. 345-410 .... **CMLC 111**
Ruiz, Jose Martinez
See Martinez Ruiz, Jose
Ruiz, Juan c. 1283-c. 1350 .... **CMLC 66**
Rukeyser, Muriel 1913-1980 . **CLC 6, 10, 15,**
27; PC 12
See also AMWS 6; CA 5-8R; 93-96; CANR
26, 60; CP 1, 2, 3; DA3; DAM POET;
DLB 48; EWL 3; FW; GLL 2; MAL 5;
MTCW 1, 2; PFS 10, 29; RGAL 4; SATA-
Obit 22
Rule, Jane 1931-2007 .... **CLC 27, 265**
See also CA 25-28R; 266; CAAS 18; CANR
12, 87; CN 4, 5, 6, 7; DLB 60; FW
Rule, Jane Vance
See Rule, Jane
Rulfo, Juan 1918-1986 .. **CLC 8, 80; HLC 2;**
SSC 25
See also CA 85-88; 118; CANR 26; CD-
WLB 3; DAM MULT; DLB 113; EWL 3;
HW 1, 2; LAW; MTCW 1, 2; RGSF 2;
RGWL 2, 3; WLIT 1
Rumi
See Rumi, Jalal al-Din
Rumi, Jalal al-Din 1207-1273 ...... **CMLC 20;**
PC 45
See also AAYA 64; RGWL 2, 3; WLIT 6;
WP

Runeberg, Johan 1804-1877 .... **NCLC 41**
Runyon, (Alfred) Damon
1884(?)-1946 .... **TCLC 10**
See also CA 107; 165; DLB 11, 86, 171;
MAL 5; MTCW 2; RGAL 4
Rush, Norman 1933- .... **CLC 44, 306**
See also CA 121; 126; CANR 130; INT CA-
126
Rushdie, Ahmed Salman
See Rushdie, Salman
Rushdie, Salman 1947- .... **CLC 23, 31, 55,**
100, 191, 272; SSC 83; WLCS
See also AAYA 65; BEST 89:3; BPFB 3;
BRWS 4; CA 108; 111; CANR 33, 56,
108, 133, 192; CLR 125; CN 4, 5, 6, 7;
CPW 1; DA3; DAB; DAC; DAM MST,
NOV, POP; DLB 194, 323, 326; EWL 3;
FANT; INT CA-111; LATS 1:2; LMFS 2;
MTCW 1, 2; MTFW 2005; NFS 22, 23;
RGEL 2; RGSF 2; TEA; WLIT 4
Rushforth, Peter 1945-2005 .... **CLC 19**
See also CA 101; 243
Rushforth, Peter Scott
See Rushforth, Peter
Ruskin, John 1819-1900 .... **TCLC 63**
See also BRW 5; BYA 5; CA 114; 129; CD-
BLB 1832-1890; DLB 55, 163, 190;
RGEL 2; SATA 24; TEA; WCH
Russ, Joanna 1937- .... **CLC 15**
See also BPFB 3; CA 25-28; CANR 11, 31,
65; CN 4, 5, 6, 7; DLB 8; FW; GLL 1;
MTCW 1; SCFW 1, 2; SFW 4
Russ, Richard Patrick
See O'Brian, Patrick
Russell, George William
1867-1935 .... **TCLC 3, 10**
See also BRWS 8; CA 104; 153; CDBLB
1890-1914; DAM POET; DLB 19; EWL
3; RGEL 2
Russell, Jeffrey Burton 1934- .... **CLC 70**
See also CA 25-28R; CANR 11, 28, 52, 179
Russell, (Henry) Ken(neth Alfred)
1927- .... **CLC 16**
See also CA 105
Russell, William Martin 1947- .... **CLC 60**
See also CA 164; CANR 107; CBD; CD 5,
6; DLB 233
Russell, Willy
See Russell, William Martin
Russo, Richard 1949- .... **CLC 181**
See also AMWS 12; CA 127; 133; CANR
87, 114, 194; NFS 25
Rutebeuf fl. c. 1249-1277 .... **CMLC 104**
See also DLB 208
Rutherford, Mark
See White, William Hale
Ruysbroeck, Jan van 1293-1381 ... **CMLC 85**
Ruyslinck, Ward
See Belser, Reimond Karel Maria de
Ryan, Cornelius (John) 1920-1974 ..... **CLC 7**
See also CA 69-72; 53-56; CANR 38
Ryan, Michael 1946- .... **CLC 65**
See also CA 49-52; CANR 109, 203; DLBY
1982
Ryan, Tim
See Dent, Lester
Rybakov, Anatoli (Naumovich)
1911-1998 .... **CLC 23, 53**
See also CA 126; 135; 172; DLB 302;
RGHL; SATA 79; SATA-Obit 108
Rybakov, Anatolii (Naumovich)
See Rybakov, Anatoli (Naumovich)
Ryder, Jonathan
See Ludlum, Robert
Ryga, George 1932-1987 .... **CLC 14**
See also CA 101; 124; CANR 43, 90; CCA
1; DAC; DAM MST; DLB 60
Rymer, Thomas 1643(?)-1713 .... **LC 132**
See also DLB 101, 336

S. H.
See Hartmann, Sadakichi
S. L. C.
See Twain, Mark
S. S.
See Sassoon, Siegfried
Sa'adawi, al- Nawal
See El Saadawi, Nawal
Saadawi, Nawal El
See El Saadawi, Nawal
Saadiah Gaon 882-942 .... **CMLC 97**
Saba, Umberto 1883-1957 .... **TCLC 33**
See also CA 144; CANR 79; DLB 114;
EWL 3; RGWL 2, 3
Sabatini, Rafael 1875-1950 .... **TCLC 47**
See also BPFB 3; CA 162; RHW
Sabato, Ernesto 1911- ... **CLC 10, 23; HLC 2**
See also CA 97-100; CANR 32, 65; CD-
WLB 3; CWW 2; DAM MULT; DLB 145;
EWL 3; HW 1, 2; LAW; MTCW 1, 2;
MTFW 2005
Sa-Carneiro, Mario de 1890-1916 . **TCLC 83**
See also DLB 287; EWL 3
Sacastru, Martin
See Bioy Casares, Adolfo
Sacher-Masoch, Leopold von
1836(?)-1895 .... **NCLC 31**
Sachs, Hans 1494-1576 .... **LC 95**
See also CDWLB 2; DLB 179; RGWL 2, 3
Sachs, Marilyn 1927- .... **CLC 35**
See also AAYA 2; BYA 6; CA 17-20R;
CANR 13, 47, 150; CLR 2; JRDA; MAI-
CYA 1, 2; SAAS 2; SATA 3, 68, 164;
SATA-Essay 110; WYA; YAW
Sachs, Marilyn Stickle
See Sachs, Marilyn
Sachs, Nelly 1891-1970 .. **CLC 14, 98; PC 78**
See also CA 17-18; 25-28R; CANR 87;
CAP 2; DLB 332; EWL 3; MTCW 2;
MTFW 2005; PFS 20; RGHL; RGWL 2,
3
Sackler, Howard (Oliver)
1929-1982 .... **CLC 14**
See also CA 61-64; 108; CAD; CANR 30;
DFS 15; DLB 7
Sacks, Oliver 1933- .... **CLC 67, 202**
See also CA 53-56; CANR 28, 50, 76, 146,
187; CPW; DA3; INT CANR-28; MTCW
1, 2; MTFW 2005
Sacks, Oliver Wolf
See Sacks, Oliver
Sackville, Thomas 1536-1608 .... **LC 98**
See also DAM DRAM; DLB 62, 132;
RGEL 2
Sadakichi
See Hartmann, Sadakichi
Sa'dawi, Nawal al-
See El Saadawi, Nawal
Sade, Donatien Alphonse Francois
1740-1814 .... **NCLC 3, 47**
See also DLB 314; EW 4; GFL Beginnings
to 1789; RGWL 2, 3
Sade, Marquis de
See Sade, Donatien Alphonse Francois
Sadoff, Ira 1945- .... **CLC 9**
See also CA 53-56; CANR 5, 21, 109; DLB
120
Saetone
See Camus, Albert
Safire, William 1929-2009 .... **CLC 10**
See also CA 17-20R; 290; CANR 31, 54,
91, 148
Safire, William L.
See Safire, William
Safire, William Lewis
See Safire, William

Saramago, Jose 1922-2010 ..... **CLC 119, 275; HLCS 1**
See also CA 153; CANR 96, 164, 210; CWW 2; DLB 287, 332; EWL 3; LATS 1:2; NFS 27; SSFS 23

Sarduy, Severo 1937-1993 .... **CLC 6, 97; HLCS 2; TCLC 167**
See also CA 89-92; 142; CANR 58, 81; CWW 2; DLB 113; EWL 3; HW 1, 2; LAW

Sargeson, Frank 1903-1982 ..... **CLC 31; SSC 99**
See also CA 25-28R; 106; CANR 38, 79; CN 1, 2, 3; EWL 3; GLL 2; RGEL 2; RGSF 2; SSFS 20

Sarmiento, Domingo Faustino 1811-1888 .... **HLCS 2; NCLC 123**
See also LAW; WLIT 1

Sarmiento, Felix Ruben Garcia
See Dario, Ruben

Saro-Wiwa, Ken(ule Beeson) 1941-1995 .... **CLC 114; TCLC 200**
See also BW 2; CA 142; 150; CANR 60; DLB 157, 360

Saroyan, William 1908-1981 ... **CLC 1, 8, 10, 29, 34, 56; DC 28; SSC 21; TCLC 137; WLC 5**
See also AAYA 66; CA 5-8R; 103; CAD; CANR 30; CDALBS; CN 1, 2; DA; DA3; DAB; DAC; DAM DRAM, MST, NOV; DFS 17; DLB 7, 9, 86; DLBY 1981; EWL 3; LAIT 4; MAL 5; MTCW 1, 2; MTFW 2005; RGAL 4; RGSF 2; SATA 23; SATA-Obit 24; SSFS 14; TUS

Sarraute, Nathalie 1900-1999 .... **CLC 1, 2, 4, 8, 10, 31, 80; TCLC 145**
See also BPFB 3; CA 9-12R; 187; CANR 23, 66, 134; CWW 2; DLB 83, 321; EW 12; EWL 3; GFL 1789 to the Present; MTCW 1, 2; MTFW 2005; RGWL 2, 3

Sarton, May 1912-1995 ... **CLC 4, 14, 49, 91; PC 39; TCLC 120**
See also AMWS 8; CA 1-4R; 149; CANR 1, 34, 55, 116; CN 1, 2, 3, 4, 5, 6; CP 1, 2, 3, 4, 5, 6; DAM POET; DLB 48; DLBY 1981; EWL 3; FW; INT CANR-34; MAL 5; MTCW 1, 2; MTFW 2005; RGAL 4; SATA 36; SATA-Obit 86; TUS

Sartre, Jean-Paul 1905-1980 . **CLC 1, 4, 7, 9, 13, 18, 24, 44, 50, 52; DC 3; SSC 32; WLC 5**
See also AAYA 62; CA 9-12R; 97-100; CANR 21; DA; DA3; DAB; DAC; DAM DRAM, MST, NOV; DFS 5, 26; DLB 72, 296, 321, 332; EW 12; EWL 3; GFL 1789 to the Present; LMFS 2; MTCW 1, 2; MTFW 2005; NFS 21; RGHL; RGSF 2; RGWL 2, 3; SSFS 9; TWA

Sassoon, Siegfried 1886-1967 .. **CLC 36, 130; PC 12**
See also BRW 6; CA 104; 25-28R; CANR 36; DAB; DAM MST, NOV, POET; DLB 20, 191; DLBD 18; EWL 3; MTCW 1, 2; MTFW 2005; PAB; PFS 28; RGEL 2; TEA

Sassoon, Siegfried Lorraine
See Sassoon, Siegfried

Satterfield, Charles
See Pohl, Frederik

Satyremont
See Peret, Benjamin

Saul, John III
See Saul, John

Saul, John 1942- .... **CLC 46**
See also AAYA 10, 62; BEST 90:4; CA 81-84; CANR 16, 40, 81, 176; CPW; DAM NOV, POP; HGG; SATA 98

Saul, John W.
See Saul, John

Saul, John W. III
See Saul, John

Saul, John Woodruff III
See Saul, John

Saunders, Caleb
See Heinlein, Robert A.

Saura (Atares), Carlos 1932-1998 .... **CLC 20**
See also CA 114; 131; CANR 79; HW 1

Sauser, Frederic Louis
See Sauser-Hall, Frederic

Sauser-Hall, Frederic 1887-1961 ..... **CLC 18, 106**
See also CA 102; 93-96; CANR 36, 62; DLB 258; EWL 3; GFL 1789 to the Present; MTCW 1; WP

Saussure, Ferdinand de 1857-1913 .... **TCLC 49**
See also DLB 242

Savage, Catharine
See Brosman, Catharine Savage

Savage, Richard 1697(?)-1743 .... **LC 96**
See also DLB 95; RGEL 2

Savage, Thomas 1915-2003 .... **CLC 40**
See also CA 126; 132; 218; CAAS 15; CN 6, 7; INT CA-132; SATA-Obit 147; TCWW 2

Savan, Glenn 1953-2003 .... **CLC 50**
See also CA 225

Savonarola, Girolamo 1452-1498 ...... **LC 152**
See also LMFS 1

Sax, Robert
See Johnson, Robert

Saxo Grammaticus c. 1150-c. 1222 .... **CMLC 58**

Saxton, Robert
See Johnson, Robert

Sayers, Dorothy L(eigh) 1893-1957 . **SSC 71; TCLC 2, 15, 237**
See also BPFB 3; BRWS 3; CA 104; 119; CANR 60; CDBLB 1914-1945; CMW 4; DAM POP; DLB 10, 36, 77, 100; MSW; MTCW 1, 2; MTFW 2005; RGEL 2; SSFS 12; TEA

Sayers, Valerie 1952- .... **CLC 50, 122**
See also CA 134; CANR 61; CSW

Sayles, John (Thomas) 1950- .... **CLC 7, 10, 14, 198**
See also CA 57-60; CANR 41, 84; DLB 44

Scalapino, Leslie 1947-2010 .... **PC 114**
See also CA 123; CANR 67, 103; CP 5, 6, 7; CWP; DLB 193

Scamander, Newt
See Rowling, J.K.

Scammell, Michael 1935- .... **CLC 34**
See also CA 156

Scannel, John Vernon
See Scannell, Vernon

Scannell, Vernon 1922-2007 .... **CLC 49**
See also CA 5-8R; 266; CANR 8, 24, 57, 143; CN 1, 2; CP 1, 2, 3, 4, 5, 6, 7; CWRI 5; DLB 27; SATA 59; SATA-Obit 188

Scarlett, Susan
See Streatfeild, Noel

Scarron 1847-1910
See Mikszath, Kalman

Scarron, Paul 1610-1660 .... **LC 116**
See also GFL Beginnings to 1789; RGWL 2, 3

Sceve, Maurice c. 1500-c. 1564 . **LC 180; PC 111**
See also DLB 327; GFL Beginnings to 1789

Schaeffer, Susan Fromberg 1941- ..... **CLC 6, 11, 22**
See also CA 49-52; CANR 18, 65, 160; CN 4, 5, 6, 7; DLB 28, 299; MTCW 1, 2; MTFW 2005; SATA 22

Schama, Simon 1945- .... **CLC 150**
See also BEST 89:4; CA 105; CANR 39, 91, 168, 207

Schama, Simon Michael
See Schama, Simon

Schary, Jill
See Robinson, Jill

Schell, Jonathan 1943- .... **CLC 35**
See also CA 73-76; CANR 12, 117, 187

Schelling, Friedrich Wilhelm Joseph von 1775-1854 .... **NCLC 30**
See also DLB 90

Scherer, Jean-Marie Maurice
See Rohmer, Eric

Schevill, James (Erwin) 1920- .... **CLC 7**
See also CA 5-8R; CAAS 12; CAD; CD 5, 6; CP 1, 2, 3, 4, 5

Schiller, Friedrich von 1759-1805 ...... **DC 12; NCLC 39, 69, 166**
See also CDWLB 2; DAM DRAM; DLB 94; EW 5; RGWL 2, 3; TWA

Schisgal, Murray (Joseph) 1926- .... **CLC 6**
See also CA 21-24R; CAD; CANR 48, 86; CD 5, 6; MAL 5

Schlee, Ann 1934- .... **CLC 35**
See also CA 101; CANR 29, 88; SATA 44; SATA-Brief 36

Schlegel, August Wilhelm von 1767-1845 .... **NCLC 15, 142**
See also DLB 94; RGWL 2, 3

Schlegel, Friedrich 1772-1829 .... **NCLC 45, 226**
See also DLB 90; EW 5; RGWL 2, 3; TWA

Schlegel, Johann Elias (von) 1719(?)-1749 .... **LC 5**

Schleiermacher, Friedrich 1768-1834 .... **NCLC 107**
See also DLB 90

Schlesinger, Arthur M., Jr. 1917-2007 .... **CLC 84**
See Schlesinger, Arthur Meier
See also AITN 1; CA 1-4R; 257; CANR 1, 28, 58, 105, 187; DLB 17; INT CANR-28; MTCW 1, 2; SATA 61; SATA-Obit 181

Schlink, Bernhard 1944- .... **CLC 174**
See also CA 163; CANR 116, 175, 217; RGHL

Schmidt, Arno (Otto) 1914-1979 ...... **CLC 56**
See also CA 128; 109; DLB 69; EWL 3

Schmitz, Aron Hector 1861-1928 ..... **SSC 25; TCLC 2, 35, 244**
See also CA 104; 122; DLB 264; EW 8; EWL 3; MTCW 1; RGWL 2, 3; WLIT 7

Schnackenberg, Gjertrud 1953- ...... **CLC 40; PC 45**
See also AMWS 15; CA 116; CANR 100; CP 5, 6, 7; CWP; DLB 120, 282; PFS 13, 25

Schnackenberg, Gjertrud Cecelia
See Schnackenberg, Gjertrud

Schneider, Leonard Alfred 1925-1966 .... **CLC 21**
See also CA 89-92

Schnitzler, Arthur 1862-1931 ..... **DC 17; SSC 15, 61; TCLC 4**
See also CA 104; CDWLB 2; DLB 81, 118; EW 8; EWL 3; RGSF 2; RGWL 2, 3

Schoenberg, Arnold Franz Walter 1874-1951 .... **TCLC 75**
See also CA 109; 188

Schonberg, Arnold
See Schoenberg, Arnold Franz Walter

Schopenhauer, Arthur 1788-1860 . **NCLC 51, 157**
See also DLB 90; EW 5

Schor, Sandra (M.) 1932(?)-1990 ..... **CLC 65**
See also CA 132

Schorer, Mark 1908-1977 .... **CLC 9**
See also CA 5-8R; 73-76; CANR 7; CN 1, 2; DLB 103

Solzhenitsyn, Aleksandr 1918-2008 ... CLC 1,
2, 4, 7, 9, 10, 18, 26, 34, 78, 134, 235;
SSC 32, 105; WLC 5
See also AAYA 49; AITN 1; BPFB 3; CA
69-72; CANR 40, 65, 116; CWW 2; DA;
DA3; DAB; DAC; DAM MST, NOV;
DLB 302, 332; EW 13; EWL 3; EXPS;
LAIT 4; MTCW 1, 2; MTFW 2005; NFS
6; PFS 38; RGSF 2; RGWL 2, 3; SSFS 9;
TWA
Solzhenitsyn, Aleksandr I.
See Solzhenitsyn, Aleksandr
Solzhenitsyn, Aleksandr Isayevich
See Solzhenitsyn, Aleksandr
Somers, Jane
See Lessing, Doris
Somerville, Edith Oenone
1858-1949 .... SSC 56; TCLC 51
See also CA 196; DLB 135; RGEL 2; RGSF
2
Somerville & Ross
See Martin, Violet Florence; Somerville,
Edith Oenone
Sommer, Scott 1951- .... CLC 25
See also CA 106
Sommers, Christina Hoff 1950- ...... CLC 197
See also CA 153; CANR 95
Sondheim, Stephen 1930- .. CLC 30, 39, 147;
DC 22
See also AAYA 11, 66; CA 103; CANR 47,
67, 125; DAM DRAM; DFS 25, 27, 28;
LAIT 4
Sondheim, Stephen Joshua
See Sondheim, Stephen
Sone, Monica 1919- .... AAL
See also DLB 312
Song, Cathy 1955- .... AAL; PC 21
See also CA 154; CANR 118; CWP; DLB
169, 312; EXPP; FW; PFS 5
Sontag, Susan 1933-2004 ... CLC 1, 2, 10, 13,
31, 105, 195, 277
See also AMWS 3; CA 17-20R; 234; CANR
25, 51, 74, 97, 184; CN 1, 2, 3, 4, 5, 6, 7;
CPW; DA3; DAM POP; DLB 2, 67; EWL
3; MAL 5; MBL; MTCW 1, 2; MTFW
2005; RGAL 4; RHW; SSFS 10
Sophocles 496(?)B.C.-406(?)B.C. .... CMLC 2,
47, 51, 86; DC 1; WLCS
See also AW 1; CDWLB 1; DA; DA3;
DAB; DAC; DAM DRAM, MST; DFS 1,
4, 8, 24; DLB 176; LAIT 1; LATS 1:1;
LMFS 1; RGWL 2, 3; TWA; WLIT 8
Sordello 1189-1269 .... CMLC 15
Sorel, Georges 1847-1922 .... TCLC 91
See also CA 118; 188
Sorel, Julia
See Drexler, Rosalyn
Sorokin, Vladimir .... CLC 59
See also CA 258; DLB 285
Sorokin, Vladimir Georgievich
See Sorokin, Vladimir
Sorrentino, Gilbert 1929-2006 .... CLC 3, 7,
14, 22, 40, 247
See also AMWS 21; CA 77-80; 250; CANR
14, 33, 115, 157; CN 3, 4, 5, 6, 7; CP 1,
2, 3, 4, 5, 6, 7; DLB 5, 173; DLBY 1980;
INT CANR-14
Soseki
See Natsume, Soseki
Soto, Gary 1952- ... CLC 32, 80; HLC 2; PC
28
See also AAYA 10, 37; BYA 11; CA 119;
125; CANR 50, 74, 107, 157, 219; CLR
38; CP 4, 5, 6, 7; DAM MULT; DFS 26;
DLB 82; EWL 3; EXPP; HW 1, 2; INT
CA-125; JRDA; LLW; MAICYA 2; MAI-
CYAS 1; MAL 5; MTCW 2; MTFW
2005; PFS 7, 30; RGAL 4; SATA 80, 120,
174; SSFS 33; WYA; YAW

Soupault, Philippe 1897-1990 .... CLC 68
See also CA 116; 147; 131; EWL 3; GFL
1789 to the Present; LMFS 2
Souster, (Holmes) Raymond 1921- .... CLC 5,
14
See also CA 13-16R; CAAS 14; CANR 13,
29, 53; CP 1, 2, 3, 4, 5, 6, 7; DA3; DAC;
DAM POET; DLB 88; RGEL 2; SATA 63
Southern, Terry 1924(?)-1995 .... CLC 7
See also AMWS 11; BPFB 3; CA 1-4R;
150; CANR 1, 55, 107; CN 1, 2, 3, 4, 5,
6; DLB 2; IDFW 3, 4
Southerne, Thomas 1660-1746 .... LC 99
See also DLB 80; RGEL 2
Southey, Robert 1774-1843 .... NCLC 8, 97;
PC 111
See also BRW 4; DLB 93, 107, 142; RGEL
2; SATA 54
Southwell, Robert 1561(?)-1595 .... LC 108
See also DLB 167; RGEL 2; TEA
Southworth, Emma Dorothy Eliza Nevitte
1819-1899 .... NCLC 26
See also DLB 239
Souza, Ernest
See Scott, Evelyn
Soyinka, Wole 1934- .. BLC 1:3, 2:3; CLC 3,
5, 14, 36, 44, 179; DC 2; PC 118; WLC
5
See also AFW; BW 2, 3; CA 13-16R;
CANR 27, 39, 82, 136; CD 5, 6; CDWLB
3; CN 6, 7; CP 1, 2, 3, 4, 5, 6 ,7; DA;
DA3; DAB; DAC; DAM DRAM, MST,
MULT; DFS 10, 26; DLB 125, 332; EWL
3; MTCW 1, 2; MTFW 2005; PFS 27;
RGEL 2; TWA; WLIT 2; WWE 1
Spackman, W(illiam) M(ode)
1905-1990 .... CLC 46
See also CA 81-84; 132
Spacks, Barry (Bernard) 1931- .... CLC 14
See also CA 154; CANR 33, 109; CP 3, 4,
5, 6, 7; DLB 105
Spanidou, Irini 1946- .... CLC 44
See also CA 185; CANR 179
Spark, Muriel 1918-2006 .... CLC 2, 3, 5, 8,
13, 18, 40, 94, 242; PC 72; SSC 10, 115
See also BRWS 1; CA 5-8R; 251; CANR
12, 36, 76, 89, 131; CDBLB 1945-1960;
CN 1, 2, 3, 4, 5, 6, 7; CP 1, 2, 3, 4, 5, 6,
7; DA3; DAB; DAC; DAM MST, NOV;
DLB 15, 139; EWL 3; FW; INT CANR-
12; LAIT 4; MTCW 1, 2; MTFW 2005;
NFS 22; RGEL 2; SSFS 28; TEA; WLIT
4; YAW
Spark, Muriel Sarah
See Spark, Muriel
Spaulding, Douglas
See Bradbury, Ray
Spaulding, Leonard
See Bradbury, Ray
Speght, Rachel 1597-c. 1630 .... LC 97
See also DLB 126
Spence, J. A. D.
See Eliot, T. S.
Spencer, Anne 1882-1975 ...... HR 1:3; PC 77
See also BW 2; CA 161; DLB 51, 54
Spencer, Elizabeth 1921- .... CLC 22; SSC 57
See also CA 13-16R; CANR 32, 65, 87; CN
1, 2, 3, 4, 5, 6, 7; CSW; DLB 6, 218;
EWL 3; MTCW 1; RGAL 4; SATA 14
Spencer, Leonard G.
See Silverberg, Robert
Spencer, Scott 1945- .... CLC 30
See also CA 113; CANR 51, 148, 190;
DLBY 1986
Spender, Stephen 1909-1995 ..... CLC 1, 2, 5,
10, 41, 91; PC 71
See also BRWS 2; CA 9-12R; 149; CANR
31, 54; CDBLB 1945-1960; CP 1, 2, 3, 4,
5, 6; DA3; DAM POET; DLB 20; EWL
3; MTCW 1, 2; MTFW 2005; PAB; PFS
23, 36; RGEL 2; TEA

Spender, Stephen Harold
See Spender, Stephen
Spengler, Oswald (Arnold Gottfried)
1880-1936 .... TCLC 25
See also CA 118; 189
Spenser, Edmund 1552(?)-1599 ...... LC 5, 39,
117; PC 8, 42; WLC 5
See also AAYA 60; BRW 1; CDBLB Be-
fore 1660; DA; DA3; DAB; DAC; DAM
MST, POET; DLB 167; EFS 1:2, 2:1;
EXPP; PAB; PFS 32; RGEL 2; TEA;
WLIT 3; WP
Spicer, Jack 1925-1965 .... CLC 8, 18, 72
See also BG 1:3; CA 85-88; DAM POET;
DLB 5, 16, 193; GLL 1; WP
Spiegelman, Art 1948- .... CLC 76, 178
See also AAYA 10, 46; CA 125; CANR 41,
55, 74, 124; DLB 299; MTCW 2; MTFW
2005; NFS 35; RGHL; SATA 109, 158;
YAW
Spielberg, Peter 1929- .... CLC 6
See also CA 5-8R; CANR 4, 48; DLBY
1981
Spielberg, Steven 1947- .... CLC 20, 188
See also AAYA 8, 24; CA 77-80; CANR
32; SATA 32
Spillane, Frank Morrison
See Spillane, Mickey
Spillane, Mickey 1918-2006 .. CLC 3, 13, 241
See also BPFB 3; CA 25-28R; 252; CANR
28, 63, 125; CMW 4; DA3; DLB 226;
MSW; MTCW 1, 2; MTFW 2005; SATA
66; SATA-Obit 176
Spinoza, Benedictus de 1632-1677 . LC 9, 58,
177
Spinrad, Norman (Richard) 1940- ... CLC 46
See also BPFB 3; CA 37-40R, 233; CAAE
233; CAAS 19; CANR 20, 91; DLB 8;
INT CANR-20; SFW 4
Spitteler, Carl 1845-1924 .... TCLC 12
See also CA 109; DLB 129, 332; EWL 3
Spitteler, Karl Friedrich Georg
See Spitteler, Carl
Spivack, Kathleen (Romola Drucker)
1938- .... CLC 6
See also CA 49-52
Spivak, Gayatri Chakravorty
1942- .... CLC 233
See also CA 110; 154; CANR 91; FW;
LMFS 2
Spofford, Harriet (Elizabeth) Prescott
1835-1921 .... SSC 87
See also CA 201; DLB 74, 221
Spoto, Donald 1941- .... CLC 39
See also CA 65-68; CANR 11, 57, 93, 173,
212
Springsteen, Bruce 1949- .... CLC 17
See also CA 111
Springsteen, Bruce F.
See Springsteen, Bruce
Spurling, Hilary 1940- .... CLC 34
See also CA 104; CANR 25, 52, 94, 157
Spurling, Susan Hilary
See Spurling, Hilary
Spyker, John Howland
See Elman, Richard (Martin)
Squared, A.
See Abbott, Edwin A.
Squires, (James) Radcliffe
1917-1993 .... CLC 51
See also CA 1-4R; 140; CANR 6, 21; CP 1,
2, 3, 4, 5
Srivastav, Dhanpat Ray
See Srivastava, Dhanpat Rai
Srivastav, Dheanpatrai
See Srivastava, Dhanpat Rai
Srivastava, Dhanpat Rai
1880(?)-1936 .... TCLC 21
See also CA 118; 197; EWL 3

Tabori, George 1914-2007 .... **CLC 19**
   See also CA 49-52; 262; CANR 4, 69;
   CBD; CD 5, 6; DLB 245; RGHL

Tacitus c. 55-c. 117 .... **CMLC 56, 131**
   See also AW 2; CDWLB 1; DLB 211;
   RGWL 2, 3; WLIT 8

Tadjo, Veronique 1955- .... **BLC 2:3**
   See also DLB 360; EWL 3

Tagore, Rabindranath 1861-1941 .... **PC 8;
   SSC 48; TCLC 3, 53**
   See also CA 104; 120; DA3; DAM DRAM,
   POET; DFS 26; DLB 323, 332; EWL 3;
   MTCW 1, 2; MTFW 2005; PFS 18; RGEL
   2; RGSF 2; RGWL 2, 3; TWA

Taine, Hippolyte Adolphe
   1828-1893 .... **NCLC 15**
   See also EW 7; GFL 1789 to the Present

Talayesva, Don C. 1890-(?) .... **NNAL**

Talese, Gay 1932- .... **CLC 37, 232**
   See also AITN 1; AMWS 17; CA 1-4R;
   CANR 9, 58, 137, 177; DLB 185; INT
   CANR-9; MTCW 1, 2; MTFW 2005

Tallent, Elizabeth 1954- .... **CLC 45**
   See also CA 117; CANR 72; DLB 130

Tallmountain, Mary 1918-1997 .... **NNAL**
   See also CA 146; 161; DLB 193

Tally, Ted 1952- .... **CLC 42**
   See also CA 120; 124; CAD; CANR 125;
   CD 5, 6; INT CA-124

Talvik, Heiti 1904-1947 .... **TCLC 87**
   See also EWL 3

Tamayo y Baus, Manuel
   1829-1898 .... **NCLC 1**

Tammsaare, A(nton) H(ansen)
   1878-1940 .... **TCLC 27**
   See also CA 164; CDWLB 4; DLB 220;
   EWL 3

Tam'si, Tchicaya U
   See Tchicaya, Gerald Felix

Tan, Amy 1952- .... **AAL; CLC 59, 120, 151,
   257**
   See also AAYA 9, 48; AMWS 10; BEST
   89:3; BPFB 3; CA 136; CANR 54, 105,
   132; CDALBS; CN 6, 7; CPW 1; DA3;
   DAM MULT, NOV, POP; DLB 173, 312;
   EXPN; FL 1:6; FW; LAIT 3, 5; MAL 5;
   MTCW 2; MTFW 2005; NFS 1, 13, 16,
   31, 35; RGAL 4; SATA 75; SSFS 9; YAW

Tan, Amy Ruth
   See Tan, Amy

Tandem, Carl Felix
   See Spitteler, Carl

Tandem, Felix
   See Spitteler, Carl

Tania B.
   See Blixen, Karen

Tanizaki, Jun'ichiro 1886-1965 ... **CLC 8, 14,
   28; SSC 21**
   See also CA 93-96; 25-28R; DLB 180;
   EWL 3; MJW; MTCW 2; MTFW 2005;
   RGSF 2; RGWL 2

Tanizaki Jun'ichiro
   See Tanizaki, Jun'ichiro

Tannen, Deborah 1945- .... **CLC 206**
   See also CA 118; CANR 95

Tannen, Deborah Frances
   See Tannen, Deborah

Tanner, William
   See Amis, Kingsley

Tante, Dilly
   See Kunitz, Stanley

Tao Lao
   See Storni, Alfonsina

Tapahonso, Luci 1953- .... **NNAL; PC 65**
   See also CA 145; CANR 72, 127, 214; DLB
   175

Tarantino, Quentin 1963- .... **CLC 125, 230**
   See also AAYA 58; CA 171; CANR 125

Tarantino, Quentin Jerome
   See Tarantino, Quentin

Tarassoff, Lev
   See Troyat, Henri

Tarbell, Ida 1857-1944 .... **TCLC 40**
   See also CA 122; 181; DLB 47

Tarbell, Ida Minerva
   See Tarbell, Ida

Tarchetti, Ugo 1839(?)-1869 .... **SSC 119**

**Tardieu d'Esclavelles,
   Louise-Florence-Petronille**
   See Epinay, Louise d'

Tarkington, (Newton) Booth
   1869-1946 .... **TCLC 9**
   See also BPFB 3; BYA 3; CA 110; 143;
   CWRI 5; DLB 9, 102; MAL 5; MTCW 2;
   NFS 34; RGAL 4; SATA 17

Tarkovskii, Andrei Arsen'evich
   See Tarkovsky, Andrei (Arsenyevich)

Tarkovsky, Andrei (Arsenyevich)
   1932-1986 .... **CLC 75**
   See also CA 127

Tartt, Donna 1964(?)- .... **CLC 76**
   See also AAYA 56; CA 142; CANR 135;
   LNFS 2; MTFW 2005

Tasso, Torquato 1544-1595 .... **LC 5, 94**
   See also EFS 1:2, 2:1; EW 2; RGWL 2, 3;
   WLIT 7

Tate, (John Orley) Allen 1899-1979 .. **CLC 2,
   4, 6, 9, 11, 14, 24; PC 50**
   See also AMW; CA 5-8R; 85-88; CANR
   32, 108; CN 1, 2; CP 1, 2; DLB 4, 45, 63;
   DLBD 17; EWL 3; MAL 5; MTCW 1, 2;
   MTFW 2005; RGAL 4; RHW

Tate, Ellalice
   See Hibbert, Eleanor Alice Burford

Tate, James (Vincent) 1943- ..... **CLC 2, 6, 25**
   See also CA 21-24R; CANR 29, 57, 114;
   CP 1, 2, 3, 4, 5, 6, 7; DLB 5, 169; EWL
   3; PFS 10, 15; RGAL 4; WP

Tate, Nahum 1652(?)-1715 .... **LC 109**
   See also DLB 80; RGEL 2

Tauler, Johannes c. 1300-1361 ...... **CMLC 37**
   See also DLB 179; LMFS 1

Tavel, Ronald 1936-2009 .... **CLC 6**
   See also CA 21-24R; 284; CAD; CANR 33;
   CD 5, 6

Taviani, Paolo 1931- .... **CLC 70**
   See also CA 153

Tawada, Yoko 1960- .... **CLC 310**
   See also CA 296

Taylor, Bayard 1825-1878 .... **NCLC 89**
   See also DLB 3, 189, 250, 254; RGAL 4

Taylor, C(ecil) P(hilip) 1929-1981 .... **CLC 27**
   See also CA 25-28R; 105; CANR 47; CBD

Taylor, Edward 1642(?)-1729 ..... **LC 11, 163;
   PC 63**
   See also AMW; DA; DAB; DAC; DAM
   MST, POET; DLB 24; EXPP; PFS 31;
   RGAL 4; TUS

Taylor, Eleanor Ross 1920- .... **CLC 5**
   See also CA 81-84; CANR 70

Taylor, Elizabeth 1912-1975 .... **CLC 2, 4, 29;
   SSC 100**
   See also CA 13-16R; CANR 9, 70; CN 1,
   2; DLB 139; MTCW 1; RGEL 2; SATA
   13

Taylor, Frederick Winslow
   1856-1915 .... **TCLC 76**
   See also CA 188

Taylor, Henry 1942- .... **CLC 44**
   See also CA 33-36R; CAAS 7; CANR 31,
   178; CP 6, 7; DLB 5; PFS 10

Taylor, Henry Splawn
   See Taylor, Henry

Taylor, Kamala
   See Markandaya, Kamala

Taylor, Mildred D. 1943- .... **CLC 21**
   See also AAYA 10, 47; BW 1; BYA 3, 8;
   CA 85-88; CANR 25, 115, 136; CLR 9,
   59, 90, 144; CSW; DLB 52; JRDA; LAIT
   3; MAICYA 1, 2; MTFW 2005; SAAS 5;
   SATA 135; WYA; YAW

Taylor, Peter (Hillsman) 1917-1994 .. **CLC 1,
   4, 18, 37, 44, 50, 71; SSC 10, 84**
   See also AMWS 5; BPFB 3; CA 13-16R;
   147; CANR 9, 50; CN 1, 2, 3, 4, 5; CSW;
   DLB 218, 278; DLBY 1981, 1994; EWL
   3; EXPS; INT CANR-9; MAL 5; MTCW
   1, 2; MTFW 2005; RGSF 2; SSFS 9; TUS

Taylor, Robert Lewis 1912-1998 .... **CLC 14**
   See also CA 1-4R; 170; CANR 3, 64; CN
   1, 2; SATA 10; TCWW 1, 2

Tchekhov, Anton
   See Chekhov, Anton

Tchicaya, Gerald Felix 1931-1988 .. **CLC 101**
   See also CA 129; 125; CANR 81; EWL 3

Tchicaya U Tam'si
   See Tchicaya, Gerald Felix

Teasdale, Sara 1884-1933 .... **PC 31; TCLC 4**
   See also CA 104; 163; DLB 45; GLL 1;
   PFS 14; RGAL 4; SATA 32; TUS

Tecumseh 1768-1813 .... **NNAL**
   See also DAM MULT

Tegner, Esaias 1782-1846 .... **NCLC 2**

Teilhard de Chardin, (Marie Joseph) Pierre
   1881-1955 .... **TCLC 9**
   See also CA 105; 210; GFL 1789 to the
   Present

Temple, Ann
   See Mortimer, Penelope (Ruth)

Tennant, Emma 1937- .... **CLC 13, 52**
   See also BRWS 9; CA 65-68; CAAS 9;
   CANR 10, 38, 59, 88, 177; CN 3, 4, 5, 6,
   7; DLB 14; EWL 3; SFW 4

Tenneshaw, S.M.
   See Silverberg, Robert

Tenney, Tabitha Gilman
   1762-1837 .... **NCLC 122**
   See also DLB 37, 200

Tennyson, Alfred 1809-1892 ... **NCLC 30, 65,
   115, 202; PC 6, 101; WLC 6**
   See also AAYA 50; BRW 4; BRWR 3; CD-
   BLB 1832-1890; DA; DA3; DAB; DAC;
   DAM MST, POET; DLB 32; EXPP; PAB;
   PFS 1, 2, 4, 11, 15, 19; RGEL 2; TEA;
   WLIT 4; WP

Teran, Lisa St. Aubin de
   See St. Aubin de Teran, Lisa

Terence c. 184B.C.-c. 159B.C. ...... **CMLC 14,
   132; DC 7**
   See also AW 1; CDWLB 1; DLB 211;
   RGWL 2, 3; TWA; WLIT 8

Teresa de Jesus, St. 1515-1582 .... **LC 18, 149**

Teresa of Avila, St.
   See Teresa de Jesus, St.

Terkel, Louis
   See Terkel, Studs

Terkel, Studs 1912-2008 .... **CLC 38**
   See also AAYA 32; AITN 1; CA 57-60; 278;
   CANR 18, 45, 67, 132, 195; DA3; MTCW
   1, 2; MTFW 2005; TUS

Terkel, Studs Louis
   See Terkel, Studs

Terry, C. V.
   See Slaughter, Frank G(ill)

Terry, Megan 1932- .... **CLC 19; DC 13**
   See also CA 77-80; CABS 3; CAD; CANR
   43; CD 5, 6; CWD; DFS 18; DLB 7, 249;
   GLL 2

Tertullian c. 155-c. 245 .... **CMLC 29**

Tertz, Abram
   See Sinyavsky, Andrei (Donatevich)

Tesich, Steve 1943(?)-1996 .... **CLC 40, 69**
   See also CA 105; 152; CAD; DLBY 1983

Tesla, Nikola 1856-1943 .... **TCLC 88**
See also CA 157

Teternikov, Fyodor Kuzmich
1863-1927 .... **TCLC 9**
See also CA 104; DLB 295; EWL 3

Tevis, Walter 1928-1984 .... **CLC 42**
See also CA 113; SFW 4

Tey, Josephine
See Mackintosh, Elizabeth

Thackeray, William Makepeace
1811-1863 ...... **NCLC 5, 14, 22, 43, 169,
213; WLC 6**
See also BRW 5; BRWC 2; CDBLB 1832-
1890; DA; DA3; DAB; DAC; DAM MST,
NOV; DLB 21, 55, 159, 163; NFS 13;
RGEL 2; SATA 23; TEA; WLIT 3

Thakura, Ravindranatha
See Tagore, Rabindranath

Thames, C. H.
See Marlowe, Stephen

Tharoor, Shashi 1956- .... **CLC 70**
See also CA 141; CANR 91, 201; CN 6, 7

Thelwall, John 1764-1834 .... **NCLC 162**
See also DLB 93, 158

Thelwell, Michael Miles 1939- .... **CLC 22**
See also BW 2; CA 101

Theo, Ion
See Theodorescu, Ion N.

Theobald, Lewis, Jr.
See Lovecraft, H. P.

Theocritus c. 310B.C.- .... **CMLC 45**
See also AW 1; DLB 176; RGWL 2, 3

Theodorescu, Ion N. 1880-1967 .... **CLC 80**
See also CA 167; 116; CDWLB 4; DLB
220; EWL 3

Theriault, Yves 1915-1983 .... **CLC 79**
See also CA 102; CANR 150; CCA 1;
DAC; DAM MST; DLB 88; EWL 3

Therion, Master
See Crowley, Edward Alexander

Theroux, Alexander 1939- .... **CLC 2, 25**
See also CA 85-88; CANR 20, 63, 190; CN
4, 5, 6, 7

Theroux, Alexander Louis
See Theroux, Alexander

Theroux, Paul 1941- .... **CLC 5, 8, 11, 15, 28,
46, 159, 303**
See also AAYA 28; AMWS 8; BEST 89:4;
BPFB 3; CA 33-36R; CANR 20, 45, 74,
133, 179; CDALBS; CN 1, 2, 3, 4, 5, 6,
7; CP 1; CPW 1; DA3; DAM POP; DLB
2, 218; EWL 3; HGG; MAL 5; MTCW 1,
2; MTFW 2005; RGAL 4; SATA 44, 109;
TUS

Theroux, Paul Edward
See Theroux, Paul

Thesen, Sharon 1946- .... **CLC 56**
See also CA 163; CANR 125; CP 5, 6, 7;
CWP

Thespis fl. 6th cent. B.C.- .... **CMLC 51**
See also LMFS 1

Thevenin, Denis
See Duhamel, Georges

Thibault, Jacques Anatole Francois
See France, Anatole

Thiele, Colin 1920-2006 .... **CLC 17**
See also CA 29-32R; CANR 12, 28, 53,
105; CLR 27; CP 1, 2; DLB 289; MAI-
CYA 1, 2; SAAS 2; SATA 14, 72, 125;
YAW

Thiong'o, Ngugi Wa
See Ngugi wa Thiong'o

Thistlethwaite, Bel
See Wetherald, Agnes Ethelwyn

Thomas, Audrey (Callahan) 1935- .... **CLC 7,
13, 37, 107, 289; SSC 20**
See also AITN 2; CA 21-24R, 237; CAAE
237; CAAS 19; CANR 36, 58; CN 2, 3,
4, 5, 6, 7; DLB 60; MTCW 1; RGSF 2

Thomas, Augustus 1857-1934 .... **TCLC 97**
See also MAL 5

Thomas, D.M. 1935- ..... **CLC 13, 22, 31, 132**
See also BPFB 3; BRWS 4; CA 61-64, 303;
CAAE 303; CAAS 11; CANR 17, 45, 75;
CDBLB 1960 to Present; CN 4, 5, 6, 7;
CP 1, 2, 3, 4, 5, 6, 7; DA3; DLB 40, 207,
299; HGG; INT CANR-17; MTCW 1, 2;
MTFW 2005; RGHL; SFW 4

Thomas, Donald Michael
See Thomas, D.M.

Thomas, Dylan 1914-1953 . **PC 2, 52; SSC 3,
44; TCLC 1, 8, 45, 105; WLC 6**
See also AAYA 45; BRWR 3; BRWS 1; CA
104; 120; CANR 65; CDBLB 1945-1960;
DA; DA3; DAB; DAC; DAM DRAM,
MST, POET; DLB 13, 20, 139; EWL 3;
EXPP; LAIT 3; MTCW 1, 2; MTFW
2005; PAB; PFS 1, 3, 8; RGEL 2; RGSF
2; SATA 60; TEA; WLIT 4; WP

Thomas, Dylan Marlais
See Thomas, Dylan

Thomas, (Philip) Edward 1878-1917 . **PC 53;
TCLC 10**
See also BRW 6; BRWS 3; CA 106; 153;
DAM POET; DLB 19, 98, 156, 216; EWL
3; PAB; RGEL 2

Thomas, J. F.
See Fleming, Thomas

Thomas, Joyce Carol 1938- .... **CLC 35**
See also AAYA 12, 54; BW 2, 3; CA 113;
116; CANR 48, 114, 135, 206; CLR 19;
DLB 33; INT CA-116; JRDA; MAICYA
1, 2; MTCW 1, 2; MTFW 2005; SAAS 7;
SATA 40, 78, 123, 137, 210; SATA-Essay
137; WYA; YAW

Thomas, Lewis 1913-1993 .... **CLC 35**
See also ANW; CA 85-88; 143; CANR 38,
60; DLB 275; MTCW 1, 2

Thomas, M. Carey 1857-1935 .... **TCLC 89**
See also FW

Thomas, Paul
See Mann, Thomas

Thomas, Piri 1928- .... **CLC 17; HLCS 2**
See also CA 73-76; HW 1; LLW; SSFS 28

Thomas, R(onald) S(tuart)
1913-2000 .... **CLC 6, 13, 48; PC 99**
See also BRWS 12; CA 89-92; 189; CAAS
4; CANR 30; CDBLB 1960 to Present;
CP 1, 2, 3, 4, 5, 6, 7; DAB; DAM POET;
DLB 27; EWL 3; MTCW 1; RGEL 2

Thomas, Ross (Elmore) 1926-1995 .. **CLC 39**
See also CA 33-36R; 150; CANR 22, 63;
CMW 4

Thompson, Francis (Joseph)
1859-1907 .... **TCLC 4**
See also BRW 5; CA 104; 189; CDBLB
1890-1914; DLB 19; RGEL 2; TEA

Thompson, Francis Clegg
See Mencken, H. L.

Thompson, Hunter S. 1937(?)-2005 .. **CLC 9,
17, 40, 104, 229**
See also AAYA 45; BEST 89:1; BPFB 3;
CA 17-20R; 236; CANR 23, 46, 74, 77,
111, 133; CPW; CSW; DA3; DAM POP;
DLB 185; MTCW 1, 2; MTFW 2005;
TUS

Thompson, Hunter Stockton
See Thompson, Hunter S.

Thompson, James Myers
See Thompson, Jim

Thompson, Jim 1906-1977 .... **CLC 69**
See also BPFB 3; CA 140; CMW 4; CPW;
DLB 226; MSW

Thompson, Judith (Clare Francesca)
1954- .... **CLC 39**
See also CA 143; CD 5, 6; CWD; DFS 22;
DLB 334

Thomson, James 1700-1748 .... **LC 16, 29, 40**
See also BRWS 3; DAM POET; DLB 95;
RGEL 2

Thomson, James 1834-1882 .... **NCLC 18**
See also DAM POET; DLB 35; RGEL 2

Thoreau, Henry David 1817-1862 .. **NCLC 7,
21, 61, 138, 207; PC 30; WLC 6**
See also AAYA 42; AMW; ANW; BYA 3;
CDALB 1640-1865; DA; DA3; DAB;
DAC; DAM MST; DLB 1, 183, 223, 270,
298; LAIT 2; LMFS 1; NCFS 3; RGAL
4; TUS

Thorndike, E. L.
See Thorndike, Edward L(ee)

Thorndike, Edward L(ee)
1874-1949 .... **TCLC 107**
See also CA 121

Thornton, Hall
See Silverberg, Robert

Thorpe, Adam 1956- .... **CLC 176**
See also CA 129; CANR 92, 160; DLB 231

Thorpe, Thomas Bangs
1815-1878 .... **NCLC 183**
See also DLB 3, 11, 248; RGAL 4

Thubron, Colin 1939- .... **CLC 163**
See also CA 25-28R; CANR 12, 29, 59, 95,
171; CN 5, 6, 7; DLB 204, 231

Thubron, Colin Gerald Dryden
See Thubron, Colin

Thucydides c. 455B.C.-c.
399B.C. .... **CMLC 17, 117**
See also AW 1; DLB 176; RGWL 2, 3;
WLIT 8

Thumboo, Edwin Nadason 1933- .... **PC 30**
See also CA 194; CP 1

Thurber, James 1894-1961 .... **CLC 5, 11, 25,
125; SSC 1, 47, 137**
See also AAYA 56; AMWS 1; BPFB 3;
BYA 5; CA 73-76; CANR 17, 39; CDALB
1929-1941; CWRI 5; DA; DA3; DAB;
DAC; DAM DRAM, MST, NOV; DLB 4,
11, 22, 102; EWL 3; EXPS; FANT; LAIT
3; MAICYA 1, 2; MAL 5; MTCW 1, 2;
MTFW 2005; RGAL 4; RGSF 2; SATA
13; SSFS 1, 10, 19; SUFW; TUS

Thurber, James Grover
See Thurber, James

Thurman, Wallace (Henry)
1902-1934 .. **BLC 1:3; HR 1:3; TCLC 6**
See also BW 1, 3; CA 104; 124; CANR 81;
DAM MULT; DLB 51

Tibullus c. 54B.C.-c. 18B.C. .... **CMLC 36**
See also AW 2; DLB 211; RGWL 2, 3;
WLIT 8

Ticheburn, Cheviot
See Ainsworth, William Harrison

Tieck, (Johann) Ludwig
1773-1853 ..... **NCLC 5, 46; SSC 31, 100**
See also CDWLB 2; DLB 90; EW 5; IDTP;
RGSF 2; RGWL 2, 3; SUFW

Tiger, Derry
See Ellison, Harlan

Tilghman, Christopher 1946- .... **CLC 65**
See also CA 159; CANR 135, 151; CSW;
DLB 244

Tillich, Paul (Johannes)
1886-1965 .... **CLC 131**
See also CA 5-8R; 25-28R; CANR 33;
MTCW 1, 2

Tillinghast, Richard (Williford)
1940- .... **CLC 29**
See also CA 29-32R; CAAS 23; CANR 26,
51, 96; CP 2, 3, 4, 5, 6, 7; CSW

Tillman, Lynne (?)- .... **CLC 231**
See also CA 173; CANR 144, 172

Timrod, Henry 1828-1867 .... **NCLC 25**
See also DLB 3, 248; RGAL 4

Unamuno, Miguel de 1864-1936 .... **HLC 2;**
SSC 11, 69; TCLC 2, 9, 148, 237
See also CA 104; 131; CANR 81; DAM
MULT, NOV; DLB 108, 322; EW 8; EWL
3; HW 1, 2; MTCW 1, 2; MTFW 2005;
RGSF 2; RGWL 2, 3; SSFS 20; TWA
Unamuno y Jugo, Miguel de
See Unamuno, Miguel de
Uncle Shelby
See Silverstein, Shel
Undercliffe, Errol
See Campbell, Ramsey
Underwood, Miles
See Glassco, John
Undset, Sigrid 1882-1949 .... **TCLC 3, 197;**
WLC 6
See also AAYA 77; CA 104; 129; DA; DA3;
DAB; DAC; DAM MST, NOV; DLB 293,
332; EW 9; EWL 3; FW; MTCW 1, 2;
MTFW 2005; RGWL 2, 3
Ungaretti, Giuseppe 1888-1970 ... **CLC 7, 11,**
15; PC 57; TCLC 200
See also CA 19-20; 25-28R; CAP 2; DLB
114; EW 10; EWL 3; PFS 20; RGWL 2,
3; WLIT 7
Unger, Douglas 1952- .... **CLC 34**
See also CA 130; CANR 94, 155
Unsworth, Barry 1930- .... **CLC 76, 127**
See also BRWS 7; CA 25-28R; CANR 30,
54, 125, 171, 202; CN 6, 7; DLB 194,
326
Unsworth, Barry Forster
See Unsworth, Barry
Updike, John 1932-2009 .... **CLC 1, 2, 3, 5, 7,**
9, 13, 15, 23, 34, 43, 70, 139, 214, 278;
PC 90; SSC 13, 27, 103; WLC 6
See also AAYA 36; AMW; AMWC 1;
AMWR 1; BPFB 3; BYA 12; CA 1-4R;
282; CABS 1; CANR 4, 33, 51, 94, 133,
197; CDALB 1968-1988; CN 1, 2, 3, 4,
5, 6, 7; CP 1, 2, 3, 4, 5, 6, 7; CPW 1;
DA; DA3; DAB; DAC; DAM MST, NOV,
POET, POP; DLB 2, 5, 143, 218, 227;
DLBD 3; DLBY 1980, 1982, 1997; EWL
3; EXPP; HGG; MAL 5; MTCW 1, 2;
MTFW 2005; NFS 12, 24; RGAL 4;
RGSF 2; SSFS 3, 19; TUS
Updike, John Hoyer
See Updike, John
Upshaw, Margaret Mitchell
See Mitchell, Margaret
Upton, Mark
See Sanders, Lawrence
Upward, Allen 1863-1926 .... **TCLC 85**
See also CA 117; 187; DLB 36
Urdang, Constance (Henriette)
1922-1996 .... **CLC 47**
See also CA 21-24R; CANR 9, 24; CP 1, 2,
3, 4, 5, 6; CWP
Urfe, Honore d' 1567(?)-1625 .... **LC 132**
See also DLB 268; GFL Beginnings to
1789; RGWL 2, 3
Uriel, Henry
See Faust, Frederick
Uris, Leon 1924-2003 .... **CLC 7, 32**
See also AITN 1, 2; AMWS 20; BEST 89:2;
BPFB 3; CA 1-4R; 217; CANR 1, 40, 65,
123; CN 1, 2, 3, 4, 5, 6; CPW 1; DA3;
DAM NOV, POP; MTCW 1, 2; MTFW
2005; RGHL; SATA 49; SATA-Obit 146
Urista, Alberto 1947- .... **HLCS 1; PC 34**
See also CA 45-48R; CANR 2, 32; DLB
82; HW 1; LLW
Urista Heredia, Alberto Baltazar
See Urista, Alberto
Urmuz
See Codrescu, Andrei
Urquhart, Guy
See McAlmon, Robert (Menzies)

Urquhart, Jane 1949- .... **CLC 90, 242**
See also CA 113; CANR 32, 68, 116, 157;
CCA 1; DAC; DLB 334
Usigli, Rodolfo 1905-1979 .... **HLCS 1**
See also CA 131; DLB 305; EWL 3; HW 1;
LAW
Usk, Thomas (?)-1388 .... **CMLC 76**
See also DLB 146
Ustinov, Peter (Alexander)
1921-2004 .... **CLC 1**
See also AITN 1; CA 13-16R; 225; CANR
25, 51; CBD; CD 5, 6; DLB 13; MTCW
2
U Tam'si, Gerald Felix Tchicaya
See Tchicaya, Gerald Felix
U Tam'si, Tchicaya
See Tchicaya, Gerald Felix
Vachss, Andrew 1942- .... **CLC 106**
See also CA 118, 214; CAAE 214; CANR
44, 95, 153, 197; CMW 4
Vachss, Andrew H.
See Vachss, Andrew
Vachss, Andrew Henry
See Vachss, Andrew
Vaculik, Ludvik 1926- .... **CLC 7**
See also CA 53-56; CANR 72; CWW 2;
DLB 232; EWL 3
Vaihinger, Hans 1852-1933 .... **TCLC 71**
See also CA 116; 166
Valdez, Luis (Miguel) 1940- ..... **CLC 84; DC**
10; HLC 2
See also CA 101; CAD; CANR 32, 81; CD
5, 6; DAM MULT; DFS 5; DLB 122;
EWL 3; HW 1; LAIT 4; LLW
Valenzuela, Luisa 1938- .... **CLC 31, 104;**
HLCS 1; SSC 14, 82
See also CA 101; CANR 32, 65, 123; CD-
WLB 3; CWW 2; DAM MULT; DLB 113;
EWL 3; FW; HW 1, 2; LAW; RGSF 2;
RGWL 3; SSFS 29
Valera y Alcala-Galiano, Juan
1824-1905 .... **TCLC 10**
See also CA 106
Valerius Maximus .... **CMLC 64**
See also DLB 211
Valery, Ambroise Paul Toussaint Jules
See Valery, Paul
Valery, Paul 1871-1945 ... **PC 9; TCLC 4, 15,**
231
See also CA 104; 122; DA3; DAM POET;
DLB 258; EW 8; EWL 3; GFL 1789 to
the Present; MTCW 1, 2; MTFW 2005;
RGWL 2, 3; TWA
Valle-Inclan, Ramon del 1866-1936 .. **HLC 2;**
TCLC 5, 228
See also CA 106; 153; CANR 80; DAM
MULT; DLB 134, 322; EW 8; EWL 3;
HW 2; RGSF 2; RGWL 2, 3
Valle-Inclan, Ramon Maria del
See Valle-Inclan, Ramon del
Vallejo, Antonio Buero
See Buero Vallejo, Antonio
Vallejo, Cesar 1892-1938 ... **HLC 2; TCLC 3,**
56
See also CA 105; 153; DAM MULT; DLB
290; EWL 3; HW 1; LAW; PFS 26;
RGWL 2, 3
Vallejo, Cesar Abraham
See Vallejo, Cesar
Valles, Jules 1832-1885 .... **NCLC 71**
See also DLB 123; GFL 1789 to the Present
Vallette, Marguerite Eymery
1860-1953 .... **TCLC 67**
See also CA 182; DLB 123, 192; EWL 3
Valle Y Pena, Ramon del
See Valle-Inclan, Ramon del
Van Ash, Cay 1918-1994 .... **CLC 34**
See also CA 220

Vanbrugh, Sir John 1664-1726 ... **DC 40; LC**
21
See also BRW 2; DAM DRAM; DLB 80;
IDTP; RGEL 2
Van Campen, Karl
See Campbell, John W(ood, Jr.)
Vance, Gerald
See Silverberg, Robert
Vance, Jack 1916- .... **CLC 35**
See also CA 29-32R; CANR 17, 65, 154,
218; CMW 4; DLB 8; FANT; MTCW 1;
SCFW 1, 2; SFW 4; SUFW 1, 2
Vance, John Holbrook
See Vance, Jack
Van Den Bogarde, Derek Jules Gaspard
Ulric Niven 1921-1999 .... **CLC 14**
See also CA 77-80; 179; DLB 14
Vandenburgh, Jane .... **CLC 59**
See also CA 168; CANR 208
Vanderhaeghe, Guy 1951- .... **CLC 41**
See also BPFB 3; CA 113; CANR 72, 145;
CN 7; DLB 334
van der Post, Laurens (Jan)
1906-1996 .... **CLC 5**
See also AFW; CA 5-8R; 155; CANR 35;
CN 1, 2, 3, 4, 5, 6; DLB 204; RGEL 2
van de Wetering, Janwillem
1931-2008 .... **CLC 47**
See also CA 49-52; 274; CANR 4, 62, 90;
CMW 4
Van Dine, S. S.
See Wright, Willard Huntington
Van Doren, Carl (Clinton)
1885-1950 .... **TCLC 18**
See also CA 111; 168
Van Doren, Mark 1894-1972 .... **CLC 6, 10**
See also CA 1-4R; 37-40R; CANR 3; CN
1; CP 1; DLB 45, 284, 335; MAL 5;
MTCW 1, 2; RGAL 4
Van Druten, John (William)
1901-1957 .... **TCLC 2**
See also CA 104; 161; DLB 10; MAL 5;
RGAL 4
Van Duyn, Mona 1921-2004 .... **CLC 3, 7, 63,**
116
See also CA 9-12R; 234; CANR 7, 38, 60,
116; CP 1, 2, 3, 4, 5, 6, 7; CWP; DAM
POET; DLB 5; MAL 5; MTFW 2005;
PFS 20
Van Dyne, Edith
See Baum, L. Frank
van Herk, Aritha 1954- .... **CLC 249**
See also CA 101; CANR 94; DLB 334
van Itallie, Jean-Claude 1936- .... **CLC 3**
See also CA 45-48; CAAS 2; CAD; CANR
1, 48; CD 5, 6; DLB 7
Van Loot, Cornelius Obenchain
See Roberts, Kenneth (Lewis)
van Ostaijen, Paul 1896-1928 .... **TCLC 33**
See also CA 163
Van Peebles, Melvin 1932- .... **CLC 2, 20**
See also BW 2, 3; CA 85-88; CANR 27,
67, 82; DAM MULT
van Schendel, Arthur(-Francois-Emile)
1874-1946 .... **TCLC 56**
See also EWL 3
Van See, John
See Vance, Jack
Vansittart, Peter 1920-2008 .... **CLC 42**
See also CA 1-4R; 278; CANR 3, 49, 90;
CN 4, 5, 6, 7; RHW
Van Vechten, Carl 1880-1964 ... **CLC 33; HR**
1:3
See also AMWS 2; CA 183; 89-92; DLB 4,
9, 51; RGAL 4
van Vogt, A(lfred) E(lton) 1912-2000 . **CLC 1**
See also BPFB 3; BYA 13, 14; CA 21-24R;
190; CANR 28; DLB 8, 251; SATA 14;
SATA-Obit 124; SCFW 1, 2; SFW 4

Voigt, Cynthia 1942- .... **CLC 30**
See also AAYA 3, 30; BYA 1, 3, 6, 7, 8;
CA 106; CANR 18, 37, 40, 94, 145; CLR
13, 48, 141; INT CANR-18; JRDA; LAIT
5; MAICYA 1, 2; MAICYAS 1; MTFW
2005; SATA 48, 79, 116, 160; SATA-Brief
33; WYA; YAW

Voigt, Ellen Bryant 1943- .... **CLC 54**
See also CA 69-72; CANR 11, 29, 55, 115,
171; CP 5, 6, 7; CSW; CWP; DLB 120;
PFS 23, 33

Voinovich, Vladimir 1932- .. **CLC 10, 49, 147**
See also CA 81-84; CAAS 12; CANR 33,
67, 150; CWW 2; DLB 302; MTCW 1

Voinovich, Vladimir Nikolaevich
See Voinovich, Vladimir

Vollmann, William T. 1959- ...... **CLC 89, 227**
See also AMWS 17; CA 134; CANR 67,
116, 185; CN 7; CPW; DA3; DAM NOV,
POP; DLB 350; MTCW 2; MTFW 2005

Voloshinov, V. N.
See Bakhtin, Mikhail Mikhailovich

Voltaire 1694-1778 .. **LC 14, 79, 110; SSC 12,
112; WLC 6**
See also BYA 13; DA; DA3; DAB; DAC;
DAM DRAM, MST; DLB 314; EW 4;
GFL Beginnings to 1789; LATS 1:1;
LMFS 1; NFS 7; RGWL 2, 3; TWA

von Aschendrof, Baron Ignatz
See Ford, Ford Madox

von Chamisso, Adelbert
See Chamisso, Adelbert von

von Daeniken, Erich 1935- .... **CLC 30**
See also AITN 1; CA 37-40R; CANR 17,
44

von Daniken, Erich
See von Daeniken, Erich

von Eschenbach, Wolfram c. 1170-c.
1220 .... **CMLC 5**
See also CDWLB 2; DLB 138; EW 1;
RGWL 2, 3

von Hartmann, Eduard
1842-1906 .... **TCLC 96**

von Hayek, Friedrich August
See Hayek, F(riedrich) A(ugust von)

von Heidenstam, (Carl Gustaf) Verner
See Heidenstam, (Carl Gustaf) Verner von

von Heyse, Paul (Johann Ludwig)
See Heyse, Paul (Johann Ludwig von)

von Hofmannsthal, Hugo
See Hofmannsthal, Hugo von

von Horvath, Odon
See von Horvath, Odon

von Horvath, Odon
See von Horvath, Odon

von Horvath, Odon 1901-1938 .... **TCLC 45**
See also CA 118; 184, 194; DLB 85, 124;
RGWL 2, 3

von Horvath, Oedoen
See von Horvath, Odon

von Kleist, Heinrich
See Kleist, Heinrich von

Vonnegut, Kurt, Jr.
See Vonnegut, Kurt

Vonnegut, Kurt 1922-2007 .... **CLC 1, 2, 3, 4,
5, 8, 12, 22, 40, 60, 111, 212, 254; SSC
8, 155; WLC 6**
See also AAYA 6, 44; AITN 1; AMWS 2;
BEST 90:4; BPFB 3; BYA 3, 14; CA
1-4R; 259; CANR 1, 25, 49, 75, 92, 207;
CDALB 1968-1988; CN 1, 2, 3, 4, 5, 6,
7; CPW 1; DA; DA3; DAB; DAC; DAM
MST, NOV, POP; DLB 2, 8, 152; DLBD
3; DLBY 1980; EWL 3; EXPN; EXPS;
LAIT 4; LMFS 2; MAL 5; MTCW 1, 2;
MTFW 2005; NFS 3, 28; RGAL 4;
SCFW; SFW 4; SSFS 5; TUS; YAW

Von Rachen, Kurt
See Hubbard, L. Ron

von Sternberg, Josef
See Sternberg, Josef von

Vorster, Gordon 1924- .... **CLC 34**
See also CA 133

Vosce, Trudie
See Ozick, Cynthia

Voznesensky, Andrei 1933-2010 .. **CLC 1, 15,
57**
See also CA 89-92; CANR 37; CWW 2;
DAM POET; DLB 359; EWL 3; MTCW
1

Voznesensky, Andrei Andreievich
See Voznesensky, Andrei

Voznesensky, Andrey
See Voznesensky, Andrei

Wace, Robert c. 1100-c. 1175 .... **CMLC 55**
See also DLB 146

Waddington, Miriam 1917-2004 .... **CLC 28**
See also CA 21-24R; 225; CANR 12, 30;
CCA 1; CP 1, 2, 3, 4, 5, 6, 7; DLB 68

Wade, Alan
See Vance, Jack

Wagman, Fredrica 1937- .... **CLC 7**
See also CA 97-100; CANR 166; INT CA-
97-100

Wagner, Linda W.
See Wagner-Martin, Linda (C.)

Wagner, Linda Welshimer
See Wagner-Martin, Linda (C.)

Wagner, Richard 1813-1883 ..... **NCLC 9, 119**
See also DLB 129; EW 6

Wagner-Martin, Linda (C.) 1936- .... **CLC 50**
See also CA 159; CANR 135

Wagoner, David (Russell) 1926- .... **CLC 3, 5,
15; PC 33**
See also AMWS 9; CA 1-4R; CAAS 3;
CANR 2, 71; CN 1, 2, 3, 4, 5, 6, 7; CP 1,
2, 3, 4, 5, 6, 7; DLB 5, 256; SATA 14;
TCWW 1, 2

Wah, Fred(erick James) 1939- .... **CLC 44**
See also CA 107; 141; CP 1, 6, 7; DLB 60

Wahloo, Per 1926-1975 .... **CLC 7**
See also BPFB 3; CA 61-64; CANR 73;
CMW 4; MSW

Wahloo, Peter
See Wahloo, Per

Wain, John 1925-1994 ...... **CLC 2, 11, 15, 46**
See also BRWS 16; CA 5-8R; 145; CAAS
4; CANR 23, 54; CDBLB 1960 to Present;
CN 1, 2, 3, 4, 5; CP 1, 2, 3, 4, 5; DLB
15, 27, 139, 155; EWL 3; MTCW 1, 2;
MTFW 2005

Wajda, Andrzej 1926- .... **CLC 16, 219**
See also CA 102

Wakefield, Dan 1932- .... **CLC 7**
See also CA 21-24R, 211; CAAE 211;
CAAS 7; CN 4, 5, 6, 7

Wakefield, Herbert Russell
1888-1965 .... **TCLC 120**
See also CA 5-8R; CANR 77; HGG; SUFW

Wakoski, Diane 1937- ...... **CLC 2, 4, 7, 9, 11,
40; PC 15**
See also CA 13-16R, 216; CAAE 216;
CAAS 1; CANR 9, 60, 106; CP 1, 2, 3, 4,
5, 6, 7; CWP; DAM POET; DLB 5; INT
CANR-9; MAL 5; MTCW 2; MTFW
2005

Wakoski-Sherbell, Diane
See Wakoski, Diane

Walcott, Derek 1930- . **BLC 1:3, 2:3; CLC 2,
4, 9, 14, 25, 42, 67, 76, 160, 282; DC 7;
PC 46**
See also BW 2; CA 89-92; CANR 26, 47,
75, 80, 130; CBD; CD 5, 6; CDWLB 3;
CP 1, 2, 3, 4, 5, 6, 7; DA3; DAB; DAC;
DAM MST, MULT, POET; DLB 117,
332; DLBY 1981; DNFS 1; EFS 1:1, 2:2;
EWL 3; LMFS 2; MTCW 1, 2; MTFW
2005; PFS 6, 34; RGEL 2; TWA; WWE 1

Walcott, Derek Alton
See Walcott, Derek

Waldman, Anne 1945- .... **CLC 7**
See also BG 1:3; CA 37-40R; CAAS 17;
CANR 34, 69, 116, 219; CP 1, 2, 3, 4, 5,
6, 7; CWP; DLB 16

Waldman, Anne Lesley
See Waldman, Anne

Waldo, E. Hunter
See Sturgeon, Theodore (Hamilton)

Waldo, Edward Hamilton
See Sturgeon, Theodore (Hamilton)

Waldrop, Rosmarie 1935- .... **PC 109**
See also CA 101; CAAS 30; CANR 18, 39,
67; CP 6, 7; CWP; DLB 169

Walker, Alice 1944- .... **BLC 1:3, 2:3; CLC 5,
6, 9, 19, 27, 46, 58, 103, 167; PC 30;
SSC 5; WLCS**
See also AAYA 3, 33; AFAW 1, 2; AMWS
3; BEST 89:4; BPFB 3; BW 2, 3; CA 37-
40R; CANR 9, 27, 49, 66, 82, 131, 191;
CDALB 1968-1988; CN 4, 5, 6, 7; CPW;
CSW; DA; DA3; DAB; DAC; DAM MST,
MULT, NOV, POET, POP; DLB 6, 33,
143; EWL 3; EXPN; EXPS; FL 1:6; FW;
INT CANR-27; LAIT 3; MAL 5; MBL;
MTCW 1, 2; MTFW 2005; NFS 5; PFS
30, 34; RGAL 4; RGSF 2; SATA 31;
SSFS 2, 11; TUS; YAW

Walker, Alice Malsenior
See Walker, Alice

Walker, David Harry 1911-1992 ...... **CLC 14**
See also CA 1-4R; 137; CANR 1; CN 1, 2;
CWRI 5; SATA 8; SATA-Obit 71

Walker, Edward Joseph 1934-2004 .. **CLC 13**
See also CA 21-24R; 226; CANR 12, 28,
53; CP 1, 2, 3, 4, 5, 6, 7; DLB 40

Walker, George F(rederick) 1947- .. **CLC 44,
61**
See also CA 103; CANR 21, 43, 59; CD 5,
6; DAB; DAC; DAM MST; DLB 60

Walker, Joseph A. 1935-2003 .... **CLC 19**
See also BW 1, 3; CA 89-92; CAD; CANR
26, 143; CD 5, 6; DAM DRAM, MST;
DFS 12; DLB 38

Walker, Margaret 1915-1998 .... **BLC 1:3;
CLC 1, 6; PC 20; TCLC 129**
See also AFAW 1, 2; BW 2, 3; CA 73-76;
172; CANR 26, 54, 76, 136; CN 1, 2, 3,
4, 5, 6; CP 1, 2, 3, 4, 5, 6; CSW; DAM
MULT; DLB 76, 152; EXPP; FW; MAL
5; MTCW 1, 2; MTFW 2005; PFS 31;
RGAL 4; RHW

Walker, Ted
See Walker, Edward Joseph

Wallace, David Foster 1962-2008 .... **CLC 50,
114, 271, 281; SSC 68**
See also AAYA 50; AMWS 10; CA 132;
277; CANR 59, 133, 190; CN 7; DA3;
DLB 350; MTCW 2; MTFW 2005

Wallace, Dexter
See Masters, Edgar Lee

Wallace, (Richard Horatio) Edgar
1875-1932 .... **TCLC 57**
See also CA 115; 218; CMW 4; DLB 70;
MSW; RGEL 2

Wallace, Irving 1916-1990 .... **CLC 7, 13**
See also AITN 1; BPFB 3; CA 1-4R; 132;
CAAS 1; CANR 1, 27; CPW; DAM NOV,
POP; INT CANR-27; MTCW 1, 2

Wallant, Edward Lewis 1926-1962 ... **CLC 5,
10**
See also CA 1-4R; CANR 22; DLB 2, 28,
143, 299; EWL 3; MAL 5; MTCW 1, 2;
RGAL 4; RGHL

Wallas, Graham 1858-1932 .... **TCLC 91**

Waller, Edmund 1606-1687 .... **LC 86; PC 72**
See also BRW 2; DAM POET; DLB 126;
PAB; RGEL 2

Walley, Byron
See Card, Orson Scott

Walls, Jeannette 1960(?)- .... **CLC 299**
See also CA 242

Walpole, Horace 1717-1797 ..... **LC 2, 49, 152**
See also BRW 3; DLB 39, 104, 213; GL 3;
HGG; LMFS 1; RGEL 2; SUFW 1; TEA

Walpole, Hugh 1884-1941 .... **TCLC 5**
See also CA 104; 165; DLB 34; HGG;
MTCW 2; RGEL 2; RHW

Walpole, Hugh Seymour
See Walpole, Hugh

Walrond, Eric (Derwent) 1898-1966 . **HR 1:3**
See also BW 1; CA 125; DLB 51

Walser, Martin 1927- .... **CLC 27, 183**
See also CA 57-60; CANR 8, 46, 145;
CWW 2; DLB 75, 124; EWL 3

Walser, Robert 1878-1956 ..... **SSC 20; TCLC
18**
See also CA 118; 165; CANR 100, 194;
DLB 66; EWL 3

Walsh, Gillian Paton
See Paton Walsh, Jill

Walsh, Jill Paton
See Paton Walsh, Jill

Walter, Villiam Christian
See Andersen, Hans Christian

Walter of Chatillon c. 1135-c.
1202 .... **CMLC 111**

Walters, Anna L(ee) 1946- .... **NNAL**
See also CA 73-76

Walther von der Vogelweide c.
1170-1228 .... **CMLC 56**

Walton, Izaak 1593-1683 .... **LC 72**
See also BRW 2; CDBLB Before 1660;
DLB 151, 213; RGEL 2

Walzer, Michael 1935- .... **CLC 238**
See also CA 37-40R; CANR 15, 48, 127,
190

Walzer, Michael Laban
See Walzer, Michael

Wambaugh, Joseph, Jr. 1937- ..... **CLC 3, 18**
See also AITN 1; BEST 89:3; BPFB 3; CA
33-36R; CANR 42, 65, 115, 167, 217;
CMW 4; CPW 1; DA3; DAM NOV, POP;
DLB 6; DLBY 1983; MSW; MTCW 1, 2

Wambaugh, Joseph Aloysius
See Wambaugh, Joseph, Jr.

Wang Wei 699(?)-761(?) . **CMLC 100; PC 18**
See also TWA

Warburton, William 1698-1779 .... **LC 97**
See also DLB 104

Ward, Arthur Henry Sarsfield
1883-1959 .... **TCLC 28**
See also AAYA 80; CA 108; 173; CMW 4;
DLB 70; HGG; MSW; SUFW

Ward, Douglas Turner 1930- .... **CLC 19**
See also BW 1; CA 81-84; CAD; CANR
27; CD 5, 6; DLB 7, 38

Ward, E. D.
See Lucas, E(dward) V(errall)

Ward, Mrs. Humphry 1851-1920
See Ward, Mary Augusta
See also RGEL 2

Ward, Mary Augusta 1851-1920 ... **TCLC 55**
See Ward, Mrs. Humphry
See also DLB 18

Ward, Nathaniel 1578(?)-1652 .... **LC 114**
See also DLB 24

Ward, Peter
See Faust, Frederick

Warhol, Andy 1928(?)-1987 .... **CLC 20**
See also AAYA 12; BEST 89:4; CA 89-92;
121; CANR 34

Warner, Francis (Robert Le Plastrier)
1937- .... **CLC 14**
See also CA 53-56; CANR 11; CP 1, 2, 3, 4

Warner, Marina 1946- .... **CLC 59, 231**
See also CA 65-68; CANR 21, 55, 118; CN
5, 6, 7; DLB 194; MTFW 2005

Warner, Rex (Ernest) 1905-1986 ...... **CLC 45**
See also CA 89-92; 119; CN 1, 2, 3, 4; CP
1, 2, 3, 4; DLB 15; RGEL 2; RHW

Warner, Susan (Bogert)
1819-1885 .... **NCLC 31, 146**
See also AMWS 18; DLB 3, 42, 239, 250,
254

Warner, Sylvia (Constance) Ashton
See Ashton-Warner, Sylvia (Constance)

Warner, Sylvia Townsend
1893-1978 .. **CLC 7, 19; SSC 23; TCLC
131**
See also BRWS 7; CA 61-64; 77-80; CANR
16, 60, 104; CN 1, 2; DLB 34, 139; EWL
3; FANT; FW; MTCW 1, 2; RGEL 2;
RGSF 2; RHW

Warren, Mercy Otis 1728-1814 .... **NCLC 13,
226**
See also DLB 31, 200; RGAL 4; TUS

Warren, Robert Penn 1905-1989 .. **CLC 1, 4,
6, 8, 10, 13, 18, 39, 53, 59; PC 37; SSC
4, 58, 126; WLC 6**
See also AITN 1; AMW; AMWC 2; BPFB
3; BYA 1; CA 13-16R; 129; CANR 10,
47; CDALB 1968-1988; CN 1, 2, 3, 4;
CP 1, 2, 3, 4; DA; DA3; DAB; DAC;
DAM MST, NOV, POET; DLB 2, 48, 152,
320; DLBY 1980, 1989; EWL 3; INT
CANR-10; MAL 5; MTCW 1, 2; MTFW
2005; NFS 13; RGAL 4; RGSF 2; RHW;
SATA 46; SATA-Obit 63; SSFS 8; TUS

Warrigal, Jack
See Furphy, Joseph

Warshofsky, Isaac
See Singer, Isaac Bashevis

Warton, Joseph 1722-1800 ... **LC 128; NCLC
118**
See also DLB 104, 109; RGEL 2

Warton, Thomas 1728-1790 .... **LC 15, 82**
See also DAM POET; DLB 104, 109, 336;
RGEL 2

Waruk, Kona
See Harris, (Theodore) Wilson

Warung, Price
See Astley, William

Warwick, Jarvis
See Garner, Hugh

Washington, Alex
See Harris, Mark

Washington, Booker T. 1856-1915 . **BLC 1:3;
TCLC 10**
See also BW 1; CA 114; 125; DA3; DAM
MULT; DLB 345; LAIT 2; RGAL 4;
SATA 28

Washington, Booker Taliaferro
See Washington, Booker T.

Washington, George 1732-1799 .... **LC 25**
See also DLB 31

Wassermann, (Karl) Jakob
1873-1934 .... **TCLC 6**
See also CA 104; 163; DLB 66; EWL 3

Wasserstein, Wendy 1950-2006 . **CLC 32, 59,
90, 183; DC 4**
See also AAYA 73; AMWS 15; CA 121;
129; 247; CABS 3; CAD; CANR 53, 75,
128; CD 5, 6; CWD; DA3; DAM DRAM;
DFS 5, 17; DLB 228; EWL 3; FW; INT
CA-129; MAL 5; MTCW 2; MTFW 2005;
SATA 94; SATA-Obit 174

Waterhouse, Keith 1929-2009 .... **CLC 47**
See also BRWS 13; CA 5-8R; 290; CANR
38, 67, 109; CBD; CD 6; CN 1, 2, 3, 4, 5,
6, 7; DLB 13, 15; MTCW 1, 2; MTFW
2005

Waterhouse, Keith Spencer
See Waterhouse, Keith

Waters, Frank (Joseph) 1902-1995 .. **CLC 88**
See also CA 5-8R; 149; CAAS 13; CANR
3, 18, 63, 121; DLB 212; DLBY 1986;
RGAL 4; TCWW 1, 2

Waters, Mary C. .... **CLC 70**

Waters, Roger 1944- .... **CLC 35**

Watkins, Frances Ellen
See Harper, Frances Ellen Watkins

Watkins, Gerrold
See Malzberg, Barry N(athaniel)

Watkins, Gloria Jean
See hooks, bell

Watkins, Paul 1964- .... **CLC 55**
See also CA 132; CANR 62, 98

Watkins, Vernon Phillips
1906-1967 .... **CLC 43**
See also CA 9-10; 25-28R; CAP 1; DLB
20; EWL 3; RGEL 2

Watson, Irving S.
See Mencken, H. L.

Watson, John H.
See Farmer, Philip Jose

Watson, Richard F.
See Silverberg, Robert

Watson, Rosamund Marriott
1860-1911 .... **PC 117**
See also CA 207; DLB 240

Watson, Sheila 1909-1998 .... **SSC 128**
See also AITN 2; CA 155; CCA 1; DAC;
DLB 60

Watts, Ephraim
See Horne, Richard Henry Hengist

Watts, Isaac 1674-1748 .... **LC 98**
See also DLB 95; RGEL 2; SATA 52

Waugh, Auberon (Alexander)
1939-2001 .... **CLC 7**
See also CA 45-48; 192; CANR 6, 22, 92;
CN 1, 2, 3; DLB 14, 194

Waugh, Evelyn 1903-1966 ... **CLC 1, 3, 8, 13,
19, 27, 44, 107; SSC 41; TCLC 229;
WLC 6**
See also AAYA 78; BPFB 3; BRW 7; CA
85-88; 25-28R; CANR 22; CDBLB 1914-
1945; DA; DA3; DAB; DAC; DAM MST,
NOV, POP; DLB 15, 162, 195, 352; EWL
3; MTCW 1, 2; MTFW 2005; NFS 13,
17, 34; RGEL 2; RGSF 2; TEA; WLIT 4

Waugh, Evelyn Arthur St. John
See Waugh, Evelyn

Waugh, Harriet 1944- .... **CLC 6**
See also CA 85-88; CANR 22

Ways, C.R.
See Blount, Roy, Jr.

Waystaff, Simon
See Swift, Jonathan

Webb, Beatrice 1858-1943 .... **TCLC 22**
See also CA 117; 162; DLB 190; FW

Webb, Beatrice Martha Potter
See Webb, Beatrice

Webb, Charles 1939- .... **CLC 7**
See also CA 25-28R; CANR 114, 188

Webb, Charles Richard
See Webb, Charles

Webb, Frank J. .... **NCLC 143**
See also DLB 50

Webb, James, Jr.
See Webb, James

Webb, James 1946- .... **CLC 22**
See also CA 81-84; CANR 156

Webb, James H.
See Webb, James

Webb, James Henry
See Webb, James

Webb, Mary Gladys (Meredith)
1881-1927 .... **TCLC 24**
See also CA 182; 123; DLB 34; FW; RGEL
2

Webb, Mrs. Sidney
See Webb, Beatrice

Webb, Phyllis 1927- .... **CLC 18**
See also CA 104; CANR 23; CCA 1; CP 1,
2, 3, 4, 5, 6, 7; CWP; DLB 53

Webb, Sidney 1859-1947 .... **TCLC 22**
See also CA 117; 163; DLB 190

Webb, Sidney James
See Webb, Sidney

Webber, Andrew Lloyd
See Lloyd Webber, Andrew

Weber, Lenora Mattingly
1895-1971 .... **CLC 12**
See also CA 19-20; 29-32R; CAP 1; SATA
2; SATA-Obit 26

Weber, Max 1864-1920 .... **TCLC 69**
See also CA 109; 189; DLB 296

Webster, Augusta 1837-1894 .... **NCLC 230**
See also DLB 35, 240

Webster, John 1580(?)-1634(?) ...... **DC 2; LC
33, 84, 124; WLC 6**
See also BRW 2; CDBLB Before 1660; DA;
DAB; DAC; DAM DRAM, MST; DFS
17, 19; DLB 58; IDTP; RGEL 2; WLIT 3

Webster, Noah 1758-1843 .... **NCLC 30**
See also DLB 1, 37, 42, 43, 73, 243

Wedekind, Benjamin Franklin
See Wedekind, Frank

Wedekind, Frank 1864-1918 .... **TCLC 7, 241**
See also CA 104; 153; CANR 121, 122;
CDWLB 2; DAM DRAM; DLB 118; EW
8; EWL 3; LMFS 2; RGWL 2, 3

Weems, Mason Locke
1759-1825 .... **NCLC 245**
See also DLB 30, 37, 42

Wehr, Demaris .... **CLC 65**

Weidman, Jerome 1913-1998 .... **CLC 7**
See also AITN 2; CA 1-4R; 171; CAD;
CANR 1; CD 1, 2, 3, 4, 5; DLB 28

Weil, Simone 1909-1943 .... **TCLC 23**
See also CA 117; 159; EW 12; EWL 3; FW;
GFL 1789 to the Present; MTCW 2

Weil, Simone Adolphine
See Weil, Simone

Weininger, Otto 1880-1903 .... **TCLC 84**

Weinstein, Nathan
See West, Nathanael

Weinstein, Nathan von Wallenstein
See West, Nathanael

Weir, Peter 1944- .... **CLC 20**
See also CA 113; 123

Weir, Peter Lindsay
See Weir, Peter

Weiss, Peter (Ulrich) 1916-1982 .. **CLC 3, 15,
51; DC 36; TCLC 152**
See also CA 45-48; 106; CANR 3; DAM
DRAM; DFS 3; DLB 69, 124; EWL 3;
RGHL; RGWL 2, 3

Weiss, Theodore (Russell)
1916-2003 .... **CLC 3, 8, 14**
See also CA 9-12R; 189; 216; CAAE 189;
CAAS 2; CANR 46, 94; CP 1, 2, 3, 4, 5,
6, 7; DLB 5; TCLE 1:2

Welch, (Maurice) Denton
1915-1948 .... **TCLC 22**
See also BRWS 8; CA 121; 148; RGEL 2

Welch, James 1940-2003 .... **CLC 6, 14, 52,
249; NNAL; PC 62**
See also CA 85-88; 219; CANR 42, 66, 107;
CN 5, 6, 7; CP 2, 3, 4, 5, 6, 7; CPW;
DAM MULT, POP; DLB 175, 256; LATS
1:1; NFS 23; RGAL 4; TCWW 1, 2

Welch, James Phillip
See Welch, James

Weld, Angelina Grimke
See Grimke, Angelina Weld

Weldon, Fay 1931- . **CLC 6, 9, 11, 19, 36, 59,
122**
See also BRWS 4; CA 21-24R; CANR 16,
46, 63, 97, 137; CDBLB 1960 to Present;
CN 3, 4, 5, 6, 7; CPW; DAM POP; DLB
14, 194, 319; EWL 3; FW; HGG; INT
CANR-16; MTCW 1, 2; MTFW 2005;
RGEL 2; RGSF 2

Wellek, Rene 1903-1995 .... **CLC 28**
See also CA 5-8R; 150; CAAS 8; CANR 8;
DLB 63; EWL 3; INT CANR-8

Weller, Michael 1942- .... **CLC 10, 53**
See also CA 85-88; CAD; CD 5, 6

Weller, Paul 1958- .... **CLC 26**

Wellershoff, Dieter 1925- .... **CLC 46**
See also CA 89-92; CANR 16, 37

Welles, (George) Orson 1915-1985 .. **CLC 20,
80**
See also AAYA 40; CA 93-96; 117

Wellman, John McDowell 1945- ...... **CLC 65**
See also CA 166; CAD; CD 5, 6; RGAL 4

Wellman, Mac
See Wellman, John McDowell; Wellman,
John McDowell

Wellman, Manly Wade 1903-1986 ... **CLC 49**
See also CA 1-4R; 118; CANR 6, 16, 44;
FANT; SATA 6; SATA-Obit 47; SFW 4;
SUFW

Wells, Carolyn 1869(?)-1942 .... **TCLC 35**
See also CA 113; 185; CMW 4; DLB 11

Wells, H. G. 1866-1946 .... **SSC 6, 70, 151;
TCLC 6, 12, 19, 133; WLC 6**
See also AAYA 18; BPFB 3; BRW 6; CA
110; 121; CDBLB 1914-1945; CLR 64,
133; DA; DA3; DAB; DAC; DAM MST,
NOV; DLB 34, 70, 156, 178; EWL 3;
EXPS; HGG; LAIT 3; LMFS 2; MTCW
1, 2; MTFW 2005; NFS 17, 20, 36; RGEL
2; RGSF 2; SATA 20; SCFW 1, 2; SFW
4; SSFS 3; SUFW; TEA; WCH; WLIT 4;
YAW

Wells, Herbert George
See Wells, H. G.

Wells, Rosemary 1943- .... **CLC 12**
See also AAYA 13; BYA 7, 8; CA 85-88;
CANR 48, 120, 179; CLR 16, 69; CWRI
5; MAICYA 1, 2; SAAS 1; SATA 18, 69,
114, 156, 207; YAW

Wells-Barnett, Ida B(ell)
1862-1931 .... **TCLC 125**
See also CA 182; DLB 23, 221

Welsh, Irvine 1958- .... **CLC 144, 276**
See also BRWS 17; CA 173; CANR 146,
196; CN 7; DLB 271

Welty, Eudora 1909-2001 .... **CLC 1, 2, 5, 14,
22, 33, 105, 220; SSC 1, 27, 51, 111;
WLC 6**
See also AAYA 48; AMW; AMWR 1; BPFB
3; CA 9-12R; 199; CABS 1; CANR 32,
65, 128; CDALB 1941-1968; CN 1, 2, 3,
4, 5, 6, 7; CSW; DA; DA3; DAB; DAC;
DAM MST, NOV; DFS 26; DLB 2, 102,
143; DLBD 12; DLBY 1987, 2001; EWL
3; EXPS; HGG; LAIT 3; MAL 5; MBL;
MTCW 1, 2; MTFW 2005; NFS 13, 15;
RGAL 4; RGSF 2; RHW; SSFS 2, 10, 26;
TUS

Welty, Eudora Alice
See Welty, Eudora

Wen I-to 1899-1946 .... **TCLC 28**
See also EWL 3

Wentworth, Robert
See Hamilton, Edmond

Werfel, Franz (Viktor) 1890-1945 .... **PC 101;
TCLC 8, 248**
See also CA 104; 161; DLB 81, 124; EWL
3; RGWL 2, 3

Wergeland, Henrik Arnold
1808-1845 .... **NCLC 5**
See also DLB 354

Werner, Friedrich Ludwig Zacharias
1768-1823 .... **NCLC 189**
See also DLB 94

Werner, Zacharias
See Werner, Friedrich Ludwig Zacharias

Wersba, Barbara 1932- .... **CLC 30**
See also AAYA 2, 30; BYA 6, 12, 13; CA
29-32R, 182; CAAE 182; CANR 16, 38;
CLR 3, 78; DLB 52; JRDA; MAICYA 1,
2; SAAS 2; SATA 1, 58; SATA-Essay 103;
WYA; YAW

Wertmueller, Lina 1928- .... **CLC 16**
See also CA 97-100; CANR 39, 78

Wescott, Glenway 1901-1987 .. **CLC 13; SSC
35**
See also CA 13-16R; 121; CANR 23, 70;
CN 1, 2, 3, 4; DLB 4, 9, 102; MAL 5;
RGAL 4

Wesker, Arnold 1932- .... **CLC 3, 5, 42**
See also CA 1-4R; CAAS 7; CANR 1, 33;
CBD; CD 5, 6; CDBLB 1960 to Present;
DAB; DAM DRAM; DLB 13, 310, 319;
EWL 3; MTCW 1; RGEL 2; TEA

Wesley, Charles 1707-1788 .... **LC 128**
See also DLB 95; RGEL 2

Wesley, John 1703-1791 .... **LC 88**
See also DLB 104

Wesley, Richard (Errol) 1945- .... **CLC 7**
See also BW 1; CA 57-60; CAD; CANR
27; CD 5, 6; DLB 38

Wessel, Johan Herman 1742-1785 .... **LC 7**
See also DLB 300

West, Anthony (Panther)
1914-1987 .... **CLC 50**
See also CA 45-48; 124; CANR 3, 19; CN
1, 2, 3, 4; DLB 15

West, C. P.
See Wodehouse, P. G.

West, Cornel 1953- .... **BLCS; CLC 134**
See also CA 144; CANR 91, 159; DLB 246

West, Cornel Ronald
See West, Cornel

West, Delno C(loyde), Jr. 1936- .... **CLC 70**
See also CA 57-60

West, Dorothy 1907-1998 ...... **HR 1:3; TCLC
108**
See also AMWS 18; BW 2; CA 143; 169;
DLB 76

West, Edwin
See Westlake, Donald E.

West, (Mary) Jessamyn 1902-1984 ... **CLC 7,
17**
See also CA 9-12R; 112; CANR 27; CN 1,
2, 3; DLB 6; DLBY 1984; MTCW 1, 2;
RGAL 4; RHW; SATA-Obit 37; TCWW
2; TUS; YAW

West, Morris L(anglo) 1916-1999 ..... **CLC 6,
33**
See also BPFB 3; CA 5-8R; 187; CANR
24, 49, 64; CN 1, 2, 3, 4, 5, 6; CPW; DLB
289; MTCW 1, 2; MTFW 2005

West, Nathanael 1903-1940 ...... **SSC 16, 116;
TCLC 1, 14, 44, 235**
See also AAYA 77; AMW; AMWR 2; BPFB
3; CA 104; 125; CDALB 1929-1941;
DA3; DLB 4, 9, 28; EWL 3; MAL 5;
MTCW 1, 2; MTFW 2005; NFS 16;
RGAL 4; TUS

West, Owen
See Koontz, Dean

West, Paul 1930- .... **CLC 7, 14, 96, 226**
See also CA 13-16R; CAAS 7; CANR 22,
53, 76, 89, 136, 205; CN 1, 2, 3, 4, 5, 6,
7; DLB 14; INT CANR-22; MTCW 2;
MTFW 2005

Wilbur, Richard 1921- .. **CLC 3, 6, 9, 14, 53, 110; PC 51**
See also AAYA 72; AMWS 3; CA 1-4R; CABS 2; CANR 2, 29, 76, 93, 139; CDALBS; CP 1, 2, 3, 4, 5, 6, 7; DA; DAB; DAC; DAM MST, POET; DLB 5, 169; EWL 3; EXPP; INT CANR-29; MAL 5; MTCW 1, 2; MTFW 2005; PAB; PFS 11, 12, 16, 29; RGAL 4; SATA 9, 108; WP

Wilbur, Richard Purdy
See Wilbur, Richard

Wild, Peter 1940- .... **CLC 14**
See also CA 37-40R; CP 1, 2, 3, 4, 5, 6, 7; DLB 5

Wilde, Oscar 1854(?)-1900 .. **DC 17; PC 111; SSC 11, 77; TCLC 1, 8, 23, 41, 175; WLC 6**
See also AAYA 49; BRW 5; BRWC 1, 2; BRWR 2; BYA 15; CA 104; 119; CANR 112; CDBLB 1890-1914; CLR 114; DA; DA3; DAB; DAC; DAM DRAM, MST, NOV; DFS 4, 8, 9, 21; DLB 10, 19, 34, 57, 141, 156, 190, 344; EXPS; FANT; GL 3; LATS 1:1; NFS 20; RGEL 2; RGSF 2; SATA 24; SSFS 7; SUFW; TEA; WCH; WLIT 4

Wilde, Oscar Fingal O'Flahertie Willis
See Wilde, Oscar

Wilder, Billy
See Wilder, Samuel

Wilder, Samuel 1906-2002 .... **CLC 20**
See also AAYA 66; CA 89-92; 205; DLB 26

Wilder, Stephen
See Marlowe, Stephen

Wilder, Thornton 1897-1975 ..... **CLC 1, 5, 6, 10, 15, 35, 82; DC 1, 24; WLC 6**
See also AAYA 29; AITN 2; AMW; CA 13-16R; 61-64; CAD; CANR 40, 132; CDALBS; CN 1, 2; DA; DA3; DAB; DAC; DAM DRAM, MST, NOV; DFS 1, 4, 16; DLB 4, 7, 9, 228; DLBY 1997; EWL 3; LAIT 3; MAL 5; MTCW 1, 2; MTFW 2005; NFS 24; RGAL 4; RHW; WYAS 1

Wilder, Thornton Niven
See Wilder, Thornton

Wilding, Michael 1942- ...... **CLC 73; SSC 50**
See also CA 104; CANR 24, 49, 106; CN 4, 5, 6, 7; DLB 325; RGSF 2

Wiley, Richard 1944- .... **CLC 44**
See also CA 121; 129; CANR 71

Wilhelm, Kate
See Wilhelm, Katie

Wilhelm, Katie 1928- .... **CLC 7**
See also AAYA 83; BYA 16; CA 37-40R; CAAS 5; CANR 17, 36, 60, 94; DLB 8; INT CANR-17; MTCW 1; SCFW 2; SFW 4

Wilhelm, Katie Gertrude
See Wilhelm, Katie

Wilkins, Mary
See Freeman, Mary E(leanor) Wilkins

Willard, Nancy 1936- .... **CLC 7, 37**
See also BYA 5; CA 89-92; CANR 10, 39, 68, 107, 152, 186; CLR 5; CP 2, 3, 4, 5; CWP; CWRI 5; DLB 5, 52; FANT; MAI-CYA 1, 2; MTCW 1; SATA 37, 71, 127, 191; SATA-Brief 30; SUFW 2; TCLE 1:2

William of Malmesbury c. 1090B.C.-c. 1140B.C. .... **CMLC 57**

William of Moerbeke c. 1215-c. 1286 .... **CMLC 91**

William of Ockham 1290-1349 .... **CMLC 32, 129**

Williams, Ben Ames 1889-1953 ..... **TCLC 89**
See also CA 183; DLB 102

Williams, Charles
See Collier, James Lincoln

Williams, Charles 1886-1945 ..... **TCLC 1, 11**
See also BRWS 9; CA 104; 163; DLB 100, 153, 255; FANT; RGEL 2; SUFW 1

Williams, Charles Walter Stansby
See Williams, Charles

Williams, C.K. 1936- .. **CLC 33, 56, 148, 306**
See also CA 37-40R; CAAS 26; CANR 57, 106; CP 1, 2, 3, 4, 5, 6, 7; DAM POET; DLB 5; MAL 5

Williams, Ella Gwendolen Rees
See Rhys, Jean

Williams, Emlyn 1905-1987 .... **CLC 15**
See also CA 104; 123; CANR 36; DAM DRAM; DLB 10, 77; IDTP; MTCW 1

Williams, George Emlyn
See Williams, Emlyn

Williams, Hank 1923-1953 .... **TCLC 81**
See Williams, Hiram King
See also CA 188

Williams, Helen Maria 1761-1827 .... **NCLC 135**
See also DLB 158

Williams, Hiram King 1923-1953
See Williams, Hank

Williams, Hugo (Mordaunt) 1942- ... **CLC 42**
See also CA 17-20R; CANR 45, 119; CP 1, 2, 3, 4, 5, 6, 7; DLB 40

Williams, J. Walker
See Wodehouse, P. G.

Williams, John A(lfred) 1925- .... **BLC 1:3; CLC 5, 13**
See also AFAW 2; BW 2, 3; CA 53-56, 195; CAAE 195; CAAS 3; CANR 6, 26, 51, 118; CN 1, 2, 3, 4, 5, 6, 7; CSW; DAM MULT; DLB 2, 33; EWL 3; INT CANR-6; MAL 5; RGAL 4; SFW 4

Williams, Jonathan 1929-2008 .... **CLC 13**
See also CA 9-12R; 270; CAAS 12; CANR 8, 108; CP 1, 2, 3, 4, 5, 6, 7; DLB 5

Williams, Jonathan Chamberlain
See Williams, Jonathan

Williams, Joy 1944- .... **CLC 31**
See also CA 41-44R; CANR 22, 48, 97, 168; DLB 335; SSFS 25

Williams, Norman 1952- .... **CLC 39**
See also CA 118

Williams, Paulette Linda
See Shange, Ntozake

Williams, Roger 1603(?)-1683 .... **LC 129**
See also DLB 24

Williams, Sherley Anne 1944-1999 .... **BLC 1:3; CLC 89**
See also AFAW 2; BW 2, 3; CA 73-76; 185; CANR 25, 82; DAM MULT, POET; DLB 41; INT CANR-25; SATA 78; SATA-Obit 116

Williams, Shirley
See Williams, Sherley Anne

Williams, Tennessee 1911-1983 . **CLC 1, 2, 5, 7, 8, 11, 15, 19, 30, 39, 45, 71, 111; DC 4; SSC 81; WLC 6**
See also AAYA 31; AITN 1, 2; AMW; AMWC 1; CA 5-8R; 108; CABS 3; CAD; CANR 31, 132, 174; CDALB 1941-1968; CN 1, 2, 3; DA; DA3; DAB; DAC; DAM DRAM, MST; DFS 17; DLB 7, 341; DLBD 4; DLBY 1983; EWL 3; GLL 1; LAIT 4; LATS 1:2; MAL 5; MTCW 1, 2; MTFW 2005; RGAL 4; TUS

Williams, Thomas (Alonzo) 1926-1990 .... **CLC 14**
See also CA 1-4R; 132; CANR 2

Williams, Thomas Lanier
See Williams, Tennessee

Williams, William C.
See Williams, William Carlos

Williams, William Carlos 1883-1963 .... **CLC 1, 2, 5, 9, 13, 22, 42, 67; PC 7, 109; SSC 31; WLC 6**
See also AAYA 46; AMW; AMWR 1; CA 89-92; CANR 34; CDALB 1917-1929; DA; DA3; DAB; DAC; DAM MST, POET; DLB 4, 16, 54, 86; EWL 3; EXPP; MAL 5; MTCW 1, 2; MTFW 2005; NCFS 4; PAB; PFS 1, 6, 11, 34; RGAL 4; RGSF 2; SSFS 27; TUS; WP

Williamson, David (Keith) 1942- ..... **CLC 56**
See also CA 103; CANR 41; CD 5, 6; DLB 289

Williamson, Jack
See Williamson, John Stewart

Williamson, John Stewart 1908-2006 .... **CLC 29**
See also AAYA 76; CA 17-20R; 255; CAAS 8; CANR 23, 70, 153; DLB 8; SCFW 1, 2; SFW 4

Willie, Frederick
See Lovecraft, H. P.

Willingham, Calder (Baynard, Jr.) 1922-1995 .... **CLC 5, 51**
See also CA 5-8R; 147; CANR 3; CN 1, 2, 3, 4, 5; CSW; DLB 2, 44; IDFW 3, 4; MTCW 1

Willis, Charles
See Clarke, Arthur C.

Willis, Nathaniel Parker 1806-1867 .... **NCLC 194**
See also DLB 3, 59, 73, 74, 183, 250; DLBD 13; RGAL 4

Willy
See Colette

Willy, Colette
See Colette

Wilmot, John 1647-1680 .... **LC 75; PC 66**
See also BRW 2; DLB 131; PAB; RGEL 2

Wilson, A. N. 1950- .... **CLC 33**
See also BRWS 6; CA 112; 122; CANR 156, 199; CN 4, 5, 6, 7; DLB 14, 155, 194; MTCW 2

Wilson, Andrew Norman
See Wilson, A. N.

Wilson, Angus 1913-1991 .... **CLC 2, 3, 5, 25, 34; SSC 21**
See also BRWS 1; CA 5-8R; 134; CANR 21; CN 1, 2, 3, 4; DLB 15, 139, 155; EWL 3; MTCW 1, 2; MTFW 2005; RGEL 2; RGSF 2

Wilson, Angus Frank Johnstone
See Wilson, Angus

Wilson, August 1945-2005 .... **BLC 1:3, 2:3; CLC 39, 50, 63, 118, 222; DC 2, 31; WLCS**
See also AAYA 16; AFAW 2; AMWS 8; BW 2, 3; CA 115; 122; 244; CAD; CANR 42, 54, 76, 128; CD 5, 6; DA; DA3; DAB; DAC; DAM DRAM, MST, MULT; DFS 3, 7, 15, 17, 24; DLB 228; EWL 3; LAIT 4; LATS 1:2; MAL 5; MTCW 1, 2; MTFW 2005; RGAL 4

Wilson, Brian 1942- .... **CLC 12**

Wilson, Colin 1931- .... **CLC 3, 14**
See also CA 1-4R; CAAS 5; CANR 1, 22, 33, 77; CMW 4; CN 1, 2, 3, 4, 5, 6; DLB 14, 194; HGG; MTCW 1; SFW 4

Wilson, Colin Henry
See Wilson, Colin

Wilson, Dirk
See Pohl, Frederik

Wilson, Edmund 1895-1972 .. **CLC 1, 2, 3, 8, 24**
See also AMW; CA 1-4R; 37-40R; CANR 1, 46, 110; CN 1; DLB 63; EWL 3; MAL 5; MTCW 1, 2; MTFW 2005; RGAL 4; TUS

Wilson, Ethel Davis (Bryant)
1888(?)-1980 .... **CLC 13**
See also CA 102; CN 1, 2; DAC; DAM
POET; DLB 68; MTCW 1; RGEL 2

Wilson, Harriet
See Wilson, Harriet E. Adams

Wilson, Harriet E.
See Wilson, Harriet E. Adams

Wilson, Harriet E. Adams
1827(?)-1863(?) ..... **BLC 1:3; NCLC 78,
219**
See also DAM MULT; DLB 50, 239, 243

Wilson, John 1785-1854 .... **NCLC 5**
See also DLB 110

Wilson, John Anthony Burgess
See Burgess, Anthony

Wilson, John Burgess
See Burgess, Anthony

Wilson, Katharina .... **CLC 65**

Wilson, Lanford 1937-2011 ... **CLC 7, 14, 36,
197; DC 19**
See also CA 17-20R; CABS 3; CAD; CANR
45, 96; CD 5, 6; DAM DRAM; DFS 4, 9,
12, 16, 20; DLB 7, 341; EWL 3; MAL 5;
TUS

Wilson, Robert M. 1941- .... **CLC 7, 9**
See also CA 49-52; CAD; CANR 2, 41; CD
5, 6; MTCW 1

Wilson, Robert McLiam 1964- .... **CLC 59**
See also CA 132; DLB 267

Wilson, Sloan 1920-2003 .... **CLC 32**
See also CA 1-4R; 216; CANR 1, 44; CN
1, 2, 3, 4, 5, 6

Wilson, Snoo 1948- .... **CLC 33**
See also CA 69-72; CBD; CD 5, 6

Wilson, Thomas 1523(?)-1581 .... **LC 184**
See also DLB 132, 236

Wilson, William S(mith) 1932- .... **CLC 49**
See also CA 81-84

Wilson, (Thomas) Woodrow
1856-1924 .... **TCLC 79**
See also CA 166; DLB 47

Winchelsea
See Finch, Anne

Winchester, Simon 1944- .... **CLC 257**
See also AAYA 66; CA 107; CANR 90, 130,
194

Winchilsea, Anne (Kingsmill) Finch
1661-1720
See Finch, Anne
See also RGEL 2

Winckelmann, Johann Joachim
1717-1768 .... **LC 129**
See also DLB 97

Windham, Basil
See Wodehouse, P. G.

Wingrove, David 1954- .... **CLC 68**
See also CA 133; SFW 4

Winnemucca, Sarah 1844-1891 .... **NCLC 79;
NNAL**
See also DAM MULT; DLB 175; RGAL 4

Winstanley, Gerrard 1609-1676 .... **LC 52**

Wintergreen, Jane
See Duncan, Sara Jeannette

Winters, Arthur Yvor
See Winters, Yvor

Winters, Janet Lewis
See Lewis, Janet

Winters, Yvor 1900-1968 .. **CLC 4, 8, 32; PC
82**
See also AMWS 2; CA 11-12; 25-28R; CAP
1; DLB 48; EWL 3; MAL 5; MTCW 1;
RGAL 4

Winterson, Jeanette 1959- .... **CLC 64, 158,
307; SSC 144**
See also BRWS 4; CA 136; CANR 58, 116,
181; CN 5, 6, 7; CPW; DA3; DAM POP;
DLB 207, 261; FANT; FW; GLL 1;
MTCW 2; MTFW 2005; RHW; SATA 190

Winthrop, John 1588-1649 .... **LC 31, 107**
See also DLB 24, 30

Winthrop, Theodore 1828-1861 ... **NCLC 210**
See also DLB 202

Winton, Tim 1960- .... **CLC 251; SSC 119**
See also AAYA 34; CA 152; CANR 118,
194; CN 6, 7; DLB 325; SATA 98

Wirth, Louis 1897-1952 .... **TCLC 92**
See also CA 210

Wiseman, Frederick 1930- .... **CLC 20**
See also CA 159

Wister, Owen 1860-1938 ..... **SSC 100; TCLC
21**
See also BPFB 3; CA 108; 162; DLB 9, 78,
186; RGAL 4; SATA 62; TCWW 1, 2

Wither, George 1588-1667 .... **LC 96**
See also DLB 121; RGEL 2

Witkacy
See Witkiewicz, Stanislaw Ignacy

Witkiewicz, Stanislaw Ignacy
1885-1939 .... **TCLC 8, 237**
See also CA 105; 162; CDWLB 4; DLB
215; EW 10; EWL 3; RGWL 2, 3; SFW 4

Wittgenstein, Ludwig (Josef Johann)
1889-1951 .... **TCLC 59**
See also CA 113; 164; DLB 262; MTCW 2

Wittig, Monique 1935-2003 .... **CLC 22**
See also CA 116; 135; 212; CANR 143;
CWW 2; DLB 83; EWL 3; FW; GLL 1

Wittlin, Jozef 1896-1976 .... **CLC 25**
See also CA 49-52; 65-68; CANR 3; EWL
3

Wodehouse, P. G. 1881-1975 ..... **CLC 1, 2, 5,
10, 22; SSC 2, 115; TCLC 108**
See also AAYA 65; AITN 2; BRWS 3; CA
45-48; 57-60; CANR 3, 33; CDBLB
1914-1945; CN 1, 2; CPW 1; DA3; DAB;
DAC; DAM NOV; DLB 34, 162, 352;
EWL 3; MTCW 1, 2; MTFW 2005; RGEL
2; RGSF 2; SATA 22; SSFS 10

Wodehouse, Pelham Grenville
See Wodehouse, P. G.

Woiwode, L.
See Woiwode, Larry

Woiwode, Larry 1941- .... **CLC 6, 10**
See also CA 73-76; CANR 16, 94, 192; CN
3, 4, 5, 6, 7; DLB 6; INT CANR-16

Woiwode, Larry Alfred
See Woiwode, Larry

Wojciechowska, Maia (Teresa)
1927-2002 .... **CLC 26**
See also AAYA 8, 46; BYA 3; CA 9-12R;
183; 209; CAAE 183; CANR 4, 41; CLR
1; JRDA; MAICYA 1, 2; SAAS 1; SATA
1, 28, 83; SATA-Essay 104; SATA-Obit
134; YAW

Wojtyla, Karol (Jozef)
See John Paul II, Pope

Wojtyla, Karol (Josef)
See John Paul II, Pope

Wolf, Christa 1929- ...... **CLC 14, 29, 58, 150,
261**
See also CA 85-88; CANR 45, 123; CD-
WLB 2; CWW 2; DLB 75; EWL 3; FW;
MTCW 1; RGWL 2, 3; SSFS 14

Wolf, Naomi 1962- .... **CLC 157**
See also CA 141; CANR 110; FW; MTFW
2005

Wolfe, Gene 1931- .... **CLC 25**
See also AAYA 35; CA 57-60; CAAS 9;
CANR 6, 32, 60, 152, 197; CPW; DAM
POP; DLB 8; FANT; MTCW 2; MTFW
2005; SATA 118, 165; SCFW 2; SFW 4;
SUFW 2

Wolfe, Gene Rodman
See Wolfe, Gene

Wolfe, George C. 1954- .... **BLCS; CLC 49**
See also CA 149; CAD; CD 5, 6

Wolfe, Thomas 1900-1938 .... **SSC 33, 113;
TCLC 4, 13, 29, 61; WLC 6**
See also AMW; BPFB 3; CA 104; 132;
CANR 102; CDALB 1929-1941; DA;
DA3; DAB; DAC; DAM MST, NOV;
DLB 9, 102, 229; DLBD 2, 16; DLBY
1985, 1997; EWL 3; MAL 5; MTCW 1,
2; NFS 18; RGAL 4; SSFS 18; TUS

Wolfe, Thomas Clayton
See Wolfe, Thomas

Wolfe, Thomas Kennerly
See Wolfe, Tom, Jr.

Wolfe, Tom, Jr. 1931- .... **CLC 1, 2, 9, 15, 35,
51, 147**
See also AAYA 8, 67; AITN 2; AMWS 3;
BEST 89:1; BPFB 3; CA 13-16R; CANR
9, 33, 70, 104; CN 5, 6, 7; CPW; CSW;
DA3; DAM POP; DLB 152, 185 185;
EWL 3; INT CANR-9; LAIT 5; MTCW
1, 2; MTFW 2005; RGAL 4; TUS

Wolff, Geoffrey 1937- .... **CLC 41**
See also CA 29-32R; CANR 29, 43, 78, 154

Wolff, Geoffrey Ansell
See Wolff, Geoffrey

Wolff, Sonia
See Levitin, Sonia

Wolff, Tobias 1945- .... **CLC 39, 64, 172; SSC
63, 136**
See also AAYA 16; AMWS 7; BEST 90:2;
BYA 12; CA 114; 117; CAAS 22; CANR
54, 76, 96, 192; CN 5, 6, 7; CSW; DA3;
DLB 130; EWL 3; INT CA-117; MTCW
2; MTFW 2005; RGAL 4; RGSF 2; SSFS
4, 11

Wolff, Tobias Jonathan Ansell
See Wolff, Tobias

Wolitzer, Hilma 1930- .... **CLC 17**
See also CA 65-68; CANR 18, 40, 172; INT
CANR-18; SATA 31; YAW

Wollstonecraft, Mary 1759-1797 .... **LC 5, 50,
90, 147**
See also BRWS 3; CDBLB 1789-1832;
DLB 39, 104, 158, 252; FL 1:1; FW;
LAIT 1; RGEL 2; TEA; WLIT 3

Wonder, Stevie 1950- .... **CLC 12**
See also CA 111

Wong, Jade Snow 1922-2006 .... **CLC 17**
See also CA 109; 249; CANR 91; SATA
112; SATA-Obit 175

Wood, Ellen Price
See Wood, Mrs. Henry

Wood, Mrs. Henry 1814-1887 ...... **NCLC 178**
See also CMW 4; DLB 18; SUFW

Wood, James 1965- .... **CLC 238**
See also CA 235; CANR 214

Woodberry, George Edward
1855-1930 .... **TCLC 73**
See also CA 165; DLB 71, 103

Woodcott, Keith
See Brunner, John (Kilian Houston)

Woodruff, Robert W.
See Mencken, H. L.

Woodward, Bob 1943- .... **CLC 240**
See also CA 69-72; CANR 31, 67, 107, 176;
MTCW 1

Woodward, Robert Upshur
See Woodward, Bob

Woolf, Adeline Virginia
See Woolf, Virginia

Woolf, Virginia 1882-1941 .... **SSC 7, 79;
TCLC 1, 5, 20, 43, 56, 101, 123, 128;
WLC 6**
See also AAYA 44; BPFB 3; BRW 7;
BRWC 2; BRWR 1; CA 104; 130; CANR
64, 132; CDBLB 1914-1945; DA; DA3;
DAB; DAC; DAM MST, NOV; DLB 36,
100, 162; DLBD 10; EWL 3; EXPS; FL

1:6; FW; LAIT 3; LATS 1:1; LMFS 2; MTCW 1, 2; MTFW 2005; NCFS 2; NFS 8, 12, 28; RGEL 2; RGSF 2; SSFS 4, 12; TEA; WLIT 4

Woollcott, Alexander (Humphreys) 1887-1943 .... **TCLC 5**
See also CA 105; 161; DLB 29

Woolman, John 1720-1772 .... **LC 155**
See also DLB 31

Woolrich, Cornell
See Hopley-Woolrich, Cornell George

Woolson, Constance Fenimore 1840-1894 .... **NCLC 82; SSC 90**
See also DLB 12, 74, 189, 221; RGAL 4

Wordsworth, Dorothy 1771-1855 . **NCLC 25, 138**
See also DLB 107

Wordsworth, William 1770-1850 .. **NCLC 12, 38, 111, 166, 206; PC 4, 67; WLC 6**
See also AAYA 70; BRW 4; BRWC 1; CD-BLB 1789-1832; DA; DA3; DAB; DAC; DAM MST, POET; DLB 93, 107; EXPP; LATS 1:1; LMFS 1; PAB; PFS 2, 33, 38; RGEL 2; TEA; WLIT 3; WP

Wotton, Sir Henry 1568-1639 .... **LC 68**
See also DLB 121; RGEL 2

Wouk, Herman 1915- .... **CLC 1, 9, 38**
See also BPFB 2, 3; CA 5-8R; CANR 6, 33, 67, 146; CDALBS; CN 1, 2, 3, 4, 5, 6; CPW; DA3; DAM NOV, POP; DLBY 1982; INT CANR-6; LAIT 4; MAL 5; MTCW 1, 2; MTFW 2005; NFS 7; TUS

Wright, Charles 1932-2008 ... **BLC 1:3; CLC 49**
See also BW 1; CA 9-12R; 278; CANR 26; CN 1, 2, 3, 4, 5, 6, 7; DAM MULT, POET; DLB 33

Wright, Charles 1935- ... **CLC 6, 13, 28, 119, 146**
See also AMWS 5; CA 29-32R; CAAS 7; CANR 23, 36, 62, 88, 135, 180; CP 3, 4, 5, 6, 7; DLB 165; DLBY 1982; EWL 3; MTCW 1, 2; MTFW 2005; PFS 10, 35

Wright, Charles Penzel, Jr.
See Wright, Charles

Wright, Charles Stevenson
See Wright, Charles

Wright, Frances 1795-1852 .... **NCLC 74**
See also DLB 73

Wright, Frank Lloyd 1867-1959 .... **TCLC 95**
See also AAYA 33; CA 174

Wright, Harold Bell 1872-1944 .... **TCLC 183**
See also BPFB 3; CA 110; DLB 9; TCWW 2

Wright, Jack R.
See Harris, Mark

Wright, James (Arlington) 1927-1980 .... **CLC 3, 5, 10, 28; PC 36**
See also AITN 2; AMWS 3; CA 49-52; 97-100; CANR 4, 34, 64; CDALBS; CP 1, 2; DAM POET; DLB 5, 169, 342; EWL 3; EXPP; MAL 5; MTCW 1, 2; MTFW 2005; PFS 7, 8; RGAL 4; TUS; WP

Wright, Judith 1915-2000 ... **CLC 11, 53; PC 14**
See also CA 13-16R; 188; CANR 31, 76, 93; CP 1, 2, 3, 4, 5, 6, 7; CWP; DLB 260; EWL 3; MTCW 1, 2; MTFW 2005; PFS 8; RGEL 2; SATA 14; SATA-Obit 121

Wright, Judith Arundell
See Wright, Judith

Wright, L(aurali) R. 1939- .... **CLC 44**
See also CA 138; CMW 4

Wright, Richard 1908-1960 .. **BLC 1:3; CLC 1, 3, 4, 9, 14, 21, 48, 74; SSC 2, 109; TCLC 136, 180; WLC 6**
See also AAYA 5, 42; AFAW 1, 2; AMW; BPFB 3; BW 1; BYA 2; CA 108; CANR 64; CDALB 1929-1941; DA; DA3; DAB;

DAC; DAM MST, MULT, NOV; DLB 76, 102; DLBD 2; EWL 3; EXPN; LAIT 3, 4; MAL 5; MTCW 1, 2; MTFW 2005; NCFS 1; NFS 1, 7; RGAL 4; RGSF 2; SSFS 3, 9, 15, 20; TUS; YAW

Wright, Richard B. 1937- .... **CLC 6**
See also CA 85-88; CANR 120; DLB 53

Wright, Richard Bruce
See Wright, Richard B.

Wright, Richard Nathaniel
See Wright, Richard

Wright, Rick 1945- .... **CLC 35**

Wright, Rowland
See Wells, Carolyn

Wright, Stephen 1946- .... **CLC 33**
See also CA 237; DLB 350

Wright, Willard Huntington 1888-1939 .... **TCLC 23**
See also CA 115; 189; CMW 4; DLB 306; DLBD 16; MSW

Wright, William 1930- .... **CLC 44**
See also CA 53-56; CANR 7, 23, 154

Wroblewski, David 1959- .... **CLC 280**
See also CA 283

Wroth, Lady Mary 1587-1653(?) .... **LC 30, 139; PC 38**
See also DLB 121

Wu Ch'eng-en 1500(?)-1582(?) .... **LC 7**

Wu Ching-tzu 1701-1754 .... **LC 2**

Wulfstan c. 10th cent. -1023 .... **CMLC 59**

Wurlitzer, Rudolph 1938(?)- .... **CLC 2, 4, 15**
See also CA 85-88; CN 4, 5, 6, 7; DLB 173

Wyatt, Sir Thomas c. 1503-1542 . **LC 70; PC 27**
See also BRW 1; DLB 132; EXPP; PFS 25; RGEL 2; TEA

Wycherley, William 1640-1716 ... **DC 41; LC 8, 21, 102, 136**
See also BRW 2; CDBLB 1660-1789; DAM DRAM; DLB 80; RGEL 2

Wyclif, John c. 1330-1384 .... **CMLC 70**
See also DLB 146

Wylie, Elinor (Morton Hoyt) 1885-1928 .... **PC 23; TCLC 8**
See also AMWS 1; CA 105; 162; DLB 9, 45; EXPP; MAL 5; RGAL 4

Wylie, Philip (Gordon) 1902-1971 ... **CLC 43**
See also CA 21-22; 33-36R; CAP 2; CN 1; DLB 9; SFW 4

Wyndham, John
See Harris, John (Wyndham Parkes Lucas) Beynon

Wyss, Johann David Von 1743-1818 .... **NCLC 10**
See also CLR 92; JRDA; MAICYA 1, 2; SATA 29; SATA-Brief 27

X, Malcolm
See Malcolm X

Xenophon c. 430B.C.-c. 354B.C. ... **CMLC 17**
See also AW 1; DLB 176; RGWL 2, 3; WLIT 8

Xingjian, Gao 1940- .... **CLC 167**
See also CA 193; DFS 21; DLB 330; MTFW 2005; RGWL 3

Yakamochi 718-785 .... **CMLC 45; PC 48**

Yakumo Koizumi
See Hearn, Lafcadio

Yamada, Mitsuye (May) 1923- .... **PC 44**
See also CA 77-80

Yamamoto, Hisaye 1921-2011 . **AAL; SSC 34**
See also CA 214; DAM MULT; DLB 312; LAIT 4; SSFS 14

Yamauchi, Wakako 1924- .... **AAL**
See also CA 214; DLB 312

Yan, Mo 1956(?)- .... **CLC 257**
See also CA 201; CANR 192; EWL 3; RGWL 3

Yanez, Jose Donoso
See Donoso, Jose

Yanovsky, Basile S.
See Yanovsky, V(assily) S(emenovich)

Yanovsky, V(assily) S(emenovich) 1906-1989 .... **CLC 2, 18**
See also CA 97-100; 129

Yates, Richard 1926-1992 .... **CLC 7, 8, 23**
See also AMWS 11; CA 5-8R; 139; CANR 10, 43; CN 1, 2, 3, 4, 5; DLB 2, 234; DLBY 1981, 1992; INT CANR-10; SSFS 24

Yau, John 1950- .... **PC 61**
See also CA 154; CANR 89; CP 4, 5, 6, 7; DLB 234, 312; PFS 26

Yearsley, Ann 1753-1806 .... **NCLC 174**
See also DLB 109

Yeats, W. B.
See Yeats, William Butler

Yeats, William Butler 1865-1939 . **DC 33; PC 20, 51; TCLC 1, 11, 18, 31, 93, 116; WLC 6**
See also AAYA 48; BRW 6; BRWR 1; CA 104; 127; CANR 45; CDBLB 1890-1914; DA; DA3; DAB; DAC; DAM DRAM, MST, POET; DLB 10, 19, 98, 156, 332; EWL 3; EXPP; MTCW 1, 2; MTFW 2005; NCFS 3; PAB; PFS 1, 2, 5, 7, 13, 15, 34; RGEL 2; TEA; WLIT 4; WP

Yehoshua, A. B. 1936- .... **CLC 13, 31, 243**
See also CA 33-36R; CANR 43, 90, 145, 202; CWW 2; EWL 3; RGHL; RGSF 2; RGWL 3; WLIT 6

Yehoshua, Abraham B.
See Yehoshua, A. B.

Yellow Bird
See Ridge, John Rollin

Yep, Laurence 1948- .... **CLC 35**
See also AAYA 5, 31; BYA 7; CA 49-52; CANR 1, 46, 92, 161; CLR 3, 17, 54, 132; DLB 52, 312; FANT; JRDA; MAICYA 1, 2; MAICYAS 1; SATA 7, 69, 123, 176, 213; WYA; YAW

Yep, Laurence Michael
See Yep, Laurence

Yerby, Frank G(arvin) 1916-1991 . **BLC 1:3; CLC 1, 7, 22**
See also BPFB 3; BW 1, 3; CA 9-12R; 136; CANR 16, 52; CN 1, 2, 3, 4, 5; DAM MULT; DLB 76; INT CANR-16; MTCW 1; RGAL 4; RHW

Yesenin, Sergei Aleksandrovich
See Esenin, Sergei

Yevtushenko, Yevgeny Alexandrovich
See Yevtushenko, Yevgenyn

Yevtushenko, Yevgenyn 1933- . **CLC 1, 3, 13, 26, 51, 126; PC 40**
See also CA 81-84; CANR 33, 54; CWW 2; DAM POET; DLB 359; EWL 3; MTCW 1; PFS 29; RGHL; RGWL 2, 3

Yezierska, Anzia 1885(?)-1970 .... **CLC 46; SSC 144; TCLC 205**
See also CA 126; 89-92; DLB 28, 221; FW; MTCW 1; NFS 29; RGAL 4; SSFS 15

Yglesias, Helen 1915-2008 .... **CLC 7, 22**
See also CA 37-40R; 272; CAAS 20; CANR 15, 65, 95; CN 4, 5, 6, 7; INT CANR-15; MTCW 1

Y.O.
See Russell, George William

Yokomitsu, Riichi 1898-1947 .... **TCLC 47**
See also CA 170; EWL 3

Yolen, Jane 1939- .... **CLC 256**
See also AAYA 4, 22, 85; BPFB 3; BYA 9, 10, 11, 14, 16; CA 13-16R; CANR 11, 29, 56, 91, 126, 185; CLR 4, 44, 149; CWRI 5; DLB 52; FANT; INT CANR-29; JRDA; MAICYA 1, 2; MTFW 2005; NFS 30;

SAAS 1; SATA 4, 40, 75, 112, 158, 194; SATA-Essay 111; SFW 4; SSFS 29; SUFW 2; WYA; YAW

Yolen, Jane Hyatt
See Yolen, Jane

Yonge, Charlotte 1823-1901 ... **TCLC 48, 245**
See also BRWS 17; CA 109; DLB 18, 163; RGEL 2; SATA 17; WCH

Yonge, Charlotte Mary
See Yonge, Charlotte

York, Jeremy
See Creasey, John

York, Simon
See Heinlein, Robert A.

Yorke, Henry Vincent 1905-1974 ...... **CLC 2, 13, 97**
See also BRWS 2; CA 85-88, 175; 49-52; DLB 15; EWL 3; RGEL 2

Yosano, Akiko 1878-1942 ... **PC 11; TCLC 59**
See also CA 161; EWL 3; RGWL 3

Yoshimoto, Banana
See Yoshimoto, Mahoko

Yoshimoto, Mahoko 1964- .... **CLC 84**
See also AAYA 50; CA 144; CANR 98, 160; NFS 7; SSFS 16

Young, Al(bert James) 1939- .... **BLC 1:3; CLC 19**
See also BW 2, 3; CA 29-32R; CANR 26, 65, 109; CN 2, 3, 4, 5, 6, 7; CP 1, 2, 3, 4, 5, 6, 7; DAM MULT; DLB 33

Young, Andrew (John) 1885-1971 ...... **CLC 5**
See also CA 5-8R; CANR 7, 29; CP 1; RGEL 2

Young, Collier
See Bloch, Robert (Albert)

Young, Edward 1683-1765 .... **LC 3, 40**
See also DLB 95; RGEL 2

Young, Marguerite (Vivian) 1909-1995 .... **CLC 82**
See also CA 13-16; 150; CAP 1; CN 1, 2, 3, 4, 5, 6

Young, Neil 1945- .... **CLC 17**
See also CA 110; CCA 1

Young Bear, Ray A. 1950- ... **CLC 94; NNAL**
See also CA 146; DAM MULT; DLB 175; MAL 5

Yourcenar, Marguerite 1903-1987 ... **CLC 19, 38, 50, 87; TCLC 193**
See also BPFB 3; CA 69-72; CANR 23, 60, 93; DAM NOV; DLB 72; DLBY 1988; EW 12; EWL 3; GFL 1789 to the Present; GLL 1; MTCW 1, 2; MTFW 2005; RGWL 2, 3

Yuan, Chu 340(?)B.C.-278(?)B.C. . **CMLC 36**

Yu Dafu 1896-1945 .... **SSC 122**
See also DLB 328; RGSF 2

Yurick, Sol 1925- .... **CLC 6**
See also CA 13-16R; CANR 25; CN 1, 2, 3, 4, 5, 6, 7; MAL 5

Zabolotsky, Nikolai
See Zabolotsky, Nikolai Alekseevich

Zabolotsky, Nikolai Alekseevich 1903-1958 .... **TCLC 52**
See also CA 116; 164; DLB 359; EWL 3

Zabolotsky, Nikolay Alekseevich
See Zabolotsky, Nikolai Alekseevich

Zagajewski, Adam 1945- .... **PC 27**
See also CA 186; DLB 232; EWL 3; PFS 25

Zakaria, Fareed 1964- .... **CLC 269**
See also CA 171; CANR 151, 189

Zalygin, Sergei -2000 .... **CLC 59**

Zalygin, Sergei (Pavlovich) 1913-2000 .... **CLC 59**
See also DLB 302

Zamiatin, Evgeny
See Zamyatin, Evgeny Ivanovich

Zamiatin, Evgenii Ivanovich
See Zamyatin, Evgeny Ivanovich

Zamiatin, Yevgenii
See Zamyatin, Evgeny Ivanovich

Zamora, Bernice (B. Ortiz) 1938- .. **CLC 89; HLC 2**
See also CA 151; CANR 80; DAM MULT; DLB 82; HW 1, 2

Zamyatin, Evgeny Ivanovich 1884-1937 .... **SSC 89; TCLC 8, 37**
See also CA 105; 166; DLB 272; EW 10; EWL 3; RGSF 2; RGWL 2, 3; SFW 4

Zamyatin, Yevgeny Ivanovich
See Zamyatin, Evgeny Ivanovich

Zangwill, Israel 1864-1926 ... **SSC 44; TCLC 16**
See also CA 109; 167; CMW 4; DLB 10, 135, 197; RGEL 2

Zanzotto, Andrea 1921- .... **PC 65**
See also CA 208; CWW 2; DLB 128; EWL 3

Zappa, Francis Vincent, Jr. 1940-1993 .... **CLC 17**
See also CA 108; 143; CANR 57

Zappa, Frank
See Zappa, Francis Vincent, Jr.

Zaturenska, Marya 1902-1982 ..... **CLC 6, 11**
See also CA 13-16R; 105; CANR 22; CP 1, 2, 3

Zayas y Sotomayor, Maria de 1590-c. 1661 .... **LC 102; SSC 94**
See also RGSF 2

Zeami 1363-1443 .... **DC 7; LC 86**
See also DLB 203; RGWL 2, 3

Zelazny, Roger 1937-1995 .... **CLC 21**
See also AAYA 7, 68; BPFB 3; CA 21-24R; 148; CANR 26, 60, 219; CN 6; DLB 8; FANT; MTCW 1, 2; MTFW 2005; SATA 57; SATA-Brief 39; SCFW 1, 2; SFW 4; SUFW 1, 2

Zelazny, Roger Joseph
See Zelazny, Roger

Zephaniah, Benjamin 1958- .... **BLC 2:3**
See also CA 147; CANR 103, 156, 177; CP 5, 6, 7; DLB 347; SATA 86, 140, 189

Zhang Ailing
See Chang, Eileen

Zhdanov, Andrei Alexandrovich 1896-1948 .... **TCLC 18**
See also CA 117; 167

Zhukovsky, Vasilii Andreevich
See Zhukovsky, Vasily (Andreevich)

Zhukovsky, Vasily (Andreevich) 1783-1852 .... **NCLC 35**
See also DLB 205

Ziegenhagen, Eric .... **CLC 55**

Zimmer, Jill Schary
See Robinson, Jill

Zimmerman, Robert
See Dylan, Bob

Zindel, Paul 1936-2003 ...... **CLC 6, 26; DC 5**
See also AAYA 2, 37; BYA 2, 3, 8, 11, 14; CA 73-76; 213; CAD; CANR 31, 65, 108; CD 5, 6; CDALBS; CLR 3, 45, 85; DA; DA3; DAB; DAC; DAM DRAM, MST, NOV; DFS 12; DLB 7, 52; JRDA; LAIT 5; MAICYA 1, 2; MTCW 1, 2; MTFW 2005; NFS 14; SATA 16, 58, 102; SATA-Obit 142; WYA; YAW

Zinger, Yisroel-Yehoyshue
See Singer, Israel Joshua

Zinger, Yitskhok
See Singer, Isaac Bashevis

Zinn, Howard 1922-2010 .... **CLC 199**
See also CA 1-4R; CANR 2, 33, 90, 159

Zinov'Ev, A.A.
See Zinoviev, Alexander

Zinov'ev, Aleksandr
See Zinoviev, Alexander

Zinoviev, Alexander 1922-2006 .... **CLC 19**
See also CA 116; 133; 250; CAAS 10; DLB 302

Zinoviev, Alexander Aleksandrovich
See Zinoviev, Alexander

Zizek, Slavoj 1949- .... **CLC 188**
See also CA 201; CANR 171; MTFW 2005

Zobel, Joseph 1915-2006 .... **BLC 2:3**

Zoilus
See Lovecraft, H. P.

Zola, Emile 1840-1902 .... **SSC 109; TCLC 1, 6, 21, 41, 219; WLC 6**
See also CA 104; 138; DA; DA3; DAB; DAC; DAM MST, NOV; DLB 123; EW 7; GFL 1789 to the Present; IDTP; LMFS 1, 2; RGWL 2; TWA

Zola, Emile Edouard Charles Antione
See Zola, Emile

Zoline, Pamela 1941- .... **CLC 62**
See also CA 161; SFW 4

Zoroaster 628(?)B.C.-551(?)B.C. ... **CMLC 40**

Zorrilla y Moral, Jose 1817-1893 .... **NCLC 6**

Zoshchenko, Mikhail 1895-1958 ...... **SSC 15; TCLC 15**
See also CA 115; 160; EWL 3; RGSF 2; RGWL 3

Zoshchenko, Mikhail Mikhailovich
See Zoshchenko, Mikhail

Zuckmayer, Carl 1896-1977 .... **CLC 18; TCLC 191**
See also CA 69-72; DLB 56, 124; EWL 3; RGWL 2, 3

Zuk, Georges
See Skelton, Robin

Zukofsky, Louis 1904-1978 ... **CLC 1, 2, 4, 7, 11, 18; PC 11, 121**
See also AMWS 3; CA 9-12R; 77-80; CANR 39; CP 1, 2; DAM POET; DLB 5, 165; EWL 3; MAL 5; MTCW 1; RGAL 4

Zweig, Arnold 1887-1968 .... **TCLC 199**
See also CA 189; 115; DLB 66; EWL 3

Zweig, Paul 1935-1984 .... **CLC 34, 42**
See also CA 85-88; 113

Zweig, Stefan 1881-1942 .... **TCLC 17**
See also CA 112; 170; DLB 81, 118; EWL 3; RGHL

Zwingli, Huldreich 1484-1531 .... **LC 37**
See also DLB 179

Literary Criticism Series
Cumulative Topic Index

This index lists all topic entries in Gale's *Children's Literature Review* (CLR), *Classical and Medieval Literature Criticism* (CMLC), *Contemporary Literary Criticism* (CLC), *Drama Criticism* (DC), *Literature Criticism from 1400 to 1800* (LC), *Nineteenth-Century Literature Criticism* (NCLC), *Short Story Criticism* (SSC), and *Twentieth-Century Literary Criticism* (TCLC). The index also lists topic entries in the Gale Critical Companion Collection, which includes the following publications: *The Beat Generation* (BG), *Feminism in Literature* (FL), *Gothic Literature* (GL), and *Harlem Renaissance* (HR).

Topic Index

SSC Cumulative Nationality Index

481

Nationality Index

SSC-156 Title Index

ISBN-13: 978-1-4144-7166-2
ISBN-10: 1-4144-7166-1

90000

9 781414 471662